# VOYAGER

## A Life of Hart Crane

John Unterecker

LIVERIGHT
New York · London

First published as a Liveright paperback 1987 by
arrangement with Farrar, Straus & Giroux

Copyright © 1969 by John Unterecker
Library of Congress catalog card number: 69–11575

**Library of Congress Cataloging in Publication Data**
Unterecker, John Eugene, 1922–
Voyager: a life of Hart Crane.
Reprint. Originally published: New York: Farrar, Straus and
Giroux, 1969.
1. Crane, Hart, 1899–1932—Biography. 2. Poets,
American—20th century—Biography. I. Title.
PS3505·R272Z797      1987      811'.52 [B]      87–4205

ISBN 0-87140-143-6

1  2  3  4  5  6  7  8  9  0

FOR

BILL BROWN, MRS. MARGARET BABCOCK (PEGGY ROBSON),
AND SAM LOVEMAN, WHO VALUED HART CRANE
AND WHOSE MEMORIES OF HIM SHOWED ME THREE FACETS
OF A MOST COMPLEX MAN

# Note

THIS book has been ten years in the making. Two years ago, when my "final" manuscript stood at half a million words and I started the process of cutting and revision that was to bring it to its present size, Robert Giroux and I agreed that the most readable format would be a text free of footnote numbers. The documentation—keyed to page references—is appended to the book, beginning on page 775.

My gratitude to Robert Giroux is very great. When I could not (I suffered a serious heart attack on January 8, 1969, shortly after releasing the corrected galleys for the body of this book), he and the staff of Farrar, Straus and Giroux saw to the preparation of the photographic inserts, correspondence concerning acknowledgments, indexing (for which I particularly wish to thank Annette Gordon), and the careful reading of page proof. But in a much larger sense I am grateful for ten years of Robert's friendship and unfailing encouragement. I wish also to express my gratitude to Michael di Capua for editorial assistance in cutting the manuscript, to Carmen Gomezplata for most sensitive copy-editing, and to Herb Johnson for the book design. The jacket drawing by Lili Réthi is, I like to think, one that Hart Crane would have admired.

Readers familiar with Brom Weber's edition of *The Letters of Hart Crane* will find that my transcriptions differ from his in minor details. Early on, I decided to draw quotations, whenever possible, from originals of both published and unpublished letters and to follow slavishly Crane's habits of punctuation and capitalization. A great many of the letters of Hart Crane that I quote are heretofore unpublished, as are almost all the letters written to him. I wish to express here my particular thanks for the courtesy and congeniality of Kenneth Lohf and Alexander P. Clark, who made my visits to the libraries of Columbia University and Princeton University memorable. At Columbia, I was given free access to the thousands of Hart Crane items housed in the Special Collections division of the library. At Yale University, I was grateful for the hospitality of R. W. B. Lewis and the cooperation of Norman Holmes Pearson and Donald Gallup, each of whom made available to me unpublished Crane manuscripts and aided me in making copies of them. I am especially grateful to Henry Allen Moe and Gordon Ray, who permitted me to examine and to quote from much of the correspondence and memoranda from the Hart Crane files of the John Simon Guggenheim Memorial Foundation. I also made good use of Hart Crane materials, and materials related to him, now owned by The Ohio State University Libraries, Fisk University of Chicago Library, the Newberry Library, Harvard University Library, the Lockwood Memorial Library of the State University of New York at Buffalo, Indiana University Library, the University of Virginia Library, Syracuse University Library, Southern Illinois University Library, the University of Texas Library, and the Library of Congress.

## Note

I cannot overstate my appreciation of and my reliance on Philip Horton's biography of Crane, Waldo Frank's early edition of Crane's poetry, and Brom Weber's critical study, his edition of the letters, and his recent edition of *The Complete Poems and Selected Letters and Prose of Hart Crane*. Without these pioneering efforts in the collection and transcription of texts and Horton's record of the fresh memories of people now dead, whole areas of Crane's life and work would presently be unavailable. Like all scholars interested in Crane's accomplishment, I look forward to Mr. Weber's forthcoming edition of the complete letters.

My greatest debt is to Crane's family, who have searched memories and attics to provide me hundreds of facts, photographs, anecdotes, impressions. This book would be thinner and duller if I had not had the fullest cooperation of such generous people as Bessie Hise (Crane's stepmother), Mrs. Elizabeth Madden and Mrs. Alice Williams (his aunts), and Helen Hart Hurlbert and Mrs. Fredrica Lewis (his cousins). His friends have been equally helpful, especially the three to whom this book is dedicated; but I could not have had a full sense of Crane as a living man without my conversations with Kenneth Hurd, William Spratling, Robert Bordner, Mrs. Richard Laukhuff, Collister Hutchison, Harrison Smith, Malcolm Cowley, Caresse Crosby, Matthew Josephson, Susan Jenkins Brown, Philip Kaplan, Charles Harris, Allen Tate, Caroline Gordon Tate, Emil Opffer, Mary Doherty, William Lescaze, Ida Scott, Eva Parker, Alex Baltzly, Bessie Breuer, Kenneth Burke, Padraic Colum, Solomon Grunberg, Isidor Schneider, Richard Rychtarik, Charmion von Wiegand, Willard Widney, Peggy Baird (Cowley), Harold Loeb, Harley McHugh, Lorna Dietz, Walker Evans, Bert Ginther, Joseph Kling, Eugene MacCown, Gorham Munson, Agnes Boulton, Stanley Patno, Carl Schmitt, Ray Sommer, William Sommer, Jr., and William Carlos Williams. I should also like here to express my appreciation for the helpful correspondence of Leslie Byrd Simpson, Nathan Asch, Claire Spencer, H. P. Collamore, Mrs. Marjorie C. Toomer, Georgia O'Keeffe, Mrs. William Wright, John Baker, George Bryan, Charles Baldwin, Mrs. Russell Cate, Val Clear, Kirby Congdon, Mr. James Fenwick, Mr. Ralph Crane, E. E. Cummings, Edward Dahlberg, S. Foster Damon, Joseph H. Dexter, Margaret Anderson, John Dos Passos, León Felipe, Mrs. Herman Fetzer, Joseph Frease, Windsor French, Alfred Galpin, Mac Hammond, Helen E. Hanley, Conrad Aiken, Raymond A. Baird, Elbert Hubbard II, Mrs. Kay Kenney Gilmore, John Lineaweaver, Harold Loeb, Arthur Koki, Archibald MacLeish, John S. Mayfield, Mrs. John W. McCaslin, Marianne Moore, Mrs. Fred Neu, Fairfield Porter, Katherine Anne Porter, Florence T. Raymond, Mrs. Reida D. Gardiner, Arna Bontemps, David Siqueiros, David W. Swetland, Frederick L. Swetland, Jr., Yvor Winters, Mrs. David Woodcock, Morton Zabel, William Zorach, Roger Zucker, Suzanne Henig, Robert Laurent, and Walter Lowenfels.

# Note

I am grateful to each of these persons for otherwise unobtainable information; I am grateful to most of them for permission to quote from their conversations with me and their letters to Hart Crane. I should also like to thank generally the hundreds of other men and women in Ohio (especially in Garrettsville, Warren, Akron, Cleveland, and Chagrin Falls), in New York City, in Hollywood, in Mexico (especially in Mexico City, Tepoztlan, Cuernavaca, and Taxco), and in Europe (especially in Paris and in Collioure), who remembered Hart Crane or who aided me in locating men and women who remembered him.

For permission to quote from published work, I am indebted to Samuel Loveman and David Mann, literary executors of the Hart Crane Estate; Mrs. Sherwood Anderson, Peggy Baird (Cowley), Agnes Boulton, Susan Jenkins Brown, Malcolm Cowley, Brom Weber, and the copyright holders listed on the copyright page. Very brief quotations I have listed by documented sources in my notes. I am also indebted to the literary executors of the Hart Crane Estate for permission to quote from unpublished Crane letters in their control, to Arthur Pell for his letters to Grace Hart Crane, and to S. Foster Damon for permission to quote from the papers of John Brooks Wheelwright at Brown University.

Had I not been able to make use of a grant-in-aid from the American Council of Learned Societies, a grant from the American Philosophical Society, and a grant from the Council for Research in the Humanities of Columbia University, work on this book would have been considerably delayed. Much of the writing of its final sections was done in 1964–1965, when I was in Ireland and France as Fellow of the Guggenheim Foundation; much of the revision of the manuscript was accomplished while I was a guest at Yaddo during the summers of 1967 and 1968. I am indebted to Columbia University's Oral History project for typed transcriptions of a number of my taped interviews with friends of Crane, as I am similarly indebted to National Educational Television for copies of interviews that I did for the documentary film *In Search of Hart Crane*.

I am also grateful to Columbia University for taking care of some of my typing costs and for financing the services of three extraordinarily gifted research assistants: Anthony Mazzella, Thomas S. Lewis, and Alan Knight, each of whom contributed significantly to the accuracy of my manuscript. I thank them for their assistance; I am grateful for their friendship.

I am also grateful for insights into the art of Crane's poetry that I gained as a consequence of long conversations with Cecil Hemley, Herbert Leibowitz, Leo Hurwitz, Michael O'Brien, Granville Hicks, and William York Tindall.

My deepest debts, however, are private and lie in that area of affection and love that is at the core of everything I have written. Out of that area comes the tone of this book. I hold responsible for that tone my wife, Ann, whose encouragement kept me writing; Bernard Heringman, who years ago first brought the poetry of Hart Crane to my attention; James N. Wise, whose copy of Crane's published letters initiated my work on this biography; Stephanie and Roderick Craib, who were the first friends with whom I discussed this book and who read page proof when I was not able to read it; Erik Wensberg, who debated with me the proper nature of biography; and Theone T. Bob, Vyvian d'Estienne, Barbara Weinheimer, and George Weinheimer, each of whom, in morning-to-midnight conversations, let me worry out a point of view, a sense of moral responsibility in dealing—as honestly as possible—with another man's life. To these good people I credit the book's virtues; its vices are my own.

John Unterecker

*New York, April 1969*

## Note for the Paperback Edition

In rereading *Voyager*, I have asked myself what, if any, changes I would make were I to start from scratch, reworking the book completely, producing a totally "new" edition. The answer is "almost none." I would, of course, incorporate into the text the letter from Gertrude Vogt that— after the book was published—arrived just in time to be fitted into the separately published notes (and which here appears on page 812), the only eyewitness account of Crane's suicide that, so far as I know, exists. And I would probably make greater use of the letters to Wilbur Underwood—letters detailing some of Crane's sexual adventures—that I had been permitted to examine only in part and that have subsequently been published in their entirety.

I would also put greater stress on Crane's growing alcoholism, which I consciously downplayed, largely because I felt too much had been made of it by other biographers and critics. During Crane's last three years, however, his drinking became progressively more uncontrolled and, though erratic, increasingly destructive. The fact that Crane—like almost everyone in his generation—did not recognize alcoholism as a disease should, I think, have been explicitly stated, and that during the last few years of his life Crane fit into many of its capricious patterns should have been said outright.

With these exceptions, however, the book as written is the book I would write today. Hart Crane's life was complex, frequently joyous, sometimes agonizingly painful. From that rich, short, intensely lived life and from an insight into the nature of history and myth, he constructed very great poetry that has outlasted his time and that will long outlast ours.

John Unterecker

Honolulu, Hawaii, January 1987

# Illustrations

FOLLOWING PAGE 48

*The young Grace Hart Crane*
*The young Clarence (C.A.) Crane*
*Hart Crane's birthplace in Garrettsville, Ohio*
*Hart Crane, as a child*
*Hart Crane, about two years old*
*The Cleveland house where Hart Crane grew up*
*The young Hart Crane*
*A reunion of the Crane family*
*Grace Hart Crane*
*Hart Crane*
*Hart Crane, c. 1916*

FOLLOWING PAGE 358

*Hart Crane's Brooklyn room*
*The view from Hart Crane's window*
*Hart Crane, c. 1924*
*Hart Crane, Allen Tate, and William Slater Brown*
*Hart Crane, summer 1924*
*Hart Crane, summer 1926*
*Hart Crane, August 1926*
*Hart Crane, winter 1923*
*Emil Opffer*
*Waldo Frank*
*Sam Loveman*
*William Sommer*
*William Slater Brown, Susan Jenkins Brown, and their son*
*William Slater Brown and Emil Opffer*
*Peggy Robson (Margaret Babcock)*
*Malcolm Cowley*
*Hart Crane, 1929*
*Constance de Polignac, Laurence Vail, Kay Boyle, Hart Crane,*
    *and Caresse Crosby*

## Illustrations

*Harry and Caresse Crosby*
*Hart Crane, February 1929*

FOLLOWING PAGE 722

*C. A. Crane and his son*
*Hart Crane, c. 1930*
*Manuscript draft of* The Bridge
*Manuscript draft of* The Bridge
*Hart Crane, c. 1930*
*Peggy Cowley and Hart Crane*
*The Siqueiros portrait of Hart Crane*
*Hart Crane, c. February 1932*
*Peggy Cowley and Hart Crane*
*Hart Crane, c. February 1932*
*Hart Crane, c. summer 1931*

# I

In "My Grandmother's Love Letters," Hart Crane faced the biographer's problem. He recognized that the biographer deals with extraordinarily fragile material: "memory" and "letters," letters

> That have been pressed so long
> Into a corner of the roof
> That they are brown and soft,
> And liable to melt as snow.

He recognized that the biographer by his very presence may distort rather than clarify the life he uncovers.

> Over the greatness of such space
> Steps must be gentle.

And he was conscious of the biographer's gnawing doubts of his own competence.

> ... I ask myself:
> "Are your fingers long enough to play
> Old keys that are but echoes:
> Is the silence strong enough
> To carry back the music to its source
> And back to you again
> As though to her?"

No biographer, or autobiographer, can encompass a life. The crucial incident—the epiphany by the river bank; the transparent, luminous dream; the word whispered to the grass, to the wind, to the sea—is never recorded. Just as the vital element escapes, so too does the trivial. The "ordinary" day—the uneventful, peaceful afternoon or evening—slips out of mind. The day when nothing special happened vanishes.

It is easy for Hart Crane's biographer to discover an avalanche of sensational anecdotes: tales of riotous drunkenness—typewriters and phonographs flying through second-story windows; of bizarre homosexual adventures with sailors in hallways and bums in public parks; of extravagant talk and extravagant dress. But only after a good deal of probing does he discover in Hart Crane not just a talented buffoon but a man who loved reading and long country hikes; who found as much pleasure in good conversation as in good drink; who found—like most men—real joy in painting a door or in planting a garden.

Most difficult of all to reconstruct—though perhaps most important—are the years of childhood and adolescence, for documents are scarce and memories—sixty years faded—untrustworthy. Hart Crane himself would have had difficulty assembling his own early memories of Garrettsville, Ohio, where, on July 21, 1899, he was born; for by the time he was five, his father and mother—ambitious for business success—had moved to Warren, Ohio.

Of course, he would have remembered his father's house, the roomy new house built as a wedding present by Arthur Crane, Hart's grandfather. And he would have remembered Arthur Crane's own house next door, big, substantial, dominated by tall trees and wide lawns. He would have remembered the bridge, a few steps down the road from his grandfather's house, that lifted over the steep banks of a narrow river and led immediately to Garrettsville's main street. He would have remembered the feed store by the bridge and the curved mill dam a few yards upstream. He would have remembered walking to town with his grandfather to see his father's uncles, Fred and Cash—probably at Crane Brothers' store, the biggest store in Garrettsville and one in which his grandfather held a controlling interest; or perhaps at the First National Bank, in which his grandfather was a director. He would have remembered the sweet steam of his grandfather's busy maple-syrup cannery on the banks of the river above the dam, from which in one particularly good year his grandfather shipped upwards of 60,000 gallons of maple syrup. And he might have remembered rides in his grandfather's buggy along the straight dusty road that led beyond the grade school to the Crane family plot in the Garrettsville Cemetery—where, now, near the graves of Arthur Edward Crane and Frederic Jason Crane and Cassius Crane, on the face of the small granite block that marks Hart's father's grave is cut in three short lines:

HAROLD HART CRANE

1899–1932

LOST AT SEA

What Hart Crane retained from Garrettsville was, however, less a sense of place than a sense of family. He never forgot that he was born into one of the "good" families of the town—a family that, on his father's side, traced its way back through merchants and farmers to distant English ancestors, to "Pilgrim Fathers" who had arrived in America on the ship *Planter* as early as 1646, to Revolutionary War heroes, and to a relative of President John Adams.

From his grandfather and from his uncles he had heard of such early settlers of the Western Reserve as Simeon Crane, who had left Saybrook, Connecticut, in 1801 and for forty days had traveled by ox-team across the half-wild country to buy a farm in the new land near Lake Erie. He had heard stories of Elizabeth and John Streator, who, two years later, in 1803, had with their sons John and Jason and a daughter, Charity, crossed the Alleghenies in a covered wagon to found a homestead in the forest that eventually was to become Windham Township. He knew that Elizabeth Streator, his great-great-great-grandmother, had lived to be a hundred and three years old, spinning wool and knitting stockings for the soldiers of the Revolutionary War, of the War of 1812, and of the Civil War. From his grandfather he had heard of "Rollin" Crane, a boy who from childhood had been in love with war and who had volunteered personally to General Grant to take a detachment of men down the Mississippi to Lower Vicksburg, where he established the Union flag.

From his great-grandmother, Sylvina Streator Crane, he had heard tales of her father, Jason Streator, who had served two terms in the Ohio State Legislature and who so prided himself on his literary ability that he had delivered original verse orations in the legislative chambers and had written his legislative reports in carefully measured stanzas. Sylvina Crane herself, who was born September 29, 1820, and lived to the age of ninety-four was filled with anecdotes of her career: stories of the way she had learned her alphabet from the Warren *Chronicle*, lying prone on the hearth before the fireplace and copying the letters out on the bricks with charcoal; of her first experiences as a schoolteacher in a one-room log schoolhouse just west of Garrettsville, where red deer scampered out of her way each morning as she walked through the forests; of her prize pupil, Lucretia Rudolph, who later married President Garfield; and of her husband, Edward Manley Crane, who had been the first white child born in Shalersville Township. His father's family had taught him to see himself as rooted in the American pioneers.

His mother's own "good" family, the Harts, had taught him to think of himself as part of the thrifty capitalist line that had turned agrarian America into a world industrial power. They traced their line back to solid New England settlers and prosperous merchants, among them Deacon Stephen Hart, one of the most active members of Reverend Thomas Hooker's Hartford congregation. They were particularly proud of the career of Hart's grandfather, Clinton Hart, a one-time schoolteacher who, deafened in the Civil War, had established himself in Warren, Ohio, as a clothing merchant and as county treasurer before moving to Chicago to become a partner in the Sykes Steel Roofing Company.

Hart learned all the Garrettsville stories about both sides of his family, but he never quite got into focus the details of his parents' courtship and marriage. By the time he was old enough to talk, his parents were already so at odds that they had little opportunity for happy reminiscences in the presence of their son.

Yet their marriage was the result of such a whirlwind courtship that the oldest citizens of Garrettsville still remember it vividly. It is Grace Hart whom they principally remember, a breathtakingly beautiful, statuesque girl who brought with her all the glamour and excitement of Chicago society when, in the early spring of 1898, she made what she expected to be a brief Garrettsville visit to her aunt, Mrs. Belden, and her cousin Mattie.

Everyone in town had watched Clarence Crane grow up and they knew what to expect of him. He was a boy sold lock, stock, and barrel on the Horatio Alger dream of business success. Ambitious and cocky, he had gone off to Allegheny College in the fall of 1892. There he joined Phi Gamma Delta fraternity and became a close friend of N. B. Madden, a fraternity brother who later married Clarence's youngest sister, Bess. But abruptly, in the winter of 1894, halfway through his second year, Clarence had come back to Garrettsville. College studies, he had decided, were too abstract. He chose instead to take a job as a salesman, traveling for the National Biscuit Company of Akron, Ohio. After this training, he felt, he could work for his father for a while and then, if luck were with him, found a business of his own.

He was good-looking, cheerful, popular. He had a flair for drama, and he used to amuse his sisters Alice and Bess by wrapping himself in one of the long window drapes of the Garrettsville house to recite comic parodies of Hamlet's "To be or not to be" soliloquy or Mark Antony's funeral oration. Like all the Cranes in Garrettsville, Clarence was proud of his knowledge of the "classics." Not as much of a scholar as his Uncle Fred, who had composed a heavy volume of his own poems and who often startled out-of-towners by his erudition when he waited on them in Crane Brothers' store, Clarence was nevertheless fond of literature and literary games and was regarded by his family as the most inventive performer in the regular winter evening sessions of charades.

An enthusiastic actor, he was a reluctant musician. Like all of Arthur and Ella Crane's children, Clarence had his instrument—a cornet—which he played grimly and loudly. Arthur Crane was a good flutist, Bess played violin, and Alice, who later studied composition and taught music, was a promising pianist. Clarence, however, was, in his sister's words, "not good" at music.

What he was good at was the organization of picnics and parties.

It was on one of the picnics that he met Grace Hart. He and his cousin Orsa Beardsley had planned an all-day expedition to

Nelson Ledges, a picnic area near Garrettsville. Clarence was to take Jessie Sykes; Orsa was to take the glamorous girl from Chicago, Grace Hart. Preparations for the trip were elaborate, with the Crane Brothers' delivery wagon decked out in flags and flowers and the horses curried and shining. The girls themselves were resplendent, and the two couples rode the five miles to the picnic ground laughing and singing. But Clarence couldn't keep his eyes off Grace; and Orsa, perhaps to his own surprise, found himself drawn to Jessie. By nightfall the exchange had been accomplished. And within a year each of the cousins had married the girl he brought home.

Grace was, however, not to be won at a picnic; and Clarence found her indecisive and hesitant answers to his repeated marriage proposals both tantalizing and exciting. He showered her with letters and gifts, swore endless devotion, and pursued her from one end of town to the other, proposing almost daily. Finally, on the last day of her visit, he leaped on the Cleveland train to carry his suit publicly to the city.

If Grace's hesitation served to increase Clarence's passion, his seemingly inexhaustible appeals through letters, telegrams, floral tributes, and Chicago visits both entertained and flattered her. Pampered from childhood and encouraged by devoted parents and devoted suitors to see courtship and marriage as a chivalric game in which the reluctant maiden finally yields her hand, if not her virtue, to the besieging knight, Grace Edna Hart at last accepted Clarence A. Crane. Soon after, on June 1, 1898, she was married to him in a large Chicago wedding.

Grace and Clarence emerged from that wedding married to virtual strangers. Deeply in love with her beauty and charm, her eloquence and wit, Clarence found incomprehensible the fact that his wife was terrified of physical love. And she, who had imagined her husband a Galahad, found what he thought to be tender advances displays of shocking brutality. From their wedding night on, their marriage was a source of mutual agony. Never entirely out of love, each found essential characteristics of the other well-nigh unbearable.

Grace had dreamed of marriage as a continuing courtship: the good provider would return home each night to be entertained by a gracious hostess. She had imagined herself singing to him in the evening, or accompanying him, handsomely dressed, to dances and parties. Crane, on the other hand, saw marriage as the end of courtship; marriage, in his dream, could provide an outlet for the frustrations of the day. It would refresh his body in the embraces of a lovely wife; it would refresh his mind by providing a listener sympathetic to his business problems.

Clarence found his wife cold and she found her husband lustful and intemperate, but they had both been trained to keep up appearances and both worked hard to put on a show of placid dignity. Though quarrels could rise to hysteria within the walls of the new home, to the public eye the young couple was perfectly matched. When, in the winter of 1899, it was clear that a baby would be born, both families rejoiced. Clarence was an only son and Grace was her parents' favorite child. Their baby would symbolize the prosperity both families expected the new century to bring.

Harold Hart Crane was born on July 21, 1899, in the fierce heat of an Ohio summer. Though not sickly, he was considered a "delicate" child and was watched over carefully by his mother and his aunts. They waited anxiously for the first signs of the allergies that plagued the Crane family—asthma, hay fever, irritating and mysterious rashes that would appear and vanish, seemingly without cause. Eventually Crane was to suffer from all of them, but in his earliest years he surprised everyone by remaining free of such symptoms.

Even in the cradle he was precocious, and he was more precocious the moment he got out of it. He walked and talked early. He learned to read early. And he learned very early that bright sayings could bring little boys all sorts of interesting adult attention. Almost everybody in his family remembers anecdotes of these years.

His Aunt Bess still recalls her embarrassment when he arrived, not yet three years old, at the head of the stairs to shock a visiting beau from Ohio State University. She had been attempting to combine baby sitting and a social evening with her young man, when Harold suddenly appeared before them in complete disarray. He marched silently downstairs and, "in perfect rhythm," accusingly announced: "My shirt is open; my vest is open; my pants are open." Mortified, young Bess hurried him off to bed to button the offending clothes.

His father used to tell of going up to the boy's room late one night, long after Harold's normal bedtime, to find him still awake. "Why aren't you asleep?" he asked. "Because I haven't yawned yet," Harold explained.

Half a dozen people remember his first trip to the Garrettsville soda fountain. The proprietor greeted the Crane family with his usual "Well, folks, what will it be?" He was proud of the fact that he had a great variety of ice-cream sodas. Harold spoke up immediately: "I'll have a codfish soda, please."

These are anecdotes his aunts liked to recall. But other anecdotes troubled them. His Aunt Bess still wonders if she was right to forbid him to play in the big bandboxes of dressmaking materials that filled an under-the-stairs closet of his parents' home. He has just turned three, when suddenly all his energy seemed to go into decoration. For days he played with the bright materials, amusing his mother by trimming and modeling her wide hats in most ingenious ways. Feathers and buttons, velvet and lace were arranged and rearranged on the broad hat brims. Soon he began to collect discarded hats from other ladies in the family. It was all right, Bess felt, for a very young boy to play with dolls, but this seemed too much—the boy playing alone in the big house, sorting through box after box of buttons and bows, watched only by an indulgent mother. When one day Harold set to work on his aunt's new hat, he sealed his doom. Bess convinced Grace that such effeminate amusements were not in the boy's best interests. "He cried for two days," she recalls; and she wonders now if "getting it out of his system" might not, after all, have been best for him.

Generally in those days he was by himself. There were other children in the neighborhood, Mrs. Scott, a Garrettsville neighbor, remembered; but Harold did not have anything to do with them. Instead, he wandered about the joined double lawns of the two big houses, stopping to admire garden flowers or to talk to his aunts as they hung up clothes on the line back of his grandfather's house. He seemed to Mrs. Scott "sweet and strange."

Only after Clarence and Grace moved to Warren, Ohio, late in 1903, did Harold discover the rough-and-tumble world outside his family circle—a world of playmates his own age and schoolground games.

The move to Warren had been planned carefully. Arthur Crane and Clarence were convinced that the best local distribution of maple syrup could be made from Warren, a town considerably larger than Garrettsville, though Garrettsville was in the heart of the producing district and had since 1840 been famous for the quality of its product. Clarence was now twenty-nine years old, and he and his father felt he should be able to handle a business of his own. Clarence had, moreover, strong objections to his father's insistence on the "purity" of his product. Clarence felt that a mixture of corn syrup and maple syrup could produce an inexpensive product of good flavor. The opportunity for him to own his own business came when Grace's father, late in 1902, sold out his steel interests to retire to Cleveland. With part of what was by this time a considerable fortune, he financed the construction of a Warren canning factory.

The business prospered beyond Clarence's expectations. C.A., as he began to call himself in these years, knew the suppliers of the raw syrup and aggressively sought new outlets. Within five years his sales were running ahead of production and he was able to sell his business to the Corn Products Refining Company of Chicago. Not only did he reap a substantial capital gain on his investment, he also persuaded the purchasing company to take him on as manager of a newly built Warren plant. Here, with a much greater opportunity to exercise his business skill, he devoted a great deal of time to the study of new ways to market sugar and to package it. (He was one of the first American businessmen to realize the possibilities of cellophane as a packaging material and imported it from France long before it was available from American suppliers.)

His new position brought him a fine salary and gave him and his wife opportunities to travel—separately. C.A. would be on the road for weeks on end, buying sugar and calling on customers. Grace would arrange for his aunts to take care of Harold in Garrettsville and would herself go to Chicago to visit relatives and friends. There she would return to the carefree life she had led before marriage.

On these visits to his birthplace, Harold charmed neighbors, grandparents, and aunts. He seemed to his Aunt Bess a child who had a "visionary aspect." He would sit for hours at the piano working out simple, delicate melodies. During one of these sessions, as she dusted the furniture, Bess stopped to listen. Harold, six or seven, worked at the keyboard, concentrating on the sounds, playing softly, barely touching the keys. "What do you call it, Harold?" Bess asked. Harold paused for a moment, his fingers hovering above the keyboard. "I call it," he began and then paused to sound a note, "I call it 'The Lamb's First Morning.' "

The image that emerges from Harold's Warren years is that of a boy eager—sometimes desperately eager—to please everyone. Accidental or deliberate wit could earn affection—as on the day young Harold amused his grandfather in the grape arbor by pointing to a cluster of ripening grapes and asking, "Grandfather, when are you going to pick your peas?" And half-conscious flattery could win affection—as on the day his Aunt Bess, concerned at his musing over his absent mother, interrupted her work to ask: "Oh, Harold, what will ever become of you if something happens to your mother?" His face luminous, the boy answered softly, "I'll always have my Aunt Bess."

But he needed more than Aunt Bess. He needed the love and affection of his parents, who seemed always out of reach and whom nothing could quite please. Here, when all else failed, illness succeeded.

His mother remembered to the end of her days the sudden attacks of nausea and fever that began in these years, attacks that no doctor was able to explain. Though in Warren Harold had at last found playmates and seemed to them a normal, well-adjusted boy, to his parents he still was "delicate." Now his abrupt ailments would be understood in terms of psychosomatic illness; but in 1906 it was not so easy to associate a casual criticism from a much-loved parent with the sudden "fit" that would follow swiftly on it.

Harold had in mother and father excellent models from whom to learn the full range of emotional disturbance. He could watch the effect of Grace's sharp tongue on his father, who, as much as

Harold, was dependent on her unpredictable affections; observing parental "scenes," he experienced at second-hand the power of her ridicule.

It was this ridicule—in her eyes gentle, in his lacerating—that accounted for the nausea that followed his delivery of birthday best wishes to the wrong Mrs. Hall. His mother had decided that a clever birthday greeting could be managed if she dressed Harold in his best and sent him off to their neighbor to present a birthday card. Harold was more than willing to go. But he misunderstood his mother's directions and went blocks away to his favorite Miss Hall, one of two maiden sisters. Miss Hall had been pleased to see him, and when he burst into "Happy birthday, Miss Mary," she, though celebrating no birthday, applauded the bright young boy. She chatted with him in the ornate Victorian parlor that always seemed to him both wonderful and mysterious, accepted the birthday card, and sent him smiling home. He strode through the front door triumphant and told his mother the full story of his mission.

Grace found the comedy of errors amusing and pointed out to him how funny it must have seemed to Miss Hall to get Mrs. Hall's birthday card. But there was no amusement in the story for Harold, and though Grace continued to regard it as a joke, Harold could not laugh. After supper, when she retold the story for C.A.'s benefit, Harold went to bed—and was soon seized by waves of vomiting and hysterical tears.

Ridicule seems also to have been responsible for a similar "fit" later that summer. C.A., in his sudden prosperity, had purchased a motorcar for himself and a new carriage for his wife. Both of them enjoyed country rides, slow drives along the winding back roads that lifted up into the shining hills of eastern Ohio. They would often drive for miles to discover a new "vista." By midsummer, however, Grace felt the need for a more social sort of holiday, and Mr. Crane arranged to take a two-week vacation on Mackinac Island.

The trip should have been a success, and in many ways it did help heal the widening split between Grace and her husband. For Harold, however, it was a source of anxiety. Grace had prepared him for the great event of life in a resort hotel by daily instruction in good table manners. In reasonably happy sessions at home he had been taught to keep his elbows off the table and his feet flat on the floor. He had been warned that a gentleman always rises in the presence of ladies and that, should ladies stop to chat, he should gracefully get up from his chair and stand by the table as long as the guests stayed.

The excitement of arrival at the gaily decorated hotel, the bustle as his parents registered, the process of being escorted to his room by a uniformed bellhop keyed up Harold immensely. Then came dressing for dinner and entrance into the resplendent dining room where, he knew, his skills were going to be put to the test. He could tell from his beaming mother that elbows and feet were behaving as they should. Then, seemingly out of nowhere, friends appeared. His father rose automatically; but Harold was busy watching his mother and sat on, admiring the ease with which she kept the conversation flowing along. In a moment the friends left and C.A. took his seat to return to his meal. Grace turned her attention to Harold; he must have waited for praise, his hands in his lap and his feet firm on the floor. He must have watched her beautiful smile tumble into laughter, realized that she was laughing at him, the awkward son who did not know enough to rise in the presence of ladies. "What will people think of you?" she asked, and the familiar, teasing ridicule began.

Harold had no defenses against her, and he would not have for years to come. One unkind word, a statement from her that he had embarrassed her or in any way hurt her would send him into deep self-accusing torments. Hadn't she told him over and over in their secret talks that he was all she had, that she counted on him to take care of her in her old age, that he meant more to her than mother or father or husband, that without him life was meaningless?

Harold sat through the rest of the meal in silence, automatically eating dessert and drinking his milk. By his bedtime both mother and father had forgotten the incident but were concerned to find Harold feverish. They questioned him in detail, searching for symptoms. Within a few hours it was clear that the boy was seriously ill and the hotel doctor was called. Yet nothing seemed to be organically wrong and the doctor was as mystified as the parents. For two days Harold lay in bed, his fever dangerously high, Grace dutifully at his bedside comforting him, reading to him, telling him of her love for him, planning adventures with him as soon as he recovered. Suddenly, as quickly as it had started, the fever broke. Only after their return to Warren was light shed on Harold's mysterious illness. Grace made a casual reference to it; Harold, in reply, referred to the incident at the table. At that point, Grace later said, the cause of the illness became clear.

Perhaps the nausea that followed Mrs. Hall's misdirected birthday card and the fever in the hotel had causes other than psychosomatic. But causes were less significant than the interpretation mother and son assigned to the illnesses. For in each case Grace and Harold came to believe that illness was a direct result of the mother's unkindness or insensitivity. And such belief strengthened the already strong bond between mother and son. Convinced that each could make the other ill simply by withholding love, they discovered the extent of their dependence on each other and something of the way their real power over each other operated. Illness could be brought on by apparent lack of love and yet be used to test love—to prove that, behind superficial slights, vast reserves of love lay waiting to effect miraculous recoveries.

C.A. and Grace also tested their love, but in far more violent ways and with far more destructive results. Perhaps the most spectacular incident took place soon after they had moved to Warren. Grace had always taken great pride in her physical beauty and no one, with the possible exception of her son, admired her more than her husband. She was also proud of her voice. She had studied singing in Chicago, where her voice had been praised for its "Italian" quality. One of her first public gestures on coming to Warren was to agree to appear in a benefit concert. C.A. thought that her performance might prove embarrassing and attempted to dissuade her from going on. As the date drew near, both Grace and C.A. became increasingly irritable, and C.A. threatened to boycott the proceedings. Finally, however, he consented to be part of the audience. He remained in his seat until Grace began to sing. Then deliberately and conspicuously he rose and left the hall. Grace never forgave him.

Too much, of course, can be made of such scenes. The melodramatic events are the memorable ones, and from such material one can turn mother or father into villain. Crane did just that, siding, through childhood and adolescence, with his mother until he had turned his father into an image of monstrous vice, a figure greedy, cruel, lascivious. Through all of Harold's early years, Grace's descriptions of C.A.'s conduct fed fuel to the fire. Her account of an ill-fated attempt at reconciliation after their divorce particularly embittered her son. "I have just read your letter," the eighteen-year-old boy wrote, "and find it hard to express my rage and disgust at what you say concerning C. A. Crane's conduct. 'Forget him,' is all I can say. He is too low for consideration. I am only quietly waiting,—stifling my feelings in the realization that I might as well get as much money as possible out of him. Why be scrupulous in one's dealings with unscrupulous people, anyway?"

When, ten years later, Hart quarreled with his mother and finally broke with her, he developed as inaccurate a picture of her as he had had of his father. He then found it possible to believe any scandal which touched her. In drunken "confessions" he told ugly anecdotes intended to prove her deceitful, even diseased. Convinced that she had withheld from him a legacy left by his grandmother, he threatened her with legal action and took grim pleasure in hiding his address from her and in refusing to answer letters she managed to get to him through friends.

In fact, neither Crane's mother nor his father was villain, though each at times cast the other in that role. To see each of them in some sort of perspective, we must free ourselves from chronology to look at the whole design of each life.

The pattern of C.A.'s career was very early established and, as he himself came later to realize, was dominated by two great drives: that toward business success and that toward the security of marital love. In falling under the sway of the first drive, Crane was a product of his times: he read and believed all the stories of the empire builders and with enormous energy fought out for himself a place in the sun. His success follows a familiar formula, in his case cracker salesman to candy executive, and though he did not rise from rags to riches (his was a rise from white collar to dress suit), he managed to give his son—and some of the employees of his Crane Chocolate Company—the false impression that he was a millionaire. At various times he had, in addition to his Cleveland factory, as many as five candy stores in Cleveland, several in nearby towns, restaurants in Cleveland, Chagrin Falls, and Hudson, Ohio, a wholesale business that included outlets in New York, Chicago, and Kansas City, and a sometimes profitable side line, the large-scale reproduction of famous oil paintings. As an employer, he was both hard-driving and fair. He worked very hard himself and he expected a good deal of his employees. Since he was in no way standoffish, he regarded most of them as his friends. He called them by their first names and worried about them in a paternalistic fashion.

His other great drive, to experience a satisfying marital love, accounts for the eighteen-year-long effort he made to find some way to please what seemed, at least to others, a beautiful but cold wife. Both sentimental and passionate, C.A. used all the instruments in his power to win Grace's affection. Yet affection of any lasting sort was what she seemed least able to give him. Even after their divorce, he wrote her flattering letters. He catered to her desire to travel. He showered her with gifts, everything from roses to automobiles. Yet, in spite of all these efforts, Grace responded only slightly. Each response, however, seemed to him a sign that the warm, full love he always wanted would eventually be his.

From Grace's point of view, however, he was an unfaithful husband attempting to buy his way back into her affections. Unwilling or unable to accept him as he was, she sought out rumors of his sexual adventures. Accusations led to quarrels and quarrels to new attempts at reconciliation.

C.A.'s divorce from Grace came in his forty-second year. After it, he was lonelier than in the days of their angry quarrels, and in the summer of 1917, only a few months after the divorce had taken effect, he came close to remarrying her. For a few weeks C.A. courted Grace almost as intensely as he had nineteen years before. And but for a quarrel over Harold's future, the remarriage might have taken place. The threat of a renewal of the old bickering was too much, however, and he abruptly left town, writing Grace a hasty note that urged her to "forget C. A. Crane."

Though C.A. was never to forget Grace, he found in Kansas City, Missouri, a woman who seemed to offer all he was searching for. One year after his angry flight from Grace, almost to the day, C. A. Crane and Frances Kelley were married. That marriage promised to be a happy one, but Frances soon suffered a series of mysterious illnesses. In the fall of 1926 it was learned that she had an incurable cancer. "I did not answer your letter," C.A. wrote his son a few days after he heard the news. "It came to me at a time when I first discovered my Frances could not recover from her present illness, and I have been so nearly crazed with grief from that day to this that I am in no condition now to write you a very satisfactory letter. . . . I hope you are well and happy. If so, you are the only member of the Crane family who is." That year and the next were for C.A. especially dark ones. As his wife lay dying, his business enterprises began to seem more and more meaningless; yet only in business could he free himself from a feeling of helplessness, and he occupied his time with plans that ranged from the construction of new restaurants to a scheme to join a Canadian mining venture.

Frances's death on January 3, 1928, drove C.A. deeper into business activity. The previous spring he had bought two neighboring cottages in the village of Chagrin Falls. These, skillfully joined, were to become a quality restaurant that could serve as many as three hundred guests at one meal and that could provide as well an out-of-town home for Mr. Crane. "This seems to be the best escape yet suggested for my troubles," he wrote his son.

His troubles soon became financial ones, for in 1929 his enterprises were threatened by the general economic collapse. Yet 1929 was for C.A. a year of great happiness. Among his associates in the firm was a young woman capable of love and devotion, outgoing and affectionate, sensible, sensitive, and mature. Late in the year he asked her to marry him; and on January 25, 1930, at the Old Stone Church in Cleveland, Miss Bessie Meacham became the third Mrs. C. A. Crane.

By now set in his ways, a businessman noted for his honesty and his tenacity, a man who had at last relaxed into a cheerful gruffness, C.A. found within his grasp everything he had always wanted. Though he was overweight and had been warned by his doctors to beware hardening of the arteries, he was apparently in good health. His wife, an excellent businesswoman willing to work as hard as he, did more than her share in supervising the restaurant. Almost to his own surprise, his son returned for a visit that was marked by mutual, and very satisfying, respect. "This turns out to be a wonderful place," Hart wrote his friend Sam

Loveman, "—such furniture (early American) and such duck and chicken! The time will pass very easily. Feel as though I had a home at last. Six great fireplaces burning—and dad's cigars!"

At the time of his fifty-sixth birthday, on April 7, 1931, Clarence Crane found that the disordered fragments of his life had pulled into focus. He had married a woman who loved him and whom he loved. His business seemed able to survive the Depression. Though he could not entirely understand the poetry of his son, who was in Mexico on a Guggenheim fellowship, he knew that it was considered good and that, in his own field, his son had become a success. He was happy. On July 6, 1931, at eight-thirty in the morning as he stopped at the Chagrin Falls post office for his mail, he suffered a stroke. Within a matter of hours he was dead of a cerebral hemorrhage.

The events of his life are clear enough. But what had C. A. Crane been?

To his sister Bess he had always been "the very best of brothers. He was so kind, so generous. Once he gave us a Packard car instead of trading it in. Another time—I remember it yet—he saw a woman crying on a street corner in Warren. She had no money; and, though C.A. had very little in those days, he took her to the store and bought her a whole load of vegetables. He loved people. He just loved them. He'd come up from Warren with his car loaded with people—just so they could have the ride."

To a man who worked for him in Cleveland at the time of the divorce, "C.A. was a bull of a man. He was big, heavy set, and he knew what he was after. Harold always thought he and his father were worlds apart, but you only had to see the two of them together to know they were father and son. And they both had the same sort of intensity, the same sort of drive; and they were both passionate men. With C.A. it was business and women. With Harold it was poetry and men. But it came to the same thing, really. They both had the same sort of drive. They were just alike."

To Grace, he had been a jealous tyrant.

To Bess, his third wife, he had been "a good man."

To Hart he had seemed at times a man guilty of "disgraceful and unaccountable" behavior, at others "of as many good inclinations as bad ones"; sometimes he had seemed "pettily dictatorial" and sometimes "much pleasanter than I expected him to be." At the end, after C.A.'s death, Hart tried to summarize his feelings in a letter to his oldest friend, William Wright. His father, he wrote, was a man of "fine qualities" with a "genuine love" for his son. "I can say that his character and the impress of it that I lately received will be a real inspiration to me."

C.A.'s life had moved from early passion to settled, happy calm. Grace Crane's life moved from sheltered, wealthy innocence to poverty-stricken and isolated old age. Just before her death, Grace, who in her youth had been regally beautiful, was working as a combination baby-sitter, cook, and scrub woman. Her money was gone. Her home and her belongings had been sold as, shifting from "desirable" to "less desirable" jobs and neighborhoods—from hotel manager to restaurant hostess to invalid's companion to drudge—she worked her way through the Depression into years of stoical resignation. "Try to see as many of the old friends as possible," she wrote Sam Loveman in the summer of 1941, "—and don't worry about *anything*. What's the use—"

Ironically, as Grace Crane lost her fortune and her looks and came finally to depend almost entirely on hard physical labor to earn enough on which to survive, she gained in dignity. In her early years, dignity had been reserved for visitors or used as a defense against domestic responsibility. In her last years there was no one left to impress and she came to an honest acceptance of the facts of her life.

She came even to accept the fact that her son had rejected her—though not the fact that his rejection would have been irrevocable had he lived. The force that gave shape and purpose to Grace's life after Hart's death was her devotion to his memory. From the time in 1932 immediately after his suicide when she had claimed his baggage, she dedicated her life with single-minded intensity to the establishment of his reputation. She began almost immediately to search for a good editor to assemble a collected edition of his poems, eventually settling on Waldo Frank for the job. She worked diligently to collect Hart's correspondence in the hope of seeing into print an edition of his letters. She encouraged Sam Loveman to give every assistance to Frank in the editing of the poems. Later she worked with Philip Horton, Crane's first biographer, to whom she gave detailed accounts of her son's early years.

In the middle thirties her concern over her final break with Hart became obsessive. She thought of nothing else and, perhaps seeking some kind of forgiveness, consulted a spirit medium who agreed to put her in touch with her dead son. For months Grace and the medium labored to compile a volume of material purportedly from Hart—consoling messages, bits of advice, even drafts of poems. The latter caused her a great deal of concern, and she suggested to Waldo Frank that he publish them as "posthumous works" in a new edition of *The Collected Poems*, a suggestion that Mr. Frank—as delicately as possible—rejected.

She died, as she had lived, thinking of her son. Sam Loveman—perhaps Hart's most faithful friend, certainly her most faithful one—had been called to Holy Name Hospital in Teaneck, New Jersey, on July 30, 1947, when it was clear that she had little time to live. She was in a coma when he arrived, but as he stood by her bed she revived long enough to tell him how she wished distributed what little remained of her property. She told Sam that she wanted him to be literary executor for her estate and for Hart's. "Who is this lady?" a nurse asked. "The mother of Hart Crane, a very great and brilliant American poet," Sam answered. As he turned back to her, Grace spoke her last words: "Poor boy."

# 2

In 1908 in Warren, Ohio, neither Grace nor C.A. could dream of death. They were far too engrossed in a bitter quarrel that towered out of control until the family was literally torn apart. Grace, suffering from a nervous breakdown and threatening divorce, entered a private sanatorium for an extended rest cure; C.A., almost equally distraught, wound up his Warren business activities and moved to Chicago to work out of the local office of the Corn Products Refining Company. Harold was shipped off to Cleveland to live with Grandmother and Grandfather Hart until some solution to his parents' problems could be worked out.

The nine-year-old who so suddenly left Warren took with him a good deal more material from which to make poetry than did the boy who had left Garrettsville five years before. Of Garrettsville, all that remains in Crane's work is a reference to an aria Grace sang:

"Connais tu le pays . . . ?"

Your mother sang that in a stuffy parlor
One summer day in a little town
Where you had started to grow.
And you were outside as soon as you
Could get away from the company
To find the only rose on the bush
In the front yard . . . . . .

But in Warren he had become a keen observer of the world he saw around him, storing up memories for the poem that was to become *The Bridge*. He remembered his father's brown tile cannery at the southwest corner of Franklin and South Pine Streets, the steaming smells of maple syrup that filtered out of it, and behind it the hoboes dotted along the freight siding:

Behind
My father's cannery works I used to see
Rail-squatters ranged in nomad raillery,

> The ancient men—wifeless or runaway
> Hobo-trekkers that forever search
> An empire wilderness of freight and rails.
> Each seemed a child, like me, on a loose perch,
> Holding to childhood like some termless play.

And he remembered details from his early reading when, as he "hurried off to school" at the old Central Grammar School on Harmon Street, he walked "with Pizarro in a copybook," and thought of Cortés and of "Priscilla's cheek" and of

> . . . Captain Smith, all beard and certainty,
> And Rip Van Winkle bowing by the way . . .

He liked grade school, and his second- and third-grade teachers, Zilla Spear and Mary Izant, liked him. Each ranked him in the "A-Division" of his class.

Like school memories, recollections of his home at 249 High Street became a part of his poetry.

> The cinder pile at the end of the backyard
> Where we stoned the family of young
> Garter snakes under . . . And the monoplanes
> We launched—with paper wings and twisted
> Rubber bands . . .

And harsher memories of the home on North Park Avenue to which his family moved in 1908, of

> . . . the whip stripped from the lilac tree
> One day in spring my father took to me

and of

> . . . the Sabbatical, unconscious smile
> My mother almost brought me once from church
> And once only, as I recall . . .

There were also friends and relatives he would not forget. There was a neighbor, Mrs. Sutcliff, a lively old lady who told stories of log cabins, bears, and Indians. There was C. Courtney Denison, a classmate in second and third grade who had lived across High Street from young Harold, and who remembered nearly sixty years later the brown-eyed, active boy whose birthday parties he had attended and who "had everything that money could buy and so easily could have been a snob" but "who never showed any signs of feeling himself better than the other boys of the neighborhood, played in all their games just as a normal member of the group, and was a favorite in that group." And there was Harold's Aunt Zell, interested in books and in painting, and her daughter Helen, a bright-eyed lively little girl.

But young Harold's principal experience in Warren was that of an outdoor world of streams and open country and forests, a world that would always be with him and that, in one way or another, he would attempt to return to for the rest of his life: by hiking down Riverside Drive when he lived in New York City; by escaping from Cleveland and Akron for long country walks along the Brandywine with his artist-friend Bill Sommer or Bill's son Ray; by trying to scrape together money to buy a Connecticut hillside; by retreating from Mexico City to the high-valley country near Tepoztlan.

It was this outdoor world that would eventually inform his poetry with an imagery of "lakes and hills," "mill-race," "dog-wood," "the loam of prairies," "cowslip and shad-blow."

"He was really just a big country boy," William Spratling, who had known him in the last year of his life in Mexico, said: "You know the type. He looked as if he'd just come in fresh off the farm."

"My memory I left in a ravine," Hart Crane wrote.

For Harold, that 1908 move from Warren to Cleveland was more than a move from small town to booming city. It was a move into new and totally unexpected freedoms. He had a room of his own, servants to wait on him, an indulgent grandmother to cater to each whim. From this time on, her house at 1709 East 115th Street would be "home."

The building itself was a large, three-story frame structure that filled most of the fifty-five-foot width of the deep lot on which it had been constructed. By far its most conspicuous feature was a pair of turrets which jutted up above the rest of the roof and which set it off vividly from the more conventional houses closely flanking it. In summer the wide front porch and second-story windows were decorated with gay striped awnings and shaded by a neighbor's young maple tree. In winter afternoons the houses across the street cast long shadows on the high-banked snow of the front yard and over the windows of the first two floors. But winter and summer the twin tall circular towers, cone-capped, accepted the full flood of afternoon light, their windows facing due west into the sunset. Harold's was the north tower. Until he was seventeen, it would be his room, and he would think of it as his room until the house was sold, a week after his twenty-sixth birthday, in the summer of 1925.

At first a good place to store his toys, this "ivory tower," as Harold promptly named it, soon became refuge and sanctuary. Cherishing its privacy, he funneled more and more of his life into it. Toys gave way to books; a desk was installed, a Morris chair, a phonograph, and finally a Corona portable typewriter. From his antique four-poster roped bed in the deep-arched alcove at the back of the room, he could look out over his private world, or, settled in his chair smoking forbidden cigars and reading forbidden books, he could experience exotic sensual delights.

Any biographical interpretation of a poet's imagery is, I think, rightly suspect. Yet towers loom ominously in Crane's life and in his poetry, and it is not unlikely that the northwest attic room was at least partial prototype for all those towers—some ivory, some steel, some flesh—that strike the perceptive reader of Crane's letters and of his poetry. From the "highest tower" of "Recitative" through all the towers of *The Bridge*—the "sea's green crying towers," "the high wheat tower," "the way-up nickel-dime tower," and the city's "ticking towers"—to the "lofty tower" of "The Broken Tower," "a tower that is not stone," one finds obsessive tower imagery and imagery obviously associated with towers— spires, cupolas (Old Mizzentop of *The Bridge* and of the vivid letters to Peggy Cowley, for instance), volcanoes, geysers, and royal palms. Cumulatively they constitute a symbol that cannot be dismissed simply as "phallic symbol." For Crane's towers merge associations that are religious, erotic, aspirational, domestic, and historical. "The Broken Tower" is not "explained" by our knowing that much of Crane's adolescence was spent in a tower room he called "ivory," yet knowing that he cherished such a place helps us sense a private world that moves behind his public poetry.

Awareness of such personal associations should not, I think, influence us in judging any poem as a work of art; but it can help us comprehend part of the poet's creative process. We can see some of the ways personal material is worked and reworked until it is no longer personal. Transformed by their setting, Crane's towers carry for the poet private values. They concern us only as we are interested in the genesis of poetry rather than the final product.

In his earliest years in Cleveland, Crane's tower room was only a place for sleeping; he spent less time there than he did roaming the neighborhood or investigating all the possibilities of city life. Cleveland was then thrusting east along Euclid Avenue, an expanding city that had just made plans for a high-speed rapid-transit system to take care of outlying suburbs, and that each year had enormously increased its rail and harbor facilities.

By taking the yellow Euclid Avenue trolley, he could explore the downtown area, its department stores and theaters. And on spring weekends and in the summer, after Fairmount Elementary School had closed its doors for the year, he could go on long walks in nearby Wade Park or, down toward the lake, in Rockefeller Park.

At home there was his grandmother, nearly seventy but still lively and spry, who bustled about the kitchen entertaining him with stories of her girlhood in Akron, her schooldays at West Farmington Western Reserve Academy, her experiences as a schoolteacher during the Civil War and her memories of marriage and motherhood. Sitting on the back porch with Harold in those days before the outbreak of World War I, she would tell stories of his mother's childhood; or, steadying the ladder for him as he climbed into the black cherry tree at the far end of the back yard, she would work out with him bright plans for his own future. In the months immediately after his arrival in Cleveland, she was for him companion, confidante, and friend. Even-tempered and cheerful, she contrasted sharply with his volatile parents.

For a time, at least, his parents themselves seemed to change. By 1909 Grace had returned home. She felt she had been "helped" by her stay in the sanatorium. She was also optimistic that in Christian Science, then a new and vital religious movement, she and her family could find relief from the emotional storms that seemed regularly to overwhelm them. Grace and her mother set themselves to study sessions, diligently working through the scriptures assembled by Mary Baker Eddy, convinced that by right-thinking Mind could triumph over the ills and the temptations that beset Flesh. Partly as a result of Grace's religious fervor, the family reassembled itself. C.A., anxious to please his wife, agreed to abandon a lukewarm family affiliation in the Methodist Episcopal Church. Harold, too, was persuaded to study Mary Baker Eddy's teachings and through the rest of his grade-school years and into high school attended, with increasing irregularity, the Christian Science Sunday school.

There were also other forces that helped bring the family together. Both Grace's and C.A.'s parents were, after 1910, in Cleveland. C.A.'s father and mother, having sold the Garrettsville syrup business, had purchased as an investment an apartment house at 2033 Cornell Road and soon after bought a house across from the Hart house on 115th Street. The major interest of both families in these years was C.A.'s new business. One of his longest selling trips for the Corn Products Refining Company had taken him across the continent to Victoria, British Columbia. There he had discovered a chocolate which struck him as outstanding. Both his father and his father-in-law encouraged him to investigate the possibilities of producing it in the Cleveland area. C.A. set to work immediately to negotiate with the Canadian manufacturer for the sale of the formula. After repeated efforts to purchase the formula failed, he had a sample of the chocolate analyzed and from that analysis developed a chocolate of his own. By April 1911 he had organized a company with a capital of about $13,000, some of the money being provided by Grace and her father.

During the two years in which C.A. organized his business— much of the time traveling to secure orders for his "Queen Victoria Chocolates"—the pattern of Harold's life settled into a fairly steady routine. School was his main concern; but more exciting than school was the public library. His first surviving letters—typed notes to his father and to his mother—reveal a good deal about

Harold's precocity and show how early had been established his interest in the arts. The first letter, dated June 2, 1910, was addressed to his father, who had taken Grace with him on a business trip to Chicago. The letter was most carefully "arranged" on the page.

My dear Father: —

I had written to Mother so many times that I thought I would write to you this time. It is raining very hard out doors. I just came home from the Library with a new book called Mr. Wind and Madm. Rain The day before yesterday I had my test in Spelling, and stood 100. I got your little note the other day and Mothers letter this morning and I am expecting you home Sunday morning to eat breakfast with us. It will seem good to have you back again. Tell Mother that I am brushing my teeth everyday. With much love to you and Mother.

Sincerely your son<br>Harold

One suspects that spelling must have been a sore subject between Harold and his father (as his tooth-brushing habits must have been with his mother). The next letter, addressed to Grace, was much more informal in tone—it was probably not written under the supervision of Grandmother Hart—and is recklessly liberal in spelling and punctuation. Dated November 5, 1910, it is written on C.A.'s old Warren stationery and typed on a machine with a vivid, purple-indelible ribbon.

My dear Mother—

I have been going to write you for a long time but I have been so busy with my home work that I have not had time.

This afternoon we all went to the Hipp. and I never saw a better show Eva Tangua was the princepul feature of the show. She was even better than I thought she would be. She had seven new gowns and the were beautiful just the kind I like.

I got your letter and we were glad to get it.

Tuesday night Grandpa and Grandma [Crane] invited me to supper and after supper we all went to here Elmensdorfs lecture on the Art Galliers in Europe He told us when all the pictures were painted and showed us the exact picture on canvass and told us much more and I enjoyed it very much. That night I stayed at Grandpas, and went to school in the morning.

Father has writen two or three letters.

We are all well and happy.

With much love<br>Harold Crane.

It is characteristic of Harold that his father's correspondence should be an afterthought in a letter that is principally about painting and theater. These interests, shared with Grace, were already of great importance. From the very beginning, Harold loved the theater—the whole business of makeup and make-believe, the effect of costume, the quality of double lives as one person for a while became another.

His interest in painting was—even in his eleventh year—completely serious. Like most children, he had amused himself with crayons and water colors; unlike most children, however, he showed talent. An impressionistic oil painting which he produced in his ninth year reveals a fine sense of muted color, and later drawings show a powerful, effective line. Almost from the beginning, he was concerned with design and composition, an interest in the formal problems of painting that never left him. Later, from the time he was sixteen until the end of his life, painters were among his closest friends; in discussions with them he evolved many of his most valuable aesthetic theories.

By the time Harold was ten he was also taking piano lessons—usually from his Aunt Alice. He was always impatient to get on to new material, refusing to work out the harmony exercises she would set for him or to practice his regular assignments. "I'm too nervous," he would explain. Instead, he would bring to her carefully practiced pieces which he had found toward the back of his graded lesson books. "He always wanted to play whatever I was working on," she recalled. "If I were working on a Chopin étude one week, I'd find him prepared the next week to play the first few bars of that Chopin étude. But he never really finished anything. He was far too impatient." What he liked were pieces with a heavy rhythmic pattern. "He liked the 'Marche Grotesque.' He'd play it over and over, each time a little louder. Grace simply couldn't stand it. 'Harold,' she said one time, 'I don't want you to ever play that piece again.'" But Harold, hammering away at the big upright piano in his grandmother's back parlor, played valiantly and loudly on.

"He was always talking about painting and writing in those days," his aunt told me. "He'd sometimes come to my studio several times a week. I think it was there, in fact, that he decided he wanted to be a poet. I had a very fine library—standard collections of all the good authors: Emerson, Whitman, Hugo, Browning. Once he stood there looking at all the books. 'This is a wonderful collection, Aunt Alice,' he said. He ran his fingers through his hair—he had a habit of doing that—and then he turned to me, very seriously: 'This is going to be my vocation,' he said. 'I'm going to be a poet.'"

But before Harold Crane became a poet he had to pass through a difficult adolescence.

On the surface, his experiences were not appreciably different from those of other boys his age. School and his music lessons took a good deal of time. Though he substituted reading for most outdoor games, he managed to see enough of the neighborhood children to become familiar with the popular eighth-grade vices. He tried out smoking—first a pipe and later cigars filched from his father's private supply. In his class at school he talked a good deal about the attractions of "the ladies." And he once disturbed his mother considerably when she found him at the end of the garden playing a little too intimately with a neighbor's daughter.

Yet, behind this superficial pattern of fairly conventional behavior, Harold was beginning to store up complex feelings of guilt and affection. Sometime between his twelfth and sixteenth years he had his first homosexual experience—an almost casual seduction by a young man who worked for the family. Too much, I think, can be made of this encounter, but that it set a pattern for Crane's later life seems undeniable. Perhaps the most accurate way to interpret his early homosexual activity, however, is in terms of adolescent experimentation. All accounts of his high-school years point to a boy overwhelmed by a sensuous world. In love with colors, smells, and sounds—the hundreds of stimuli which touched his body—he found the body itself miraculous. In these years his sexual experiences were part of a general exploration of the possibilities of flesh, part of a constant search for new ways in which to gratify the senses. They were not involved with any feeling of love. That experience, more terrible and far more devastating, would be reserved for later, and would be for Hart deeply traumatic. His early encounters were, so far as can now be determined, chiefly important in furthering in Crane a kind of secretiveness. Deliberately, carefully, he began in these years the construction of an elaborate series of public and private personalities. These masks, remarkably successful, presented to each of his worlds a different face. At school, where his interests, according to his Aunt Alice, had already drifted away from "fact" toward "imagination," he was a polite, quiet boy, unobtrusive and inconspicuous. At home, especially for his mother, he played the role of young artist. To some of his friends he was a boy philosopher. To others, he was expert at retelling the sophisticated tales he was already reading. Only in the security of his room did he have to deal with reconciling the different faces he presented the world. He must have struggled with the problem of his "real self" and felt the tug of sharply divided loyalties: loyalties to the "vices" he had to hide from mother and father and grandmother; and other loyalties, more complex still, to the three people in whom his life was centered.

Certainly he came to feel deeply the division between his father and his mother. He was no longer the little boy who used to endear himself to Grace by coming to her bedside and standing silently beside her in the dark on nights when C.A., angered by a quarrel, had marched out of the house; yet he was still caught up inextricably in her charms. He told her that she was more beautiful than any of the girls his own age—his real sweetheart, he said. He felt that she was much more in need of his protection than any "common girls" could ever be. So long as he could count on her affection, he once told her, he could do without puppy love.

And yet he responded also to his sometimes serious, sometimes humorous, and always unpredictable father, who, frequently out of town on his business trips, wrote regularly and warmly to wife and son. Harold had to find ways to reconcile that father, whom he loved, with the domineering husband Grace sometimes spoke of, for speak of him she did, working out her own problems in conversations with her son.

He had, also, to try to understand the sort of activities he enjoyed—to explain to himself why, instead of playing baseball with the neighborhood boys, he would retreat to his room to read or go on solitary walks to University Circle to watch the fountains, fascinated by the shimmer of light on the water.

And he had, finally, to face the fact of death; for on January 23, in the hard winter of 1913, his Grandfather Hart died. Though Harold had never been as close to his grandfather as to his grandmother, he was jolted by the experience of watching a man sicken fatally.

The death of Mr. Hart had several consequences. An immediate one was the decision of Grace and C.A. to make the Hart house their permanent home. A long-range one involved a legacy of $5,000 that was to be held in trust for Harold until the death of his grandmother. Giving him always the illusion of security, yet for years tantalizingly unavailable to him, the money was a mixed blessing. He was sometimes able to use it as security for loans to tide him over temporary financial crises. But it was the focus of his last, terrible quarrel with his mother and the ultimate reason for his breaking with her.

In 1913, when he first knew of the legacy, Harold was scarcely aware of money; all his needs and more were provided by his father's booming business. Harold's was the problem of an eighth-grader's day-to-day living. The Cleveland schools in those years were run on a semester basis with graduations both in January and in June, and Harold was making plans for registration in high school in January.

East High School, which he entered in January 1914 and which he attended intermittently for the next three years, was one of the show places of the Cleveland educational system. It was good-looking. Its wide lawns set it far back from the respectable middle-class houses of 82nd Street. But, of greater importance, it boasted a fine faculty and was proud of the fact that an unusually high number of its graduates went on to college.

Harold was not active in school. He can be located in his freshman- and sophomore-class pictures, a serious "firm" look on his face; but he joined none of the many school clubs, he played in

none of the organized sports, he wrote for neither the school newspaper nor the school yearbook. In all his years in school there is
only one reference to him in any school publication, a "bright
saying" that appeared in the humor section of the 1916 East High
School *Annual*:

Miss M. Peters: What is a partitive genitive?
Harold C: It is a part of which the whole has been taken.

In school, he registered for the "Classical" program, the standard college-entrance course that included—in addition to algebra,
geometry, English, and physics—three years of German (where
he met Miss M. Peters) and three of Latin. His record, though
not a bad one, is complicated by excessive absences. He was frequently out of school because of Southern and Western trips with
his mother, and he often missed examinations or failed to turn in
assignments. As a result, his record is spotted with a number of
"Pass" grades, East High's solution for the problem child who
was too bright to deserve a failure but who had done so little work
that his grades couldn't honestly be calculated. In the first semester of his freshman year, he seems to have been present for all
classes and to have built up a fairly conventional record: Algebra,
85; English, 90; German, 77; Latin, 75; and Physical Training, 79.
In his second semester, however, the fall of 1914, Algebra, Latin,
and German are all graded P and no grade at all is recorded in
English. His single numerical grade is an 85 in Physical Training,
the one subject in which no final examination could have been
given.

The rest of his record is equally spotty and is complicated by
withdrawals and reentries. For almost the entire spring semester
of 1915 he was out of school, visiting his mother and grandmother
on the Isle of Pines, just south of Cuba. His announcement in a
letter to his grandmother in February 1916 that he was at last
"a Junior (capital) in high school" represents—if his record means
anything—considerable generosity on the part of the school system. It is no wonder that he found school distasteful. Having difficulty keeping up with his classmates—not because he didn't
study or because he wasn't bright enough, but simply because he
was never in Cleveland for a whole school year—he came more
and more to be dependent on private study for his lessons and on
a few close friends for companionship.

When he did go to school, he tried—except in the English class
taught by Mrs. Marian Wright Warner—to be as inconspicuous as
possible. Eleanor Claridge, a member of his class, remembers him
as quiet and introspective, a "silent boy." She was herself interested in writing and had been attracted to him. She did her
best to lure him into conversations, but Harold, though polite,
seemed not to care for girls—at least not to care for them "seriously." From his friend William Wright she had heard of his poetic

accomplishment. "Even in those days," she remembered, "Bill regarded him as a genius."

Only in Mrs. Warner's class was he an active participant. He had read far more widely than most students, and his teacher, years afterwards, remembered him in terms of "his shining brown eyes as he argued with eager interest about everything that came up for discussion." He wanted, she remembered, "so much to find out about things."

But it was less in class than in full, long, and easy talks with his close friends that Harold was able to bring together his knowledge. Of those friends, William Wright was most important. Superficially, the boys were as different as night and day. Wright was, in his high-school years, an animated extrovert, a cheerful boy involved in almost everything the school offered. Member of half a dozen clubs, manager of the football team, writer and editor for the yearbook, he seemed always to be bubbling over with vitality. Short, thin, and blond, he raced about the school corridors, joking about his activities with the husky football team, outlining debate speeches, supervising in one way or another most of the activities of his class. Crane stood by in silent, amused detachment, participating in nothing.

Beneath surface differences, however, the two boys shared identical dreams. Each hoped to become a poet. And each found in the other an audience for a lively wit that was lost on the rest of their schoolmates.

Perhaps because the tragic element shows up so strongly late in Crane's career, and because he wrote more of his troubles than of his joys, we are likely to get a distorted picture of Harold Hart Crane—to see him as the brooding, gloomy figure of the David Siqueiros portrait. Most of his closest friends remember him in terms of laughter and good humor. "I am going to take the liberty of believing (at least until I have seen better evidence to the contrary than has appeared so far) that Hart was not essentially an unhappy man," Wright wrote Grace Crane in the year after Hart's death.

> He had difficulties of a colossal nature sometimes and moods when undoubtedly things must have seemed very dark indeed. But to my mind he was not morose nor very often wholly despondent. I consider that, on the whole, for one of his gifts and his temperament he was rather more stable and better-balanced than one would have a right to expect. Is this nonsense? *I* don't think so, at least. Perhaps I saw only one side of him. But at least that side existed, since I saw it. And I must say I never saw him totally unhappy.

Wright was a good observer. But his remark that he may have seen only one side of his friend's personality is truer than he realized. For, by the time he had reached high school, Harold had become adept at compartmentalizing his life. Later, as he came to know a wider range of men, his adaptation would become spectacular. He would be able to be as rough or as tough as the roughest sailor. With his aunts in Cleveland he would be polite, charming, genuinely innocent. He would be for his grandmother, to the end of her life, an irrepressible, high-spirited boy. With a heavy-drinking friend, Hart would be able to follow or lead, drink for drink, or, if need be, seem completely drunk without benefit of alcohol. For serious writers and for painters, he would be poet and / or aesthetician—and sometimes mystic seer. None of these personalities was in any sense false. The "real" Hart Crane was any one of them or the whole series of them. Each friend saw him as something uniquely his own.

Sam Loveman once remarked that it was exhausting being with Hart because he demanded so much emotional involvement. "It was as if he were devouring you," Sam said. "It was overwhelming." Literally dozens of people—people who knew Hart in all sorts of connections: writers, painters, sailors, storekeepers—still, more than thirty-five years after his death, think of him as "my best friend." The driving intensity, the demanding intimacy of his personality made some men—like the writer Nathan Asch, for instance—reject him; but those who rejected him found him unforgettable and those who did not reject him found themselves completely captivated by his encompassing personality. "Not a small section of my own mental landscape has always been concerned with Hart," wrote William Wright.

> Even though I sometimes didn't exchange letters with him for a year, and didn't see him for three or four, still he was always present as a unique and personal phenomenon; a something that belonged to me and to only a few others . . . After all, there are few who have the privilege of knowing a great man; and knowing him so closely, and personally, as I have known Hart, almost from boyhood.

"Do you know where I first met Hart?" Wright wrote Mrs. Crane. "I *think* it was at Eleanor T. Flynn's dancing school. Romantic days!" On their first meeting they had walked to the pond in Wade Park, comparing notes on their families. The friendship was very quickly established and each boy looked forward to the good talks Saturdays would bring. "I am quite sure that I still wore short trousers," Wright wrote in another letter.

> We walked along the edge of Wade Park near the old apartment building known as Whitehall one day early in our acquaintance. It must have been on Saturday afternoon, for that was the day we went to dancing school. We had, I think, our dancing pumps dangling from our arms in black silk bags. Those were tense days, war days, and even boys of fifteen were talking of their

future. I had no idea what mine should be, but I believe I said I expected to become a lawyer. It was then that Hart first confided his conviction that he had discovered his bent, and that he would be a poet. . . . It was a very different world then . . . a world in which boys of fourteen and fifteen respectively carried little black silk bags to dancing school!

Grace Crane, in her own visits to the dancing school, always created a sensation among the girls, for they admired her faultless carriage and her magnificent clothes. They respected the dignity and austere beauty of their teacher, her high-necked full silk dress shining under the bright lights, but Grace Crane's beauty was breathtaking and the rumors of her marital difficulties, which all the boys and girls knew about, contributed in the children's eyes an element of mystery to her loveliness.

Harold himself was felt to be something of a catch. Neither rough nor rude, always immaculate in his dress, he seemed to at least one girl in the class, young Hazel Brown, "shy and diffident, lonely," and very nice.

It was, however, her sister Vivian, a beautiful girl, dainty and graceful, fragile as a Dresden doll, her long hair worn loose to her waist and accented by a light-blue hair ribbon, her long-waisted full skirt tied round by a light-blue sash, who attracted Harold. It was Vivian whom he dated, and it was to Vivian he brought what her sister still remembers as a most remarkable gift—a large box of his father's candy divided across the middle, on one side "the most delicious chocolates" and on the other, fresh from the florist, a delicate corsage. "Both mothers were pleased to see them going out together," her sister remembered. "She was the only girl he ever took flowers to."

"I was not in love with him," Vivian wrote me. "I felt very sad when I read of his miserable life after it was ended. I do think he would have been a fine man if his boyhood had not been as it was. He was bitter even at that age."

But though Harold attended dances and shows with Vivian Brown and with other girls, it was with several boys, particularly with Wright, that he worked out his plans for the future.

They met regularly, not only at the dancing school, but also at East High School. "Hart's 'home room' . . . was on the second or third floor, mine on the first," Wright wrote. "He used to come down during recess periods and we would walk together through the halls . . ." One day, after dancing school, Hart invited Wright to come home with him. "It must have been February or March, for the snow was melting backward and showing dirty edges along the sidewalks and there was something of spring in the air."

From that time on they were inseparable companions, eager and enthusiastic readers who almost daily compared notes on their

literary discoveries. Harold's room was well stocked with books.
"I have often wondered what happened to his books," Wright
wrote.

> He once had a great many of them; and very fine ones. I re-
> member being in his room on . . . East 115th Street a good many
> times; and seeing his fine collection. I hope they have not been
> scattered. He had a small victrola and some very good records;
> and the room always smelled of good, strong tobacco. What a
> pleasant place!

Though most of the books are, in fact, scattered, a few, some
dated with the year of their purchase or bearing the "Harold
Crane" signature that identifies them as being from a time earlier
than the summer of 1917, have survived to indicate how wide
Crane's early reading was.

During his first year in high school he was investing his spare
cash in books. In that year he bought the Everyman editions of
*Plutarch's Lives* and of Balzac's *About Catherine de Medici*, a
copy of Voltaire's *History of Charles XII, King of Sweden*, and
Dowden's substantial edition of *The Poetical Works of Percy
Bysshe Shelley*. In the back end-pages of the Shelley volume
Crane scrawled what for him must have seemed prophetic lines:
"For, truly, at the call of love, / What nobler gift can be."

He already owned by this time—1913 Christmas presents from
his mother and grandmother—the handsome leather-bound three-
volume set of Caffin's histories of Dutch, Spanish, and French
painting , and he would soon add to his library Hawthorne's
*Mosses from an Old Manse* and Oscar Wilde's *Lady Windermere's
Fan*.

By 1916 he had invested in a history of medieval Europe, a
biography of Goethe, a collected Lionel Johnson, the Everyman
*Coleridge, Pelise: A Book of Lyrics Chosen from Algernon Charles
Swinburne*, and *Edgar Allan Poe's Tales of Mystery and Imagination*, on one of the end papers of which he had jotted down
what looks like an analysis of the short story "The Oval Portrait":

> Simone's death is caused by the annihilation of her beauty in
> the portrait and as useless beauty vanishes so her spirit takes
> wing and only the casein [?] on the portrait (really the perfect
> reproduction of her soul and form) remains to mock the artist,
> her husband.
> The artist poses her as *Destiny* although he never can know
> destiny; he is so absorbed that he does not notice how she
> [is] melting and like a crimson rose brushed [?] by the frost
> she wilts and passes.

Crane was not much given to marking up his books, but annotations such as this one, in which he focuses on the triumph of art

over life, are characteristic of the kinds of material to which he was drawn. In the same edition of Poe, Crane marked passages concerned with the nature of artistic composition. *What art is* and *how art is made* were for him serious matters.

The extent of his library in the years he attended East High School was considerable enough to impress not only Wright but another close friend, the boy who lived next door to the Cranes, Kenneth Hurd. What Hurd recalls is "a fairly large library of ultra modern (at least it seemed so to me) verse."

Kenneth, in spite of the fact that he was interested more in radio than in poetry, was a frequent visitor to Harold's tower room and had an opportunity to watch the would-be poet at work. Surrounded by his books, and perhaps recollecting passages such as those pertaining to the divine madness of poets in the Socratic *Dialogues* (which he had marked carefully with a double underlining of red ink), Harold would use whatever stimulants were at hand to put him into a properly "poetic" mood. "Smoking a cigar (cigarettes were unknown in those days) would put him into a trance," Hurd recalled; and if he weren't able to get a cigar, his mother's new perfume would do as well. All odors in those days excited him. Sweat was as attractive as cologne. Once, Hurd told me, Crane dashed out of the door of the tower room where they had been chatting and into the other tower room, at that time the bedroom of the Cranes' heavy-set maid. Harold came back carrying a pair of her oldest shoes. Settling down in his Morris chair, pencil and paper by his side, he sniffed long and lovingly at the broken-down, sweat-stained leather. "These inspire me," he told his startled friend, and plunged into the labors of composition.

Harold's more spectacular pursuits of inspiration were undoubtedly intended for show. But he was moody and shifted rapidly from high elation to deep depression. Some of these moods found release on the family piano. "Harold used to improvise beautifully," Hurd told me. "He would play as long as anyone was willing to listen, loud or soft, depending on his mood."

His earliest poems, if we can judge from one survivor, were long Swinburnian rhapsodies. "They were filled with references to gods and goddesses—all kinds of myth," Hurd said. Harold was always willing to recite—though never willing to explain—them. "What does it mean?" Kenneth once asked him at the end of a particularly dark recitation. "Oh, I don't know," Hart said. "I don't know."

Yet, if he chose to be mysterious about the meaning of his work, he was quick to respond to a poetic phrase—even one not his own. Once, as they walked through the park, Hurd pointed to a flurry of autumn leaves: "Look at those leaves chasing each other." Harold paused for a moment to think about his friend's remark.

"Why, that's beautiful," he said. Kenneth, flustered, was quick to say that he'd read the phrase somewhere, that it wasn't original. "But it *is* beautiful," Harold insisted.

Most of the time their walks through the park were in pursuit not of autumn leaves but of empty tennis courts. Both were determined players, Harold making up in violent energy what he lacked in skill. "He did love to play tennis. His motions were certainly not graceful or effeminate but rather erratic and awkward with lungings and futile wavings of his racket."

Even in the park, Harold always carried with him the book he was currently reading. Once, in fact, his book scandalized his friend and the girl who had come with them. Perhaps because they were accompanied by a young lady, they had been driven to the tennis courts in Rockefeller Park near the lagoon in Harold's mother's electric runabout—a very special concession. As Harold and Kenneth left the car, Harold turned back and handed his book to the girl. "Here. You can read this while we're playing," he said, and marched happily off, leaving the sixteen-year-old his brand-new "complete and unexpurgated" *Decameron*.

For all the Cranes, these were years of hectic activity. By the time his son had entered high school, C.A.'s business had become an established Cleveland fixture. His "Mary Garden Chocolates"— the singer's name was secured through a business arrangement— were of high quality and their packaging lavish. One box, for instance, boasted a cover by Maxfield Parrish (the original of which hung above Harold's piano) and another, patterned in musical notes, linked art and appetite: "Music by Mary Garden. Candy by Crane." Even summers—usually a slack season for the candy industry—were booming, for Mr. Crane had just invented "the candies with the hole," Life Savers. At first punched out for him on a pill machine by a pharmaceutical manufacturer, the candies caught on—perhaps because of C.A.'s ingenious wrapper, an old sailor cheerfully tossing a life preserver to a young lady swimmer: "Crane's Peppermint Life Savers . . . 5 cents . . . For That Stormy Breath." (Crane, usually astute in business matters, several years later sold the trademark and the formula to Edward J. Noble for $2,900.)

All the family at one time or another took a hand in the stores. Grace briefly supervised the setting up of a restaurant in one of them, and Harold frequently went with his father on the daily visits to each store and to the factory.

Yet Grace grew restless; her husband in his new affluence had even less time to devote to her than he had had in Warren. In the winter of 1914 she took six weeks to visit her mother at the Isle of Pines and in the summer of that year she insisted on the need for a trip East. Taking Harold with her, she visited Boston and Rye Beach, stopping, as always, at the best hotels. Harold, just turned fifteen, was now no longer the sensitive child of Mackinac Island but a presentable escort who knew how to carry on extended witty conversations and how to lead his mother as they danced to after-dinner waltzes in the airy hotel ballrooms.

All through the fall of 1914, family tiffs proved a steady irritation; and they grew in intensity after Harold's grandmother—the strongest steadying influence in the family—left for her little plantation on the Isle of Pines. By Christmas, both Grace and C.A., their nerves frayed, decided that their best bet would be a holiday trip to visit Mrs. Hart on her island home. A few weeks of rest and relaxation, they hoped, would enable them to rediscover the love each of them had once felt for the other.

Harold looked forward to the trip: the long train ride to Florida, a stay at Jacksonville, a steamer ride first to Cuba and then to the Isle of Pines, and finally—at journey's end—his grandmother waiting to welcome him to the plantation he had heard so much about. All of it added up to an adventure almost as exciting as those he read about in his books. And though he was fearful of becoming seasick (his fears proved well grounded), he was sure, as he told friends and relatives, that the journey would be "broadening."

Broadening it was, though not in the way Harold had expected it to be. Almost from the beginning, the island trip was doomed. C.A. was concerned about Harold's absence from school and his own absence from business—particularly about some up-in-the-air plans to make a long sales trip to California. Grace, on the other hand, was anxious to prolong the visit. Finally, in mid-January, C.A. insisted that they should return to Cleveland. But Grace refused to leave until they had taken an auto trip to the mountains in the interior of the island. The excursion, she felt, would do them all good. What started as a minor quarrel soon exploded into a public scene with shouted insults and hysteria on both sides. In the end C.A.—fiercely angry—took the Sunday-night boat for the mainland, leaving Grace and Harold to amuse themselves as best they could. ("As long as I live," C.A. wrote her later, "I'll never forget your words in your bedroom—'We may never talk again.'")

As in most of their difficulties, as soon as they were separated, C.A. was overcome with remorse and quickly accepted all the blame. The next day he wrote from a hotel in Jacksonville a long, anxiety-laden letter.

My Dear Girl: —

At this same desk I've written you many letters. At the same telephone here in the corner last year came a message that gave my heart an extra pulsation, but today how very very different!

If my absence from you in the past has caused you the same feelings I've had since Sunday night, I'm forever sorry and in the future we will go and come together. I've seen you all the long way up the Coast. I still see you ready for the auto trip . . . —I can't tell you how I feel. I'm only ashamed of my weakness. . . . If I'm cast off, say the word and I'll drown my feelings the way the weak generally do. Now please write me often—tell me the truth—and if your love for me has faded away—say so. I've never been so utterly miserable in my life . . .

When you get tired of the mountain and the climate and really want a husband, I hope I'll be presentable.

With infinite love and assurance that this is the last bark of the dog, I am,

Yours in wedlock<br>CAC

With it he enclosed a note for his son.

Dear Harold: —

I guess you must have thot that dad behaved very badly. Last year we lost mother for six weeks but you were with me and this year I lose you both and she seems to think you won't be home for so long that I'm fearful dad is going to be all busted up.

I'm hoping that you'll both realize that I'm worth saving and come back a good deal sooner than April 1st. Tonight I start north and Thursday will be in my office. I shall appreciate more than ever before in my life your letters so try and write me by every boat. Life wouldn't be worth but very little without you both and it's worth something to have your father feel that way, isn't it?

Take good care of yourselves and come back to me as soon as you *can*.

With love,<br>Papa

For the next week C.A. kept up a barrage of letters, usually two or three a day. By January 29, five days after he had left the island, he was hopeful that Grace would consent to his coming back as early as March 2. The next day, a Saturday, he wrote her three letters, a card, and a cablegram, most of them in celebration of the arrival of a batch of mail from her. Even before the postman arrived, he had gotten off a note urging her immediate return: "Grace honey, I do sure need you *bad. I am not* going to let you stay until the middle of *March* or anywhere near that— Don't you think a *real* devoted husband is worth more than those mountains?"

The minute her letters arrived, he sat down to write a long letter of his own, this one filled with joy that she had shown some tenderness: ". . . Your letters have just arrived and I've fairly eaten them up. Do you really care for me, dear, and does this separation mean anything to you? I'm all busted up and I'm going home tonight to read them again and again. . . . Please tell me . . . what I want to hear and come home as soon as you can." Sunday, which he spent at home, was a day of agony: "I've praised the island to the very skies . . . but I do hope those bugs you write about will drive you off the place. Your letter today did me lots of good and I do so want to believe you when you tell me that I am dear to you, but how can I reconcile your cheerful absence for so long when I want you here so badly."

On Monday, knowing Grace's passion for motoring, C.A. went out to price automobiles: "I just about bought a Cadillac 8— . . . and if I just knew that you were my true devoted wife and would come back to me very soon I'd close up the bargain. But I don't want to own a machine to ride around alone so I'm going to wait and hear when you are coming back."

Grace's letters were a mixture of casual gossip about island affairs, plans for attendance at island dances, and vague promises of an eventual return. She protested, also, about the deluge of letters she was receiving.

By this time everyone in the family was upset. Harold, deciding to take matters in his own hands, wrote his father a particularly disturbing letter in which he carefully ignored the letter that his father had sent him. "I was *so* disappointed in Harold's letter today that it busted me all up," C.A. wrote Grace. "I had looked forward to hearing from him and especially the first letter. But it was a scant page—never a word of missing me or recollecting that my heart really broke when I left him. Never a suggestion of my letter to him and our good time together. A dog and I can harness the horse and goodbye. *Well*, I guess I'm getting foolish in my old age but I won't annoy him with a reply."

Yet it was impossible for C.A. to stop writing letters, "dreadful letters," he told his wife. "I know just how bad and how frequent they are." But day after day, the flood of mail continued.

> It was two weeks ago that I "sailed out to sea" and to me it was like "Crossing the Bar." . . . If we ever do get together again, let's make up for this by less friction, for I surely do love you enough to give my life or its service for you. I realize how dependent I am upon you for my sole satisfaction and encouragement to succeed. Please do hurry back for I need you more than you know. . . . Every day I resolve I won't write, but it's no use. I've played solitaire until my brain reels. . . .

On the island itself, things were hardly any better. Mrs. Hart and Grace spent much of their time trying to amuse the by now thoroughly despondent Harold, taking him alternately to beaches and mountains, having friends in and going off to visit other friends. Grace, as compulsive as her husband, found it impossible not to talk to her son about marital difficulties; and the more she talked, the more depressed he became and the more he irritated her by his disobedience.

It may have been in these days early in February that Harold made what he later told his friend Bill Wright were two suicide attempts: one by slashing his wrists with a razor and one by swallowing all he could find of his mother's Veronal sleeping powders. Though the account sounds melodramatic, there is every reason to believe the suicide attempts really took place. We know, for example, that his mother's entire supply of the sleeping powders disappeared, for she wrote a hasty letter to her husband asking how many packets he had sent (he had sent eighteen) and asking him to send her more immediately. Mrs. Crane never spoke of those suicide attempts, but she did tell Philip Horton of an incident in which Harold, roused from sleep to drive off a midnight invasion of their neighbor's cattle, had raced shouting into the night, to disappear for the better part of an hour. When he returned, he was gasping for air, unable to speak. Before she could question him, he fell to the floor and remained unconscious until she and her mother had carried him by mule cart to a native doctor. According to Grace, Harold volunteered no explanations and she asked for none.

Probably it was in response to this incident that Mr. Crane on February 8 wrote Grace: "Dear: I've just received your two letters and a sad one from Harold. I'm sorry now I spoke of his letter to me. Don't say anything to him about it. I've written him a comforting little note and let it pass."

Whatever happened on the Isle of Pines late in the winter of 1915, the events seem to have created in Harold psychological wounds of almost incalculable severity. C.A. and Grace were able to recover from their spats with remarkable resiliency (as C.A. put it in a letter of February 10, 1915, "When we are together we sometimes disagree but apart I feel a devotion for you that I'm sure you would be glad of if you knew its intensity"). But the boy—conscious only of family violence and of a sense of indescribable wrong—would for days after a parental quarrel find himself emotionally and physically ill.

"It is difficult to recover Hart's own words when he described the childhood incidents that affected his later emotional life," Allen Tate told me.

Once in Paris he did talk about this to me; but . . . I can't remember how he put it. It was to the effect that the constant quarreling of his mother and father, and the violent sexual reconciliations (which lasted only a day or so), had given him a horror of the normal sexual relation. Apparently his parents made no effort to conceal this. One must, of course, take all this with a large grain of salt. I am sure that many young men have had parents like the Cranes but did not become homosexual. At any rate, Hart took the side of a mother whom he neither liked nor respected; and this must have had a very bad effect on him.

Perhaps because the anger of his parents had hurt him so deeply, Crane cultivated for the rest of his life a public manner of buoyant optimism, of cheerful good will. Only when he had been drinking heavily would the mask shatter and a tortured, fierce personality break free, a personality almost paranoid in its insistence on the "disloyalty" of friends and family, a personality that could and on rare occasions did become obscene and vicious.

There is no question that the island wounds helped shape this "underground man" in Crane. Nevertheless, on his return to Cleveland late in the spring of 1915 he had for his classmates only praise for the island's balmy climate, its charming natives, its beautiful, strange, misshapen mountains.

For C.A., Grace, and Harold finally did go home together. C.A.'s avalanche of letters triumphed—though for a while he had had doubts of ever seeing his family again. On February 17, Grace relented, telling him that he could come down. They would probably return with him.

Grace's decision to return may well have been prompted by her son's dangerous rebelliousness. A letter she received from Cleveland—a letter she kept to the end of her life—may also have had a hand in it. "Well, we will be glad to see you," her correspondent wrote. "Mr. Crane is alright now. I think he puts on a lot to make you feel badly and also I know he is lonesome. But I think if I were you, I would make it the last time to go so far and so long unless he can go and stay also. I can understand your position, you are between two fires, but I think husband comes first."

Whatever the reasons, late in March the Cranes were back in Cleveland, with Harold hard at work preparing for June examinations. "He was very brilliant, of course," Vivian Brown commented, "or he could not have kept up with his classes."

He did keep up with his classes, though, and even managed to work at his poetry. By the summer of 1915, when he celebrated his sixteenth birthday, he was confident of his ability.

He needed encouragement beyond that of his high-school teachers, however. He had met only one professional writer, Elbert Hubbard, whom his father admired and who had once written enthusiastically of C.A.'s spreading business ventures. Hubbard in his Cleveland visit must have seemed to young Harold artist incarnate: eloquent, lordly, and "artistically" unkempt—his unpressed jacket set off by a flowing Windsor tie and a long, carefully mussed shock of leonine hair. Almost weekly after Hubbard's return to East Aurora, New York, where he ran what for a time was an internationally famous inn-farm-workshop-publishing house loosely modeled on William Morris's ventures in late-nine-teenth-century England, Harold had badgered his parents to let him visit the great man. Finally, probably in the fall of 1914, they had consented, Grace most reluctantly.

Though the visit seems to have been disillusioning, it gave Crane an insight into the practical side of a successful writer's life. Living, as most of the apprentices did, with the Hubbard family, working mornings in the Roycroft book bindery (where he helped produce sumptuous editions of Hubbard's own works) and afternoons on the spreading, level farms associated with the inn, Harold came to hear at first-hand how manuscripts could be marketed, how newspaper editors could be cajoled into accepting columns, how books could be publicized. Like Harold's father, Hubbard was a phrase maker. His books, abounding in quotable "sayings," seem now the product of an extrovert ad-man, but at the time they struck many Americans as mines of profundity. Though at first attracted to Hubbard by his praise of Emerson, Whitman, and Poe, Harold returned home convinced that Hub-bard's output was pompous and shallow. Ironically, C.A.—who had been unsympathetic to the visit to East Aurora—later regu-larly quoted Hubbard in letters to his son, usually on the im-portance of a steady job and cash in the pocket.

Harold's second experience with a professional writer—again, thanks to his father's business associations—was a good deal more satisfying. One of the Chicago outlets for Crane's Mary Garden Chocolates was a catering business run by Harriet Moody, widow of the University of Chicago poet-professor William Vaughn Moody. Mrs. Moody, a sensitive critic and seriously concerned about the future of poetry in America, listened sympathetically to C.A.'s acccunt of a disturbing but obviously talented son. C.A., dubious of the possibilities of Harold's making a living as a poet and yet proud of the fact that Harold seemed capable of good work, talked out his dilemma: he wanted his son to go to college; he wanted his son ultimately to work with him in the candy business, but only if he were really interested in it; he wanted his son to make a good living, yet he wanted him to continue to write if his happiness depended on it.

Mrs. Moody proved to be an ideal listener. She was acquainted with many of the major poets of the day. She had been hostess both to Rabindranath Tagore and to William Butler Yeats in their visits to Chicago, and she was an admirer of poets as different from them as Carl Sandburg and Vachel Lindsay. Her advice, necessarily general in nature, was that Mr. Crane should do his best to encourage Harold's interest in poetry but that he should also see that Harold enter college. She asked to see samples of Harold's work.

The samples must have been impressive, for she arranged to talk with Harold on a Cleveland visit late in the winter of 1915–

1916. During their conversation, Harold confessed to her that, come what may, he intended to "give all" for poetry. Though at the time she hesitated to encourage so extreme a step, a long letter and another sample of his poetry convinced her that perhaps Harold was making the proper move. "I have a deep conviction that you are following the real right lead for you," she wrote back.

The poem Harold had sent her was called "Nocturne," and she was very careful to say in response exactly how she felt about it. Praising it for "very true . . . mood" and "pictures," she went on to add, "The realization in phrase is not quite equal in quality, it seems to me, to the quality of the verse melody and the mood." But she asked to see more poems and promised to send him copies of new work by other poets who interested her. One of her first gifts, sent soon after their correspondence started, was a copy of her husband's selected letters.

By the summer of 1916, Harold and Mrs. Moody were in regular correspondence, though her catering business sometimes delayed her replies. ("I am always afraid my long silences after you send me a manuscript," she wrote on July 2, 1916, "may seem discouraging, and that would be a real pain to me.") She had come by this time to think of Harold not as a business acquaintance's son but as a poet. "This last is far the best of yours I have seen," she wrote. "Indeed I find it beautiful, tender, and sincere." She was a good teacher, asking for revision or clarification whenever she had difficulty with the sense of a line, as in one poem in which she asked for a prose paraphrase of two lines and an explanation of an "obscure" one: "For murmur of mine has found a shore."

His letters to her were full of problems. He hoped to get away from Cleveland and the difficulties of his parents long enough to produce a small volume of poems, and Mrs. Moody did her best to locate friends with whom he could stay. For a while it looked as if she might find a place for him with her friends the MacKayes at Cornish, New Hampshire, where he would be able to write in undisturbed seclusion and complete his schoolwork under the direction of a tutor. When the plan fell through, she asked him to visit her in Chicago. "When your father comes to Chicago some time, come with him and stay with me while he is here." And she regularly provided literary news:

> Padraic Colum is bringing out an anthology of the poetry of the young Irish revolutionists.
> It will probably be good.
> Do you know the work of Sandburg? That is good too, in a different way from yours and mine.
> Better read it.

Throughout their correspondence it is less news of the literary world than good advice on the careful testing and revision of poetry that characterizes her letters: "Love of your work, and work, will give you your full voice."

This sort of advice was what he most needed. One of the earliest surviving poems, probably a product of the months just before he met Mrs. Moody and almost certainly one of the poems he showed her on her visit to Cleveland, "The Moth that God Made Blind," suffers greatly from a verbosity that Crane would never again be guilty of. Though material that would reappear in much of his early work (a moth / flame motif, sea imagery, a sight and insight theme) is already apparent, the whole poem falls apart. Of more biographical than literary significance, it is an allegory of the poet as visionary artist. The poet is like a moth, blind to things around him and despised by his fellows but able— because of that blindness—to rise into the bright light of the sun. "Still lonely" after his flight, the moth-artist falls back to earth, in the last lines becoming identified with the author.

> My eyes have hugged beauty and winged life's short spell.
> These things I have: —a withered hand;—
> Dim eyes;—a tongue that cannot tell.

If "The Moth that God Made Blind" was written just after Christmas of 1915, Crane had every reason to be melancholy. His schoolwork was giving him a good deal of trouble, and he was having a difficult time getting on with his schoolmates. His parents, exhausted by the Christmas rush in Mr. Crane's stores, were preparing once more to head south to the Isle of Pines, where his grandmother had already taken up residence—only this time they were going without Harold, having decided that their own troubles might be lessened if they could be free, for a little while, from an overly demanding son.

On the fifth of January, Mr. and Mrs. Crane left Harold with his aunts, a very unhappy, brooding boy. Determined to be lonely, he was; within two days he wrote his grandmother a sad little note full of the news that he was "so lonesome" and hopeful that "perhaps this lonesomeness will wear off in a little while as it usually does you know." By the end of the month, however, his mother and father returned; and Harold's letters to his grandmother took on a considerably more cheerful and decidedly more "literary" tone. Fascinated by words, he was now spending much of his spare time poring over his dictionary and his father's thesaurus. "Your letters would augur a fairly favorable winter and good conditions on the island," he wrote on January 26, and, two weeks later:

> It is strange, in view of the fact that last winter I defended the desirability of northern winters to the expense of much discomfiture from other arguers, that the whole illusion has melted away and I have often this winter thought of the South with

longing—yes, even Florida. My blood, I guess, has been thinner or digestion poorer. Some of these days have cut me thru and thru so that I have for the most part of the season been exquisitely uncomfortable, "Once south has spoilt me" as they say.

The conflict between school and his writing forced him to make compromises with both. He expended a great deal of energy cramming for January examinations. ("We had *English* today and Latin and Geometry are due tomorrow. They are my hoodooes and so I am not a little worried tonight about the outcome.") Yet as soon as the examinations were over he was ready to rush back to poetry.

My writing has suffered neglect lately due to study for examinations, but I will soon resume it with vehemence as I am intensely,—grippingly interested in a new ballad I am writing of six hundred lines. I have resolved to become a *good* student even if I have to sit up all night to become one. You will undoubtedly wink when you read this state declaration so often made but this time it is in earnest.

Disturbed by his parents' quarrels when they were with him and lonely when they were away, unable or unwilling to make himself popular at school, sixteen-year-old Crane shifted moodily from extreme self-pity to extravagant elation.

A February 10, 1916, letter to his grandmother is typically full of these extremes. He begins: "I have just returned from the store and got so car-sick on the way home, I haven't recovered yet"; promptly announces with a good deal of excitement that he has passed his examinations with fine marks and so entered the junior class; goes on to tell in great detail about the activities of Dora, their cook, who "has been working in the store kitchen for the past few days . . . and she has literally bubbled over all the time for her excitement and love of the work"; and then in the midst of a recital of his day busy with the lives of people—his mother, whom he has just left at the store; Dora; "Alice," whom he likes "better always"—suddenly announces that he is completely isolated from human companionship.

It is surely lonely for me here, eating alone and seldom seeing any one but in the darkness of morning or night. If you were here it would be so different, but I am consoled amply by knowing of your comfort and welfare where you now are. I have been working hard lately at my writing but find it doubly hard with the task of conjoining it to my school work. They are so shallow over there at school I am more moved to disdain than anything else. Popularity is not my aim though it were easy to win it by laughing when they do at nothing and always making a general ass of oneself. There are about two out of the twelve hundred I would care to have as friends.

Alternately posturing and sincere, shy and aggressive, in this awkward year he makes a fiction of his life, acting the young writer, adapting the cliché stances of fictional heroes to his own needs.

But it is not fiction that he spent a good deal of that winter more or less by himself. His parents were occupied with business affairs through all of December; they were away on what turned out to be a hasty southern trip from the fifth of January until some time near the twentieth; as soon as they returned to Cleveland—almost before they had unpacked their suitcases—they left for New York and stayed through the end of the month. And through most of February they worked regularly in the company office or in the stores.

It is no wonder, therefore, that he felt abandoned by parents and that in his letters to Mrs. Moody he planned to get away as soon as possible from what was not always a happy home.

Except for a short visit to Chautauqua, New York, probably just before his seventeenth birthday, his hope of leaving home to be "on his own," a hope that he and Mrs. Moody corresponded about, simply did not materialize.

The Chautauqua visit, though brief, was a real holiday, since it represented Harold's first completely independent excursion. Invited by their friends the Brown girls to see the wonders of America's cultural center, Harold and his close friend George Bryan set out by train for Jamestown, New York. Though George and Harold had gone to different schools, they had grown up in the same neighborhood and had become fast friends at about the time Harold registered in East High School. At first entertaining themselves by pure deviltry—as when they "executed" all of George's older sister's dolls by decapitating the lot of them (the heads came off under a big rocking horse, Harold rocking madly away and George feeding dolls to the rocker guillotine)—they came later to be valuable companions, confessing those fears and ambitions they could not talk about to their parents. It was to George that Harold poured out in full the story of his parents' unhappy marriage and of his own confused "support" of his beautiful and talented mother, and it was with George that he would later in New York try to sort out other feelings about his home and family. "Harold in those days was very impetuous and was in hot water most of the time," George remembered. "And when he was corrected by his mother or Grandmother Hart, he was pouty and sulky to everyone."

Chautauqua was a pure delight. "We had a dandy time," George wrote to me, "and I attributed it to the fact that [Harold] was away from his parents and grandparents who never allowed him much freedom at home." The Browns had a small cottage at the lake, and though the boys took many of their meals at the cottage, they stayed at a nearby hotel. ("We were very unpopular with their Mother," George later remembered. "She watched them like a hawk.") Swimming, loafing in the sun, squiring the girls and their mother around the extensive grounds of the Chautauqua Foundation, where an almost constant program of lectures and concerts was available, Harold managed to forget the conflicts of home. "Harold was a shy, awkward boy," Vivian Brown wrote, recollecting his visit, "but [he] had a fine sense of humor."

The fine sense of humor almost deserted him when he returned home to accompany his mother on a guided tour of the West. Convinced that he was old enough to travel by himself, he rebelled all the way across the country at sharing a compartment with her, at first shocking and later amusing her as night after night he hurled his clothes out of his upper berth past her lower one, all the while shouting mild oaths.

Though he did his best to convince his mother that he was on the trip only to please her, withdrawing much of the time to the observation platform by himself, or refusing to join her until he had finished one of the dozens of books he had brought with him, the trip was for both mother and son a significant opportunity to enjoy life together. Both of them freed from responsibilities, they came to see each other as young companions rushing from a narrow, confining world, Harold visualizing himself as older and more mature than he was and Grace, just turned forty, trying to recapture the fading glow of her girlhood. In Yellowstone Park they got up at dawn to take the earliest coach drive through the pine forests, bundling themselves in sweaters and scarfs against the chill mists, and climbing up beside the driver to enjoy the best view. Together they gasped in astonishment as Old Faithful drove its tons of steaming water into the sky. And at night they listened to rangers by the campfire telling of grizzly bears and elk and of the days—not so far back—when Indians had moved silently through the dark forests.

They crossed the continent. In San Francisco they admired the Golden Gate, danced far into the night at a gala hotel ball, explored Chinatown together, and together rode the spectacular cable cars that lifted them up San Francisco's vertical streets.

On the return trip they swept through the Pacific Northwest and up into Canada, where at Banff they swam, played tennis, rode the looping bridle trails that carried them above Lake Louise and descended to the rim of the magnificent lake.

In all these travels Crane was assembling material that would wait until *The Bridge* for final expression. The country itself, "a body under the wide rain," gradually unfolded to him, "her yonder breast / Snow-silvered, sumac-stained or smoky blue." Like the "hobo-trekkers" he celebrated in "The River" section of his long poem, Crane had covered the continent and stored up memories of the land.

... I have trod the rumorous midnights, too,

And past the circuit of the lamp's thin flame
(O Nights that brought me to her body bare!)
Have dreamed beyond the print that bound her name.
Trains sounding the long blizzards out—I heard
Wail into distances I knew were hers.

But it was not the continent he would write of when he returned from the Western trip. As a poet, Crane was still entangled in the diction of the nineties, and his verse, carefully made, reflected themes and techniques that he found in Swinburne, Symonds, Dowson, and Wilde. Wilde was the subject of his first published poem, "C 33," a thirteen-line lyric that appeared in the Greenwich Village *Bruno's Weekly* of September 23, 1916. Its title the number of Wilde's cell in Reading Gaol, the poem praised Wilde for having "woven rose-vines / About the empty heart of night" and went on to see the jailed poet as a penitent artist, a creator of "song of minor, broken strain." As Brom Weber convincingly argues, the poem is almost certainly a product of the first half of 1916, its subject suggested by a series of articles in *Bruno's Weekly* of January and February 1916 which had sympathetically related some of Wilde's prison experiences.

By the late summer of 1916, when he submitted "C 33" to *Bruno's Weekly*, Crane had no hesitation in calling himself a poet. Not only had Mrs. Moody praised his work, but she had asked other poets to examine it, among them Rabindranath Tagore, the 1915 winner of the Nobel Prize for literature, who, during a 1916 visit to Cleveland, included Crane in a list of writers and newspapermen to whom he granted brief interviews.

It was Wilde, however, who meant most to young Crane. At about the same time that he sent his homage off to *Bruno's Weekly*, he wrote a letter of praise for another Greenwich Village publication, Joseph Kling's *The Pagan*: "I am interested in your magazine as a new and distinctive chord in the present American Renaissance of literature and art. Let me praise your September cover; it has some suggestion of the exoticism and richness of Wilde's poems." Impressed, Kling printed Crane's letter in his next issue. The September cover which Crane had celebrated was an ornate woodcut of a large white circle festooned with birds and flowers and bearing in the center an appropriately pagan motto:

Hang your lantern in your nook
Drink and laugh at Priest and Shah.

In Kling's magazine were short stories by Sholom Asch and Theodore Dreiser and an impassioned letter from Margaret Sanger asking for cash contributions for the dissemination of information about birth control. The same issue included a strong attack on Christian Science ("a rotten, idiotic creed," according to Kling) which must have brought a sardonic smile from young Crane, still an occasional visitor to the local Christian Science Sunday school.

Crane had discovered *The Pagan* and *Bruno's Weekly* in Richard Laukhuff's bookstore in downtown Cleveland's Taylor Arcade. But more important to Crane than any of the books or magazines he found there was Richard Laukhuff himself.

The son of a German organ builder, Laukhuff had spent three years in France and three in Italy as a journeyman working for organ builders. The languages he had picked up in these trades proved useful to him when he came to the United States, especially when in 1916 he decided to start the bookstore, using as a nucleus his own library of six thousand books. At first he planned to sell only Continental literature, but he soon felt it was important to support contemporary writers. Laukhuff was an enthusiastic reader, a man in love with ideas; and it was evident from the beginning that the bookstore had in it the makings of an informal educational institution. Any time of day one could drop in on what became a kind of continuing seminar. The chairs at the back of the store were always occupied, though the occupants varied from hour to hour. Here literature became a living force as ideas were debated and styles of writers analyzed. Laukhuff, who knew the works in the original, could be counted on to solve problems created by a translation or to summarize untranslated work.

A store that began as a connoisseur's library, Laukhuff's gradually built a national reputation. Laukhuff sold only books he could respect and rigorously excluded popular fiction and popular magazines. But there were collections in all fields of the humanities and liberal arts and a fair sampling of "little" magazines. During the early years there were also exhibitions of the work of important local artists, such men as George Henry Keller, Charles Burchfield, and William Sommer. Until his death on July 15, 1957, Richard Laukhuff served the cause of literature. "Nothing pleased him more than to have a customer express surprise at finding some obscure classic on his shelves," noted the Cleveland *Press* editorial at the time of his death, and then went on to quote his typical comment: "Why not? THIS is a BOOK store."

Crane, at first a timid and later an enthusiastic member of the group of readers, writers, and artists who gathered there, was active in the back-of-the-store seminars. Here he and his friend William Wright would pore over the little magazines just in from Chicago and New York, studying them as possible markets for the poetry both boys were now producing, and enthusiastically questioning Laukhuff about the great European writers to whom they were being introduced.

Crane found at Laukhuff's an island of peace. In the troubled autumn of 1916, Europe was engulfed in the most destructive war of its history and the United States was moving closer to active participation. Crane's secure world of high-school friendships was already—like the world around him—disintegrating. At home, his parents daily insulted each other, then quickly sought reconciliation. Harold was their conflict's focus and its victim, for both mother and father saw each other as inadequate parents. And school, which before had seemed to Crane of little value, became now a mockery. By the end of September, a writer with work published in "advanced" magazines, he saw school as a hindrance to the vocation he had set for himself.

Increasingly he immersed himself in writing. Harold had never been conceited about his work, Kenneth Hurd remembered; but now poetry came to be the only thing he was sure of. "He wasn't lazy," his friend recalled. "I was a radio bug in those days and my room was, also, like Harold's, on the third floor. Late at night, I'd look out of my window and still see the lights on in his room next door. Harold would be reading or working on one of his poems." Of course it was equally true, Hurd remembered, that Harold "did no physical work of any kind if he could help it"; but he did work steadily at his poetry.

In these difficult days the one member of the family both Grace and C.A. regularly turned to was Harold's Aunt Zell, a brilliant, sophisticated woman both of them respected. Zell's first husband had been Grace's brother Frank. After his death, she had remarried. Her second husband, Will Deming, was the publisher of the Cheyenne (Wyoming) *Tribune* and Zell assisted in the management of his other newspaper, the Warren *Tribune*. In very short order she assumed full responsibility for its publication.

Intense and witty and devoted to the arts, she welcomed visits from young writers and painters and especially from Harold. At her house in Warren he had met several art students, among them John Lloyd, a boy near his own age who briefly worked as houseboy for Harold's parents. At Zell's home he also met a young painter just ten years older than himself, Carl Schmitt. Schmitt, well on the way to establishing a name as an artist, had been sponsored to a year's study in Europe by Mrs. Deming and had already set up a studio in New York City. Ambitious and hardworking, he was also an extraordinarily good conversationalist.

Though Schmitt must have seen relatively little of Crane in these visits, his importance cannot be overestimated. He was the first of a series of artists who helped Crane work out a basic aesthetic. Recognizing that the boy had an artist's enthusiasm and an artist's concern for form, Schmitt explained details of a metaphysical scheme for the relationships among the seven arts that he had evolved for himself while he was a student at the

*The young
Grace Hart Crane*

*Both photos: collection of
Mrs. Elizabeth Madden*

*The young
Clarence (C.A.) Crane*

The house in Garrettsville, Ohio, where Harold Hart Crane was born on July 21, 1899. This photograph was taken during the following August

The earliest surviving photographs of Harold Hart Crane

*Harold, age two or so*

1709 East 115 Street: the house in Cleveland where Hart Crane grew up. He indicated his tower bedroom ("sanctum de la tour") on this postcard photo in 1928, when the house was sold

*Collection of H. B. Collamore*

Hart    C.A.        Grace

Top: *C. A. Crane*. Back row: *A local dentist, Arthur Crane (C.A.'s father), Fred Crane (Arthur's brother), Mr. and Mrs. Madden's maid, Ella Crane (C.A.'s mother), Lotta Crane (Fred's wife), Grace Crane.* Front row: *Hart Crane, Fredrica Crane (Fred's daughter), Byron Madden holding Betty Madden, Bess Madden (C.A.'s sister), Jack Madden (Bess's son), Margery (Fred's daughter)*

*The young Hart Crane*

Grace Crane and Hart, photographed by the same Cleveland photographer, Frank Moore

*This photograph was probably taken in 1916, not long before
the seventeen-year-old Hart left home for New York*

National Academy of Design. He encouraged Crane to adapt these general theories of aesthetics to his own poetry.

The trips to Warren were for Harold and his mother and father a respite from their troubles, but nothing Mrs. Deming could do— or any of their relatives could do—was able to save the foundering marriage of Grace and C.A. Quarrels piled onto each other, increasing in intensity. Finally, on a night late in November, the end came. C.A. packed up and moved out of the house.

Though she had been angered by his presence, Grace was enraged at C.A.'s "desertion" and rushed to Mr. John J. Sullivan, the family lawyer, to ask him to file for a divorce. Charging C.A. with "gross neglect of duty," she asked Mr. Sullivan to arrange a settlement that would give her enough money to live comfortably for at least five years and give her as well complete "custody and control" of Harold.

Closer to her in these years than ever after, Harold was entirely sympathetic to his mother. Together thcy made plans for a life in which they could pursue common dreams. And as an omen of success, the November issue of *The Pagan* printed Harold's imagistic lyric "October-November."

Elated both by its publication and by the fact that his mother was finally treating him as a man, Harold jubilantly wrote his friend Carl Schmitt: "I don't know whether or not I informed you in my last letter of the step mother and I have taken. —Next week mother files her petition in court for her divorce from father. In this I am supporting her. So the first thing to do was to secure some employment. Your poet is now become a salesman, and (it might be worse) a job at selling pictures at Korner & Wood's has been accepted."

Events at the end of 1916 moved swiftly. Harold, at last having a legitimate excuse to quit school, withdrew from East High School.

On December 11, 1916, Mr. Sullivan, acting as attorney for both parties, drew up and filed an annuity agreement acceptable to Mr. and Mrs. Crane. All of Mrs. Crane's demands were generously agreed to. As alimony, she was to receive $20,400 in cash over a five-year period: $200 a month in 1917, $300 a month in 1918, and $400 a month in 1919, 1920, and 1921. In addition she was to have all the furniture at 1709 East 115th Street, plus a cash award of $210 to take care of immediate needs. C.A. agreed also to pay all court costs and an attorney's fee of $1,000, which was to take care of his and of Grace's debt. He also agreed immediately to pay back to Grace with full accrued interest the $5,000 he had borrowed from her in establishing his business.

Provisions for Harold were similarly generous.

In addition to the foregoing, the said husband shall maintain, support, and clothe their said son Harold Crane, until he is of

age, whether said son shall reside with his mother during the
years of his minority or any part thereof, or elsewhere and shall
give to said son the privileges of a full college and education
and pay all legitimate and necessary expenses therefor, and
during any time in the minority of the said son that he shall be
or reside with his said mother, the board and lodging expenses
of said son, shall be paid to said mother in behalf of said boy.

With Grace occupied with legal matters and C.A. living at
his club, Harold found the time of the divorce action not chaotic
but peaceful. "With pipe, solitude and puppy for company," he
wrote Schmitt, "I am feeling resplendent. After a day's work in a
picture store selling mezzotints and prints, you may not think it,
yet there comes a great peaceful exaltation in merely reading,
thinking, and writing. For occasionally in this disturbing age of
adolescence which I am now undergoing, there come minutes
of calm happiness and satisfaction."

Perhaps Crane's estimate of himself in this letter is the best we
will ever have for these years. For though the "disturbing age of
adolescence" produced in him complex emotions, involved passions that would later lead him to intricate love affairs with several
men and a strange, parallel series of near-love-affairs with married women, the years of adolescence in Cleveland were years
of high spirits, joy, and hope.

If we are to see this seventeen-year-old boy accurately, we
must see not just the product of a dominating mother, a doting
grandmother, and a father ambitious for worldly success, but a
boy who kept before himself two bright dreams.

One dream involved a glorification of friendship. It was a grand
and idealistic dream, a vision of almost total communication between himself and good friends who would know him to the
core. To those friends he would be able to confess everything—
hopes and ambitions, secret sins, fears. He would be able to count
on them in any emergency. Numbered among them were such
boys as George Bryan, Kenneth Hurd, and William Wright and
such young men as Carl Schmitt. To the very end of his life,
similar friendships—both with men and with women—would provide the stability he could only sporadically find in his own family and in himself. They gave him, to use a word that would be
for the next ten years his key to life and art, "balance."

His other dream involved an unqualified spiritual commitment
to art. Just as friendship could provide the balance that would
resolve all the tensions of disordered life, so art could express
those tensions and resolve them into some permanent form. The
making of a poem, the "composition" of all its scattered com-
ponents—ideas and emotions, images and statements, rhythms
and rhymes—could only be achieved through balances as delicate as those which in the real world produced friendship. "I have

had tremendous struggles," he wrote Schmitt, "but out of the travail, I think, must come advancement. . . . Carl, I feel a great peace; my inner life has balanced, as I expected, the other side of the scale. Thank God, I am young, I have the confidence and will to *make* fate."

That the fate he made was not the fate he anticipated is self-evident; his best-laid plans could not include all the incalculable forces that moved about him. "Someday, perhaps next summer," he wrote Schmitt, "I shall come to you and we may work together. You understand, I know." But fate hurried him along, and within a week—not within the six months he had expected—he was on the New York train. C.A., Grace, and Zell had decided—perhaps as a kind of Christmas present, for he left just after the holiday—that he should be given the opportunity to prove himself in New York City.

# 3

It is impossible now to reconstruct the emotions of the seventeen-year-old who, just after Christmas of 1916, boarded a train for New York in search of the kind of freedom he had never known at home. Behind him he left the warm security of his grandmother's home, the few close friends he had made at school, and the shocked relatives of his father, who, upset by Grace's divorce action, were further disturbed to learn that Harold, supervised only by a young painter and by Mr. Crane's business associates, was to be allowed to descend on the wickedest and cruelest city in America.

To some extent Harold must have shared the doubts of his relatives. He knew that his father and mother were anxious to see him register at a college. Yet, better than either of his parents, he knew how unlikely it was that, with his incomplete school record, he would be accepted by any college. For the next six months he diligently wrote Grace and C.A. details of his tutoring for a Columbia University entrance examination, but within weeks after his arrival in New York he had adjusted his lessons more toward preparing for the life of a poet than for the life of a scholar.

When, twelve hours after he left Cleveland, he got off the holiday-crowded train to enter the bustle and rush of Grand Central Station, he must, for a moment at least, have doubted the wisdom of his move. In New York City he knew personally only his "guardian" Carl Schmitt. He had instructions from his mother to call on several of her friends and from his father to visit the Crane Candy Company's office at 18 West Thirty-third Street, where he soon established himself as a favorite with Mr. Crane's New York representative, Hazel Hasham, and with Miss Bohn, whom, a week after his arrival, he describes to his father as "a dandy," a person who "has a very sweet way, sincere, and earnest." Harold had made plans to spend some time in the office-bookstores of his "New York editors," Guido Bruno and Joseph Kling. But he did not know anyone within ten years of his own age. And in his first month in New York he would not become closely acquainted with any young people at all. Consequently, whereas his early letters home are filled with references to his busy efforts to soak up New York's culture, after the first week more and more space is devoted to requests to his mother to "write me often," explanations to his father that "While I am not home-sick, I yet am far from comfortable without letters, and often, from you," and pleas to his grandmother to urge his friends to keep up their correspondence.

To his new acquaintances, most of them in their late twenties and early thirties, Crane was a lonely, bright young boy. Some of them saw him as a protégé, a discovery whom they were willing to teach or to help, but he was also frequently a barely tolerated pest, always underfoot when work was to be done. "I felt sorry for him," Joseph Kling told me. "He'd come in and hang around the office half the day. He never had anything to do." Carl Schmitt, burdened by too many visits from his young friend during Crane's first months in New York, took to locking his door and refusing to answer it. "He'd take all of your time if you'd let him," Schmitt recalled. "He was a wonderful person to talk to. He'd talk to you for hours; but I had work to do, and sometimes I had to pretend I wasn't home."

In Crane's first month in New York City, however, he and Schmitt were the closest of companions. Crane went from the train directly to Schmitt's studio at 308 East Fifteenth Street, and the two set out quickly to find Crane a room of his own nearby. The one they located, at 139 East Fifteenth Street, dark, dirty, and cold, was to be only a temporary expedient—but the rent was low and the neighborhood colorful. Summing up the room's advantages and disadvantages in a letter to his father, Crane explained, "The room I have now is a bit too small, so after my week is up, I shall seek out another place near here, for I like the neighborhood. The houses are so different here, that it seems most interesting, for a while at least, to live in one." Crane spent well over a month in the room on Fifteenth Street, but by the end of the first week he was depressed by rooming-house grime. Trained to be fastidious, he had done his best to clean and polish everything that could be cleaned, but the hall bathroom was beyond his control. "The bath-rooms in the boarding-house are a nightmare, they are so filthy," he wrote his mother. On the same day, in a man-to-man letter to his father, he hinted that his discomfort was the consequence of a small allowance: "I do most of my bathing and dumping over at Carl's, as these rooming-house privys, and bathtubs are frightful. Sometime later I expect to be able to afford a small bath-room of my own. Bedbugs, too, have been an awful trial; but never you fear, I am having some fine experiences."

The most vivid of those fine experiences was Crane's encounter with the city itself. On the last day of 1916, for instance, he had set out in style to ring out the old and ring in the new. "I have just been out for a long ride up Fifth Ave. on an omnibus," he wrote his father. "It is very cold but clear, and the marble facades of the marvelous mansions shone like crystal in the sun."

New York at the turn of that year was indeed a glittering place. And though *The New York Times* the next day reported that the Sunday New Year's Eve had made for a gentle celebration, "The Great Cabaret Belt" comparatively quiet and only modest crowds gathering in Times Square to watch the "great ball of incandescent lights" descending on the Times Building pole, for Harold the city was a place of wonder.

It is true, of course, that he was no stranger to city life or to the arts. All through his last year in Cleveland, he and Bill Wright had gone downtown to see visiting road companies or to attend vaudeville performances at the Hippodrome.

But here in New York everything was available at once. That Sunday afternoon when Harold had admired the marble façades of Fifth Avenue, Damrosch was at Aeolian Hall leading the New York Symphony in a performance of one of Harold's favorite pieces of music, Dvořák's "New World." Nearby, at Carnegie Hall, Fritz Kreisler played before a standing-room audience; and that evening, as Harold watched Times Square fill with its "modest crowd," Efrem Zimbalist packed 4,000 people into the jammed Metropolitan Opera House. Music, in this heyday of the soloist, seemed to be everywhere: Leopold Stokowski was about to bring the Philadelphia Orchestra to Carnegie Hall for an afternoon concert with soloists Josef Hofmann and Fritz Kreisler, Alma Gluck was soon to be heard with the New York Symphony, and Karl Muck was scheduled in mid-January to lead the Boston Symphony in a sure sell-out, his soloists, top drawing cards Paderewski and Kreisler.

Broadway was also booming, all the popular stars having returned to capitalize on the city's prewar swirling prosperity. One of Crane's first efforts at self-education was, as a matter of fact, at the theater. "Last night," he wrote his mother early in his stay, "I saw Warfield in 'The Music Master.' It was tear-moving." He had had a wide choice of plays, for William Faversham was at the Booth in Shaw's *Getting Married*, Anna Held was playing in *Follow Me*, Maude Adams was at the Empire in J. M. Barrie's *A Kiss for Cinderella*, Ruth Chatterton was playing in *Come Out of the Kitchen*, Laurette Taylor was at the Globe in *The Harp of Life*, and, twice a day at the New York Hippodrome, Anna Pavlova was appearing in *The Big Show*, an extravaganza that claimed "1000 people" in its production and that featured in second billing to Pavlova a "New Ice Ballet." In Greenwich Village, the Washington Square Players were presenting a bill of four one-act comedies.

The young motion-picture industry was also putting its best—
or its most spectacular—foot forward, the 44th Street Theatre advertising Geraldine Farrar in Cecil B. DeMille's *Joan the Woman*,
"proof that the Motion Picture is an Art!" For those interested in
more mundane things, Burton Holmes was conducting trave-
logues in Carnegie Hall, and at the old Madison Square Garden,
"the Crystal Palace of America," for fifty cents one could attend
the annual poultry show.

Progress and prosperity were everywhere. The boom times almost crowded off the front pages Europe's contradictory war
news, rumors of impending peace flanked on one side by the
Kaiser's New Year proclamation to his troops that "you are vic-
torious in all theaters on land and sea" and on the other by accounts of a German famine, hints of German revolution, and a
story about the soon-to-be-rejected German "peace note." Possible Russian revolution threw a long shadow across the foreign
news ("Duma Denounces 'Dark Forces' "; "Revolution Aimed at
Sinister Influences Undermining Russia's War Efforts"). Local political corruption and a lurid murder ("Find a Girl Model
Strangled to Death") offered readers the diversion of scandal.

At first, Crane was struck by the crowds he found everywhere.
"Well, I haven't seen anybody as fine as you, Mother, and probably won't," he wrote home. "But I am meeting humanity here;
all kinds of it; and it is absorbing." *Humanity*, in fact, became a
principal theme in many early letters. "I took a long ride on an
omnibus out into the Bronx and back," he wrote his mother a
little later, "and saw all the fashion on Fifth Ave. When you see
the display of wealth and beauty here, it will make you crawl.
It is the most gorgeous city imaginable, besides being at present
the richest and most active place in the world. The swarms of
humanity of all classes inspire the most diverse of feelings: envy,
hate, admiration and repulsion. But truly it is *the* place to live."
And to his father, more directly, Crane did his best to explain the
importance of the multitudes. Somewhere in the crowd, Harold
felt, he might discover his "lost identity": "It is a great shock, but
a good tonic, to come down here as I have and view the countless
multitudes. It seems sometimes almost as though you had lost
yourself, and were trying vainly to find somewhere in this sea of
humanity, your lost identity." Alone, in the room he came to hate,
he worked the material of these letters into "The Hive," the first
of his poems written and published in New York. It appeared in
the March issue of *The Pagan* and identifies the city-world with
the poet's heart: "Humanity pecks, claws, sobs and climbs" up
the "chasm-walls" "Of the hive of the world that is my heart."
From this violence, mercy and love emerge, "And I watch, and
say, 'These the anguish are worth.' " As much a product of Crane's
careful study of turn-of-the-century Symonds and Yeats as it is of
his experience of multitude, the poem nevertheless reveals clearly

that Crane knew what he was talking about when he wrote his father that he would soon make "serious efforts" to become a professional writer: "If you will help me to the necessities, I think that within six months I shall be fairly able to stand on my own feet. Work is much easier here where I can concentrate."

Crane began quickly to work hard at his writing, his principal teacher being Carl Schmitt. Harold was a daily visitor in Schmitt's Stuyvesant Square studio, where the talk would inevitably center on problems of aesthetics. Schmitt, an enthusiastic theoretician, stressed the significance of balance in the finished work of art, an idea that Crane had taken to in their earlier Warren conversations and in their correspondence before Crane's arrival in New York. The art object—whether painting or poem or symphony—was, in Schmitt's view, achieved through an intricate set of precise and delicate balances. These balances operated, Schmitt liked to say, in an "area of expediency" which could be visualized in terms of the intersection of a vertical spiritual plane and a horizontal material one:

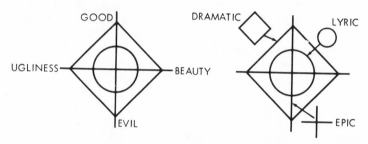

The spiritual plane in this diagram governed the whole range of moral experience and the material plane the whole range of sensuous and aesthetic experience. Since man's life is always compounded from a mixture of good and evil, beauty and ugliness, spirit and flesh, his art can exist only in the core of the diagram, the "area of expediency." (No man can, for example, experience absolute beauty. Similarly, no man and no art can be absolutely free of spirituality, or, for that matter, absolutely free of materiality.) As the French symbolists had insisted, even though all of man's art, even music, is of necessity grounded in the material plane, spiritual correspondences do exist and can be evoked through the harmonious arrangement of material symbols in the formal work of art.

All these ideas were meat and drink to Crane. "Nearly every evening since my advent," he wrote his father,

> has been spent in the companionship of Carl. Last night we unpacked some furniture of his which had arrived from his home, and afterward talked until twelve, or after, behind our pipes. He has some very splendid ideas about artistic, and

psychic balance, analysis, etc. I realize more entirely every day, that I am preparing for a fine life: that I have powers, which, if correctly balanced, will enable me to mount to extraordinary latitudes. There is constantly an inward struggle, but the time to worry is only when there is no inward debate, and consequently there is smooth sliding to the devil. There is only one harmony, that is the equilibrium maintained by two opposite forces, equally strong. When I perceive one emotion growing overpowering to a fact, or statement of reason, then the only manly, worthy, sensible thing to do, is build up the logical side, and attain balance, and in art,—formal expression. I intend this week to begin my studying,—Latin, German, and philosophy, right here in my room. They will balance my emotional nature, and lead me to more exact expression.

Readers of Crane's poetry are usually struck by pyrotechnical displays of synesthesia. Crane studied this deliberate confusion of the senses in the French poets he laboriously translated, but a groundwork for the technique was offered in his conversations with Schmitt. For in Schmitt's scheme all the arts were necessarily interrelated; and part of the artist's problem was the calculation of the proper degree of "borrowing" from sister arts to make any particular work most expressive. How much should such "space" arts as painting and sculpture draw on the elements that logically dominate the arts that can only be experienced in time (literature, music, etc.)? How much rhythm—essentially a property of the "time" arts—can be incorporated in a painting before the painter's special concern, vision, becomes distorted? Using his own canvases for illustration, Schmitt taught Crane how to see.

"Carl is a more wonderful man than you have any idea. A tremendous thinker!" Harold wrote his mother. To his father he praised Carl for being "very good to me, giving hours of time to me, advising . . ." Almost every night they met for supper in a nearby Italian restaurant, then returned to Carl's roomy studio to "spend the evening in aesthetic talk."

Schmitt—a born teacher—was determined that Crane master not only a general theory of art but the particular techniques of poetry as well. Crane had brought with him to New York a group of poems that seemed to Schmitt metrically and imagistically awkward. What Crane needed, he felt, was a set of technical exercises designed to give him the feel of musical language. Play with words, Schmitt urged. Learn how the sounds of poetry counterpoint the sense or how they carry independent melodies of their own. Substitute nonsense words in favorite poems to find out what the sounds themselves are doing. Crane at first howled with pain as Schmitt dismembered Poe's "Ulalume" by substituting "darn tanks of lager / In the misty mud regions of beer" for Poe's "dank tarn of Auber" and "misty mid region of Weir." Yet he soon delighted in bringing to Schmitt ingenious rhythmical exercises and displays of alliterative nonsense. Sample for sample, Schmitt would match Crane's work, the two men scribbling far into the night on either side of Schmitt's studio table. Crane's efforts have all vanished, but one of Schmitt's survives to reveal the ingenious rhymes and rhythms he pressed on his young protégé. Titled "A Caution," it was printed in the November 1918 issue of *The Pagan*, where Crane, by that time associate editor of Kling's magazine, did his best to immortalize his friend's comic efforts.

> I would rather keep my wife,—
> Lead an awful lawful life,
> Than give up eats
> And die like Keats,
> Or suffer like poor Shelley.
>
> If you'd be like William Shakespeare
> Cultivate the guy that makes beer: —
> Even Dante drank chianti, so they say—bum, bum.
> And Milton in his early teens
> Had foaming ale with ham and beans: —
> That's why they're great,—they simply ATE!
> They had three meals a day!
>
> Don't end up E. A. Poe-ical,—
> Live right on earth, heroical,—
> You needn't starve your soul to feed your belly,—tra-la-la.
>
> I would rather cast my lot
> With a waffle awful hot,—
> Than give up eats,
> And die like Keats,—
> Or suffer like poor Shelley.

Not all of Crane's work with Schmitt centered on technical exercise, however. Schmitt was a sensitive and careful reader who was familiar with the work of most of the major English and Continental poets, and with a good many of the obscure ones as well. A devout Catholic, Schmitt was particularly fond of Dante and would be one of the first Americans to discover and admire Hopkins.

What Crane wanted, though, was the conversation of living poets. This, too, Schmitt could provide. A friend of Padraic and Mary Colum, Schmitt arranged for Crane to pay a visit. "Really," Crane wrote his mother, "as I expected, I am right in the swing. Tomorrow I call on the noted Irish poet-dramatist, Padraic Colum. Then I shall meet Frank Harris, editor of 'Pearsons,' and friend-biographer of Oscar Wilde. . . . Within a few weeks I expect to be printed in the columns of the 'New York Evening Sun.' Fine, isn't it."

His meeting with the Colums—postponed a few days—was even more satisfying than he had expected it to be, for not only had Schmitt spoken well of him but so had Crane's literary correspondent, Mrs. Moody. "Today has been both rainy and busy," Harold wrote his mother on January 5:

> that is, "busy" in the most pleasant sense of the word. This afternoon I made a call on Padraic Colum, whom I mentioned to you before. We shall be great friends, I think, and he has asked me to call again on next Monday afternoon. In the conversation I found that he is a great friend of Mrs. Moody, so that added a great interest in our acquaintanceship. Also I was much pleased, on mentioning her name, to hear him quote some lines of my verse, which she had evidently shown him, and which he seemed to think excellent.

Two days later he wrote his grandmother: "Things are progressing splendidly; I am striking up a real friendship with Padraic Colum, who is really enthusiastic about my work, and whose wife is a dear, red-haired, cultured Irish-woman."

Though the dear, red-haired, cultured Irishwoman never really took to Crane's poetry, feeling that at no time did Crane "give an emotional significance to words or perhaps an emotional significance to his mind or to his life," she did find him fascinating as a type of American would-be intellectual. She saw him as "gangling, semiliterate" and was amused by his arrival, for after a few minutes' conversation he pulled out from his pocket a sheaf of verses which he read "in a dull voice and in an embarrassed way." Gradually she came to pity him because of the obstacles that both her husband and she could see in his path. "He would come round to see us about twice a week and talk about poetry, never getting over his excitement at how much we seemed to know about it. 'How do you know all this?' he would ask gravely as he helped me with household chores and to make tea and scones." At first they talked of writers the Colums knew, and Crane was encouraged to study Arthur Symons's book on the Symbolist movement. In time Crane came to use his sessions in the Colums' kitchen as part of the informal education he was organizing for himself. Delighted that Mary Colum could quote whole poems in French, and entertaining her with what she felt was his "queer pronunciation," he would put her through her paces on Baudelaire, Rimbaud, and Verlaine. By the end of January, accepted by Padraic and Mary as a friend of the family, Crane proudly wrote his mother that he had sent to Mr. Sullivan, the lawyer who had arranged Grace's divorce, "a choice volume of Irish songs autographed by one of the principal literary figures in America today, Padraic Colum."

I have invited Colum and his wife to dine with me tomorrow night at Gonfarones, an Italian eating-place, where the table d'hote costs only 60 cents per plate, and where the food is fine. Colum says I should have a volume of verse out in two years without any difficulty, and has offered to write a preface for it also. He has seen, as I said before, all my work,—nearly all, and admires it.

Another poet who had seen some of Crane's work was Conrad Aiken, who, in New York on a one-day visit, spent an afternoon in his friend Schmitt's studio talking informally with the poet and the painter. And though Crane was never to become close to Alfred Kreymborg, Kreymborg did look at Crane's work with a view toward publishing some of it in *Others*. Meeting through Schmitt or Mrs. Moody such artists as Jerome Blum, such poets as Ridgely Torrence, and such popular idols as Earl Derr Biggers ("Earl Biggers, the author of 'Seven Keys to Bald Pate,' was in for some grub, and I was shocked nearly off my feet by the quietness and un-worldliness of his behaviour"), Crane felt "everything is optimistic." "At this age," he wrote his grandmother, "there is no necessity to drudge, when so much awaits me in the future."

Most days, in spite of a scattering of lonely hours, were for Crane full ones. He planned a reading program and was for a while faithful to it, spending part of each day at home with his books or at The New York Public Library at Forty-second Street. As soon as he found a friend with a piano, he sent to Cleveland for his music. He attended as many concerts and lectures as he could afford.

Schmitt, the Colums, and—on her infrequent visits—Mrs. Moody did their best to see that he used free time profitably. "Mrs. Moody gave a fine dinner," he wrote his mother on the first of February, "and I can't tell you how many distinguished people were there. Then there was music in the evening up at Mr. Moody's old apartment on Washington Square, and Mr. Colum read from his last book." By the middle of February he could write his mother: "People here have surely treated me splendidly; Mrs. Moody, Carl, the Colums, and last but not least, the Lords [parents of the young woman who was to marry Carl Schmitt], people you have yet to meet in order to become fully convinced." By way of summary, he explained his immediate plans:

I wish above all other things that you could be here this week, for there are several big things that I have been invited to. The initial exhibition of the choicest of Chase's pictures is to be privately (by invitation) opened tomorrow afternoon from four until six. The greatest painters of the day will attend. Carl having given me his invitation, I am going to take Mr. Colum and perhaps his wife. Then Mr. Colum has given me a ticket to the reading by Vachel Lindsay of his own poems at the Princess

Theater. Also, on Thursday, I shall attend the meeting of the Poetry Society of America, which is quite exclusive.

On the surface all seemed to be well. Yet Crane was experiencing a series of complex and disconcerting emotional upheavals, most of them the direct result of pressures unintentionally imposed on him by his divided parents.

For he corresponded with both his father and his mother and acted for each as the principal agent of news about the other. Too involved in their tangled feelings to judge either parent dispassionately, yet trying to help both of them, he was baffled by their alternate praise and condemnation of each other.

At times it must have seemed that the divorce action would be called off, so affectionate did Grace and C.A. appear to be. On January 30, for instance, Grace wrote Harold: "Your father sent me your letter to him. I thought it was a fine one and remember always to write him just as good ones. Who knows but what our separation is as much of a tragedy to him as to me. We have both suffered much and perhaps have some sorrow yet to overcome." Three days later his father wrote: "You must be careful to write [your mother] often for she misses you and I know has much to contend with in the matter of her own trials and tribulations. I would arrange to write her at least twice a week always, and make her feel that you are just as interested in her as you always have been, and are not unmindful of the fact that she is going through one of the hardest trials of her life." Yet within a week of her earlier letter Grace shifted from praise to blame: "Your father's provision for me has been very small everything considered. Everyone says that, but he refuses to do more and so if he is content to send me away after nearly twenty years of service, I say Amen—I will manage some way—and if I can only get strong I can work and he is welcome to his money and all it may bring him."

Other concerns also were very much in Crane's mind. He was worried about his grandmother's health. All through January, Grace explained to her son, Mrs. Hart had suffered from a severe cold, and afterwards from a bilious attack. "These kept her in bed some days and made it hard and confining for me. . . . She has failed a great deal lately but still insists that she is in the ring."

But he was even more worried about his mother's unstable emotions. Her anxiety over the divorce, he felt, might lead directly to another breakdown. He recognized the warning signs. She was convinced that a recent operation had been unsuccessful. Her doctor, she wrote, was "fearful of an adhesion." Yet she immediately set out on a set of erratic and unsatisfactory journeys.

The first of them had occurred just after Crane left Cleveland for New York, Grace packing quickly and heading for Chicago with Molly, the Cranes' maid-of-all-work ("one of the few," according to Harold). "I shall think of you especially on New Year's Eve in the big City," she wrote her son. "I shall be in Chicago and grandma and your father here. What strange positions fate places us in."

No sooner had she written than she had evidence of the melodramatic pattern of her "fate." For a farewell note arrived from C.A. as she and Molly were about to leave for the train. Accompanied by a corsage of violets that enclosed a single rose, it must have seemed in many respects an epitome of her painful, passionate marriage—romance and tenderness and jealous possessiveness entangled in strands of vanity and affection.

"For *old* love's sake—Love sings a song
  Amid the ruins where the garden bloomed with beauty—
    when life was young and fair.
  And on its broken statue's brow—a rosied wreath he binds.
  Love isn't love that alters—when it alteration finds."

Surely no words of my own framing could express my heart as these do. Please wear this rose out of Cleveland, and if my thoughts and true desires help at *all*—you'll find solace and health. I shall think of you each hour and pray for you each night.

                                As always
                                Clarence

And I've opened this again to tell *you* that you're leaving with my heart and my *affection* tucked away where its been for twenty years.

Her first letter from Harold must also have deepened her consciousness of the inextricability of her involvement. In one sense, Grace Crane's life was dominated by a headlong search for a free companionship. She had hoped to discover it with her husband, then with her son, then with a second husband, and at the end of her life with the memory of her dead son. Yet, instead of the free affection she yearned for, she was burdened with responsibility that she was temperamentally incapable of shouldering. Rather than contributing to the rest and relaxation she had hoped to find in Chicago, Harold's letter only reminded her how important his claims on her were. "You are in Chicago, as I suppose from your letter today rec'd.," he wrote.

How I do long for your ultimate, complete happiness! You are a queen, and you shall have it too. Often I have come across the most charming, odd apartments in my walks and I like to think of you calmly happy in one of them, happy with me and Grandma, in a few clean rooms.

Separated, mother and son grew closer than ever before. "You will never know how happy your letters, which came to me today, made me," she wrote back, insistently repeating, "Your letters were a joy." From this time on, her letters are not signed simply "Mother" as in the past, but "From your Dearest, Grace." His letters to her frequently begin "My dear, dear Mother." "If he seemed to dislike his father," Mary Colum wrote, remembering this time, "he was psychologically, though perhaps not emotionally, so involved with his mother that he doubted if he could ever pull himself free of her."

This long-distance involvement grew as mother and son exchanged increasingly intimate letters. Chicago, Grace soon decided, was not really satisfactory, so within a week she and Molly returned to Cleveland. "Your father is going away somewhere soon from what he said to me over the phone," she wrote her son, "and soon you will be almost a real orphan. The old home looks lonesome enough now and I am anxious to arrange my affairs to go east to live with you." But before she came to join him in New York, she felt, she should go to Florida to get the rest she had not yet been able to find. Still, whether in Chicago or in Florida, she would be, she made clear, a changed woman. C.A. had been the center of her life. Harold would now fill that spot.

> Harold perhaps it will be a satisfaction to you [to] know that I am really happy and that my dear son has with his own courage and philosophy done almost all there was to do to bring me to that state of mind.
>
> You, in my trouble, have been able to pay me for all the care and anxiety I have had for you since you came to me nearly eighteen years ago. I am expecting great things of you and when we see each other again we can talk over our plans which look very beautiful to me now.
>
> I am asking you to send me your love every day as I shall you. Write me often at the Royal Poinciana. I shall think of you, on the night of the 23rd when the three Jannotta boys from Cornell and Verna and Mildred Ross are there and shall be saying to myself—How much I wish you all could see my boy—. If we dance my partner will not be there—but I shall dance and be happy thinking of how rich I am in having you.

There is no question that Grace did often think of Harold while she was in Florida, and there is also no question that in the first few days she found the sort of distraction she had been searching for. She had gone to Palm Beach to help celebrate the Golden Wedding of her friends the Skiffs, and she soon went through an exciting round of parties: "I have never done any letter writing under such disadvantages as here. It is almost impossible to snatch a moment to write to any one—so much to see, hear, and do, and one feels extravagant to miss any of the attractions that are here when it costs so much to stay at the hotel which provides them." To keep up with the crowd, Grace had invested in a new wardrobe: "I wish you might see me my dear, for I have some very pretty sport clothes and this is the place where one has to have them." She participated in the hotel Cake Walk, spent evenings in ballroom dancing, took trips to the Lake Worth oyster beds, became a "regular" at the afternoon "tea dansants" at Cocoanut Grove—"the loveliest spot imaginable." She danced, as she had predicted, with the young sons of her friends the Jannottas, but, as she quickly pointed out to her son, "I did wish for you."

Letters of this sort entertained and disturbed Harold, for he was painfully envious of his mother's easy entry into high society. And though he was careful to write mother, father, and grandmother of his excitement over his suddenly achieved independence, he was also uncomfortably aware that in order to entertain his new friends in even modest ways, he had to make do with only the barest necessities. (Mute evidence of his efforts to keep track of the sums his mother and father sent him can be found in margins of manuscripts and letters, as, for example, at the bottom of the telegram he received from Grace on January 23, the day after her arrival at Palm Beach. While blizzards howled outside his room, he read her night letter: "MOTHER AND I ARRIVED HERE THIS MORNING WAS SO DISAPPOINTED NOT TO FIND A LETTER FROM YOU HERE DO WRITE ME SOON I AM THINKING OF THE LAST TIME YOU AND I WERE HERE HOPE YOU ARE WELL AND HAPPY WEATHER HERE JUST LIKE SUMMER LOVE GRACE." Beneath it in neat pencil Harold had calculated his week's spending: $2, 5, 2.50, 2.50, 1.25, 1.50, 1.25, 1.75, .50, 4.00, 4.00, .50, totaling it as approximately $28.00, and adding beneath it $30—perhaps his budget for the coming week.)

His financial difficulties—and he had many—were partly the consequence of the stratagems he had used to convince the members of his family that he should come to New York. He had told his mother that he intended to tutor for enrollment at Columbia and that he chose New York as the place for his study because of its cultural advantages. Knowing that his father would be unlikely to respond to a plan of this sort, Harold had told him that it was his "avowed intent" to get something to do in New York, preferably on a magazine. He may have intended to carry out both plans; but if so, his early talks with Carl Schmitt had put both projects out of mind. For Carl felt that the artist could accomplish more through independent study than in any institution: Harold's proper program was neither to work nor to go to school, but rather to engage in a private campaign for self-improvement.

Almost immediately, Harold ran out of money. In desperation, he turned to his father, suggesting that the best arrangement might be private study in New York until college opened in the fall. C.A., no doubt startled at Grace's extravagant spree and

Harold's sudden and expensive change of plans, mailed off $25 to meet current expenses and did his best to offer good advice: "It is all right for you to stay in New York for a while, and get an experience there, but I do not think it is the right place for you to stay until next fall, provided you are not employed."

Like Grace in her letter in answer to the same proposition, C.A. emphasized the importance of college.

> You do not have to make plans for your maintenance or come to any understandings after you have obtained the age of 20. If you had followed my desires, you would plan on a splendid college career, the better to prepare yourself for what I think you are perhaps best adapted to. I scarcely [know] how you can gain the result desired unless you do have that college education.

C.A.'s immediate suggestion must have made his son's aesthetic hair stand on end: "How would you like to go to Calvert or some military school this summer, where you would get a liberal amount of outdoor exercise, as well as some book work, and perhaps prepare yourself to enter college or some preparatory school this fall?" It seems unlikely that the alternative suggestion his father made several weeks later, that Harold return to Warren, Ohio, to work on his Aunt Zell's paper, met with a happier reception.

If the preparation of a budget satisfactory to his father worried him, letters from his mother did little to make Harold's days brighter. Grace soon became dissatisfied with her splendid vacation. A siege of cold weather ("terrible weather—so cold that all the shrubbery froze and the only place that one could be really comfortable was in bed"), her mother's worsening health, rumors of United States' involvement in war that "stirred everyone up," particularly her wealthy friends ("As this is the most fashionable resort and consequently many moneyed people here, there is much excitement and concern. . . . They tell me that 40% of Wall Street stocks was manipulated from here, so that shows who's here"), all combined to ruin Grace's holiday: "I feel as if I were out of touch with everything and everybody here and would be happier to be somewhere where it would be possible for me to get home overnight if necessary." To cap everything, Harold's letters became disconcertingly brief. Grace feared he was drifting away from her.

> You and I will have to have some serious talks about our plans for the future when I see you. For it is my earnest desire now to arrange things in Cleveland so that by next fall at the farthest I may join you in New York. In the midst of your enjoyment and enthusiasm of your new environment, I don't want you to be entirely unmindful that you have a duty to me

as well as I have toward you. After nineteen years of married life I am obliged to admit that it spells *"Failure"* for your father and me. For him it does not mean *all* because his business has been his profession, but for me it means all but you, for marriage has been my profession. Most of the time I am optimistic about my future because it lies with you I *hope*, but once in a while I must confess I lose hold of myself and let me tell you my dear boy that those hours are real agony. Not that I wish to return to your father nor do I regret the step I have taken, but rebellion, resentment, malice etc. for the manner in which I have been treated, come forth for me to fight back, about every so often, no matter how hard I try to keep them out of my consciousness. Being physically weak makes it the harder for me to fight these moods. Health is such a wonderful thing and in that I am almost bankrupt. So I am asking you to write me often Harold because your letters even though short are a stimulus to me and surely you love me enough to do what you can to help me fight my way back to peace, happiness, and health. . . . For awhile I shall have to spend money and take life easy—for the effects of my operation and all that followed are manifesting themselves now more and more.

Now no more of this—only one thing more. Do not allow yourself to become [an] egotist and unmindful of others. But just remember that true happiness is largely due to "service" and no matter how rich your day may have been in opportunities, it is not entirely complete unless you have done or thought of someone else. Please write me often. You have no idea how much you help me in so doing. We are planning to leave here the thirteenth, stop a few days in Washington, and then I am coming to see you and I want you to be glad to see me. It has been so long since anyone has been *glad* to see me.

Anxieties more than counterbalancing the attractions of Florida, Grace hurriedly packed, bundled her mother on the train, and rushed to Cleveland. Harold, alarmed about Grace's emotional stability, quickly answered her letter: "I am supposing that this will find you at home by several days, and hoping that you will not remain there very long, but come and see your anxious son as soon as you can." He alone, he felt, could bring her the peace neither mother nor husband, travel nor wealthy friends could offer. And to lure her to him he listed all the delights of the city he had come to find so fascinating.

But then, when you do come, there will be hosts of . . . things to do, as no one in New York is ever without some new place to go, or some event to witness. If you want a quiet time that can be easily had too; and I am not making any definite plans for you, as I want you to be unencumbered by any engagements during your stay. It will be enough to me to talk quietly with you, and have you with me. I am inquiring about schools etc. and we can also discuss that definitely when you arrive. N.Y. is overflowing, so let me reserve rooms for you ahead.

From the time he first arrived in New York, he had been intrigued with the variety of its restaurants. "Bun-shop food," he had written his father, "has really made me quite magnificent and fat." And earlier he had written his mother of the inexpensive splendors of New York's foreign restaurants: "Carl and I dine around the corner nearly every evening on a sumptuous meal (no fooling) for 50¢. I never found anything like it in Cleveland for the money: it includes soup, entree, roast, dessert and demitasse." Now he was quick once more to list such pleasures: "Last night I took dinner with Harold Thomas and Carl in an Italien restaurant where you have to speak Italien to get anything at all to eat. They cook everything in olive-oil so that one has a good cathartic with his meal besides a splendid gratification of the palate." Though the splendors of the "Italien" restaurant and its double-barreled delights may not have been much of an inducement, his urgent "Am so anxious to have you settle here, and I know you will be happy" undoubtedly turned the trick. In any event, in her next letter Grace announced that she would soon descend on New York. Elated, Harold wrote her in return a letter in which the loneliness that he had been carefully camouflaging finally broke through.

> Your good letter I have just read, and it cheered me up a good deal. You know, I am working hard and see very few people and even now haven't had more than a half-hour's talk with anyone for over a week. My work, though, is coming along finely, and I shall be published both in "Others" and again in the "Pagan" this next month. Yesterday was a day of tremendous work. I turned out in some ways, the finest piece of work yet, beside writing a shorter poem also.
>
> Mother, you do not appreciate how much I love you. I can tell by your letters that there exists a slight undercurrent of doubt, and I do not want it there. If you could know how I long to see you perhaps that might make some difference.
>
> Now everything is in truth going splendidly, only I get terribly lonesome often when I am through working. A man *must* wag his tongue a little, or he'll lose his voice. Hurry, so that we can both wag!

On February 26 she wrote the letter he had been waiting for: "Don't delay at all in making a reservation for me at the Waldorf Astoria for [a] single room, *with bath.* . . . I want a hotel for awhile, a week at least, and feel most at home at the Waldorf." "I must be absolutely comfortable," she had earlier explained, "and have a large part of my mornings undisturbed for a while.

I am very uneasy and cannot promise you how long I will stay—but if I find I am happy there may make you quite a visit and you and I have many things to discuss and some to settle. You have written me so little about *yourself* that I can hardly realize I have a boy." She criticized him—but she made clear that, like him, she had no one else to turn to: "It seems very lonely here without you, and it isn't home anymore."

Harold, who had been in his new room at 54 West Tenth Street for only a week, immediately set about putting it to rights. Though as a child he had been compulsively neat, during parts of his adolescence he affected an "artistic" disarray. ("Harold's room at their residence at home was very untidy all of the time but he would make a small pretext of tidying up a bit when he had company," his friend George Bryan remembered. "At his room in New York on the several trips that I visited him, it was about the same; very untidy in 1917–1918.") Having assured his father that he was achieving "a fair amount of bodily cleanliness for health" and having been warned by his mother that he had best be careful to keep "body and mind clean," he had no alternative but to make his quarters presentable.

A touchier matter would face him when his mother arrived: explaining his falling out with Carl Schmitt. The reason was simple enough, for the friendship had cooled as a result of Crane's hero-worship—but Harold had difficulty seeing it in those terms. Always delighted to be in Schmitt's company, he had begun to extend the length of his visits to the studio, sometimes arriving early in the morning and staying far into the night. When Schmitt took to locking the door, Harold assumed his friend was out. But on one visit he heard Schmitt walking about in the room. The moment was awkward. Crane had arrived bearing a potted Easter lily, a present intended in part to compensate his friend for hours of advice and aesthetic instruction. "You can't imagine how guilty I felt when I finally opened that door," Schmitt recalled. "There sat that lonely plant. It troubled me for years." Schmitt tried the next time he saw Harold to explain that sometimes he had to isolate himself in order to accomplish his day's painting, but Crane's feelings were hurt and he wrote his father a long letter complaining of Carl's "betrayal" of friendship. C.A. did his best to bring the friends together again and was pleased at last to hear from Harold that things had improved. "I am glad to hear you say what you do about Carl," C.A. replied. "He is struggling for an existence and I would think you were very foolish not to make every effort to like him and especially appreciate his position. You are often a victim of moods, and sometimes they lead us to depths that are hard to understand when they have passed away." Though the friendship was patched up, the two young men were never again so close as they had been in Harold's first month in

New York. Unable to see how anyone could experience too much friendship, to the end of his life Crane would find both wounding and incomprehensible such "betrayals."

When, shortly after the first of March, Grace checked in at the Waldorf for what was to be a three-week visit, Harold had already lined up a series of dinners with his friends the Colums, with Schmitt, and with the Cleveland dramatist-essayist-philanthropist, Charles Brooks. Grace had known the Brooks family in Cleveland, but it was not until this visit that Harold had had an opportunity to spend much time with the urbane playwright. At the age of thirty-nine already a successful businessman, a founder of the Cleveland Playhouse, and the author of *Journeys to Bagdad*, Brooks provided for Crane and for his mother an easy entry into a group of upper-middle-class sophisticates, comfortably well off and talented. Here, in dinner conversation about current Broadway hits, Grace did her best to steer Harold back toward a college career, offering Yale-educated Brooks as a model of the successful college-graduate author.

Harold was never more than mildly amused by Brooks's literary accomplishments, but he enjoyed the dinners and was happy to find that Grace approved of his companions. ("I was delighted that you were with the Brooks," she wrote on her return to Cleveland, "also Mr. Colum and when we are back in New York again together we will have quite a little colony of friends.")

It was Carl Schmitt, however, briefly ranking high in Harold's affections because of his gallant devotion to Mrs. Crane, who was at the center of their social life. Handsome, witty, and still a bachelor, he seemed to Grace a personification of the hometown boy turned accomplished New Yorker. "Dear Carl! How glad I am you have him," Grace wrote. "It has meant so much to you to have such a friend and neither of you can possibly understand what it has meant to me. I shall hope that the future holds many good times for us three."

Certainly in her short visit she crowded in a maximum of good times. "You know Mother has been here," Harold wrote his father at the end of her stay, "and we have been so busy there has been no time spent here in my room at all." Accompanying her to theaters, concerts, and galleries, going with her on shopping expeditions, and even arranging for her to take lessons in "rhythmical physical culture," Harold saw to it that her days were full. To thank him for his efforts, she praised New York by disparaging Cleveland: "I was so glad you had not returned with me when I got off the train the other morning. The town looked so empty and dead and I knew your heart would have gone into the depths." A few days later she took up the same theme: "People look too fat and slow and sleepy here for me, and my heart and desires are with you back there. I wonder how it ever looked good to me. So you may count on my being at least a neighbor of yours just as soon as I am free to do so."

Part of the excitement of Grace's visit involved the still-pending divorce action. Convinced that C.A. was preparing to fight the divorce, Grace persuaded herself that she was being followed by private detectives. Her arrival therefore had a cloak-and-dagger secrecy. "Keep the news of my arrival to yourself and Carl. Will explain when I see you," one letter ended; and an earlier one warned Harold not to mention her coming to anyone associated with C.A., particularly Hazel Hasham: "I would prefer the priv-ilege of going and coming without being watched—just as your father does." Even after she returned to Cleveland, secrecy seemed called for: "Please refrain from talking over personal mat-ters with any one."

But not talking about personal matters proved for Harold more easily said than done. In escorting his mother to dinner and the theater, he had in the first few days of her visit exhausted his small cash reserve. Too proud of his independence to ask her to advance him money and forbidden to write C.A. that she was in New York, he began a series of secret moves of his own, dropping in at C.A.'s office whenever he ran out of cash to borrow as much as he could against his still-to-be-established allowance. The system worked well until just before his mother's return to Cleve-land. (Harold in the course of two weeks borrowed from Miss Hasham the sum of $168.) On March 21, however, C.A. got word of Harold's debt and of Grace's visit. He summoned his son to re-turn to Cleveland within a week's time.

Although no record of Harold's subsequent conversation with his mother survives, one can with no difficulty surmise the gist of their talk. For suddenly her visit is cut short, and Harold is again the model of a hard-working student. "Your telegram has just come telling me to be home in a week," he wrote his father,

> but I really must stay now, for I have begun tutoring for the summer course at Columbia, and there is no time to waste now in preparation. I shall have to cram day and night to attain the examinations at all, and so you see it is impossible to return just now.
>
> I sincerely want to get something done now in some direc-tion and I realize it is time to go about it. This tutoring is the only way to begin, leaving off in school as I did, and assured of approval in your eyes I have begun. I do hope it will be satis-factory to you. The catalogue of the summer course will be is-sued soon and then I shall send it to you so you can see all about it.

Grace, meanwhile, was in consultation with the family lawyer, Mr. Sullivan. Immediately after receiving C.A.'s wire, Harold had inquired of a local lawyer just what C.A.'s financial responsibility toward him was and what right C.A. had to call him home. In Cleveland, Grace had been asking the same question: "I have told Mr. S. your situation exactly and I feel quite sure you can trust your case in his hands. . . . The laws for Ohio are not the same as New York so New Yorkers are hardly capable of giving advice as to what to do. Of this one thing be assured and that is Mr. Sullivan is *your friend* and *admirer* and any advice coming from him you may rely upon." Basically, Mr. Sullivan's advice coincided with Grace's: Harold should stay in New York. "He is glad you did not come home with me, but thinks you have done the right thing in getting started upon your college work and seems to have every confidence that you will reach your goal. He admires your pluck and determination to succeed."

Fortified by Mr. Sullivan's advice and perhaps nettled by Grace's recommendation that he trim his budget ("get your living expenses down where you can show what your money goes for"), Harold set out to locate the least expensive tutor in New York (a budget sent to his father a little later put his weekly tutoring fees at $2) and prepared separate lists of living costs for mother, father, and grandmother. C.A., though concerned about "a boy of 17 years of age living a practically free life in New York City," finally consented to the study project: "If you can do it, and accomplish good work, you will surprise me. But I am willing to be surprised." C.A. found the debt run up at his office hard to take ("Hazel has become hopelessly confused in the matter of advancing you money," he explained to Harold and went on to point out that in an incorporated business even the president's son has to have some reason for drawing on office cash), but he seemed perfectly willing to cover all reasonable bills that his son might incur. Suddenly, to Harold's surprise, it was Grace who wanted a strict accounting. "My dear Mother," he wrote on April 3,

Carl has just come over with Grandmother's letter. My board costs at least $11.00 per week

room ————————————————————————6.00

laundry————————————————————1.50

And the clothing, I can't say.

I repeat again after my letter Sunday that I am not denied money by Father any more. At least the office gives it to me, and he sent a check of twenty-five two weeks ago.

But why all this list business? Isn't he supposed to pay what is reasonable until I am twenty-one without any such business as this? Grandma hasn't made it very plain in her letter what you want this for. Don't make any stipulation about what I am to be paid if you don't have to.

Grace, of course, wanted a detailed account of Harold's expenditures so she could present them in the impending divorce action, which moved to a rapid settlement. On April 6, three days after Harold had written his father, C.A. wrote Harold a long and affectionate letter, pointing out that rather than separating mother and father, the by-then-granted divorce had mysteriously brought them close once more. "If mother keeps up her present friendliness for me, I think we will both have performed a miracle in that we have come out of our troubles willing to forget and forgive, and nothing would please me better than the opportunity of not only doing for 'her, but going to see her as frequently as she might ever wish it."

Harold, his father indicated, was to continue along his present path as long as it gave him satisfaction.

> I want you to study hard, and accomplish all that you set out to do. To finish something is the greatest thing in the world, provided you finish it well and to your own satisfaction. If your forte is along literary lines, I am willing to lend my support that you will accomplish what will give you the greatest pleasure. I know how devoid of pleasure my work would be here if I could not inject into it some of the things which I like, even though my tastes may be quite plebeian.

> By the terms of the contract, you are turned over to your mother in the matter of custody; but that need make no difference, and I do not intend that it shall. We are both centered upon you, and your success will be our happiness.

Perhaps part of C.A.'s shift in tone toward his son's literary plans was a consequence of the success Harold seemed to be having. Though he was never to be published in *Others*, for months Crane was convinced that he would be. Almost everyone associated with the magazine had been bombarded by Crane with samples of his poetry. Even before his arrival in New York, William Carlos Williams had written him, praising his poems.

> Damn good stuff. "Others" is in a state of transition—to say the least, so— We'll keep your things in the hope that someday—someday—when we get some money—we may print them.

At the end of his first week in New York he had reported to his grandmother that William Carlos Williams and Kreymborg had accepted for publication one of his lyrics. By mid-April such publication seemed inevitable. In the same mail with the encouraging letter from his father came a cheerful note from Williams promising certain publication in the uncertain future.

> "Others" is floating precariously somewhere under and somewhere over something. It's lack of money as anyone can guess and yet we are alive!

> I like your things very much. The first 25 bones I touch shall

go into a miscellaneous issue in which as a newcomer you shall appear but—when?

If you want to see your work in print soon and have the opportunity to put it in some other magazine I advise you to do so.

I'm glad to hear from you and I'll see you sooner or later if you remain in N. Y.

*The Pagan*, however, offered Crane more than promises. Its end-of-March publication of "The Hive" brought joy to Crane's mother and grandmother. Here was real evidence that Harold's stay in New York was worthwhile. The marked copy of the magazine had arrived in Cleveland just after Grace's return and just before her birthday. It reminded her both of the pleasures of the city and of the promise of the son who would write "the world such poems." Celebrating, she put into practice the exercises she had learned at the "rhythmical Physical Culture" studio in New York:

To be serious, Harold, I was so proud at seeing you appear in the Pagan which arrived yesterday, that I straightway turned on the Victrola and expressed my delight in the most original dance you have yet to see. The only trouble was that my bedroom being small and very full I had some difficulty and was obliged to restrain my feelings more than I would have had there been more space. Your grandmother is always my most interested spectator, and once yesterday in my effort to get on the other side of the room avoiding both bed and bureau in my flight she looked a bit frightened. But she was soon herself again and tried some of the fancy steps herself. Last night before retiring we both played caterpillar and spring flowers etc. Mother informed me this morning that part of her bunion left in the night—so I think she is a very apt pupil. We can't be poets but we are doing our best to be nimble and keep up with the latest ideas.

She tried to make her son's way easy with his father by telling Harold to send the published copy of the poem to all of C.A.'s close relatives. ("It would please them and that is almost always the thing to do.")

Part of Harold's troubles, of course, can be traced to Grace's picture of herself as frustrated artist. Painfully conscious that she had been trapped by time and circumstance into a domestic round that destroyed her talent and her beauty ("I have grown very thin and look like a girl until you get a good look at my face," she had written her son), Grace did everything in her power to make sure that Harold got the opportunities she had lacked. Though she had still not entirely given up the dream of making a career for herself in musical comedy or in motion pictures, one career was immediately open to her: she could be the mother of a poet, smoothing his path, making a home for him in which he could entertain brilliant, witty friends. In her visit to New York they had talked over the sort of house or apartment they might get, Harold voting for suburban life, Grace for life in the city. "If your father should come to see you," she had written as soon as she returned to Cleveland, "try and get him to go to Gramercy Park and look at some studio apartments that will do for you and me. . . . Everyone I talk to that understands the conditions says that down town is the place to live rather than out."

Making a home for him was one way Grace could share her son's success; another more public way of sharing that success would be through his name: Harold Hart Crane. She had given the world a poet. The least he could do would be to give the world her name. On March 28 she had taken her copy of *The Pagan* to her friend Mrs. Baker to show her Harold's poem "The Hive." "Mrs. Baker is strong for Harold Crane," Grace wrote him the next day.

> By the way, writing that name brings to mind this question— In signing your name to your contributions and later to your books, do you intend to ignore your mother's side of the house entirely? That was the only thing I criticized about it. It seems to me that Hart or at least H. should come in somewhere. I understand that the Cranes say you get all your literary talent from them—uncle Fred, for instance, being the example they point to. If you feel that way, leave "Hart" out—but if not, now is the time to fix it right. How would "Hart Crane" be? No partiality there. You see I am already jealous, which is a sure sign I believe in your success.

In later years, after his final break with his mother, Hart would assure Lorna Dietz that it wasn't his mother's letter that had induced him to change his name but rather his hatred of the shrill "Haaaarooooold" she had used through his childhood to call him in from play. But for whatever reason—and affection is the most likely one—the next poem he published was signed *Harold H. Crane* and all subsequent ones *Hart Crane*.

Ostensibly to help his mother and grandmother close up their house in preparation for their move to New York, but more likely merely to enjoy a holiday with his at-last-happy family, Harold made a short visit to Cleveland, picking out the books he wanted later to be shipped to him both from his own library and from C.A.'s. As they looked through the books and talked over future plans, C.A. did his best to recollect his own college experiences and to offer Harold such advice as he could give.

Undoubtedly, they also spoke of the war; for only two weeks before, on April 6, the United States had officially declared war on Germany, and every city and town in America was suddenly alive with marching men. Soon after his visit, Harold, in a letter now lost, announced his intention to volunteer and C.A. in his answer counseled a watch-and-wait policy: "Now I want you to get over all this disturbance in your mind. The war need cause no such turmoil.as you indicate. If the time comes when our country needs us, why we will both go. I would make a very poor marcher, but some one has got to drive automobiles and I can do that." Meantime, as C.A. indicated, Harold had his study to keep him busy and C.A. had his business.

His business at this time was of some concern to C.A., for with the arrival of warm weather in the first months of war the candy business came to a standstill. "How is business?" Harold wrote soon after his return to New York.

> The war seems to put the blink of everything in the confectionary line, but you will have to suffer no worse than the rest. They are all getting out patriotic packages now, and you had better do the same. Pictures of Lincoln and Washington seem to be on all the boxes here, and they are tying them with red-white-and-blue ribbons. If the candymakers are to live at all now, they have GOT to be patriotic.

Harold was searching for a place in which his mother and grandmother could comfortably live; but as late as the day of their arrival, just after the first of May, he had found nothing that pleased them. Grace's heart, as she had made clear earlier, was set on Gramercy Square—and for nearly all of a rainy week, Grace and her son sloshed from one brownstone to the next, diligently looking for an apartment. "We certainly have had bum weather since Mother arrived," Harold wrote his father. "This was on last Tuesday, and it has rained ever since." Finally, in the second week of May, they located just what Grace wanted, an apartment at 44 Gramercy Square (135 East Twenty-first Street), in the same building with their Cleveland friends, Mr. and Mrs. Brooks. Subletting for the summer months, the two ladies and the boy settled in, Grace and her mother taking the bedroom and Harold sleeping in the living room. The little apartment was crowded, but it was comfortably furnished and it was in a good neighborhood, Gramercy Park still retaining much of the fashionable charm that had made it a turn-of-the-century showplace. Tenants of the buildings on the Square were entitled—as they still are—to gate keys to one of the finest private parks in the city, a two-block oasis of green. Here on sultry summer evenings Grace and her mother could rest on the neat benches beside formal gardens or chat with neighbors strolling clean gravel paths.

But finding a place to live did not solve all of Grace's problems. In the first few weeks Grace became increasingly moody. Though Harold and his grandmother did their best to divert her from her own troubles, neither trips to the theater nor automobile rides about the city in Hazel Hasham's car were of any great help. It was consequently with relief that Harold found that his mother and grandmother, in conversations with Mrs. Brooks, had once more developed an interest in Christian Science and were making serious efforts to put into practice the mind-healing principles of that creed.

Not even Christian Science, however, could distract Grace from money worries. Never before in her life having had to plan her finances, she now found herself suddenly operating with a generous but decidedly fixed income. Monthly bills always exceeded monthly income. As her own costs went up, so did her son's. "Mother and I must eat together now," he wrote his father, "and I cannot economize now on food so much as before." So awkward, in fact, did things become that Grace, Harold, and Miss Hasham all sat down one day to compose separate messages to C.A., each urging him to come to New York to help straighten out their difficulties. ("I do wish you would hurry and come," Harold's letter said. "There are so many things I want to discuss with you, which cannot be satisfactorily done in letters. I have to accept much money from Mother for expenses, and she really can't afford it at all.")

C.A. was about to set out from Cleveland on a business trip, but he took time to compose a long letter to Grace, making suggestions and outlining in some detail the allowance he proposed to give Harold. His letter, however, was never sent, Mr. Sullivan having suggested that there was nothing to be gained by "continued communications" between C.A. and his wife. Instead, C.A. wrote a brief note to Harold, explaining that he would advance him $140 a month for living expenses, $40 of which was to represent Harold's share of the rent.

This is your allowance for the time being. Whether it is ever increased or decreased depends entirely upon conditions under which your father has to submit. If you are conversant with what I am paying mother, what I have returned in interest, etc., and the monthly drain upon me, together with my own expenses, you will believe me when I say that it is in excess of my income, and I have had to borrow for it.

I want you to make progress, for what I am allowing you now represents $1680.00 a year—much more than anyone in my employ outside of Ervin and Hazel Hasham, and it is yours for the development of your education and under such conditions as I have never known of before. My two years at Allegheny College did not represent what this does in one year, and I am perfectly willing that you may have the experience, only I want you to know that your father is doing it because of his affection for you and not because any Court would grant you such an allowance under such conditions as exist. I am hoping that war-time conditions will not strand me, although we are dealing in very high class luxuries.

I am quite certain that this answers the question that your mother wished answered, for I know of nothing else between us to be discussed other than your welfare.

With much love, I am<br>Your father

The combined effects of Christian Science, C.A.'s letter, a three-week visit from Harold's Aunt Zell, and *The Pagan*'s publication of two more of Harold's poems brought a temporary harmony to the apartment at 44 Gramercy Park. The poems, both "night pieces," are strikingly different in tone and in structure. "Annunciations" builds to "high cries from great chasms of chaos outdrawn." The structurally much simpler "Fear" has night licking windows behind which a speaker is disturbed not so much by fear as by "demands." Less ambitious than "Annunciations," "Fear" is, I expect, for most readers a good deal more successful and for poets a good deal more interesting, the echoing half rhyme of "Give me your hands, / Friends" clear evidence of Crane's accurate ear.

Responding to pressure from his mother and his grandmother, Harold spent much of the first two weeks of June with his books and with his tutors. He was concentrating particularly on preparations for a Columbia qualifying examination in algebra that would be given at the end of June, but he was also trying to get his languages in shape for autumn examinations. His arrangement with Columbia involved his successfully passing examinations covering fifteen units of work, at which point he would be considered for admission to Columbia College; he was also attempting to supplement his high-school German and Latin with a reading knowledge of French.

In spite of these preparations, however, he was devoting more thought to the army than to college. A letter of June 5 to his father reveals the "uncertainties" he was doing his best to avoid. "Just what college-life during the next few years is to be, is very indefinite," he wrote. "Some have already been practically left empty, as Dartmouth, and there are large contingents going both from Yale and from Harvard. But I expect to go right ahead, and prepare myself, not allowing uncertainties to affect me at all."

With Grace apparently reconciled to her divorce and Harold busy at his studies, Mrs. Hart felt that she could return to Cleveland. Harold and Grace were both sorry to see her leave, yet both celebrated the freedom her absence gave them. Mrs. Crane could now go dancing with Cleveland visitors, and Harold enjoyed the luxury of weekends at the Connecticut home of his friends the Lords.

Perhaps Mrs. Hart's return to Cleveland was premature. As soon as her restraining presence was withdrawn, Grace and Harold turned in their private conversations to the divorce.

Most of her husband's troubles and her own, Grace felt, were caused not so much by incompatibility as by "nerves." And in the long run her diagnosis may not be far from the mark. Grace and C.A. spent a good deal of time and money treating ailments which could have had psychological rather than physical origins, and both of them recognized that Harold's "moods," his nervous irritability, and his severe attacks of hives might be the product of delicately balanced emotions. "He is looking fine now," Grace wrote C.A. in the middle of July, "although more or less nervous at times, a condition which he comes naturally by and will likely always have to struggle with more or less."

"Nerves" were also undoubtedly at the root of some of the ailments that plagued C.A. "I have had much trouble with my eyes for weeks," he wrote, "and the congestion in my head and neck which you are familiar with. At present I am going to the Osteopath twice every day, and once last week, I think he was scared; but this will pass away, and no doubt I am in for just as many years as the rest of you." Like his father, Harold enjoyed his illnesses. "I finally had to go to a doctor about my rose fever and some lung or palate trouble (I don't know yet which it was) and of course did not get away from him without undergoing some sort of operation," Harold wrote C.A. "He slyly reached in and cut my palate so that it was sore all day, which may have helped in alleviating an incessant cough I had, but which is better now. I never before had such a cold, and blow and sneeze all through these fine warm summer days. But in every other item of health I seem to hit a high mark."

If, Grace felt, "nerves" were responsible for her troubles with C.A., perhaps a new attitude on her part and on his—the sort of attitude she detected in his warm and sympathetic letters to Harold—might heal the wounds they had inflicted on each other. She was enthusiastically seconded by her son. His letters from his father had been congenial, and the two—separated by nearly 500 miles—seemed to draw much closer together than when they had lived in the same house. "Now I am awaiting your long letter promised in the last you wrote," Harold ended one letter, "but it will have to be pretty darn good to beat that last."

Grace, too, felt that she should make some effort, and a cheerful letter to C.A. brought a quick reply: "Your letter of the 7th came in the late mail last evening. It is the most pleasant occurrence I have had for some time, for it gives a promise of our ultimately becoming good friends, and that is what I have desired more than anything I can imagine."

Letters from Grace, C.A., and Harold are now newsy and af-

fectionate. C.A. tells of a visit with Maxfield Parrish, of a trip to
the Seiberling estate in Akron, and of changes he is planning
for his Cleveland stores. Harold recalls the winter before, when he
worked for Korner and Wood, and encloses newspaper clippings
that he thinks will interest his father. And he thanks him for a
"generous" gift of money for a new suit ("I shall get it tomorrow.
One really can't get along very well with one suit for every day
including Sundays"). Grace writes of a brief trip she made to
Newport, of her disappointment at failing to see Chicago relatives
("However, I am glad that Harold and they were able to see one
another"), and of her gratitude for C.A.'s gift of a large box of
candy. Grace and Harold make a point of stopping off at a Broadway photography shop to have a postcard portrait of themselves
prepared, a "splendid" one according to C.A., who sets it up on his
office desk.

As letters passed back and forth, Harold's mother and father
felt once more drawn toward each other. "If out of all this curtain
fire of trouble," C.A. wrote her, "we can emerge, seeing the best
in each other and blinded to the mistakes and hasty utterances,
I shall have much satisfaction and confidence that perhaps life
is really worth living." Grace, making plans for Harold's eighteenth birthday, found it impossible to write of her son without
thinking of her husband.

> On Saturday the twenty-first Harold will have reached his
> 18th year and I am planning some sort of a celebration which
> will suit my pocketbook and his pleasure. I often wonder if you
> realize what a fine son you have, and what possibilities he has
> for success along his chosen line of work. Of course you do not,
> for you are not with him as I am or in a position to see how he
> is regarded by others. To study Harold, to right as far as pos-
> sible any wrong ideas which he might have, about Life and
> people, and make up for my share of the unhappiness which has
> come into his young life, has been my chief object in being in
> New York. I feel that it is not too much to say that I am suc-
> ceeding, and that sometime if you are not already, you will be
> very proud of him. Of course he has his faults, but in most in-
> stances I recognize that they are only reproductions of yours
> and mine. . . . I am doing the best I know how, feeling per-
> fectly sure that the time will soon come when you will realize
> that your obligations towards Harold are not possible to be
> represented by money alone and that a perfect understanding
> between you two will be one of the most satisfying forces that
> can come into your lives. For after all, one's greatest and sur-
> est claim to posterity is through one's children, and I feel that
> whatever mistakes you and I may have made, Harold was not
> one of them.

Whatever happened between mid-July, when Grace drafted this letter to C.A., and August 1, when, after a visit home in the company of his mother, Harold returned alone to New York, the events were certainly not so simple as they later became in Grace's mind. By autumn of that year she had brooded long and hard over those two weeks and had begun to distort them. When Philip Horton talked to her nearly twenty years after, she had reduced the story to a simple one in which she was the victim, Harold an innocent bystander, and C.A. the villain.

In that account, Mrs. Crane had returned toward the end of the month to visit her mother, leaving behind her in New York a boy who sensed in her action a "longing for reconciliation" with C.A. After several days, Harold received a wire calling him home. He was pleased to find his parents happily making plans for the future: "his father, impetuous as a young suitor, boisterously insisting upon an immediate marriage, and his mother once more swept away by her husband's dominance. Apparently the best had happened. A few days later Harold returned to Gramercy Park where, it was planned, his parents, after a quiet civil ceremony, would join him to celebrate the beginning of a new life. But he waited at the apartment in vain. Shortly before the proposed ceremony his father disappeared, leaving a curt note for Mrs. Crane to say that he had changed his mind and definitely abandoned their plans for remarriage. There was no further explanation."

The main pattern of events is accurate enough: Grace and Harold did return home at the end of July, C.A. did urge remarriage, Harold did return to New York, and C.A. did leave town after writing Grace a short note telling her to forget him. But some recently discovered correspondence between Harold and his father throws a different light on those troubled days.

Grace's return to Cleveland was undoubtedly prompted by C.A.'s renewed cordiality. In the three months that followed the divorce, C.A., at the advice of Mr. Sullivan, had steadfastly refused to visit Grace, though on several occasions she had begged him to talk to her. The warm tone of their July correspondence, however, seems to have softened his resolve. In the letter in which she announced her plans for Harold's eighteenth birthday, not only did Grace stress her desire that Harold and his father achieve "a perfect understanding" but she repeated her conviction that in conversation other difficulties could also be ironed out: "I have long felt that a personal interview with you would be to the advantage of all three of us." At that time she had no plans to go to Cleveland. Her decision to go may well have been a result of C.A.'s now lost letter in response to her own. Within two or three days after July 21, Harold's eighteenth birthday, she and Harold were both in Cleveland, almost certainly invited there by C.A. as a birthday present for his son.

During that week remarriage must have seemed inevitable. Grace and C.A. were devoted to one another, and Harold basked in their love. Plans were made for remarriage and for a New York honeymoon. In the midst of those plans, however, the three fell into a complicated and bitter quarrel involving both Harold's maintenance in New York—which C.A. felt was too high—and Grace and Harold's insistence that New York was the only place for the two of them to live. Tempers rose to the breaking point. Harold apparently screamed that he was "through" with both his parents and rushed off alone to catch the midnight train to New York. Grace took to bed in sheer hysteria, and C.A. stormed back to his rooms at the Cleveland Athletic Club.

For the first few days afterwards it seemed to both Harold and his father only a repetition of dozens of other such scenes, and though both were wounded, both were prepared to forgive and forget. The next morning C.A. wrote an extraordinarily sympathetic letter to his son, suggesting that their differences could be adjusted and that Grace, who had already telephoned him, was in a much happier frame of mind than on the night before.

August 1st, 1917.

My dear Boy:

This morning you woke up in New York, and by this time you are back in your chosen haunts, bag and baggage, after a visit at home.

You know I recall, and always will remember, the pleasure I had in coming back after my first few experiences at Meadville. Father used to talk expenses to me and a few other things that were not just to my liking, but just the same, home-coming is a good thing—even dogs wag their tail when they get in sight of the old farm house.

This visit has meant much to me. You are the only treasure I have on God's green earth, and whatever has or ever does happen, I want you to know that your father's love for you is equal to any emergency.

Do the work that is before you, with the sincerity which will bring the very best results. It isn't at all necessary that you should achieve great financial success, but it is necessary that your own peace of mind should never be disturbed, and the building of character is the only thing that will possibly insure it.

Your mother called me up this morning, and seems to have spent a very comfortable night, and is in a good frame of mind. My visits to the house will be much less frequent now that you are away, but I hope I have impressed you with the fact that I wish every good thing in the world for her.

With my love, I am
Your father

Harold's answer and C.A.'s return letter are missing, and Harold in a letter a week later mentions that "I have been diabolically nervous ever since that shock out at the house." But his tone is entirely sympathetic to his father.

I feel so near to you now that I do hope that nothing can ever again break the foundation of sincerity that has been established beneath our relations. Never has anyone been kinder than you when I was last home. I want you to know that I appreciate it, and also your two fine letters.

Grace, it is clear, has suffered a nervous breakdown; and Harold urges his father to avoid seeing her as long as she is upset.

I am very, very sorry that things are going so badly with Mother. I guess there is nothing for her to do but to get back here as soon as is possible and try to re-instate herself in poise and health. I look for her this week. At least I see no reason why she should linger longer. But I have received no word from her and am uncertain as to much of the true state of affairs with her. I only hope you are avoiding any meetings as much as possible, for as I said, it is now too early,—she is not yet established well enough to endure the strain which you know any contact causes.

As this letter indicates, Harold had expected Grace back in the middle of August. Yet she delayed her return until at least a week later, having spent most of her time at home under the care of her mother. C.A., perhaps accepting Harold's suggestion that he avoid meetings, seems to have urged her in phone conversations to remain in Cleveland, apparently with little success. The next surviving document is C.A.'s "curt note" of August 21. By this time all communications between the two had broken down: C.A. heard of Grace's plans through Hazel Hasham in New York. Once again, however, Grace decided to attempt to "talk things over" with C.A., though she remained adamant in her plan to live in New York with Harold. C.A.'s note, more resigned than unfriendly, was intended to put an end to what he had come to regard as a hopeless effort at reconciliation.

Grace:

I'm leaving town tonight for my vacation. Since I've talked with Hazel I've decided that a further meeting just now is unwise for she tells me you are now decided on your going to N.Y. and my coming so often disturbs your *resolves*.

Keep the promise you made yourself. Pluck wins—wins everything. Forget C. A. Crane does or ever did *live*.

Get busy with things that make for *your* happiness. There is a sunny side to every *street*. You're due to cross *over*.

Good luck
CAC

Grace was, understandably, humiliated and resentful. Within a few days she once more packed her belongings and, accompanied by her mother, returned to New York. Here, she told Philip Horton, she again suffered a breakdown. This time Harold extended his full sympathy.

When she returned to New York under the care of her mother, who dared not leave her alone, the boy's indignation flared into rage at the sight of her suffering. During the succeeding weeks all their efforts to achieve an ordered and happy life at the apartment were futile. Despite the distractions and amusements Harold and his grandmother contrived, she could not shake off the obsession with Mr. Crane's last injustice. Incessant brooding aggravated her condition, so that much of the time she was confined to her bed. There, as in years before, Harold again took up his post, sitting beside her in the darkened room for hours, his spirit once more wrenched from the pattern of its own growth and inflamed by the old wounds of humiliation and resentment. That his father had again shattered their prospects of stability and happiness seemed to him a gesture of deliberate malice; and his offer of remarriage now appeared to have been a diabolical plot to bring about their present mortification. In the face of such maneuvers his own efforts to maintain a just balance of affection between his parents seemed naïve, and thenceforth he made no attempt to control or conceal his true feelings.

Grace's memory may here also have distorted the real events. Undoubtedly she was emotionally exhausted when she returned to New York, but her mother's conviction of the efficacy of Christian Science seems to have persuaded her that the proper course was one of loving forgiveness. Some miracle—perhaps brought about through Harold—might still salvage her lost marriage. Her attitude toward her husband, Harold wrote his father on September 18, had become one of "forgiveness, tenderness, mercy, and love." Clearly, on this date both Harold and Grace were hoping against hope for reconciliation. A week later the lease on their sublet apartment would expire, Grace and her mother would return to Cleveland, and Harold would again be alone in New York.

The letters and postcards C.A. sent his son in the course of his vacation have all disappeared—destroyed either by Harold or, after his death, by Grace. But C.A. kept to the end of his life one extraordinarily eloquent letter from his son. It was in answer to a "good letter" from C.A. that must in passing have made a slighting reference to Grace, and it is worth quoting in full, as it shows the kind of relations that still prevailed between father and son and the extent of Harold's involvement in his parents' problems.

My dear Father:—

Your good letter rec'd yesterday. From what Hazel says I presume this will find you back in Cleveland, and busy looking over what has happened while you have been away. I haven't written more because, as you can readily perceive, I haven't known your address most of the time, but once again you may expect my regular letters.

This one thing though, I am going to ask of you. If, when you write me, you are thinking of Mother in a distasteful way, please conceal it, remaining silent on the subject. And if, in thinking of her, one kind thought should occur (as I know it does) express it. You remember that when I last was home, I said that I "was through." —That was possible with me for but one hour. My heart is still as responsive to both your loves, and more so, than ever. I have seen more tears than I ever expected in this world, and I have shed them through others' eyes, to say nothing of my own sorrow. And now, when I hear nothing but forgiveness, tenderness, mercy, and love from one side, how can [I] bear resentment and caustic words coming from the other without great pain? Happiness may some time come to me, I am sure it will. But please, my dear Father, do not make the present too hard,—too painful for one whose fatal weakness is to love two unfortunate people, by writing barbed words.

I don't know how long we three shall dwell in purgatory. We may rise above, or sink below, but either way it may be, the third shall and must follow the others, and I leave myself in your hands.

Write soon. I do hope you come to New York.

Affectionately,
Harold

It was C.A.'s answer to this letter, not anything that had happened in Cleveland during the summer, which precipitated scenes, angry words, and Harold's decision to side with his mother.

Whatever C.A. said, it was enough to shake Grace free from her Christian Science-inspired mood of forgiveness and love. Infuriated, she wrote an angry, accusing letter which survives only in a copied draft and may never have been sent.

September 23, [191]7.

Clarence:

Harold received your letter yesterday and last night read it to me.

Because it contained remarks concerning your mental attitude toward me, I am now going to write you what I trust will be my last communication to you for quite some time.

In a few days I shall return to Cleveland to live, and take my place among my friends and begin to enjoy life as I have not done for many days.

When I was last there you made a spectacle of me and yourself before the neighborhood, my family, our son, and our mutual friends, and after forcing your attention and devotion upon me until I forgave you every confession of wrong you *voluntarily* made me and all past wrongs, at your own repeated requests I consented to once more become your wife.

As you well know, we painted a beautiful picture of our future together, in which all mistakes of the past were to be avoided, Harold made happy and successful through our united efforts, and love of the highest order for you and me.

All of this would have been possible and just as it should have been, but just at this point you chose to change your mind, leaving me with nothing but a cruel, hard note telling me of your departure and a request to forget you. If you can explain this procedure even to your own satisfaction you can do more than any one else can who is conversant with the facts.

I will not tell you of the agony and struggle that has been mine during the following weeks, nor how *earnestly* Harold has hoped that he might see his father and mother once more happy together.

From what he saw and heard you say when he was last home, his faith in your affection for me was so strong he felt there was surely reason in appealing to you as he did.

I think he would have been the happiest boy in America if he could have been the means of bringing his father and mother once more into harmonious relationship.

In the letter he received yesterday you struck your boy the hardest blow you have ever dealt him.

Being familiar with both sides of the case, he has not forgotten what you said to him about how much you still cared for me, and he knows all too well what sincere unselfish devotion I have always had for you.

Clarence you have put my affection to every test and it has endured through everything. Such love does not come to everyone and never twice to the same person. You have thrown mine away, and if you ever regret it or other things which may follow, you have no one to blame but yourself. The door between your life and mine is closed, locked and the key thrown away.

If it is ever unlocked it will be you who does it, and I am quite sure you will never be able to find the key. Do not pity me. I shall be quite content and go on my way rejoicing. My happiness no longer depends upon one person.

As you may not always know my address in the future, I am asking you to kindly send my checks to Mr. Sullivan, whom I will always try to keep informed as to my whereabouts

This letter needs no reply, and I earnestly ask you to refrain from trying to communicate with me in any way excepting about Harold, and only then when it is of a serious nature.

I am leaving you absolutely devoid of any malice, and hoping that you will soon find the road that leads to real happiness.

Two days later, Grace returned to Cleveland and a month's accumulated gossip. Rumors of all sorts were circulating. Some of the most vicious she attributed to a man on C.A.'s office staff. It was he, she wrote her son, who had poisoned C.A.'s mind against her. "Forget all the past and leave C.A. to that bastard" was Harold's quick rejoinder. Now, for the first time in his correspondence, Harold's name is changed; his letter is signed "Hart," a clear indication to his mother that the break with his father was to be permanent. "You have all my love, and if I *am* a little reckless, you shall find in the end some wisdom," he wrote her. No longer, he assures her, will C.A. hear much of his son; and, as for Grace, her best bet is to put her husband completely out of mind. "I . . . find it hard to express my rage and disgust at what you say concerning C. A. Crane's conduct," he writes. " 'Forget him,' is all I can say." Grace should center her mind elsewhere: "You have lived too long in a house of shadows, ignoring the pulse and vivacity of life around you, and it is time to forget."

At first, however, it must have seemed to both Grace and Hart that forgetting would be impossible. On the same day that Hart wrote to Grace, she wrote to him: "If I have much time to think it is not good for me and I always get my thoughts centered upon your father. My love for him is not the kind to leave when bidden, but unless he can feel different and treat me as I feel I should be treated I never wish to see him again."

Yet slowly Grace and Hart discovered that they could get along by themselves. Grace found therapy in redecorating her home. She turned C.A.'s room into a guest room, using for it much of her own furniture, and brought down to her own room Hart's four-poster bed and his dresser. Hart again busied himself with tutoring, independent study, and renewed literary efforts. Soon mother and son—Grace in Cleveland and Hart in New York—were involved in the social round both enjoyed, Grace caught up in plans for the wedding of a friend's daughter, and Hart a frequent breakfaster and supper guest with the Brooks family.

High-strung, Crane and his family had seen their problems in a melodramatic light. Grace and Hart especially were given to Wagnerian outbursts. Yet the normal day-to-day business of life tempered and tamed their outraged emotions.

Hart, in fact, for all his words, had never lost a fun-loving nature. A week after his summer quarrel with mother and father, he had cheerfully written C.A. to thank him for purchasing one of Carl's paintings. ("Its name is 'Olga', and I am sure you will like her very well. . . . You have pulled [Carl] out of a very serious difficulty.") His letter described in eloquent detail a hot day's trip with Carl and another friend to Long Beach: "If you could shake responsibilities like this for a week or so, it would work inestimable good upon you. You cannot worry on such a beautiful beach with the sound of waves in your ears. We all get to thinking that our heads are really our bodies, and most of the time go floating around with only our brain conscious, forgetting that our bodies have requirements also." Through the difficult summer he carried out a normal correspondence with Cleveland friends—with Bill Wright; with another high-school friend, George Skeel; with John Lloyd. Even on the September day when he had passed on to his mother the letter from C.A. that had so enraged her, he had sat down casually to renew his correspondence with the doll-beheading friend of his childhood, George Bryan. "I was sorry to have missed your call when I was last home. I think you came just after I had left for the station. I don't know much about you. You may not be at home to receive this, but wherever you are, please write your *old faithfull* soon and tell him about yourself."

His consciousness that he was building a reputation as a poet contributed as much as anything to his recovery from the troubles of his parents. Indeed, the day after his mother left for Cleveland he had a most encouraging meeting with Maxwell Bodenheim, who not only was willing to read his work but praised it. He "complimented my poetry excessively," Hart wrote, "and has taken several pieces to the editor of the 'Seven Arts,' a personal friend of his."

Bodenheim, one of the strangest figures of recent American literature, wore in those days the mantle of world-weariness. Still in his early twenties, he struck most of his friends as an eloquent, exhausted misanthrope. To Alfred Kreymborg, Bodenheim seemed to speak "with the weariness of an aged man, and his pale eyes gave forth the insistent impression that for him life had sounded the ultimate disillusionment." To Crane, however, he represented the poet who, "through the adverse channels of flattery, friendships and 'pull,'" had finally succeeded "after four years of absolute obscurity" in getting his work published. He was, Crane felt, "a first-class critic . . . and I am proud to have his admiration and encouragement."

Bodenheim planned to show Crane's work to James Oppenheim at *The Seven Arts*; he also assured Crane that the long-delayed *Others* publication would at last take place: "As soon as 'Others' begins again this winter, he says I shall have an organ for all of my melodies, as he is one of the editors." Bodenheim's opinion of editors was, however, a low one. "Editors," he told Crane, "are generally disappointed writers who stifle any genius or originality as soon as it is found. They seldom ever trouble to read over the manuscript of a 'new man.' "

Crane's own experience with editors was more encouraging. Kling was rumored to feel Crane was "the equal of any American lyricist of the day." ("I don't trust Kling's criticism very far, judging by the 'tone' generally prevalent in the magazine," Crane wrote Schmitt, repeating the rumor. "But I *am* improving and would just as soon be deceived a little as not.") Kling had already accepted for his next issue of *The Pagan* Crane's graceful lyric "Echoes," its musical internal rhymes binding together an imagery of "slivers of rain"—jade-green laced with the yellow of sunlight—and the "opal pools" of a lover's eyes. And he would print in the following December issue Crane's "The Bathers," a fragmentary poem perhaps founded on a memory of the Isle of Pines, certainly founded on its scenery. There was also every reason for Hart to assume that Margaret Anderson and Jane Heap would soon print in their *Little Review* his poem "North Labrador."

Crane's admiration for *The Little Review* had begun in Cleveland when he found the Chicago publication among the magazines in Richard Laukhuff's bookstore. Already a distinguished, though never widely circulated, publication, its contributors included such established writers as Edgar Lee Masters, Carl Sandburg, Amy Lowell, Vachel Lindsay, and John Gould Fletcher, and a long list of soon-to-be-important newcomers—among them Witter Bynner, H.D., Sherwood Anderson—and Maxwell Bodenheim. Crane had followed the evolution of the magazine with something of a lover's zeal; when, just three months after his arrival in New York, Miss Anderson and Miss Heap brought the magazine to New York and very nearly to his own doorstep, Crane was delighted. Through the summer months he made a steady pilgrimage to 24 West Sixteenth Street, where, in the then-down-in-the-mouth building that had once been the home of William Cullen Bryant, *The Little Review* had set up its offices.

The summer of 1917 was an exciting time for the magazine's editors; for Ezra Pound, in April named "foreign editor," was bombarding the New York office with an outpouring of major English and Irish work. In addition to his own poems, Pound sent in work by T. S. Eliot, W. B. Yeats, and Wyndham Lewis, all of which appeared in the summer issues of the magazine, and would soon arrange for the serial publication of Joyce's *Ulysses*, which began in the March 1918 issue and ended—after four issues had been seized by the Post Office Department and the editors brought to trial for the publication of "obscene literature"—with the September–December issue of 1920.

Crane, who now spent much of his free time at Joseph Kling's bookshop-office, used to provoke the man who was publishing him by describing his efforts to break down a competitor's barriers. "I go up there day after day," he told Kling. "But the door is always locked. What do those women *do* in there?" What they did a large part of the time was to paper the walls. "It took several months—" Margaret Anderson remembered, "first to find the money, then the time. We bought gold Chinese paper at a Japanese paper shop, in long oblong strips. Papering the walls with these required Chinese patience, as they were disposed to tear under the most delicate touch. The woodwork was pale cream, the floor dark plum, the furniture old mahogany. The feature of the room was a large divan hung from the ceiling by heavy black chains. It was covered with a dull-toned blue and on it were four silk cushions—emerald green, magenta, royal purple, tilleul. Between the windows was a large reading table with a lemon yellow lamp."

Finally, when the decoration of "Jane's beautiful gold room" was completed, Crane—along with other young poets and painters —was admitted to what would become a series of almost always exasperating but always stimulating evenings. "To tell you the truth," Miss Anderson wrote me, "I was never a great fan of his poetry, and I remember that our discussions were mostly on this prejudice of mine."

Nevertheless, for a while at least, it looked as if "North Labrador" would be accepted by *The Little Review*. In mid-September, Crane wrote a jubilant letter to Schmitt—then vacationing in Warren—that he was sure to be published beside Yeats and Pound. Publication plans, however, were suspended after a hot discussion about Norwegian ice. The poem "contained a vague reference to the immaculate white ice of Norway," Miss Anderson wrote in *My Thirty Years' War*, her account of those days, and she went on to quote Jane Heap's crushing comment: "Immaculate is a dirty word to use. . . . That ice is so white it looks black." After criticism of this sort, Hart would "sometimes leave us in fury"; but he always came back, usually bringing poems.

Finally his persistence was rewarded. In the same September week in which his mother returned to Cleveland, he found an acceptance letter waiting for him in his mail.

> Dear <u>Hart</u> Crane, poet!!
> I'm using "Shadow" in the December issue, now going to press. It's the best you've sent yet: I'll tell you details of just why when you come. It's quite lovely.
> Hurrah for you!!
>
>                                                      MCA

"In Shadow" was to be subjected, after its publication, to Pound's most scathing satire. (An "Easter sonnet" addressed to Crane pointed out: "Beauty is a good enough egg, but so far as I can see, you haven't the ghost of a setting hen or an incubator.") Crane took the criticism in his stride, remarking only that it was "too good a douche to waste on one novice," and reiterating his admiration for the work of Pound. Although the poem is not as strong as those Crane was later to write, it is no mean accomplishment for an eighteen-year-old: it is an account of a love affair presented in terms of an afternoon-to-evening transformation, a tracery of internal rhyme and near-rhyme reinforcing the last stanza's late/wait rhymes.

All things considered, there was every reason for Hart to exclaim to his mother that, despite his concern about family problems, "Success seems imminent now more than ever. I am very encouraged, poetically, at least."

In other ways, too, he felt he was reaching out to conquer new horizons. His landlady, a Mrs. Walton, had discovered that her new boarder at 25 East Eleventh Street was a poet, and she outlined for him her own literary activities as a scriptwriter for the rapidly expanding motion-picture industry. Here, she pointed out, money was to be made, and she offered to help Hart work up plots which could be used either for fiction or for film scripts. Together they planned a novel.

"The plot is already thick in my head," Hart wrote his mother, "and tonight the first chapter will be written off,—at least in rough draft. It is a story whose setting is to be Havana and the Isle of Pines." The hero of the book would be based on Walter Wilcox, the handsome tenant-farmer of Crane's grandmother's small estate, "and the heroine is a N.Y. society maiden who is attending the races."

But for an act of God, Crane might have written his novel. However, on the day on which he outlined for his mother the plan for the would-be best seller, Grace was sitting down to write him of a disaster: ". . . a letter from Walter Wilcox came today telling us of the most terrible hurricane that the Island has ever experienced, and our place, with the exception of the house alone, is in total ruin. The house is some damaged and was almost blown off the foundation. Many families are destitute. No boats have been heard from. . . . Can you imagine how discouraged and heartsick Grandma and I feel? So much money sunk in that place, and now no hope of ever getting a cent out of it. Walter is utterly discouraged and disgusted and will leave for the north as soon as we write him what to do about our house."

It is no wonder that Crane in his reply noted: "My novel about the Isle of Pines has been somewhat blown to pieces by that blasting letter of yours."

Yet, if he abandoned his barely plotted novel, he did not abandon all hopes of making a living as a writer. Mrs. Walton continued to offer him encouragement, and while she agreed that in view of the island disaster a romantic novel about his grandmother's fruit grove might not be the wisest project, she did feel that Crane should use prose to bring him an income, poetry to bring him fame. Short stories for The Smart Set magazine might be a profitable venture. Crane wrote his mother his new plan: "I am busy thinking up plots for Smart Set stories. You see, I want to make my literary work bring me in a living by the time I reach twenty-five and one cannot begin too soon." But after a weekend of plotting short stories he felt there must be easier ways of making a living. By Monday morning he had once again changed his plans: "Mrs. Walton and I are working out movie scenarios. She has had considerable experience and is of great help to me."

Movie scripts soon joined *The Smart Set* stories and the island novel in Crane's growing collection of bright hopes blasted. The only remnant of his enthusiastic plans was a lingering hope that Mrs. Walton might somehow find a place for Grace—still a would-be actress—in one of her scripts.

Yet Crane was not despondent. His principal feeling in these cool October days was buoyant confidence such as he had seldom known before. His poetry was building a reputation, his parents' troubles had freed him for what he felt was true independence, and the war promised a sure escape should all else fail. Shining through the letters of this time is an eighteen-year-old's discovery of his own possibilities: he really could lead a *private* life. "O if you knew how much I am learning!" he exclaims to his mother. "The realization of true freedom is slowly coming to me, and with it a sense of poise which is of inestimable value. My life, however it shall continue, shall have expression and form. Believe me when I tell you that I am fearless, that I am determined on a valorous future and something of a realization of life."

# 4

When Harold Crane arrived in New York in Christmas week of 1916 he was a boy. Ten months later, in October 1917, Hart Crane was sure that he had somehow become a man. Without his being aware of it, perspectives had changed; the world seemed different. "The smallness of hitherto large things, and the largeness of hitherto small things is dawning," he wrote his mother. "I am beginning to see the hope of standing entirely alone and to fathom Ibsen's statement that translated is, 'The strongest man in the world is he who stands entirely alone.'"

It is easy now to look back and to pinpoint the moments of change: divorce, reconciliation, rejection of father. And, with just a shade more subtlety, it is easy to fill in the slow, continuing forces of change—the year of near independence in a strange town, the turbulent violence of the war to end all wars that filled newspapers with screaming headlines and streets with cheerful yet desperate parades. Even the growing confidence of the would-be poet is easily enough tracked down, as hope in early letters is replaced in late ones by certainty.

But who can presume to uncover the reality of change, the trick transformations of recollected dream, or dream itself, or the world of otherwise-lost conversations that live on in memory alone or that coil around objects to give them strange, irrational importance? What biographer—however meticulous his search—can hope to locate, in the thousands of casual acquaintances a man makes, the imperative voice, the important word? We play games with our mothers, our fathers, our wives, our children, and, sometimes, ourselves. Who doesn't withhold his profoundest convictions from nearest and dearest, yet spill them out to a stranger on a bus, a scrubwoman leaning on her mop?

How much did Crane's sense of newly discovered independence depend on an end-of-September excursion to Staten Island with Stan and Anna, friends he had met during the summer, whom he visited regularly through the autumn and winter?

Stanislaw Portapovitch, a dancer in Diaghilev's great Ballet Russe, had accompanied Crane and Schmitt to Long Beach in the summer months. Crane would later celebrate him in his lyric "To

( 92 )

Portapovitch (*du Ballet Russe*)." Though best remembered by a few of Crane's friends as the man who taught Crane to dance the "gotzotsky," to Carl Schmitt, at least, he was memorable in his own right. "You mustn't underestimate the importance of that dancer," Schmitt insisted. For Portapovitch, like Schmitt, demonstrated both in conversation and in art the crucial importance of balance. It was inevitably after his visits with Portapovitch that Crane would be most filled with an ebullient sense of life's possibilities.

"I have never felt as encouraged, as free or as clean," he wrote his mother the day after the Staten Island trip. "Think of me often as such or not at all, for I hope you will understand me."

The events of the day had on the surface been trivial enough. He had joined Anna and Stan just after lunch. "We ferried to Staten Island and back, had dinner, and then I took Anna to the Strand, as Stan is dancing every evening from six until two at Healy's Restaurant (100 dollars per week). Surely, you will say, he *has* earned it. What a diabolical profession! And yet he likes it. I suppose that the occasional opportunity for expression is the scant reward."

In his long day's talk with the young couple, the fragments of Crane's life had seemed to fall together into a coherent pattern. He returned to the boarding house planning not only to stand free from his father but as well to begin the intricate process of untying—as gently as possible—the apron strings of grandmother and mother.

He had already shown some independence by dismissing M. Tardy, his French tutor, and hiring in his place another boarder at Mrs. Walton's, Madame Eugénie Lebègue. Now, he decided, the sooner he made a permanent break with Cleveland, the better; he urgently requested his mother to send on his books. ("They might just as well be here, and needless to say, I need them.")

Though he was aware that his mother was making plans once more to join him, he did his best to hint that for a while at least a bachelor life might be the best thing for his work. ("I am alone a good deal of the time and am glad of it. My work will always demand solitude to a great extent in creative effort. Your son is improving every day, so don't worry one moment about me.") He discreetly failed to reply to her plans for his spending Christmas in Cleveland.

In spite of all of his resolutions, he realized that complete independence would be impossible so long as his father continued to pay for his room and board; and with some relief, he accepted his mother's suggestion that he make one more friendly gesture toward the father he had so recently disowned. Grace's complex feelings both toward C.A. and toward her son are nowhere clearer than in this letter, as she does her best to explain to Hart exactly why she feels it is morally right for him to take advantage of the man she urges him to despise:

> I do not know whether you have written him or not since I left —but if not you must. You can and should write him a courteous letter giving him your address and some idea of what you are doing. As long as you receive and accept his support, you must do that at least and I beg of you not to be foolish and cut off your nose to spite your face. I appreciate more than I can say your loyalty to me and it comforts me in many a lonely hour. . . . You are entitled to his support—*Take it!* Only remember that you have a certain duty towards him also. My affairs need never again be mentioned between you. Far better not. You know now what he is capable of being with one whom he proposed before every one, to love better than life. It is horrible to think such natures exist and we have to cope with them—but they do and you *know* it, so be *wise*—and don't allow your feelings to cheat you out of what is *rightfully* yours. All this can be accomplished without being a hypocrite either.
>
> So far as I am concerned, I must *forget* him. It will not be easy—but it must be accomplished one way or another and that is my first task. I want to accomplish it without either hate, revenge, or malice, so that he may some day look back upon himself with condemnation, and upon me with admiration. No matter what misfortune may be mine, I want to always remain true to my ideals. That is about all there is left for me. . . .
>
> I hope sometime to receive through you from your father his part of the last month's rent and also the amount I spent for your clothes. As I have nothing whatever to say to him it is up to you to inform him of what he does not know. . . .
>
> My most devoted love is yours and you are always my dearest sweetheart—
>
> > As Always—
> > Grace—
>
> My best regards to Mrs. Walton. If you or she can get me a job in the movies, just wire me and I'll be there the next morning. Write *often*, or I shall be miserable.

Hart's letter to his father has been lost, but the tone of it seems evident from C.A.'s reply: "Your letter of October 8 was duly received. It is the first one that you have written me for three weeks, so I can easily understand that I am not to receive communications from you frequently." Yet, swallowing his pride, C.A. did his best to come to some understanding with his difficult, suddenly aggressive son. And though Hart cannot be imagined to have responded to his father's suggestion that the two of them "ought to talk together as two business men," he does seem—for a while at least—to have accepted as reasonable his father's explanation that "the obligation which I have with your mother the next year, under the conditions, will represent more than fifty percent of my income, and we must all have a care as to the future."

What C.A. found most difficult to stomach was the fact that, though his son was tutoring for only one hour a week, both Grace and Hart continued stoutly to maintain that Hart was in New York in pursuit of an education. Surely, C.A. argued, "if you are only devoting $2 a week to tutoring, you must have a large amount of time on your hands." He recommended that Hart look for "some employment for, say, half the time each day. . . . That would give you some revenue and more than the revenue, it would give you independence, which you must absolutely crave, to the extent of buying a few things without asking father for the money."

C. A. Crane was, in his own eyes, unreservedly truthful when he explained to Hart: "Your father wants to do everything for his only boy that he should do." Yet he found it hard not to balk at Hart's paying $11 a week for his room at Mrs. Walton's when C.A.'s own rent in Cleveland was only a dollar a week more! Hart, he felt, needed to accept a greater degree of financial responsibility. To illustrate what he meant, he recapitulated the years just after his own marriage:

> My younger life was not one of privation, but it surely was not one of "easy-going." If there is any one thing that I can thank my father for, it was the willingness on his part to let me know the value of money and to get a taste of how it was acquired. When you were a baby in arms, I moved to Warren with less money than I give you every four months, and with a full responsibility of a family. It has always meant that there was earnest work for me at every sunrise. I have now reached an age when I think more seriously than ever before. I have gone through experiences which tell me every day that "life is earnest."

After C.A.'s letter arrived, Hart was for a time polite to his father, yet resentment was easily kindled. Grace passed on to him so many Cleveland rumors that Hart soon wrote angrily to Carl Schmitt: "I understand that my male parent has spoken of me to several mutual friends as being a weakling, and totally incapable of anything at all. Knowing this, I can understand a great many more of his actions than I have heretofore." Memories of early slights were now joined to new ones. Hart, in Mary Colum's kitchen, puzzled over his father's character, recollecting the time he had first broached the suggestion that C.A. support him until he could make a living as a writer.

> To his mind, fed on literature, being a poet was a distinction to any family. To his father, poetry writing was a sissy game, and he lectured the boy in contemptuous words. "Do you see

that girl out there?"—pointing through the glass partition to a secretary in an outside office. "She has more real manliness and independence than you have."

A further source of irritation was the money Grace advanced for Hart's fall and winter wardrobe. Offering to repay the debt, Mr. Crane asked for an itemized account. As the letters went back and forth (and the itemized list grew), tension rose on all sides, Mr. Crane apparently withholding the money in the hopes that Hart would be forced to find some sort of employment. "However," Hart wrote Schmitt, "I am not going to seek work and drudge at completely foreign tasks as long as I can help it, and I am pursuing the old course of self-culture with reading, etc. I don't want to have to go to court, but if any more pressure is brought to bear, I'm afraid it will be inevitable." Melodramatic as it seems, Grace finally did convince her lawyer to go before a judge, as evidence a sheaf of bills for Hart's clothing, and collect the several hundred dollars that was due her.

By this time Hart had given up the pretense of preparing for Columbia. The entrance examinations had been completely forgotten in the weeks of family turmoil. Even if they had been remembered, Hart's erratic tutoring could scarcely have prepared him for them. In a letter to Carl Schmitt, he blamed his father's strict allowance for his failure to matriculate. ("I must explain to you that on twenty-five dollars a week, Columbia is out of the question. That is all I am to get,—clothing and everything. While it will do for decent living, it really is too meager for any college.") But Hart did not want to attend college. His plans were set for a year of intensive reading and writing.

It was now his mother who threatened to make his plans go awry, for she refused to send his books and she declared her intention once more to return to New York. In letter after letter he begged for the books and hedged against getting a room for her. The world that had suddenly opened up to him in his long, late talks with Stan and Anna seemed about to close in again. For Grace's focus was persistently on her son. ("Dear boy, I miss you *so much* I hardly know how to stand it.") She urged him to arrange with Mrs. Walton for a room near his own. She would come to New York, she wrote, sometime before Thanksgiving, stay on with Hart until just before Christmas, and then return with him to Cleveland for the holidays.

Finally he decided toward the end of October that it might be best for her to come. She had described to him a siege of nervousness that made it, she said, impossible to write letters; she needed to talk to him. With remarkable tact for an eighteen-year-old, he extended to her his fullest sympathetic understanding: "Don't write, Mother, if it makes you nervous. I can readily understand how that might be, for I myself have often felt so about it. Especially letters." Though he still recommended that she get a room in the neighborhood rather than at Mrs. Walton's, he did offer his room as a place for entertainment: "My room is quite lovely and whenever we want to have a few people in, it can be done here. I have lately discovered that I can have an open fire in the grate, anytime I want it. When Carl returns, I may be able to procure a few of his pictures and that will add much."

Confident of his new maturity, he explained to his mother that he might be able to get a job for her through Mrs. Walton—perhaps, this time, as a dancer. His own success seemed certain: "I am really getting a reputation for poetry and can find space now in at least two magazines for most of my better work." She would, he told her, fit in well with his growing circle of friends. Only the day before, an acquaintance had given him tickets to a concert at Aeolian Hall and he had been able to invite Mr. Brooks as his guest. "We enjoyed it very much, afterwards meeting Mrs. Brooks and dining at Gonfarones. . . . I nearly laughed myself ill during the evening, and then returned and wrote a poem." Through Stan and Anna he had finally met people of his own age, and a phone call from his boyhood friend George Bryan—passing through New York on his way to school in New Jersey—assured him at least one old friend near enough for weekend visits.

"We shall have no more melancholia around now," he wrote his mother. "I am sure I shall never let you succumb to that again. . . . The freedom from responsibility which you will have on your future visits here will make it seem very comfortable for you, I am sure."

Grace, too, as plans jelled for the New York trip, grew confident. And when Hart wrote her that he had changed his mind about finding her a room nearby, that he would instead give her his own room and himself take another in the same house, she was delighted: "Your letter . . . has been a great relief to me—both because I did not want you to leave there and because it opens a possibility of our being together in the location which we so much desire."

In these days her mood shifted abruptly from despair to elation. She had returned to active work with a Christian Science practitioner who advised social activity and generous thought and did his best to bring her around once more to sympathy for C.A. She was quick to pass on to her son her changed attitude.

> Think as kindly of your father as you can—write him as often as you feel you should, and above all say nothing to anybody against him. It looks now as though he and I were perfectly able to live without the society of each other, and I am getting a better grip upon myself. You won't have such a droopy mother to manage when I come back to you, I feel quite sure, and there are good times and plenty to eat in store for us. . . .

Now dear boy keep a level head as you most always have, and try to be charitable and fair to your father. Although he is fast passing out of my life, I want always to give him credit when credit is due, and I find hating anyone or resentment are very disastrous things to one's health and in fact to one's whole life. I will not go further into this matter until I see you. . . .

I shall have much to tell you when I return and I want you to be happy thinking of the good times in store for us. Don't let your nature be embittered by anything you hear or see, but always know there is a sane way out of every difficulty.

Some profit, even, might be drawn from their troubles, she felt— for what else does a writer deal with if not raw human emotions? "All your trials," she wrote her son, "can be turned into valuable results in your line of work if you will only look at it that way. *Human* nature and *Human* experience are with us constantly and we do not have to go far away to study them."

When Grace arrived, she and Hart had opportunity to spare for the study of human nature. He had assured her she would experience "no more melancholia" and she had promised him "jolly good times," but in fact their holiday together proved a nightmare of hysteria and violence.

Almost all records of the months between Thanksgiving of 1917 and Easter of 1918 have vanished, perhaps destroyed by Grace before her death. (She went through her own and Hart's correspondence in the Leonia, New Jersey, home of her friends the Dexters, where she "spent some days reading letters, many of which she destroyed after reading.") A few very long letters from Mrs. Hart to Grace have survived, however, and these, supplementing the account Mrs. Crane gave to Philip Horton, allow some notion of the events of these troubled months.

Soon after her arrival in New York, Mrs. Crane told Horton, Hart was taken seriously but mysteriously ill. The attending physician could find "no recognizable symptoms," and Grace ascribed the ailment to the "obscure nervous disorders" that had plagued him from his youth. Fearing that a crisis beyond her control might arise, she telephoned C.A. in Cleveland and urged him to come to New York. C.A.'s answer, as Grace recollected it, was a flat reply "that he would not come to New York even if his son were dying."

Worried and upset by Hart's seizure and infuriated at C.A.'s response to her call, Grace spent the day brooding angrily. By evening, she told Horton, her own tensions had reached the breaking point, and as she was about to retire, she was "seized by a sudden attack and lost consciousness. For two days she lay in a curious state of coma, insensible to what was going on about her." Hart, himself ill, did not know what to do. Finally he decided to wire his Aunt Zell in Warren, Ohio. She had been concerned, as always, about Grace's stability and had given Hart instructions that if any serious problems should arise he was to telegraph her.

That done, he sat down by his mother's bedside to listen to her recriminations and to write his friend Carl Schmitt: "There is no one in the world whom I have to explain things to but you. One cannot explain to any but those who have understanding. So do not be too critical of my confessions." His greatest concern was that in her breakdown Grace seemed to have made her son the principal cause of her collapse. "The hardest thing for me to bear is the blame that Mother puts on me as being in a major way responsible for her present condition. You know how hard it has been for me, and was last summer. This trouble will never, never end, I'm afraid, or if it does, it will be in insanity. I no longer anticipate, there is enough, it seems, in the present." Grace, Hart wrote, was "in a worse state" than ever before. As for himself, Hart was "holding on to health and sanity with both hands."

Zell's arrival brought enough order out of the chaos into which Grace and Hart had fallen to let them get their things together and return to Cleveland for the Christmas holidays. In the preparations for the week of gift-giving and relative-visiting, both Grace and Hart regained a good deal of their lost composure. By New Year's they felt well enough to accept C.A.'s invitation to a New Year's Eve party of relatives and friends. C.A. named them "guests of honor" and so celebrated them that Grace once more concluded that her affection for him had returned.

Grace's renewed fondness for her former husband must have seemed to Hart the height of folly. When the two of them had once more returned to New York and C.A.'s packages of candy were met always with an enthusiastic response on her part, Hart grew passionately indignant. He went so far as to sign his letters to Carl Schmitt *Harold Hart*, and stormed about their rooms in angry denunciation of his mother's vacillation.

Grace and Hart in these months came to see each other with new eyes. Hart's independence, of which he had been so proud, seemed to her proof that he had become an insolent, undutiful son. And her shifting attitudes toward C.A., which frequently brought on passionate outbursts of affection or hatred and ended almost always in tearful exhaustion, seemed to Hart evidence of increasing and frightening mental instability. Not that he loved her less. If anything, George Bryan felt, his affection for her during these trying months deepened. But he was painfully aware that nothing he could do seemed to help her.

By mid-February a crisis developed. The details are missing, but the root of the trouble was financial. C.A. was apparently determined to withhold payment for Hart's expenses until he heard that Hart was employed. Grace, convinced that she could win back C.A.'s affection, tried to persuade Hart to go to work for his father—or, failing that, to make another display of affection for him. Hart grew furious with both his parents.

He now refused to go on any longer with the fiction of college preparation. He walked out on his tutor, in the process confiding his troubles to Mrs. Walton and thereby causing Grace to brand both him and Mrs. Walton "disloyal." And he firmly refused to work for C.A. or even to speak to his mother about her latest dream of remarriage.

After a bitter argument, Grace took to her bed and Hart threatened to move to other quarters. Two days later he announced that he was going to break for good with her and with C.A.

This quarrel was far more serious than the Thanksgiving one, for Zell was not free again to pull the family together. This time there was no one to help. C.A. refused to come to New York to try to solve Grace's problems. And Hart's grandmother, seventy-nine years old and in a state of near collapse, was physically incapable of a journey anywhere.

To Mrs. Hart, alone in Cleveland, Grace's reports of angry debates with Hart and her frequent announcements that she couldn't live without C.A. spelled certain destruction of what little remained of her family. She consulted one friend after another. She routed Mr. Sullivan out of a sickbed, and she spent long hours with Mr. Ely, her Christian Science practitioner, noting down his advice and urging him to pray for Grace and for her family. A good deal of her time seems also to have been spent writing to Grace: "I wrote you such a long letter yesterday, I exhausted my resources and perhaps your patience in reading it, but these are such anxious moments of waiting, that I feel I must be doing, or saying something to cheer and help you to gather up courage, so the only resource I have is to write." Mixing prayer, Christian Science dogma, and practical advice into an emotional rush of words, she tried to accomplish via the U.S. mails what might have been easy had she been able to talk to Grace.

> All of us come up to conditions that can only be met by our own personal efforts. This is *yours*—and it would or might seem to be superhuman if viewed from your personal standpoint.

Through faith, Mrs. Hart argued, Grace might gain the strength to solve all her problems.

> Then will the power be given to go on to a glorious victory. And you have tried various ways and means—but there is one thing to decide on—that there is only *one* power, *one* mind, *one* God—who never fails. Stick close to the winning side and you are safe. I feel sure you will do this, dear, because you have tried everything else. March on and meet the foe at every step with the faith you will be carried safe through, as surely as the Israelites did when they were bidden to pass through the Red

Sea. They obeyed—but when they got there the waters parted and they passed through dry shod and so will you. You must take the *stand*—or you will never conquer. You do so bravely many times—but there seems to come a time you cannot meet. Let this be the time you can say—I have won—and won *forever*. Then will you not only be redeemed—but your Darling boy will be assured you have gloriously won out.

If only Grace would shut her eyes to the past "and *absolutely refuse* to see, hear, or talk, or even *think* of it," there might be some hope that she would solve her problems. In this way, Mrs. Hart felt, Grace might be able to bring Hart to something like his earlier devotion.

Do not mind Harold's seeming sadness—but remember—the best medicine for him is to see you have decided to throw off this past grief. You never can get anywhere by nursing it. You will soon see how your boy will change when he sees you have dropped it. Why deny him this spark of comfort? He thinks and worries more than he tells you, only he has a different way of showing it or working it off—. There is no reason why you and Harold should not be happy together. It may be best for a while you be not in [the] same house together until you have worked yourself up to a better state of feeling. Grace, you have done much for yourself in the past, yet you have not quite established yourself—but I feel sure you will see the necessity of a greater effort just at this critical time.

Knowing Grace's weaknesses, Mrs. Hart urged her to make up her differences with Mrs. Walton: "Try and overcome any ill feeling towards Mrs. W. Let her see you are nice and doing your part. Avoid talking over the subject with her, and she will be drawn to you—and be nice." Habitually suspicious of others, Grace had in the past broken with friends over imagined slights. Now, her mother felt, there was a danger of the same pattern reestablishing itself: "We can imagine so much when we are looking for trouble, don't you know? How much better to be looking for good in everybody. How much happier we are not to be distrusting everybody." Rather than leaving Mrs. Walton's as she had threatened, Grace should do her best to be up and about ("It's the only way to drive off troubles"); for were Grace to move out, she would be "much more lonely—and I think Harold would feel badly to have you leave so comfortable a place and location."

Mrs. Hart's letter was postmarked February 22, 1918. Three days later, in answer to a special-delivery letter from Grace, she sent off a desperate special delivery of her own in which, even more strongly than before, she urged Grace to abandon what now seemed a meaningless, hopeless infatuation for her former husband. Though the letter is extraordinarily long, only the full text of it conveys the spiritual chaos into which the whole family had now drifted.

My Dear Grace:

Your S. D. just received and read. Its contents *paralyze* me—after my long waiting, watching, and agony of mind. Now I can see no way to have this problem work out, for you and Harold to be brought together, but for *you* to *forever* leave C.A. out of your *thoughts*,—or talk—and take a stand for your boy, so decided that he will *know* he will never be annoyed by any thought of reference to him again. It is this that has brought this about more than anything, and it has now reached the point where he thinks if you are still undecided in your mind whether you are going to still cling to the faint possibility of getting him back or be wretched if you do not, he will leave all and go it alone. He is no worse than lots of boys who have to make their way unaided in the world—and he would feel far happier to do it than live under the constant fear of a constant breakdown from you. You are only making it worse for him by trying to bring them together. The more you try it the worse it makes it for Harold—and as far as feeling he—C.A.C.—cares for you, what does it amount to, when he will torture you as he has for the past year. It now is up to you to show Harold by *word* and *action* that you have taken the stand to stay by him—and that never more will you give way or show that you care for him—for I have heard Harold express himself that it was like a dagger thrust through and through him when he sees you are letting down—and this is the point he will make, if it is put to the test, that was what laid him out. And hard as it may seem to think this is so, we *have* to face facts some times that never occurred to us it could be possible—but the deep underlying current of your love—for him—C.A.—has led you to do things—seemingly through interest for Harold—that has every time failed, as you say. And it does seem that it is not to be. And rather than lose my boy, I would take the stand now and for good that I shall pick up myself and go on—with my boy—and take up my work where I left off. Even though you may feel no interest or heart in it, *do* it, with a determination you have cut loose from him every tie—and this decision, and this only will bring you the victory. It only wants the *courage* and *determination* to do it. You will be blessed the moment you do it. Then let Harold for the time being alone, to work out his problem which by letting him see you are letting go—from your hold—he thought of any future hold on him (C.A.C.). He will gradually see that you mean to stick to it, and then he will turn again to you. It may be some little time before he may be himself. And Grace do not lose the *only chance* for you to win him back because it is a *"struggle"* for you, and sit down in despair.

That will never win out, you know, and it is now time to *act*. I know Harold thinks you would have been stronger long ago if I had not sympathized with you so much—but I have meant to do right, and it has failed, and you have called me hard hearted when my heart was bleeding for you. You know that, and no one can ever know how I have suffered the last few days—at not hearing one word. I am sorry Harold does not care to get my letters. I've tried to advise him the best I know how. I want to get this off today, so I will have to hasten. After I read your letter and could gain sufficient strength to ask myself what to do, I thought I would call Mr. Sullivan at his office. His girl said he would not be in his office today. I said, could she reach him? She said if he calls up I'll tell him you want him. But I finally called up at his house, and *she* answered and said he was ill, could she take the message. I said no! it was something very necessary for me to tell him. Finally he answered the phone— and I said I had a very important letter from you. I saw by his voice he was a sick man. He says, *tell* me *something*—what it is. I told him you wanted advice about Harold—as things were in a very serious condition, and you did not know what to do. He says, well I am in bed—and am in danger of taking my death of cold by coming to the phone. I have left word at [my] office that I am out of [the] City so no one would find me. He says, tell Grace *not to worry* about Harold—that if she will do this and go on and take care of *herself*—it's the best thing she can do. I am going to see if Mr. Ely will come out this PM and tell him the situation, but if C.A. has refused you to go to N.Y. there is no earthly use of my trying to see him, and will only compli- cate matters more for Harold. What if he did say he was going to use Harold to deliver goods? If Harold could get the use of the car, he could learn to drive it himself and might be a good thing to get him out, and forget himself, but I don't hardly think he will do it, but the more you press C.A. about Harold— the worse and harder it will be for him—both for you and he, for it may be the means of driving him away. Just be as *gentle* and *prudent* as you can *now* until this is tided over—and the first and most important step is to guard yourself—by not letting down—and in this you go to Mr. Estey. You need tell him of only present conditions. Your past is not necessary for this present emergency. Rae says he is so gentle and kind—and gives you all the time you want and as often as you desire—and that she thinks he is just the one for you. And this will give you some where when you are so distressed to go to. Go often. Don't, I beg of you, give up. It means a terrible tragedy to us all. Don't sit and brood over your troubles, it is paralyzing to you. Fight to the bitter end for courage and strength to pull you through, and you *will* win—and this is something no one can do for you. We can go only so far—but you *must* reach for the life lines *yourself*—and grasp with a death grip and *hang* on. I am suffering for you equally, and helpless to do anything without your concentrated effort. Let's pull together—and help will come, but not perhaps in the way you have planned. Clarence seems to have taken a very stubborn stand. Let him go— He may have to reap the whirlwind after you have passed in to quiet waters. He will certainly have to reap the harvest he has sown, and after he has paid the penalty come out of it a better man and return to his former love at last. But be assured—God will not accept until the last penalty has been paid. Take courage— brace up—every hour you delay is dangerous. Do I beg of you see it before it is too late. I *know* your freedom of mind will come when you make the sacrifice and decide you will cut loose from CA. That is all that holds you and separates you from your boy. Just say to him, Harold, I have been foolish long enough. I have made my friends wretched, by my hanging on to one who has brought us both so much unhappiness, and most of all my dear boy. I see it now—forgive me—and I will try from now on to forget the past and stand by my child. *Believe me!* and help me to stand firm. There is yet happiness in store for us. Do not mind if he seems to doubt it. *Show* him by every day['s] life you mean what you say, even though you mark the way by bleeding footsteps. You *will* have your support by the way if you reach out for it. Just think what it will mean to all concerned. While you think you are the only one who suffers, it is not so. We, all, every one of your friends will gladly stand by you. Besides, by so doing you will bring together the remnants of your family into peace and joy and harmony we have not known for many years. You will be made richer in happiness for the struggle and victory, and have redeemed your boy to be an honor to you in your declining years. You may live to see the day when you will bless D.L. for all this suffering. Try it, as long as there is life there *is* hope. Don't let your name and heritage go down unhonored. Carry your standard bearer high above the smoke of conflict. And try my way and the way Mr. Ely and Mr. S. has directed you to do. You have side tracked them, by trying to work for Harold. You know Mr. Sullivan has told you it would *never* work—and you have proven it out. The only thing that will ever convince C. that he doesn't know what he is doing and will repent it later on is to let him prove it out, and also to show him that he has made the mistake of his life by turning down one who was noble and brave enough to live above it. This suffering of mine won't follow you any longer than when you have decided to make the sacrifice. Then stand *firm*. It's all up to *you*, and yours is the *victory* as sure as the day follows the night. I've just talked with Mr. Ely. I've told him all the conditions and also what I have written you. He says, it's the one and only thing for you to do—

is to stand *firmly* up—and he will work most *earnestly* for you
to make the decision—for you to *remember* he will give you his
*best* efforts right along—that you may have wisdom given you
to handle Hart just right, for you not to be discouraged if he
seems indifferent for a time, that he may be that way until he
feels you are safely established. And go on quietly each day
about your work asking no favors of him—so [he] has no
chance to refuse—and do no talking with *any*one over the case.
Try and keep your thoughts in the right channel. Shut out all
thoughts of either one that will destroy his efforts. Make yourself go out as much as possible—and do not allow Hart to know
you are grieving. It only worries and drives him away. Let him
rest from study awhile, but keep things from Hazel as much as
possible so C.A. won't get hold of any more—and don't worry
if H. has to work a little. He has much to learn, and he is none
too young to learn it. And I have done all I can see that would
be of any avail and as I have said before it remains for you to
take up the work that no one but *you* can do, and when you do
it in earnest you will soon be relieved of this terrible depression.
It is the Devil fighting you to the last ditch, and when he sees
he has no power to further win, he will leave you forever alone.
Oh I beg! of you to let us all help you—to do this—for your
*own* sake—for *Hart's*, and for *Mother's*. Let me not go down to
my grave in sorrow over something I am not to blame for. If
when all is over, and we have failed here of happiness, we are
no better than we were before before the end—besides the penalty of not having used our blessings and talents to any purpose.
And after reading this letter ponder it well—see if it is not the
best *and* only way left for harmony to be established between
you and Hart. You have tried various ways. Come back to the
starting point, and accept the advice of everyone who is interested and loves you and wants to see you pick yourself up
and make yourself over into a noble, courageous, grand woman,
one upon whom God has lavished rare and beautiful gifts.
Don't spurn them and turn them down as for naught and
worthless. Don't *force* Harold to do anything, or overurge him
against anything he does not want to do, but just lead him
gently. He is remorseful perhaps. You can better afford to do
this than to have him feel you are hurt by it. I'm sure my dear
girl now after all I have written that some of it may help you
to feel it is worth the while to try this way—and remember Mr.
Ely is heart and soul working that you may be able to overcome
this mental state you are in and the light *will* come as soon as
you are willing to see the light. When you have the terrible depression return remember he is trying to help you to be rid of
it, and also remember you are nearing the time of your men-
strual period and I will admonish him to work along that line
so you may be reinforced by that time in advance. And here

I send my whole heart of love to you—hoping you will not deny me a letter telling me that you do feel some better. It's almost impossible for me to stand this strain much longer in my weak condition. Love to Hart. I am sorry he has gone back on Grandma. John comes tonight. Don't forget Mr. Ely is making a mighty effort for you. Every *day.* So don't feel you are alone. Work with him. Please wire me you feel some better. All will go well as soon as you pick up.

Grace, however, did not pick up—at least not for some time. Finally, she and Hart decided that it might be best if he looked for a less expensive room and she returned to Cleveland.

Through the worst days of her troubles, she had come increasingly to rely on the help of a Mrs. Spencer, an active Christian Science practitioner, once a resident of Cleveland and now a friend of the Brooks. Thanks largely to the efforts of Mrs. Spencer and her daughter Claire, Grace and Hart were finally reconciled enough to be able to deal with one another. "He had a most heavy and distressing mother complex," Claire Spencer recalled, "which resulted in his homosexuality. This thing he fought for awhile."

Hart may, in fact, have fought his homosexuality during these difficult months by persuading himself that he had fallen in love with Claire. "I remember his coming to our house when I was married to Harrison Smith," she recollected, "and telling me that I had done this thing to him because of my treatment of him." Born only a few months apart, they shared not only an interest in literature but as well an excited volubility. On their long walks through the twisting streets of Greenwich Village, Hart would escape from his concerns about his mother in wild flights of laughing anecdotes—half fiction and half fact—about the writers who congregated about the *Little Review* office or at Joseph Kling's bookstore. More often than not, their walks would take them to Churchill's, where, after a light supper, they could dance the evening out. "He always wore sailor trousers then," she told me, "as he liked the way they flared out at the bottom as he danced."

Claire soon came to be his most sympathetic listener. Shifting from cheerful banter to grim recollections of childhood, Hart would say how much he had come to hate Cleveland—not so much because of anything repellent in the city but because of all the grim associations of his early years. "His youth must have been very painful," she remembered in 1962, "his father not at all in sympathy with him or his poetry. His mother played on his emotions as only an unhappy and foolish woman could. After Hart died she called me up in New York and asked me to come and see her. I just couldn't do it. By this time I was sure that it was all her fault—his drinking, his conscience, his sexual troubles."

However much Hart had fallen in love with Claire Spencer— or however much he had imagined it—for Claire herself he was only a very good companion. "I was totally unaware that he had any feeling for me at all. I did see a lot of him, it's true. But I was never aware of any emotion being there."

After Grace, near collapse, returned to Cleveland, Hart moved to a new room at 78 Washington Place, between Sixth Avenue and Washington Square. Here, as he wrote his friend George Bryan in a cheerful invitation to join him for a weekend, "all the twentieth century luxuries" were available in a room considerably bigger and cheaper than his other one: "plenty of room . . . running water, double bed, stove, closet, etc."

Though much concerned over his mother's welfare, he was relieved to return to the pattern of life that had preceded her Thanksgiving arrival. He again looked up Stan and Anna, and he began again to drop in regularly on the offices of *The Little Review* and *The Pagan*.

So much of his time, indeed, was spent in Joseph Kling's establishment that Kling suggested Crane might as well make himself officially useful. Accordingly, the April–May issue of *The Pagan* listed on its masthead "Associate Editor—Hart Crane" and was crammed with his material—two poems, a drama review, and a commentary on the war-inspired popular reaction against Nietzsche. "Such a burst of trumpets," Hart wrote Schmitt, "cannot fail to arouse the relatives of a slim, sleek youth of eighteen, I am sure."

Even before the trumpets, Hart had been able to ship home a few flute solos. In the January issue of *The Pagan* had appeared "Modern Craft," his elegantly ironic portrait of the wide-eyed flapper who "hazards jet; wears tiger-lilies," and who, "Drowning cool pearls in alcohol," becomes a paradoxical figure of "innocence dissolute," the Greenwich Village girl who, substantially unchanged, can still be found in Bleecker Street coffee houses. In some ways anticipating the middle of "For the Marriage of Faustus and Helen," "Modern Craft" shows how far he had come since, nearly two years before, he had submitted to Guido Bruno "Carmen de Boheme." That gaudy poem, winding cello tones "sinuously" through a room "On smokey tongues of sweetened cigarettes" and including in its last stanza a picture of a gypsy wagon that "wiggles, striving straight," appeared suddenly—to Crane's surprise—in the March issue of *Bruno's Bohemia*. As Crane told an Akron reporter a little over a year later, the poem, a product of a sixteen-year-old's "white-hot imagination," had been forgotten almost as soon as he shipped it off. "Two years after that when he went to New York," Crane's interviewer reported, "he turned the pages of a current issue of the magazine's and stared at his poem—with his name signed!" Laughing "heartily" and "tolerantly," Hart dismissed it as accidentally surviving juvenilia.

The poems that appeared in the April–May issue of *The Pagan* were an altogether different matter. "Carrier Letter" achieves ironic juxtapositions that hint the intricate structures Crane would later build. "Postscript," rooted in personal material (his recent break with his mother?), shows that he is already able to turn private sorrow—a private life that is "foregone though not yet ended"— into effective public poetry.

Though his editorial post on *The Pagan* earned Hart not a penny, it did offer him a supply of passes to the newly established Village theaters and to many of the uptown concert halls. One immediate consequence of these passes was a brief signed review of Village theater activity. Crane praised Eugene O'Neill's *Ile*, "a picture of the silence, solitude, and desolation of northern waters," which was appearing, in a bill of two plays, at the Greenwich Village Theatre. Most of his space, however, was devoted to the group of one-act plays presented by The Other Players. Edna St. Vincent Millay's *Two Slatterns and a King* seemed to him dramatically the most satisfying part of the program. ("Although slightly reminiscent of Anatole France, its medieval satire was gratifying.") But he was really more interested in Alfred Kreymborg's *Manikin and Minikin* and *Jack's House*. He praised Kreymborg's innovation of "a sort of lyric-dramatic dialogue" and William Zorach's "futuristic scenery."

Though Crane worried about his family, wrote poems literally despite them, lived—as who doesn't?—vicariously in the lives of his closest friends, shifted rapidly from brooding introvert to extrovert dancing-companion, the public world that surrounded him was unavoidably part of his consciousness. The war forced its way into his private life. His *Pagan* essay on Nietzsche was "about" the war, as was a little editorial note by "H.C." which reported that the editors of the magazine had had reservations in printing a patriotic poem.

Nevertheless, it is difficult to discover exactly what Crane's reaction to war was. Certainly it was not the reaction of Ernest Hemingway—another young writer who was ultimately, for far different reasons, to prove a suicide, and who was born on the same day in the same year as Crane to a mother named Grace in Grace Crane's home town. Hemingway, who suffered from defective eyesight (Crane did also), had moved heaven and earth to enlist in the war—and failing enlistment had settled for overseas duty with the Red Cross. "Delirious with excitement," he had marched down Fifth Avenue from Eighty-second Street to the Battery in an end-of-May parade that Crane might well have watched from the curb, his own contribution to the war effort in his pocket, a brand-new Liberty Bond.

Crane—who at various times tried to enlist in the war, not for patriotic reasons but to escape—had seen all the parades. In the fall he had "witnessed the great red-cross parade on Fifth which took three hours to exhaust itself," and a little later had written home ironically of another day on the curb—this one a rainy day during which he "barely escaped ruining" his "beautiful felt hat in the rain": "Parades,—parades,—parades! I am so tired of them. All the firemen in town, undaunted by the rain, insist on parading up Fifth Ave. and blockading traffic so that one can't get . . . a 'bus or reach the subway. There have been nurse parades, and dog-parades and cat-parades and all to that eternally rapturous and boresome melody, 'Over There.' "

It is easy, from passages like this one, to turn young Crane into a pacifist; but in fact he seems to have been neither pacifist nor ardent nationalist. Convinced, if one can judge from the tone of his letters of this time, that Germany had to be defeated, he was nevertheless disturbed by the jingo patriotism he saw all around him. He had been particularly upset by something he had heard of on his return to Cleveland at Christmas time, a series of war-inspired slanderous attacks on his friend Richard Laukhuff. Laukhuff's German background had made him an easy butt for vicious rumors that hinted he might be a German spy.

It may have been with this in mind that Crane wrote for *The Pagan* his defense of Nietzsche, for Nietzsche—one of Laukhuff's intellectual heroes—was currently being attacked as "the herald of modern Prussianism." Pointing out how ironical it was that Nietzsche, who had admired things French, who had "denied his German origin, and declared himself a Pole in all his views and sympathies," and who in *Menschliches, Allzumenschliches* had made a "direct arraignment of Prussianism," should somehow be regarded as the philosophical spokesman of political Germany, Crane did his best to defend a philosopher he had learned to admire and attacked those people who could not distinguish a man's national origin from his intellectual attainment.

The Nietzschean influence can be overrated. (Almost all literary or philosophical influence can, in Crane's case, be overrated, since he valued an artist's personality quite as much as his ideas.) But it is true that Crane found in Nietzsche's Apollonian-Dionysian dichotomy a satisfying explanation for the nature of man, and particularly for the nature of the artist. Feeling his own orientation to be Dionysian, Crane came increasingly to believe that he had been destined for the role of wine-inspired prophet-poet. A glass of wine in hand, he found suddenly that the shyness and awkwardness that had always troubled him would miraculously disappear and the words which, cold sober, he had fought for would come effortlessly to his lips.

By the spring of 1918, Hart felt, if not on top of the world, at least very much a part of it. His sense of well-being came, as always, from improved relations with his family.

Grace, in Cleveland, was making a slow but steady recovery from her breakdown. By Easter she felt well enough to wire her

son a carefully worded telegram: "I AM SENDING YOU MY LOVE AND
EASTER GREETINGS WITH ALL THAT THE TERM MEANS AM FEELING
BETTER AND HOPE YOU ARE WELL AND YOUR PLANS WORKING OUT TO
PLEASE YOU." Soon mother and son were again in active correspondence. Grace told him that she hoped to become a member
of the Cleveland Little Playhouse ("which has a mission something like the Greenwich Theatre in New York") and recommended to him the film of *The Blue Bird*, in which Stan had
briefly appeared ("but they reeled the film so fast that he was not
like most of the others given a fair chance to be appreciated").
Though the earlier warmth of their letters, the gossipy intimacy,
had disappeared, Grace and Hart were doing their best—in rather
formal prose—to heal the wounds of their recent break. "I want
you to know that I have certainly appreciated your good letters
and assurances of affection," Grace wrote, "that I miss your comradeship very much but hope you will write often and let me
know what you are doing and your plans. Please know that I always love you and feel that you will before long find your right
place and an opportunity to express yourself to your own satisfaction." Sometimes, of course, Grace lapsed into self-pity and
recrimination. "I got a letter from home yesterday as doleful as
usual," Hart wrote his friend George Bryan after one of Grace's
tirades. "In fact I have had 'the blues' nearly all day as the result
of reading it last night just before sleeping." But most of her letters
were now cheerful ones, happy accounts of motor trips with her
mother and Mrs. Baker. A week's outing to Saegertown, Pennsylvania, had especially delighted her. A long walk in the spring
sunshine had reminded her of her youth, when, accompanied by
her infant son, she had wandered through the same fields: "Once
you may remember you fell in the river close by here and were
fished out by a Jap. I am sure if you were here now, a wonderful
poem would be the result." Though New York seemed too much
for her at this stage, perhaps Hart could be persuaded to come to
Cleveland for his summer vacation. "I am thinking of buying
a 'chummy Roadster,'" she wrote, offering to let him learn to
drive it "and motor for diversion."

Hart's father had also developed a more tolerant attitude toward his son. He was especially pleased that Hart had briefly
held a position as salesman in the basement of Brentano's bookstore. Though most of Hart's customers wanted books "on wet
nursing, care of mothers during pregnancy, the Montessori
method, and how to know the wild flowers," the job gave Crane
easy access to books he wanted to read and enough pocket money
sometimes to entertain Claire Spencer, sometimes to make payments on the Liberty Bond he had purchased "at a 'dollar down'
etc.," and sometimes to splurge extravagantly by putting up visiting friends.

One of these friends was George Bryan, whose proximity (he

was attending Carleton Academy at Summit, New Jersey) made visits possible.

Hart had had no real difficulty in talking about his troubles with Claire Spencer or with his friend Stan, but the presence of someone who had grown up with him and who knew intimately the members of his family gave Hart an opportunity to unburden himself completely. "I haven't had as much pleasure and happiness in two years as was crammed into those few hours you were here," Hart wrote after one Saturday visit. "I am sure you cannot say as much but you must remember George I have been practically starved for any happiness whatever for a long long time." Composing his note in elegant green ink ("Now don't remonstrate against this ink. I tell you it is Spring and green is the only proper color"), and pleading, "Write soon, George, because you are the *one* person who brings me some sense of restfulness and satisfaction," Hart did his best to convince his friend to return again two weeks later—this time for a full weekend, possibly with an evening's double date for dancing or the theater.

In the meantime, events in Cleveland had been moving swiftly ahead—so swiftly, in fact, that Grace had scarcely been able to keep up with them. Though she had heard that C.A. had met in Kansas City a young woman of whom he was inordinately fond, the announcement of his impending marriage to Frances Kelley— a clear-skinned, pale, black-haired Irish beauty, gentle, affectionate, and soft-spoken—threatened to destroy the tranquillity Grace had only recently regained. Striving very hard to remain calm, she sat down to compose one of the hardest letters of her life, an urgent, roundabout attempt to lure (not "command") her son to return to Cleveland, so that he could be by her side at the time of C.A.'s marriage.

> Now I am going to make this *suggestion*, notice I do not command. There is a good home awaiting you here and food that you have forgotten how good it tastes. There are also plenty of jobs if you want them and a warm welcome for you if you should decide to spend the summer here instead of hot New York.
>
> I am thinking very strongly of buying a car, and as I wrote you from Saegertown you may learn to drive it.
>
> The war now is a real issue and there is no dodging one's duty towards helping in one way or another. I think I have found where I can be active and not depressed.
>
> Whether you are in N.Y. or here, the Government demands that all young men 18 or over be occupied in some way. Don't you think that during the summer it would be a good change to come back here and get a job of some kind and have the use of an auto on Sundays? You have within your grasp the privilege

of making me very happy by having you with me for a while during a time which may be very trying and hard for me to bear.

You have often said you considered it a privilege to live. Then thank your father and mother for that and repay them for their desires for your happiness and welfare by doing something for them. It may be that your father has selected a wonderful woman for his second wife—or at least one who will make him happy. I am not going to say that I am glad that he is to be married so soon—because I had thought that someday with the necessary separation and time to view things more broadly we might all three again be happily reunited. But it doesn't look that way now. However you have no quarrel with your father over that anymore than if I should take the same step.

So please write him a good letter to that effect very soon. I know he does care for you and you for him. Then if you see nothing more tempting, accept my suggestion and return here to the best bed and meals and the most devoted hearts [that] await you. Wire me your decision when you have made it. This plan is only for the summer you know.

I was delighted to know you had stopped smoking—no wonder you feel better. My best love to the Spencers. Molly says if you come home bring a Pomeranian dog with you. You can't buy them here. My what a summer with dog, fleas, gasoline, and poetry!

If you decide to come you can likely store your desk, bookcase, and *objet d'art* at your father's office—bringing such books as you may need here back with you in your little trunk.

Love from us all—

> Devotedly your
> Mother Grace—

Hart, for the first time actively busy with literary matters, did his best to delay the trip home. As soon as it came off press, he sent the April–May issue of *The Pagan* to his mother, hoping perhaps that such clear evidence of his success—his name on the cover as Associate Editor—might convince her of the wisdom of his remaining in New York.

But Grace had withdrawn into a flurry of activity, "getting very busy," as Hart's grandmother wrote him, "which is her only salvation." Attending play rehearsals three nights a week, taking riding lessons in the Armory, taking driving lessons every morning, selecting and finally purchasing her car, Grace rushed from one project to another. "They say her car is the handsomest in Clev. —and they wanted to show it in the window," Hart's grandmother wrote. "It is very plain but elegant and nobby." Hart, his grandmother implied, would not really have to come to Cleveland. "Everybody is lovely to Mother and are trying to plan things for her pleasure," she told him. "So don't worry. She is thinking lovely things of her boy if she does not write—and feels sure of his final success."

Hart held out in New York until the end of May, doing his best to convince himself that *The Pagan* could not get through the summer without him. "I should certainly like to get out of the city this summer," he wrote George Bryan, "but at present I fail to see any way. If you come to work here, as you said you might, I suggest that we take conjointly a really good room out farther in the city." But George did not join him, and finally there seemed nothing to do but to go back to Cleveland, settle in at home, and look for a job.

His first work in Cleveland was at a munitions plant, where, tightening bolts on machine parts, he watched a seemingly endless procession of objects pass before him on a conveyor belt. For a while he was proud of his contribution to the war effort and surprised to find himself happy in the rough comradeship of physical laborers. But he began to dread his nightly return home; for Grace, edgy as C.A.'s marriage drew near, fretted over trivialities.

When Grace suggested a long motoring tour through New England, Hart encouraged her to make the trip. He could not, he explained, go with her; every person counted, whether tightening bolts or fighting in the trenches; he was needed in his work. His real vacation, consequently, began on the afternoon of July 4 as his mother and grandmother and Charles, their driver, walked out the front door to get into Grace's handsome new car.

Letters from his grandmother were encouraging. They told of Grace's good spirits and of their continued affection for him. "I think of you very very often," his grandmother wrote from New York, their first extended stop, "and hope you are not unhappy— or at least are resting more quietly—since our departure—for it was anything but restful there."

Hart must have found ironic the good wishes his grandmother passed on to him from Grace, who, according to Mrs. Hart, "feels badly that you are not with us—but feels very proud of you for being so brave—to stick to your work." For on the day before he received the letter, he had resigned from his job at Warners, the ammunition factory, his resignation to take effect on July 18. He may have had a moment's twinge of conscience when he read that, but what he did upon quitting his job was to write his friend William Wright, then working at a boy's camp near Cleveland, to invite him to come for a weekend visit. Crane knew there would be no problems in his finding new employment, and he set about the search in a holiday mood. "I . . . shall spend the rest of the week in looking around and deciding on another occupation," he wrote Wright. "Perhaps it will be marriage, —I can't yet determine. Do you know of any lonely young lady (or old) with a lot of money?"

Hart's nineteenth birthday fell on a Sunday in the weekend of Wright's visit, and the two boys spent the day reminiscing over old times.

Since his high-school days, Crane had felt the need for very close friends. With these as confidants, he could relieve the pressure of family problems and later of problems created by complex and sometimes awkward sexual adventures. In New York his confidants had been Schmitt, then the ballet dancer Stan, then Mrs. Walton, then Claire Spencer, and finally George Bryan. Each of them was gifted with a sympathetic capacity to listen; their lives—steadier than his own—offered a vicarious strength that he felt he could rely on in times of crisis.

In Cleveland, especially while Crane was in his teens, his best listener had been Bill Wright. Cocky, cheerful, outgoing, Wright never failed to bring Crane successfully through his deepest depressions. Now, discussing the relationship between "life" and the poetry that each of them wrote, the two friends planned a summer of literary achievement.

Though his own poetry was moving in a different direction, Crane was fond of Bill's work and wanted to see it in print. Thanks to his position on *The Pagan*, he was able to arrange for the July publication of Wright's short poem "Mood." The first stanza—derived from Verlaine—had the sort of lushness that Crane was carefully excising from his own verse, but he must have liked—at this stage of his development—the open, relaxed statement of the second stanza. Because we do make poetry first for our friends and then for the world, it is worth looking carefully at the work Hart's best friend in Cleveland was producing.

Mood

The moaning of a violin
Somewhere
In the heavy etherial incense
Of the rose-scented darkness
Drifted softly, languidly,
Into my soul.

And it was as if
My fingers lay
In the soft cool hand of Pan;
And he led me,
Gently,
Into the far reaches
Of the dreamy sky.

To see similarities and differences between the work of the two young men, one has only to turn to Crane's "Forgetfulness," a poem almost certainly composed during this same summer and published in the next issue of *The Pagan* (Aug.–Sept. 1918). "Forgetfulness" has a good deal in common both with the approach to poetry of Wright's second stanza and with the tone of the entire poem. One can imagine, after comparing the two poems, the kind of criticism Crane must have been tempted to make of his friend's work ("try it without *the far* in the second last line"; "try *dreaming* instead of *dreamy* in the last line"). With such changes, Wright's second stanza could have been written by young Crane. But, jealous of a poet's integrity, Hart printed his friend's poem intact— no matter what revisions he would have been tempted to make were it his own.

If the two boys talked about poetry, they must have also talked about prose—and one prose work in particular; for a long letter from Crane in defense of Joyce's *A Portrait of the Artist as a Young Man* was printed—under the caption "Joyce and Ethics"— in the then current issue of *The Little Review*. Defending Joyce against the attacks of a "Los Angeles critic" in an earlier issue of the magazine, Crane particularly objected to the association of Joyce and "decadence." "Sterility," Crane insisted, "is the only 'decadence' I recognize. . . . A piece of work is art, or it isn't: there is no neutral judgment."

Contemptuous of a critic who could not distinguish between the literary values of Wilde, Baudelaire, Swinburne, and Joyce, Crane did his best to rank these writers. Swinburne he dismissed as a poet of "beautiful, though often meaningless mouthings," a poet of "sound," famous for "irrelevant metaphors." Wilde, too, he ranked low: "after his bundle of paradoxes has been sorted and conned,—very little evidence of intellect remains." Baudelaire and Joyce, however, were very different literary craftsmen. "Let Baudelaire and Joyce stand together, as much as any such thing in literary comparison will allow. The principal eccentricity evinced by both is a penetration into life common to only the greatest." That penetration, achieved through a thrust that reveals "entrails," must not be regarded as immoral or obscene. "The character of Stephen Dedalus is all too good for this world. It takes a little experience,—a few reactions on his part to understand it, and could this have been accomplished in a detached hermitage, high above the mud, he would no doubt have preferred that residence." If comparisons have to be made, it is not Wilde or Swinburne who should be compared to Joyce, but rather professed moralists, writers concerned with the nature of the spirit of man. "*A Portrait of the Artist as a Young Man,* aside from Dante, is spiritually the most inspiring book I have ever read. It is Bunyan raised to art, and then raised to the ninth power."

While Hart read and wrote about Joyce, made halfhearted attempts to find work, and made rather formal duty calls on his father in the factory office of the candy firm, Grace continued her New England tour. By the first week in August, Hart's friend Bill Wright had returned to Springfield, Ohio, where his family had moved, and Hart was plainly bored. "The most momentous news that I can summon to report," he wrote Wright, "is that my teeth are repaired and one of them duly crowned."

The return of Grace and Mrs. Hart put an end to boredom: "Mother and Grandma returned yesterday [Aug. 8]. The house is in uproar,—-descriptions, and relations spattered all over ceilings and walls. —It must have been a wonderful trip!!!" For the first few days of their return Hart was in good spirits. The Cranes' heavy-set cook was off to a mountain vacation, and Hart wrote Bill Wright a cheerful note in which he imagined accidental meetings between the two: "Now I hope that you are going to a cool place, there in the mountains. Molly, our cook, is also about to journey thither and gives favorable accounts of the climate and scenery. Perhaps you will meet in some thick-wooded lane or by some trout-stream (I can picture her coyly wading), and if such should occur, remember home and mother ignoring, mon vieux, her seductive girth.—Jesus! God-Almighty! Yours, etc. Harold Hart Crane."

For several days Grace and Hart got on well together, but soon her extravagant praise of men in uniform and her prodding reminders that Hart was still unemployed and consequently a drain on her resources began to be the occasion for short and painful arguments. "You know, Mother," he wrote her the next spring, "I have not yet forgotten your twitting me last summer at my not paying my board expenses when I was at home, and I don't welcome your generosity quite so much now on the possibility of a recurrence of such words at some future time." Four days after Grace returned, Hart decided to take matters in his own hands. Rushing downtown to the army enlistment office, he attempted to volunteer for immediate overseas duty. His heroic gesture, painfully ill-timed, had coincided with a government decision to prohibit minors from enlisting. "I . . . was not permitted even to enter the office," he told Wright. "The guard at the door said to 'look in the paper,' which I did, and found that all minors are to be excluded from 'volunteering,' and, if drafted at all, will be apprenticed in machine shops, etc., during the war period."

Wright himself had considered, as an alternative to the draft, the wisdom of entering the ambulance corps. This, Crane felt, would be pointless: "I think by the way things look at present, ambulance service, after the time necessary for training, transportation, etc., would be a little superfluous. (Some would call me a demon of the Huns for whispering this in your ear.) I really believe the war isn't to last much longer." Besides, Crane added, since

Wright had already been accepted as a freshman at Yale, he had no real worries. "You won't be drafted for anything. But you will have to undergo some discipline, as Mother, who visited no less than twelve Eastern colleges in her last expedition, states."

His own move, Crane said, had been a result of boredom and exasperation. "Heat and conditions at home (both of which you comprehend, I'm sure) drove me to the deed from which I was frustrated this morning. I take no credit for patriotism nor bravery. Neither," he added, "was it an attempt to get into a uniform before the war is over for certain effects with the ladies."

> I am really sorry I couldn't get in, principally, I suppose, because I had made my mind up, and disposed of so many seductive distractions, such as, (well—) love, poetry, career, etc. Now the damned things come back again, sporting about me with all too much familiarity.
>
> I may go to New York,—I may remain here, I may explode, Lord knows. Thank your stars that you have a settled course to follow, and write soon.

The home Hart returned to that night was, in fact, not far from explosive. C.A. had already left Cleveland for Kansas City, where, two days later, he would be married. Grace, in an agony of nervous irritability—resenting the calls of sympathetic friends and regarding as unsympathetic those friends who, tactfully, did not call—saw Hart's recruiting misadventure as a deliberately planned affront. And Mrs. Hart, concerned that mother or son, or both, might fall again into an emotional collapse as they had in New York, fluttered helplessly between them.

More to escape his home than to earn a living, Crane decided to answer one of the shipyard ads that daily called for manual workers on the waterfront. He presented himself as physically fit and willing to work and was quickly signed on as a riveter. For three weeks he crawled—not always efficiently, for the hay-fever season was in full swing—from girder to girder of the tankers then being rushed to completion in the Cleveland docks. Hay fever, however, put an end to his riveting career. His doctor declared that his long bouts of sneezing, his running nose, and his swollen eyes were incompatible with the delicate and dangerous work in which he was engaged.

No sooner had he left the shipyards than the apparently impossible happened. "I am included in the 18–45 draft," he wrote Schmitt, "and sincerely wish to be taken soon to be a 'rough . . . common . . . soldier.'" Of course, he cursed the unpredictable government; but he was not above seeing the ironies of his situation: "I have skidded about at one thing and another most all summer and feel prepared and even enthusiastic. They say that all grouches stand excellent opportunities for promotion, so my ambition is becoming dreamily tickled at the prospect."

The ironies of his efforts to turn himself into a soldier were only beginning. After writing all his friends details of the way in which he had been frustrated at enlistment and then abruptly drafted, he found his draft call maddeningly delayed from week to week as the end-of-the-year influenza epidemics closed one camp after another. Finally, when it seemed inevitable that he would leave for camp, November 11 arrived, the Armistice was signed, and all draft calls were abolished.

The week of the Armistice was for Crane a busy one, for he had managed—perhaps on the strength of an "Armistice" sonnet—to get a cub-reporter job on the Cleveland *Plain Dealer*. He was also assembling a group of his best lyrics to be submitted to a Cleveland minister, the Reverend Charles C. Bubb, who, as an avocation, ran The Church Head Press, a small publishing house. Crane probably heard of Bubb through Laukhuff, for he left at Laukhuff's store the half-dozen poems he hoped Bubb would publish. ("While they are few in number, I thought that they might possibly be equal to the boundaries of a modest pamphlet. 'Six Lyrics', or some such title might be used for the booklet.") Nothing came of the publication plans, but Crane and Bubb began a literary correspondence that continued into the next year.

Crane's experiences on the *Plain Dealer*, though by no means disillusioning, were for the first month comparatively tame. He worked at a desk job in the city room, hobnobbing with reporters but never going out on a story. Finally, on December 12, his chance came. "I really feel as though I had been initiated into the reporting game after the experience I went through last Thursday night," he wrote George Bryan.

> There was a horrible automobile smash-up on the west side in which 6 people were killed,—and about 4 badly injured. For about 3 hours five of them remained unidentified at the morgue, and I was sent down there to assist in the operation. There I had to watch the bloody corpses being undressed, washed and laid out on slabs. I didn't puke nor anything else, but for a first experience it was a trial.

As the holidays drew near, and with them holiday violence, Crane spent more and more time in the *Plain Dealer* office or out on similar "identification" chores. He was on duty all of Christmas morning and afternoon and all of New Year's evening in what was by now a grisly routine. "I spent New Year's evening at the morgue," he wrote Bryan, "trying to identify some woman who celebrated the holiday season by throwing herself into the lake."

By the second week of January, Crane was beginning to tire—physically and emotionally. "The work has been rather stupid in the office for the last few days," he wrote Bryan on January 7, "and I can't help longing for the time when I shall be out of it." The next day Crane resigned, his resignation to take effect immediately.

Though the holiday season had been a busy one for Crane, one of new sights and new smells, he found time to polish his first book review, a careful and very just evaluation of Lola Ridge's *The Ghetto and Other Poems.*

Published in the January issue of *The Pagan*, it praised her poems for the "dramatic quality" of "personal utterance"—exactly Crane's project in his own poetry of the time—and warned against "barren cleverness." Perhaps of most interest to the student of Crane's verse is an image that Crane selected for quotation.

> Over the black bridge
> The line of lighted cars
> Creeps like a monstrous serpent
> Spooring gold. . . .

For it reveals something of great importance in Crane's poetic technique: his habit of adapting other people's imagery and other people's themes to his own purposes. Crane delighted in literary adaptation and literary allusion. He committed to memory the most brilliant lines of poems he admired, or copied them out in the loose-leaf notebooks he kept with him always. And sometimes, altering them almost but not quite beyond recognition, he would fit them into his own verse. Though no critic could fail to see the relationship between Miss Ridge's lines about the serpentine cars that cross the black bridge and Crane's adaptation of the image in the brilliant "Proem" he was years later to write for *The Bridge* ("Again the traffic lights that skim thy swift / Unfractioned idiom, immaculate sigh of stars, / Beading thy path— condense eternity"), no critic could honestly describe Crane's lines as in any way "derivative" from Miss Ridge's. Achieving relationship only, Crane barely echoed—certainly not borrowed.

He had used his review of Miss Ridge's book primarily as a vehicle for an opening statement about the nature of the modern world, a statement he was, in one form or another, to return to in much of the poetry he subsequently wrote. "Extremities," he insisted, "clash in a close proximity" in our world, "so that there is a finer, harder, line than usual to divide them. There is a cruelty in this,—a kind of desperation that is dramatic." Illustrating his point with science—he might well have chosen science's product, modern industry—he pictured a science "grown uncontrollable" and wearing on its face "a grin that has more than threatened the supposed civilization that fed it." "Science has brought in light," Crane admitted, but he went on to insist that it "threatens to destroy the idea of reverence, the source of all light. . . . In one sense it has become a gargoyle."

During the time that Crane worked on his review—and worked for the *Plain Dealer*—he had been in steady correspondence with George Bryan, who, recently moved to McKees Rocks, Pennsylvania, was well within easy travel distance of Crane's Cleveland home. Offering Bryan another evening of intimate talk ("You know, or ought to know, that I am always with you in whatever troubles or 'blues' you may be having"), Crane arranged to spend Christmas evening with his friend.

For Crane that year neither family gifts nor religious sentiment made Christmas memorable: it was rather George's visit—the best present anyone could give him. Meeting after Crane was through at the *Plain Dealer*, the two young men began a conversation that ran on into the night. Crane poured out all his accumulated bitterness against his father—he still regarded him as having "betrayed" both himself and his mother—and his increasingly intricate feeling of exasperated affection toward his mother, whom he still admired above all other women but whose temperamental instability could be counted on to drive him into agonizing depression.

Not talked out until dawn, Crane spent the rest of the week recovering from the emotional exhaustion of their conversation. It wasn't until Saturday, December 28, that he thanked his friend for his good and helpful listening: "One night of happiness,—that was Christmas night! I was tired next day until about six o'clock, but after that I began to revive somewhat, and by midnight I never felt finer in my life." Tiredness, Crane concluded, is only a state of mind. "I believe we can think so much about being tired and that we *ought* to be tired after only 1 hour's sleep, etc., etc., that we *are* tired, whereas, if we are so busy as to not have any time to think about ourselves at all, we soon feel as fine as ever."

When Crane quit his $20-a-week job on the *Plain Dealer*, he was once more at loose ends. He expected to find work of some kind and to save enough money to be able to return to New York in the spring—April or May, he told George Bryan. But work, with veterans returning, proved considerably harder to find than it had been at the time of the Armistice. Under the circumstances, C.A. offered to support his son for "a while" and Hart began a rapid rearrangement of plans. On January 12 he expected to be leaving for New York at the end of two weeks; on February 4, within a week or so; and by February 15, at no foreseeable date. He reached New York on February 21.

The six weeks at home began well. Crane settled down again to compose movie scripts as he had earlier in New York. Somewhat to his surprise, he found the writing easier than it had been, and he was enjoying the experience—but he regarded it as merely a stopgap until his allowance was arranged and he was able to leave.

Before he could work out anything with his father, however, Grace—worried about an income for herself and for her son—again took to bed. And though her illness was of comparatively short duration, Crane called off a projected visit to his friend William Wright, writing him on the Sunday that he was supposed to be visiting in Warren, Pennsylvania.

> The sky is cleared somewhat. I hope my tempestuous letters have not struck you as being too eccentric. Indeed I feel some assurance as to that in your generous and sympathetic responses. You're a brick! And this is not the first time I have had occasion to say so. Mother is fully recovered again and seems to be on her feet. Quite naturally she has had periods of strenuous fears but, as some one of her friends assured her:—What is the use of holding up one's hands at a column of figures?

Though Crane did his best to be cheerful, his mother's depression was infectious. "Your letter was a real comfort, George," he wrote George Bryan in the middle of the month. "It came at just the time that I felt discouraged enough to kick the bucket. Mother had one of the spells you know about and every . . . other imaginable thing happened. As a result I had [to] give up my visit to Bill Wright, and I haven't had the confidence in circumstances again to make a single plan."

He did finish the scenario he had been working at and, on the morning of the fifteenth, shipped it off to a motion-picture company. "Now," he told Bryan, "I cannot breathe real easy until I get some kind of an answer. A story that's worth anything at all is worth a good sum of money, and money being the commodity I am in great need of at present, I am naturally very much interested in how my poor little story is treated."

Since he wasn't happy, Crane during these days began to amuse himself with a kind of professional unhappiness, exaggerating the pose of a bitter young man—largely for his friends' entertainment. "I am primarily distinguishable these days as 'the man with a grouch,'" he wrote Bill Wright in a short note urging a weekend visit. "Still, as this mood has never been so totally foreign to my conduct, such good friends of mine as yourself would doubtless find me recognizable. I would like you to make me a visit (if it can be fairly soon) just to try out the experiment as 'Dr. Wright' (who sets things right) (awful, I know, but premature dotage!) stopping at 1709 E. 115 St. where all will be found of placid pleasures procurable in these days of lusty Bolshevism and the young 20th Century. I promise solemnly that order will be maintained throughout the sojourn and bid your parents divest themselves of all apprehensions as to your safety while in 'Fourth City.'

I am smoking again, full tilt, and promise you numberless Cincos to pass the time away."

But before Wright could arrive for his visit, Grace suddenly snapped out of her depression, C.A. set a figure for Hart's allowance, and Hart himself took the evening sleeper for New York.

# 5

When Crane stepped out of Grand Central Station on the morning of February 21, 1919, he stepped into a deluge of winter rain. Nevertheless, he was happy. "Just arrived," he wrote George Bryan on a picture postcard of one of his favorite buildings, the recently opened Public Library at Forty-second Street. "It sure seems good to be back in the old town."

Rushing all over the city in his search for old friends, he stopped in to see Mrs. Walton and Madame Lebègue; spent part of the afternoon with Joe Kling, who invited him to a performance of the visiting Chicago Opera Company later in the week; and called on Mrs. Spencer, who told him details of Claire's recent marriage to Harrison Smith. But though his friends, as always, meant a great deal to him, it was now the city itself which was most exciting. Suddenly old faces and even old streets took on a different appearance.

> The city is ablaze with life, even in this rainy weather. The avenues sparkle and money seems to just roll in the gutters. I am looking on it all with different, keener, happier eyes than ever before. In a way it is just like coming the first time, as I seem now to have been looking at different things before. Of course the truth is, I am looking at things (the same things) *differently*.

Convinced that Grace, with the assistance of the Christian Scientist Mr. Ely, had made a miraculous recovery from her nervous breakdown, Crane took seriously what before he had regarded as a convenient superstition, a hocus-pocus by which his mother could be distracted from her troubles. The efforts of Grace and his grandmother and Mr. Ely to make him see the light were in New York continued by Mrs. Spencer. "After the dishes were cleared away we sat before the wood-fire and talked Science," he wrote his mother on the evening of that first long day in the city, "and I played the piano while she washed the dishes. She tells me some astounding stories about the numerous demonstrations she has made."

For two weeks Crane regularly visited Mrs. Spencer's home, going over with her—sometimes in the company of Mr. and Mrs. Brooks—the wonder cures her Christian Science practice had effected. As he listened and tried to believe, he felt that his own personality was suffering a change for the better. "It must be due to a change of disposition within myself," he wrote his mother, "but I find the Brooks's much more cordial and agreeable." And he went on to summarize Mrs. Spencer's conclusions.

That I, myself, am largely responsible is borne out by what Mrs. Spencer told me the other day. She said that Mr. Brooks had remarked about the astounding change in my manner and disposition, and said that I was now quite a delightful personality. I should blush to tell this on myself were it not such an interesting testimony to the influence of Science.

His enthusiasm, however, began to cool under increasing pressure from Grace and Mr. Ely that he make a public commitment, and a few days after his pleasant talk with Mrs. Spencer, he did his best to free himself from what threatened to be an uncomfortable long-distance entanglement. "I wrote Mr. Ely yesterday," he told Grace on March 11, "and so that is off my conscience. I would prefer that you discontinue his treatment of me, as I feel quite able to stand on my own feet and demonstrate the truth without assistance from without."

Neither Grace nor Mr. Ely gave up their efforts to win the near-convert; and Crane grew resentful of what he came to regard as an invasion of his soul. "I think you are holding the wrong and un-Scientific thought concerning me and my attitude toward Science," he finally wrote his mother, adding testily:

The fact that I do not talk and write about it continually is no sort of testimony that I am not as much interested as ever in it. You know that I am not and probably never will be one of those who make the matter a complete obsession, reducing every subject and thought and description to the technical language of the textbooks. I have met a number of Scientists who by such procedure managed not only to bore me and others quite dreadfully, but also to leave one with the impression that they were scared to death about everything and found it necessary to maintain a continual combat against every aspect and manifestation of life in general. Perhaps it may serve as sufficient testimony to the efficacy of right thought, etc. that I am finding far less problems and fears that demand denial. I certainly have not felt quite so well or quite so clear-headed for several years, and that is, or ought to be enough to reassure you and alterate your somewhat morbidly anxious fears for me which have leaked into your last few letters. I again beg you to relax from such fears, etc. which seem to have you in their power enough to prompt you to such seemingly strenuous conflicts of resistance and denials. Your letters seem to be prompted by some fear (I mean certain references in them) that seems to me entirely un-Scientific. Please do not mistake me and become hurt or offended. I only feel that you have not overcome, not quite, what might be called "the fear of fear" which is an ultimate Scientific triumph.

Exactly one month later, with a sigh of relief that—had Grace had her ears cocked—might have been heard in Cleveland, Crane finally took his stand. "No:—at present I am not a Christian Scientist," he wrote in answer to a set of "very vital questions" put to him by Bill Wright.

I try to make my Mother think so because she seems to depend on that hypocrisy as an additional support for her own faith in it. So,—mum's the word to her. If it weren't very evident how very much good it has done her I should not persist in such conduct,—lying to both Lord and Devil is no pleasure . . . However, Bill, I have unbounded faith in its efficacy. Not that a normal optimism will not accomplish the same wonders,—it is a psychological attitude which will prevail over almost anything, but as a religion, there is where I balk. I recommend it to you if you are nervous, etc., though, as a cure, and the best and only one to my knowledge. What it says in regard to mental and nervous ailments is absolutely true. It is only the total denial of the animal and organic world which I cannot swallow.

Almost parallel with his growing disillusionment with Christian Science was a growing irritation with the mother he could never understand, who seemed closer to him than any of his friends, yet seemed to dominate him with a possessiveness none of his friends exercised.

Grace's reconciliation with C.A. was now impossible. But Hart felt that if she could find a companion she would be freed from what he recognized was an unhealthy dependence on himself. "How did you like Mr. Darling?" he asked hopefully, a week after he arrived in New York. "Don't be too shy, that is, if you like him. I hope you won't continue to miss me with all the lovely friends and invitations you are having. You know, it's only an erroneous 'claim' that demands my presence."

Yet even as he urged her to move away from her single devotion to him, he wanted her to know how much he valued her, continuing to send her the "Sunday specials" she treasured and staying home Sunday nights to await her special-delivery letter. "Your letter has not arrived as yet," one of his own letters ended, "but I am expecting it before bed-time." He went on, as before, to urge her to free herself from any supposed obligation and in the next sentence to remind her how important she was to him: "Hope you are having a real good time now all the time, not saying 'no' to anything good that comes down the line. I got your picture put into the loveliest little frame yesterday that I ever saw, and as a result the landlady went into ecstasy no. 2 about your beauty."

At Easter he wrote her a long, warm letter: "Were I in Cleveland today you should have flowers instead of this poor letter, but as it is I'm afraid I haven't anything better to offer than lots of love and optimism, which, even so, can't be amiss. I shall celebrate the day by wearing one of the splendid neckties you sent me, and maybe write a poem. . . . I am hoping that you will not think I have neglected you. Still, I know you won't think so, and rest, assured."

By May, however, a number of minor irritants had added up to a frustrating sense of parental domination. Not all these irritants were directly the responsibility of either Grace or C.A., but Crane associated all of them with his free yet dependent status. There was, for example, the matter of his lodgings. When he arrived in New York, he went back, at Grace's suggestion, to Mrs. Walton's at 25 East Eleventh Street, settling into a small, inexpensive room, clean but inadequately partitioned off from the rooms on either side. Crane could hear everything that went on around him, and his neighbors—who soon complained to Mrs. Walton—could hear all too clearly his midnight typing.

After a day devoted to a search for other quarters ("I must have walked, in all, 20 miles today. I never dreamt that I would experience such difficulties in finding a room"), Crane found a place at 119 West Seventy-sixth Street that would fit into his dollar-a-day maximum. Grace was disturbed to see him move away from a neighborhood familiar to her, but she became reconciled to the wisdom of his move. Two weeks later she had to go through the process again. This time, Crane explained, there had been no difficulties of space or soundproofing—the large front room had been adequate enough—but he had run into painful difficulties with his landlady. "The landlady has committed enough atrocities since writing you last to fill a book, and I have found another room which I expect to move into some time next week. In all truth she is quite insane." Crane listed all her distressing symptoms: she had a habit of entering the room without warning, rushing up to an empty space on the floor, "pointing to some unseen object and inquiring 'Is that yours'." And at other times she would arrive to announce "in a hushed voice, 'It's down there'. That would be all one could get out of her as to what was 'down there':—letter, caller, or delivery man, and several times it has been nothing at all." She also told everyone who telephoned Crane that he wasn't there and had never been there.

Once again Grace advised Crane to stay where he was; but

after a third week of his landlady's peculiarities, Crane accepted
the suggestion of another roomer that they share a nearby apartment. "The room I have secured is better than the one I have:
—on the first floor, front, and much roomier. One of the fellows in
the house here, a Harvard man and lieutenant just out of service,
has roomed there before and swears to the complete sanity and
integrity of the little Irish woman that runs the place."

The front basement apartment at 307 West Seventieth Street
("practically three rooms,—one of them immense") into which he
moved also cost a dollar a day, but by sharing the rooms he
could bring his weekly rent down to $3.50. Grace was reluctant
to have her son move in with a man she did not know; but the
lower rent—which she was at the moment paying out of her own
pocket—and Crane's enthusiasm for his new roommate, both in
letters to her and in letters to his friends, was enough to convert
her. As "a lieutenant just out of the army, a Harvard grad. and a
champion tennis player," Alex Baltzly had all the qualities Grace
most admired. He was also, Crane assured her, "very much a man
of the world (in the finer sense, I mean) and his conversation
is extremely stimulating to me, especially as he has a wide knowledge of literature and art, and a thorough appreciation of music."
With Baltzly introducing Crane to some of the Romantic poets,
and Crane instructing Baltzly in the glories of Cézanne and the
Post-Impressionist painters, the two young men managed to have
a comfortable, casual, mutually satisfying friendship. They were
both too short on cash to attend the theater—though they wanted
to—and so they settled for long walks by the river; visits, Baltzly
remembered, to "dozens of movies"; and window shopping in
bookstores and such print shops as the Fifty-seventh Street gallery run by "Putzi" Hanfstaengl, later famous for his piano sere-
nades to Hitler. (Hart purchased a reproduction of a Cézanne
still life and Baltzly one of a Dürer engraving.)

Baltzly, a historian by training, tried at first to bring their conversations around to politics or the war that had just ended, but
Hart made it clear that such subjects were for him duller than
dishwater. Literature, art, music delighted him, but he preferred
reading the dictionary to reading the newspaper. "He wasn't much
concerned with the meaning of words at all, you know," Baltzly
recalled, "but he did love the sound of them." Gradually, as they
came to know each other, Hart began to talk about painful recollections of his childhood, and about more recent sessions with his
mother, who, having taken to bed with the sick headaches that
marked her "spells," would insistently go over years-dead quarrels with C.A., reliving in the darkened room the pattern of arguments and reconciliations that had marked her married life. As he
talked out his problems, Crane came to a temporary detachment,
a detachment he may have unconsciously expected Grace to
share. He wrote her that his association with Baltzly was for him

most valuable because Baltzly was "someone completely outside of any knowledge of me or my family." Luckily, no matter
what she felt, she was wise enough to keep her opinion to herself,
accepting without comment Crane's summary judgment: "I am in
wondrous luck to have found such an extremely suitable person."

She did not accept without comment Crane's next decision to
move, a decision prompted toward the end of May by Baltzly's
leaving for Boston to take a job in an insurance firm. Having accepted without her consent Harrison Smith's offer to share a
studio above the *Little Review* offices, Crane had recklessly
written home to break the news and to ask her to send several old
rugs stored in his grandmother's attic. Her answer, obviously an
acid one, has disappeared; but Crane's response survives.

> I see you are displeased at my having changed rooms, but
> I would like to ask you what you would have done faced with
> a like situation at the time I was. I felt indeed very fortunate to
> have located so successful a bargain as the two rooms here on
> the top floor of 24 West 16th St., for ten dollars per month. It
> only costs me that because Hal Smith uses one of the rooms as
> a study separate from his apartment to come to for his writing,
> and so I have the use of his room as well as my bedroom. When
> I told Hal and Claire of my predicament, Claire rushed to the
> cupboard and the result was that a bed was bought for me
> and temporary bedding loaned. Hal also sent over other furnish-
> ings etc. which has made the place livable and even comfort-
> able for me. I see no reason for returning now to a rooming
> house, and shall probably remain here for some time to come.

Perhaps Hart's letter is testy because he was beginning to chafe
under the ambiguous and erratic allowance that Grace made
available to him. When he left Cleveland, he had been under the
impression that an arrangement had been made by his father to
advance him a flat sum of $25 a week. After several weeks in
New York, however, he discovered that his mother wanted him
to keep a record of his expenses and forward them to her at the
end of every other week. She in turn would send them to C.A.;
C.A. would then send a check to Mr. Sullivan, who would send a
check to Grace, who would in the meantime advance Hart what
he needed for the next two weeks. Though the arrangement was
cumbersome, Hart did his best to adjust to it, noting only in his
first itemization that it might be wise "to make it a monthly arrangement of payment . . . and not bother Sullivan with too frequent duties about such details." His intention, he said, was to be
"pleasant and duteous" to Grace. He found it awkward, however, to have to remind her in his first letter about the matter:
"I shall need some money now as soon as you can send it." Such
reminders, which gradually increased in frequency, began to color

the tone of their correspondence, though—as he told George Bryan early in his stay—he certainly regarded himself as "damned lucky" to have "a dependable allowance."

His problem was that neither allowance nor expenses were dependable. Grace would neglect to forward Hart's itemizations to Mr. Sullivan and was almost always late in sending his check; and Hart, who did his level best to keep costs at an absolute minimum, was not able to avoid small but critical expenses. "I have had to buy a brief-case and a new hat this week," he reported on April 12, as he set out on an ill-fated career as "Advertising Manager" for *The Little Review*, "and so the fifty you sent last Monday will hardly carry me for the usual two weeks. I wish you would kindly send me an extra $25 Monday, if possible. You haven't told me a thing about whether you have succeeded in collecting anything yet, and I wish you would."

In his first month in New York he had found it a game to get by on his allowance, proudly sending Grace itemizations like this one:

The following is a list of my complete living expenses covering the two-weeks period extending from March 7th, '19, to March 21st, '19.

| | |
|---|---|
| $14.00 | room rent |
| 24.50 | board |
| 3.00 | laundry |
| 1.50 | suit-cleaning and pressing |
| 2.35 | car-fare |
| .25 | telephone calls |
| .68 | postage stamps |
| .35 | tooth brush |
| $46.63 | sum total |

But as March wore into April and April into May, and as Hart began to wear out his welcome as dinner guest at Mrs. Spencer's, at Claire and Hal Smith's, and at the Brooks', and as all his sincere efforts to earn a living fell through, what had been a game became cumbersome routine. Finally he wrote an angry Decoration Day note in which he unburdened himself of his sense of accumulated wrongs. Grace, it turned out, had all along been advancing Hart money from her alimony rather than collecting it from Mr. Sullivan. With mingled humiliation and indignation, he pleaded with her to take some definite action.

I have cashed the checks you sent as there is no use in my being foolish about such matters when I have only fifteen cents in my pocket and a very empty stomach. I do [not?] ask you for more, however. I am very much against your sending me money from your personal allowance. It seems to me that it would not be very much trouble to go down and see Sullivan for a half an hour for a few days and get sufficient results from the enactment of a perfectly just and practical contract so that I would not be due to hear within a few years the accusation of having made you economize and scrimp your own pleasures for my assistance during this trying time when I am making every possible effort to get started in something.

It had not been easy to beg and borrow from friends who knew him to be the son of a wealthy father and a well-to-do mother or to accept their generosity endlessly without sometime making a token repayment. "I have found out recently what it is to be like a beggar in the streets," he wrote, "and also what good friends one occasionally runs across in this tangle of a world."

Even the failure of his quixotic effort to turn the "Advertising Department" of *The Little Review* into the magnificently profitable enterprise of his dreams seemed in the bleak days toward the end of May somehow a failure not just of himself but of the mother and father who had made available to him nothing more than "complete inexperience."

The *Little Review* project had begun in a shimmer of glory. Discouraged because his topical movie scripts had not found a producer (the plot of one of them climaxed in a shipyard strike), Crane had given up his plan "to have a kind of fleet [of them] going around from office to office." Though it saddened him to think that he might not be able to cash in on the easy money one of his friends seemed to have available ("A writer friend of mine has just been offered $2000 for a scenario that won't take him over a day to write"), he recognized that his own gifts lay in different directions. In early March he decided to turn to advertising. "I expect to enter the advertising writing game," he wrote George Bryan. "I should like it much better than newspaper work, and I have always had a hunch that I could write interesting ads,— and,—there is a lot of money waiting for the man who can write good ads."

Any job at all, of course, was at this time a little unlikely. "You have no conception of the difficulties here in finding work of any description just now," he told Grace. "Every day a couple of troopships dumps a few thousand more unemployed men in the town, and there really is danger of a general panic and much poverty as a result unless the government takes a hand to assist in the matter." A week later he repeated much the same news to George Bryan.

Don't give up your job until you have to, is my advice these days to almost everybody. The situation of employment here in New York is quite critical at present. There have been so many thousands of soldiers landed here from overseas that have decided to settle here in preference to returning to their home towns in the west that the place is choke-full, and I am having a devil of a time to find anything at all to do. . . . Why you cannot even get a job as a waiter or street-cleaner. This isn't saying that I have applied for these elevated positions as yet, but you can see that the situation is pretty bad when such conditions are existent.

It was in the midst of sad talk of this sort that Margaret Anderson and Jane Heap had suggested that Crane might want to work on a commission basis soliciting ads for *The Little Review*. Though he was at first cautious about committing himself, the temptation of working in the same office with Miss Anderson finally turned the trick. As he wrote Grace: "One good thing about it will be the advantage it will give me of association with influential people who have to do with The Little Review and also a certain amount of personal freedom to develop my own talents along with the other work." He could, he decided, earn "at least as much per week even from the start" as he had earned on the *Plain Dealer*. "There is no reason why The Little Review could not be developed into as paying a periodical as The New Republic, The Nation, or The Dial," he continued. "All it has lacked from its inception has been someone with business initiative ability to develop the advertising and subscription departments of the magazine."

Two weeks later, he had secured only one ad, the announcement of "Stanislaw Portapovitch—Maître de Danse" which appeared in the June issue. Crane's poem in celebration of his friend's ability had been published in the delayed February number of *The Modern School*; Stan obviously had no choice but to place an ad in *The Little Review*.

No more ads came in. Crane, nevertheless, had for a few days a starry-eyed "subordinate" with several years' experience in the field. Together they planned a comprehensive attack on "all the great establishments on Fifth Ave." The two young men concluded that these establishments could be counted on to negotiate year contracts "of no less than $480 each," and to net Crane alone "$4,000 per year on commissions." But his subordinate, the congenial advertising man, vanished, as Crane sadly told his mother, "on a spree," never to reappear in the *Little Review* office.

Rather than making money in his new position, Crane soon found himself spending even more than he had spent before. By the end of May he was busy "looking for something else . . . every day,—anything that comes along,—with the intention of one way or another, establishing my independence from all outside assistance." "The advertising world," he wrote his mother, "is a good field for money,—but it's the hardest thing in the world to get worked up."

Earlier, he had told Bill Wright of the psychological difficulties of the work: "You have no idea how hard it is to even break into some of these huge and ominous mechanisms, New York offices. It ought to toughen me a little and perhaps that is what I need. It is a very different matter when one approaches with the intent of selling, and selling the appealing article,—space." Only the elusive vision of "over four thousand per year" convinced him that "perhaps I am not wasting my time after all."

He finally not only did not earn four thousand a year from *The Little Review* but in fact had nothing more than office space, free stationery, and the small commissions from the series of full-page ads placed by his father. Crane—who had to blame some-one—decided that his mother was responsible for his failure.

Unhappy, unsuccessful, he found intolerable the letters from her that urged him on to success and that asked for more frequent reports on the "progress" which in fact he was not making. "Your letter was filled with the customary complaints about my not writing oftener," he grimly began one letter. "Now I admit that the last two weeks have been poorer in letters from me than usual, but you seem never to have realized, Mother, that there is absolutely nothing to fill up the three-or-four-letter-a-week program which I have been trying to conduct,—even were my days filled with tremendous action. A couple of letters a week will contain all the news worth telling, and whether you have appreciated that fact or not, the truth remains."

Truth, he decided, was the one thing Grace had always run from. Perhaps it was time she heard it. With a brutality that in the end he acknowledged, he catalogued, in a two-page, single-spaced letter, all the affronts and indignities that his family—and Grace especially—had subjected him to. Her harassment over his correspondence, his rooms, his allowance, his unemployment were all ticked off. Behind them, he made clear, was a much larger, much more painful, much uglier indignity—one which, try as he would, he could never get out of his mind.

> I don't want to fling accusations etc. at anybody, but I think it's time you realized that for the last eight years my youth has been a rather bloody battleground for your's and father's sex life and troubles.

It was this, not his irregular schooling or his irregular employment, he insisted, which had been the destructive agent of his childhood and which was destroying him now. Neither ignorance nor indolence had kept him out of college; rather, his futile wanderings in New York were the direct responsibility of the reckless parents who persisted in making plain to a teenage boy the intimate details of their passions.

With a smoother current around me I would now be well along in some college taking probably some course of study which would enable me upon leaving to light upon far more readily than otherwise, some decent sort of employment. Do you realize that it's hard for me to find any work at all better than some manual labor, or literary work, which, as you understand, is not a very paying pursuit?

Emotionally exhausted, Crane tried to salvage the core of love that he still felt for Grace.

For some time after your letter I was determined not to write rather than compromise with hypocrisy or hurt your feelings. If this letter has wounded you, then I am ready to beg your pardon in apology with the understanding that I write no more, for I have discovered that the only way to be true to others in the long run, is to be true to one's self.

The spring of 1919 seemed to Crane something of a muddled, directionless time. Yet he found almost as much joy as despair; for his near poverty forced him into close friendships. By far the most important was the one with Claire and Harrison Smith, who, back from their honeymoon, settled down in an apartment that Crane and Mrs. Spencer had helped furnish. Soon their regular dinner guest, Crane delighted in acting the role of bachelor friend. "I dined with Hal and Claire last night at the first dinner given in their new apartment, only two others," he wrote his mother. "It was lots of fun to assist Claire as butler,—cutting bread, (which for once I did properly as all agreed,) and pouring the wine,—(yes, we had a little). Claire cooks better than the average newly-wed."

Harrison Smith must, for a while at least, have seemed in Hart's eyes something of a rival—the man who got the girl—but soon the marriage became for Crane a model of what a literary person's should be: "Hal is, I find, one of the kind that improves with acquaintance. He is writing a novel now,—something about sea life, and we intend to read some of it when I come up for Sunday evening tea."

By mid-April Hart was very nearly a part of the family, dining at least twice a week with the young couple; going with them to cabarets, where he "drank beer and ate cheese dreams," to the circus ("a great success"), and to the theater ("The play was a rollicking farce, written by that same man who wrote that funny story we all read a few weeks ago in the Saturday Evening Post, Sinclair Lewis, who is, by the way, Hal Smith's best friend"); and discussing with them endlessly the writers he was then most interested in—particularly Joyce and Pound, whose *Portrait of the Artist* and *Lustra* he asked Grace to send on to him ("up in my room on front shelves"). "Claire and Hal come into my letters so often of late that I am beginning to fear boring you," he wrote, "but as long as they are responsible for so much of my pleasure I shall have to include them anyway."

They provided a good deal more than pleasure; for Hal Smith shared Crane's room above the *Little Review* office, and Claire Smith did her best to make it livable. "Hal rented him a room in the Village," she wrote me. "He, Hart, was completely broke. I remember helping him clean the place up. At that time he took most of his meals with us."

Something of the flavor of these days and that room can be re-constructed from Charles Brooks's urbane and comic essay, "A Visit to a Poet," a thinly disguised account of Brooks's call on Crane in his new quarters. Brooks, then in his early forties, an elegant and dapper man-about-town, described his ascent past the undertaking establishment and the embalmers' school, past the office of *The Little Review* (in his account, *The Shriek*), where, stopping to ask for his poet-friend, he was met by the proprietor of the magazine.

> A young woman's head in a mob-cap came into view. She wore a green and purple smock, and a cigarette hung loosely from her mouth. She looked at me at first as if I were an old-fash-ioned poem or a bundle of modest drawings . . . There was a cup of steaming soup on an alcohol burner, and half a loaf of bread. On a string across the window handkerchiefs and stock-ings were hung to dry. A desk was littered with papers.

Trapped into buying a subscription to the magazine, he went on to the poet's top-floor quarters, where, in the back-room "studio," surrounded by stored embalmer's supplies, he was encouraged to admire the "view," a vista of one abandoned bathtub, a shabby tree, a washstand on its side, and the rear windows of a ladies'-garment factory. Here he and Crane discussed art and letters and particularly the magazine's latest discovery, Baroness Elsa von Freytag von Loringhoven, whom Brooks, evading libel, named "The Countess."

> "The Countess wears painted stockings."
> "Bless me!" I cried.
> "Stalks with flowers. She comes from Bulgaria, or Esthonia, or somewhere."

Brooks in his essay made much of the Baroness, turning to her to end his piece.

> As I was opening the street door, a woman came up the steps. She was a dark, Bulgarian sort of woman. Or Esthonian, per-haps. I held back the door to let her pass. She wore long ear-rings. Her skirt was looped high in scallops. She wore sandals —and painted stockings.

Nothing Charles Brooks or anyone could write would do justice to the Baroness in the flesh. She had first appeared in the *Little Review* offices in a costume that Margaret Anderson was never able to forget.

She wore a red Scotch plaid suit with a kilt hanging just below the knees, a bolero jacket with sleeves to the elbows and arms covered with a quantity of ten-cent-store bracelets—silver, gilt, bronze, green and yellow. She wore high white spats with a band of decorative furniture braid around the top. Hanging from her bust were two tea-balls from which the nickel had worn away. On her head was a black velvet tam o'shanter with a feather and several spoons—long ice-cream-soda spoons. She had enormous earrings of tarnished silver and on her hands were many rings, on the little finger high peasant buttons filled with shot. Her hair was the color of a bay horse.

Soon a regular contributor to *The Little Review*, she became for all the members of the staff an endless source of anecdotes, each more outlandish than those that had gone before, and all filled with the breathtaking audacity of a woman they came to accept as a half-mad, half-tragic artist, a brilliantly inventive poet and painter, but an even more brilliantly inventive human being. Who, having experienced it, would not remember to the end of his days the time she arrived in the office, her shaved head lacquered a bright vermilion, her body sheathed in a crepe stolen from a house of mourning? "She came to see us," Margaret Anderson recollected.

First she exhibited the head at all angles, amazing against our black walls. Then she jerked off the crepe with one movement. It's better when I'm nude, she said.

Returning to the Smiths' after such days at the *Little Review* office, Hart, roaring with laughter, would pantomime in extravagant detail all the Baroness's gestures and imitate broadly her heavy, strong, insistent speech. One time, Claire Spencer remembered, "the Baroness took Hart's typewriter, which was really Hal's, and Hal and Hart went to call on her and planned to get the typewriter and bring it back. They came away without it, though. They sat and talked with her about an hour. On the table was the typewriter. But neither of them had the nerve to even mention it." Later in the week Hal quietly purchased another typewriter.

Though most of Crane's evenings were spent with the Smiths, many of his days—particularly early in the spring—were spent at Joe Kling's bookstore, where, surrounded by the graphic art Kling was most fond of and much of which he reproduced in his magazine (work by George Bellows, John Sloan, Stuart Davis, Auerbach-Levy, Gaudier-Brzeska, Paul Signac, and William Gropper), Crane would debate the relative merits of the artists. "He fancied himself an art critic," Kling said, "and a music critic, and

a literary critic." The two men differed strongly on the importance of a good many writers—particularly Maxwell Bodenheim,
whom Kling came increasingly to admire, though he had printed
without cuts in the February issue of *The Pagan* Crane's patroniz-
ing review of *Minna and Myself*. (Bodenheim's poems, Crane had
said, "are often little heaps of images in which the verbal element
is subordinated, making for an essentially static and decorative
quality." Bodenheim's aesthetic theories, his conviction that "true
poetry is . . . unconnected with human beliefs or fundamental
human feelings," had seemed in Crane's eyes "inordinately precious.")

The most important consequence of Crane's association with
*The Pagan*, however, was neither his acquaintance with Kling nor
even the publication of his early poems and reviews; it was his
meeting with Gorham B. Munson. Munson, young, enthusiastic,
freshly arrived in the Village, was, like Crane, a devoted admirer
of Wyndham Lewis, Pound, Yeats, and Joyce, and already a contributor to *The Pagan*. (His fable "The King of the Strange
Marshes" had been printed in the same February issue that included Crane's Bodenheim review and that was already on sale
when Crane returned to Manhattan.) When Kling introduced the
two young men, they immediately fell into conversation about
their favorite writers, and particularly about Joyce, whose
*Ulysses* was then appearing in *The Little Review*. Munson remembers that he was most impressed at that time by Crane's
volatile literary enthusiasm, but the fact that Crane—not yet
twenty—had himself been published by *The Little Review* contributed in no small part to Munson's admiration.

By the middle of March they were fast friends, meeting almost
every day in Kling's store. The April issue of *The Pagan*—promising great things—listed four Associate Editors, including both
Hart Crane and Gorham B. Munson. With the first *Pagan Anthology* in print (it included Crane's "October-November" and
"Fear") and the *Second Pagan Anthology* planned ("Forgetfulness" would be Crane's contribution), it did seem likely that
something of real importance might evolve. "The magazine has
grown," Crane wrote his mother soon after his return to New
York, "and I'm pleased to say, there is much to support the hope
of immediate further improvement." With Munson's help, he felt,
it might be made into a major publication.

By the end of May, however, Munson and Crane were looking
for other literary outlets, and the two summer issues of the magazine carried none of their work and credited them with no editorial activity. They had by this time grown to depend on each
other's literary judgments, Crane especially coming to count on
Munson for detailed and sympathetic criticism of all his work.
"Gorham was really his first critic who examined every poem,"
Allen Tate told me, "—I should think more than half the poems in

*White Buildings* and the early parts of *The Bridge*. Gorham's criticism was . . . invaluable to him."

Crane in the spring of 1919 was seldom lonely. Though he might write George Bryan, "I find all my old friends either married or making loads of money,—seldom both," and though he found some friends strangely changed ("Stan and Anna no longer interest me very much. They are quite incommunicable and smug, having settled into married life and a flat"), the only waking hours he spent entirely by himself were early morning and late night, when, reading in his room, he reexamined *The Complete Poetical Works of Swinburne* and sampled a "rather diverse" list of major figures: "Chaucer, D. H. Lawrence, Cervantes, Henry James, Plato, and Mark Twain."

"The last few weeks have been just one round of dinner engagements," he wrote Bill Wright. "I am not a guest at many tables, but am frequently at a few, which, you see, is rather complimentary." Though it is true that he ate regularly with only a few friends, he paid duty calls on most of his mother's Cleveland acquaintances. (He went to the ship to see Mr. Brown off to Europe: "I never dreamed that Mrs. Brown would be so fearful of her husband's safety as her actions at the time indicated." He visited a Mrs. Gardiner, one of Grace's literary acquaintances: "I was Mrs. Gardiner's guest for dinner at the Pen and Brush Club." And he squired his Aunt Zell on a shopping spree about town: "I being the clothes-model" for her purchases for her son-in-law.) He also did his best to capitalize on a rather slight acquaintance with writers: "Supped with Mr. and Mrs. Kreymborg" (Kreymborg later recollected that at the time he was not much impressed with Crane's work); "this afternoon took tea with Ridgely Torrence and his wife, who were extremely gracious to me"; "I met Robert Frost's daughter at a theatre party the other evening, and had the pleasure of taking the very interesting and handsome young lady back to her Columbia dormitory." And he did his best to keep track of his own Cleveland friends, who, drifting in and out of New York, reminded him of different—if not happier—days at home. An afternoon with Roger Zucker's mother induced a nostalgic letter to Bill Wright. A telephone call to Alice Calhoun, once a high-school friend but in New York a promising motion-picture actress, reminded him how quickly fame could come to the very young—the very young of his own acquaintance: "She is now engaged in her first big picture, and is very busy, she tells me. . . . Alice certainly is pretty enough for success in the movies, and young enough (only 18) to develop a good deal of dramatic talent."

He was hardly aware of it most of the time—and to almost every one of his friends, to the end of his life, he remained "a Cleveland boy, a mid-Westerner"—but to himself he was imperceptibly becoming a New Yorker. He responded rapturously to the delicate huge grace of the city's spring: "The days are amazingly beautiful and the night's superb. Last night I took a long walk up Riverside Drive which is just around the corner from my rooms, and the Hudson was beautiful with the millions of tiny lights on the opposite shore." Even a late spring blizzard, "a terrific blizzard of snow which has continued for twenty-four hours," had in it elements of a fierce beauty, the snow swirling in gigantic gusts up the Hudson and through the steep aisles of downtown Manhattan. And if, in the bright days of spring, he looked forward to getting out of the "crowded metropolis" to some place cool where he might "see the moon and stars and hear the frogs croak," if the city took on "the look of a desert,—a devastation" to his eyes, it was a desert in which illusions rather than realities withered and died: "Illusions are falling away from everything I look at lately." In spite of the fact that life in the city was for Crane "rather hard at best," "still," he felt, "there is something of a satisfaction in the development of one's consciousness even though it is painful."

> There is a certain freedom gained,—a lot of things pass out of one's concern that before mattered a great deal. One feels more freedom and the result is not by any means predominantly negative. To one in my situation N.Y. is a series of exposures intense and rather savage which never would be quite as available in Cleveland, etc. New York handles one roughly but presents also more remedial recess,—more entrancing vistas than any other American location I know of.

As summer approached, Crane once more toyed with the idea of registering at Columbia for a quick, practical course of study that might prepare him to earn a living. His mother, eternally optimistic, had suggested that he might study at the Columbia School of Journalism; but this, Crane knew, would be out of the question. In answer to Bill Wright, who during a Cleveland visit had talked with Grace about the problem of his friend's education and who would himself begin a year of study at Columbia in the autumn, Crane grimly explained: "I don't plan to take up any journalistic course anywhere. I understand that the course at Columbia demands two previous years of college anyway, so it looks as though that were out of the question. Mother has often talked about that plan, but I cannot seem to convince her of the attendant impossibilities." He might register for "a short course in business and advertising, . . . which might possibly be continued next fall." The problem here would be financial. He had no money of his own to contribute to the tuition. Grace felt that his education was his father's responsibility and neglected to volunteer the funds, and C.A.—though Hart hinted broadly— not only did not offer tuition, he even failed to pay for the most recent "Mary Garden Chocolates" ad Hart had placed in *The Lit-tle Review.*

Hart was tempted to press his father for the money to attend the Columbia courses. There was the prospect of being again enrolled in the same school with Bill Wright and the prospect of seeing more of a new acquaintance, Matthew Josephson, then a student at Columbia College and an irregular visitor in the *Little Review* offices. But the overpowering temptation of spending a seashore summer with Hal and Claire Smith lured him away from education and all the hazily dreamed-of financial rewards that might come of it.

All through that unsatisfying spring the Smiths had been trying to "do something"—anything—for Crane. Fond of him for his high spirits, his wild bursts of laughter, his thigh-slapping story-telling, his uninhibited delight in literature and art, they felt gradually more and more responsible to get him through the black depression that would descend when, his check delayed, he would come to them for the loans he always repaid and always had to reborrow, or for consolation when, after a morning's effort to screw up his courage to try to sell another *Little Review* ad, he would be turned away by secretary or office boy.

One thing, they found, always worked. Crane, in spite of rose fever, loved the country; and the Smiths, who soon after their marriage began to spend weekends in Mrs. Spencer's little cottage in West Englewood, New Jersey, regularly invited him to join them. Returning from his visits well-fed and rested, he was able even to forgive his mother for her ambitious plans. ("Hope you'll go out and see my mother if you get time," he wrote Wright after one such weekend. "We have had some differences of late, but my fundamental feelings toward her are not in the least altered.")

In early July, the call of the sea triumphing over the call of the West Englewood wild, Hart and the Smiths set out for a Fourth-of-July drive to Brookhaven, Long Island, where the Smiths had heard of a "barnstead" that could be rented for the summer. It was, Hal and Claire agreed, an ideal summer home, and Hal rented it on the spot, inviting Crane to join them in the first month of their stay. Crane, when he returned with them to New York to pack up the belongings he would need, could talk of nothing else but the "endless munificence" of his friends. "I am going along as their guest," he wrote his mother, "although Hal lightened any embarrassment I might have felt . . . by suggesting an office for me as handy man about the place,—gardener, chauffeur, etc. My duties will be light, however, as they are taking the Japanese cook along too, and so I am anticipating soon idyllic days of sailing, bathing, romping and reading."

The house he would live in was "simply superb," and he catalogued for his mother all its excellences.

The owners, (now in California) were evidently art lovers, for the place bears ample proof of it. . . . An old immense barn has been changed into a most romantic and ample house, with the living room extending in the center to the roof, and a gallery around the second floor containing about eight bedrooms that on one side look down into the living room below, and on the others have a view of the country around. There is also a library (already stocked) and servants' quarters with private bath on the side. A lovely orchard of peach and apple trees and a rose garden surround the house which is quite a distance from the road and its unpleasant traffic of continual machines.

There was, Crane explained to Grace, no reason for his not going. "I may never again have such an opportunity and as the city offers me at this time nothing better than a machine shop job, I don't feel that the time is wasted. Work will be easier to find next fall, without doubt, and meanwhile I see no reason for denying myself this pleasure."

Crane spent just under a month at Brookhaven, much of it filled with the pleasure he had anticipated. Afternoons and some mornings were devoted to reading, working on poetry, or simply loafing in the sun. On moon-flooded summer evenings, Claire Smith remembered, they improvised five-minute dance solos—each a twelve-inch-record long: "We had lots of wonderful times. He had brought with him a lot of Wagner records. We used to drag the victrola out on the grass nights and both of us would dance, and looking back it seems to me in a most affected manner. All this sounds so petty and childish. But we were both very young then." Wagner, "and especially a record named *Valse Bleu*, also *Valse Triste*," would spread music across the moon-dappled lawn; leaping, whirling through the summer night, Crane would lift out of himself into something he dreamed of being.

Dancing in just this way, Crane may on July 21 have celebrated happily his twentieth birthday. Or he may have celebrated it in quite a different manner. For, in spite of the Smiths' tact, Crane found his position awkward. Unable to reciprocate their generosity, he began to suspect that he was unwanted, imagining veiled insults when none had been proffered. Claire herself found tact stretched to the limit: "I was pregnant then and in a state of nasty irritation. So our fights were quite often. Hart kept a diary and always left it around open so that I would read what he had put in it, especially when he referred to my rudeness. All this didn't make for much peace in the house. But Hal was always the man of kindness and always asked me to apologize—which I did. And Hart to show his forgiveness usually read his poetry to me—which made me mad all over again."

Hart himself got mad enough to pack his trunk only once during his stay, but he chose the middle of the night to do it, awakening the whole household as he struggled to drag his belongings thumping and bumping down the stairs that led from gallery to living room. There, in a tearful scene of forgiveness, everyone excused everyone else for insults real and imaginary. And Hart returned to his room to fill one more page of his diary with a detailed account of the event, as usual leaving the diary open for Claire to read the next day.

Hart through the summer devoted considerable time to calculating ways in which he could work himself into the advertising business. Here, he was still convinced, money could be made —enough money to support himself comfortably and afford a little extra for his mother and his grandmother. He knew that neither of them had anything to worry about, Grace's alimony and Mrs. Hart's investments providing a more than ample, steady income. But one of his mother's principal pleasures was spending money; and he knew she would spend it neither wisely nor conservatively. (Years later he was to enliven a drinking bout with friends by detailing a whole series of accusations against her—the principal one being that she had squandered on dresses and fur coats the money that should have been used to send him to college.) His problem was both simple and unsolvable. He needed a job that would support him and that would at the same time be light enough to allow him unlimited time for reading and writing; his shyness, his lack of experience, his limited schooling made it most unlikely that he would ever locate such a job.

Grace, meantime, kept up a steady pressure ("things look so dark"), fretting each time Hart requested his allowance, yet always assuring him of her unlimited faith in his eventual success. Though at the time he had left New York for Brookhaven his own future looked dark, Hart had done his best to explain to his mother exactly where he stood.

> During the last two months I don't feel that I have called heavily upon your funds. I have done all I could to locate work that I respect, but haven't been successful . . . I have been to advertising agencies, and publishers but, as I said, in vain so far. I can always find work in the machine shop and shipyard but cannot help avoiding them as a last resort, as they would merely suffice to keep breath in the body and get me nowhere in particular.

A letter from George Bryan which arrived while Crane was finishing his own letter to Grace renewed Hart's hope for a job with the Thomas Cusack advertising agency (George was then working for the Denver branch, run by his father). But it was neither George nor Crane's friends who found work for him, but his own father.

Hart had heard relatively little from C.A. after his second mar-

riage. He had, late in the spring, received a friendly letter, the one
in which C.A. offered to take a *Little Review* ad—only to hear
nothing from him for the month following. ("Of course all my
friends think his treatment of me is disgraceful and unaccountable," he had written his mother. "My own opinion is hardly less
reserved, as you know, but I try my best to turn my thoughts to
other channels as much as possible. It is only when hunger and
humiliation are upon me that suddenly I feel outraged.") It was
therefore a surprise when, at the end of Crane's second week at
Brookhaven, C.A. not only volunteered the money for the *Little
Review* ads which had already appeared and for those which
would appear during the rest of the year, but also recommended
that Hart return immediately to New York to be interviewed at
the offices of Rheinthal and Newman, the firm which supplied
Mr. Crane with the Maxfield Parrish reproductions he featured on
his boxed candies.

Hart's July 29 interview with Mr. Rheinthal was "very satisfactory," largely, Hart felt, because of his father's generous recommendation. "Everything," he wrote his mother on the thirtieth,
"is pointing toward very friendly relations with C.A. in the future." Crediting his father's change to the intervention of C.A.'s
New York office staff, which, Hart felt, had supplied "a more
adequate understanding of my motives, interests, character and
position," and as well to "a certain pride . . . in the position of his
only son," Hart concluded optimistically: "I am not building
many air castles, as I have learned too much already for that,—
but it is hopeful, at least, with present relationships prevailing."

Whatever his relationship to his father was to be, Grace, Hart
felt, would have to accept it. Too often, perhaps because of
the extent of Hart's "affection and love" for her and the extent
of her "interest" in his career, Grace had attempted to manipulate
his feelings. Now once more she suggested how Hart should deal
with his father. Hart's response was firm.

> Your letter dated the 28th has just come . . . At best I
> think your words are a little unkind and very inconsiderate. I
> will not attempt again to reckon with your misunderstanding
> etc. of the part you and I together, and as individuals, have
> played in relation to C.A. You either have a very poor memory,
> or are very confused when you think you have a right to accuse
> me of either a wrong or a right attitude toward him,—an un-
> friendly or [a] friendly one,—after the continually opposite
> statements and accusations you have made to me for the last
> four years yourself. At one time you have recommended a
> course of diplomacy toward a veritable devil, and five minutes
> later a blow in the face and scorn of any relationship whatever.
> And now you suggest a wily and conniving attitude toward a
> character which you claim as fundamentally good. With such in-

consistencies in memory I fail to see how you have adequate reasons for 'accusing' me of a 'wrong' attitude toward him, whatever position I might have taken. It has all been very hard, I know. Probably the truth consists more moderately in the estimate of him as a person of as many good inclinations as bad ones. Your feelings as a woman lover were bound to be dangerous in diverting you from an impersonal justice, and, however much I may have been blinded by my own relationship with him, I cannot deny having been influenced by your sufferings and outcries. There are reasons for acts and prejudices which cannot always be justified by the turn of the moment, but look hard enough, and substantial roots will be found.

Hart had intended to wait until the beginning of September to begin his new job, but a quarrel of unusual intensity at the Smiths' sent him packing, this time for good. (Hart was soon writing Margaret Anderson a note about the "vast irritations" that had been brought on by his "Brookhaven abdication," enclosing with it his father's check for the *Little Review* ads, a check large enough to help "a lot" with the September issue, and a big box of "beautiful Mary Gardens," which, she assured Hart, "filled us all with joy.")

Hart started his job at Rheinthal and Newman during the second week of August, convinced—as he was in starting almost every job he tackled for the rest of his life—that after brief training he would quickly rise to the managerial level, there to find time to write poetry in the well-paid leisure the future always seemed to offer.

It is easy to see Hart Crane either as a poet who celebrates industrial America or as a poet who is in perpetual rebellion against the crassness and vulgarity of a capitalist society, a society symbolized by the uncomprehending businessman father. Some of Crane's own remarks support both pictures. But, like all simple diagrams intended to explain human conduct, both pictures are false. And no one was more aware of the falseness of such distortions than Crane himself. As he had explained earlier that year to Bill Wright, "I agree . . . that for such as ourselves business life is not to be scorned. The commercial aspect is the most prominent characteristic of America and we all must bow to it sooner or later. I do not think, though, that this of necessity involves our complete surrender of everything else nobler and better in our aspirations." The trick, he felt, was to be a part of the commercial world, yet privately to lead a life independent of it.

He did not, however, rise quickly to the top at Rheinthal and Newman; by late October his job in the "order department" —a job that combined the least attractive elements of office boy and stock clerk—became more than he could bear. Though he had liked his employer—a man, genial and considerate, who had done his best to explain father to son and son to father—there was no possibility for him to amount to anything if he stayed with the company. His leave-taking was friendly ("Mr. Rheinthal has been very decent, and I am going over tomorrow morning to have a pleasant talk with him"), but he felt great relief as he walked out the door: "My working there has certainly been to no advantage beyond that of a purely diplomatic nature. Three months of tiresome and unprofitable work. Any child could do it that had sufficient muscular strength, and toward the last the insult that it branded on my intelligence grew rather painful. Whatever I do now I am sure will be much better. I want a job where I can have a chance to use my brains a little. They have become very heavy and rusty lately."

He had not entirely neglected his brains, however. One of his first evening calls after taking the job was at the office of Joseph Kling, where he picked up for review a copy of Sherwood Anderson's *Winesburg, Ohio*. Crane had read Anderson's stories as they had appeared separately in *The Little Review*, but the published book seemed greater than the sum of its parts. "Beyond an expression of intense gratitude to the author, it is hard to say a word in regard to a book such as Sherwood Anderson's *Winesburg, Ohio*," he began his review. "The entire paraphernalia of criticism is insignificant, erected against the walls of such a living monument as this book." Comparing it to Balzac for revelation of character, to Edgar Lee Masters for its exploration of Midwest America, to Maupassant for its subtle structure, and to Lucretius for its "exquisite" novelty, Crane found it a book of "flawless" style and of "significant material." "America should read this book on her knees," he concluded. "It constitutes an important chapter in the Bible of her consciousness."

Faced with such praise, Anderson initiated what was to be an extended correspondence.

> Some friend has sent me your review of Winesburg Ohio, in The Pagan.
> How can I hope to express my appreciation of your generous words. Surely it is to the minds of such men as yourself the American workmen in the arts must look for new fuel when his own fires burn low.
> Again I thank you for your good words.

The Anderson review had appeared in the September issue of *The Pagan*, but well before it was published Crane was looking for another outlet for his poetry. The one he found—*The Modernist*—was a new magazine edited by James Waldo Fawcett, a casual acquaintance of Crane's and a friend of Munson's. In a now-lost letter Munson had inquired about Crane's success in placing a poem with Fawcett, and Crane—on a prophetic postcard of the Brooklyn Bridge ("Knowing your predilection for bridges, I send you this!")—had explained that his new job, then two weeks old, was keeping him very busy: "Haven't been over to see 'The Modernist' but suppose it is racing along as usual."

By early October, and probably well before that time, Crane had made visits to 25 East Fourteenth Street, where the magazine was published. The first issue (November 1919) carried three of his lyrics: "North Labrador" (at last finding a publisher); the slight, carefully constructed "Interior" with its image of love that blossoms "like a tardy flower" in a lamplit, world-excluding room; and "Legende," a compressed statement of "tossing loneliness" built, like many of Crane's best poems, on what became for him the obsessive image of the sea. (A brave poem, "Legende" marks a step forward for Crane. When he describes his shell-like heroine as "a pathos," he begins the exploration of the possibilities of language that is characteristic of his strongest work.)

Fawcett, whom Crane liked—but only, as he explained to Munson, with "a kind of dumb-animal affection"—wanted his magazine to appeal to everyone and signed up a large staff of assistant editors, associate editors, and contributing editors. (Gorham Munson, closest to the top of the masthead, was one of two assistant editors; Crane joined a small crowd of contributing editors at the bottom.) Selling for twenty cents and dedicated to a platform that would break any publication ("Radical in Policy; international in scope. Devoted to the common cause of toiling people. Opposed to Compromise; pledged to truth. Dedicated to the task of overthrowing old falsehoods. A forum for active minds and vital art. A better and freer magazine"), *The Modernist* gave birth to its one and only issue and disappeared. "I was quite astonished by the amount of literary rubbish [Fawcett] had managed to get into its confines," Crane wrote Munson. "There was hardly a gleam of promise through it all." Crane must have watched the disappearance of *The Modernist* with relief. For he felt responsible not only for his own contributions but for those of his friends as well, some of whom had been turned down by Fawcett without consultation with the editors who had persuaded them to submit work. Matthew Josephson, for instance, had at Crane's and Munson's suggestion submitted some material, only to have it abruptly returned. "You evidently were not consulted about the Josephson mss.," Crane wrote Munson, "as I saw one of them returned the day I left New York."

Josephson, Crane knew, would be blisteringly indignant ("Josephson's opinions of 'The Modernist' will more than match your own, I think," he wrote Munson), but he was less sure of the reactions of other friends, among them Charmion von Wiegand, a young poet, one of whose "Egyptian Sonnets" Crane had accepted for the magazine. He had met her in the spring through his roommate Alex Baltzly, but he had long before heard his father speak of her and her husband, Hermann Habicht, an executive in the import-export house of Habicht-Braun, one of Mr. Crane's chief suppliers.

Hart enjoyed his evenings with the young couple, and in Charmion particularly he found a person eager to discuss poetry and painting. Never so intimate with Charmion and Hermann as with some of his other friends, he seems to have relied on them for casual, comfortable visits and stimulating correspondence, in his letters playing the teacher and advisor. ("Any of the works of André Gide are good, same of older ones like Rimbaud, Laforgue (Jules) and Guillaume Apollinaire. . . . I am mad about Laforgue, but he is hard to translate and very acid.")

When Hart returned from Brookhaven to his rooms above the *Little Review* offices, he was prepared for his usual siege of early September hay fever—a fine stock of handkerchieves were purchased especially for it—but he was not prepared for an invasion of bedbugs that for weeks made life miserable. Exhausted from sneezing and sleepless from midnight-to-dawn bedbug pursuits, by mid-September he found himself compelled to take a week off from Rheinthal and Newman.

In spite of sneezes and scratches, his week of freedom was a pleasant one. It ended in a delicious cold snap that drove off the bedbugs and diminished the pollen count. He also reestablished friendly relations with Hal and Claire Smith. Hal brought in from the West Englewood bungalow a supply of furniture to supplement the bed, dresser, and table that until this time had been Crane's principal furnishings. As they hung a mirror above the room's small mantelpiece and arranged ("pretentiously," Crane wrote his mother) a fire screen below it, the two friends agreed that for the time being Crane should keep the rooms entirely for his own use. Consequently, Crane once more sat down to request his mother to send on "the old dining room rug (third floor) to stop my bed from singing and knocking so much on this bare floor."

The fall months were also made pleasant by the arrival of Bill Wright, who had enrolled at Columbia and could join Crane for Sunday strolls on Riverside Drive or Saturday-night sprees on Broadway. On one such weekend, accompanied by their visiting Cleveland friend Roger Zucker ("enthusiastic and excited as a young calf"), "the boys," as Crane wrote his mother, spent a full day cavorting through the city. "We went to 'Chu Chin Chow' Sat. night and they were all aglow with the beauty of the theatre and the performance. William, in spite of an heroic attempt at boredom, was confessedly impressed, and Roger has been gasping 'My God' at everything since his arrival. . . . I took them to Churchills after the show, and we ended up merrily with beer and sandwiches and cabaret music."

Yet happy weekends with Bill Wright, and pleasant dinners with the Smiths and the Habichts, and long, good talks with Gorham Munson and Matthew Josephson were not enough to make Crane feel that his time was well spent. He had floundered from a job that had existed largely in his imagination ("advertising manager" of *The Little Review*) to the meaningless job at Rheinthal and Newman, and now—at the end of October—to no job at all. He was even without a place to live, for the cold snap that drove the bedbugs out of his unheated rooms finally drove him out as well, his tentative home being a furnished room at the Hotel Albert in the Village.

His father, radiating confidence, wrote him stories of success crowned with success. Letters arrived from all over the country— Kansas City, Chicago, San Francisco—recounting business triumphs and evenings of happy recreation at the theater or concert hall. "He speaks of going into the publishing business (perhaps with M. Parrish) and also the soft drink business," Hart summarized for Grace. "As his business is now well beyond the million mark, he says he [is] planning on the second. His plans sound stupendous and certainly command much admiration. I can honestly flatter him in many ways." Though Hart, in fact, chose not to flatter his father, he was pleased when C.A. went out of his way to search for job opportunities for his son and, when none could be found in New York, offered to pay his way home for a serious talk about Hart's gradually working his way into one of his own booming enterprises.

Perhaps to his own surprise, Hart accepted the offer. "I leave for Cleveland tomorrow night," he wrote Charmion von Wiegand on the evening of November 5, "and am very anxious to get off." He would, of course, miss New York. "Let's write occasionally and be as metropolitan as possible," he told her. For though he would soon be "out in those great expanses of cornfields so much talked about and sung," he would no longer be able to do without Manhattan friends: "You can't very well dispense with me even though you do live 'in the big city.' "

He would miss "the big city," yet there were many things he looked forward to in Cleveland. He had become increasingly preoccupied with his family, and it seemed to him—uncomfortably isolated from them—that unsuspected qualities in his mother and father were gradually coming to light. "Thank you for your fine appreciation of my poems which came this morning," he had written his mother just a week before his decision to return. "It is good to know that you like them, and that your interest in me extends even to my efforts in that line of work which is not generally of much interest to you." His father's letters about the theater and about music had also seemed significant to Hart; and though he knew that the full-page ad for Mary Garden Chocolates that for many months would be the *Little Review*'s chief source of advertising revenue did not make C.A. a patron of the arts, Hart did value the fact that his father's payments helped keep the magazine alive.

His grandmother especially had been in his thoughts. Gentle and generous, she had drifted through his childhood as the always present, soft-spoken mediator in his parents' quarrels, an endless supplier of buttermilk cookies and cinnamon-scented, mouth-watering apple pies. Perhaps, he felt, she would like a little poem in her honor. "I am beginning something in an entirely new vein with the luscious title: 'My Grandmother's Love Letters,'" he soon wrote Charmion von Wiegand. "I don't want to make the dear old lady too sweet or too naughty, and balancing on the fine line between these two qualities is going to be fun. I hope that living close to her in the same house won't spoil it all."

# 6

Whatever else Cleveland meant to Crane on the morning of November 7, 1919, it meant an end to the restless, irresolute independence he had had for a year. For better or for worse, he had decided to cast his lot with his father. He would work in his father's business, learning, as his father wanted him to, the whole structure of the company from the bottom up.

In many ways, he accepted this decision with relief. For, in spite of all of his free time in New York, he had been able to produce only a few poems, none of them, he knew, of the quality he aspired to. He had met some writers and editors, and he had made two or three close friends. But he had been rootless. And no matter how much he enjoyed the "metropolitan" whirl, the "great expanses of cornfields" which he referred to in his letter to Charmion von Wiegand were inescapably involved in an image he was beginning to construct, an image of the complex interrelationship of rural, metropolitan, and industrial America out of which, he hoped, a new kind of poetry could evolve. When he stepped off the train that morning, these were only half-formed feelings, but in the months immediately following they came to dominate much of his thinking.

For the first week in Cleveland, however, he enjoyed what he felt was a well-earned holiday. He was pampered by mother and grandmother, who competed with each other to see that he was stuffed with good home cooking. And his days were filled with visits to such old friends as Richard Laukhuff in his shop at 40 Taylor Arcade, where, Crane wrote Munson, *The Modernist*—unavailable anywhere in Cleveland—had better be sent: "The Pagan, he tells me, is getting too tame. He also says that the Little Review has suffered neglect since the last Baroness contribution. The B. is a little strong for Cleveland."

But the principal business of that first week involved him in a discussion with his father concerning plans for his future. Those plans, he told Munson, were rosy.

> The size of my father's business has surprised me much. Things are whizzing, and I don't know how many millions he

will be worth before he gets through growing. If I work hard enough I suppose I am due to get a goodly share of it, and as I told you, it seems to me the wisest thing to do just now to join him. He is much pleasanter than I expected him to be, and perhaps will get around after [a] while to be truly magnanimous.

Together, Hart and his father toured Mr. Crane's Cleveland plant and his local retail stores; but it was on a trip to Mr. Crane's newly opened Akron store that Hart was most impressed with his father's accomplishment. "I was down there with him yesterday," Crane wrote Munson, "and find that he has a wonderful establishment,—better than anything of its kind in New York." When Mr. Crane suggested that his son might begin his work there, Hart jumped at the opportunity. The hours would be spectacularly long—"six in the morning until eleven at night"—and Sunday the only day off. But the job was forty miles away from home. He would have little parental supervision.

And besides there was Akron itself, in 1919 a town booming more spectacularly into a city than any other community in America. Akron was the birthplace of the rubber tire, and America had just committed itself to the automobile. The town seemed in Crane's eyes a frontier city reborn, but this time an industrial frontier—the rubber barons rolling in wealth, outdoing each other in the construction of palatial estates, and the immigrant laborers tough, sure of themselves, swearing, joking, brawling in streets that were alive with raw life.

> The place is burgeoning with fresh growth. A hell of a place. The streets are full of the debris from old buildings that are being torn down to replace factories etc. It looks, I imagine, something like the western scenes of some of Bret Harte's stories. I saw about as many Slavs and jews on the streets as on Sixth Ave. Indeed the main and show street of the place looks something like Sixth Ave. without the elevated.

As if to confirm his own observations, the Akron *Beacon Journal* on Friday, November 21, just three days after Crane had settled into his room in the Hotel Akron, ran a front page account of the new Chamber of Commerce report. "AKRON IS HALF BILLION CITY," the headline trumpeted. Not only had the annual value of manufactured goods increased in one year from $411,119,800 to $522,-436,020 but the number of building permits had reached an all-time high, 6,418 permits representing $23,172,380: "This amount is almost twice the value of building permits ever issued in Akron in any one year."

Like other local merchants, C. A. Crane fitted his advertising to the theme of community self-praise. *Akron Must Go Forward!* blared one ad for his new store. Beneath the headline was a photograph of the store, on one side of the central aisle the glistening, mirrored, extravagantly long soda fountain and, on the other side, counter after counter of loose and boxed chocolates. Mr. Crane, in a hymn to Akron's progress, caught the boom-town tone the city thrived on:

> Akron cannot exist half county seat and half metropolis. It must be one or the other—and it is going to be a metropolis.
>
> The business houses must keep pace with the manufactures.
>
> One store that is representative of the future Akron is
>
> ### CRANE'S
>
> A store that would be distinguished on Fifth Avenue.
>
> Designed especially as an answer to Akron's demand.
>
> Beautiful surroundings, a luncheon service that cannot be judged by previous Akron standards and a complete line of
>
> CRANE'S
> WONDERFUL CANDIES

It was not, however, in this store that Crane spent most of his time, but rather in the Portage Drug Store, where, behind a specially installed counter, he sold Christmas boxes of Mary Garden Chocolates. His father had at the last minute decided to expand his Akron operations and Crane was assigned the one-man stand. His hours were just a little better than they might have been in the main store, "about 14 hours every day" he told Munson, but he chafed under his isolation.

There were compensations, however. Because Mr. Crane neglected to advertise "our Portage Drug Store stand" until two days before Christmas, business was anything but brisk; and Crane was able to take long lunch hours. He would browse through the poetry shelves of the Temple Book Store, or stop off to chat with Herbert Fletcher, a young bookdealer who prided himself on his acquaintance with the best in new literature.

Behind his counter, Crane set up a book niche which, in the first week, housed Pound's *Pavannes & Divisions*, the current *Little Review*, T. S. Eliot's *Prufrock and Other Observations*, and a volume of Maupassant stories. Here, sometimes leaning on the counter and sometimes—when he thought he could get away with it—seated cross-legged on the floor, Hart would study the structure of poems, a Cinco cigar clamped between his teeth, happily oblivious to the surrounding world of aspirin and Mary Garden Chocolates.

Crane in these days attacked a poem the way hundreds of other young men in Akron were attacking the motors of their fathers'

Fords. He tinkered, calculated, adjusted, balanced. He fussed until it hummed. Making a poem was for him—then and to the end of his life, perhaps as it is for every good poet—a matter of pushing and pulling, chopping and pounding. "I wrote a short affair last night that I may hammer into shape," he wrote to Munson in that first week, and went on to talk about the difficulties of composing in his spare time what he recognized as a major effort, "My Grandmother's Love Letters." While he was in Cleveland, "contact with the dear lady" had made work on the poem impossible. And now that he was at a distance from her, time itself limited him: "Grandma and her love letters, are too steep climbing for hurried moments, so I don't know when I shall work on that again. As it is, I have a good beginning, and I don't want any anti-climax effect. If I cannot carry it any further, I may simply add a few finishing lines and leave it simply as a mood touched upon." Though he did not significantly lengthen the poem, he worked on it in much of his free time, shipping off copies to Munson and Josephson and to Sherwood Anderson, with all of whom he was now in regular correspondence, as each variation was tried out. "I enjoyed your letter with its encouragement to Grandma and am sending you a record of her behavior to date," he wrote Munson at the end of November. "She would get very fretful and peevish at times, and at other times, hysterical and sentimental, and I have been obliged to handle her in the rather discouraging way that my words attest. However, I think that something has been said, after all, although the poem hasn't turned out as long as I had expected."

Not everybody responded to the poem. Sherwood Anderson's first reaction to it, for instance, must have been something of a jolt: "Let me speak of your poem. I can speak frankly because I have so little knowledge. It does not give me anything of yourself, the bone and flesh and reality of you as a man. Your letter does that so your letter is to me the better poem." And though Anderson in a postscript concluded: "The poem seems beautiful to me," he made clear that in his opinion its strength was not a consequence of technical precision—all the labor of composition that Crane had put into it—but rather a consequence of personality, that it was achieved "through the realities of you the man." But Munson and Josephson, as Crane wrote Bill Wright, were enthusiastic: "The poem . . . has won praise from two of my severest N.Y. critics. I finished it down here in Akron, and didn't know whether it was any good or not, but Josephson says that it's the best thing I've done, and urges me to continue in somewhat the same vein on a variety of subjects." At the end of January, when, after being rejected by *The Little Review*, it was accepted by *The Dial* and Crane for the first time in his life was given a cash payment for a poem—all of ten dollars—he was sure he had reached a turning point in his literary career. He was, at last, a professional writer.

The perceptive reader probably hears faint echoes of Eliot's "Preludes" in the poem, but it was Wallace Stevens who was most in Crane's mind as he brought it into final shape. "New theories are filling my head every day," he wrote Munson. "Have you given the poems of Wallace Stevens in the Oct. 'Poetry' any attention? There is a man whose work makes most of the rest of us quail. His technical subtleties alone provide a great amount of interest. Note the novel rhyme and rhythm effects." Not so much modeling his poem on Stevens, for only in the last line of the third stanza is there a hint of imitation, but rather adapting to his own purposes what Stevens was doing, Crane expanded the second stanza's partial rhymes (enough, Elizabeth, roof, soft, mother) into a structure of sound for the entire poem, intruding "soft" into the first stanza, and anticipating the repetitions of "enough" and "roof" in the final two stanzas. Like Stevens, Crane recognized the power that sudden fully rhymed couplets can have in such an apparently open poem, and like Stevens he made poetry out of what at first seem deceptively simple, prose-like statements.

He had also learned how to produce poems that were not "about" people but rather that were in a way "equivalents for" people. "My Grandmother's Love Letters," for instance, evoked the grandmother rather than described her, defined her by assigning her qualities to remembered stars, to soft rain, to insubstantial snow, to gentle steps, to "invisible" white hair, to webbed birch limbs, to gentle laughter, to music thought about—not played.

While "Grandmother" matured, Hart's reading program went on. Josephson encouraged him to read the Elizabethans and the Metaphysicals; Sherwood Anderson, busy attempting an oblique definition of America in the "New Testament" he was writing, urged Crane to investigate Paul Rosenfeld, Van Wyck Brooks, and Waldo Frank, none of whom Crane had read at all carefully. Anderson had for some time been corresponding with Brooks about the still-unpublished *Ordeal of Mark Twain* and now that it was scheduled for January publication he recommended it to all young writers. "It should be a remarkable fine piece of work," he told Crane, comparing it to Waldo Frank's *Our America*, a book he had a week earlier recommended not only to Crane but, through him, to C.A. as well. Brooks, Anderson explained, "has not Frank's flame in criticism but he has a remarkable mind. In a way I respect it more than any other mind in America."

But it was Frank's book, not Brooks's, that was for Crane a revelation, for it suggested a way in which industrial America, in which Crane felt himself inextricably enmeshed, might be somehow transformed into a better world. Only by the artist's involvement with it, Frank suggested, might the artist—inheritor and transmitter of the culture of the past—triumph over the barbarism of an industrial society: in no respect could he ignore it. In letters to Bill Wright and to Munson, Crane immediately began to adapt Frank's ideas to his own needs.

He urged Wright, discontented at Columbia University, not to make the mistake of cutting himself off from formal education.

> You might as well fight things out for yourself on the campus as anywhere else, and you will get enough and far too much of the stolid and narrowing influence of mercantile life after you are out . . . I hope you won't worry too much about the 'practical value' of your education in relation to your future business and pursuits. The vice is rampant already in America. Most Americans are mad fanatics on pragmatism. Good God,— isn't a little seasoning of culture the most precious and scarce quality in our world today! I grant you that even the colleges are against it,—they have all turned into business institutions run by successful-business-men-trustees, but still there is a lit- tle wine in the grape if it is squeezed in the right way, and you, I think, are one who really has a hungering for the best flavor. I do not know about the monetary situation that you are in, but if college is a comfortable possibility for you, I would remain in the regular B.A. program even though I didn't intend to be a writer, diplomat, jurist, or scholar. Excuse this harangue, please, and when I send you a book I have been reading you will perhaps understand me better.

With Munson, he debated in some detail the pros and cons of that book. "Waldo Frank's book IS a pessimistic analysis!" he ex- claimed in one letter, and then went on to discuss the possible consequence to young writers of such accurate pessimism.

> The worst of it is, he has hit on the truth so many times. I am glad to see justice done to Sherwood Anderson, but this ex- treme national consciousness troubles me. I cannot make myself think that these men like Dreiser, Anderson, Frost, etc., could have gone so far creatively had they read this book in their early days. After all, has not their success been achieved more through natural unconsciousness combined with great sensitiveness than with a mind so thoroughly logical or propagandistic (is the word right?) as Frank's? But Frank has done a wonderful thing to limn the characters of Lincoln and Mark Twain as he has,— the first satisfactory words I have heard about either of them. The book will never be allowed to get dusty on the library shelves unless he has failed to give us the darkest shadows in his book, —and I don't think he has.

If ten years later, when he had come to regard Frank as a spiritual brother and a very close friend, Crane ever thought back to his first reactions to Frank's book, he would perhaps have been struck by the pattern of accidents that had drawn not only him but Munson into the circle of young writers aided and in some ways dominated by Frank. Munson, caught up in the enthusiasm he shared with Anderson and Crane, was soon to publish the first book-length critical study of Frank's work; and Crane, carried along in the tide of Munson's interest, would finally be indebted to Frank for friends, for ideas, for editorial assistance, for help in securing financial grants in days when such grants were harder to come by than now. But perhaps Crane—at the end of his life involved in accidents far more fierce, far more brutal, than any that could have been experienced by the boy in Akron, elbows on the candy counter, *Our America* propped open on a box of Mary Garden Chocolates—perhaps Crane, looking back, could have seen neither pattern nor meaning in any part of his life; and perhaps he would have been hard put to calculate the ways in which the reading of any one book would shape his life.

Certainly not all his reading at this time was of the sort I have been discussing. Crane read everything that came his way: he read the Akron *Beacon Journal*, he read (and enjoyed) his dictionary, he read (and later fitted references to them into poems) streetcar ads and highway billboards. Over the Thanksgiving holiday, Crane, spending the day in Cleveland, read and—roaring with laughter—quoted to his mother and grandmother long passages from *The Young Visiters*, the next day recommending the book to Munson: "Have you read 'The Young Visitors' by Daisy Ashford (alias Sir James Barrie) yet? I don't know when I have been more delighted. Subtle satire par excellence!" He did not, however, take back to Cleveland with him, nor quote to mother or grandmother, another book he had recently been given by his Akron bookseller friend, Mark Twain's suppressed *1601*. Crane explained, in a note to Munson that accompanied a copy of the book, that it had been written in one of Twain's "ribald moments," and went on to say, "it gives me a stronger light on some of the reasons for Mencken's enthusiasm for the writer. The grand ejaculatory climacteric speech of Queen Bess is magnificent. You will regard the book as quite a treasure."

Able, through books, to keep his mind off a dull job—at breakfast, lunch, and dinner; in the drugstore; at night jackknifed up in his hotel bed, reading by the suspended overhead lamp—Crane always seemed to have a book within reach. "If you feel 'blue' read good old Rabelais, Mark Twain, or a novel by Conrad," he wrote Wright. "I have 'gone to the books for the doctor' so much that I know the remedial shelves quite well."

Blue he may sometimes have been, but he solved problems of loneliness quickly. Wherever he went, he managed to associate himself with a group of writers and artists; and Akron was no exception. Soon he had made friends with the steady customers of his bookseller, among them several reporters on the two Akron papers. Perhaps it was through these acquaintances that Alice Chamberlain, a columnist of the Akron *Sunday Times*, heard of him and arranged to publish in the issue of December 21 a long two-column interview. Crane took the interview lightly, describing it to Munson as "an agreeable joke and an anachronism in Akron," as "silly enough, but forced upon me, and misquotations as well," but his father saw it as a not-so-veiled attack upon all he held most dear. "The pater was furious," Crane told Munson, "at the headlines in particular, and I spent a nervous day yesterday with him in explanations etc. Sic semper." The headline, *Millionaire's Son Is Clerk In An Akron Drug Store*, spread out above a staring photograph of Crane, did ignore Crane's poetic ability—the subject of the article—and did perhaps suggest that C. A. Crane was a penny-pinching tyrant. At least C.A. read that suggestion into it and found support for his reading in Miss Chamberlain's statement that "Hart Crane doesn't like the idea very well" of going into business. Her direct quotation from Hart was still more upsetting: "The modern American artist must generally go into business life. He is often forced in anyway by necessity."

Of course, rather than attacking the idea of the businessman-artist, Crane had been doing his best to justify it. "What I mean," he had told Miss Chamberlain, "is that the artist's creation is bound to be largely interpretive of his environment and his relation to it; and living as we do in an age of the most violent commercialism the world has ever known, the artist cannot remain aloof from the welters without losing the essential, imminent vitality of his vision." Only by being a part of the business structure of industrial America could the would-be "American" poet, painter, novelist, or musician have any notion of the real world that he was supposed to be shaping.

"Of course he must see much farther than the edge of his desk. He must fight against much of the oily smugness he sees around him. His sympathies must not be blunted and he must have patience—patience to wait for America's great economic growth, eventually to complete a structure that will provide a quieter platform, as it were, for the artist and his audience.

"We will then perhaps, achieve a national culture. At present we have Robert Chambers' whilers-away of evenings in pullmans. However, there is a growing discontent among us with these purveyors of mush. We want more solid food and some is being offered. Have you read Carl Sandburg's 'Cornhuskers,' Dreiser's novels, Edgar Lee Masters' poems, or Sherwood Anderson's masterpiece, 'Winesburg, Ohio'? These men have recognized realities that are close to us and our present day life, and we cannot afford to ignore them."

It was up to the artist, then, to achieve a precarious balance between the tough-minded business community and an equally tough-minded fraternity of critics of that community. The artist had to cultivate a deliberately split personality. He had to be "two different people," as Crane told his interviewer. One of his lives, if it was to be meaningful, had to be devoted to business; another, to art. And the two lives, "art and business," had to be kept "entirely separate."

If Crane was here proposing for himself the sort of life that Wallace Stevens eventually came to lead, he had every reason at this stage to expect that he could bring it off. His father, in spite of doubts raised by Crane's interview, was pleased to have his son working for him, and he assured Hart that in the not-too-distant future both Hart's free time and his income would increase enough to allow for the double life Hart dreamed of. "I expect I will have a real job in time," Crane told Munson. "I like to think that I can keep on writing a little, at least, of good quality, until,—someday when I shall start up a magazine that will be an eyeopener. I feel in a Billy Sunday mood this evening . . ." His father's business seemed to be opening branches all over the country, and Crane saw an unlimited possibility of places to work in: "I won't be in Akron long. After that it may be Kansas City, Frisco, or even New York." Before he left the area, however, he would put in some time working for his father in Cleveland. There, for much the same pay that he was earning in Akron but with shorter working hours, he could count on free evenings and a Saturday half day.

Perhaps no one was more surprised than Crane at his ability to get on with his father. The two violently disagreed, of course, on almost all literary matters; but influenced by Sherwood Anderson, who "explained" father to son and who had been instrumental in driving Crane toward his businessman-artist position, Hart came increasingly to respect C.A.

"About your father," Anderson had written. "One is at a disadvantage there. Fathers, American fathers, can't be dismissed. I wish I knew him as well as you. I would like to work with him for an afternoon as well as with you." Even C.A.'s views on the arts, for Anderson, made a kind of sense.

> The arts he ridicules have not been very sturdy and strong among us. Our books are not much, our poetry not much yet. The battle has scarcely begun. These men are right too when they ridicule our pretentions.

What was needed in the arts, Anderson argued, was something like the individualism of American businessmen! America no longer needed artists working in groups, men banded together in Chicago or New York, but "much more now what is wanted is the reality of individuals." If the artist could define his own uniqueness, then he might find a way of communicating to other isolated artists.

> I hope to express much of the vague, intangible hunger that constantly besets me as it must you. One doesn't hunger to defeat the materialism of the world about. One hungers to find brothers buried away beneath all this roaring, modern insanity of life.
>
> You in Akron, another man in California, a fellow like Fred Booth, shivering in some cold room in New York.
>
> The land is indeed vast. In an odd way groups defeat growth. We must remain like seeds planted near each other in a field. No voice any of us may raise will quite carry across the spaces. . . . I want to send the voices of my own mind out to the hidden voices in others, to do what can't be done perhaps.

Driven by such observations into a reexamination of his own experiences in New York, Crane did his best to work out the reasons for his return to a home town that he didn't really like but that was somehow necessary to him. For one thing, he had explained to the young woman who had interviewed him for the Akron *Sunday Times*, bad as Cleveland and Akron were—and he objected strongly to their industries and to their gross commercialism—they were not quite so bad as such a place as Greenwich Village. For though they were vulgar, they had at least a vulgar honesty about them. Greenwich Village, on the other hand, he saw as simply "deplorable."

> "It is utterly self conscious, because it has been so much in the limelight. With so many uptown visitors coming in to observe from mere curiosity, and with so many 'artists' who are not artists at all living there, the Greenwich village of a few years ago is gone. All of the real artists are moving out."

Crane clearly was trying to associate himself with men like Anderson and Frank, men who insisted that the American artist define himself in terms of the evolving American character; but there is also no question that, like many other young men of the times, he saw his private tradition to be quite as much European as American. In his own eyes, he was torn between the way Anderson was traveling and the way Josephson was traveling. For Josephson, quick-witted, wry, ironic, writing letters that seemed to Crane "charming with a peculiar and very definite flavor to them," managed an air of worldly sophistication altogether different from the moral earnestness of Anderson and Frank and Brooks. Josephson's tone—assured, brittle, casual—fascinated Crane. "He says he has had a falling out with Amy Lowell, but a falling in with T. S. Eliot by way of compensation," Crane told Munson. He came increasingly to count on his correspondence with the "particular, hierarchic Josephson" for "fascinating" gossip about local writers and about the French writers whom Josephson was reading.

Caught in the double pull of personalities, Crane saw not only his literary style but also his personality as an odd amalgam of Josephson and Anderson. "[Anderson] and Josephson are opposite poles," Crane wrote Munson. "J., classic, hard and glossy,— Anderson, crowd-bound, with a smell of the sod about him, uncouth. Somewhere between them is Hart Crane with a kind of wistful indetermination, still much puzzled."

Though Crane had relatively little free time in Akron, he did meet and later come to know well another young man "in Akron exile from N.Y.," Harry Candee, "a very sophisticated and erudite fellow" to whom he had been introduced by Herbert Fletcher. Drawn to each other by a mutual interest in literature and painting, they had arranged to spend together the Sunday afternoon immediately before Christmas. Their afternoon, once it got under way, swept spectacularly into what Crane came to think of later as his "one purple" evening in Akron, a progression that started in the kitchen of a Roumanian family locally famous for the quality and quantity of its prohibition wine, then moved on— jugs of the wine bundled under their overcoats—to Candee's boarding-house room, and ended when Crane, "dreadfully drunk on dreadful raisin brew," he confessed to Munson, "puked all over" the halls of the boarding house.

For Crane, the evening had been a holiday from respectability, wonderful glimmering moments of improbable delights tucked into it. Candee, fresh from European travel, had presented him "one of the cigars made especially for the Czar, defunct, of Russia." Cigar clamped in his teeth, a glass of the raisin wine in hand, Crane listened fascinated as Candee quoted "an opus by Eugene Field,—very exclusive,— . . . quite strong," displayed "a rare and wonderfully complete edition of Catullus," and discussed the merits of decadent and brilliant Edgar Saltus. "You will believe me an ox when I tell you that I was on the job again next morning," Crane told Munson, "and carried the day through with flying colors."

Eventually turning his purple evening into plain poetry, Crane drew on it for the happy central section of his poem "Porphyro in Akron":

> I remember one Sunday noon,
> Harry and I, "the gentlemen,"—seated around
> A table of raisin-jack and wine, our host
> Setting down a glass and saying,—
>
> "One month,—I go back rich.
> I ride black horse. . . . Have many sheep."
> And his wife, like a mountain, coming in

With four tiny black-eyed girls around her
Twinkling like little Christmas trees.

And some Sunday fiddlers,
Roumanian business men,
Played ragtime and dances before the door,
And we overpayed them because we felt like it.

Once the Christmas rush was over, Crane found his work load
drastically reduced. Most of his evenings were now free, and he
spent a number of them with Candee. Crane had moved to
"Akron's newest commercial hotel," the Bond, and either there or
at Candee's rooms the two friends, sometimes meeting with
Fletcher, discussed life and literature. Crane was working his way
through a reading list that included Somerset Maugham's *Moon
and Sixpence*, Edgar Lee Masters's *Starved Rock*, "Pound and
Eliot and the minor Elizabethans"—which he turned to increasingly, he said, "for values"—and work by Djuna Barnes and Ida
Rauh. He was fascinated to discover that not only had Candee
been reading many of the same writers but that they had one spectacular writer as a common acquaintance.

I was suddenly surprised last evening (Candee and I have
been in the habit of talking until two and three in the morning) to hear him mention the Baroness. It seems he knows her
very well. Knew her before she came to the Village and Margaret Anderson got hold of her at all, and believe me he had
some surprising tales to tell. He goes on for hours telling of
exotic friends of his and strange experiences. He knows Europe
well, English country house parties, and Washington society,—
prizefighters, cardinals, poets and sculptors, etc., etc., and the
wonderful thing is to find him here in Akron, forced to earn his
living as secretary for some wheezing philanthropist.

After Crane went back to Cleveland, he saw Candee only intermittently. But he did manage, whenever the pressure of work or
family proved too much for him, occasional trips south on the
high-speed Interurban trolley for overnight visits with his friend.
Such visits, which sometimes turned into literary and alcoholic
debauches, were for Crane inevitably refreshing. At the end of the
Easter rush in his father's factory, for example, Crane allowed
himself such a luxury. He went, as he told Munson, "armed with
two bottles of dago red," but that proved only a starter.

That didn't seem to suffice . . . and a quart of raisin-jack was
divided between us with the result that the day proper (after
the night before) was spent very quietly, watered and Bromo-
Seltzered, with amusing anecdotes occasionally sprouting from
towelled head to towelled head. The bath in the unconscious

did me good, though, and was much better than the stilted parade and heavy dinner that my home neighborhood offered.

Just before he left Akron, Crane had made another friend, a much older man, the photographer H. W. Minns. Crane, improving on nature, did his best to turn Minns into something of a character, describing him in a letter to Munson as a "filthy old man." Minns was in fact, according to those who remember him best, nothing of the kind. He was, one friend remembered, "a lovely man, generous, intelligent, sharp-eyed, thoughtful. You could never call him a filthy old man. That's just not true." He was, however, "a marvelous photographer." Crane, excited at the thought of a major discovery in Akron, told Munson all about him. Minns was the only photographer in America, Crane wrote, "to hold the Dresden and Munich awards." A man "written up" in *International Studio*, he had been ranked by "authorities" with Coburn and Hoppé of London.

> . . . and there is no one in New York who compares with him. He used to read the Little Review, knows Marsden Hartley,— and lives in a tumble down old house in the center of the city. I expect the pictures of me that he takes to be wonders. He refused to take the "rubber-king," F. H. Seiberling, for love nor money, simply because he thought his face without interest. He confided to me yesterday that he was an anarchist, and I picture with some pain the contrast in his circumstances here with what acclaim he would achieve in [a] place like London. He has always been afraid of N.Y.—and wisely,—for probably he would have long since starved there.

Crane was soon shipping off to editors samples of Minns's work, doing his best to get his new friend the public acclaim he felt Akron had deprived him of. And in part Crane succeeded. Margaret Anderson, badgered until she agreed to consider publishing some photographs, by the end of summer had contracted not only to print two in *The Little Review* but also to print Crane's one-page evaluation of Minns's work. Probably written in early August, a month Crane devoted to catching up on Henry James, it praises Minns for exactly the sort of personality delineation Crane admired in James's prose and strove for in his own poetry. Minns's " 'arrangements,' " Crane said,

> are not the empty, obvious contortions of so many modern photographers. He plainly could not content himself with that. There is, in his faces, the urge of an ethical curiosity and sympathy as strongly evident as in the novels of Henry James. Undoubtedly his portraits are deeper, more vivid, than the daily repetitions of his sitters in their mirrors give back to any but themselves, but this is only to mention again the creative ele-

ment that gives to his portraits such a sense of dramatic revelations.

It was, however, neither Minns nor Candee, neither his correspondence with Josephson nor that with Munson, and it was none of the books that he read that made Akron a memorable place for Crane. Akron was memorable because there Crane for the first time fell hopelessly, absolutely, recklessly in love.

Crane had had more than his share of emotional involvements. He had joked with Bill Wright, constructing from the girls they knew an ideal woman with whom he might fall in love; and in New York he had, in fact, persuaded himself that he was in love with Claire Spencer. He had had awkward, not always pleasant, "affairs" with other boys and with men; and he had habitually idolized his friends, both men and women, elevating friendship to a plane of deeply felt Platonic love. But not until his stay in Akron did he experience a love so obsessive as to obliterate reality, so obsessive as to make itself the only real thing in an otherwise incoherent universe.

He first mentioned his love affair in a letter to Munson: "I have lately begun to feel some wear from my surroundings and work, and to make it worse, have embarked on a love affair, (of all places unexpected, here in Akron!) that keeps me broken in pieces most of the time, so that my interest in the arts has sunk to a rather low station." His life, he explained, had become "quite barbarous."

Unable to talk openly with any of his friends about the sort of love he was experiencing, he managed, nevertheless, to convey to most of them the tone of his feelings. On the day after he had written Munson he wrote a letter to Bill Wright that hovered just short of the open confession he might have made had Wright —still at Columbia University in New York—been within conversational reach.

> I have my little Corona with me once again, so you will not have to struggle through this as you did my last communication. Of course you are excused. I am very sorry to hear of your sickness, which I hope will have completely vanished by Christmas. And do, when you come back afterwards, let down a little from the strenuosity of your work. I wish you had more outside friends (from the college, I mean) to help you neglect your *conscience and work* a little more. I can understand you, I think, because in many ways we are alike. We demand so much from life, and so seldom are we satisfied. Grey, grey days,—I have had even more of them than yourself, I think.

At about the same time he must have written Sherwood Anderson, telling none of the details of his love affair but much of his feelings, for on December 17, Anderson—who had still not met

Crane—commented on the way in which the love affair made his unseen correspondent more real: "It is odd how the fact of your being in a love affair vivifies you. My mind shall play with your figure at odd moments—you hungering and being defeated and arising all the time to new days."

Finally, however, Crane decided to tell someone the truth about what was happening to him. It must have been with considerable relief that on Saturday, December 27, he sat down at his typewriter in Akron's Hotel Bond to break the news to Munson that the love affair which by now he saw as the richest emotional experience of his life was an affair not with a woman but with a man.

> So many things have happened lately with the rush of Christmas, etc. that I am tired out and very much depressed today. This 'affair' that I have been having, has been the most intense and satisfactory one of my whole life, and I am all broken up at the thought of leaving him. Yes, the last word will jolt you. I have never had devotion returned before like this, nor ever found a soul, mind, and body so worthy of devotion. Probably I never shall again. Perhaps we can meet occasionally in Cleveland, if I am not sent miles away from there, but everything is so damned dubious as far as such conjectures lead. You, of course, will consider my mention of this as unmentionable to any one else.

Munson, though at first surprised because in all his dealings with him Crane had seemed so aggressively "normal," proved an ideal confidant, discreet and sympathetic. Like the other friends who eventually came to know of Crane's sexual adventures, Munson accepted Crane's affairs as "normal for him."

Altogether too much, it seems to me, has been made of Crane's homosexuality. Crane himself was partly responsible for his reputation. In the mid-twenties, when he had returned to New York, his affairs became an open secret. After one drink too many, he would become compulsively confessional, offering any sympathetic listener detailed and often lurid anecdotes. But as anyone who has even glanced into psychoanalytical case histories knows, the sexual histories of most "normal" persons—when they are available for biographical summary—show such elaborate variation as to suggest that Crane's record is unusual only because so much of it has become public property. The normal man, if Kinsey's statistics are accurate, indulges secretly in such a wide range of "vices" that, in some ways, Crane's affairs seem bland.

It is important to realize, I think, that had Crane been just a little more discreet; had he, say, been able to afford an analyst to whom he could privately pour out his troubles; or had he simply not put in writing details of his homosexual activities, not only would we be unable to document any of this, we would almost certainly construct an inaccurate "reality." We would visualize a virile young man, a bachelor disillusioned by his parents' unhappy marriage and himself unlucky in love (Claire Spencer's marriage would loom large in such a biography), a lonely man finding at last—as Crane, in fact, did—a satisfying, whirlwind romance in the final love affair with Peggy Cowley.

Yet in spite of the fact that we do know a good deal about Crane's sexual activities—the letters have, after all, been published and many anecdotes have become public property—we should keep in mind that sex was not the only business of Crane's life. Sex was, as it is for most men, important. But his life did not revolve exclusively about it. The same letter to Munson in which Crane made his confession of homosexual love was filled with details about his work for his father, his correspondence with Sherwood Anderson, his opinions about all the books he had been reading.

It is important too to realize that Crane's was a real love affair, not just a sexual adventure. Like most men, Crane had had his share of sexual adventures; but such adventures meant little to him because there was no emotional involvement. They provided only physical satisfaction.

This love affair was genuine. Crane was twenty and he was in love. And when he told Munson that not just body but soul and mind as well were committed to his lover, he meant exactly what he said. For the two months in which it was most intense, Crane's affair transformed his world. He could suddenly without difficulties get through what he regarded as a meaningless day at his father's store, because waiting for him at the end of his day would be passion, tenderness, compassion, and shared devotion. "Akron has, after all, afforded me more than N.Y. would under present circumstances and times, and, odd as it may seem, I have almost no desire for an immediate return there. Of course," he explained to Munson, "I suppose my 'affair' may have a good deal to do with my attitude."

After his return to Cleveland, when he could see his lover only on weekends—and not every weekend, at that—Crane counted the days between visits. "My love affair is affording me new treasures all the time," he wrote Munson.

> Our holidays are spent together here in Cleveland, and I have discovered new satisfactions at each occasion. . . . I live from Saturday to Saturday. Gold and purple. Antinous at Yale. So the wind blows, and whatever might happen, I am sure of a pool of wonderful memories. Perhaps this is the romance of my life,—it is wonderful to find the realization of one's dreams in flesh, form, laughter and intelligence,—all in one person. I am not giddy or blind, but steadier and keener than I've ever been before.

While it lasted, the love affair seemed to Crane a miracle. Everything went right. When he returned to Cleveland, fearful that so close to home his affair might be discovered, he was startled but pleased to find his mother sadly telling him that he would have to get a room by himself for a month or two; she and his grandmother had decided to spend the rest of the winter on the Isle of Pines. On January 11, when he moved from his Akron hotel to 11431 Euclid Avenue, he was sure his new quarters were a godsend. And for a few weeks they were. But finally they became more of a prison than his father's factory. For his lover proved untrue, and the wonderful weekends stopped. By March 6, upset and worried, he was writing Munson details of his loneliness: "My Akron friend has not been able to see me for some four weeks, and I am in need of a balm, spiritual and fleshly. I hope next Sunday something can be arranged." But Sunday led into Sunday without the expected visit; postponement piled on postponement. Finally, by the end of April, everything that had once been miracle had become, without his quite realizing it was changing, as empty as the empty air. "I have gone through a great deal lately," he confessed to Munson, "—seen love go down through lust to indifference, etc. and am also, not very well."

# 7

Though in one sense the first six months of 1920 were for Crane a period of marking time—he spent almost all of it in his father's factory "learning the business" as a combination stock boy, handyman, office helper, and replacement clerk—it was also a period in which Crane had the opportunity to think through his own views on life and art.

The discovery that he could become so involved as he had with his Akron lover, so entangled in a mesh of idealized, self-less love, of passion, and of lust, shocked him. It is no accident that one of the poems he composed in these months was "Episode of Hands," or that the first draft of "Garden Abstract," another poem of this time, struck Matthew Josephson as evidence of Crane's turning to a "phallic theme," or that Crane recommended naturalism to Gorham Munson as "the only foundation left for serious and interesting modern work."

In this discovery of the body, entertainments which a year before would have seemed vulgar were now satisfying. "Last night was made enjoyable by the spectacle of a good prize-fight," he wrote Munson one evening early in March. Not every match, he admitted, was worth looking at

> . . . but provide two sublime machines of human muscle-play in the vivid light of a "ring,"—stark darkness all around with yells from all sides and countless eyes gleaming, centered on the circle,—and I get a real satisfaction and stimulant. I get very heated, and shout loudly, jump from my seat etc. and get more interested every time I go. Really, you must attend a bout or two in N.Y. where a real knock-out is permitted.

Perhaps responding to the fight because, as he explained to a new acquaintance nine years later at another prize fight, this one in Paris, "Boxing matches always make me feel homosexual!" but more likely in 1920 responding in terms of aesthetic excitement, Crane considered the possibility of turning his experiences into poetry. "There is something about the atmosphere of a ring show that I have for long wanted to capture into the snares of a poem," he wrote Munson.

I shall not rest easy until I do, I fear. To describe it to you,—what I mean,—would be to accomplish my purpose. A kind of patent leather gloss, an extreme freshness that has nothing to do with the traditional "dew-on-the-grass" variety conveys something suggestive of my aim. T. S. Eliot does it often,—once merely with the name "Sweeney" and Sherwood Anderson, though with quite different method in a story of his in "The Smart Set," some time ago, called, "I Want To Know Why," one of the greatest stories I ever expect to read,—better even than most of the Winesburg chapters.

His new poetry, Crane hoped, would be "harder" than anything he had yet done, hardened in part at least by the detachment of ironic laughter. It is not surprising therefore that the names of Mark Twain and Rabelais begin to pepper Crane's correspondence. "The modern artist has got to harden himself," he explained to Munson,

> and the walls of an ivory tower are too delicate and brittle a coat of mail for substitute. The keenest and most sensitive edges will result from this "hardening" process. If you will pardon a more personal approach, I think that you would do better to think less about aesthetics in the abstract,—in fact, forget all about aesthetics, and apply yourself closely to a conscious observation of the details of existence, plain psychology, etc. If you ARE an artist then, you will create spontaneously.

This was exactly Sherwood Anderson's point of view, and Crane was delighted several weeks after he wrote Munson to find Anderson writing him a similar note: "I am in truth mightly little interested in any discussions of art or life or what a man's place in the scheme of things may be. It has to be done I suppose but after all there is the fact of life. Its story wants telling and singing. That's what I want—the tale and the song of it, I suppose."

The two poems in which Crane struggled to "harden" his work were both eventually dropped by him as inferior. "Episode of Hands" was never offered for publication, and "Porphyro in Akron," though eventually printed, was deleted by Crane from the *White Buildings* collection.

The first was a direct result of the excitement Crane found in physical contact and was little more than a versification of an experience he had had in his father's factory. A young factory worker had cut a finger and had come to Crane, "the factory owner's son," who "knew a grip for books and tennis / As well as one for iron and leather," to have the wound bandaged. As Crane wound the gauze strips around the finger, "factory sounds and factory thoughts / Were banished from him by that larger, quieter hand / That lay in his with the sun upon it." The poem ended exactly as the incident had, in a sudden moment of silent communication. While the bandage knot was being tightened, "The two men smiled into each other's eyes."

When Crane sent copies to his friends, he was sure the poem was a failure or needed a great deal more work. And yet, as he told Munson, the experience had been so moving that he had been compelled to turn it into poetry.

> It is interesting to me,—but do I succeed in making it of interest to others? . . . Much remains to be done on it yet,—but enough is done with it at present to detect the main current of it, which is principally all that worries me. . . . This piece was simply a mood which rose and spilled over in a slightly cruder form than what you see. It happens to be autobiographic, which makes any personal estimate of it all the more dangerous.

Anderson and Munson wrote back with strong criticism of the poem, Anderson's response being almost total rejection and Munson's qualified by doubts of the poem's economic significance. The latter seemed to Crane not really pertinent, and he accurately put his finger on the real problem.

> The poem fails, not because of questions, propagandistic and economic, which you mentioned, but because of that synthetic conviction of form and creation, which it lacks. . . . As it stands, there are only a few fragments scattered through it to build on, —but I may make something of it in time. However,—if it does evolve into something,—it will be too elusive for you to attach sociological arguments to, at least in the matter of most of the details you have mentioned.

"At present," Crane went on to say, "I feel apathetic about it." Had he known that in the same day's mail he would be receiving Sherwood Anderson's even stronger objections, apathy might have given way to hopelessness. "I hope you'll forgive me if I use the surgeon's knife on the wounded hand poem," Anderson wrote.

> The owner's son and all that is a bit patronizing. Doubt laborer's caring much for it. There is a beautiful passage about the wound itself, pure poetry,—the light among the tangle of wheels, . . . light going down into the pool of blood. I like that more than I can tell you. It's beauty and poetry. All the rest seems to me at once not intimate enough and too precious[?]. . . . You'll forgive me the attack on the poem, won't you?

Finally, Crane rescued from it those lines which Anderson admired, working them a year later into his unpublished poem "The Bridge of Estador," itself a mine for several subsequent poems.

"Porphyro in Akron," a good deal more ambitious, was, like "Episode of Hands," or, for that matter, like "My Grandmother's Love Letters" (in Crane's opinion his best poem to date), founded directly on real experience. Any successful poem, Crane felt, had to be grounded on the substance of the poet's life. It had—somewhere at its core—to be personal. It is perfectly true, he argued, that this in itself is not enough to produce a poem. The poet has to build a structure equivalent to but not descriptive of the experience on which the poem is founded. But he must never lose sight of the personal feeling which initiates the poem and which gives it much of its life.

"Porphyro in Akron," looser than most of Crane's poetry, anticipates the time transplantation he would later draw on in "For the Marriage of Faustus and Helen," Crane here casually tossing the romantic hero of Keats's "Eve of St. Agnes" into present-day industrial Akron. Seeing his poem as "a set of sketches connected with Akron life," Crane may have used the construction of it as therapy for his disintegrated love affair. "I don't much care whether anyone will care for it or not. What I seem to want to do more and more as time goes on," he wrote Munson, "is to preserve a record of a few thoughts and reactions that I've had in as accurate colors as possible for at least private satisfaction." He nevertheless worked on the poem all through the summer and fall, regularly submitting it to magazines until it was finally published in the August–September 1921 issue of the *Double-Dealer*.

"Garden Abstract" was perhaps the most important of his new poems. Dissatisfied with early drafts, Crane decided to "make something interesting out of it, after all." Week after week rearranging lines, shifting point of view, turning what had started as personal poetry into a little drama of Eve and the apple, he came finally to feel that he was working on a poem almost as important as "Grandmother's Love Letters." "The 'Garden Abstract' has got hold of me now," he wrote Munson. "It is carrying me on with all the adventuresome interest that 'Grandmother's Love-Letters' did, and I am very hopeful." But, to his surprise, the poem was rejected by *The Dial*, *The Freeman*, and *The New Republic*. He could see why the last two of these might not like the poem ("the theme was pure pantheistic aestheticism,—and I suppose they would say that it was too detached from life, etc."), but he found it harder to accept the rejection by *The Dial*. Not until midsummer did he send it out again, this time in response to Margaret Anderson's cheerful request that he "send on anything you think of interest." Accepting both it and his note on Minns for the September–December issue of *The Little Review* and encouraging him to continue in the same vein (" 'Garden Abstract' one of the best, I think, but not yet quite all I want from you. Send more"), she helped make his summer pleasant.

Before summer, however, Hart's time in Cleveland was little else than casually dull. He spent most days in his father's factory, where "packing cases and moving heavy cases of chocolate, barrels of sugar etc." reduced him to near exhaustion. Only "much camaraderie with the other employees" permitted him to "humanize" the job and so find day-to-day "salvation." After work, his mother's neighbors served him home-cooked dinners, and a "mild patroness of the arts" saw to it that Crane met the brother of the painter Warshawsky, himself a painter and a pleasant conversationalist. Hart spent the rest of his free time in the company of Cleveland and Akron newspapermen whom he had known in his days as a cub reporter and such new acquaintances as Herman Fetzer, who, as "Jake Falstaff," was just beginning the "Pippins and Cheese" daily column that for years would brighten the Akron and Cleveland papers.

In order to counter this routine dullness, Hart invented a secret life, a life purely of the imagination. No matter how many people he talked to in a day's time, he told Munson, he felt untouched.

Of course I am utterly alone,—want to be,—and am beginning to rather enjoy the slippery scales-of-the-fish, continual escape, attitude. The few people that I can give myself to are out of physical reach, and so I can only write where I would like to talk, gesture, and dine. The most revolting sensation I experience is the feeling of having placed myself in a position of quiescence or momentary surrender to the contact and possession of the insensitive fingers of my neighbors here. I am learning, just beginning to learn,—the technique of escape . . .

In such self-conscious isolation, Crane more and more fell back on his correspondence with friends; and letters to Munson, Anderson, and William Wright are in the early months of 1920 particularly numerous.

No letters of this time reflect his feelings better than those to Wright. Always at ease with this friend of high-school days, Crane projected in letters to him a revealing mixture of sophistication and naïve innocence. Take, for example, a letter of February 24, 1920, in which twenty-year-old Crane shuttles, almost from sentence to sentence, between ironic man-of-the-world and confessional teenager. Nineteen-year-old Wright, halfway through his sophomore year at Columbia, was properly shocked, concerned, and amused as Crane danced from role to role.

Yes,—whatever else New York may fail in, it is sure to offer excitements, whether in the form of dormitory kleptomania or Greenwich Village Follies, and I am glad to know by your last letter that you are in the midst of them. Take a layman's word of advice and remain in your present surroundings as long as possible and extract the full amount of enjoyment from them while they last. It is not very exciting to arise and essay forth to ten hours dull and exasperating labor every morning at five-thirty and return home at night with a head like a wet muffin afterward. And that is the routine that I am enmeshed in at present, to say nothing of trying to exist on starvation wages. It's the old bunko stuff about "working from the bottom up" and "earning an honest dollar" in practice, and if there are not some enlivening changes in it soon, I am liable to walk into the office and tell the amused and comfortable and rich and thriving spectator that "the joke's up." Catullus uses somewhere in his epigrams about a man that he was "fucked flat," meaning I suppose a reference to emaciated thighs, etc., but the phrase is none too vivid for me to use at present in reference to my nervous and intellectual state. Add to this, an uncomfortable room, cold, etc., and a routine of hasty and inadequate meals snatched from chance lunch counters and there is further evidence for the state o' things. I've been much revived, however, by the recent news that Mother expects to be back in Cleveland by next Tuesday, and that means that the house will be re-opened and things restored for me to a more sane basis. This isn't much of a letter to send to an ambitious sophomore but it's the best I can do tonight, and I take it that you'd rather hear from me than not in spite of it. I certainly hope that we can get together next summer (it can't be before), but it may be that you, being the freer agent, may have to consent to a visit in Cleveland. If you want to see me bad enough, you will survive even that calamity. My poem in "The Dial" ["My Grandmother's Love Letters"] ought to be out any day now. I corrected the proof they sent me as much as two weeks ago, and you will be sure to get it in the basement of Brentano's on Fifth Ave. around Twenty-sixth St. The subway stands used to handle the magazine, but I don't know about that now. Write me what you think of it. It is quite a feather in my cap to appear in the assemblage that "The Dial" claims now, and I am quite encouraged about myself. All I need is time for a small amount of leisure, and time when I am not all tired out from previous exertion, mental or physical, it makes no difference, and I would turn out better stuff than even this opus.

Crane was physically tired. But another kind of tiredness was produced by his efforts to adjust to the inexplicable variations in the characters of his parents.

Most of the time now his father seemed to him "impossibly tedious and 'hard' . . . insistent on starvation wages." And though Crane talked him into a $5 a week raise, he could not help but regard the conversation as a "long and hypocritical conference." Yet he responded to his father's praise. On April 1 he reported to Munson that his father "seems to be very much satisfied with my present devotion to office hours, etc." In fact, Crane speculated about the possibility that C.A. might allow him to spend one of the summer months working in the New York office, in spare time free to "snoop about,—etc.,—and get a glimpse of some of my friends." In a burst of zeal, Crane for two weeks after his talk with his father took on every assignment C.A. proposed— only to come down with sore abdominal muscles which he immediately diagnosed as "an incipient rupture caused by the incessant heavy lifting at the factory." In spite of the pleasures of a week free to read in bed, Hart, encouraged by his mother, was "furious with resentment against all those concerned in the circumstances of its cause." When the rupture proved a false alarm, he returned to work, docile, a shade more cautious: "I am quieter, now that the affair has not been so serious as I first suspected. I am back at it again today,—but shall in the future take more precautions against strenuosity."

If Hart found his father "cold," he found his mother all too "warm." So long as she was on the Isle of Pines, she seemed to him a pleasant, companionable woman, witty, congenial. Though his tone is condescending, a January 28 note about her is intended as praise: "I am beginning to discover that I enjoy her society,—I have worked over her for three years painfully,—and the result is a woman of more interest than I had dared to hope for." But when she came home and Hart was once more established in his own room, she was the mother he had always known.

Well,—my mother is at length returned and the house open again. At present, however, the domestic vista appears a desolate prospect to me,—a violent contrast to the warm pictures that the former rooming-house room had conjured up as anticipations. I wrote you a while ago that I had gotten 'round to enjoy my mother's companionship. That illusion, at least for the present, seems to be dispelled. She left here two months ago, a rather (for her) ductile and seductive woman with a certain aura of romance about her. She comes back now, satisfied, shallow, unemotional, insistent on talking food receipts and household details during meals. The weight of this terrible Christian Science satisfaction I feel growing heavier and heavier on my neck. Tonight I am distraught after a two-hour's effort at camaraderie and amusement with her. "Dutiful son," "sage parent,"—that's nice,—and a pat on the back and the habitual "goodnight kiss." I give my evenings to her to hear advice about details in business affairs which she knows nothing about. Mon Dieu!!! And there is Grandmother in a loud background to add to the confusion. Exhausted as one may be from an inhuman day, one must beam out the dinner and evening in proper style or there are exclamations culminating in excruciating tears. However, I mind it most when I am alive, like tonight,—not tired, stupid, mild, as on "week nights."

Much of the time withdrawing from mother and father, though superficially dutiful to both, Crane saw himself as an emotional sleight-of-hand man. "I don't know, G.," he wrote Munson, "whether I'm strong and hardened or not. I know that I am forced to be very flexible to get along at all under present conditions."

Yet he realized that his problem was entirely personal, that nowhere he could go and nothing he could do would in any way change the tangle of his life. "I read the *Times* often enough to realize that music is the only extra stimulus that N.Y. has to offer above Cleveland in these dry days," he wrote Matthew Josephson. "As I've said before, I don't especially long for N.Y. as of yore, except once in awhile when an overwhelming disgust with my work afflicts me and I want to lose myself in the chill vastness of the old place. (I should better have said 'find myself,' for I play a business part so much and so painfully that the effort wears.)"

Even music could be had on phonograph records. It had been his phonograph, in fact, that he had missed in his boarding-house room more than any of the other comforts of home. "I cannot write much now," he had explained to William Wright, "cramped in this rooming house room, but when . . . I am re-installed in my own room with my little Victrola, I hope to revive my intimacy with la Muse." It is no surprise that as soon as he was reestablished he purchased a new recording of the Processional from *Parsifal*.

When music failed, Crane had his books: Rimbaud, Apuleius, Rabelais, Villon, Eliot, Vildrac, Baudelaire, Saltus, James, Mencken. The lists ramble on from letter to letter. "Have been reading Stendhal's 'Chartreuse de Parma,' 'Noa Noa,' 'Way of All Flesh,' and 'Landor's Conversations,'—a strange mixture." A little later: "Did I tell you how I have been enjoying the letters of Henry James? Also, Aldous Huxley's 'Limbo,' and the Noh plays of Fenollosa and Pound. Conrad's 'Nigger of the Narcissus' seems to me all polyphonic prose, plus the usual quality of Conrad characterization etc. Then I've read most of the tales in James's 'Better Sort' vol." He read all the little magazines in Richard Laukhuff's bookstore, often writing Munson and Josephson detailed critiques: "I like Marianne Moore in a certain way. She is so prosaic that the extremity of her detachment touches, or seems to touch a kind of inspiration. But she is too much of a precieuse for my adulation. Of this latter class even give me Wallace Stevens, and the fastidious Williams in preference."

Though not by any means a recluse, Crane did in his last year of adolescence enjoy moments which must have seemed to him very like a hermit's. "In my limited surroundings I grow to derive exceptional pleasures from little things such as a small Gauguin I have on the wall," he told Josephson, "Japanese prints, and Russian records on the Victrola, in fact, the seclusion of my room." Withdrawing into that room, pipe in one hand and book in the other, his Victrola drowning out the conversation of mother and grandmother that filtered up from the living room, Crane could experience inner freedom. Here he could relax or, seated in front of his portable typewriter, pour out long, chatty letters to distant friends.

He was not really unhappy in Cleveland, but, particularly this year, he was bored. "My mother is able to offer me only the usual 'comforts of home' combined with stolid, bourgeois ultimatums and judgments which I am learning how to accept gracefully." There were times when he was tempted to pull up stakes; but he remembered the disappointments of his previous year in Manhattan. And so he was only mildly regretful when he turned down Matthew Josephson's suggestion that the two of them get away from middle-class stupidities by joining the artists and writers who were already forming a floodtide of émigrés to Europe. "Your suggestion of a flight to the walks of Chelsea or the Mediterranean tempts me exceedingly. I should like to be rash. I assure you that if I were in your position I should do just such a thing, but I feel too much bound by responsibilities in connection with my Mother's fate, to more than dream of it. However, I wish we could get together for a while next summer. Perhaps you could make me a visit here. . . . I can offer you no woodland retreat or metropolitan carnival,—only a very middle-class house and dull conversation,—but the time we had to ourselves would be very interesting to me, at least." If he couldn't travel, others might travel to him. Crane wrote almost identical invitations to Bill Wright, Gorham Munson, Sherwood Anderson.

Meanwhile, he went through a round of family social affairs, sometimes going out of his way to be unpleasant. He found himself one evening escorting his mother to a Warren Society dinner. When they arrived, Crane stared out over a sea of middle-aged couples, locating only one person anywhere near his own age. As he stood talking to her (the daughter of a family friend), he made no effort at conversation; instead he poured out a stream of cynical invective, uncomplimentary remarks—not even amusing, she remembered—about everyone in sight. At about the same time, he told Munson, he had been "beset by two terrible occasions,—a Crane-grandparent-golden-wedding celebration, and a collegiate ball. The terrors of the first were alleviated by some real champagne, but the second was aggravated by auto trouble on the way home with two hysterical, extremely young and innocent females under my care at three in the morning."

Throughout his life Crane would be torn between the middle-class values that he liked to satirize and the bohemian values he sometimes plunged into—and sometimes shudderingly withdrew from. When in a joking letter to Bill Wright he interrupted a flow of nonsense to exclaim "You are an old romantic codger," he was thinking as much of himself as of his friend. Both of them lived in a world of kaleidoscopic possibilities. "Your imagination is as profound as mine," Crane wrote. And he whirled off Bill's possibilities: a waiter, "living perchance at the old collegiate chambers for a touch of austere distinction or the handy shower baths"; a bus conductor, "helping middle western dowagers up the spiral bus-stairs, gasping to view New York!" "But if, on the other hand, old habits and memories have driven you thoroughly revolutionary and 'bussy' to the extent of change of residence into Bleecker St. or Old Bowery, it would be wise and kind to appraise me of that finality . . ." For no matter how wild their dreams or ambitions, how comically mundane their accomplishment, they had lurking at the back of their would-be-bohemian minds one most outlandish dream of all, the dream of becoming a part of the world they so recklessly attacked: "And now I dream of becoming a business man! And I suppose someday I shall even meditate marriage! (My epitaph shall be:—'Il fumait sa pipe.')"

But his epitaph, of course, was "Lost at Sea."

# 8

All through the winter and spring of 1920 Crane had chafed at his job in the candy factory, convinced that he was caught in a round of exhausting and meaningless activity. He had managed, however, to come to life almost every weekend, taking trips to Akron, dropping in at Laukhuff's bookstore, hobnobbing with newspaper friends and with new acquaintances— actors and actresses from the Cleveland Playhouse. But by the middle of April he was thoroughly depressed, and a note from Bill Wright did nothing to bring him out of his gloom.

Wright, who had seemed to him the model of cheerful self-sufficiency, whom he had always counted on for encouragement and sympathy, had suddenly fallen into a melancholy as dark as Hart's own. He could see no reason to continue in college; could, in fact, see little reason to live. Crane, obviously worried about his friend, got off a letter that was intended to be cheerful but that soon dropped into a parallel melancholia.

Monday—April 19th—20

Dear William—

So far as news goes I haven't a postcard full, but I want you to know that I enjoyed your letter and am thinking of you. Was tired to death last Saturday, having had two carloads of boxes to unload and arrange in storage space . . .

I think that the Spencerian School plan might work out well for you. If I am still in Cleveland when you come, you must plan to stay with me. You might stay out at the house, or, if I am living by myself, as I sometimes meditate, we could bunk together. As I see it, your college life is meaning nothing to you, and in that case, probably it would be unwise for you to continue it longer than this term. But I don't attempt to offer advice to anyone about anything. I have encountered so much misunderstanding from even those who had every reason for fathoming me the most successfully, that I realize my own limitations in such respects. I think a summer spent in the country at work on a farm might be what you need,—anything that will revive your faith in life, a lack of which you seem to be suffering from. That is what I would like to do,—but it seems at present a very remote possibility. Write me soon, and remember me as always your affectionate frater,—

Harold

Though Crane did not spend the summer on a farm or in Cleveland with his friend—though he did not see Wright until the very end of summer, and then only briefly—from the time of their exchange of letters Crane's spirits began to rise. Life was no easier at home with his mother, but his father seemed to have a growing respect for him. He often went out of his way to praise Hart's diligence at the factory, and he began once more to speak of assigning Hart several weeks' work in the New York office. In June he had an even better idea. For Hart's twenty-first birthday was approaching, and C.A., thankful that some of their misunderstandings had been cleared up, decided to celebrate by giving Hart a two-week vacation, pay in advance, and a generous cash bonus to go with it. Hart's announcement went out to every friend in Manhattan. His letter to Munson is typically exuberant.

As the plans are at present I shall almost assuredly be in New York for two weeks beginning about the first of next month. I shall not have anything to do with sales matters or the office, but shall devote all the time to as much of a "whooping time" as my resources will admit. Will you be there to go swimming and sunning on the Long Island shore with me? We must have a Sunday morning breakfast at the Brevoort etc. I shall not forgive your absence under any conditions. After that, unless some very tempting literary job in N.Y. should offer itself, I expect to return to the old job here. That,—or I might get a job "stewarding" to England. But we'll have some talks anyway. . . .

From the time his sleeper pulled into Grand Central at 10 A.M. on Sunday, the Fourth of July, until he returned exhausted to Cleveland two weeks later, Crane lived at top speed, trying to crowd into his days visits to theaters, concerts, beaches, speakeasies, friends' homes, restaurants, parks, bookshops, waterfronts, editors' offices, and art galleries. Staying at the Prince George on Twenty-eighth Street, he devoted his mornings to writing, his afternoons to sightseeing and shopping, his evenings to visiting such friends as Charmion von Wiegand, Alex Baltzly, and Joe Kling, and his nights—at least some of them—to good-spirited carousing. Though he was determined to have fun, he found more fun in conversation than in any other activity. His best times were spent in what he insisted on calling his "parlors" at the Prince George with Gorham Munson, who joined him to work line by line through their most recent poetry and to talk over Munson's projected article on Pascal.

Crane returned to Cleveland just in time for his birthday and a long talk with his father about the future. He was, they agreed, to work in the factory until fall, at which time he would be sent out to open up a new sales territory—"the territory around Washington, D.C., Norfolk, Richmond, Va." Responsible for his own success or failure, he would be able to "rise and retire at later hours, and have a drawing account at the bank." He would be given a "good percentage commission" on everything that he could sell. And perhaps best of all, he would be in a position to prove that C.A.'s confidence in him was justified. "He even made the unhoped-for concession of mentioning that he had chosen this territory for me on account of the better sort of business type that is in Washington," Hart wrote Munson, "and also on account of Washington's 'literary and Journalistic associations.' "

Celebrating, Crane shipped off two boxes of his father's best Mary Garden Chocolates to the offices of *The Little Review*, one addressed to Margaret Anderson and one to the Baroness—who never got hers. ("I must be a pig or an idiot," Margaret Anderson wrote back, "but I spose I opened the last two Mary Gardens so eagerly that I saw nothing indicating that one was for the Baroness. I just thought you were being specially 'sweet' to us, and we shared with Djuna Barnes, but the poor Baroness suffered. I'll try to make up to her some day by buying her one.")

On September 8, Crane left for Washington with the high hopes that marked every move he was ever to make. He was sure that his new surroundings would be "much better than this smug atmosphere around here," and he was confident that they would lead to "revived inspiration." He had, he wrote Munson, "a lot of doubts" about his capacities for salesmanship, but the possibility of free time, "more leeway for whatever reading or writing I may want to do," made the prospect of his new job bright. Besides, Washington was 300 miles nearer New York than Cleveland was. He would, he reasoned, be within striking distance of old friends.

Crane spent the first few days sightseeing and room hunting. His expense account, though adequate, could not keep him for long in a downtown hotel, and he soon rented a room "in an unexceptional maison in a row of other rooming houses." There were, he explained to Munson, "charming places" in Washington, but the row house at 1310 L Street was not one of them. If he did not care for the room he had found for himself, he did do his best to like the city. "There is a certain easiness about it," he wrote, "and geographically it is, I should judge, the nearest like Paris of any American city. An endless number of parks and monuments, and all the streets are lined with trees. At least it is more elegant than any other American city and with a very different psychology than N.Y., Cleveland or Akron."

But trying to like a city and liking it are two altogether different things, and Crane was never able to stir up any affection for Washington. "I am not in the type of Washington life that offers material or incentive for writing," he confessed to Munson several weeks after he arrived.

> The diplomatic circles have all kinds of scandals waving around which I generally hear a whisper of from the fringes, but there is really no cafe life here or factory or shop life worth mentioning. Thousands of clerks pour out of government offices at night and eat and go to the movies. The streets are beautiful with many parks etc. but it is all rather dead. . . . I don't even get a sip of academic tea nor advice from President Wilson.

His final reaction to the six weeks he spent there was summed up in a note to Munson. Washington had offered Crane only a "ghastly time."

Part of the trouble was his failure as a salesman. Even before he approached his first prospect, he knew enough about himself to realize exactly what he would go through. "I dread this tramping around trying to sell Crane's candy," he wrote Munson. Like many people who are normally extroverted, cheerful, outgoing, but with strangers are introverted, almost terrorized, Crane found nothing more difficult than walking through an office door to face buyers, business executives, presidents of corporations. Perhaps in his mind transforming them all into carbon copies of his buyer, business-executive, president-of-corporation father, the man he admired, loved, and feared more than any other man, Crane would pace the streets before their offices, sometimes for hours. By the time he had gathered up courage to plunge through the closed door, he would be in a cold sweat, excited, half inarticulate. "I've been running around talking, talking, talking and waiting for the proper persons to arrive at their offices etc. etc. etc. all week," he wrote Munson on the evening of his fifteenth day in the city, and yet he had managed to open up only two new accounts. Four days later, trapped in "postponed July," an Indian summer heat wave that sent temperatures soaring into the nineties, Crane again temporarily abandoned his career as a candy salesman. "It's too hot to write and too hot to sell candy," he wrote Bill Wright, "but I hope you'll be more interested in my attempt at the former than most people I approach are interested in [my] failure in the latter. . . . The last few days I scarcely dare to open my samples for fear of finding them grey with sweat." By mid-October he was completely disheartened. "I'm proving to be, thus far, quite a negative sort of salesman and how long my father's patience will last I don't know. I satisfy myself as much as possible by working hard at it all the time and at least I want to be able to swear to a certain amount of effort."

On October 27 Crane was allowed to return home. "I find agreement from my father that my lack of results here has not been so much a matter of personal inadequacy as the weather and general slowness of business here at this particular time."

In Cleveland once again, Crane realized what part of his troubles had been. Really alone in a really strange city, he had come down with an overwhelming case of homesickness. From the first day in Washington, when he had experienced "a terrible vacuity about me and within me and a nostalgia for Cleveland," the hunger to be back in familiar scenes with familiar people, who no matter how insensitive or dull were at least his own, had daily grown worse. Cleveland, when he came back, was not beautiful; and the back-breaking work at the factory was as hard as ever— but Crane was happy. "Yes, 'Jurgen' has been breathing his *native* Ohio air for two weeks now," Crane wrote Munson, "and is elbow and knee-deep in shipping and packing at the factory. The Christmas rush has already begun and I'm tired to death tonight after a rush since five this morning." Yet he was relieved to be "back into the usual smoke and tawdry thoroughfares."

Does one really get so used to such things as, in time, to miss them, if absent? I am sure I should not miss factory whistles in Pisa or Morocco, but I frankly did miss them in Washington. Anyway, they were more enlivening (and the people they claim) than anything or anyone that I saw in W. which seemed to me the most elegantly restricted and bigoted community I ever ventured into.

Homesickness and his failure to secure orders for his father's company account for much of Crane's dislike of Washington, but his total revulsion was founded on more complex experiences.

When Hart had gone to Washington, he could hardly have been called innocent. He had already turned twenty-one. He had been through one serious love affair. He had seen a little, at least, of the seamier side of life in New York. But his emotional experiences—violent enough, and frequently unconventional—were based on passion. He had had relatively little experience with men or women whose whole lives revolved around casual sexual gratification. In Washington he was thrown into such a circle. Both fascinated and repelled by these people, he had attended orgiastic parties, wild evenings of intricate debauchery where, at first observing, he ended participating. One man who met him soon after he returned to Cleveland remembers to this day his shocked surprise as Crane recounted anecdote after anecdote of improbable adventure. However funny—and spectacular—these anecdotes were, and many were both spectacular and funny, the experiences that led to them were for young Hart profoundly disturbing. By the time he left Washington, he had been touched, he felt, by an unwholesome world that before his visit had had literary reality only. He was disgusted at the possibilities of his own corruption.

He had drifted into the group easily. Washington was full of soldiers and sailors on leave, and from them and from other new acquaintances he had heard of what must have seemed to him a city within a city. "I am really more interested in the soldiers and sailors that one meets than anything else," he wrote Munson. "They have a strange psychology of their own that is new to me. This sounds bad, and perhaps it is so,—but what should one do with the reported example of ———— ———— scenting the air as it does. From what I'm hearing, about every other person in the government service and diplomatic service are enlarged editions of Lord Douglas. Amusing Household! as Rimbaud would say." Munson, answering him, spoke of his own uneasy nights; Crane insisted on a significant difference in their experiences: "My nights are uneasy also. But you ought to pity me more than yourself,—my satisfactions are far more remote and dangerous than yours, and my temptations frequent, alas!"

The details of Crane's experiences—though they can be uncovered from unpublished letters and from the recollections of friends to whom Crane confided—are unimportant. What is important is Crane's mixed response to them. He was far too much a product of Cleveland and its moral code to turn against it lightly, and what he could not help but regard as his own moral transgression was to torture him until the day of his death. In later years, when companionable drinking would drift over the line into drunkenness, he would drag out for friends the details of his sins, sometimes bragging of them, sometimes defending them, always hounded by them.

And yet, perhaps because he did until his dying day possess an elemental innocence, a purity which none of his adventures could corrupt, his closest friends still think back on him as almost miraculously untouched by the chaos of a life he never successfully controlled. Sam Loveman, who was to meet him in Cleveland and to know him perhaps better than any man, tried once to tell me how this sort of innocence could transform innuendo into Gargantuan comedy. We had been talking into a tape recorder, and I had mentioned Hart's once speaking of Sam's fondness for long walks. Loveman said:

I love to walk. I can't walk much now. This damn physical condition. Well, I'll wait. I can walk in heaven. Yes, we walked— on Sundays. It was wonderful to be with him because certainly I was never bored. . . . And riding on the subway was just one holocaust of laughter because he saw double meanings in all the ads, and usually obscene meanings. He claimed that most of them had some sexual or phallic undercurrent of meaning. I doubted that, although very frequently he was right or seemed to be right. He didn't have a pornographic mind, though. He was one of the cleanest human beings I have ever met in that sense. No matter what his life was, he was a very clean human being and completely wholesome.

Another man—the ship's officer for whom the "Voyages" poems were written—in trying to sum up his relationship with Crane saw it as passionate enough, ecstatic, sometimes violent. "But one thing it was not. It was never *dirty*."

It was dirtiness, however, that Crane had discovered in Washington, and the sense of that kind of dirtiness lurking within him—perhaps within all men—sickened, fascinated, and disgusted him.

He had not, of course, been completely isolated from conventional society. Given his gregarious nature, he would have gone mad if for six weeks he had been unable to discuss literature, art, music, the theater. Armed with a letter of introduction from his Akron friend Harry Candee, Crane soon after his arrival had paid a call on Wilbur Underwood, a minor government official in charge of "all the official communications etc. that come into the state department." Considerably older than Crane, Underwood had an interest in all the arts and an apparently inexhaustible fund of literary and political gossip. "He has proved a charming person," Crane told Munson, "and has introduced me to several other interesting people. He is one of the few who is thoroughly cognizant of what is going on abroad, knows some things weeks in advance of the newspapers and, of course, a great many things that never come out. His opinion of most of Europe, especially the greedy tactics of some of the freshly hatched nationalities, is below cynicism."

Underwood and Crane regularly attended the pre-Broadway tryouts of new productions. They agreed that Emily Stevens saved the musical *Foot-Loose*, and they were both surprised to find Walter Hampden's *Merchant of Venice* far below their expectations. "The way it was done, setting, costumes, speech, gestures,—everything was sickening," Hart wrote Munson. "Hampden, in one scene only,—the tantrum with Tubal,—was good, everywhere else his acting was indifferent. I cannot understand how a man of his intelligence,—for I remember his Hamlet as being quite good,—will venture forth with such a cast of burlesque queens, (his Portia!!!) and bitches. The worst examples of antiquated theatricality, and mouthing of words! And the audience was ample and enthusiastic,—a true barometer of the American stage at present."

The more Crane saw of Underwood, the more he regarded him as a man who should have been an important literary figure. That same American society which could not distinguish between good drama and bad was responsible, Crane concluded, for Underwood's lack of success. As a young man, little older than Crane, Underwood had published in England two volumes of verse. Both had been well received. But there was no money to be made in poetry, and Underwood had settled into the security that government bureaucracy offered. Though Crane had not yet read Underwood's poems, he easily identified with him. "What pathos there is in these sudden flashes on forgotten people," Crane wrote Munson, "forgotten achievements and encounters!"

> Here is this man, Underwood, with the beauty and promise of his life all dried and withered by the daily grind he has had to go through year after year in the State Dept. with a meagre salary. A better critic and more interesting person one seldom meets, yet the routine of uninteresting work has probably killed forever his creative predispositions. A very few friends is all that life holds for him. Yes, Pound is right in what he says in his "The Rest,"—"O helpless few in my country, O remnant enslaved! . . . . You who cannot wear yourselves out by persisting to successes."

Underwood no longer produced poetry but he read it, and Crane showed him everything he had written. Underwood, in turn, made available to Crane his extensive library of rare books, many unobtainable in America. "I have just been enjoying to the full his copy of the 'Satyricon' of Petronius (Arbiter), a . . . completely unexpurgated Paris edition, purported to have been translated by Oscar Wilde, although it seems to me too fine a job for what I imagine Wilde's scholarship to have been. Also, I am enjoying 'The Golden Ass' of Apuleius, and some Saltus vols. that he has."

Perhaps during discussions of such exotic classics or perhaps on the midnight walks the two men took after their evenings at the theater, Crane once more risked confessing details of his emotional and sexual involvements. Underwood was an ideal confidant. Too much a man of the world to be shocked by anything Crane could tell him, he proved in Washington, and in the long correspondence that continued until Crane's death, always sympathetic, always understanding. From this time on, it was to Underwood that Crane would in long letters pour out details of his secret life.

> NEWS! News! NEWS!—The "golden halo" has widened,—descended upon me (or "us") and I've been blind with happiness and beauty for the last full week! Joking aside, I am too happy not to fear a great deal, but I believe in, or have found God again. It seems vulgar to rush out with my feelings to anyone so, but you know by this time whether I am vulgar or not (I don't) and it may please you, as it often might have helped me so, to know that something beautiful can be found or can "occur" once in awhile, and so unexpectedly. Not the brief and limited sensual thing alone, but something infinitely more thrilling and inclusive. I foolishly keep wondering,—"How can this be?—How did it occur?" How my life might be changed

could this continue, but I scarcely dare to hope. I feel like weeping most of the time, and I have become reconciled, strangely reconciled, to many aggravations. Of course it is the return of devotion which astounds me so, and the real certainty that, at least for the time, it is perfectly honest. It makes me feel very unworthy,—and yet what pleasure the emotion under such circumstances provides. I have so much now to reverence, discovering more and more beauty every day,—beauty of character, manner, and body, that I am for the time, completely changed.—But why aren't you here to talk with me about it! How I wish you were here.

. . . I have told you all that has happened. The rest would merely be to mention details of ungodly strain and hours of "Christmas rush" at the factory,—seventeen hours [at] a stretch sometimes. When I have had time I have spent it with Dostoievsky's *Les Freres Karamazov* which I like even better than *The Possessed*. The beautiful young Alyosha, and Father Zossima! Dostoievsky seems to me to represent the nearest type to the "return of Christ" that there is record of,—I think the greatest of novelists. But I am forgetting Frank Harris, who, you know, comes second to the "woman taken in adultery."

My mother leaves for her southern island in ten days, and I am taking a room for the rest of the winter. Write me here for the present, anyway, and it will be faithfully forwarded with the "seal secure."

# 9

The first few months of 1921 were halcyon days for Crane. Though snow piled hip-deep on Cleveland streets, though winds whipped in off the frozen lake, and though gray, blustery days succeeded one another in a procession of snow and more snow, Crane's private world opened into something like radiance. He was in love—and love made all the difference.

His mother and grandmother were 1,500 miles away; the Christmas rush at the store was over and his father was frequently out of town. He had an apartment of his own, and a host of new friends. With a convenient supply of cigars in his father's office humidor, a supply of homemade wine in the "Little Italy" section of Mayfield Road, and the latest books and magazines in Richard Laukhuff's bookstore, Crane settled down to three solid months of the good life.

"He was a wonderful guy to be with in those days," Harley McHugh told me. McHugh had worked with Crane in his father's factory and in the store on Thirteenth and Euclid Street, and he had every opportunity to watch Crane in these happy months. "He was never the same from one day to the next. One day he'd have the highest enthusiasm and the next day the deepest depression. But he was always worth being with."

During this time Hart went to work only when his father was in town. Alan Howard, then assistant to the superintendent at the factory, remembered that every time Mr. Crane left the city he made a point of saying, "See that Harold gets down to work." But he also remembered that in practice "this was an impossibility . . . Harold came in to work only when out of funds." When he did appear, however, he was extraordinarily popular with everyone in the factory. Like the rest of the workers, Hart—officially a shipping clerk—would carry his lunch, once in a while on his lunch hour offering to read to Alan Howard or to McHugh one of the poems from the manuscript notebook he sometimes brought with him, but more often laughing and joking with the other men.

At work, but even more at play, Hart struck his friends—perhaps even struck himself—as a Rabelaisian character. On the

nights of his visits to Little Italy, he would always be in a roaring
good humor. During one bout, McHugh remembered, Hart insisted that the evening be "formal" and rushed back to his apartment in the Del Prado to struggle into his tuxedo, then to his
mother's house, where he "borrowed" the Baker electric auto that
was her pride and joy, and then back again to meet his friend for
a wild and wonderful drive down snow-swept Euclid Avenue.
On another night the two of them, burning bright on red wine,
descended on a touring opera company that featured, of all
women, Mary Garden. Louder almost than the opera star, Crane
'ust missed being expelled from the theater, his not very well
suppressed snorts of laughter bringing stares from neighboring
patrons of the arts and then a visit from a much concerned
usher. (After the performance, Crane, all propriety, introduced
himself to Mary Garden as son and heir of the manufacturer of
Mary Garden Chocolates and told her how much he admired her
bright, lyric style.)

Bert Ginther, another friend of those days, had been introduced to Hart by the photographer Hervey Minns, and his memories too are of laughter and of good humor. After their first
casual meeting in Crane's apartment, Ginther invited Crane to
join him for a Sunday breakfast in his own apartment: "Came
Sunday and our friendship got going with a flourish—very likely
an eyeopener or two of prohibition red eye or white mule—Hart
at table reading to me from his pocket-size Satyricon—and I enjoying with all my might my introduction to Petronius and Hart's
infectious loud-and-ready laughter for Trimalchio, Giton, et
cetera, Inc."

Sam Loveman, when he met Crane for the first time in Laukhuff's store, was, he felt, almost literally snatched up and hurried off to the Del Prado, there to be regaled by shocking stories
of life in Washington, quizzed about his literary interests, and introduced to Hart's latest discoveries. "And I must say," Loveman
recollected, "there were many people in literature that I was
unacquainted with or knew only in a cursory sort of way. Hart
had . . . an amazingly broad knowledge of modern literature. . . .
I recollect one [writer] in particular—Edward Thomas, who was
a friend of Frost's, a protege of Frost's—who I think did better
poetry than Frost ever could write and who was killed during
the First World War. Hart read an extract of him to me and I
liked it so much that I went out and got a copy and I've had it
ever since." Their afternoon together, like dozens of other afternoons and evenings in this golden time, was crowded with
easy, spontaneous good cheer.

Mindful of his own Gargantuan laughter and seeing the boy
he had fallen in love with as a kind of Pierrot, Crane—who in
these days was much too caught up in a shining existence to find
time for writing—cheerfully remarked to Munson:

Here is my sum poetic output for the last three months,—two lines—

> "The everlasting eyes of Pierrot,
>     And of Gargantua,—the laughter."

Maybe it is my epitaph,—it is contradictory and wide enough to be. But I hope soon to make it into a poem, and thereby, like Lazarus, return.

Crane's Pierrot—in the eyes of most of Hart's acquaintances a shy, retiring boy altogether unlike his extroverted friend—was neither "literary" nor "artistic." A pleasant young man, he seemed in no way extraordinary. But to Hart he was a miracle of grace and beauty. When on February 11, after an evening of wine and laughter and love, Hart sat down to write to Munson, his "subconscious rioting out through gates that only alcohol has the power to open," he found himself breathless before the experiences he had recently been living through.

> The fact is that I am entirely engrossed in personal erotic experience lately . . . O if you had ever seen the very soul of Pierrot (in soul and incarnate) you would at least admire. Never, though, has such beauty and happy-pain been given me before—which is to say that my love is at least somewhat requited. You and one other are the only ones to know now or later of this, so do not think me silly or vulgar to tell you. . . . Never have I suffered so, or reached such moods of ecstasy.

Moods of ecstasy, however, came and went; and it would be unfair to suggest that all of Crane's hours were ecstatic. Although he often found excuses for not showing up at the factory, he did— whenever his father was in town—do his best to put in an appearance and, more often than not, to put in full days of work.

Though Hart was only vaguely aware of it, his father was much concerned about his son's welfare. Reports of Hart's sprees, both emotional and alcoholic, had begun to work up through the office grapevine. Finally C.A. called in Ed Morgan, one of his oldest friends and, like the lawyer John J. Sullivan, one of the few men who was regarded with real admiration by all three of the Cranes—C.A., Grace, and Hart. Morgan, who apparently talked to C.A. for hours, seems to have advised him to accept the fact that his son really did want to be a poet and not a manufacturer. His recommendation must have been persuasive, for shortly after their talk Hart himself was called in. Both C.A. and Hart left the office feeling that a great deal had been accomplished. "A talk with my father last week settled things more definitely for me than many months have afforded," Hart wrote Munson.

> I shall remain in my present capacity at the factory indefinitely until I find a job at some more "literary" work, when my father

and I will more-or-less conclusively part hands so far as a business connection is concerned. . . . You see I have not said anything to him about my personal interests for almost two years, leaving him only what details of indifference to business as naturally revealed themselves throughout my association with him, to judge from. I long ago "gave up" talking over such sores with him,—and it has amused me vastly to find that at last the attitude aroused him to seek such indirect solutions to the "enigma." Now I can hope to get a little reading and writing done before spring here in some sort of tranquility. Before the summer is over I may have found me a journalistic job,—but the main point under either drudgery is that I accomplish some real writing.

Meanwhile, C.A. continued to search for a job that his son might find to his liking. By the middle of February, Hart was once more transferred: "I'm now keeper of a warehouse which handles bulk supplies for my father's various Cleveland stores. My own boss, and not rushed, and even have time for occasional half-hours of reading. At present, then, I'm somewhat more satisfied."

That job lasted all of ten days. Hart was again transferred, this time to the basement of his father's restaurant on Thirteenth and Euclid. Here, too, he was in charge of a storeroom; and for the first few weeks, at least, he was pleased with his job. He had hardly anything to do, and he spent his time reading and writing. Across a basement corridor from him were the restaurant kitchens, where Hart delighted in the relaxed, free, good times of the Negro cooks and dishwashers. Grace, when Hart wrote her of his transfer, felt that C.A.'s assigning Hart to this job in this place—particularly because Hart had replaced a discharged Negro handyman—was a deliberate effort to humiliate son and mother; but Hart, lacking Grace's prejudices, managed to thrive on the underground life. For the first time in months he set to work on a poem and in the leisure of his storeroom turned out the first drafts of "Black Tambourine," a study of the store's porter, who, "forlorn in the cellar," seemed caught between two unavailable worlds: lost Africa nothing more than racial memory, and the white, smiling world of the restaurant upstairs barred to him by "the world's closed door." Aesop, at the poem's middle, reminds us that this fable has a moral, that it carries a "tardy judgment" on those who close doors. Pleased, both with his poem and with himself, Crane shipped off a copy to *The Dial*, which promptly rejected the poem, and another to Munson. "You see," Crane explained, "my present job allows me more time while 'at work,' and I may even do more,—for better or worse, according as you feel about it."

As February drifted into March and March into April, Crane came to regard his basement storeroom as a sanctuary. He could drop into the kitchen at any time of day for coffee and cakes; he got on well with everyone in the restaurant; he even got on well with his father. Though he did not for a moment abandon his plan to seek work elsewhere, he was contented. And he was also reconciled to Cleveland. "You know there is precious little for me to build on here," he could write Munson; but he could as easily write Underwood, "I don't want to move out of here for a long time,—I'm so tired of moving, moving uncertainly from place to place these last six years."

Nothing remained now but the memory of that time in early winter when he "ran gait" at the factory "at the rate of fourteen hours straight per day of rushed and heavy and confusing labor," when he had been "very morose and irritable" under the "pressure of exertion, not to mention disgust and boredom," and had summed up his experiences neatly in a sentence: "Our age tries hard enough to kill us, but I begin to feel a pleasure in sheer stubbornness, and will possibly turn in time into some sort of a beautiful crank." With "no time, literally, for poems, to say nothing of energy," with "not love enough in me . . . to do a thing," he had felt only passive despair. "I don't believe in the 'sublimation' theory at all so far as it applies to my own experience," he had written Munson. "Beauty has most often appeared to me in moments of penitence and even sometimes, distraction and worry. Lately my continence has brought me nothing in the creative way,—it has only tended to create a confidence in me along lines of action,—business, execution, etc." But now, freed from physical labor, freed from almost all parental supervision, assured that he would be allowed to escape from his father's business, and experiencing in his new love "the strongest incentive to the imagination, or, at least, the strongest in my particular case," Crane set to work on a number of literary projects.

One of these, a "poem on adolescence,—which, very adolescently, I have never finished," is of interest principally as the source for a phrase in the "Faustus and Helen" poem that two years later would come into being. Explaining to Munson that the four lines he quoted represent "somewhat my mood," Crane dismissed his experiment as showing too much the influence of Eliot and Huxley.

> "The mind shall burst its aquarium vagueness,
> Its melon opacity of graduate dawn";—
> Wise-youthful prophecy to the tired pillows
> Resentful of the room and shades,—still drawn.—

Altogether different from this poem and well worth more work was "Black Tambourine," which he continued steadily to revise. "Black Tambourine," he felt, lifted above influence to be "something definitely my own. . . . I am getting nearer to what core I have, right along, I think." Like every young poet who admires, and yet wishes to be different from, the dominant poetic voices of his time, Crane did his best to calculate how each of his contemporaries got his effects—and then to discover parallel but different techniques of his own. When in the autumn of 1920 he first read Huxley's *Leda* poems, for instance, he knew he was in the presence of work that somehow he must account for: "They strike me as dry and very clever,—but is real poetry so obviously clever? Modern life and its vanity seems to me to be responsible for such work. There is only a lime or a lemon to squeeze or a pepper-pot left to shake. All the same I admire his work very much. He comes in the line of Eliot and Sitwell. Eliot's influence threatens to predominate the new English." William Carlos Williams also was a voice Crane felt compelled to deal with; his *Kora in Hell*, which Crane bought late in January, seemed "a book for poets alone, as I see,—meaningless to a large extent to most people, but very suggestive and, to me, stimulating."

Doing his best to steer a course somewhere between Eliot on the one hand and Williams on the other, Crane worked hard to evolve his own style. Not all his friends grasped what he was getting at. Sherwood Anderson, for example, saw "Black Tambourine" primarily in sociological terms.

It seems to me that your poem has now real charm and meaning.

Still I wonder if the American negro is quite lost in mid air between Africa and our stupid selves. Sometimes I think he alone is not lost. I don't know.

Doesn't one have to be careful here? A figurative impulse comes that has beauty as a figure. Perhaps that is enough but I have never found it to be enough for me. . . .

Still I don't quarrel with your conception. It may be the true one and you've got beauty into the singing of it. Remember only that the black man above all men knows song physical. The tambourine cuts small figure with him.

Munson had almost as much trouble with the poem as Anderson, finally asking point-blank for an explanation. Crane's answer was carefully phrased. He wanted, he made clear, not to be limited by a single "meaning"—the sort of meaning, for instance, that Anderson had found. Instead, he wanted the poem to be viewed as an object. Crane, who by the time he wrote Munson had met and already been greatly influenced by the Cleveland artist William Sommer, insisted that the basic achievement in the poem was an achievement in presentation—and he explained himself, as he would increasingly from now on, in terms borrowed from the fine arts.

The Word "mid-kingdom" is perhaps the key word to what ideas there are in it. The poem is a description and bundle of insinuations, suggestions bearing on the negro's place somewhere between man and beast. . . . The value of the poem is only, to me, in what a painter would call its "tactile" quality,— an entirely aesthetic feature. A propagandist for either side of the negro question could find anything he wanted to in it. My only declaration in it is that I find the negro (in the popular mind) sentimentally or brutally "placed" in this midkingdom . . .

Perhaps the strangest poem he turned out in these ambitious days was "The Bridge of Estador," a pastiche of lines rejected from other poems, fragments of work in progress, and fragments that would eventually be worked into as yet unwritten poems. Crane, conscious that he was assembling a literary collage, merrily subtitled it "An Impromptu, Aesthetic TIRADE," and above the title put a symbolic little diagram that looked like a ten-spoke bird cage settled onto a horizontal cross. At the intersection of the cross Crane drew a nice, firm X. Though in itself a minor effort, his poem acted as a reservoir for the future. Bits of "Episode of Hands," and the Gargantua-and-Pierrot phrase I have already quoted (eventually part of "Praise for an Urn"), were thrown in with lines that would later be crucial to "Faustus and Helen," "At Melville's Tomb," and *The Bridge*.

Crane put so much local scenery into "The Bridge of Estador" that a realistic reading almost forces itself on one. All the sun and moon references, which culminate finally in Gargantua's laughter and Pierrot's happy-sad eyes, give one element of the poem away. And the warehouse, the factory, and the lake bordering Cleveland offer another. So when Crane admonishes in his second stanza "Do not think too deeply, and you'll find / A soul, an element in it all," he probably means what he says. The soul of "Beauty's fool," the poet, the man who is "twisted with the love / Of things irreconcilable," finds himself caught up in a love affair involving all the opposites of his world. Gargantua's sun wars with and loves Pierrot's moon. The sun-streaked factory wars with and fits into a landscape of slant moon and slanting hill. Linking the opposites will be imagination's "bridge of Estador / Where no one has ever been before," but from which the poet—the lover of irreconcilables—can achieve his necessary perspectives and so bring order into chaotic daily life.

With considerable time on his hands, Crane turned to a widening group of friends both for companionship and for literary and artistic discussions.

"Literary" acquaintances were at first in the minority, though one of them, Sam Loveman, proved in the long run to be a most dependable friend. Ten years older than Crane and recently discharged from the army, Loveman was in many ways diametri-

cally opposed to his enthusiastic, unpredictable young acquaintance. A man widely read in French and English literature, particularly in the Romantic poets, Loveman at first struck Crane
as "a poet who can do nothing but sigh out 'Keats' and 'Swinburne' in depreciation of anything modern you show him." Both
Loveman and Crane were born storytellers, and between them
they shared a whole world of literary gossip. Crane had at
his fingertips all the most recent anecdotes passed on by Munson
and Anderson; and Loveman, at work on a biography of the
novelist Edgar Saltus, could reconstruct eloquently the flavor of
an earlier literary generation. The friends met often at Laukhuff's bookstore, where they were sometimes joined by Bert
Ginther, and then went either to Crane's apartment at the Del
Prado or to Ginther's apartment, debating endlessly the virtues of
traditional and modern literature.

Crane was deep in a systematic reading of Dostoevsky. Earlier he had read *Crime and Punishment* and *The Possessed*;
now he turned to *The Brothers Karamazov* and J. Middleton
Murry's study. Munson had suggested the project, and all through
the early months of 1921 Crane faithfully reported his reactions.
"He *does* give one more life than my mundane world supplies,—
and stimulates. He makes you forget yourself (should I better say,
lose) in the life of his characters for days at a time. And how few
writers can do that!" "What marvelous psychology!!! A careful
reading of 'Dosty' ought to prepare one's mind to handle any
human situation comfortably that ever might arise." "He is all-
absorbing, and somehow his offering is such a distinct type of itself that one doesn't want to mix any other kind of reading with
it."

Crane did, however, interrupt his pursuit to read Sherwood
Anderson's *Poor White* and then was delighted to hear from
Anderson that Dostoevsky was his own favorite author. ("Had I
known you had not read him I should have been shouting at
you long ago. . . . There is nothing like *Karamazov* anywhere else
in literature, a bible. . . . I have always felt him as the one
writer I could go down on my knees to.") Crane was quite as
enthusiastic about *Poor White* as he had been about Anderson's
earlier work. "It fascinated me as much as 'Winesburg' and this
in spite of a great fear of disappointment," he wrote Munson.

> I wish after you have read it we might have a fireside hour
> over the book. We might agree perhaps on the exquisite work
> of such scenes as the description of the murderer-saddlemaker
> sitting by the pond and rocking gently to and fro (the sim-
> plicity of A's great power of suggestion is most mocking to
> the analyst)—and the scene where the sex-awakening girl
> hears the men in the barn in speaking of her say,—"the sap
> is mounting into the tree." Nature is so strong in all the work

of Anderson, and he describes it as one so willingly and happily surrendered to it, that it colors his work with the most surprising grasp of what "innocence" and "holiness" ought to mean. Also, his uncanny intuition into the feelings of women (a number of women have remarked to me about this) is very unusual.

Crane's own letter to Anderson is missing, but something of its quality can be suggested by Anderson's response: "When a man publishes a book there are so many stupid things said that he declares he'll never do it again. The praise is almost always worse than the criticism but you know how to take a story naturally and simple and how to react naturally and simple. It does one good."

His range of reading broadened by the recommendations of Anderson, Munson, Loveman, and Laukhuff, Crane found himself reexamining aesthetic values. But not all his ideas came from literature. Like many other men of his generation, Crane expected the fine arts to point a new direction for the arts in general. Here his conversations with Minns were of the greatest importance. After each visit to Akron he would return filled with new ideas. "When you get a chance, see the new monograph on Jacob Epstein including fifty photos of his works," Crane wrote Munson. "He seems to be much better than most of Rodin, and I'm enthusiastic almost to the point of silliness."

But there was plenty in modern art that he disliked. He particularly objected to the excesses of the new Dada movement. "I hear 'New York' has gone mad about 'Dada,'" he wrote Josephson, "and that a most exotic and worthless review is being concocted by Man Ray and Duchamp, billets in a bag printed backwards, on rubber deluxe, etc. What next! This is worse than The Baroness. By the way I like the way the discovery has suddenly been made that she has all along been, unconsciously, a Dadaist. I cannot figure out just what Dadaism is beyond an insane jumble of the four winds, the six senses, and plum pudding. But if the Baroness is to be a keystone for it,—then I think I can possibly know when it is coming and avoid it."

Making a special trip to Akron to discuss Dada, Crane was overjoyed to find Minns echoing his own contempt. "I read him the opinions of Man Ray," Crane told Munson, "whereat he flew into a holy rage. 'There is no sense in the theory of interesting "accidents."' And I am with Minns in that. There is little to [be] gained in any art, so far as I can see, except with much *conscious* effort." Man Ray, they agreed, "seems to have done much good work so far, but it has been in spite of his 'ideas.'" And they agreed too that "if he is just recently infected it is too bad, because there is less chance of him sustaining his qualities under such theories." "If he doesn't watch his cards[?]," Crane concluded, "M. Ray will allow the Dada theories and other flamdoodle of his section [to] run him off his track." Though their final products might resemble one another, Crane's art would be an art of deliberate arrangement—all of its effects calculated; the Dadaist's anti-art, spontaneous enough but essentially meaningless, would be capricious, by its very nature trivial.

Dada, nevertheless, was riding high; and in letter after letter Crane went out of his way to renew his attack. Munson and Josephson, both interested in the new movement, continued to pass on to Crane samples of recent Dada accomplishments, entertained always by Crane's vehement outbursts against "the wet-dream explosions" of writers like Robert McAlmon. "Their talk is all right,—" he explained, "but what is true of it has been said adequately before,—and all they can seem to add is a putrid remnant or two."

> Perhaps I am on the downward grade, but when I come to such stuff as theirs I can only say, "Excuse me." I will be glad to receive stimulation from the sky or a foctid chamber or maybe a piss-pot, but as far as I can make out, they have wound their *phalli* around their throats in a frantic and vain effort to squeeze out an idea. In fact they seem very "Dada" in more sense than one.

Crane reacted strongly to this and other European art movements, but it was the artist Bill Sommer, whom Crane met through Sam Loveman, who had the most lasting impact on his aesthetic development. When, toward the end of March, Loveman showed Crane some of the drawings and water colors Sommer had given him, Crane was beside himself with excitement. Here, he felt, was an extraordinary talent that was known to no one outside a small circle of friends; he begged Loveman to arrange a meeting.

Sommer himself, older than Crane's father, seemed to Crane, when they finally met, artist-incarnate. Unpretentious, cheerful, interested neither in fame nor in money, Sommer asked only to be allowed to devote all his free time to painting. Sketching anywhere and everywhere he went, he would cover envelopes, menus, backs of letters with drawings, all the time carrying on a conversation studded with quotations from Blake, Roger Fry, Cézanne, and Clive Bell.

Discovering him in Cleveland seemed to Crane pure miracle, and within a week he had shipped off extravagantly enthusiastic letters to everyone he knew in New York City who conceivably might be of use in building for Sommer a national reputation. Letters went out to such likely persons as Joe Kling, still editor of *The Pagan*, and also to such relatively unlikely ones as Josephson, Anderson, and Munson. Everyone Crane knew who might publicize or purchase Sommer's work eventually heard from him.

Something of Crane's feeling can be caught in an April 10 letter to Munson.

I have lately run across an artist here whose work seems to carry the most astonishing marks of genius that have passed before my eyes in original form. That is,—I mean present-day work. And I am saying much I think when I say that I prefer Sommer's work to most of Brzeska and Boardman Robinson. A man of 55 or so—works in a lithograph factory—spent most of his life until the last seven years in the rut of conventional forms—liberated suddenly by sparks from Gauguin, Van Gogh, Picasso and Wyndham Lewis etc. I have taken it upon myself to send out some of his work for publication, an idea that seems, oddly, never to have occurred to him. An exhibition of his work in N.Y. would bring him in something and I wish I could only be there to do something for him. . . . If I ever get time I want to send some of his better things to the Dial and give them some *real* material for reproduction. They have, so far, brought out only a few worth while things in drawings. What a damned pity there are so few channels for such work to get to people here.

Spending as much time as he possibly could with the older man, Crane listened sympathetically to Sommer's life story. He had been born in Detroit in January 1867, the first son of a pair of cheerful, easygoing German immigrants. He had little formal schooling, having been forced to withdraw from school halfway through his thirteenth year. His art training had, however, begun well before that time in Julius Melchers's Sunday morning art class. It was Mr. Melchers, father and first teacher of the American artist Gari Melchers, who persuaded young Bill that in one form or another drawing was to be his life work. And when Bill's father was no longer able to contribute the seventy-five cents a month fee for the lessons, it was Mr. Melchers who had announced, "Well, you come anyway, Bill," and had talked Bill's father into apprenticing his son with the Calvert Lithography Company for a seven-year term. Here, sketching and drawing, Bill learned his trade. He left home as soon as that apprenticeship was over, going first to Boston as a journeyman lithographer, then to New York and poster illustration, then, in 1890, to England. There, after a year's work in London and in Nietherfield, he ran into a remarkable piece of good luck. A close friend, Fred Hager, had come into an inheritance and insisted on using part of it to finance several years of art study for Bill at the art school of Ludwig von Herterich in Munich. Refreshed but impoverished, Sommer returned to New York, once more turning to lithography for a living. Here, at the age of twenty-seven, he met and married Martha Obermeyer, did his best to provide her with the funds to raise their three sons, and exasperated her regularly with his forgetfulness, his irresponsible rejection of all household chores, and his occasional drinking sprees. She was, however, the cornerstone of his life, quiet, always dependable. It was as much to earn her a present as for any other reason that in 1907 Sommer accepted a job with the Otis Lithography Company of Cleveland, the company guaranteeing transportation for the family and, as a bonus, a $500 fur coat for his wife. Working six days a week and painting on Sundays, Sommer debated theory and technique of painting with his shopmate, William Zorach, and with their friend Abe Warshawsky, just back from Paris. When Zorach took off for Paris and returned with news of the abstract art that was sweeping all before it, Bill immediately responded to the new stimulus, producing sketches and water colors altogether different from most of the work being produced in America. Years later, after Sommer's death, Zorach tried in a letter to reconstruct the feel of these years: "Bill was always interested in new developments," he wrote, ". . . and asked me at length what was going on and what was doing in Paris. (Remember this was before the Armory Show and even the impressionists were considered wild men in art circles in New York and only a very small group knew of what was going on in Paris at this time.) . . . Bill immediately swung into the more abstract type of painting—and I remember how fed up he got working day and night in the shop . . . how depressed he was and how desperate to get some painting done on Sundays—and holidays."

By 1914, through industrious skimping, Bill and his wife had managed to save $1,200. They used all of it to buy a house for themselves and, nearby, an abandoned one-room schoolhouse. Here, in the rolling farm country along Brandywine Creek, Sommer established his studio. Jugs of cider, apples from the orchards that came right up to the schoolhouse, a wind-up phonograph that groaned out Wagner and alternated with a pianola as a source of music, pipes in ashtrays, horses and cows grazing in the orchard, the visiting Dominski children, Mrs. Sommer peeling potatoes— all became subjects for Sommer's Sunday painting.

A short, wiry man of enormous creative vitality, Sommer, by the time Crane knew him, had built up a local reputation; but it was a reputation for friendship, generosity, philosophical curiosity (his studio was littered with scraps of paper bearing quotations from Kant, Hegel, Nietzsche), for fellowship with younger artists and writers.

Crane determined to put this situation to rights. Sommer, he felt, deserved recognition; Crane was the man to see that he got it.

Before Crane could do more than get his project under way, however, he found himself again caught up in difficulties with his father and mother. He had had his emotional holiday, days of happiness that he would always look back on, days of un-complicated security and good will. Then the old chaos descended. In early April his mother returned from her winter vacation to open up her house, and Crane moved out of his apartment and set-tled once more in his third-floor tower. Mother and son talked over at great length the kinds of work he had done for his father, the significance of his current job in the basement of the Euclid Avenue store, the indignities real and imaginary that had as a result come his way, the reaction of friends and neigh-bors to his failure to be promoted in the business.

Word quickly filtered back to Mr. Crane that mother and son were resentful of the "mistreatment" of Hart. And Mr. Crane, who had in fact in these months been leniency itself, decided once more to look into his son's affairs. On one visit to the store he found Hart comfortably settled in his storeroom, book in hand, notebook propped up beside him. Hart, his father decided, had become too lax. Hart was told that he was hired to work, not to loaf, that there would be no more on-the-job reading and writing. Visibly upset, Mr. Crane marched out of the store. For a week the divided family held itself in an armed truce. Then, on the morning of April 19, Hart's seething feelings and his father's came to a head. The truce ended. Insults and shouts, wounded vanities, fears, jealousies, resentments had their day.

# 10

What was said by Hart and by his father on that April morning in 1921 will never be known. Whatever it was, it was enough to cut off communication between them for two years.

Nearly fifteen years after the event, Grace Crane tried to reconstruct it for Philip Horton's biography. Hart, she said, had wandered from the storeroom to chat with his friends in the kitchen of the store and to join them for a late breakfast of toast and coffee. As they talked, their jokes and stories filled the big kitchen with good-natured laughter, and none of them saw Hart's father descend the basement stairs.

C.A. may have seen Hart's performance in the kitchen as a serious loss of dignity for himself; but since C. A. Crane was known by most of his staff as a congenial employer, himself fond of making jokes and telling stories, the severity of his reaction seems out of character. In any event, he reprimanded Hart, ordered him to return to the storeroom, and, as Hart turned to go, added that since Hart was again living with his mother, he could eat his meals with her, too.

Hart interpreted the remark as an attack both on himself and on Grace. He whirled to face his father, threw the storeroom keys on the floor, and, in front of the other help, yelled that he was through with C.A. for good. C.A., by now as angry as his son, turned white with rage, shouting that if Hart didn't apologize he would be disinherited. Hart climaxed the scene by screaming curses on his father and his father's money and rushing blindly from the store, his face beginning to break out with red hives.

By the time he reached home, Grace remembered, his face was distorted almost beyond recognition. He ran past her, slammed up to his room, and refused to answer her pleas to let her in. Finally she persuaded him to allow her to put him to bed, and as she pulled the shades and straightened the room, she listened to his almost incoherent account of the morning's confrontation.

For the whole day Hart lay in bed fretting about the scene, going over the charges and countercharges, doing his best to justify his violence. By the morning of the next day, he had managed to see his stand as heroic. By afternoon, he was almost gleefully hearing reports of C.A.'s anger. By evening, he was sitting down to write Munson an exultant account of what he now saw as a brave and necessary act of defiance. The entire letter is worth quoting, for it reveals the self-dramatization Hart was capable of and at the same time his capacity to drop out of his posture of righteous indignation into a casual discussion of his latest literary effort.

April 20th

Dear Gorham: —

Your letter did me good, and has left a good hangover for me for the last few ungenerous days. I left my father's employ yesterday *for good*—nothing, I think, will ever bring me back. The last insult was too much. I've been treated like a dog now for two years,—and only am sorry that it took me so long to find out the simple impossibility of ever doing anything with him or for him.

It will take me many months, I fear, to erase from memory the image of his overbearing head leaning over me like a gargoyle. I think he had got to think I couldn't live without his aid. At least he was, I am told, furious at my departure. Whatever comes now, is much better than the past. I shall learn to be somewhere near free again,—at least free from the hatred that has corroded me into illness.

Of course I won't be able to get to N.Y. now for any summer vacation. You know what a privation that means to me. I have nothing in sight in the way of employment,—and as times are so bad,—I don't know when I shall. A job as copywriter for an advertising house will probably be open to me about June 1st. And there is a new newspaper opening out here soon,—perhaps that may yield me something. I have a roof over my head and food anyway—here at home—and maybe I shall write something. The best thing is that the cloud of my father is beginning to move from the horizon now. You have never known me when it has not been there—and in time we *both* may discover some new things in me. *Bridges burnt behind!*

Glad you like "Estador." I'm beginning to myself. I cannot quite accept your word changes although I'm far from satisfied with it. But the more I work over it the less I seem likely to be,—so I'm going to try it on the "Dial."—Anything for some money now.

Write soon<br>Hart

Through most of the time he spent at home, Hart's feelings toward C.A. continued to be harsh; but he consoled himself by gradually shifting all responsibility for his quarrel away from himself and his mother and over to C.A. "I am also glad, in a way, that I gave him the trial I did," Hart wrote Munson. "I should always have felt rather dis-satisfied without having done so." A little later, Hart would be more explicit in his denunciation: "Two years thrown away at the feet of my father without the gain of a jot of experience at anything but peon duties in a shipping room! I can never forgive him, nor my own foolishness."

For several weeks Hart's mood of heroic defiance held. Encouraged by his mother to rest and to read, he settled comfortably into his room, and though he wrote Munson that he was "facing . . . the acutest difficulties of unemployment," that, if nothing else turned up, he might "take work running automobiles around a garage," his efforts to find work were relatively feeble. He had good reason to hope that the copy-writing job he had mentioned would in fact materialize; in the meantime, he took what he privately felt was a well-earned vacation.

By the end of a month's unemployment, however, he was becoming restive, and Grace was going out of her way to remind him that her own resources were not entirely unlimited.

He had, as a matter of fact, picked a particularly bad time to break with his father. America was caught in the midst of a brief but severe postwar depression, and almost all industries were laying off rather than taking on men. When Crane wrote Munson, "There is absolutely nothing doing here," he was not exaggerating. Even his expectations of landing the replacement job in the local advertising firm were beginning to fade, for friends, he realized, sometimes promise more than they are able to deliver: "Most friends and friendly offers have proved themselves such slippery fish!"

Early in June he did finally put in a few days with the local advertising house, but he found himself in no way ready to do the work expected of him. Officially a copy writer, he was immediately reduced to a glorified office boy and was then dropped from the staff. "No job in sight even now!" he wrote Munson. "I'm about convinced of the hopelessness of the advertising plan. Business gets worse and worse and they haven't enough to do to keep a new man busy."

All through June, July, August, September, October, and November, Crane trudged a dusty, hopeless round, pursuing faint leads that vanished before he could get them fairly in sight. In this six-month period his total income from "productive labor" was precisely $2.50—earned on October 5, when, for that day only, as "foreman" of three men distributing advertising matter, he "walked untold miles of city blocks." (Memories of those miles undoubtedly convinced him a few months later to withdraw an application for work as a Cleveland postman.) A one-week career as commission real-estate salesman for the S. H. Kleinman Realty Company netted him, early in November, nothing at all.

It is no wonder that Crane was discouraged. "I feel terribly in the dark at present," he wrote Munson on the first of November. "Can't write a thing,—and no work and worried. Wonder if this sitting on the wall will ever end for me—?" Three weeks later his spirits had dropped lower still: "There is nothing but gall and disgust in me,—and there is nothing more for me to tell you but familiar, all-too-familiar complaints. I wish I could cultivate a more graceful mask against all this."

Crane did, however, put himself briefly to school. His painful experience in June had convinced him that something more than self-education was needed for a potential copy writer, and in the autumn of 1921 he registered in a Western Reserve evening-school course which, he hoped, would ready him for the only kind of work he could at this time visualize for himself. The course met two nights a week, ran through May of the following year, and offered at its completion "a diploma which, I understand, has a real value." (Several years later Crane was to cite as college background this "diploma" from Western Reserve when he applied for a job—successfully—with the New York advertising firm of J. Walter Thompson.) The course, he felt, was "very good." "I am now pretty sure of making advertising my real route to bread and butter, and have a strong notion that as a copy writer I will eventually make a 'whiz.'" Eventually, of course, Crane did become a copy writer—and, though not a whiz, he earned most of his lifetime's bread and butter in one advertising firm or another.

In the spring of 1921, however, work of any kind was more than half a year in the future for Crane, and in his enforced leisure he consolidated his close friendships with Bill Sommer, Sam Loveman, Bert Ginther, and Richard Laukhuff; and he went on to meet and see a great deal of a wide circle of new friends.

It was at this time that he first met Hazel Hutchison, then an active member of the Cleveland Playhouse and later, as Collister Hutchison, an eloquent poet. At this time, too, he met a young Russian librarian, Peter Keisogloff, and shared with him enthusiastic conversations about literature and about the paintings of Bill Sommer, which they both admired. Kay Kenney, a vivacious, enormously talented girl who seemed the focus of every group in which she moved, was often in these days Crane's happiest companion as, singing, laughing, alive with irrepressible wit, they would turn their troubles into comedy. "The great laughter which was Hart's most distinctive and charming feature," she recollected in 1962, "has never, to my knowledge, even been touched. Not really. And yet, it colored and saved, (I am certain,) him to the end of his life."

Certainly it was this laughter rather than Hart's troubles which all the friends of this time recall most vividly. For Bob Bordner, a young newspaperman and art enthusiast, who, with Jake Falstaff and Jake's wife, Hazel Stevenson, would come up from Akron on Sundays to meet at Bill Sommer's Brandywine studio, Hart was a person of riotously happy good times.

There in Sommer's studio, the pot-bellied stove roaring in winter and on brisk spring days, every window flung wide on summer afternoons and nights, the crowd of Cleveland and Akron artists and writers would congregate. It was always a meeting of easy informality, Crane sometimes wandering off for long walks along the Brandywine with Ray Sommer, Bill's youngest son, or sometimes joining Edwin to haul in wood and coal for the kitchen range or, in autumn, jugs of cider, apples, and big jars of honey. The Sommer boys were all close to Crane's age—young Bill three years older, Edwin precisely Crane's age, and Ray three years younger—but it was Bill himself whom everyone came to see, and the boys—on visitors' days—more often than not made themselves scarce. William Jr., in fact, remembers only one real meeting with Crane. "I remember I had just finished a kidney tilt top table of walnut with tripod legs that tapered toward the toes and I was proud of it and took it down to show my father. Crane was there and my father was anxious for me to leave. At other times when Crane was there my mother would say not to go to the studio."

Bill's sons and his wife, all of whom worked hard to keep the family from going under, must sometimes have resented the crowds who would assemble these weekend days around the big studio table; but if they did, they managed not to show it. Bill was the star of the family: tilted back in his chair, a pitcher of cider on the floor beside him, he held court. In the background was Martha, who—earthy, warm, generous—saw to it that everyone had enough to eat. Sommer's visitors once in a while came equipped with jugs of prohibition wine, but they brought little else. It was Martha's garden in summer, and in winter the spare cash she got from selling cider and vinegar, which really fed the visitors.

Sommer and Crane, both walking anthologies of the poetry they had memorized over the years, would alternately declaim verses and analyze them. For a while at least they devoted some of these sessions to a calculation of how the visual, verbal, and musical arts are interrelated. These meetings, Bob Bordner said, were for everybody great times of "mighty talking" that would often begin at noon and go on until it was time to hike the two miles down the road to the Interurban stop and there catch the last trolley to town. I asked Bob if he could put down for me his recollections of one of these midnight walks, and he answered that no two visits to Sommer's place were alike, that no visit was "typical." One night, however, did stand out in his memory.

Crane, Sommer and I were walking on the dirt road under a starry early winter sky from Brandywine to the Interurban car line. (We used to have to light a torch of newspapers and wave it so the motorman would stop.) We had been listening to Bill's Bach records, and Bill was declaring he could SEE in color the various movements of the music as it was played.

Bill would bellow out certain of the phrases and holler "Seee. See. That's red shading off into purple now," and so on.

Crane was fascinated and we got into whether poetry could be heard in colors too. . . .

They saw possibilities in my notion there might be mathematical relationships between the lengths of certain wave lengths of sound and light, or between speeds, or frequencies . . .

We wished we had a real musician to see if he could HEAR color, maybe.

But that hollering of Bach up a lonely night road, and arguing about such fantastics, was fairly typical of the highfaluting level of our youth.

For Crane these visits with Sommer were numbered among the great events of his life. He wrote of them, at length, to everyone he knew, so that all through 1921 and 1922 and well into 1923 his correspondence is dominated by Sommer's name. If Crane can be said to have had a "teacher," Sommer was that teacher. Sommer acted as surrogate father, counselor, drinking companion, confidant, infallible conversationalist. In Sommer, Hart found an equal, a man of genius whom he could talk to with absolute ease. Spiritually they were contemporaries, though Sommer was able to draw on fifty years of thinking about art, Crane on fifteen.

The intellectual foundation for their discussions could, of course, have been discovered by Crane in many places. At its most abstract, it was the long Hermetic tradition, the "neo-Platonic" tradition that runs as a fairly steady current beneath a wide range of Western painting and writing. Crane had already found some of its outcroppings in the English Romantic poets and the French symbolists—particularly Rimbaud—and he would soon be plowing through Ouspensky's *Tertium Organum*, an effort to support it in terms of current scientific theory. Later, encouraged by the poet Jean Toomer and Munson, he would look into—and reject—its emergence in the Gurdjieff movement.

For Crane was suspicious of any aesthetic theory that moved too far away from the real world. And in this he was seconded by Sommer. Both of them were convinced that any successful art must find a form inherent in things—a notion Sommer had discovered in Clive Bell and Roger Fry—but Crane and Sommer went on to emphasize that though form was crucial, the things in which the form was discovered were of equal consequence. Sommer's water colors—apples heaped on a plate, the children of his Polish neighbors, cows and horses in a field—were never so far from representational as to be unrecognizable . . . but they were also never so representational as to be photographic. And Crane's poetry—which relied for much of its strength on human character, on personality, and which gained its power by translating personality into the interrelated metaphors of poetry—superimposed an abstract, almost geometric, imagistic structure on a conversational, casual surface. Three of the thousands of passages Sommer invented or copied out from his books and which after his death littered his studio are pertinent.

Art is no longer a sensation that we take up with the eyes alone. Art is the creation of our spiritual, inward vision, nature just starts us off, instead of working with the eyes we conceive with the *subconscious* and thus the complete changing of nature.

. . . I take my pen drawing home and start in with color, and in the peace and quiet of the studio (I try for unity in the relationship of colour planes, keeping out shadows, not shading), prolonging forms that touch each other and in this way build a oneness that can be felt out of a Bach fugue or choral which has no beginning or end, just an arrangement of line and colour. Style can not be forced from our hand, it must come of itself as we see and drag the forms out of nature, the forms as we need them, not an imitation . . .

Everything that happens is intrinsically like the man it happens to. Intrinsic, inward, essential, real, inherent—within.

Building out of ideas like these an aesthetic which sought simultaneously for formal elegance and private vision, Sommer offered Crane wisdom. And Crane, who recognized in Sommer and in his art a brilliance that made everything else being done in America dull by comparison, accepted it with great humility.

If he was humble before Sommer's mind and art, he was not, however, humble before the man. Even before he had begun to make Sunday visits to Sommer's studio, Crane had arranged to spend one evening a week with Sommer in Cleveland. They would meet for dinner, often inviting Kay Kenney along. When Kay joined them, they would go to an inexpensive restaurant, "under the sidewalk," Kay recollected, where they could talk undisturbed for hours.

When they ate alone, Sommer and Crane would go up afterwards to Crane's room. "We do all kinds of stunts," Crane wrote Munson, "from Chopin Ballades and Heine lyrics to sparring with an old set of gloves I have." At one of these sessions Crane unearthed some of his schoolboy drawings and paintings and was thrilled to hear Sommer say he showed promise as an artist. Sommer particularly praised the freedom of line in some of Hart's sketches, and soon, under Sommer's casual direction, Crane was working on sketches and water colors.

The biggest events, however, were the Saturdays and Sundays at Sommer's studio. Though the paintings he had seen in Cleveland should have prepared him for those he was to see on his first visit, the sheer quantity and quality of Sommer's assembled work that he saw that day always remained in Crane's memory. He had spent all that bright June Saturday at Brandywine and when he returned at midnight to his tower room he was still drunk with excitement. "Well—it has been a day I shall not soon forget," he wrote Munson.

> I have just a little time since returned from my first visit to the Sommer farm and studio—about half way between here and Akron in a beautiful untrodden valley. He has an old old-fashioned school-house for his studio—the walls all white and hung with such an array of things as you never have seen. Forgive my enthusiasm—I have been so dazzled for the last 8 hours that I may seem somewhat incoherent in my expression. . . . I could picture a dozen N.Y. picture dealers in that studio today—radical or pedantical—all tearing each other's hair for the first chance of exhibiting such stuff. I feel convinced now that all that needs be done is to get some samples of this work before them,—and if they have any sense at all— either artistic or commercial—they will seize upon it.
>
> The oils are superb—and there are a great number of them. . . .
>
> "Dynamism" is the splendid and fitting word for Sommer— the word I had been looking for and got only as far as the adjectival use.

Finding in each of his visits "new wonders," "inspiration," "a breath of fresh air," "one gorgeous surprise after another," and pronouncing his friend a man "burgeoning every day the more with the wonderful genius he has," Crane devoted his free time to "placing" Sommer in a New York gallery.

The letters that he had sent off announcing his discovery were now rapidly followed by drawings and water colors to Kling's *Pagan* (which printed a drawing), to Margaret Anderson's *Little Review,* and to the editors of *The Dial* and *The Liberator.* But Crane needed someone who could act as a New York agent for Sommer; and he nominated Munson for the job.

> I have got Sommer to take some photographs of some of his oils, and as soon as they are out I want to send you copies. I feel sure of S's work as as important as any contemporary work anywhere, and I'm very interested to hear what you will

think. I wish I were better trained for analysis of this kind of work,—but as it is I can only "feel" the power of it.

Munson was almost as enthusiastic as Crane; and the two were soon making plans to launch Sommer as a major new discovery. Sommer turned over to Crane all the business details, even the pricing of the individual drawings and paintings. ("I do not claim any judgment on this myself," Crane explained to Munson, "but I don't want to put so large a price on his things at first as to deny all possibility of sale.") After a good deal of soul searching, Crane settled on a scale of $20 for life drawings, $25 for water-color portraits, and $30 for water-color "compositions."

By the end of June, Munson was able to make a progress report. He had bought one of Sommer's drawings himself, and he was doing his best to get DeZayas to exhibit a large selection or to see that someone else did. The project had about it a wonderful innocence, since neither Sommer nor Crane nor Munson knew quite how to go about interesting potential dealers. Letters asking questions and offering good advice shuttled back and forth, sometimes three or four a week. "Find out, if you can, what system these dealers are in the habit of using regarding framing etc.," Crane suggested. "Are pictures sent to them already framed, or, in some cases, are they framed at hanging, and at whose expense?" There was also the problem of the proper gallery, and the unsolvable problem of the "in" that would open the proper gallery to the paintings: "I am sure that if Bourgeois and Daniels could see them they would fall like rocks."

Munson—dutifully carrying drawings and water colors from potential customer to potential customer, though with never an immediate prospect of a sale—suggested that if the prices could be cut he would be able to place a few of the drawings with friends no wealthier than he. Some of the dealers had also rebelled at what they felt were high prices for an unheard-of artist. Crane, indignant, argued that by that kind of logic the paintings and drawings would eventually have to be given away.

> What you say about prices is right, but I cannot but think that $10.00 is a slaughter price for most of the things I'm now sending. Really—to offer such irreplaceable creations for the price of a silk shirt is too much! . . . It isn't going to be any point for S. to sell his stuff without realizing on a whole batch of things more than $100.00. . . . These prices as they are are what I should call vulgarly "dirt cheap" and in compromise satisfactory in a way—but *no lower*. These picture dealers are quite shrewd businessmen after all, I suspect.

For a few days toward the end of June, letter piled on letter. Crane would rush from the mailbox at home down to the Otis Lithography Company, where he would join Sommer for a quick

lunch, then home again to get off to Munson the latest suggestions or to pack up and send new drawings and paintings. Though
he didn't have the money to be a patron of the arts, Crane did
have the energy and enthusiasm to be the next best thing: a passionate propagandist. And his enthusiasm was infectious. He was,
he felt, for once in his life engaged in a noble undertaking. "Your
letter of this morning is encouraging," he wrote Munson on the
twenty-ninth.

> I have written DeZayas that you will bring in the 26 pieces
> you have no doubt received by this time, and that he is to keep
> them for a while to show to his clients, selling as many as he
> wants at the *net return of the price on each to the artist*. Aren't
> you delighted with this bunch!? .... Both S. and I are very grate-
> ful for all you have done about this matter and it is all the
> better that as you say, you have enjoyed it. I shall keep in
> touch with DeZ. and Daniel now and perhaps we can get an
> exhibition next fall. If we could realize enough to give Sommer
> a year's freedom from the drudgery of the lithograph fac-
> tory,—he would then have a real opportunity to realize his tre-
> mendous reach.

For all of Crane's enthusiasm, however, the project fell
through. Munson in midsummer returned the drawings he still
had and sailed for Europe. Slowly the drawings that had been
sent to magazines began to come back to Cleveland, too. Crane
told friends who were headed for New York to ask for the drawings that were still at the DeZayas gallery, but month after month
went by with no report from the gallery owners. His interest
in Sommer's work did not flag, but he was rapidly running out
of acquaintances. An August 13 letter to Charmion von Wiegand was one of his last attempts that year to interest a New
Yorker. Describing Sommer as a great painter, "really a master,"
he wrote for her what by now had become a form-letter capsule
biography: "He has worked most of twenty years, after studying
in Munich and Strassburg,—in a tiresome lithograph factory
here,—has lately become radical, (freed by Wyndham Lewis, Picasso, Roger Fry, Bell, etc.) and is turning out (really) superb
things. DeZayas and Daniel are enthusiastic about some of his
work that I sent the former, and if you care to go into DeZayas'
gallery and see some of his work it is there. Ask to see the drawings and water-colours by WM. SOMMER."

Just how enthusiastic DeZayas was, however, is open to question. Soon after getting Sommer's work he had shown it to Man
Ray, who did not care for it. From that time until mid-September, when Crane indignantly demanded its return, it had apparently remained in an unopened portfolio. This, Crane decided,
was the way of all dealers. "DeZayas has proved a fizzle," he wrote
Munson.

I wrote him at periods of a month apart three letters about the drawings—and without hearing a thing. Finally I wrote, asking him either to acknowledge the receipt of them or send them back. He wrote me then,—that he was sending them back. But that was two weeks ago—and they haven't arrived yet. Never again will I entrust those scurvy picture dealers that suck their sustenance by putting themselves between the artist and the public and bleeding them both. I shall be thankful to get the drawings after since hearing more about their sort, to which, I hear, there are few exceptions. This is too bad after all your work, Gorham, but I know you will take it as *fatefully* as the artist and I.

If, in 1921, "the artist" always seemed to be William Sommer, Sommer was by no means the only artist Crane was acquainted with. Perhaps the one he saw most frequently was a young man very close to his own age, a man "just eight months out of Paris, half Swiss, who is sophisticated in all the latest fads and who has helped me a great deal in my French reading." This was the architect William Lescaze, at that time a "promising young man" who had arrived in Cleveland in 1920—Cleveland, because once in Geneva he had owned a "Cleveland" bicycle.

Soon after his early-spring meeting with Crane in Laukhuff's bookstore, Lescaze had organized a weekly gathering of young men and women interested in the arts. Members of this new circle included a good many of Crane's friends—among them Bill Sommer and Sam Loveman—and new acquaintances brought in by Lescaze, among them Charles Harris, Lescaze's roommate, an engineer who in his free time composed poetry. Also through Lescaze, who was an excellent violinist, Crane became acquainted with Jean Binet, who in 1919 had come to America from Switzerland to teach eurythmics at the Cleveland Institute of Music and to study composition with the Cleveland Orchestra's new composer-conductor, Ernest Bloch. Six years older than Crane, Binet had already established a local reputation. "I am to meet him tonight," Crane wrote Munson on October 6, "and with some anticipations, as I am told he is a remarkable and inspired amateur pianist, playing Erik Satie, Ravel, etc. to perfection." The close friendship that developed continued until Binet returned to Switzerland in 1923.

Lescaze's group was always ready to engage in any sort of discussion about the arts, and though its meeting places varied—sometimes, Charles Harris remembered, dinner meetings would be held under the beamed ceilings of the New Amsterdam Hotel ballroom, and at other times, Sam Loveman remembered, there would be Saturday lunches among the potted palms of Klein's restaurant on Prospect Street—the tone of the meetings was always much the same. "We'd sit there for two hours, three hours, till the middle of the afternoon and then disperse," Loveman recalled. "And there was no dominating figure. I wouldn't say that Hart was the dominating figure. But everybody conversed, and everybody was happy. These things are very common in periods of creative activity, where a group springs up like a mushroom out of nothing. . . . They function for a certain amount of time, and then, like these natives that are born in the South Seas, they simply die of malnutrition. They disperse."

Crane was Lescaze's most faithful attendant, though he sometimes had reservations about just how much artistic progress could be accomplished at a party. "Tonight I attend the weekly 'salon' that Lescaze gives to his friends," he wrote Munson just before one of them.

> There will be banter and chatter enough to be tiresome. Somehow, when there are women present (the kind one has around here) no conversation can be had uninterrupted by little compliments, concessions to them etc. They insist upon being the center of attention irrespective of their ability to take part in any argument. Consequently there are interminable innuendoes and clucking and puffings that never terminate anywhere. One of the few women who would carefully avoid this kind of thing is Margaret Anderson. Homage to Margaret!!

He had no doubts at all about the private meetings with his new friend. "Lescaze has proved an inspiration to me," he wrote. "Knowing intimately the work of Marcel Proust, Salmon, Gide, and a host of other French moderns, he is able to see so much better than anyone else around here, the aims I have in my own work. We have had great times discussing the merits of mutual favorites like Joyce, Donne, Eliot, Pound, de Gourmont, Gordon Craig, Nietzsche etc. ad infinitum. After this it goes without saying that I never found a more stimulating individual in N.Y."

Sometimes, driving into the country in his mother's car, they would for hours wander the back roads, Crane quoting his favorite Elizabethans and Metaphysicals and Lescaze countering by quoting in French and then translating Baudelaire and Mallarmé. At other times, their conversation would turn to painting. "It amuses me to see Lescaze praise Sommer's work," Crane wrote Munson, "—there is all the differences between them that distinguish Baudelaire from Rabelais." Feeling that Lescaze's painting showed "a peculiar sharp diabolism in it," Crane considered him, after Sommer, one of the few painters of his acquaintance worth serious attention: "His work at a local exhibition here recently caused a terrible furor, being in company with Burchfield's, the only work worth looking at." Crane was therefore flattered when, on a Sunday morning in October, Lescaze paid a visit to his turret room and offered to make a sketch of him. Gleefully Crane changed records, smoked cigars, read samples of his poetry aloud, and speculated about the significance of Lescaze's art. When the portrait was done, he was overjoyed. "I have recently had myself futuristically sketched by Lescaze," he wrote Munson. "When I get some money I intend to have a few photographs made of it, and will send you one: I like the thing very much, although most of my friends insist on saying that I never look quite so insane as the picture suggests."

Feeling that he was part of an active, productive group of writers, painters, and musicians, Crane—on the surface, at least—led a happy, relatively uncomplicated existence. He managed in the spring and in the autumn to attend concerts by the Cleveland Orchestra, sometimes joining the musicians afterwards to discuss the merits of the performance. With Binet or with another new acquaintance, the composer Gordon Hatfield, whose cycles of art songs had just been published, Crane would talk about the correspondences he had discovered between poetry and music and would explain in detail his method of "translating" into poetry the music that roared out of his wind-up phonograph.

This was a year of discovery and consolidation for Crane. Only toward the end of the year did he write poetry worthy of his philosophy of art. He had managed early in the spring to assemble the graceful little poem "A Persuasion." But it was not, Crane felt, much of an accomplishment. Its best lines were recovered from discarded poems and its manner was reminiscent of a style he had already mastered. "Perhaps it seems a bit tame to me on account of having used several phrases coined some years ago in it," he explained to Munson. He submitted it first to *The Dial*, which rejected it, and then to *The Measure*, which somewhat to his surprise published it in October, probably through the intervention of Padraic Colum, who had admired the poem. Crane finally excluded it from *White Buildings*.

Though Crane produced no important poetry, he did write a little criticism. Late in May, the editors of the *Double-Dealer*, accepting "Black Tambourine," asked him to submit articles on contemporary writers. The first one he completed was on Sherwood Anderson. (He for a while also toyed with an article on Joyce, but he felt that his lack of formal academic training incapacitated him for the broad historical criticism that a Joyce piece might demand.)

In putting together the article on Anderson, he relied for a good deal of his material on chatty summaries of Anderson's correspondence. He also worked into his article his own new aesthetic preoccupations. When he praised Anderson for having achieved "work of distinct aesthetic achievement, an example of synthetic form," readers of Clive Bell and Roger Fry could nod their heads in happy agreement. Finding in Anderson not just realism but "a lyricism, deliberate and light, as a curl of milk

weed seeds drawn toward the sun," Crane discovered precisely
the qualities he was hoping to incorporate in his own poetry:
eloquence, precision, coherence. Most of all, he discovered a sincerity that produced unsentimental treatments of potentially sentimental material: "In Anderson there has been some great sincerity, perhaps the element of the 'soil' itself personified in him,
that has made him refuse to turn aside to offer the crowds those
profitable 'lollypops' that have 'made' and ruined so many other
of our writers."

Though Crane was finally persuaded by Munson and by Lescaze that the article was not very good (Lescaze, he told Munson, said that "reading it gave him the impression of a young
man inflating and playing with a series of variously colored bal-
loons in the boredom of his chamber"), Anderson and Basil
Thompson, an editor of the *Double-Dealer,* were enthusiastic.
What made Crane enthusiastic was being paid for something he
had written. Though $20 fees would hardly make him rich, they
would at least reduce his humiliating need to beg his mother for
spending money.

He got under way, at this time, a whole series of "free lance"
projects: a translation from Vildrac, "which, in the original
at least, is fine for the *Double-Dealer;* an article on Pound which
he hoped to be able to write in a style "suitable" for the popular magazine *Shadowland;* a play "on or around the figure of
John Brown." Most of these projects, Crane admitted, were begun
"for mere commercial reasons," and he worked on them only intermittently. Finally, offended by the kind of writing he saw in
the magazines he most admired, he decided good work was
more important than cash, and he discarded all thoughts of becoming a commercial success. "As a matter of fact," he wrote,
"I am continually being more and more horrified at what names
we had always been accustomed to hoping rather much of,—
are rushing into print with, and obviously out of the urgent need
or desire of mere money." Though he was now listed on the
stationery of the *Double-Dealer* as a regular contributor, he felt
no joy in his fame: "To my mind almost every issue has been
largely filled with utter weakness and banality." And yet this was
one of the best of the American magazines! The more popular
ones—neither fish nor fowl—tried to cross liberal politics with
"democratic" literature and produced, Crane felt, a mishmash of
jumbled prose. "Sommer said you had something in a very recent 'Freeman' which I've been trying to get, but guess I'm too
late," Crane wrote Munson.

> Sometimes I get so exasperated with the "intellectual" attitudes
> of these papers like the "Freeman," "New Rep.," "Nation," etc.
> where everything is all jumbled together,—politics, literature,
> painting, birth control, etc., etc., etc. that I ignore them for a

time and probably miss some good things. It's the way they are served that I object to—I'm beginning to be somewhat pained by this "Intelligencia" mood when it comes upon me. This probably indicates that I am not a very responsible individual—and truth is—*I'm not.* How tired I am of the perpetual ferment of the New Rep. Those fellows are playing a creative game nonsense. Does anything they ever say have any concrete effect? Old Washington goes on just the same on the old rotten paths. These gentlemen are merely clever at earning their livelihood in clean cuffs. But hear me rant on!!! I don't care two pence for the whole earth and heavens and least of all for politics. It's only when the political gentleman's Irish potatobeds obstruct my view of my petunias and hollyhocks that I'm thus aroused,—and even that is a small complaint in the long list of larger ones I have.

One of Crane's complaints was that he remained in Cleveland while all his friends were enjoying the heady Continental pleasures of the expatriate, Lost Generation. Almost everyone he knew was that spring packing his bags and heading for the docks. Josephson, Munson, Anderson, Kreymborg were all in Europe by midsummer. ("They all are—alas—but me," Crane wailed.) Charmion von Wiegand and her husband had been there, had returned, and were making plans to go back. And everyone wrote full, enthusiastic accounts of the good life that was to be had, of the carefree world where artists were respected, where living was cheap, where good wine—not the prohibition rotgut Crane was forced to search for in cellars and back alleys—could be had for a song.

For everyone else, the trip to Europe was so casually, so effortlessly accomplished that Crane, hard put to travel the twenty miles to Sommer's studio on the Brandywine, was green with envy. "A friend asked me to go to Paris and London in May and I decided to do it," Anderson had written, and then had sailed. Munson, one day a schoolteacher in Ridgefield, Connecticut, was a week later a "Citizen of the world!" ("There are so many things you will be doing and planning and seeing from now on that I'm afraid my letters will touch you weakly if at all. . . . But you must preserve the record of many a choice moment by writing me about it anyway," wrote Crane from his Cleveland attic. And he added, in a note written just before Munson sailed, "What a breath you will take!") With all the New World heading for the Old, Crane did his best to joke about the exodus ("Everyone seems to be going either sick, mad,—or to Europe. I much prefer the latest alternative"), but there was always the parallel theme: "How I envy you." "Living *is* at last becoming quite impossible. At least here," he wrote Munson.

When you get to Italy I advise a permanent residence there for you.

Later, perhaps I'll come over and join you. In time there may be only D. H. Lawrence, the Rainbow, and Capri left. I shall (with my millions acquired by that time in flattering biographies of rich businessmen)—I shall rejuvenate the baths and temple there of Tiberius and we shall live in state,—waited on by the only fair and unsullied youths and maidens then procurable in Europe.

Forgive my "alas-es" tonight and my dreams. I am more in need of the latter than the former, I fear.

He tried to imagine himself with his friends: "Everything must be very clear and bright,—I can picture myself quite dazzled, like an old bespectacled 'prof' crawling out of his study hole into an April day (of the better sort)." But he ended always with reality in front of him: "Yes,—we are, on this side, getting farther and farther away from the old world tang of cheese and wines. That is what makes the sky so blue over the Mediterranean—the diet affects the eyes."

"Yes," he wrote Munson, "I much wish I could share your horizons,—instead of retracing day after day a few familiar circles of routine and thought. Keep on writing me your bright kindly letters, they are a lantern of hope and a warmth to the heart. I sometimes wonder if, without you, I should have kept writing so long."

"I envy you." The note runs through all of the correspondence. But beneath it runs another note, a note of hope and of optimism. For Crane was, after all, a young man of twenty-two. He had ahead of him, he was sure, a full, long life. All of the Cranes lived long, long lives. "I envy you," he wrote his friend. "But,—someday—I have much time,—I'll take wing, too." For time, Crane felt, still lay ahead of him, who had consumed already all but a third of his days.

# I I

Europe seemed all the more attractive because in Cleveland Crane was putting in most of his free time "at the mercy of every domestic want that comes up." Fussed over by his grandmother and gently prodded by his mother into job-hunting expeditions, he was "in turn chauffeur, parlor maid, dish-washer and errand chaser." "And I really," he complained to Munson, "have been 'busy' in these foolish ways and directions."

Through all his time at home, but particularly during his extended unemployment, Crane was torn by complex feelings toward his mother and grandmother, especially toward his mother. In all their talks about C. A. Crane, talks more open even than those that had followed the divorce, Grace stressed the element of mental cruelty; and Hart, convinced that he had been victimized while he had worked for his father, supported and deepened her resentments. At the same time, however, he chafed under Grace's dinner-table conversation. He found especially hard to take her delicate reminders of his growing household debt. "Life here so close to my family is proving very hard," he told Munson, and went on to say that the "occasional spree" he used as a "protest" seemed to be about his only accomplishment. But even that was only momentarily satisfying: "I feel like a pauper in more ways than one, and long for some kind of job, enough money to buy smokes again and a new suit."

Summer brought hay fever, mosquitoes, and, in his attic room ("the only place in the house where I can escape constant interruption"), "inhuman heat." Under the circumstances, both mother and son saw far too much of each other. Each tried to make the best of a bad situation—sometimes gritting teeth to control frayed tempers—but finally each recognized that their hoped-for warm companionship was not, except on rare occasions, going to materialize. Crane never ceased admiring his mother for her fortitude, her "bravery," her willingness to sacrifice herself for his comfort and sometimes for his convenience; but he also, more and more, found himself telling friends of the little ways in which her anxiety for his happiness created, in fact, unhappiness for him.

Life with mother—especially during the early prohibition days of economic depression—made Europe seem attractive to him. But the decision of the town fathers to celebrate Cleveland's 125th anniversary on his own twenty-second birthday was for Crane the crowning, crashing climax to his pointless Cleveland life. "The 'march of events' has brought upon us Cleveland's 125th anniversary with all its fussy and futile inanities and advertisements to make hideous the streets," he wrote Munson.

> Blocked, and obliged to wait while the initial "pee-rade" went by today I spent two hours of painful rumination ending with such disgust at America and everything in it, that I more than ever envy you your egress to foreign parts. No place but America could relish and applaud anything so stupid and drab as that parade—led by the most notable and richest grafter of the place decked out in Colonial rags as the founder of the city Moses C. Ah—the Baroness, lunatic that she is, is right. Our people have no *atom* of a conception of beauty—and don't want it. One thing almost brought tears to my eyes, (and I hope you do not think me too silly in mentioning it)—the handful of Chinese who came along in some native and antique vestments and liveries to prostitute themselves in the medley of trash around them. To see them passing the (inevitable) Soldiers' Monument ablaze with their aristocratic barbarity of silk, gold and embroideries *was* an anachronism that could occur *only* in America. And the last of their "section" brought a float with a large "melting pot"—its significance was blazoned in letters *on* it!! All I can say is—it's a gay old world! If ever I felt alone it has been today. But I must encounter fireworks, bawling "choruses" and more "pee-rades" for 7 more days—as the community believes in celebrations that are productive of business.

Like it or not, Crane was, he realized, doomed to spend the immediate future in Cleveland . . . and in his mother's home. By the end of summer he was, if not reconciled, at least doing his best to put into practice the resolution he had made earlier in the year: "to regain a mental and spiritual status that has been lost to me for over a year. What I want to do is gather up the threads again and go on, to put it stale-ly. I have reached such blind alleys and found no way out of them that there is nothing at present for me to do but laugh a little and *endure*— which I hope to do."

As summer days shortened to autumn ones, Crane drifted into a mood that began to look, even to him, like happiness, tentative, provisional, but real. Early in August he could report to Munson, "I learn a Scriabin Prelude,—make a drawing,— stroke my black cat (a recent acquisition) and read intermittently." By the end of the month he could say, "My news is thin,—only I'm a little encouraged lately by having a poem (the last one you read) taken by 'The Dial,' and 'Porphyro in Akron' has lately come out in the 'D.D.' and in the place of honor. . . . Still out of work, but more resigned—and if my luck in mss. continues,—I may even become self-satisfied." By October he had lifted completely from gloom: "My terrible hay fever days are over, and the fine autumn weather that I like the best of the year has arrived to console me. My mood is neither happy nor desperately sad. It will best be conveyed to you by the quotation of a new poem, 'Chaplinesque'—only started (if I can help it) as yet . . ."

For finally it was his ability to write, once more to make words behave, that pulled him into a musing ease. In September he produced two of his finest poems ("Chaplinesque" and the first version of "Voyages I," "The Bottom of the Sea Is Cruel"), a translation of Gourmont's "Marginalia on Poe and Baudelaire," and a review of Shaw's *Back to Methuselah*. He was riding high. Regularly in attendance at his advertising course, playing piano, working hard at his painting—"I may (softly now!) send them [*The Dial* editors] a really good futuristic picture of mine (pastel-watercolor)"—reading, and, most important, writing, he felt not just busy but productively busy.

For "Chaplinesque," Crane knew, was in many ways a major accomplishment. The ingredients that went into it are easy to locate, most conspicuously those associated with Chaplin himself, whose *The Kid* had just been shown in Cleveland. Crane described his poem as "a sympathetic attempt to put [in] words some of the Chaplin pantomime, so beautiful, and so full of eloquence, and so modern," to find verbal equivalents for "the arrested climaxes and evasive victories of his gestures." "Comedy, I may say, has never reached a higher level in this country before. We have (I cannot be too sure of this for my own satisfaction) in Chaplin a dramatic genius that truly approaches the fabulous sort." When Munson described *The Kid* as sentimental, Crane was quick to defend the film. "Chaplin may be a sentimentalist, after all, but he carries the theme with such power and universal portent that sentimentality is made to transcend itself into a new kind of tragedy, eccentric, homely and yet brilliant." He saw in Chaplin's treatment of America a technique for turning the raw materials of American life—Cleveland's anniversary celebration, say—into an indigenous art.

If Chaplin and his "pliant cane" provided inspiration and framework for the poem, a good deal of private material was also worked into it, even such very private material as the pun on Crane's own name in the line "What blame to us if the heart live on." (That the pun was deliberate is made clear in a letter to Munson.) The third stanza's rejection of the businessman's money-counting gesture ("that inevitable thumb / That slowly chafes its puckered index toward us") probably linked, in Crane's mind, to his recent rejection of his father and his father's values. Even the "famished kitten" of the second and last stanzas seems to have been suggested quite as much by the stray black cat Crane had rescued from a Cleveland alley as by anything he had seen in *The Kid*. (When I asked Sam Loveman about the black kitten, he remembered not only how Hart had found it but even the circumstances of his naming it. "Oh, yes, a little vagrant kitten appeared on the scene—black like pitch, dark like midnight. And I said, 'Well, what are you going to call her?' He thought for a minute and he said, 'Agrippina.' . . . A few days later I said, 'How's your cat?' 'Oh, well,' he said, 'I'm not going to call her Agrippina. She's a male. I'm going to call her Agripenis!' ")

That the material of the poem had personal roots is of biographical interest; but what Crane made of it is infinitely more important. "I have made that 'infinitely gentle, infinitely suffering thing' of Eliot's into the symbol of the kitten," he explained to Munson, and went on to say that kitten linked to poet: "the pantomime of Charlie represents fairly well the futile gesture of the poet in U.S.A. today, perhaps elsewhere too."

Most of Crane's Cleveland friends found the poem difficult, and of his correspondents only Sherwood Anderson responded with unqualified enthusiasm. Bill Wright, who in a visit before returning to school had spent considerable time with Crane, regarded it as altogether mysterious.

Though the poem is difficult, it is not—as Crane's reply to Wright's letter makes clear—an impossible exercise.

> As you did not "get" my idiom in "Chaplinesque," I feel rather like doing my best to explain myself. I am moved to put Chaplin with the poets (of today); hence the "we." In other words, he, especially in "The Kid," made me feel myself, as a poet, as being "in the same boat with" him. Poetry, the human feelings, "the kitten," is so crowded out of the humdrum, rushing, mechanical scramble of today that the man who would preserve them must duck and camouflage for dear life to keep them or keep himself from annihilation. . . . I have tried to express these "social sympathies" in words corresponding somewhat to the antics of the actor. I may have failed, as only a small number of those I have shown it to have responded with any clear answer,—but on the other hand, I realize that the audience for my work will always be quite small. I freely admit to a liking for the thing, myself . . .

Part of what he liked was an achievement of an altogether technical nature. When he sent "Chaplinesque" to Wright, he had enclosed with it a short, chatty note. The poem had just been completed, and Crane had only two things to say about it: that he was still near enough to it to be enthusiastic, and that he was particularly happy about its subtle partial rhymes: "When I get near-rimes like 'pockets' and 'deposits' I am always gleeful."

Just as he felt his experiments with partial rhyme accounted for a significant part of the success of "Chaplinesque," Crane must have felt that his experiments with synesthesia in the somewhat slighter poem, "Pastorale," gave it such strength as it had. "Pastorale," which had been written in the spring and accepted by *The Dial* in midsummer, rendered autumn in terms of painting ("the year / Broken into smoky panels") and music ("this latter muffled / Bronze and brass"). Oddly related in its imagery to a passage from *Poor White* which Crane had quoted in his article on Anderson and praised in a letter to Munson (the passage which culminates in the phrase "the sap has begun to run up the tree" and which Crane associated both with sexual passion and with all "animal and earthy life"), the poem was, Crane felt, "more perfectly done" than "Chaplinesque" but "not so rich."

"The Bottom of the Sea Is Cruel," roughed out toward the end of September, was, on the other hand, Crane felt, "not nearly so good, to my mind, as my start on Chaplin, but has a certain crispness to recommend it." Discouraged by his own estimate and by a similar reaction from Munson and Anderson, Crane tucked his "sea poem" into his "incomplete" file. There it remained for two years until, resurrected as "Poster," it appeared in *Secession No. 4.* Even then, its career was not over. Never for long out of Crane's mind, it eventually became the first of the "Voyages" group, crucially important in introducing all the major themes, setting most of the principal images, and establishing a dominant tone of witty seriousness.

The route by which Crane had reached these new poems was in part a consequence of his reaction to the Dada movement. All through the year Crane and Josephson had carried on an erratic correspondence about the values of Dada, Josephson arguing that it offered the artist the possibility of working in new forms, Crane questioning just how valuable, in themselves, new forms were. ("The Dada dramas are tres amusant," Crane had written Munson, "—but—well—alright56789_____*!!") Nevertheless, Josephson's enthusiasm for Dada and his own doubts about it forced Crane to work out in some detail a theory of poetry that would allow for maximum "verbal richness" and yet express "modern moods."

I can say with J that the problem of form becomes harder and harder for me every day. I am not at all satisfied with anything I have thus far done, mere shadowings, and too slight to satisfy me. I have never, so far, been able to present a vital, living and tangible,—a positive emotion to my satisfaction. For as soon as I attempt such an act I either grow obvious or ordinary, and abandon the thing at the second line. Oh! it is hard! One must be drenched in words, literally soaked with them to have the right ones form themselves into the proper pattern at the right moment. When they come, as they did in "Pastorale" . . . they come as things in themselves; it is a matter of felicitous juggling!; and no amount of will or emotion can help the thing a bit. So you see I believe with Sommer that the "Ding an Sich" method is ultimately the only satisfactory creative principle to follow. But I also find that J. stirred up a hornet's nest in me this summer with his words about getting away from current formulae, from Heine to Wallace Stevens, by experimentation in original models, etc. and my reaction to this stimulation is to work away from the current impressionism as much as possible. I mean such "impressionism" as the Cocteau poem (trans.) in *The Little Review*, which you have probably seen. Dada (maybe I am wrong, but you will correct me) is nothing more to me than the dying agonies of this movement, maladie moderne. I may be even carried back into "rime and rhythm" before I get through provided I can carry these encumbrances as deftly and un-self-consciously as, say, Edward Thomas sometimes did. I grow to like my "Black Tambourine" more, for this reason, than before. It becomes in my mind a kind of diminutive model of ambition . . .

If Crane's new poetry was to be in part a reaction against Dada, it was also to be in part a reflection of the best of the past. Here too Josephson was important to Crane, for his enthusiasm for the Elizabethans brought Crane to a more careful reading of them than he had made earlier. "I've been having a wonderful time diving into Ben Jonson," he wrote Munson.

After one has read "Bartholomew Fair" it isn't so hard to see where Synge got his start,—a start toward a husky folk-element in the drama. I can see myself from now rapidly joining Josephson in a kind of Elizabethan fanaticism. You have doubtless known my long-standing friendship with Donne, Webster, and Marlowe. Now I have another Mermaid 'conjugal' to strengthen the tie. The fact is, I can find nothing in modern work to come up to the verbal richness, irony and emotion of these folks, and I would like to let them influence me as much as they can in the interpretation of modern moods,— somewhat as Eliot has so beautifully done. There are parts of his "Gerontion" that you can find almost bodily in Webster and Jonson. Certain Elizabethans and Laforgue have played a tremendous part in Eliot's work, and you catch hints of his great study of these writers in his "Sacred Grove" [sic].

I don't want to imitate Eliot, of course,—but I have come to the stage now where I want to carefully choose my most congenial influences, and in a way, "cultivate" their influence.

What Crane now wanted to write was poetry subtly flavored by the past (poetry of allusion rather than imitation), poetry that made use of variations on traditional forms and practices (partial rhymes, sprung rhythm, etc.—devices which extended traditional patterns rather than broke with them), poetry that allowed the poet to speak in a recognizably personal voice. He wanted his reader, coming on a new poem, to be able to say with assurance: Ah, this is by Hart Crane! When Crane wrote to Bill Wright, "I am only interested in adding what seems to me something really *new* to what *has* been written," he was speaking not of an extreme break with the past but of the careful transformation of the past which every major poet necessarily makes. That act of transformation, he felt—and here he is echoing Bill Sommer— could be accomplished only if the poet presented an "intensely personal viewpoint" in a "personal idiom." Otherwise, he would run either toward the pointless exhibitionism of the Dadaists or toward the slavish imitations of the hide-bound traditionalists. Wright, who felt Crane's poetry was "needlessly sophisticated," had compared it unfavorably to the clarity of Edna St. Vincent Millay. But Miss Millay, Crane felt, achieved her clarity at the sacrifice of individuality.

Unless one has some new, intensely personal viewpoint to record, say on the eternal feelings of love, and the suitable personal idiom to employ in the act, I say, why write about it? Nine chances out of ten, if you know where in the past to look, you will find words already written in the more-or-less exact tongue of your soul. And the complaint to be made against nine out of ten poets is just this,—that you are apt to find their sentiments much better expressed perhaps four hundred years past. And it is not that Miss Millay fails entirely, but that I often am made to hear too many echoes in her things, that I cannot like her as well as you do.

Crane made out for his friend two reading lists: one of poets who, in his opinion, were members of the "unusable" past; the other, of poets who were, for his purposes, of crucial significance:

I can come half way with you about Edna Millay,—but I fear not much further. She really has genius in a limited sense, is much better than Sara Teasdale, Marguerite Wilkinson, Lady Speyer, etc., to mention a few drops in the bucket of feminine lushness that forms a kind of milky way in the poetic firmament of the time (likewise all times);—indeed I think she is every bit as good as Elizabeth Browning. And here it will be probably evident that most of her most earnest devotees could not ask for more. I can only say that I also do not greatly care for Mme. Browning. And on top of my dislike for this lady, Tennyson, Thompson, Chatterton, Byron. Moore, Milton, and several more, I have the apparent brassiness to call myself a person of rather catholic admirations. But you will also notice that I *do* run joyfully toward Messrs. Poe, Whitman, Shakespeare, Keats, Shelley, Coleridge, John Donne!!!, John Webster!!!, Marlowe, Baudelaire, Laforgue, Dante, Cavalcanti, Li Po, and a host of others. Oh I wish we had an evening to talk over poetic creeds,—it is ridiculous to attempt it in a letter. . . . I am fond of things of great fragility, and also and especially of the kind of poetry John Donne represents, a dark musky, brooding, speculative vintage, at once sensual and spiritual, and singing rather the beauty of experience than innocence. . . .

Just for fun, look up the poems of Donne in the Library and read some of the short lyrics like The Apparition, A Jet Ring Sent, The Prohibition, The Ecstasy, and some of the longer things like The Progress of the Soul, etc., if you feel intrigued.

Refreshed by good weather, good literary production, good friends, and good reading, Crane set out once more in search of employment. Christmas was coming, and with it the possibility of temporary jobs. This time he was in luck. Korner and Wood, where five years before he had sold reproductions of paintings, had an opening in the book department.

In one respect, Crane's new job was an eye-opener. All his previous dealings with books had been as writer or as reader. Now, for a change, he was selling them.

Two weeks of book-service to the "demands of the public" in a store have bred curious changes of attitude toward the value of popularity (of the slightest sort) in my mind. The curious "unread" that slumber lengthily on the shelves, and whose names are never called, are much nearer my envy than I had once thought they might be from the mere standpoint of neglect. This pawing over of gift-book classics in tooled leather bindings etc. etc. is a sight to never forget. Poor dear Emerson must slumber badly. Aristocratic is Whitman, though,—no one ever calls for that "democrat" any more than for Landor or Donne. And Edgar Guest and Service, deaths heads both, are rampant.

A passing benefit of his job was the "company discount." Putting a healthy percentage of his salary back into the firm, he purchased, among dozens of other volumes, Wyndham Lewis's *Tarr*, Ben Hecht's *Erik Dorn* ("The book still puzzles me, which makes me dislike it a little more than ever. As a whole it is deficient, but I have always admitted certain parts good"), Sherwood Anderson's *The Triumph of the Egg* ("He has written of ghastly desolations which are only too evident in my own experience and on every hand. I am more enthusiastic than ever in my praise for him although I feel, in an odd way, that he has, like a diver, touched bottom in a certain sense, and that his future work must manifest certain changes of a more positive character than the bare statement of reality, to conclude his promise"), and Rémy de Gourmont's *Un Coeur Virginal.*

Crane was pleased to find Gourmont's book in Cleveland, though he was surprised that it had not been seized by the "jealous Puritan" censors who had made the *Little Review*'s serial publication of *Ulysses* such a capricious shambles: "I have snatched it up against its imminent suppression along with 'Jurgen' and other masterpieces. If this is a fair sample of its author, and it's supposed to be, I cannot see how his 'Physique d'Amour' translated by Pound and to be published by Boni & Liveright, will ever get beyond the printer's hands. Yet how mellow and kindly is the light from de Gourmont! One hates to see him on the tables with Zane Grey and Rex Beach."

Suppression was then very much in the air, and Crane, in his correspondence, fulminated against the dirty-minded guardians of the American public's morals. He was especially indignant at the shabby treatment that was being given *Ulysses*. Early in the year, as soon as publication of the first edition was announced, he sent in a reservation for a copy. But month after month went by, one delay after another pushed back the publication date, and the clamor for its banning rose to a crescendo. Like many other writers who regarded Joyce as the supreme genius of twentieth-century literature, Crane decided that the only way to get a copy was to have one smuggled in. "The 'Ulysses' situation is terrible to think on," he wrote Munson. "I shall be eternally grateful to you if you can manage to smuggle my already-subscribed-for copy home with you. . . . I *must* have this book!"

When at the end of 1921 Crane summed up the gains and losses of the year, gains, he was pleased to conclude, far outran losses.

There had been terrible times. During his unemployment he had been "weary and tormented"; the break with his father had produced much more of an emotional shock than he had anticipated; living at home with his mother—never easy for Crane—had been made even more difficult by his constant need to borrow from her; the second love affair of his life, though not so searing as the first, had worn gradually from passion into casual friendship.

But he had survived, and he had gained from the year lasting things. His friendships with Bill Sommer and Sam Loveman would be lifelong friendships. His recent work was, he knew, far above anything he had ever been able to produce before. He had gained enough of a reputation, both as a poet and as a personality, to have editors asking him to submit material—and he had had the great pleasure at one point of being able to report that every poem he valued was in print, that he was "sold out."

He had also managed with his recent earnings to pay back the most pressing of his debts and to be left with "a little change to spend during the last few weeks which has worked unbelievable miracles on my spirit." There was even a chance not only that his job selling books would continue but that he would have a choice of jobs. For his instructor in the advertising class liked him and went out of his way to recommend him to the Corday and Gross agency. Interviewed by "the 'authorities'" of the company on—of all days—Christmas morning, he had, he felt, made a very good impression. "If I can only manage to write them the proper kind of letter and 'sell myself' as they ridiculously put it, I may secure myself something profitable." The company, he told Munson, was a "very high-class" one that had "the best connections with the largest agencies in New York and elsewhere."

His life, compounded from friendship and from art, from affection and from words, was "a little better" than it had been. He was in good health and in good spirits, and though he lacked that essential commodity, "time (a natural requirement with me for all writing or thought) to sit Buddha-like for a couple of hours every day and let things sift themselves into some semblance of order in my brain," he had a great many of the other ingredients of happiness.

For he felt that at last he was part of a world of artists and writers of potential greatness. Some of them—Anderson, who had just won the *Dial* prize; Padraic Colum, with whom he was again in correspondence—were men of established reputation. Others, he was sure, would soon establish themselves—Josephson, for instance, who seemed to Crane a man "cold as ice, having a most astonishing faculty for depersonalization,—and on the other hand . . . a certain affectionate propensity in his nature that is doubly pleasant against the rather frigidly intellectual relief of the rest of him." Still others, he knew, would achieve fame only if someone pushed them to it. (In the last group was Bill Sommer. "If I were only in N.Y. I should see to it that S's work were given its due,—but that time will have to wait.") His friends, he felt, blazed with creative power.

Not the least of these friends was Gorham Munson, whose letters of encouragement and information—gossipy, cheerful letters—were for Crane documents to be saved and savored. It was to Munson in Europe that Crane turned when, on Christmas day 1921, in the midst of "a houseful of indiscriminate relatives," he catalogued the profit and loss of that year, and it was Munson, in his final ordering of acquaintances and friends, who was awarded top place.

Your letter arriving a few days ago, of the 5th, and the note of the seventh announcing my presence on the boulevards (in Chaplinesque attire) have provided me with rich materials for a kind of Christmas tree, at least as thrilling as any of remotest childhood memories. Names and presences glitter and fascinate with all kinds of exotic suggestions on the branches. I can be grateful to you for the best of Christmas donations, as I can thank you for the main part of my mental and imaginative sustenance of the last six months . . .

Your figure haunts me like a kind of affectionate caress through all sorts of difficulties. You are always my final and satisfactory "court of appeal," and it is useless to attempt to tell you how much this means to me. So believe me when I tell you that I love you, and plan and plan for the glorious day when we shall get knees under the table and talk, and talk, and talk.

# 12

Crane's career in advertising began on January 3, 1922. Though he was never to rise to any eminence as an "ad man"—never, in fact, to make more than a bare living at this profession—he entered on his apprentice job at the direct-mail house of Corday and Gross with the conviction that he was on the sure path to success. His "position" was once more at the bottom of the ladder. His salary was an absolute minimum. (During the eight months he worked for the firm, his highest take-home pay was $25 a week.) But advertising, he felt, was one of the few fields in which native wit might compensate for nonexistent academic training. "One year of this and I shall probably be trained in a profitable vocation that can be practiced anywhere," he wrote Munson. "It's what I've wanted to get into, you know, for years. So I'm pleased. With the burden of continual fear and depression lifted, I *may* now begin to write a little."

The emphasis in Crane's note to Munson is, however, on writing —not copy-writing. Much as Crane anticipated his job, and much as he expected to enjoy the work, a job, any job, was by now in Crane's eyes only a means to an end. He knew that, whatever else he did, his real vocation would be poetry. And since poetry could bring no man a livelihood, he would have to achieve a balance between work and creative work. "When out of work," he explained to Sherwood Anderson, "I am not able to rid myself of worries enough to accomplish anything. Some pecuniary assurances seem necessary to me to any opening of the creative channels. Now things begin to look a little better for me."

By the end of his first month he was able to send off a round of letters to all his friends congratulating himself on having found a job he could turn to with pleasure rather than loathing: "I grow more pleased with my work and treatment there every day. In short, I rather begin to feel sort of human again." "Never guessed a commercial institution could be organized on such a decent basis. And they actually will come of their own accord and tell you that they are pleased with the work you are doing for them!!!!!!!!!!"

As Crane's spirits lifted, his interest in the world around him became once again as intense as it had been during his first few days alone in New York City. Now, however, it was Cleveland that opened to him:

> There are so many rather interesting people around this winter that there is always something or other doing. A concert to go to, a soiree,—and then since I have been writing ads a certain amount of hangover work to be done evenings sometimes,—that altogether I don't like it. But I like my work and am wonderfully treated at the office. . . . I pass my goggle-eyed father on the streets now without a tremor! I go on mad carouses with Bill Sommer wherein we begin with pigs' feet and sauerkraut and end with Debussy's "Gradus ad Parnassum" in the "ivory tower." Around Ernest Bloch at the Institute of Music here are gathered some interesting folks from all over everywhere. There is even a French restaurant here where the proprietress stands at the cashier's desk reading La Nouvelle Revue Française and where wonderful steaks with mushrooms are served—alas, everything, including real garçons, except vin. The place looks like a sentence without any punctuation, or, if you prefer, this letter.

As life around him became enjoyable, Crane's desire to escape America for the wonders of Europe drifted into the background. He wrote Sherwood Anderson that at the end of December he had been "all ready to scrape around for money enough to start for Europe." Munson's and Josephson's letters, he explained, had been tantalizing: "letters that made me foam at my moorings." But then "this job came along, and I thought I had better take it." Now, however, as winter softened into spring, and as the round of parties and concerts intensified, Crane found satisfactions triumphing over discontents: "Ernest Bloch . . . conducted two weeks ago his 'Trois Poèmes Juifs' which were magnificent enough for Solomon to have marched and sung to. I occasionally pass him on the streets or in the aisles of the auditorium, and realize that genius, after all, may walk in Cleveland."

For there was, Crane felt, a mood stirring in America that was, though still imprecise, still superficially meaningless, altogether different from and perhaps ultimately more important than the postwar gloom so riotously displaying itself in Paris. His ideas— tentatively expressed at first in letters to his friends—emerge as significant elements in the ground plan of "For the Marriage of Faustus and Helen" and later still in the initial plan for The Bridge.

At first he was most impressed by the postwar boom which so rapidly had succeeded postwar depression and in which he was now completely caught up.

Everyone is suddenly so enormously *busy*—making money, attending teas, motoring, starving—God knows what all. It makes me reel! Life is too scattered for me to savor it any more. Probably this is only on account of my present work which demands the most frequent jerks of the imagination from one thing to another, still,—the war certainly has changed things a lot here. The question in my mind is, how much less vertigo are we going to suffer in this latter whirl than we did in the first blows and commotion.

Crane became obsessed with this American "vertigo" and when, late in the spring, Munson returned to New York, Crane very seriously asked him to sum up his first reactions as he compared Europe to America, and, explicitly, Paris to New York: "There must have been some new aspects of the place awaiting you. I know that even a few months in the West Indies and Canada open your eyes to new things on your return." What Crane really wanted was corroboration for a growing conviction that out of American crassness and vulgarity a new kind of art—an amalgam of sensuality and elegance, of boldness and delicacy— was likely to arise.

The world is becoming fast standardized,—and who knows but what our American scene will be the most intricate and absorbing one in fifty years or so?

Something is happening. Some kind of aristocracy of taste is being established,—there is more of it evidenced every year. People like you, Matty and I belong here. Especially Matty, who was doing better work last summer before he got in with the Paris crowd than I suspect since.

He grew indignant at the efforts of his friends to "place" themselves—and him along with them—in one Continental literary camp or the other. And so, in spite of the fact that never before or after did he theorize more persistently about the structure of his own poetry, he felt compelled to say to Munson that he was "hopelessly tired of Art and theories about Art."

I can't quite account for it—never having suffered from indigestion like this before. It is, after all, I suppose, because I have nothing of my own to "give," and therefore feel so little at stake in all the deluge of production and argument that I grow either bewildered or else indifferent. I am going through a difficult readjustment right now besides meeting a period in my so-called "creative life" where neither my conscious self nor my unconscious self can get enough "co-operation" from the other to do anything worthwhile. I wrote something recently which I thought, on the moment, was good. Today I have faced it as a hopeless failure, disjointed and ugly and

vain. I am only momentarily depressed by these facts, however, as I am kept so busy with my ad writing that I haven't
time to think much about it.

Josephson provoked Crane into repeated efforts to define, if
not the kind of work he hoped to do, at least the kind of work he
hoped to avoid. The literary world, Crane felt, was becoming
entangled in a set of fashionable attitudes—all of them of European origin, all easy to imitate and some, at least, of no lasting
value. Yet it was precisely these fashionable attitudes which Matty
Josephson seemed to be supporting wholeheartedly; and Josephson, Crane felt, was carrying in his wake a great many of the
young writers Crane had admired. Crane was particularly disturbed when Munson, who had met Josephson in Europe, seemed
suddenly to reflect Josephson's championship of Dada and emerging Surrealism. "I have a bone to pick with you," Crane wrote
soon after Munson reached America, "or a misunderstanding to
unravel. I am hoping you come to Cleveland soon,—it can't
be too soon for me." Face to face they could thrash out their differences in regard to the champions of anti-art.

All this talk from Matty on Apollinaire—about being gay and
*so* distressingly and painfully delighted about the telegraph,
the locomotive, the automat, the wireless, the street cars and
electric lamp post, annoy me. There is no reason for *not* using
them,—but why is it so important to stick them in. I am interested in possibilities. Apollinaire lived in Paris. I live in Cleveland, Ohio. These quotidian conveniences so dear to him are
not of especial pleasure to me here. I am not going to pity myself—but, on the other hand, why should I stretch my face continually into a kind of "glad" expression. Besides,—sadness
(you will shrink in horror at this) has a real and lasting appeal
to me.

I am stubborn—and grow indifferent at times about all this
mad struggle for advance in the arts. Every kind of conceivable work is being turned out today. Period styles of every description. Isn't it, after all, legitimate for me to write something
the way I like to (for my own pleasure) without considering
what school it harmonizes with?

I'm afraid I don't fit in your group. Or any group, for all
that.

When Crane spoke of the "difficult readjustment" he was going
through, he referred, I think, to the shift in poetic technique which
became visible in "Black Tambourine," which was developed in
"Chaplinesque," and which would be characteristic of much of his
best verse from 1921 on. It was, to oversimplify, the imposition
of a metaphysical technique on poetry that was written from a
symbolist point of view. Its subject matter was almost always

drawn from contemporary American life. Its imagery, though public enough, was frequently charged with private significance. The tightly knit poems that resulted were, for most of his readers, enigmatic but strangely meaningful. This "significant denseness" was no accident. It was something Crane worked very hard to achieve. It was in part, he explained to his friends, a consequence of a complicated formal structure, a structure compounded from rhymes and near rhymes, carefully adjusted rhythms, intricate multi-dimensional puns, and a system of deliberate "echoes," repetitions, and cross references.

Until January 1922, he had been feeling his way. But at that time he began to systematize his theories under the stimulus of conversations with Sommer and Lescaze—and remembered conversations with Ernest Nelson, one of Sommer's co-workers at Otis Lithography, whom Crane had met through Sommer and Sam Loveman and whose death, the result of a street accident (he was struck by a passing auto just after he stepped off the curb), shocked all his friends, and shocked Crane into poetry.

Nelson's importance to Crane is almost impossible to assess, but there is no question that it was considerable. Six months after his death Crane was still troubled by regrets that their long conversations had so suddenly been cut off. "I think," he told Underwood, "he has had a lasting influence on me." Though Crane knew him for only a few months, they were from the beginning the closest of friends. Crane classed him, as he said, as "one of the best-read people I ever met," a man of "wonderful kindliness and tolerance and a true Nietzschean."

Nelson was then in his fifties. Despite a life of considerable hardship, he had not lost the buoyant good spirits of his youth. Born in Norway, he had rebelled against family religious restrictions and at the age of fifteen had set sail for America. For a short time he went to art school in Washington, D.C., where, Crane wrote, he "won some kind of distinguished medal." But, as soon as he was through school, "an aunt of his in America who had been paying his tuition abruptly withdrew all her help and forced him into the prostitution of all his ideals and a cheap lithographic work that he was never able to pull out of afterward." Before he had married, Crane went on, Nelson had written several good poems, good enough to be published in the best magazines of the day; but by the time Crane met him, Nelson had given up hope of a career either as poet or as painter. "Living in seclusion for a number of years," he had become, Crane felt, "one of many broken against the stupidity of American life in such places as here."

Though broken as an artist, he had been in no way broken as an amateur scholar, for he had put a great deal of his earnings into a fine private library. This was open to his friends, Crane among them.

When Nelson died—the week before Christmas 1921—Crane was overwhelmed by the loss, but the funeral—one of rare dignity—seemed to cancel out the pathos of an accidental death and to replace it with a distillate of love, honor, friendship, affection, respect. "Bill and I were among the pall-bearers at this funeral," Crane wrote Munson, "where there were only a few others present, although all appreciative of what the man was. I can't go into detail, but the affair was tremendous, especially the finale at the crematorium. It was beautiful, but left me emotionally bankrupt last Sunday, the day following. That funeral was one of the few beautiful things that have happened to me in Cleveland."

From the funeral, Crane believed, a tribute to Nelson ought to arise—a tribute worthy of the man and of his ideas. It should achieve the significant denseness Nelson's own poetry had never attained but which his thought seemed to drive toward.

The memorial poem Crane finally wrote, "Praise for an Urn," was not begun until well into February, but all through January he discussed the theories of artistic structure that were to be drawn on in the poem. Some of these evolving theories were worked out in letters to Munson and to Josephson. But, oddly, it is in a letter to Sherwood Anderson, whom he did not expect to be sympathetic to his views, that Crane most carefully spelled out his intentions.

In my own work I find the problem of style and form becoming more and more difficult as time goes on. I imagine that I am interested in this style of writing more than you are. Perhaps, though, we include the same features under different terms. In verse this feature can become a preoccupation, to be enjoyed for its own sake. . . . For instance, when I come to such a line as the following from John Donne, I am thrilled—

"Thou shallt not peep through lattices of eyes,
   Nor hear through labyrinths of ears, nor learn
   By circuit or collections to discern; etc."

Or take another, called The Expiration

"So, so break off this last-lamenting kiss,
   Which sucks too souls and vapours both away:
Turn thou, ghost, that way, and let me turn this,
   And let ourselves ; night our happiest day;
We ask none leave to love; nor will we owe
   Any so cheap a death, as saying, go.

Go; and if that word have not quite killed thee,
   Ease me with death by bidding me go too;
Or if it have, let my word work on me,
   And a just office on a murderer do;

Except it be too late to kill me so,
Being double dead, going, and bidding go."

What I want to get is just what is so beautifully done in this poem,—an "interior" form, a form that is so thorough and intense as to dye the words themselves with a peculiarity of meaning, slightly different maybe from the ordinary definition of them separate from the poem. If you remember my "Black Tambourine" you will perhaps agree with me that I have at least accomplished this idea once. My aims make writing slow for me, and so far I have done practically nothing,—but I can wait for slow improvements rather more easily than I can let a lot of stuff loose that doesn't satisfy me. There is plenty of that in the publishing houses and magazines every day to amuse the folks that like it. This may very well be a tiresome ranting for you, but I think you will like the quotation anyway.

Crane devoted a great deal of his limited free time in February and March to discussions of these and related ideas and to working out as a concrete example "Praise for an Urn."

This is one poem that Crane's bibliographer will have no trouble dating. On Saturday, February 11, 1922, Crane wrote Munson, "I haven't done anything in poetry for some time, but may resume again when I get a breeze in my sails." On Monday, two days later, just before joining Bill Sommer for lunch "at the joint around the corner" from Corday and Gross, Crane stole a few minutes from his ad-writing to drop a short note to Bill Wright, who, now a senior at Ohio State University, had just paid Crane a visit. The note not only lets us date almost to the hour the inception of the poem on Nelson but also lets us have a good view of the way Crane wrote his poetry. Friend after friend has spoken of his method of composition, a kind of darting into and out of the poem, usually with orchestral accompaniment from the wind-up phonograph. This time, however, the stimulus to poetry was poetry itself.

I have just finished a very quiet Sunday, reading Webster's wonderful "Appius and Virginia." I shall enjoy that recently acquired set of Webster that I showed you. Did you ever read Taine's History of English Literature? I turned to the Age of Elizabeth last night and found some extremely sensitive estimates of my present enthusiasms, Jonson, Webster, Massinger, etc. I kept getting up out of bed to add words and phrases to a thing I hope may turn into a poem,—but we'll see. I seem to be very dry of late. Perhaps the Spring may bring me a renewed pulse.

Though he didn't wait until spring to finish his poem, he did spend the better part of a month on it.

The finished poem was well worth the labor of composition. At last finding a satisfactory use for his line from "The Bridge of Estador," "The slant moon with the slanting hill," and again—though here in an altogether different context from their earlier appearances—combining Pierrot's eyes and Gargantua's laughter, Crane assembled in two dozen lines many of the significant oppositions that constitute life; from those stark oppositions, he made death meaningful. One has only to quote out of context the words on which the poem is suspended to lay bare both method and theme: "time," "space"; "sun," "moon"; "living," "dead." Once these are fixed in mind, the inherent oppositions reveal themselves—youth and age (the "gold hair" he must have had as a boy, opposed to the "broken brow" of the dead man); joy and sorrow (sunlight's laughing Gargantua opposed to Pierrot, the moon's sad-eyed hero); body and soul (the dead man in the crematory and the boy he once had been, opposed to "his thoughts," "assessments of the soul"). Working with a series of grim paradoxes (we "scatter," for instance, not Nelson's ashes but the "well-meant idioms" of funeral orations and poems into the suburbs, "where they will be lost"), Crane wittily avoided sentimentality without sacrificing seriousness or sincerity.

The poem was, Crane suspected, so difficult that most editors would automatically reject it; so he took a chance and sent it off both to *The Dial* and to the new magazine *Secession*, which, largely under Munson's direction, was being readied in Europe for its initial appearance. To his consternation, it was accepted by both magazines, and almost simultaneously. The *Dial*'s acceptance, however, arrived several days before Munson's. Much embarrassed, Crane withdrew the poem from his friend's magazine.

The elaborate story of the emergence of *Secession*, the conflicts that developed among its contributors—particularly the conflicts between Munson and Josephson—should sometime be dispassionately analyzed; but this is hardly the place for such an analysis. In *Life among the Surrealists*, Josephson's account of his time abroad, Munson is presented as a young innocent who, enthusiastically recommended by Crane, came one day to discuss literature and left fired with the ambition to publish a great new literary magazine. Josephson, recollecting in 1962 his first reactions to Munson, pronounced him a person who suffered from an "evident lack of critical acumen and literary taste." When he first met Munson, Josephson said, Munson "thought the style of Theodore Dreiser could hardly be improved upon, and that Waldo Frank was 'the greatest American novelist.' In a word (so it seemed to me), Munson scarcely knew the difference between Marianne Moore and Thomas Moore." Munson saw their meeting in quite different terms: "I met a rather stiff young man, narrow in his interests, brittle in his thinking, and at moments charmingly pompous in speech. A certain pathos in his character was appealing. I looked at his verse. It impressed me without, I must say, taking my breath away." These were the co-workers: Munson, founder and editor of the magazine, and Josephson, at least in his own mind, the power behind the throne, the moving force who brought to the magazine its most illustrious contributors. ("I labored to prepare the first two issues of our review; made translations of pieces by Aragon, Éluard, Soupault, Tzara, and Breton; and wrote a short essay on Apollinaire which embodied our 'platform,' our ideology of experiment and innovation," wrote Josephson, still indignant forty years after the event. "Inasmuch as mail from the United States followed Munson rather slowly, he was obliged, for want of other manuscripts at the time, to make up the first two issues principally out of material supplied by . . . Matthew Josephson. Munson then named himself sole editor of the publication, though about sixty per cent of its text, at the start, consisted of my contributions.") The great miracle, of course, is that the Josephson-Munson "collaboration" lasted as long as it did—for by the end of the first few months it had reached a breaking point. By the end of the second year it had resulted in a heated meeting of the contributors to *Secession* and to *Broom* (Harold Loeb's elegant magazine to which both Munson and Josephson had contributed, Josephson eventually serving as associate editor). Finally, several years later, the quarrel ended in an elaborately staged—and often reported—fistfight on the rim of a swamp in Woodstock, New York.

Whatever the facts of Munson's and Josephson's collaboration on *Secession,* Crane's sympathies were from the beginning with Munson. Munson was editor of the magazine; Munson financed the magazine; Munson had assembled—sometimes with, sometimes without, Josephson's help—a distinguished list of contributors. In spite of his sympathy, however, Crane at first urged Munson to think twice before committing all his spare cash to the venture.

And now, mon cher, willy-nilly as it all may be, we come to your magazine. I don't want to hurt you at all, but I must confess to little or no enthusiasm at the prospect of another small magazine, full of compressed dynamite as yours might well be. Unless one has half a million or so, what's the use of adding to the other little repercussions that dwindle out after a few issues!? Don't waste your time with it all, is my advice. Much better sit down and pound on your typewriter, or go toting mss around to stolid editors. Listen,—there is now *some* kind of magazine that will print one's work however bad or good it is. The "arty" book stores bulge and sob with them all. I pray you invest your hard-earned money in neckties, theatre tickets or something else good for the belly or the soul,—but don't throw it away in paper and inefficient typography. Don't come home three months sooner for the prospects of that rainbow. No one will especially appreciate it and it will sour your mouth after all the vin rouge you have been drinking.

The notion of Josephson's acting as a kind of literary advisor for Munson's new project may also have encouraged Crane to take a dim view of it. Dada in its own place—in Paris—might be well and good; but what was the point in ramming it down supersensitive American throats?

By all this you must not think that I have joined the Right Wing to such an extent that I am rollicking in F. Scott Fitzgerald. No,—but by the straight and narrow path swinging to the south of the village DADA I have arrived at a somewhat and abashed posture of reverence before the statues of Ben Jonson, Michael Drayton, Chaucer [and] sundry others already mentioned. The precious rages of dear Matty somehow don't seem to swerve me from this position. He is, it strikes me, altogether unsteady. Of course, since Mallarmé and Huysmans were elegant weepers it is up to the following generation to haw-haw gloriously! Even dear old Buddha-face de Gourmont is passé. Well, I suppose it is up to one in Paris to do as the Romans do, but it all looks too easy to me from Cleveland, Cuyahoga County, God's Country. But Matty will always glitter when he walks provided the man in front of him has not sparkled,—which we hope he never does, of course—and so I am happy to hear from him always about his latest change of mind.

Munson's enthusiasm, however, soon reconciled Crane to the magazine, and he offered *Secession* the soon-to-be-withdrawn "Praise for an Urn." "Your list of contributors to your magazine is indeed a galaxy. And when you so insistently and delightfully invite me to join the crew I am full of all kinds of yearnings to do so. But what if I have nothing to send! There is only one *possible* thing, and I am enclosing it. I am not at all certain that you will like it, but use it if you want to. It seems to be my limit these days." By the end of March the magazine had been named and the flyer circulated which proudly announced price ("20 cents"), program ("It will . . . expose the private correspondence, hidden sins and secret history of its American contemporaries, *The Dial, Little Review, Broom, Poetry,* et cetera. It already notes in current literature very much that demands hilarious comment"), and contributors ("the youngest generation of American writers who are moving away from the main body of intelligent writing in the United States since 1910. . . . Slater Brown, Kenneth Burke, Donald B. Clark, Malcolm Cowley, Hart Crane, E. E. Cummings, Matthew Josephson, Marianne Moore,

Wallace Stevens, and . . . certain allied Frenchmen, Guillaume Apollinaire, Louis Aragon, André Breton, Paul Éluard, Philippe Soupault and Tristan Tzara"). As soon as the flyers reached Crane, he began distributing them among his friends. "You know I shall talk it up," he explained to Munson, "—but the worst is that most of my acquaintances are totally unfitted for enthusiasms of this sort. The indifference you will encounter when you return to these States you must be prepared to face."

When the first copy reached him in mid-April, Hart sent off a long critique of the issue: a poem by Tristan Tzara struck him as "perfectly flat"; he liked a prose work by Louis Aragon ("in its odd way, a quite beautiful thing"); a poem by Malcolm Cowley was "encouraging" (he quickly added, "although dreadfully alike something he had published in one of the last L.Rs.").

> But what has happened to Matty!?! And,—just *why* is Apollinaire so portentous a god? Will radios, flying machines, and cinemas have such a great effect on poetry in the end? All this talk of Matty's is quite stimulating, but it's like coffee,— twenty-four hours afterward not much remains to work with. It is metallic and pointillistic—not derogatory terms to my mind at all, but somehow thin,—a little too slender and "smart,"—after all.

For Charmion von Wiegand, then traveling in Europe, Hart summed up his impressions of that first issue. "I am skeptical about all such dear, darling and courageous and brief attempts, but shall do my best to make his magazine a success, despite my literary and philosophical differences with him in this project."

Much as Crane was interested in the progress of his friend's magazine, far more immediate problems took up most of his time. Most pressing were the ones which involved family finances, for his mother's alimony was running out and Hart and Grace began to spend long evenings trying to calculate ways in which she and her mother might be able to survive. They were, of course, not penniless. Mrs. Hart owned the home they lived in; she had enough of an income from securities to take care of most of her own needs. Grace, however, had never been a money manager. Until this time sheltered by wealthy parents, a wealthy husband, or her substantial alimony, she had often used spending sprees to overcome emotional problems. These sprees would have to be curtailed. She feared that her elegant wardrobe would drift from the height of style to a shabby gentility, that her excursions to Chicago and New York would no longer be happy vacations at the best hotels but instead penny-pinching visits at the homes of relatives and friends. Hart, at least for the present, could be counted on for no more than his own maintenance, and Grace did not dare dip deeply into her already reduced savings. Finally she decided that she would have to find some kind of dignified employment: hostess in a restaurant perhaps, assistant in one of the city's hotels, anything that would let her draw on the only assets she had, her charm and her beauty.

As she and Hart would talk through her problems, both of them would look back fondly to Hart's childhood, to the days when financial security seemed limitless—the good times of gardeners, maids, cooks, chauffeurs, handymen, tutors—until, magnifying the past out of all proportion, they would make the present unbearable. For just across the street from them were Hart's *other* grandparents—C.A.'s mother and father, comfortably well-off, regularly visited by C.A. and his handsome new wife, living symbols of a lost, luxurious world.

It is easy to understand how Hart—in spite of a job he liked, good friends, and success in his literary ventures—still was hard put to find enough time free of anxiety for the production of poetry. At a time when the world had conspired to make him happiest—the first crocus pushing up through disappearing snow, cherry buds in his grandmother's back yard swelling toward blossom, the ice in the lake breaking up under the pressure of soft breezes from the south; the whole generous, natural world lifting into spring—Hart fretted, worried, "discussed," endlessly, money. "Just now, I apologize for it," he wrote Munson on a bright, blustery twelfth of March. "I am so much worried by family finances that it's hard for me to do anything more than my work."

My mother's alimony has reached its limited time and she is preparing (at 45 yrs. of age!) to go out into the world to learn to make her living!

I, naturally, shall henceforward be called upon not only to "keep" myself, but to lend as much of a helping hand as is possible in this predicament. So, it's hard work for some time ahead for me, I guess. My present wages *just* suffice for my own limited requirements. My pater is too much of a cad to really do anything for his former wife except what the agreement between them says. The fact that this was made when she was partially out of mind and very ill, makes no difference to him.

However, I shall not resign myself to the proverbial and sentimental fate of the "might-have-been" artist without a few more strenuosities. I will have to expect a certain tardiness of gait, however.

Trying to be as good as his word, Crane got underway several "easy" literary projects—the revision of two abandoned lyrics and the translation of a group of Laforgue poems for the *Double-Dealer*, still the best-paying outlet he had discovered. (The proceeds from the poems and the translations would, he wrote Wright, go toward the purchase of "a new pair of shoes and a hat.") He also worked steadily at his home-study project on Elizabethan poetry, and as usual read widely in recently published literature. (Aldous Huxley's *Crome Yellow*—"one of those things that evokes much quiet laughter and holds delightful savours, at least for a contemporary, between its covers"—particularly pleased him.) But that spring he also read Gogol's *Taras Bulba*, a series of books on Egyptian and Greek art, and—perhaps most important—*Moby Dick*.

He continued, of course, to be actively interested in the fortunes of his friends. Through Charmion von Wiegand, he arranged for a German translation of work by Sherwood Anderson, a project that kept him all spring and summer in a fairly steady correspondence with Anderson, Miss von Wiegand, Huebsch (Anderson's publisher), and Emil Reeck, the German friend of Miss von Wiegand who prepared the translation. He volunteered detailed, and very perceptive, criticism of Bill Wright's poetry and prose; and he even did his best to cheer him through a painful love affair, warning him, in passing, of the dangers of "unmellowed ladies" who "know not and care not what they do" and cheerfully pontificating about the proper place of women in a man's world: "They have the faculty of producing very debilitating and thoroughly unprofitable effects on gentlemen who put themselves too much in their hands. Woman was not meant to occupy this position. It was only the Roman Catholic Church who gave it to her. Greeks, Romans, and Egyptians knew better how to handle her. . . . All this suffering is quite romantic and beautiful, you know, but you pay a stupid price for it."

For in Crane's vocabulary "love" was becoming more and more difficult to define. Both of his serious homosexual love affairs had drifted into purely sensual gratification; and he was reasonably sure—on the basis of such experiments as he had made—that he could expect little more than sensual gratification from any woman with whom he might become involved. "Involvement," in fact, was for Crane the great drawback in any experience of love—paternal, maternal, homosexual, heterosexual. For the lover, Crane began to feel, always loses. He opens himself completely to the beloved—Crane could visualize no possibility of a "tentative," of a "reserved" lover—and so invites, if not the worst risk—the false lover's calculated betrayals—the accidental betrayals that time and space force on us all: unintentional slights; the thousand distractions of a pushing world; petty jealousies, envies, greeds. "Betrayal" came in his mind to be the necessary companion of "love," always following hard on love's footsteps. "I have been through two or three of these cataclysms myself," he wrote Bill Wright, "harder than yours because of their unusual and unsympathetic situations. Maybe I have gained something by them, I don't know,—but it is certain that I lost a great deal too."

For a while he believed that he had "cured" himself of all emotional entanglement. Gratification of the flesh was, in one way or another, easy enough to come by; one need make, if one were tough enough, no spiritual commitment of any kind. He could take care of needs of the flesh, he told one friend, by wandering the parks at night; the spiritual side of love could isolate itself in friendship. Love's two divisions need not share one flesh.

But, of course, his project failed. ("He once confessed to me," Sam Loveman said, "that he couldn't live if he weren't in love. He said he couldn't stand the loneliness.") Spring came, and spring upset all his plans. "With the banal arrival of spring and weeks of rain and cloudy skies," he wrote Munson, "I have again fallen in love! I guess I might about as well take up quarters at La Rotonde and be done with it. However, *somethings* must be indulged in to make Cleveland interesting."

# 13

Despite family problems and his efforts to "discipline" his emotions, Hart approached his twenty-third birthday with the kind of assurance in his own powers that he had never had before. His job, for one thing, was going very well. Though he had not yet been given a raise, he had been allowed to work up in some detail several of the direct-mail catalogues which Corday and Gross specialized in. Activity of this sort not only gave Crane a good deal of confidence; it also provided the incidental benefit of company-financed travel. He enjoyed several three-day trips to Jamestown, where, as he told Munson and Wright, he devoted himself to " 'investigation of the product,' in ad. lingo," by interviewing executives of his clients, the Art Metal Company ("puzzling my head over blue prints and figures until I have become somewhat dull"). These trips, his first expeditions from Cleveland in over a year, so refreshed body and soul that he toyed briefly with the notion of bolting for New York City and a real holiday (" . . . *almost* kicked the traces of home, family and Co."); but discretion—and plans for a company-sponsored trip to Pittsburgh—lured him back to the straight and narrow.

Just as his travels refreshed him, so too did his extensive correspondence with new friends and old. Of the new friends, one man would ultimately be of great importance to him in helping to shape his literary ideas. That was Allen Tate, at this time a student at Vanderbilt University. There, as the only undergraduate member of the "Fugitive" group, he was actively participating in the editorial work that led to the April publication of the first issue of the group's magazine.

When I spoke to Tate, the circumstances of his first correspondence with Crane were still vividly clear to him. I asked if he recollected when the first letter had arrived:

> I remember exactly. It was in May, 1922. One of the first poems I had in print was in the May issue of *The Double Dealer*—it was called "Euthanasia"—typical youthful title. Crane wrote me a letter. . . . He said that evidently I'd been

reading T. S. Eliot, and he gave me some "signals," which I didn't understand at that time. He said, "I admire Eliot very much too. I've had to work through him, but he's the prime ram of our flock," which meant that in those days a lot of people like Hart had the delusion that Eliot was homosexual. "Ram of our flock" I didn't get onto until later, and when I knew Hart, much later, we joked about it.

Then, right after that, he sent me in typescript his poem "Praise for an Urn," which appeared in the *Dial* a month or two later. I thought it was a very beautiful poem. Even now, I'm astonished that a boy of 21 or 22 could have written it.

Tate's return note to Crane initiated a correspondence which for two years was for both young men satisfying and helpful. In Tate, Crane found a brilliant, sympathetic writer, a man interested in the sort of technical problems he himself responded to; while in Crane, Tate found a man of erratic, perceptive genius who, though nowhere near so well schooled as himself, was nevertheless "usefully" educated. "In fact," Tate recalled, "when I first knew him, even in the first letter that I received from him, I was astonished at his precocity. Although he'd never been to college, and I think only about three years to high school, he had a much greater literary sophistication than I did, and I had a much better education." The kind of reading Crane did, the values he extracted from his reading, continued all through their friendship to interest Tate; for Crane's unpredictable but careful kind of study was, Tate concluded, in its own way remarkably efficient: "He knew exactly what he could use. . . . For his purposes, he was very well read, but from the scholarly point of view, not. The scholars wouldn't have acknowledged his reading at all." This "useful" reading was a specialized, productive consequence of the accidents of his life.

It's curious—I don't think Hart ever read any of the great masterpieces through. I mean things like *The Divine Comedy* or Blake's *Prophetic Books*. I'm not sure he'd ever read all of Shakespeare. He didn't read, you know, for historical knowledge, from that point of view. He read for shock, for language. It was reading for sensibility. What he could use. His instinct as a poet led him to that kind of thing.

For example, he more or less identified himself with Rimbaud. There's some reason for that. . . . But he didn't read all of Rimbaud by any means. Rimbaud's awfully difficult and Hart's French was limited.

Until the correspondence with Tate began, Munson had been Crane's principal literary critic. Now Tate began to take on this function of correspondent-critic, and soon Crane and Tate were working out together the literary stances they wished to take.

Crane had from the very beginning felt that Tate's poetry paralleled his own. ("It is because your poem [in the *Double-Dealer*] seemed so much in line with the kind of thing I am wanting to do, that I felt almost compelled to write you.") Both admired the French symbolists; both were interested in, and to some extent influenced by, the Elizabethans; but it was less this than a rejection of Dada and its attendant nihilism that at first seemed to Crane to be the most important link in their work.

Crane's problem as a poet, he wrote Tate, was that he wanted at the same time to deal with modern themes in a modern manner and to reflect the best qualities in the long literary tradition that T. S. Eliot was defining. He did not want, nevertheless, to be caught up in fashionable pessimism, attractive as it might be.

> The poetry of negation is beautiful—alas, too dangerously so for one of my mind. But I am trying to break away from it. Perhaps this is useless, perhaps it is silly—but one *does* have joys. The vocabulary of damnations and prostrations has been developed at the expense of these other moods, however, so that it is hard to dance in proper measure. Let us invent an idiom for the proper transposition of jazz into words! Something clean, sparkling, elusive!

Though this mid-May letter to Tate is the first explicit statement of what for the next few years was to be for Crane a compelling aesthetic, it had been evolving through the entire winter and spring. He had all this time been searching for the framework of a poem that, much earlier, he had talked over with Gorham Munson. The poem was "For the Marriage of Faustus and Helen." On the same day that Crane wrote Tate, he described it to Munson as "a metaphysical attempt."

From this moment, when he decided to "transpose" jazz into words, Crane knew exactly where he was going. His only problem was to find time to work on the poem. Through much of the summer it was a regular weekend project, blotting out "quotidian complaints" about his family. On June 4, for instance, he got off a quick note to Munson offering him the latest version.

> I want you to see the new coin from the mint enclosed herewith.
>
> I have been at it for the last 24 hours and it may be subjected to a few changes and additions, but as I see it now in the red light of the womb it seems to me like a work of youth and magic.
>
> At any rate, it is something entirely new in English poetry, so far as I know. The jazz rhythms in that first verse are something I have been impotently wishing to "do" for many a day. It is the second part of the (three section) "Marriage of Faustus and Helen" that I must have tired you with mentioning.

The other parts are entirely unlike it, and God knows when they will be done. The first part is just begun. However, I have considerable ambitions in this opus, as I have told you.

Something of the excitement Crane must have felt about the poem shows up in a note to Bill Wright. He apologizes for his tardiness in answering letters by saying that he is so "immersed" in his poem that he has no opportunity for social amenities of any sort. The day after he wrote Wright, he told Tate that the poem would use the techniques of Eliot for altogether different ends than those to which Eliot put them. Tate, who had just discovered Eliot, had spoken of the impact of a first reading. Crane acknowledged Eliot's power.

What you say about Eliot does not surprise me,—but you will recover from the shock. No one ever says the last word, and it is a good thing for you, (notice how I congratulate myself!) to have been faced with him as early as possible. I have been facing him for *four years*,—and while I haven't discovered a weak spot yet in his armor, I flatter myself a little lately that I have discovered a safe tangent to strike which, if I can possibly explain the position,—goes *through* him toward a *different goal*. You see it is such a fearful temptation to imitate him that at times I have been almost distracted. He is, you have now discovered, far more profound than Huxley (whom I like) or any others obviously under his influence. You will profit by reading him again and again. I must have read "Prufrock" twenty-five times and things like the "Preludes" more often. . . . In his own realm Eliot presents us with an absolute *impasse*, yet oddly enough, he can be utilized to lead us to, intelligently point to, other positions and "pastures new." Having absorbed him enough we can trust ourselves as never before, in the air or on the sea. I, for instance, would like to leave a few of his "negations" behind me, risk the realm of the obvious more, in quest of new sensations, *humeurs*.

Jazz rhythms and Eliot transformed were two of the ingredients that went into "Faustus and Helen"; a third was alcohol. The kinship with Rimbaud which so forceably struck Tate was, in part at least, associated with Rimbaud's prescription for concocting poetic language: to build poetry through a systematic derangement of the senses. Rimbaud tried drugs. Crane, more conservative, settled on wine—though he could in lucky moments, as all his friends have attested, grow drunk on language alone, piling up in the excitement of good talk wonderful, extravagant phrases, inventive, witty, evocative, until, reeling with them, he would rush from the room to hammer out a few on his typewriter. These, in less heated times, would be used as raw material for poems.

Good conversation sometimes set in motion Crane's inventive faculties; but wine, Crane found, was far more easily come by. In part, certainly, the power of wine went with its surroundings; for, by the accident of prohibition, wine could be easily had in Cleveland's "Little Italy," where, homemade, it was served in the back parlors of immigrant workers' homes. Here, in a world of good feeling uncomplicated by the rigid propriety of his own home, Crane could imagine what it might be like to have been born into a happy family not driven toward success and social conformity but relaxed into sensual enjoyment, into love. There is no question that later in his life alcohol nearly destroyed Crane. But in the social drinking of Cleveland's "Little Italy," it was in every sense a liberator.

Some of the quality of this liberation—and some details about its effects on his work—shows up in a wonderfully open, scrawled, happy letter to Munson, probably written on June 18 but headed only *Sunday midnight*, and above that the huge announcement— from one side of the page to the other:

> *"Apologies Later!—"*
>
> *Sunday midnight*

Dear Gorham: —

I have been in a house up in "Little Italy," a section of Sicilian immigrants very near our house where one can get good three-year Chianti,—and, incidentally, am feeling very fine as Sunday evenings go. *There* is the place to enjoy oneself in the family parlor of a pickslinger's family with chromos on the walls that are right in style of Derain and Vlaminck. Bitch dogs and the rest of the family wander in while the bottle is still half empty and some of the family offspring. Tristram Shandy read to a friend with a Spanish Bolero going on the Victrola sounds good in such a milieu! I never should live without wine! When you come here we shall make many visits to this charming family. You will like my classic, puritan, inhibited friend, Sam Loveman who translates Baudelaire charmingly! It is hard to get him to do anything outside the imagination,—but he is charming, and has just given me a most charming work on Greek Vases (made in Deutschland) in which Satyrs with great erections prance to the ceremonies of Dionysios with all the fervor of deGourmont's descriptions of sexual sacrifices in "Physique de l'Amour" which I am lately reading in trans.

I am glad you like Lescaze's "portrait" of me. He *has* an athletic style. Your criticism of painting et al strikes me as very exact and appreciative—at least, as far as I am able to justly criticize it. He hates Cleveland with all the awareness of the recent description of this place accorded in the last "Masses" or *Liberator*, as I understand. Just now I am in too banal a mood to give sympathy to anything. At times, dear Gorham, I feel an enormous power in me—that seems almost supernatural. If this power is not too dissipated in aggravation and discouragement I may amount to something sometime. I can say this now with perfect equanimity because I am notoriously drunk and the Victrola is still going with that glorious Bolero. Did I tell you of that thrilling experience this last winter in the dentist's chair when under the influence of ether and *amnesia* my mind spiraled to a kind of seventh heaven of consciousness and egoistic dance among the seven spheres—and something like an objective voice kept saying to me—"You have the higher consciousness—you have the higher consciousness. This is something that very few have. This is what is called genius."? A happiness, ecstatic such as I have known only twice in "inspirations" came over me. I felt the two worlds. And at once. As the bore went into my tooth I was able to follow its every revolution as detached as a spectator at a funeral. O Gorham, I have known moments in eternity. I tell you this as one who is a brother. I want you to know me as I feel myself to be sometimes. I don't want you to feel that I am conceited. But since this adventure in the dentist's chair, I feel a new confidence in myself. At least I had none of the ordinary hallucinations common to this operation. Even that means something. You know I live for work,—for poetry. I shall do my best work later on when I am about 35 or 40. The imagination is the only thing worth a damn. Lately I have grown terribly isolated, and very egoist. One has to do it [in] Cleveland. I rush home from work to my room, hung with the creations of Sommer and Lescaze—and fiddle through the evenings. If I could afford wine *every* evening I might do more. But I am slow anyway. However, today I have made a good start on the first part of "Faustus and Helen." I am, needless to say, delighted that you like the second part so well. The other two parts are to be quite different. But, as yet, I am dubious about the successful eventuation of the poem as a *whole*. Certainly it is the most ambitious thing I have ever attempted and in it I am attempting to evolve a conscious pseudo-symphonic construction toward an abstract beauty that has not been done before in English—at least directly. If I can get this done in the way I hope, I might get some consideration for the Dial prize. Perhaps I'm a fool for such hopes—but sooner or later I expect to get that yearly donation.

I can't give you any encouragement for a position in *my* own Co. for a position for the summer, but you might find a good place somewhere else here as—on a new Cleveland paper that has just started up—or why not work in a factory here this summer? It's only a few weeks. Certainly, somehow or other, dear Gorham, you must come. I will pay your way back—no need to worry about that! In the meantime don't let me languish too long!

Yours,<br>Hart

Allen Tate's address is:
2019 Broad St.
Nashville, Tenn.

---

Please write him and send a copy of "Secession"—the poor boy has T.B. and genius, and is isolated from all the world we know. He has done wonders considering his handicaps. His letters to me of the last month prove this.

H.C.

I am not going to read this over in the clear sober light of the dawn. Take it for what it is worth tonight when I seal the envelope—*if* you can read it!

Though a few days later Crane apologized for the letter ("I must have insulted you to the limit with that letter of Sunday night"), he made clear that he had no apologies for his "condition," that, in fact, the condition was closely related to his progress on the poem, which, on a sober Thursday, was giving him "a terrible time." "The best way for me to speed up, I guess," he finally decided, "is to forget all about time and be quite indifferent." His drinking bout he passed off cheerfully: "When I am filled up I am feeling too good to be taken seriously."

As he predicted, work on the poem did go slowly. It was not finished until well into the winter. Meantime, both Munson and Tate sent careful critical reactions as draft after draft reached them, and Sherwood Anderson applauded Crane's summary of his plans. ("I'm interested in what you are shooting at in poetry. It isn't easy I know but it looks like a man-size job, doesn't it?" For Anderson, what was of most importance was the magnitude of the task: "What I suppose is worth while in life is just having something like that to go after.")

Neither Anderson nor Crane could have suspected at this time that their friendship would soon come to an end—and at their first meeting. Yet it happened within weeks of the arrival of Anderson's letter, when three friends descended at one time: Munson, making his much-postponed trip from New York; Bill Wright, arriving to spend an afternoon and evening on his way home, his diploma from Ohio State University fresh in hand; and Anderson, arriving unexpectedly from Chicago.

Munson reached Cleveland first, soon after Crane celebrated a three-day Independence Day holiday. Crane welcomed him,

Munson remembered, with great enthusiasm and took him home proudly to meet mother and grandmother. As Munson and Crane settled back after supper to recall their days in New York—telling anecdotes about Joe Kling and Margaret Anderson and the other friends they shared—Mrs. Crane joined in with her own memories of New York: the theater and her first love, opera and light opera. Munson immediately took to Hart's grandmother, who, pert and cheerful, struck him as "bright"; but Grace seemed to him cloying, her efforts to get reassurance about Hart's literary abilities evidence, Munson felt, of her own doubts about it. "It was plain she didn't believe in him," Munson told me. "She was baffled by his writing and she wanted a convincing recommendation. She wanted some kind of confirmation of Crane's own high opinion of his work."

When the two friends ascended to Crane's tower bedroom-study —which Munson shared during his stay and where he spent most of his time while Crane was at work—the flavor of the conversation changed. Here, isolated from the rest of the family, the two could pore over the wonders of *Ulysses*, which Munson had at long last delivered—"one of the dozen or so copies that have, so far, been smuggled into U.S.," Hart proudly wrote Bill Wright.

The book was soon to become for Crane a kind of Bible; he would study it as if he were in fact studying a sacred book. Joyce, both young men agreed, was the great formal master of twentieth-century prose; the book, Crane soon asserted, was "the epic of the age."

Tying in both Joyce's book and Joyce himself with his own recent preoccupations, Crane, at that moment exactly halfway through his "Faustus and Helen" poem, decided that *Ulysses* could best be compared to Goethe's *Faust*, "to which it has a distinct resemblance in many ways." It was, he felt, a book of "marvelous oaths and blasphemies," of "sharp beauty," of "sensitivity." And yet its author, he was told by both Munson and Anderson, rarely talked about books ("I like him for that," Crane wrote Underwood), sometimes got drunk, dressed "quietly and neatly," was "very quiet in manner," and, as Crane hoped to be, was "steeped in the Elizabethans, his early love." Like Crane, also, Joyce was "still very poor." But primarily, above and beyond personality and the circumstances of life, Joyce, who in a chaotic world ended his great book with a triumphant *Yes*, was for Crane a symbol of what the modern artist could and should be: a man who could present the grimness of reality as something shot through with significant light. "He is," Crane said, "the one above all others I should like to talk to." Munson, who had talked to Joyce, seemed, so far as Crane was concerned, to have chatted with God.

Not all their conversation was, however, about Joyce; for Crane was at last able to confess the details of his emotional in-

volvements and to tell some of the funny—and some of the painful—adventures his sexual pursuits had gotten him into. He was
always quick, Munson remembered, to see the comic side of
situations which, potentially dangerous, sometimes resolved in
abrupt withdrawals from startled gentlemen with ruffled dignities.
Crane could not resist taking those risks, which sometimes got
him into serious trouble. Only a short time before Munson's arrival, Hart had found himself caught in a petty blackmailer's
trap and was being forced at irregular intervals to part with
hard-won ten-dollar bills. Munson still recalls Crane's nervousness one night during the visit when a payment came due. "He
was frightened," Munson said; for it was Hart's first experience
with a blackmailer—he would have other such experiences later
—and he was troubled by fear of exposure and by fear that the
payments might have to be continued endlessly.

Most of the time, however, Crane was in good spirits. He
liked his job; and he was proud to introduce Munson to such
Cleveland friends as Richard Laukhuff, Sam Loveman, William
Lescaze, Alfred Galpin—then a young scholar interested in
translating French poetry—and especially Bill Sommer. Sommer
and Munson, as Crane had predicted, were from the beginning
drawn to each other; one of the high points of the visit was a
trip out to Sommer's studio. Sommer seemed to Munson on this
visit "relaxed yet vital, simple, humorous."

Since Crane had to be at work from nine to five every day and
since Munson was himself busy on the study of Waldo Frank
which he would soon have ready for publication, the two
friends, except for occasional luncheon meetings, saw each other
only in the evenings. A few of these evenings were devoted to
sightseeing and casual visits, one of them to Crane's friend
Dominick, the son of Simoni, the Italian Chianti-maker of Little
Italy—a memorable visit during which Crane, urged on by Loveman and Munson, composed five then unprintable limericks,
each one a celebration of the accomplishments of a contemporary
poet (the range was wide, Crane's targets extending from Maxwell
Bodenheim through Edna St. Vincent Millay to Ezra Pound).
On the whole, however, their time together was devoted to literature.

It may have been during these conversations, Munson be-
lieves, that Crane began urging him to look into P. D. Ouspensky's *Tertium Organum*. This strange book, which at first glance
seems to cross theosophy and popular science, had come into
Crane's hands through his acquaintance of Akron days, Harry
Candee. Proclaiming the reality of a fourth dimension—a realm
of that "higher consciousness" which Crane had already referred
to in connection with his dentist-chair vision—Ouspensky stressed
the importance of the creative artist as forerunner of a new race
of supermen. The artist, Ouspensky maintained, had an inkling

of the world of the higher consciousness in which opposites were reconciled and creative activity was accomplished through the motive force of love. Citing samples of both Eastern and Western mysticism, Ouspensky concluded his book with a quotation from R. M. Bucke's *Cosmic Consciousness*, adding, almost as an afterthought, that had Dr. Bucke—an admirer of Whitman—not spent the evening on which he discovered cosmic consciousness "reading poetry in the company of men of high intellectual and emotional development" but had instead played cards, written a newspaper editorial, or worked on a night shift in a factory, "then we may declare with certainty that no cosmic consciousness would have appeared in him at all. For it undoubtedly demands a great freedom, and concentration on the inner world."

Now, Crane was in most ways a cheerful skeptic; but he was also a dedicated poet, a man with an unshakable belief not just in the dignity but in the efficacy of the artist. The artist was good because good art was good for people. It made them better human beings. The trouble was that not all people had an interest in or a desire for good art. Most people, in fact—like Crane's parents, like the men and women with whom he worked—set a primary value not on art but on family, business, politics. They were not, as Ouspensky was, concerned with the intersection of space and time in an illumination of reality, but rather with the day-to-day Cleveland-bounded reality of making a living. Crane, however, lived in both worlds.

Perhaps it was only at the end of the book, when Ouspensky hinted at a new world in which superman poet would joyously communicate with superman poet, that Crane succumbed to the temptation of joining Ouspensky's visionary group; but succumb he did. Passages like the following may have helped win him over:

> A higher race is rapidly emerging among humanity . . . It will be truly a HIGHER RACE—and there will be no possibility of any falsification, any substitution, or any usurpation at all. It will be impossible for anything to be *bought*, or *appropriated* to oneself by deceit or by might. . . .
>
> The men approaching the transition into a new race begin already to know one another: already are established passwords and countersigns. And perhaps those social and political questions so sharply put forward in our time may be solved on quite another plane and by quite a different method than we think—may be solved by the entrance into the arena of a new race CONSCIOUS OF ITSELF which will judge the old races.

Obviously, Ouspensky's no-nonsense approach to what was essentially a religious problem pleased Crane, and his formulation of consciousness in terms which drew on the limiting factors of both time and space only finally to abolish them was attractive to a poet arranging the mystical marriage of medieval Faustus and classical Helen in a setting which bore a likeness to one of the yellow Euclid Avenue streetcars Crane daily took to work.

But it was less dogma than imagery that Crane extracted from Ouspensky, though in his talks with Munson, and later with Jean Toomer and Waldo Frank, dogma was what he discussed. "You cannot," Munson insisted to me, "overemphasize the importance of that book. Crane hounded me to read it. And he kept after me to read it until I finally did." When, months later, Munson got around to the book, he and Crane—by that time again in New York—were prepared to find its secret admirers everywhere and to respond to those "pass-words and countersigns" (if they could just figure out what they were) with which Ouspensky said those with the "higher consciousness" were to greet one another. Ultimately, Crane abandoned Ouspensky's "philosophy," as, indeed, he abandoned every other formal system that he gave brief allegiance to. While he subscribed to it, however, he knew he was close to the core of a company of the elect.

One person who turned out not to be of the elect was Sherwood Anderson. Crane had already begun to feel that Anderson's recent literary production was not up to the quality of *Winesburg*, but he had charitably decided that Anderson was printing potboilers written earlier. In January, for instance, he had written Anderson a note about the story "The Contract," which had just appeared in *Broom*. "It may be an infraction," he said, "but if it is I want to ask your forgiveness. This story in some ways strikes me as inferior to the intensity and beauty of your other recent work, and I have an idea that it [is] something you wrote quite a while ago." Making an awkward comment worse—since the story was Anderson's *newest* work—Crane went on to say: "Coming from anyone else, I would think, 'This is good; but this fellow is trying to imitate Anderson and can't quite do it.'" Crane's comment must have struck far more deeply than he realized, for Anderson *was* beginning to imitate himself. He was at the peak of his popularity, writing very rapidly, and he dismissed both the story and Crane's reaction: "It doesn't seem to come off, does it? I rather thought it did when it was in manuscript but when I saw it printed felt very much what you have said. There will be a story in the Feb. Dial that you will, I'm sure, find charming." But Crane did not find it charming; soon after he read it he mailed Munson a clipping, "the first peck at Anderson to my knowledge, from the native Huebsch nest," adding that though Anderson deserved the "wholesale praise" he had recently been getting, that praise was "too uniform."

When, however, Crane received a telephone call from Anderson one day in the third week of July—perhaps on Hart's birthday—

temporary reservations were abandoned in favor of present delights. A man he regarded as a great writer had arranged to be in
town especially to meet him. They would have dinner as soon
as Crane was finished at the office. After dinner, he would bring
Anderson home not only to meet Munson, Grace, and Mrs. Hart
but to examine the paintings by Sommer and Lescaze which now
covered the walls of his bedroom.

The dinner went very well. Crane's earlier enthusiasm for Anderson bubbled to the surface, and they talked at length of
Crane's efforts to arrange for the German translation of Anderson's work. After dinner, however, conversation declined. By
the time they got to the tower room, they were almost talked out.
But Anderson did seem interested in the paintings by Sommer
and Lescaze and soon was striding through the room uttering,
Munson felt, judgments that were neither sincere nor particularly
valid. "I just thought he was pretentious," Munson told me. "I had
already begun to question his fiction. Certainly I wasn't as enthusiastic about it as Hart was at this time. And I was annoyed
by the way he walked around the tower room, looking at the
paintings. He'd look closely at a painting, pace back a few steps,
admire it for awhile and then praise the color: 'What color!' "

Despite Munson's discomfort, however, the evening might have
gone off fairly well if Munson hadn't taken exception to Anderson's high praise of the critic Paul Rosenfeld, one of Anderson's
closest friends. As soon as Munson said that he didn't think
much of Rosenfeld, Anderson flared. "You must be a colossal
egotist," Anderson said. Munson, angry, stuck to his guns. The
more they talked, the more upset they became. Soon Waldo
Frank's name entered the argument, Anderson having sided with
Rosenfeld in an attack on Waldo Frank's *Dark Mother*.

Crane, meanwhile, was hard at work trying to keep the evening he had so looked forward to from degenerating into a brawl.
At last he got all tempers tentatively under control. "We did finally recover from the spat," Munson remembered, "though not
very much. Crane was a little distressed, and Anderson was quite
mad."

For the rest of his short stay in Cleveland, Anderson went
out of his way to avoid Crane. On the last day he got off a note:

> I'm sorry indeed that this note will reach you after I am
> gone. The only thing I regret about my conversation with your
> friend was my own stupidity in being drawn into a literary ar-
> gument. It is the sort of thing I like least in the world but do
> not blame him. It was my own affair to stay out of it.
>
> If you care to send some of the watercolors I'll be very glad
> to show them to Paul. However I'll not be in New York for at
> least 2 or 3 weeks. Then you can send them c/o B. W. Huebsch
> —116 W. 13th St.

I am sorry I have not seen more of you but unfortunately I came to Cleveland in a rather tired bedeviled mood. That has led me to hunt solitude for the time. Really I am, ordinarily, a much more social being.

The outburst in Crane's tower room continued to echo all through the twenties, both for Munson and for Crane. When Anderson returned to New York, Munson recollected, he told a number of the writers associated with *The Dial* what a difficult man Munson was. Rumors of those remarks finally reached Waldo Frank, who worried that the first important study of his own work might be launched under inauspicious circumstances. "Frank was upset about it," Munson said, "and questioned me, I remember, for several hours." A little later, *Secession*, still under Munson's editorship, attacked both Rosenfeld and Anderson.

The quarrel just about ended Crane's hopes of finding, by way of Anderson, a New York market for Sommer's paintings; but, as he told Munson, he decided nevertheless to send off a group of them on the off-chance that something might come of the gesture.

I sent 27 Sommer things off to Anderson last Saturday, feeling very much as though I were delivering Plato into the hands of the Philistines. Anderson has been nasty besides being "just another fool." I have been shocked, sensation very rare with me, with the contents of your letter relating his maneuvres. He is evidently none too sure of the quality of his work so highly praised by Rosenfeld. I realize that he insulted me while he was here—it wasn't necessary to tell fibs to avoid my company—but I shall beam on until all hope of his getting Bill an audience has vanished. In that event, I judge by your letter that we can depend fairly certainly on Frank, and Stieglitz, perhaps. I haven't much hope in Anderson's interest in anything connected with us now, after disgracing himself the way he has. Encore, regardez, mon ami,—don't let kittens out of the bag before they have claws again if you want to be an effective iconoclast.

Anderson continued to create difficulties for Munson and Crane. And though Crane assured Charmion von Wiegand that during his visit "the man's personal charm supported the impressions his letters had given me," he felt compelled to add that he had been "very disappointed in him since he went down to N.Y. . . . and stirred up a petty rumpus in the Dial office—about something that Munson told him on the subject of Rosenfeld's position as a critic, etc." The story wasn't worth going into, Crane said, "but it showed Anderson to be surprisingly petty and malignant, not to say untactful. La-La! Well,—he hasn't yet destroyed my taste for some of his work yet—despite that most of my friends don't value his work above a Russian rouble."

As Crane expected, the reception of Sommer's paintings was anything but enthusiastic. Anderson's note, pleasant enough in itself, seemed to Crane to carry undercurrents which had little to do with art criticism, for its clipped, businesslike tone was in sharp contrast to the chatty letters Anderson had written Crane before they met.

> I got the water colors and drawing before Rosenfeld and two other painters under what I thought favorable conditions but didn't get much of any favorable reaction. They all said about the same things—not any distinct personality coming through—the animal pieces apparently felt. They all liked them.
>
> The other drawings reminiscent of a half dozen modern men. No distinct personal note going through yet. They all seemed to think the man unable to paint a head of anything, animal, man or woman.
>
> A distinct sense of caricature. Some individuality in that. Not a notable man at all.
>
> You see, Crane, I am giving you just the gist of comments picked up from Rosenfeld and the others as I stood about. My own feelings do not go into this. The drawings are being sent back to you insured, from Westport, Conn. . . .
>
> I'm really sorry I went into this but suppose I should have been glad if the comments I got had been more favorable. I hate having anything to do with any unfavorable judgment on any man's work. Do understand I only acted as your agent in this.

Crane, furious, blamed Anderson for the "betrayal" of Sommer and nominated Paul Rosenfeld as chief prosecution witness at what he called Sommer's "trial." Though angry, he felt there might be techniques of retaliation: "Let us create our own little vicious circle! Let us erect it on the remains of such as Paul Rosenfeld."

Anderson's visit may have impaired his friendship with Crane, but it in no way impaired Crane's creativity. For Crane suddenly was caught up again in "Faustus and Helen," so much caught up that he almost completely disregarded Munson, who, himself trying to write, found exhausting the whirlwind cycles of Crane's Victrola playing, typing, revising, rewinding, replaying. Crane quite literally almost always worked his poems out of the structure of congenial pieces of music, sometimes playing the same five-minute record over and over, a dozen, two dozen, three dozen times. On the last two nights of Munson's visit, while Crane fought through lines of the second-to-last stanza of the first section of "Faustus and Helen," Munson was driven, he said, nearly wild by Crane's hammering typewriter alternating with his loud trial reading of the lines and their variants, all the time in the background the same record grinding over and over through its five-minute cycles, Crane racing to wind up the machine or, if the writing were going well, letting it nightmarishly wind down in its hissing, clicking final grooves.

When on July 26 Munson returned to New York, Crane was deeply involved in his poem, his study of *Ulysses*, his discovery of E. E. Cummings's *The Enormous Room*, and a careful reading of Clive Bell's *Since Cézanne*. He was about to begin a one-week vacation, and he anticipated—as he wrote Underwood—"fresh violences," both alcoholic and sexual. But if they materialized, their record has disappeared.

What seems rather to have occupied most of his vacation was a search for a new job. Crane enjoyed his work at Corday and Gross, but he was becoming concerned about promotion in a small organization. Crane therefore set about getting together samples of his advertising work, lining up references, and making casual inquiries about firms in and around Cleveland that might soon be taking on new employees. His "vacation," he told Munson, "went like nothing at all."

> I sold about 60 dollars worth of second hand books and paid some bills,—but the best part of it was a day and a half that I had out in the country with the Sommers. That will last a long time. . . . After you left I asked for a raise, and received no satisfaction. Now I think I have got something with a fresh competitor of the Co.'s that will supply me with 50. per week instead of 25. and with more copy writing and less mail clerk work.

The job lead which so interested Crane had come through the intervention of Leonard Smith, a friend of Crane's mother's who was much respected in Cleveland advertising circles and who was convinced that Grace's son was a genius. When he heard that Crane was looking for a better-paying job, he took it on himself to get in touch with Stanley Patno, then a partner in a new direct-mail advertising firm that would eventually become the Roger Williams Press of Cleveland. Crane, he told Patno, was not only a good copy writer but a poet with an established reputation. Somehow the fact that Crane had once had a poem turned down by Ezra Pound seemed to count as much in Smith's eyes as that he'd been published in the country's best little magazines, for Patno still remembers Smith's lively account of Pound's rejection of the poem.

On the strength of Smith's recommendation, Patno invited

Crane in for a talk. Patno realized at once that Crane's advertising experience and his samples counted for very little, but the two young men got on very well; almost without their realizing it, their conversation shifted from advertising to literature. "Crane was a good talker," Patno remembered. "I liked Sherwood Anderson; and, of course, Crane had known him. And he was wild about Joyce. In fact, he persuaded me to buy a blue-paper-cover 1922 *Ulysses* through Laukhuff. I paid $25 for it. I suppose it's worth more now. . . . I really hired him on the basis of conversational ability."

Crane struck Patno as a "nice, well-balanced person." He was full of enthusiasm, Patno told me; and as they would drive home together, since Patno's route took him near Crane's home, they would talk not company business but literature and painting. "He'd quote at length from Eliot." Patno remembered Crane's excitement about a poster he had collaborated on for the annual ball of the Kokoon Club, Cleveland's society of artists, Crane contributing as text for the poster his roof-garden dancers from the second section of "Faustus and Helen":

> White shadows slip across the floor
> Splayed like cards from a loose hand . . .

If Hart had been hired for conversational ability, conversation may have been his chief contribution to the firm. "It probably galled him to write advertising copy," Patno told me. For Crane, he felt, really had no selling instinct: "He could do nothing with headlines, and he'd labor endlessly over the copy. He'd spend half a day brooding, groping for the right word, sitting there in front of his typewriter trying to get a poetic delicacy into ads that didn't require it. I'd always work out for him the basic plan of the ad, and usually I'd do the headlines as well, since I knew what trouble they gave him. Then I'd let him fill in the copy. For instance, in an ad for Pittsburgh Plate Glass I'd set up a photograph of a cigarette on a mahogany desk with a headline: 'Somebody forgot a cigarette!' Then Hart was supposed to do the body of the text, pointing out how a plate-glass desk top would prevent burns. Well, Hart wanted to turn that copy into imagist poetry, and worked at it endlessly." As Hart put it in a letter to Charmion von Wiegand: "There are birth pangs to go through with, even in so staid a thing as advertising copy and ideas. I hammer my forehead for hours some days trying to get an idea that will be read, and loosen purse strings."

Of course, Hart was not all of the time so diligent. Sometimes he solved dilemmas of ad-writing by writing poetry. "Once, I remember," Patno said, "I'd given him full materials for a Pittsburgh Water Heaters ad—headlines, sub-heads, etc. When I came in to see what progress he'd made—we were already past our deadline—Hart had stepped out; but there in his typewriter was what he'd in fact been working on—one of his own poems!"

In spite of awkward moments of this sort, employer and employee got on very well. Hart managed to do the work he was hired to do, not always brilliantly or promptly, but adequately. The copy for Pittsburgh Water Heaters and for Pittsburgh Plate Glass, the copy for Fox Furnace Company and for Seiberling Tires eventually was produced. Hart was cheerful and, in spite of minor lapses, dependable. There was never, for instance, in the whole term of his employment, any time missed because of his drinking, which he did his best to keep secret from mother and grandmother but which his employers certainly were well aware of. Later he was to have a reputation as a destructive drinker, violent and unpredictable, but that sort of destructiveness was never in evidence in Cleveland. "Hart enjoyed drinking," Patno said, "and when he got drunk he was happy. I remember one party when he ended up jumping up and down on the table with exuberance. Of course, I knew he did a good deal of drinking. But he always got to work on time."

# 14

Toward the end of August 1922, when Crane started getting to work on time for Stanley Patno, he felt as secure as he was ever to feel. His salary had been doubled; his mother and grandmother were pleased with his business success; the first two sections of "Faustus and Helen" were nearly complete. He had established himself close to the center of a group of young artists and writers in Cleveland, and he was in communication with a rapidly expanding circle of nationally known literary figures. He was on very good terms with Dominick and his red wine in Little Italy and, in a different neighborhood, with a devout gentleman who was able to deliver rabbinical sherry by the gallon.

Among his friends, there was a steady round of parties. Every time one of the Cleveland artists or writers had a visitor, the entire group was called together. One such visitor was the poet James Daly, a friend of Charles Harris's, and another was H. P. Lovecraft, the writer of horror stories and weird tales, who came to see Sam Loveman and Alfred Galpin and who described for his aunts in Providence, Rhode Island, the Loveman-Crane-Sommer-Lescaze circle:

> As for the kind of time I am having—-it is simply great! I have just the incentive I need to keep me active and free from melancholy, and I look so well that I doubt if any Providence person would know me by sight! . . . The companionship of youth and artistic taste is what keeps one going! The programme of the past few days is much like that of the days previously chronicled, but last night was rather unusual. We held a meeting here of all the members of Loveman's literary circle, at which the conversation covered every branch of aesthetics. . . . It gave one a novel sensation to be "lionised" so much beyond my deserts by men as able as the painter Sommers [sic], Loveman, Galpin, etc. I met some new figures—Crane the poet, [Edward] Lazare, an ambitious literary student now in the army, and a delightful young fellow named Carroll Lawrence, who writes weird stories and wants to see all of mine. . . . All the circle say they like my stories—

which duly inflates me with pride. . . . Tonight Galpin, Crane, I, and a fellow I have not yet met are going to a concert held in the art museum building. Great days!!

It was during these "great days" that Crane began to visit the home of Charlotte and Richard Rychtarik, soon to be among his most intimate friends. Rychtarik, a Czechoslovakian artist recently arrived in Cleveland, was making a reputation for himself with the bold designs he prepared for Cleveland Playhouse productions. Cheerful, generous, and warm-hearted, he contributed to the circle's gatherings a steadying humanity. It was in Charlotte, however, that Crane found a companion to whom he could pour out the problems that continued to nag at him. For Charlotte was in many ways very like himself. Outgoing, fun-loving, talented musically, sympathetic to the poetry Crane was trying to write, she was able to offer the considerate understanding he needed and to match him in wit.

"Lately time flies," Crane wrote Bill Wright, and he obviously meant it. There had been a host of "excitements," not the least of which was the new poem. "I have had a somewhat long poem on hand all summer that has taken the kick out of everything else for me—and will continue to until it is finished. I never have had as steady an interest in my writing as lately—all of which proves that it was a good thing for me to have got away from my father who was so antipathetic to it."

For by this time "Faustus and Helen" had become obsessive. On a Friday night at the end of August, for instance, Hart received Munson's critique of the "final" versions of Parts I and II and got off a draft of the first lines of III in the return mail.

> Of course I'm enthusiastic about Faustus and Helen now! Who wouldn't be after your comments. However,—when it comes to the last section—I think I shall not attempt to make it the paragon of SPEED that I thought of. I think it needs more sheer weight than such a motive would provide. Beyond this I have only the surety that it is, of course, to include a comment on the world war—and be Promethean in mood. What made the first part of my poem so good was the extreme amount of time, work and thought put on it.

By the second week in October, Part I had been shipped off to *The Dial.* ("I'm impatient for the money,—besides that I feel that it is complete and might as well be out and aired. Having it around stagnates new ideas for me.") But *The Dial*—though it kept the manuscript for a month—wasn't interested. ("Evidently Mr. Watson, Jr. has something to say about things as [Gilbert] Seldes mentioned that he was obliged to keep it overtime in order to show it to Mr. Watson, concluding with, 'Regrettably, we cannot use it.' ") Crane was annoyed ("I would like to make a vow,

if I felt capable of keeping it, not to send anything again to the
Dial for two years. But, of course, I am merely cutting off my
own nose with such tactics"), but he had another likely place
of publication. For while Part I was being rejected by Seldes,
Josephson, in the Berlin office of *Broom*, was persuading Harold
Loeb that Part II—which months earlier Crane had sent off under
the title "The Springs of Guilty Song"—should be printed by the
magazine. As soon as Crane got word that the second part was
likely to be published, he sent along Part I. ("This latter [Josephson]
will probably find too emotional or old fashioned to praise, but I
thought I'd submit it anyway.") By December, Crane was reasonably sure that *Broom*, rumored to be failing, would be out of business before his work was printed. "I always (almost always)
hop on just about as the ship is sinking. I shall probably fool
around a year or so before those two poems get printed. Matty's
too evident predominance in the pages has been a bad thing for
Broom. At least I know a number of people who have resented it
highly." Crane's fears about the poem lying fallow for "a year or
so" were, as it turned out, unjustified, though it might have had a
happier publication history had that happened. For *Broom* revived
just as Crane completed Part III, printed Part II as if it were an
independent poem, and neglected to do anything about Parts I
and III. Now Crane could find no magazine that would publish the
entire poem. Finally, in September 1923, *Secession* accepted it—
and, once more, printed only part of it. Munson and Kenneth
Burke, acting as American editors, had shipped off to the European
editor, John Brooks Wheelwright, a complete and correct draft of
the poem, only to have Wheelwright—pressed for space—abandon
the second part (on the theory that it had, after all, been published) and allow the rest to go into print unproofread. Not until
the winter of 1924—more than a year after it started its published
career—did "Faustus and Helen" finally show up, complete at last,
in the seventh issue of *Secession*.

This first of the three major poems on which Crane's reputation rests was, therefore, not publicly known until his other two
principal enterprises—"Voyages" and *The Bridge*—were well under
way. Even in its manuscript circulation, however, "Faustus and
Helen" managed to travel far enough and wide enough to gain
Crane a reputation as a "most promising" young poet.

No one, so far as I know, has more successfully explicated his
poem than Crane himself did when, in 1924 or 1925, he set down
in "General Aims and Theories" the basic plan from which he
worked. "When I started writing Faustus & Helen," he wrote, "it
was my intention to embody in modern terms (words, symbols,
metaphors) a contemporary approximation to an ancient human
culture or mythology that seems to have been obscured rather
than illumined with the frequency of poetic allusions made to it
during the last century." His problem was to steer away from a

Greek Helen and a Teutonic Faustus, to find instead a scenery in which modern Faustus and Helen might walk. He had, he decided, to reconstruct in believable modern terms "the basic emotional attitude toward beauty that the Greeks had."

So I found "Helen" sitting in a street car; the Dionysian revels of her court and her seduction were transferred to a Metropolitan roof garden with a jazz orchestra; and the *katharsis* of the fall of Troy I saw approximated in the recent World War. The importance of this scaffolding may easily be exaggerated, but it gave me a series of correspondences between two widely separated worlds on which to sound some major themes of human speculation—love, beauty, death, renascence.

Crane was never to offer a more detailed analysis of the poem, but these remarks and his description of the poem as "metaphysical" should give us all we need in the way of guidance. With this much information and the text before him, any man should be able to see the basic structure of the set of lyrics; for Crane's "metaphysical" process—as the passage from Ben Jonson's *Alchemist* hints—is nothing more than the alchemy poets have always delighted in: the linking of several apparently unrelated human experiences through the "magical" action of shared imagery. In this way the "baked and labeled dough / Divided by accepted multitudes" of Crane's poem operates through the entire work not only as a communion image (reinforced by later references to Helen's "white wafer cheek of love" and Faustus's "bartered blood"), but also as an image for an altogether different sort of experience: the buying and selling which characterizes modern life and which finds its logical epitome in the transactions of the manipulators of metaphorical dough—hard cash—on the stock market.

Finding his way out of the "dimensional" world of stock markets and streetcars through human communion—eyes that meet, if only in dream or metaphor; hands that find "some way" to touch and so spread "ecstasies" through flesh—the Faustus of the poem reconciles the irreconcilable things of the world—love and death, for instance—thanks both to his mortality and to the immortality that love and art confer.

Crane does just what he had planned to do. He adapts the technique of Eliot to a point of view altogether different from Eliot's: for working with the mess of modern life—"smutty" business, orgiastic binges, the cataclysmic violence of world war— he lifts above that mess, above the despair of his times, through an imagination which "spans beyond despair," "outpacing" the businessman's "bargain," the jazz singer's shrill "vocable," the "religious" gunman-pilot's "prayer."

It is no wonder, therefore, that in November, when Crane for the first time had a chance to read *The Waste Land*, he found Eliot's poem "good, of course, but so damned dead"; for it was in this month that he was feverishly polishing his own "answer" to Eliot. And yet, if he was "rather disappointed" in *The Waste Land*, it was only because he valued Eliot so highly. And though Crane was wrong in concluding that *The Waste Land* failed to "add anything important to Eliot's achievement," he was absolutely right in seeing Eliot as the coming giant of the twenties.

I do not want to suggest that Crane, in the autumn of 1922, had delusions of grandeur, that he thought of himself as a rival to Eliot. He knew very well that the best he could then claim was a reputation as a minor poet. Yet he knew too that the only way he could become a major poet was through ambitious projects. Major poets, he recognized early on, are poets who set themselves tasks which stretch their powers to the breaking point.

He had not, however, done at all badly that year in building a good though small reputation; and when, at the end of October, William Stanley Braithwaite asked permission to reprint "Praise for an Urn" in an anthology, Crane was flattered. This was only one in a series of pleasant incidents. Louis Untermeyer had singled Crane out as a young man who would bear careful watching and had gone so far as to write a note asking if he might meet Crane in his next Cleveland visit. But perhaps the pleasantest event of all was a note from Charlie Chaplin, a "most delightful acknowledgment" of "Chaplinesque," which Crane had sent to him in the spring. Thrilled to have been in direct communication with "the greatest living actor," the man he regarded as modern civilization's "prime interpreter of the soul," Crane showed the letter to all his acquaintances.

He had also managed to have some work published. *Gargoyle*, to which early in the summer he had sent "The Great Western Plains"—a poem which feebly drew on material he would later use in "The River" section of *The Bridge*—included in its autumn issue both the poem (Crane was paid, "with apologies," one dollar) and Lescaze's "futuristic" portrait drawing of Crane glaring from a heavily accented right eye. Amused with the drawing, Crane told his friends that Lescaze had discovered in him Jakob Boehme's visionary man—the right eye focused on both future and eternity, the left turned backward into time. Crane, of course, had arranged for the publication of the drawing and—as soon as it was printed—saw to it that *Gargoyle*'s editors had a set of reproductions of Bill Sommer's work. Another set went to the editors of *Broom*.

His support of his friends also involved him in a tiff with *The Little Review*, which in the spring had gone out of its way to attack Munson's *Secession*. What he described to Munson as a "slight reprimand" was intended, he said, to keep Jane Heap "aggravated" enough to continue the attack and give the magazine much-needed publicity. Crane's letter, with precisely the kind of rejoinder he had expected, appeared in the autumn 1922 issue of *The Little Review*—the Joseph Stella issue—accidentally forging one more link between Crane and the Brooklyn Bridge which Stella so frequently celebrated and which Crane was still to turn to.

But not everything that Crane wrote immediately found a publisher. "Sunday Morning Apples," which he had dashed off on a happy summer day (the first Saturday in August), was to wait for first publication until 1924. This poem, as Crane told Munson, had been written "out of sheer joy" and Crane at first dismissed it as "a homely and gay thing" in praise of his friendship for Bill Sommer. Celebrating Sommer's greatest strength (his "rich and faithful strength of line") and listing some of Sommer's favorite subjects, the poem manages to deal as well with the "seasonable madness" that animated both painter and poet. For Crane, in describing one of Sommer's paintings, had very carefully drawn from it the country man's progress through the natural year— perhaps Crane's own most persistent preoccupation (one that would determine, for instance, a great deal of the imagistic structure of *The Bridge*). At the heart of the poem, "spring" gives way to summer ripeness (the "ripe nude"), which itself merges unobtrusively into autumn's "purple shadow" to burst finally "on the winter of the world." Dealing with man's "spontaneities," his free gestures in a world of fixed, recurrent cycles, both Crane and Sommer celebrate the "explosion" of delight an artist's "inquiries" can produce when, with understanding eyes, he arranges a still life or abstracts from the moving pattern of life the design joy scrawls on time—as when, for instance, "A boy runs with a dog before the sun." Casual in tone, cheerful, yet elegantly formal, the poem illustrates that which it preaches, maneuvering finally its real subject—Bill himself—into the very heart of his illuminating subject matter: "The apples, Bill, the apples!"

"Sunday Morning Apples" would wait two years for publication. The poem that would become the first of the "Voyages" set was, on the other hand, well on the way to the public eye by the middle of autumn. "The Bottom of the Sea Is Cruel," as it was then called, was one of several poems that Munson had taken back to New York and that he was showing to other writers and editors. One of them, Kenneth Burke, then associated with *The Dial*, was particularly impressed and spent a little time with Munson suggesting possible improvements in the poem. Though Crane was reluctant to accept the suggestions, he was more than pleased that Burke, whom he admired, was interested in his poetry. "I'm glad that Burke meets you in approving the 'sea' poem, and I'm sorry that it is, or at least appears to be beyond me to make changes in it," he wrote Munson, adding that

it was a poem about which he had never been "very enthusiastic."
Like the jazz-dominated second part of "Faustus and Helen," it
was a formal exercise in a medium too little tapped by poetry.
Here the medium was advertising.

> Its only value in my mind rests in its approach to the "advertise-
> ment" form that I am contemplating and, I think, spoke to
> you about. It is a kind of poster,—in fact, you might name
> it "Poster" if the idea hits you. There is nothing more profound
> in it than a "stop, look and listen" sign. And it is this concep-
> tion of the poem that makes me like the last line as I do—
> merely bold and unambitious like a skull and cross-bones in-
> signia.

When "Poster" was accepted by *Secession* for its January 1923
issue, Crane was certainly not visualizing it as the first in a set of
six related lyrics. Only much later—after the sixth, tentatively
titled "Belle Isle," had been written—did he find a subject and
an imagery to link the two ends of what would become an in-
tricately integrated group.

During the autumn and early winter of 1922, however, it was
not so much writing as day-to-day good fellowship that filled
Crane's relatively limited spare time. Nothing of world-shaking
importance seemed to happen, but all the hours were filled up.
A little work, a little wine, a little writing, a very little love affair,
a little effort, now and then, to bring eligible middle-aged men
home to meet his mother: this was the pattern of Crane's life.
Though he signed a mid-September note to Munson "hastily, unusually so—," the letter betrays nothing of a pressing nature.

> I'm about fed up on furnaces and hot water heaters. I've
> been very attentive to the little ad. stories now for quite awhile.
> It's about time that I did something about F and Helen again.
> To make things better or worse (I don't know which yet) I've
> almost fallen in love. I may add, an object more than usually
> responsive this time.
> So picture me as imbibing much at Simoni's, but otherwise,
> feeling rather middle aged. I've rushed through this while
> Mother powdered her nose to go and see "Orphans of the
> Storm." O yes,—Fitts wrote me about contributing to his mag-
> azine. I've nothing to send him however.

For a time there were only trivial crises. Crane drifted along
through pleasant, relaxed days made eventful only by the com-
ings and goings of friends and relatives. When William Lescaze
announced his intention of returning briefly to Europe, Crane
began taking orders for copies of *Ulysses* which Lescaze was
supposed to smuggle into the country. "He is going to try to
bring back a raft of 'Ulysses' for frantic Clevelanders including

our friend Loveman who often speaks of you," Crane explained to Munson. (The "raft" of copies of the banned book finally turned out to be two.)

Another traveler was Grace Crane, who for a month in September and October "did" New York. She at first intended to spend only a few days vacationing—seeing shows, shopping, resting at the Waldorf, the one hotel in New York that she liked—but she soon decided that she might look for work of some sort (which she never found) and extended her stay from week to week.

Her visit was good for both mother and son, for it gave each the perspective they found it hard to retain under the pressure of Cleveland intimacies. There is no question, I think, that Hart had been doing his best gradually to ease Grace's dependence on him. Though they joked about the "suitors" who still escorted Grace to theaters and to parties, Crane would have been glad to see his mother married to any of them. For he felt that her anxiety about dwindling cash reserves and about her son's "development" might both, if she were to set up a household of her own, be brought under control. Less selfishly, he was pleased to see his mother able to regain—if only for the month in New York—the high spirits of earlier years, when on holidays and long vacations Grace and Hart had lived in the height of style. Even their letters begin to sound like the letters that half a dozen years before a very different seventeen-year-old had exchanged with a different mother. "Am anxious to hear *all* about things," he wrote her on October 7, just before her return.

> Have a good time right up to the last minute. Chuck your thoughts about anything so drab as work—and laugh with 'em all!
>
> I'm glad everyone has treated you with such affection. Give all *eligibles* my regards. . . .
>
> Grandma has been chipper and quite unruffled!

Unruffled Grandma must have been ignorant of Hart's consumption of rabbinical sherry, for he was at this point buying a gallon a week. Two days after he posted the note to his mother, he got off a letter to Charmion von Wiegand in which he described himself at his ease in his tower room, "sipping some delicious old style sherry as I write that's only supposed to be sold to rabbis and catholics for ceremonial purposes." Its function, as he explained, was to nudge inspiration along: "You see the muse has been taught to slip a few things over on the guardians of the faith." Three days later—on Thursday, October 12, the day of his mother's return—he killed the bottle and presumably got rid of the evidence, though not without regrets for its passing. As he explained to Munson, "It's as smooth as Prufrock and is only supposed to be sold to *rabbis* for religious purposes. Rabbi Crane! What strange conversions there are."

Grace's return was an occasion for celebration, her trip having made her, Crane said, "almost too rejuvenated to suit my jealous disposition." Not only had she done all the things Crane longed to do; she had even managed to visit most of his friends. Munson's wife—whom Crane had not met—was, she told Hart, " 'a faun,' a lovely 'gazelle.' " And she described in great detail a meeting Munson had arranged for her with Isadora Duncan and her "delightful" husband.

Crane, who had never seen Isadora Duncan dance, immediately secured tickets for her impending Cleveland visit. She more than lived up to his mother's description of her. "She gave the same program (All Tschaikowsky) that she gave in Moscow for the Soviet celebration," he wrote Munson.

It was glorious beyond words, and sad beyond words, too, from the rude and careless reception she got here. It was like a wave of life, a flaming gale that passed over the heads of the nine thousand in the audience without evoking response other than silence and some maddening cat-calls. After the first movement of the "Pathétique" she came to the fore of the stage, her hands extended. Silence,—the most awful silence! I started clapping furiously until she disappeared behind the draperies. At least one tiny sound should follow her from all that audience. She continued through the performance with utter indifference for the audience and with such intensity of gesture and such plastique grace as I have never seen, although the music was sometimes almost drowned out by the noises from the hall. I felt like rushing to the stage, but I was stimulated almost beyond the power to walk straight. When it was all over she came to the fore-stage again in the little red dress that had so shocked Boston, as she stated, and among other things, told the people to go home and take from the bookshelf the works of Walt Whitman, and turn to the section called, "Calamus." Ninety-nine percent of them had never heard of Whitman, of course, but that was part of the beauty of her gesture. Glorious to see her there with her right breast and nipple quite exposed, telling the audience that the truth was not pretty, that it was really indecent and telling them (boobs!) about Beethoven, Tschaikowsky and Scriabin! She is now on her way back to Moscow, so I understand, where someone will give her some roses for her pains.

Soon he persuaded himself that he had singlehandedly been responsible for the final ovation that a few hundred souls had given her. To friends who hadn't been there, he described how his applause had turned the tide of the departing crowds, catching the final stragglers to bring them back to the front of the auditorium. As the story improved—in each telling, Hart's applause got louder —Sam Loveman, who had been with him, found Hart's role almost as interesting as the dances themselves had been. "Hart had a very curious way of believing that he was the prime instigator in any movement," Loveman told me. "For instance, when we went to see Isadora Duncan . . . she was hissed, she was hooted, she was booted, they threw things at her, and left the hall. There were a few hundred people who stayed. Well, now, Hart claimed that his hand-clapping had forced the acclamation that was heard by the few hundred that remained, which was not true. I'm sure that it took more than Hart's hand-clapping." Responsible or not for Isadora's rescue from the Philistines, Hart remembered the evening and the figure of the heroic dancer to the end of his life, fitting her—along with the Walt Whitman she had celebrated—into the gallery of Olympians with which, in epigraph and reference, he decorated *The Bridge*.

In spite of such visits as Isadora Duncan's—or perhaps because of them—Crane began to grow restive. In letter after letter to friends in New York or on the Continent, he made plans for the day when he would again break free from what he now considered a thoroughly stultifying middle-class society. He was far too sensitive not to realize that a great deal of his poetic strength came precisely from his own experience as a part of that society, but he felt he needed the private freedom—the anonymity—that only a large city could offer. He was troubled, too, because rumors of alcoholic sprees had drifted not just through his office but into his home. And Grace Crane—in many ways a most tolerant person—was intolerant of her son's private and public sherry parties. After doing her best to ignore the all too obvious evidence of Hart's drinking, she announced that she would no longer allow him to have alcohol of any kind in her home. Her ultimatum—coming on the same day that had seen Hart's applause for iconoclast Isadora Duncan—was more than he was willing to take. "I am in great ferment," he wrote Munson, and went on to say that he had moved to a hotel until he could become calm enough to talk to his family. A host of irritating annoyances—as much Hart's making as Grace's—had plagued both of them. "They are little things, mostly," he wrote, "but such little things accumulate almost into a complex that [is] too much for me to work under. There is no use in discussing them here, but just the constant restraint necessary in living with others, you may appreciate, is a deadening thing. Unless something happens to release me from such annoyances I give up hope of doing any satisfactory writing."

Yet Crane did return home. For Christmas was less than two weeks away, and Grace and Hart were determined to be forgiving. Beneath superficial good spirits, however, Hart was unhappy, more and more frequently finding escape in drinking—away from home. It was, perhaps, neither himself nor the city that was at fault, he explained to Bill Wright, who, now out of college and settled with his family in Warren, Pennsylvania, had written to tell Hart of the boredom of life in an even smaller town than Cleveland. The real trouble, Hart sighed, was in the fabric of the modern world.

> However much boredom you may find in Warren—I assure you, it will not be as strenuous as the hot water I am stewing in. The Pittsburgh Water Heater surely has been on my mind the last three weeks, and the burden is still unshifted. I am growing bald trying to scratch up new ideas in house-keeping and personal hygiene—to tell people why they need more and quicker hot water. Last night I got drunk on some sherry. Even in that wild orgy my mind was still enchained by the hot water complex—and I sat down and reeled off the best lines written so far in my handling of the campaign. All of my poems in the future will attest this sterilizing influence of HOT WATER!
>
> Nothing happens here, either. I am grateful only for wine. I have neither women or song. Cleveland street car rides twice a day take out all hope of these latter elements. I think of New York and next summer when the present is too sharp (or is it dull!). But the main faults are not of our city, alone. They are of the age. A period that is loose at all ends, without apparent direction of any sort. In some ways the most amazing age there ever was. Appalling and dull at the same time.
>
> You have my pulse. I wish I had something more inspiriting to offer. But not today.

Christmas week brought Crane briefly improved relations with his mother (along with a new walking stick and puce-colored gloves). "I cannot remember a more hectic month than the last," he wrote Munson at the end of the first week of 1923, "unless I recall some of the old bivouacs of New York days, when I rico-chet-ed 'from roof to roof' without intermission." For though he might enter the new year "flabbergasted and dull," he had be-hind him memories of "two rush campaigns to write, gifts and remembrances to buy and send to far too many people—sup-pers, parties and evenings—much tossing of the pot,—'prison, palace and reverberation'!" And before him—literally before him, a copy beside his typewriter—he had the almost completed draft of "Faustus and Helen": "My carousing on New Year's Eve had one good outcome; it started the third part of 'Faustus and Helen' with more gusto than before. When I catch my next breath I hope to carry it on to the end."

# 15

Though it may be idle to speculate about the sources of that "gusto" which Crane did indeed recover early in 1923, and which was responsible not only for the last section of "Faustus and Helen" but for most of the initial planning of *The Bridge*, some credit for it should go to Bill Sommer and to the long fruitful discussions he and Crane shared. These discussions —about the nature of art and about the state of mind of the artist—are reflected in Crane's correspondence and in the voluminous notes that Sommer, an eloquent, perceptive man, jotted down on scraps of paper—backs of envelopes, grocery bags, blank space at the end of letters. One can only guess at the date of composition of most of the surviving fragments, many of them decorated with casual sketches in pencil or in ink. Yet among them one can trace parallels between Sommer's reading and Crane's. Hunter Ingalls, who in preparation for his fine study of Sommer's work searched carefully through these notes, discovered numerous quotations from Crane's favorite authors and from work in which we know Crane was interested. Passages from Wyndham Lewis, from Ezra Pound's essay on Gaudier-Brzeska, from Ouspensky's *Tertium Organum*—usually on the nature of artistic form or on the nature of the artistic experience— are quoted at length.

From Ouspensky, Sommer carefully copied out a dramatic presentation of a four-dimensional world:

> The snail feels the line as space, i.e., as something constant. It feels the rest of the world as time, i.e., as something eternally moving. The horse feels the plane as space. It feels the rest of the world as time.

Wyndham Lewis is quoted at length on the "accidental rightness" of good painting. And passages from Gaudier-Brzeska alternate with Pound's comments on Gaudier, Sommer sometimes going to the trouble to check dictionary definitions of terms. ("Great gift of Gaudier's—Synthesis" is followed by Sommer's careful transcription of a dictionary definition of the word.) But more often than not, Sommer interlarded quoted passages with his own observations: "Ideals are like nuts—their contents become moldy in time and hollow—therefore we must use our Ideals in the present moment and keep gathering new ones." His theme, in original as well as in quoted passages, was the supremacy of the arts: "The fates gave us art so that we could find ourselves and be free from the turmoil of life, the world as it ought to be is here, our world is an error."

Almost as interesting as the evidence of Crane's influence on Sommer is the evidence of reverse influence. I have already mentioned Crane's diligent reading of Clive Bell's *Since Cézanne* —Sommer's "bible," according to William Milliken. But this is only one example among many. In the autumn and winter of 1922, Crane steeped himself in art books, all of which he shared with Sommer. As soon as higher salary checks had started rolling in, Crane had sent off to Germany for a number of such books. By early October he was the proud owner of "a beautiful German monograph on Etruscan art," and fretful about other books which had not yet arrived: "God knows,—I suppose the post office found something 'obscene' in the Japanese landscapes somewhere, or the Chinese temples,—or the Egyptian monuments!!" One by one, however, they came: "the most prodigious book on Egyptian sculpture that I've ever seen" capping the batch. This book convinced Crane—as perhaps it had convinced Sommer— that "the children of the Nile completed every possibility of sculpture long before the Greeks began to work. . . . It's largely the spacious austerity of Egyptian art that particularly hits me." A volume on African primitive sculpture and a set of books on Cézanne—the latter a gift from Charmion von Wiegand—completed the collection.

Crane was not only learning a good deal from Sommer; he was also continuing to sell his friend's work. As part of this project, he had persuaded Munson to invite Sommer to do a cover drawing for *Secession*. His principal activity on his friend's behalf, however, was a four-way interchange of letters involving Crane, Munson, Sommer, and William Carlos Williams. After his earlier efforts to persuade a New York gallery to exhibit Sommer had fallen through, Crane decided that perhaps the second-best procedure would be to place Sommer's paintings with a number of influential writers and editors. Munson was to act as an unpaid agent. Williams, one of the first men Munson approached, liked a small water color—a dramatic grouping of three dark figures against an angular, expressionistic landscape—which, after a good deal of confusion, he eventually purchased and which until the time of his death in 1963 was displayed in a second-floor bedroom of his Rutherford home. As Crane explained in his reply to Williams's first letter, Sommer was pleased to place the painting with Williams: "He likes your poetry and felt flattered at the interest of a man who could appreciate painting as well as your Matisse poem showed in 'Contact.' "

The confusion over the painting arose because no one was willing to fix a final price for it: Munson recommended $20, Crane recommended $25, and Sommer advised Williams to pay what he thought it was worth. For a while letters came and went every day: "Ye Gods! don't ask me what price to make it," Crane finally exclaimed to Williams.

> Sommer himself can't be made to care very much since it is going to a fellow artist. He's baulky as hell about letters, simply gets the d.t.s at the thought, but, between ourselves and whether he writes you or not, I wish you would make it $25 if you can. Considering the current prices of most work infinitely inferior to his, it's certainly worth it, and he needs the money for canvas. . . .
>
> I wish you could meet old Sommer. We want to get him out of that union labor hell-hole lithography factory before it's too late. Make any noise you can about your picture to the right people, *please*, and let me know of any friends of yours that might care to see more of his work, either to talk or buy.
>
> There's nobody in this country that's got certain line qualities that Sommer has. I wish you could see some of his things around the walls of my room! But they're practically buried here.

Williams's reply was warm in tone, generous in praise. Crane paraphrased this letter for Munson: "Williams . . . said that Bill got under his underdrawers!—and went on to say that he was potentially greater than Marin. It has heartened Bill wonderfully. Such a letter was worth more than the plaudits of a hundred Rosenfelds."

Crane immediately invested in a set of photographic reproductions of six of Sommer's best paintings. This was part of a new campaign that had as its object a monograph on Sommer and a related gallery exhibition. Munson had agreed to discuss both ventures with Alfred Stieglitz and William Fisher. The hope was that Fisher, who had just seen through the press a monograph on Kuniyoshi, might consider doing a similar work on Sommer. Stieglitz might be able to arrange a gallery show.

"If Stieglitz becomes interested," Crane wrote, "please assure him that I shall be glad to send him originals, etc." Even if both monograph and exhibition fell through—as they did—the photographs could be used in selling individual pictures. "Keep them as long as you want and show or send them anywhere that you think advisable."

The next purchase of a Sommer drawing was made by Sibley Watson of *The Dial*, who had regularly been turning down

Crane's own work. Watson's payment was the same as Williams's —$25—but carried with it rights to reproduce the work in the magazine without additional payment and rights to buy similar work at a similar price. Crane rushed back a note to Munson saying that Sommer had no objections to the attached strings. Though, as Crane explained, Sommer's gratitude to Munson would "never reach the frenzied pitch of a letter," the realization that there was a possibility of finding a large audience for his work was for both Sommer and Crane a great spiritual boost. "I must admit," Crane wrote, "that I personally got a greater 'thrill' out of the news than any personal acceptances have given me for many a day."

By now Crane was completely committed to an aesthetic he and Sommer had worked out together. It drew into focus a great deal of the reading they had been doing in common—Clive Bell, Wyndham Lewis, Ouspensky—but more importantly it founded itself on an essential optimism, a celebration of life that both men shared and that was more fundamental than the accident of their reading. What they felt they had experienced on both their alcoholic and their aesthetic benders was a glimpse into the heart of things. There, beneath the disordered surface of the modern world, they looked into a coherence which gave them the courage not to deny their artist's vocation. For only the artist and the mystic, they felt, could penetrate to that ordered place—and only the artist in his structured works could reproduce for the rest of the world something of that inner world's glowing possibilities.

It was to the timeless elements in painting and poetry that Crane and Sommer turned, each hoping to discover a continuity of technique and of vision in his own medium. Each was very much a man of the times, willing to adapt new techniques to what he regarded as essentially unchanging aesthetic ends, unwilling to capitalize on fads and fad techniques for the sake of popularity. Sommer, like Crane, saw Dadaism and its excesses as pointless virtuosity, pointless because surface disorder was made to seem essential rather than superficial. Crane probably also talked to Sommer about his rejection of Eliot's view of the world. For Eliot's vision, he felt—and it is important to remember that he was thinking this at the time of *The Waste Land* and not, say, at the time of *Four Quartets*—ignored "spiritual events and possibilities." Though Crane would never find in orthodox faith the spiritual events he had in mind—spiritual events that arose in this world and not in any other and that could be reduced to something so simple as human affection, human communion, human love—he knew precisely the sort of experience he was talking about, an experience that sometimes involved sex and as often as not didn't: an experience that he would find as he sat up to all hours with Bill Sommer trying to calculate how a Bach fugue, a Chinese painting, a Donne sonnet all irrationally illuminated one another; or the experience later in the year, in an old house halfway up the side of Woodstock's dominating mountain, of hammering out with Slater Brown and Edward Nagle a diagram to explain the structure of "reality"; or of sudden shattering love which reduced him, later still, to early-morning drunken howls—"I love you! I love you!"—before the New York apartment of one young man whose startled mother, roused from sleep, gave Crane a last quick touch of beloved flesh when she forced her sleepy son ("Send him home, whoever he is! What will the neighbors think!") to descend to the street and lead Crane away from the door. Even in Crane's darkest days of disillusionment, experiences of this sort would lift him into productive intensities—in Mexico, for example, when participation in Indian religious rites and participation in rites of love with Peggy Cowley could lead him to "The Broken Tower."

It was with Sommer that Crane most fully talked out his ideas. And it was in defense of Sommer's art that Crane defined his own. Part of a very long letter to Munson beautifully illustrates this habit of thought.

> Stieglitz voiced an old feeling of mine about Bill's work—the lack of finish evident in so much of it. This has always pained me. As a whole, his comments seem very just. But I tend to differ with him on one point in common with other critics who are so obsessed with the importance of current developments in art that they fail to recognize certain positive and timeless qualities.
>
> I refer to the quality of line in Sommer's work. That has, in particular, nothing more to do with modern work than the draughtsmanship of Michelangelo. It is something that may not distinguish a man as a great innovator or personality—but it is, for all that, a rare and wondrous quality. From what you write Stieglitz has the sense to recognize this quality and to value it. But a person like Georgia O'Keeffe, who has so distinctly her own horn to play, is scornful of everything short of evolution and revolution.
>
> It is a relief once in awhile to detach one's judgment from such considerations as hers, and to look at a piece of work as totally detached from time and fashion, and then judge it entirely on its individual appeal. I think that in Sommer's case, you, Williams and myself are appreciators of this kind. I can enjoy Bill's things regardless of their descent, evident or otherwise, from French or German artists of the last generation. He has certain perfections which many of the most lauded were lacking in. God DAMN this constant nostalgia for something always "new." This disdain for anything with a trace of the past in it!! This kind of criticism is like a newspaper, always

with its dernier cri. It breeds its own swift decay because its whole theory is built on an hysterical sort of evolution theory. I shall probably always enjoy El Greco and Goya. I still like to look at the things Sommer makes, because many of them are filled with a solid and clear beauty.

. . . Please let [me] know what you find in Eliot. With your head knocked against Burke's over such a topic there ought to be some fine illuminations. You already know, I think, that my work for the past two years (those meagre drops!) has been more influenced by Eliot than any other modern. He has been a very good counter-balance to Matty's shifting morale and violent urgings. . . .

There is no one writing in English who can command so much respect, to my mind, as Eliot. However, I take Eliot as a point of departure toward an almost complete reverse of direction. His pessimism is amply justified, in his own case. But I would apply as much of his erudition and technique as I can absorb and assemble toward a more positive, or (if [one] must put it so in a sceptical age) ecstatic goal. I should not think of this if a kind of rhythm and ecstasy were not (at odd moments, and rare!) a very real thing to me. I feel that Eliot ignores certain spiritual events and possibilities as real and powerful now as, say, in the time of Blake. Certainly the man has dug the ground and buried hope as deep and direfully as it can ever be done. He has outclassed Baudelaire with a devastating humor that the earlier poet lacked.

After this perfection of death—nothing is possible in motion but a resurrection of some kind. Or else, as everyone persists in announcing in the deep and dirgeful Dial, the fruits of civilization are entirely harvested. Everyone, of course, wants to die as soon and as painlessly as possible! Now is the time for humor, and the Dance of Death. All I know through very much suffering and dullness (somehow I seem to twinge more all the time) is that it interests me to still affirm certain things. That will be the persisting theme of the last part of "F and H" as it has been all along.

While Crane was busy with friends, his mother was doing her best to see that he kept in touch with relatives close to his own age. His cousins Joseph and Hurxthal Frease and another cousin, Joseph Frease Smith, were consequently frequent guests at the lavish Sunday dinners Grace and Hart's grandmother would serve.

Joe Smith and Joe Frease were both attending Case Institute of Technology, and though they had little in common with Hart, all the boys—Hart included—shared a fondness for Hart's grandmother's cherry pies. They also shared recollections of happier days when Grace, C.A., and Hart would drive down to Canton to visit the Frease boys' Aunt Rachel, Mrs. Frease-Green (like Grace, she was a singer, but, unlike Grace, she had for years studied opera in France and Germany and on her return had made something of a reputation as a soloist). Yet the Sunday evening visits of Crane's cousins were often awkward affairs. "I was not interested at the time in writing poetry," Joseph Frease recollected, "and he was not interested in engineering—which I was studying at the time." Even Hurxthal, who had once tried his hand at short stories and poetry and who was precisely Crane's age, found relatively little to discuss. Joseph Frease wrote me that only once had Hart really bothered to talk about literature to him: "Hart made one attempt one weekend to be pleasant to me—taking me to dinner and imbibing in port wine—somewhat scarce at the time (Prohibition times). It turned out somewhat unpleasant for me and I do not recall much of anything about what we may have discussed except that he did suggest that he was going to get me a copy of a book by James Joyce. This never occurred."

Through much of this time Crane kept himself busy, but there were a few rough February days when the kind of love he thought he was finally free of suddenly returned with all its devastating violence. "You see, for two or three years I have not been attacked in this way," he explained to Munson. There had been infatuations which Crane felt bordered on love—infatuations with both men and women; but they involved no deep commitment on either side. And there had been quite a few loveless erotic adventures. When Crane refers to these adventures in his letters—as in some of the unpublished letters to Wilbur Underwood—he almost always adopts a bragging yet ironic tone. He tells such stories, I think, more for literary effect than for any other purpose, usually trying both to shock his correspondent and to make him laugh. His efforts to "educate" Cleveland's truck drivers into the combined mysteries of sex and literature—especially his father's truck drivers—are recounted with such evident good humor that no one (except possibly the truck drivers) could be offended. Even when the adventure is summed up in a good deal of graphic detail, it sounds less like an erotic triumph than like a demonstration of metaphysical wit. A cheerful note to Underwood that begins with a sweeping *Whoops!* is characteristic of this sort of correspondence. Crane is talking about some late-night visits to the Cleveland parks: "The first night brought a most strenuous wooing and the largest instrument I have handled. Europa and the Bull are now entirely passé. As this happened only two nights ago, I am modest and satisfied. Still, I am uneasy. I fear for all the anticlimaxes that are surely now in store for me. Like Alec, I yearn for new worlds to conquer, and I fear that there are only a few insignificant peninsulas and archipelagoes left."

Nevertheless, adventures of this sort—or encounters like the one with "an athlete—20 only—dark haired—distinctly Bohemian" who one Saturday night made love to him—were, Crane realized, essentially empty, nothing on which a man could found a life. Such relationships were doomed to disintegrate when the adventure itself disintegrated. There is a muddle of braggadocio and self-contempt when Crane sentimentally writes of the affair with his Bohemian athlete: "I hope it will last a while—I deserve a little kindness and he *was* so kind!" For when love wasn't available, kindness sometimes was—and kindnesses of the sort Crane had in mind could alleviate lust.

Yet lust was—halfway through Crane's twenty-third year— omnipresent. All summer and autumn he had been driven by desires that more often than not he diligently stamped down. "But how I am stalked by lust these dog days!" he wrote Underwood early in September. "And how many 'shadowy' temptations beset me at every turn! Were I free from my family responsibilities I would give myself to passion to the final cinder. After all— that and poetry are the only things life holds for me."

For "love," Crane had convinced himself, was impossibly dangerous, not so much in that it might be discovered—which was dangerous enough—but in that it threatened to dissolve the hard, ironic armor he had devised to shield himself from a wounding world. Yet when love did come, Crane was always vulnerable.

No wonder, then, that his midwinter, fragmentary love affair, which was so tenuous that it barely existed, should nevertheless move him deeply. He had congratulated himself, he wrote Munson, that two or three years free of love had "cured" him, had built up a "security against future outbreaks of the affections." Yet the modeling of a face, the hint of a gesture, were enough to destroy all his defenses.

> A recent evening at a concert some glances of such a very stirring response and beauty threw me into such an hour of agony as I supposed I was beyond feeling ever again. The mere senses can be handled without such effects, but I discover I am powerless as ever against those higher and certainly hopeless manifestations of the flesh. O God that I should have to live within these American restrictions forever, where one cannot whisper a word, nor at least exchange a few words!

Crane, however, must have managed his few words, for within two weeks he was writing Underwood a rhapsodic, sometimes incoherent account of an evening which had lifted past casual affection. This interlude, Crane knew, would end, and soon, because this time the lover was not a stranger but a boy Crane had been acquainted with for years. There was far too much risk for anything more than a quick caress, a touch in the dark.

Yet that touch created for Crane indissoluble bonds. Perhaps the experience was so overwhelming because so brief, perhaps because for once Crane did not have to be the aggressor: an "impossible" love had approached him and demanded a return of affection. "Those who have wept in the darkness sometimes are rewarded with stray leaves blown inadvertently," he wrote Underwood. "Since your last I have [had] one of those few experiences that come,—ever, but which are almost sufficient in their very incompleteness." The night before, he wrote, he had gone to a vaudeville show with the boy, who had "manifested charming traits before" but had never been alone with Crane. Very little had actually occurred, but a kind of communication had been established, a fragile communication, playful and delicate. Crane, with no trace of irony, saw it as wholesome. "Last night," he wrote, "—it sounds silly enough to tell (but not in view of his real beauty)—O, it was only a matter of light affectionate stray touches—and half-hinted speech. But these were genuine and in that sense among the few things I can remember happily."

The boy became an image of idealized grace.

> . . . you must think of someone mildly sober, with a face not too thin, but with faun precision of line and feature. Crisp ears, a little pointed, fine and docile hair almost golden, yet darker,—eyes that are a little heavy—but wide apart and usually a little narrowed,—aristocratic (English) jaws, and a mouth that [is] just mobile enough to suggest voluptuousness. A strong rather slender figure, negligently carried, that is perfect from flanks that hold an easy persistence to shoulders that are soft yet full and hard. A smooth and rather olive skin that is cool—at first.

Though Crane recognized that his passion would come to nothing, it nevertheless left behind it a residue of joy. Crane was just drunk enough when he described the boy to make the shift from the particular experience of love—ecstatic and rich—to the spiritual consequence of love: his poetry. For love, he felt, put him in touch with those forces he and Sommer had been talking about as they read Clive Bell and Ouspensky. Knowing what we do of Crane's thinking at this time, it is easy to see how Bell's abstractions about the pure forms of art and Ouspensky's celebrations of a continuing strain of mystical vision merge with this new ecstasy to nudge Crane into a productive frame of mind. The wild transitions of the rest of his letter are not, therefore, quite so wild as they might at first appear.

> Excuse this long catalog—I admit it is mainly for my own satisfaction, and I am drunk now and in such state my satisfactions are always lengthy. When I see you ask me to tell you

more about him for he is worth more and better words, I assure you. O yes, I shall see him again soon. The climax will be
all too easily reached,—But my gratitude is enduring—if only
for that *once*, at least, something beautiful approached me and
as though it were the most natural thing in the world, enclosed
me in his arm and pulled me to him without my slightest bid.
And we who create must endure—must hold to spirit not
by the mind, the intellect alone. These have no mystic possibilities. O flesh damned to hate and scorn! I have felt my cheek
pressed on the desert these days and months too much. How
old I am! Yet, oddly now this sense [of] age—not at all in
my senses—is gaining me altogether unique love and happiness. I feel I have been through much of this again and again
before. I long to go to India and stay always. Meditation on
the sun is all there is. Not that this isn't enough! I mean I find
my imagination more sufficient all the time. The work of the
workaday world is what I dislike. I spend my evenings in
music and sometimes ecstasy.

He goes on in the same letter to say that most evenings are
spent in composition, that he has been "writing a lot lately,"
that he feels he is bringing much into contemporary verse that
is new: "I'm on a synthesis of America and its structural identity
now, called *The Bridge.* . . ."

If we can see all the ecstasy, the theorizing, the reading, the
job satisfactions, the relatively peaceful life at home playing one
against the other, we should be able to sense the climate that led
Crane to his great poem. Of course, we should have to recognize,
as Crane did, that each of these elements was in some ways a distraction. His love affair was as destructive as it was creative:
"Passions of this kind completely derail me from anything creative
for days,—and that's the worst of it." But they were necessary
distractions—in the long run as functional as eating and sleeping. They were parts of a wholeness which he was determined to
incorporate into poetry.

A different sort of ingredient—one much more susceptible to
analysis—was the literary correspondence that Crane had for
years been carrying on with Munson, that he had recently begun
with Tate, and that he was just beginning with Waldo Frank. In
long, gossipy letters to these friends, Crane fell into the trick of
working out for himself the shifting trial outlines for the poem
that would become, he knew even then, a major work. These
correspondents were not just confidants but something more:
that real audience, the friends of good taste, for whom every
artist works.

It is true enough, I suppose, that ideally the artist creates his
work for the anonymous audience that survives him and that, if he
is lucky, becomes his future. But most artists in the here and now

bring off their grand effects not for their "public," which they seldom meet, but for sympathetic parents, wives, lovers, friends. Though Crane's parents were each sometimes sympathetic, they were hardly an audience for his poetry. His lovers, with two known exceptions, found the poems—even those written for them —mysterious. Yet in literary friends, especially at this stage of his career, Crane had the happy fortune to know the sort of men whose response to drafts of his work would help define its final shape. I don't want to suggest that an unfavorable comment from, say, Tate would cause Crane to destroy a section of a poem. It would not. But it would cause him to make a reappraisal of work not yet completed; it would kick into action his own critical faculties.

Of these letter-writing friends, the newest one, Waldo Frank, had the most immediate impact on Crane's work. Thanks to Munson's enthusiasm, Crane had for several years been reading Frank's novels and articles. Yet not until he had carefully read Munson's study did Crane begin a systematic investigation into the ideas of the older writer. Munson's book, which Crane planned to review for the *Double-Dealer*, had been sent on in galleys in the hope that Crane might be able to persuade Richard Rychtarik to collaborate with him in working out a cover design. The book, Crane felt, was not only "exact and fair" but "dramatic" as well. But it was really the subject of the book in whom Crane was at this time most interested, and in very short order he had laid the foundations for a friendship that would continue through the rest of his life. "We never quarrelled," Frank recollected. "He did quarrel with a number of his friends, but that was usually after he had been drinking a good deal . . . But he kept that side of his nature away from me."

Their correspondence had begun with a letter from Hart. "Waldo Frank wrote me a very cordial letter in answer to my written praise of 'Hope,'" Crane wrote Munson. It was, however, a second letter from Frank that set the tone for much of their correspondence: "You are a genuine poet. No doubt of that at all," Frank wrote. "A passionate abstraction takes the place in your work of the rhetoric, the clang-tricks, the ancient associations so usually found in verse even of the best sort." The second part of "Faustus and Helen," which had just appeared in *Broom*, seemed to him altogether successful: "I do not know when I have seen the raw and sophistical qualities of jazz and dancing and repressed debauch so amazingly made into an aesthetic form. . . . You have a genuine vision, and an amazingly honest form for it." He felt, on the other hand, that parts of "Stark Major," an early draft of which Crane had enclosed with his second letter, were far less successful, objecting particularly to a "jumbled" second stanza: "Wont you, after a bit, be making your strange steel-sure abstractions more malleable than they are

here? Of course, that you have made the concrete into the abstract essence proves you an artist . . but the somewhat brittle
state of the transformed stuff gets in your way . . ."

It was this sort of detailed yet sympathetic criticism that Crane
had long needed. Now, he felt, it came from all sides. "Everyone writes me such encouraging notes about F and H," Crane
told Munson, "that I am doubly sorry that I ever sent any to
BROOM for publication."

> Frank wrote me a very shrewd appreciation of Part II which he
> probably repeated to you. Untermeyer's mention of me among
> the New Patricians prompted me to send him a copy after
> reading his article on Eliot in a recent Freeman. I disagreed
> with him openly on many points, but the substance of his last
> paragraph made me think he would be interested in reading
> the poem. I was rather foolish to follow such an impulse, but
> his answer was quite decent. He made the charge of a new
> type of "rhetoric" however, which is just what Frank took
> pains to mention as fully absent. . . . Allen Tate writes me the
> most glowing praises possible, calls me the greatest contem-
> porary American poet, etc. etc. so I feel about ready to de-
> liver myself of my memoirs and expire in roses. And then, your
> appreciation has especially been enjoyed. You "get" the form
> and arrangement of the "Stark Major" poem much better than
> Frank does, but he is right about the second paragraph being
> too complicated and vague and you are wrong about the
> last verse being redundant. When I get the second verse worked
> out to suit me I'll send you another copy.

The fact is, early in 1923 Crane was at last hitting his stride;
everything in his environment helped him to write well. Not just
major projects, but minor ones also seemed to tumble from
him. The comic imitation of E. E. Cummings—"America's Plutonic Ecstasies"—with its parody ads and its ironic contrast
of classical aesthetic purgations (the Dionysian revels of "the one
goat . . . / that kicked out long ago—") with contemporary
American pluto-water ones ("all america is saying / 'how are
my bowels today?'"), was a January product immediately accepted by Norman Fitts and immediately published in *S4N*.
("*S4N*," Crane explained, not very helpfully, to Charmion von
Wiegand, "has naught to do with the Ku Klux Klan. Nobody
seems to be certain what it does mean—perhaps the insignia of a
war-time mosquito fleet, which I like to imagine anyway, as it
is so apropos.") A similar but less finished poem, "Euclid Avenue," was done at about the same time, though it waited for publication until long after Crane's death. And a host of very minor
efforts—a layout for Munson's study of Frank, a review of Munson's book for the *Double-Dealer*, a satirical cartoon of Paul

Rosenfeld—were all underway. The cartoon of Rosenfeld—public-enemy number one in Crane's efforts to place Sommer's paintings—was accepted by Jane Heap and Margaret Anderson for *The Little Review*, where it appeared with the title Hart had assigned it: " 'Annointment of our Well Dressed Critic, or Why Waste the Eggs'—three dimensional vista by Hart Crane."

As his letters make clear, Crane was at this time also at work on "Stark Major," that arrangement of birth and death which may have been a consequence of his early infatuation for Claire Spencer. This poem, founded on the dawn-to-dawn structure that Crane had used in "Faustus and Helen" and that he would draw on far more elaborately in *The Bridge*, was of considerable importance to Crane, though not to *The Dial*, which turned it down.

All this activity, however, was nothing to the ferment in Crane as he began to assemble the ideas and feelings that seven years later would yield *The Bridge*.

Almost as soon as he settled on the title, he began sending his friends notices that a major project was underway. The materials he drew on had been collected—some quite consciously, some unconsciously—over most of his adult life. The commitment to write the poem, however, is easy to date. On February 6, 1923, Crane sent off one letter to Munson, one letter to Tate—the "public" announcement to the readers who mattered—saying that the project had begun. To Tate he explained, "I'm already started on a new poem 'The Bridge' which continues the tendencies that are evident in 'Faustus and Helen,' but it's too vague and nebulous yet to talk about." In the note to Munson, Crane was more cautious: "It will be exceedingly difficult to accomplish it as I see it now, so much time will be wasted in thinking about it." Yet less than a week later, Crane ended a long letter to Tate with the first four lines of his new poem:

> The ads are calling, so Addios. I feel like quoting the first verse of *The Bridge* for a snappy close: —
>> Macadam, gun grey as the tunny's pelt,
>> Leaps from Far Rockaway to Golden Gate,
>> For first it was the road, the road only
>> We heeded in joint piracy and pushed.
>>> La-La
>>> Hart.

He was never to lose the theme announced in these lines—or the first two lines themselves. He was never to deviate from the initial vision of the poem.

It is easy to see in his correspondence of these weeks how his reading helped shape the poem. ("You may be indisposed to Waldo Frank," Crane writes Tate three days after the letter in which he quotes the opening lines, "but I must recommend to you 'City

Block' as the richest in content of any 'fiction' that has appeared in the American 20th century. Frank has the real mystic's vision. His apprehensions astonish one.") We can smile as Crane echoes Frank's remarks about Crane's own "mystic's vision," or as, in a long, excited letter to Munson several days later, he echoes Frank's terminology—the need to cast work into an "abstract," a "symphonic" form. But if a single force had to be found for initiating The Bridge, that force probably would be Waldo Frank.

By mid-February, when an attack of the flu gave Crane a few days at home for almost exclusive work on the poem, the large design was clear in his mind. The design, he explained to Munson, could in many ways be traced to the vision of American possibility Frank had opened to him. "I do want to thank you, Gorham," Crane wrote, "for your constant interest in interpreting me to others whose added interest all makes me confident that I have more to offer than I once supposed. And I am even more grateful for your very rich suggestions best stated in your Frank study on the treatment of mechanical manifestations of today as subject for lyrical, dramatic, and even epic poetry. You must already notice that influence in 'F & H.' It is to figure even larger in 'The Bridge.' The field of possibilities literally glitters all around one with the perception and vocabulary to pick out significant details and digest them into something emotional." For The Bridge, Crane explained, was to discover in the American past the roots on which a future might be founded.

A good deal of the initial planning, Crane told Munson, had taken place during a mighty binge on the evening of February 16, when in the company of his Cleveland friends he had begun to define the shape of the final poem.

> Your summary of praises for "F and H" was such a fine tribute that it might account for my backache and confinement to the bed yesterday. But the more probable cause for that, however, is liquor and the cogitations and cerebral excitements it threw me into regarding my new enterprise, "The Bridge," on the evening precedent. I am too much interested in this "Bridge" thing lately to write letters, ads, or anything. It is just beginning to take the least outline,—and the more outline the conception of the thing takes,—the more its final difficulties appall me. All this preliminary thought has to result, of course, in some channel forms or mould into which I throw myself at white heat. Very roughly, it concerns a mystical synthesis of "America." History and fact, location, etc. all have to be transfigured into abstract form that would almost function independently of its subject matter. The initial impulses of "our people" will have to [be] gathered up toward the climax of the bridge, symbol of our con-

structive future, our unique identity, in which is included also our scientific hopes and achievements of the future. The mystic portent of all this is already flocking through my mind (when I say this I should say "the mystic possibilities," but that is all that's worth announcing, anyway) but the actual statement of the thing, the marshalling of the forces, will take me months, at best; and I may have to give it up entirely before that; it may be too impossible an ambition. But if I do succeed, such a waving of banners, such ascent of towers, such dancing etc., will never have been put down on paper! The form will be symphonic, something like "F and H" with its treatment of varied content, and it will probably approximate the same length in lines. It is perhaps rather silly to go on this way before more than a dozen lines have been written, but at any rate it serves to excuse my possible deficiencies in correspondence in the near future, should the obsession carry me much further. I hate to have to go to work every day!

This sense of riding the crest of an enormous emotional wave carried Crane through the last two weeks of February and into March. He rushed through his hours at work, turning out the best copy he had ever produced. After work, he would dash home to sort through the day's mail, eat a hasty meal, rush out again to join the Rychtariks, Loveman, Harris, or Sommer for an evening of wine and high talk or a night at the theater or at the concert hall. And, late in the night, he would fight through new plans for his poem, answer letters, dream of the complex satisfactions that an "inspired" art and an inspiring love—the one that had begun at a vaudeville performance—were offering him.

The letters from Frank were especially fruitful; Crane actually memorized passages from them and even from his own responses. "Such major criticism as both you and Gorham have given my 'Faustus and Helen' is the most sensitizing influence I have ever encountered," Crane wrote him. "It is a new feeling, and a glorious one, to have one's inmost delicate intentions so fully recognized as your last letter to me attested. I can feel a calmness on the sidewalk—where before I felt a defiance only."

The letter referred to had indeed been enthusiastic. Frank praised "Faustus and Helen" first for its "solid, luminous DENSE texture" and went on to celebrate it for its analysis of America: "You have made me see the very stuffs of our beloved hated life, hereabouts, take on glittering and parabolic significances . . not take on, but reveal them inwardly." The poem, Frank said, was "a sort of marriage of heaven and hell . . . the hell of our modern mechanized world suddenly bearing as its essence an antique beauty which certain Elizabethans glimpsed for our language: and which you will also find fleshed in Racine."

Praise of this sort convinced Crane that he was no longer an isolated poet writing a poetry altogether out of key with modern pessimism, but that he had found fellow workers, moving, though in different forms, in directions he wished to take. "And better than all—" he told Frank:

> I am certain that a number of us at last have some kind of community of interest. And with this communion will come something better than a mere clique. It is a consciousness of something more vital than stylistic questions and "taste"; it is vision, and a vision alone that not only America needs, but the whole world. We are not sure where this will lead, but after the complete renunciation symbolised in "The Wasteland" and, though less, in "Ulysses" we have sensed some new vitality. Whether I am in that current remains to be seen, —but I am enough in it at least to be sure that you are definitely in it already. What delights me almost beyond words is that my natural idiom (which I have unavoidably stuck to in spite of nearly everybody's nodding, querulous head) has reached and carried to you so completely the very blood and bone of me. There is only one way of saying what comes to one in ecstasy. One works and works over it to finish and organize it perfectly—but fundamentally that doesn't effect one's *way* of saying it.

Frank, Crane confessed to Munson a week later, seemed to him "an extremely mystic type," who had, in their brief correspondence, accomplished "a world of good." "As I wrote him, now I feel I can walk calmly along the sidewalk whereas before I felt only defiance. He gripped the mystical content of the poem so thoroughly that I despair of ever finding a more satisfying enthusiast."

On the surface, at least, things were never better, but there are hints in Crane's correspondence of difficulties brewing under the surface, difficulties that would soon send him, except for brief visits, permanently away from Cleveland.

For one thing, Crane had been indiscreet in confessing to friends details of his sexual adventures. Too many people, he felt, knew far too much about his private life. It must have been with horror that he read a note from Munson that asked if he had any objections to Munson's talking about some of those exploits. It was fine and good, Crane felt, to lead the liberated life; but it was an altogether different thing to become a symbol of it.

> And now to your question about passing the good word along. I discover that I have been all-too easy all along in letting out announcements of my sexual predilections. Not that anything unpleasant has happened or is imminent. But, it does put me into obligatory relations to a certain extent with "those

who know," and this irks me to think of sometimes. After all, when you're dead it doesn't matter, and this statement alone proves my immunity from any "shame" about it. But I find the ordinary business of "earning a living" entirely too stringent to want to add any prejudices against me *of that nature* in the minds of any publicans and sinners. Such things have such a wholesale way of leaking out!

Going on to name a poet and a painter famous in bohemian circles for their flamboyant conduct, Crane made very clear that he didn't want to be thought of as a member of their entourage—or, for that matter, of the entourage of any other homosexual "leaders" ("the list too long to bother with"). "I am all-too free with my tongue," he added, "and doubtless always shall be—but I'm going to ask you to advise [me] and work [to make] me better with a more discreet behavior."

There were also minor but persistent irritations at home. Splendid as his revels were, inevitable morning-after excuses always had to be made for late arrivals, for irritability at breakfast, for after-midnight bouts of Victrola-accompanied writing.

And the end came to Crane's brief interlude of love.

The turbulence of these days—days in which he nevertheless continued to work on *The Bridge*—is most evident in Crane's last letter to Munson from Cleveland.

For some odd reason I feel a great desire to write you although I have nothing to offer, or little anyway, beyond the reflection of a most annoying week. There is, however, a paradoxical qualification to add to this statement in the mention that the last several days have been equally among the most intense in my life. The annoyance comes in only on the scoring of a repressive *fate*. To be stimulated to the nth degree with your head burgeoning with ideas and conceptions of the most baffling interest and lure—and then to have to munch ideas on water heaters (I am writing another book for housefraus!) has been a real cruelty this time, however temporary. The more I think about my Bridge poem the more thrilling its symbolical possibilities become, and since my reading of you and Frank (I recently bought City Block) I begin to feel myself directly connected with Whitman. I feel myself in currents that are positively awesome in their extent and possibilities. "Faustus and Helen" was only a beginning—but in it I struck new *timbres* that suggest dozens more, all unique, yet poignant and expressive of our epoch. Modern music almost drives me crazy! I went to hear D'Indy's "II Symphony" last night and my hair stood on end at its revelations. To get those, and others of men like Strauss, Ravel, Scriabin, and Bloch into *words* —one needs to *ransack* the vocabularies of Shakespeare, Jonson, Webster (for theirs were the richest) and add our scientific, street and counter, and psychological terms, etc. Yet, I claim that such things can be done! The modern artist needs gigantic assimilative capacities, emotion,—and the greatest of *all—vision*. "Striated with nuances, nervosities, that we are heir to"—is more than a casual observation for me. And then—structure! What pleased me greatly about Frank's comment was the notice of great structural evidence in "F & H." Potentially I feel myself quite fit to become a suitable *Pindar* for the dawn of the machine age, so called. I have lost the last shreds of philosophical pessimism during the last few months. O yes, the "background of life"—and all that is still there, but that is only three-dimensional. It is to the pulse of a greater dynamism that my work must resolve. Something terribly fierce and yet gentle.

# 16

That "background of life" that he had spoken of in his letter to Munson moved abruptly into the foreground when, early in March 1923, Crane lost his job at Stanley Patno's advertising agency. Apparently he was dropped not because of any failings on his part but simply because there was not enough work for him. Years later Patno described Crane's leaving as "an amiable parting of the ways," and it was evidently just that.

It produced, however, something of a crisis in Crane's life, for his work had had real value to him as an aid in healing the wounds made by the break with his father. So long as he was "successful" in some sort of a career, he could manage the occasions when they would meet. As a man with a profession, Hart felt he could earn his father's respect if not his love. Now, when this neat structure was threatened, Hart went to extraordinary lengths to make sure that word of his "failure" would not reach the Cranes.

His mother and grandmother, his closest friends, even Mr. Patno himself were all sworn to secrecy. Officially, Hart would be sent on a three- or four-week "business trip" to New York City, where he would find work. He would then "resign" his job in favor of the better position.

While this scheme was being set up, Hart put in a very painful time. He made a point of going across the street to pay a courtesy call on his Crane grandparents, explaining about the business trip and chatting about their own plans to move into a small apartment. He also went through everything he owned and packed a very large trunk with his most precious possessions. This would be sent on later. In order to support the illusion of a short trip, he would carry only several light suitcases.

During this last week in Cleveland, Crane was alternately restive and wild with anticipation. Fits of gloom would settle over him—fears that he would never be able to hold any job, doubts about the quality of his poetry. As Saturday night, when he would leave, approached, he became increasingly edgy. His mother and grandmother, even Allen Tate in Nashville, grew concerned over these black moods. Tate, indeed, was worried enough to get off several letters one after the other, anxious notes in which he did his best to calm Hart. On March 26, Crane's last letter from Cleveland reached Nashville. Tate answered immediately: "Your note almost alarms me, but I know it is simply haste and perhaps uncertain prospects in New York; so I'm allaying any incipient fears."

On the night of his departure, however, Crane was in a good mood. His last Cleveland evening was spent with his mother and grandmother and the Rychtariks, by now his closest friends. Their talk was of the success they were sure he would have— success both in his profession and in his career as a poet—yet there was an undercurrent awareness that he would never again live in Cleveland. This time he was making a break for good. Therefore, though there was much joking and good will and talk of triumphant returns, there was also a good deal of sadness when Crane swung up into his pullman and bent down to take the cakes Charlotte Rychtarik had baked for him, the drawings and paintings Richard had put in his charge, the little farewell gifts from mother and grandmother.

But the railroad tossed him an omen of good luck. He wrote the next day to Charlotte and Richard:

> Did you see the name of the car I rode here in? It was called "The High Bridge"!
> What do you think of that??!!??!! Wonderful??!!??!!
> Your cakes are all gone. Both Gorham and Eliza think they are *great*. Richard's pictures, too!
> I am quite happy. A long walk this afternoon in salt air and clear sunlight. Everyone carrying canes and wearing bright clothes. Lunch tomorrow with Waldo Frank. Munson is enthusiastic about my staying with them. They have a fresh and charming apartment with room enough for me, so everything is FINE.
> I sat a long while thinking about how beautiful you both were when I left you last night. Yes,—of course, Life is very beautiful when there are such people to meet and love as I love you both. Be very happy. Along with me. I never felt better before.

A series of letters of this sort to Crane's mother and grandmother, to Tate, to the Rychtariks allowed all these worried people to relax. "Your very interesting letter of Monday was thoroughly enjoyed at the breakfast table this morning," Hart's grandmother wrote, "and made us very happy to note the cheerful state of mind it reflected all through." She made clear that there was no sign that anyone suspected he had lost his job: "We are carrying out our plans we made before you left in regard to your business trip etc., so no one questions us."

But much as Hart's mother and grandmother tried to encourage him in his job hunt, it was hard not to beg him to return. "We are both well, and gradually overcoming the terrible loneliness we felt after you left," his grandmother wrote. Grace was more direct.

> I wouldn't want you to know how lonely I am without you, or how much I miss you nights—and mornings. No one to bring me a cup of coffee—and no victrola and tramping overhead,—just deathly still and deadly dull—I *hate* it!!

Even the family canary—so Grace would have it—was saddened: "Clip misses you I feel certain. He does not sing as much and especially from six to eight—the time you were around."

There is no question that letters of this sort moved Crane deeply. In spite of all the annoyances of living at home, his attachment to his mother and grandmother was the strongest tie he had to anyone in the world. He was in New York because he felt he had to prove himself to his father. But he knew he had his mother's love, and he knew that his love for her was quite as strong as hers for him. If he also half guessed that it was impossible for them to go on living under the same roof, then that was a guess he resolutely suppressed. His problem was to keep up her spirits; her problem was to keep up his.

Yet both of them played dangerously on each other's weaknesses, Hart hinting of the happy time when they would be together in New York, Grace—perhaps unconsciously—luring Hart back toward Cleveland, listing in her letters the friends made lonely by his absence, over and over stressing her own loneliness. She told of plans for the annual dinner-dance of the Warren Society of Cleveland, which she would have to attend without him.

> I shall be very forlorn without you. In fact I am all of the time—I miss you terribly—but I am to be happy if you can get located in New York in the advertising business. You have no idea how happy I shall be when I know you are really settled, or how much interested I am in your success. . . . I dropped in on Sam [Loveman] one afternoon about a week ago. He was very nice—and said he missed you more and more. . . . Remember you are to write often—whether your news is good or not.

She listed the friends who had stopped by to inquire after him— the composer Jean Binet; the Rychtariks; Kay Kenney; Charles Harris; William Lescaze; the writers Ted Robinson, Charles Baldwin, and James Daly; their neighbors the Hurds; all the relatives; all of her friends and the friends of friends. To those who were not in on the secret, her statement, she told Hart, was always the same: Hart is in New York on business; it is not certain when he will be back.

Just as Grace made an effort to keep in touch with Hart's friends, Hart begged his friends to stop in to see her as often as they could. "Keeping down the worries at home is the greatest problem I have," he wrote the Rychtariks, "otherwise I should be absolutely certain of staying on here." When Charlotte sent Grace flowers on Easter Sunday (which, in 1923, happened to fall on April 1, Grace's birthday), Hart got off a letter of effusive thanks: "How can I thank you enough for being so *very* thoughtful as to send my mother those Easter flowers! Her letter that has just come in was full of the pleasure that they gave her, and you know how much her happiness and satisfaction mean to me."

Perhaps some of the pleasure mother and son found in their correspondence was due to the game of deception in which they were engaged. For even a month after Hart had gone, his father's family was still in the dark about the true reason for his absence. Grace and Mrs. Hart now were spending a good deal of time at the front window, the sale of the Crane home having finally taken place.

Preparations for moving are going on over across the street, but I think their troubles have only begun. Mrs. Crane does not gain very fast—and today she is down in bed again. Bess is there helping and the doctor also. Frances [C.A.'s second wife] is very *scarce*. . . . It will certainly be a very acceptable change to me, to have them off of the street.

Two weeks later the Cranes were gone. Grace grimly summarized the leave-taking.

The Crane mansion across the street is almost a thing of the past. The wreckers have been busy for nearly three days and the house is roofless, doorless, windowless and nearly sideless. They make an awful lot of dirt and muss, and you would think you were in the factory district, the way things look at present in our immediate vicinity.

The family moved out early Wednesday morning, and right in the midst of the muss, they brought out your grandmother Crane, and took her in C.A.'s car over to the apartment. She certainly was a pathetic sight, so weak she could scarcely walk, and weeping as though her heart would break. She felt very badly to leave this house—for I think she has cared the most for this place of all the homes she has had. I don't believe she will ever be happy where they are—but she is too much of an invalid now to [have] anything to say about where she is to live.

Frances has been down in bed again—nervous breakdown so I hear.

Well anyway we are as free from the sight or sound of them now as if we lived in another town.

It took Hart more than two months to find employment in New York. Though he did not spend all day, every day looking for work, and though he did not accept the offers made by his Aunt Zell and by Allen Tate to arrange interviews with New York newspaper publishers, Crane's search for work was diligent, exhaustive, and exhausting. He turned down the newspaper offers—as gently as possible—for the best reason in the world. He had had his share of newspaper experience in Cleveland; the work, he felt, was both degrading and brutalizing. The newspapers fed their readers a steady diet of violence, of scandal: a diet of sudden death and gossip. He wanted no more visits to the morgue.

What Crane knew he needed at this time was a job in advertising—and preferably in a good agency. Only by establishing himself as a man moving steadily ahead in his profession could he show father, mother, grandmother—perhaps most important of all, himself—that he was no longer a boy floundering from one job to another, that he was mature enough to be respected as a man.

Crane's job hunt began where it ended: at J. Walter Thompson's agency. At their first meeting, Waldo Frank had offered to write him a letter of introduction to an old friend on the Thompson staff. Crane followed it up immediately.

He had expected that his first interview would land him a job; but he learned rapidly that more was involved than a pleasant chat. "Everybody tells me that I ought to plan on at least three weeks before possibly getting a job," he wrote the Rychtariks at the end of a week and a half of fairly industrious searching. "It takes such a long time to travel over the great distances here between agencies that I only get to see three or four people a day. Sometimes not that many, as so many times the persons I need to talk to are busy or out."

Hart's first three weeks in New York went by quickly, but then a series of "sure things" that fell through threatened to break his buoyant spirit. "It is a dark, cold and horrid day," Crane wrote the Rychtariks in mid-April. "I am staying in and waiting to hear from an agency in regard to a job. *That* particular job will be *known about* before evening. If I get it—very good. If I don't, it means that I must start out looking again. In this last case they seemed so certain of giving it to me that it seemed foolish to look around other places until I get their decision. But there is something here, I know." Unfortunately, there was not.

Crane counted the weeks. So did the Munsons. Not that Crane was initially a difficult guest; he really was not. But a third person in a small apartment was bound to create a certain awkwardness. In addition, his presence had forced his hosts to postpone an invitation to the Negro poet Jean Toomer, whose *Cane* was published that year. Toomer had been in correspondence with Munson for some time and was scheduled to meet him on a brief visit. Week by week, as Crane's visit lengthened, Toomer found his invitation moved back. "Crane is a bully chap," Munson explained, "and I look forward to your gusto coming into contact with his gusto"; but since the Munsons had limited space, the meeting of gustos had to wait until Crane vacated the spare bed. Both Munson and Crane believed Toomer would prove one of the strongest workers in the Frank-centered movement of which they now considered themselves leading members. He was, they felt, an important poet and a perceptive critic. "Your critique of my Study [of Frank]," Munson noted in one of the many visit-postponing letters, ". . . is, as Hart Crane would say, the cat's cuffs."

Thompson's, in the meantime, kept calling Crane back for interviews with various members of the staff. "The copy director at J. Walter Thompson is trying to find a way to work me in there despite a well-filled copy dept.," Crane wrote Charles Harris. "I feel quite flattered although only mildly hopeful."

When Crane first approached the Thompson agency, he filled out a long questionnaire about his background, his experience, and his interests. Stretching truth a good deal, he described himself as a June 1921 graduate of Western Reserve University. (He modestly assigned himself only a Bachelor of Arts degree, going on to point out that after graduation he had taken extension work in advertising at the same school—in reality, of course, the only studying he had ever done there.) The rest of his application form was entirely truthful: he said that he read French and German "moderately well"; that he had a considerable knowledge of art; that his favorite subjects in school were history, psychology, and literature. He explained that he had left his last job at the Roger Williams Company in Cleveland in order to come to New York to look for a better one, that his pay had been $50 a week when he left, and that he had been employed as a copywriter. His duties he described simply: the production of "good copy, which was all that was required." The work at Corday and Gross had been, he said, "mostly apprenticeship" and he had left the job in order to get the higher salary at the Roger Williams Company. He made no reference to his work for his father. Such other employment as he had had, he explained, was "retail selling in bookstores" during school and at other times. Crane's references— the most prominent men of his close acquaintance—were Harrison Smith, H. C. Candee, and Gorham B. Munson.

Part of the application form at Thompson's was a set of comments on recent ads. Crane's were on a Cyclone fence ad, a "Barreled Sunlight" paint ad, and an American Radiator ad that had appeared in *The Saturday Evening Post* of April 14, 1923 (the week, apparently, in which Crane came in for one of the half dozen interviews he went through before landing the job). His comments were, I was told by an executive at J. Walter

Thompson's who was kind enough to get out the file and study it for me, "not bad, sensible and to the point." Crane, he felt, knew what he was talking about; he implied that even today a young man with similar experience who filled out an application more or less along these lines would be given serious consideration.

By the end of April, not just Crane but everyone associated with him was restive. "Hart Crane is hanging on indefinitely at Gorham's," Waldo Frank wrote Jean Toomer, "and (this is confidential) is making it very hard for the dear man to work consistently." The confidential comment was, however, open knowledge. "Crane has completed his fifth week of job-hunting," Munson himself wrote Toomer. "I am way behind on my assignments, and everything is in a mess."

By early May, Crane was deluged with good advice. "Put an advertisement in the Times and perhaps the Monitor," his mother wrote. His Aunt Zell renewed her offers for newspaper jobs. "I cannot imagine how you are getting money to buy food or pay car fare by this time," his mother added. "I *do* wish you would take *any* job to meet expenses until you get one you want."

Crane, meantime, attempted to conserve what little money he had been able to borrow from friends; tried, as well as he could, to keep out from under foot at Munson's; and did his best not to let each gesture toward a job raise his hopes too high. "I have bids in for jobs at two very good agencies," he explained in a long letter to Bill Sommer. "The thing is a farce, however, the way you are kept waiting to know the outcome of one interview after another with various executives. J. Walter Thompson have had me on the string now for three weeks, and a letter this morning tells me that within the next few days I must drag myself up there again for another interview with one more Thompson executive. It is the same way at Batten's." The Thompson letter was especially irritating; it asked Hart to wait by his telephone all day Thursday on the chance that an executive who was "away from the city a great part of the time" would be in town long enough to talk to him. If he didn't get a phone call Thursday, the personnel secretary cheerfully explained, he would probably get a letter Friday. With this kind of delay, Hart told Sommer, "I shall have to cast about for anything available from stevedoring to table-waiting." "Every few days," he fretted to Charles Harris, "I am called up to meet another one of the firm, and then, I am left to puzzle around while they stroke their chins together in a semi-circle. . . . Nothing is more exhausting than job-chasing."

Finally, toward the end of May, waiting turned into working— and none too soon; for Hart was down to his last pennies. It was at this point that he got off an urgent letter to Richard Rychtarik. He was "trying to scrape enough money together to take a furnished room." His first pay check wouldn't arrive until June. "As I have nothing in the meantime I am wondering if you would send me $10.00 which I will send back as soon as the end of June anyway. . . . Moving around so much and trying to get clean clothes, shoes fixed, hair cut, and all with my new job on my mind makes it impossible for me to be a good letter writer. . . . I've been through so much lately however that I'm *very tired* and can't sleep. The job is a *good one.*"

Along with the money from Rychtarik came a five-dollar bill from Bill Sommer, who was making the first installment of repayment for the photographs Hart had paid for, and a note from Hart's mother that under the circumstances must have seemed comic.

> The other night when looking at some of your book[s] in your room . . . I picked up one of those small Shakespeare volume[s] and out fell a $20 bill. What do you want me to do with it? I can send it registered or my check for that amount, or keep it to pay on some of your bills here. Let me know what to do.

Though Crane had certainly felt his credit was stretched tight, and though sometimes he was embarrassed never to be able to return the hospitality all his friends extended him, he generally managed to be in very good spirits. He spent some time looking up such old friends as the Habichts, "who serve wonderful sherry and Benedictine." He visited Harry Candee, who had just returned from a trip to the Far East and who showed Hart "the most wonderful silks, beads and jade, ornaments and costumes that I have ever seen. Some things belonging to former emperors. Chinese, of course. He brought me a wonderful old brown jade Buddha from the Han Mountain that is perfection itself." From Candee, Hart bought a present for the Rychtariks, a smock which, he explained to Richard, "I am sure you will like to wear when you paint." (It was Charlotte, however, who ended up wearing it; Richard made a drawing for Crane of the smock in action.) There were also friends from Cleveland who arrived for short visits, which were for Crane always happy ones. He chatted with Charles Harris; went uptown to call on his high-school friend Bill Wright, who was living near Columbia University; had dinner one night with James Daly; met William Lescaze one afternoon at a coffeehouse. Lescaze was just back from Europe with the two copies of *Ulysses* that Crane had arranged for friends to purchase. "I'm very much excited over the arrival of 'Ulysses,'" Tate wrote him, "and you may be sure that I'm going to take the copy."

Of all Crane's visitors at the time, Richard Rychtarik was the one he most enjoyed seeing. "There are so many things to look at," he had written well in advance of Richard's arrival. "The weather then will be just right,—warm, yet not too warm—and clear as only ocean air can make things clear." He especially wanted to show Rychtarik the life of the streets: the immigrant sections and the financial district, the docks and Fifth Avenue. But the two friends had time only to scratch the surface. "It was fine to have him here for even a little while," Crane wrote Charlotte on the evening of Richard's departure, "and I am hoping that when he comes again it will be for a longer time, because you simply cannot 'see' New York in a week or two weeks, you can only 'feel' a few chords of the life that is so various, noisy and rich." They had accomplished a good deal, however, visiting galleries, meeting some of Crane's new friends. "Most complete of R's experiences, I think," Crane said, "was the Picasso exhibition and the afternoon with Stieglitz."

When he brought Rychtarik to visit Stieglitz, Crane himself was paying only a second call. Yet he approached Stieglitz as an old friend. For their first meeting—only two weeks before, at an exhibition of Stieglitz's photographs—had exploded into mutual admiration.

Crane had arrived at the gallery set to meet the man he regarded as one of the high priests of art. He did not, however, expect quite so immediate a response from Stieglitz. For within minutes Stieglitz was praising him. As they walked about the gallery, Crane managed to say all the right things. The next day he got off a quick note.

"Dear great and good man, Alfred Stieglitz," Crane began, "I don't know whether or not I mentioned to you yesterday that I intend to include my short verbal definition of your work and aims in a fairly comprehensive essay on your work. I had not thought of doing this until you so thoroughly confirmed my conjectures as being the only absolutely correct statement that you had thus far heard concerning your photographs. That moment was a tremendous one in my life because I was able to share all the truth toward which I am working in my own medium, poetry, with another man who had manifestly taken many steps in that same direction in *his* work." In the fragment he enclosed—with a plea that it be kept secret—Crane described Stieglitz's art in terms of captured motion: "Speed is at the bottom of it all— . . . the moment made eternal."

Crane's note had been enthusiastic; Stieglitz's return letter bordered on the rapturous. Crane could come to visit him at any time; he could bring Munson with him, "or any one you may wish to bring." Between them absolute communication had taken place.

> The document you sent me I treasure. No one shall see it through me except O'Keeffe.—She is a rare person—an integral part of myself.—She says that what you wrote is so concrete yet so intangible that one becomes full of wonder.—

—The moment before the Apples and Gable will remain
with me for all time.—There was never truer seeing.—I am
very glad you are. Because of all of us.

Though Crane was to visit Stieglitz infrequently, they became
steady correspondents, Stieglitz turning, in letter after letter, to
Crane's extraordinary response to the apples and gable picture.
Crane was proud as a peacock that he had penetrated to the
center of a great artist's work. "Alfred Stieglitz says I am the
first one to discover the secret of his marvelous photos," Crane
wrote Charles Harris. And, soon after, he began shipping off to
Stieglitz typed copies of his strongest poems, poems which Stieglitz in turn praised and which he went out of his way to read
aloud to such visiting artists as John Marin: "And all felt something deeply moving and all wished to read again and again.—
And that is significant as we, none of us, are so ready to wish to
read again and again that which is written today."

Not everyone, of course, responded in the same way to
Crane's work. "Meeting some of the older poets and writers down
here is an odd experience," he wrote Charlotte Rychtarik. "Most
of them are very disagreeable, and don't talk the same language
as we do, they are not concerned with the same problems." On
one of these evenings, at a party in the Village, Crane had been
asked to read some of his recent work and had settled on "Faustus and Helen." The response had been totally cold: "Very few
of them, of course, understood anything that I was talking about.
If it weren't for the praise and understanding I have received
from people like Frank and Munson and Allen Tate, etc. I would
begin to feel that I might be to blame. But this 'new consciousness' is something that takes a long while to 'put across.' " New
York's literary circle, Crane wrote Tate, had in it all too many
"fat-heads."

Disagreeable as some of the evenings were, Crane did manage
to meet many important writers. Louis Untermeyer, John Dos
Passos, Marianne Moore, E. E. Cummings, Kenneth Burke, and
Slater Brown—the last three soon to become Crane's close
friends—were all new acquaintances. Crane even found himself
sitting down, on one of these occasions, next to "the beloved
Paul Rosenfeld." After Crane's first onslaught, Rosenfeld much
later recalled, Hart fell peaceably to eating cheese and crackers by
his side.

The richest of Crane's new friendships was with Slater Brown.
Crane had unlimited admiration for men like Frank and Stieglitz,
and he found himself enormously stimulated by conversations
about literature and the arts with Munson. But with Brown he
could relax into wit-exploding, devil-may-care good times. The
two were almost precisely of an age and they both were out to enjoy

life to the hilt. Brown seemed, in Crane's eyes, to have discovered the right way—a golden way—to live in the world. Describing Brown to Underwood, Crane heaped praise on top of praise—carefully pointing out, however, that this time his affections were totally platonic: "quite unsensual."

On the same day that Crane wrote Underwood about his new friend, he answered a letter from Bill Sommer. His subject was Slater Brown.

> At LAST! a letter from you!!! And let me mention that it was one of the most beautiful I ever got from anyone. AND I am expecting more. I read it the second and third times during my meal last night down in one of the Italian restaurants on the lower East Side. There you get a bottle of wine (fine, too!) and a good meal (that delights the eyes as well as the stomach) for about $1. And such service! The waiters all beam and are really interested in pleasing you. As Rychtarik said when he was here last week, it's just like Europe. I don't know where I should have been by this time, however, had it not been for three or four very fine people,—Gorham and his wife, and Slater Brown (the friend of Cummings, "B" in the "Enormous Room") who, in spite of knowing me only a couple of weeks, has put me up nights in his room during the recent spell of grippe in the Munson household, and who has kept me in funds, poured wine into me, and taken me to the greatest burlesque shows down on the lower east side that you ever imagined. We went to one last night, and I so wished you were along. (They do everything but the ACT itself right on the stage, marvelous jazz songs, jokes etc. and really the best entertainment there is in N.Y. at present.)

It was this side of New York—a tough, vital one—that Crane had always liked best; but in the past he had often wandered the streets alone. With Brown, he could enjoy the "really stupendous place" as it should be enjoyed. For New York, Crane told Sommer, "is the center of the world today, as Alexandria became the nucleus of another older civilization."

> The wealthier and upper parts of the city have their own beauty, but I prefer as a steady thing the wonderful streets of this lower section, crowded with life, packed with movement and drama, children, kind and drab looking women, elbows braced on window ledges, and rows of vegetables lining the streets that you would love to paint. Life is possible here at greater intensity than probably any other place in the world today, and I hope and pray that you will be able to slip down here for a week or so during the summer. You must plan on it. Later on I shall probably take a small apartment

with Brown, and then there will be plenty of room for you to stay with us at no expense at all.

Cautioning Charles Harris at the end of another letter, "Please be very quiet about the 'high-life' details of this note," Crane recounted some of the wilder exploits of the past several weeks.

I'm taking a day off the much beaten path in sheer desperation at my unanswered mail. Naturally you are one of the first casualties, and if the pen is mightier than the sword you won't be able to stand this fire-farting of mine very long. I am in a mood for superlatives ever since the water closet over-flew at maison Munson the other day before I could collect my drawers around my hips. But that's not the haff of it,—such a round of hospitality as I've been undergoing lately is very strenuous, and if this letter smacks of a "hang-over" I'm not the one to cry surprise. I'm just discovering what a rich place this village is, I mean the whole town, of course, from Battery to Bronx. It is rich in good dispositions, by which I mean that if you haven't enough to buy a bottle there is always someone near to help you. Wish I could tell you about some of the recent evenings, midnights and dawns. I've been so much the guest of Slater Brown . . . and he is so remarkably fine that my sorrows and foot blisters have been much alleviated and I can look the whole world in the face, a drunkard and a man! Policemen here don't mind if you step up and occasionally use their tummys as tom-toms, neither do neighbors mind your "early" shouts from windows hailing far from gently all the dawn. Or if you care to you can suspend yourself outside, feet raking up the clapboards and nothing is felt to be amiss. As I wrote Kathryn (the famous vaudeville songster) [Kathryn Kenney] I have slept on everything but walls and danced the gotzotzsky so much that my calves almost refuse to function. The zimbaloon at Moscowitz's is responsible for even more, but details involve me in lengthy convolutions.

Though he had no trouble writing letters while he was unemployed, Crane did find writing poetry next to impossible. He was either excited by the prospect of work or depressed by the prospect of continued unemployment. And in both situations he lacked the peaceful atmosphere that he felt he needed. "What I want in the end," he wrote to Rychtarik soon after arriving in New York, "is a decent room with plenty of quiet to work. I never before felt TIME as I do now. It is the most precious thing in the world. I long to get into my 'Bridge' again, but it will be many weeks probably." Other than a cheerful consequence of a night on the town, a postcard to Charlotte Rychtarik which Crane headed "WELL/WELL/NOT-AT-ALL" and ended "pffffff!" and which neatly announced:

Yakka-hoola-hikki-doola
Pico-della-miran-dohhh-la
leonarda-della-itchy-vinci
es braust ein ruhf vie
        *DONNERHALL*

—other than this brief "lyric," only six lines of verse (a fragment about dancing children, tucked in at the end of a long letter to Charlotte Rychtarik) can positively be identified as from this period. And even the six lines seem thin in contrast to Crane's comment on them: "The children in springtime come out and dance on the streets of the crowded city. Why in hell can't we older people have the same freedom, to join the rhythm of life?"

Though Crane produced no work of any significance in this time, he did find himself in print; *S4N* brought out, in its May-published March–April number, a review of *Eight More Harvard Poets* that he had written just before he left Cleveland. Crane singled out for praise two poets of considerable promise: John Brooks Wheelwright and Malcolm Cowley. Crediting Wheelwright with "stertorous drive" and "real emotional significance" and Cowley with "a faculty for fresh record, city and road panorama, and ironic nuance," he more or less accidentally initiated one of his richest friendships, that with Cowley. Wheelwright, on the other hand, would very shortly be mistreating "Faustus and Helen" in *Secession* and thereby bringing down on his head the combined wrath of Crane and Munson.

As soon as the review was published, Cowley wrote Wheelwright a note in which he said Crane's piece was "about the only intelligent criticism" the anthology had had. Several days later Cowley decided that he ought to say the same to Crane and sent from France, where he was then living, a most perceptive letter about Crane's own poetry: "You write with a bombast which is not Elizabethan but contemporary, and you are one of two or three people who can write a twentieth century blank verse, about other subjects than love, death and nightingales and in other patters than ti tum ti tum ti tum ti tum ti tum. Salutations."

On the first of June, with a good job at last secured, Hart's spirits soared. He moved from 4 Grove Street, where he had been staying with the Munsons, and settled in briefly with Brown at 6 Minetta Lane, only a few doors away. When the windfall money from the Rychtariks, from Sommer, and from Grace arrived, he took a room at the Hotel Albert for a few days. "It certainly is wonderful to have a room by myself again where I can take a bath and have quiet when I want it. All this would have been impossible," he wrote the Rychtariks, "if you had not been so wonderfully kind. I am getting back all my usual confidence again."

Hart was indeed getting back his confidence, his letters ringing a

chorus about the *fine, fine, fine* world. "The job is fine and I am
working with fine people. So is N.Y. fine these days when the
streets are full of life, color and sunlight and everybody is out.
They have lemon-yellow shades on all the lamps on Fifth Ave.
and it gives the street and everybody the color of champagne in
the evening. How fine it is that I am here and settled *for good!*"
And yet, and yet. The letters from Cleveland drifted back, filled
with a tangle of joy and pathos. Grace wrote that she was thinking
of selling their house, since it now seemed Hart would never return to it. This letter—full of the details of house cleaning,
rides in the country, luncheons at the Union Club—must have
seemed to Hart a letter from a lost world.

> It is a warm beautiful day and I feel as if I had been born
> again, after this long gloomy cold winter and spring.
> The yards around here look beautifully green and fairy like.
> Margaret and another woman are washing the porches and
> their furniture and by night the swing, chairs, awnings, rugs
> etc. will be in their old places once more and you can picture
> us sitting there evenings and every spare minute we can.

Grace did her best to sustain a light tone, but at the end it broke:
"I get terribly hungry to see you dear, and I do not see how I am
going to get along this summer without you. There is no one I
love so much as you—you know, don't you?"

There were also letters from Hart's grandmother, long, rambling letters in an angular, cramped handwriting—letters much
too long to quote in full but that even fragmented carry something of the message that Hart reduced to a chorus of a single
word: loss, loss, loss, loss . . .

> My Dear Hart:
> My thoughts are upon and with you so much today, that it
> seems to me I must have a little chat with you—and tell you
> how much we (*I*) miss you, especially when I am alone. When
> I knew you were up in your room even tho' I didn't see you, I
> knew you were there.
> I miss you *very very* much dear, and now that I know you
> have decided to stay in New York, I wonder if I will ever see
> you again.
> Your room looks so pretty now that it is all dolled up—but
> it lacks something that no one can supply but you.
> Your [special delivery letter] came yesterday p.m. Mother
> was not at home—so I did not open it until she came. . . .
> When she read it I saw the tears come to her eyes—and we
> said you were mighty brave to go through what you have and
> not give up—and we feel mighty proud of our Hart.
> I am glad Mother did not know all this—until it was over,

for she felt badly enough as it was and I had hard work to cheer her up many times. . . .

I am wondering how you are putting in the day—-but you have no lack of places to go in N. York.

And dear Hart, I want you to take good care of yourself. Health is a great asset and you must try not to take things too strenuous. . . .

Everybody is going along in the same old way here. Nothing new. We never see any more of our old friends across the way—but we are not mourning at all. And goodbye dear with my best love which you always have—

Grandma

Don't scold at this long letter.

"Please see lots of my Mother and grandmother," Hart ended his next letter to the Rychtariks. "They are very fond of you both. Again, a thousand thanks for all your love and friendship. And remember, please to write me soon . . ."

# 17

Hart tried hard to like his new job. He had been taken on in the statistical department at a salary of $35 a week, something of a cut from his Cleveland pay and prestige; but he had hopes of moving up to the copy department. "They employ a lot of real writers as copy writers at Thompson's," he explained to his mother, "and have an entirely different feeling about art and business than you encounter any place west of N.Y. In fact it's a feather in your cap if you know a little more than you're 'supposed to' here."

Though he did his best to glamorize office life for his mother (describing "the company, its offices, personnel and methods" as "clean and courteous"), Crane soon found that beneath a surface "as smooth as glass," jealousies and rivalries were as real as they had been at all the other firms he had worked for. Until his promotion to the copy department (a promotion that carried no raise in pay), he managed to ignore the simple facts of corporate organization. "There's no atmosphere of *fear* around," one early letter noted. "The sun streams in the windows onto the heavily carpeted floors and very simply, everyone seems to be doing what he is supposed to do without any fuss or rush." As soon as Hart began turning out copy, however, a different tone dominated his correspondence. He was still "officially" pleased ("things look stimulating enough as regards the immediate future here"), but he was upset to see his copy rewritten, and he was troubled because he was assigned no regular accounts but rather asked to take care of spot work of an insignificant nature.

Perhaps he was also afraid that in some way he didn't quite grasp he had bungled his first important assignment—an assignment that in midsummer had taken him to Buffalo and Chicago in connection with the "Barreled Sunlight" advertising account of the U. S. Gutta Percha Paint Company. Hart, who usually enjoyed travel, had hated the trip. Chicago was hot ("I thought I would be melted to nothing before I got away"), and wet ("There was a good deal of steaming rain"), and confusing ("I found it hard to find my way around"). The hotel to which he had been assigned was altogether too grand ("I felt very uncomfortable and out of place"). Perhaps worst of all, he had no way of judging company response. "I guess my work has been entirely satisfactory," he reported to his mother, explaining that on his return he had been "very cordially greeted" by his superiors. Nevertheless, from that time until the end of October, when he resigned, steadily mounting doubts about the quality of his work plagued him.

Initially, the most attractive part of his job had been its promise of letting Crane live as a professional man during the day and as a free-living writer at night: "I have a job and a totally different world to live in half the time." Yet this neat separation of interests proved impossible to manage. The evening freedoms all too frequently gave him morning hangovers. Even worse, the daytime job cut in on his evening pleasures in ways he had not anticipated. For Crane—like many organization men before and after him—found it impossible to leave his office concerns at the office. Night after sleepless night would be devoted to Barreled Sunlight and Naugahyde suitcases. Yet in the mornings, worn out, he would produce copy in no way more interesting than that produced at the other desks on the fourteenth floor of 244 Madison Avenue.

Crane attributed his growing restiveness, his growing irritability, to everything except work: "I came near a collapse near the middle of the week—the trip, hot weather, etc. certainly tested me and worries keep me from much sleep . . . NY is bad in the summer anyway—takes all the vitality you have to give and gives you back nothing to build with or repair." When his mother hinted that perhaps he disliked his job, Hart was grouchily defensive.

> I feel one hundred per cent better since I got back to copy work. . . . I'm far from being dissatisfied, as you suggested. The plain fact was, and still is—that New York takes such a lot from you that you have to save all you can of yourself or you simply give out. I need a good bed, but it will be a long time before I can get one unless you feel like shipping that little brass bed on the third floor down here to me sometime. That would be fine, and could serve me always here, but you'll probably think it out of the question to send it.
>
> It doesn't make much difference how early you go to bed if you can't get to sleep—you know that. And that has been the state of things with me for some time here. However, I'm really feeling all right. It [is] just tiredness—and worry that you are very, very unhappy—what to do—etc.

There were, on the other hand, bright spots in Crane's summer. Early in June, before Slater Brown left town, Crane, Brown, and Sue Jenkins had spent marvelous evenings together. Sue frequently invited Crane to join her and Brown for Sunday dinners, the preparation of which sometimes began on Saturday afternoons. In these early summer days, New York still held wonderful unexplored areas. "Really, I'm having the finest time in my life," he wrote home.

> There's no use trying to describe the people I go round with. Not that there are so many—there could easily be, but I'm always cutting down on all but the few I like the most. Last night marketing with Sue and Bill Brown, down in the Italian section (where everyone looks so happy!) was a perfect circus. We carried pots and pans, spinach, asparagus etc. etc. from place to place—only buying one kind of thing in each store—jostling with the crowds etc. I've never been with young people I enjoyed so much, and they, of course, have had real lives.

For a while Crane was engaged in so much of a social and creative whirl that he neglected writing most of his regular correspondents. "I am swimming, neck-high, in a sea of activities here," he explained to the Rychtariks, "that almost makes correspondence impossible. I am writing on the 'Bridge' again which is very absorbing, and there is always someone wanting to lunch, and to dine,—and you know how long wine keeps you sitting and talking at the table. Evenings pass in a flash, before you know it!!! In truth, I am enjoying myself, and *growing* as I have never done before and it's all rather intense. But you both know what a capacity I have!"

So long as friends were available and he was able to work on his poem, New York seemed magnificent. It was a place, Crane decided, where his work counted for something. Munson, Toomer, and Frank were all enthusiastic about the progress he was making on *The Bridge*. Frank, especially, went out of his way to praise the poem. It was, he wrote in one note, "a body amazingly simple, fecund and grandiose." Crane and his work were both "tremendously important."

Lifted by praise of this sort, Crane jealously guarded the time available for the poem. "I've been trying for several days to get something to you," he told his mother shortly before the Fourth of July, "but with my head simply bursting with the 'Bridge' poem which has been coming out simply by leaps and bounds, with the laundry to travel for, the suit to be pressed, the room to be dusted up and cleaned, and friends coming around to invite me out to eat every evening—all this added to my duties and time at the office has made it impossible." As a result, he explained, "my correspondence all 'roun' is dropping off, and must continue if I keep on at my present rate of writing—for it is very hard, extremely painful to tie your mind down to anything as personal as a letter when you have the drive of a hundred horse power steed propelling your brain in other directions."

Crane was now settled into a room at 45 Grove Street that he had sublet from Louis Kantor, a European-bound reporter on the New York *Tribune* and a friend of Slater Brown's. So long as the weather remained cool, Crane found that it perfectly suited his needs. "A fine large room, just repainted in grey and white, with running water and right next to a bath," it had cross ventilation, a plentiful supply of "all black" furniture and "a fine large table to write on." The one indispensable item that it lacked—a Victrola—was provided by Crane's friends, who together had purchased one as a moving-in present. "I can't tell you how fine I feel to get my feet on the ground again and put my nose up into the sky again for a few minutes with the 'Meistersinger' Overture," Crane wrote the Rychtariks. Best of all, the room had privacy. There was no longer any possibility of "an inquisitive landlady always looking through the keyhole."

With its high white ceiling, its light gray walls, and black floor, the big square room seemed ideally suited as a gallery for the works of his friends. Three weeks after moving in, Crane wrote his mother that he had succeeded "in changing things around and in 'making it my own.' . . . There are Lescazes, Sommers and Rychtariks on the walls, besides a very large oil painting by Edward Nagle, two of whose drawings you may have seen in the last *Dial* if you opened it."

But by mid-July, though Crane could not have begun to guess it, most of his good times in New York were at an end. He still had ahead of him a weekend of pleasant good times at Rye, New York, visiting friends of William Lescaze, enjoying "the sweet clean air of woods and water" and a picnic dinner on a two-masted sailboat. ("We took our dinner along, having cocktails, chicken, sandwiches, ice cream etc. I nearly burst—my appetite was so stimulated after my swim, salt air, etc.") And he had ahead of him two happy days as the guest of Waldo Frank at Darien, Connecticut; but both these excursions were trips away from the New York City that at the beginning of summer had seemed so attractive.

Of course, he realized that much of New York's charm lay not in its cosmopolitan life but in the friends he had discovered there. What he found hard to realize was that, with the friends gone, all the beauty and magic and wonder would disappear from the streets and in the place of beauty and magic would be violence, swirling dust, and noise. But while they were still with him, the friends transformed the place. "You must plan to come here sometime," he wrote Charlotte Rychtarik.

The intimacies, lights, shades, and interesting points of conversations cannot really be preserved. And I am having so much good talk here that I am very pleased. Really, I haven't been to a concert or theatre since I came, but with good wine and interesting friends, what more do you need.

It was out of these conversations, and out of this Manhattan opened up through affection and love, that Crane constructed— while he could—first the end and then some of the beginning of *The Bridge.* The good times that these friendships created dominate a letter to Charles Harris.

There is a regiment of various voices, noises and instruments from behind and before assailing me through the two windows that open on two courts. The little vengeance that this machine offers these assembled Victrolas, arguments and domestic accidents entitles lady Corona to a name for modesty, I assure you. In the face of such a din, she is always faithful, too,—which is more than I can say for my mind under such circumstances, so if this *is* typewritten it doesn't necessarily mean that it is a letter, or the epistolary answer, at least, that you deserve. But it IS a BEE-OOtiful DAY!

And last night was a beautiful night. As usual I was dissolved in several bottles of wine,—this time in company with Munson, Mrs. M, and Jean Toomer (whom you have probably seen in old "Brooms"). . . .

You should have heard from me before if I had not been so furiously busy. One takes more time for meals, dressing, brushing one's teeth, farting, etc., here than in the spacious middle zest. But things are keyed up more . . . and I'm always catching up, either in time or money.—or correspondence. If my days are casually pleasant with amenities,—they are also limited in moments, and when dinner, wine and conversation consume about three hours every evening, and you work at an office another eight,—you haven't time for much else but poetry. I really have been working however silly I sound, on my Bridge poem. It's just begun—the end written—and now I am starting on the beginning. Its inception is constantly attended by sharp arguments with Burke, Brown, Munson, Frank, Toomer and Josephson on all kinds of things that have much or little to do with it. I occasionally get very tired of it, and draw in my tongue. Josephson I can scarcely tolerate and he generally spoils my digestion when he is present,—but as personalities I am very fond of Burke and, especially, Slater Brown (whom you'll never read much of—because he is dilatory about his writing and one of the most pleasantly lazy people in the world. He also has the champion bladder, winning all endurance tests and in altitude rivalling the City's C.F. D.'s ladder towers. G——— S——— and T——— once tried to outdo him, but no fires were put out.)

If friendship and love initiated—and I am sure they did—
much of *The Bridge*, other elements of it can be traced to ideas
Crane had discussed earlier with Carl Schmitt, with Bill Sommer,
with Gorham Munson, and more recently with Waldo Frank and
Alfred Stieglitz. These initiating ideas, which dealt both with the
structure of the arts and with the structure of "reality," were important to Crane. Yet the worst possible mistake would be to read
the poem as if it were an exposition of these ideas. At best they
are philosophical abstractions. They are structurally important,
but they are not the poem. They are no more and no less important than the system of sounds on which it is built, the system
of linked images, the alternate moods of hope and despair, the
intricate sets of chronologies and spatial relationships, the "characters" who are chosen less for their own interest than as figures
in a deliberately arranged microcosm, or than that other microcosm, the self—a self whose typical day Joyce had drawn on in
*Ulysses* and William Carlos Williams would later draw on in
*Paterson*, Leopold Bloom, Dr. Paterson, and Crane's man-on-the-
bridge all being ordinary men who, doing very ordinary things,
manage to follow in the footsteps of mythic absent giants.

When Stieglitz wrote Crane, "This country is uppermost in
my mind—what it really signifies—what it is—I am not trying
much analysis—I do not arrive at my results that way," Crane
must have echoed a profound *amen*. For the analysis, the philosophical argumentation, is in the long run more important to
the man than to his work. The argumentation gives the man
maturity. It gives him a way to deal with the world. In Stieglitz's
terms, "to *understand* anything [the artist] . . . must endeavor
to have [his] *inner* house in order—without becoming *self-
conscious*."

When Crane's inner house was in order, he found it easy to
write. When it wasn't, he often tried to set it to rights by getting
off long letters to friends. A Fourth-of-July letter to Stieglitz is
both an announcement of accomplishment and an effort to put
himself in shape for new production. "You should have heard
from me much before this if I hadn't been neck high in writing
some climacterics for my *Bridge* poem," Crane wrote. "That simply carried me out of myself and all personal interests from the
dot of five until two in the morning sometimes—for several days
during which I was extremely happy."

Happiness was not always easy to retain. An argument with a
friend would leave Crane angry and unproductive: "The thing
which hurts me now that I have the time to write letters, is that
I not only have left the creative currents that would have
prompted me to better statements than I am usually equal to,
—but also that I'm in a low state of reactions towards everything,
following an evening with Mr. Josephson." For Josephson, a good

friend of Cowley's, whom Crane was fond of, had devoted the evening to a detailed attack on Munson, Munson's ideas, and Munson's magazine. The day after Josephson's visit, Crane was still upset.

> Malice seems to settle inertly but very positively in some people, and as he is somehow attached to several really fine friends of mine whose company I would hate to forgo on such account, I suppose I must learn to face this little clown with better results. So far, I can only say that wine is no ally against such odds. It even turns to vinegar! and that is much less pleasing than pure water. I don't need to say any more to you about this man, his vacant mind, vague eyes and empty hands. We've given that enough attention. I rant here merely because I have been cheated (willy-nilly) of pouring out a clearer cup today . . .

Perhaps Crane had especially resented Josephson's remarks about Munson because he resented Josephson's ideas about art, ideas in fundamental opposition to the visionary idealism shared by Munson, Crane, and Frank. Josephson, whose satirical wit was frequently used to rip to shreds the optimistic fabric of Crane's aesthetic, had been Dada's champion, Crane sometimes felt, because he was at heart anti-artistic; his real commitment was to the mundane world rather than to the world of the spirit. It was people like Josephson, Crane wrote Stieglitz, whom he had to "combat."

> I have to combat every day those really sincere people, but limited, who deny the superior logic of metaphor in favor of their perfect sums, divisions and subtractions. They cannot go a foot unless to merely catch up with some predetermined and set boundaries, nor can they realize that they do nothing but walk ably over an old track bedecked with all kinds of signposts and "championship records." Nobody minds their efforts, which frequently amount to a great deal,—but I object to their system of judgment being so regally applied to what I'm interested in doing. Such a cramping cannot be reconciled with the work which you have done, and which I feel myself a little beginning to do. . . . We answer them a little vaguely, first, because our ends are forever unaccomplished, and because, secondly, our work is self-explanatory enough, if they could "see" it.

Though their media were different, Crane felt he and Stieglitz shared "common devotions . . . a kind of timeless vision." This vision was grounded in the world: "I feel more and more that in the absolute sense the artist *identifies* himself with life." Yet in their representation of the world, artists of Stieglitz's sort,

Crane felt, always attempt to suggest an inherent order behind the superficial disorder of represented objects. It was because of this shared belief that Crane could write Stieglitz, as he said, "very egotistically," for he really felt that their ideas about art coalesced in work which in a real sense they created *together*: "You will understand that I am always seeing your life and experience very solidly as a part of my own because I feel our identities so much alike in spiritual direction. . . . In the above sense I feel you as entering very strongly into certain developments in 'The Bridge.' May I say it, and not seem absurd, that you are the first, or rather the purest living indice of a new order of consciousness that I have met? We are accomplices in many ways that we don't yet fully understand. 'What is now proved was once only imagined,' said Blake."

Crane found a good deal of relief in writing out his troubles to Stieglitz and in talking them out with Munson and Brown— for troubles were beginning to bulk larger in his life than joys. "The city," he wrote Stieglitz, had become "a place of 'brokenness,' of drama." As one friend after another moved out of town, Crane's productivity fell off. Instead of pleasures, his days were filled with petty annoyances. Filth, noise, disorder crowded in on him. Entangled in the city's corruptions, he began to discover corruptions in the persons he had seen as closest to him.

There seemed also to be a conspiracy of inaction from the people he most loved in Cleveland. Little matters swelled to disproportionate size. The Rychtariks were subtly torturing him by ignoring his regularly repeated requests that they send on to him a box of books; Bill Sommer, who still owed him $15 for the photographic reproduction of paintings, was selfish and self-centered. (Crane got off an angry letter to Sommer's youngest son asking him to see that the money was paid—and soon—or to stop by at Crane's Cleveland home to remove all of Bill's paintings that still remained there.) Even Crane's mother and grandmother came under fire. Hart fretted about correspondence that was not forwarded to him and the trunk that by mid-July had waited nearly four months in his attic bedroom. "I'm all ready for my trunk now," one letter ended, as Hart begged for at least minimum summer necessities:

Please include following items particularly:

1. bathing suit
2. Indian bed cover
3. 2 old pillow cases
3. white linen pants
4. my last year's straw hat
5. 2 or 3 old saucers or such for pipe ashes

The rest you will find already in the trunk. *Do not* send my dress clothes or fine dressing gown! . . . Tennis racket, case and balls, too, *please*!

On the evening of Saturday, July 21, 1923, Crane settled down with nothing more for company than a bottle of wine. Every one of his New York friends was by now away for the summer. In the whole city there was no person to say "Happy birthday!" Hart was miserable.

He was also suffering from a guilty conscience. In spite of all his irritable remarks to family and Cleveland friends, it was they who had remembered him. The long-delayed trunk had been delivered, stuffed with birthday gifts and affectionate notes from Crane's mother and grandmother. "Both you and Mother have my most spontaneous enthusiasm and gratitude for your most appropriate (and needed!) gifts," Hart quickly wrote his grandmother.

> There was so much love expressed in that trunkfull that in taking things out, seeing familiar objects, putting them around my room etc. I had one of the pleasantest evenings I have had for months. There was not an extra or useless thing in it, and you don't know how much is added to my satisfaction and ease by all your thoughtfulness. The socks are superb, the shirts just right in every way, and you sent me the first fresh ties that I have had for many months, for I've bought no clothing since I came down here. The famous 21st will be spent quietly but "richly and luxuriously" thanks to you dear ladies.

On the morning of his birthday, cards had arrived from almost all his Cleveland friends, and birthday letters from Charles Harris and Charlotte Rychtarik. Hart read them on his way to work, reread them at lunch, read them again over a bottle of wine in a little restaurant on Prince Street, "the place where Richard ate with me," he wrote Charlotte Rychtarik. And then he poured out to Charlotte the tangle of emotions that had been troubling him for the last year. "Yes, it is my birthday," he confessed, "and I must be a little sentimental." For pages and pages the letter went on—an account of the leave-taking of his new friends "for places more cool and green and watery"; comments on the heat ("a frightful day, torrid and frying"); questions about Charlotte's mother, whom Crane and Richard had seen off on her return trip to Prague; apologies for his frequent notes about his books; announcements of plans for the publication of a collection of his poems; a summary of the still-unwritten Stieglitz essay; an account of the conflict between job and *The Bridge* ("I am forced to be ambitious in two directions, you see, and in many ways it is like being put up on a cross and divided"); a résumé of his weekend at Rye. But through this enormous letter—

no matter what the subject of the separate paragraphs—runs a
thread of agonizing self-analysis and self-justification: his new
poem would validate the pain his absence was causing his mother
and grandmother; for in ways they would never be able to grasp,
mother and grandmother—Cleveland itself and his friends there—
had combined to produce the poem that could be written only
in isolation from those beloved, ruinous persons. Stripped of its
chatty context, this theme could not be more clear.

Dear Charlotte:
     Your lovely letter came to me this morning. . . . And I am
full of happiness that you think of me as you do,—both you
and Richard. . . . And I have just come back from a lonely
meal in Prince Street . . . Ah, yes *there* is wine, but what is
wine when you drink it alone! Yet, I am happy here in my room
with the Victrola playing Ravel,—The Faery Garden piece
which you and I heard so often together up in my room in
Cleveland. When I think of that room, it is almost to give way to
tears, because I shall never find my way back to it. It is not
necessary, of course, that I should, but just the same it was the
center and beginning of all that I am and ever will be, the center of such pain as would tear me to pieces to tell you about,
and equally the center of great joys!
     The "Bridge" seems to me so beautiful,—and it was there
that I first thought about it, and it was there that I wrote
"Faustus and Helen," which Waldo Frank says is so good that
I will be remembered by that, whether or not I write more or
not. And all this is, of course, connected very intimately with
my Mother, my beautiful mother whom I am so glad you love
and speak about. Indeed it was fine of you to go over and see
her as I asked you to do, Charlotte and Richard! And may I
also say, in the same breath, that your letter was very painful?
It really was,—because I have known all the things you said
about her unhappiness for many, many months. *And* there is
really nothing that can be done: that is the worst of it. I am sure
if you think a minute about my Grandmother's age you will
realize from that alone that my Mother could not possibly leave
her to come here or anywhere else. And my Grandmother, at
her age, cannot move. My mother has had her full share of suffering and I have had much, also. I have had enough, anyway,
to realize that it is all very beautiful in the end if you will
pierce through to the center of it and see it in relation to the
real emotions and values of Life. Do not think I am entirely
happy here,—or ever will be, for that matter, except for a few
moments at a time when I am perhaps writing or receiving a
return of love. The true idea of God is the only thing that can
give happiness,—and that is the identification of yourself with
*all of life*. It is a fierce and humble happiness, both at the

same time, and I am hoping that my Mother will find that *feeling* (for it need not be a conscious thought) at some time or other. She must *accept everything* and as it comes (as we all must) before she can come to such happiness, glorious sorrow, or whatever you want to call it. You must never think that I am not doing all I can to make my Mother's life as bright as possible, even though I do not always succeed. I am doing work of a kind which I should not choose to do at all except that it makes me (or will make me) more money in the end than the simpler things which would satisfy my own single requirements—and just because I want to provide for my mother's future as much as I can. We shall be together more and more as time goes on, and this separation at present is only temporary. You don't know how grateful I am that you have given her your sympathy and love, and that has been *real* or she would not have confided in you the way she has.

. . . Mother sent me my trunk (that much debated question which you will remember!) this week, and it was full of all kinds of dear familiar things that you have seen and touched in my room. There is that ivory Chinese box, for instance, which is here before me as I write. It looks very charming on the black table next to the jade Buddha that Harry brought me from China.

I have not written much this last week . . . But I am sending you a copy (to keep) of the last part of "The Bridge" which is all that I have done so far, that is, in a lump. You will remember enough of what I told you a long time ago about my general ideas and the plan of the entire poem to understand it fairly well anyway. It is sheer ecstasy here,—that is, all my friends who have seen it, say that. It was written verse by verse in the most tremendous emotional exaltations I have ever felt. I may change a few words in it here and there before the entire poem is finished, but there will be practically the same arrangement as what you see. If I only had more time away from office work I should have made much faster progress,— but I am perfectly sure that it will be finished within a year,— and as it is to be about four or five times as long as the enclosed fragment when it is complete,—I shall have been working about as fast on it as I have ever worked in the past.

. . . You mustn't think I don't want your letters or as many as you can write! I only meant that I cannot always get around to answer them as soon as I would like.

Love to Richard, too—your

Hart

It was one thing for Crane to love his mother; it was an altogether different thing to deal with her. He realized that she was close to another nervous collapse, and he saw what most of the contributing factors were: his own absence, his grandmother's minor but confining illnesses, and Grace's steady, draining conviction that her movements were spied on by the entire Crane family. Though he could offer her affection ("I'm only 8 hours riding distant, and *eventually* your next-bedroom neighbor!") and assurances that his grandmother's health would improve, he had real difficulty discovering an attitude toward his father and his father's family that would satisfy her.

What he did finally do was simply echo Grace's sentiments as, from day to day, they changed. In June, when she was startled by an unannounced visit from C.A. and Frances and decided to "punish" them with an air of icy haughtiness, Crane approved her behavior.

> I really can't understand *why* the Cranes should have called on you (from such a distance!) unless from an unsupportable accumulation of curiosity. If they did it from any other motives, I certainly feel sorry for them as snubbed people, doubly-snubbed! I'm not at all worried about C.A.'s manipulation of any tricks with me down here. He knows better, I'm sure, than to risk making himself very foolish, and would be afraid on other grounds anyway. I hope you impressed them with my "luck." Of course,—I *really* don't care anything about it, except they realize that they won't see me sweating any more in Cleveland.

Yet he could as easily echo her concern when his Crane grandparents were taken ill and be as happy as she to hear that they had recovered. When she rather lightly dismissed C.A.'s failure to get in touch with his son on New York visits, the light tone was reflected in Hart's reply: "I have been rather expecting a ring from C.A. all week, but have decided that he has passed me by this time. It's just as well that I didn't know when he is around anyway, as the knowledge carries with it a number of tremulous forebodings which are better explained in the science of psychoanalysis than in common language."

What most disturbed Hart, however, was his mother's frequent announcements that the Cleveland house would soon have to be sold. As the summer wore on, her letters became more desperate: she couldn't stand Cleveland; she couldn't bear Hart's absence; she could no longer take care both of her mother and of the routine housework. If she could just persuade Mrs. Hart to sell the house, they could settle down in an apartment—perhaps in New York.

Hart did everything he could to ease her tensions. He begged her to consider renting the house. He continued to plead with Sam Loveman and the Rychtariks to keep in touch with her. ("My mother is again very unhappy. I do hope that something happens to straighten out her matters soon—loneliness is the greatest. It makes it terribly hard for me to think about my work when I hear her speak as she did last week in a letter.") He even managed to pay her a weekend visit early in the autumn. Nothing, however, seemed really to aid her.

The combination of loneliness, discontent at work, and worry about his mother was capped when Crane discovered that his copy of *Ulysses* had been mysteriously removed from his Cleveland bedroom. Hart went wild with indignation. Convinced that a friend had stolen the book, he managed, before he was through, to alienate half his Cleveland friends and to persuade the other half that they had in their midst a "crooked," "dishonest," "unbalanced," "nutty," "terrible," "abominable snake." Over a three-week period, he stuffed the post box with letters to Cleveland and worked himself into one of his most spectacular cases of hives, only coming out of it when he confronted the man he was convinced had stolen the book and extracted from him a written "confession."

Violence of one kind or another seemed all summer and autumn to be flickering at the edges of Crane's world. Grand battles over *Secession* and *Broom* were building up, and Crane was caught in the cross fire of insult and counter-insult that touched Munson, Burke, Wheelwright, Josephson, Cowley, Brown, Nagle, Glenway Wescott, Isidor Schneider, Robert Sanborn, James Light —and their wives and women.

Crane's initial involvement came as a consequence of Wheelwright's revisions and deletions of the first *Secession* printing of "Faustus and Helen." As soon as the European galleys arrived, Munson had rushed to Crane with the strange version of the poem in hand. Together, they agreed that the best bet was, if possible, to withdraw it. In a blistering letter to Wheelwright, Munson announced: "Apparently, you don't care in what light Burke and I appear before our contributors and our public. The first result of this is Hart Crane's request to return Faustus and Helen since I can offer him no guarantee as to the manner in which it will be presented nor guarantee the freedom from editing it is entitled to nor even its freedom from damaging misprints." In mid-October, after many of Munson's letters had gone astray, been ignored, or been returned unopened, a letter from Wheelwright arrived detailing page-by-page plans for the issue. Munson was roaringly angry: "Crane, you see, was right to demand the withdrawal of Faustus and Helen from your hands. . . . As I have written you, we went to the trouble of getting Loeb's permission to reprint part II because Broom had had the poor taste to print only that part, thus bitching Crane's poem as a symphonic unit. I stressed the unity of the whole poem and pointed out that we were deliberately rectifying Broom's unjust treatment. . . . You must not print Faustus and Helen, that's all." By this time Crane had thrown up his hands in despair. "Your note . . . is certainly appalling. I *may* cable but I'm inclined to think the overt act is already accomplished!!!" For there was really nothing Munson or Crane could do about the poem: "I can only gnash my teeth about my 'F & H'—at last completely slain! People now will never get the correct impression—that it *wasn't* written like a patched blanket. O, well—on the other hand I'll have a book some day." Ten days after Munson had written Wheelwright and Crane had wired, the misdated and misnumbered copies of *Secession* came floating in from sunny Italy. Munson decided the time had come for drastic action.

> The only decent thing I can do for Crane is to shear off the first two pages. You were given explicit directions for the running of his poem. Also I object to your lack of conscience in quoting me. Didn't it occur to you that I was not, in my letters to you, writing for publication in Secession and that I might pass remarks to you which, in public form, I would develop in 500 or 1000 words? Here again I resent being dragged into public view in a half-dressed condition.

Crane, who had for nearly a year been looking forward to the publication of the full text of his poem, did his best to dismiss the matter. There was, after all, nothing he could do. "Cheero, old bird!" he wrote Munson.

> I have just seen the "last" Secession! and I am in no position, I must admit, to quarrel with you about your decision to destroy the garbled pages of "Faustus and Helena." A beautiful bit of business—"blues in your breasts," and the two lines that our hero decided were inessential to the poem! That damned note at the end with its ill-advised quotation from your personal comment is still worse. But never mind, I don't care at all if you will make the necessary clipping. Some few friends of W's have probably already received copies to treasure as their vision may permit, but I should like to keep as many people in America free from misconceptions about me as possible. Why don't you wire the consulate in Florence to stop W from any further rape of S—it is a positive elopement that seems to have no prospect of termination. I am thinking of starting abroad with the DIAL, calling it "The Pile," hemorrhoid, or something like that! My cable, of course, failed.

Wheelwright was perhaps the only participant in the *Secession* battles to remain comparatively calm—and that was only because he was in Florence rather than in New York. Yet even Wheelwright was finally disturbed. In an autobiographical "comment" that is to be found in the file of his papers at Brown University, Wheelwright sometimes ironically, sometimes in earnest, evaluates his past actions. Attached to one of the letters from Munson is a very full statement not just about Crane as a writer but about Crane as a person. His note on the "Faustus and Helen" incident reveals a great deal about both men.

> In what I did to Hart Crane's poem, I was absolutely unmoved by any personal consideration. What I had seen of him I had liked. All the Secessionists highly disapproved of what I did. That made me very sorry. No sooner had I landed in New York than I told Hart Crane so. No sooner had I told him than he thrust out his arm at me and shook hands and absolutely and completely forgave me in the sweetest manner. Later, he told me that he had been extremely angry and unhappy and that as soon as I had told him I was sorry, he had found it impossible to feel either unhappy or angry any longer.
>
> I am sorry to say that although I did immediately and have constantly recognized this to have been one of the most beautiful acts I have seen outside of my family circle, that the light in which it placed myself by contrast is so unpleasant to me, that I have since then been unable to enjoy Hart Crane's company and find him, drunk or sober, extremely tiresome. Since this change of feeling for him, I have found his poetry readable and myself rather guilty for not being able to read more of it.

The week that the copies of *Secession* arrived was the week of the gala *Secession–Broom* meeting, hurriedly called by Malcolm Cowley in the hopes of salvaging from the sparring members of the two magazines some sort of program to which they could all subscribe. The meeting took place on October 19 in the Italian speakeasy on Prince Street to which Crane had taken Rychtarik. Crane—rightly, as it turned out—had considerable misgivings about it. Munson, who had been recovering from a serious illness, had—after picking up the ill-fated *Secession* copies—returned on doctor's orders to Woodstock, New York, and further convalescence. Jean Toomer was in Washington. Waldo Frank was unable to attend. "So I seem," Crane wrote Munson, "to be the only delegate from the higher spaces at the Broom conclave." Crane was especially perturbed that wives had been invited. "If those . . . women . . . are present—you can depend upon it nothing worthy of recording will transpire. I don't approve at all of making it so feministic. I told Cowley, who has kept urging me, that I have a very slight interest in the meeting—and am unconcerned with its issues. I am really going only for the lecture on reasonable affabilities. Very likely I'll play the most contrary rôle —make a scene or something before we get through. I hope Brown is there—and certainly Burke. Otherwise there'll be simply *no* reason for the affair."

Malcolm Cowley, who in *Exile's Return* gives a cheerful blow by blow account of the proceedings, reports that the meeting got underway with his reading of an angry letter from Munson, much of it a diatribe against Matthew Josephson. Halfway through his reading, Cowley saw comic possibilities in the letter: "I began to read it seriously to my audience, but . . . I was overcome by a sense of absurdity and began to declaim it like a blue-jawed actor reciting Hamlet's soliloquy." It was at this point that the battle began to rage. Crane, as he had predicted, was Munson's chief advocate. Soon everybody was shouting—or else preparing, like Glenway Wescott, to beat a dignified retreat. "Glenway Wescott rose from the table," Cowley recollected, "very pale and stern. 'How can you people expect to accomplish anything,' he said precisely, 'when you can't even preserve ordinary parlor decorum?' He swept out of the restaurant with the air of one gathering an invisible cloak about him. . . . Hart Crane, with red face and bristling hair, stamped up and down the room, repeating 'Parlor, hell, parlor.' More bottles appeared on the table."

Josephson, who sent off his own account of the evening to Harold Loeb, saw it as a victory, if rather a Pyrrhic one. Though the projected unification was clearly impossible, at least everyone now knew where he stood. From Josephson's point of view, Munson's letter had turned the trick.

> The attack was so manifestly unfair and unjust that it, of course, damaged Munson considerably, as foreseen by us in reading it. His growing breach with the group named has widened and he has lost all hold save on Toomer, W. Frank, and Crane. The latter, a most likable boy, made great speeches against me; he is intensely loyal to Munson, blindly so, and I like him for it. After the meeting we nearly had a street fight. Although I had answered none of Munson's accusations, which merited no reply, I told Crane he was a liar, and hit Light in the scuffle. But Crane, who is an old friend of mine, couldn't fight me.

It began to seem to Crane that not just Josephson but the entire group of friends that he had once visualized as working harmoniously together were now at each other's throats. Even Stieglitz, who generally acted as peacemaker, found himself at odds with Waldo Frank. "By the end of a summer in New York everybody is at the limit of endurance," Crane wrote home.

Crane could find no happiness in New York, but neither was there ease when he looked toward Cleveland. Though his grandmother assured him that Grace's state of mind was improving, Hart knew that with her money slipping away in little extravagances, her health untrustworthy, and insidious wrinkles intruding on her beauty, his mother was building toward hysteria.

She was intolerably lonely. In the first years after her divorce, she had been amused by still-eligible bachelors competing to invite her to dances, concerts, the theater. Yet without her really noticing, the invitations had fallen off steadily. Now she was reduced to one gentleman caller and one gentleman she refused to see. "I feel sorry that Mother has so little come into her life to cheer or happiffy her," Hart's grandmother wrote. "She has no one to come to see her but G——— and he is so *poor* that we have to do all the entertaining, and that she tires of—but as she says it's better than not to have any one to hang onto." The gentleman forbidden entry to the house, who was separated from his wife and promised much in the way of divorce but performed little, was now, Mrs. Hart said, "squelched" for good. "She has forbidden his coming time and time without number, until he has a right to come. I am glad she has taken the stand. I think she has offended him now so he understands what she means."

There seemed no hope of remarriage in Cleveland. But perhaps—though she talked much of remarriage—what Grace wanted was less a husband than an escort. Possibly, if all her wishes were granted, the escort would in fact be her son. "She does miss you so much—you will never know, or how your letters cheer her," Mrs. Hart wrote. "Don't deprive her of them. Promptly—no matter who else falls short. You should see how she brightens up after getting a letter from you. It makes it much easier for me to get along."

Hart had no difficulty seeing where the unrelated statements in his grandmother's letters were leading: "We miss you more than you can guess. I want Mother to get out of this town. She will never meet any one here that will benefit her any. Too many of the Ex's around. . . . If I thought it would do Mother any good—to take a little trip to N. York—or make her any happier to have a little visit with you, I would be glad to make it possible for her to go . . . She would only stay a few days—at most. . . . Don't hint that I have said anything when you write nor worry about her. She is all right, only at times gets very lonely and discouraged." And there were Grace's restless notes about the house: it was too big for two women; it was too much work; if Hart weren't coming back . . .

Quite as much as Grace and her mother needed Hart, he needed them, but in Cleveland, not in New York. In Cleveland, they were his "anchorage." "I am glad to think of you as located for the winter," one letter hopefully began, "putting in coal, and assured of the comforts that I know you ought to have." In New York, he said, there was no real stability. Landlords raised rents without warning. Tenants, such as the Munsons (who were apartment hunting), were suddenly forced to pay sky-high rents or to go through the disorder of emptying out one cramped apartment only to stuff their belongings into another, no more spacious one.

But they [the Munsons] may not move at all—so discouraging is the search. That's one of the banes of New York—one is on a moving cloud here most of the time, for, either the house you live in is being torn down for an apartment, or else the landlord is gouging you constantly for the last cent. I never want to have any of us without some property of our own—land and building—whether we live in it or not, but just so that "we have it" and are not entirely subject to the whims of fortune. If I ever get any money, I know that I shall attend to that investment before I travel or anything else. You've got to have an anchorage somewhere if you are ever to have any repose of mind.

Yet anchorages were for Crane hard to come by and repose of mind impossible to find. "I've been in such despair," Hart wrote Stieglitz. And though his despair was despair at ever finding time to work on his poem, it was closely related to that other despair for his mother's happiness, a despair he could never long keep down: "If I can once get certain obligations disposed of in my family, I shall certainly break loose and do only such simple labor for my room and board as will not come into my consciousness after 'working hours.' Streams of 'copy' and ad layouts course through my head all night sometimes until I feel like a thread singed and twisted in the morning. This has been, very likely, as strenuous [a] year and as wasteful a one as I shall encounter for a long time, although you can never foretell such things as long as you have a family and connections."

Perhaps the prospect of a visit from his mother did it. Perhaps it was the request for a raise—which he did not receive. Or an all-night visit from Charlie Chaplin. Or a long talk with Waldo Frank which that visit led to. Or a combination of these forces—or none of them. But very suddenly Hart decided that he had to get out of New York. He didn't care where he went. All he knew was that he had to leave.

The evening with Chaplin obviously reminded Crane that he was a poet who ought to be getting on with an important poem. "He remembered my poem very well and is very interested in my work," Hart wrote his mother. "I am very happy in the intense clarity of spirit that a man like Chaplin gives one if he is honest enough to receive it. I have that spiritual honesty, Grace, and it's what makes me clear to the only people I care about."

Chaplin's visit was unannounced and unplanned. Crane's account of it, which he asked his mother to preserve ("Save this letter—I want it as a memo-souvenir"), carries all the surprised delight six superb hours produced.

Grace, dear!

I had just got my pajamas on last night when there was a rap on the door. I opened and in walked Waldo Frank—behind him came a most pleasant-looking, twinkling, little man in a

black derby—"Let me introduce you to Mr. Charles Chaplin,"
—said Waldo, and I was smiling into one of the most beautiful
faces I ever expect to see. Well!—I was quickly urged out of
my nightclothes and the three of us walked arm in arm over to
where Waldo is staying at 77 Irving Place (near Gramercy).
All the way we were trailed by enthusiastic youngsters. People
seem to spot Charlie in the darkness. He is so very gracious
that he never discourages anything but rude advances.

At five o'clock this morning Charlie was letting me out of
his taxi before my humble abode. "It's been so nice," he said
in that soft crisp voice of his, modulated with an accent that is
something like Padraic Colum's in its correctness. Then he,
blinking and sleepy, was swung around and was probably soon
in his bed up at the Ritz.

I can't begin to tell you what an evening, night and *morning*
it was. Just the three of us . . .

It must indeed have been a good evening. Crane talked about
"Chaplinesque" and what the poem meant to him, and about
his plans for *The Bridge*. Waldo Frank began to outline some of
the ideas that would go into his yet unwritten *Virgin Spain*. Chaplin explained what he had been trying to accomplish in *A Woman
of Paris*, which had opened at the Lyric Theatre a week before.
Soon, however, their conversation shifted to much more personal
matters. "Our talk was very intimate—Charlie told us the complete Pola Negri story—which 'romance' is now ended. And there
were other things about his life, his hopes and spiritual desires
which were very fine and interesting. He has been through so
very much, is very lonely (says Hollywood hasn't a dozen people
he enjoys talking to or who understand his work) and yet is so
radiant and healthy, wistful, gay and *young*."

By dawn Crane felt that in Chaplin he had discovered another
of those friends on whom, literally, his life depended. "We (just
Charlie and I) are to have dinner together some night next week,"
Crane told his mother. "You cannot imagine a more perfect and
natural gentle man. . . . Stories (marvelous ones he knows!) told
with such subtle mimicry that you rolled on the floor. Such graceful wit, too—O that man has a mind."

Even though no real friendship developed from Crane's meeting
with Chaplin, the visit did serve to strengthen his determination
to escape the straight commercial path he saw before him. If an
artist were to achieve anything of merit, Crane concluded, he had
to do his best to keep clear of the bickering into which the
*Broom–Secession* group had fallen, and at the same time had to
keep clear of entrapment in those businesses that dissipate creative energy. Working out these ideas, Crane thought how the artistic potential of his dead friend Ernest Nelson had been ex-
ploited and finally destroyed and how, in the same lithography

factory that had consumed Nelson's art, Bill Sommer was still wearing himself out. It was all meaningless, exhausting grubbing for money—money which, in the long run, did nothing but pull friends apart. He thought over his own blunders: he had allowed a missing book to destroy a friendship; his anxiety over Sommer's tiny debt had very nearly alienated one of his closest friends.

Well, some damages could be repaired. Hart bought a picture postcard of the Woolworth tower, strolled on to a restaurant, and sat down to one of his favorite Italian dinners. He read over a letter from Stieglitz that had arrived that morning—a long letter in large part about the healing forces of art and nature: "Most of the summer has been quite an ordeal. But it did not quite get me under. My work finally saved me. And with that came the clearing all about. I have done some real things." Stieglitz was writing from his summer place on Lake George; and as Crane read the letter, the roaring elevated at the corner shaking the little restaurant, the ironies of his situation must have cut deep. Stieglitz would be coming back to town as late as possible that year: "It's too glorious here, and the Silence is perfect." Never, he said, in all his sixty years had he been so struck by the beauty of the natural world. He had been taking nothing but "'sky' pictures . . . that are truly beautiful and are *new*—different from anything the eye has seen in any medium.—But that happened. Life compelled me into the doing—that's all." One day, he told Crane, he and O'Keeffe had hiked up to the top of a neighboring mountain— "only 1800 feet high." Yet the excitement he experienced had been overwhelming.

> In fifty years I have been up there at least fifty times—and I have seen some marvelous pictures from there—but on this occasion nature actually vied with art and I feel that all the pictures I ever saw put together could not hold a candle to what lay there at my feet—as I turned around 360 degrees!—An unforgettable hour.

One's life doesn't have to be grubby; there are ways to fight the corruption, Crane thought. He could make a beginning by reminding one friend—as he had been reminded by Chaplin's visit and by Stieglitz's letter—that the artist is of some importance not just to the world but to particular men and women. A postcard to Bill Sommer might repair a little damage, might remind Bill of his own value.

Dear Bill:
Gaston Lachaise, Charlie Chaplin and others have praised your pictures on my wall. I hope you are continuing to *work* and to *purify* yourself. Love—

　　　　　　　　　　　　　Hart

He could repair broken friendships. And with luck and good counsel, he could do something about his own pointless existence.

His first step was to get in touch with Waldo Frank. Crane wanted to talk over the strategy by which he might free himself of his job and discuss the places he might go when he was no longer tied to Manhattan. At this point he was willing to admit that—except for the friendships with Brown, Toomer, and Frank —New York had offered him nothing. "The situation for the artist in America seems to me to be getting harder and harder all the time," Crane had recently written the Rychtariks.

> Most of my friends are worn out with the struggle here in New York. If you make enough to live decently on, you have no time left for your real work,—and otherwise you are con- stantly liable to starve. New York offers nothing to anyone but a circle of friendly and understanding brothers,—beyond that it is one of the most stupid places in the world to live in. Of course, one's friends are worth it,—but sometimes, when you see them so upset by the fever and crowded conditions, the expenses and worries—you wonder whether or not there is much use in the whole business.

"I want to keep saying 'YES' to everything and never be beaten a moment, and I shall, of course, never be really beaten," he wrote Richard and Charlotte; but he was frightened by the pos- sibility of being "beaten" if he didn't take quick and forceful action.

The scheme that Frank and Crane worked out was, on the surface at least, a sensible one. Crane should take advantage of the family house on the Isle of Pines. By telling J. Walter Thomp- son that family business demanded it, he would be able to get a leave of absence. He could then go to the island, live cheaply, work on his poem in undisturbed leisure—and have a job to fall back on if island living were no better than life in New York. He would not really plan to support himself; if the poem were going well, he would ask his family for a loan to tide him over until he could begin writing reviews and articles.

"The N.Y. life is too taxing," he wrote Munson, "—and while I am perfectly solid—more so than ever in certain ways—the impact between the inner reality and the consciousness around me threatens to shatter my nerves and health. It is too early for that to happen. . . . I can finish the 'Bridge' there and write my Stieglitz article—drink gallons of orange juice, bathe and play tennis. I need these things badly. I haven't had any vacation, you know, for five years."

Two days later, Crane wrote a similar but much fuller letter home. In it he tried to sum up not just superficial discontent but the real truth of his situation: he had become extraordinarily edgy ("nerves and insomnia" were threatening to push him into "a real breakdown"); there was "no prospect" of a raise in salary; he hated life in New York City; he would not return to Cleveland ("I'll never consider living in Cleveland again permanently—no matter what happens").

Most of all, he was anxious to head off Grace's threatened visit . . . or the even more disastrous possibility that she would force the sale of the house and settle in New York. He was, of course, protecting a hard-won freedom; but he was also very much concerned for Grace's welfare.

> I think this and other letters of mine have said enough about living conditions in New York as it has now become—to make it plain that you will never want to settle here. I have never accented these points in any particular relation to you—but I am more and more certain that you will never want to *live* here. Rents are terrific, food very high and unless you have unlimited funds you have to content your self with trying to keep clean in a dinky stuffy apartment without a porch or any of the outdoor privileges that go with the poorest shanty.

He explained that though he was not feeling well he did not want her to "waste a lot of money" coming to New York in the belief that he needed "bedside attention." All he wanted was the chance to go to the Isle of Pines for a little recuperation.

> Please don't think that I'm flat on my back or anything like that—by what I've said. I have been at the office every day and doing my regular work. It's the steady and growing strain of it all that I feel—without relief or rest, and I don't want to disregard too many red signals . . .

Grace answered with a letter any mother might be expected to write—urging caution, forethought, prudence. Hart's reaction was what one might have anticipated of any spoiled son: he went to his supervisor and turned in his resignation, asking that it be regarded as a leave of absence since he might wish to return in the spring. He would, he said, finish out the week's work. "It simply had to be," he wrote Munson from his office that afternoon. "I got so I gagged every time I sat down here." The letter to Grace and his grandmother that he turned out that night was grimly factual. He would need about $200 to settle his debts and to pay for second-class fare to the island. "And if you don't feel you can raise that amount I shall borrow it at 6 per cent. But if I have to do this, I shan't be able to afford a trip to Cleveland to see you." Grace wrote back that he could not go to the island. Their house there was up for sale. They might very well not own it when Hart arrived. She enclosed enough money for train fare to Cleveland.

Grace's letter reached Hart on the morning of October 26. Angry at her and much in need of some outlet for his frustrations, Crane may at this point have taken action against his sea of troubles somewhat as Matthew Josephson tells it: "He was assigned to writing the literature of cosmetics. Thinking to inspire him, his superiors placed on his desk numerous vials of strong perfume, whose odor he was supposed to capture in words. But the perfumes nauseated him and so one day, when he had come to work with a bad hang-over, he snatched up the whole collection and threw them out of his office window. After that he was done for at the agency and forced to take refuge in the country, at Woodstock, New York . . ." Maybe it did happen that way—though if Crane tossed out of windows everything that his acquaintances have him tossing, most of America, half of Europe, and all of Mexico would still be littered with far-flung typewriters, perfume bottles, dogs, radios, manuscripts, books, and former friends.

What his mother's letter did produce was despair. "I hardly know how to begin—such confusion reigns at present," Hart wrote to Stieglitz that evening. Once again he told the whole story. His nerves were "frazzled." "In fact they got so on edge writing that damned advertising under the pseudo-refined atmosphere of the office I was working in that I had to resign the other day to save my mind. I have the prospect of coming back after a six week's vacation if I want to—but I don't want to, and as things stand at present haven't got the money to carry me through the rest and contemplation that I need. Rather wound up, you see!" He told also of his mother's attack on his island plans: "If I can get somebody to lend me the money, however, I may possibly go right ahead, regardless. Both of my parents are interested in money only in connection with my actions, and I have never been persistent enough in the past to really clear that notion away."

Mention of both his parents in his letter to Stieglitz might have prompted Crane to write a quick letter to his father, the first letter he had attempted in that direction for some three years. It was a history of his advertising career, his decision to devote some time to his long poem, his critical need for financial support. He didn't expect an answer.

By this time, very late at night, Crane had worn out most of his irritations and had settled on his immediate plans. He would accept an invitation that had arrived some weeks before from Edward Nagle and Slater Brown, who could put him up in the house they had rented in Woodstock. He would as politely as possible make clear to Grace that he intended from here on (with her help!) to lead his own life.

I am not going to the Island, but I expect to go up state to Woodstock for 6 weeks, leaving late next week. . . . Please arrange to send me $15.00 per week while I am there. That will buy the necessary food, etc. When I get my rest and come back to town I expect to try some other kind of literary work, maybe with a publishing house, before accepting Thompson's offer again. They pay so damned little and expect so much—that I might do better another place.

At any rate I am going to have some time in the country and in the open air. Just now I am very exhausted, as I have said. Thank you for inviting me back to Cleveland, but you know there are too many people to talk to there and, after all, it's city life too. My present plan is much cheaper and better. The Island would have been best of all . . .

Grace made an attempt to dissuade Hart from his Woodstock visit. If he had been fired from his job, she said, he should diligently search for another. If he felt he needed a little rest, he should visit the mother and grandmother who loved him rather than run off to new acquaintances. "You must not fool yourselves that I was fired at all," Hart rather helplessly answered. "If that were so I shouldn't hesitate to admit it, but my run-down state and a certain distaste it developed for advertising work in general simply made it impossible to go [on] indefinitely there without at least a temporary relief."

I am depending on you to help me some, as I said in my last letter. I think you will agree that a thoroughly out-of-doors life for a month is not only a sensible thing for me, but really due me after all the time I have denied myself such a natural privilege. If you don't understand such a rightful desire on my part, then I can only say that your vision is warped. It was fine of you to ask me home, but I know you will realize that the atmosphere of Cleveland is anything but conducive to rest *for me*. The amount to which I am asking you to help me will not exceed the carfare to and from Cleveland—at most. Brown is poor and can only offer me the hospitality of the house he has taken,—any extra board he is unable to provide, so I am anxious to do my part and be decent about not stretching his hospitality unreasonably. So please send me fifteen dollars in cash or check at Woodstock sometime next week. Even if you have to pinch a little bit, I think that the things I am trying to do deserve a few sacrifices. I make as many as I can myself, and still keep sound and living,—and I hope you will [be] faithful enough—whether you see my complete ends or not— to lend me some assistance.

I hope you are both well and happy. Don't worry about me. I know damned well what I'm doing. I'll write you as soon as I get to Woodstock.

The next evening—Crane's last in New York—was devoted to a gloriously drunken farewell party. Such friends as Crane could assemble rallied round. Free spirits, even if all of them were broke, had to celebrate the triumph of art over advertising! When the party ended, Crane wandered out for a stroll through the night streets.

# 18

Whatever Grace Crane thought of her son's decision to abandon his advertising career in favor of the Woodstock hills, from Hart's point of view it made the best kind of sense. To produce the work he was capable of, he needed not only time but good times. Brown and Nagle were able to provide these. Though only two finished poems resulted from his visit, the well-being during the two months gave Crane a notion of the sort of life he wanted to lead.

The euphoria had begun the evening before he left New York. Though it is impossible to reconstruct, enough of a dreadful yet splendid nature took place to set Crane, for over a month, trying to capture the experience in a poem. In a letter to Underwood, he hinted of an "appalling tragedy"—presumably sexual—that had taken place. Yet the evening's "tragedy" was shot through with illumination. Writing to Jean Toomer, Crane speaks of that night as "sad and wondrous."

> It keeps coming to me, though, in a kind of terrific rawness. And as I said, it is nothing to be overcome or superseded—its causes were outside of myself—and its gift a broken thing. It does cry for words, however,—and I'm wondering if I am equal to such an occasion, such beauty and anguish, all in one.

Three weeks later Crane was still attempting to fit it into a poem. It had involved a boy—perhaps a sailor—and a "boat for Antwerp." The experience, Crane told Toomer, continued to "haunt" him, and fragments of the evening had begun to collect into poetry. "That poem has been my only immediate concern," Crane wrote.

> It is growing very slowly. I doubt the possibility of ever printing it, but don't care. Significances gradually lift themselves from the trial lines. I send you some of the poem as it stands at this hour, as you are fine enough to be concerned. It was great to have your inquiry about it. I think I shall call it "White Buildings" perhaps. Certainly it is one of the most consciously written things I have ever attempted, whether or not it has any

sense, direction or interest to anyone but myself. Let me know if anything in it gets through at all to an outsider.

So far as I know, the poem was never completed. Yet it has some importance, for—in addition to bearing the "White Buildings" title—it incorporates material Crane would later draw on for "Recitative," "Passage," "Voyages IV," and the "Harbor Dawn" section of *The Bridge*. It is useful, too, as a demonstration of the way in which personal subject matter gradually becomes depersonalized by Crane's technique into something independent of its origins. In this poem the process isn't quite completed; the human element bulks very large—a meeting on a misty November night and an early-morning sense of loss when the speaker finds himself no longer communicating by way of words and arms but instead engaged in dialogues with a beam of sunlight and the sheet of paper that will become the poem. But the transforming devices are already beginning their processes: the morning sun acts as a link to an eastward-sailing lover, and though its beam of light may strike the speaker of the poem with something not far from the impact of a baseball bat, it does also serve to illuminate the "normal" life of everyday events (the washerwoman at her tub, the wash that decorates the courtyards between apartment houses). Crane told Toomer, "I think I ought to apologize for this page as it stands!" The page, however, merits reproduction.

> This way where November takes the leaf
> to sow only disfigurement in early snow
> mist gained upon the night I delved, surely
> as the city took us who can meet and go
> (who might have parted, keen beyond any sea,
> in words which no wings can engender now).
>
> For this there is a beam across my head;
> its weight not arched like heaven full, its edge
> not bevelled, and its bulk that I accept,
> triumphing not easily upon the brow . . .
>
> And, margined so, the sun may rise aware
> (I must have waited for so well devised a day)
> of the old woman whistling in her tubs,
> and a labyrinth of laundry in the courted sky;
> while inside, downward passing steps
> anon not to white buildings I have seen,
> leave me to whispering an answer here
> to nothing but this beam that crops my hair.
>
> (other verses even less developed—poem
> ends with following lines:

Vaulted in the welter of the east be read,
"These are thy misused deeds."—
And the arms, torn white and mild away, be bled.

Crane's last night in New York had given him an unfinished poem. His first night away from New York gave him a new friend. For he had been invited to make his way up to Woodstock by way of Ridgefield, Connecticut, and the home of Eugene O'Neill.

Crane's introduction to O'Neill—like his introduction to a number of other people who would later be very important to him—came about through Sue Jenkins, one of the few of Crane's friends who had spent most of the summer in New York. A widely read, perceptive, cheerful person, Sue had the capacity of being both a good listener and a good storyteller. Much of Hart's talk with her, of course, was about their friends: Slater Brown, whom Sue would soon marry; Brown's friend, E. E. Cummings, whose poetry Crane admired and sometimes parodied; and the members of the Provincetown Playhouse, where James Light, Sue's husband, was working as a director and Eleanor Fitzgerald—generous and beautiful—was business manager. Ivan Opffer, a talented artist whose drawings would soon be appearing in *The Bookman*, was often at Sue Jenkins's house during this time, as was his brother Emil, whose career in the merchant marine had already begun and who would entertain Sue and Hart with anecdotes from each of his ports of call.

O'Neill had known Sue Jenkins and James Light for years and through them had read some of Crane's poetry. But until a week before Crane left New York City, the poet and the playwright had never met. When they did meet, they got on very well, O'Neill urging Crane to spend the weekend at Ridgefield and offering to drive him on to Woodstock on Sunday morning.

Crane, who needed no second invitation, found O'Neill a superb host. The visit, he reported to Toomer, had been "A roisterous time! Cider, belly dances and cake walks . . . and we didn't go to bed until daylight." O'Neill seemed to Crane a dream come true: he was the uncompromising writer who led a full, wild, "real" life, yet who managed to turn it into both good and profitable art. "Drunk on cider most of the time," Crane was, nevertheless, alert enough to admire the way O'Neill had assembled everything a man might want: "He has a huge place in the country with a charming wife who loves to flirt, an enormous grey Irish wolfhound dog (bigger than a man) and a housekeeper that brings your breakfast to your bedside every morning."

After such celebration, one might have expected Crane to be ready for a letdown; but in his two months with Brown and

Nagle it never came. For the first time in years he managed—almost all of the time—to put worries out of mind.

Hart liked everything about his visit. He liked the house and its location—on a dirt road running north from the Saugerties highway and not far from a small cottage where the poet Richard LeGallienne lived. He liked the artist Edward Nagle, who—tall, thin, myopic, and dressed like a *fin de siècle* poet with a flowing black tie—would amuse Hart and Brown with his exaggerated ineptitude in practical household affairs and with his exaggerated cleanliness. ("In Woodstock, Hart and I remarked that he spent much of his time sweeping the studio floor," Brown wrote me, "employing his broom more frequently than he did his brush.") Best of all, Hart enjoyed the easy conversations with Brown. "Hart was very happy to be in Woodstock," Brown recalled, "—it was a wonderful, unspoiled place then with serious and intelligent artists about."

It is that tone of happiness that shows up in every Woodstock letter Crane wrote. Even a random sampling displays it.

November 4—to Jean Toomer:

Long walks today, wrestling matches and hide and seek on the lawn. My biceps are certainly swelling. The house is just right . . . I can see some sturdy days ahead, even though no pen shall touch the paper and the typewriter remains click-less.

November 8—to his mother and grandmother:

Felling trees and piecing them up for warmth is a new sport to me, but I have taken to it with something like a real enthusiasm. This is my fourth day here in the mountains, but already I feel like a new person. My muscles are swelling and my blood simply glowing. . . . Certainly I should like to become a giant again in health, as I naturally am. And I have never had an outing like this before in my life.

November 10—to his grandmother:

It is a rainy day, but the last two days have been superb. We climbed up halfway on one of the mountains near here one afternoon. You could see for miles around, the same as the postcard that I sent you shows. I am getting myself hardened up—not wearing too much clothing and keeping meanwhile in motion a good deal.

November 13—to Sue Jenkins:

Life is very pleasant here, despite all the guests that we have been having, and it is no less ardorous. My biceps are larger and my cheeks are much bekindled, but as for TIME—His shoulders are more narrowed than the spirit of the necktie counter's tender on a Jan. evening. I have not even had a moment to do the three briefers for the DIAL that I took up here as a precautionary measure. Letters likewise. Meanwhile the fireplace glitters and the stove consumes, and we eat enormous meals.

November 16—to the Rychtariks:

There is much to be done every day and every hour. We chop down trees in the woods which surround us, then saw them up. It is very cold already up here, and it keeps us busy just doing that. Then there are the meals to get. I didn't know that I could do so many things in that way. I made some fine gravy that was praised not only by the immediate household, but by Gaston Lachaise and his Mme. who are here also for the winter and who dropped in that evening for dinner. . . . To speak briefly, I have never felt so fine in my life before. So quiet it is here! No cats fighting, people quarrelling or subways beneath you to make the ground tremble. . . . If I can I shall stay out here all the winter with Brown and Nagle. Certainly they are wonderful people and make me want to live with them forever.

November 21—to his mother and grandmother:

After you have carried 150 pounds of log on your shoulder and sawed about a quarter of a cord your system steams up with abundant heat. . . . And in view of the very salutary results I am going to remain here until January first. . . . Of course I shall not be home for Christmas, but you will be jolly enough at Zell's without me this time. . . . I fried some apples this noon for lunch in the fat left over from some pork sausage. I have been rather surprised how I have remembered some of the ways you cook things without my ever having been conscious when I was home as to just what was done . . . Last night we had Gorham and his host, Fisher, who live about half a mile through the woods from here, in to dinner. I never ate so much in my life, great quantities of ham, baked potatoes, and the sweetest beets ever cooked. The weather and the exercise breed tremendous appetites.

November 23—to Jean Toomer:

I really am happy to hear the wind in the boughs, use the axe and saw, and even enjoy the bit of cooking which I share in doing. There is not much time for other things except on rainy days like the last, when I sat reading the Golden Bough and alternating black cat "Jazz"—or tiger "Chauncey Depew" (on account of his dinner visits across the fields to neighboring plantations) in my lap, now well protected with corduroy.

November 27—to his mother:

It has not been as cold here yet as I had expected. However, a few flakes of snow are liable to start down at any time and I shall welcome them. The mountains around here are so beautiful in their various aspects and under the different skies that everyday brings—I haven't been here long enough yet to ignore them from habit, and doubt if I ever should be indifferent to their presence. For one thing, they are not too picturesque in the obvious way so that they stand up and shriek for your attention all the time. They are very much an easy and careless part of a natural landscape.

December 5—to Alfred Stieglitz:

We're about a mile and half from the village and very much by ourselves. My first taste of the country for years—and a month of it has put me in a steadier mood than I remember since childhood. . . . When your letter came yesterday I felt and still feel very remiss, the most so now that my imagination, sunk in a kind of agreeable vegetable existence, refuses to offer you any real evidence that life in the country has been of personal benefit to me. But it's rather pleasant to be irresponsible and purely bovine once in five years or so. About all I am doing besides the many chores is—grow a mustache (very slight so far!).

December 5—to his grandmother:

It is raining steadily today, and you can't even see the mountains through the overhanging mists. I like this country here more and more. In all kinds of weather it has unique beauties and I shall be sorry to leave it in January, which I must do, of course, as I must find some kind of work again.

December 10—to Malcolm Cowley:

The gentle melancholy of your card was gracious and welcome; reassuring to know THE CITY is a little away from me yet.
"I SHALL HAVE SPEECH WITH YOU IN BABYLON" would start a good poem, perhaps, were not Babylon so outspoken already. Meanwhile the much-vaunted sexy stories refuse to be born. I draw pictures, cook, sweep and masturbate the cats.

December 14—to his mother:

I have just come back from the village whither one of us has to go at least once a day to get the mail, milk, and groceries. It is so fine to walk through the quiet woods and meadows quite alone by oneself and watch the clouds floating over the edge of the mountains like white chariots in the sunshine! There isn't any more beautiful country in this continent than right here. Sometime it would be fine for you to come here for the summer and live in one of the modest houses, costing very little, and you could dress as you damned pleased, read and sleep and take long walks on level or hilly land, as you chose. I have never looked so well in my life as I do now, and I'm strong as an ox with the fine exercise I have been having. I think city life is a fake and a delusion, and I'm certainly going to see to it that I see more of this sort of country in the future.— Only three hours from New York, too. . . . Time flies even faster out here than it seems to in the city—I don't quite know why except that I am always so happily busy.

Though there was relatively little drinking during the Woodstock holidays, a certain amount of the "happy" life can be attributed to the presence in the cellar of a barrel of elderberry wine, the unintentional contribution of "old man Rector," an erratic inventor from whom Brown and Nagle had rented the house. In spite of the fact that Hart proved allergic to the wine—breaking out from head to foot in what Brown remembered as one of the most "terrific" cases of hives he had ever seen—the three conspirators very nearly managed to kill the barrel before Mr. Rector arrived to spend a few days making adjustments on his most recent achievement, a kerosene-burning automobile. Each evening after supper Mr. Rector—a pint measuring cup in hand— would descend to the cellar while Crane, Brown, and Nagle, in whispered consultations punctuated by Crane's whooping laugh, would speculate whether the barrel had finally gone dry. "Because we'd really been swilling it!" Brown remembered. Each evening, however, Mr. Rector emerged triumphantly and carefully measured out into his best stem glasses one drink apiece and one only. "Herr Rector is still with us!" Hart groaned to Sue Jenkins. "I'll be glad when either he gets his damned kerosene fliv going, or else it blows him into Norway."

Finally Mr. Rector vanished down the road in a swirl of fume-laden dust, and Crane, Nagle, and Brown settled into weeks of high talk about art and life. "The three of us got drunk on the wine filched last night from the private cellar of the owner of this house," Crane wrote Toomer late in November. "Great defense of the MACHINE by Brown opposed by Crane and Nagle. Went furious to bed. The night before it was Marinetti, John Brown, KKK and Jesus Christ." A few fragments of their talks survive, for some passionate notetaker at these sessions scrawled crucial phrases on sheets of typing paper. One of those sheets drifted into Brown's papers, where it remained until 1958. Although the penciled phrases have smudged badly and one word is illegible, the sheets capture a bit of what must have been a glorious debate.

Energy is essentially without direction.
This we imbibe, as artists.
Power is energy in direction.
This we dispense, as artists (as transformers)

Nagle says "all Art is economy of energy."
B. says "if as N. says Art is economy of means, then e. of m's can only be judged by its purpose."
Nagle says, "but why?"
B. says, "Machine [illegible word—replies?] with definitions of purpose in mechanical terms.

---

You can have direction without purpose.
Matter has rhythm, not essentially direction.
Art has direction without necessary purpose
purpose of art is unity—
Art is a measurement and to that extent an imposition (H.C.)

(X) Life is made is made of objects
(Y) objects are made of straight line, square and circle. S.B.

---

$$\frac{X}{Life} = \frac{object}{Y}$$

$$Y = a+b+c$$

$$a+b+c = X$$

$$a+b+c = Y$$

Brown adds *"recognition"* as a
*component factor*

---

A work of art is nothing but a fulcrum (of shifted energy) H.C.

---

At first glance the argument sounds wild enough (and *looks* it: type cannot reproduce that desperate scrawl), but the positions which lie behind it are familiar to any writer or painter, for Brown and Nagle and Crane were struggling with fundamental problems of aesthetics.

Other evenings were a good deal more lighthearted. Crane occasionally entertained Brown and Nagle with parodies of contemporary poets, several of which still exist in manuscript. One brilliant parody of Cummings manages to combine an assortment of sexual references with startlingly relevant imagery of a "piping" hot dinner—"applesauce," "celery" ("creamed"), and some "corking" wine. In passages worthy of Joyce, Crane traces the meal through the "belching" and "fumbiguts" of the intestinal tract and into a final "semi-colon."

There was even a little time for Crane to work at serious poetry. He continued to polish "Recitative," a poem begun about a month earlier and into which he now incorporated some of the material from the "White Buildings" poem. The reworked version, he explained to Munson, was "more metaphysical and restrained" than an earlier draft, a "confession" which he now regarded as a product of the "somewhat flamboyant period in NY." Even after his "tentative" draft appeared in the spring 1924 issue of *The Little Review*, however, Crane continued to doctor the poem, adding three stanzas and revising many of the lines before he established the final *White Buildings* text of 1926. Interesting not only because it uses bridge-tower imagery but also because Crane designed it as a deliberate self-portrait, the poem mirrors the essentially opposed halves of man's nature: that of the lust-driven, darkness-seeking animal, the ape, bestial and corrupt, whose parted lips break into a "fragment smile" of certain innuendo; and the ape's opposite, the "white buildings" of day that transform phallic imagery into imagery appropriate to the soul. What the poem asserts, then, is nothing less than the naked truth about Hart Crane—and, he believed, the truth about every man. Each part of man's body participates in his double nature: and a single smile can be both the "crucial sign" of his lust, his "blowing leaves," and simultaneously the "crucial sign" of an entirely spiritual communion. For the body *bridges* spirit and flesh, and man must learn to "walk through time" in the single stride which incorporates into one action his double nature. Though avoiding a discussion of the rather obviously Freudian "reflexes and symbolisms" of the poem, Hart spelled out as much of the structure of "Recitative" as he discreetly could for Allen Tate.

> It *is* complex, exceedingly,—and I worked for weeks, off and on, of course,—trying to simplify the presentation of the ideas in it, the conception. Imagine the poet, say, on a platform speaking it. The audience is one half of Humanity, Man (in the sense of Blake) and the poet the other. ALSO, the poet sees himself in the audience as in a mirror. ALSO, the audience sees itself, in part, in the poet. Against this paradoxical DUALITY is posed the UNITY, or the conception of it (as you got it) in the last verse. In another sense, the poet is *talking to himself* all the way through the poem, and there are, as too often in my poems, other reflexes and symbolisms in the poem, also, which it would be silly to write here—at least for the present. It's encouraging that people say they get at least some kind of impact from my poems, even when they are honest in admitting considerable mystification. "Make my dark poem light, and light," however, is the text I chose from Donne some time ago as my direction. I have always been working hard for a more

perfect lucidity, and it never pleases me to be taken as wilfully
obscure or esoteric.

During this time, Crane also made minor revisions on "Possessions," a poem constructed from almost precisely the same
materials as "Recitative"—the "partial appetites" of "lust" and
"rage" which oppose the spiritual ecstasy that burns like an "in-
clusive cloud / Whose heart is fire." As in the other poem, dark
(the "black foam" of a midnight thunder storm) is opposed to
light (the cleansing "white wind" of spiritual regeneration) and
again a single object symbolizes the two sides of man's nature (a
"fixed stone of lust" transformed to "bright stones wherein our
smiling plays"). Pleased that Tate and Toomer liked "Possessions" (Toomer found it "a deep, thrusting, dense, organized,
strong, passionate, luminous, and ecstatic poem"), Crane sent
it off with its companion piece to Margaret Anderson, who soon
printed the pair in *The Little Review*.

Most of the writing Crane did at Woodstock was, however, not
intended for publication, though it included some of his best
work: I mean, of course, his superb letters. Compared to one
product of these months, the minor lyric "Interludium" (which
Crane wrote in honor of a work by Lachaise and published in
the July issue of *1924*—and later suppressed), the letters seem
especially rich, revelatory, and eloquent.

Because the times were happy ones, most of these letters are
full of bubbling gaiety. Crane tells all his friends, for example,
about the riotous preparations for a gala Thanksgiving dinner
that was planned weeks in advance and that subjected its hosts to
the problems of a constantly changing guest list and a consequently changing menu. Finally there were only six guests—from
the Woodstock area, Lachaise, his wife, and Marjorie Spencer;
from New York, John Dos Passos, Stewart Mitchell, and Elaine
Orr—but there must have been enough food for a small army and
enough preparation of food for a large one. Contributions came
from all over. Madame Lachaise several weeks in advance had
shipped from Maine two barrels of Northern Spy apples; Grace
Crane sent a large fruitcake; the New York guests came armed
with Marsala wine and cherry cordial; Brown and Nagle had purchased a full barrel of hard cider; someone contributed a supply
of locally brewed red wine (the elderberry wine was long since
gone).

After much consultation, Crane and Brown and Nagle had decided to hold the festivities in an attached studio, where Nagle
sometimes painted and where they would be able "to have the
most room possible to spread out in." Tuesday morning they went
out in the woods to cut "fragrant pine boughs" to line the overhanging balcony and the stair railing. In the afternoon the ad-

vance cooking began. What with Nagle's efforts to keep the kitchen neat (his "great vice" of "super-neatness," Crane wrote, kept him "always whirling around with a broom or wash pail"), Brown's eloquent suggestions, and Crane's determination somehow to evolve applesauce—"a tremendous quantity of it"—from a mysterious assembly of raw materials (the only information he lacked, he told his mother, was "how much of water, sugar, cinnamon or anything to put into it"), it is a miracle that anything was accomplished. But by Thanksgiving eve, they were set to go: "We had all the walls hung with candles as well as the table."

The party was a great success, even though at the last minute someone noticed that the turkey, which was supposed to arrive cleaned and stuffed, was empty. Crane heroically rose to the occasion by creating pot-luck stuffing: "It was left to me entirely. You should have seen me going at it, sewing it up tight afterward and everything!" They roasted the turkey in front of the big fireplace in a "wonderful roasting machine" that Lachaise had bought in New York City. "You put the bird on a long spit which had a crank and catches. One side of the cage was entirely open and that was turned toward the fire." Finally, no more than two hours behind schedule, dinner got under way.

> The meal began with potato and onion soup made by Nagle. Then turkey with mashed potatoes, cranberry sauce, squash and gravy. Celery too. Then I made some fine lettuce salad with onions and peppers and French dressing. Dessert was composed of pumpkin pie and mince pie and the marvelous fruit cake. . . . Nuts, raisins, etc. . . . Sat down at five and didn't get up to dance until eight. I danced fat Mme. Lachaise around until we both fell almost exhausted. Then there was a girl who could match me on my Russian dance and we did that together at a great rate. I forgot to mention that we had a Victrola, of course, which Lachaise bought in Kingston just the day before. Lots of jazz records, etc.

By 3:30 A.M. the guests were exhausted, the turkey was picked clean, and, after a brief funeral address by Crane, its bones were consigned to the fire.

Parties of this sort were as exhausting as they were entertaining, and it was always with relief that Crane and his hosts settled back to their wood chopping. On most nights, with Lachaise and Fisher within easy reach, there was no shortage of good conversation and—from Fisher's library—good books. Fisher's library also included five notebooks that Crane found fascinating. These comprised the "Greenberg manuscript," a body of poetry written by a tubercular boy who had died, at twenty-three, in Manhattan State Hospital for the destitute, on Ward Island.

Crane saw the notebooks for the first time shortly before he returned to New York. He had been invited to join Fisher for tea; but, as he reported to Munson, the manuscripts so fascinated him that he "stayed until nearly midnight."

> This poet, Grünberg, which Fisher nursed until he died of consumption at a Jewish hospital in NY was a Rimbaud in embryo. Did you ever see some of the hobbling yet really gorgeous attempts that boy made without any education or time except when he became confined to a cot? Fisher has shown me an amazing amount of material, some of which I am copying and will show you when I get back. No grammar, nor spelling, and scarcely any form, but a quality that is unspeakably eerie and the most convincing gusto. One little poem is as good as any of the consciously conceived 'Pierrots' of Laforgue.

What Crane found in the manuscripts was not finished poetry but the stuff from which poetry could be made. Samuel Greenberg's primitive, half-formed work showed an artist's vision but a vision relatively unshaped by technique. Had he lived, had he had time to read, time to perfect his art, he might, Crane felt, have become a poet much like Crane himself. The same interest in language, the same exploration of the possibilities of metaphor showed up in the tumbled-out phrases, and as Crane laboriously copied them he was swept with pity for their maker.

It was perhaps as much in homage to Greenberg as in an effort to create an independent poem that Crane during the next month assembled "Emblems of Conduct," a collage put together from fragments of four Greenberg poems. Though Crane made no effort to publish the poem, he foolishly let himself be persuaded to include it in *White Buildings*, little calculating that after his death its origins would be uncovered and a small crowd of diligent scholars would set off on the trail of other Greenberg references in his work. Although much energy has gone into the search, the best that can be said is that Greenberg's work entered Crane's mind in much the same way that Eliot's, Stevens's, Donne's, Whitman's, and Poe's had. Faint echoes of Greenberg—and many other writers—show up in early drafts of the "Voyages" poems, in "Lachrymae Christi," and in *The Bridge*. As Mark Simon's recent study of the manuscripts demonstrates, Crane paid Greenberg the high compliment of sometimes paralleling his imagery; but that parallelism—and "Emblems of Conduct"—constitutes the "Greenberg influence."

As December drew toward an end, Crane reluctantly began to plan his return to New York.

For a week or so, however, it looked as if he might not have to. A hike earlier in the month had taken him to the top of Overlook Mountain, where he had talked with the caretaker of the burned-out hotel that is still one of the local Woodstock "sights." The caretaker was fed up with his job and urged Crane to get in touch with the owner of the property and offer his services. The pay was $40 a month, but groceries were provided—and of course there was no rent for the caretaker's cottage. "It would be a hard winter, perhaps a terrific experience," Crane wrote Munson. Yet there was a beautiful view ("I could see clear across the Hudson valley and miles up and down the river") and though the only company would be the cow, the two horses, and the chickens that went with the cottage, Hart would have a chance to test his fortitude as the country man he always dreamed of being. "I'm strongly tempted," he wrote Malcolm Cowley, "and would like to try out Loneliness and hurricanes and drifts at the pleasant risk of only monthly or bi-monthly visits to the nether world of common speech."

But the job fell through, and the very meager support that Crane's mother and grandmother had been providing came trickling to an end.

Crane had had no reason to assume that his family would support him indefinitely; but he had hoped that they could understand the kind of exhaustion which had forced his move on him. Instead, most of their letters were full of the plans for selling out and getting out which had so distressed Crane the previous summer. "Wouldn't it be easier and better to rent the house furnished and let that pay for a comfortable apartment for you and some of your expenses than to sell it outright?" Crane wrote his mother. "I am not trying to 'run affairs,' (especially as you have never taken me into any of the family financial discussions that I have an interest in) but only want to suggest what seems to me the better way. If you part with both the Isle of Pines place and 1709, I think you will feel pretty much on the high seas, while perhaps a little more effort in another direction less drastic would prove much better in the end." Grace retaliated by announcing that she had had to get a job, implying that Hart's wasteful ways, his cavalier abandonment of a good position, had forced her to work in his place. Munson, as usual, was Crane's confidant.

> The folks at Cleveland have disappointed me much, not only by sending me only half as much money as I asked for and require, but by a great deal of wailing. I guess I told you before you left here that my mother has taken a position, since explained to me as helping a friend of hers in a very de luxe antique and what-not establishment just started. It involves nothing but standing around and talking to people, I'm sure, yet mother is reported to return home every night so exhausted and wrecked that she cannot hardly speak. She has not per-

sonally written me for a month now. All the reports and symptoms come from my grandmother. But would it have been so much different had I been at Thompson's during these two months, I am tempted to ask. They won't stop to think or plan,—either of them,—beyond the next day ahead. And woes continue indefinitely.

Though Crane was disappointed in Grace's behavior, it did not really surprise him. What did surprise him was to find himself once more in communication with his father. For C.A. answered the curt note that Hart had sent shortly before quitting his job.

C.A. did his best to write a cheerful and affectionate letter, but painful memories rankled: "It is now almost three years since you left my store with strange words and strong determination to never again be associated with me. In those years no word has come to me that you have felt differently, no change of attitude on meeting, and no favors asked or given." He went on to say, however, that he had faith in Hart's "sterling qualities," his "good mind," and his "good morals." And he did his best to make it possible for his son to turn toward him.

This is not the only case of its kind in the wide world, and if you have a real desire to mend it now, you will find me in the same receptive mood that I have been all of this time, but don't expect your gray-haired father to "jump through the hoop." Do your full share and I will try to do mine. Write me when you have time, and believe me, always your father.

Crane's reply is missing, but it must have been congenial enough, for C.A. wrote that Hart's letter was "much more gratifying" to him than any Hart had written "for a long time." Though Hart rather gruffly dismissed his father's letter when he discussed it with his friends ("My father says he expects to arrive in NY early in Jan.," he told Munson, "but from his last letter I surmise he is as hopeless as ever") and though he growled to Nagle and Brown about his father's habit of dictating personal letters and then filing the carbons, it is abundantly clear that their exchanges had worn down most of the edge of antagonism that still remained between them. Hart was, of course, convinced that neither his father nor his mother understood him; but he found himself now drawn almost equally to both—even as he rejected them. "My family is still much on the shelf with me," he wrote Munson, but immediately intruded qualifications—"as far as I can keep up the pretence to myself, at least."

Crane meant it, however, and without qualification, when he told Munson: "I don't think that either side will be able to induce me back to Cleveland again to stay." His time in Woodstock had given him a chance to get on his feet again. He didn't know what he would do when he returned to New York ("I shall stave off my landlady as long as possible, and then take up a bench in Battery Place or embark on a ship"), but he was sure that he would not be employed by J. Walter Thompson. In his conversations with Brown and Nagle and in his correspondence with Frank, Toomer, and Stieglitz, Crane had tried to establish a correct attitude toward his real work—his poetry. He decided that only by being faithful to his vision could he accomplish significant art.

One can watch him trying out this attitude on old friends. By the end of a gossipy letter to Charlotte Rychtarik, for example, he is ready to hazard a definition of himself.

> You should not forget me. I am free now—at least more so than ever before in my life, but that doesn't mean that I forget such people as you and Richard who have been so fine to me and whom I shall love always—even though I haven't any way of proving it but to just keep on saying so. I hear that my Mother has taken a Job of some kind and is working very hard. I am sorry to hear it, but I also know that she did not need to do it unless she felt like it. Everything is being sold as soon as possible. Only I refuse to sell myself any longer than I absolutely have to. I shall beg and steal when necessary to avoid it.
>
> . . . I do hope that you will write me soon—if you feel like it—and tell me all about yourselves, how you are playing and how R is painting. I am sure you are gaining on Time! One must.

Hart was free. He had only to grasp his freedom, he must have thought in these happy months, and then for sure he would have it. He might even give that freedom to himself as a Christmas present. He might, with a loving gesture—with all the love that still rode powerfully beneath his fear of domination—free himself from his mother and his grandmother. On December 21, he wrote a Christmas letter home, asking to be accepted as a poet; asking for understanding, even if "certain ardors" which sometimes gripped him would be little understood in Cleveland; and—most desperately—asking his mother to free him from her dream of "success." As in his letter to Charlotte Rychtarik, Crane held off as long as he could the statement he had to make. But he needed the gift of liberating love Grace could offer him far more than the checks she and his grandmother would be slipping into their own Christmas letters the next morning. And though he said—as he had to say—"I'm going back to NY on the second or third of January (if I can get the carfare) and after that I won't ask for any more money," his real request was far more important.

I don't know what I'm going to do, but I can probably wash
dishes or work on the docks or something to keep skin and
bone together. I shall keep my old room at 45 Grove Street
(which is as cheap as any that can be found anywhere) as
long as I can bamboozle the landlady. After that I'll have to
depend on my good coat, or the kindness of friends. I've been
able to store up a sufficient reserve of physical and nervous
force while out here in the country to last me quite awhile, I
think. I am not at all discouraged about anything, and I think
that if you and Grandma will use your natural wits at a little
better planning—you'll be able to get along fairly comfortably
without working so hard. One can live happily on very little,
I have found, if the mind and spirit have some definite objective in view. I expect I'll always have to drudge for my living,
and I'm quite willing to always do it, but I am no more fooling
myself that the mental bondage and spiritual bondage of the
more remunerative sorts of work is worth the sacrifices inevitably involved. If I can't continue to create the sort of poetry
that is my intensest and deepest component in life—then it all
means very little to me, and then I might as well tie myself
up to some smug ambition and "success" (the common idol
that every Tom Dick and Harry is bowing to everywhere). But
so far, as you know, I only grow more and more convinced
that what I naturally have to give the world in my own terms—
is worth giving, and I'll go through a number of ordeals yet to
pursue a natural course. I'm telling you all this now, dear, because I don't want you to suffer any more than inevitable from
misunderstandings—for once we see a thing clearly usually
nine-tenths of our confusion and apprehension is removed.
Surely you and I have no quarrels, and I think you understand
me well enough to know that I want to save you as much suffering from Life's obstacles as can be done without hypocrisy,
silliness or sentimentality. You may have to take me on faith
for some things, because I don't know whether it is possible
for all people to understand certain ardors that I have, and
perhaps there is no special reason why you, as my mother,
should understand that side of me any better than most people. As I have said, I am perfectly willing to be misunderstood,
but I don't want to put up any subterfuges before *your* understanding of me if I can help it. You have often spoken to me
about how you lamented the fact that you didn't follow certain convictions that you had when you were my age because
it wasn't easy enough; and I know what strong obstacles were
put in your way. I, too, have had to fight a great deal just to
*be myself* and *know myself* at all, and I think I have been
doing and am doing a great deal in following out certain

natural and innate directions in myself. By Jove—I don't know of much else that is worth the having in our lives. Look around you and see the numbers and numbers of so-called "successful" people, successful in the worldly sense of the word. I wonder how many of them are happy in the sense that you and I know what real happiness means! I'm glad we aren't so dumb as all that, even though we do have to suffer a great deal. Suffering is a real purification, and the worst thing I have always had to say against Christian Science is that it willfully avoided suffering, without a certain measure of which any true happiness cannot be fully realized.

If you will even partially see these facts as I see them it will make me very happy—and we can be much closer and more "together" that way than merely just living in the same house and seeing each other every day would ever bring about alone. I have been thinking much about you and about dear Grandma —and I shall have you with me much on Christmas day.

And then it *was* Christmas, with the checks and letters from Grace and her mother, and a check from Hart's Aunt Zell, and a little check from the Rychtariks. And at Woodstock there was a week of little celebrations: "Mme. Lachaise gave me a harmonica, Nagle a pipe, and Brown a horn and an embroidery set! . . . We had a fine Christmas tree which we went up on the mountain and chopped down ourselves. The Lachaises brought all kinds of toys and silvery bubbles, etc. with real candles first ignited on the Eve of Xmas when we roasted a chicken before the fire and danced and drank wine and cider." At all the parties there was dancing and song, wine and—since it was 1923 nudging into 1924—girls in bobbed hair and short skirts. Hart was "free" and happy. "I'm the acknowledged crack dancer everywhere now." Everyone was very, very happy and very, very free. Hadn't Lachaise at one of the parties even suggested that Hart be sketched "quite nude"?

From Cleveland, Grace Crane wrote how "lonely and forlorn" she was without her son.

I had expected you on Christmas ever since you left us last March. I do not think you should be away from us so long at a time. You will see a big change in your grandmother, and I feel you should be with her as often as you possibly can, and do all the nice things you can to make her happy. Her stay is short now, and I realize more each day what a superior wonderful woman she is. . . . It is a shame for us to be separated, anyway. Mother told you about losing dear little Clip. I feel just terribly about it, and can't get used to doing without him. He was the bravest, loving little spirit up to the very last minute, and I shall never forget him nor the lesson he taught me.

In Woodstock, Crane valiantly whirled toward the New Year, a "grand dance with every sort of drink known" putting a period to the best time of his life.

What could he ask the future to give him? "I hope that '24," he wrote Munson, "—well, what shall we *hope* for? I don't think I know enough to hope for anything."

# 19

When Crane returned to 45 Grove Street, to the room that had in his absence been taken over by Kenneth Burke, he felt for a while like a man from another world. Everyone in New York, it seemed to him, was rushing about pointlessly; and though he joined the flight from party to party—though he drank more, laughed louder, danced more wildly, debated more passionately than any of his friends—he nevertheless felt, he soon wrote Munson, "as solitary as I ever felt in my life." He saw, he said, "an outward chaos around me—many things happening and much that is good, but somehow myself out of it, between two worlds."

Yet his days and nights and early mornings were crammed with activity.

> I've lunched and dined with Burke and the Cowleys, seen the new Stieglitz clouds, Sunday-breakfasted with Jean [Toomer] and Liza [Munson], argued an evening with Rosenfeld and Margy [Naumburg], chatted with O'Neill, [Eugene] Mac-Cown, and R. Edmond Jones—Wescott, Matty, Light and been to concerts with Jean—etc. etc. All this besides running around and looking for jobs.

New York, he explained to his mother, was "abristle with its first acceptance of European art and artists." Like everyone else in town, Crane argued the merits of Matisse, Picasso, "and all the other cubists." Also like everyone else, he found himself "plunging into a lot of varied company, meeting new people and revisiting the old, dining here and there and enjoying free tickets to modern concerts, plays and exhibitions of modern painters, etc." He knew what everyone was doing, had an opinion on everything. He was not, however, uncritical. Ignorant or informed, everyone, Hart protested, devoted too much time to "talk, talk, talk!!!"

This hectic artistic climate revived Crane's worries about how the contemporary "tone" of artists like E. E. Cummings and Gertrude Stein could be adapted to his own essentially "classical" orientation. Yet adapted it had to be. For one must live in one's own time, and there were elements in Cummings and in Stein—just as there were elements in Eliot—that most accurately caught the spirit of the twenties. "My approach to words is still in sub-stratum of some new development," he wrote Munson, "—the same as it was when we talked last together—and perhaps merely a chaotic lapse into confusion for all I dare say yet. I feel Stein and E.E.C. as active agents in it, whatever it is . . . Suffice to say that I am very dissatisfied with both these interesting people and would like to digest their qualities without being too consciously theoretical about it."

Theory, however, was about all Crane produced early in the year; his efforts to find work and his energetic reappraisal of his relationship with his father were consuming most of his free time.

The inception of this new stage in that relationship is easily dated, for on the afternoon of Sunday, January 6, C.A. telephoned Grace to ask exactly what Hart's situation was. Grace, at first startled and then rather pleased, explained that Hart was out of work but that he could return to J. Walter Thompson's if he found nothing more to his liking. There was, C.A. said, some possibil-ity of an opening in his business that Hart might want to con-sider: what did Grace think? Sensibly, Grace recommended that C.A. make his offer directly to Hart. She then composed a tele-gram that obviously baffled her son. Hart wrote her: "Your strange telegram came last night and I'm writing merely to thank you and to say that I haven't seen or heard of C.A. so far. . . . I take it that he phoned you to say that he was leaving Cleveland Sunday night, etc. or something like that." On Wednes-day morning C.A.'s letter arrived, "offering me a position with him as a travelling salesman!" "This is unacceptable, of course," Hart wrote Munson, "even though I now can't complete the rent on this room for the rest of this month and simply don't know what is going to happen."

"I see through every sentence of the letter a stiff and after-all unyielding disposition to reduce me to a mere tool," he wrote Grace. "I see through all the words, my dear!" Nevertheless, Hart felt, there was a chance that his father actually was trying to help rather than control him, so he decided to follow a course as devious as the one he believed his father was following.

> Not yet are things ripe; but, on the other hand, I am not going to destroy the bloom of the fruit. I shall reject this offer in a most tactful way. If my father really has an affection for me he will not resent my explanation that I value my career as a writer more than anything else in my personal life and he *may* understand that from diverse other explanations that such a position as he offers now is incompatible with those interests (even though in the end it might offer me more money).

I shall ceremoniously thank him (I could not be more "ceremonious" than his calculating letter, threatening me with this as the last business offer he will make me, if I don't accept it at once!) No, dear, if I starve I don't get led into such a false and artificial life as he would guide me into with that letter! But, as I said, I shall not offend him. There is no object in that. I am no mere cog in one of his machines and I shall answer more cleverly than to be included in such a category. And so, again, I want to thank you for your good sense—to have left the thing entirely to me and to have kept us both pure from misinterpretations on his part!

Had C.A. been able to read this letter, he would probably have fallen into a justifiable rage; for his offer had been open and generous. The business was expanding; he was pleased to be on good terms with his son again; perhaps, after all, son and father could work together. He had also delicately attempted to feel out Hart's attitudes toward him.

> You have never indicated that you wanted to come back into the Crane Chocolate Company. . . . I do not want to try to make you over into something which does not appeal to you, for now as never before our business must show progress and profit, and it is only by my association with people who are genuinely interested in accomplishing this that the desired results will be obtained.
>
> I just seem to have the feeling that if you are ever to take up this work, that now is the time to do it, and if you feel that you have something else in prospect or in mind that is better for you, I strongly advise you to turn a deaf ear to this and go on with your work, whatever it may be. In other words, in later life I do not want you to feel that if your father had not been in the candy business that you might have developed into a real advertising success. . . .
>
> Write me just how you feel, and if you would like to come into the organization and spend two or three years in direct constructive work upon the road, then I feel you would be set to be of great service to me here.

Hart devoted three days to composing an answer, finally deciding that truth could accomplish more than ingenuity. "I have written father, as my last letter indicated, that I would not be doing fairly either by him or myself to accept the position," Hart told his mother. In the same mail he sent off to C.A. a three-page, typewritten, single-spaced document in which he attempted to say to his father all the things that face to face he had always been too frightened or too angry to put into words. He said he would have to turn down the job offer ("kind as it is") and went on to say that his reasons for turning it down were complex.

In what follows, father, I hope that you will take my word for it that there is no defense of my personal pride involved against any of the misunderstandings that we may have had in the past. I have come to desire to talk to you as a son ought to be able to talk to his father, that is, in a pure relationship, without prejudices or worldly issues interfering on either side. That was the basis of my first letter to you in three years—that I wrote a little over two months ago, and I hope it may be the basis of your interpretation of what I am writing you now. I, at least, am doing the most honest thing I know to do in whatever I have said to you and in whatever I may say to you since that time. That's a pledge from the very bottom of my heart.

Hart referred to C.A.'s advice that he "turn a deaf ear" to the job offer if he felt advertising likely to prove more enjoyable or more profitable.

But if there had been any chance to tell you before I should have stated to you I had no interest in advertising beyond the readiest means of earning my bread and butter, and that as such an occupation came nearest to my natural abilities as a writer I chose it as the quickest and easiest makeshift known to me. Perhaps, in view of this, it will be easier for you to see why I left my position at J. Walter Thompson's at the last of October, unwise as such an action would be understood from the usual point of view. I went to the country because I had not had a vacation for several years, was rather worn with the strain of working at high speed as one does in such high geared agencies, and above all because I wanted the precious time to do some real thinking and writing, the most important things to me in my life.

Though there was a chance that he might be able to return to his job, Hart said, he was not sure he would want to go back. "I told Grace that they had asked me to return definitely because I didn't want her to worry about me: she has enough worries as it is." His real concern, however, was to convince his father that his devotion to writing was compulsive, obsessive, inevitable.

I think, though, from the above, that you will now see why I would not regard it as honest to accept your proposition, offered as it was in such frankness and good will. I don't want to use you as a makeshift when my principal ambition and life lies completely outside of business. I always have given the people I worked for my wages worth of service, but it would be a very different sort of thing to come to one's father and simply feign an interest in fulfilling a confidence when one's mind and guts aren't driving in that direction at all. I hope you credit me with genuine sincerity as well as the appreciation of your best motives in this statement.

You will perhaps be righteously a little bewildered at all these statements about my enthusiasm about my writing and my devotion to that career in life. It is true that I have to date very little to show as actual accomplishment in this field, but it is true on the other hand that I have had very little time left over after the day's work to give to it and I may have just as little time in the wide future still to give to it, too. Be all this as it may, I have come to recognize that I am satisfied and spiritually healthy only when I am fulfilling myself in that direction. It is my natural one, and you will possibly admit that if it had been artificial or acquired, or a mere youthful whim it would have been cast off some time ago in favor of more profitable occupations from the standpoint of monetary returns. For I have been through some pretty trying situations, and, indeed, I am in just such a one again at the moment, with less than two dollars in my pocket and not definitely located in any sort of a job.

He was not, however, without hope, Crane went on to say, for his poetry was at last beginning to be recognized. He listed all his literary and artistic references, the "many distinguished people" who were his friends and admirers; and in case his father didn't grasp their accomplishments, Hart took the trouble to spell them out. It was an impressive list: Eugene O'Neill ("dramatist"), Waldo Frank ("probably the most distinguished contemporary novelist"), Alfred Stieglitz, Gaston Lachaise ("the sculptor who did the famous Rockefeller tomb at Tarrytown"), and Charlie Chaplin ("who is a very well read and cultured man in 'real life'"). These were men who agreed that he was "making a real contribution to American literature."

I wish you could meet some of my friends, who are not the kind of "Greenwich Villagers" that you may have been thinking they were. If I am able to keep on in my present development, strenuous as it is, you may live to see the name "Crane" stand for something where literature is talked about, not only in New York but in London and abroad.

Hart realized, he said, that his father was "a very busy man," his mind "filled with a thousand and one details and obligations which clamor to be fulfilled." Yet, he went on, he had to take up a little of that time to make his own case. "I couldn't see any other way than to frankly tell you about myself and my interests so as not to leave any accidental afterthought in your mind that I had any 'personal' reasons for not working in the Crane Company."

Hart was his father's son, however, in more ways than he

might have been willing to concede. For he was a salesman born. All his adult life he had been selling an image of art and the artist; at the end of this long letter he tackled his toughest customer with the most eloquent sales pitch he could devise.

> And in closing I would like to just ask you to think some time,—try to imagine working for the pure love of simply making something beautiful,—something that maybe can't be sold or used to help sell anything else, but that is simply a communication between man and man, a bond of understanding and human enlightenment—which is what a real work of art *is*. If you do that, then maybe you will see why I am not so foolish after all to have followed what seems sometimes only a faint star. I only ask to leave behind me something that the future may find valuable, and it takes a bit of sacrifice sometimes in order to give the thing that you know is in yourself and worth giving. I shall make every sacrifice toward that end.

For a while, Hart's letter did establish a really friendly relationship with his father. C.A.'s return letter, long and affectionate, was accompanied by a generous check. ("And I want you to feel that this is not given in any spirit that you would not like.") His concern, he said, had been to make sure that Hart had not changed his mind about leading a "commercial life." If Hart ever had such interests in the future, there would always be an opening for him in C.A.'s company. So long as he was sure that Hart was determined to be a writer, he would do his best to be of help.

> Your letter made a deep impression upon your father, for I realized profoundly that you are determined to follow out a life work which is quite different from what has been mapped out for me. I am not telling you your work is wrong; your letter convinces me that your decision is right, and if followed with the clear, honest purpose that is indicated, I feel very certain that you will at least be satisfied with the results you propose to obtain. . . .
> There is such a thing as one branch of a family digressing from the usual channel and upholding the intellectual reputation. I rather feel this morning that your choice is not an unwise one, and that you will be able to make a mark along more satisfactory lines than your father. . . .
> In conclusion, Harold, let me say that I thoroughly appreciate, in every detail, your splendid letter, and you and I can turn over a new leaf in our lives so far as they concern each other. I will endeavor to keep my attitude altruistic, as well as fatherly. There is much more in this world than money, and while I perhaps may have the reputation of considering that

element as quite essential, it is not for the love of money that I have ever worked. I do like accomplishment, and I have recognized the fact that my nature continually urges me on in that direction, just the same as yours urges you on in another.

I don't want your present financial status to keep you from having good food and lodging. I think it is only foolish tradition that tells us that all authors write better if they are starving. So long as you are a man in effort and good morals, you are entitled to "he" food, and your father will endeavor to be helpful.

Hart was deeply moved. Not only did he immediately write his father, he also got off a letter to his mother ("I have such good news to tell"). Though he was still careful not to let himself wholly believe in this new father, he wanted to believe in him.

> Yesterday morning came the finest letter from CA that I have ever had. To put it briefly, he has finally come around not only to accept my interests in writing as genuine, but he actually commends them and says that he wants to help me some in the future. How quick he may reverse his opinions, is, of course, not to be conjectured, but I am glad that I wrote him the letter I did containing such a thorough explanation of myself, and his reply seems a sincere and cordial document— including a check which, along with your recent generosity, helps me out a great deal just now. He didn't seem to resent my refusal of his offer at all. Altogether, I've felt unusually jolly for the last 36 hrs.

Crane soon had several opportunities to test his new relationship with his father, for within a month after C.A.'s letter he found and lost one job, lost out on a second job that almost seemed a sure thing, and was once more completely without funds.

The job he found and lost—with an advertising agency, Pratt and Lindsey—had seemed very nearly ideal. Hart liked Mr. Pratt, who had hired him, and he found the work he was to do entertaining.

> I always get mixed up in some strange topic. This time it is a book on cheese, how happy it makes you and how good it is for tissues, stomach, and bowels, etc. A large importing house wants it, and I've been having to write it in no time.

When his "cheese book" went to the printer "without any changes whatever," Crane—who had been taken on in a probationary arrangement—was sure there would be no unsolvable problems.

Perhaps what pleased him most, however, was to be interrupted at work by a telephone call from his father. C.A., who was in town on business, asked if Hart would spend part of Saturday afternoon with him.

We talked from 3 until five—and in the end it was very satisfactory. He began in the usual arbitrary way of inquisition into my attitude toward business life, etc. just as though there had been no exchange of letters and recent understandings on that subject, and did his best to frighten me into compromises. I parried these thrusts very politely, although it was very hard many times not to jump up and begin declaiming. However, I realized this time that my ordinary language about such topics is simply beyond his comprehension, so I quietly kept on doing my best to explain myself in terms that he would understand and not resent any more than possible. He finally ended by accepting me quite docilely as I am . . .

C.A. even went so far as to ask Hart's advice about publicizing a new product. "He is going to send me data on the subject, and wants me to write some ads for him about it!" This, so far as Hart was concerned, was the clinching gesture. "You see," he wrote his mother, "from this alone (and I have also other grounds to judge by) that he really respects me." Father and son parted good friends. C.A. had inquired about Grace and her mother ("and seems to have the right sort of interest"), had praised Hart's stubborn dedication to his private vision ("He also came around to agree that I was quite exemplary of both sides of my family in not being made of any putty—knowing what I want to do, and sticking it out despite adversities"), and as he was walking out the door had "thrust a greenback" in his son's pocket.

When, after only two weeks at Pratt and Lindsey, Hart was fired, he was afraid that he might lose his father's respect. He was convinced—perhaps rightly—that he had been dropped because there wasn't enough work for him to do. "The man who had employed me," Hart wrote his mother, "couldn't say a thing against my work or copy as an excuse, but he had to invent some fantastic pretenses that I saw through right away as grounds; it was a dirty deal . . ." For months Crane brooded about it, only relaxing a little when late in the spring he heard from another man in the office that he had been hired "on the momentary whim of the president, and that as soon as the secretary and treasurer found out about my presence he raised a hell of a row, all of which resulted in my dismissal."

Crane's immediate problem was finding work. For a little while there was a good chance that he might get a position with the publisher B. W. Huebsch, a job he had been dickering for even before he accepted the copywriting one. But Huebsch settled on another man. "My only regret at getting one good man," he wrote Hart, "is that I have to pass another by."

After some soul-searching, Crane decided to ask his father for a loan—a hundred dollars at six percent. As day after day passed without a reply, he became desperate. "I don't know what on earth I am going to do," he wrote his mother. Though he was able to eat, thanks to the generosity of Sue Jenkins and the Munsons—who regularly had him in to dinner—and Eugene O'Neill, who at the beginning of the siege of joblessness had him up to Ridgefield for the better part of a week, Crane was often literally without carfare.

Finally he heard from his father. He wrote, Hart explained to Grace, "a really sincere and fine letter, explaining that he had been out of town when my letter came, and enclosing at least half the amount I had asked him for as a loan."

There is no question that Hart was tempted to use the money to buy a train ticket to Cleveland and the security Grace and C.A. were extending to him. He was suffering, he told his mother, from a real "attack of homesickness." And yet, paradoxically, he was afraid that if anything might endanger his new alliance with C.A. it would be his own presence.

> I have a terrible fear of the reaction I would have to Cleveland,—after I had been there a month or so! And, also, somehow I feel that at the present stage of my renewed relations with CA it is better that I be not too close to him! He has gone far enough to say that—even though he does disagree with me on my chosen career, etc. that it is none of his business, and he doesn't make any of the old stipulations on my conduct, location, etc. etc. that he used to. It marks a real advance, I think, either in his spirit or in his diplomacy (I am not sure which it is, so far).

One imagines Hart, his mother, and his father during this period as moving along terribly private paths—each concerned with immense problems anxiously kept from the other two and yet each guessing, and misunderstanding, the motives and actions of the others.

Hart pretended that he had to stay in New York for the sake of his writing; in fact, however, he hated the city. He had to stay in New York neither for writing nor for employment; he had to stay because he had fallen more desperately in love than ever before. Yet how could he talk about the problems of this kind of love to his father or—in spite of all the delicate hints and preparations he had made—even to his mother?

Grace Crane wrote Hart long letters about her hopes that he would eventually find congenial work. What she did not discuss was her anxiety about what would happen to her when her mother became so ill as to be unable to take care of herself. A trap seemed to have closed on Grace. It was the house they were afraid to sell, afraid to keep; the house that was much too big for two strong women and that would be impossible if one of them were bedridden and doctor bills were consuming the money that now went to pay the once-a-week maid. Only marriage,

Grace felt, might save her. Yet how could she tell her son that she had been systematically searching for a husband and that there was at last a prospect in view? How could she admit that she was trying to make herself fall in love?

And C.A.—who seemed to Hart so cavalier about answering letters and so ruthlessly focused on business and money—had no way to spell out to son and former wife his growing concern for his new wife's health.

All their guesses about each other were wrong; all their dreams for each other, nothing but wish-fulfillment dreams. "It has been like spring here," Hart wrote Grace.

> The weather veering from bright skies into showers. The wind blew a little snow this morning, but not a handful, and now there is brilliant sunlight, the wind continuing in almost a gale. It is always so pleasant to hear you mention spring in your letters: the note is so genuine. . . . It always makes me hope that we shall have a place in the country some time where I can come and go, and bring friends occasionally that will charm you, while you can have endless days and weeks for quiet reading and gardening. That beats life in the city all to pieces!

Dreams of this sort, Hart must have felt, were better than truth; for truth cut too deeply, was, in all its intricacies, far too much for one young man to understand, let alone a broken family of three high-strung and independent persons. He had even, he decided, been a little foolish in sending his mother carbon copies of some of his letters to his father. Certainly, he felt, it would be unwise to show her both sides of the correspondence.

> My dear, you know I can't tell you much more about CA's letters than I have been doing without retyping them or forwarding them on for you to return. I am telling you all there is in them that is definite enough to matter, and while I have thought of sending them to you to read successively as they came,—something has made me feel that while there might be no harm in it nor real injustice, at the same time and in the sum of things, I think it a little confusing, somehow not quite right. I can't put it into better words, but perhaps you will feel what I mean, and not misunderstand and think me obtuse or ungrateful, or unfeeling toward you. You see, it's just because this present relationship between himself and myself was started on such an entirely fresh basis, without any more elements of the past entering into it than could be helped. And also, because, really I don't yet have much idea as to how he really feels about me. He is a long time answering my letters, and I now haven't heard from him for over two weeks and don't know when I'm going to. I don't feel that there

is anything at present between us but a fragile thread of feeling and communication: perhaps there never will be anything more. At any rate we can speak on the street without getting upset about it.

By the beginning of April, however, Hart was sure that the fragile thread of communication had once more snapped. He was penniless again, and C.A. was again not answering mail. Hart admitted to his father that he had had to spend most of the money that had been sent him to pay back debts and to pay advance rent on a furnished room at 15 Van Nest Place (a room that had once been Waldo Frank's and that Hart had taken when Louis Kantor reappeared at 45 Grove Street). When his letters went unanswered, Hart decided that his father had given up all expectations of Hart's ever finding work and that he was withholding further loans in the hope of forcing Hart into the family business. ("He may be trying to draw me back to Cleveland by these tactics, but he's a long way from the right method, I can only say!") Rumors that his father had had a nervous breakdown were, Hart decided, obviously inaccurate.

> CA's silence can mean only one thing to me now—an absolute denial and confession of complete indifference—if not enmity. I don't mind about the money,—but he has not even written me any kind of words,—and right on top of the most evidence of cordiality that he has ever put on paper to me! Well, so it goes. . . . He is the strangest animal I ever heard of.

Hart found it impossible to understand his father's apparently erratic reversals of feeling, and he despaired over Grace's wild plans. For now she talked of selling the house, hiring a caretaker for the island property, and moving to California.

> Of course I can't understand why you want to go out to California when you have such a perfectly lovely place in the West Indies,—all your own, with certain traditions and associations, and with (after all) as pleasant a group of people as you will run into in Cal. to associate with. And for me to be struggling around here in dirty NY when money is actually being paid out of the estate to *hire* strangers to live in such a delightful place as the Island—is one of those jokes of fate that make words seem futile! But everything in my family on both sides seems always to have been "balled up," and that's one reason why I begin to feel no use in worrying about responsibilities toward such a waste of time, energy and emotion,—to say nothing of money. I'll probably end up quite a bum,—but I shall try to keep enough at a distance so that you won't feel too compromised.

On the same afternoon that Hart wrote his melancholy letter to Grace, however, he landed a job at Sweet's Catalogue Service.

Though it is true that the interval between jobs had been a long and difficult one, Hart had never seriously doubted that he would find something he could do. Halfway through his search for a position, he had written home a long account of all the offices which had almost but not quite hired him; but he had meant it when he said, "Still, I am not discouraged; I don't think I ever get discouraged any more in that black-as-night way that I used to." Even though he had to move from room to room and finally parcel out his belongings with friends and move in with Sue Jenkins and James Light at 30 Jones Street, he had not been discouraged. Someone was always able to help him.

For in this cold spring of 1924, "dirty NY" was for penniless Hart Crane a place of apple-blossom sunrises, of gulls pinwheeling outward into a sky of blue and delicate oblivion. Hart was in love. He had to turn down his mother's requests that he come home.

> I *might* come home after two weeks more or so. But I can say nothing definitely, absolutely nothing. Don't worry about me any more than you can help: it's not so bad to miss a few meals, and there are one or two people in New York that I can't make up my mind to leave without trying a little longer.

No matter how much Hart complains about the peculiarities of his parents or about the vagaries of the business world, a recurrent celebration of life runs through the letters of these months: "I have a revived confidence in humanity lately, and things are going to come very beautifully for me—and not after so very long, I think. The great thing is to Live and Not Hate."

"If [my friends] had not been so very fine," Hart wrote the Rychtariks, "I should have had to go back to Cleveland long before this. Instead of which I was treated to wine and food and even fell in love." When Hart's cousin Helen Hurlbert returned from a New York visit, she told her Aunt Grace that she thought Hart was in love. Grace misunderstood.

> Helen says you are looking very well—and seem happy. I asked her if you kept your mustache trimmed—and she said *no*. Now Hart—get busy with the scissors and trim it. You look so much better when you do. She also says you are in love—I will address you in that connection when you come home. You haven't been very confidential with us in that respect. I do not care how much you are in love, just so you do not *marry*. You know that would end your writing career and other ambitions. *So keep your head.* Love is a *sickness*.

The feelings Hart was experiencing were so different from everything he had ever meant by *love* that he found himself tongue-tied even to catalogue the symptoms; and while the words he settled on—*pure, profound, lovely*—caught some of its qualities, the essential joy escaped description: "I shall never, of course, be able to give any account of it to anyone in direct terms."

Perhaps the best place to look for a description of what Crane was experiencing is in the *Phaedrus*, where Socrates—accepting everything—speculates about the possibility of that open, generous, affection we call Platonic love. It was something of this sort that Crane and Emil Opffer found themselves caught up in, an enormously heightened friendship characterized by mutual understanding and devotion. "There was nothing dirty in it," Opffer told me, just as thirty-six years before Crane had told Waldo Frank that the relationship was founded not so much on sex as on "a purity of joy."

For many days, now, I have gone about quite dumb with something for which 'happiness' must be too mild a term. At any rate, my aptitude for communication, such as it ever is!, has been limited to one person alone, and perhaps for the first time in my life (and, I can only think that it is for the last, so far is my imagination from the conception of anything more profound and lovely than this love). I have wanted to write you more than once, but it will take many letters to let you know what I mean (for myself, at least) when I say that I have seen the Word made Flesh. I mean nothing less, and I know now that there is such a thing as indestructibility. In the deepest sense, where flesh became transformed through intensity of response to counter-response, where sex was beaten out, where a purity of joy was reached that included tears. It's true, Waldo, that so much more than my frustrations and multitude of humiliations has been answered in this reality and promise that I feel that whatever event the future holds is justified before hand. And I have been able to give freedom and life which was acknowledged in the ecstasy of walking hand in hand across the most beautiful bridge of the world, the cables enclosing us and pulling us upward in such a dance as I have never walked and never can walk with another.

Miraculously the fragments of Hart's existence fell into order. He walked across the bridge, and it was as if the world began composing his poem for him; he moved out of Sue Jenkins's and James Light's apartment and into the world of the bridge, which he would share with his new friend.

"Note the above address," he wrote Waldo Frank from 110 Columbia Heights in Brooklyn, "and you will see that I am living in the shadow of that bridge." Though it has since changed in some ways, in 1924 the Columbia Heights neighborhood was an oasis of quiet respectability. "It's really a magnificent place to live," Hart told his mother. "This section of Brooklyn is very old, but all the houses are in splendid condition . . ." It was its quiet, however, that Hart, as in his letter to Waldo Frank, returned to again and again; near his new home, the sea could speak.

It is so quiet here; in fact, it's like the moment of the communion with the 'religious gunman' in my F and H where the edge of the bridge leaps over the edge of the street. It was in the evening darkness of its shadow that I started the last part of that poem. Imagine my surprise when Emil brought me to this street where, at the very end of it, I saw a scene that was more familiar than a hundred factual previsions could have rendered it! And there is all the glorious dance of the river directly beyond the back window of the room I am to have as soon as Emil's father moves out, which is to be soon. E will be back then from S America where he had to ship for wages as ship's writer. That window is where I would be most remembered of all: the ships, the harbor, and the skyline of Manhattan, midnight, morning or evening,—rain, snow or sun, it is everything from mountains to the walls of Jerusalem and Nineveh, and all related and in actual contact with the changelessness of the many waters that surround it. I think the sea has thrown itself upon me and been answered, at least in part, and I believe I am a little changed—not essentially, but changed and transubstantiated as anyone is who has asked a question and been answered. . . . Just now I feel the flood tide again the way it seemed to me just before I left Cleveland last year, and I feel like slapping you on the back every half-hour. . . . And my eyes have been kissed with a speech that is beyond words entirely.

Hart, who had moved to Columbia Heights shortly before Easter, had thought of celebrating with a literal communion; but Prohibition "dago red" triumphed over sacramental wine. "I had intended to attend mass at St. Patrick's," he wrote his mother:

. . . but a drinking bout with some Danish friends of mine last night proved too much for an early rising. Emil Opffer, an old man but very distinguished as an editor and anarchist, and whose two sons, Ivan and Emil, Jr. I am very fond of, dines at a certain Italian restaurant on West Houston St. every evening, and it was there that the party was held. In fact he is the same old fellow whose room I am to have in this same house when he moves out at some indefinite date, but soon. I have a small room in the front now, which is quite clean and comfortable. But when I get his present room on the back of this same floor, I shall have the finest view in all America. Just imagine looking out your window directly on the East River with nothing intervening between your view of the Statue of Liberty, way down the harbor, and the marvelous beauty of Brooklyn Bridge close above you on your right! All of the great new skyscrapers of lower Manhattan are marshalled directly across from you, and there is a constant stream of tugs, liners, sail boats, etc. in procession before you on the river!

It is easy to understand how Crane neglected his letters to his mother (". . . right here my dear I wish you to realize that you treat me very badly indeed. . . . It isn't fair at all to me, Hart . . . dead silence for two weeks . . . Now I won't *have* such neglect—and I won't love you at all any more if you ever repeat this indifference. It's the only responsibility you have toward me—and I think you should not overlook it"). Nevertheless, he tried to get to Sweet's on time and he struggled with *The Bridge* and his new "Voyages" lyrics, now planned as a set of six poems ("they are also love poems") that would define the world of the sea Emil seemed to carry with him.

Crane did not, of course, isolate himself from friends. He kept in touch with all his correspondents—with Waldo Frank, traveling in Spain; with Allen Tate, whom he would soon meet for the first time; with the Rychtariks, Stieglitz, Brown, Lachaise, Sam Loveman. But his letters were spaced out, for his days were richer than they had been before.

His friendships were now centered on Sue Jenkins, Emil Opffer, and Eugene O'Neill, through whom Hart came to know most of the "regulars" at the Provincetown Playhouse. He could count on passes to the theater and invitations to cast parties and smaller spontaneous gatherings in the apartments of Sue Jenkins and Eleanor Fitzgerald. When in early summer Allen Tate finally made his New York visit, Hart, after finding him a room in Brooklyn Heights, took him to meet Sue Jenkins and then Malcolm Cowley and Kenneth Burke.

By now there clearly was a feeling of a group, though rather a loose one, nothing so formal as the group that had assembled once—and once only—to attempt to merge *Secession* and *Broom*. Crane's new circle was held together by a number of shared beliefs and feelings—and by very good times. "Our group, if it could be called that, was sort of miscellaneous," Tate recalled in 1962, "people from all over the country. Malcolm Cowley said in a piece in *The Sewanee Review* a couple of years ago that it was only some years later that he knew where I was from. He knew I was from the South by the way I talked, but that was about all he knew. We never inquired into the origins of our friends."

Aside from casual parties in each other's apartments and occasional trips out to Ridgefield to spend weekends with the O'Neills or trips to New Jersey to visit Kenneth Burke, the most common meeting places were Village coffeehouses and the back room of John Squarcialupi's Perry Street restaurant. There, Peggy and Malcolm Cowley, Sue Jenkins, James Light, Burke and Tate when they were in town, Crane, and sometimes Matthew Josephson and E. E. Cummings would meet. "I think we were drawn together by three things," Tate told me. "We were young, we were poor, and we were ambitious. That is, we thought that the older generation was pretty bad, and we were later going to replace them."

Of all his literary friends, Crane was in closest contact, during this year, with Malcolm Cowley. It was Cowley who had persuaded Sweet's Catalogues—where he was working—to take Crane on, and it was Cowley who helped break Crane in to the rather different type of copywriting he would be expected to do for the gigantic architectural and engineering catalogues the firm produced. "He wasn't really a *good* copywriter," Cowley recalled, "but his work was adequate and that was all that was demanded of him." Crane, I suspect, felt pretty much the same way about it. He was no longer concerned with becoming an executive; he was happy enough to get a weekly pay check. "The work involves no extraneous elements like 'human interest' and such bosh," Hart wrote Waldo Frank at the end of his second week, "albeit a great deal of care and technical information: but so far I've been able to straddle it, and here's hoping."

As Crane came to spend more of his time with Sue Jenkins, James Light, and Cowley, his visits to the Munsons began to slack off. In part this was because Munson was deeply involved with the Gurdjieff movement, then at its height, a discipline initiated by the Russian mystic who had formed, in France, a colony of disciples dedicated to arduous physical and spiritual exercises. At first Crane had been as excited about the program as Munson, for Ouspensky had given it his blessing and it promised the sort of revelations Crane had always been drawn to. Together they had attended a demonstration by some of its members. "Things were done by amateurs which would stump the Russian ballet, I'm sure," Crane told his mother. There were "some astonishing dances and psychic feats."

But Crane was far too involved with his own psychic feats— feats of love and affection in his dealings with Emil and with his father—to link himself to any organized movement. Though he still saw Munson now and then, their literary alliance was considerably dissipated. After one evening together, Crane spoke of "a gratifying sense of excitement when I left that recalled some of the earlier Munson-Burke-Toomer-etc. engagements that took place before the grand dissolution, birth control, re-swaddling and new-synthesizing, grandma-confusion movement"; but he also admitted having been present at a coffeehouse discussion of a new satirical magazine, *Aesthete, 1925*, that was expected to contain not

At *110 Columbia Heights, Brooklyn,* c. *1924.* Above, left: *Hart's room.* Above, right: *The Manhattan skyline from his window.* Below: *Hart on the roof, the Brooklyn Bridge behind him*

Left: *Hart Crane, Allen Tate, and William Slater Brown; February 1925.* Below, left: *Hart, the summer of 1924.* Below, right: *On the Isle of Pines, summer 1926; Hart holding "Aunt Sally" Simpson's pet owl*

 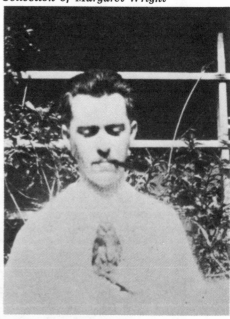

Left: *On the Isle of Pines, August 1926.* Below: *In Woodstock, New York; winter 1923*

Above, left: *Emil Opffer, c. 1924, on the roof of 110 Columbia Heights.*
Above, right: *Waldo Frank, c. 1930. Below, left: Sam Loveman, c. 1930.*
Below, right: *William Sommer*

Above, left: *William Slater Brown, Susan Jenkins Brown, and their son in May 1928.* Above, right: *Slater Brown and Emil Opffer, c. 1930.* Below, left: *Peggy Robson (Margaret Babcock), c. 1934.* Below, right: *Malcolm Cowley, 1931*

Left: *Hart Crane at Le Moulin, the Crosbys' retreat near Chantilly, in 1929.* Above: *On top of Le Moulin: Constance de Polignac, Laurence Vail, Kay Boyle, Hart Crane, and Caresse Crosby; 1929.* Below: *Harry and Caresse Crosby, 1927*

*In Paris, February 1929*

only onslaughts against Ernest Boyd, at whom the magazine's single issue was "aimed," but against Munson and Frank as well.

When Crane and Munson met to talk about the matter, they found they simply were not communicating. The next day Crane spelled out his role in the plans for the impending publication.

> When this came up at the coffee house a week since yesterday I at once interrupted it by offering to withdraw from any participation in the issue whatever. Allen Tate was there at the time, and as a fairly neutral party I think you can rely on him to check my statement as a fact. At any rate I hope you will ask him about it when you next see him. I have so consistently defended you and Waldo in that particular company that I have so far derived little from the meetings but an unnecessarily aggravated state of nerves and feelings.

Crane went on to say that he found both sides of current literary debates very near unbearable. "Issues are not at all clear, and I am disgusted most of the time." He could not, however, bring himself to take quite so severe a stand as that which he felt Munson was insisting on.

> Regardless of these issues you will be assured, I hope, that I have so far found nothing in either your work or Waldo's which I would wish to attack. Your generosity, meanwhile, certainly deserves my thanks for appreciating the sometimes necessary distinctions between a personal friendship with a man and one's opinion of his work.
>
> My rewards or discredit from participation in a magazine issued by your enemies will be bound to be, to a certain extent, somewhat embarrassing, yet, as you recognize, I still feel that I can owe myself that freedom on a clear responsibility. I am growing more and more sick of factions, gossip, jealousies, recriminations, excoriations and the whole literary shee-bang right now. A little more solitude, real solitude, on the part of everyone, would be a good thing, I think.
>
> Let us have lunch together soon.

Their second meeting proved no more successful than the first. Crane prepared to be dropped by the man who a year before had been his closest friend.

> Reflecting on our conversation at lunch today I have come to feel bound to suggest that you take whatever decisions or formalities are necessary to "excommunicate" me from your literary circle. How much further you may wish to isolate me depends entirely on your own personal feelings, but I am not prepared to welcome threats from any quarters that I know of—which are based on assumptions of my literary ambitions in relation to one group, faction, "opportunity," or another.

Though six months later the wounds would heal, Crane and Munson would never again be the intimate friends they once had been.

The shifts in Crane's friendships during 1924 were part of a larger change in the rhythm of his life. In spite of his feelings of communion with Emil Opffer, he spoke in a number of letters of a need for "brokenness," though perhaps what he was talking about was less a need than an experience he couldn't avoid. By "brokenness" Crane meant the deliberate fragmentation of life, a system of parceling life out into little units relatively isolated from one another: in his own case, job, literary friends, non-literary drinking companions, Grace and her family, C.A. and his family, Cleveland friends. Crane had always achieved privacy by this sort of division; but now the process was accelerated.

Perhaps consequences, perhaps causes of this brokenness were the wildly shifting moods of elation and despair that almost all of Hart's experiences now induced in him.

Half a dozen times after their first meetings, Hart found himself buoyed up by what he was sure were positive signs of his father's affection, only to be shattered afterwards by some evidence of coldness or what he took to be contempt. After each of these occasions, Hart would write his mother painful analyses of the father-and-son relationship. "I shall keep on doing my best to NOT DENY him anything of myself which he can see as worth realizing (which means *possessing*, also)," he wrote, "meanwhile not depending on him either in thought or deed for anything whatever. . . . His problems are many, and I think he may realize in time that they are more than strictly those concerned with his business, however much and fast they multiply." A month later Hart spent a full day with his father—lunch at the Commodore, theater in the afternoon, dinner at one of the city's best restaurants, theater again in the evening: "He was . . . more companionable than I seem so far to remember at any time in the past. Told stories, talked about his business, enthused about NY as a splendid candy market . . . and he mentioned pleasantly as I put him on the train that we had had 'quite a reunion.' " But Hart still had doubts. "It will probably take a number of years to convince me one way or the other on that matter—after the way I have seen things turn out in the past."

True to Hart's prediction, the barometer of affection between father and son did for a number of years continue to vacillate. When Hart fell ill—as he did several times during the summer and autumn of 1924—he could count on chocolates (which his father advised him not to eat: "Live as much as possible on milk") and pleasant letters of good advice; but most of the time C.A. and Hart each had difficulties thinking of enough to fill a page. "Hay fever and uric acid are at least two subjects that we can have in common," Hart wrote his mother, "and if I were only constantly racked by one or the other of these diseases I'm sure we might have a much more ample correspondence. . . . Now that I have to answer his letter in some sort of equal physical measure I'm at a loss to know what 'all' to fill it with. In a way, it's funny." Yet it was never funny when C.A. visited New York and failed to call his son. Though Hart wanted to feel complete independence from his father, he was in no way willing to accept the fact that C.A. had the right to complete independence from him: "On going up to 'headquarters' the other day for chocolates for my friends, I learned that CA had been here during September,—just how long I didn't ask. Which shows that I'm to expect the complete 'go-by' from him in the future. He must be mortified about something—too much so to show his head. I'll send him a Christmas card once a year, and bless his soul!"

Hart experienced far greater peaks and depths of elation and despair in his friendship with Emil Opffer. When Jean Toomer wrote a curt note asking if Hart's failure to answer letters was to be interpreted as an end to their correspondence, Hart answered entirely in terms of his own complex feelings.

> I have not written—even an answer to your note of last— I don't know how many weeks ago. And I can't answer yet. Heaven and Hell has transpired in the meantime, but I hope to know them both better before I get through, and before I say good-bye to you.
> . . . Life is running over me and destroying me. That I confess, and you can boast about indifferences or immunities or victories as much as you wish. I have not gone this far for any kind of victories.

The pattern of Hart's world was for a little while clear. He saw himself as bound in a "blood-brotherhood." During the ten-day periods between Emil's voyages, Hart and his friend would meet for dinners and, when they could afford them, concerts. When cash was low, they would listen to records or stand in the wings at the Met if Lauritz Melchior, a friend of Emil's, were singing.

While Emil was at sea, Hart—badly troubled by jealousy— would sit in his room trying to push ahead the "Voyages" poems or go out on the town for an orgy of carousing. Drinking sessions of this sort produced the "acidosis" that troubled him for the rest of his life and for which his parents would diligently prescribe inefficient remedies. One binge, however, was worse than the rest and Hart was seriously frightened. "As for myself this last week," he wrote his mother a month before his twenty-fifth birthday, "I've been most unhappy."

My uric acid resulted in urethritis which has been very painful and nerve wracking. A steady diet of buttermilk has finally relieved me, however, and I am going to continue it for some time yet. I'm looking better now than when you saw me in Cleveland but get neuralgic immediately as soon as I deviate the slightest from my diet. I was in a perfect panic for several days, fearing I had a venereal disease but a complete examination of my body and urine disproved any trace of that. I know now, however, just how one is paralyzed with fear at any such suspicion. Believe me, it's awful! The whistles are tooting midnight, and as this is the latest I've been up for a week now, I'd better turn in. Don't let my news alarm you. I'm practically mended already—am working everyday at the office, etc. I certainly do realize better than before that I must be careful.

It was during that time of agony, when Hart believed he had "spoiled" his body and would have to give up not only Emil but all his friends and acquaintances, that he had written Jean Toomer his "Heaven and Hell" letter. "I do not even remember my precise statements," he wrote a little later. "It was written and mailed in a state of almost hysterical despair." As soon as he learned that his "venereal infection" was only illusion, Hart swore off "beckonings and all that draws you into doorways, subways, sympathies, rapports and the City's complicated devastations" and turned with renewed vigor to the composition of the poems that would, he hoped, give an enduring stability to his friendship with Emil—a stability that might, with luck, outlast both of them.

I feel very much at peace with experience, so-called, which at present I feel inclined to believe, is the effort to describe God. Only the effort,—limitless and yet forever incomplete. But I want to elaborate my ideas a little longer before I admit that as complete. It is so much a matter of terminology, after all. I try to make my poems experiences, I rather don't try, when they are good *they are*—like "Possessions." And bright stones —in the end.

Enclosing with this letter to Toomer an early draft of "Voyages IV," Hart described some of the emotional forces that had brought it into being.

I shall probably never be able to be very personal about it, yet sometime I'll have more to say to you than now and here, about the maelstrom of the last three months,—what unbelievable promises it has not only fulfilled, but what complications, also, it has placed and replaced again and again between such beautiful realizations as it has, in the end, accomplished. And to *know* that such a love would forever be impossible

again—that it would never be met with again, if only because one knew that one would never have the intensity to
respond to a repetition of such even though it seemed worthy
enough! I have not the initial exaltation (which you may see
in the poem enclosed) but at least as much in some other way
—which is new to me. I have never been given the opportunity
for as much joy and agony before. The extreme edges of these
emotions were sharpened on me in swift alternation until I
am almost a shadow. But there is a conviction of love—that
is the only way I can name it—which has somehow arrived in
time, and which has (now so much has proved it) an equal
basis in the both of us.

Writers work up their material in many ways. Yeats constructed
poems from his own diaries and from spirit messages. Other poets
have combined drugs and—thanks to tape recorders—effortless
automatic writing. Crane gathered his raw material, as Malcolm
Cowley has pointed out in *Exile's Return*, under the combined influence of alcohol and music, getting just tight enough to link
phrases effortlessly. These he would type up to whatever music
came to hand. That music could be anything, Slater Brown told
me; songs from *Hit the Deck* or the symphony by César Franck
would work equally well, or not at all. Afterwards, after the
phrases had been assembled pell-mell, Hart would work and re-
work them for months, now cold sober, diligently calculating
relationships until he was sure he had built a secure structure.
"What he really had as a writer," Cowley told me, "was a capacity to follow a line of thought *harder*, more persistently, than
most of the men we knew. Hart wouldn't let go until he had every
word—and the right word—exactly where he wanted it."

But before the first part of this process began, Hart often dealt
with his material in another way. By defining his feelings—as in
some of his letters to Toomer and Frank and Munson and a
few of the letters to his mother and to Brown—he would roughly
shape phrases that later under the pressure of alcohol and music
would amalgamate into poems. It is in these letters that the tone
of the relationship with Emil most clearly shows up, the tone that
underlies "Voyages" and parts of *The Bridge* and that picked
up much of its character from the area of Brooklyn Heights
where the two walked whenever Emil was in town. Crane recorded the neighborhood in all seasons and at all hours of the
day. He caught it on spring mornings when it came to life "with
occasional trees jutting up an early green through the pave-
ments," with "tulips dotting the edge of one of the several beautiful garden patches that edge the embankment that leads down to
the river," and at spring twilight when, dropping into Emil's
father's room, he could watch the sweep of the foggy river drifting
into night.

Everytime one looks at the harbor and the NY skyline across the river it is quite different, and the range of atmospheric effects is endless. But at twilight on a foggy evening . . . it is beyond description. Gradually the lights in the enormously tall buildings begin to flicker through the mist. There was a great cloud enveloping the top of the Woolworth tower, while below, in the river, were streaming reflections of myriad lights, continually being crossed by the twinkling mast and deck lights of little tugs scudding along, freight rafts, and occasional liners starting outward. Look far to your left toward Staten Island and there is the Statue of Liberty, with that remarkable lamp of hers that makes her seen for miles. And up at the right Brooklyn Bridge, the most superb piece of construction in the modern world, I'm sure, with strings of light crossing it like glowing worms as the Ls and surface cars pass each other going and coming. It is particularly fine to feel the greatest city in the world from enough distance, as I do here, to see its larger proportions. When you are actually in it you are often too distracted to realize its better and more imposing aspects.

That summer, though it was a bad summer for Crane— "anvil weather" and hay fever and loneliness—there were still Sunday afternoon walks near the docks, and evenings on the roof, where he and Emil—in port for an "indefinite brevity"—could watch the flickering lights of the bridge and plan voyages they might make together. Crane now talked constantly of quitting his job, of breaking free and sailing out of the harbor that had become nothing less than a gate opening and closing on the finest friendship he had ever known. "My happiest times have been with Emil," Hart wrote his mother. "He is so much more to me than anyone I have ever met that I miss him terribly during these eight-week trips he takes for bread and butter."

By autumn Crane was installed in the room that had been Emil's father's, with the whole spread of the harbor before him. But he had moved in under the grimmest of circumstances. The room became available when Mr. Opffer died. His hospitalization, an operation, and his death all took place during one of Emil's times at sea, and it was with an agony of concern that Hart and Ivan Opffer met the returning ship. "His father's death and the shock of first knowing about it at the pier almost transformed him all the while he was here," Hart wrote his mother. "It was something of a strain on me, also, to be with such an unhappy man and to be able to do so little."

Hart had a week's vacation in October, the best days of which, he told friend after friend, were spent in front of his window polishing the nearly completed set of poems and planning minute corrections of the early drafts of The Bridge. "There's no stopping for rest . . . when one is [in] the 'current' of creation, so to speak, and so I've spent all of today at one or two stubborn lines. My work is becoming known for its formal perfection and hard glowing polish, but most of those qualities, I'm afraid, are due to a great deal of labor and patience on my part."

Now it was the autumn light which Crane celebrated, a light altogether different from that which had thrown a haze across the soft evenings of spring, a light crisp and aggressive as the late October air.

> The last day of my vacation, and somehow the best! So cold and sharp it is, you might think it time for turkey. You know how keenly brilliant the atmosphere around these parts can be—frequently in any season. On such days one gets an even better edge to this glorious light here by the harbor. The water so very blue, the foam and steam from the tugs so dazzlingly white! I like the liners best that are painted white—with red and black funnels like those United Fruit boats across the river, standing at rest. And you should see the lovely plumes of steam that issue from the enormous heights of the sky-scrapers across the way.

Rain offered riches also.

> It darkened before five today and the wind's onslaught across the bay turns up white-caps in the river's mouth. The gulls are chilly looking creatures—constantly whirling around in search of food here in the river as they do hundreds of miles out at sea in the wakes of liners. . . .

> My—but how the wind is blowing. Rain, too, on the window now! There was a wonderful fog for about 18 hours last week. One couldn't even see the garden close behind the house—to say nothing of the piers. All night long there were distant tinklings, buoy bells and siren warnings from river craft. It was like wakening into a dreamland in the early dawn—one wondered where one was with only a milky light in the window and that vague music from a hidden world. Next morning while I dressed it was clear and glittering as usual. Like champagne, or a cold bath to look [at] it. Such a world!

Such a world, indeed—the world of the "Harbor Dawn" section of *The Bridge*, caught in these letters almost as vividly as in the poem.

Crane came to love the room from which he observed the harbor. All his treasures were on display, and he allowed himself three red roses—purchased weekly from the little old lady who had a hole-in-the-wall stand near the subway entrance—to decorate the window. Luxuriously happy, Hart felt there was little more that life could give him.

I've been toasting my feet at an electric stove, a kind of radio heater that I have in my room, and glancing first at the bay, then with another kind of satisfaction at my shelves of books and writing table,—for a long time unable to think of anything but a kind of keen sensual bliss, that is in itself something like action—it contains so much excitement and pleasure.

Settled down in the expensive dressing gown his mother had given him for his birthday ("She absolutely squandered her money on it!" he told Emil), he felt himself "well arranged for a winter of rich work, reading and excitement." All aspects of his poetry were going well. "Just now I am doing a great deal of writing (for me)," he wrote the Rychtariks, "and every time I get near my desk I begin to complete (or try to add to) some poem. There are at least 4 lying around, still unfinished at present."

Perhaps some of these good spirits can be linked to encouraging news that Sam Loveman brought him from Cleveland. Sam had decided to move to New York and he came bearing information about Grace's stepped-up social life. She had a real *beau*, a Mr. Curtis—considerably older than she—who was showering her with attentions.

Rumors about Mr. Curtis had already reached Hart by way of his grandmother, who would dash off confidential reports whenever Grace was out of the house. "Grandmother's charming letter of last Sunday tells me that Gracie is having a few attentions paid her these days,—" Hart had written his mother early in September, "and I was certainly made gay and glad to hear of the pleasant 'doings.' 'Gracie' must write me some of the details very soon,—if, indeed, she is ever intending to write me again. When you say that you are really in love, then I'll forgive you all kinds and lengths of silence."

Grace withheld comment for some time, but the reports from Mrs. Hart continued to arrive, usually accompanied by warnings that Hart was not to breathe a word about the source. Some days Grace would no sooner get out the door than Mrs. Hart would be at her writing desk: "Mother and Mr. Curtis [have] just left for a drive and later [to] have dinner at Hotel Cleveland. Nothing *too good* for Mother these days. Quite a change for her for which I am very glad. He certainly knows how to court the 'Ladies.' "

Sam Loveman assured Hart that there was not only courtship on Mr. Curtis's part but a genuine response on Grace's—that, in fact, she had confessed to him that she thought she might be falling in love. If this were true, all sorts of freedoms would be available to Hart. If Grace were to marry, the need for him to stay in a "good" profession would disappear. Hart had always remembered—no matter how much he tried to suppress them—childhood promises made at his mother's bedside: she need never fear a poverty-stricken old age; he would always be at hand, ready to provide her a retreat where they could always be together.

If she were to marry, however, the promises of a ten-year-old boy would lose their irrational hold on the twenty-five-year-old man who "knew" with his conscious mind that they had no force, that in fact he *was* free.

In one year to regain his father's love, or at least to come close to the promise of it; to find a perfect friendship, a friendship that asked nothing of him but the return of love and understanding; and to break free at last from the maternal bonds that for so long had suffocated yet sustained him!

No wonder Hart sat down on September 14 to compose with deliberate care a letter quite as tactful as the one he had written to his father the previous spring. If he had then been able to discover in C.A. a father he didn't have to hate, perhaps now he could find in Grace a mother willing to accept love from some man other than himself.

He began his letter with a full account of Sam's first days in New York. But it was not Sam that he wished to talk about, rather what Sam had had to say.

So far, [Sam's] most coherent and welcome conversation has been about you, Grace, and several matters that you seemed to think were inadvisable to put on paper to me.

But why you have been so cautious, or sweetly shy, I'm at a loss to understand, because I certainly would never be timorous about writing you any news about myself, however intimate, and feeling quite sure enough that you would not be apt to quote it either far or near—just from the very facts of our relationship. However, I don't want you to think that I in the least minded hearing such delightful news quite orally from dear old Sam: good news is too welcome, only too welcome, however it comes. And now I want you—or rather want to reassure you about something that I have intended to write for some time, and in which you must believe my fullest and most intense sincerity is voiced.

When grandma wrote me awhile ago about Mr. Curtis and his devotion to you—describing as she did, such a human and very loveable person, I was exceedingly happy. But when— later in the course of the letter she mentioned that you felt that no alliance was worth anything that "broke" our relationship— that made me very worried and sad. (I have spoken to you about this attitude of your's before, and you should not persist in assuming what I feel is a somewhat biased and unnatural attitude toward it. I also feel that you are unduly influenced by what Zell [Deming] has to say on such subjects, and you should know that she is a very different type of personality than you and is in a very different relationship to life. . . .) What I want to repeat to you again—and with emphasis—is that I, first, have an incessant desire for your happiness. Second, that I feel you are naturally most happy—or would be, given the proper opportunity—as a married woman. And thirdly, that I have perfect faith in your ability to select a man that loves you enough, and who has spirit and goodness enough to not only make you happy,—but to please *me* by his companionship. And you must remember, that *whoever you chose and no matter what the circumstances might be, no such element could ever affect our mutual relationship* unless you positively willed it,—which doesn't seem likely by the undue circumspection you feel about the matter.

You must remember, dear, that nothing would make me happier than your marriage—regardless of such matters as money. And for God's sake don't marry—or at least *seek* to marry a mere moneybag. It has always hurt me to hear you jest about such matters. A few material limitations are not so much to the heart that is fed and the mind that is kept glowing happily with a real companionship. That's what I want to caution you now,—and I must speak plainly before it is too late, because you have made as many mistakes in your life as the average, and I don't want you to persist in what is a very sentimental attitude, I fear, regarding my reactions to your natural inclinations. As the years go on I am quite apt to be away for long periods, for I admit that the freedom of my imagination is the most precious thing that life holds for me,—and the only reason I can see for living. That you should be lonely anywhere during those times is a pain to me everytime I contemplate the future; you have already had a full share of pain, and you must accept—learn to identify and accept—the sweet, now, from the bitter. And that you are able to do that if you follow your trained instincts—I have not the slightest doubt. I'm not urging you to do anything you don't want to; you, I hope, will see that clearly enough. I only want you to know that life seems to be offering you some of its ripeness now, and that if you will stop trying to reconcile a whole lot of opposing and often very superficial judgments—and recall some of the uninjured emotions of your youth which have revived, very purely in your heart, I know—you will better decide *your happiness* and *mine* than if you allow a clutter of complex fears and unrelated ideas to determine your judgment. I shall always love you just the same, whatever you do; and you know that. I can't help but say that I shall respect you even more as a woman, however, if you learn to see your relationship to life in a clear and coherent way; and you are doing that, I must say, with more grace and rectitude every day.

Do not, please, hesitate to write me your feelings after this. You should not fear—and you should trust to my understanding at least as much as to anyone I know.

My everlasting love,—
your Hart

Though Grace did not write Hart a full account of her feelings—perhaps she never faced them long enough to define them—she did treat her "romance" somewhat more openly. She told of the dances, the dinners, and the parties she and Mr. Curtis attended and of their long drives in the country, one of them including an overnight stay in Canton, Ohio, where they were royally entertained by her cousins, the Smiths and the Freases.

Hart did his best to encourage Grace's romance, even going so far as to send a letter now and then by "the new aerial mail," which that summer made it possible for his Sunday special-delivery note to be written as late as Saturday afternoon. If Grace were willing to subject Mr. Curtis to the inspection of a dozen cousins, certainly, Hart concluded, wedding bells must not be far distant.

Your recountal of the Canton social excursion was delightful, in fact all your letters lately are filled with the kind of charm that emanates from a gain in happiness and a victory over stubborn and harsh memories. You don't know how happy it makes me! You seem to become more and more your essential self. It takes someone's real affection to do that for you—to permit the condition, at any rate, for such a rejuvenation of the spirit—and you know how much I have been hoping that you would let nothing come in your way to keep you from responding completely to your happiness. I know you are quite in love, so you need not bother to spoil it all by keeping on saying that you are afraid that you are "going to." Most women never know when they are really in love anyway—but you can't fool me any longer about yourself, madame, because I'm too delighted to be able to encourage you in this happy direction.

Finally Grace herself announced that she felt "something" was happening.

Your references to my being in love and it being so traceable in my recent letters, certainly makes me smile. Purely imagination on your part my dear, *purely imagination.* I've written you just as cheerfully many times before, although I may not have been able to recite so many pleasant experiences or attentions as have been mine in the last two months. Yes, I think I am in love or something, and I do not want to be—it is slavery. But Chas. is so thoughtful and considerate of me that I just feel myself slipping slipping slipping. Maybe my wise, sophisticated son can offer me the proper advice for the situation. Please do answer my "S.O.S."

Hart answered it enthusiastically. Come Christmas, he would get a day off from his work, take the night train, and be in Cleveland for the celebration of what he hoped would be a new life both for his mother and for himself: "I shall bring two quarts of something good from the metropolis and you'll BOTH have to break ALL THE RULES! I also want Mr. Curtis to join us during part of it. I'm sure to like him and we'll tching-tching your health."

"I am counting the days until Christmas and nothing must be allowed to keep you away from me on that day," Grace answered.

> Yes we will all drink out of the bottle you bring along—and we will have as gay and happy a Christmas as we've ever known and probably the most so of all. I do not know just what your opinion of Mr. Curtis will be—but Hart he has a wonderfully gentle nature, big heart and great tolerance—most unselfish and is devotedly in love with me. He is a thoroughbred—altho' a little bit old fashioned in his type. Loves life and beauty— music and art—and all of the best things that life has to offer. He plays poker—dances—swims—is 64 and the figure of a youth. He is prepared to like you and is only worrying about whether you will like him or not.

Hart did arrive in time for Christmas. And mother, son, grandmother, and suitor did drink out of those bottles Hart brought with him. But Hart's own celebration had begun long before that time, back in the early autumn, when rumors of Grace's romance had first come through from Cleveland. Freedom had then first opened up before him, and freedom demanded its rites.

# 20

No one can, of course, fix the hour and day when Hart Crane became a "serious" drinker, yet it seems likely that the summer and autumn of 1924 was the time when occasional, and finally frequent, sprees became very nearly habitual. But these were a far cry from alcoholism. I do not want to perpetuate the false picture of Crane as a thoroughgoing alcoholic, a lush desperately fighting for the next bottle. He was never—even after his trip to Europe, when he was drinking heavily—what anyone would think of as a "classic" alcoholic.

During the very brief visits Hart paid to Cleveland in 1924, whenever he did become tipsy he was careful to stop drinking as soon as the singing and dancing stages set in. He no longer attempted to hide his drinking from his mother, but he did his best to persuade her—as he himself believed—that he was indulging in the "harmless gambols of an exuberant nature." Perhaps to counter the rumors that he knew were circulating, he wrote her about current and past celebrations. He shared with her, he felt, a capacity to enjoy a "lyric evening," and though he couldn't help regarding her, he said, as an "inbred Puritan," he knew she could be sympathetic to his own boisterous inclinations. At one of the dances Charles took Grace to, she had met Hart's former employers from the Cleveland advertising agency headed by Stanley Patno; her account led Hart to fond recollections of his time there. His employers had been, he said, "good sports too . . . and unusually merry bosses. I still like to think of those five o'clock booze parties we had in the office and how giddily I sometimes came home for dinner. You were very charming and sensible about it, too."

In New York, however, Hart's exploits seemed to many observers more than "harmless gambols." When Howard P. Lovecraft, the horror-story writer—considerably more of a puritan than Grace Crane—came to town to visit his friends Sam Loveman and the book dealer George Kirk, Crane's binges were already part of the literary gossip of Greenwich Village. In one of his long diary-like letters Lovecraft describes Crane as "an egotistical young aesthete who has attained some real recognition in the Dial and other modernist organs, and who has an unfortunate predilection for the wine when it is red." Lovecraft notes that Hart is now "a little ruddier, a little puffier, and slightly more moustached than when I saw him in Cleveland two years ago." A little later, he reported a visit to Hart's apartment: "We found Crane in and sober—but boasting over the two-day spree he had just slept off, during which he had been picked up dead drunk from the street in Greenwich Village by the eminent modernist poet E. E. Cummings—whom he knows well and put in a homeward taxi." Lovecraft, disapproving, settled on a moralizing tone: "Poor Crane! I hope he'll sober up with the years, for there's really good stuff & a bit of genius in him."

Hart was, however, in this happy time nowhere near ready to sober up. All through the autumn and winter of 1924 and well into the spring of 1925, he dashed from party to party at an accelerating gallop. "I've been just too rushed to even brush my teeth!" he exclaimed in one letter. There was a trip "into the New Jersey hills to visit Kenneth Burke and family"; on another night, "a wild jubilee with Tate"; on still others, sessions with the Cowleys, with Sue Jenkins, and, when they came to town, with Jean Toomer, Waldo Frank, and Eugene O'Neill. The quick trip to see Burke was typical: "His farmstead, wife and kids made us welcome—including a collie dog and tom cat who sleep, eat and play together. We consumed six quarts of fine home made blackberry wine in the evening and then all went out and made the roads and hillsides resound with songs and merriment. I sat down in the wrong place once, and in the darkness whacked my head against a tree—which I felt the next morning. But our hilarity was worth remembering."

From Christmas in Cleveland until New Year's Day in New York, Hart caroused steadily. On January 4—a Sunday morning—he explained to his mother that he hadn't written for the simple reason that "this is the first 'day of rest' that I've had since I came back,—but fortunately that doesn't mean that I am all fagged out by any means. I've managed to get some regular sleeping hours, have curtailed my liquor rations (since New Year's eve) and am feeling as well as anyone could ever ask."

When Crane went on to say, "I am very happy these days and the more so because I trust you are," he meant exactly that. His New Year's celebration—though spent with friends who had never met either his mother or his father—was clearly a private celebration of his new congeniality with his father, his mother's coming marriage, and his own consequent release from "responsibility." "You must tell me . . . what you did on New Year's eve," he wrote Grace, and then summarized his own evening.

Our party at Squarcialupi's (what a name!) was a delight. I was sent out to get some more Victrola needles about midnight, and before I got back the whistles began to blow. Even though it was in an uncrowded neighborhood—people began throwing their arms around each other, dancing and singing. Whereat I went into such an ecstasy as only that moment of all the year affords me. I hugged my companion and started singing Gregorian chants or something of my own version approaching them, and I hope in good Latin. O New York is the place to celebrate New Year's! There is such spirit in everyone, such cordiality!

One party ran into the next. There were big parties and little ones, sessions in restaurants and speakeasies. Hart, who drank everything available, sometimes criticized the Prohibition combinations—but downed his drinks manfully.

Imagine making anything fit to put in one's stomach out of two quarts of heavy cream, a dozen eggs and a bottle of Johnny Walker whisky! It was the richest and most disagreeable egg gnog I have ever had, and it tasted just like ivory soup melted down in a wash tub. Saturday and Sunday I spent as quietly as possible—that is, as previous engagements would permit me—and I must say that I am far from desiring any excitement further this week or next.

But as soon as one hangover lifted, Hart prepared to fit the next one on. When, on the last day of February, he congratulated himself on finally spending a "quiet and economical Saturday evening" at home writing letters—among them one to the Rychtariks—he was in the next sentence prepared to admit that his chances of repeating the performance were unlikely.

I owe enough answers to letters to keep me in a week, but I know well enough that tomorrow night will find me in a Spanish restaurant near here, recently discovered, which serves the finest ruby-colored and rose-scented wine in N.Y. . . . Waldo Frank knows Spanish very well, and was able to convince the management, thereby, that we were not revenue officers. Since then life even in "my" retired neighborhood in Brooklyn has been gay. I know you think me terrible, and given over entirely to pleasure and sin and folly. Certainly I am concerned a great deal with all three of these—and even so, don't get *all* I want.

Not until very late spring did the "usual jamborees and dinner parties" begin to taper off; and though Hart made an occasional resolution to behave himself ("I can see where I had better plan on another respite from friends and celebrations unless I want to be uncomfortably on the edge of things"), a telephone call, a note in the mailbox, a friend met on the way to dinner would be enough to start the ball rolling. ("There certainly was much rum and running about during last Sat. and Sunday!") During all this time, Hart suffered from a nagging awareness that his social life was leaving him no time for writing. He could take the hangovers. He found it more difficult to take the self-examination that letters from Cleveland friends forced him to make; their faith in his artistic powers must frequently have seemed to him in painful contrast to his actual production.

With most of his New York friends, Hart defended his sprees as in some way or other "necessary" to his art. With such Cleveland friends as the Rychtariks, he was willing to face facts. When he got right down to it, the sprees were just sprees.

> As you picture matters, the usual bacchanale of life around here and among my friends still occupies me a good deal. Some of it is sweet and clarifying—but as time goes on I tire of certain repetitions that occur in it and seem to be developing certain reactionary tendencies toward solitude and more austere examinations of myself. Above all, with the regular amount of highly detailed work I have to do every day at the office,—the "grind" in other words, and all the tempting other activities outside my real self, I feel worn out most of the time and so distracted that I lack the reflection and self-collection necessary to do the work, the *real* work that ultimately concerns me most. Still, considering the slight time which I have for any real freedom I think I have done a good bit of work during the last two years. But I cannot profess to any real ability in measuring it. One struggles along blindly most of the time.

In April 1925, when he wrote the Rychtariks, Hart was at long last pulling his work together for a first volume. Originally he had expected the book to end with a rising sequence of poems: "Faustus and Helen," the "Voyages" set, and *The Bridge*, a group arranged in terms of increasing density and length. But with *The Bridge* expanding each time he worked on it, he soon decided that he would have enough for a book if he published a collection of his best work to date, reserving *The Bridge* for a second volume. *White Buildings* drew its title from Crane's unpublished 1923 poem of that name; but the phrase, as he later told Caresse Crosby, had been initially suggested to him by the paintings of Giorgio di Chirico. ("I . . . never met him. It was my early enthusiasm for his style of painting that inspired me with the name 'White Buildings' years ago.")

Though it is a small point, it is worth establishing that almost as soon as he started to gather his poems, Hart began to think of them as *a book* and not *a collection of poems*, for he recognized far better than most of his critics that the interrelationships between the separate poems were of great importance. "You know one makes up one's mind that certain things go well together—make a book, in fact—and you don't feel satisfied until you have brought all the pieces to a uniform standard of excellence."

Hart's springtime orgy of revision and organization was brought on because he had for the first time met a man interested enough in his work to offer to publish it. That was Samuel Jacobs, the owner of The Polytype Press on West Eighth Street in Greenwich Village. Jacobs, who had done the typesetting on Cummings's *Tulips and Chimneys* and whose "notably beautiful books" Crane had admired, felt that a privately printed edition of five hundred copies could be produced for as little as $200, most of that going for binding. (Jacobs had volunteered to donate his own services as compositor.) The only problem would be time, since Jacobs would have to work on Crane's book when his press was not otherwise engaged.

Though Crane and Jacobs knew that work on the book would be slow—its production might take the better part of a year— Hart finished most of his revision by the beginning of March. "I have revised a good many poems," he wrote his mother on Washington's birthday, "and had to complete others that were half finished, and it all takes a great deal of work."

One of the poems on which Hart worked most diligently was "Lachrymae Christi," which he had started more than a year before and which—before he was finished—incorporated materials from earlier, abandoned work (the mill, for instance, from "Episode of Hands"). It was probably "Lachrymae Christi" Crane was thinking of—he had been working on it, off and on, for about five months—when he wrote Jean Toomer that he felt poetic "experience" was "the effort to describe God." In any event, the completed poem is certainly that, for it makes very neatly the Christ-Dionysus link. Spring's "lilac-emerald" breath transforms dead winter into life; the "tinder" eyes of Christ force an "unmangled" smile from the "charred and riven" face of destroyed Dionysus.

Playing the sort of literary game his readers had come to expect from him, Crane brilliantly assembles a body (that of reborn Christ-Dionysus-earth) from the natural scene—the "smile" of a factory windowsill, "fox's teeth," "flanks" of hillsides, "eyes," "tongue," "palm," and earth's "tendoned loam" compounding into the refreshing experience of spring which can "anoint with innocence" and through sacrifice—"the year's / First blood"— clear the artist's tongue of "death" and "perjuries," free him from the domination of "vermin and rod." (Ultimately, scholars should calculate the impact of a submerged distillery—colorless benzine, for instance—gradually becoming blooded to the sacramental wine that is carried in "the grail / Of earth" and that through the "Compulsion of the year" transforms everything.)

Brom Weber, citing a "Word made Flesh" passage in one of

Hart's letters, remarks that the real source for the poem can be found in the fact that "the cloud of fire had swept over him— Crane had fallen in love." Weber is, I think, absolutely right. The regeneration Crane deals with in this poem is the same sort he deals with in the exactly contemporary "Voyages" set. Even though that suite of poems drew on two lyrics Crane had written before he met Emil Opffer, the few phrases that can be tracked back to Samuel Greenberg, and an imagery that was explicitly calculated to link to the larger unit of poems that would constitute *The Bridge*, any biographical view of "Voyages" has to see it as a tightly knit structure which is privately, as Crane told everyone he knew, a literary "equivalent" for the complex relationship of friendship, affection, and love that he felt for Emil—"an 'even so' and 'All hail!' to a love that I have known."

Publicly, however, the poems were meant to link love and sea and death into a dense, affirmative design. Moving out from land and innocence in the first poem, Crane gradually extends the reach of his sea, from the second poem's "Carib fire" of the West Indies to the last poem's white Belle Isle, an island off the coast of Labrador. Crane's geography is also vertical; in the third poem he explores the bottom of the sea and in the last the rainbows that lift above it. For he wishes to reveal the whole broad "spectrum of the sea," which is nothing more nor less than the spectrum of love. In order to identify *sea* and *love*, he constructs a body / sea in exactly the way he constructs, in "Lachrymae Christi," a body / earth. This identification of sea and body permeates all six of the poems, but it is concentrated in the third, where the "theme of you" is assigned an infinite blood-relationship, an "infinite consanguinity," with the sea. A wave becomes a breast (while the trough of the wave becomes the breast of a loving sky); the sea is given hands and even feet (the "lithe pediments" of those pillars of light which extend into it), so that finally the *I* of the poem may voyage—like the light which wrestles through it—into the fleshy body of the sea: "Permit me voyage, love, into your hands . . ."

This experience has in it something of death, though a death on the order of the "little death" of Elizabethan and Jacobean poetry —the calm that follows love. But the other death is there too, for human love does die. The farewells that announce a voyage announce as well the separate and separating lives of people who, in the communion of love, had become one in body and spirit. The poet's task, therefore, is to make spiritual union survive the divorce of flesh. And his technique is the poem. Through his power—that of the "imaged Word"—he translates the "silver snowy sentences" of the sea, its very "signature," its "superscription," into a poem that defines in quite a literal way the "incarnate word" which is, of course, "creation's . . . word"—the spirit of God made flesh. It is a "word" spoken through flesh; and it can be "answered," Crane asserts, only by the artist:

> The imaged Word, it is, that holds
> Hushed willows anchored in its glow.
> It is the unbetrayable reply
> Whose accent no farewell can know.

There is no question that Crane was thinking of these poems in his "General Aims and Theories" essay, a most careful statement of his aesthetic which was written during the months that he worked on "Voyages."

Just exactly when Crane started work on "General Aims and Theories" is difficult to pin down. Horton dates the essay 1925 and Weber speculates that it was intended as a guide for a preface to *White Buildings* that at one point early in 1926 O'Neill was supposed to write. My own guess is that Crane may have begun thinking about the essay somewhat earlier—when he was asked to contribute to a "final" symposium number of *Broom* back in the spring of 1924. On March 8, 1924, Munson wrote Toomer listing the contributors who had agreed to participate (Crane, Wescott, Brown, Nagle, Burke, and Munson) and defining very loosely the kind of document each had been asked to write ("anything from 50 to four or five hundred words in the form of a statement, entertaining or otherwise"). Whenever he wrote the essay, it defines most accurately Crane's own stand as an artist, and it helps the reader unadjusted to the symbolist tradition to comprehend the "logic of metaphor" that Crane employed most conspicuously in the "Voyages" set.

What the "logic of metaphor" finally achieves, in Crane's view, is precisely the sort of enduring statement articulated by the "imaged Word" that he turns to in the last stanza of the last "Voyages" poem. To put it most simply, the total poem defines a feeling in exactly the way a word defines a concept. When Crane says, "It is as though a poem gave the reader as he left it a single, new *word*, never before spoken and impossible to actually enunciate," he is asserting both the structure and the utility of the poem. The poem's great value is that it is "a stab at a truth," in exactly the way a single word accurately used is a stab at a truth. The poem, however, must operate in a territory where no defining word exists: it must spell out a feeling so accurately that when we put down the poem—its harmonic structure of interrelated images flowing together into a significant pattern—we acknowledge its metaphoric statement as emotionally *true*. Consequently, as Crane says, "the terms of expression employed are often selected less for their logical (literal) significance than for their associational meanings. Via this and their metaphorical interrelationships, the entire construction of the poem is raised on the

organic principle of a 'logic of metaphor,' which antedates our
so-called pure logic, and which is the genetic basis of all speech,
hence consciousness and thought-extension."

Crane uses several examples from his own poetry, the most
telling, I think, from "Voyages II": "When . . . I speak of 'adagios
of islands,' the reference is to the motion of a boat through islands clustered thickly, the rhythm of the motion, etc. And it
seems a much more direct and creative statement than any more
logical employment of words such as 'coasting slowly through
the islands,' besides ushering in a whole world of music."

Perhaps this is the place to say that Crane never intended his
poems to be used in quite the way I have been using them here.
That is, he did not want us to read the poems as confessions. That
they were, Crane was as quick as any other honest man to admit.
But he knew that their confessional function was of value only to
himself: it was what got him going; it was his "secret" motive. For
example, we know that Emil Opffer talked about the sunken city
off San Salvador and that Crane worked it into his poem because
he was working Emil's sea into the poem. This kind of fact,
Crane might have said, is historically interesting; but it has nothing whatever to do with the final success or failure of the poem.
It helps us know a little about how the poem was put together and tells us something about its author. But that is the
most you can say for information of this sort. The poem itself,
Crane insists, must lead an independent life: "I would like to establish it as free from my own personality as from any chance
evaluation on the reader's part. (This is, of course, an impossibility, but it is a characteristic worth mentioning.)" Though the
"Voyages" set is a consequence of a love for a man, its subject
matter is love itself. Crane would have been the first to be
distressed if the poems were read simply as an account of a private
love affair. He was writing poetry, not autobiography.

One result of Hart's decision to bring his finished poetry together in one volume was that work on *The Bridge* was virtually
suspended. There had been several sessions in 1924 when the
poem had seemed to race along, but more often than not Hart
felt day-to-day pressures that made composition intolerably slow.
"There are days when I simply have to 'sit on myself' at my desk
to shut out rhythms and melodies that belong to that poem and
have never been written because I have succeeded only too well
during the course of the day's work in excluding and stifling such
a train of thoughts," Hart wrote toward the end of September.
"And then there are periods again when the whole world couldn't
shut out the plans and beauties of that work—and I get a
little of it on paper. It has been that way lately. And that makes
me happy."

Even when circumstances forbade work on *The Bridge*, its

quality, as I have already suggested, intruded itself into Hart's letters. It also shows up, rather sweetly, in a scrap of occasional poetry done as a bon voyage present for his Aunt Zell. Hart's little poem, as it turned out, included some errors, Grace having misunderstood her sister-in-law's itinerary. "I nearly sank with mortification when she informed me casually that she was not even going near *Spain* and had not intended to from the outset of her plans," Hart later wrote home. "How did you ever get so bawled up on her plans as to write me about that as you did? I finally explained the joke of my verses to her on that score, as I thought she would enjoy them all the better, maybe when she found them in her stateroom."

What Zell—who was taking a holiday from her duties as publisher of the Warren newspaper—found in her stateroom was a twenty-line poem, "To Zell, Now Bound for Spain," surmounted by a photograph of Hart at his Brooklyn Heights window. She had asked for a literary send-off. "Knowing how hard such 'occasional' pieces are for me to write," Hart confessed to his mother, "I worried considerably. But it's not so bad for a piece of pure invention."

> From Brooklyn Heights one sees the bay:
> And, anchored at my window sill,
> I've often sat and watched all day
> The boats stream by against the shrill
> Manhattan skyline,—endlessly
> Their mastheads filing out to sea.
>
> And just so, as you see me here
> (Though kodaked somewhat out of focus,
> My eyes have still the proper locus)
> I'm flashing greetings to your pier,
> Your ship, your auto-bus in France—
> All things on which you glide or prance
> Down into sunny Spain, dear Zell.
> Good berths, good food and wine as well!
>
> I hope to know these wishes a true
> Forecasting. Let me hear from you.
> Enclose some petals from a wall
> Of roses in Castile, or maybe garden stall;
> While I'll be waiting at this old address,
> Dear Aunt, God-mother, Editress!

Understandably, as soon as Hart completed the revisions for his book, he grew impatient with delays on Jacob's part. Finally, early in spring, Hart and his publisher had a long and serious discussion. Jacobs was still willing to do the book, but he couldn't guarantee publication for at least a year. Perhaps, he suggested, Hart could find another publisher willing to bring the book out, with Jacobs still taking care of composition. This, both men reasoned, might speed up matters.

Hart quickly agreed to this scheme—largely because he knew that private publication would be the worst way to launch himself. "That would suggest to the general public, whether true or not, that I had paid to have the book brought out myself, which makes a bad impression on reviewers, and puts me in an unpleasant position. That's one thing I would never do,—at least with a first book. It's enough to put good food on the table, without having to rub people's noses in the plate who don't want to eat!"

Some sense of Hart's indecision and hesitation during these months can be caught in a letter he got off to his mother and grandmother just after Easter. He was trying, that spring, to be "sensible." He wanted desperately to quit his job, join Emil on a coastal steamer, and taste again the open, non-literary life that he knew accounted for a great deal of his work's vitality. Yet reason dictated that he stay close to the literary market, where he had one man committed to his book and several friends willing to push it with commercial publishers.

> I have been able to lift my head with a little more calm and cheer since a week of almost sanatorium regime—going to bed early and what is better, sleeping soundly again. I have been letting the dreams of voyages etc. subside for awhile under the illusion (for illusion I suspect it to be) that my book may appear by next fall and that [it] is advisable for me to stick around and correct proofs etc. . . . Waldo Frank is going to do what he can to influence Boni and Liveright, his publishers, to make the investment. But all this is a little late to bring them now, as I understand—so that it may be this time next year before the book actually comes out.

As the book began to make its rounds, Hart brightened a good deal. Just having the book in shape gave him confidence. "Getting that wad of my past work into permanent collection and out of the way, so to speak, is an hygienic benefit."

When Waldo Frank reported that Horace Liveright was in no mood to tackle a volume of verse and that Hart had best wait until autumn to approach him, Hart sent the manuscript to Thomas Seltzer. "It takes long enough to find a publisher, as a rule," he explained to his mother, "without depending on the moods of any one of them." When Thomas Seltzer did not come through, Hart tried Harcourt, Brace, where his friend Harrison Smith worked as an editor.

Hart felt that the book really had to appear by the summer. "I'm figuring that publication in book form will give me at least enough prestige to get a little money for my magazine contributions. Besides this, I have begun to feel rather silly, being introduced everywhere as a poet and yet having so little collected evidence of the occupation. There won't be any explosions of praise when the book appears, but it will make me feel a little more solid on my feet."

Hart's friends were doing everything they could to help. Waldo Frank and Eugene O'Neill had offered to write "blurbs" for the book jacket and for the publisher's announcements, and half a dozen of Hart's other friends had promised to do reviews. Yet nothing came of their aid. The book circulated slowly from publisher to publisher, always being awarded praise but never a contract, and Hart came to feel more and more, as he kept repeating to Cowley, "caught like a rat in a trap."

Part of his problem had to do—as always—with his job. The one at Sweet's kept him alive, but it offered nothing in the way of satisfaction, not even the satisfaction of decent pay. After a full year, Hart was still pulling down only $35 a week, just what he had earned at J. Walter Thompson's. At those wages, even overtime amounted to very little. "It takes this night work at the office to make me continually sulky," Hart complained, "and with two more nights of it again this week in prospect, don't blame me if I'm not exactly gay." Bad as work was in the spring, it would be worse, Hart knew, once summer sweat brought out his hives and summer pollen started the sneezing and snorting that would not let up until September.

For a while, there had been a bright dream that Emil would come into enough of an inheritance to be able to invite Hart on a trip to the Scandinavian countries, but that, like other dreams, fell through.

Hart's summer plans vacillated. When his mother encouraged him to find a job as a ship's writer ("it would be a wonderful experience for you and you can afford to do a little adventuring in the next five years"), Hart came close to leaving Sweet's. But a nibble of interest sent him scurrying to a publisher, and the ship sailed. There was also the possibility that Grace might allow him to use the house on the Isle of Pines, in which case he would certainly plan to spend his summer there. Early in May, the Lachaises invited him to join them in Maine. By this time, however, he had changed his plans so often that he had no notion what he wanted to do. The Lachaise offer, he told his mother, was tempting.

> Just a mile from the ocean—and a wonderful beach set in a cove of rocks topped by pines! How I would love to go—and I really may decide to. As I have been mentioning, the summer at the office and the extra night work required looms up before me as almost unthinkable. I have asked for a raise—but it has not been settled as yet. I think I impressed it upon the boss, however, that if it isn't forthcoming I have other plans. I in-

quired again yesterday, but have been put off until Tuesday.
Well, we'll see. I have got into such a rut of repetitious feeling,
thought and dissatisfaction with myself that it seems the only
salvation to break away for awhile into some change of work
and environment.

Hart continued to hesitate until the very end of May. By then,
all his closest friends were leaving or about to leave town.
The Cowleys had moved out to Staten Island; the Burkes were
at their farm in Jersey; Slater Brown had bought a run-down
farm in Pawling, New York; Waldo Frank had moved up to
Massachusetts for the summer; Emil Opffer was in town only on
short visits between voyages. Only Sam Loveman was likely to be
spending the summer months in New York, and even Sam
talked of returning to Cleveland.

It was at this point that Hart himself almost returned to Cleveland, for he suddenly had two tempting job offers.

The first came from William Freeman, under whom he had
worked at Corday and Gross. Hart told his mother of the offer.

Then [Freeman] went on to say that The Corday and Gross
Company needed someone of my type in their copy department
very badly, and that they would be glad to connect with me
in case I cared to go back. He further mentioned that I was
the one "brilliant" copywriter they had ever had there, that the
company had fully realized, long since, that they made a great
mistake in letting me be lured away without raising my salary,
etc. etc. Well! I must say it was a satisfaction to be so spoken
of. I was glad to know, too, that such an opportunity will always be at least plausibly open to me in case I am ever again
located in Cleveland for any length of time.

The second offer came from his father. C.A., in New York on
business, made another spur-of-the-moment attempt to bring Hart
back into his firm. Though he did not know it, he had caught his
son at a particularly vulnerable time, for Hart's raise had not come
through, and he had just turned in his two-week notice at Sweet's
Catalogues. The meeting began on a very friendly note, dinner
at the Waldorf and C.A.'s best cigars lulling father and son
into a congenial mood. Finally, as Hart told his mother, "C.A. . . .
offered me a job which I was all ready to take. Whereupon he became so pettily dictatorial that I withdrew quickly. . . . I'll write
more about it later. We parted on friendly enough terms, I guess."

What happened, Emil Opffer told me, was that Hart had been
overwhelmed by the generous offer his father had made and had
accepted the job without reservation; they were busy going over
the responsibilities it carried when C.A. casually mentioned that
one of them would be decent grooming: Hart would have to get
rid of his mustache! Hart jumped to his feet, shouted that he'd be

damned if he'd work for a tyrant, and marched out of the restaurant. When he had a chance to think about it, however, the
incident seemed so heroic and so comic that he was able to telephone his father and patch up the quarrel—without, however, accepting the "dishonorable" job.

By the last week in May, Hart had his immediate problems
solved. Emil had agreed to take over the room at 110 Columbia
Heights. A telephone call to his mother and grandmother—the
first long-distance call Hart ever made—had helped calm their
apprehensions about his impending unemployment. And he had
a place to stay:

> Later on in the summer I may take a boat job on the South
> American or West Indian Routes, but at present I have been
> very lucky in being invited out to a lovely farm near here,
> (Brewster, N.Y.) to spend a month or so. Brown has just
> bought it, and has urged me to come out and help him plant
> the garden, etc. And this is just what I have been needing,
> exercise, open air, and relaxation from the tension of the desk
> (which had become very threatening to my health and nervous
> stability, I can assure you).

Perhaps, as Hart packed his things, he tried to sort out significant events of the past six months. But, if he did, chances are he
could make neither head nor tail of the jumble. *White Buildings*
had for a while seemed certain to be published: now nothing
could seem less certain. He had broken with Munson, his oldest
"literary" friend, yet the "break" seemed meaningless ("Gorham, of
course, I don't see at all, nor hear much about. . . . and I strangely
enough, don't miss seeing him half as much as I had once thought
I would under such circumstances. Of course, I'm really his friend,
as I know he is mine, but it may do us good to separate a little
while"). Then there was his mother's happiness in what was by
now an "unofficial" engagement to Charles Curtis. There were
the meetings at Squarcialupi's. There were visits to the theater
as O'Neill's guest, and trips to the opera with Emil, and one
visit to a concert at which Stravinsky conducted his own work.
("But he disappointed both Waldo and myself by not including
the 'Sacre du Printemps' on the program. I don't care for
what I heard of his *latest* work. Indeed, the 'Petrouchka' was the
only fine thing on his program.")

But who knows where significance lies? Perhaps altogether
different memories drifted back as Hart went through the "real
turmoil" of the first three days of June, packing for shipment or
for storage everything he owned. Maybe he remembered the day
of the earthquake, when, halfway through a letter to the Rychtariks, the paper started bobbing under his hand and—halfway
through a word—he took off for some place safer than his fourth-
floor room.

WELL! It isn't often that one gets an earthquake inside a letter, but this letter carries the evidence of one to you this time! Thank God I'm living still to finish the ending of that last sentence. I had, as you see, just started the word "few" meaning to follow it with "poems"—when the room began swaying frightfully and I had the most sickening and helpless feeling I hope to ever have. By the time I got down the stairs people were coming out of other rooms all over the house, etc. . . . The feeling was simply frightful.

Or maybe he remembered the days of "the great unprecedented fog," when the harbor had come alive with warning noises: "Well, it's just been hell for me over at Columbia Heights. I haven't had 6 hours of solid sleep for three nights, what with the bedlam of bells, grunts, whistles, screams and groan of all the river and harbor bouys, which have kept up an incessant grinding program as noisesome as the midnight passing into new year. Just like the mouth of hell, not being able to see six feet from the window and yet hearing all that weird jargon constantly." Or perhaps Hart remembered the end-of-January eclipse of the sun, when everyone in his office had dashed to the windows: "I saw it from a fire escape (21 flights above Bryant Park and the Library at 42nd St.) and the queer green light that spread over everything—the total darkness and stars at the moment of totality—the mad crowds in the subways on the way to see it—etc. made a great impression."

Or did significance rest in persons who show up only in parentheses in Hart's letters—Stewart Mitchell, for instance, who had helped Hart between jobs and whom he sometimes visited, a generous, good friend—or those other persons, casually described, whose names have vanished? Perhaps, on that last day of sweaty packing, he thought as much of the flower seller he'd no longer greet twice a day—on his way to work and on his way home—as he did of anyone else. Hart had always bought from her whatever seasonal flowers were cheap.

> . . . have bought some gay marigolds and narcissi from the funny little florist woman nearby who has a regular case on me, or rather has an amusing way of flattering one. She's a sight, alright! Bumpy body, pocked face, mussy hair and a voice that simply barks at you it is so raucous. I can't be seen passing her place without her glimpsing me, and signaling. When I enter she jumps at me with such phrases as—"Well my handsome Good Looking again!, How's my big boy?; Ain't he a dandy!", etc., etc., etc. I generally get enough from her to make my room gay on a quarter . . .

Or perhaps on June the fourth, Hart's thoughts were altogether different. He told his mother that they were only of relief at finally escaping the city.

Practically everything is packed up. There has been a real turmoil, too, I can tell you. The frightful and sudden heat of the last 3 days brought on a fearful attack of uric acid trouble —headaches, bladder trouble and urethritis. No sleep for three nights and I have been dieting on buttermilk and crackers. Besides trying to complete all arrangements by Saturday and still give some time to the office, I have had 3 engagements with the dentist. I thought one tooth had an abscess and had to have an x-ray taken to find out that it hadn't. There is one more trial with a filling tomorrow and then I'll be through. I'm about done out, however, and a feather could knock me over. Furthermore all these exigencies have about used up all the money I had saved up, little enough!

But I'm sure the change and exercise will do me up, and it's better to be a pauper with health than a near-pauper and a perfect wreck here in the city.

# 2 1

The six weeks that Crane spent in Brown's old farmhouse on "Tory Hill" in Pawling, New York, were—like his time visiting Brown at Woodstock—among the happiest, the least harried of his life. "You have no idea how busy we have all been," Hart wrote his grandmother at the end of the first week.

> There has been a great deal—tons—of wood to clear away from the house, rubbish, also, and a lot of old plaster they threw out in making alterations. Then we have been building bookcases, shelves and tables for the inside, as well as scrubbing and rubbing down floors. Getting up every morning at five-thirty. The air is so fresh and the birds so sweet that you simply can't stay in bed a moment longer. And how good breakfast tastes! We have bought a good oil stove, which works on about 10 cents a day. All our cooking and lamp-oil comes to much less cost than similar means in the city would cost. Brown has a Ford which he got for 35 dollars! We go marketing about 7 miles away to the nearest town every three or four days. This place, you know, is quite delightfully isolated from other houses. It's about 150 years old—and did I tell you that a lot of wonderful old rope beds and furniture came right along with it?

In all his time in the country, Hart's enthusiasm never faltered, never diminished. He was amused when his grandmother seemed surprised to find him committed to clean air and open space ("It seems so strange however that you can be content with such surroundings—one who has been used to being in the rush of city life so long"), but he assured her that, given the opportunity, he would settle down in such a place forever. Soon she began to pick up in her own the tone of his letters. She had "caught," she told him, "the inspiration of the place"; the "veritable tonic" of that second-hand country air led her to reconstruct fragments of her own childhood.

> Oh you ask me if I knew anything about rope bedsteads. I should say it bro't very vividly to mind when my father had the job housecleaning time of tightening up the ropes, and he

would say to me Come here "Sis" and walk over these ropes, one at a time and stretch them and then he would stretch each one around the pin in the side of the bed—then over several times until they were tight as a drum.

"Life has been going along here at Brown's farm," Hart answered her, "as pleasantly as anyone could wish." Even a touch of rose fever could not mar days that were full from sunup to sundown.

We have the house painting almost finished. I've already mentioned how I enjoyed doing that. Brown and I have been making screens the last couple of days and now I defy a mosquito to attack my slumbers or a fly to fall into my soup. Although planted very late in season Brown's garden is about up, peas and beans, and soon will follow a whole menu of delicious vegetables for the table. . . . Yesterday afternoon we picked blueberries—about four quarts in an hour—and there's nothing better to eat with cereals for breakfast I can tell you. It's pleasant to pick them, too—great patches of bushes laden to bending with the beautiful milky-blue fruit that looks the freshest thing on earth. The huckleberries will be out later—and there will be simply bushels of them. Brown also has great quantities of raspberries, blackberries, currants and gooseberries—as well as elderberries on his place. Also plenty of sap maples and walnut trees. I haven't yet stopped enthusing about the place, you see . . .

When there was no work to be done on the house, there was wild country to be explored—abandoned farms, dilapidated and grown over, returning slowly to a woodland not much different from what it had been in pre-Revolutionary days: "I walked over twenty miles yesterday over the ridges of the hills into neighboring valleys. It made me so sleepy that I went to bed at the fall of darkness." And there was a marvelous fireplace to brighten the chilly early summer evenings. "We have a bright merry fire in the big fire place," Hart wrote his grandmother on one of those nights. "It has a Dutch oven along side—do you remember any like that?"

Celebrations were relatively calm weekend affairs. The Fourth of July, however, proved spectacular enough for everyone to remember some of it—and a few people, Hart among them, to be unable to remember all of it. What he remembered was, however, vivid enough. "Nothing could beat the hilarity of this place," he told his mother, "—with about an omnibus-ful of people here from New York and a case of gin, to say nothing of jugs of marvelous hard cider from a neighboring farm." Allen Tate, who intended to discuss the possibility of Hart's contributing to *The Fugitive*, found poetry driven out of his mind in a whirlwind of singing, dancing, and community wrestling that reached one peak in an impromptu orange-peel-tossing contest.

Hart thought it was the pleasantest drunk he had ever been on. Though he censored slightly, he hit off for his mother most of the high spots.

You should have seen the dances I did—one all painted up like an African cannibal. My makeup was lurid enough. A small keg on my head and a pair of cerise drawers on my legs! We went swimming at midnight, climbed trees, played blind man's buff, rode in wheelbarrows, and gratified every caprice for three days until everyone was good an' tired out. The guests are still recovering, I understand, in their separate abodes in the city. It certainly is infinitely pleasanter drinking and celebrating on a wide acreage, like this farm, than in the tumult and confusion of the city. Aside from this one blowout I have not had a drop since I have been here—and have not felt like drinking, either. The desire for booze in the city comes from frayed nerves and repressions of the office, I'm sure.

It was parties of this sort which helped establish Hart, in the eyes of his friends, as the "Roaring Boy." Malcolm Cowley, in *Exile's Return*, reconstructs this time, when the atmosphere was one of "youth and poverty and good humor." At their parties, Cowley said, Hart "would laugh twice as hard as the rest of us and drink at least twice as much hard cider, while contributing more than his share of the crazy metaphors and overblown epithets." Yet out of Hart's wildness, the draft of a poem would sometimes emerge.

Gradually he would fall silent, and a little later he disappeared. In lulls that began to interrupt the laughter, now Hart was gone, we would hear a new hubbub through the walls of his room —the phonograph playing a Cuban rumba, the typewriter clacking simultaneously; then the phonograph would run down and the typewriter stop while Hart changed the record, perhaps to a torch song, perhaps to Ravel's *Bolero*.

If the alcohol, the friendship, and the music accomplished their magic, Hart would appear in kitchen or garden—wherever his audience had settled down—". . . his eyes burning . . . He would be chewing a five-cent cigar which he had forgotten to light. In his hands would be two or three sheets of typewritten manuscript, with words crossed out and new lines scrawled in. 'R-read that,' he would say. 'Isn't that the grreatest poem ever written?' " They would read it, of course, "Allen Tate perhaps making a profound comment," and the rest responding to its rhythms and its vivid images. "But we would all agree that it was absolutely superb. In Hart's state of exultation there was nothing else we could say without driving him to rage or tears."

Yet, as Cowley points out, this was by no means the end of

the story, for Hart, cold sober, would eventually hammer his poems into final shape.

The long search for *findrinny* is a good example of Hart's persistent attention to the language of his poetry. The search had begun in early drafts of "Voyages II," while Hart was working at Sweet's Catalogues, and it continued well into the summer.

"I've told this story, but there's no use not telling it again," Cowley explained to me. "He wrote the line 'seal's findrinny gaze toward paradise.' Bill Brown—Slater Brown—told him that he couldn't find *findrinny* in any dictionary. So Hart began looking for it—looked for it in the big Webster's and the big Standard dictionary, which was Webster's rival at that time, couldn't find it, cursed, looked through books for it, finally changed the line to 'The seal's wide spindrift gaze toward paradise.' " While it lasted, Hart's search, Cowley said, had taken him to the public library (on office time) and South Street speakeasies (on his own time). But neither the books that he consulted nor the sailors offered him the word he was after. All summer long, Hart insisted "It's a *real word!*" Yet, as Cowley reports, " 'findrinny' he could never find." The word, of course, exists. After Hart's death, Brown noticed it in *Moby Dick*, where Hart might first have seen it, though it is as likely that he saw it in Yeats's "The Wanderings of Oisin," a poem he had read in high-school days.

Though Independence Day was the most spectacular day of Hart's stay with Brown, the really important days, in Hart's mind, were those devoted to plans for his own permanent emigration to the country.

I have already spoken of Hart's need for an "anchor," his persistent fear that wandering might overwhelm and finally destroy him, that the voyages of his life would be nothing more than helpless, uncontrolled drifting unless somewhere he could be sure of a piece of land that was his own, a place—after all the voyages—to which he could return.

Dylan Thomas—another voyaging poet—found for a while an anchor of a sort in wife and children, an anchor that held him for a little time in one place before the great drifting began. Hart Crane was not so lucky. He was sure by this time that he would never marry. The best he could hope for would be a piece of ground not far from friends to whom he could turn for a kind of second-hand participation in family life.

Perhaps it is this drive that accounts for Hart's intense relationships with the wives of many of his friends. Claire Spencer, Mary Colum, Charmion von Wiegand, Charlotte Rychtarik, Sue Jenkins, Peggy Cowley were, each in turn, enormously valuable to him; he could confess to them his darkest fears. Sitting in kitchens, talking to them as they prepared dinners, or shopping with them, he could worry out feelings about his parents and even, in his most intimate conversations, try—not always successfully—to explain just what it was that he experienced in homosexual encounters.

When Brown suggested that Hart might want to settle nearby, it was almost as if an impossible dream had come true. It must have seemed to Hart that he was to be an auxiliary to a couple —a part of their life, yet free to lead his own life in his own way. But he couldn't afford the luxury of his dream unless, by some miracle, his family could be persuaded to find a way to subsidize him for at least part of each year. Before he was finished, he tackled, one after another, mother, grandmother, father, and aunt. Each offered good wishes and good advice, and his father contributed $50 toward current living expenses. But the dream remained a dream.

The scheme he suggested to his mother was perhaps the most ingenious of all. Grace, who had been seriously ill during the spring, was in Chicago visiting her wealthiest friends. Perhaps, Hart suggested, she could persuade them to support her starving artist-son.

> Have a good time in Chicago, and, by the way, why don't you explain my case to the Ross's—that is,—if any opportunity appears. They give thousands to charities every year—and boast about being patrons of art. Why don't they keep some artist who is trying to live—and still get something done? A small allowance for me six months of the year would mean almost nothing to them—and it would keep me alive and productive in some cheap place in the country. You might mention Frank's and O'Neill's and Anderson's admiration for my work, —and that I have a book about to be published. . . .
>
> Everyone thinks it a crime the way I have been treated. I'd be glad to work six or eight months of the year if I could have the remaining time for my natural creative activity. Please see what you can do about this.

Grace did nothing.

Hart's approach to his grandmother was a bit more devious. He knew how concerned she was about his health, and in letter after letter he stressed his improved eating, sleeping, and breathing habits. He also dropped increasingly broad hints that a country retreat might save him from the destructive horrors of New York City. In July, for example, he noted:

> This is the kind of place I am going to have when I can afford it. Perfect quiet and rolling hills, almost mountains, all around —with apple orchards and lovely groves of trees and rocky glens all about the house. . . . Brown has even been so nice as to offer me a strip of land as my own and a great pile of cut

timber to build me a cabin—if I will stay here with him and Sue. You can't beat his affectionate generosity in any friend on earth. I wish you could know Sue, also. Well, someday you will, I'm sure, as I'm not likely to lose my enthusiasm for them very soon. . . . If I could pay my share in household expenses here I should like to stay all summer as I have certainly been made to feel extremely welcome. Otherwise I can't go on accepting things as they are.

But it had taken every penny of his grandmother's spare cash to send Grace to Chicago; and Grace herself, as Hart's grandmother made clear, had by now run through everything she had. Her medical bills had cleaned out her savings, and—in spite of the temporary happiness Chicago might be giving her—the prospects for her health looked none too good.

I think the reason she is in the shape she is is because she is so homesick to see you and to help you but she hasn't a cent to help herself—and I am trying to do all I can for her but it is mighty little and that won't be long—but there is always a way out, someway—and I am going to know that if we live right, we are not going to suffer.

Be a good boy dear and write me soon all about your dear self—

Love by the bushell<br>Grandma

The hardest letter was, of course, the one to C.A. Yet there had been moments of unexpected generosity, and perhaps if the hint were phrased just right, C.A. might come through with the wherewithal for a cabin in the wilderness.

I left Sweet's Catalogues as I had expected, about two weeks after your visit. No raise in sight and the heat and rose fever getting on my nerves. There is, to my great relief, none of that pestilence up here—on account of the high altitude, I suppose, and I have been having great days out of doors, working in the garden and painting the house, etc. I feel about made over.

I could stay here indefinitely as far as my hosts are concerned; they have even offered me a strip of land and the timber wherewith to build me a comfortable cabin, but one can't live long on ferns and wintergreen, and so I suppose I'll be jogging back to New York in about three weeks. I'll probably take a boat job then and say good-bye to the U.S. for awhile.

But even before Hart's father had the chance to answer (he did not offer to help Hart finance the cabin), the blow Hart had for years been dreading finally came. The Cleveland house was to be sold—and soon: just six days after Hart's twenty-sixth birthday. He would be needed, his mother made clear, in

Cleveland; the house had to be emptied before the first of September.

Hart dreaded going back to Cleveland; yet in one respect he was anxious to go. Though there was now no way of saving for himself and his family the home he loved and could never bear to stay in, there was at least a chance that he could persuade his mother and grandmother to keep their property on the Isle of Pines. All that year negotiations between the governments of the United States and Cuba had gone on regarding the return of the island to Cuba. Grace and her mother, like many other American owners, were convinced they should sell quickly and get out. Hart was quite as convinced that this would be the worse possible move. There, at least, an anchor might hold; a piece of sustaining land might allow him to function as he needed to function. "Someone was telling me about reading that the paper had left the Island and that settlers were pulling up by the wholesale," he had written home earlier in the spring.

> Have you got any such news as yet? It all sounds perfectly plausible to me. But a few Americans less on the Island would certainly not spoil it for me, and we're all fed up on papers anyhow. For heaven's sake let us not donate the place to charity—better let it rot and keep the land. To own a grass plot even that far away gives one a relieved feeling . . .

For over a year, he had been encouraging his mother and grandmother to take pictures of the Cleveland house and yard. He wanted to preserve it in all seasons and shadows. ("The photos of the cherry tree in bloom were a joy to have and keep. I liked especially the one with yourself, Grace, standing underneath. The attitude and expression you took were gracious and lovely. The tree and the entire yard, for all that, have a great place in my memories, and now that the place is liable to be sold at any time I'm especially glad to have the pictures.") Now, with arrangements for the sale virtually completed, there was nothing left for Hart but to make private farewells. "I would like to say 'goodbye' to the property (wherein have occurred so many intense experiences of my life) and I would like to sort out a few articles for preservation that have especial personal associations for me."

Hart's five days in New York on his way to Cleveland convinced him that the sooner he got back to Tory Hill and "Robber's Rocks" (by now Brown's house had been christened), the better. "After the quiet and freshness of the country the New York or rather Manhattan mid-summer seems more than ever intolerable," he wrote Waldo Frank. "Rather ghastly, in fact. But Cleveland won't be much better." He stayed at his old room in Brooklyn Heights, seeing a little of Emil Opffer, who had now taken over publication of *Nordlyset*, the Danish-American newspaper his father had started. But by now Hart's earlier emotional involvement seemed to have drifted into casual friendship, and he spent little more time with Emil than with other friends. He talked briefly to Jean Toomer and Gorham Munson, who offered him a letter of introduction for a possible publicity job with Henry McBride; he joined Sam Loveman for dinner and for a long walk on which he talked out his worries about his mother and grandmother; he checked in with everyone he could locate. Nobody struck Hart as especially happy or especially well:

> Dos Passos has just come back from the hospital, after about two months of some influenza complication which has almost finished him. Cummings looks bilious and harried. His connections with Vanity Fair are broken and like the rest of us he is looking for pennies. Jimmy Light has just sailed past Columbia Hts. for England where he expects to put on some O'Neill plays.

Gloomy at the thought that in Cleveland a routine of deception and money-grubbing would begin, Hart settled down to drink his problems out of sight. ("I can't at present see my way to make any definite plans without risking some kind of unpleasant entanglement," Hart had written Waldo Frank just before leaving Brown's place. "I wish that 'wile' and 'guile' were easier instruments for my imagination to use!") Hart's binge was, however, only temporarily satisfying, and the physical suffering that it induced was enough to bring him to swear off liquor for a while. "I cannot resist longer in describing my torments from my week of debauchery (wine-bibbing only) (O yes, there was one pleasant occasion—) enroute through NY," he wrote Bill and Sue, weeks after. "I'm just getting over it, and am still on the strictest diet. It has led to a final resolution to hop the water wagon until my next birthday, at which time I shall bound down with a crash—but not until then! What is life without a bladder!"

Hart returned home with mixed feelings, drawn there by a desire to see the Rychtariks and Bill Sommer and especially anxious to spend as much time as he could with his grandmother, now well into her eighties. Her fondness for Hart never slackened, nor his for her. Her letters had filled him with sadness, as more and more she focused on her death. Though she wrote about drives in the country with Charles and Grace, her mind was on her grandson, not the scenery.

> We rode 155 miles that day—. We had a beautiful day. No dust, just cool enough to enjoy every minute—but dear don't you know we missed having you with us? We miss you *all the time*. It isn't right for us to be separated so long. We must ar-

range to see each other oftener. These precious years are going so fast, and I want to see you oftener . . .

Hart's principal business at home, however, involved problems that had to be thrashed out with Grace. She had made up her mind to use the money her mother would get from the sale of the house to speculate in Florida real estate. Once she made a killing in the Florida boom, she had written her son, all their problems would be solved. She had an inside "tip," she explained, that a section near Miami would soon be developed. If she put into it every penny they had, within months the money would be doubled. As a bonus, she and her mother would have the pleasure of a winter in the Florida sun.

Hart did his best to head off the scheme. In a long letter, he begged her to reconsider or at least wait until he arrived in Cleveland before committing herself.

This Florida plan of yours prompts me to worry a little, Grace. You must certainly be cautious about investing your money there the way things are going at present. Of course I have been hearing all that you have about the tremendous sums exchanged there in real estate, and maybe more than you. That information is certainly nothing that one has to be "tipped on" these days. Everyone—even the farmers around here—are scraping their coins together and rushing down to Miami to buy little lots, and I know well enough that at least *some people* have made and are making fortunes there. But doesn't such a great campaign of advertising as this now seems to be—doesn't it arouse your suspicions as to the validity of the proposition to the small investor? Remember, Grace, that the stock market is run on the same plan and with the same tactics—and the daily crop of suckers can be reaped in other fields and byways than Wall, and often is. If you had thought of investing in Miami property a year or so ago it would undoubtedly have meant a considerable profit. But—as I see the situation now—the whole proposition there is like a whirling roulette wheel that with every revolution spins a higher figure—but which has already begun to slow down. I don't see how the situation can be otherwise when there has been such a wholesale flux of gamblers to the place as there already has been. For certainly there is a limit to the value of property—and there is a limit to the present national craze of flocking to Miami. I may be wrong, of course, but it seems to me that most of the fruit down there has been picked up already. . . . In such "gold rushes" watch out for the boom psychology that animates everyone concerned—even the losers—into bursting their voices with salutary legends of their luck and the general prospects of the place. It amounts to as much a conspiracy as

though they had all sat down together at a great mass meeting
and agreed to swear they each saw Jesus bathing on the beach.

Hart's alternate suggestion was the one he always made: if Grace
really needed a trip south, she should go to the Isle of Pines.
But Grace, as he found out when he arrived home, was as dedicated to living in Miami as Hart was to living anywhere except
Cleveland.

The labors of packing up and selling off what amounted to
two complete households of furniture did not help Grace's temper.
Sometime during his visit she told Hart that she could never stand
living with him for more than short periods. And when Mrs.
Hart, who had nursed Grace through three unrelated spring ailments, fell ill, Grace screamed that she had had all she could stand
of a nagging old mother and an ungrateful son. It was at this
point, Hart later told friends, that he was put in charge of bedpans
and hot-water bottles.

It was easier, finally, to give in to Grace than to try to reason
with her. Florida would, of course, be the best place for both
ladies.

"I have been trying to get time and clarity to write you for
the last two weeks," Hart wrote Waldo Frank,

> . . . but the nightmare hurly-burly and confusion here inter-
> cepted me consistently. Three more weeks of it and I shall be
> able to get back to Brown's place in the country and collect my-
> self. Our old home will be rented by its new owner to a fra-
> ternity, my mother and grandmother will be leaving for Miami,
> and Cleveland will become for me, I hope, more a myth of
> remembrance than a reality, excepting that my "myth" of a
> father will still make chocolates here.

As piece after piece of furniture was carted away, the house
took on a strange bareness—almost as if it were drifting toward
the lost past when Grace and Hart and C.A. had been moving
furniture in, preparing to make a "fresh start" on a very unsound
marriage.

Although much of the household goods went into storage, some
things never to emerge in Hart's lifetime and in Grace's lifetime
only when they were sold for storage charges, Hart's possessions
had somehow to be "available." Yet he had no place to store
them and there was little likelihood that he would have in the
near future. Nevertheless, he fought for everything, arguing
with his mother that sometime he would certainly want his bed,
his chair, his bookcase, his desk. He won the battle of the desk.
He couldn't be talked out of his books. He even triumphantly preserved one box of phonograph records. But there was no way to
save his tower bedroom. Depressed, he marched across the

street, backing onto the apartment-house lawn where his grandfather Crane's house had once stood, to take a last photograph.
And in his bedroom he found a dozen picture postcards of the
house, which he sent to his best friends, photographs of "the vanishing stronghold (see other side)." On Bill Brown's, Hart drew a
firm arrow toward his attic room, the "ivory tower" that had enclosed his childhood; "Sanctum de la tour," he scrawled across
the face of the card. On the card to Munson, Hart recalled the
visit that had been so productive for both of them: "Perhaps you
would like a picture of the departing 'tower'—in which you
worked for a while."

By the third week of August, so much had been sold or given
away, and so wildly, that Hart resorted to dark-of-the-night
"thefts" of the few remaining treasures. "I only hope I shall be able
to get away with another Indian rug," he wrote Bill Brown.

> The last was a pretty clean haul, nobody having missed the
> article even yet,—which is possibly an improvement even on
> my biscuit snatching famous by this time at Sherman central
> emporium. But there is so much hysteria around here that I
> doubt it would be noticed much if the house slid en masse for
> fifty feet. . . . Meanwhile you must begin plans for an exten-
> sion to your house to accommodate the Crane antiquities, por-
> traits, libraries and knick knacks from Halifax.

What he shipped off to Brown seemed little enough: "5 cases
of books; 1 trunk (filled with blankets, china, pictures, etc.); 1
desk; 1 chair." Seeing his Cleveland life reduced to objects left
him a little awed, a little frightened. "Believe me," he wrote
Brown, "I'm in a strange state."

Hart had hoped to have long talks with each of his old friends in
Cleveland. He would be there, after all, nearly a month and a half.
Yet, as it worked out, nearly all his free time was devoted to his
family—and half a dozen sessions at the dentist. He did manage
one quick visit with Charles Harris, a fine full day with Bill Sommer, and—toward the end of his stay—a number of meetings
with the Rychtariks; but these were his only escapes from family worries and family responsibilities.

The "one bright afternoon" with Sommer was in some ways,
as Hart wrote Waldo Frank, the happiest of the six weeks.

> The old baldpate was asleep on a sofa when I looked through
> the screen door and knocked. Arose a great bulk in white un-
> dershirt and white duck pants—the black eyes revolving in the
> pallid or rather, dusty-white miller face like a sardonic Pier-
> rot's. The few hours I was there were spent with him out in the
> old school-house studio, surrounded by a flower garden and
> filled with plentiful new wonders of line and color. I wish you
> could have seen several of the oil childrens' portraits that he has

been doing! And there is a line drawing of a head and hand that I am bringing back to New York that you will greatly care for. While we were both chewing, smoking and listening to the crickets I finally found out why Sommer has been so remiss about joining in with me in my several efforts to expose him to fame and "fortune." He hates to let his pictures leave him. Against that impasse, I guess, nobody's efforts will be of much avail. It's just as well, of course, if he has triumphed over certain kinds of hope. I admit that I haven't, at least not entirely. I still feel the need of some kind of audience.

There was, of course, every reason for Sommer to be pleased with his own work. He had always had a superb sense of line and an extraordinary feel for composition; but now a new kind of life was entering his painting. He was fast approaching his peak, and he must have had a luxurious delight in his own facility. Crane recognized in Sommer an artist who had already accomplished what Crane knew—given the right time and place—he could also accomplish.

But Crane—his belongings reduced to a few crates on a railway siding—had nothing at all in the way of "place." Sommer, "at his country place," had what Crane yearned for. "I was almost made to feel as I have on Tory Hill," Hart wrote Brown. "The country around his place ('Brandywine') is so similar to yours." Now more than ever, Hart realized that what he wanted was a country home of his own. And he again set about getting one.

Two days before he left Cleveland, he got a hasty note from Sue Jenkins saying that an eighty-acre tract near Tory Hill was available for $400 and that "Uncle Charlie" Jennings, Brown's landlord, would loan him $200 on a three-year mortgage. "There are several fine sites on it, and enough trees to make a log cabin, if you wished—certainly enough stones to build a stone house," Sue reported. "I doubt if another such opportunity will ever be found in this section of the country. . . . Bill is very anxious to have you get this place. Jennings has taken a great shine to you, apparently. He told us that this year he would press cider only for himself, us and you. . . . To the naked eye Jennings looked perfectly sober, and the offer was made in the presence of Bill, me and his wife."

Hart nearly went wild in his efforts to raise the remaining $200. He began by tackling his mother and grandmother, but Grace pointed out that they would need every penny from the sale of the house to get established in Florida. In any event, she argued, Hart was hardly in a position to take on more debts. He turned next to his Aunt Zell, begging her to keep his request confidential. Zell proved no more interested in his proposition than Grace, however—and went on, apparently, to recommend that Hart find a good job and settle down. Her letter arrived soon after he reached New York. "I had expected a refusal," he wrote the Rychtariks,

> but I'll be damned if I had calculated on such a lot of insulting assumptions and advice as she packed onto me. The letter is enclosed for your amusement. It is a perfect document of typical American conduct and should be preserved in a museum. Well, I'm through with her. In a way, too—it's a relief. There need be no more useless simpering, smiles and hypocritical assumptions between us. In other ways, too, the Cleveland trip did me good by opening my eyes more fully than ever. I'm glad of it on the whole. My aunt knows what I think of her by this time: I answered at once.

By this time Hart was running out of people to whom he could appeal. He had hoped to turn to O'Neill, but he was neither in Ridgefield nor in New York City. Another friend, unnamed— my guess is Stewart Mitchell—was also out of town and not expected back for some time.

"I am so afraid that the land up there will get away from me before I get there that I can hardly sleep nights," he wrote the Rychtariks; and though he knew they couldn't afford to lend him money, he finally accepted the offer they had made in Cleveland: if everything else failed, somehow they would scrape up the cash. "If I can hear from you by next Friday or early the following week it will be a Godsend. . . . I shall write you again as soon as I get there and look the situation over."

When Crane reached Brown's place, the situation had changed. The land he was hoping for had been put into the hands of a real-estate agent and another offer had been made for it. For several days Hart paced Brown's lawn, afraid to put in a bid and so raise the price of the land, afraid to let it go without an effort. Then Rychtarik's check for $225 arrived.

And then a miracle occurred. Not the piece he wanted but a better one—at half the price—suddenly was available just across the state line, in Connecticut. Hart got off a jubilant note to the Rychtariks.

> A friend of Brown's, Miss Bina Flynn, has just bought a lovely place within a half mile from Brown's place, wonderful old Dutch house in good condition and built about the time of the American Revolution and with 160 acres of land around it. She needs money to help pay for it and has offered me 20 acres of the best of her land for $200.00. The piece that I have picked to buy is on the top slopes of a hill that overlooks the valley and it contains several open fields and a great deal of forest land. As it is much more convenient (within better access from the main road) and as it contains no useless swamps or

wasteland as the other property included I think I am getting as much of a bargain, if not more. Twenty acres is plenty to spread out in anyway, and there will be plenty of room on it for whatever place you would want, too.

Miss Flynn is out here today transacting the purchase of her property and I expect to settle with her very soon. More and more I become convinced that this is the only way for me to live, that is, when I can make arrangements to afford it as a permanent way of living, and I am sort of planning to come out here next summer and put up a temporary cabin which will at least do during the warm weather. I shall roll in the grass with prayers and pleasure when I really get this tract of land for my very own.

On October 13, 1925, Hart got his "twenty beautiful acres of country land," his "anchorage," the piece of earth that was supposed to be roothold and sanctuary against the chaos and disorder of his life.

And he needed it. He was about to enter on a dreadful time, weeks when it must have seemed as if all his worst fears would be realized: that he would be torn from all connections, disowned by mother and father, rejected by both families, forced finally to stand completely alone in a world in which he could find no kind of employment. Though he would later go through worse ones, the six weeks from the middle of October until the first of December were more agonizing than anything that had come before.

# 22

Perhaps Hart's bad time seemed so very bad because it represented such a fall from the joys of Tory Hill. For he had returned to Brown's farmhouse, after the chaos of his Cleveland expedition, as if he were returning to a lost paradise.

Cleveland had been a nightmare of arguments and illnesses and sleepless nights. And five days in New York seemed nothing more than a busy unreality of quick visits to friends and heroic feats of self-control. Hart, still gallantly on the wagon, had been proud of himself. Not even Emil's invitation to visit a Danish ship for dinner followed by a "spree on the real stuff" ("Those shipboard dinners are marvelous affairs from all I have heard!") could lure Hart from the path of temporary virtue. ("I was too afraid of it to go along.")

What he yearned for was what he found when he returned to the country—open space; friendship; a relaxed life, calm and happy. "I'm feeling, gradually, myself again," he wrote the Rychtariks. "I walked 14 miles through the hills and back day before yesterday. The air is sharp, the wood smells so good burning in the fireplace, the trees are beginning to turn the most wonderful colors." Even though there had been a light frost, the garden he had helped plant that spring was still productive. "I had a regular spree one day on tomatoes and paid for it dearly," he wrote at the end of his first week back. During most of his autumn visit, Hart managed to confine his sprees to fruits and vegetables. "When I arrived I found . . . a large crock of home-made ale that just makes your mouth water. Bill and I sat late by the fire last night—but he was the only one to retire tipsy. I couldn't be tempted by the best cider in the world."

Day after perfect day drifted by. Even when a "lively" crowd of weekend visitors showed up at Eleanor Fitzgerald's place, or when Emil arrived to visit his mother, who had just bought a house "in easy sight just across the valley from us here," Hart limited himself to discreet sips of Bill's ale. Hart was drunk with the land itself, and he could manage without alcohol. Every few days he would hike up to the hill he was purchasing from Bina Flynn and come home to write friends progress reports on the changes of leaf color, the bite of frost in the air.

Soon, Hart knew, he would have to return to New York and to his job hunt. Soon he would have to get in touch with his mother, who might already have left for Florida and whose strange silence —he had had no letters at all—was threatening his hard-won calm. But the calm held marvelously and he sank into it, postponing until the last possible minute his departure from the healing, luxurious land.

> Today it is raining, but the ten days before it have been as divine as anyone could wish for. We have had big fires in the evenings, long walks, big meals (almost entirely of lettuce, carrots, beets, turnips, squash etc. just taken from the garden). Sue seems to be very contented out here and is busy every moment making jellies, jams, pickles, etc. The hills are covered with wild grapes, elderberries and apple orchards. Don't you think the quince is a beautiful fruit? There are about a dozen quince trees on Brown's property—all loaded with their sort of kid glove golden fruit. Yesterday we had a great time making six gallons of ale. It must ripen for about five days in a warm corner of the chimney in a huge crock, and then we can begin to drink it. Brown also has a complete distilling outfit out in the shed. He makes wonderful apple jack from cider. But this is a forbidden drink for me these days!
>
> All my furniture and things arrived in perfect condition. In addition I have been making tables and cupboards from old loose wood that has been lying around for years. They really look like antiques, all right! But I do love the weather stains and silver streaks on the surfaces. Most of the wood is oak and quite strong.
>
> So you see how the days go . . . In addition I am getting back to enough poise to read a good deal. It's funny! Here I've been for over two weeks, now, and without a cent of money to my name. But I haven't felt uncomfortable by any means. I know I can go back to a job now with a much better feeling of independence than before.

When Hart did go back, however, it was not to a job; and his feeling of independence soon became a feeling of isolation.

Once arrived in New York, he celebrated the purchase of his land. In no time flat, celebration put an end to abstinence and for nearly a week Hart roamed from Village party to Village party. One night he went out with friends from Woodstock who, he reported to Brown, "nearly killed me . . . with some abominable apple jack." One other night, he dropped in on Sam Loveman and a group of friends, among them Howard Lovecraft.

At one time Loveman had a caller in the person of his bibulous fellow-poet Hart Crane, (formerly of Cleveland) who was just back from the country and only about ¼ "lit up" by his beloved booze. Poor Crane! A real poet and a man of taste, descendant of an ancient Connecticut family and a gentleman to his finger-tips, but the slave of dissipated habits which will soon ruin both his constitution and his still striking handsomeness! Crane left after about an hour, and the meeting proceeded. . . .

During several of these nights of wandering, he found himself in the company of the poet Laura Riding (Laura Gottschalk); and for a while he encouraged his friends to speculate about a romance.

There have been numerous "celebrations" besides the already recounted one (by Bina) on the great transaction, and the Punch Palazzo has had due patronage. The engrossing female at most of these has been "Rideschalk-Godding," as I have come to call her, and thus far the earnest ghost of acidosis has been kept well hence.

Hart had no trouble filling his evenings. Emil took him to see *Arms and the Man*, which Hart found "very amusing, if ancient." And on other nights he visited the Tates, parents of a newborn girl. It was the days Crane hated, the long waits to be interviewed for jobs that did not come through, the meetings with magazine editors he did not particularly care for, but who just might be willing to assign a little book reviewing. "Mrs. Boving [Emil's mother] tells me you have been pressing apples, grapes and everything in sight," Hart wrote Brown. "I wish I could be with you. The city certainly is not pleasant for long."

Though his disappointments and dissipations had so far been only minor ones, Hart was already drawing on his Tory Hill memories and the reality of his piece of land to get him through the meaningless days and hectic nights. "I have been back in town for about two weeks now," he wrote Bill Sommer, "looking around for a job for the winter." But it was Tory Hill that was on his mind. (Crane, who did not pay taxes but who did get mail, always described Brown's farmhouse and Addie Turner's, both on South Quaker Hill, in terms of their Patterson postal address. The houses were in Pawling; Hart always spoke of them as in Patterson. To avoid confusion I shall follow his practice.)

This is the pleasantest time of the year in New York, but I was sorry to have to leave the fields and woods and my cosy friends, Sue and Bill, and their delightful abode with open fireplaces,—cider and free life. There are only about two places in America (sifting them all down) where I care to live. One of them is here, back in the room I told you about, overlooking the terrific N.Y. skyline, bay, etc. and the other is out there near

Patterson, N.Y. in the lower valleys of the Berkshires. And even though I haven't a cent now and am on others' charity, it feels good to know that I have secured 20 acres out there for my very own. On top of a hill with a wonderful view over two valleys, and mostly covered with splendid woodland, etc. Next spring I plan to go back there and put up a small cabin. From that time onward, even though I may have to live elsewhere for my living, I'll at least feel that I have "headquarters"—a place to keep my books and pictures without worrying about landlords and rent and moving, and a place to come to—no matter how poor I am—to think, read and create. For it costs almost nothing to live there if you have your own garden.

Of the jobs that did not materialize, the one that perhaps most disappointed Crane was on a ship bound for Martinique.

I just missed getting the pick of jobs of the S. Am. line, last steamer—said occupation being deck yeoman at 20 minutes work a day, all freedom of ship, mess with officers or any first class passengers that seemed colloquial, white uniform, brass buttons, cap, meditation on the sun deck all day long, and seventy-five dollars a month clear sailing! The chief officer had already approved me, but before I could get over to the offices for final approbation they had already sent someone else over to the ship. We must have passed under the river. However, I noticed that my questionnaire (filed last June) had won an OK sign in the upper right corner, and I have been told to come around again on the 26th when the next boat arrives. I'm not waiting for that, however, as I need instant cash and there is not one chance in a hundred of a similar vacancy soon.

The little notebook in which Hart kept track of what he owed friends was beginning to accumulate an agonizingly long list of uncrossed-out items.

When his final lead, to an advertising job, petered out, Hart began an all-out campaign to put into shape and sell his few unpublished poems. Though he knew these couldn't yield more than a few dollars each, a few dollars would allow him the self-respect of a meal bought with his own funds.

Because of his work on *White Buildings*, Hart had made little effort to place his most recent poetry. Allen Tate, however, as an editor of *The Fugitive*, had taken for the September issue the fragile lyric "Legend," that mirroring gesture toward self-definition which Hart had been working on the preceding October, and "Paraphrase," a poem which defines the fear of death in terms satisfactory both to medicine and to prosody. When Crane came to working up recent poems, therefore, all he had to work up were

"Lachrymae Christi," which Tate accepted for the December *Fugitive,* and two products of the summer: "The Wine Menagerie" and "Passage."

Both these poems were consequences of that remarkable Fourth of July party at Bill Brown's house. Soon after Hart's "cannibal" dance, Malcolm Cowley remembered, "with the nail keg still perched on his head and his face still daubed with house paint, red and brown, he sat by the lilacs in the dooryard, meditatively pouring a box of salt on the phonograph." Near him was a cedar tree, and Hart would occasionally glance up into its branches. "One of the wives, pregnant and stark sober, heard him repeating time and again: 'Where the cedar leaf divides the sky . . . where the cedar leaf divides the sky . . . I was promised an improved infancy.'" These lines, of course, begin "Passage." By Sunday afternoon, "The Wine Menagerie" was also underway, "an intoxicated version," Cowley recalled, that "was nearly incomprehensible, except for a few magical phrases." Working to phonograph accompaniment, Hart assembled disjointed fragments that he had been collecting on scraps of paper over the preceding months.

When he was in Cleveland in August and early September, Hart had continued to work on these poems. Bert Ginther, who saw him at this time, remembered one evening in particular. "When Hart pressed the front door bell of Florence Manor, I pressed the door release and waited. And I heard Hart coming along the hallway to my apartment—and shouting with mirthful voice his derision of the imitation marble walls of the hallway. The words that Hart shouted are these: 'Painted emulsion of snow, eggs, yarn, coal, SHIT.' The last word fortissimo; and not *manure* as in 'The Wine Menagerie.'"

Under the pressures of poverty, however, Crane tamed his emulsion—and Marianne Moore tamed the whole menagerie. For when T. S. Eliot rejected the poem for *The Criterion,* Crane offered it to *The Dial.* By that time—the last week of November— he was desperate for cash. Marianne Moore said she would publish the poem if he would accept a few editorial changes. Crane, without a murmur of protest, agreed to the arrangement. Only after he left Miss Moore did he fret about his decision. He had already, he shouted to one friend after another, corrupted body and soul for the sake of physical survival; now he was being forced to corrupt his art. "The Dial bought my Wine Menagerie poem— but insisted (Marianne Moore did it) on changing it around and cutting it up until you would not even recognize it," he wrote the Rychtariks. "She even changed the title to 'Again.' What it all means now I can't make out, and I would never have consented to such an outrageous joke if I had not so desperately needed the twenty dollars." The more Hart talked about it, the more upset he became. Finally he turned to Matthew Josephson and begged for help. Josephson, much moved, volunteered to do what he could, at which point Hart threw himself on the Josephsons' bed and burst into a fit of tears, sobbing until he fell into a tossing sleep.

The rest of the story becomes a jumble of badly managed gestures of good will. Josephson wrote Miss Moore, offering to buy back the poem for what she had paid for it; Hart repudiated Josephson's letter; Kenneth Burke—Scofield Thayer's secretary on *The Dial*—was accused of being a "spy," though for whom and of what he was never sure; and Marianne Moore—genuinely unaware that her well-meant efforts to improve the poem had not been appreciated—couldn't understand what all the fuss was about. "Hart Crane complains of me? Well, I complain of *him*," she said, years later, in a *Paris Review* interview.

> He liked *The Dial* and we liked him—friends, and with certain tastes in common. He was in dire need of money. It seemed careless not to so much as ask if he might like to make some changes ("like" in quotations). His gratitude was ardent and later his repudiation of it commensurate. . . . He was so *anxious* to have us take that thing, and so *delighted.* "Well, if you would modify it a little," I said, "we would like it better."

The version that appeared in *The Dial* in the May 1926 issue was modified enough for Kenneth Burke to remark that Miss Moore had taken all the Wine out of the Menagerie.

Ultimately, Hart restored the original. In *White Buildings,* with its alcoholic companion poem, "Recitative," it helps prepare the reader for the imagery and theme of "Faustus and Helen." In Crane's *Collected Poems* it anticipates *The Bridge.* For the serpent that is transformed through "wine talons" into a creature of the "feathered skies" and the corrupt, flirting couple who are transformed through a "receptive smile" into innocents of "new purities" are recurring motifs of considerable importance in those major works.

It is the transforming wine, however, that is the central concer.. of "The Wine Menagerie," the wine that masks the speaker in "dominoes" not unlike those half-masks of costume balls and ancient rituals, dominoes which enable him, disguised, "to travel in a tear . . . within another's will." He is able, thanks to wine, to escape his own skin and experience the menagerie of animal lusts that drive other men and women. If, at the end, this Petrushka's make-believe world collapses and he exits alone, he has at least been permitted a vision of communion and a momentary taste of that innocence which flickers within even the most corrupt soul.

Like "The Wine Menagerie," "Passage" had been rewritten in Cleveland, where old photographs and old memories contributed to that "Memory" which in the poem Crane "com-

mitted to the page." He submitted the poem, as usual, to Marianne Moore, who rejected it. "We could not but be moved, as you
must know, by the rich imagination and the sensibility in your
poem, Passage. Its multiform content accounts, I suppose, for what
seems to us a lack of simplicity and cumulative force. We are
sorry to return it." Crane, who found her letter amusing, couldn't
resist quoting it to Waldo Frank—and then adding: "It seems
almost as though Miss Moore might be rather speaking of her
own poems with such terms . . ."

"Passage" was, for Crane, "the most interesting and conjec-
tural thing I have written," and he was hard put to accept it as
disorganized. In his letter to Frank he went out of his way to
stress what had apparently struck Miss Moore as its least distinguished element: "I'm particularly anxious to know what you
think of its form?"

At first glance, the "form" of the poem seems loose indeed, the
stanzas ranging from four to seven lines and the lines themselves
from dimeter to hexameter. Yet it is a tight structure, tight in exactly the same way that "Faustus and Helen," the "Voyages"
poems, and *The Bridge* are tight. That is, it is organized by the
double passage through time and space with which Crane's
reader should by this time have become familiar. The tem-
poral pattern is that of a day, a year, twelve years, probably a
lifetime, and perhaps an eon. The progress of day is worked out
in terms of dawn ("sapphire arenas"), afternoon with its length-
ening shadows, "evening," and night, when the significant con-
stellation Serpens swims "a vertex to the sun." Serpens, conveniently for the poem, is midway between the pole and the equator
and midway between the points where the sun appears on the
first day of spring and fall. The year and the dozen years are
suggested by the "dozen particular decimals of time," as well as by
a number of autobiographical references. The lifetime is suggested by the "improved infancy" that carries through to the
present, when time returns the narrator to the ravine in which
memory finally "breaks." And the eon is indicated by those "ages"
known to man that sweep from "the Ptolemies" to the "abyss"
of the future. Space is also carefully split up into its elemental
parts: earth (the "hills" and "valleys"), air ("entrainments of the
wind"), fire (that "burned" the summer), and water (the "sea"
itself and each of the "ravine," "rain," "fountains" and "beaches"
references).

The experience of "Passage" is, however, more than its machinery. The experience is that pathos felt by the remembering
man, the man who gathers up his past and discovers that his
progress through time and space has been nothing more than
"transience" and "fleeing," that his "improved infancy" has developed into corruption and questions. Like many of Crane's

best poems, this is an innocence-and-experience document, personal in its recollections of an Ohio boyhood, Crane's "stolen book," and his "too well-known biography," but universal in its picture of the "chimney-sooted heart of man," which can be refreshed by the "fountains" of ecstasy, driven wild by the "iron coffin" of deceit and smiling betrayal, terrorized by the "icy speeches" of winter, hatred, death.

Good as this poem seems now, in the difficult autumn of 1925 Crane could not find either an American or an English publisher for it. T. S. Eliot turned it down for *The Criterion* quite as firmly as Marianne Moore had for *The Dial*.

Nothing seemed to work out for Crane during this bad time. A project to translate some of his poetry into Hungarian—initiated during his Cleveland visit by a friend of the Rychtariks—produced translations but they were not published. An article by Allen Tate on the "Voyages" set that was intended to accompany the poems in *The Guardian*, a Philadelphia magazine, never appeared, though a disastrous advance announcement did. (The magazine folded before printing either the poems or the article.) "Since the last (yesterday) Guardian has come out *without* the Voyages I am thinking of trying to become a literary ex-patriot," Hart wrote the Browns. "It's just as tiresome as ever. This issue contains a lot of tommy-rot by Seaver and an 'announcement' in the bargain that reads unforgivably:—'Voyages, four remarkable poems by Allen Tate' will appear in the next issue!"

Even such brand-new poems as "At Melville's Tomb," begun on the morning of October 26 and revised each time an editor returned it, could find no publisher. Nor, for that matter, could Hart's book find a publisher. The manuscript of *White Buildings* had been circulating, in one form or another, for the better part of a year; though most editors found "promising" elements, it was always returned unaccepted.

Perhaps the most discouraging of the rejections was the one sent that summer by Hart's old friend Harrison Smith. Rejecting the book for Harcourt, Brace, he professed admiration for those passages he could understand but then went on to dissect in some detail "Recitative" and "Faustus and Helen," both of which, he explained, puzzled him. Finally, commenting that "one has to live in a mundane world," Smith turned down the manuscript.

So I am afraid that we will have to pass up "White Buildings," with a good deal of sorrow on my part because I feel certain that you are a genuine poet—and there are not many genuine poets lying around loose these days. . . . It is really the most perplexing kind of poetry. One reads it with a growing irritation, not at you but at himself, for the denseness of one's own intellect.

By midsummer even Crane was reading his manuscript with "a growing irritation," though not the sort Harrison Smith had felt. "I am dissatisfied with at least half the poems," Crane told Waldo Frank, though he went on to add that he could not revise endlessly. "Reason seems to dictate, then, a certain amount of necessary indifference, that is, if I'm ever to print any collection of poems before the grave."

Crane had, of course, done his best to be heartened by Frank's assurance that *White Buildings* "contains some of the truest poems ever written in our land" and by his certainty "that their publisher *exists*." Yet month after month went by and that publisher did not appear.

There seemed to be agonizing delays everywhere. Eugene O'Neill had volunteered to write "some kind of notice" for the book early in the summer, but by early autumn neither Crane nor Waldo Frank had succeeded in getting in touch with him. Horace Liveright, who had rejected the book in the spring but who had suggested that Crane let him look at it again a little later, was just as elusive. On October 21, when Waldo Frank did finally corner him and persuade him of the wisdom of Boni and Liveright's bringing out Crane's book, Liveright said he would do so only if O'Neill—still out of reach—would write "a preface or short foreword."

For weeks Hart, Frank, finally Liveright himself attempted to get a commitment from O'Neill. "They have lost so much money on the better kind of poetry (which simply *doesn't* sell these days)," Hart explained to Bill Sommer, "that they want to hook the book up with an illustrious name and catch the public that way as much as possible."

Finally O'Neill consented to tackle an introduction. But by this time Liveright had again soured on the idea; not even O'Neill's name, he decided in mid-November, could sell the volume.

Though Hart's poverty, his inability to find a job, and his publication misadventures were enough to depress him, the worst blow was to be his discovery that the Florida expedition of his mother and his grandmother had ended in disaster. Both women were eventually stranded in separate towns—Mrs. Hart in Winter Haven and Grace in Miami—both desperately ill.

Hart had been doubtful about the trip from the beginning. And Grace's first reports from Florida had done nothing to encourage him of its advisability. As soon as she arrived, she had set about "establishing" herself with local real-estate firms. Apparently her method was to hint that she would put her money into any corporation that would take her on as a saleswoman. In some communities, the plan might have been a sensible one. But Miami was a boom town and Grace was traveling in very fast company.

During her first few weeks in Miami, her letters to Mrs. Hart

were full of anecdotes about the young real-estate promoters who
had suddenly come into her life.

> There are men men men everywhere, young and old, and it
> has been my very good fortune to meet a number of very
> high type ones. One is connected with the Coral Gables out-
> fit—very high type, and is from Cleveland and knows who I
> am and many of my friends. He stands very close to the powers
> that be at Coral Gables, and is interested in getting me on the
> sales force in a high type plane and is getting the stage all set
> to introduce me to his boss at the right time. In the meantime,
> other things are presenting themselves—and I am trying to let
> it all soak in and determine if I really have an opportunity,
> just which is the best. These men have been wonderful to me
> and I go out to dinner with some of them every night. Last
> night I went to the Hotel Antilla at Coral Gables and danced
> and dined until 10:30—later to the beautiful new Coral Gables
> Country Club—for concert and more dancing, and always
> meeting more people. . . . Sunday I am going to drive to Palm
> Beach, Fort Lauderdale and Boca Raton. We will be gone all
> day and these two men (young chaps) are simply doing it
> without any idea of selling me property but simply because I
> expressed the wish that I could see it. . . . Send this letter to
> Hart. I will write him as soon as I can but time is too valuable
> now to spend in writing long letters. . . . I may be able to drive
> up to see you some time after you get to Winter Haven—be-
> cause if these men down here like you they will let you lead
> them around by the nose—

In letters of this sort, which came to him by way of his grandmother, Hart sometimes found a phrase or two of gratitude for
his own letters and once in a while an indication that his mother
remembered she was soon to be married ("I had a nice letter
from Hart today and a dear one from my beloved Chas. Bless his
heart—I think of him often. There is a side of this he would so
love—the wonderful evenings—palm trees flowers moonlight,
sea, and dancing. I will write him tomorrow"). But from her son's
point of view, far too much of Grace's correspondence was now
concerned with those armies of "men men men" she seemed
constantly to be dancing with. She disapproved, of course, of the
ways in which some of the lady real-estate dealers operated ("I
never would stoop to the kind of selling these women who are
down here are doing. They look like freaks—hang around the
hotel lobbies and approach men until the whole thing is quite
disgusting"). But Grace, Hart knew, was susceptible to flattery.
And soon, he was afraid, she might herself join the lobby ladies.

Most of Hart's correspondence was with his grandmother, who
was still in Cleveland, where she had recently suffered a very painful attack of acidosis. "I, of course, have not said a thing to

Grace about it," Hart told his grandmother; he urged her to be very careful of her diet and especially urged that, when she did go south, she stay in Winter Haven.

I'm glad to hear that you are going to such a lovely place, and on the other hand I hope you will be able to stay there as long as possible instead of rushing away to Miami—which sounds like a perfect madhouse to me. I don't even like the idea of Grace's staying there very long. It's not the kind of place for people like us. Meanwhile there is plenty to think about with the Isle of Pines property—I hope she stays there long enough to really inspect conditions and rest up a little from the insane flurry of a place like Miami.

When he wrote to Grace, Hart repeated, as delicately as possible, the same suggestions. He begged her to leave Miami, for he could not bring himself to ask her to stop flirting with strange men. "I hope you will give plenty of time to the Island in preference to this insane Florida territory. If I were you I wouldn't waste another minute or dollar around Miami. It isn't the place for people like us, at all."

Hart ended that letter of October 24: "Love, and take good care of yourself." As it turned out, love and good care were what Grace would be in need of, for she failed to take the ship to the Isle of Pines as she had intended and was soon too ill to write anyone anything. Hart continued to send letters to their island home, but after three weeks of silence on Grace's part he decided that she must have been offended by his good advice and by his hints that he was in need of financial assistance. ("No job has eventuated as yet," he had planted in one letter, "and I'm obliged to sleep in three different places and always dine as guest.")

He heard nothing from Grace but far too much from his grandmother. No sooner had she stepped onto the train that would take her to Winter Haven than she realized she was too ill for any sort of traveling. Though she wrote Grace a deceptive note about the "clean" train and the pretty flowers she saw on the way down, she confessed the truth of her situation to Hart.

Tuesday 8 p.m.

Dear Hart

Your good letter was a great joy to me today, for it has seemed as if I was deserted by God and man. Instead of the beautiful setting you placed me [in], I have not even been able to step outside the door since I came—and am in bed under a Dr's care, and have suffered more than language can express —and have had no letter from Grace—except a night telegram next morning I got here. I did not let her know my condition for I supposed I would be better very soon—so put the best side on—not to cause her worry—but did suppose she would write me. Every mail I have looked for word from you and her but you say she has gone to the Island, is the reason, and I would suppose she would have informed me before leaving. I never want to be caught this way again. Imagine how I feel to be here with none of my kin, a care on a friend, who has no girl, but she is very kind to me and Dr. says I will have to lie in bed a few days. . . . Don't worry. I'll be all right soon. Write me every day dear. I am so lonesome. . . .

Wed 9 a.m.

Had a fairly good night, and think I am on the mend but must keep off my feet until the bladder heals up which depends on how still I keep. It is tedious but not serious, Dr. says—

The sun is shining and everything is beautiful outside but quite cool from the effects of cold up north. I wish I could give you part of a beautiful bouquet of large red roses—half-blown. They are enough to make any one feel well to see them. A young lady sent them to me. They are just gorgeous.

And don't forget to write me often. You are the only one I am in touch with. Don't worry. I'm sure I will soon be all right. Can you read this?

Grandma

And then there was silence from Hart's grandmother as well as from his mother. Letter after letter would go out to them—and always silence in return. All sorts of wild fantasies now occurred to Hart. He told one friend he was sure that his mother had poisoned his grandmother's mind against him and that they were refusing to write because they were afraid he would ask for money. And he speculated to another friend about his grandmother's dying while his mother tripped the light fantastic in luxurious Miami. But, in fact, he knew nothing. And finally his own letters—which could chronicle nothing but poverty, hopelessness, and despair—also stopped.

He was now destitute; and he turned—as he always did when everything else failed—to the father he had so often disowned. Too upset to think of consequences, he wrote a foolish, angry letter, demanding and contemptuous.

Though C.A. was deeply offended—and said so—he sent Hart enough money to keep him alive. But he also made very clear that there was a limit to his patience.

I did not reply to your letter of November 4th, as in a letter where you ask money assistance from your own Father, I think it is quite unnecessary that you should stoop to refer to him as a disgruntled, narrow-minded commercialist. In other words I still appeal to the old adage "You cannot catch flies with vinegar."

It seemed to him, he said, that he and Hart were destined always "to travel different paths, and to have different ideas of what constitutes a wonderful existence." Though he did wish his son well in the "literary success" Hart had bragged about, C.A. found it impossible not to be upset by the tone of Hart's correspondence and by vague reports that drifted back from friends and relatives.

> Unfortunately you have to endure the parents you have until Providence shall provide you with others, but I have never written you a letter which upbraided you for your shortcomings, and I never expect to. . . .
>
> According to my narrowed and bigoted way of looking at things you have pawned your birth right to my accomplishments in life at a very low figure, but fortunately I have found another young man who wants to carry on my work and singularly enough seems to feel that it is worth while.
>
> Whether it is calling at my sisters or elsewhere, I learn your true opinion of my existence, and I have come to accept it as something which I cannot correct, at least at my advanced age. . . .
>
> Anyway it is a check that you want so I am enclosing you $50.00.

Harsh as parts of C.A.'s letter were, Hart valued it more than the check it contained. The fact that C.A. could take the trouble to be offended by his son's thoughtlessness was, Hart felt, a gesture of love and he said as much in the letter he wrote in return. While rifts of misunderstanding would continue to trouble them, it was really this Thanksgiving of 1925 that marked a new relationship between father and son. For Hart at last accepted the fact that, in spite of differences, affections and sympathies bound them to each other.

> I was very glad to hear from you and it was generous of you to thus come to my aid. The only pity is that artificial theories and principles have to come so much between us in what is, after all, a natural relationship of confidence and affection.
>
> You may not believe it, father, but in spite of what opinions you may hear that I have against you (and not knowing what is told you, I still refuse to acknowledge them either way) I still resent the fate that has seemed to justify them and God knows how much we all are secretly suffering from the alienations that have been somehow forced upon us. If we were all suddenly called to a kind of Universal Judgment I'm sure that we would see a lot of social defenses and disguises fall from each other and we would begin from that instant onward to really know and love each other.

I feel rather strange these days. The old house sold in Cleveland; Grandmother ill in Florida; Mother somewhere in Cuba or the Isle of Pines; and I not hearing from either of them for the past month. Altogether, it's enough to make one feel a little foot-loose in the world. But I'll have a job soon, and will probably be reassured in the mail that everything's alright. At such times, though, I realize how few we are and what a pity it is that we don't mean a little more to each other.

Though C.A.'s return letter was not quite so gracious as his son's, he was willing—gruffly at first—to accept Hart's gesture of love.

It may be that after a certain time you will get some of the cobwebs off of your eyes and realize that families while broken up and discarded really do mean something to us after you grow old and feel the coldness of the outside world.

Of course he still could not understand, he wrote, how Hart hoped to earn a living as a poet; but he was willing to be convinced. He felt that Hart had had far too little in the way of material reward to show for his literary triumphs. "It is just a question of whether Harold Crane can make a living following out his pet scheme of life or not. . . . So far as the success you claim for yourself having been already attained, and being the greatest in your class since 1852, I can hardly see it that way, but probably I am not informed."

Both son and father did their best to cut through dense webs of misunderstanding. "You made a statement in your former letter which I unqualifiedly denied," C.A. insisted.

I have never said that I was not interested in you. I have told you that I was not interested in your work, and I am not interested in it because it does not bring you a livelihood. I have used the expression before and again say it. Writing to most people should be an avocation not a vocation.

Their most serious differences, however, were the insubstantial ones: the insulting remarks that gossiping acquaintances carried from father to son, son to father. For, although the rumors had a basis in fact, they were not fact itself.

At least C.A. was now able to spell out what was troubling him.

For the past nine years you have had a very poor opinion of your Father and you haven't hesitated to feed the flame of discontent and continually pity yourself for having such an unsatisfactory parent.

For a while you even changed your name, but I note for some reason or other you have gone back to it.

One thing is certain. Your father can get along just as well without you as you can get along without him, and that is for you to find out, if you have not already arrived at that decision. . . .

No "Fate" has caused you to suffer from any existing conditions between us. That has just been a matter which you choose to build up in your consciousness and if it has gotten now to where it is difficult to see over it you yourself must tear it down and make the correction. . . .

I do hope that you will get better news from your mother, and you can rest assured that any advances you wish to make to me toward getting on more friendly terms with your Father will be met with a hearty response.

Before Hart could answer this letter, other blows fell. Mr. Curtis telephoned from Cleveland to say that Hart's mother and grandmother were bedridden and that he was leaving immediately for Florida to bring Mrs. Hart home. A series of jobs for which Hart had been interviewed fell through, all the polite discouraging letters arriving within a few days' time. And Liveright made one more "final" announcement that he would not bring out *White Buildings*.

Hart carried his father's letter about with him, forcing himself to read it and reread it. For after all, what had he accomplished? Unemployed, sponging off friends, he wandered streets he despised and despised himself for waterfront vigils that would bring him drunkenly home more lonely and more desperate than when he had shrugged abruptly into his overcoat to rush away from startled new acquaintances or ironically smiling old ones into the private darkness of winter nights. "This filthy mess" that his life had become must have seemed, on hangover mornings in late November, so meaningless, so corrupt, so hopeless that mere existence was a nightmare chore.

It was out of this chaos that on December 1 he wrote the Rychtariks:

I have kept putting off writing you because I wanted to have some kind of pleasant news to report, but it seems useless to defer any longer; I certainly have thought of you often enough . . .

The facts are hard, but true. I have not yet succeeded in finding myself a job, and even after trying every sort of position, like selling books in stores during the Christmas rush, ship jobs, etc., etc., and I have just been kept going by the charity of my friends. The nervous strain of it all has about floored me, and I feel as though the skin of my knees were quite worn off from bowing to so many people, being sniffed at (to see whether I had "personality" or not) etc. How I shall love it when, some day, I shall have a little hut built on my place in the country to live in—and get out of all this filthy mess!

Even the publication matter of my book of poems has not come through the way I had expected. O'Neill is writing the Foreword, after all, but he took so long to notify Liveright (the publisher) about it that I must now try to place it somewhere else. This may not be so hard, but it probably means that it will not come out until at least next autumn, and I had so hoped to have it printed before that . . .

So you see how it's been! I don't mean to wail, but it is hard to keep up and going sometimes. To make matters worse, my mother and grandmother have both been sick in bed (grandmother seriously) at Miami. . . . Neither of them have written me for many weeks, and I have even myself stopped writing them. They could have at least answered my letters, I think, and what it is that they are angry about I really don't know. Their whole trip has ended just as badly as (you'll remember) I predicted. And what my mother wants to remain down in that silly and expensive place for any longer I can't guess.

It was out of this chaos that he tried to persuade his father not to judge him but to love him.

Dear Father:

Your letter was appreciated in many respects and I don't want you to think that I wasn't glad to hear from you. But there were recriminations in it which assumed a basis for apologies and regrets on my part which I don't feel I at all suggested in my last letter and which I certainly cannot acknowledge now or later. In fact, you always seem to assume some dire kind of repentance whenever I write you or call on you, and so far as I know I have nothing in particular to repent. I simply said I was sorry that you could not see me in a clearer light, and it seems I shall have to go on lamenting that to some degree for the rest of my life. If I began to make recriminations on my behalf there wouldn't be any use writing at all, for though I have plenty to mention, I don't see what good it would be to either one of us to embark on a correspondence of that sort. My only complaint right now is that you seem determined to pursue such a course, and I can only say that if you persist I have no answers to offer. You and I could never restore our natural relationship of father and son by continually harping on all the unnatural and painful episodes that life has put between us via not only ourselves but other people during the last ten years, and if you are not willing to bury such hatchets and allow me, also, to do so, then I'll have to give up.

For the last six weeks I've been tramping the streets and being questioned, smelled and refused in various offices. Most places didn't have any work to offer. I've stepped even out of my line as advertising copywriter, down to jobs as low as twenty-five per week, but to no avail. My shoes are leaky, and my pockets are empty: I have helped to empty several other pockets, also. In fact I am a little discouraged. This afternoon I am stooping to do something that I know plenty of others have done whom I respect, but which I have somehow always edged away from. I am writing a certain internationally known banker who recently gave a friend of mine five thousand dollars to study painting in Paris, and I'm asking him to lend me enough money to spend the winter in the country where it is cheap to live and where I can produce some creative work without grinding my brains through six sausage machines a day beforehand. If he refuses me I shall either ask Eugene O'Neill who is now writing the Foreword to my book and won't refuse me for some help to that end, or I'll take to the sea for a while —for I'm certainly tired of the desolating mechanics of this office business, and it's only a matter of time, anyway, until I finish with it for good. I can live for ten dollars a week in the country and have decent sleep, sound health and a clear mind. I have already bought ten acres near here in Connecticut and it's just a matter of time until I have a cabin on it and have a garden and chickens. You see I have a plan for my life, after all. You probably don't think it's very ambitious, but I do. As Dr. Lytle said to me when I was last in Cleveland, "What does it all amount to if you aren't happy?" And I never yet have spent a happy day cooped up in an office having to calculate everything I said to please or flatter people that I seldom respected.

I wish you would write me something about yourself these days. Let's not argue any more.

Yours always,
Harold

# 23

The letter that Crane wrote to Otto Kahn just after he wrote his father was a shot in the dark, even though it had been initiated in conversations with Waldo Frank and Eugene O'Neill. I doubt, however, that Crane really expected Kahn to respond either as quickly or as generously as he did. Within three days of writing his letter, Hart had visited Kahn's home at the corner of Ninety-first Street and Fifth Avenue and after a three-hour interview had been offered not just the thousand-dollar loan he had requested but an additional thousand payable when the first loan ran out.

Hart's letter to Kahn had been scrupulously accurate. He told of the plans for the publication of his first volume, of his career as a copywriter, and of the difficulties of simultaneously writing poetry and advertising. ("What real writing I have done has had to be accomplished after office hours and sometimes at the risk of losing my position.") He told also of the past two months of fruitless job-seeking, "endeavoring by every means to secure work again as a copywriter," and of his very real hesitation in applying for a loan.

As a supplement to his letter, Hart had quoted brief notes specially prepared for him by Frank, Tate, and Munson and had volunteered as additional references O'Neill, James Light, and Eleanor Fitzgerald; at the interview, he added the names of Marianne Moore, Jane Heap, Harrison Smith, and Paul Rosenfeld. But it was neither his admirers nor his past accomplishments that Crane talked most about with Kahn, but rather his plans for *The Bridge*. As he explained to Kahn, with sufficient freedom he was sure he could produce a poem that would "enunciate a new cultural synthesis of values in terms of our America."

Kahn was impressed by the support Crane had been able to assemble and by his ambitious plans, but his real response—as he later told Waldo Frank—was to Crane himself, his enthusiasm, his freshness, his intensity.

When Hart walked out of Kahn's mansion late in the afternoon of December 6, he walked on air. Yet during the week that followed, a week of celebrations, packing, letter writing, and planning, he found it almost impossible to grasp the fact that for a little while at least he would be, as he told one friend, "paid" to produce poetry.

Some of his most burdensome worries also evaporated during that week. Two days after his conversation with Kahn, he at last heard from his mother, a cryptic telegram sent from Miami: "AM STILL CONFINED TO MY ROOM AT HOTEL STRAND MIAMI FLO AND AM STARVING FOR SOME NEWS FROM YOU WIRE ME AT ONCE ANY CHANGE OF ADDRESS AND HOW YOU ARE THAT I MAY WRITE YOU GRANDMOTHER BACK IN CLEVELAND AT MANOR ALL MY LOVE GRACE."

Hart's answer was full of anger that for "almost six weeks, now" neither Grace nor his grandmother had written him; no matter how sick they had been, he wrote his mother, they should somehow "have taken pen in hand and at least have written me once . . . especially, it seems to me, since you knew by my several last letters that I was having a difficult time and was without funds entirely." His letter summarized the bitterness of the summer in Cleveland, the "disgust" Grace had told him she felt toward him.

Yet tact triumphed over anger. Hart announced his good fortune and spelled out his plans for the immediate future; and Grace wired details of the mixed-up correspondence and of her own illness: "YOUR FIRST LETTER IN TWO MONTHS RECEIVED THIS MORNING AM ALMOST WILD WITH JOY OVER WONDERFUL NEWS AM STILL BEDRIDDEN AT STRAND I HAVE NURSE SOME TIME YOU WILL KNOW HOW VERY ILL I HAVE BEEN I ALWAYS WILL LOVE YOU HOPING TO RETURN TO CLEVELAND FOR XMAS WILL WRITE SOON WIRE ME ANSWER GRACE."

Assured of his mother's love, Hart went ahead with a tentative plan to join the Tates in the country. Even before Hart had approached Kahn, he had been invited to share the house that Tate had rented not far from Brown's Tory Hill farmhouse. But uncertain of an income and afraid that his mother's and grandmother's illnesses might force him to return to Cleveland, Hart had hesitated to accept the offer. Now that there was nothing to stand in his way, he paid back all but one of his debts—the substantial one to the Rychtariks for the purchase of his land—and packed his bags. His joy—as the following letter from Tate suggests— was infectious.

Dear Hart:
    You who have lately been plunged head over keel into miseries unutterable, and suffered the direst anguishment of body in conflict with the uncalculated measurements of the soul, you who have even been oftime sad, but are now the darling of princes and, as it were, the delight of kings—you I solicit for a little task most humble to be performed, should it be impossible for William and me to meet you Saturday at the station,

before you leave Patterson for these parts, a task moreover which, by its contrast with magnificence, will cast in bolder relief its quality, now so eminently possessed by you (the delight of kings), and isolate your flexible virtue for the instruction of men and the admiration of women; to wit: the purchase, in the shops of Patterson, of (1) one broom, (2) one pound of raisins, (3) a discreet quantity of carrots, (4) a similar portion of turnips, (5) and two pounds of dried apples. . . .

"And yet
The homeliest duties on himself did lay." . . .

The upstairs room is ready for you—the finest room in the house, albeit not the warmest. But add the little inner warmth by means of Bill's cider and vinelli, or of his beefsteak from the one-half cow which he bought recently, and you'll be all right. Altogether we should have a fine time.

We are all settled. The boxes came Monday. We unpacked yesterday. We seem always, thank heaven, to have been here!

We are expecting you Saturday: don't fail us. And do try, please, to have at least half your money left by the time you get here. You may need it to build houses, etc.

Love from us all,
Allen

Hart's first act on joining the Tates, nearly a week late, at Mrs. Addie Turner's house down the road from Brown's, was to begin the process of making his rooms—the two upstairs front bedrooms—livable. Since he planned to stay at Mrs. Turner's until he could erect on his own property "one of the small partitional houses that are made in sections," Hart had brought with him everything he owned. "My pictures and knickknacks look wonderfully jolly on the simple kalsomined walls," he wrote the Rychtariks, "and the books fairly glisten on the shelves." The larger of the two rooms Hart used as a study; he brought down from Brown's house his little drop-leaf desk and arranged in its pigeonholes his current correspondence. In this study, "spacious and light, in which the sun streams every morning," Hart was for months happily to "research" *The Bridge* and to get underway rough drafts and detailed outlines of a substantial part of it.

The smaller room was Hart's bedroom, and he filled it with the treasures he had packed up in Cleveland the summer before. "It is extremely pleasant to have familiar quilts, blankets and comforters on my bed," he wrote his grandmother. "Your knitted shawl, of the many colored insertions, has been admired by legions. I have it hanging outspread on the wall . . . It is so cheerful and homelike." "Around me always," he soon wrote Grace, he kept photographs of his grandmother. "Lovely old daguerreotypes taken at different times—which I snitched from the family archives at various times through the past!" For Mrs. Hart was still seriously ill and her grandson, thinking of her as a citizen of a more gracious time than his own, nearly turned his bedroom into a shrine dedicated to her memory. "It is marvelous the way my brave hearted good Grandmother keeps her character and fibre through everything. I am more proud of her than she knows!" Nothing pleased Hart more than when Mrs. Turner, who already regarded him as her favorite tenant, told him he could use as his own an antique "sleigh bed" something like one his grandmother had once described.

Mrs. Addie Turner and Hart had taken to each other immediately. "I think she was really more than half in love with him," Mrs. Tate told me. To Malcolm Cowley, Mrs. Turner was "a grass widow of sixty with a whining voice and a moderately kind heart." To Allen Tate, she was "a New England farm woman, and extraordinarily stupid, but motherly and kind—just a 'character.'" But for Crane, Addie Turner became a confidante with whom he could share troubles and joys. While the Tates were writing or doing chores about the house, Hart, more often than not, would be catching up on local gossip in the section of the house everyone called "Mrs. Turner's part." Here he would sit stroking one of her cats while she peeled potatoes. They would talk about the weather (it was especially cold that winter, so there was always weather to talk about), about the fact that Hart had been "swindled" in his purchase of a 50-gallon drum of "bad kerosene," and sometimes about the difficulties he had in adjusting to Mrs. Tate's writing habits. For he had established the disturbing custom of charging in for a chat with Caroline Gordon (Mrs. Tate) while she was at work on her novel; though she was too polite ever to ask him to leave, he did sense a coolness on her part.

I asked Allen Tate to tell me a little about a normal day's routine in Hart's Patterson life, but it was so uneventful that reconstructing it was something of a chore. "It's hard to remember," Tate said.

> When we lived up in the country, Caroline and I, he usually spent the day upstairs in his room. He'd come down at lunchtime, and we ate together, at first. Then later he had Mrs. Turner prepare his meals. He was very child-like. One of the difficulties of having him in the house was that he would suddenly burst into the room with some idea, be very enthusiastic, and interrupt other people at their work.
>
> Then in the evening, if there was anything to drink, he would get a little drunk. Now, up in the country it was sometimes hard to get anything but bootleg whiskey or rum. He liked rum particularly. We had cider, hard cider, and that was very bad for him. He would get very drunk on it, and be ill

afterwards. But usually the normal day, such as I described, he would work in the morning or read. Then as a rule he'd go to the Browns' house in the evening. On weekends people from New York would come up. But on the whole, it was a rather quiet time. Everybody was working at something.

In his early months there, it was certainly an aura of peace and mutual productivity that surrounded Crane. Almost cut off from the rest of the world by the cold that reduced to a minimum the supply of visitors, the Tates, Crane, and the Browns formed an island of literary activity. Holidays seemed only slightly more eventful than any other days. Hart's Christmas night letter to his father, like his New Year's Eve letter to the Rychtariks, told not of wild doings but of long walks. "From the window of my study on the second floor I can look out on a valley, white with the moonlight on the snow," Hart wrote.

> Flakes have been falling intermittently all day, then it cleared toward sunset, and a long walk over the hills was about the most pleasant thing imaginable. We had a regular Christmas Dinner at noon, I assisting Mrs. Tate to the extent of making cranberry sauce and plum pudding sauce which I managed to do pretty well considering my lack of previous experience.

New Year's Eve was as peaceful as Christmas. "Here I am at this date," he wrote the Rychtariks, "and sixty-six miles from a drink. Isn't it tragic! And there will not be a whistle or a shout to tell me it is a new year. I shall probably be fast asleep, unless I get scared and stay up blinking over a book—for it must be a bad omen to be asleep at the switch of the new twelvemonth."

"I pray for heavy storms," Hart wrote on New Year's Eve, for he had invested in a spectacular pair of snowshoes which he was desperate to try out. Eva Parker—a long-time resident of the area whose dry wit made her especially popular with Hart—recalled some of his practice sessions in Mrs. Turner's kitchen. One afternoon, she told me, he marched the whole half mile to Brown's, the snow less than an inch deep in the ruts of the dirt road.

When they arrived, the "heavy storms" arrived with a vengeance, and Hart's "scrumptious snow shoes" came down off the wall. Andy the mailman was unable to make his rounds; and Hart, "despite the amiable jeers from the natives," gallantly trudged a mile cross-country to the nearest main-road farm to pick up mail.

Much of that mail was pleasant enough—a postcard from Laura Riding, who, on board the ship that was taking her to England, looked back fondly to the "two mad weeks" of Hart's New York–Patterson transfer; a Christmas check from his father; letters from Grace and Mrs. Hart, first with small Christmas checks and then with thank-you notes for the substantial checks that Hart had sent them. Grace, still convalescent but returned to Cleveland, had settled down in a room at Wade Park Manor near the room in which day and night nurses tended her mother.

Though Hart ruefully told Charles Harris that as a consequence of Otto Kahn's support "my various relatives are becoming 'aesthetic' in their reactions!" he was really very pleased to be on good terms with all of them. Only his grandmother's continuing ill health now worried him; for the better part of January and into February he made a point of getting a letter off to her at least once a week.

Toward the end of January it seemed most unlikely that his grandmother would live, and Hart spent days indecisively readying himself for the call that would summon him to Cleveland. During much of this time he wandered from room to room of Mrs. Turner's "part," did his best to forget his troubles by joining Sue Jenkins and Slater Brown in the weekend parties that preceded the Browns' trip to Montreal, and took long country walks with Tate. Armed with "The White Powder Wonder," a shotgun Tate purchased, they would range the hills searching for small game. (If Crane's letters are an accurate index of their hunting prowess, their entire take consisted of one squirrel: "We had an exclamatory time over the stew it made.") Though Hart did devote himself conscientiously to background reading for *The Bridge*, he was having a hard time forcing himself to turn to the poem itself.

On a few lucky days, however, he wrote furiously. "One really has to keep one's self in such a keyed-up mood for the thing," he told his grandmother, "that no predictions can be made ahead as to whether one is going to have the wit to work on it steadily or not." In fact, however, its progress correlated closely with Mrs. Hart's illness. When her recovery seemed likely, Hart was able to turn to his poem; when she had a setback, the poem too had a setback. Just after Grace reports that Mrs. Hart is making a substantial improvement from a serious relapse ("she is getting along slowly toward where she was a week back"), Hart writes in return:

> There isn't much news—only the good news (to me!) that I've been at work in almost ecstatic mood for the last two days on my Bridge. I never felt such range and symphonic power before—and I'm so happy to have this first burst of substantiation since I had the good luck to be set free to build this structure of my dreams.

But when Grace writes one week later that she is utterly discouraged—both about her mother's recovery and about her remarrying—Hart drops all work on his poem for a holiday in New York.

It is impossible to underestimate the impact of Grace's letters on Hart or to fail to see how quickly he reacts to her comments on his grandmother and her sometimes very reckless gossip about his father. Though Grace almost always urged Hart to think well of C.A., she could not resist quoting remarks by him that, taken out of context, were bound to seem unbearably cutting. Hart had told both Tate and Brown that he felt things were at last settling down between him and C.A. and that he appreciated C.A.'s thoughtfulness toward his grandmother. Yet a casual aside in one of Grace's letters very neatly destroyed much of the affection that was being built up.

Yes, it is very amusing and very evident how your father feels —now that you have the interest and support of a prominent person. He said to me over the phone when I was thanking him for the roses—that he sent mother for Xmas,—he said— "I understand Harold has a new Daddy"—an expression which revealed a whole lot to me—(both jealousy and fear). I told him I thought it was about time and was of course very happy over it, not any more on account of the money, than for the recognition of your ability by a man of such "intelligence and influence."

I think he is just a little bit puzzled as to just how to act. Well, be as it may, I am glad through and through for your good fortune, and hope your attitude to all your family will be entirely free from bitterness, as it is a dissipating force you don't want to get into your thoughts now. This next year is a most important year and you want to satisfy your benefactor that you are using his help to the best of your ability no matter if you do not set the world on fire.

Grace's bouts of melancholia also inevitably set off a parallel reaction in Hart. The letter that provoked his New York trip was full of regrets about the sale of their Cleveland house; it catalogued her troubles in a fashion Hart was more than familiar with and which, when he was within reach of her, always sent both of them to the brink of hysteria.

What a tragic time I have had since leaving 1709—I've wished a good many times I were back in the old home. It is so much harder to be sick in a hotel. I am so broken down physically and mentally—so depressed and confused that I do not amount to anything, and it is hard for me to believe that I ever [can] take any interest in anything or ever be myself again. I feel so thoroughly whipped that I can't imagine my ever enthusing about anything again. If I can only get strong enough to get work and earn something in some way that I can become absorbed, I believe that will be my only salvation in the future, and it is going to be work or marry. I have never felt I would be willing to marry to escape work. Chas is wonderful—but he is not young and not rich—and there is going to be little left for me when mother goes.

One glance at this letter was all Hart needed. He had an invitation to drive down to New York with friends; he was packed and ready in a matter of hours.

His "vacation" served its purpose and Hart returned to Patterson pleasantly exhausted. Though he was away from the country for only five days, he was glad to get back to "the peace and beauty of cleanliness." As he explained to his mother, "They are obliged to use soft coal throughout the City now, and great clouds were blowing everywhere, sooty and dark."

New York had been "a swirl of errands and social engagements," from which one glorious afternoon emerged. Fortified with wine and carrying his Otto-Kahn-fattened checkbook, Hart stopped off to admire the primitive-art treasures housed in a Columbia Heights shop. He spent $100 that afternoon, Brown remembered, as he roamed about examining the big rhinoceros-hide shields and long spears. This was well before the vogue for primitive art had gathered force and Hart was able to make his money go a long way. "My study now is a picture to enjoy," he wrote his mother. "When I was in New York I bought some beautiful and rare Congo wood carvings—and added to my Sommer paintings and your photograph they make a marvelous room." The details of that room, in fact, were to become fixed in the memories of Hart's friends, just as later his room in Mexico was to make a vivid impression on visitors, and after his death, Hart's mother's room—at the end of a long corridor in a dingy hotel—was to blaze for Lorna Dietz with those of Hart's glittering treasures that Mrs. Crane had recovered from customs, from friends, from all the casual storage places into which Hart thrust them.

But in Patterson, six years from the date of his death, Hart was at the height of his pride and his power. He was determined to construct a world for himself in the two Patterson rooms, a place where music, light, art, fresh air, friendship, and wine could merge into poetry. Here he would entertain not only his own friends but visitors of the Tates' and the Browns' and, later, friends of the Cowleys'. The study, Cowley recalled, "was always neat when I saw it, the drop-leaf oak desk bare of papers, the books—not many of them—on their shelves, and the snowshoes crossed on the wall, not far from a carved wooden panoply of African arms." By mid-February, Hart had added to this collection a small sculpture by Gaston Lachaise, a seagull which the artist had offered him shortly after his poem on Lachaise appeared in print.

After Hart's return from New York, the routine of the household settled down into a congenial dullness. Though Hart sometimes complained that he was "a little bored with this ultimate privacy of a rural winter—supplies and mail so difficult of access and stiff fingers and chilblains," and though more than once he longed for "a few cocktails and taxis for a change," he had to confess that "this is the place for me to work—and I'll be here indefinitely and unregretfully."

By the second of March, with snows still blocking the road, Crane and the Tates were ready to make summer plans. "Spring will be marvelous here," he wrote the Rychtariks, "—and we are going to have a large vegetable and flower garden. I'm *planning* to get up at dawn every day and cultivate it!" He was now responding very well, Hart was pleased to say, to the combination of "temperate living," "good sleep," and "considerable outdoor exercise." And though he was still given to wild dashes through the Tates' kitchen on his way to the pump, he had simplified everyone's life by deciding to take his meals with Mrs. Turner. He would often stop by, nevertheless, to help Mrs. Tate dry dishes, or join her and Allen in cross-country hikes. After one of these hikes, Mrs. Tate recalled, they sat together in the kitchen soaking their chilblain feet in tubs of steaming water, while Hart ironically declaimed the passage from "Voyages II" in which he celebrates the "poinsettia meadows" of the ocean tides. "Charming and imaginative" were the words she used to describe Hart on afternoons of this sort. "He was a wonderful storyteller, able to turn a walk down the road into a heroic adventure." In these conversations he loved to sing the virtues of his friends. He would return from a visit with Brown full of praises for his wit and for his wife's insights. "A woman of Proustian imagination!" Hart would shout. Sue would grow old magnificently, he assured the Tates, letting his own imagination run wild as he visualized for them her progress into a fabulous old age.

Even on his way to the pump in the morning, Hart would more often than not be full of cheerful—and loud—accounts of how the corrupt kerosene he burned in his stoves had nearly asphyxiated him or how Mrs. Turner's cats, "tramping up and down the stairs," had kept him from sleeping. Still wearing his grandmother's shawl and the toboggan cap in which he had spent the night, Hart would speculate about the weather, the likely dates for the start of their garden, the hangover advantages of rum as compared to hard cider.

Yet Hart was working. Everyone was. "Hart studied all the time," Mrs. Tate told me, "a writer's kind of study, a real immersion in the background reading that he was doing for *The Bridge*." Mrs. Tate's novel was also moving along well and Tate, as Hart reported to friends, had "suddenly spurted" into poetry and criticism.

As long as the weather remained cold, Hart spent most of his time with his books. "I've been delving into everything from Spanish history to New Bedford Whaling records, from D. H. Lawrence to Lord Bacon," he told Charles Harris. All this reading was directly related to the poem, for Hart was at last sure of the materials he needed. Though details of the outline of *The Bridge* changed frequently over the next three years, the list of "strands" that would go into it was in mid-January 1926 virtually complete. At that time Crane wrote a note to Waldo Frank in which he spoke of the last section as recapitulating all the principal motifs of the earlier ones, then largely unwritten. This last section, he explained, "is symphonic in including the convergence of all the strands separately detailed in antecedent sections of the poem— Columbus, conquests of water, land, etc. Pocahontas, subways, offices, etc. etc. I dare congratulate myself a little, I think, in having found some liberation for my condensed metaphorical habit in a form as symphonic (at least so attempted) as this."

Crane outlined for Frank the symbolic transformations he hoped to work on his dominant image. "The bridge in becoming a ship, a world, a woman, a tremendous harp (as it does finally) seems to really have a career." He wanted to induce the "feelings of elation, etc.—like being carried forward and upward simultaneously— . . . in imagery, rhythm and repetition, that one experiences in walking across my beloved Brooklyn Bridge." Crane anticipated at this early stage of the poem an objection that some of his critics would raise. The final section, he told Frank, "seems a little transcendental in tendency"; but he was quick to insist that no section of the poem could be read independently of any other. Though the last section by itself might seem "transcendental," "the pediments of the other sections will show it not to have been."

Hart's heavy reading program was serving a double purpose. Not only did it give him useful facts; it also brought to mind half-forgotten experiences that could be made poetically functional. "I have been reading the Journal of Christopher Columbus lately— of his first voyage to America, which is concerned mostly with his cruisings around the West Indies," Hart told his now recovered grandmother. "It has reminded me many times of the few weeks I spent on the Island to hear him expatiate on the gorgeous palms, unexpected pines, balmy breezes, etc. which we associate with Cuba." Columbus's landing place took on for Crane—and eventually for his readers—the character of Mrs. Hart's plantation on the Isle of Pines.

Almost everything could be helpful. The *Oresteia* of Aeschylus suggested patterns of metaphor; Whitehead's *Science and the Modern World* suggested patterns of "reality"; and Waldo Frank's *Virgin Spain* suggested patterns of historical design. From Lawrence's *The Plumed Serpent*, which Crane was reading in March, he took more than eagle and serpent; and from historical works (such as Prescott's *The History of the Reign of Ferdinand and Isabella*, a book on Magellan by Hildebrand, and George

Francis Dow's *Whale Ships and Whaling*, "a marvelously illustrated book on whaling and whaling ships, published by the Marine Research Society, Salem, Mass."), Hart noted down those "facts" (the names of ships with literary associations, for example) which might be raised to symbols. "Studying," as Caroline Tate pointed out, "all the time," Hart stuffed his mind with Melville's sea (*Moby Dick, White-Jacket,* everything else by Melville he could buy or borrow) and did his best to "incorporate" Marco Polo into "the subconscious." He read Eastern philosophy, he proudly reported to Malcolm Cowley, "until I actually dream in terms of the Vedanta scriptures."

Through such gatherings, he was able to make "the scaffoldings for the Bridge jackknife upward a little."

The more Hart worked on his poem, the more monumental the task seemed. "At times the project seems hopeless, horribly so," he wrote the Rychtariks, "and then suddenly something happens inside one, and the theme and the substance of the conception seem brilliantly real, more so than ever!" Whether a success or a failure, it would be, he realized, the grandest project he could tackle. "At least, *at worst,* the poem will be a *huge* failure!"

"In a way," he was soon explaining to Munson, his poem was "a test of materials as much as a test of one's imagination." For Crane's difficult project was that of creating an affirmative statement from contemporary life. He couldn't guarantee that he could work it out, but he was able at this stage to say, "I know my way by now, regardless. I shall at least continue to grip with the problem without relaxing into the easy acceptance (in the name of 'elegance, nostalgia, wit, splenetic splendor') of death which I see most of my friends doing."

Though most of Crane's time was devoted to *The Bridge*, he did try his hand at a now vanished "burlesque" article, which he submitted unsuccessfully to *Vanity Fair*, and he was in erratic correspondence with Eugene O'Neill, who was still trying to convince Liveright to bring out *White Buildings*, preferably without a foreword by himself. Crane, always a little awed by O'Neill, was sometimes baffled by O'Neill's friendly gestures. When, for example, Hart explained that Liveright would probably not be doing the book but that he hoped O'Neill would still do the foreword, O'Neill wrote back that he felt "rather diffident" about writing his "first and only foreword" for any other publisher. A month later he sent an even more enigmatic note from Bermuda.

I saw Liveright the day before I left. I think from the way he talked there is no doubt about his doing your book in the fall. He seems to think he needs more stuff for a volume and that your new work will do this trick for him. So that's that. There seems to be nothing for you to worry about.

"Nothing, indeed!" Hart roared. Was he supposed to have *The Bridge* ready for autumn publication? Was there a foreword to the book or not? Would Liveright again turn the book down if "more stuff" were not forthcoming?

Meanwhile, Hart's friends were doing their best to help establish his reputation. Malcolm Cowley's poem "The Flower in the Sea" was dedicated to him; Allen Tate revised and again offered for publication his article on "Voyages"; and Gorham Munson put together an extended critical study that he described to Crane and that Crane asked to examine.

Almost immediately after Munson's essay arrived in Patterson, Hart—essay in hand—descended on New York. A note from Grace had announced that her wedding would soon take place and that he was needed in Cleveland. Deciding to combine family duty and New York pleasure, he planned to spend several days in Manhattan before going out to Ohio.

Though he talked with Munson, Hart was hard put to recollect what had been said about aesthetics in the course of their "rummy conversation." The night before he met Munson, he had joined Malcolm Cowley in "part one" of a three-day bout that ended only on the morning of his Cleveland arrival, when Hart— to his considerable astonishment—discovered that his mother had the potential of a fine amateur bartender. "My mother knows how to mix the best cocktails I ever drank!"

In spite of the fact that she had no objections to serving her son an 11 A.M. pick-me-up, Grace saw to it that the rest of his visit was reasonably sober and comparatively tranquil. He put in five days of wedding discussions—where, when, who would be invited—with Grace and his grandmother.

Hart left Cleveland in good spirits, cheered by a "dear little note" that his grandmother had slipped into his suitcase and determined for her sake to be "strong and good enough to match the ideals you have for me someday." One day in New York City was all he needed to put those ideals quite out of his head. He told his grandmother that it was "hectic"; he confessed to Malcolm Cowley that it had a good many orgiastic elements ("After a perfect spasm of sentiment and 'inspection' I was released from the fond embrace of my relatives in Cleveland—only to fare into rather more than less spasmodic embraces in N.Y.—a one night spree—on my way back"). And he told Waldo Frank that it had culminated in a "hideous experience"—and a very bad cold.

Crane never quite knew how to explain his own feelings to other people, although he certainly talked a lot about them. When he was drunk, he often became abusive about his homosexuality, Tate recalled, sometimes going out of his way to be insulting to the wives of his friends; when he was sober, his homosexuality became the source of a collection of riotously funny anecdotes.

But his real feelings on those nights when he pursued lust, not love—when he got drunk in order to free himself to search the sailor bars on Sands Street—those desperate feelings seemed, once they had passed, like fictions lived by an invented character rather than by the flesh-and-blood man who tried to calculate what precisely had driven him to the gestures he had made, the words he had said, the brute violence of sudden passion or the risk of the more brutal violence that sometimes left him black and blue and penniless, an object dumped in an alley for the early-morning policeman to discover and haul off to the station house.

During the last years of his life, Crane found a few close friends to whom he spoke as openly as he knew how about the forces that drove him; but he could find no easy answer for his "condition," and the friends—Solomon Grunberg, for example—could offer him no easy solution to his difficulties. If he found it awkward to speak to friends about his feelings, he found it almost impossible to speak of them to his family. But one letter of this time, a letter to his mother, at least attempts to prepare her for the stories that he knew would sometime or other drift back. He tried to suggest the complex experience of holding not just a few but dozens of conflicting values. But as always he was unable to do more than hint the truth of his life.

> I, too, think I made my visit at just the proper time. I'll never forget how really eloquently Grandma looked, how intelligent and fresh. And *you* looked so good to me, too! Remember, that suffering does, if borne without rancor, it does build something that only grows lovelier with time—and it is a kind of kingdom among those *initiated*, a kingdom that has the widest kind of communion. You and I can share our understanding of things more and more as time goes on. I loved you *so much* for many of the things you said when I was with you.
>
> Yes, I hope you never will turn your back on me, as you say. And this is not to say that there may come occasions for it —but there may, after all, be times of temporary misunderstandings as there have been before. I can be awfully proud of *you*, however less occasion I may [have] to feel similarly about myself. I do some awfully silly things sometimes—most of which you don't know about, but which I sometimes (not always) regret. Don't let this stir your apprehensions any, however. I'm in no particular pickle at present.

Though Hart was in no moral "pickle" at this time, he was in an intellectual one; for the aesthetic and philosophical assumptions on which he had founded *The Bridge* were being attacked by a number of his friends.

Munson, for example, had praised Crane in his article; but, Crane felt, for the wrong reasons. "You arbitrarily propose a goal for me which I have no idea of nor interest in following." That goal—roughly, the sympathetic establishment in poetic terms of a "new synthesis of reasonable laws which might provide a consistent philosophical and moral program for our epoch"—was, Crane argued, simply not his. Such a system was bound to be dominated by philosophical abstractions, not by the physical and emotional detail that for Crane in large part constituted a poem.

Dominated neither by abstract theory nor by literal description of objects, his poetry, Crane insisted, would have to survive through the articulation of powerful metaphors into an experience of coherence.

Munson, Crane felt, was asking poetry to take on extra-poetic functions. "When you ask for exact factual data (a graphic map of eternity?), ethical morality or moral classifications, etc. from poetry—you not only limit its goal, you ask its subordination to science, philosophy." The problem is that science "is in perfect antithesis to poetry. (Painting, architecture, music, as well.) It operates from an exactly opposite polarity, and it may equate with poetry, but when it does so its statement of such is in an entirely different terminology." The two disciplines might possibly achieve similar effects; but their methods, Crane felt, were bound to be opposed.

If science's method could not be the poet's, neither, Crane argued, could philosophy's:

> What you admire in Plato as "divine sanity" is the architecture of his logic. Plato doesn't live today because of the intrinsic "truth" of his statements: their only living truth today consists in the "fact" of their harmonious relationship to each other in the context of his organization of them. This grace partakes of poetry. But Plato was primarily a philosopher, and you must admit that grace is a secondary motive in philosophical statement . . . No wonder Plato considered the banishment of poets;—their reorganizations of chaos on bases perhaps divergent from his own threatened the logic of *his* system, itself founded on assumptions that demanded the very defense of poetic construction which he was fortunately able to provide.

Crane did not want his work to be judged as science or philosophy. Neither did he want it to be judged as autobiography. "What I'm objecting to," Crane wrote Munson, "is contained in my suspicion that you have allowed too many extra-literary impressions of me to enter your essay, sometimes for better, sometimes for worse."

Of greater concern to Crane were the literary differences he sometimes had with Allen Tate, Slater Brown, and Malcolm Cowley. Very close to all of them in aesthetic theory, he argued with them endlessly about the optimistic orientation of *The Bridge*. Tate, especially, found it impossible to accept Crane's use of Whitman as a figure symbolizing "The Spiritual body of America"; but almost all the literary men Crane was now closest to—Waldo Frank was the only significant exception—objected to the vaguely Whitmanesque tone that Crane planned to impose on his poem. "Why he wanted to identify himself partly with Whitman, I don't know," Tate told me. "Hart had a sort of megalomania: he wanted to be The Great American Poet. I imagine he thought that by getting into the Whitman tradition, he could carry even Whitman further. And yet there's another thing we must never forget— there was the homosexual thing, too. . . . I don't think he was wholly conscious of it, but it must have had some influence. The notion of 'comrades,' you see, and that sort of business."

Though they did not discuss this psychological motivation, Tate and Crane did go over—hot and heavy—an outline of the poem that, toward the middle of March, Crane prepared for Otto Kahn. Their differences, though they were not so clearly formulated in the spring of 1926, were essentially those Tate was later to draw on in an essay about his friend's poetry. In that essay, Tate maintained that the poem as a whole suffered from a "lack of a coherent structure, whether symbolic or narrative . . . The historical plot of the poem, which is the groundwork on which the symbolic bridge stands, is arbitrary and broken, where the poet would have gained an overwhelming advantage by choosing a single period or episode, a concrete event with all its dramatic causes, and by following it up minutely, and being bound to it. In short, he would have gained an advantage could he have found a subject to stick to."

Almost as often as they talked about *The Bridge*, Tate and Crane talked about what Crane insisted was T. S. Eliot's death orientation, his "pessimism," a pessimism that Crane felt most of his friends—Tate included—shared. From Tate's point of view, however, "There was a fundamental mistake in Crane's diagnosis of Eliot's problem."

> Eliot's "pessimism" grows out of an awareness of the decay of the individual consciousness and its fixed relations to the world; but Crane thought that it was due to something like pure "orneryness," an unwillingness "to share with us the breath released," the breath being a new kind of freedom that he identified emotionally with the age of the machine. This vagueness of purpose, in spite of the apparently concrete character of the Brooklyn Bridge, which became the symbol of his epic, he never succeeded in correcting. The "bridge" stands for no well-defined experience; it differs from the Helen and Faust symbols only in its unliterary origin. I think Crane was de-

ceived by this difference, and by the fact that Brooklyn Bridge is "modern" and a fine piece of "mechanics." His more ambitious later project permitted him no greater mastery of formal structure than the more literary symbolism of his youth.

Though Crane was eloquent in defending his position, he found that his arguments with his friends did nothing to push on the poem itself. Instead, all too frequently they left him and his friends so grouchy that trivial incidents could create unpleasantnesses that would last for days.

By the beginning of April, Hart's frustrations over the sections of the poem he could not get underway were overwhelming. Irritable and fault-finding, he became convinced that his friends were engaged in an intellectual conspiracy against him. "I have been having an awful time (like constipation) getting the first part of The Bridge (Columbus episode) to move," he wrote the Rychtariks. And it is clear that he feels this "surprising problem" is as much due to the reactions of his friends as to the mechanics of putting the poem together. "People like Waldo Frank will probably like it—that is, they'll be interested in the content and presentation, but most of my younger associates and friends will probably be pretty doubtful about it. Well, one has to face such things with a confidence superior to a lot of contingencies."

Not even the fact that the Cowleys would soon arrive could shake Hart out of his depression. At best he could count on only "a few 'animations' with Malcolm before I, the climate, the solitude or whatever it is, drives him into the kind of shell that Brown and Tate seem to have retired into lately. My mood being preeminently N. Labrador these days—I should like a little good company immensely."

By the second week of April the N. Labrador mood had permeated the entire household. Spring thaws had set in and the landscape was a sea of mud that made any outdoor activity impossible. Indoors, Hart found himself able only to "drone about, reading, eating and sleeping." If he had been able to drone quietly, the oncoming difficulties might have been averted; but Hart was never one for quiet droning. He was now all over the house, bringing Tate intricate diagrams of the ways in which subjective and objective imagery operated, bursting in on Caroline—it seemed to her—almost every time she spread out her manuscript on the kitchen table. Neither gentle hints nor gentle requests for privacy were of any avail.

Finally Mrs. Tate put a lock on the door. Hart, in grim silence, retaliated by taking soap, razor, washcloth, and towel from their niche beside the pump and installing them in Mrs. Turner's kitchen. "Why this should make them mad, I don't know," Hart wrote his mother, "and why it should make them mad because

I immediately began avoiding their parts of the house *completely* (not being invited to do otherwise) I can't see either."

This sort of behavior, of course, did make the Tates angry—as did Hart's sullen withdrawals every time he met them on the road or in the yard. But they all might have settled down into something like their earlier close friendship if, early on the bright, cold morning of Friday, April 16, Hart and Mrs. Turner had not made a tour of the back yard. Hart's account of it differs considerably from the—I suspect, more accurate—recollections of Allen Tate and Caroline Gordon. "Matters came to a climax day before yesterday, shortly after breakfast," Hart wrote his mother.

> I had been talking to Mrs. Turner around on "our" side of the house about some plans for cleaning up some rubbish, etc. when suddenly a door opens from the Tate's kitchen and Allen shouts out, "If you've got a criticism of my work to make, I'd appreciate it if you would speak to me about it first!" Then the door savagely banged, and Mrs. Turner and I (who hadn't mentioned him or anything that concerned him) were left staring at each other in perfect amazement. I can't easily describe how angry I was. I felt myself losing all control—but I managed to address the Tates without breaking anything. Mrs. Turner came in with me and corroborated the facts of the matter, and it turned out that the Tates hadn't heard actually a thing I was saying—their imaginations, they evidently felt, were perfectly justified in building up a perfect tower of Babel out of nothing.
>
> Nothing was touched on at that fiery moment but the immediate circumstances of what I had said and what I hadn't. Tate finally admitting that he was all wrong. My feelings remained little cooled, however. The rest of the time since then has been simply hideous.

What the Tates remember hearing through their bedroom window on that cold morning was Hart elaborately calculating just how much work he and Mrs. Turner would have in raking up the wood chips Tate's industrious firewood chopping had produced. "Of course, our quarrel came about over the chopping of the wood, which he didn't like to do," Tate told me. "Malcolm said that Hart told him that chopping 'constricted his imagination.' That was all right. But when Hart walked around the yard after the thaw came, and all the chips of wood were there, and he said the yard was very dirty—well, I was annoyed, because he hadn't helped put any of the chips there!" Caroline Gordon still remembers Tate's anger as he threw off the covers of their warm bed to stalk angrily through the frigid house muttering, "What the hell does he mean that that woodpile isn't neat?"

Several months later, after Hart and the Tates were again close friends, Tate could recognize that the incident had "its extremely comic side. And I think Hart felt that too." But during the few days before Hart left, everyone involved was hopping mad. For Hart did leave, but not before he had comforted weeping Mrs. Turner, who volunteered a room on her side of the house and absolute privacy, or before the Tates—unable to sleep and worn out from trying to guess what Hart's next move might be—had gotten out of bed in the middle of the night, each to type up separate accounts of their feelings and slip them under his door. The substance of both notes was that they had invited Hart to live with them while he was still penniless, but after his affluent arrival he had "spread" himself and his possessions "all over the house, invading every corner; and so on . . ." "I must say I'm stumped," Hart wrote his mother. "How can I . . . persist in staying here after such an insulting statement from the Tates to the effect that I was originally their guest and that I was invited on the grounds of charity rather than from any other motives?"

Hart realized, of course, that he ought to follow the advice his mother soon gave him: he ought to patch up his differences with the Tates and get on with his poem. Otto Kahn had just forwarded another $500 for his summer expenses, and the costs of a move to another part of the country would wipe out most of it. Yet, if he stayed on, would he get any work done? Most likely not. No, he wrote his mother, he would have to get away.

> Try and not think hardly of me. Life is awfully hard on all of us. I've been in a terrible state of mind—I guess you got that from my letter, and saw the reasons plainly enough. I've tried to give every consideration a thorough test—and while I could bury my pride and beg the Tates to become reconciled, they really wouldn't you know, and Mrs. Tate especially. I couldn't get any work done in such an atmosphere.

By this time Hart had returned to New York, made plans for a major move, and come back to Patterson to pack his belongings. He had tried time and again to write Tate a letter defining his attitudes. It wasn't just woodchopping that was behind their difficulties, Hart felt; it was something deeper. I have no notion if he sent any of the drafts he wrote—certainly there is none among the letters Tate generously made available to me—but some impression of what he *might* have said can be gained from a much-revised fragment of one of the unsent ones. It begins halfway through a discussion of the philosophical differences that Hart thought needlessly separated him from his friend.

> You expect me to "welcome" failings that haven't yet appeared in your work merely because I detect a certain narcissism in the voluptuous melancholies of Eliot—which you admire, and I don't—. We should be able to agree to disagree about such

matters without calling in dish pans, saws, and slop jars. You claim I have involved these factors in my relations with you—. I have torn up a letter, long and tiresome, detailing my own convictions that my notions have been more detached and less ridiculously subjective and selfish than you assume.

It's all wrong—all the way through—and unfortunate. Although I have no apologies to make—because I can't see my frequent vulgarities and assumptions as totalling the *real* causes you and Caroline have mounted against me—I don't see any use in being either defensive or ironic. These are easy and obvious modes and I think it better to let the matter rest as you want to believe it.

I'm sorry for my failings wherever they have incurred your inconvenience and displeasure, and ask you to forget them and me as soon as possible.

Hart Crane

# 24

As soon as Hart became convinced that there was no possibility of working on his poem if he remained in Patterson, he began casting about for a place to go. At one point he toyed with the idea of renting a cottage at a seaside resort; but he realized quickly that there was only one place in the world he wanted to be. "If you feel at all sympathetic to this situation of mine I wish you *this time* [would] be generous enough to let me go to the Island and finish my poem there," he wrote his mother. He knew what objections she would make: "Summer in the tropics isn't of course the paradise of the winter months, but it is a thousand times better than a hall bedroom in New York without light or air, to say nothing of the fact that it might cost me a hundred or so of what I have left just spent in *looking* for work. You know how long it is sometimes."

Hart was desperate, and he wasn't above using threats. "I'm asking you for this refuge," he wrote. "I've always been refused before. If you deny it now I'm not sure how much farther away I'll go to accomplish my purposes. Perhaps to the orient, even if I have just enough to get there and no more." Indeed, he might go further than the Orient: "If I can't somehow succeed in taking advantage of this one opportunity given me by Mr. Kahn, I don't know how I'll feel about life or any future efforts to live . . ."

Grace, as Hart explained to the Rychtariks, "made a terrible fuss" when he proposed his island expedition. It was only when he told her he was going—with permission or without—that she most reluctantly offered to let him stay in the house his grandfather had built and from which Hart, as a boy, had run suicidally into the night. "I'm *terribly sorry* that I can't get you to fully agree with me about this matter," he wrote her, "but you'll see it work out much better than you may expect."

"I realize it's hard for her to think of me as so far away," he explained to the Rychtariks, "—but I'll be still farther away, I think, if my Bridge breaks down entirely. I can't allow it all to be the victim of malice, envy, jealousy and petty-mindedness."

Grace was always unpredictable, and never more so than in the week of Hart's leave-taking. No sooner had she become reconciled to his going to the Isle of Pines than she abruptly canceled all the elaborate plans she and Mr. Curtis had made for their marriage, bundled a surprised bridegroom onto the train, and took off for New York. Hart had to be at her wedding, Grace felt; and if that meant a breathless ceremony in New York's City Hall two days before Hart departed, then that was how it would be.

For three days Hart lived in a cheerful nightmare. "I spose Bina [Flynn] has already told you the details of the parental wedding in NY," Hart wrote the Browns. "Those last . . . days in town were mad ones for me. Sibyl Fiske, Agnes' sister, gnawed at my hand for quite a while at the dinner with the Cowleys. I don't remember what it was all about, but I think we fell in love with each other. I finally brought the bridal pair to lunch with Lachaise and Mme. A good time was had by all."

The only bad time was at a performance of Eugene O'Neill's *The Great God Brown.* During the second-act intermission, Grace recklessly attempted to persuade Hart to change his Isle of Pines plans. Their argument, Grace later recalled, was intense enough to delay the performance for several minutes. Hart finally ended the debate by dashing out of the theater. Nevertheless, the next morning she received, she told Philip Horton, "a dozen penitent roses, and on the heels of the messenger who brought them, Hart himself, haggard from a sleepless night." Hart, she said, flung himself on her and wept for forgiveness.

In spite of that evening, the wedding—from his point of view—was a success. "We had some good hours and happy ones together in NY," he was soon to write Grace. "Charles was such a good sport and you looked so scrumptious!" Yet Hart was not sure, when his boat pulled out, that the wedding would bring his mother happiness. There was, he told Waldo Frank, far too much of a difference in age between Grace and Mr. Curtis. And though Mr. Curtis seemed eligible—"a very dapper gentleman," Waldo Frank told me—Hart was certain that Grace had married for all the wrong reasons.

Hart had ample opportunity to talk to Waldo Frank, for Frank had accepted his invitation to join him for a few weeks on the island. Hart could not have chosen a better companion. As always, he was steadied by Frank's reasonableness. They had perfect weather on the trip down, and as their ship steamed along the coast, Hart managed to shake himself free of most of his worries. It was, he wrote his mother, "a wonderful sail; smooth as glass and the usual increasing blue." Hart paced the deck, watched flying fish, tried to photograph a porpoise, chatted with the passengers. In no time at all, he was "picking up wonderfully."

Because prohibition had dominated Hart's adult life, he found it a novel experience to have wine casually, not secretly, dispensed. "We've had a little drink, but not much. What we have had has been straight from Europe and openly served on our table. Makes you feel rather civilized to have some genial real St. Julian and a cordial in the smoking room afterward." A good Cuban cigar in one hand and his cordial in the other, Hart leaned back contented, letting his conversation with Frank drift along as effortlessly as the high banks of clouds that seemed always to line the eastern horizon.

Though much of their talk was of Hart's plans for *The Bridge*, they also tried to calculate how long he could make his money last. He had already made two very large dents in the $500 that had just been advanced by Otto Kahn. The ship passage was responsible for the first and another—almost as big—was made when he decided he had to pay back $100 of the money the Rychtariks had loaned him for his hilltop "anchor." Yet Hart wanted to spend a full year on the Isle of Pines. His problem was how to stretch his remaining money as far as possible—to make it last, say, until early August, when he hoped he could ask Kahn for the final $500 of his "loan." By the time that was gone, *White Buildings* might at last be published—or at least close enough to publication to justify his asking for an advance. And if worst came to worst, he could always sell his $200 worth of Connecticut back to Bina Flynn. With good luck—and the sale of a few poems and a few reviews—Hart might be able, the two friends decided, to achieve his year in the sun.

The first economy measure came on their two-day layover in Havana: Waldo Frank's proficient Spanish allowed them to spend all their time in Cuban hotels, bars, and theaters. Latin American vitality was for Hart a sensuous revelation—not always pleasant, but always exciting. "We didn't visit an American haunt except the steamship office," he wrote the Browns. Everywhere there were crowds.

> . . . blacks, reds, browns, greys and every permutation and combinations of southern bloods that you can imagine. Corona-Coronas, of course, for 15¢, marvelous sherry, cognac, vermouth and "Tropical" (the beer that I was talking about). . . . Then we went to the Alhambra, a kind of Cuban National Winter Garden Burleque. Latin "broadness" was somewhat veiled for me as far as the dialogue went, but actions went farther than apparently even the East Side can stand.

But it was the street life that was most exciting.

> Gratings and balconies and narrow streets with plenty of whores nodding. The day of our departure a great fleet of American destroyers landed. Streets immediately became torrents of uniforms—one sailor had exactly the Chinese mustache effect that I aspire to. . . . Taxis anywhere in town for only

20¢ . . . Great black bushed buxom Jamaican senoritas roared laughter at us, old women hobbled up offering lottery tickets (I finally got one on a hunch). The whole town is hyper-sensual and mad—i.e. has no apparent direction, destiny or purpose; Cummings' paradise.

Though on this first visit Hart dismissed the Cubans as a "trashy bastard people" and the town as "a funny little metropolis . . . more like a toy city than a real one," Havana would later become a place he hungered for. Now, however, it was only a way-stop to the Isle of Pines, which was "enough Eden" for his present purposes.

All the way down he speculated on what his grandmother's house would be like, for his memories of it were a tangle of hatred, violence, and terror. The house, he discovered, though badly run-down and in need of repairs, its gardens overgrown, its roof leaking, was "much more spacious" than he had remembered, a perfect place, he decided, for his work. Low and rambling, it offered him both privacy and—in the person of its caretaker, Mrs. Simpson—a tough, brilliant, cheerful companion.

It was, in fact, Mrs. Simpson from whom Grace had been "protecting" Hart whenever he tried to sail away to the Isle of Pines. She was, Grace had told him, an old woman of "whimsical temper" who would be certain to be irritated by his presence and who might, in a moment of anger, leave him to fend for himself in the jungle, the summer heat of which would, Grace was sure, destroy him. In such a situation, she wrote, Hart would be a helpless prey to the elements.

Mrs. Simpson, however, turned out to be "goodness itself," "really lovable and quite the contrary of all I had expected." She was "very sociable and jolly"; she encouraged Hart to smoke after-dinner cigars (Grace, who objected to them, had assured him that Mrs. Simpson would tolerate no cigars anywhere in the house); and she saw to it that he was well fed. "We really like her very much, her wit, her good sense and lack of all sentimentality."

"After Grace's warnings I was quite dubious about getting along with Mrs. S.," Hart wrote his father, "but I find her very pleasant indeed and things promise well." She escorted Crane and Frank on drives around the island, took them swimming at her favorite beaches, joined them on picnic excursions to the interior of the island, and made sure that they were entertained by all her friends.

When, at the end of two weeks, Waldo Frank returned to New York, Mrs. Simpson—by now "Aunt Sally"—began to assume even more importance in Hart's scheme of things. He had been dreading her response to what he knew was inevitable: his first binge. But when it came, she took it in her stride. "Yesterday I got tight for the first time, on Bacardi. Cuban Independence day," he explained to the Browns. "Falling in with a flock of goats on my way home (I was trembling at what Mme. Sampsohn would say) I stubbed my toe and skinned my knee. Arrived home in a somewhat obvious condition, there was nothing to be done but have it out with Mme. . . . We had it fair and square. It is now established that I can drink as much as I damned please. A couple of murdering desperadoes got loose from the penitentiary here recently—and I think she's glad to have my company. But she's been so damned pleasant and considerate that I haven't any reason to think she doesn't like me on less fearful grounds."

Mrs. Simpson did indeed like Hart. She had the capacity to live and let live, to accept any person she liked wholeheartedly, exactly as he was, without trying to "improve" or reform him. Valuing independence and honesty, she could be completely sympathetic —and responsive—to Hart's shifting moods. When he wanted to be alone, she would scrupulously avoid his side of the house (the two west bedrooms), "and without there being, so far as I know, any misunderstandings about my occasional withdrawals, silences, etc." All in all, Mrs. Simpson, he concluded, "has displayed the most unusual sensibility and tact in many ways, and while I thought for awhile that her voice and her parrot (which sounds the same) would become unbearable in time, I find that altogether I couldn't hope to find a greater aggregate of sense, understanding and goodwill in any woman I know of."

One of the first things Hart and Mrs. Simpson talked about was the future of "Villa Casas"—what it would cost to repair the roof and pump, what could be done to rehabilitate the overgrown groves that, crushing up against the house, produced a better crop of mosquitoes than of grapefruit. ("It is, of course, a great mistake to have planted so many fruit trees so close to the house," he wrote to his grandmother. "They give practically no shade—and simply stifle every breeze that approaches.") Hacking away with an ax at the dead and dying orange trees that cluttered the front yard, Hart opened up enough space to do some replacement planting, putting royal palms in place of the oranges. "How I wish you had thought of planting some of these perfect delights when the place was being built," Hart wrote home; "they are the one perfect sort of tree to have round a house, their ornamentation, stateliness and open-airyness can't be surpassed."

As his muscles toned up under the pressure of the first physical labor he had done in months, Hart found himself responding to the island life. He fell in love with its exotic fruits.

I feel like a gastric museum at present, a cross cut of Tahitian stomach coast—but not in especial distress—at least so far. Uric acid won't have a whispering chance in a few days what with all the strange fruits and vegetables I'm trying. Casvas, guavas, bread fruit, limes, cumquats, kashew apples, cocnuts, wild oranges, bananas, God I can't remember any more of the damned names. O yes, mulberries and avacadas and papayas! And mangos! Maybe I don't get enough of it yet! Tamarinds . . . pomgranates . . . guabanas . . . O sacre Nom de . . .

Everyone got a letter about mangoes; finally he wrote a poem, "The Mango Tree." "I'm wild about them," he wrote his grandmother. "The finest fruit I ever ate—excepting grapefruit, which are impossible to get now." Even Hart's father got a note about mangoes, Hart speculating about the commercial possibilities of shipping them north.

I am astonished to find how little of the Island I really saw when I was here before. The variety of vegetation, fruits, flowers and woods in general—all is the more amazing now because of the season. Everything but the citrus fruits is in full harvest or approaching it. For instance, I never had any ripe mangos when I was here before. It would take millions of dollars to advertise them enough in the north (as with any new fruit) to make them initially acceptable even as a gift—but once tasted, people would come back for them like wildfire! They're the most delicious fruit I ever tasted. I haven't eaten meat more than once since I hit the island, and I don't want it again. Not that the cut wasn't good, but such an abundance of fruits and vegetables makes it completely superfluous.

Dressed in his island finery (sailor pants, a T-shirt, and hemp-soled shoes, "the kind the peasants of Spain have worn for centuries and they are the coolest thing on a hot road that you ever tried"), Hart amused himself talking to Attaboy, Mrs. Simpson's screaming parrot, and Pythagoras, a baby owl "no bigger than a fat sparrow" which had blundered onto the porch one of the first days of Hart's stay and which immediately became part of the household.

The island overwhelmed him with its luxurious vitality. "To me, the mountains, strange greens, native thatched huts, perfume, etc. brought me straight to Melville. . . . Oleanders and mimosas in full bloom now make the air almost too heavy with perfume, it's another world—and a little like Rimbaud." Then, as he became used to it—its magnificent skies, the sudden views of the sea through tropical vegetation, the tearing storms—he relaxed into an easy contentment. In spite of Mrs. Simpson's having given him permission to do as much drinking as he wanted to, he now found that he didn't want to drink. "Nothing 'happens' down here," he wrote to Bill Wright.

There's everything fine in the world to drink—but nobody to drink with—so I haven't even sampled the many various labels that deck the bar—beyond some delicious Bacardi (15¢ a throw) some French cognac and beer, the latter my staple beverage. Strange, too, how the removal of all *verboten* signs vitiates one's appetite.

In this happy summer of Hart's life, there is both a tangled nostalgia for lost days and a real recapture of them. In one respect, he may have turned back to earlier times because his quarrel with the Tates and simple physical distance isolated him from most literary friends. There were still occasional letters to the Cowleys, numerous letters to Waldo Frank, and frequent ones to the Browns. Yet most of Hart's New York acquaintances were now classed by him as either insincere or vicious. "It has been so disgusting to note the sudden turns and antics of my 'friends' since I had the one little bit [of] help I ever had toward my work in the money from Kahn," Hart wrote Wilbur Underwood. "Everytime I came into N.Y. from the country I'd hear new monstrosities of fables going about town as to how I was squandering money on pâté de foie gras, etc. And worse whisperings. It's all been very tiresome—and I'd rather lose such elite for the old society of vagabonds and sailors—who don't enjoy chit-chat."

It was, in fact, two of Hart's sailors who were responsible for much of his correspondence while he was on the island. And it was in them that he found unexpected loyalties. One had traveled all the way to Patterson from Norfolk, only to find Hart gone, and for no other reason than a happy memory of "two evenings in Brooklyn last January." "I was very touched," Hart told Underwood and then went on to celebrate his memories of waterfront nights.

Immortally choice and funny and pathetic are some of my recollections in each connection. I treasure them—I always can—against many disillusionments made bitter by the fact that faith was given and expected—whereas, with the sailor no faith or such is properly *expected* and how jolly and cordial and warm the touseling *is* sometimes, after all. Let my lusts be my ruin, then, since all else is a fake and mockery.

If New York sailors heard more from Hart than New York literary friends, friends of Cleveland days suddenly found themselves in active correspondence. Of these, Bill Wright, his oldest and in many ways his best friend, especially helped him recover past times. As a "leap in the dark," Wright had sent a note to 1709 East 115 Street, in hopes of again getting in touch with the good friend he had lost track of. The fraternity boys who had taken over the 115 Street house finally mailed it to Grace at Wade Park Manor and eventually it reached Hart, who responded with a brief history of his life, starting with the advertising job in Cleveland.

I've really thought quite often of getting in touch with you; last summer when I was out in Cleveland helping the family move I tried to get in touch with the Lovell's and failed otherwise, too, in getting any trace of you—excepting that you had gone to Pittsburgh. Some reporter or feature writer on the Cleveland Times—a friend of Kathryn Kenney's, but whose name I forget, told me this much, but no more. I am very anxious to know what you have been doing and how your parents are. Hasn't it been a long, long time since any news united us! I should have to write you a book to tell you all that has happened . . .

Though Hart didn't quite write a book, he did work through the jobs he had held, the publication plans for *White Buildings*, his hope of soon returning to *The Bridge*, his mother's remarriage, his grandmother's illness and her recovery. But it was friendship he was writing about. Wright's letter had been an unexpected manifestation of "loyalty," the loyalty Hart valued more than intellect or wit. "Do write me soon, and lengthily, the leap in the dark of your words is certainly welcome."

Wright seems somehow—more through good luck than by design—to appear on the scene whenever Hart needs him. He was, during Hart's difficult high-school years, the single confidant Hart could count on; after the divorce, he was inconspicuously present in New York whenever Hart needed someone to talk to; he reappears as a correspondent during Hart's island summer, when Hart had most need of old friends. Four years later it is to Wright that Crane turns when he is desperate for money; and when C. A. Crane dies, Margaret and Bill Wright are the friends Crane visits on his trip north from Mexico. Perhaps because neither Hart nor Bill ever asked much more of each other than understanding, they got on without an extensive correspondence. They shared—Wright felt it and I am reasonably sure Crane had some sense of it too—an awareness of each other as totally dependable.

They had an altogether generous friendship; they always wished each other well. When Bill, in one of his letters to the island, announced that he was about to be married, Hart's enthusiasm could not have been more sincere.

By your letter I see you have been through some strenuosities too! But I'm glad that you haven't encountered anything more fatal than the wedlock vows which you seem destined to make. Good luck to you, Willy and may you live to see all your grandchildren riding over the North Pole on weekends. I have hovered on the brink several times—but finally decided that I was too ridiculously romantic for marriage—which shows me to be cautious and wise in the extreme!

That last sentence is an honest one. Crane had thought of marriage on more than one occasion, always rejecting the idea as an impossibility. In high school there had been girls whom he wished he could have fallen in love with; there were several married women—among them, Claire Spencer—whom he did half fall in love with. Hart's orientation, as his friends have attested, was toward a "normal" middle-class life. That he felt he could not lead such a life did not lessen his desire for it.

Hart's correspondence with old friends, his long conversations with Mrs. Simpson, his efforts to make the house livable, his wild sessions with the out-of-tune piano, sessions that Mrs. Simpson encouraged—all helped him forget his painful exit from Patterson. And yet that exit rankled. Sometime in July he got off a gloomy note to Wilbur Underwood.

> I have not been able to write one line since I came here—the mind is completely befogged with heat and besides there is a strange challenge and combat in the air—offered by "Nature" so monstrously alive in the tropics which drains the psychic energies.—And my poem was progressing so beautifully until Mrs. Tate took it into her head to be so destructive! How silly all this sounds! Howsoever it's a cruel jest of Fate—and I doubt if I shall continue to write for another year. For I've lost all faith in my material—"human nature" or what you will—and any true expression must rest on some faith in something.

Hart's prophecy was inaccurate, for he was about to enter the most productive period of his life. It was a combination of several factors that finally brought him to write, one of them undoubtedly his mother's silence. Grace, busily adjusting to her second marriage, had been writing only the briefest of notes. She was well; she was busy putting away the wedding presents; she would be writing soon. For nearly two months, Hart assumed he would not have to worry about Grace's problems.

Another contributing factor involved him in considerable physical pain. Hart, who had always wanted to be a sailor, made the mistake of taking a pleasure trip to Grand Cayman Island.

> Thursday (June 3rd) I'm sailing on the schooner for Grand Cayman. There are two days on the water each way, and I may spend a week on the island if the boat stays that long. I'm looking forward with great glee to my first real sail—and they tell me that Cayman is lovelier· than anything around. Bread, cheese and cookies are to be packed by Mrs. Simpson and I'm hoping not to feed the fishes. If I do,—well then I'll have at least found out that I'm a goodfornothing landlubber.

There was a Grand Cayman poem ("The Air Plant") as a direct consequence of the trip, and others that derived incidental imagery from it. When the ship *did* sail, as he told Waldo Frank, Hart enjoyed himself immensely.

> The motion made me anything but sea-sick, with a good wind the rhythm is incomparable. More gorgeous skies than even you saw, acres of man-sized leaping porpoises (the "Huzza Porpoises" so aptly named in Moby Dick) that greet you in tandems (much like M. and Mme. Lachaise if you have ever seen them out walking together) and truly "arch and bend the horizons." One enormous shark, a White-Fin, lounged alongside for awhile.

But far too much of the time the schooner went nowhere. Between head winds and calm, Hart had an unexpected total of eight days at sea.

> And let me tell you that to be "as idle as a painted," etc. under this tropical sun with thirty-five cackling, puking, farting negroes (women and children first) for a whole day or so (the water like a blinding glassy gridiron) is a novel experience. . . . Vile water to drink, etc. etc. . . . And the much bruited Grand Cayman was some torment, I can survive to tell you. Flat and steaming under black clouds of mosquitoes, and not a square inch of screening on the island. I had to keep smudge fires burning incessantly in my room while I lunged back and forth, smiting myself all over like one in rigor mortis and smoke gouging salty penance from my eyes. The insects were enormous; Isle of Pines species can't compare in size or number. After nine days and nights of that I staggered onto the schooner —and here I am—with a sunburn positively Ethiopian.

Hart emerged, however, "rather toughened and well. The exasperations and torments of such a siege make one grateful for modest amenities. Mrs. Simpson yesterday for the first time appeared to me as the Goddess of Liberty." Yet for weeks his sunburned skin peeled and his ears began to puff up alarmingly—and painfully.

While Hart's "double-barrelled, non-pareil earache" gradually eased off, he compensated for physical pain by going through a spiritual purgation. Like much else these days, it seems to have been part of an emptying out into hopelessness, a welcome sweep through discomfort and despair that would end with his again being able to work on the long poem.

He had reason enough for one kind of despair—he was out of money. The combination of the Grand Cayman trip and an expedition to a Havana doctor had used up the last of Kahn's second contribution. He was determined, however, to stay on the island until he had written something, so he got off a note to Bina Flynn, asking her to buy back his twenty acres of mountaintop.

But that netted only $100, since he now repaid the Rychtariks the rest of his debt.

It was at this point that he read Oswald Spengler's *The Decline of the West*. For a few days it seemed to blot out the optimistic vision that lay behind *The Bridge*. Crane worked through that massive study, seeing Spengler's public theories in terms of his own private literary failings both in Patterson and on the island. Part of his trouble, Crane felt, was a loss of faith in man; this he attributed to the "disloyalty" of literary friends, but he recognized also that the despair he had earlier assigned to Eliot could now be found in himself as well. Spengler defined for Crane something he had not until this time been able to accept. "This man is certainly fallible in plenty of ways," he wrote Waldo Frank, "but much of his evidence is convincing—and is there any good evidence forthcoming from the world in general that the artist isn't completely out of a job? Well, I may not care about such considerations 2 hours from now, but at present and for the last two months I have been confronted with a ghostliness that is new."

In this letter Crane anticipated the philosophical, historical, and psychological attitudes that many of his critics would draw upon to attack the intellectual foundations of *The Bridge*—and acknowledged them as, for the moment, valid. No one, in fact, has subsequently so efficiently attacked Crane's basic assumptions as Crane himself did here.

The darkness is part of [the artist's] business. It has always been taken for granted however, that his intuitions were salutary and that his vision either sowed or epitomized "experience" (in the Blakian sense). Even the rapturous and explosive destructives of Rimbaud presupposes this, even his lonely hauteur demands it for any estimation or appreciation. (The romantic attitude must at least have the background of an age of faith, whether approved or disapproved no matter.)

All this is inconsecutive and indeterminate because I am trying to write shorthand about an endless subject—and moreover am unresolved as to any ultimate conviction. . . . Emotionally I should like to write the bridge; intellectually judged the whole theme and project seems more and more absurd. A fear of personal impotence in this matter wouldn't affect me half so much as the convictions that arise from other sources . . . I had what I thought were authentic materials that would have been a pleasurable agony of wrestling, eventuating or not in perfection—at least being worthy of the most supreme efforts I could muster.

These "materials" were valid to me to the extent that I presumed them to be (articulate or not) at least organic and active factors in the experience and perceptions of our common race, time and belief. The very idea of a bridge, of course, is a form peculiarly dependent on such spiritual convictions. It is an act of faith besides being a communication. The symbols of reality necessary to articulate the span—may not exist where you expected them, however. By which I mean that however great their subjective significance to me is concerned—these forms, materials, dynamics are simply non-existent in the world, I may amuse and delight and flatter myself as much as I please—but I am only evading a recognition and playing Don Quixote in an immorally conscious way.

The form of my poem rises out of a past that so overwhelms the present with its worth and vision that I'm at a loss to explain my delusion that there exist any real links between that past and a future destiny worthy of it. The "destiny" is long since completed, perhaps the little last section of my poem is a hangover echo of it—but it hangs suspended somewhere in ether like an Absalom by his hair. The bridge as a symbol today has no significance beyond an economical approach to shorter hours, quicker lunches, behaviorism and toothpicks. And inasmuch as the bridge is a symbol of all such poetry as I am interested in writing it is my present fancy that a year from now I'll be more contented working in an office than before. Rimbaud was the last great poet that our civilization will see—he let off all the great cannon crackers in Valhalla's parapets, the sun has set theatrically several times since while Laforgue, Eliot and others of that kidney have whimpered fastidiously. *Everybody* writes poetry now—and "poets" for the first time are about to receive official social and economic recognition in America. It's really all the fashion, but a dead bore to anticipate. If only America were half as worthy today to be spoken of as Whitman spoke of it fifty years ago there might be something for one to say—not that Whitman received or required any tangible proof of his intimations, but that time has shown how increasingly lonely and ineffectual his confidence stands.

There always remains the cult of "words," elegancies, elaborations, to exhibit with a certain amount of pride to an "inner circle" of literary initiates. But this is, to me, rivalled by numerous other forms of social accomplishment which might, if attained, provide as mild and seductive recognitions. You probably think me completely insane, talking as obvious hysterics as [a] drunken chorus-girl. Well, perhaps I need a little more skepticism to put me right on the bridge again . . . I am certainly in a totally undignified mind and undress—and I hope to appear more solidly determined soon.

Please don't think . . . that I [am] burning manuscripts or plotting oriental travels . . . Desolately I confess that I *may* be writing stanzas again tomorrow. That's the worst of it. . . .

—All this does not mean that I have resigned myself to inactivity . . . A bridge will be written in some kind of style and form, at worst it will be something as good as advertising copy. After which I will have at least done my best to discharge my debt to Kahn's kindness.

Reading Spengler had forced Crane to question the assumptions behind *The Bridge*, but it was his triumph over his doubts that helped him return to work on the poem. By the middle of August—his creative forces in full flow—he again wrote Waldo Frank about the book that two months before had so unsettled him.

Yes, I read the whole of Spengler's book. It is stupendous, —and it was perhaps a very good experience for ripening some of the Bridge after all. I can laugh now; but you know, alas, how little I could at the time. That book seems to have been just one more of many "things" and circumstances that seem to have uniformly conspired in a strangely symbolical way toward the present speed of my work. Isn't it true,—hasn't it been true in your experience, that beyond the acceptance of fate as a tragic action—immediately every circumstance and incident in one's life flocks toward a positive center of action, control and beauty? I need not ask this since there is the metaphor of the "rotted seed of personal will," or some such phrase, in your Spain.

I have never been able to live *completely* in my work before. Now it is to learn a great deal. To handle the beautiful skeins, of this myth of America—to realize suddenly, as I seem to, how much of the past is living under only slightly altered forms, even in machinery and such-like, is extremely exciting. So I'm having the time of my life, just now, anyway.

Spengler was one of many factors that thrust Crane into his greatest productive bout. The immediate catalyst, however, was almost certainly Allen Tate's offer to Horace Liveright to ghost-write O'Neill's preface for *White Buildings*.

When Crane heard of it, he was overwhelmed with contrition and gratitude. Here was loyalty that exceeded even the sailors', that lifted above the silly quarrel and angry words that had driven him from Patterson, above arguments over Eliot's "pessimism" and Whitman's "optimism," and represented, Crane felt, a demonstration of selfless good will the like of which he had seldom seen. "The news of Allen Tate's generosity refreshed me a great deal," he immediately wrote Waldo Frank, "truly beautiful of him."

For Tate had broken through the deadlocked publication plans. The important thing, Tate reasoned, was to get the book into print. If O'Neill couldn't write criticism, Tate could. He would do the foreword; O'Neill would sign it; and Liveright would publish the book. Separately and together, Waldo Frank, James Light, and Tate met with Liveright. Finally, from their meetings emerged a sorely needed check for $100—Crane's advance from Liveright—and a new offer from O'Neill, this time to write a short statement for the book jacket. And Liveright cheerfully agreed to Crane's request that the foreword be signed by Allen Tate. "I'm very glad things have turned out this way," Crane wrote his mother. "My umbrage toward Allen is erased by the fidelity of his action, and I'm glad to have so discriminating an estimate as he will write of me."

While the arrangements and persuasions were taking place in New York, Crane, on the Isle of Pines, celebrated his twenty-seventh birthday with an orgy of writing. If a week before he couldn't bring himself to think about his poem, now he could hardly tear himself away from it. He revised the dedicatory "Proem" to *The Bridge*—written earlier in the summer—and immediately went back to the "Ave Maria" section, rewriting and reorganizing it. Within a week he was at work on the "Cutty Sark" section and preparing plans for "Powhatan's Daughter."

By the end of July he was literally enraptured by his own work. He could talk of nothing else, think of nothing else. "I've meant to write you for a long time," he apologized to his grandmother, "but about the time I got over my ear agonies I began to swarm with ideas and I've been writing like mad for the last two weeks. I'm so glad I don't know what to do—for I began to fear that I never would be able to work down here." The next day he sent a long note to his mother. He thanked her for a birthday check, then quickly turned to his obsession.

I'm feeling quite well now—all but sleep, and whether that's due to the heat, chronic insomnia or my present ferment of creative work, I don't quite know. . . . In all other ways this is the most ideal place and "situation" I've ever had for work. Mrs. S——— lets me completely alone when I'm busy; lets me drum on the piano interminably if I want to—says she likes it—and has assumed a tremendous interest in my poem . . . She reads and sews a great deal and just talks enough to keep on splendid and equable terms with me. She's a perfect peach, in other words. The result is—that now that my health's better I'm simply immersed in work to my neck, eating, "sleeping," and breathing it. In the last ten days I've written over ten pages of the Bridge—highly concentrated stuff, as you know it is with me—and more than I ever crammed in that period of time before. I can foresee that everything will be brightly finished by next May when I come north, and I can make a magnificent bow to that magnificent structure, The Brooklyn Bridge when I steam (almost under it) into dock! For the poem will be magnificent.

During this time of hectic production, Crane was indeed writing day and night. When his energy flagged, he prepared transcripts of the poem for such friends as the Cowleys and Waldo Frank. ("One never knows what may happen, fires burn the house here, etc. and mss be burnt or otherwise lost.")

By the end of the month Crane was so engulfed in his work that he found it impossible to believe he would ever want to stop writing. "I feel an absolute music in the air again, and some tremendous rondure floating somewhere," he wrote to Waldo Frank. "My plans are soaring again, the conception swells. Furthermore, this Columbus is REAL. In case you read it—(I *can't* be serious)— observe the water-swell rhythm that persists until the Palos reference. Then the more absolute and marked intimation of the great *Te Deum* of the court, later held,—here in the terms of C's own cosmography."

With the "Ave Maria" section finished and "Cutty Sark" underway, he amused himself by noting for the Cowleys that "in the middle of *The Bridge* the old man of the sea (page Herr Freud) suddenly comes up." He then went on to explain that the research he had begun at Patterson was at last being used. ("It happens that all the clippers mentioned were real beings, had extensive histories in the Tea trade—and the last two mentioned were life-long rivals.")

The swirl of activity carried well into August. Crane began the month by trumpeting to Waldo Frank: "I feel as though I were dancing on dynamite these days—so absolute and elaborated has become the conception. All sections moving forward now at once!" At this time he set up a group of footnotes to the completed sections, more or less on the order of Eliot's for *The Waste Land*. Almost as soon as they were written they were abandoned. "However," he wrote Frank, "the angle chart from the Scientific Am. embodies a complete symbolism of both Bridge and Star, even including the motif of the 'holy tooth.' And I should like to use it on the cover." A week later he announced that he was deep in the "Powhatan's Daughter" section: "It ends up with the prodigal son from the '49. There's to be a grand indian pow-wow before that. Two of three songs have just popped out (enclosed) which come after Cutty Sark and before the Mango Tree. The last, 'Virginia' (virgin in process of 'being built') may come along any time." Now that the entire poem was clear in his mind, Crane felt under no constraint to confine himself in any way.

I skip from one section to another now like a sky-gack or girder-jack. Even the subway and Calgary Express are largely finished. Though novel experiments in form and metre here will demand much ardor later on.

I'm happy, quite well, and living as never before. The accumulation of impressions and concepts gathered the last several years and constantly repressed by immediate circumstances are having a chance to function, I believe. And nothing but this large form would hold them without the violences that mar so much of my previous, more casual work. The Bridge is already longer than the Waste Land,—and it's only about half done.

His poem, he told the Rychtariks, was "becoming 'divine.'" As August drew to a close, he focused on the elements of his life that were to serve as a private substratum for the elaborate framework of the "public" poem. This process—not unlike surgery, he told Waldo Frank—forced him into dispassionate analyses of himself. He was not trying to "justify" his career; he was now trying simply to see it and, reorganizing scraps of memories, to use it.

Work continues. The Tunnel now. I shall have it done very shortly. It's rather ghastly, almost surgery—and, oddly almost all from the notes and stitches I have written while swinging on the strap at late midnights going home.

Are you noting how throughout the poem motives and situations recur—under modifications of environment, etc.? The organic substances of the poem are holding a great many surprises for me . . Greatest joys of creation.

Working at fever pitch, Crane found all his faculties keyed up. He heard, saw, and tasted more acutely, he thought, than ever before. His letters are filled with the riot of color and sound that the island offered him. Much of this color and sound is worked unobtrusively into *The Bridge;* some spills over into poems like "The Idiot," a poem anticipated in an August 19 letter to Waldo Frank.

Here, too, is that bird with a note that Rimbaud speaks of as "making you blush." We are in the midst of the equatorial storm season; every day, often at night, torrents engulf us, and the thunder rods jab and prospect in the caverns deep below that chain of mountains across. You can hear the very snakes rejoice,—the long, shaken-out convulsions of rock and roots.

It is very pleasant to lie awake—just half awake—and listen. I have the most speechless and glorious dreams meanwhile. Sometimes words come and go, presented like a rose that yields only its light, never its composite form. Then the cocks begin to crow. I hear Mrs. S——— begin to stir. She is the very elf of music, little wrinkled burnous wisp that can do anything and remembers so much! She reads Dante and falls to sleep, her cough has become so admirably imitated by the parrot that I often think her two places at once.

I have made up a kind of friendship with that idiot boy,

who is always on the road when I come into town for mail. He has gone so far as to answer my salutations. I was unexpected witness one day of the most astonishing spectacle; not that I was surprised.—A group of screaming children were shrieking about in a circle. I looked toward the house and saw the boy standing mostly hid behind the wooden shutters behind the grating; his huge limp phallus waved out at them from some opening; the only other part visible was his head, in a most gleeful grin, swaying above the lower division of the blinds.

When I saw him next he was talking to a blue little kite high in the afternoon. He is rendingly beautiful at times: I have encountered him in the road talking again tout seul and examining pebbles and cinders and marble chips through the telescope of a twice-opened tomato can. He is very shy, hilarious,—and undoubtedly idiot. I have been surprised to notice how much the other children like him.

By the end of August, having worked himself into exhaustion, Crane decided he deserved a vacation. The principal sections of *The Bridge* were either completed or carefully outlined. In addition, he had written "The Idiot," "The Mango Tree," and the richly eloquent "O Carib Isle!" And he had drafts of "The Air Plant" and "Royal Palm," the latter no more extraordinary for its Freudian overtones (a tower, and a gray trunk "that's elephantine" and that rears "fruitless" into the sky even though it is pressed by the jungle's "hot love / And tendril" until it is "unshackled" to become "a fountain at salute") than for the fact that it is dedicated— perhaps with a trace of irony—to Grace Hart Crane.

In a cheerful note to her, Hart announces his plans for the immediate future.

Grace,—you naughty old thing!

Why don't you write me a line or so: *stingy!* You'd think you had some choice secret or so—that you wouldn't part with for the world!—while I sit here sweating out masterpiece after masterpiece! Well, I've got the main outline sections of the *Bridge* already done, and I'm going to Havana for a week, even though I can't afford it; just for the change of scene. One can't even take a walk here or budge out of one's corner without being consumed by bugs; this for the summer, anyway . . . My hay fever has reached a crisis lately, on top of which I'm very tired from doing more writing than all the last three years together (a glorious triumph!)—so I think I deserve a little variety. I'm going to see a few bad shows—and come back next week. . . .

Love to Grandma, you—and my best to Charles—

Hart

Mrs. Simpson sends you her best, and she's a dear, AND you owe her *seven* letters!

The Havana interlude proved refreshing. Hart ran out of money, of course; but he had expected to when he took the boat, so temporary poverty left him untroubled. There was always the promise of another $500 from Otto Kahn; Mrs. Simpson had assured him that she could keep him in cigars until he sold a poem; and there was the lurking possibility that C.A. might come through with a helping hand.

It was, in fact, the "fifty dollars or so" that C.A. might contribute that prompted Hart to write him a casual, happy note full of references to hay fever and the "little vacation" of a week at the "Isla de Cuba" Hotel ("grandes departamentos con servicio sanitario privado y elevador").

Though Hart explained that "it's great fun walking the quaint old streets and alleys—you don't need any company," the fact was that, on a "long cool drive along the Malecon," he was not alone. The night after writing his father, as he sat in the "Gran Cafe, 'La Diana' (abierto toda la noche)," Hart wrote on the back of a menu a more accurate account of his holiday. He posted it to Waldo Frank that night.

I'm having my last bottle of "Diamante" before leaving for la Isla tonight. A pestulant Abbe is gulping olives at the next table, and my waiter is all out of patience with him. But I cannot conceal my mirth—cheeks bulge and eyes strain at suppressions. "Fuck la Cubana!" says the waiter who is Spanish. Well I never had such a fiesta of perfect food and nectar in my life. Furthermore, if you were St. Valentine—well, maybe you are! So here goes—even if you call my little story stale.

Perhaps you have also experienced the singular charm of long conversations with senoritas with only about 12 words in common understanding between you. I allude to Alfredo, a young Cuban sailor (most of them are terrible but Alfredo is Spanish parentage, and maybe that explains it) whom I met one evening after the Alhambra in Park Central. Immaculate, ardent and delicately restrained—I have learned much about love which I did not think existed. What delicate revelations may bloom from the humble—it is hard to exaggerate.

So there have been three long and devoted evenings—long walks, drives on the Malecon, dos copas mas—and a change from my original American hotel to La Isla de Cuba, sine commotion, however.

I'm going back much relaxed. I got on a terrible tension—not a tennis court on the island! Just day after day in the heat and the house. Now I shall get a fresh view of what I have written and have still to write—and with an internal glow which is hard to describe. Silly of me to say so—but life can be gorgeously kindly at times. I'll hope to find word from you.

Once he returned to the island, memories of the satisfying week persuaded Hart to settle down with a dictionary to learn "the most beautiful language in the world." And he did manage a few heroic Spanish sentences before breaking down. "Caro Hermano," he wrote Waldo Frank.

> Estoy en casa ayer de madrugada. No dormaba la noche a bordo mar. Mucho calor, y pensaba en el carinoso Alfredo y los calles blancas Habaneros, de consigniente dulces con Mi Bien. Encontreremos de nuevo en Deciembre . . . Busco en dicionario y gramatica, sudo, raspo pelo de suerte que el tierno Cubano-Canario (parentela los Canarios) mi carta apprenderá.

Though he told Frank about a new project that was supposed to put to use the Spanish he would learn ("my next piece of work just apprehended in the form of a blank verse tragedy of Aztec mythology—for which I shall have to study the obscure calendars of dead kings"), a series of painful letters from his mother soon put all plans out of his mind. For her long silence was at last broken—and with it any hope Hart had of accomplishing any more creative work until he could find a way to help her with her problems. Grace's second marriage was foundering, and she wrote out for her son erratically spaced outpourings filled with minute accounts of her sufferings. Weeks later—after his return to New York—Hart tried to describe for Charlotte Rychtarik something of his response as he had tried once more to face a chaos that had become an inescapable part of life.

> I have no idea of just what the situation is at present with my Mother, but I have been terribly worried about it for many, many weeks. The result has been that there was only about four weeks on the Isle of Pines that I managed to accomplish any work at all; my mother's unrestrained letters, the terrific heat and bugs, etc., nearly killed me. . . .
> I don't want to do anything to hurt *anyone's* feelings, but I think that unless I isolate myself somewhat (and pretty soon) from the avalanche of bitterness and wailing that has flooded me ever since I was seven years old, there won't be enough left of me to even breathe, not to mention writing. If I could really do anything to help the situation it would be different. But it's a personal problem, after all. I'm doing my best—and I'm grateful to you for appreciating it.

Grace's letters have vanished, but their tone is suggested by two of Hart's. The first—written two days after his return to the island from Havana—deals with plantation problems. Obviously, he is trying not to be disturbed by the announcement she must have made: she has decided to leave her husband. He does, however, let feeling break through at the beginning and end of the long letter.

I was awfully glad to get your two letters on my return from Habana last Saturday, though I am deeply affected by many of the facts therein. I think you are very brave, I'm proud of your spirit, and you must not fail to maintain it steadily.

. . . I'm glad you have the good sense to take the matter as you do. Keep as cool as possible, mentally, I mean, and stop thinking about everything being "all over" for you! A good long rest (it's coming someday) and you'll think differently. Meanwhile, let it just be "all over," perhaps,—that's one way of most economically bearing the burden. Both of us are too strong-fibred to die easily, or resign under any circumstances, even though we think we have sometimes.

His second letter—written on September 19, nearly two weeks after the first—is similar in tone. But by now Grace's letters had become far more desperate.

It's hard to answer your last two letters with any real equanimity, I'm too sympathetic to all you're going through. There isn't much to say except that it's all evidently got to be faced, and the calmer the better for you, and what you'll gain after all, by having braved it. And you will gain something out of it, if you face it in the right, square way, one always does. I think of you a great deal these days, and if I sometimes seem indifferent, remember that I'm attempting a titanic job myself, and if anything of that is to be accomplished there must be some calm and detachment sought for.

Hart was trying to finish *The Bridge*. Yet whenever one of Grace's letters arrived he was thrown off his working schedule for days. He managed, nevertheless, to be encouraging. "I'll write again soon. Brace up, dear, and don't think so much about melodramatic things like old ladies' homes. This is a stiff year for both of us." He chatted about old friends, told of his new poem's progress, and assured Grace that *White Buildings*—so long delayed—was going to come out at last. "It won't be necessary for you to inquire any about my book because I have already left an order with Laukhuff to deliver you a copy as soon as it appears, which probably won't be until December. I haven't even had my proofs yet for correction."

Meantime, there were financial problems to deal with. With Grace separated from her husband, he could count on no help from her, and he had heard nothing from his father since he had written to him from Havana. Finally he decided to apply to Otto Kahn for the last installment of his loan. ("I can warn you," Hart wrote, "albeit with no excess of modesty, that the poem is already an epic of America, incomplete as it is. And it is well worth the faith which you have so kindly volunteered,—a little of which on the part of my father, who still stubbornly sulks, would also be welcome.") But Kahn was traveling and did not get his letter until well into October. By that time, Hart had written a second, more desperate, note.

> You can see the situation is a little harrowing, especially as I am ill, entirely without funds, and need to get to a cooler locality. The summer here according to the natives has been the hottest in twenty years. With my work on my mind (of which I have done considerable) and the pestilence of heat and insects, I'm completely exhausted.

Not even a cheerful letter from Malcolm Cowley, to whom he had sent a copy of the most recent draft of his poem ("I'll confine myself to saying that I think The Bridge a magnificent piece of work," Cowley wrote), could bring Crane out of this gloom.

What did lift Crane from gloom was a hurricane. In the third week of October, one whirled into the island, uprooting trees, washing out roads, unroofing houses. Hart enjoyed every minute of it. As soon as the wind began to blow and the rain to fall, he tore through the house slamming shutters, bringing in furniture and tools from the yard, sticking pots and pans under the leaky roof. When the wind reached hurricane force—plaster bulging out from the walls and patches of ceiling falling—it seemed the better part of valor to join Mrs. Simpson, Attaboy, and the other household pets under the biggest bed. There, the house shaking to pieces around them, Hart and Mrs. Simpson reminisced about all of the wild times of their lives, Hart squirming out at periods of comparative calm to bring food and drink, Victrola and records into comfortable reach. The wilder the wind, the wilder their stories and laughter. The night was a high point of Hart's life; and it was unforgettable for Mrs. Simpson. "Think I had rather to go through a hurricane every day with you who could at least laugh a little," she later wrote him. From the islanders who decided to stay on, she explained, she heard "nothing but laments and complaints." During the winds, Hart had roared, of course, but he had roared eloquently—as when, on a quick trip out of doors for the satisfaction of natural functions, he found that a most violent gust of all had blown his clothes away. "The picture of Adonis striding through the tall grass garbed 'a la natural' often comes to mind," Mrs. Simpson wrote, "and makes me wonder how we both came out so well. Instead of 'laying me flat' I think those tempestuous tirades, gasps and groans of yours served to draw you nearer to me—but for your sake, I hope you never repeat them."

The morning after the storm had been all celebration, survival calling for a dance. Balancing soggy cushions on their heads— masters of the semi-Spanish one-step—Hart and Mrs. Simpson swirled through "Valencia" and might have gone on to the rest of Hart's records had there not been so much debris in the yard that demanded cleaning up. And the next day brought the icing on the angel food. A contingent of sailors from the U.S.S. *Milwaukee* reached town, carrying enough "rescue" food and drink to stock a day-long party for all concerned. Hart had never found sailors so spectacularly available. If surviving photographs of the sailors mean anything, Operation Rescue became one of the finest picnics the U.S. Navy has ever sponsored. Hart summed up the hurricane and its aftermath: "Certain of the actors in this melodramatic episode of wind, rain, lightnin', plaster, shingles, curses, desperation and sailors—never will leave my mind."

But neither hurricane nor celebration could go on forever; and Hart was soon suffering from a combination of hangover, sinus headache, and hay fever that could at night be alleviated by Veronal but that each morning was back more thumpingly than ever—accompanied by occasional dizziness brought on by one Veronal tablet too many.

There was, Hart and Mrs. Simpson decided, little point to his staying on the island. It would be months before the house was habitable; he was flat broke; he felt rotten. It would be best, they agreed, if he returned to New York, tried to get his final $500 from Otto Kahn, and if possible settled in with Mrs. Turner in Patterson. Mrs. Simpson—almost as short of funds as Hart himself—scraped up enough to pay his passage. Taking only his manuscripts and such clothing as would fit into one suitcase, he abandoned forever the remains of his wardrobe, two trunks, and many of his books. His "texts," those books he still needed for his work on *The Bridge*, he set aside for forwarding to wherever he might next hang his water-soaked and very battered hat.

# 25

Crane reached New York on October 28; he checked in at the Hotel Albert in Greenwich Village, wrote a note requesting an interview with Otto Kahn, and telegraphed his mother that he had survived the hurricane. The next day was spent with old friends. Hart was relaxed and happy. The telegram that reached him on October 30 put a period to relaxation.

> YOU WILL NEVER KNOW HOW RELIEVED I AM IN RECEIVING YOUR WIRE FROM NEW YORK HAVE BEEN PROSTRATE IN BED FOR 2 WEEKS IN HOSPITAL THINGS IN TERRIBLE SHAPE HERE SEE KAHN HES BEEN WONDERFUL NO ONE INTERESTED HELPING ME BUT BANK AND KAHN WRITE DETAILS WHEN YOU FEEL ABLE
>
> GRACE

Before he could do anything about his mother, whose illness, he feared, was more emotional than physical, Hart had to find some source of money and he immediately made a gracious, veiled plea to his father. He explained that many letters had gone astray. ("This is due, I understand, to the corrupt manners of the Havana postoffice. Letters are often opened in the hope of finding American currency, and not reforwarded.") Perhaps letters from his father had been among them: "So, in view of this, I feel prompted to at least express my regrets to you—in case you have been as mystified at *my* silence as I have been at yours."

Before Hart could hear from his father, however, he had a cordial letter from Otto Kahn, who, apologizing for having been out of town at the time of Hart's return, suggested a brief visit. ("I am overwhelmed with accumulated work and engagements but shall be pleased to see you for an interview, which unfortunately can only be of limited duration, if you will call at my residence, 1100 Fifth Avenue, at eleven o'clock tomorrow, Tuesday.") In the course of the interview, Hart learned about Grace's requests for help for herself and for assistance in determining if Hart had been among the storm victims. Though he had not yet received the letter, three days earlier Mrs. Simpson had written Hart: "I heard today (through a man from Havana) that inquiries had been sent from Washington to the American embassy asking for news of Hart Crane; did you hear anything about it? The man could tell me nothing more." A week later she would add that Kahn's delayed telegram had at last arrived: "A telegram came for you from O.K.—say isn't he well named?"

Though the interview with Kahn was friendly, he was surprised to find that *The Bridge* was not yet ready for publication. (As usual, it was Mrs. Simpson who rose unhesitatingly to Hart's defense. "I am awfully sorry O.K. was disappointed but he won't be long. What does he expect? One can't write like a streak of lightning, although you came near doing so when you did write; and you will again when you get started. I feel sure of you.") Kahn's check for $500 was, however, promptly mailed out.

In the same mail was a check for $25 from Hart's father and with it a jolting letter. The man whom Hart sometimes pictured as unfeeling, cold, ruthless turned out to be, like his son, capable of compassion and sorrow, anguish and heartbreak.

My dear Harold:—
I have your letter of October 31st. I did not answer your letter to the Isle of Pines. It came to me at a time when I first discovered that my Frances could not recover from her present illness, and I have been so nearly crazed with grief from that day to this that I am in no condition now to write you a very satisfactory letter.
I believe your mother is passing through a very serious and unsatisfactory condition herself, both mentally and physically. I think you should come home and see her and perhaps be helpful.
As far as I am concerned, I am so nearly broken that I don't know whether I can bear up through the valley that is ahead of me or not. Your letters have always been sent to your mother for she requested that.
Am glad to know you escaped any misfortune in the Isle of Pines disaster, and I hope you are well and happy. If so, you are the only member of the Crane family who is. I am enclosing you a check for $25.00 in case you care to come home, and will be glad to know what your plans are.
With much love<br>Your Father
Your mother called me up and is much disturbed about you. Now please *write me* all particulars about yourself so I can act intelligently. I know nothing at all what Kahn is doing for you or what your needs *are*.

Hart decided, after much soul-searching, to postpone as long as possible his return to Cleveland. His presence, he felt, could do little to aid either his mother or his father. Their proximity might end his work on *The Bridge*. By the end of the first week of November, he had settled down in Patterson with Mrs. Turner and her cats. As soon as he moved in, however, wintry winds began to blow and he found himself virtually isolated. Weekends, when there were visitors at the homes of his friends, he could be counted on as an inevitable guest; and he did his best to persuade old friends to visit him on other weekends. But few visitors arrived.

Hart was lonely—and Cleveland news became considerably worse. His father now offered to help him with his living expenses —and eventually put him on a fairly dependable allowance—but the weight of gloom under which C.A. lived dominated their correspondence.

> My own condition remains as despairing as ever, and I have nothing to say which is either comforting or cheerful.
> . . . I know that you will recover your physical and mental poise as soon as you get in the quietude of your old haunts, and I only hope that things look brighter for you than they do for me.

From his mother, Hart received reports of never very clearly defined ailments, pleas for his quick return to Cleveland, and vituperative accounts of the ways in which she had been mistreated by both her husbands. Then for a month and a half he heard nothing at all.

Though Hart talked out fully with the Browns and with the Cowleys all his concerns over his family, the most direct recipients of his worries were those surrogate mothers, Mrs. Turner and Mrs. Simpson. There is no way now to recover the conversations with Mrs. Turner; that they were interminable, confessional, and frequently emotionally exhausting is one fact, though, on which everyone who saw Hart that winter is agreed. But a few of his letters to Mrs. Simpson are preserved and almost all her letters to him, letters that reveal the tough fiber of her character and that speak eloquently of her determination to help free him from what had become a nightmare bondage to parents he could no longer bear to be with yet whom he helplessly continued to love.

Of all the people he knew, he found Mrs. Simpson—with the possible exceptions of Bill Wright and Bill Brown—easiest to talk to. Many of his earliest letters to her are dominated by discussions of the amount he owed her, Hart calculating it as $250 and she insisting that it was a good deal less. ("Say boy you must be a 'rapid calculator'! How do you make out you owe me $250? I didn't make any note of it, but it surely can't be as much, so get an adding machine and figure it over again.") But it was Hart's doubts about his conduct toward his parents that provoked her most pointed rejoinders:

> Got your nice letter of Nov. 3 today. I am so happy to know
> you are feeling better. As yet I've not heard from Cleveland!
> But don't you worry; and hang on to your money awhile
> longer. Give them plenty of time, for they owe it to you and
> then some. . . .
> If I were you I would not go to Cleveland unless 'tis abso-
> lutely necessary. . . .
> . . . I'll write you just as soon as I hear anything; in the
> mean time "lay low," don't worry and please tear this up as
> soon as read.

It was his first duty, she insisted, to get on with the poem that
had so nearly been completed on the Isle of Pines. There, it had
been worries about Grace's dissolving marriage that had forced
him to interrupt work. What would happen to his poem, Mrs.
Simpson asked, if he had face-to-face meetings with Grace and a
grief-stricken C.A.?

> Suppose by now you are on The Bridge again. I do hope noth-
> ing happens to knock you off again for you got such a hard
> bump down here. I think you are right about staying away
> from Cleveland and conserving your money. Is your mother in
> hospital? I have written her three letters and I've not had a
> word from her. . . . I had thought of writing to Mr. Curtis
> asking if your mother is sick but since getting your letter I'm
> glad I didn't; too bad things are in such an uproar but I can't
> see what good I can do so 'tis best to keep quiet.

In spite of Mrs. Simpson's encouragement, however, Hart could
not press on with the remaining sections of *The Bridge*. But he
could work on the other poems he had started on the island. It
was again Mrs. Simpson, I think, whom he had to thank for the
work he turned out during these months, since her letters about
the places and persons he had known kept them constantly in
his mind. She told him how the idiot boy had survived the hurricane.

> Mrs. ——— and the "wit" had an amusing experience. They
> got out of the house just as it went down and took refuge in
> the privy, both with suit cases packed. The privy went over
> and they lost their suit cases and had to hang onto the grass
> until daylight.

In later letters, casual references of this sort helped Hart remember not a tropical world of heat and hurricane but one of joy.
"It made me feel good to know you feel a slight homesickness
for the tropics," she wrote. "I was afraid you would hate the
tropics and everyone down here, the ——— kid included. I see
him occasionally and he still wears the smile that won't come off."
Thanks to letters like this one, Hart was able to put in order

462 V O Y A G E R

some of the feelings the summer had given him. "I am hoping that your country retreat is as pleasant to you as mine is to me," he wrote Waldo Frank toward the end of November, but it was the island that was most alive in his mind. "It seems marvelous to sleep again, buried under the sound of an autumn wind—and to wake with the sense of the faculties being on the mend. Now I can look back and enjoy 'every moment' of the summer Carib days—so gracious is the memory in preserving most carefully the record of our pleasures, *their* real savor, *only*."

In the edgy quiet—with no word from his mother or father— Hart managed subdued celebrations. Thanksgiving came and went, a day spent with the Browns. It was now, however, not to his mother but to Mrs. Simpson that he wrote the detailed story of turkey, stuffing, cider, song and dance. Mrs. Simpson, who had spent the day at a baseball game and for dinner had cooked herself a slab of bacon, could not have been more pleased with the story.

I am so glad, boy, you had such a nice Thanksgiving dinner, but it almost made me weep when I read you were to have cider. If I could have a barrel of cider and a good long straw by my bedside I wouldn't want to wake up after the cider was all gone. I don't blame Sue and the others for liking those dance records. They even made my old feet tingle and at times I did some great maneuvers out in the kitchen where you couldn't see.

Her eight-page letter, like most of those she was to write that year, was full of hurricane information.

Yes, I saw the picture, in the Sunday Times, of the 2x4 blown through the royal palm. In looking over the yard here I found a piece of board 8 inches wide sticking out of the ground. I tried to pull it out but couldn't, so got a pick and dug it out; 'twas almost 3 feet in the ground. Just think what force it must have taken to drive the square end of an 8 inch board into the ground that distance with one blow.

In his answering letter, Hart summarized recent events. He hoped for immediate publication of *White Buildings*. Progress on *The Bridge* was slow ("but I'm not worried. Eventually it's going to be done, and in the style that my conception of it demands"). He had entered on a correspondence initiated by Yvor Winters from which he was getting "most stimulating criticism." But it is really Hart's awareness of climate that makes his letter most interesting; tropical hurricane versus New England blizzard fills his mind. The immense variety of the world sweeps through this letter, the letters to other friends written in the same period, and the tropical poems which Hart was putting in final shape and already beginning to send out.

Sunday—December 5th, 1926

Dear Aunt Sally:

From hurricane to Blizzards—all in six weeks! The fates sure do give me immoderate changes. It's "two below naught" outside, as they say in Hicksville; snowdrifts on the hills and windows, and my room isn't so warm but what tickling the typewriter keys is a stiff proposition. My nose got so cold last night it kept me awake, besides I could hear the congealing water click into ice in the pitcher on the washstand, ticking, ticking—every few moments. But my kerosene stoves are doing better than last winter—better oil, and I think with considerable economy I'll be able to finish the winter here, if I'm not called back to Cleveland. . . .

Got a letter from Alfredo (you remember the Havanese sailor?) yesterday. The second since I got back. I have a great time translating his Spanish—without a dictionary of any size. Once he got his niece to write me a letter in (broken) English. One of the statements ran, "Maximo Gomez, my ship—him sink in ciclon. All my clothes drowned." . . . I'm still bent on learning Spanish as soon as my fortune or inheritance permits. With enough Spanish and enough reputation as a poet,—someday I might be appointed to sell tires or toothpaste in Rio de Janeiro! . . .

I'm glad you have got under a good roof again. You're such a good brick, you ought to get dried before some of the rest. I hope you got my letters, especially the one *containing* the check. . . .

I'm eating like a horse, losing my becoming tan, and getting fat, I fear. How I would like—at the present moment—to step into a grove of royal palms, doff these woolens—and have a good glass of Cerveza with you! The storm is increasing, howling loudly. It looks as though we were to be snowed in for the rest of the winter. Really!

The blizzard howling, Hart sent off to Harriet Monroe at *Poetry* magazine the revised version of "O Carib Isle!" ("Slagged of the hurricane—I, cast within its flow, / Congeal by afternoons here, satin and vacant"), then waited for her letter, one that would demand that he justify the poem by explaining its meaning. (He had already been through a similar exchange during the summer, when he had sent her "At Melville's Tomb." Explaining in comprehensive detail his theories of the "logic of metaphor," Crane ultimately persuaded her to publish in the October *Poetry* not just the poem but her letter to him, his long reply, and her rather grudging last word.) When "O Carib Isle!" was accepted, Mrs. Simpson summed up Hart's feelings as well as her own: "I remember your correspondence with Harriet Monroe. Hope she gave you a good price for ["O Carib Isle!"]. I have her sized up as not a very generous creature." Though Miss Monroe turned out to be generous enough, "O Carib Isle!" sat in her office for the better part of a year before she got around to printing it.

There were other hurricanes brewing in Crane's poetry besides the one that ripped through the last lines of "O Carib Isle!" "The Air Plant" is nothing more nor less than a tour-de-force "objective correlative" for a hurricane, as its last line makes clear. And though the hurricane fragment "The Return" was not published until after Crane's death, it is likely that it and the also pos - humously published "Eternity" were drafted, at least in part, in Patterson in the winter of 1926–1927. "Eternity," probably the clearest statement of his hurricane recollections Crane ever set down, pictures the battered town and the battered Crane house, where he and Mrs. Simpson "shoveled and sweated." Its high point, however, is the scene in the bar, where, using sailors as emissaries from a calm and different world, Crane finds a way to define island chaos and simultaneously lift out of it.

> . . . In due time
> The President sent down a battleship that baked
> Something like two thousand loaves on the way.
> Doctors shot ahead from the deck in planes.
> The fever was checked. I stood a long time in Mack's talking
> New York with the gobs, Guantanamo, Norfolk,—
> Drinking Bacardi and talking U.S.A.

If Mrs. Simpson's correspondence helped give Crane themes for his poetry, the impending publication of *White Buildings* gave him a literary security he had never known before. He was sure that at least a few reviewers would write favorably of it. Waldo Frank had already sent him a copy of the review he would print in *The New Republic* and Yvor Winters had requested Harriet Monroe's permission to review the book. (She had already printed a passage from Winters's note in the October *Poetry*, his remark that "Faustus and Helen" should be considered "one of the great poems of our time, as great as the best of Stevens, or Pound, or Eliot." When Hart quoted such advance comments to Mrs. Simpson, she tried to keep them from going to his head. "I'm glad you are getting at last what you deserve—Praise; but don't let it spoil you. 'Twas useless for me to write that—you are too reasonable and level headed to be spoiled by well merited praise.")

Though *White Buildings* arrived in Patterson early in December, the book was not available to the public until well after Christmas. Crane, who really had attempted to control his excitement, regarded it as "a beautiful book" and immediately set to work sending out copies. Luckily for his strained finances, a good many of the recipients were literary critics who could be sent books for review. Even so, Crane proved to be his book's best customer; relatives and such close friends as Bill Sommer, Mrs. Simpson, Bill Brown, and the Rychtariks all received appropriately autographed copies.

Yet neither Mrs. Simpson's letters nor the publication of his book were enough to keep Crane from brooding over family troubles. "Nothing but illness and mental disorder in my family," he wrote Wilbur Underwood on December 16, "—and I am expected by all the middle-class ethics and dogmas to rush myself to Cleveland and devote myself interminably to nursing, sympathizing with woes which I have no sympathy for because they are all unnecessary, and bolstering up the faith in others toward concepts which I long ago discarded as crass and cheap." For Grace had again turned toward Christian Science as a solution for emotional troubles; this time, however, it seemed to her son that she was doing so for un-Christian and unscientific reasons. When she wrote him a long letter just before Christmas, spelling out once again all the "wrongs" that had been done her, Hart found himself unable to resist a frank answer.

> Your letter came yesterday and I am glad that you can once more write. Yes—it is a very melancholy Christmas for all of us. . . . I am certainly anything but joyful.
>
> Insomnia seems now to have settled on me permanently—and when I do "sleep" my mind is plagued by an endless reel of pictures, startling and unhappy—like some endless cinematograph.
>
> Am making as much effort as possible to free my imagination and work the little time that is now left on my Bridge poem. So much is expected of me via that poem—that if I fail on it I shall become a laughing stock and my career closed.
>
> I take it that you would not wish this to happen. Yet it may be too late, already, for me to complete the conception: My mind is about as clear as dirty dishwater—and such a state of things is scarcely conducive to successful creative endeavor. If it were like adding up columns of figures—or more usual labor—it would be different . . . Well, I'm trying my best—both to feel the proper sentiment to your situation and to keep on with my task. "The Bridge" is an important task—and nobody else can ever do it.
>
> My "White Buildings" is out. A beautiful book. Laukhuff has been instructed to send you out a copy as soon as he receives his order.
>
> Do write to Mrs. Simpson—Box 1373 Nueva Gerona—and tell her what to do with the house. She has written you many times asking. There won't be a timber of it left in a few weeks if someone doesn't live in it.

I'm glad you have taken up C.S. again. You never should
have dropped it. But it seems to me you will have to make a
real effort this time—with no half-way measures. It isn't anything you can play with. It's either true—or totally false. And
for heaven's sake—don't go to it merely as a *cure*. If it isn't a
complete philosophy of life for you it isn't anything at all. It is
sheer hypocrisy to take it up when you get scared and then
forsake it as soon as you feel angry about something. Anger is
a costly luxury to you—and resentment and constant self-pity.
I have to fight these demons myself. I know they are demons—
they never do me anything but harm. Why look at yourself
as a martyr all the time! It simply drives people away from
you. The only real martyrs the world ever worships are those
devoted exclusively to the worship of God, poverty and suffering—you have, as yet, never been in exactly that position.
Not that I want you to be a martyr. I see no reason for it—
and am out of sympathy with anyone who thinks he is—for
the *real* ones don't think about themselves that way—they are
too happy in their faith to ever want to be otherwise.

If this sounds like a sermon it's the best I offer sincerely.
I'm not well and still have the tonsillitis. Write me again as
soon as you feel able. . . .

If you see Grandma give her my love—I don't know where
to write her . . . I can't understand why you have to move at
once. Chas. wrote me that he was paying the rent on your
aptmt. until *Oct*. And isn't a husband *obliged* to pay the expenses—or half his income—until at least such time as a divorce has been enacted?

It is no wonder that Hart had written Underwood that he dreaded
the thought of a return to Cleveland. "Whether I can do it or not
is the question. It means tortures and immolations which are hard
to conceive, impossible to describe. There seems to be no place
left in the world for love or the innocence of a single spontaneous act."

But Hart could still count—for a few years more—on friendship. He spent Christmas Day at Eleanor Fitzgerald's house, just
down the road from Mrs. Turner's, in the company of the
Browns and friends who had come up from New York. And he
ended 1926 in a burst of letter-writing to those old friends with
whom he had fallen out of touch. For each, he provided a summary of his extraordinary year. "A mad year," he wrote Alfred
Stieglitz, "—one of every possible extreme, physical and psychic!"
Visits to friends helped; letters from friends helped. Yet at
year's end Crane was intolerably lonely. A guilty sense that somehow he had failed to do enough for his family hounded him all

through the holidays. And though a long letter from Mrs. Simpson helped persuade him that he had been wise in avoiding the temptation to go home for Christmas, it also kept fresh his feeling of a responsibility inexplicably botched.

> Does Mrs. Turner take good care of you? She'd better. Poor boy, I know just how worried you are over conditions in Cleveland but 'tis nothing you've had a part in bringing about and I can't see how 'tis going to help matters any to have you go to Cleveland. If you were "flush with cash" I'd say go at once. You do just what *you* think is right in the matter regardless of what others say; how I wish it were in my power to help you, but my purse is just as lank as yours and just now I see no way of it ever becoming any plumper. But I'm not going to lie down and mourn over it. Do your mother's friends say what is the matter with her? Surely 'tis something more serious than a swollen leg. . . . Do they say anything about your Grandmother? . . . Now as the Cayman people say "buck up." If *you* feel you must go to Cleveland do so, but go with the determination to grab the "bull by the horns" and do what you think just; sometimes a severe lesson is a good thing, and remember you always have my love and sympathy. Tomorrow is Xmas. I am to go to Miller's for dinner and had 7 invitations for tomorrow and regret exceedingly my inability to accept them all. "Louie the Chink" gave me a bottle of wine. I'll open it when "the Jones" come. Then we'll talk of you as we sip our wine. They both like you. . . .

With Christmas over, and the houses of all his friends shut up for the coldest months, Crane wandered through the empty rooms once lived in by the Tates, chatted in her kitchen with Mrs. Turner, tried to make himself write new sections of *The Bridge*, failed, tried to come to some decision regarding Cleveland, failed, tried to study Spanish, marched through the snows to the warm kitchen of the local bootlegger, marched back to Mrs. Turner's house and his chilly second-floor room, where, going through his address book, he turned again to very old friends, friends he had known in Cleveland, who would understand the forces that kept him from action of any sort. One of these letters—a note to Sam Loveman—catches accurately, I think, the special kind of loneliness through which Crane was moving, a loneliness that would dominate his days increasingly.

> Dear Sam: —
> It's frightfully cold out here—and I've had tonsillitis for two weeks. Everyone but the old woman and the cats has gone into town for the rest of the winter.
> How have you been? Do wish you would write me once a

year or so. Have you forsworn all correspondence? I have so little news that there is no excuse for this except it's Christmas time and I want to wish you the best for 1927.

Complications in Cleveland seem endless—and I may have to give up everything and go out and struggle some more in that chaos. As it is—I can't get my mind free enough of it to accomplish any work here . . . Yes "God is love"—as Mary Baker Eddy says!

As ever—
Hart.

# 26

For nearly a month Hart settled into an uneasy routine of reading most of the night and, in the early afternoons, writing letters—many of them attempts to sell the island poems and the finished sections of *The Bridge*. A series of ailments—most of them, as he himself recognized, of psychological origin—began to plague him. The insomnia that had earlier troubled him was now almost unbearable and it was complicated by his tonsillitis, which finally disappeared only to be followed immediately by an attack of conjunctivitis. Though he enjoyed talking about his ailments to Mrs. Turner and the townspeople, he hungered for the easy evenings of wit and good fellowship that he had once known in Cleveland, that he had always had with the Browns, and that, to his surprise, he had recaptured with Mrs. Simpson on the Isle of Pines.

It was, however, worry that his Christmas letter had permanently offended his mother that most troubled him. Yet as week after week went by without an answer, he began to daydream that if he were totally cut off from his family, financially and emotionally a free agent, he might become a writer able to travel unimpeded through the world. That was a dream. Reality, of course, was his empty wallet and the Cleveland silence that built a wall between him and the poem he wanted to finish. "Unable, for various reasons, to carry my work any further—I spend the time reading and studying Spanish," he wrote to Wilbur Underwood.

Yes—I hope to live in some other country someday. Or if not to live—at least to make a long visit. Spain and Mexico, Peru, etc. fascinate me. What little of the Spanish character I saw in Cuba I liked and the language is quite beautiful. Someplace where there is some liberty of action, where one can take one's time—and perhaps have something good to drink. All this is a dream—of course.—I'm already looking around for a job in N.Y. Money is low, etc. But I have to have something to think about besides The Times and H. G. Wells' prophecies.

Finally, in the third week of January, Crane received a long letter from his grandmother and, immediately afterwards, a "good" letter from his mother. Though the news they brought was in no sense good, the very fact of the letters gave reassurance of love; and he hurried to explain to his mother—as much in need of affection as he was—that his harsh Christmas note, while critical of her actions, should in no way be considered a rejection. He had hoped, he said, that she and her second husband could be reconciled, not so much because their marriage was founded on love as because it had seemed founded on a community of interests. Though he said nothing about them, he must also have remembered the crises she had gone through during her first divorce.

> The delay in the divorce proceedings may mean that Charles is reconsidering—and it might be just as well all around if he did. I have the idea that you both care for each other more than you thought you did. Such thoughts are neither here nor there, however, and I'm in no position to form judgements or advise. I've never been able to figure out what the quarrel was 'all about'—i.e. the issue involved. . . . But you must get something to do as soon as you are physically able . . . I mean—that without some kind of activity you'll remain in a morbid condition—and your viewpoint will become more warped all the time. People just have to have some kind of activity to remain healthy-minded.
>
> But you seem to [be] already much better; and I'm enormously glad. Don't think I don't care for you,—I can't help it, no matter how I feel about some things.

Grace's letter eased Crane's anxieties enough to make it possible for him to return to *The Bridge*. On the day he answered her, he got out the manuscript to copy for her the dedicatory first section; four days later he mailed off the "Ave Maria." ("Here is the first section of The Bridge—Columbus meditating at the prow on the return from his first trip—he thought he had found the way to India, you know. It's been hailed as a masterpiece by more than one. I wrote it on the Island.")

The letters from home also brought news that explained his father's silence; they told of the death of C.A.'s second wife. "I had heard nothing about the death of Frances until Grandmother's letter reached me, last Friday, I think," he explained to Grace. "CA did not trouble to answer the letter I wrote him in November, and though I shall probably not hear from him, even now, until God knows when—I wrote him a short note of condolence as soon as I heard" In fact, it would not be until the last day of March that Crane would hear from his father, a welcome letter that would send him rushing to Cleveland for the reconciliation he both feared and hungered for; in the intervening months, he failed to guess the simple explanation for his father's failure to write. Perhaps, he speculated in an end-of-February letter to his grandmother, C.A. was resentful that his poet-son had produced a volume of poetry. "I suppose, or am left to suppose, that the publication of my book has so angered him that I need not expect to hear from him again. I have written him two letters, neither of which he has answered, so I can't do more." Even when Grace explained that C.A., shaken by the death of Frances, had been put on a regimen of sedatives, the true cause of that disturbing silence eluded Hart.

I took enough veronal powders on the Island during those mad last days to convince me that there's nothing worse. And they didn't even give me sound sleep! The feelings next day were weird in the extreme. I hope that CA won't keep them up very long. His attitude and emotions toward life would probably make one gasp if one could get a cross section of them. For a long time he has seemed to me as thorough a specimen of abnormality as I have ever heard of. I've given up even trying to imagine how he sees or thinks. I probably shall continue to not write him until he answers some of my former letters— or gives me some sign that he wants to hear from me. I sent him a copy of the recent New Republic, but without any note or comment. He probably likes to build up the picture that he's creeping around in utter disgrace on account of the public 'disgrace' his son has made of himself. Well, the thirty thousand people that read the New Republic probably wouldn't give him much sympathy—regardless of their estimate of my particular value.

The notion that C.A. was grief-stricken seems to have been something Hart could not face up to. For he had visualized his father as a man of passion, not as a man of sustained tenderness and affection.

That he would soon acknowledge how wrong he had been is a credit both to his honesty and to his insight. When he returned to Cleveland that spring to spend two weeks, not with his mother but with his father and his young cousin Fredrica, he came to know and understand C.A. better than ever before. Perhaps most important of all, he realized belatedly how different C.A.'s life and his own might have been had the marriage to Grace been as satisfying as the marriage to Frances.

I asked Fredrica Crane, who lived with C.A. and Frances during the last year of Frances's life, to tell me what she could of their marriage. Her answer indicates, I suspect, much that Hart himself became aware of in those April weeks when he and C.A. learned again to talk to one another. Frances Crane was born Frances Kelley, Fredrica told me, "Frances Kelley from Kansas City. C.A. met her there in the years when he had his candy factory. He built a branch in Kansas City." She was a typical Irish beauty. "She had the very dark, almost black, naturally wavy hair, and great big blue eyes, very blue eyes, and long dark lashes and brows, and white, white skin. She was quite stunning." But beyond being beautiful, she was, Fredrica said, "one of the sweetest, dearest people I've ever known in my whole life." It was this tenderness that C.A. responded to; and, as in everything else he did, he responded to it overwhelmingly. "He absolutely adored her. I think—I think his love for Frances was—was *the* most important thing in his life. You see, his life with Grace was one long battle. That was a mistaken marriage from the start. . . . But Frances was the love of his life. There's no question in my mind about that. He worshipped her."

But in February all Hart knew was that C.A. had not written him of Frances's death and that neither *White Buildings* nor the reviews he had dutifully clipped and mailed had been acknowledged.

Though C.A. said nothing about *White Buildings*, other Clevelanders did. "I'm very much amused at what you say about the interest in my book among relatives and friends out there in Cleveland," Crane wrote his mother shortly before the book was published. "Wait until they see it, and try to read it! I may be wrong, but I think they will eventually express considerable consternation; for the poetry I write, as you have noticed already, is farther from their grasp than the farthest planets. But I don't care how mad they get—*after* they have bought the book!"

When it did appear, some Cleveland relatives found it, though mysterious, strangely satisfying. It was not the kind of poetry they were used to, but they could recognize references to persons and places with which they were familiar and they did their honest best to be proud of the book. C.A.'s two sisters, the Aunt Alice and Aunt Bess that Hart had as a child been close to, displayed the book on their living-room tables. Another aunt, who worked in a bookstore, sold it to every customer who was a reader of poetry and to a few who were not. If not every Clevelander he was acquainted with bought the book—or having bought it, understood it—Crane could not blame his family for failing to support him. "What you say about the reactions to it on Cornell Road are both amusing and touching," he wrote Grace. "And when I read about Mrs. Jackson taking a copy to read to the Garrettsville Federated Women's Clubs I rocked with laughter! The poor dears will never, NEVER know what in hell to make of it all! I'm awfully grateful to Aunt Alma for having sold so many."

And there were congratulatory letters, of course, from such Cleveland writers as James Daly, Kathryn Kenney, and Bill Wright. Wright's letter undoubtedly meant the most to Crane. Wright had been the first person to be in touch with him after the summer hurricane—producing a long letter, in some ways an awkward one. He was plainly worried that Hart had been one of the storm victims and yet he was attempting to be cheerful.

He had, however, been going through an emotional hurricane of his own, periods of intense depression alternating with the happiness of his recent marriage. He was sure, he wrote, that Hart had survived. "With all your internal combustion, you oppose too much resistance to the cosmos; and you are too tough a knot spiritually to be much troubled by a mere physical tempest." From all apparent evidence, indeed, it should have been Hart rather than easygoing Bill Wright who would suddenly be unable to cope with private feelings. But that was not how things worked out.

> Don't accuse me of being "hearty," Harty. I've grown much less so in the last few months, by the way, the nervous storm that has been sweeping me having now turned its attention to my digestive system and reduced my weight to somewhat less than it has been in several years. However, I am somewhat recovered now, am able to eat with some assurance that I may digest the meal, and seem to be getting a little of my vitality back. I'm such a melancholy devil, though, that I completely go to pieces under the strain of physical weakness and get under the influence of all kinds of crotchets and phobias.

Wright faced at this time an impending nervous collapse, one that he had hoped would be forestalled by marriage.

> I've been married since I wrote you last, too. I hesitated a good while on account of my physical and mental state, but I decided to go on with it immediately since there was everything to gain and nothing to lose and since Margaret was anxious to get on a somewhat more settled basis. It was consummated in an Ohio farmhouse (her grandmother's) on one of the starriest nights I ever saw, with the 96 year old gammer sitting by like a veritable Cumaean sybil while the bans were pronounced. We avoided the ceremonial display by turning a rehearsal the night before into the act itself.

Settled in Warren, Pennsylvania, Bill and Margaret had tried through quiet living to ease some of the tensions Bill was suffering from.

> My job is not over-strenuous and if I succeed in overcoming my many indispositions I shall look forward to a comparatively calm season for a few years. It is very brave country hereabouts, and just now we are watching the last fires of autumn die out. I want, if I am able, to do some shooting during November. After that we hole in for the winter. When you return to these U.S. I hope, providing we are both of the living, you will come to see us.

Hart, not quite sure what tone would be proper, had held off answering. All he had been able to manage was a postcard: "Safe and sound though the roof and chimneys came off. Am getting settled back in the country. Working hard to finish my poem before Xmas. Thanks for your good letter—will try to answer it soon. Best to you, Margaret.—Hart."

When Bill Wright's second letter arrived—shortly after the publication of *White Buildings*—Hart had no choice but to answer it, for Wright's nerves had grown worse. "He was married last Fall," Hart explained to his mother, "and apparently hasn't been well for the last several years. He is just now returning from some sanitarium in Clifton Springs, NY where he's been undergoing treatment for nervous indigestion and complications. That nervous breakdown he had at Yale seems to have permanently crippled him. He wrote me a rather pathetic letter congratulating me on my book—which he said he'd seen and bought."

Wright had become Hart's last link to his childhood. Both of them had, of course, changed since the days when they walked home together from Eleanor T. Flynn's dancing school, their heads full of poetry and promise. Yet there was a core of shared life that was different in character from that experienced in any other friendship either of them ever made. It was, perhaps, the idealized brotherhood Hart hoped for with each new friend. But with Wright it actually existed, and there is in the letters they exchanged a careful effort not to tamper with the past. Most of their letters are, therefore, oddly formal; it is only when one of them is in serious trouble that the sustaining core of friendship reappears. It reappears vividly in the letter Hart composed on March 11, 1927. He told first of his life in Patterson and ended by saying that he was sending a copy of Hemingway's new novel, *The Sun Also Rises*. But the heart of the letter is memory—and the different kinds of suffering that they shared.

> I feel very guilty for not having more adequately answered your good long letter of hurricane days. I've been laboring under a number of disabilities however,—insomnia (induced by tropic suffocations, I guess) a whole train of minor ailments besides, and last but not least a rather overwhelming accumulation of family worries and concerns. I refer to my mother's second excursion to the divorce courts in Cleveland, my grandmother's continued critical condition, etc., etc. It's so maddening not to be able to be of any help or use in such situations—which have been rather chronic in my family since I was seven. . . .
>
> Your letter came just before I left on a ten-mile trudge to town today (for lemons and tobacco!)—and along the way I had time to think over a lot of our bygones together in Cleveland, and later in Warren and NY. I'm very sentimental, and though I won't burden you with much of it on paper, I won't promise not to let loose on you sometime when I have your

ear again. Let me only say that your letter with its generosity and kindly interest meant a great deal to me; in the mood I was in I didn't deserve so much. It's a shock to learn that you're so seriously laid up. It must be hellish. You are extremely modest about details—but I'll venture that whatever it is you'll come out all right. Modern medicine and surgery effect more wonders every day; this sounds like a bromide, but it's my honest impression at any rate.

For weeks, nostalgia for lost days, induced by the letters from Wright, dominated Crane's feelings. And it was reinforced by some photographs Grace found among old papers and sent him. One was of the house in Warren, Ohio, in which Hart had spent many of his early schooldays. The photograph, now lost, brought back a flood of memories—"sentimentalities," Crane confessed—that were too immediate for poetry, though they would eventually appear as a series of private references in the childhood sections of *The Bridge*. "That was a happy thought," he wrote her, "—sending me the picture of the Kinsman house. It is particularly beautiful."

What of Zell and Helen these days? I haven't of course, corresponded with Zell since our little blow-up of nearly two years ago. Every once in a while I have a dream with Warren scenes in it. Hall Kirkham, Donald Clark, Catherine Miller, Leonard Bullus, Mrs. Potter with her great heart-shaped bosom—and Mrs. Gilbert gasping with her goitre—what has become of them all, I wonder. I once wrote a poem with Mrs. Potter as the subject—but it didn't turn out to be much of anything but a sentimentality, and I guess I threw it away.

It was in this fashion—suffering from minor ailments, reliving the past, writing when the rare calm letter from Cleveland would give him freedom to write—that Hart spent the winter. "It's sixteen below and the sun brightly shining," he wrote Waldo Frank one late-January afternoon. "I'm living in practically one room— the kitchen—with the old lady these days—to keep warm. Writing a little again on the Bridge and studying Spanish."

At the end of February, Hart and Mrs. Turner were snowed in. A week later, however, in the first pre-spring thaw, Hart went sloshing through soft snowbanks and ankle-deep puddles to the Browns' hillside farm.

There is a vague roar of snow water streaming the valley so the roads may open soon if we don't have another inundation soon. I've just come back from a moonlight tour of Tory Hill—the Ford (with its ditty box and rear parts quite gone) looks rather lonely. I was tempted to steal the shovel lying in the coal pile, but desisted. Everything looks well around the house—outside at least. The spring gurgles. . . .

There is no particular news except the recent terrific enlargement of Señora Turner (I hope you won't inflate this mention into a myth of carnality on my part!) and I'm much tempted to recite her the limerick on the young lady from Thrace, where belly rhymes with Nelly, etc. She is knitting a crimson scarf for her next winter's use which Bloody Mary would envy . . .

Give Malcolm my best . . . I hope you and Sue decide to come out to the woods fairly early, however uncertain the prospects of my continuance here are.

But thaw gave way once more to winter weather. "Spring was really with us—but has left," Hart told Wilbur Underwood on the first calendar day of spring.

Every kind of bird was in full choir around the valley last week. Now there is no sound but the cold wind full of icicles. Last week I planted lettuce in the cold-frame. I long for green things again. The old lady is going to look for cowslips as soon as they are likely to sprout. I never ate any—but they sound to me always as good as some Shakespearian lyric.

At last winter wore down into spring, Hart having taken only one ten-day "vacation" in New York during the whole time between his return from the Isle of Pines and his April trip to see his grieving father. The New York vacation—though ostensibly an effort to find work and to discuss with Liveright the critical reception *White Buildings* was getting—may have been suggested by a January 17 letter from Gaston Lachaise, who asked to borrow for an exhibition at Stieglitz's gallery the sculptured seagull he had earlier presented to Crane. Though he found no job, Hart did see Cowley and the Browns and spent quite a bit of time with Isidor and Helen Schneider, both of whom he had come to know well.

There was also a publisher's cocktail party for Hart to attend, a section of *The Bridge* having earned him the invitation. "I am so glad that you enjoyed the Columbus part," he wrote to Grace nearly a month after the New York hangovers had subsided.

It is coming out next September in The American Caravan, a yearbook of American letters, just started by Paul Rosenfeld, Alfred Kreymborg and Van Wyck Brooks, and published by the Macauley Co. When I was last in NY the owners of the Macauley Co. gave a large party to all the contributors up in a huge but unbelievably vulgarly furnished and expensive apartment on West End Avenue. There seemed to be everybody there I'd ever heard of. Enormous quantities of wine, cocktails and highballs were served. I had just landed in town after three months with the bossy cows—and I had my share.

A literary cocktail party was not, however, Hart's favorite kind of dissipation; after an evening with the intellectuals, he needed the tough company of waterfront dives. He summed up for the Browns the end of his vacation and the return to the country.

The last two nights in town were mainly spent on the Hoboken waterfront, where you want to go (though it's for men only) if you want the good old beer, the old free-lunch counter and everything thrown in—for 15¢ a glass. Whiskey and gin are also much superior to the other side of the River and cheaper. Take the Christopher St. ferry. Walk up *past* Front St. There are three in a row. Begin with McKelly's—or some such name.

The last night went flying back to Brooklyn with a wild Irish red-headed sailor of the Coast Guard, who introduced me to a lot of coffee dens and cousys on Sand Street, and then took me to some kind of opium den way off, God knows where. Whereat I got angry and left him, or rather Mike Drayton did. . . .

Mrs. Turner was laid up all day Monday from an excess of oatmeal eaten at breakfast in celebration of my return. Went up to Tory Hill yesterday and found everything just as I left it. Encountered Mrs. Powitzki at the Jennings and think she is marvelous. Did you ever talk to her? I never heard such loluctions. I should love to tickle her. Since which I've been reading the Cock also Rises (sent me by a Cleveland friend) and have developed a perfect case of acidosis. No wonder the book sold; there isn't a sentence without a highball or a martini in it to satisfy all the suppressed desires of the public. It's a brilliant and a terrible book. The fiesta and bullfight best. No warmth, no charm in it whatever, but of course Hemingway doesn't want such.

When the Browns finally put in an appearance, toward the end of March, for a weekend of house-opening chores, Hart was more than eager to do his part in welcoming them. They had come up with other neighbors—owners of several barrels of home brew—and all of Hart's acquaintances soon heard about the first day of their visit: an "authentic" typewriter fling. It all started, Slater Brown recalled, after everyone had gone off to sample some of Bina Flynn's wine. Hart, who more than sampled, eventually made everyone promise to write to Mexico's President Calles, whom he admired. Since he and Brown had been studying Spanish together, Hart reasoned, each of them should be able to produce a masterful document. And Hart dashed home to begin work on his. But, alas, the Spanish wouldn't flow; Hart, furious, tossed his typewriter out the window. After he'd dashed down, rescued it, and returned to his second-floor study, he discovered that it still wouldn't write Spanish and he tossed it out the window again. This time, however, Mrs. Turner had beaten him to the snowpile in which the typewriter had landed and was tenderly carrying it toward the house. Hart was desperate to compose his letter and Mrs. Turner was desperate to save the typewriter, so within seconds the two of them were rolling around the yard wrestling for the machine. Hart himself wrote out the story for Allen Tate.

> B———s and Browns drove up Saturday and left last evening. The B——— casques are 150 gallons full of successful and highly combustible nectar.—I celebrated to the full—returning to my boudoir late Saturday night and knocking Señora Turner down besides hurling my Corona from the window in a high dudgeon because it wouldn't write to President Calles automatically in Spanish and express my "untold" admiration for his platforms.

"The next day," Slater Brown told me, "I walked down towards Hart's house and I saw all the trees below his window festooned with the typewriter ribbon." Brown, about to leave for New York, offered to take the typewriter with him. "Bill has taken it to the hospital for long and I fear expensive treatment," Hart wrote Tate. But the typewriter was well beyond repair, and Brown eventually arranged to trade it in on a new one. "I remember I had great difficulty in explaining what had happened to the typewriter because it had dirt and grass in it—in its works."

After two weeks of handwritten letters, Hart—swearing vows of moderation—typed up on his new portable a spate of important letters. For Edgell Rickword, editor of *The Calendar*, had asked if Hart would be interested in having the new firm of Wishart and Company distribute *White Buildings* in Great Britain. Though the offer, which had been arranged through Allen Tate, finally came to nothing (Liveright was not able to supply sheets), for months Hart looked forward to wide distribution.

He also entertained himself—sometimes disturbed himself—with the reactions of reviewers and friends. At first, *White Buildings* had nothing but praise. On January 23, he had written his mother:

> It is going to get some excellent and laudatory reviews. Waldo Frank's in the New Republic (a full page) ought to be out any day. Matthew Josephson is reviewing it in the NY Herald, Yvor Winters in the Dial, Archibald MacLeish in Poetry . . .

Yvor Winters, who is a professor of French and Spanish at the Moscow University, Idaho, writes me the following:

"Your book arrived this evening, and I have read it through a couple of times. It will need many more readings, but so far I am simply dumfounded. Most of it is new to me, and what I had seen is clarified by its setting. I withdraw all minor objections I have ever made to your work—I have never read anything greater and have read very little as great." Etc. So you see what kind of a review he is apt to write.

Waldo Frank ends his article in the New Republic by saying:

"At present Hart Crane is engaged in a long poem that provides him with a subject adequate for his method: the subject indeed which Mr. Tate prophecies in his introduction. Yet already White Buildings gives us enough to justify the assertion, that not since Whitman has so original, so profound and—above all, so important a poetic promise come to the American scene."

Five days later, in a letter to Frank, Crane added to the list of "wonderful reviews" a new group by other well-known writers. In addition to the "great explosion" that Hart expected Yvor Winters to provide, there would be "another from Mark Van Doren (of all the unexpected!) in the Nation this week." "Seligmann," Crane continued, "has written a sincere and just estimate in the Sun; Josephson in the Herald Tribune; MacLeish in Poetry; etc. I don't know any further, but there may be other surprises. I certainly feel myself very fortunate, considering the type of stuff in WB."

By mid-February, reactions had begun to come in from English and European writers and editors. Eugène Jolas, who had just translated "O Carib Isle!" into French for an anthology of modern American poetry, asked if he might publish the poem in the first issue of *transition* and went on to sum up *White Buildings* as an "immense" book. The London *Times* published a favorable review; other foreign criticism was similarly enthusiastic. But in America Crane had surprises that were not pleasant. *The New York Times* gave very little space to the book. (The review was printed "along with several others," Crane explained to Grace. "They often bunch them that way.") And in reviews by friends and acquaintances strange last-minute revisions proved jolting. Waldo Frank's review in *The New Republic* had been condensed, with the passage Crane had quoted to his mother among the editorial casualties. "The one quotable paragraph (from the publisher's standpoint) has been lopped off: the last, with the allusion to Whitman," Crane wrote Tate. "The rest will be a sufficient warning to most readers not to read the book, for it's one long dissertation on the subject of obscurity." Crane was fully conscious of the immediate impact of such a review.

The genial tactics of the editorial proofreader have even helped Frank on a little by falsifying his ms.—at least the copy I hold. For instance, 'the obscure poet he is likely *for long* to remain' has been changed to read '*ever* to remain.' This not only alters the time-limit before my possible admission to the panting bosom of the generous reader, but changes the emphasis of the context in such a way that the reader infers the

reviewer's prophecy to be that I shall probably *never* write anything that is comprehensible! With the world all flying into
trillions of tabloids I probably shall not!

There were other disturbing shifts. *The Dial*, which was to run
Yvor Winters's review, printed instead an unsigned *"briefer"* in
which Crane was accused of producing poetry that was "what
one might call high class intellectual fake." The note, Crane and
Tate agreed, was probably written by Conrad Aiken, but was not,
Crane argued, something that either he or Tate should reply to.
"I do not feel . . . there is any particular justification for attacking
him. He has a perfect right to claim that many of the poems are
specious . . . He may quite well believe that he is right on this
score. For years, remember, perfectly honest people have seen
nothing but insanity in such things as The Tiger—."

Irritated by the way his book had been misunderstood, annoyed by lady editors and ladylike male editors who, unable to
distinguish between ironic wit and sentimental self-pity, rejected
poems for all the wrong reasons, Crane threw up his hands in
mock despair. "What strange people these old virgins (male and
female) are. Always in a flutter for fear bowels will be mentioned, forever carrying on a tradition that both Poe and Whitman spent half their lives railing against—and calling themselves
'liberals.' " "The Dance" section of *The Bridge*, which Crane had
left at *The Dial* offices, would, Crane predicted to Tate, probably
be rejected. "I've had to submit it to Marianne Moore recently,
as my only present hope of a little cash. But she probably will
object to the word 'breasts,' or some other such detail. It's really
ghastly. I wonder how much longer our market will be in the
grip of two such hysterical virgins as The Dial and Poetry!" But
*The Dial* and *Poetry* were only symptomatic of an editorial tradition that, rightly or wrongly, Crane regarded as effete, precious,
at its worst coy and saccharine. "I envy buckandwing dancers
and the Al Jolsons of the world sometimes. They don't have to
encounter all these milksops . . . and they do *please*. They're able
to do some 'good' to somebody and when they laugh people don't
think they are crying."

Feelings of this sort—almost always instigated by a condescending rejection—sometimes persuaded Crane that the sacrifices
he made for the good poems he knew he could write were, after
all, pointless. If editors preferred mediocrity to excellence, what
hope was there of building an audience of good taste? "Out here
one reads the paper—one sees evidence mounting all the time,"
he wrote to Tate, "—that there is no place left for *our* kinds
of minds or emotions." There was even the dreadful possibility
that people with "our" kinds of minds and emotions had become so blasé that they were incapable of pleasure and unlikely

to apprehend truth. "Unless we can pursue our futilities with some sort of constant pleasure there is little use in going on—and we must apprehend some element of truth in our mock ceremonies or even our follies aren't amusing." Spelling out in letters such as this the feelings that the "Quaker Hill" section of *The Bridge* would give form to, Crane was obviously working—though inconspicuously—much harder at his big poem than anyone realized.

Yet if a rejected section of *The Bridge* could bring gloom, a favorable review could change his entire view of the world. Two weeks after his disheartened letter, a set of clippings about *White Buildings* was sent to him; again he reported his feelings to Tate.

> Altogether, I think that this is the last time in our lives to be badly discouraged. The ice is breaking—for both of us, as near as I can see—in several different quarters—and I'm beginning to detect many salutary signals. Apparently our ideas and idiom evokes some response—however slow. And what we do win in the way of intellectual territory is *solid*—it can't be knocked over by every wave that comes along—as could Masters, Bodenheim, Lindsay, etc. We wouldn't believe the developments of the next five years if they could be detailed now!

While Crane would certainly not have believed the developments of the coming five years, the last of his life, at the moment he was far more concerned with money than with prophecy.

Money, of course, was always a problem for Crane—but in these months he was especially troubled. For he could no longer hope for assistance from either his mother or his father, and he had exhausted the last of the promised "loans" from Otto Kahn.

Though the small sum Mrs. Simpson realized from the island sale of Hart's trunks was some help—as was a loan she advanced him—and though he sometimes earned ten or twenty dollars from the sale of a poem, most of the time he was desperately poor. When, for example, Isidor Schneider, toward the end of February, wrote of a possible editorial position on *The New Yorker*, Hart found himself incapable of getting together the price of a train ticket.

Of various get-rich-quick schemes he invented, Hart's most ambitious was a plan to do a biography of John Augustus Roebling, the designer of the Brooklyn Bridge, who had once lived in the room Hart had occupied at 110 Columbia Heights. Hart, indeed, worked up enough enthusiasm to set Allen Tate on the trail of Roebling's heirs and a possible publisher. The point, Hart told his friends, was that the biography would help sell the poem and the poem would help sell the biography. Though his project never got past the talking stages, dwindling in Hart's correspondence from a "burning" idea to a "promising" one to an idea likely to be impossible to carry out, for a while at least it seemed a way to combine work on the poem with an income-producing activity.

What put a stop to the plan was C.A.'s letter of March 31 offering his son "much love," railroad fare to Cleveland, and news of Grace's improved spirits.

> I have not written you for more than weeks. There is little to say. We are all of us trying to make the best of a bad situation and Fredrica, Frances' brother and myself are living at the apartment. I have been paying but little attention to the business, some days working less than two hours, and have been putting in most of my time where roads were good and trying to get my mind on something besides my troubles.
>
> The first of May I am going up into the far North; well up toward Hudson Bay, and investigate a mining property which I have acquired a small interest in . . . If I do this we will close up that flat when I go away, and then I will decide when I am gone what I will do on my return, but before we do this it occurs to me you might want to come home for two or three weeks, and now is a good time for you to do it. There is plenty of room in the house and you could spend as much time with me as you wished, for time hangs heavily on my hands. I am enclosing you a check which will enable you to find your way here if you are so inclined; if not, you can use it for things which you need.
>
> I should have written you under ordinary circumstances long ago that your book of poems has raised much favorable comment from my friends who are capable of understanding it. As for myself, I have not read it for my mind is only on my troubles and even a magazine article has failed to interest me, or anything which pertains to an outside matter.
>
> Mr. Morgan was in the office Tuesday and said he would soon write you a congratulatory letter. I showed him the article by Mr. Frank and he thought it an excellent one.
>
> I hear from your mother through Bessie and Byron [Madden] and they tell me she is in a much better frame of mind and, no doubt, will be glad to see you, for Bessie told me not more than an hour ago she is very lonely and has little to take up her time. All things considered, it looks like an advantageous hour for you to come back . . .
>
> Your father has had a blow that has staggered him, and I shall be glad to have you put in some time with me, for I am lonesome enough even under conditions which could not be bettered, or with friends who help all they can.
>
> With much love, I am
>
> Your father,<br>CAC

Hart read the letter, walked to town to cash the check, bought a ticket for Cleveland, returned to Mrs. Turner's to pack enough clothes to last him for two or three weeks, paid several weeks' back board money, and set out immediately for Cleveland and reconciliation. He was about to make his first visit under his father's roof since that day, more than ten years earlier, on which he had hurriedly been packed off to New York so that father and mother might, in his absence, end the marriage that had brought him into the world.

He was returning, of course, to help his mother through her second divorce and to help lighten his father's grief at the death of a second wife. It must have seemed a return to a kaleidoscope Cleveland, the fragments of his youth waiting for him but their design drastically, irrevocably altered, and himself altered too, though it would take other eyes than his own to see each of the changes.

# 27

Crane's April visit to Cleveland was one he both yearned for and dreaded, for he knew how unstable Grace would become as her second divorce drew closer. Letters from his grandmother and occasional letters from Grace had reflected her shifting feelings about leaving Charles Curtis, her distrust of friends, her terrors of poverty-stricken old age. Hart had also been the recipient of harsh words; his remaining in Patterson was, she felt, a "betrayal." Consequently, his letters in the month before his return are filled with reassurances of love and pleas that she remain calm. "I don't want you to think that you haven't my sympathy these days," he had written on March 1.

> You don't know how horribly upset I am—and have been for many months. I could not withhold my sympathies from you—no matter how much I might disagree with you on the question of your judgement etc. which brought about the present state of affairs. Affection is something that overrules reason always and I suffer with you much more than you think.
>
> There seems to be only one thing to do. Face the situation, and make it as simple as possible by putting all unessentials out of mind.
>
> By this I mean—put out of your thoughts the reactions of all your former "friends"—ignore them. I know it isn't easy. But you are not going to have to live in Cleveland always.
>
> Get up your ire enough to dominate the court. You ought to get some alimony—*don't* urge any lump settlement. But get so much per month if you can.
>
> For the present we'll have to be separated. . . . If I can get anything in N.Y. I'll send you something from that. I'm trying as best I can to get a connection.

During this month, the barometer of Crane's feelings—his capacity for work—responds precisely to the tone of Grace's letters. When she is optimistic, there is real hope that his poem will again flower. "Your splendid long letter of last week will have to be answered a little later when my eyes are better," he wrote her from the midst of his conjunctivitis. "I [am] immensely glad to know—and the tone of your letter shows it—that you are facing things with energy and courage. It helps me a lot, and I 'may be able to get to work again on my poem when I get rid of this eye trouble." A few days later he explained that her good letter had helped not only his writing but his vision: "Nervous crises always affect my eyes." He was, he said, at work again on *The Bridge* and was elated over selling "Powhatan's Daughter" to *The Dial*.

Similarly, it is no accident that immediately after getting a "bad" letter from Grace he abandons work on the poem and his exploratory work on the biography of Roebling. "Such stories as got circulated concerning me by that crazy ———, rattle headed ———, and scared Chas Curtis would make one lose faith in every one," she had written. She had become convinced that one friend was spreading rumors that she was a drug addict and that another had made disparaging comments about the troubles she had had with her leg. Only escape from Cleveland—perhaps to her son—might ease her mind. And yet there seemed to be no way for her to leave.

> My divorce case is liable to come up any day now, and I am just sitting on the edge all the time—nervous and unsettled and still dazed somewhat at the whole turn of affairs.
>
> I wish I didn't have to live here in Cleveland another day— I just despise the place in every way—but I can't budge on account of mother. She has *no one* but me. My mind is so confused about things pertaining to myself that I can't see anything clearly, can't formulate any plan that seems right or that will solve my problems.
>
> I certainly wish I might have a visit with you . . .

That Grace was not faring well, he realized as soon as he paid her that visit. She was near exhaustion, both from the emotional stresses of the divorce and from the physical demands of caring for her mother. Though Mrs. Hart was almost as pert as always, she was much of the time bedridden, and her daughter had become her principal companion.

His efforts to help his mother filled Hart's daytime hours. Together, they made elaborate plans for the day when her divorce would become final. She had been invited by wealthy Chicago friends to spend some time with them and Hart encouraged her to make the trip. Afterwards, he felt, she might come to Patterson and spend at least part of the summer with him at Mrs. Turner's house.

Hart's presence was also good for Mrs. Hart, who seemed to gain in strength and vitality so long as he stayed in Cleveland. She was sure, she said, that she would be able to get along very comfortably as a boarder in the house of an old friend while Grace recuperated in Chicago.

If he was helpful in cheering up his mother and grandmother, his father was helpful in easing some of Hart's problems. C.A. proved, to Hart's surprise, to be most congenial. The superficial gruffness and bluster of his manner, dispelled by grief, had been replaced by an almost awkward gentleness. He tried to make his son comfortable in the huge apartment that now housed only himself and his niece, Fredrica. And Hart, in turn, did his best to ease his father's grief. "C.A. was in a broken-hearted state," Fredrica remembered, "and he was so happy to have his son with him. . . . The two of us were really concentrating on trying to help C.A. to adjust a little. C.A. appreciated this effort on Hart's part. There was a real mellowness there that there never had been before. They were more back on the basis that they might have been on, perhaps, a good many years earlier, of father and son, and gentle kidding, and jokes and fun and normal—more or less, at least—superficially normal—father and son family relationship."

Hart spent almost every evening with his father, going out alone only when C.A. had to spend an evening out. Even then it was usually Hart who got home first. One such night was particularly vivid in Fredrica's memory. She had seen relatively little of Hart; Western Reserve drama courses and rehearsals took up many of her evenings. On this night, however, she found him settled in the living room, a copy of Marlowe's *Dr. Faustus* in hand. "Of course, I didn't know a thing about Hart's background. I was young and naïve, and to me he was just a perfectly wonderful older cousin that I was beginning to know for the first time. And he treated me like a sort of long-lost little sister, like 'why haven't I ever found out I had a young relative like this before?'" They began talking about the Elizabethan dramatists and soon began reading through *Dr. Faustus*, Hart, with all the gusto in the world, roaring out one after another of Marlowe's great oratorical speeches. "He was . . . gay and jolly and having a wonderful time," Fredrica recalled. "He was reading *Faustus*— tramping up and down this long, long apartment—it was enormous—and then he'd break that mood, and sit down at Frances's piano. Frances had a beautiful Steinway Grand, which was one of the very lovely things that C.A. had bought for her, a magnificent instrument. He sat down and played away. I'd never heard him do this before, because I hadn't known him really before. I was astounded. I remember saying to him, 'Hart, why don't you do something with this? You play magnificently.' He just laughed. This was just one of the things he did for fun, and he could never in the world be serious about it. He said, 'Ask Aunt Alice what a rotten music pupil I am'—that sort of thing. Because he was a trial. She used to try to teach him, apparently, when he was a little boy, and he just would not do his scales and exercises." I asked if she could recall anything he had played, but her memory was only of rich variety. "It was all improvisation."

As April 19, the date for Grace's divorce hearing, drew near, tension mounted in both households in which Hart spent his Cleveland hours. Never was his role-playing so intricate as it now became. In the mornings and afternoons, Hart Crane discussed with his mother her divorce and his literary career. In the evenings, Harold Crane discussed with his father C.A.'s business projects and his own prospects in advertising. For, of course, at 5 P.M. every day, Crane changed not just parlors but names.

Grace wanted Hart to stay in Cleveland through the hearing, but she was also anxious to have him avoid the courtroom and the accounts of what had gone on. Finally they agreed that the day might be less painful if he accepted C.A.'s invitation to join him on a trip to New York. Father and son left the day before the hearing commenced.

Perhaps, for once in his life, Hart had made the right move. The newspaper headlines were brutally sensational. "Denied Car, She Seeks Divorce," blared the Cleveland *News*. "Says Mate 67 Let Love Cool," announced the Cleveland *Press*. Though the stories themselves were relatively tame, Grace and her friends found them a horror. The account in the *News* particularly upset her; it was, she wrote her son, "as ridiculous as it is false. You know I never asked Chas to drive his car in all my life, nor wanted to. The Judge asked me if I did, and I said no—I used the street car or taxi as the occasion demanded." The story, however, had given an altogether different impression.

Complaints by Mrs. Grace Hart Curtis 51 that her husband Charles E. Curtis 67 wouldn't allow her to use his automobile, thus compelling her to use taxi-cabs and pay for them out of the $150 a month "pin money" he gave her, featured a contested divorce hearing Tuesday before Common Pleas Judge Erving.

The two were married April 29, 1926, and their marital venture went on the rocks November 10, 1926, when the wife filed a divorce petition charging neglect and cruelty. The husband countered with a cross petition which made like charges in his own behalf.

Mrs. Curtis, who now lives at 2057 E. 100 St., testified that Curtis, an insurance adjuster, left her November 9, 1926. In his cross petition he asserted he came home from a business trip about that time to find she had left their Wade Park Manor home and quartered herself in Hotel Statler for two days.

That seemed to have angered him, although she says she explained that she had been ill and she felt she could get better attention at the downtown hotel.

Curtis, she testified, paid all the bills at the Wade Park Manor home and allowed her the sum of $150 a month as "pin money." Since their separation she testified he has paid her $250 a month which she finds insufficient.

Declaring that she lives in "a garrett" and in a manner such as she has never been accustomed to, she has asked the court to fix alimony comparable to her needs.

The Cleveland *Press* story, which Grace found "different but equally silly and untrue," and which she did not send on to Hart, turned the divorce action into drama. "Cooled ardor of 67 year old husband drove Mrs. Grace H. Curtis, 51, from a palatial suite in E. 100th St to a one-room apartment at 13732 Euclid Avenue," it began. Eventually Hart himself was worked into the story.

Last October Mrs. Curtis was ill. Her son, Hart Crane, former Cleveland newspaperman, was in the Isle of Pines. There was a storm there. Mrs. Curtis charges Curtis refused to get a message from her son for her.

The newspaper reports told so little of the real events—just as the court presentation itself had—that Grace found it impossible to believe she could have said what was attributed to her. For months she would relive her day in court, second-guessing the things she had said and reviewing what had been said about her. But at first her reaction was shock and anger. "I *never* put in such a day as I did on Tuesday—all day from nine to six in that court room on and off of the witness stand. I was a rag . . . Since then, I have been expecting hourly to receive the verdict . . . but Saturday came and went and no word. So I am still on the anxious seat and nervous is no name for it. I feel I must scream—. Ever since last Oct. I've been thinking of this night and day, and never dreamed of all this trouble at the last." The hearing, she told her son, had been "a very tense nerve racking thing. I was on and off the witness chair three times, and it certainly was hard to be composed when they told things that were untrue."

There had been only one bright consequence: the warmth and affection shown Grace by C.A.'s sisters, Bess and Alice; Alice had even taken the witness stand on her behalf. "Alice Crane stayed right in court all day with me," she wrote Hart, "and testified as to my condition when she came to my home after Chas. had left." This generosity moved Grace deeply; for months she felt closer to C.A.'s family than to any other Clevelanders.

For a little while, indeed, the divorce had drawn Grace and C.A. and Hart into something like the semblance of a family. Though he tried to avoid discussing Grace with Hart, C.A.'s attitude toward her and her problems was charitable. He was also anxious to aid his son. As they sat in the smoking car of the train, enjoying his best Havana cigars, C.A. offered to give Hart a steady allowance, enough to pay for board and room with a bit left over for cigars and postage stamps.

When they reached New York, they checked in at the Hotel Roosevelt, each agreeing to visit his own friends but to meet for dinner and for after-dinner talk. Hart, however, managed only a day and a half visit, a frantic time in which he attempted to see every friend in Manhattan and a few in Brooklyn. For his own part, C.A., still gloomy, was packing bag and baggage only a few hours after Hart had taken his train north.

Out of their trip came a restoration of affection. Just before he took the train, C.A. wrote his son a quick note: "Am leaving for home on the 6:30 and so ends this N.Y. trip. I am none the worse and no better for it unless it has in a small measure contributed to your joy. . . . Am leaving without seeing anyone for my mind isn't in accord with things in general. Write me once a week. I'll do the same. With love, Your father, CAC."

Hart's answer, signed "with much love," had a warmth that was, for the first time in years, unforced.

I am still thinking about some of the pleasant hours we had together recently. Altogether it was the most satisfactory visit we have ever had together. And this, despite the fact that, as I well realize, you were far from gleeful much of the time. If I was able to alleviate, even for only a short period, some of [the] depression that you were struggling under, I shall feel very happy—for it is a good thing to be of some use to one's father, especially when he's been so good to me as you have.

He was happy to be on good terms with his father, but he was even happier to find himself caught up once more in a very different kind of affection. For he was now able to breathe "I love you" into the empty Patterson nights, knowing that on some weekends there would be ears to hear his words, eyes to smile back affection and good will.

It is very easy to see Hart's affairs as sordid liaisons, grubby and desperate and corrupt. Once in a while they were just that. But most of them—and there were not really many significant ones—were open, generous, buoyant. What he wanted, and what he sometimes found, was a comradeship that could rise to passion but that could also be both casual and intimate. It was intimacy that he wanted most of all; for by now almost all his close friends were married, most of them happily. Though Hart joined them for long talks that drifted through the summer nights of their youth (they were all, like the century itself, still in their twenties), the time always came for the talks to end and his loneliness to begin. When, therefore, he found someone to whom he could talk as easily as to his close friends but who could also offer him ecstasy, his isolated world became a little more like their everyday one. He could relax. He could write. In the enjoyment of life, he could free himself from worries about money and mother and father.

Father, ironically, was indirectly responsible for the affair that made the late spring of 1927 one of the pleasantest times of Hart's life. If C.A. had not encouraged Hart to join him on the New York trip, he would certainly not have met—late on the night of April 19—a sailor whose wit and eloquence matched Hart's own and whose carefree affection and good looks turned him into another "Phoebus Apollo." By the morning of April 20, Hart was exhausted, happy, relaxed. He canceled plans to look up the Tates and took the first train to Patterson, where he immediately made new plans—thanks to his father's allowance—to return periodically to New York for "a summer of 'roses and wine.'"

Hart was well aware that he sometimes turned his love affairs into "entertainments" for his friends; this time he did his best to keep his excitement private. He made four "secret" trips to Manhattan during May, happily using up every penny of the $50 his father had advanced. He borrowed small sums from the Browns; he again went into debt to Mrs. Turner. When June arrived, bearing with it an accumulation of debts and hay-fever sneezes, Hart suffered. But the memories were marvelous, and the mood they engendered was, I think, responsible for Hart's abruptly producing—in mid-June—the bulk of "The River."

Though Hart told no local friends about his new sailor, he could never manage to be without at least one confidant. The record of his happiness shows up in letters to Wilbur Underwood, who, in Washington, would not be likely to spread rumors. The fragments of these letters that follow speak for themselves. Interwoven with Hart's letters to his parents, they show clearly how, for Hart, love could lead to poetry.

Perhaps the best place to begin tracing this joy is in a letter to his mother written a week after his return to Patterson and a week before the first visit to New York, on May 3. Hart is answering her letter about the divorce hearing; in it, Grace had spoken of going to Chicago, though she hinted rather broadly that she would prefer an invitation to Patterson. Hart deftly avoided an immediate invitation, tried to cheer his mother, and could not avoid suggesting his own happiness.

> By this time, even though I have of course not heard, you must have received the judge's verdict: and whatever it is, I hope you will go out to Chicago with Blanche and Frank for a couple of weeks—hop on the train as soon as you can pack, and let Cleveland go hang for awhile. . . .
> The clipping you enclosed from the News was actually not as bad as I feared it might be. It seems worse to you than it

would naturally seem to others . . . At least nothing was said about 'dope'—by which I take it that no such fool accusations came up in court. They certainly would have been liable for a charge of slander and libel if they had dared to bring it up. You must write me a few details . . .

A nice letter from CA came along with yours of yesterday. I can scarcely believe that he has so revived his interest in me. The skies are again blue today, after several gloomy days of unbelievable cold and rain. . . .

The woods are full of shad-blows and the loveliest cowslips! Mrs. Turner has been cooking me bushels of fresh dandelion greens!

When, a day later, Crane got a "victory" telegram from Grace, he sent off a congratulatory note.

Your telegram—and the letter following—have made me fairly whoop for joy! And I am *so* glad that you started off for Chicago at once. It was just the thing for you to do. . . .

I'm sure you are having a good time by now—and the lovely attentions of the Ross's will go a long way toward making you smile again. Write me soon.

On the same day Hart must have written to Underwood, outlining plans for a Tuesday visit to New York, for the next Wednesday morning, May 4, he wrote to thank Underwood for his best wishes. Hart had spent the night at the Hotel Albert.

I think you must have offered the requested Tues-night prayer! At any rate the gods were never so good—indeed I think Apollo himself may have been sojourning in gob blue— but that aloof rather chilly deity would hardly have qualified as well!

Am leaving for the woods this afternoon—a great time— yesterday afternoon on the U S S [illegible] marvelous old Johnny Walker and Bacardi from the officers—such hospitality!

It's nice to be in love again . . .

He would be returning to New York in another week. He had only to fill up the days between. He set to work in Mrs. Turner's garden.

Not even a generous but upsetting letter from his father and a depressing one from his mother could darken Hart's cheerful mood. At almost any other time, either letter would have been enough to set him brooding for days.

C.A.'s, which arrived first, offered his own kind of love—for he wanted to buy for himself and his son a country restaurant-hotel, a place in the Ohio hills where they could live and work together. Father and son would settle down, C.A. said; and if

neither would raise a family, they could at least arrange for C.A.'s
dog to have one.

This tavern is very old—more than one hundred years. Your
grandfather and grandmother attended dances there before
they were married. During the past two years it has been put in
very good shape by the new owner, and if one wants an old
tavern I have never seen a better one. Surrounding it are sixteen acres of splendid land, part of it in fruit. . . . I am almost
inclined to close the deal. There are fifteen rooms, which probably would not be in great demand, but it is a marvelous place
for you to live and if I buy it I am going to ask you to come
back and make that your home. You can earn your board and
keep in any number of ways. Be assured of a jolly life, with
woods and acres to roam in and write all the poetry you want.
We would take Sing there for his home, provide him with a wife
and insist on a family. I would not give up a Cleveland room,
but would expect to spend most of the time there myself. . . .

I can think of no reason why you would not think this an
admirable place for you. Ed Morgan went out with me yesterday and then walked three and one-half miles over the hills to
his home in Hiram. You are not much interested in stores, but
this might be something your father could leave you that you
would appreciate.

I would not ask you to do the cooking or to milk the cow,
but you would probably have to earn your board and keep
by attending to certain duties. Among them, we are going to
have the best barbecue that was ever built.

Think this over and write me if you are willing to come out
and assume some share of the burden, if I undertake it.

Our work for a year would be in revamping the place inside
and out, building huge fireplaces and getting the ground in
shape for outdoor entertainment.

It really seems to me this is the answer to the wearisome
days ahead of me . . . It would not have to make a lot of
money to satisfy me, and the chances are I will go ahead with
it.

Hart, of course, turned C.A. down, though not without regrets.
In lieu of the truth, he invented reasonably good excuses. There
was his hay fever, for one thing. "It has so happened that for a
number of years you haven't seen me under the benign influence
of Ohioan pollens during the months of June, July, Sept. and
October,—so you probably don't so sharply recollect what a miserable looking critter I become during those twelve or so weeks
every year. Cleveland is severe enough, but what those months
would mean right out in the hayfields—I dread to contemplate."
There was also *The Bridge*, which Crane was still telling himself
he would finish by autumn. "It will take all the concentration I

can give it to accomplish this. And if I came out behind-hand on it I would disappoint Boni & Liveright, my publisher, very much: he wants it to appear by next spring."

If he couldn't bring himself to leave a hard-won independence, he could at least wish his father well and promise to see a great deal more of him than in the past.

So you see how things stand . . . It would be folly for me to add complications, however fine it would be to live in such a lovely place as you describe and be with you. Get the farm though, I think it's a fine idea, and you will get a great deal of pleasure and relaxation out of it. One doesn't lose money often on that kind of real estate, and as for someone good to run it— the range of your acquaintance will probably suggest a number of capable people: Morgan has the necessary personality, as well as Fredrica, and the latter could be completely trusted, I'm sure, to hold her head much better than the average female. Besides, she would be able to make it a homelike place for you. Then I will visit you at some sneeze-less time—like midsummer or late fall—and tell you about all the latest farm improvements in New York and Connecticut! . . .

There is little news here excepting wonderful weather and continued application to my work. We have ploughed the garden and I am about to plant. . . . I looked for the May check in today's letter. Hope you won't forget it before plunging into the Canadian wilds as I have obligated myself somewhat for oil and other supplies on the pleasant prospect of being solvent. The Tates are definitely decided against coming out here this summer, so that makes it possible for you to comfortably visit me here whenever you feel like it. I wish you would consider it and come!

Crane may really have been tempted by his father's letter to return to Ohio, but if so, that temptation was driven away by his mother's gloomy note. The most she could elicit from him was a promise to make a Cleveland visit in the autumn and a most casual invitation to her: "If you feel like coming east here with me for a visit you'll be very welcome." He hoped, he wrote, that she would not let herself be embittered by her second divorce. ("I hope you will not think about it any more than you can avoid: bitterness will only warp your viewpoint and make matters all the harder for you.")

Hart had every reason to warn Grace against bitterness, for he recognized in her letter the signs he had seen far too often in his childhood. In Chicago she had so diligently attempted to forget her troubles that she had pushed herself into exhaustion. And with exhaustion had come a return of hopelessness and self-pity. Her eight-page letter swirls with agony. Even random paragraphs reveal her frame of mind.

Your two nice letters have been received and they were welcome I assure you—even though I am visiting and supposed to be enjoying life. If I do not it's my own fault—as the whole Ross family are kindness itself. But I doubt if any of them or you either, with the conditions both mental and physical that I have to contend with, would be very conscious of anything but *self*—and all of the complications that seem to be present. I think I have *never* been so restless and uncertain of everything—especially myself. One of the worst things that can happen to one, I think, is to lose self confidence. That is what I seem to have done—and I just feel like a know nothing in my own estimation most of the time.. . . .

I suppose your father will soon be on his way to Canada if he is not already. Gee, it makes me shiver to think of it—it is plenty cool enough for me *here*. I am so pleased over the conditions which seem [to] exist between you and your father, and I really believe the war is over for you two. If you can only keep him from marrying now, and prevent a new state of affairs and complications from arising, from having a wife's whims to cater to and be influenced by.

As for myself—I cannot imagine anything worse than marriage. I feel toward that subject as I do when I've been made ill by overeating. It nauseates me and I still agree with your poetess friend—"They make me sick, they make me tired." I view all men, at present at least, with entirely new eyes— totally incredulous as to actions or sayings toward women. I certainly have not an illusion left in that respect, but I must not show it I suppose—but go on listening and pretending to believe the *darlings*! . . .

I hope you will send grandmother a telegram for Mother's Day, the eighth, on Sunday. I feel just like crying every time I think of her. Although she's been *such* a trial and so difficult *always* for me, and has been responsible for so much trouble, yet I realize she didn't do anything maliciously and she now sits alone in a strange place—so many many hours in which to reflect—and nothing around her to remind her of the long life she's almost ended, except *me*, and you, and what we can bring to her from the world outside, of which she still is so fond. I wish with all my heart that I could see my way clear to put her in a little home again and surround her with the old things that are so familiar and with which she has seen around her for so many many years. I, too, miss my home—and never shall be happy until I can have another, no matter how modest. In fact that is about half what is the matter of me—*I can't get adjusted to this way of living in someone else's house!* You will feel that way too, some day when you grow older. It is my strongest sense of security—a place that is mine to manage and be what I want to within its four walls.

Hart gave her his good advice about avoiding bitterness, reported on the weather ("gorgeous"), provided details about local
bird life ("there's a whip-poor-will that sings until about ten
every evening"), and rather ironically summarized C.A.'s recent
offers. ("He has not gone to Canada yet—and probably won't.
In the meantime he has almost dragged me into two other different enterprises of his, but I keep fighting shy—and it has so happened that in both cases the propositions finally failed to interest
him.")

C.A., in the meantime, gracefully accepted Hart's decision to
stay in Patterson, congratulated him on his good intentions ("It
is refreshing to know with what enthusiasm you are entering into
your work on your return to the old lady and the cats"), and sent
a check.

It arrived on the morning of May 12. The same afternoon Hart
wrote an exultant note to Underwood.

> I'm going in for the weekend to see Phoebus Apollo again. I
> quote the close of a letter just received: 'If you are in the city
> I should like very much to see you. I cannot come to you; for
> the last silver dollar is squandered and gone. Yet, omnia vincit
> amor. It is a little life and tomorrow—we may die. Dum
> vivimus, vivamus. May I see you? A morte . . .'
>
> He is in the quartermaster's div. and has brains as well as
> beauty and ———! Dear Wilbur, you must get well and fall
> in love again!

Hart would now let nothing interfere with his joys. He thanked
his father for the check and explained that a host of debts had
suddenly fallen due. These "debts" were covered by C.A. a week
later. ("I have your letter of May 12 and I am enclosing you a
check which will clean up your obligations.") Hart, of course,
raced for the first train. This time he had more than a happy
binge to report to Underwood, for, almost reluctantly, he found
that the sense of ease love gave him was again nudging him
toward poetry.

> . . . I brought my phoenix directly back with me to the coun-
> try—in company with two quarts of Johnny Walker—and he
> spent the weekend with me under the apple trees. Life is worth
> living at times.
>
> Since then I've been planting a vegetable garden! The first
> I ever 'did'—as well as the first spring I ever had in the
> country.
>
> There's no particular news: I am trying to get settled down to
> the summer's work, i.e. fighting out the rest of my problems
> concerning The Bridge. I am almost tired of being a poet!

He also wrote to thank C.A. for the check that had made the weekend under the apple trees possible. It had arrived, Hart explained,

"just in time to stave off a suit on account of an old bill for books." To such uses do literary men put literature!

Hart was on top of the world. He really couldn't feel upset when his mother—after several weeks of silence—suddenly bombarded him with nineteen pages of advice and self-congratulation. Grace had ended her Chicago visit by permitting herself to be subjected to a "psychoanalysis 'vocationgram.'" Convinced that it had finally revealed to her her true nature, she sent Hart her only copy (". . . but you must not lose it, and please do not keep it long") and outlined for him exactly how he must behave toward his father in the future.

> I've neither seen nor heard from C.A. and do not care. I do hope you will not take him seriously in regard to his promises, but will keep right along your line of work and accomplish what you've started and what your friends are expecting you to [do]. You'll have a life of regret if you do otherwise. You've made a fine beginning. Your father has many good qualities and much real talent, but he is so very unreliable in his plans that he is very unsafe to *listen to*, even. I really feel sorry for him. He is getting nothing out of life—doesn't understand himself or anything—just working hard and hitting wild. I really wonder where he will end up. He hasn't any philosophy, no plans, no friends, no love and no hobbies. I've never seen anyone like him. I really think you can do more for him today than anyone. You know how to give advice without his discovering that it is advice or that you are questioning his wisdom. . . . In the meantime don't let C.A. sidetrack you with any of his overtures for getting you to live with him or be employed by him, and don't count a great deal upon his help. Work and plan independently. Then anything he gives you will be that much extra.

That Hart had been following her advice in his own way was not, I think, entirely apparent to him. He must have smiled, however, as he wrote C.A. his reason for delaying an answer to C.A.'s most recent note. "I should have answered your letter sooner, but I've been immersed in the Bridge at which times personal matters are always neglected."

Immersed in love, Johnnie Walker, and sometimes cider, Hart had nothing but best wishes for everyone. "I can't help including some rhymes coined recently by a number of us at a cider party." For C.A., he knew, was as amused by light verse as he was. The nonsense verse, Hart explained, "might be called 'Sweeney's Answers to the Sphinx.'"

> Did you ever see Amanda Swope
> Riding in a calliope—

Eating iced cantalope?
. . . . Nope
Did you ever see old England's Queen
All dressed up in bombazine—
Riding in her limousine?
. . . . Nope
Haven't you seen Edwardus Rex
Wearing his new gold-rimmed specs—
Riding into Waco, Tex?
. . . . Nope

As to C.A.'s new plans for a country restaurant, which now centered on the little town of Chagrin Falls, Hart, though wanting none of them, was pleased to encourage them. "It will give you as much as you probably want of the country, going back and forth to the office, and the rest of the time you will have a real home, built exactly as you would wish it, with just enough business in connection with it to make it seem additionally 'homelike' to you."

After borrowing enough from friends for one last New York fling at the end of May or early in June, Hart returned to Patterson, his vegetable garden, and Doughty's *Arabia Deserta* ("such prose!"). His "Phoebus Apollo," shipped off to California, left behind one photograph and a host of delicious memories. "I'm still in a doting daze," Hart confessed to Underwood early in June. He told his mother a week later: "I'm writing no more than a word today. I've been in a productive mood—the usual kind of dream state—for several days, and for the first time in a long while am getting some real work done on the Bridge. I'll write more later when my head is less busy."

It is foolish, of course, to imagine that any one element in a poet's life brings him to the point of writing, but it is clear enough that for Crane "being in love" was a key element. Another was some sense of stability in his relationship with his mother and father. Though there were inevitable ups and downs during these days, on the whole he found his mother's divorce "good" for her; and he found his father's well-meaning and frequently generous letters a pleasant surprise. By now Hart had spent and overspent every penny C.A. had given him; finally, rather grimly, he asked for a loan. C.A.'s response was quick. "I do not want you to be financially embarrassed, and do not want you to think that your father is stingy . . . You do not have to borrow money from your father. As long as I have any I shall be glad to see that you are provided for, and your idea of giving your mother a little diversion by living with you is not out of line at all. So let your mind rest easy regarding this matter for the time being, and I will do the needful."

Before C.A.'s check arrived, however, Hart found himself caught up in his mother's tangled finances. Several weeks earlier she had returned to Cleveland and had written asking for aid; his grandmother had taken a turn for the worse and at the same time was forced to leave the home in which she had been living. Hart, at precisely the same point, had written Grace telling her how deep in debt he was. What happened, of course, was that Grace and Hart immediately sent each other small checks, which, while in transit, left them penniless. The money matters were soon straightened out, both Grace and Hart being able to think well of themselves. (As Hart wrote, though the checks "practically offset each other," the final effect represented a gain for mother and son. "In the true sense . . . they aren't self-cancelling, *are* they?")

Mother and son were both worried about money, but what they really feared was that another move might be very bad for Mrs. Hart. Though they said nothing of it, they were trying to prepare themselves for her death. Fears that she might die brought Hart and Grace once more into complete sympathy. "I am very much moved by the state of things," he wrote, "—and you must believe that I am ready to do anything I can." But since all anyone can do in such a situation is offer affection, Hart—out of the reserve of his own joy—offered love to his grandmother and to his mother. "Don't let [what may happen] blind you with its weight and shock, however, to the rest of your life and the many thoughts and experiences that it can hold for you," he wrote Grace. "You have the Hart courage and beauty of attitude— which that marvelous Mother of both of us has to such a great degree. The victory of life is love, I know it more each year."

# 28

While the combination of love and relaxed family tensions helped bring Crane back to the poem he now was sure would be the making or breaking of him, purely literary activity defined where he was going.

The reviews of *White Buildings*—most of them enthusiastic, but almost all of them shy of what Crane considered accurate analysis of his aims—were a source of continuing fascination. I don't mean to say that he agonized over reviews; but he did read them most carefully, particularly those written by acquaintances.

Two of these reviews obsessed him, those by Yvor Winters and Edmund Wilson. Wilson's, in *The New Republic*, had scattered praise and advice in something close to a 50-50 ratio. The praise pleased Crane, who quoted it to his mother: "Edmund Wilson (a very fastidious sceptic) recently began his review of the season's poetry in The New Republic by saying: 'When one looks back on the poetry of the season, one is aware of only two events which emerge as of the first interest: "The King's Henchman," by Miss Millay, and "White Buildings" by Mr. Hart Crane.'" What he did not quote was Wilson's comment that Crane was at times willful and at other times "curiously vague." The trouble with much modern poetry, Wilson felt, was that it was isolated from society. Crane, a modern poet, by implication shared this isolation.

Winters, who had praised Crane in public and criticized him in private, seemed to Crane to belong in Wilson's camp. Since at this time Crane valued Winters's opinion more than that of any other critic, he felt compelled to spell out his objections to the way in which the two men were pigeonholing him. Each of them, Crane felt, was anxious to make him over into his own image—or at least his own image of Major Poet. Yet each, Crane felt, demanded of him a kind of conformity, a social adjustment, that was not just repellent but literally impossible.

The letter he wrote Winters so accurately defines Crane's position that it deserves extensive quotation—for Winters, in insisting that major poetry could be written only by "complete" men, was, Crane felt, ultimately attacking not just poetry written by homosexuals, but as well all that makes any man's art individualistic.

The great strength of any art, Crane believed, is private vision. That a man has not been born, say, Shakespeare or Chaucer in no way negates his artistic potential. He is not a lesser artist, only a different one.

You need a good drubbing for all your recent easy talk about 'the complete man,' the poet and his ethical place in society, etc. . . . Wilson's article was just half-baked enough to make one warm around the collar. It is so damned easy for such as he, born into easy means, graduated from a fashionable university into a critical chair overlooking Washington Square, etc. to sit tight and hatch little squibs of advice to poets not to be so 'professional' as he claims they are, as though all the names he has just mentioned had been as suavely nourished as he—as though 4 out of 5 of them hadn't been damned well forced the major part of their lives to grab at *any* kind of work they could manage by hook or crook and the fear of hell to secure! Yes, why not step into the State Dept. and join the diplomatic corps for a change! indeed, or some other courtly occupation which would bring you into wide and active contact with world affairs! As a matter of fact I'm all too ready to concede that there are several other careers more engaging to follow than that of poetry. But the circumstances of one's birth, the conduct of one's parents, the current economic structure of society and a thousand other local factors have as much or more to say about successions to such occupations, the naive volitions of the poet to the contrary. I agree with you of course, that the poet should in as large a measure as possible adjust himself to society. But the question always will remain as to how far the conscience is justified in compromising with the age's demands.

The image of 'the complete man' is a good idealistic antidote for the horrid hysteria for specialization that inhabits the modern world. And I strongly second your wish for some definite ethical order. Munson, however, and a number of my other friends, not so long ago, being stricken with the same urge, and feeling that something must be done about it—rushed into the portals of the famous Gurdjieff Institute and have since put themselves through all sorts of Hindu antics, songs, dances, incantations, psychic sessions, etc. so that now, presumably the left lobes of their brains and their right lobes respectively function (M's favorite word) in perfect unison. I spent hours at the typewriter trying to explain to certain of these urgent people why I could not enthuse about their methods; it was all to no avail, as I was told that the 'complete man' had a different logic than mine, and further that there was no way of gaining or understanding this logic without first submitting yourself to the necessary training. I was finally left to roll in the gutter of my ancient predispositions, and suffered to receive a good deal of unnecessary pity for my obstinacy. Some of them, having found a good substitute for their former interest in writing by means of more complete formulas of expression have ceased writing altogether, which is probably just as well. At any rate they have become hermetically sealed souls to my eyesight, and I am really not able to offer judgement.

I am not identifying your advice in any particular way with theirs, for you are certainly logical, so much so that I am inclined to doubt the success of your program even with yourself. Neither do you propose such paradoxical inducements as tea-dansants on Mt. Everest! . . . I am suspect, I fear, for equivocating. But I cannot flatter myself into quite as definite recipes for efficiency as you seem to, one reason being, I suppose, that I'm not so ardent an aspirant toward the rather classical characteristics that you cite as desirable. This is not to say that I don't 'envy' the man who attains them, but rather that I have long since abandoned *that* field—and I doubt if I was born to achieve (with the particular vision) those richer syntheses of consciousness which we both agree in classing as supreme, at least the attitude of a Shakespeare or a Chaucer is not mine by organic rights, and why try to fool myself that I possess that type of vision when I obviously do not!

I have a certain code of ethics. I have not as yet attempted to reduce it to any exact formula, and if I did I should probably embark on an endless tome with monthly additions and digressions every year. It seems obvious that a certain decent carriage and action is a paramount requirement in any poet, deacon or carpenter. And though I reserve myself the pleasant right to define these standards in a somewhat individual way, and to shout and complain when circumstances against me seem to warrant it, on the other hand I believe myself to be speaking honestly when I say that I have never been able to regret—for long—whatever has happened to me, more especially those decisions which at times have been permitted a free will. (Don't blame me entirely for bringing down all this simplicity on your head—your letter almost solicits it!) And I am as completely out of sympathy with the familiar whimpering caricature of the artist and his 'divine rights' as you seem to be. I am not a Stoic, though I think I could lean more in that direction if I came to (as I may sometime) appreciate more highly the imaginative profits of such a course.

You put me in altogether too good company, you compliment me much too highly for me to offer the least resistance to your judgements on the structure of my work. I think I am quite unworthy of such associates as Marlowe or Valéry—except in some degree, perhaps, 'by kind.' If I can avoid the pearly gates long enough I may do better. Your fumigation of the Leonardo legend is a healthy enough reaction, but I don't think your reasons for doubting his intelligence and scope very potent. I've never closely studied the man's attainments or biography, but your argument is certainly weakly enough sustained on the sole prop of his sex—or lack of such. One doesn't have to turn to homosexuals to find instances of missing sensibilities. Of course I'm sick of all this talk about balls and cunts in criticism. It's obvious that balls are needed, and that Leonardo had 'em—at least the records of Florentine prisons, I'm told, say so. You don't seem to realize that the whole topic is something of a myth anyway, and is consequently modified in the characteristics of the image by each age in each civilization. Tom Jones, a character for whom I have the utmost affection, represented the model in 18th Century England, at least so far as the stated requirements of your letter would suggest, and for an Anglo-Saxon model he is still pretty good aside from calculus, the Darwinian theory, and a few other mental additions. Incidentally I think Tom Jones (Fielding himself, of course) represents a much more 'balanced' attitude toward society and life in general than our friend, Thomas Hardy. Hardy's profundity is real, but it is voiced in pretty much one monotonous key. I think him perhaps the greatest technician in English verse since Shakespeare. He's a great poet and a mighty man. But you must be fanatic to feel that he fulfills the necessary 'balanced ration' for modern consumption. Not one of his characters is for one moment allowed to express a single joyous passion without a forenote of Hardian doom entering the immediate description. Could Hardy create anything like Falstaff? I think that Yeats would be just as likely—more so.

That's what I'm getting at . . . I don't care to be credited with too wholesale ambitions, for as I said, I realize my limitations, and have already partially furled my flag. The structural weaknesses which you find in my work are probably quite real, for I could not ask for a more meticulous and sensitive reader. It is my hope, of course, not only to improve my statement but to extend scope and viewpoint as much as possible. But I cannot trust to so methodical and predetermined a method of development, not by any means, as you recommend. Nor can I willingly permit you to preserve the assumption that I am seeking any 'shortcuts across the circle,' nor willfully excluding any experience that seems to me significant. You seem to think that experience is some commodity—that can be sought! One can respond only to certain circumstances; just what the barriers are, and where the boundaries cross can never be completely known. And the surest way to frustrate the possibility of any free realization is, it seems to me, to willfully direct it. I can't help it if you think me aimless and irresponsible. But try and see if you get such logical answers always from Nature as you seem to think you will! My 'alert blindness' was a stupid ambiguity to use in any definition—but it seems to me you go in for just about as much 'blind alertness' with some of your expectations.

If you knew how little of a metaphysician I am in the scholastic sense of the term you would scarcely attribute such a conscious method to my poems (with regard to that element) as you do. I am an utter ignoramus in that whole subject, have never read Kant, Descartes or other doctors. It's all an accident so far as my style goes. It happens that the first poem I ever wrote was too dense to be understood, and I now find that I can trust most critics to tell me that all my subsequent efforts have been equally futile. Having heard that one writes in a metaphysical vein the usual critic will immediately close his eyes or stare with utter complacency at the page—assuming that black is black no more and that the poet means anything but what he says. It's as plain as day that I'm talking about war and aeroplanes in the passage from F & H (corymbulous formations of mechanics, etc.) quoted by Wilson in the New Republic, yet by isolating these lines from the context and combining them suddenly with lines from a totally different poem he has the chance (and uses it) to make me sound like a perfect ninny. If I'd said that they were Fokker planes then maybe the critic would have had to notice the vitality of the metaphor and its pertinence. . . . If I am metaphysical I'm content to continue so. Since I have been 'located' in this category by a number of people I may as well go on alluding to certain (what are also called) metaphysical passages in Donne, Blake, Vaughan, etc. as being of particular appeal to me on a basis of common characteristics with what I like to do in my own poems, however little scientific knowledge of the subject I may have.

I write damned little because I am interested in recording certain sensations, very rigidly chosen, with an eye for what according to my taste and sum of prejudices seems suitable to—or intense enough—for verse. If I were writing in prose, as I sometime shall probably do, I should probably include a much thicker slice of myself—and though it is the height of conceit for me to suggest it, I venture to say that you may have received a somewhat limited idea of my interests and responses by judging me from my poems alone. . . . One should be somewhat satisfied if one's work comes to approximate a true record of such moments of 'illumination' as are occasionally possible. A sharpening of reality accessible to the poet, to no such degree possible through other mediums. That is one reason above all others—why I shall never expect (or indeed desire) *complete* sympathy from any writer of such originality as yourself. I may have neglected to say that I admire your general attitude, including your distrust of metaphysical or other patent methods. Watch out, though, that you don't strangulate yourself with some countermethod of your own!

Thanks to love, relaxed family tensions, and perhaps to the self-definition that he had accomplished in his letter to Winters, Crane was suddenly able to write. In the first three weeks of June, he re-organized the sketchy drafts he had made of the "River" section of *The Bridge,* adjusted the neighboring sections so that they could accommodate the newly drafted one, and revised a number of poems he had written on the Isle of Pines. It was "The River," however, that was the center of his activity and he sent copies of it to his mother, his father, and his "Aunt Sally," each of whom figures in the poem. Indeed, he even goes out of his way to ask permission to use the name "Aunt Sally," seeing her as a surrogate mother-and-grandmother all in one. He had talked over the plan of *The Bridge* with her the summer before. Now he explains how "The River" links "Van Winkle" and "The Dance" and how his reference to her functions.

Sunshine and a certain amount of heat seem to stimulate me to writing, that is, judging by the intensive work I did on the Island with you last summer, and by the returned activity I've been having lately. We haven't had any particularly hot weather, but it's been warm enough to sweat a little, and that seems to be good for me. As a little evidence of my activities I'm enclosing a new section of the Bridge, called The River. . . .

I'm trying in this part of the poem to chart the pioneer experience of our forefathers—and to tell the story backwards as it were, on the 'backs' of hobos. These hobos are simply 'psychological ponies' to carry the reader across the country and back to the Mississippi, which you will notice is described as a great River of Time. I also unlatch the door to the pure Indian world which opens out in the Dance section, so the reader is gradually led back in time to the pure savage world, while existing at the same time in the present. It has been a very complicated thing to do, and I think I have worked harder and longer on this section of the Bridge than any other.

You'll find your name in it. I kind of wanted you in this section of the book, and if you don't have any objections, you'll stay in the book. For you are my idea of the salt of all pioneers, and our little talks about New Orleans, etc. led me to think of you with the smile of Louisiana. I continue in a kind of 'heat'— and I may have another section or so finished up before August. I sure want to get it *all* done by December. . . .

Wish I could read *The River* out loud to you as I used to do last summer! Too damned bad the hurricane came—I liked my little study room there so much, with the mango tree to look at through the back window . . . I achieved some triumphs in that little room.

Though a letter to his father in which Hart comments on the presence of C.A.'s cannery in "The River" has disappeared, C.A.'s answer survives.

> I received your letter the middle of last week, and the enclosure was, I believe, the best I have ever seen of your work. When I say the best it more nearly approached that low standard which I could understand. Something of this nature, in my humble opinion, would sell better than other things I have seen; it does not leave quite so much to the imagination.

Grace Crane figures in the poem in terms of the real trip across America that, with Hart as companion, she had taken years earlier, and though Hart never specifically identifies her, he must have hoped that she would recognize her "contribution." "The reader is really led back to the primal physical body of America (Pocahontas)," he writes her, "and finally to the central pulse and artery, the Mississippi. The description of that great river of time is one of the stateliest things I've done, I think. Read it carefully, and tell me what you think of it. The introductory speedy vaudeville stuff (what comes before the line beginning 'The last bear . . .') is a kind of take-off on all the journalism, advertising, and loud-speaker stuff of the day."

His Aunt Bess and her husband, Byron Madden, would, Hart hoped, also see how he was fitting his Midwestern background into a poem that celebrated those elements of the land he and all the Cranes loved. "I wish you would give Bess, Byron and the rest of the Crane family my best when you see them," he writes in one of the letters to his mother that enclosed a section of "The River." "I often think of them . . . Byron and Bess ought to like this better than my earlier stuff." For they were also part of the private world that lay behind the public world of *The Bridge* and it was important to Crane that they recognize their part in the harmony he was attempting to create.

Indeed, *The Bridge* and "family" merge in Crane's correspondence of the early summer, his thoughts flickering back and forth, in letter after letter, between the poem and the persons who had been most important to him during early childhood. "I guess I haven't been wandering around entirely in the dark all this time," he wrote Grace in the letter that enclosed the finally completed "River." "The sincerity of my vision and technique evidently has made an impression. It certainly takes work though, and unflagging self-criticism. I was so glad to get such a good letter from you, and to know . . . that you and the Maddens are on good terms again. I can't help liking them all—the whole family. Give them my best, won't you, when you see them."

Simply from a literary point of view, it was important to Crane that his family appreciate and understand his poem. They were typically "American"; if they couldn't feel what he was doing, what was the point of doing it? He tried to clarify his work for them. In many letters, he linked the poem to those current events that he knew his Cleveland relatives would be discussing. If they could read it in terms of Lindbergh's transatlantic flight, for instance, then they could see what in the American character he was trying to celebrate. "I don't wonder that business is depressed," he wrote C.A.

> For over a month we haven't heard, read, eaten or been permitted to dream anything but airplanes and Lindbergh. After reading a good deal about it I've decided that the world is quite mad. I'm sure it will take months for people to get their eyes out of the sky and their necks uncrooked and back to their stomachs. Time and Space is the myth of the modern world, however, and it's interesting to see how any victory in that field is heralded by the mass of humanity. In a way my Bridge is a manifestation of the same general subject. Maybe I'm just a little jealous of Lindy!

By midsummer a good deal of the poem was in print or scheduled to be. *The Dial, Poetry, transition, The Calendar,* and the first and second editions of *The American Caravan* had all accepted sections. In mid-August, T. S. Eliot asked if he might print "The Tunnel" in his *Criterion*, for Crane the greatest honor that had yet been paid his work.

With "The River" out of the way, Hart tried to prod along *The Bridge* by revision of such earlier poetry as had still not been printed, but he allowed most of the summer to drift aimlessly by. Mornings he spent chatting in Mrs. Turner's kitchen or joined her in weeding that garden he had once so enthusiastically planted. "Have almost got to the point of enjoying it, though I'll ever be anything but a farmer," he wrote Underwood. "Occasionally I have a cider spree with neighboring friends around here, and go swimming in a small lake nearby. The rest of the time I try to write." With his note, Crane included a copy of "The Air Plant," "a tropical effusion, a left-over memory of my ferocious experience in the West Indies last summer." During these months and a bit earlier, "To Emily Dickinson," "Old Song," and "March" were published and he got ready the group of island poems that in December would appear in *transition* 9 under the collective title "East of Yucatan." Though he was proud of most of them, he was now impatient with anything that distracted him from *The Bridge*.

But distractions were easy to come by. "All my activities can be summed up in a few lines of verse—and then not very good," Crane by mid-August was writing Underwood.

> It's no use to tell you how futile I feel most of the time—no matter what I do or consider doing, even. Part of the disease of the modern consciousness, I suppose. There is no standard of

values in the modern world—it's mostly slop, priggishness and sentimentality. One had much better be a wild man in Borneo and at least have a clear and unabashed love for the sight of blood.

There were, nevertheless, fewer money problems, since C.A. had faithfully, if sometimes belatedly, made his contributions. "I've had a perfectly terrible time getting my father to keep his promise about the allowance," Hart wrote the Rychtariks, "—and am just as uncertain and worried about the next meal as ever. *Sic semper!*" The checks—$50 a month—did continue, however, well into the autumn, Hart, at the beginning of each month, always writing a reminder and C.A., toward the middle of each month, always responding with a check.

The trouble, of course, was that, with no other source of income, Hart found every weekend in New York a matter of debit financing that would leave him penniless.

He knew also that he could never again count on help from his mother. The alimony from her second divorce was $150 a month and was to last only two years. And even at the beginning she had difficulties collecting it. "The check from Chas. has not arrived yet this month," she had written in mid-July, "and I nearly went wild trying to locate enough money to pay the rent gas ice etc. here. It makes me fearful of the future . . ." For the first time in his life Hart did without a birthday present from her: "I have no material gift to send, but I *do* send you a great deal of *love,* and my *sincerest* wishes for your *success, happiness* and *health,* and a *long useful life.* I am also very happy that I am your mother and that I have a dear son of whom I am so proud and who I know loves me." There was, however, a gift of a rug, a contribution from his grandmother, who, according to Grace, had devoted weeks to making it—"finished and lined, every stitch her own." It was one of the last active gestures of Mrs. Hart, who, increasingly frail, would soon limit her world to a chair by the window. "I am glad you like your rug," she wrote. "It is only just something to remember Grandma by. I could do better with another one, but I'm quite satisfied not to try it again. Most too heavy work for hands that have been idle so long." And there were letters from friends, including a long, gossipy one from Mrs. Simpson: "Did you have a nice birthday? I thought of you—a kid, yet; only 28 years—and yet you have done more than many twice your age."

But neither a birthday "dancing party" nor cider sprees, neither gardens nor letters could re-create for Hart the relaxed joy that had earlier permitted him an easy entry into the life of his long poem. Instead, frustrations and worries—Grace again unhappy and anxious to leave Cleveland, his grandmother obviously failing, his poem completely stalled—spurred him into a series of tentative and unworkable plans. He would return to New York and try to get a job. He would go back to the Isle of Pines. He would make a trip to Martinique. He would go to Europe. Every person he talked to offered different advice, and Hart, for a day or two, took each suggestion with the utmost seriousness. "I have been in swimming only twice this year," he wrote the Rychtariks. "There is no water near here but a tiny lake full of snakes. *Someday* I hope to spend a summer by the sea. Maybe when I go to Spain and Majorca! I was greatly surprised to find out that some people in Madrid have taken an interest in White Bldgs. . . . Maybe I will find some good company when I get there." But the real likelihood, as he told everyone, was that he would reappear in New York City.

On August 12, Hart made his decision. He would look for a New York job, probably at the end of September or early in October. In the meantime, as he explained to his father, he had to be sure he could afford the move.

Life goes on here pretty evenly and monotonously. I have managed to do a good deal of writing, but not as much of it is on The Bridge as I would have liked to have finished by this time. Difficult is no word to describe the sort of things I'm trying to 'put across' in that poem, and I've been rather too much on a tension of worry lately about a number of things to give it the requisite concentration. Grace and her present pathetic circumstances is one cause and my own arrangements for the coming fall and winter is another. It's obvious that I must get a job in town, and I'm casting out lines now even—for it generally takes ages to get anything definite worked up. I'm not asking for reassurances, but I do hope that I can count on your assistance to the extent of the monthly amount until I can get something on my hook—for otherwise I may not have the necessary carfare to ride in when the time comes for the preliminary interview!

I certainly never fancied that my poems would suffice to keep me 'going' anywhere, but my market returns have certainly been much less for this summer than I had expected. One magazine in England that owed me about $50 has just suspended publication, and it doesn't look as though I'd get anything from them, and I've saturated most of my American market for some months to come, occasionally five or ten dollars will drift in, but not much.

C.A.'s return letter was exactly what Hart needed to help him make definite plans. Not only did C.A. guarantee the continuance of the allowance, he also showed the sort of sympathetic interest in his son that always—though not always for long—lifted Hart's spirits.

C.A.'s own spirits were, for the first time in months, really good. His construction of the Chagrin Falls restaurant had been the best sort of therapy. "Whatever happens to it after it is done, I can truthfully say it has helped me this summer in keeping my mind occupied, which otherwise would have been in a sorry state." He was, however, quite as much concerned with Hart's state of mind.

Now regarding yourself, which is the paramount issue. I am perfectly willing to continue for an indefinite period the allowance of $50.00 a month. If I understand you correctly this pays for your board and gives you an overage of $20.00 a month. You have, at different times, written me of sales of your articles, but I note from your letter that they are not forthcoming as expected. I do not want to say anything more than I have in the past regarding your mode of living, but it is necessary that people earn a livelihood, and if writing will do it then you have chosen a much better vocation than I: If it won't do it, then a job is the right thing to think about. I know you are not interested in things I am doing and so much of my life is now in a ship-wreck that I cannot say the example is a good one for you to follow. About all that the Lord can do with my soul when it comes to the final accounting is to say that I worked hard and accomplished little.

I read a very interesting article in the morning paper. J. Ogden Armour died yesterday in London. From the second richest man in the world his fortune dwindled until less than $20,-000.00 of it remained at the time of his death, but through it all he stood up like a soldier and took his medicine which was dealt out to him. I have not been as brave as that with my calamity, but I have been dealt a bitter blow for some reason or other and if you can avoid those things in life I do not blame you for roaming the wild wood and getting all there is in the broad expanses of nature. However, we are born under a certain star and are probably influenced naturally by conditions not altogether under our control. The great thing in life is to be able to choose the right way; the way that leads to peace and comfort and satisfaction to yourself when you reach the declining years.

I can think of no reason why I cannot keep up the allowance I am giving you, providing it adds to your comfort and helps you do the things you want to do. . . .

In spite of his best efforts to find work—and he did try—none of the "lines" Hart put out in search of a job landed anything. At the beginning of September, he decided that he would once more appeal to Otto Kahn.

Hart's letter to Kahn included, as had earlier letters, a progress report on *The Bridge*. This time, however, Hart wrote so comprehensive an account that after publication of *The Bridge* he offered a copy of it to Eda Lou Walton, then teaching a course in modern poetry at New York University, as a reasonably accurate statement of his intentions. Somewhat later, he revised the note, probably with the hope of publishing it.

His method, he explained to Kahn, was "architectural," in that it attempted to weld into a coherent whole a group of independent lyrics. Though each of the sections of the poem could stand by itself, a tissue of interconnected material—words, themes, images, symbols—bound them together into the larger structure, *The Bridge*. Forging these links had been the greatest problem, for they had to be inconspicuous in order to be effective. Eventually, of course, Crane hoped for readers who would study his poem as carefully as he himself had studied Donne and Eliot; but that kind of analysis was, he knew, secondary. He pointed out to Kahn: "It might be better to read the following notes *after* rather than *before* your reading of the ms. They are not necessary for an understanding of the poem, but I think they may prove interesting to you as a commentary on my architectural method." That method, he insisted, was itself basic. *The Bridge could* be read as separate sections, but to read it in that fashion would be destructive. It should be seen as a form made up of unique forms, a grand composition made up of separate but associated designs. "For each section of the entire poem has presented its own unique problem of form, not alone in relation to the materials embodied within its separate confines, but also in relation to the other parts, *in series,* of the major design of the entire poem. Each is a separate canvas, as it were, yet none yields its entire significance when seen apart from the others. One might take the Sistine Chapel as an analogy."

Crane devotes most of his letter to the just completed "Powhatan's Daughter" section—and so misleads some of his critics into thinking that the themes developed there are more significant than those of the rest of the poem. But as he explains, "I don't wish to tire you [with] too extended analysis of my work, and so shall leave the other completed sections to explain themselves."

What Crane particularly hoped to make clear to his benefactor was the way a group of integrating devices holds his poem together. Most basic of these is the "music" of the poem, Crane deliberately referring to his rhythms in musical rather than literary terms. He contrasts "The Harbor Dawn" to its surrounding material: "Here the movement of the verse is in considerable contrast to that of the Ave Maria, with its sea-swell crescendo . . . This legato in which images blur as objects only half apprehended on the border of sleep and consciousness, makes an admirable transition between the intervening centuries." In the "Van Winkle" section, "the rhythm is quickened; it is a transition between sleep and the immanent tasks of the day. Space is filled with the music of a hand organ . . ." "The River" begins with "a great conglomeration of noises analogous to the strident impression of a fast express rushing by. The rhythm is jazz." "The Dance" is just that—a dance. "Indiana" is a "lyrical summary" of the conquest of the West. "Cutty Sark" is "built on the plan of a *fugue*."

Patterns of space and time are also consciously used. "Van Winkle" is intended to give the impression "of the whole continent —from Atlantic to Pacific—freshly arisen and moving," while "The River" uses trains and hobos to "carry the reader into interior after interior." All kinds of space and all kinds of time have to be made to function if the poem is to achieve its purpose. Crane wants his poem to deal not only with historical time but with the time of any man's life, a pattern that begins in "The Harbor Dawn" and works through "Powhatan's Daughter" and indeed through the entire poem. Commenting on "The Harbor Dawn," he explains: "The love-motif (in italics) carries along a symbolism of the life and ages of man (here the sowing of the seed) which is further developed in each of the subsequent sections of Powhatan's Daughter, though it is never particularly stressed. In 2 (Van Winkle) it is Childhood; in 3 it is Youth; in 4, Manhood; in 5 it is Age. This motif is interwoven and tends to be implicit in the imagery rather than anywhere stressed."

When Crane wrote his letter to Kahn, he was quite sure that he would soon bring *The Bridge* to a successful conclusion. He knew, of course, that family problems could always interfere; but he hoped he might solve some of them by taking a trip out of the country and so escaping direct involvement in the complex affairs of his mother and father. It was not, needless to say, in these terms that he explained to Kahn his desire to leave America. "Even with the torturing heat of my sojourn in Cuba I was able to work faster than before or since . . . The 'foreignness' of my surroundings stimulated me to the realization of natively American materials and viewpoints in myself not hitherto suspected, and in one month I was able to do more work than I had done in the three previous years. If I could work in Mexico or Mallorca this winter I could have The Bridge finished by next spring."

If Kahn were not willing, however, to contribute money for travel, Crane would have to find a place to live. A letter from Sam Loveman, still at 110 Columbia Heights in Brooklyn, must have seemed providential. Though the friends had had a confused falling out—over an unpaid debt, Hart assumed—the letter was warm and generous, as was the note Hart wrote in return. Discreetly, he hinted that he might like to join Loveman in his old quarters. "Circumstances compel me to find work in NY as soon as possible, and if I can find a little corner in your neighborhood again I shall feel more at home than elsewhere in Babylon. . . . I have had plenty of time to myself, but have been the victim of too much worry to have turned it to much advantage."

Hart's time to himself was, however, finished. Within the next two months a whirlwind of activity returned him to New York, rushed him off to Cleveland, and finally shipped him across the continent to California.

# 29

Crane's plans, as he prepared to leave Patterson, could charitably be described as fluid, and not only because of the round of cider parties that preceded his exit. In the same week that brought him a letter from Otto Kahn offering "another $500" and a set of leads to New York jobs, he had a note from his mother announcing her immediate departure for California.

Grace Crane had apparently not really thought through this move, for she had made no coherent plans concerning Mrs. Hart. But she knew that she had to leave Cleveland and she knew that she would not leave until she had seen her son. In the next mail, Hart heard from C.A.

> This morning I have a letter from your mother, asking if I will furnish the money to have you come home because she expects to go to a far away city very shortly and does not expect to have the opportunity of seeing you again for a very long time.
>
> I do not take much stock in this, for her obligation to her mother is such that she could not do this without bringing much criticism upon herself. I think this is simply a case of an idea which will probably disappear as soon as she gives it much sober thought.
>
> However, if she writes you she is positively going and wants to see you, you can act on your own judgment about coming home and I will be glad to pay your fare out and back . . .

Hart decided that he had no choice in the matter. He wrote Kahn to postpone the discussion of his latest subsidy until early October, then grimly packed up most of his Patterson belongings and set out for Cleveland.

Though for Hart and his mother the whole episode bordered on melodrama, to some of his friends it became one more scene in an endless tragi-comedy. Even C.A.—sending off the check that made the Cleveland farewell possible—could not resist an ironic tone.

> I have your letter this morning and note that you really desire to come to Cleveland to see your mother before she departs for her new location. . . .

I have not been informed when she expects to go, or whether, but I suppose these are dark secrets that will, in time, be revealed.

There were really no dark secrets about Grace's plans, just unlimited uncertainties. Nevertheless, the week Hart spent helping his mother pack was one he would not forget. Every other minute, she would tearfully change her mind. Finally she did leave, accompanied by her invalid mother and about half her earthly possessions. She was on her way to visit relatives near Los Angeles.

Hart was now living on nerve alone. Exhausted by his mother's leave-taking, still with no prospects of work, he was literally down to his last penny. Unwilling to beg more from his father, he turned again to the Rychtariks, asking for enough to keep him going until he could collect the money from Kahn.

When he got back to New York, he accepted Sam Loveman's invitation to live at 110 Columbia Heights. On good days, Hart tried to talk out with Sam the confusion and unhappiness his last Cleveland visit had thrown him into. But on bad days, talk was not enough; Loveman soon found himself searching Brooklyn waterfront bars for his sometimes abusive, sometimes roaringly good-natured, always lonely friend who was now doing everything in his power to see that alcohol blotted out private pain.

Hart managed, however, to pull himself together for the interview with Kahn. And he emerged from it full of hope. For Kahn encouraged him to follow through on the travel plans that months earlier he had vaguely formulated in long evenings with the Browns. Their recollections of Martinique had persuaded him that one island paradise, at least, might be real. There, he felt, freed from a too familiar world and its too familiar problems, he would really write. He explained all this to his father.

I have just had an interview with Otto Kahn, following his reading of the manuscript of 'The Bridge.' Kahn is very enthusiastic about what I have accomplished and is most anxious that I keep on with the composition without interruption until it is finished. I told him about your willingness to extend me the assistance of the monthly allowance of $50 and he has come forward with an additional $300 which will provide me with the necessary boat-fare to Martinique for the winter. That is a much pleasanter island than the Isle of Pines and I will also be able to learn French and Spanish there, which will make it possible for me [to] earn my living up here later by translation work.

I know enough about Martinique from people who have recently been there to be sure that the allowance you have been giving me will cover my living costs there. The winter season will insure me against any of the excessive heat that I experienced on the Isle of Pines and I shall be able to get much more accomplished.

I shall probably sail on the 20th (Furness-Bermuda Line) and arrive about 8 days later. . . .

C.A. sent off a check for $100: "In order that you may have plenty of cash to start off with, I am giving you two months' allowance now and hope to hear from you frequently when you are established in your winter home."

But neither C.A. nor Hart had counted on the consequences of Grace's cross-country train trip and her efforts to find housing for herself and her mother. She was on the verge of a complete breakdown, she wrote. She begged Hart to remain in the United States. She was afraid that if she became ill, Hart's grandmother, who could not be expected to live long, would be left without anyone to care for her. Frustrated and baffled, Hart returned his steamer ticket and set out to look for a job. Almost immediately, he located one in a gloomy Fifty-seventh Street bookstore.

In the meantime, he managed briefly once more to offend his father. C.A., who was to be in New York on a business trip, had asked Hart to meet him at the Waldorf Astoria so that they might talk over Hart's confused plans. "You can drop over there at ten or eleven and we can have a chat," C.A. had written, explaining that he would be at the hotel on October 19. Hart failed to show up. After sitting in the lobby for the better part of three hours, C.A. was furious.

Again Hart found himself writing the familiar letter of apology and explanation.

> I was sorry to hear that I had put you out waiting for me when you were last in New York. I had supposed, however, that you would be *registered* at the Waldorf, and that I should first get in touch with you over the telephone. After three efforts —each time being told that no such name was registered —I concluded that you simply hadn't come, or else had gone to another hotel. . . . Perhaps the Desk or the phone girl were to blame. Anyway, I certainly was most sorry to miss you.

Worried over Grace, fearful that he had alienated his father, hating his bookstore job (he gave himself such severe eyestrain, attempting to read in the near-dark, that for days, he told friends, he suffered an excruciating headache), Hart felt that the trap that always seemed about to close on him had this time really sprung shut. "Family worries too complicated to explain make it seem useless to attempt—at least for the present—any sort of creative work," he wrote Underwood, adding as an afterthought the phrase "far or near."

Though Hart was hopeless, his best friends were not. Several attempted to find a position for him that would provide the security he needed to be able to write. It was Eleanor Fitzgerald who came to his rescue this time, just as in future years it would be she who, when other friends had dropped him, would see that he had a roof over his head. She introduced him to Herbert A. Wise, a wealthy young man whose doctor was sending him to California for a six-month rest; Hart, she felt, might make a congenial companion on the trip.

At about the same time, Grace wrote that she had rented a Hollywood bungalow. She seemed, so far as he could tell, in comparatively good spirits.

Hart at first couldn't believe his own good fortune. For a week, he tried to hold down euphoria. He might, after all, do something to offend Wise. But by the first week in November he was sure that he would be invited to make the trip, and he got off an exultant letter to Grace.

My letters recently have been pretty meager, but when you have finished all I have to tell you in this one you will see to a large extent why this has been so. For until circumstances took some more or less definite sort of shape I haven't wanted to say anything about them, for the news is exciting, I warn you, and even though there is *still* some chance of a miscarriage, still I can't suppress it any longer. All this has occupied my mind so completely during the last ten days that I haven't been able to think of much else to write you. So draw in your breath now and hear!

On the fourteenth of this month I am leaving for Pasadena. This was decided yesterday in a final conference with Herbert A. Wise, a Wall Street millionaire . . . I am to be his secretary and companion. He is a very cultured man, interested in my work, and is giving me almost complete freedom to pursue my inspiration, though I have been cautioned by his physician and nurse to exercise as sedative an effect on him as possible.

I have been most excited, I assure you, while my probation period has been progressing! Dinners, luncheons and rides with him during as much time as I have been able to spare from my bookshop duties. He has travelled everywhere, and if our friendship proves to be a success there is a possibility of its including such things as travel with him in Europe, etc. On the other hand, if either of us at any time feels that we are getting on each other's nerves the understanding has already been established that we can part immediately without argument or strain. . . . He must, at all costs, secure a minimum of irritations—and if his physician should recommend it, I might well be left behind. But so far as I can see I am going to see you soon—and under the most amazing circumstances. . . .

He is taking his car and chauffeur along, as well as his valet and wine cellar. A regular 'establishment,' in fact. I certainly shall have every comfort imaginable, probably too much. I have the privilege of ordering a great quantity of books for our reading and I shall have the chance to play all the tennis I've been longing for so long. *But* don't think that I haven't some responsibilities, all the harder because they are indefinite in that I really have a 'patient' on my hands!

Now you have most of the points on the situation. Almost incredible, isn't it?

There were, of course, likely to be drawbacks. Crane was never a man who enjoyed being waited on, and he rather dreaded the entourage of servants who would staff the overgrown "bungalow" his employer had rented. There was also something of a problem regarding his position. He couldn't determine exactly what his job was. A "companion" could be everything or nothing. He finally decided that he was to be a "secretary" who could "talk . . . about Eliot, Spengler, metaphysics and what not."

And there was the problem of Grace Crane, soon, as Hart wrote his father, to be "within whistling distance." He was fearful that she would not fit easily into the sophisticated life of his new employer. It would be best, he decided, not to mention her to Wise until the move had been undertaken. Hart did his best to explain this to Grace herself. He asked her to say nothing to C.A. and then went on to ask of her more general discretion.

Also, please say nothing to the Harts or anyone else out there until I tell you to. I have had to use tact—a great deal of it—in this affair, and you must be ready to observe a certain amount of discretion along with me. I have not even mentioned that I knew anyone on the West Coast as yet, though in due time I intend to tell [Wise] that my mother is in Los Angeles. I can't explain now why these points are important, except that until he understands me better I don't want to introduce any features into the situation which might complicate matters. On the other hand, please don't feel the least bit uncomfortable—there will be no difficulty in my spending a fair amount of time with you. I shall probably tell him about that side to the situation before we arrive.

Also, remember to be prepared to hear that this has been suddenly called off, in which case I'll wire you. —But I've just had to tell you! *Ain't we got fun! ! ! !* . . .

Love, love and more love!

Hart

During the two weeks before his departure, Hart celebrated. A letter from his father capped his happiness, for Hart had been more than fearful that C.A. would not be sympathetic to another "unproductive" job. As it turned out, he was pleased: "It is certainly very marvelous that you can go to California the way you have outlined it. You will be with your mother, which is another satisfaction, and yet nicely situated I imagine from what you tell me. I hope everything will come out well . . ."

There were, of course, farewells to be said to friends, among them a recently acquired sailor. Hart told Underwood about him: "I've been having the liveliest time with a sailor kid—a kind of gamin who wakes up after about the third—and asks me who's my doctor. 'Why?' 'Because I'm love sick about you.' Etc. He'd wear me all out if I'd let him. His affection also includes a certain amount of gold-digging. But he's worth it." Less amorous farewells were extended to the Browns, by now Hart's closest friends; to Isidor and Helen Schneider, with whom he was developing a very warm friendship; and to E. E. Cummings and his wife, Anne, until this time rather casual acquaintances but ones in whom Crane delighted.

It was with Cummings and his wife, indeed, that Crane had started one of his wildest evenings, an evening that improved gradually in the telling until, in California, he heard second-hand of escapades that had grown to monstrous proportions. For the facts themselves were spectacular enough. Just before he left for the West Coast, he wrote a summary for the Browns.

Traintime approaches, but I hope life does not continue to grow accordingly more hectic, as has been the rule so far! Several times I have all but lost my ticket, presented several days ago. Notably Tues. night in jail. . . .

After a riotous competition with Cummings and Anne in which (I don't *know* but I'm sure) I won the cocktail contest I found myself in the Clark St. station along about 3 o'clock playing with somebody's lost airedale. The cop who rushed at me, asking me what I was doing is reported to have been answered by "why the hell do you want to know? ! ! !" in a loud tone of voice, whereat I was yanked into a taxi and was sped to the station (slyly and en route tossing all evidence such as billet doux, dangerous addresses, etc., out the window) and the next I knew the door crashed shut and I found myself behind the bars. I imitated Chaliapin fairly well until dawn leaked in, or rather such limited evidences of same as six o'clock whistles and the postulated press of dirty feet to early coffee stands.

I was good and mad. Made an impassioned speech to a crowded court room, and was released at 10 o'clock without even a fine. Beer with Cummings in the afternoon which was almost better than the evening before, as C's hyperbole is even more amusing than one's conduct, especially when he undertakes a description of what you don't remember. Anyhow, I never had so much fun jounced into 24 hours before, and if I had my way would take both C'gs and Anne along with me to heaven when I go.

Though Crane himself made the most of such wild days, turning them in the telling into spectacular confrontations between himself and a baffled world, they were isolated peaks on a much more peaceful landscape. Much of the day after his night in jail, for example, was spent shopping for small presents for his friends and for the Browns a not-so-small edition of the paintings of Brueghel (". . . a belated wedding memento which I hope will bring warmth to your lips and a smile to your hearts occasionally"). He had tried, he later said, to find something that caught the spirit, the humor, of the many days and nights he'd spent in their company. "Its humor really belonged to you, if you get what I mean, and you therefore were more capable of 'owning' it than anyone I ever knew. If you were dead and gone, I think it would have been a better commemoration than flowers—so take good care of it—and hand it on to your grandchildren."

At first, Hart was overwhelmed by California: "The drives are so many and superb and everywhere such beautiful bodies, faces!" Not only was he easily able to get from Wise's house in Altadena to Hollywood for visits to his mother; he was also free to spend a great deal of time by himself. When the luxuries of his new home threatened to pall, he could find earthier company in San Pedro. The sailor whom he had been so fond of in the spring showed up for several weekends, even inviting Hart to spend a day with him on the *Arizona*. For two weeks solid, Hart wrote the Schneiders, he devoted himself to "flying around" the California roads on a whirl of sightseeing: "movie studios, cafés, bootleggers, golf links and warships."

After every eventful day there was his extraordinary new home to return to, "all bad furniture and bathrooms."

I luxuriate every morning in a shower of matchless brilliance and every evening in port . . . The third cook proved Viennese and satisfactory and I'm adding an irresistible five pounds to my pulchritude each day. What I'll do when faced again with Mrs. Turner's cold turnips I don't know!

It's hard to think of Christmas, though I believe in Santa Claus more than ever.

It really seemed a miracle. Three weeks earlier, Hart had had no notion where his next meal was coming from. "It is wonderful to live in such comfort for awhile," he wrote the Rychtariks, going on to detail for them, as he did for all his friends, the splendors of his new situation.

I hope you'll forgive me all this whooping and hurrahing—but what else can one do—with two cars to ride around in, mountains to climb, seas to swim in, books to read, sailors to talk with, warships to visit, skies to fly in, roses to pick (they climb all over the roof), walnuts to crack, etc., etc., etc! ! ! ! . . . My boss is only 34, a bachelor, and has a furious love of excitement, so there may be some amusing developments. But at present, it's part of my 'task' to keep him quiet on a more-or-less intellectual and sedentary diet. Well, well—not at all! Where will I be next? Tahiti? It's not so far from here!

Though few people had a greater capacity for life lived at a fever pitch, even Hart—after several weeks of unmitigated sensation—began to yearn for the opportunity to "read and think some." Before his arrival he had had misgivings about the Los Angeles area, fearing that it would be a retired businessman's dream world. Once there, he found his "most cherished prejudices" confirmed. "California," he told the Schneiders, "is one great pink vacuum. Miles and miles of marvelous blvds. and pink sunsets and millions of happy vegetables, aroused only on the rumor that somebody is sinning."

Sin—at least the relatively mild variety that Hart indulged in—was comfortably within his means; and he took the opportunity for self-indulgence more often than not. "I've done my best in this respect to stimulate the populace, but I can also say that I haven't been alone in my efforts." For the combination of a bottomless wine cellar and dozens of invitations to spectacular Hollywood parties threw Hart into a hedonistic orgy from which, panting, he would occasionally emerge for letters to friends and visits to Mother.

"One can't seem to wake up out here without the spur of Scotch or gin," he explained in one letter to the Browns.

> There has been plenty of that—in fact last Saturday night I danced the "Gotzotesky" right on Main St. Los Angeles, while ———— ————, an aviator from Riverside and a Kentuckian— danced the Highland Fling—or as good an imitation of it as he could manage. This after having invaded the Biltmore ballroom and dancing with fair ladies of the haute mondaine. Albeit— and having got our waiter drunk and having left in high dudgeon—I don't think I dare attend their supper club again.

There were also a number of parties that Crane did not very much care for but that he sometimes attended. These were raw affairs organized by the most aggressive of Hollywood's homosexuals. In spite of being disgusted by "these Hollywood fags" ("I never could stand much falsetto, you know"), he couldn't help but be amused by their extraordinary evenings and by the tight little world of gossip and vanity in which they lived. Their parties seemed to last forever. One could leave at midnight, be gone for three days, and return to find the same crowd caught in the same fierce carousing. "Whoops! and Whoops again, dearie, and then more warbling, more whiskey and broken crockery and maybe broken necks, for all I know, when I get back and view the ruins!" One of these "girls" fixed on Hart so persistently that he decided the best part of valor was a weekend isolated from everybody.

The present "star" was once "Ariel" in the "Tempest"—and though she still makes the welkin ring I fear her voice would never do again. She has adopted the pronoun "we" to signalize her slightest thought, whim or act—and her conceit was so wounded on spying my "Chaplinesque" during the course of her drunken and exclamatory rampage through "Edificios Blancos" —that she nearly passed out—and insisted on the spot that I make instant amends by composing a sonnet to her superb P.A. (Hollywood shorthand for "physical attraction") . . . Hence here I am by the sea—and mighty pleased until the storm subsides . . .

Even in this crowd, however, Hart made some friends—writers and actors, rather like himself, who didn't have the cash to give parties and who went, therefore, where they were invited. Nearly two years later, when Hart had just arrived in Europe, one of these friends—an actor, more successful and rather wealthier than most —wrote him a letter that in its wit, its despair, its ironies suggests the quality of a part of Crane's Hollywood life. Though the full letter cannot be quoted, a sampling will reveal something of the world through which Crane moved, a world that disgusted and fascinated him.

Dear Hart—
Went to rehearsal of "——— ———" yesterday in which I'm supposed to play and C——— and B——— were there, both playing a part. I will get them to write you. They are both well, but W——— is in the Bastille again.

They told me that F ——— has been in much dirt since he left my ménage and was in jail twicet. Hope you are over there next June (1930). Am coming there to live—will take a flat in London and make it my head brothel. Somehow I'm used to London—narrow and cold as the English are. . . .

Main Street is full these nights—just as of old, but there is a concerted drive against *Queens* in *Cans*. Many go in, and all are taken.

Did I tell you in my cups, of my diamond ring? Well, it looks as tho I will get it back. The police say it's in hock for $500, but I think they have it, and are double crossing me so as to get $500. . . . If it is $500, then the God damned thing can stay in hock, tho it cost me $2000.

Had a grand time last Sat.—three gentlemen called on me, and 2 more on Sunday afternoon until I felt like M. Goddddam. How do you do Curly Craft from Cupid's College? How is the

$10 you took from Madame Crane, in my villa? And how do *you* do Madame ———? How air your diseases and your great villas, and your retinue and your "*lovers*"? J——— had some dirt and left the ménagerié. Miss F——— had her nose broken through the windshield and served 30 days on one count, God, she wasn't so bad off with me, at that. But it is much better to live alone, and cheaper dearie. . . .

Hart, don't send me postal cards because they go to Mother's office and she reads them, and when you write, mark letters "Privée." Savvy?

I am feeling fine but not working, still I don't care a damn. Am just biding my time. La ——— is a building of a villa in Pasadeny, I hear, and still has that poor little faggot with him. God! Main Street is as brilliant as ever and poor Maw still drives up and down in her chariot, bowing left and right.

My God, remember the night at the apt., when I flew—Oh, God 'elp us all. . . .

My God Hart I am so tired of it here. Nothing but bloody movie news in the papers. Movie everything. It's bloody terrible but I'll end it soon. Things are coming to a head with me and next year I fly hence and be no more seen. My God, I hope you are there then. Remember the great fight, Hart? And the great plucking of bracelets and wrist-watches, and the great massacre of Mother and the ripping of sweaters? Like monkeys dismembering a lobster at Marguerey's. Write your old Maw soon—she air doing her washin' today, towels, dearie, and has ter go shoppin' agin Saterday. One hairy gaffer guv me a hammock and mattress. My God what'll I do with it? And another one an ash tray with royal Hawaiian coat of arms and yet another one, a little box and a wedding ring of beads that he made for "G———." God 'elp me for accepting gifts, but when you get to be an ancient light like myself, it's nice ter be remembered with Gold, Frankincense and Myrrh and a little clout on the chops once in awhile.

Write yer old Maw soon, chile. She air cravin fer news of the big town.

Resp.<br>G.

My respects to Mme de Rochefecauld or whatever her name is.

Yrs etc.<br>G.

Though Hart hinted at this part of his life to a few friends ("I'll have to save the most amusing details until I see you, on account of the Censor," he explained to Sam Loveman), he was usually discreet enough to confine anecdotes to conversation. An unwatered ninth Scotch, however, released for Bill Brown a casual, lilting letter that shows how effectively Hart kept in focus—if not always in control—the powerful and satisfying forces of lust, love, wine, friendship, and art.

I am above all, anxious to hear about Sue and the enfant sublime! My blessings—from the fairy God Mother in her native clime, here where the evenings are made lustful and odorous with the scent of lemon flowers and acacias on the sea-salt air!

A paean from Venusberg! Oy-oy-oy! I have just had my ninth snifter of Scotch. O shades of Bert Savoy! They say he had a glass eye as the result of some midnight with a mariner. But I have had no such dire results as yet. OH BOy! Try to imagine the streets constantly as they were during that famous aggregation last May in Manhattan! And more, for they are at home here, these western argosies, at roadstead far and near—and such a throng of pulchritude and friendliness as would make your "hair" stand on end. That's been the way of all flesh with me . . . And wine and music and such nights—*WHOOPS!!!!!!!*

Besides which I have met the Circe of them all—a movie actor who has them dancing naked, twenty at a time, around the banquet table. O André Gide! no Paris ever yielded such as this—away with all your counterfeiters! Just walk down Hollywood Boulevard someday—if you must have something *out* of uniform. Here are little fairies who can quote Rimbaud before they are 18—and here are women who must have the tiniest fay to tickle them the one and only way! You ought to see Betty C——— shake her tits—and cry *apples* for a bite!

What can I write about? Yes I am reading Wyndham Lewis' "Time and Western Man," Fernandez' insufferable "Messages" and all the other stuff. But I would rather do as I did yesterday —after a night of wine—wake up at dawn and dip into "The Tempest," that crown of all the Western World. What have I to say after that event, I wonder. ? ? ?

> —The charm dissolves apace
> And as the morning steals upon the night,
> Melting the darkness, so their rising senses
> Begin to chase the ignorant fumes that mantle
> Their clearer reason. . . .

Maybe with me someday, as good Prospero says. Perhaps—as Ceres says in the same play—

> Spring come to you at the farthest
> In the very end of harvest!
> Scarcity and want shall shun you;
> Ceres' blessing is upon you.

But you will tear this up—and keep me true, Bill. And if I come back to you and the dear hills of Connecticut again, as I hope to, I shall have a cargo for your ears.

More often than not, the situations in which he found himself
could not be set down on paper, but Hart did put the tone of
these swirling days into letters. He succeeded in documenting,
superbly, the surface of the hedonistic world into which he had by
the beginning of 1928 become almost completely incorporated.
The lush sensuality of Southern California, its corrupt "artists," its
vivid fakes and frauds, its patently false values both attracted and
repelled him. It is this, rather than the particular details of his life,
which fills his California correspondence. One letter to the Cowleys,
written on the last day of January, epitomizes these experiences.

Writing is next to impossible—what with the purling of fountains, the drawling of mockingbirds, the roaring of surf, the
blazing of movie stars, the barking of dogs, the midnight shak-
ings of geraniums, the cruising of warships, etc., etc., not to
mention the dictates of the Censor, whose absence will be welcome sometime, I hope, when we get together at the Dutchman's
or some rehabilitated Punch Palace where I'll at least be able to
offer some new words to the (albeit) ancient tunes! My phil-
osophic moments are few, but when they do occur it is almost
always possible to turn on the radio and immediately expose my
soul to the rasping persuasions of Aimee McPherson, eternally
ranting and evangelizing to packed houses at the great palm-
flanked arena of Angelus Temple. She broadcasts the news that
people are frequently carried out in pieces, arms broken, heads
smashed in the stampede for salvations which she almost nightly
stages, thereby emphasizing the need of arriving early (so as
to save one's body as well) and thereupon lifts her voice into a
perfectly convulsing chant, coaxing and cuddlingly coy about
"Come, all ye—" (You can catch her in it on the Victor) the
chorus of which would make a deacon's bishopric leap crimson
and triumphant from the grave. . . . I haven't seen her, but
they say she has beautiful long, red, wavy tresses. . . .
The peculiar mixtures of piety and utter abandon in this
welter of cults, ages, occupations, etc., out here make it a good
deal like Bedlam. Retired schoolmarms from Iowa, Kansas and
all the corn-and-wheat belt along with millions of hobbling
Methuselahs, alfalfa-fringed and querulous, side by side with
crowds of ambitious but none-too-successful strumpets of
moviedom, quite good to look at, and then hordes of rather
nondescript people who seem just bound from nowhere into
nothing—one can't explain either the motives nor means of
their existence. One can generally 'place' people to some extent;
but out here it's mostly nix. One begins to feel a little unreal as
a consequence of this—and so much more, like the perfect
labyrinth of 'villas'—some pseudo-Spanish, some a la Maya
(the color of stale mayonnaise), others Egyptian with a simply
irresistible amphora perched on the terrace, and some vaguely

Chink. Our house, a large *U* with patio and fountain, rambles all over the place, and is almost vertical to the observatory on Mt. Wilson. Plenty of roses, camellias, oleanders, acacias, etc., as well as a good wine-cellar. I've just been interrupted by the butler bringing in a makeshift for champagne, composed of carbonated apple-juice with a sling of gin; so all attempts at epistolary consecutivety are hereby and henceforth abandoned! No, I'd better give up—I was just about to say something about the pool rooms down at San Pedro where the battle fleet rides close at anchor. Gradually I'm becoming acquainted with all the brands of bootleg that the Westcoast offers. I haven't been blinded by anything yet but beauty and sunshine, however; but I did have to get glasses to shield me from the violet rays, which are terribly strong out here. I'd better stop, I guess.

Love to you both and peace to all our bladders!

When Hart returned to the East Coast, he was surprised to find that his letters had reinforced many of the legends already forming about his name. Men who knew him only slightly felt that they had heard, through him, of a real never-never land and they came to see him as its spokesman. The writer Nathan Asch, for example, in the summer of Hart's return a tenant at Mrs. Turner's Patterson house, found Hart himself even more difficult to comprehend than the stories he had heard about him. Years later, Asch set down his recollections of his brief acquaintance with Crane; they reflect the nightmare quality that Hart's accounts of that life must have had.

From what Hart told us, I built up a picture of Hollywood as a voluptuary's dream place, where all the senses are satisfied; I don't know why I thought of where he lived with his rich patron as a sort of incense-laden seraglio, with couches on which reclined beautiful youths, and where even the ordered spaces of time meant nothing, so that day and night did not have ordinary connotations; breakfast was not served in the morning, and the first meal of the day was not breakfast; liquor flowed, and bodies met and penetrated in an atmosphere of music; and this Hart told us: once during a party . . . he found himself in the bathroom with a strange and beautiful looking man, worn looking too, who insisted on going down on him, and when he raised himself, showed himself to be a famous and already aging star . . .

But not all of Hart's California time was devoted to rum and riot. During the first few months, he took many long walks by the sea. "It has been good to come over here where places are rather deserted of crowds," he wrote Slater Brown during one Santa Monica weekend, "and hear the gulls cry overhead and watch the solemn pelicans eye you awhile and then hawl up their legs and sprawl into the air." There was also a really good supply of recorded music. "Wise is buying all the albums of symphonies, quintettes, concertoes and what-not on the Victor list," Hart told Sam Loveman. "So I'm living on intimate terms for the first time with Brahms and Beethoven—the two most exciting of all to me."

But, as always, it was literature that was the real center of Hart's life. It offered him pleasures quite as voluptuous as those he found at the dinner table, in speakeasies, or even in the various beds easygoing California made available to him.

When anyone was willing to talk seriously about the arts, Hart pounced on him. "God! you never know who you're meeting over here," he wrote Slater Brown.

> . . . First there was a snappy collegiate hanging around the studios, who turned out to know Allen [Tate]—and then today on the beach a mile below here, at Venice, I found myself talking literature, Spengler, Kant, Descartes and Aquinas—to say nothing of Charles Maurras and Henri Massis—to a Bostonian of French descent who knows Stewart Mitchell, and especially his Aunt, very well! He turned out to be one of the best scholars I've ever met—a great reactionary toward the same kind [of] classicism that Eliot and Lewis are fostering in England. I had him spotted as a Romantist [Romantic?] in less than five minutes—but he wouldn't admit it until we parted. The dialectic we had was more rousing than the aforesaid tonic combustions of alcohol . . .

There was also Yvor Winters, with whom Hart spent four days of Christmas week. Their conversation was of literature—and of a major figure Crane was until then unfamiliar with. "I'm terribly excited about the poems of Gerard Manley Hopkins," he wrote Loveman. "Winters loaned me his copy recently (I had never read any of Hopkins before) and I have discovered that I am not as original in some of my stylisms as I had thought I was. Winters tells me that the book (Oxford edition, edited by Robert Bridges) is now out of print. I'm simply wild to secure a copy—and am wondering if you could locate me anything around New York. I'm willing to pay anything up to $10.00. Failing this, I think I shall go to work and type out the whole volume, for I've never been quite so enthusiastic about any modern before." Though he regarded Crane as a man of "more or less manic-depressive make-up" and though he was shocked to find that "his hair was graying, his skin had the dull red color with reticulated grayish traceries which so often go with advanced alcoholism, and his ears and knuckles were beginning to look a little like those of a pugilist," Winters was caught up by Hart's literary sensitivity and his enthusiasm: "I would gladly emulate Odysseus, if I could, and go down to the shadows for another hour's conversation with Crane on the subject of poetry."

When there was no one for Hart to talk to, he could always

write out for friends summaries of his reading and his off-the-cuff reactions to it. "Richards' 'Principles of Literary Criticism,'" he told Brown, "is a *great* book. One of the few—perhaps the only one in English excepting stray remarks by Coleridge—that gets to bed rock." He had also been looking into Eliot's sources: "Weston's book, 'From Ritual to Romance,' was quite fascinating—but Winters claims that scholars regard half her data and deductions as imaginative bunk." And he had read a number of recent novels, one of which seemed to him outstanding: "Did I rave to you about Elizabeth Madox Roberts' new book—'My Heart and Flesh'—before! . . . I think it a great performance." Before he left California, he also read Glenway Wescott's *The Grandmothers* ("damned fine, although I think it weakens toward the last; Wescott seems to lose his grip"), the most recently translated volume of Proust's great novel, and Gide's *The Counterfeiters.* "I also am," he wrote Sam Loveman, "now introduced to Heathcliff (whom I have put beside Ahab) thanks to your mention of 'Wuthering Heights.'"

And of course there were the little and not so little magazines, the ones that had published him and that continued to publish his friends. These Crane studied carefully, sometimes taking time to write out a commentary for one friend or another; for, in a very literal sense, they were his "professional journals." Though he was rarely altogether pleased with the work they printed—much of it, he felt, was in one way or another hysterical or pretentious—he read and reread all of it. "Every week," he wrote Brown, "I scour the pages of the New Rep., Nation and Herald-Tribune for the names of our 'rising generation.'" He was surprised that he'd seen nothing recently by Malcolm Cowley and asked if that meant that Cowley had been ill. He then went on to summarize his reactions.

> Much by Robert Penn Warren, but little by his friend Tate, excepting a recent review of Winters which I thought excellent. Slater Brown, I long since neglected to mention, scored keenly in tussle with the milksop critic of Estlin C'gs in the Canby Crap Can. "The point was well taken," as my grandmother would say. And how is C'gs? for I think you told me he was pretty hard up. [Stewart] Mitchell seems to be bursting with new energy by the evidence in recent numbers of the Dial. And last, but not least in this litry column, how goes it with your translations . . . I must say that I haven't yet been able to decipher that defense of me by Laura [Riding], published in Transition along with Kay Boyle's explosive boil. I wrote her promptly, thanking her for her sentiments, but questioning her style. Her latest book announced by Jonathan Cape, is "Anarchy Is Not Enough"—and so she seems to be maintaining her consistency.

In her commentary on "my grandmother and her grandson's poems," Hart wrote Isidor Schneider, Miss Boyle had made a wholesale condemnation of his work. "We were both damned together—for trying to 'climb up onto another plain' or something. Laura Riding's defense of me was and still remains a vast mystery. In the final paragraph I am made to feel that I'm a good kid alright, alright, and hardly a speakeasy. But that's all I can make out."

Seeing his name in print again—in *transition* and also in *The Dial*, which in February had published "The Air Plant"—reminded Crane that he was indeed a poet, one who had on his hands an almost completed major poem.

California, however, was no place to work on *The Bridge*, though it represented an aspect of America that he knew he would sometime have to touch on in his poem. Recent books defining the present and anticipating the future—books that might seem pertinent to some of his themes—were a hindrance of another kind. For none of them seemed grounded in the real soil of a real country; none of them seemed to be in touch with 1928. "I often wish I had the scientific and metaphysical training," he wrote Schneider, "to appreciate and judge all these Whiteheads, Bradleys, Fernandez, Wyndham-Lewis-es, etc., who keep drumming up new encyclopedias of the Future, Fate, etc. And now Waldo has written another, especially devoted to America."

> I read them, puzzle and ponder as best I'm able, but Spengler was about the only one who flattered my capacities to the least extent. They are all so formidable, bristling with allusions, statistics, threats and tremors, trumpets and outcries on the least splitting of a hair which I can't locate through the labyrinth of abstractions. I'm afraid I'd better give up trying to make any headway in their direction—or else relinquish all attempts to do any writing myself. For about all they really net me is a constant paralysis and distraction. I think that this unmitigated concern with the Future is one of the most discouraging symptoms of the chaos of our age, however worthy the ethical concerns may be. It seems as though the imagination had ceased all attempts at any creative activity—and had become simply a great bulging eye ogling the foetus of the next century . . . I find nothing in Blake that seems outdated, and for him the present was always eternity. This is putting it crudely; but when I get some of these points a little more definitely arranged then maybe I'll have more nerve to continue my efforts on the Bridge.

If Crane could not finish his own major work, he could at least do his best to get back into print the work of Hopkins, a major artist incomprehensibly neglected. As in his earlier campaign to teach America to see the excellences of Bill Sommer's painting, he diligently propagandized Hopkins's worth to all the editors and publishers he knew. Before he returned Winters's copy of the poems, he made typewritten copies of a number of them and even

committed several—including "The Wreck of the Deutschland"—
to memory.

Copies of the typed copies were shipped off to friends, usually
with a brief critical introduction to make sure that the recipient
looked for the right things in the sample. Introducing "Pied
Beauty" to Isidor Schneider, for example, Hart explained: "Hopkins does incredible things with rhythms more essentially modern
than any I have found. Yet he evinces at the same time some of
the deepest traditions of English prosody. His nearest relations
(as to attitude and metaphor) seem to be Herbert and Donne."
Everyone Hart met that spring had the opportunity to hear about
the wonders of Hopkins's formidable technique, everyone from
script writers to Bennett Cerf. "I suggested to Bennett Cerf when
he was here that Hopkins would be a good man for the Nonesuch
Press to re-issue," Crane wrote to the Schneiders, "but Cerf apparently has no ear nor mind for any poetry. I found him pleasant,
urbane—but very superficial; a 'type' all too common in every
metropolis nowadays."

During his six months in California, Hart became casually ac-
quainted with several hundred people. But almost all of that time
he was painfully lonely. Even men he had known on the East
Coast seemed, in California limelight, difficult to talk to—even
Charlie Chaplin, whose all-night conversation years earlier in
Manhattan had made him, Hart felt, a blood brother. But when
the two men finally met again, it was, as Hart explained to Waldo
Frank, a "rather disappointing experience."

> During my first month on the Coast I happened to meet him
> sitting in his favorite restaurant one evening. I had a friend
> with me and he was also engaged, but I stopped for a moment
> in passing to say hello—identifying myself with you (whose
> address he wanted immediately). I later sent him an inscribed
> copy of White Buildings along with a letter, but never got any
> response further than a formal letter from his secretary ac-
> knowledging receipt of same, etc. As I had already urged him
> to dine with me (my boss, Mr. Wise, was simply wild to meet
> and entertain him) I couldn't press matters much further. He
> was simply too busy otherwheres to be interested—that was
> obviously it—and all the stars have built walls of mystery about
> themselves as impregnable as Carcasonne! Just try to get them
> on the phone sometime! But Charlie surely was never so radiant
> and handsome as when I saw him. . . . Hair snow-white, which
> means almost as white as the smiling flash of his teeth, and
> those same eyes of genius.

The only close friend who showed up in California was Emil
Opffer, but their March weekend proved to be such a shambles
that they had hardly an opportunity to talk. It even began badly.

Each of them had arrived, Emil told me, bottles of good fellowship in hand—at wrong addresses and at wrong hours.

For Crane had a week earlier left his job with Herbert Wise and had moved into the Hollywood cottage rented by his mother. Though he had sent a ship letter to Emil, explaining his move and suggesting that they meet at the dock, it failed to arrive. To further complicate matters, the *California*, on which Emil was working as a waiter, docked early. Consequently, while Hart was hurrying down from Hollywood, Emil was on his way to Altadena—and eventually on to Hollywood and Mrs. Crane, who sent him back to his ship. Hart, meanwhile, paced the docks, accompanied by a young French sailor, who helped kill one bottle and put a severe dent in another. When Emil showed up, all bottles were empty. That was, however, no real problem, since he had just won $100 in a pre-docking shipboard crap game. Arm in arm, the three young men headed for the nearest speakeasy.

Hart's version of the weekend forms the core of a long letter to Sue and Bill Brown:

> Life is nothing if not exciting whenever Emil happens to land, if only for a few hours. It took him (or his presence) to arrange the most harrowing week-end yet, and I'm only praying that he's still alive, for when I left him in his berth in the "glory-hole" of the "California" last Sat. night he looked as though he were nearing the Pearly Gates. We were held up and beaten by a gang in San Pedro . . . The story is complicated and lengthy— and Emil will probably give you the full version or as much as he can remember when he sees you.
>
> I left Wise's ménage a week ago today. However, as E somehow failed to get my ship letter announcing same and the hour at which I would meet him—he flew right up to Altadena, leaving me to wait a *full 8 hours* by the gangway . . . By that time I had about finished a half pint of alcohol which I had bought for our mutual edification . . .
>
> *Scene Two.* Speakeasy joint with booths. Many bottles of dubious gin and whiskey—with much "skoling"—Emil flashing a fat pay roll—and treating three or four still more dubious "merry andrews" who had invited themselves to our noisy nook. It being midnight, all ordered out.
>
> *Scene Three.* A street, or rather, several streets. Our "guests" very insistent on taking a hotel room in which to finish the fire water. Emil and I both reeling but refractory. I finally noticed Emil being spirited away by three of them, while it was evident that I, who had been more emphatic in my wishes, was being guarded by two others. I broke away—and had just caught up to Emil who was being put around a dark corner—when all five started slugging us. I put up quite a fight, but neither of us were in much condition. They all beat it as a car turned on a nearby

corner. Both of us were robbed of everything, and E practically unconscious. After reporting at police headquarters I don't know how I would have got E back to his ship without the help of a sailor friend of mine whom I had run into earlier in the evening while waiting for E. We roused several of his shipmates —and I'm only hoping that his bumps and bruises haven't been any more fatal than mine. I finally had to finish the night in a ward of the Salvation Army Hotel, and it was five o'clock Sunday before I got enough money to get back to Hollywood. On his way back from Frisco I'm hoping to see E again—but not in Pedro! . . . I don't mind my losses but I feel terribly about Emil's luck. He always seems to get the hardest end of things.

Aside from his watch, Hart lost little more than his dignity, and that was a loss he had learned to adjust to. He had not lost Emil's friendship. He counted himself, all told, lucky.

For by the end of March, friendship had become for Hart a matter of capital concern. In spite of the presence of his mother— perhaps because of it—he was desperately homesick for the places and faces he associated with happiness. Friends who had not heard from him for months—some who had not heard from him in years—suddenly found themselves again in correspondence. Waldo Frank, Gorham Munson, Gene Toomer, Gaston Lachaise, Mrs. Turner, Mrs. Simpson, Sam Loveman all had letters beneath which ran a common theme: "God bless you, Sam! I've been homesick to see you more than once. There may be roses, surf and sunshine out here—but so far as I've yet been able to discover, there are very few people as yet!" His real family, he came to feel, was an amalgam forged from the affection of the men and women who knew his mind, who smiled into his eyes. He felt closer to Sue and Bill Brown than he had ever felt to his father or, toward the end of his California stay, than he felt to his mother. "I get terribly homesick out here," he wrote the Browns—from his mother's home.

And yet, of course, it had been primarily to be close to his mother that he had taken the position with Wise and that later— as Wise prepared to return east before going on to Europe—he had resigned, preferring to risk unemployment so long as he could remain with Grace and his grandmother. But, as in all his recent dealings with Grace, delight gave way to irritation. The variant in the pattern this time was that when Hart left her house in mid-May, he left it forever, furtively climbing out of his bedroom window to tiptoe away from the bungalow, baggage in hand, long after she had gone to bed. He left only a note on the pillow, saying he had "gone East." Though mother and son corresponded for several more months, and though each, for a little while, expected their misunderstandings to heal, soon—with the death of Hart's grandmother—a new crisis developed, Hart finally cutting himself

off from his mother completely, hiding his address from her, refusing to answer the pleading letters that found their way to him.

Neither Hart nor Grace was ever able adequately to explain
the swift disintegration of their affections. It was six months, almost to the day, from Hart's November 3 letter, in which he jubilantly announced his impending arrival in California ("But I've
just had to tell you! *Ain't we got fun!!!!. . . .* Love, love and more
love!"), to the day when he ducked into a Hollywood travel
agency to purchase a one-way ticket to New York. In mid-November, Hart, newly arrived, resplendent in new clothes, had brushed
tears of joy from his eyes as he covered the faces of his mother
and grandmother with kisses; on a mid-May evening, after a goodnight kiss to his grandmother, Hart and Grace, for the last time in
their lives, looked coldly at each other's lips, eyes, arms, hands.

Only fragments of the record of that growing mutual irritation
remain. For his own part, Hart scrupulously avoided writing of it
to anyone but his most intimate friends, and even then he was
careful to confine himself to the broadest generalizations. Fragments of letters to his Aunt Zell Deming, to whom he turned for
counsel after his return east, survive. But most of the correspondence that touched on these days was, after his death, systematically destroyed by Mrs. Crane: the letters that he wrote her
after his return east, her own letters to him, letters from his friends
that most directly dealt with Grace, letters from him to other
friends that, after his death, had come into her possession.

What is left is a tangle of Hart's references to "difficulties," some
vaguely remembered conversations, an account that Grace wrote
out for Sam Loveman, and a patchwork of implications that show
up in a few of the letters from Hart's friends.

These, assembled, represent neither "truth" nor "reality." The
most one can discover is evidence that Grace and Hart were under very great emotional pressures and that neither handled these
pressures especially well. Concerned for each other's welfare, each
grew furious when the other ignored the much too frequently
proffered good advice that each of them was happier to give than
to receive.

In the beginning, things had gone well. Grace and Mrs. Hart
had been little more than settled into their apartment when Hart
put in an appearance; both women were still delighted by California sunshine, friendly neighbors, and winter flower gardens,
and Hart congratulated them on their escape from Cleveland
cold and Cleveland gossip. By the end of his second week in
California, however, he had already begun to detect signs of trouble. "I have been over to see my Mother and have had lunch with
her several times," he wrote the Rychtariks. "She is looking very
well, and, of course, seems to be pleased that I'm so near. . . .
Grandmother is failing, but still lively, and incidentally very hard
on my mother's nerves. I think it is doing mother good, however,

to get away from all the ghosts of her past—but life isn't easy anywhere."

One of the reasons life was not easy for Grace was that she had again almost exhausted her available funds. She still, however, owned some acreage on the Isle of Pines, near the house owned by Hart's grandmother. Unfortunately, land values on the Isle of Pines had for years steadily declined and it was now unlikely that—as she hoped—she could realize enough cash to give herself and her mother one or two more years of security. Hart was properly disturbed that they had foolishly held the land when they could have sold it for a really substantial sum; but he agreed to ask Mrs. Simpson to put his mother's land on the market at $3,000. Her reply—that there was little possibility of selling the house for half that price and that there was no chance at all of selling the entire property—must have been responsible for at least one grim interview between Hart and his mother.

For Grace's real problem—and to a considerable extent, Hart's—was the memory of former affluence. Neither could face squarely that in the time of the country's greatest prosperity their annual incomes held them in virtual poverty. Each of them found it easier to eat badly than to dress badly. "Keeping up appearances" was for Grace not just a casual compulsion but a life-and-death matter.

And yet there was no way for her to keep up appearances. Mrs. Hart's doctor bills and the salary of the woman who acted as cook-maid-housekeeper-companion took every penny of the alimony from Grace's second marriage. She and her mother survived by selling off, one by one, their remaining stocks and bonds, the precarious "security" of dividends and interest that they had counted on to support them in California retirement.

By the beginning of February, tensions in the little bungalow-apartment were building toward a breaking point. Mrs. Hart seemed cheerful, but she was bedridden much of the time and needed constant attention. Their overworked housekeeper complained steadily that she had been misled as to the extent of her duties. Grace herself frequently took to bed, suffering, she explained to Hart, from the emotional exhaustion of more illness and unhappiness than she could cope with. "I see my mother on the average of twice a week," Hart at this time wrote to Sam Loveman.

She is located so far away that it takes a good two hours to reach her, so it nearly always means devoting practically a whole day to the occasion. My grandmother is better off than at any time for the last three years—the climate has done wonders. They have a small cottage and would be quite comfortable were they more satisfied with the general temper of the woman they brought out here to live with them. I'm not capable of judging the situation very accurately, but there's been a good deal of fretting and umbrage, very discouraging indeed to me at times. Wise has practically asked me to accompany him to Europe in the Spring, but their situation may deny me that opportunity.

All through February and well into March, Hart tried to make up his mind what he should do. As he had anticipated, he was asked to return east with Wise and then go on to Europe. But Grace begged him not to desert her in what both recognized would be the year of Mrs. Hart's death. With the motion-picture studios booming, Hart would surely be able, she felt, to find congenial work, perhaps as a writer, perhaps even as an actor. For Grace had never been able to free herself from the glamour of the movies. All through her youth she had dreamed of becoming a great singer—perhaps not in opera, but surely, granted the opportunity, in musical comedy. When that dream faded, she quickly replaced it with a dream of becoming a motion-picture actress. She wouldn't, of course, demean herself by pounding on studio doors, but perhaps she would be "discovered"; that dream had brought her to Hollywood. And it too proved nothing more than a dream. Hart, on the other hand, might well succeed in films, she speculated, for already he had made "connections" with writers and actors. Hart himself had no illusions on that score. His relationship with most of the actors he knew could hardly have been called—except in the very broadest sense—professional.

It may, indeed, have been Grace's persistent requests that he introduce her to his friends in the motion-picture industry that persuaded Hart to have a long and very serious talk with her about the nature of homosexuality and the problems of the homosexual. Whatever the occasion, it is certain that they had such a talk. Just how Grace reacted to it is far less certain. Hart told one friend that after growing visibly upset, she rushed from the room and that for days afterward she seemed to him cold and contemptuous. He had been quite sure, he said, that she already suspected his sexual activities; he had felt, therefore, that she would be sympathetic to his honesty. According to him, she was not.

Grace's version of the conversation survives in letters to Sam Loveman that were written after Hart's death and in the account she gave to Philip Horton. Hart, she said, had invited her to Altadena for a weekend. On the first evening of her visit he had found an opportunity to tell her "in a matter-of-fact way, calculated to diminish the shock of the announcement, that he was homosexual." Horton's summary reconstructs Grace's memories:

He explained the aberration in its simplest terms, and went on to mention certain experiences of his adolescence which had conditioned him towards it; he described the years he had suffered from the sense of his difference from other men and the corrosive consciousness of guilt; he told also of his vain efforts to cure himself by attempting normal relationships; and he concluded by insisting vigorously—too vigorously to be convincing—that he was no longer ashamed of it, that in his reading on the subject he had learned to recognize it as a common phenomenon of all societies and all races. Needless to say, it was not by any means true that he had come to accept his status with complete equanimity, and doubtless his mother realized this. In any case, she understood her son well enough to know that any expression of horror or remonstrance on her part might well destroy the relationship which had bound them together so intimately since his childhood. Without committing herself either to approval or disapproval, she gave Hart to understand that she concurred with him in his attitude toward the subject, and promised faithfully to read the books on it that he recommended to her. The only false move she seems to have made lay in her sudden decision to spend the night at a hotel in town rather than with Hart, as she had originally planned.

Grace suggested to Horton that she left the Altadena house because "she wanted to be alone after experiencing such a profound shock." Whatever the motives for her bag-and-baggage departure, Hart interpreted her sudden change of plans as one more in the crippling series of attacks that, he decided, she had for years been making on his personality.

He could not, however, bring himself to leave her when, several days later, she told him that, no matter what direction his sexual life had taken, she was still anxious for him to join her and her mother in Hollywood. Though Hart might well have resigned his position without Grace's urging (he had, really, no stomach for the kind of luxurious living that it entailed), her pleas and his desire to make his grandmother's last months happy ones persuaded him that the move was morally unavoidable. By March 20, he had left Altadena and settled in the apartment at 1803¾ North Highland Avenue, Hollywood. "Yes, I have moved over to my mother's place," he told Isidor Schneider, "—from courts and halls and stucco walls to a very modest bungalow. . . ."

> The more I saw of my mother's situation here and the necessity of her constant attendance on my grandmother (who is practically a centenarian) the more out of place I felt in my position with Wise. And the folly of returning east with him and of putting myself at such a distance from her and her problems was all too evident: I'm too much needed here to have much peace of mind elsewhere. So maybe I'll turn native for awhile. At present I'm prospecting for some scenario or other mechani-

cal work with the movies. Work isn't easy to find out here just now, but then I can't remember when or where it has been a cinch to find!

Whatever position he took, he told the Browns, it would not be another job as secretary-companion to a wealthy traveler. Though he was able to say of his former employer, "we are still friends so far as I know," he could not have brought himself, he explained, to stay on indefinitely.

> The situation became too strained to be continued. If I had only had some definite duties I could have kept my self-respect, but the tip-toeing, solicitous, willy-nilly uncertainty of every-thing, besides his interminable psycho-analysis of every book, person, sausage and blossom got to giving me the heeby-gee-bies. . . . Such circumstances don't promote a very lively morale —and it's probably better for me to lose a little of the attendant avoirdupois in favor of a more exhilarating outlook.

While Crane did not look forward to the prospect of unemploy-ment, he was at least better able to face it than at many times in the past. For one thing, he still had several hundred dollars of the sum Otto Kahn had advanced him; and for another, Kahn was about to arrive in Los Angeles and might reasonably be expected to help Hart find a position that would make use of his talents. Shortly before leaving Wise, Hart had written to Kahn, explaining his situation and asking for an interview.

The meeting took place at 10:30 A.M. on the morning of March 26. Though Kahn's recommendations to influential men at the studios—Jesse Lasky, William Fox, someone at Paramount—ulti-mately led to nothing, his interview with Hart did provide a diverting morning. While the two men sat chatting in the patio of the Los Angeles Ambassador Hotel, "Pathe news-reel or some such torture swooped down on us . . . and for all I know we may be thrown upon the screen together all the way from Danbury to Hong-Kong and Mozambique!" Advising the Browns not to be shocked should they see the newsreel ("I'm wearing horn-rims now"), Hart ruefully noted, "At least I have 'broken in' the movies in one way."

It very soon became obvious that this was the only way he would be part of the movie industry. He applied to the major studios. He visited the men Kahn had suggested and also those suggested by Isidor Schneider. Absolutely nothing came of his efforts.

In the meantime, Hart's grandmother took a turn for the worse, and Hart was called on to put in at least a part of each day as companion and nurse. Though he might not be able to find work, he explained to his friends, and though *The Bridge* seemed for the time being hopelessly bogged down, he was doing what he had to do. "The experience of the last two years has taught me the futility of any retreat from what I, after all, must regard as my immediate responsibilities. The further I might go from the actual 'scene' of operations," he wrote to Waldo Frank, "the more obsessed I tend to become by the inert idea. . . . When all this is over—someday —I may be able to regain the indispensable detachment from immediate concerns that such a work as my Bridge demands."

But for the moment, the routine of bedside and bedpan became the center of Hart's world. Grace herself suffered an extended "nervous collapse" and Hart, as the only functioning member of the household, was saddled with most of the nursing duties. Able to escape only on Grace's infrequent "good" days, he carried his grandmother back and forth to the toilet, cleaned house, cooked meals, and tried—for Grace's sake and for his grandmother's—to be encouraging, cheerful, witty.

Considering his circumstances, his chaotic and unhappy life, it is not surprising to find Hart suffering from what we so elegantly name "a loss of values." He had read all the books his friends had recommended—books "everyone" was reading—and had found them either unrealistic or, for all their fine abstractions, trivial. "I have tried reading Fernandez' *Messages* and Lewis' *Time and Western Man* without being able to wholly approve a single page of either . . . Beginning with . . . Spengler and Wells," he wrote Frank, "this age seems to [be] typically encyclopedic. . . . God knows, some kind of substantial synthesis of opinion is needed before I can feel confident in writing about anything but my shoe-strings. . . . These Godless days! I wonder if you suffer as much as I do. At least you have the education and training to hold the scalpel."

Gorham Munson sent him a copy of his new book, *Destinations*, which incorporated the article he had written about Hart's poetry two years before. At that time it had seemed to Hart to misrepresent the core of his art; now he was not so sure. "As for Hart Crane, I know him too well to disagree on as many points as I once did." For the whole of Munson's book, Hart had less to say. But he praised what he could.

> With the general exhortation of your book (as a whole) toward more definite spiritual knowledge and direction I find myself in close sympathy. The spiritual disintegration of our period becomes more painful to me every day, so much so that I now find myself baulked by doubt at the validity of practically every metaphor I coin. In every quarter (Lewis, Eliot, Fernandez, etc.) a thousand issues are raised for one that is settled and where this method is reversed—as with the neo-Thomists—one has nothing as substitute but an arbitrary dogmatism which

seems to be too artificial [to] have any permanence or hold on the future. This "future" is, of course, the name for the entire disease . . .

Meanwhile, his situation grew grimmer, Hart managing such spiritual balances as he achieved by contemptuous analysis of the corrupt world in which he was still attempting to make a place for himself. For he was running out of money and there were no income-producing prospects in sight. He knocked at the right doors; he went to some of the right—for "right" read "most barbaric"—parties. Yet he found neither employment nor distraction. Able to escape from his mother's watchful eye neither in his writing nor in a job nor in polite society, he finally devoted most of his comparatively rare "free" time to the pursuit of sailors and the patronage of bootleggers. And then the sailors sailed away and alcohol lost its kick. On April 27, he sent off to Slater Brown a disconsolate "spasm" of a letter, ironic, helpless, and angry.

> Since the Fleet with its twentyfivethousand gobs has left for Hawaii I have had a chance to face and recognize the full inconsequence of this Pollyanna greasepaint pinkpoodle paradise with its everlasting stereotyped sunlight and its millions of mechanical accessories and sylphlike robots of the age of celluloid. Efforts for a foothold in this sandstorm are still avid, but I have had little yet in encounter. "Crashing the gate" is a familiar expression out here, and it seems to be exclusively applied to the movie industry. To cap the climax I have to endure my mother's apparently quenchless desire that I become an actor! But if I can hold on until the middle of May I'm due for an interview with Jesse Lasky (HIMSELF) and maybe through that entree I can creep into some modest dustpan in the reading dept. of Paramount. . . .
>
> Have just discovered the presence here of Mrs. Alice Barney, the world-famous grande dame and mother of Nathalie Clifford Barney of Paris, friend of Valéry, translator, . . . etc. As she is a great friend of Underwood of Washington, I have been invited to her next weekly "evening." She ought to be a little different than the typical Hollywood hostess—perhaps mildly Proustian. God knows I need some sort of diversion besides bus rides and the rigor mortis of the local hooch.

Hart found particularly ironic a letter from his father; for C.A., who was completely unaware of the reality of Hart's life and Grace's, cheerfully wrote: "I had a letter from your mother, in which she indicates she is roaming around among flower beds and enjoying life to the fullest in Hollywood. I hope she won't pick up a bumble bee in her quest for happiness." *Flower beds*! Hart must have exclaimed to himself as he thought of how he circulated through the wailing bedrooms of the bungalow.

C.A., excited by the boom psychology that caught most businessmen in these months, reported: "The financial situation in business is such that most anything could happen without alarming
us greatly. I see that General Motors stock has climbed from a
low of twenty-five to a high of two-hundred." He had just returned from New York, where, hoping to bolster his wholesale
business, he had introduced a new line of packaged chocolates.

> Your father is now Mr. Cartier, a Frenchman with a gay
> moustache and several years lopped off his countenance in
> order to make him more attractive to the buying public.
> Mr. Cartier lives in New York. The father whom you have
> known is residing at Canary Cottage, Chagrin Falls Village. We
> have at last gotten around to impersonating Dr. Jekyll and Mr.
> Hyde. You will not be surprised to know that I have a grown
> family in New York, and chow pups in Chagrin.

Hart—living a much more vivid Jekyll-and-Hyde life than his
father could ever have imagined—could not bring himself to answer that letter, the happiest from C.A. in years. It was difficult,
in fact, to answer any of the optimistic letters that everyone
seemed suddenly to be sending him. The Schneiders were off to
Europe, excited at the prospect of leisure and travel. Waldo Frank
had rented a cottage on Bailey Island, off the coast of Maine,
where he hoped to put in shape a book of essays and to renew
work on a novel. "If you have no plans for the summer, why not
come up to Bailey Island?" he wrote. Gaston Lachaise sent an
announcement of the opening of his New York show, regretting
that Hart couldn't make it.
"From what I have heard and read," Hart wrote Munson, "it
has been a wonderful winter season in NY—unprecedented as far
as music goes, at least." But there was neither music nor wonder in
California.

> The aridity of social life out here is simply appalling. The near-
> est thing to reality is the greasepaint and vulgarity of the boule-
> vard that runs through Hollywood. Broadway around Times
> Square at any time of the day is better. Expensive cars by the
> legion—and frizzed poodles and parading vampires. . . . Thank
> God the sea is near, that's all I can be grateful for.

From Bill Brown he heard of the opening of E.E. Cummings's
*him*. The whole group of Patterson friends had attended. "Your
salute to the comments of the ny critics' cracks at *him* displayed
more life than I have seen around here since I arrived," Hart answered. "Although I am still holding my sides, I'm a little sad; for
I would have liked to have been there. Especially with Anne
[Cummings] drinking gin and Emil sporting his shiners and shirt
front and all the tumult and guzzling there must have been afterward! . . . It's good to think of you as back near Patterson. I had a

good letter from Malcolm. It all makes me homesick. Things like that croquet game in the rain, the afternoon at the cider mill, the skeleton surrey ride and the tumble down the hill!"

Lacking friendship and love, lacking a job, lacking a world that in any respect seemed meaningful, Hart faced a bitter fact; now that he could not write, he was being asked to submit poetry to the best of the new magazines. "I haven't a thing to send for the *transition* Am. issue. I can't imagine ever having anything to say out here except in vituperation of the scene itself."

Had Hart found work, had his grandmother died in May of 1928 rather than in September, had Grace Crane found strength to carry on at least some of the household chores rather than taking to her bed—had any one of these happened, the design of the rest of Crane's life and his mother's might have been drastically different. But Hart did not find work; Mrs. Hart, in great pain and in constant need of attention, lived until September; and, about the first of May, Grace took to bed, making explicitly clear that Hart would have to remain within call.

As might have been expected, the consequences were ruinous. Grace accused Hart of callous indifference each time he spent an evening out. Hart—more and more certain that her illness was largely a matter of acting—became convinced that Grace kept him busy waiting on her so that he would have no opportunity to visit waterfront bars.

Months later, he told the Schneiders that the early weeks of May had been "intolerable," weeks when "excessively hysterical conditions arose between me and my family." Behind the stories he told friends, one can sense Crane's growing conviction that his mother's love for him had degenerated into a brutal possessiveness. He knew all too well what such a feeling was, but he was shocked to find it dominating a relationship he had always idealized as pure and selfless. Not only did he discover that Grace was jealous of his love for his grandmother; he also discovered—recalling his past—a lifelong pattern of jealousy: Grace "guarding" him from any deep affection for his father, for his other relatives, for the girls whom, in a more conventional boyhood, he might have come to love. She loved him, he knew; but she did not love his freedom. She was as jealous of homosexual attachments as of family ones; every trip in and out of the house had become a subject of close questioning. She would never voluntarily, he felt, allow him to love anyone other than her; nor, he was sure, would she ever allow him a life substantially independent of her. Each move on his part toward an evening's freedom found her "collapse" worsening. Each effort on his part to talk out his problems honestly or to define for her his feelings was greeted by attacks on his "disloyalty." Then would come her inevitable shuddering, sobbing retreat to her room, where, helplessly, he would eventually come to apologize.

There is no way to know how long this pattern might have continued had not Hart, in the midst of one of their most violent exchanges, stalked angrily from the house. His mother—as often before—had ended her catalogue of accusations by telling him that she wished he had never come to live with her, that she wished he would go back to those friends he loved so much more than he loved her, that she hoped he would get out and leave her in peace. This time, anger carried Hart to a travel agency, where he inquired about the price of a one-way ticket to New York. He had just enough money left to pay for it. He selected a complicated route that would take him by rail to New Orleans, then by ship to New York. His itinerary would delay his exit for a week or ten days. If he were being hasty, he would have a week to test his resolve.

Months later, in New York City, he wrote to his Aunt Zell, offering her an account of those last few days in Hollywood. He was still shaken by memories of a week of lies and deception. All through the spring, Grace had badgered him to try his hand at acting. His first performance and his farewell one were played during that week. For audience: a dying old lady; another lady, middle-aged, baffled into hysteria by too much love.

> I was desperate, and desperately firm. I could not take the chance of being frank, for it involved the hazard of other wild demonstrations, perhaps even worse than the last. Grace was walking about again two days before the date on my ticket. I had never acted before, and in the process I discovered that she was doing a good deal of it herself, timing her recovery by gradual degrees, quite confident, in fact, also—that she had completely subdued me to a kind of idiotic jelly of sympathetic responses. Well, I carried it through—packing by infinitesimal degrees and labyrinthine subterfuges (it sounds like a comedy, but I was ill and nearly dead for sleep) until on the appointed hour the taxi drove up with darkened lights—and I was on my way—'home'—the only one I ever hope to have—this supposedly cruel city, but certainly better for me than either of my parents.

# 30

Hart's exit from California was the first of a series of flights from his mother, flights that would punctuate the rest of his days and that would leave him each time shaken by bitter memories of her demanding love. He was never again to see her, but each flight—prompted always by terror that she might persuade him to return—led to an orgy of drunken escape and complex moves from place to place as, swearing friends to secrecy, he attempted to cover his trail. In these voyages of retreat there were intervals of pure horror, times of sobbing confession to his oldest friends of a love he could not—no matter how hard he tried—transform into the hatred he had "rationally" convinced himself his mother deserved. Driven by this storm of feeling, he first fled to New York, soon after to Europe, and finally to Mexico. But no matter where he went, he found himself pursued by her letters and by memories that would not let him rest. So long as she lived, he felt, she would continue to hunt him down. "If he had lived," Sam Loveman told me, "he would have had to go back to her. He loved her more than he loved anyone else. He couldn't live without her." But he could not live with her, either.

At first, however, Hart persuaded himself—and even persuaded Grace—that all would be well. Though "a coolness," he told friends, had colored their correspondence after his return east, he and his mother did continue to exchange letters through the summer and early autumn of 1928.

During the long trip from Hollywood to New Orleans, Hart gradually relaxed. A group of New Orleans reporters who admired his work met and feted him as he lay over for a day before the departure of his ship. ("I . . . was treated like a senator by some writers on the *Times-Picayune* who had a considerable enthusiasm for my poetry.") And five days at sea on the way to New York gave him leisure to plan a program of writing and working.

New Orleans—"a beautiful old town, full of history and with the kind of mellowness which I prefer to all the boomed-up modernity of Los Angeles and environs"—had been a revelation. Its leisurely pace, the gentle May breezes that carried up from the Gulf a salt flavor, the Old World atmosphere that, in spite of 1928, still permeated the French Quarter were for him much needed proof that

America could not be entirely defined by Hollywood standards. "The old French quarter of New Orleans with its absinthe speak-easies and wonderful cooking seemed unspeakably mellow and gracious after all the crass mechanical perfection of Hollywood," he wrote the Schneiders, "and the six hours on the great delta were even more symphonic than I had expected." That vast mouth of the Mississippi, he explained to his father, was quite as compelling as he had pictured it in *The Bridge*: "The boat ride down the delta of the Mississippi (we were from 10 till 5 p.m. completing it) was one of the great days of my life. It was a place I had so often imagined and, as you know, written about in my River section of *The Bridge*. There is something tragically beautiful about the scene, the great, magnificent Father of Waters pouring itself at last into the oblivion of the Gulf!"

Hart arrived in New York rested, well fed, and impoverished ("I was grateful that meals had been included in my ticket, for I only had $2. and an entirely disproportionate appetite"). After several days visiting friends, he gratefully accepted Waldo Frank's offer to pay his way up to Patterson and to advance him enough money to keep him solvent until he could locate employment. It was at this point that he decided to write out for his father a much watered-down account of the failure of the California adventure, an account that led to another request for a subsidized summer.

> It's going on to three weeks since I got back here in the country, and in spite of my sincere fondness for certain features of the coast I can certainly say that I feel more in my element here in the East. Maybe it's my room—with my desk and my books— or old friends nearby—or the more stimulating mental atmosphere. But at any rate I don't miss the parade of movie actors nor a lot of other artificialities of Hollywood, though for a time I was rather amused by such matters. . . . Living isn't so cheap as it's cracked up to be out there, and though Grace was very generously inclined and urged me to stay I felt that it was taking too big a chance. So when you come down to New York next time perhaps we can get together for an evening.
> . . . Although I'm not as keen about New York as I once was, it looked damned good to me. People aren't as indifferent and impersonal there as they are in the west despite all the slogans and catch-words to the contrary. I soon had the carfare to complete my journey out here—and here I've been ever since, thanks to my good credit with the old woman and the famous cat! There seems to be no possibility of finding any kind of work until after the election, but at least I can live here at the most utter minimum of cost imaginable. I hope you can help me out a little as you did last summer. It's just a question of your interest in the matter, for I'm not claiming that you necessarily ought to. . . .
> I neglected to mention how much I enjoyed your last letter.

You must be getting a lot of real satisfaction out of your country retreat *this* summer, now that it is really a completed article and in all probability running pretty smoothly. Recently I came across the enclosed poem by Guest in a newspaper. I don't know whether or not it tells of *all* the trials of a confectioner or not, but at any rate it certainly suggested that Eddie had recently been sampling some of *Crane's Best.* Which reminds me that I'm sort of candy-hungry these days, as well as the old woman. And I can't help recalling the delicious assortment we received from you last summer.

Please give my best to all the folks including Joe—and do let me hear from you real soon.

Though C.A. may have suspected Hart's reasons for so abrupt a return, in his answer he made only very guarded references to Grace. ("Write me how your mother and grandmother are getting along. Is Mrs. Hart confined to her bed, and do they intend remaining in California indefinitely? You never refer to them in your few letters, and I am commencing to think it is a secret.") Instead of talking about Grace, C.A. summarized for his son the one visit he had made to Grace's California relatives.

Perhaps you had the same experience that I had. Thirty days at Mr. Hart's palatial residence cured me of ever wanting to live there. Of course, anyone of us would like to be adopted by George Hart and enjoy some of the fruits of his wonderful prosperity. I am not referring to the hospitality, but only to the continual sunshine; the same bird perched on the same spot every morning, singing the same song. In a short space of time I grew weary of such a methodical climate. However, I would imagine with your desire to write, and with your willingness to do so, entertaining a great many privations, that the California climate would appeal.

C.A., obviously seeing through Hart's letter, hinted that he would like a little more detail about his son's activities.

I had always imagined that California, with its limpid climate, moving picture stars and shady nooks, was an ideal stamping ground for a vagabond. I can't imagine you ever leaving that for the wild country around New York City. . . . Your letter does not indicate what you intend to do, but I suppose you will resume your writing and chop wood for the coming winter.

For all his irony and piqued curiosity, however, C.A. was a generous man. It must have amused him to write out his check and wind up his letter with "fatherly advice."

All are usually well here and Joe is still my secretary. I will ask him to prepare a two pound Cartier La France and forward [it] to you today.

Yesterday was Father's Day, so it is opportune that I should enclose a check to help you get settled again in the old home . . .

You are getting to be a big boy now, so don't go around with your pants unbuttoned, and write your old decrepit father whenever you have a stamp with which to mail it.

C.A.'s check helped solve Hart's immediate problems, but his letter did not make it easier for Hart to work on *The Bridge*. For very much in Hart's mind was the specter of his abrupt departure from Grace, whose oddly formal letters rehearsed old accusations and chronicled new sufferings. Hart read them, his friends recalled, over and over. "You are right about your mother," Mrs. Simpson wrote on Hart's twenty-ninth birthday, "no one can help her. She is afflicted with self pity (the worst disease in the world) and as you say 'tis up to her and her alone to overcome it. . . . You *must* throw it and all other worries off your mind until you get the Bridge finished."

Throwing off worries, in spite of good intentions, is, however, not easily done. And Crane's good intention of devoting himself to the assembly of his poem evaporated in the pursuit of pleasure. At first he turned down all tempting invitations. Waldo Frank again suggested that Hart come to Maine, but on June 12, Hart denied himself the trip.

It's nice, damned fine, of you to ask me up—maybe I'll be able to make it along in August. But it's a slim chance. I want above all things to get the Bridge completed this summer, and aside from the necessity of taking any work which may come along I'll need to keep my head or rather my nose away from too tempting horizons. But at least I *trust* we'll have a reunion and a long visit in the Fall.

When, several weeks later, Charmion von Wiegand invited him to join her and her husband for a weekend at Croton-on-Hudson, he was still hopeful that he would soon be into a writing session.

Certainly it sounds alluring—and I shall look forward to calling on you later on in midsummer, perhaps, if the invitation extends that far. Right now I'm too miserable with my spring installment of hay fever to be good company for anyone but a wood louse. Even so, it's good to get back east—leaden skies and sneezes—and all. . . .

I'm going to try to make up a lot of lost time so far as writing goes this summer. Have done nothing for a year. So there is little or nothing, alas, to send you.

By the middle of July, however, the steady barrage of offended letters from his mother was taking its toll. "I hope you are doing more writing than I am," he wrote the Schneiders. "I have made my ninety-ninth resolution to round up *The Bridge* this summer and fall, but it doesn't look very likely as yet." Instead of writing, he had, he confessed, squandered almost all of his first six weeks in Patterson on a round of parties, for friends were within very easy reach.

> The Asches are inhabiting the former "Tate's part" of the house. The Josephsons are nearby, down the road. Cowleys stet, ditto Browns; and Fitzi will return from her Riviera visit to the Vails next month.

When there were no parties to keep his mind off his troubles, he was able—even at night—to find his way to "a marvelous boot-legger on a neighboring hill, who makes better beer than I've had north of Cuba!"

He had taken his first trip up this hill with Nathan Asch. Through all the early days of the summer they had remained virtual strangers, but on one memorable day they walked up Rattlesnake Mountain together.

> He had the best, the corner room in Mrs. Turner's house; and . . . it was hung over with weird African fetishes and masks, this being long before the days when everybody's rooms became over-hung with masks; and when I came in it produced a weird feel-ing in me, as if I who was living only beyond the wall had trav-elled to a barbaric country. I felt on formal behavior. I spoke in a different tone of voice. It must be understood that we were never informal with one another; and once when Hart seriously misbehaved he wrote Lysel [Mrs. Asch] a formal letter of apology —I have the letter—which reads as stilted as those letters usually read. I came into his room only when he invited me, or when he gave a party in it; otherwise it was there—as strange to my awareness even when he was in New York and the room was simply shut up, as when I heard him creaking there, or type-tapping. Lysel and I had two rooms; we had no couch in the living room, but only a wrapped over mattress on the floor; and I have the same feeling now I had then, when I, lying near the floor on the mattress reading, heard Hart's knock, called *Come in*, and watched him looking over me through the open door. He had heard there was a new bootlegger opening up on Rattlesnake Mountain; it was a couple of miles away, the day was lovely, did I want to walk up? We walked over the unscraped, ungraded road, past long-abandoned and now stone-scattered tobacco fields, through the ruined New England air, passing shacks in which the farmers, who with their ancestors had lived there for hundreds of years, seemed settled as impermanently as squat-ters. . . . The bootlegger's name was W——— V———; I have written about his death elsewhere [*The Valley*]; when Hart and

I first came on him, he was already dying of the disgrace of having been cashiered from the Army, of being married to a bitch so vulgar she should have been murdered on the spot. V——— was all tentative implicitness, she was all common explicitness, all obviousness; the word vulgarity has been so ruined, it probably doesn't evoke her. Anyway, V——— hated women because he had her, Hart felt nothing at all about women; the two of them hit it off pretty well, drinking up V———'s gin that he mixed out of alcohol tins in the wood-shed.

Other weird characters from Rattlesnake Mountain showed up; there were legends there were fugitives from justice among them; V———'s wife served them. She was a dressmaker in NY, who had come down long enough only to see him settled, in her silk dress, with the whalebone stays of her corset showing, with her hips wriggling, delighting the mountain derelicts. I was neither a despairing poet, nor a disgraced army officer, nor was I hiding from the police, so I stumbled back down the mountain in the dark, while Hart did not come back for two or three days of quiet for me, and when he did there was quiet for another day of his sleeping it off; and then again that God-awful New World Symphony resounding through the house, and the typewriter in the next room rattled. It sounded to me mysterious, as if with the ghostly artifacts staring down, demonology were being practiced there. Indeed, something like it was. Sometimes, Hart gave a party; we, the writers rejected by New York booming with the market of the twenties, consoled ourselves with the gaiety we could engender ourselves. We drank the liquor from either V———'s or one of the other bootleggers, and then we shouted and then we danced. I always felt both sillily self-conscious and utterly unself-conscious at these times, because we did nothing orderly or sensible or rational. We did not speak to each other, but rather each of us howled out, and we did not dance with our wives or even with each other, but whirled around Hart's room, faster and faster, as if we were truly possessed. I, who was doing what the others were doing, always wondered at the time whether we were showing off a phony anarchy, or were we actually at the time a part of some primeval horde? Exhausted, we would fall down on the floor, and after jerking, collapse. . . . It probably wasn't that the room was bewitched, possessed, but rather, op-positely, it was a place where there was utter meaninglessness, anything went there, because nothing was important, nothing mattered; after all of the transcendent strain and effort of living, it was in this room that everything collapsed.

So that the room itself was an extension of Hart, an additional stretch of one part of him, and I who did not understand what he was about did not like to go in there. I preferred my own way.

Perhaps it was during one such party that Hart, "drunk and shouting and breaking things," burst in on Mrs. Turner, who had taken refuge in the kitchen clutching her cat Tiger to her bosom. Asch couldn't remember why Crane had gone to her. But he remembered her terror. "Oh, Mr. Crane, Mr. Crane," Asch heard her moaning softly. Yet, though Addey Turner dreaded Crane's violence and during the worst of it did have to hide from him, she was, everyone knew, his greatest defender. Asch was certain that had he asked Mrs. Turner to choose either Hart or himself as a boarder, "for all that we were no trouble to her, while Hart was an agonizing problem in her life, there was no question but that she would prefer Hart." For both she and Hart had now come to accept the fact that her ramshackle house was his only home. "If she didn't understand him any better than his candy manufacturing father did," Asch felt, "at least she was not in a position to put any pressure on him; she loved him and fussed over him and was mistreated by him and was his victim."

When he was not drinking—when stories of his bad behavior drifted back to him and, humiliated, he would come to apologize to his "victim"—no man had greater warmth or charm. Only once in this time did Addey Turner fail to forgive him. Though records of the violence are gone, chances are that it had something to do with his twenty-ninth birthday party. In any event, five days after that party, Hart found himself compelled to write from Fitzi's home, several miles down the road toward nearby Gaylordsville, Connecticut, an embarrassed letter to his father.

> I'm sorry that hay fever has bothered you so much this year. But it isn't the roses, for if they had anything to do with it I should have "died the death," as Mrs. Hurd used to say, in California. I lived surrounded by them in the Pasadena villa. Which reminds me that I might have missed a good many of this year's sneezes if I hadn't lingered on out there after my boss left—with the vain delusion that I might be of some help to Grace. Just had a letter from him recently from one of the mountain resorts in the Swiss Alps. And at present I haven't a place to lay my head.
>
> I oughtn't to say that, I suppose, for I really have been made perfectly welcome. However, I'm far from comfortable and really don't know where to turn. Mrs. Turner decided that she couldn't extend my credit any longer although I had paid her up to the last three weeks and she has never suffered from her trust in me in the past. . . . I've never felt quite as humiliated. I can't ask you for anything more, and I'm not. The above is about all the news there is, however, and it might have been better not to have written you at all just now, I don't know.

This letter was difficult to write, for only three weeks earlier Hart had written C.A. outlining—for the last time—plans to purchase a house of his own. With C.A.'s backing, he would make a down payment on a nearby farmhouse. He had offered, as security for C.A.'s loan, the inheritance that would come to him when his grandmother died. Owning a house, he made clear, would give him the rootedness that he longed for and that he had so often in the past been denied.

There was, however, another reason for wanting to tie up in Connecticut property the inheritance that could not be granted until some time in the indefinite future. He had been fearful, he later told a number of people, that if he did not quickly put the money into local property, his resolve might weaken and he might again join Grace in California. For this, of course, was her great hope, a hope that was at the heart of each of her letters: they would use his inheritance to purchase a California home; they could live at their ease and enjoy to the fullest each other's company.

Needless to say, Hart had not been able to explain any of this to his father. To C.A., the plan to purchase a Connecticut farmhouse with an unawarded legacy was one more example of Hart's careless-ness in money matters. Though he was sympathetic, his *no* was firm.

Now, Harold, your second letter dwelling on the purchase of a home cannot possibly gain my interest at the present time. There are many reasons for it. Since 1922 my business has consumed at least one-half of what I was worth. During the war period we built a very satisfactory enterprise, but through taxes, falling off of business, mis-judgment in a lot of matters, it is keeping my nose well to the grindstone now to meet the pressing demands of the present. . . .

Besides, I question very much the advisability of your invest-ing your anticipated five thousand dollars in that locality. There are always homes for sale. It may not be this one, but one that will amply suffice for your requirements.

When you get your money from the Hart estate you can invest it as you see fit. I surely have little ownership or interest in that treasure.

If you are suffering from hay fever there as badly as you do here, why don't you pick out a place in Michigan where the weather might be more propitious and equally as pleasurable?

I never owned any real estate until I was fifty-one years old. That is not an argument for not doing so; in fact, I think it is a mistake not to own your own home and have a place where your feet are firmly planted on the ground, but I cannot take on anything new as long as I have a sizable mortgage and a bank loan to face every three months. . . .

Now I am sorry that I cannot write you more encouragingly regarding your acquiring a home, but this is the first indication I have ever had that you had a tendency toward settling down, and maybe by the time you have fully convinced me that you want to I will be in better shape.

"Michigan!" Hart had bellowed when he first read the letter. And then had come a letter from Grace inviting him to return to California for his grandmother's last days. And then "his" house—the last anchor he would try for—had been sold. Then there had been Rattlesnake Mountain, the ill-fated birthday celebration, Mrs. Turner's tearful request that he look elsewhere for a place to live, Fitzi's rescue, and the down-and-out plea to C.A., not so much for money as for sympathy. And all within three weeks.

Though C.A. again came through with money, he was becoming impatient with a son who seemed able neither to hold a job nor to write. The letter that accompanied his $50 check was long, but the gist of it was simple: no one can survive indefinitely without some source of income. "Of *course* you don't know where to turn," C.A. exclaimed in the midst of it.

You don't seem to have enough of the earnest side of life in your make-up. You and I agree now as never before that your father has made a failure of his life because he has paid too much attention to hard work and not enough to play. I have been too ambitious for things that really did not amount to anything at all, and now when I analyze it all I cannot quite understand why I have been so foolish.

Unlike Hart, young C.A. had found work to be his only satisfaction.

It was born in my father to be saving and energetic. All of my younger life he kept me at it until I got the same impression of things. . . .

Now, I don't want you to do this way, for I have lived to see the folly of it all, but I want you to get it out of your head that you can live in this world and be a good citizen without paying your way in the legal tender of the realm. . . .

You tried to work with your father, but you didn't want to work. You didn't see the sense of it all. . . .

I think you write well, and unquestionably have better than an average ability for it, but no business is any good unless it pays a dividend and if writing does not pay a dividend then you have to do something else.

You know I would not be very happy to have you hungry, or to have you go along and not pay your honest obligations. I am trying my best to do that much, if nothing more. . . .

I cannot tell you what to do. On that subject my advice has been all wrong for many years. I would have turned from my own business many times in the last seven years could I have done so, but like the shoemaker I must stick to my last and not follow strange Gods during poor times at least.

When he got letters of this sort, there seemed to be so wide a gulf between himself and his father that Hart felt it might never be bridged. And yet it was for his father that much of his poetry had been written. If it were good enough, it would give Hart fame and fame might bring him enough money to buy that home of his own he longed for. He knew it could happen. It had happened to some of his friends. When he was independent and famous, then perhaps his father would admire him. In the meantime, what was left to tell C.A. but the truth?

> Your check alleviated my distress and extreme embarrass-ment. After paying up, I had about $15.00 left, and decided I had better clear out before I repeated any of my obligations. I am going to the City without any prospects whatever, and as my funds won't last very long I shall have to take anything on land or sea that I can grab. Patterson is the only address I can give as I don't know where or with whom I shall bunk. But the old woman will always forward my mail wherever I may be.
>
> Thank you a great deal for the help. Someday I shall have a little place of my own away from all the contention and fret that have beset me so the last three years. Then maybe I can hang up my few pictures, lay down my rug, set my books on a shelf —and know that I can really sit down and concentrate on my work for awhile. I'm tired of having to leave my few possessions scattered in all corners of the western hemisphere. I know, you think I'm just lazy. But there are other sides to the matter which are evidently impossible to make clear. Anyway, I'm grateful for your affection and maybe I'll someday be able to prove myself less trivial and inconsequential than you think.

Having, as he told his father, no place to bunk, Hart decided to visit Charmion von Wiegand for a few days at the house she had rented in Croton-on-Hudson. The spot was beautiful; the big, U-shaped building surrounded a garden, beyond which fields and apple orchards stretched down toward the Hudson. When Charmion picked him up at the station, she was shocked to see how trans-formed he was: "His hair was white; he'd lost weight; he'd aged tremendously." He was insistent that he wanted to write, but he was clearly so exhausted that writing was nearly impossible.

He did, however, manage a few fitful work sessions, the good food and the good company doing a great deal to restore his spirits. ("You don't know what a good time I had with you!" he wrote Charmion a week later, "—and how fortunate I feel to have had your cheerful company at a time when I felt the impulse toward anything but gaiety!") One afternoon the two of them went out to work in the orchards, he to write and she to paint. But, instead of writing, he spent the afternoon reading aloud from *The Bridge,* pausing now and then to comment on the structure of "The River" and to praise the painting on which she was working.

The next day Hart and Charmion went to a party in New City, New York, across the Hudson, a gala affair at the home of Maxwell Anderson. Just before they left to drive down to the ferry, Hart took her aside. "You keep an eye on me and see that I don't get too drunk, because I do awful things when I get drunk." But the party was a big one and she soon lost him in the crowd that milled about on the Japanese-lantern-decorated lawn.

Hart seems, however, to have done nothing really "awful" that evening. The guests who remember meeting him were struck, for the most part, by his rather formal grace and rather stilted eloquence. Among these was the novelist Bessie Breuer, who was pleased, late in the evening, to find that he had drifted back to the kitchen. She had gone there to talk to two Negro maids, both old friends. For the first time, she felt, she saw Hart relax. Dancing uninhibitedly with the maids, he was just drunk enough, she told me, to lose his self-consciousness but not drunk enough to lose his dignity.

The dance that had started in the kitchen then moved to the living room, where a number of partygoers had collapsed. But not Hart. "Suddenly there was a space in the middle of the room, and there was Hart dancing with abandon by himself," Charmion recalled. "And he really had such a rhythm. I knew he was tight, but it was very beautiful. Because he had absolute abandon and, at the same time, a certain control of his movements. He was like a ballet dancer swinging there—and he was having a gorgeous time."

The nearest Hart came to committing his "awful" act was well along toward morning. Sometime after midnight, he had told Eda Lou Walton that if he could get away by himself he might be able to do a little writing and she soon saw him marching off, a candle in one hand and a bottle of wine in the other. "When he had been gone for a long time," I was told by Suzanne Henig, Miss Walton's biographer, "Eda Lou felt she might look for him. She found him drinking alone and writing by candlelight." He must have found a radio or a phonograph, for Miss Walton remembered that the room was full of music. "She said he became so incensed at her seeking him out that he picked up the nearest object at hand, an Australian boomerang, and chased her with it through all the rooms. He would throw it and then pick it up and throw it again. Finally he returned to the room and slammed the door. Eda Lou, somewhat unnerved, returned to the living room . . . and found herself a corner in which to fall asleep. She remembered that several hours later she was awakened by Crane tugging at her shoulders. He had knelt down beside her and, overcome by extreme remorse and guilt, was begging her to excuse his behavior." In spite of this incident, Crane and Miss Walton became good friends.

It was good friends, certainly, who helped solve Hart's problems when he finally reached New York City, for Malcolm Cowley and his wife suggested that Hart settle into their small apartment at 501 East Fifty-fifth Street. They would be spending the rest of the summer in the country. Good friends also saw to it that he had enough to eat. The Munsons encouraged him to stop by for dinner. Sam Loveman made him several small loans. And Lorna Dietz, a friend of the Cowleys, brought him fresh-baked pies and chocolate cakes.

With no job in sight, he decided that perhaps he could once more persuade his father to contribute $50 toward the cause of American literature. His approach was indirect but obvious.

I've been cooking my own meals and doing my best without the help of a flatiron to keep myself looking spruce, but my shoes are giving out as well as the several small loans that friends have given me—and so far I haven't been able to make any connections with ad work. I guess I'll have to give that up.

I agree with you completely in what you say about learning a trade; in fact I have wanted to learn some regular trade like typesetting, linotyping, etc. for a long time back. However, connections that pay anything whatever while learning these trades are hard to find out about. And, of course, I need something more than air to live on in the meantime. I'm going to do my best during the next few days to find a job as a plumber's or mechanic's helper. The work is physically heavier than I have been used to for a long time, but I fancy I can make the adjustment . . .

On August 16, two days after he posted this letter, Hart was routed out of bed by a telegram: "AM SENDING YOU THE MONEY TO COME HOME AT ONCE. FATHER." A letter arrived on the eighteenth.

My dear Harold:

I have your letter of August 14. I judge that you are coming to realize now that one has to have some money to get along in this world, and that they cannot eternally borrow from their friends and remain in good standing.

Your letter indicates you are so nearly on your uppers that I am sending you the money to come home and try a job I have for you here. In that way I think you will be well cared for, have enough to eat and a good place to sleep.

I am enclosing [a] check for forty dollars and will expect to see you either Saturday or Sunday morning.

With love.
Your father,
CAC

By that evening, Hart had come up with employment—a temporary, part-time bookstore job, but enough to give him an excuse to remain in New York. Not that New York was attractive to him.

Rather, it was the only place left, he felt, where he was still "acceptable" and where he could have some anonymity. Granted his circumstances, he wrote Underwood, there was "nothing left to struggle for except 'respectability.'" Liquor wasn't what it used to be. And even sex seemed to be fading fast. "Occasionally some sailor gives me a jolt—but I guess I'm getting old."

The letter he wrote to his father was different in tone.

> I hope you won't blame me for utilizing the check enclosed in your letter for some immediate necessities, without which my first pay day would seem even longer away! I can refund the money to you later. Meanwhile it will seem good to have something definite to do—as well as something definite to eat.

Though his new job, he explained, was only the shadow of a job, it would do for the time being. Beyond this job, in the far distance, were the really good jobs Hart always held out to himself: "As there are two or three real possibilities hanging fire here—and of considerable ultimate importance,—I feel that I am justified in staying on the ground. One in particular, the editorship of a magazine, I should hate to risk missing."

How very intangible his job was is indicated by what Hart wrote Charmion von Wiegand the next day: "I've been in the toils of seeking toil—still am in fact." Apparently he did put in a few hours a day for a few days—clerking during lunch hours—but soon he located a more attractive temporary position. This one was with an advertising firm, Griffin, Johnson & Mann. "It looks like a very decent outfit to me," he wrote Malcolm Cowley, "but they may not have more than three or four weeks' work for me at most. At any rate I've been taken in under the enthusiastic auspices of a former copy-chief of mine in Cleveland. I'm expected to perform prodigies, but I feel as rickety as a cashiered V———. Maybe I'll limber up in a day or so. Of course they *would* put me to writing on wedding rings the first day!"

The check his father intended for train fare, the pay from the week or so of bookstore work, and the prospect of regular pay for the better part of a month gave Hart enough confidence to look for a room. More than most people, he needed a place of his own—and preferably in familiar surroundings. There was no question where he would look for housing. "Tomorrow afternoon," he wrote Cowley on a day late in August, "I may find a room over on Columbia Hts. if the patron saint of rooming houses (St. Anne, I believe!) is feeling commodious. I may continue to use these quarters occasionally, however, as you suggested. . . . Mrs. Turner will know whatever new address I may have."

The first mail to reach him at his new address, 77 Willow Street, Brooklyn, was a telegram from Grace Crane, forwarded by Mrs. Turner. It was dated September 5: "Mother passed away tonight.

Funeral here. Advise later. Grace." It was a telegram Hart had for months been expecting, a telegram he had dreaded; for in many ways he had been closer to his grandmother than to any other member of his family. It was also, however, a telegram that for months he had guiltily desired. With the death of his grandmother, he would come into the long-delayed $5,000 bequest from Grandfather Hart. Freed from job hunting, free to put down roots, he would be able to finish *The Bridge*. Grace herself, released from the pressure of Mrs. Hart's illness, might again become an amiable companion. Perhaps she would come east to live near him, perhaps with him.

For a few days, swept by sorrow yet planning the future, he was in buoyant mourning. Because the telegram had been delayed, he barely had time to wire flowers for the funeral and flowers for his mother. He, of course, immediately sent her a telegram of sympathy and wrote her a long, compassionate letter. He could not, he explained, come to California; he had hardly enough money to keep himself alive. But he was concerned for her welfare and hoped sincerely that with the strain eased she would be able to make a fuller life for herself.

As soon as he had mailed this letter, he wrote his father. He knew that his grandmother's estate would be enough to take care of his own legacy and to provide a small income for Grace, but he also knew that his mother had exhausted her own funds. Until the estate was settled, Grace would be in a very awkward financial position. This, Hart explained to his father, would be greatly alleviated if C.A. would volunteer a small loan.

C.A.'s answer was the first of a series of shocks that would turn Hart's next three months to horror—the mildest of these shocks, in fact, for those yet to come were from Grace and were far more jolting.

I try to imagine Hart's reaction on reading his father's letter, but I cannot. Like almost all of C.A.'s letters to his son, this one had been dictated to a secretary, who typed it on company stationery, two embossed cranes pecking away on either side of the letterhead and in large italics across the bottom of the sheet the new company slogan: *In All the World No Sweets Like These*. No sweets like these, indeed, Hart may have thought as he read his father's businesslike note.

> I have your letter of September 9, and on my return home from a business trip last Sunday my sister Bessie told me of the passing of Grandmother Hart.
>
> Of course, this had to be expected for she had long since lived out her usefulness, either to herself or to others. I think your mother will be much relieved now that she does not have the responsibility of Grandmother Hart to reckon with.
>
> Now, regarding finances: I appreciate the fact that your mother is having a hard time, but I am not disposed to send her

funds for she has all kinds of relatives in Warren who are abundantly able to take care of their own family. Matters with me are not easy at all. I have tried to tell that to you in a frank manner, and your mother's future existence will have to be worked out by herself, without any support or advice from me.

I am glad that you have found work which is more pleasing to you, and will be glad to know of your progress whenever you feel inclined to write.

I am having the hay fever worse this year than for five years past, and will be anything but comfortable until frost.

Though Grace's letters of this period and Hart's answers have vanished, the effect of her letters remains vivid in the memories of his friends. In her first notes, apparently, she renewed her pleas for his return to the West Coast, initially playing on his sympathy and then—he thought threateningly—pointing out that she was too ill to take care of the settlement of his grandmother's estate; his inheritance would have to wait until she was better or until he could come out to help take care of the legal details. Finally she stopped writing. Hart's letters—at first concerned, then demanding —went unanswered. Grace's silence, he was sure, was punishment for his failure to come to California. By refusing to answer his letters, she was administering chastisement calculated to drive him wild.

During this time, Hart paid several more visits to the summer home of Charmion von Wiegand. Here, in the gentle hilly country above Croton-on-Hudson, he and Charmion discussed at length modern painting. These were discussions of technique and form similar to those Hart had had years earlier with Bill Sommer. She urged him to search out the Brooklyn Bridge paintings of Joseph Stella, some of which were in the Brooklyn Museum. Stella, she felt, captured the same forces Hart was attempting to draw on in his poem. Indeed, after she and Hart had talked long enough about *The Bridge*, Charmion herself set out to do a painting based on it —not of the Brooklyn Bridge, for that was obviously Stella's territory, but of the symbolic Indian landscape. "You couldn't have tickled me half so much by painting my feet (alias Mr. Buddha's) as by the news that you've painted my Indian Maid in symbolic repose by the Mississippi," Hart wrote her. "I'm dying to know more about her; to see her! . . . I made a pilgrimage to the Brooklyn Museum one afternoon last week—wandered around hours because someone gave me the wrong guidance—and got there just as they were closing. So I've yet to see the Stellas."

Almost all of Hart's visits to Croton were pleasant, but during one, Charmion remembered, Hart stepped across that line of drunkenness he had warned her about. He had seemed absolutely exhausted when she picked him up at the station, his face gaunt and drawn. This was almost certainly during his bitter correspondence with Grace, for soon after his first glass of wine he was full of talk about the perfidy of women. In no time at all, Charmion recalled, he became "frightfully drunk," emptying glass after glass. "He went straight through half a gallon of red wine." He insisted that they dance together. But he became so caught up in the dancing that he did not hear the music end, the phonograph needle scratching on and on. Finally he dashed over to put on a new record. He kept railing about the untrustworthiness of women, then, after they stopped dancing, began a lecture on the essential ugliness of women as opposed to the essential beauty of men. To illustrate this lecture—the phonograph in the background roaring out jazz tunes—he extracted from his wallet and lined up on the piano photographs of men he had loved. He praised their muscles and hard flesh, sneering at the flabby buttocks and breasts of women. Then Hart and Charmion danced again, Hart's dancing, frantic and desperate, ending in collapse. She rushed out to call her Irish housekeeper, and the two women attempted to drag him up the stairs to his bed, while the phonograph scratched away in the record's last grooves. Halfway up the stairs Hart came to his senses long enough to snarl, "I'll kill you if you touch that phonograph." "I'm not easily frightened," Charmion von Wiegand told me, "but I was frightened then." The next day—barely aware that he had been drunk the night before—Hart was all smiles, all radiant charm.

Frequently during this time Hart also turned for companionship to Lorna Dietz, whose sense of humor matched his own and whose Midwestern background, he often told her, gave them "much in common." Just what, she could never be certain, she told me, except that they had been brought up in the same sort of middle-class, success-oriented world. But sometimes Hart told her that she reminded him of his mother, on one evening adding, "my mother on *good* days."

Lorna Dietz, who was a trained musician, told me about Hart's fervent performance of such works as "Too Much Mustard." "He had a fine sense of rhythm," she said, "but he had no feel at all for a melodic line." Only after Hart's death, when Miss Dietz met Grace Crane for the first time, did she realize how he had been persuaded to believe himself a man of infinite potential in all the arts. No one would have found it surprising for his mother to praise him as a great poet, Miss Dietz told me. But in rapid succession Grace had announced to her that he could have been a great dancer, a successful actor, a great painter, a major concert pianist. Miss Dietz changed the subject. Hart had many talents; but she had *heard* "Too Much Mustard."

Both Hart and Lorna loved vaudeville, Hart usually timing his arrival so that he could sit through two shows. On one evening, however, they had barely settled into their seats when he was seized with laughter. A juggler was on stage, working furiously. No one else in the theater seemed to think there was anything funny about his performance; certainly Miss Dietz did not. But Hart was swept with laughter. Finally he caught enough breath to yell, "He's an armadillo!" and again fell into wild laughter, repeating over and over, "He's an armadillo!" Miss Dietz could see no resemblance between the juggler and an armadillo. Neither could the ushers who dragged Hart up the aisle. By the time they got to the door of the theater, Hart was filled with righteous indignation. "They can't do this to us. I'll show them that they can't do this to us. I'll make something out of it they'll never forget!" Miss Dietz rose to the occasion. "Oh, let's not, Hart. I'm hungry!" Hart was delighted. The idea of not getting into a fight because you were hungry was even funnier than a juggling armadillo. With a grand shrug of the shoulders, he consented. "O.K., let's not." Laughing, the two of them swept out into the Broadway crowd.

Visits to Charmion von Wiegand, a quiet evening with Gene Toomer ("an exceptionally fine evening," Toomer wrote Hart. "Whole passages of 'The Bridge' are still vivid in my mind and feelings"), a weekend in Connecticut with the Cowleys, evenings with Lorna Dietz and with Eleanor Fitzgerald, who, recently back from Paris, was full of gossip about Paris writers and artists—these offered Hart the distraction he needed to keep from thinking too long about his mother's new and ominous silence.

Yet everything conspired to remind him of his mother. Lorna Dietz sounded like her. Sam Loveman defended her. Everyone he knew solicitously inquired about her. The very fact of his debts forced him to think about her.

Among other debts, there was the one he had owed the Rychtariks for over a year. Long before his grandmother's death, they had written reminding him of it. When he finally answered—a few weeks after her death—he had fallen into a form letter of apology: as soon as his grandmother's estate was settled he would see to it that they were promptly repaid. It was the unpleasantness of having to write letters of this sort as much as anything else that made him impatient with Grace. The least she could do, he felt, was to expedite the settlement of the estate.

All through September and into the middle of October her silence continued, Hart alternately storming against her and falling into brooding terror that she might be so ill she could not write. Yet there were second-hand accounts from Hollywood that she was up and about and looking well. He had heard from visiting Clevelanders that she had answered letters of condolence. Her silence, he finally decided, meant only one thing: she was scheming to cheat him out of his inheritance. Perhaps she was already spending his money.

These were terrible days for Hart, and he packed them with activity. His object was to cram the minutes of every hour, the hours of every day; he sought out people constantly. One of these people was William Carlos Williams, whom he had sometimes written to but never met.

> At times I'm prompted to wonder why in paradise we don't once in a while get together. Especially since I'm told that you frequently get over to Manhattan. I'm a stranger in New Jersey. But from what Nathan Asch says, it's a good place—and you live on a magistral hill in a venerable mansion, not to speak of governmental rations. No, that's not what I mean . . .
>
> But do look me up sometime. I know how busy you are—and perhaps the liveliest man in America. Phone me at Vanderbilt 2970 between dawn and dark, please, sometime when it's convenient. There are so many things to talk about—with you.

Neither visits with old friends nor visits with new ones, however, could lighten Hart's conviction that doom was hovering over him. When life should have been easiest, it had become most difficult. Day after day he would rush home from work to see if there was a letter from Grace. But he was always disappointed. Cut off from both mother and father—for he had refused to answer the cold letter C.A. had written at the time of Mrs. Hart's death—Hart turned to the only person he could think of who might be able to act as an intermediary, his Aunt Zell.

At first, apparently, his letters were cautious inquiries. Had she heard anything from Grace? Did she know anything about the settlement of his grandmother's estate and the fate of his inheritance? Did Grace herself have enough ready cash to get along? But soon he had occasion to involve her more directly in his affairs. For on October 15 Grace sent him a telegram—a series of imperatives: "COME AT ONCE DESPERATELY ILL AT HOME ALONE ONLY YOU CAN HELP ZELL IN NEW YORK ANSWER AT ONCE. GRACE." Hart sent a reply saying he could not come. He had no money and no way to get money. He begged her to write.

While he waited for the letter that never arrived, he got in touch with his aunt at her Manhattan hotel. Beyond having heard Grace's familiar complaints of exhaustion, she knew no more than Hart. She promised, however, that on her return to Ohio, she would do her best to find out what was happening. If Grace were seriously ill, Hart would, of course, have to go out. But there was also the possibility, they agreed, that Grace might be using her illness as she had sometimes used it in the past, to avoid an action she did not want to take. For Grace might really be attempting to block his inheritance. Both of them knew how much she feared Hart's independence. She might be trying to persuade him to come to California—through love or, if necessary, through a sense of duty —in order to reestablish the ties that Hart's leave-taking had broken.

In fact, Grace was confined to her bed and attended by a nurse
—perhaps not as ill as she thought but almost certainly more ill
than Hart believed. For immediately after he received her telegram,
he received a letter from California friends who reported that she
was rumored to be in very good spirits.

For a few days he tried not to believe that Grace was deceiving
him. He waited for the letter from her that did not arrive. He
waited for news from Zell. He waited to hear what Sam Loveman,
returned to Cleveland for a short visit, might be able to pick up
from mutual friends.

Though he talked to everyone about his problems, he needed
most to talk to his oldest friends—people who had known him in
what now seemed the happy days of the past, people who had
known the good times of the 115th Street house, his grandmother's
bustling hospitality, Grace's bright charm. For that had been real
too. But now he was heartsick, and he had no one to talk to.
Charlotte Rychtarik, who had answered his apology for the delayed
repayment of the loan with a long, sympathetic letter, received
from him a letter full of the swirling chaos of his life.

> Sam is in Cleveland this week, and maybe you have already
> seen him. Anyway, he said that he was going to phone you. If
> you do see him he can tell you more about my life the last year
> than I could get on paper in three weeks . . .
>
> Your letter made me feel a lot better. It lifted a load from my
> spirit that I had felt for many months. I really need to *see* you,
> *talk* with you to explain what a hell the last two years have
> been. Perhaps you'd then see how it has been almost impossible
> for me to write anyone. For who wants to hear nothing but
> troubles? I've waited, putting off writing again and again, hoping
> to have something interesting to offer—for that is what such
> friends as you and Richard deserve. . . .
>
> There is much to say, but little to tell,—if you get what I
> mean. I haven't had a creative thought for so long that I feel
> quite lost and *spurlos versenkt*. My present job lasts another
> week, and then I must tramp around again to find another.
> Moving around, grabbing onto this and that, stupid landladies—
> never enough sense of security to relax and have a fresh thought
> —that's about all the years bring besides new and worse mani-
> festations of family hysteria. It's a great big bore! I feel like say-
> ing what the Englishman did: "Too many buttons to button
> and unbutton. I'm through!"

Though Hart was discouraged, it is a mistake, I think, to accept
his own evaluation, to see him as accomplishing "nothing" during
that summer and autumn. For the "typetapping" that had driven
Nathan Asch wild did have some consequences. There were frag-

ments that would later be worked into finished poems—or at least poems good enough to be sent out. There were ideas for *The Bridge* that seemed worth jotting down. He continued polishing the unpublished island poems, sending them out, as they were readied, to an assortment of magazines. Harriet Monroe asked that one be rewritten—"just a little changed"—and went on to volunteer to consider it for publication if Hart would "throw a sop to Cerberus by pointing out verbs and subjects." *The Dial* published the slight lyric "The Mermen" in its September issue and agreed to print in the winter issue Hart's drawing of Slater Brown. It was probably during this time also that Hart put into final shape, for the spring issue of *The Dial*, the very fragile lyric "A Name for All." He was, indeed, planning beyond *The Bridge*, trying to assemble from the Isle of Pines material a substantial section of a new volume.

Another publication project—not his own—involved the poems by Malcolm Cowley that would become *Blue Juniata*. As early as the middle of July, Hart had written to the Schneiders about them: "I have it at least in mind to try my best to get his poems accepted by some publisher or other before a twelvemonth. He'll never do much about it himself, as you know, and his collection is really needed on the shelves these days." During the late summer Hart had worked through the poems with Cowley, making suggestions about the sequence, questioning lines that he felt needed more attention. When, at the end of October, the poems had not yet found a publisher, Hart again asked to be given the opportunity to work on them. He would be out of a job within a week; he had heard nothing from his mother or his aunt or his father or even Sam Loveman. He badly needed literary activity to keep him from brooding.

Hart was a perceptive and careful editor and, when it came to poetry, absolutely sure of his taste. During late autumn evenings, he reexamined the poems, discussed with Cowley the structure of the book, and—at the end of November—spent two days typing the manuscript. He delivered one copy to Gorham Munson, then an editorial advisor for Doubleday, Doran; another, he explained to Cowley, he would attempt to place with an English publishing house. Just as he had been anxious to make a structure for *White Buildings*—something more coherent than a mere "book of poems" —so too, in Cowley's manuscript, Hart searched for ordering materials. Though Cowley, as he told me, finally put together his own book, he was grateful for Hart's suggestions. Hart himself felt the draft was a great success.

> It has been a pleasure for me to spend part of the last two days in typing the mss. of your book. Certainly I have been on more intimate terms with the poems than ever, and my en-

thusiasm has been heightened thereby rather than in any way diminished. . . .

Really the book as we now have it has astonishing structural sequence. Most of the more doubtfully important poems come in the central section. There is the fine indigenous soil sense to begin with in the Juniata, and the eloquent and more abstract matter mounting to a kind of climax toward the end. Hope you don't mind my enthusiasm!

The next summer, when Cowley sent him proofs of the about-to-be-published book, Hart congratulated him on it and then went on to congratulate himself.

Since reading the proofs I'm certain that the book is even better than before. And the notes!—When you first mentioned them to me I admit having trembled slightly at the idea. But since seeing them I haven't a doubt. The maturity of your viewpoint is evident in every word. Humor and sincerity blend into some of the cleverest and [most] adroit writing I know of, leaving the book a much more solidified unit than it was before. . . . Really, Malcolm—if you will excuse me for the egotism—I'm just a little proud at the outcome of my agitations last summer. "Blue Juniata" will have a considerable sale for a long period to come, for the bulk of it has a classical quality—both as regards material and treatment—that won't suffer rejection by anyone who cares or who will later care for American letters.

Working on Cowley's poems could not, however, fill all of Hart's time—nor, of course, could it provide him a living. When he heard of an opening for a file clerk in the brokerage house of Henry L. Doherty, he jumped at the opportunity.

The job, like most of his jobs, came through the good offices of a friend, this time the photographer Walker Evans. Though Crane had heard of Evans before the autumn of 1928—his father was a Cleveland acquaintance of Crane's father—they did not become friends until Crane returned to Columbia Heights. There, where Evans was living and where he put in as much time as he could photographing the neighborhood, they saw a great deal of each other, Hart strolling along on photography afternoons.

Evans himself was working at the brokerage house as a stock clerk; his brother-in-law was personnel manager. In no time at all, Hart had a job.

He held it less than a month, which, considering his frame of mind and the quantity of alcohol he consumed to ease that frame of mind, was something of an achievement. For his nights were now blazing ones. He drank to blot out thoughts of the mother who refused to write him and who seemed bent on indefinitely holding up his inheritance. He searched the Sands Street bars for companions willing to shoulder toward oblivion insomnia hours. The letter Malcolm Cowley received soon after his manuscript reached Hart is a fair sample of Crane's early-morning, still-tipsy prose.

the 20th of the 28th at the A.M. 7-thirtieth

Dear Malcolm:

After the passionate pulchritude of the usual recent maritime houreths—before embarking for the 20th story of the Henry L. Doherty Co's 60 on Wall Street story—I salute your mss which arrived yesterday morning—as well as the really cordial apologies accompanying them for the really unhappy hours inaugurated last week by the hysteria of S. God damn the female temperament! I've had thirty years of it—lacking six months—and know something myself.

It's me for the Navy or Mallorca damned quick. Meanwhile sorting securities of cancelled legions ten years back—for filing —pax vobiscum—With Wall Street at 30 per—and chewing gum for lunch—

But here I am—full of Renault Wine Tonics—after an evening with the Danish millionaire on Riverside—and better, thank God, a night with a bluejacket from the Arkansas—raving like a 'mad. And it's time to go to work. So long. . . . I'll be careful with the mss. And your book'll be out within 7 months. . . . About time! God bless you and give my love to Peggy! And as W. J. Turner says:

"O hear the swan song's traffic's cry!"

When Hart left his job, early in November, he left it gloriously. As on several bad mornings, he showed up around noon, still drunk, still in the clothes he was wearing when he left the office the night before, clothes now rumpled and bedraggled. Evans remembers him marching through the startled office, straight up to one of the big windows that opened out onto "financial" New York. Hart peered out intently. By now the whole office was his audience. "There's Scott's Emulsion!" he roared. His fist swung up in an arc and came crashing down onto a pile of stocks and bonds that, scattering, littered the floor. "There's Scott's Emulsion!" he roared again. "I never took a drop of that and I never will as long as I live!" Turning, he strode through scattered securities, past gaping secretaries, until he was framed in the office door. "Never!" And he was gone.

There are dozens of anecdotes from this period of Crane's life, grand comic scenes that Hart played with an almost professional elegance; and there were less comic ones, as when, at a more crucial stage of drunkenness, he would haggle with cab drivers, all of whom, he was convinced, were conspiring to cheat him—scenes that often ended with Hart sporting a black eye or a bloody nose.

For day after day after day went by with no word from Grace. Finally, on November 8, there was a telegram from his aunt in

Warren, Ohio: "DONT WORRY THINK IT ONLY MELLOW DRAMA AM
WRITING. ZELL." If this telegram were right, it would confirm the
worst of Hart's suspicions. If it were right, his mother would be precisely the fraud he was beginning to accuse her of being, the deceitful woman determined to reduce her son—one way or another—to
a helpless creature forever tied to her apron strings.

Hart now sent off a letter of inquiry to the Guardian Trust Company, which was, with Grace, co-executor of his grandmother's
estate. He was told that his mother had wired that she was too ill to
write or even to sign the papers that would make available to him
his inheritance. But if she were too ill to sign her name, how, Hart
reasoned, could she arrange to send a telegram to the Guardian
Trust Company?

The letter from his aunt did nothing to make him more sympathetic to his mother's situation. Though Mrs. Deming's note has
been destroyed—probably by Grace—some notion of its contents
can be reconstructed from Hart's correspondence with Mrs. Simpson. Hart told her what he really believed: that in the few months
he had known her she had been a far better mother to him than his
own, that living in her company he had been able to write more
productively than at any other time in his life. Part of her answer
is a response to this praise.

> I've just reread your last letter, and boy you are some flatterer I'll
> say; if I were not so old and time hardened I might have burst
> with pride, as it is I swelled considerably—but I like to get 'em
> just the same; your letters I mean.

Mrs. Simpson minced no words about Grace.

> . . . I don't know what to think of your mother's actions. If she
> is insane or really sick she is to be pitied, but if she is merely act-
> ing for effect she deserves to be utterly ignored. Yes, you told me
> your Grandfather Hart had left you $5,000; now maybe your
> mother has used the money and is only acting so, so as to gain
> time and put off the evil day as long as possible. I have heard of
> people doing such things but it seems to me as if such is the case
> the much saner plan would be to confess at once and relieve the
> tension on both sides. I can just imagine how wrought up you
> are all the time. I think Waldo gave you excellent advice when
> he said for you to go to some quiet place where you can write
> unmolested and keep your whereabouts a secret. I'd miss hearing
> from you but I'd know it to be for your good, so let's pray you
> get your inheritance soon or enough money in some way to en-
> able you to find that "secluded spot." You know the real worth-
> while things never come to one without a struggle and the harder
> the struggle the greater one appreciates what he gets in this
> world. You and I both have a HELL of a time getting along but

I do not know of anyone with whom I would change my lot entirely, do you?

. . . Now please don't worry over things that you cannot help; you are doing the best you can and that is all that should be expected. Your mother certainly knows you have no money to travel across the continent at every whim of hers. I really can't understand the case; perhaps your mother has had plenty and her own way for so long that 'tis crushing her to give up both. Keep up your courage, boy; it can't go on forever, and I am sure things will adjust themselves soon in a way profitable to you. Write when you can.

Before he received Mrs. Simpson's letter, Hart again wrote to Zell. He was now attempting to work out an attitude that would let him escape from what was, he was certain, an altogether unhealthy domination by his mother.

I feel very sorry for her, for certainly she is miserably unhappy, but on the other hand I think that commiseration only renders her more helpless. She is profoundly attached to me, really loves me, I know. But there are mixtures of elements in this attachment that are neither good for her nor for me. Psychoanalysis reveals many things that it would be well for Grace to know. But I think she is at present too prejudiced to give ear to any counsel. I'm really alarmed. But what can I do? I now live in that constant state of wondering 'what next?'. I shall not be surprised at almost anything.

Nevertheless, I am now making a strong effort to discipline myself against the obsession with this and other wasteful family problems that have robbed me of my vitality during the last twelve years—unmanned me time and again and threatened to make me one of those emotional derelicts who are nothing but tremulous jellyfish might-have-beens. I may already be in that latter class, although I have done already too much solid writing to believe that to be true. I can't continue, however, to harbor this insatiable demon of morbidity without committing myself to destruction.

One's conscience ripens somewhat by the age of thirty. I must respect my emotions or I can't feel the necessary solidity to create anything worthwhile. It is a spiritual crisis. Really serious. Perhaps you understand what I mean. If I am to continue in my sympathies for Grace she must not abuse the confidence that I would like to place in her sincerity. I won't be dragged into hell—and live there forever for anybody's joke—not even my mother's. That is, not unless the hold is already too strong on my unconscious emotional nature, for hope of escape, —which remains to be proved. If she continues with her present methods she may drive me to drastic methods of isolation.

Hart was trying very hard to understand exactly what it was that had bound him so closely to his mother, that had made him so jealous of his father's business success yet so unwilling to follow in his footsteps. He was even cautiously beginning to probe into the forces that drove him to find sexual gratification with burly sailors and spiritual gratification on alcoholic binges, subjects that, except in comic anecdotes or drunken confession, he usually shied away from with his "literary" friends. In Solomon Grunberg, however, who had bought into Sam Loveman's new bookstore, Hart found a man he could trust, a man who proved to be perhaps his most sympathetic, most casual, and most knowledgeable listener.

For Grunberg—witty, eloquent, thoughtful, in love with music, attracted to philosophy—had recently become a student of the works of Freud and Jung and Adler. At the time Hart knew him, he was already practicing as a lay analyst. Though Hart declined Grunberg's offer to explore his mind ("If I let myself be psycho-analyzed, I'll *never* finish *The Bridge!*"), he did, on long walks, take advantage of Grunberg's listening silences, his offhand leading questions, his summaries of pertinent "classical" cases.

During the warm October afternoons and wet November nights, they must have covered, Grunberg told me, hundreds of Manhattan miles, Hart puffing away on big black cigars or chewing plug to-bacco. Afternoon walks would take them to Automats—where they could sit for hours over cups of steaming, then cold, coffee—or to five-and-ten-cent stores that Hart loved to wander through, an admirer of kitchenware, cheap toys, pencil sharpeners, ribbons, inner-tube repair kits, hair curlers, and shoelaces. In late November, when they drifted into the Broadway five-and-tens out of swirling snow, the Christmas goods were on display and Hart—with a professional eye—evaluated ribbon candy and peppermint candy canes. When their night walks took them to Grunberg's apartment, Hart would sometimes bring along a bottle of wine. After a couple of drinks, Hart would on these nights grow "fidgety," Grunberg said, until with mumbled excuses about a forgotten ap-pointment he would shuffle into his ill-fitting, out-of-style overcoat and rush out. "I don't think he ever went out after the sailors until he'd had something to drink," Grunberg told me. "Hart's drinking and his homosexuality were all tied up in each other."

During these months, Hart worried incessantly about his rela-tionship to his mother and father, Grunberg said; and once, on one of their meanderings, Hart talked about the nightmares he had been having, nightmares that made insomnia preferable to sleep. Hart would not let Grunberg comment directly on the dreams. Per-haps he realized that comment was not necessary; for Grunberg had already talked enough about the language of dreams to make the sense of them obvious.

Like other dreams Hart later talked out, these had classical features. One of them seemed to Grunberg clearly about Hart's father and about Hart's own sense of inferiority. Grunberg said he was sure Hart was well aware of its symbolic content. It involved a river, Hart told him. Hart had somehow gotten into a little boat—a rowboat or a canoe—and was floating down the center of the river. He could see the shores on either side and far in the distance he could hear a waterfall. Though his boat floated along very peacefully, he began to worry as the noise of the waterfall got louder. Finally he became frightened. The boat had picked up speed. As it was swept closer and closer to the waterfall, he suddenly saw, standing on the shore just above the falls, an enormous naked Negro. Hart could not keep his eyes off the Negro's huge penis. Even though the noise of the falls was deafening and he was thoroughly frightened, he kept watching. Suddenly he realized that he was naked, too. The boat was at the very brink of the falls now and he felt himself covered with shame. His own penis was tiny, he knew, as tiny as a baby's, and he forced himself to look at it.

The other dream was even more vivid; he had the feeling, long after he was awake, that it was something he had actually experienced. He had gone to bed exhausted, and when he woke up, he was in his old room on 115th Street. He got up, remembering that he had to hunt for something in the attic, and as he stumbled through the dusty attic—half awake—he kept trying to remember what he was looking for. Whatever it was, it was in a trunk. He was sure of that. It was very dark in the attic, but when he found the trunk, there was enough light for him to see that it was full of his mother's clothes. He started rummaging through them, looking for whatever it was he was looking for, pulling out dresses, shoes, stockings, underclothing. But the trunk was so full, it seemed he would never find what he was after. There was so much to look at that when he found the hand, he hardly realized it was a human hand; but when he found another hand and a piece of an arm, he knew there was a body in the trunk. He kept pulling out piece after piece of it, all mixed in with the clothing. The clothing was covered with blood. It was not until he had almost emptied the trunk that he realized he was unpacking the dismembered body of his mother.

Toward the end of November 1928, Hart's nightmares were hardly more horrible than reality. For the life-and-death struggle with Grace now came out in the open. Sickened as much by his own actions as by hers, Hart decided to demand that the Guardian Trust Company give him the inheritance he had waited for so long. He telephoned the Cleveland office and said he wanted five hundred dollars immediately, the rest of the five thousand dollars within a week.

He was told what for months he had dreaded to hear. The bank could do nothing until Grace signed the papers; she had written to say that she would not sign until her son joined her in California. The man Hart talked to tactfully suggested that it might be best if

Hart gave in to her. She was grief-stricken at the loss of her mother; she had told the bank that she could not understand his cold refusal to come to her.

Fiercely angry, Hart sent a telegram ordering Grace to sign the papers at once or be prepared to face legal action.

A day later he had Grace's equally fierce telegram. The papers were now signed. But he would live to regret that he had forced her to sign them. She was going to urge C.A. to use his influence at the bank to prevent Hart from collecting any money. They would not turn over money, she threatened, to a drunkard.

So far as Hart was concerned, this exchange ended his dealings with Grace. Only once more in his life, on a wild spree in Paris, would he write to her: a postcard announcing his departure for "the Orient." He signed it "Atlantis."

"Grace will probably never hear from me again," he now wrote Zell. "Nervous strain or simple hysterics could never explain the underhanded and insatiable vanity that has inspired her to attempt to crush her nearest of kin. And all for a bucketful of cash! I think I can say that my part in this long melodrama is almost over. I shall try to remain as unconcerned about the rest of it as possible." He asked Zell to show his father his correspondence about Grace; if she attempted to interfere with his inheritance through C.A., Hart's side of things would have a fair hearing.

There was no longer any doubt in Hart's mind as to his next step. A continent between himself and his mother would hardly suffice. He had to place an ocean between them as well.

He immediately went to the offices of the Cunard Line to book passage to England. At this point he had no plans for what he would do once he arrived. He told Slater Brown and Waldo Frank that he was eventually going to Spain, there to study Spanish and to attempt to recover the desire to write. But he really did not care where he went so long as it was far from Grace Crane.

Only a few days before he left, his plans were still up in the air. For his money had not yet been released, and he was unable to pay for his ticket. "I hope to get off next Saturday," he wrote Malcolm Cowley.

The bank behaves too strangely—now ignores my letters not to mention telegram. The meddlesome old nanny that is handling the matter there will soon hear from me through a lawyer if things don't take a new turn by Monday. That's the only way to handle it, I guess. I'm to see Art Hays Monday and talk it over. At any rate, I think it would be foolish to bring my troubles over to London with me and have them poison my first impressions of the place.

In the meantime—footloose, if not fancy free—Hart tried to forget that he had a mother, a father, an aunt—even an inheritance. His friends helped.

Herbert Wise, back from Europe, took Hart to see *Show Boat*: ". . . the beautiful new Ziegfeld Theatre has them all beat—and the settings, songs, costumes and glistening lithe girlies! Like greased lightning—the suave mechanical perfection of the thing."

On the last night of November, less than a week before his ship sailed, Hart and Lorna Dietz started out for the movies. But Hart found a bottle and they were sidetracked to a speakeasy. From then on, Miss Dietz—restraining when she could and riding with the tide when she couldn't—tried to keep Hart from being beaten up by taxi drivers and jailed by the police who were called by his Columbia Heights neighbors. At one point, she recalled, she had to sit on his chest to keep him from smashing all the china in Sam Loveman's apartment. Hart's version, gaudy enough, omitted that detail. "Lorna and I went on the best bat ever last night—Sam's old place—finally two cops came in and joined the party at three o'clock—asked Lorna to marry me and live with me in Spain—but she's got to wait for her divorce from the Danish gaucho now on the pampas." The bucketful of ice water that she doused him with in a relatively futile effort to get him sober enough to go to bed, he also omitted from his account.

At last Hart got word that some—not all—of his inheritance could be immediately collected. Since none of his friends could match his new wealth, he financed his own going-away party. It took place the night before his departure at Bauer's restaurant downtown on Third Avenue. He had invited everyone he liked: Charmion von Wiegand, Sam Loveman, Solomon Grunberg and his wife, the Cowleys, E. E. Cummings and his wife, Lorna Dietz, Walker Evans, the Schneiders, the Munsons, the Browns, Eleanor Fitzgerald—perhaps half a dozen more. Though not everyone showed up, there was a fair-sized crowd. Hart, Lorna Dietz recalled, was in his best form. He recited his latest limericks. He danced with all the ladies and then by public demand danced the "gotzotsky." Even without public demand, he played "Too Much Mustard" on the tinny piano and—with a whisper to Walker Evans ("I fake it")—something that could have been Debussy. "He was all laughter and happiness, that night," Miss Dietz told me.

Yet when the party was over and almost all his friends had gone their way, happiness gave way to despair. Hart was nearly in tears. He had "faked" more than Debussy. "The party was a failure," he moaned. "It was awful, awful!" Mony Grunberg was baffled. "But, Hart, it was a wonderful party! Everybody had a wonderful time. *You* had a wonderful time." But Hart would not be consoled. "Cummings didn't show up. He didn't show up and he didn't even say he couldn't make it!"

In the taxi, on the way home, Hart complained again and again about the betrayals of his friends. Cummings's "betrayal" was as bad as his mother's—and as he said it, he broke into sobs of grief. For no party could cover his agony, no laughter could blot out the horror of the insults he had traded with Grace Crane, the price in love he had had to pay for the bequest from Grace's father to his only grandson. After all the years of waiting, he would now be able to put the money to only one use: flight, flight across space, across time, secret flight from the consuming love of a mother he could never put out of mind.

Yet flight brought no peace. Whenever he risked a letter to his oldest friends—Bill Wright, the Rychtariks—his admonition was always the same: You have no notion where I am. You haven't heard from me. Even at the end of two full months in Europe, his obsession was flight; his demand, secrecy. "First of all—before you read another word of this—you must swear to me not to repeat to *any*one that you have heard from me, not even that you know where I am," he wrote to the Rychtariks. This was at the end of February, yet Hart was still concealing his address, his mail being forwarded to him by the bank to which he told his friends to write. To make sure that the Rychtariks believed him, he told part of the story of his disintegrating relationship with Grace Crane.

I hate to begin my letter so seriously, but in time you will know more about *why* I don't want my family to find my whereabouts right now. I am very serious about this request, and I'm sure that you have enough interest in my work to abstain from any action which would cripple me. . . .

I scarcely know how to begin to tell you all that's been happening to me during the last year. But here's a brief summary, omitting thousands of details, all of which, however, are really important. . . . During my sojourn with the millionaire in California last winter my mother made life so miserable for me with incessant hysterical fits and interminable nagging that I had to steal off east again, like a thief in the night, in order to save my sanity or health from a complete breakdown. I went back to Patterson and tried to pull myself together, without money or prospects of any kind. Then in September, after I had secured a good job in an advertising agency, my Grandmother died, leaving me the inheritance which my grandfather bequeathed me over fifteen years ago.

Of course there had been a coolness between my mother and me ever since I left California. The net result of this was that (being co-executor of the estate with the Guardian Trust Co) she held back her signature to the papers for weeks, pretending to be too ill to sign her name. And finally she threatened to do all sorts of things if I did not come at once to California and spend it with her—among which she said she would write to my father and try to get him to intercede with the bank against paying me! This could have no effect whatever, but you may gather a little bit from what I have said about just how considerate and honest she was! I can't begin to tell you about all the underground and harrowing tactics she employed. Got people who were practically strangers to write me threatening and scolding letters, so that I never came home from work without wonder and trembling about what next I should find awaiting me. She had, through abuse, destroyed all the affection I had for her before I left the west; but now she made me actually hate her. I finally had to consult a lawyer, who directed his guns on the bank. This finally brought results. In the meantime I had given up all my plans about buying a little country place in Connecticut, for her ultimate home as much as mine. There was literally no other sensible plan but to take my money and get out of communication as soon as possible.

After having received written promise from the bank (as well as an advance) that the money would be in my hands by a certain day, I went ahead and engaged steamer passage to London. But the bank did not even keep its word, and I did not actually get the money until a few hours before the boat sailed. You can imagine my state of mind. I got on the boat more dead than alive. And I have not since had the least desire to know what is going on in California, and doubt if I ever *shall* care. Since my mother has made it impossible for me to live in my own country I feel perfectly justified in my indifference. I have had no particular quarrel with my father, and shall write him sometime after the Bridge is done and I don't fear mental complications. Meanwhile I'm so sure that she has carried out her threat and written him certain things that I'd rather keep out of it all. Twenty-five years of such exhausting quibbling is enough, and I feel I owe myself a good long vacation from it all. Neither one of them really cares a rap for me anyway. . . .

Whether or not Grace actually wrote C.A. about those "certain things" is now impossible to determine. (If she did, C.A. was wise enough, when he next saw Hart, to steer clear of a discussion of them.) But as far as Hart was concerned, the threat of so terrible a betrayal of confidence was enough. He would avoid her for the rest of his life.

Hart sailed to London, drifted to Paris, to Marseilles, briefly to Spain. When he returned to America, he hid from her. His year in Mexico was, in part, a way of avoiding her. His return from Mexico ended in suicide.

Halfway around the world in California, Grace Crane did what she could to repair her life. For months she had lived under medical care, dosing herself with sedatives, on the worst days arranging for a nurse to come in. She tried, rather helplessly, to trace her son, writing to those of his friends who might give her information of some sort. The return letters—when there was an answer—told much the same story: Hart was traveling, no one knew for sure where.

Like Hart, Grace saw only one side of their struggle, but she was able to hope that everything would be well when she finally found him. In the meantime, she faced confusions and fears quite as painful as those Hart saw ahead of him. A letter to Sam Loveman shows an edge, at least, of a precipice that for months she had walked. It is dated January 24. By that time Hart had moved on from England to France; so far as Grace knew, however, he was still somewhere on the East Coast.

My dear Sam: —

I am just beginning to recover from a very serious illness which struck me shortly after my mother's death. I still have to have a nurse. During most of this time I've had no word from Hart, excepting that very vicious telegram he sent me concerning his inheritance, which he seemed to think I was holding up intentionally. My reply was equally vicious—and I want Hart to write me at once and get on our old loving basis. I cannot live without his love, Sam, and I'm sure he needs mine. Will you tell me how to get in touch with him, and give him this letter if he is anywhere near you. My mother's death left me a broken hearted woman. My constant care of so many years being suddenly taken away from me made me feel my utter loneliness to the point where I became very ill. With Hart away and mother gone, I feel like a wanderer on the face of the earth. I can't bear it. I must know where Hart is and that he still loves me. Hoping this finds you well and that I may hear from you soon—

I am as ever—
yours sincerely,
Grace H. Crane.

Loveman, who would help take care of Grace in her old age, who would be with her at her death, who would attend to her cremation and to the distribution of her ashes from that Brooklyn Bridge her son had so admired and so celebrated, was perhaps the person most likely to have been able to reconcile mother and son. But he knew that, with Hart's violent feelings, a long lapse of time would have to intervene. He could understand Hart's feelings; he could understand Grace's. He loved both of them. He wrote her a compassionate letter, explaining that he had no precise knowledge of Hart's whereabouts but that he was sure Grace would eventually hear from him. Her return letter is, in quality, like literally hundreds that over the coming years she would write to her own friends and especially to Hart's, letters filled with agony, blurred with hope.

My dear friend Sam : —

Your letter came this morning and I was indeed glad to hear from you, although you were unable to supply me with Hart's address. I had begun to think that you had entered into some agreement with Hart, not to let me know his whereabouts.

Just a few days back, I learned from my sister-in-law, Mrs. Deming of Warren, Ohio, that he had gone to Europe on a slow-moving boat. He dropped her a card at Halifax simply stating that he was on his way to Europe. I presume he counted upon her informing me sooner or later. As I do not have any correspondence with his father, I do not know whether he knows anything about Hart or not.

When my dear little mother passed on, I supposed that he would be glad to come out and help me through the sad ordeal of taking her remains back to Ohio to their last resting place. You see, I am absolutely alone—and I certainly needed his moral support at this time. I wired him to come and he flatly refused. Shortly afterwards I was taken ill. The reaction from so long a strain of caring for mother, and the loneliness I was obliged to endure through the ordeal of disposing of all of mother's things —simply put me to bed with the worst breakdown I've ever had. I still have a nurse and am just beginning to walk out. I've been for weeks in a very serious condition and I wonder how I've been able to pull myself together again as far as this. I miss my dear mother so, it just breaks my heart to go through her personal belongings and dispose of them. It would have been such a comfort to have had Hart near me, and I feel that for all of the many years of constant devotion to his interests in every way, regardless of what sacrifices it meant for me, Hart should have stood by and seen me through. I have not even had a line from him since last October.

Well Sam, this is a hard life for most of us, isn't it? It takes great courage to go through the trials and disappointments that confront us. It seems as if mine would never cease.

I can only hope that Hart will find himself while abroad and settle down to do some really constructive work. "The Bridge" should have been finished long ago, it seems to me. . . .

As soon as it gets warmer back in Ohio and I get stronger, I shall probably take mother's body back to Ohio to our family burial lot in Warren. Then I do not know what next. I am a ship without a rudder. I must seek employment of some kind right away, as my share of the estate was *very* small. It is very difficult for a person of my years to find anything to do that will support one, even modestly. This country has about ten people for every job. It is a beautiful country though and extremely interesting in many ways. Hollywood of course is the very center of the "Movies" and in fact that industry is the most important one out here. They simply rule the whole place, and you see them everywhere. I wish you might have been out here when Hart was. I was so in hopes he might make some connection with the writing end of it—"title writing" or something along that order. There's big money in it.

I hope this finds you in better health, and that business will be better *soon*.

You will find as you grow older that the strenuous life in a big city is very wearing—*also* that it is very comforting to be near your family if possible. I do not like Cleveland because I've seen so much trouble there, and the long cold winters are hard for me to endure—but Ohio is my native state, and where I've spent the greater part of my life, and I find it hard to get it out of my system.

I have only a few relatives and friends left and they are all in or near by Cleveland. I do not know how I will feel when I go back.

Let me hear from you again real soon, and if you have any news from or about Hart, let me know immediately. I wish we could all be back again in our old home on 115th St.

With all good wishes, I am as ever,

Affectionately yours
Grace H. Crane

But the house on 115th Street was, for Grace as well as for Hart, long since part and parcel of lost days. Nothing of hers remained in it, not even a package of her mother's letters in the attic or a trunk filled with her own old clothes.

# 31

The Cunard Line's *Tuscania*—a ship that made a series of American, Irish, and French ports before finally arriving in England—allowed Crane two solid weeks at sea.

Fresh air, new faces, and good food were what Hart needed, and as soon as his hangover lifted, he was one of the ship's most active passengers—diligently pacing the deck or, settled into a corner of the lounge, reading the Melville that Sam Loveman contributed as a going-away present. Hart had always dreamed of the joys of a life at sea; now he was able to experience them. "Ahoy Sam!" one of his first letters begins. "The ship is rearing like a high-strung broncho—and I'm out walking the quarter deck much of the time —enjoying the rhythmical lift and plunge of it. We've had high seas running and sleet and rain since Sandy Hook but I've been down for every meal. O it's great! The bad gin pains are leaving my head—and taking only the bad memories with them—*not* the pleasant thoughts of you and Mony [Grunberg] and others."

Hart soon discovered he was the only United States citizen in the tourist-class dining room. The other passengers—"such nice people"—were Irish, Australian, and English, "all of them the pleasantest crowd I've ever met." "Some of the people on board you'd love," he wrote Bill Brown, "—Mr. Pickwick, actually, to say nothing of Falstaff and Mrs. Gamp." "One old squire," he told Charmion von Wiegand, "took me for a Cambridge man—and I admit that after a day or two in confab with some of these natives one does tend to lose one's 'middle-western accent.'"

By the end of the trip, Hart had made himself universally popular. He had been careful to keep his drinking under control; even when his consumption was high, he found that—with no immediate worries—he remained cheerful to the end of the bottle. "The whiskey . . . is like balm of Gilead—or whatever Poe said," he wrote Loveman. "A little goes a long ways—and really doesn't sadden one." For when Hart was at ease, alcohol made the world glow. "You must excuse my exuberance momentarily at least," he wrote Charmion. "I can't stop being tremendously pleased at the wonderful ale, . . . the balmy spring air, and the prospect of meeting more of such people soon on foreign shores. I feel really rested now, despite a hectic round of pleasures."

Hart's pleasures were not only hectic but—within the limits of the ship—comprehensive, extending from the first-class salon to the sailors' quarters. "I *would* be given the one really handsome English waiter in the salon," he had exclaimed soon after the ship left New York. When it approached the coast of Ireland, he catalogued the joys that the "R.M.S. Rumrunia" made available to its passengers: "The trip has been one song and dance practically all the way. Rum—which wasn't even priced on the wine list—is now the favorite with the quarterdeck and high cabin folks as well as the foc'sle—where, as you might imagine, I've paid my respects."

Before the *Tuscania* reached its first Irish port, there was a gala evening, many of the passengers assembling from each other's wardrobes impromptu fancy-dress costumes. "My performance given at the Anderson party last summer was but a slight forecast to the splendors of my behavior night before last—when at a bal masque, dressed in a red coat of a sergeant-major, sailor hat, shark swagger stick, etc.—I essayed a dervish whirl." His "dress breeches" were "lined with rum and brandy" and he capped his dance by offering the lining all around.

All the way across, the weather—the air "like April"—had been "gorgeous." As the ship neared Plymouth, Hart got off one last postcard: "Today is like the 'Tristram' verse of Swinburne. Millions of sea gulls following us and soaring overhead with such a flood of golden light as seems tropical."

But England in winter was England in winter. Hart stepped off the ship into a cold rain, chills, and fever. Fighting off "incipient flu" with "good Jamaica rum and quinine," he swayed slowly through the pre-Christmas London crowds.

During his first few days in London, Hart devoted himself to locating friends and acquaintances. He visited Paul Robeson backstage (Robeson was starring in *Show Boat*) and at the "sumptuous home" Robeson had rented from "an ex-ambassador to Turkey." And he met Edgell Rickword, who had printed his poetry in *The Calendar*. But it was Laura Riding and Robert Graves who were Hart's most enthusiastic welcomers. "Delightfully hospitable," they suggested that he join them for their Christmas festivities.

After three days of wet sightseeing, Hart felt that Christmas evening with cordial, witty people would be a godsend. And in fact it was. Hart reported the next day to Sam Loveman "the most unique Xmas I ever had." He had begun the day with a long walk by the Thames ("white swans in the water and beautiful fleets of hardy rowers"). When he got to Graves's houseboat, "at Hammersmith in front of Wm. Morris' old headquarters," he was set down before "a most luscious plum pudding" and a long session of casual drinking and good talk.

Long after Hart's death, Laura Riding tried to recollect what his stay in London had been like. It seemed to her that Hart had alternated between "great affection" and "incoherent attack." She remembered his heavy spending while he was drinking, spending that sometimes ended with him accusing his companions of cheating him. It seemed to her that Hart was unreasonably moody.

If she had mixed feelings about Hart, Hart had mixed feelings about her. "London, I can still believe, might be delightful under proper circumstances," he wrote the Schneiders. "I had incipient flu before I landed, then the raw cold of the particular season, the bad hotel accommodations, the indigestible food AND Laura's hysterical temper at the time—all combined to send me off with no particular regrets."

Yet there were certain elements of London that he had admired. "I loved its solid, ponderous masonry—and the gaunt black-and-white streakings and shadings. It's a city for the etcher." The green of its wet winter was startling. "No snow here at all," he had written Waldo Frank a week after his arrival, "—and the grass as green as summer in the parks. I've already seen a great deal—tramping around by myself, drinking Australian wine with old charwomen in Bedford Street—talking with ex-soldiers, and then the National Gallery with its marvelous 'Agony in the Garden' of El Greco. The beautiful black and white streaked stone façades of the buildings made me quite sentimental. London is negative (as Laura says) but one gets a chance to breathe and deliberate. And there is something genuine about nearly every Englishman one meets."

Perhaps the high point of his stay in London was his visit to Limehouse. Limehouse at this time meant, to every red-blooded American, Fu Manchu and Dr. Moriarty. "Expecting to be black-jacked, etc.," Hart explained to American friends, "I drank so many Scotch-and-sodas during a game of darts in one of the pubs, that I frightened people, actually scared some of the toughs about —all of whom struck me as being very pleasant people." The "dangerous" section turned out to hold not the "exciting adventures" Hart had anticipated but rather a population of young hoodlums who "drank only lemonade . . . O life is funny!"

As for the rest of London, "the damp, raw cold was like a knife in my throat—and the hotels like cellars." On the whole, it seemed to Hart "a wonderful but sad, heavy city." On January 6, 1929, he left for Paris.

If London was heavy, Paris was "incredibly free and animated." Even at the very beginning of his stay, it was for Hart a city designed for casual friendships, its cafés and parks crowded with easygoing, pleasure-loving people, an international group swept together in the last great boom year of the twenties. All barriers were down. The good life in this last gay year was one's own, a life lived at whatever pace one could manage, in whatever style one wished. As early as his second day in Paris, Hart crowed over the new largeness that had entered his life: ". . . one can behave so naturally here!"

Unlike London, Paris was a haven for people Hart had heard about, people he wanted to meet. Some of them also wanted to meet him. First on Hart's list was Eugène Jolas, who months before had enthusiastically welcomed him to *transition* and who now undertook to see that he was introduced to all the right people. Less than forty-eight hours after he arrived, Crane could tell Sam Loveman, "Am meeting Wescott for lunch tomorrow and there have been all sorts of others, Edgar Varèse, Eva Gauthier, Soupault, Laurence Vail, etc." Within ten days, Hart was acting as unofficial consultant for coming issues of *transition*.

Jolas also saw to it that Hart had lunch with Harry Crosby. For Crosby, whose Black Sun Press would soon print sections of Joyce's *Finnegans Wake*, was, Jolas realized, the one man in the world with the good taste, energy, money, and enthusiasm to bludgeon Crane into finishing *The Bridge*. Jolas prepared Crosby for the meeting by telling him that a great poet had just arrived in Paris.

Crosby's reaction to Crane was just what Jolas had hoped for. Mrs. Crosby still remembers her husband's enthusiastic return home. "I've met the most wonderful poet! He's going to come to dinner tonight. We have to get a bottle of *Cutty Sark*. That's what he likes to drink."

Within a few days, Crane was very much part of the Crosbys' world. On January 19, for example, Harry Crosby recorded in his diary: ". . . there were people for cocktails Jolas, Allanah Harper, Crouchers, I forget who else, then CC left for London and I went with Jolas to the Deux Maggots where we found Hart Crane and all three of us to Prunier for oysters and anjou then to see CCC and when I got home I read Hart Crane's White Buildings and to-day is the first day this year I have not walked to the Pôteau de Perthe or climbed to the top of my Suntower."

Two days after he read *White Buildings*, Crosby invited Jolas to tea, obviously intending to find out what publishing arrangements Crane had made for *The Bridge*. Jolas ("always dynamic and inspiring," according to Crosby's diary entry for that day) must have been eloquent, for several days later Hart was again asked to visit the Crosbys, this time to talk about his unfinished poem. Crosby had already seen several sections of *The Bridge*; after listening to Hart read excerpts from the poem and talk about his theories of aesthetics, he decided on the spot that he would be the poem's first publisher. "Hart Crane for luncheon and he says he will let us edit his long poem on the Brooklyn Bridge fragments of which have appeared in the Criterion the Dial Transition but it is not yet finished (he is thinking of going to Villefranche to finish it) and then he showed me a MSS of poems Blue Juniata by Malcolm Cowley and

then the frotteurs came to frotter the floors and they made a great
noise and broke a huge glass and I kicked them all out."

Startled by the fact that *The Bridge* was likely to appear in print
—and disconcertingly soon—Hart hesitated to announce the event.
He was, however, feeling better than he had felt in years, and he
wanted somehow to let the world—that world he had abandoned—
know. A postcard to Sam Loveman, written at his hotel (Hôtel
Jacob) after the luncheon with the Crosbys, lists Parisian delights,
more or less in ascending order: "Dinners, soirées, poets, erratic
millionaires, painters, translations, lobsters, absinthe, music, prom-
enades, oysters, sherry, aspirin, pictures, Sapphic heiresses, editors,
books, sailors, *And How!*"

Though sailors helped Hart enjoy the first few days in Paris,
literature was his primary concern. He and Crosby had made plans
for possible formats for *The Bridge*. Hart especially wanted as a
frontispiece a full-color reproduction of one of Joseph Stella's
Brooklyn Bridge paintings. Though neither of the Crosbys was
familiar with Stella's work, they were caught up in Hart's enthusiasm. This enthusiasm was also transmitted to Jolas, who accepted
Hart's suggestion that *transition* try to secure an essay Stella had
written and the rights to reproduce three of his paintings. The essay—a privately printed monograph—had been given to Hart by
Charmion von Wiegand; its publication in *transition*, he felt, would
be one way of attesting to the aesthetic standards he and his
friends shared.

Though the frontispiece for *The Bridge* never worked out, the
*transition* issue with the Stella paintings and essay did. "*transition*
is able to pay little or nothing now for contributions," Hart explained to Stella, "but, since our friend Varèse has told me that
your essay has never been printed in any journal, we feel that so
splendid and sincere a document should have wider circulation
than private printing has allowed it."

In asking that Stella permit the use of his painting as a frontispiece for *The Bridge*, Hart made clear that such a "private favor"
was prompted by his recognition of public parallels in their work.
"It is a remarkable coincidence that I should, years later, have discovered that another person, by whom I mean you, should have
had the same sentiments regarding Brooklyn Bridge which inspired
the main theme and pattern of my poem." When, a year later, he
met Stella for the first time, the poet and the painter spent an entire
evening, Charmion von Wiegand recalled, in animated discussion
of literary and artistic relationships. "They were both tough-minded
when it came to art," she told me, "and each of them was able to
appreciate the technical accomplishment of the other."

Not only did Hart arrange for the Stella reproductions, but he
contributed to forthcoming issues of *transition* some material of his
own. From Brooklyn memories and his notebook, he unearthed for

the February number the very slight poem "Moment Fugue." For the fall issue he offered "The Mango Tree," one of the few Isle of Pines poems that had not yet been published.

Another literary project that consumed Hart's Paris time was Malcolm Cowley's *Blue Juniata*. As Crosby's diary indicates, Hart at their second meeting had shown him the manuscript. They talked about it in great detail during several later meetings. There was, indeed, a real possibility that at Hart's insistence Crosby would have undertaken its publication had not Hart finally heard from Cowley that the book was to be published in America.

All of Hart's literary activity in Paris was carried out casually, much of it at "teas" and supper parties. " 'Teas' are all cocktails here," he explained to Cowley, "—and then that's just the start of the evening. And as lions come these days, I'm known already, I fear, as the best 'roarer' in Paris." And yet, as Caresse Crosby recalled, "Hart was never really *terribly* drunk when he was with us. He was slightly tipsy a lot of the time—most of the time, really— but he never passed out; he never had to be dumped into a car and sent home. He'd get to the edge of drunkenness without going under. And at those times he'd be a wonderfully witty, charming person."

At some of his meetings with the Crosbys, Hart talked about himself. ("Hart Crane for luncheon and a long talk on poets and sailors he is of the Sea as I am of the Sun," Harry Crosby wrote.) But on other days their talk was of the art of poetry; for Hart had again begun to work—erratically, it is true—on *The Bridge*.

At this time the Crosbys lived surrounded by their friends. On the first weekend in February, Hart was invited, along with a number of other people, to pay a three-day visit to Le Moulin, their country retreat. Hart was enormously impressed: "Have just returned from a weekend at Ermenonville (near Chantilly) on the estate of the Duc du Rochefoucauld where an amazing millionaire by the name of Harry Crosby has fixed up an old mill (with stables and a stockade all about) and such a crowd as attended *is* remarkable." In some ways, Hart had been the bright particular star of the weekend. "Le Moulin Hart Crane here and much drinking of red wine and he reads aloud from Tamburlaine and he is at work on his long poem The Bridge," Harry Crosby noted. Then he went on to list a few of the other highlights of the day: "And CCC arrives with a goose and I made fire-oblations by throwing glasses of red wine into the fire and there was a goddess in the flame and her name was Trinitrotoluol." On the third of February, the party hit its peak: "Mob for luncheon—poets and painters and pederasts and lesbians and divorcées and Christ knows who and there was a great signing of names on the wall at the foot of the stairs and a firing off of the cannon and bottle after bottle of red wine and Kay Boyle made fun of Hart Crane and he was angry and flung the American Caravan into the fire because it contained a story of Kay

Boyle's (he forgot it had a poem of his in it) and there was a tempest of drinking and polo harra burra on the donkeys and an uproar and confusion . . .'"

Hart described it as a weekend of "new atrocities—such as getting drunk yesterday and making violent love to nobility. As le comte was just about to marry, I couldn't do better, though all agree (including Kay Boyle and Laurence Vail) that I did my best . . ." By the end of the weekend, Hart was certain that Crosby would withdraw the invitation proffered at the beginning of it. ("I'm invited to return at any time for any period to finish *The Bridge*, but I've an idea that I shall soon wear off my novelty.") Crosby, however, proved to be a man of his word. On the tenth of February, Hart arrived for a two-week visit.

By this time Hart's Parisian pace had slowed to a mere dash. Nevertheless, he kept up with things. Between visits to Le Moulin, he had been invited to have an apéritif with Gertrude Stein. At first he was amused by her circling pink "a rose is a rose is a rose" notepaper and then, when he arrived "Tuesday afternoon about five," by Miss Stein herself. "One is supposed to inevitably change one's mind about her work after meeting her," he told Waldo Frank. "I haven't, but must say that I've seldom met so delightful a personality. And the woman is beautiful! AND the Picassos!"

When Hart returned to the mill, Crosby was ready for him, having put in a new supply of Cutty Sark. Crane, who had no way really to reciprocate such favors, did what he could. "He was always bringing us gifts," Mrs. Crosby remembered, "a necklace for me, some moccasins for Harry that he'd bought from a sailor." Hart's real gifts, however—ones that the Crosbys treasured—were manuscript copies of some of his poems. On the sixth of February, Crosby noted, "Hart Crane came to tea and he gave us the MSS of his O Carib Isle (one of the five best poems of our generation) . . ."

Crane, who was now really anxious to get back to *The Bridge*, looked forward to an escape from Paris. "For I haven't got down to work yet," he told Waldo Frank, "and probably won't do so until I get off to some quieter place in the country. This City, as you know, is the most interesting madhouse in the world. . . .Paris really is a test for an American, I'm beginning to feel. And I'm so far from certain that I'm equal to it in my present mood that I'm quite uneasy."

At first he had planned to take a trip to Villefranche and then perhaps to Cannes—but as he explained to Frank, "After last weekend at Ermenonville I changed my mind. The beautiful grounds of the Chateau, donkeys and bikes to ride, a whole tower to myself and all the service that millionaires are used to having—all that is very alluring, and I would be quite alone except for the gatherings on weekends. . . . I feel a great need to get into myself again, and into my work. When I consider that it has been over a year since

I have written anything longer than scratch notes for the Bridge I'm almost overwhelmed. What a year it has been, too! It has been the most decisive year of my life in a number of ways. But I also find that I now need more strength than ever."

Before Hart could find the repose he longed for, however, he had to survive another weekend of visitors. This one, as Harry Crosby's diary indicates, began with a February 10 blizzard.

> Snowstorm—Hart Crane and the Jolases arrive Croucher arrives and there was a great drinking of red wine and the Empty Bed Blues on the Graphophone and a magnificent snowball fight and we rode donkeys and we pulled the old stagecoach out into the centre of the courtyard and a mob for supper and I take a lantern and walked out through the storm to the Pôteau de Perthe . . . and when I got back the wild mob had left.

The "wild mob" gone, Hart settled in to enjoy the first isolation he had experienced in over a year. With only a skeleton staff of servants and his case of Cutty Sark to keep him company, he decided to tackle the "Cape Hatteras" section of his poem. He worked, as always, in erratic bursts, tearing out into the empty park to hike through the snow, then rushing back to build up huge fires in the tower fireplace. (Crosby, in Paris, observed that it was a week of "intense cold—the coldest I have ever known it in France and all the pipes are frozen and bed is the only nice place in the world—.") In spite of the fact that Hart knew what he wanted to do with "Hatteras," the words proved stubborn. At the end of a week's work, beyond some careful notes on the history of the airplane and a few new phrases jotted down in his notebook, he had relatively little to show anyone.

The poem nevertheless was underway, a fact that becomes evident from the tone of Hart's correspondence. On February 13, when he wrote to Bill Wright, he was obviously avoiding mention of his poem. He was at best hoping to get work done.

> I'm out here in the country, near Chantilly, resting up after a month of Paris with something of London (almost including the flu) to begin with. Tate, who is living in Paris on a Guggenheim scholarship which he was recently awarded, handed me your letter the other day. I must say that I'm happy about your keeping me in mind.
>
> I thought I sent you my address from California last winter . . . so maybe it's your fault that we've kept such quiet between us. However that may be, I *do* feel guilty for not ever writing decent letters to anyone any more. . . . I don't wonder much any more that people don't answer.
>
> No use to try to tell you all that's happened . . . Most of it is censored anyway, as I have cut all cables with my family now—

and part of my object these days is to forget (or stall off) as much as possible some of the tiresome and harrowing episodes of the last two years. Otherwise I'll *never* do any more writing or accomplish anything. For this reason I must ask you to keep my address entirely to yourself. And it might be just as well if you failed to mention that you'd heard from me at all. I'm not shame-faced—but I just want to be let alone for awhile. Perhaps you understand. . . .

I'm having the time of my life—only—I left America so ex-hausted that I haven't had time to get myself really together yet. However, things look propitious. I never thought I'd be living within sight of the old Radziwill's chateau, in a forest like that in Pelléas et Mélisande, with a roaring fire burning all day long in the fireplace and old peasant servants to bring me red, red wine, etc.

If I can stay long enough and get a bit rested I ought to get some work done here. Anyway I plan to stay over here (in France) for at least a year.

As I have noted before, Hart's oddly formal letters to his oldest friend almost always signal important events in his life—times of crisis with his family, moments of uncontrollable homesickness, celebrations of accomplishment. Here, it seems to me, homesick-ness and impending accomplishment fall together. He is not quite ready to announce that the end of *The Bridge* is in sight. He has cried wolf far too many times in the past. Yet he is announcing an intention to get to work.

Four days later there is no doubt that "Hatteras" is going well—for "Hatteras" is the Whitman section and Hart is busily sending off cheerful postcards to two men whom he always associates with Whitman—Alfred Stieglitz and Waldo Frank. He does not say that he will soon have a draft of "Hatteras" (he will, however, have it within two weeks' time), but his tone of satisfaction is unmis-takable: "Salutations—dear Stieglitz! I seldom write because I fear I have little or nothing to say. But if something is not hap-pening now—it will—someday! Can I help loving France! *Now!* Here is peace, wood-fire, sweet food and wine—and solitude in an old mill tower—what more can I require? Love—Hart Crane. Write me please! Ask Waldo for address—isn't room here." The card to Waldo Frank as good as continued the message to Stieglitz: "Yes, how can one help loving Europe! And after such barbarous crudities—en famille—as I have tasted! Here I am in an old mill tower with an old peasant couple bringing me wood for the glorious hearth, and food and delicious wine—all by myself for a whole week of solitude and study! I walk in the beautiful snow-clad park of the chateau and dream of getting back to myself—and you! Which means healing strength and love (another word for faith).

You understand? Hart." When Harry Crosby sent a letter asking if Hart were enjoying himself and if he were warm enough, the return telegram absolutely shouted happiness: "YES AND HOW SHALL HAVE THE WHOLE FOREST DOWN YOUR HART."

A short visit to town sent Hart back refreshed. His poem was now moving rapidly ahead. "I'm quite mad about Paris," he wrote the Rychtariks. "One can take long walks without ever being depressed, for you can't walk a single block without encountering something gracious to the eye." He had long since repaid his debt to them. Now he was anxious for mail. "Write me soon, and I promise to do better about answering than before. And lots of love!" He got back to the mill just in time for another wild Sunday: "Polo with golf sticks on donkeys! Old stagecoaches! Skating on the beautiful grounds of the chateau! Oysters, absinthe, even opium, which I've tried, but don't enjoy." From such delights, more postcards emerged, among them a tipsy one to Sam Loveman: "Water Boy! What the hell's the matter with you—and you won't ever write a word! Here I'm in marble halls and palace walls with my bad reputation on walking terms with the Comte du Rochefoucauld all through his magnificent estate, swans, sheep, pheasants and all— and deep on the 'Road to Xanadu' and kindred matters." But then followed one more week of solitude: "five days out there working all by myself . . . Meanwhile I dream of how fine they've promised to publish the Bridge—on sheets as large as a piano score, so none of the lines will be broken . . ."

Harry Crosby—"heir to all the Morgan-Harjes millions," as Crane told his friends—was doing himself proud. When a chimneysweep whom Hart imported for an evening's pleasure left "the blackest footprints and handprints" on a pale pink bedspread, on a white chenille rug, "up and down the curtains" and even on the wallpaper and the ceiling, Harry—rather than admonishing Hart—marveled. What is a country estate good for if not to be enjoyed? When Hart borrowed half the mill's furniture to make himself a bedroom fit for a king, Harry, returning with the phonograph needles Hart had requested ("Columbia, loud tone ! ! ! !"), took the rearrangements in stride. For Hart was producing, and the job of the world is to permit artists to produce. Crosby did what he could, which, as it turned out, was everything. Even when Hart wanted companionship, he knew to whom he should turn.

> Also, if it appeals to you, call up Eugene MacCown—and ask him out over the week end. But not please, unless it distinctly interests you to do so. My rudeness, in this case, is propelled by something you once (recently) suggested as to such an invitation.
>
> He's at 101, rue de la Tombe-Issoire (1 Villa Seurat) *Gobelins 40-61*.
>
> Crouch, Grouch, Couch is just leaving—after the most

amusing lunch in my life—I'm still a bit dizzy. He's great. So are you. So is Caresse. . . . . And HOW!

All best to the fleet.

I AM NOW BUSY.

When Hart went back to Paris—exhausted, mostly from writing —he was caught up in the same vortex that nearly three weeks earlier he had escaped from: "I've never been in such a social whirl —all sorts of amusing people, scandalous scenes, café encounters, etc.," he wrote the Rychtariks. "Writers, painters, heiresses, counts and countesses, Hispano-Suizas, exhibitions, concerts, fights, and —well, you know Paris, probably, better than I do. I had originally intended to stop here only two or three weeks on the way to a permanent location at Mallorca, one of the Balearic Islands (Spain). But I've fallen so much in love with the French and French ways that I've decided to stay here until summer anyway, and try to learn the language before leaving."

This time he could with reason feel that he had earned a holiday. Two days earlier he had delivered to Harry Crosby the first draft— still short several stanzas—of "Hatteras" and the day after had received an enthusiastic reaction. Answering Crosby's note, Hart looked forward to his next visit: "Yes, I'm longing for le Moulin, and anytime like next Thursday suits me perfectly. Meanwhile I'll try to add a few more paragraphs to the flying machine, scream awhile, dream awhile, etc. Your praise is very stimulating. My confidence revives! Love to Caresse!"

But well before that Thursday, Crosby called to say there was a party on, this time in Paris. As usual, he recorded the high spots.

Party on the Boat—Kay Boyle Laurence Vail Evelyn Nada Carlos Hart Crane a Dolly Sister Croucher H and C Etcetera Etcetera and Hart Crane tattooed his face with encre de chine and little Masie Mousie little Mousie Masie was afraid of all the people and the D.S. was the Lady of the Nombril and there was champagne and music and I was glad for a pill of black idol and there were cascades of diamond clouds crashing over a mountain of emerald the spray of the clouds flew off like sea-gulls and there were silver stars done up in red ribbons and a giant crane swinging iron baskets of orange suns and there was a catapulting through tunnels of delirium into a bed of fire.

Before the opium pills and the bright dreams, Harry had again praised "O Carib Isle!" and Hart decided that he might relish a manuscript copy of the Grand Cayman draft. (This version, which was published in *transition*, is drastically different from the one printed in *The Collected Poems*, in that it presents the "Brutal necklaces of shells" in terms of "clean enamel frames of death.") He sent off the manuscript the day after the boat party. Crosby's response was delivered by Auguste, his chauffeur.

Paris First of March 1929

Hart what thunder and fire for breakfast! "Such thunder in
their strain!" by Christ when you read something like that all the
dust and artificiality and bric a brac are swept magnificently
aside and one becomes clean like those "clean enamel frames of
death" you talk about. I am so damn glad to have this poem in
MSS—someday when we are all dead they will be screaming and
cutting each other's throats for the privilege of having it. It is
sure as Kubla Khan is sure as Blake is sure as Ozymandias and
Anabase are sure and that can't be said of many things. I am
no critic but I know gold when I see it. You write from impulse
and imagination not by rules—everyone should of course but
they simply don't—the result is you have a clean virginity of
language, a male strength, which the cérêbralè writers lack
(Valéry for instance—the Cimetière Marin) and I agree with
Tate: "the energy of Crane's vision." And it has that Timeless
quality without which nothing can endure. It is thoroughbred
poetry and that too is a rare quality. I read in Ossian "the song of
the feeble shall pass along; they shall not know where the
mighty lie." I disagree.—The song of the mighty (O Carib Isle!)
shall pass along; they shall not know where the feeble lie. Well
give 'em hell. I shan't try to thank you for the MSS; you must
know how damn glad I am to have it and how delighted Caresse
is.

Hart, I have to fly to Croyden and back to-morrow. If you
have nothing better to do I invite you to come. We leave here
6:30 in the morning. I'll come in the car for you and we get back
to Paris at 4 in time for your sailor! Just tell Auguste yes or no
as I have to get the tickets. Now that the Aeroplane part of
your poem is written it might amuse you. We could take a bottle
of Cutty Sark! And get Ossified! At all events give 'em hell—we
are going out to the Mill Thursday and hope you will come out
with us. Just let us know an hour ahead of time. Thursday we
leave here at six.

Well give 'em hell for the third time and a thousand thanks for
the MSS.

Harry

Though Hart did not join the flight to Croyden, he did make it
out to the mill for a series of parties in March and early April.
But with his French slowly becoming bearable (early in his stay, he
had arranged for lessons and for a while, at least, kept at them
faithfully), Hart felt freer to wander off under his own power. The
Crosbys were important to him, but they were now no longer the
center of his world. Except for an entry on March 3 ("To-day
drank sherry and champagne and a glass of Cutty Sark and Hart
Crane appears and talks about sailors and hurricanes and about the
Bridge and about how Otto Kahn gave Crane money so that he

could write the Bridge . . ."), Hart vanishes from Crosby's diary for the better part of four months. There are still notes back and forth—a thank-you note from Caresse for a bouquet Hart sent her ("I adore the first sweet peas of Spring—you are very darling! Will you *please* come out to the Moulin with us on Saturday A.M. . . ."), invitations to cocktail parties, and so on. But there is no question that Hart's circle of friends is by this time widening considerably. There is also no question that some of his more spectacular escapades at the mill are returning to haunt him. Caresse never forgot the circumstances of one of his late-evening decisions to return to Paris. Only one person was going in, a lady who was a close friend of Caresse's. That night she had met Hart for the first time. Though they barely spoke all the way to Paris, he made an indelible impression. For at one point he abruptly roused himself from his alcoholic fog, thrust out his arm in an imperial gesture, and loudly commanded, "Stop!" Auguste stopped. With regal dignity, Hart alighted, marched briskly forward, did an about-face, unbuttoned his fly, and urinated toweringly into the glare of the headlights. Casually buttoning up as he returned, he swept into the back seat, nodded cheerfully to Caresse's friend, and turned to the chauffeur. "Proceed," Hart commanded. Nature satisfied, he fell asleep. Hart forgot the incident but his new acquaintance did not. "Who is that *horrible* young man?" she asked Caresse the next time they met. The story—as all the other stories about him—eventually drifted back to Hart.

As he moved away from the Crosbys' circle, Crane fell in with a group of young artists and writers—Americans and Frenchmen who were just beginning to produce good work. Cocktail parties with Alan Tanner, his sister Florence, and Elsie Arden now filled much of his free time. Soon the painter Eugene MacCown, a member of this circle of friends, suggested that Hart move in with him at the Villa Seurat. Crane—tired of life at "that damned hotel," where typing and music at 4 A.M. were frowned on and where he was forced to live in a dismal back room—was overjoyed to move. MacCown's first-floor spare bedroom was light and airy. "So far as quiet goes," he explained to the Crosbys, "it's almost as good [as] *le Moulin* and I'm getting into some work again. I'm sorry about having left so much trash of mine out at *le Moulin* but maybe next week I can get out with you and remove it."

Hart now traveled very much with the Tanners and MacCown, and one of the places they traveled to was the home of Willard Widney and his wife. The Widneys, Americans who had settled in Paris five years earlier, did a great deal of casual entertaining. At Mrs. Widney's salon, young writers and painters could meet such established figures as Pavel Tchelitchew, Ford Madox Ford, and Ernest Hemingway. Mr. Widney—less interested in parties than his wife—was in the habit of taking as many of the guests as he could persuade to join him to prize fights and other sports events; Crane made several such trips. Once on the way home, Widney recalled, Hart suggested that the group stop at MacCown's apartment for a nightcap. They tiptoed in, Hart having warned them that there were light sleepers in the building. He was determined, however, to hear some music. "He put an ordinary straight pin in the machine and placed his ear over the sound box. I thought it was pathetic," Widney remembered, "and i·ı a way rather beautiful—his hunger for good music."

At most of the places where Bill Widney saw Crane, silence was no problem. Nor, for that matter, was dress or manner. Hart had by this time become considerably more aggressive in his homosexuality than he had been in America. Here, he was given, after too much to drink, to embarrassing displays. Even when he was not drinking, he felt free to talk about his sexual conquests, usually great sagas of seldom unrequited pursuit.

Sex, which was everyone's topic of conversation, also gave Hart opportunities to establish himself as one of the crowd's wittiest citizens. At Tchelitchew's, Widney recalled, Hart once became involved in discussing with Florence Tanner the proper limits of "legitimate sex." Widney, called on to define the term, said that he felt sex was legitimate "where both enjoy it." Hart knew better: "It's legitimate if only one does." At other times and places, Hart dusted off his store of unpublished limericks. "He told them very well, using exaggerated speech, savoring every nuance." Two of them proved unforgettable to Widney:

> About the poet Burns
> The research worker learns
> That the skin of his ass
> Was too tender for grass.
> He had to use maidenhair ferns.

> Elizabeth Browning Barrett
> Was found by her maw [Hart drew out "maw"] in the garrett
> Placing a dime in
> As far as her hymen
> And ramming it home with a carrot.

Such limericks—part of Hart's considerable store for special occasions—were never offered for publication.

Too much partying, however, took its toll. Hart began writing notes to friends, regretting his inability to make appointments, even pleasant ones: "Am feeling too bum—with acidosis—to go anywhere this weekend." Finally, in mid-April, he decided it was time once more to pack his suitcase. A bad stomach, a bad head, and a very sore throat persuaded him to try the South of France; at MacCown's suggestion, he made a reservation on the night train to Collioure. Two short notes mark his farewell. The first, to the Crosbys, is dated April 13.

I hear from Kay Boyle that you are leaving for Berlin next Monday. So I may not see you again before I leave for Collioure (near Perpignan) as it's only a matter of ten days or so before (I hope) I get off. How long I stay depends on a number of things—and I may get over into Spain since it's so near.

Anyway I'll be hoping to hear from you. Either this address or Guaranty Trust will be good.

Yes, I'm over my tonsillitis, thank God. First time I've been really laid up for several years. It was nice of you to think of calling.

The second note, sent a week later, is a hurried response to Caresse Crosby's suggestion that he spend his last weekend with them. She very much wanted, she said, to talk about *The Bridge*. Since recent progress was non-existent, Hart may have moved his departure forward in order to avoid the discussion. In any event, he sent posthaste a brief reply.

Am leaving 9:15 tonight for Collioure—so can't spend the week-end with you as I should so like to. But thank you a million times!

Am anxious to know what you've decided about The Bridge. Will you write me soon, c/o Guaranty Trust Co.?

Had Hart known what Caresse Crosby wanted to say about *The Bridge,* he might have delayed his trip. Rather than to ask about unfinished sections, she had wanted to suggest that he publish *The Bridge* as it stood. The draft manuscript that he had some weeks before delivered to them seemed to the Crosbys as "finished" as any work they knew. Caresse wrote on Shakespeare's birthday: "I wanted to say about 'The Bridge' that when I saw it, it seemed already to be one poem. Why do you think it must be added to? It is eternal and it is alive and it is beautiful—why don't you let us print it as it is? Afterwards if you add more you can have a second edition. If it seems too fragmentary to you it is because you already know the pieces that should fit in—but I feel that if you published it now, it would give you a fresh impetus for the rest! Think it over."

Two days later, her letter reached Crane in Collioure. He answered immediately. If he could not write the final sections, make final links, by the first of September, he would agree to publication of the existing parts.

Your suggestion about immediate publication for the Bridge is very generous, indeed inspiring. I'm so glad to know that it strikes you as being already so organic as to satisfy the requirements that its general form demands. The fact of your having stated this may help me to relax my concern about the rest of it enough to possibly stimulate me to quicker results with the remaining projected parts. We'll see. At least I'm becoming weary of the burden and am ready for almost any compromise.

Suppose, then, that I agree to turn the thing over to you by the first of September, regardless of my success in the meantime? By that time we'll possibly all be in Paris (I *may* be much before) and can see the thing through the press together. If you like I'll give you my word about the matter, especially as I know you run your press on business principles and like to know your schedule sometime in advance. As you say, there can always be a second edition incorporating additions. For all I know, the *Bridge* may turn into something like the form of "Leaves of Grass," with a number of editions, each incorporating further additions.

Hart felt a little like a traitor to his poem. But he was not writing —even the "Hatteras" section was still incomplete—and so long as nightmares about his mother, his father, and his grandmother continued to plague him, there seemed little likelihood that he would find enough repose in which to turn out any work. For nightmares that had begun in England would not let go; only alcohol could briefly blot them out. It was from this perspective that he wrote a long-delayed answer to the letters the Schneiders had kept sending him since his departure from New York.

> . . . I've been late in answering—hoping, in point of fact, that I'd have more "progress" to report than the usual preoccupations of a typical American booze-hound in Paris. But alas, I must bow my immodest head in resignation, while you must credit me with more attachment and affection than has seemed evident to judge by my responses. . . . However, as regards creative writing—I can't say that I'm finding Europe extremely stimulating. I left home in a bad state of nerves and spirit and haven't exactly recovered yet, so perhaps my reactions are not as fresh as they might be. Perhaps a few weeks of the quiet of places like this ancient fishing port may change my mind—but at any rate I haven't so far completed so much as one additional section to the "Bridge." It's coming out this fall in Paris, regardless. Limited edition of 200 copies, Black Sun Press (Harry and Caresse Crosby)—which won't complicate my contract with Liveright in any way. If it eventuates that I have the wit or inspiration to add to it later—such additions can be incorporated in some later edition. I've alternated between embarrassment and indifference for so long that when the Crosbys urged me to let them have it, declaring that it reads well enough as it already is, I gave in. Malcolm advised as much before I left America, so I feel there may be some justification. The poems, arranged as you may remember, do have I think, a certain progression. And maybe the gaps are more evident to me than to others . . . Indeed, they must be.

In the meantime, though he did no writing, Hart did slowly relax. Collioure, the luminous village that had offered its brilliant light to Juan Gris, to Matisse, to Braque, and to the hundreds of other painters who had followed them to its twisting alleys and tiny beaches, gave him, for a few weeks, peace.

He had registered at the Hôtel Bougnol-Quintana, a very modest place that had become widely known as a one-building art colony. The first week, he spent days and nights walking the village's three beaches and climbing into the vineyards that lift abruptly above the town toward the bare rock of the Pyrenees. "First impressions are great!" he wrote on the day of his arrival. "It looks as though I might stay awhile. Primitive is certainly the word. Just re-read MacLeish's 'Hamlet' down by the water. It takes on new values suddenly."

Hart had reached Collioure at precisely the right time. The spring blossoms were just beginning to fade from acres of apple and pear and cherry; the bay sky was filled with high-blown flights of swallows. All night long, behind his hotel and high into the mountains, there was a rolling, endless, constantly changing carol: "Nightingales all night and the sound of surf all day! I don't know what could rival this spot for form and color."

On days when the wind—Collioure's most spectacular commodity—let up, Crane stretched out on the flat sands between castle and church. "I'm beginning to feel my feet a little nearer to ground already," he wrote Caresse Crosby. "Hot suns and rural surroundings and the sea can almost always be counted on to relieve that suspended feeling that cities generally induce . . . So maybe I can get some work done, after all. At least I don't feel as doubtful now as I did a week ago." The only unfortunate feature was the presence of crowds of painters, all anxious to theorize about art and all frantically working. "Living at that one-and-only boarding house at Collioure," he later noted, "—with an international colony of painters—got on my nerves. To see them so busy every day with every nook and corner of the 'picturesque' gave me the 'willies.' " Of course, he acknowledged to Caresse Crosby, they had reason to be enthusiastic. "Every nook, corner, alley, turret, parapet and sailboat simply screams to be painted. It's alright for me. But if I were a painter I'd be damned scared of the place. It certainly has spoiled all stage sets for me. They'll never be able to equal the genre of this place."

Too many painters—and too few friends. These were the drawbacks of the most magnificent spot Crane had visited. Since for Crane the real pleasure of beauty was in the sharing of it, his enjoyment was tempered by the absence of those people who should have marveled with him. Yet he did what he could. He wrote more letters and postcards in a week's time than he had written in the month before he reached Collioure or than he would write in the month after he left it. Bill Brown got one of those notes.

Why the hell don't you write to me? You used to. And here I am, sitting by the shore of the most shockingly beautiful fishing village—with towers, baronial, on the peaks of the Pyrenees all about, wishing more than anything else that you were on the other side of the table.

This begins to look as good as the West Indies. Maybe—if I could talk Catalan it would be better. I began to feel as you predicted about Paris. Wish you were with me! I don't know whether you want to hear from me or not—since you have never written—but here's my love anyway, Bill—

Even Gertrude Stein—who had told Hart that Collioure's sewage system left something to be desired—got a postcard: "There has been too much wind to notice odors. I like it, so far, and expect to stay awhile. Feel quite indigenous since spending last night out on a sardine schooner. The dialect isn't so easily assimilated."

But no place could satisfy Crane. Homeless, he longed for the home he had never had—or for that second-best home he had located in the hearts of his Patterson friends. He tried to sum up Europe for the Schneiders, who a year before had written to him reactions not significantly different from his own.

As for Paris, I'll have to wait until I see you to touch the subject. Phillipe Soupault and his wife were about the most hospitable French people I met, and Gertrude Stein about the most impressive personality of all. The marvellous room of hers, the Picasso's, Juan Gris and others (including some very interesting youngsters) on the walls! Then there were Ford Madox Ford, Wescott, Bernadine Szold (just back from the orient), Richard Aldington, Walter Lowenfels (who has an interesting book of verse coming out in England—(Heinemann)), Emma Goldman, Klaus Mann, Eugene MacCown, Jolas (whom I like very much), Edgar Varèse, Rene Crevel, Kay Boyle, (who has decided she likes me) and a hundred others just as interesting, or more so, who aren't particularly known. The Tates are living in Ford's apartment while he is away, and declare they never want to leave Paris. I like it all too well, myself, but would have to live there a long while before I could settle down to accomplish any work, I fear. And lately—all cities get on my nerves after a few weeks. I'd never want to settle down for good over here like many do, however,—town or country. For even here by the blue inland sea, with ancient citadels and fortifications crowning the heights of a lovely, white-walled village—I can't help thinking of my room out there in Patterson. Silly, I know ... but what can one do about it?

My plans are vague. May stay here two months more or only two weeks. Spain is very near, but also, I hear very expensive. I'm crossing over to a nearby town to see a bull fight in a couple of days. But I may not explore it much further at the time, re-

gardless of my intense interest. There are other small ports between here and Marseille which are very intriguing. I can't regret
not seeing everything this trip—or even never. You see I like
France pretty well!... Write soon—please!

Though Hart did get in his trip to Spain—a day in Figueras, an
hour and a half away from Collioure on the slow train that crosses
the border at Cerbère—he was too restless to stay. He had come
to see the bullfights ("Six bulls; four with much esprit. I've decided I like it, gore and all"). But the bullfights were the only
Spanish sight he was willing to look at. As for Collioure, once the
wind died down and the painters took to the beaches, he decided
that perhaps Gertrude Stein knew whereof she spoke. "I'm moving
north along the coast soon," he wrote Harry Crosby. "—Cette,
Martigue and maybe across Marseille to the other places. They
crap all over the beaches here, and I want pure salt water if none
other . . ." Yet even worse than sewage is silence. Hart was lonely
for friendly voices. "I've thought of you," he wrote the Crosbys,
"—Sundays out at le Moulin—and the cannon, vodka, donkeys,
Médoc. . . ."
Hart had been lonely in Collioure; he made up for it in Marseilles. In that international port, English was a second language,
and the waterfront bars had a speaking likeness to those of Brooklyn and Hoboken. Hart arrived in the middle of May.

> Marseille is a delightful place—to me—and I want to stay a
> week or so longer. Thank God, there's nothing much to gape at
> —museums or otherwise—and the people seem (I mean the
> citizens and residents) less French than anywhere else I've been
> . . . Here there is no one building that one wants to look at
> twice. It's dirty, vulgar, noisy, dusty—but I claims wholesome.
> Had a great time last Saturday visiting the whorehouses with an
> English sailor—whose great expression of assent and agreement
> was "heave ho!" And a row with one of the officers later in the
> evening—a true Scotsman—who said he would give the 16 (why
> 16 I don't know) remaining years of his life to see America
> "humbled in the dust." He was a fine looking old codger—with
> upturned whiskers and eyebrows—looked like a triton or Nep-
> tune but had too much beer in him to float . . .

The only trouble in Marseilles, indeed, was hay fever. "I'm having
my usual spring touch of that down here—though I can't see any
*fields* around here. No, Europe isn't my cure, after all! Even though
someone sent me some damned-fool clipping from the 'Tribune,' reporting me as 'convalescing' at Collioure, 'a tiny village far in the
Pyrenees'! Christ Almighty! Save me from such mention!"
Marseilles did have one beneficial effect. "I can think of my
work here—get my feet more on the ground—and dress and do as
I please," Hart wrote the Crosbys, and then went on to ask

exactly when they wanted him to supply the manuscript for the printer. At the mill he had made a careful study of Coleridge, a study that persuaded him that an accompanying gloss of the "Ancient Mariner" sort might be a useful device to bind together the early sections of *The Bridge*. He was now trying to construct one. The problem was just how extensive to make it—and how far to continue it. For Hart wanted his gloss to lead the reader into the poem, not to become a substitute for the text. "I'm trying to write a gloss," he explained to Crosby, "—but it's not easy to be consistent about it, as the poem is developed not on narrative lines nor dramatic . . . Shall we try to help the poor public or not? That's the question!"

Perhaps Marseilles also encouraged Hart to work because there he had run into two very productive artists: the painter Marsden Hartley and the poet Roy Campbell.

He had known Hartley casually back in Brooklyn. There, listening to Hart's record of Ravel's *Bolero*, they had tried to analyze the nature of "absolute music," that ideal sound that Hart maintained paralleled the "absolute poetry" every poet strives for and never attains. Their meeting in Marseilles was sheer accident. Hartley, sitting at a café terrace, saw Hart frantically dashing up the street, stepped out to say hello, and within minutes was engaged in a detailed discussion of *The Bridge*'s structural problems. Hart, he later recalled, was worried over the relationship of the "Three Songs" to the rest of the poem. "National Winter Garden" was the item of major concern, and Hart whipped out a copy to ask Hartley for his opinion of its role in the larger poem. Hartley's answer was probably the wrong one—that he did not think it had either the grandeur or the sweep of the rest of the poem but that if Hart thought it belonged, then obviously it had to go in—for Hart quickly changed the subject. When they met again on the next Sunday to watch a harbor water carnival, Hart spent most of the time trying unsuccessfully to persuade Hartley to join him in a visit to Campbell and his wife.

If second-hand reports can be trusted, the Campbells were relieved when, at the end of two weeks, Hart went tearing back to Marseilles. He was never an easy visitor and the isolation of the house that the South African poet had rented at Martigues—the desolate and beautiful flat lands where wild ponies and nearly wild cattle are herded by hard-riding French cowboys—alternately stimulated and depressed Crane. "Swimming isn't good there," he explained to Tate, then hinted there were "other features" that made Martigues unattractive.

Yet if the particular landscape troubled Crane, the area was compelling. "I have come to love Provence, the wonderful Cezannesque light (you see him everywhere here) and the latinity of the people. Arabs, Negroes, Greeks, and Italian and Spanish mixtures." It was, he decided, the one part of France to which he might someday return: "When I come to France again I'll sail direct for Marseille—and it's certainly my intention to come again!"

But Hart was unable to appreciate any spot for long. As the deadline for the manuscript of *The Bridge* approached, he found that no place and no activity satisfied him. Indeed, he realized one bright June day, no place and no activity had seemed for the past two years in any deep sense valuable.

Perhaps, he concluded, he might after all be better off settling down in America rather than France. At the very least, he would have fewer difficulties cashing checks. For again he was having problems extracting from his New York bank the remains of his much-fought-over inheritance. His money was in a savings account. He had neglected to bring his bank book to France. He had run out of traveler's checks. Borrowing enough from the Tates to get from Marseilles to Paris and in Paris eventually borrowing enough from the Crosbys to pay for his return passage to America, Crane—for the first time in his life in possession of a substantial bank balance —was both penniless and in debt.

He did not, of course, starve. Nor did he die of thirst. So long as they were both in Paris, he could count on Harry Crosby's generosity to solve problems of eating and drinking. "Hart Crane back from Marseille where he had slept with his thirty sailors and he began again to drink Cutty Sark (the last bottle in the house)." Though Crane had initially alternated between praise for Marseilles's sailors and Roy Campbell's poetry ("wonderful," "splendid"), by the time he left Crosby, he was barely able to comment on anything.

He had, of course, been drinking heavily since his first arrival in Europe, but the binge that started on Crosby's last bottle of Scotch was monumental. Not until days later was Hart coherent enough to make apologies. "A thick fog still envelops my 'memory' of the latter hours at your side last Saturday! I think Cutty Sark won that bout without the slightest doubt!"

For much of that first week of July, Hart drifted from bar to bar, looking for people to talk to. The Crosbys were now out of town, and he felt himself at loose ends: "Paris is . . . more lonesome than I thought." Tired of hotel life and rather pointedly not invited to return to Crosby's country house, Hart asked MacCown if he could again use the room in the Villa Seurat. There he wrote Joseph Stella another inquiry about the frontispiece to *The Bridge*, revised the gloss of the opening sections, and let Malcolm Cowley know publication plans: "The Crosbys are bringing out the Bridge in December or January—that is, it'll be finished and on sale by that time. Yes, you can have a copy—but don't tell anyone about it. I don't get very many gratis—and I might like to sell a half dozen of them myself. Why not?"

In these unhappy days Hart lived from moment to moment. At first he intended to sail for New York during the last week of

August, but he soon realized that neither friends nor borrowed cash would hold out that long. ("Perhaps it's just as well that a good part of my money is tied up in a savings account in New York and inaccessible to me here," he explained to Cowley.) Until the return of the Crosbys, however, Hart could do nothing about purchasing his ticket. Though they had volunteered to loan him what he would need, they had neglected to make the money available through their bank. Impatient, Hart devoted himself to a clinical study of the bottom of the bottle. For he was still persuaded that alcohol gave him inspiration. Night after night, Mac-Cown recalled, Hart would come reeling back to his room, diligently to jot down phrases and revisions of phrases—all or almost all of which would in the morning be assigned to the wastebasket. His inability to write or revise made him so touchy that many acquaintances who already knew his temper was undependable came to feel, during these final Paris days, that they were dealing not with a congenial companion but with a most demanding, most insulting man. "I felt toward the end that he was just using all of us," Willard Widney told me. "He had a fierce megalomania, and when he had been drinking hard it became damned offensive."

Hart's wild days at the beginning of July might nevertheless have come to nothing more than an unusually grim hangover had he not one night dropped in at the Café Select. He was not drunk when he arrived, his late afternoon and early evening having been devoted to conversation with the friends and acquaintances who drifted in and out of the little cafés along the Boulevard Raspail. When he reached the Select, however, he settled into more serious drinking, soon assembling in front of him a considerable pile of saucers. Then came his bill and the discovery that he had no more than fifty centimes in his pocket. At first the waiter and then the proprietress stood over him demanding payment. Hart was reasonable. He would return the next day with ready cash. They were adamant. He would cross the street to borrow the sum from a friendlier bartender. They were still unmoved. Finally Hart began shouting denunciations of French waiters and French café owners. "Madame Select," a woman never kindly disposed toward Americans, ponderously announced that she had had enough: Hart would not be permitted to leave his table; she would call the police.

What had been until then a mildly entertaining show seemed now doomed to turn into disaster; other Americans in the café—among them, MacCown—took up a collection to pay Crane's bill. At this point, however, "Madame Select" wanted nothing less than vengeance. She refused the cash, phoned the police, and ordered a waiter to collar Crane, who, wildly angry, floored in rapid succession the first waiter, several others who came hurrying from the rear of the café, and, triumphantly, the gendarme who arrived to investigate the disorder. It is one thing to knock down a crowd of waiters; it is quite another—at least in Paris—to attack the police. Within minutes a larger force of gendarmes arrived. Though Crane managed to smash chairs and bottles over their heads, he was finally clubbed into insensibility and dragged off, feet first, his head bumping over the curbstones. At La Santé, he was subjected to a methodical beating with a rubber hose, dumped into a cell, and held for several days incommunicado.

MacCown, meanwhile, was doing what he could to secure Hart's release. With other friends, he set up a defense fund (Bill Widney recalls contributing a thousand francs), hired a lawyer, and began collecting "character references" from writers such as Cocteau and Gide. Crane, they maintained, was a major artist wrongfully imprisoned.

Word soon reached the Paris offices of the *Herald Tribune*. Whit Burnett, then a young reporter, got in touch with MacCown to ask how he might help. With E. E. Cummings, who had recently arrived in Paris, and with others of Hart's friends, they stormed the office of the Chief Prefect of Police. Angered as much by the "character references" as by their loud protests, he refused to release Crane without a trial. Harry Crosby, who might have been able to use pressure to get an early one, was touring the French countryside. The best Crane's lawyer could do was arrange for it to take place about a week after Crane had been imprisoned.

By the hour of the trial, all his friends were mobilized. Crosby, who had returned to Paris the night before, spent most of the day racing from place to place, gathering new character references, picking up money to pay Crane's fine, and at one point in the trial getting himself thrown out of court for being a one-man cheering section. His diary describes some of the minute-by-minute chaos of the roughest July 10 of Crane's career.

> To the Black Sun Press (I am doing a second edition of Transit of Venus and a miniature edition of The Sun). Then to take a taxi to see McGowan [MacCown] about Hart Crane. I arrived in front of the Deux Maggots and hailed a taxi. Just then McGowan stepped out of the café with Vitrac and a girl called Kitty Cannell. We drove off to the Palais de Justice. It was quarter to one. I had a date with Marks at the Ritz Bar so I rushed off and got him (we drank two cocktails) and brought him back with me to the trial. Hart was magnificent. When the Judge announced that it had taken ten gendarmes to hold him (the dirty bastards, they dragged him three blocks by the feet) all the court burst into laughter. After ten minutes of questioning he was fined 800 francs and 8 days in prison should he ever be arrested again. A letter from the Nouvelle Revue Française had a good deal to do with his liberation. They wouldn't let him out right away so I went with Marks to Le Doyen to eat and to drink sherry cobblers in the sun. We got tight and he went off to see Eugene O'Neill [MacCown?] and I went to the bank.

On my way back I started off towards the race-ticker bar on the Rue Cambon to see if Tornado had won, but on the way I saw a pretty American girl, so I talked to her and we went to the Ritz for a sherry cobbler (her name was Sheelah—I like it) but I had to rush off to the Conciergerie where I found Vitrac and Whit Burnett. Apparently Hart had been sent back to the Santé so Burnett and I drove over there (we saw a truck run over a cat) and here we had to wait and to wait from six until long after eight (we spent the time drinking beer and playing checkers and talking to the gendarmes). At last the prisoners began to come out, Hart the last one, unshaved hungry wild. So we stood and drank in the Bar de la Bonne Santé right opposite the prison gate and then drove to the Herald office where Burnett got out to write up the story for the newspaper, Hart and I going on to the Chicago Inn for cornbread and poached eggs on toast (Ginetta and Olivares were there and Ortiz) and Hart said that the dirty skunks in the Santé wouldn't give him any paper to write poems on. The bastards.

Hart's time in prison, however, left him only momentarily subdued. After a few days of quiet respectability, reading and writing in MacCown's apartment, he again picked up the roaring life that had been his downfall. But, before that, he went with Harry Crosby to a travel agency and booked passage to New York on the *Homeric*, the first departing ship that had a second-class cabin.

It was easy enough for those who saw Hart only during Parisian evenings to assume that he never wrote a word. But even such people noticed that he now displayed—at least early on—the shadow of discretion. Bill Widney recalled that during one night in the Dingo Bar Hart actually went out of his way to avoid a fight. A pair of American college boys—further gone than either of them—had been staring disapprovingly throughout Hart's loud, laughing account of life in a French prison. Widney, irritated, stared pointedly back until the heftier of the two boys lumbered over to lean on the table and demand: "Want to make something of it?" Normally this would have been Hart's cue for action, but he now realized too much was at stake. "Look," he said, trying hard to seem the model of sweet reasonableness, "I just got out of jail, and I don't want to go back again. I really don't want to make *anything* out of *anything!*"

What he wanted, of course, was quickly to finish his Paris commitments. No matter how "full" his evenings were, he did his best to appear at Harry Crosby's home or office for morning discussions of the *Bridge* format and last-minute revisions on the manuscript. He was not always in good shape and his revisions were not final ones, but he did show up to deliver them.

Hart appeared rather the worse for wear. He had been up all night in Montmartre. He had all sorts of stars and anchors pinned to his sweater and the dactylo appeared to work on The Bridge and Hart read his poems aloud and declared that there was no greater poet than he and he played the Graphophone and talked of Marseille and of Roy Campbell of the Flaming Terrapin . . .

Finally Crane sailed back to America, "launched" a few days before his thirtieth birthday by Harry Crosby, who presented him with a farewell bottle of Cutty Sark. By careful rationing, Hart made it last three days.

# 32

On the pier, beside Harry Crosby, had stood a young Danish boy. "Please ask Harry if he can think of any job for that nice Danish boy I introduced him to the morning I sailed," Hart was soon writing Caresse Crosby. "He's without work or funds—and starving. He's an expert trainer and keeper of horses (Danish Royal Artillery) and speaks English fairly well. . . . Honest, industrious, and will do anything that's honorable." During the next few years, Hart would infuriate some of his friends, first by sending his young acquaintance ten-dollar checks, then by advancing him $150 for a trip to America that never took place. ("He wasn't any good; he was just after Hart's money," one friend assured me.) "He *needed* the money," Hart explained to those friends who complained that it was being thrown away.

"I must add one word of warning dear boy," "Aunt Sally" Simpson had written in a birthday letter that arrived just before Hart left France, *"don't be too free with your cash."* Yet, Hart must have brooded, what is cash good for? He had spent nearly half his inheritance; all it had gained for him were some hangovers, a week in jail, and eight months of unprofitable wandering through England and France. He had substituted scenery for a home, a crowd of bright, busy acquaintances for the close friends that had formerly made his disordered life meaningful. "You'll soon have another birthday," Mrs. Simpson had written. "I wish you all good luck and happiness and hope you live to enjoy many more *happier* ones." He carried her letter with him to the ship; he thought about her and about his Isle of Pines interlude as the *Homeric* worked slowly across an Atlantic "smooth as castor oil and sunny." When Harry Crosby's Cutty Sark ran out, Hart turned to bourbon and soda, a drink, he noted in a letter to Crosby, he had not had since his "sweaty days" in the West Indies. "It almost makes me see palm trees on the horizon."

As soon as he landed in America, Hart wrote Mrs. Simpson a long letter. He enclosed a check for twenty-five dollars, a birthday present for the one person who had remembered his own birthday. By giving some of his money, Hart now decided, to those friends who needed it more than he, he could justify the battle that had brought it to him. Such gifts were made most casually. "I have more than I need," he seems to have told Mrs. Simpson, for she soon wrote: "Hope you didn't skimp yourself to send it. You said in your letter you had plenty and I don't doubt you but I sincerely hope you told the truth; and may you always have plenty."

He must have pictured himself to her as a new man—a man no longer troubled by the family he had isolated himself from, a man who in Europe had chatted casually with millionaires and who was now readying for publication the book on which he had so long labored. "I am so glad for you," she wrote. "I cried for joy when your last letter came; at last you have achieved what you set out to do. I knew you would, and I am doubly glad you have got control of yourself and will not let other people's affairs worry you. Aren't you just stepping on the high places?" But Mrs. Simpson was shocked by the heavy lines in the smiling face that looked out of the photograph he had sent and by the streaks of gray hair that two years before had been solid brown. "I didn't like the picture very well; somehow it didn't look like my boy poet.—Are you really gray, Hart? I am almost snow white."

For absent friends, Hart tried to seem wealthy and wise; for local friends, he tried to seem absent. There had been, he felt, far too much humiliating publicity concerning his brush with the French courts and his week in jail. Earlier incidents involving the law had been occasions for comedy, but his French experience was not of this kind. He was, he believed, disgraced by a story that had appeared in The New York Times just after his Paris "trial." Headed POET SEES "LEFT BANK"; NOW HE MUST STAY DRY, it had described in vivid detail his drunken brawl, his stay in jail, and the "joyous laughter of the whole court" as the magistrate of the Thirteenth Correctional Court of Paris told him that for the rest of his time in France he would either stay sober or face another week in prison. For several weeks after he got back to New York, Hart avoided friends he would normally have turned to. Not until he ran into Slater Brown on the street and was assured of their continuing affection did he feel confident enough to approach the group of writers and artists with whom he was most intimate.

Another motive may also have been involved in Crane's decision to evade old friends. He realized that he no longer had any option about publishing The Bridge; in some form or other, it would soon be in print. Though he would be free to make revisions for the Liveright edition, he would be judged, he knew, by the one Caresse and Harry Crosby would publish. Since convivial Paris had not moved the poem to completion, perhaps Brooklyn isolation could accomplish the wonders he felt were needed.

And indeed his first few days in Brooklyn—he had returned, this time to 130 Columbia Heights—were productive. ("I can't help thinking [the gloss] a great help in binding together the general theme of Powhatan's daughter," he wrote Caresse Crosby. "As for the Columbus note, it simply silhouettes the scenery before the colors arrive to inflame it.")

When he was not working, Hart was reading Donne's *Devotions* or visiting, alone, the "wonderful" beaches of Brooklyn and Queens (beaches, as he noted, "packed with pulchritude").

He was now in weekly correspondence with Caresse Crosby about typography for the book. He had also begun dropping in on booksellers who might be able to place part of the planned edition of 250 copies. At this time—early in August—Hart was determined to have the first edition published by Christmas Eve, perhaps even by Thanksgiving.

For once, no one could accuse him of failing to work. He carted his manuscript everywhere. When Patterson friends persuaded him to make a two-week visit, he spent much of his time on the "Cape Hatteras" section, expanding and revising what he had written in France. His letter to the Crosbys are filled with inquiries about the progress of the typesetting, suggestions for page size, revision of material already in type, drafts of new sections, revisions of those drafts. Now it is Hart who presses for speed: "I'm passionately anxious to hear from you as soon as possible."

As he looked toward the winter of 1929, the whole world seemed—for a change—to be conspiring to aid his literary progress. He received requests for unpublished *Bridge* material. Liveright notified him that the 500-copy first edition of *White Buildings* was exhausted and that a second printing was on the way. He was conveniently housed. "I'm settled at last in a comfortable furnished apartment—not far from the navy yard. . . . I can buy corn whiskey from my janitor for only $6. per gallon! No more querulous, farty old landladies for me for awhile . . . Liveright is issuing a second edition of White Buildings—Vanity Fair bestows laurels in the Sept. issue—Eliot urges me to contribute as well as old Mamby Canby of the Sat. Review, the old enemy camp. So I'm feeling optimistic to a large extent." To cap that frame of mind, he had a long, flattering letter from Paul Rosenfeld, asking him to contribute the "Machine Age section" of his poem to the fourth *American Caravan*.

Hart was working so well, indeed, that by the end of September he felt able to promise Caresse Crosby "two final sections" within a week's time. Once again he was caught up in the productivity that had first appeared on the Isle of Pines. Whole days were now spent in working and reworking, Hart hating even to take time out for progress reports to the Crosbys. ("I have more to send," one such report notes, "—and it's very important. I am working like mad since I've found this apartment where I can keep my own hours, etc. I'm too rushed to type you out a final copy of this finale to the 'Cape Hatteras' section yet, but you can get some idea of what I'm accomplishing by the muddled copy I'm including herewith. . . . It looks pretty good to me . . .") He launched into both "Quaker Hill" and "Indiana" even before "Hatteras" was in final shape ("The book must have these sections") and he soon began a rapid integration and linkage, rewriting "finished" work to accommodate that which was still taking form. ("I forgot to include this new version of 'Cutty Sark' in the earlier letter sent today. I have changed very little—what little has been only to promote clarity—which includes a more generous sprinkling of punctuation. So please use this instead of the version you've had. . . . Hope this doesn't put you out!") In mid-September, New York's heat—and perhaps the desire to consult the "Quaker Hill" landscape—had sent him up to Patterson for a week, but it had not slowed down what he described accurately as "fevers of work." "I sent you, registered, the 'Cape Hatteras' last version. But retyping it for a magazine, I couldn't help glimpsing some necessary improvements. So please use this *second* version, as enclosed. I vow that you'll be troubled by no further emendations—excepting perhaps a comma or so on the proofs." His poem was falling into place, the parts linking exactly as he had hoped they would:

> Since I'm writing I can't help saying that I'm highly pleased with the way I've been able to marshal the notes and agonies of the last two years' effort into a rather arresting synthesis. . . .
> Gosh, how I'd like a bottle of Cutty Sark tonight to soothe my excited nerves!

Of course, his happiness did not last. The crash that very nearly finished *The Bridge* came in the first days of October. Hart had returned from Patterson more sure of his prowess, more sure of his poem, than he had been for years. But suddenly he found himself stymied. Everything that had worked to pull the poem together now seemed to pull it apart. Panicky, he rushed from friend to friend, manuscript in hand, trying out each new phrase, blaming the friend when he himself found a passage unbearable. Nearly hysterical, he decided that inspiration would have to come from the bottle—and stepped onto a treadmill helpless round that carried him from bootlegger to speakeasy to waterfront dive.

It was difficult in these October weeks to be with him and almost impossible to escape him. All his closest friends were subjected to desperate telephone calls; those who were most easily available also received middle-of-the-night visits. These friends— among them Evans, Loveman, and Lorna Dietz—fought Crane's battles with taxi drivers and responded to pre-dawn "emergency" calls. Brown recalled one of them in which Hart, convinced that he was dying, demanded that Brown come to him immediately. Hart's "death" turned out to be no more than an unusually bad hangover.

None of these friends ever shrugged his shoulders and went back to bed. For there could be a time, they knew, when Crane would really be in jeopardy. More than once he arrived at Loveman's apartment badly beaten by sailors who did not want to play. And more than once Lorna Dietz sat through the night by Hart's bed attempting to hush his terrified screams as waves of delirium tremens brought a nightmare world before his staring eyes.

For nearly three weeks in October, Hart drank, raged, rioted. On the *Bridge* deadline that he had really expected to meet, he sent the Crosbys a cable: "HAVE BEEN ILL YES SOON LOVE—HART—" Finally, as much disgusted by what he saw in the mirror as by drunken visions, he returned to Patterson for a week of outdoor recuperation. "I was a wreck when I left town," he wrote to Loveman, and to Lorna Dietz he sent a letter that was apologetic yet tentatively hopeful.

> I've been *weltschmerzing* a little bit all by myself here since last Saturday afternoon, when I suddenly picked up and left town. I've never seen such color as this year's autumnal shades, but the storm that began this morning after three wonderful days of sunshine probably won't leave so much on the boughs to be gazed at . . . Nevertheless I'm staying at least until next Monday—and maybe somewhat longer. I feel quite rested already, but I know that I need a little "reserve" after the way I've been acting. I'm *hoping* also, to complete the last two sections, God 'elp me! And then to come back to town and see you again in your sweet, new, cheerful, rosy little nest!
>
> You've possibly seen Emil, who left Monday for a few days with his mother.
>
> Lots of love, Dear!

Hart had known Lorna Dietz, of course, for several years, but during the weeks of heavy drinking he had come to value her in an altogether new way. He saw her as a guardian companion, a person who would not fail him, no matter how outrageously he "tested" her. A survivor of his worst binges, she joined the select inner circle of friends for whom, in an entirely literal way, he stayed alive.

When Hart returned from Patterson at the very end of October, he found a cable from the Crosbys, telling him he must choose immediate publication of his book or postponement until February. He had completed the "Indiana" section during that week, but not "Quaker Hill." He had to decide—and quickly—to do without "Quaker Hill," to send in a fragmentary version in the hope that he could revise on galleys, or to accept a three-month delay.

Before he could make up his mind what to do, he suffered two serious frights. His health—bad when he had left town—seemed abruptly to deteriorate. At the same time he learned that his mother now knew his whereabouts and was planning to return to the East Coast. Hart's fears for his health and his fear that he might again become involved with Grace coalesced into terror. If he could not deal with her when he was well, how, he reasoned, could he cope with her when he was ill? After a day's brooding, he was near panic. Finally, late at night, he broke down and, in a fit of tears, telephoned his father. C.A., though startled to hear from Hart after a year-long silence, said what needed to be said: "You come home right away, Harold. We'll talk it all out once you get home."

It was not until the next day that Hart realized what he had committed himself to: if he returned to Ohio, publication of *The Bridge* would definitely be delayed. As usual, he consulted friends, particularly Miss Dietz. Encouraged by her to make peace with C.A., if not with Grace, he wired the Crosbys: "DEFER PUBLICA-TION LOVE—HART," and then composed a long, explanatory letter. "I really do want to see at least the bulk of the poem in proofs," he wrote. He then went on to make plans to see the Crosbys between Thanksgiving and New Year's, when they would be visiting America, to discuss last-minute corrections. "Haven't been well lately," Crane told them, "but hope to improve as soon as I can get the 5-year load of The Bridge off my shoulders. You can't imagine how insufferably ponderous it has seemed, yes, more than once!" He had had, he explained, a particularly difficult time with the "Indiana" subsection, a part of the poem most of his friends regarded as decidedly inferior and one which, Crane feared, the Crosbys would also object to. And yet the design of the poem—as Crane well knew—demanded precisely the tone and method he had settled on. There had to be a "letdown" between the rhetorical language of "The Dance" and the very different but equally rhetorical language of "Cutty Sark"; "Powhatan's Daughter" had to be "completed" by being gently brought down to modern times, its "continental" imagery transformed into that of the surrounding sea. What made this structuring so difficult was the need to keep all the sections of the poem subtly interconnected. "The symbolism of Indiana (metamorphosis of Pocahontas (the Indian) into the pioneer woman, and hence her absorption into our 'contemporary veins' [)] is, I hope, sufficiently indicated without too great sacrifice of poetic values," Crane wrote. "It does round out the cycle, at least historically and psychologically—one leaves the continent surrounded by water (pure space) as one found it in the first place (Harbor Dawn), and Cutty Sark quite logically follows as 'space' again."

Edgy from worry over the way his poem was fitting together and more than edgy at the prospect of his mother's arrival, Hart set off with altogether mixed emotions for a two-week visit to his father's house. And yet, as it turned out, the visit was one of the happiest times in Crane's "home" life; for he found his father very much at ease as proprietor of Crane's Canary Cottage, the handsome restaurant that had by now been opened in the village of Chagrin Falls.

Not only was C.A. at ease, he was in love and—as Hart soon learned—about to announce his impending marriage to Bessie Meacham, a young woman who had worked with him in his business enterprises and whose congenial good humor and generous, outgoing nature complemented her quiet beauty.

Hart immediately relaxed. In the evenings, after the last diners left the restaurant, he was able to settle down before one of the huge fireplaces to read far into the night. For the first time in his life, he found it almost pleasant to talk with his father, Miss Meacham acting as catalyst. The three of them planned a future in which Hart could come and go as he wished, a welcome son who had proved himself as a writer, one who would not be expected to take over the family business. After the first few days, indeed, it was taken for granted that a room and bath on the second floor of the north wing would permanently be "Harold's rooms," his to live in whenever he could come home. "This turns out to be a wonderful place," he wrote Sam Loveman. "The time will pass very easily. Feel as though I had a home at last. Six great fireplaces burning and dad's cigars!" Hart was now almost excessive in his praise for the father whom ten years before he had condemned as a man of neither taste nor honor. Now his father's honor seemed self-evident and his taste—in furniture, at least, and food—superlative. "Father's collection of early Am. clocks, desks, chairs, tables, beds and highboys makes my eyes water and my head swim," he wrote Bill Brown. "Wish you were here for some of the superb duck and chicken!"

The people of Chagrin Falls who remember Crane from this visit and the ones that followed remember him in terms of laughter and good will. When he isolated himself in his room to write or read, he went out of his way to make clear that he was avoiding no one, that he retreated to his room to accomplish the only kind of work that meant anything to him. "Girls, if I don't show up, just go ahead," he told the waitresses. "I might be up there three or four days—but I'll be down for meals, you'll be able to see me at dinnertime!"

He was now full of stories of his adventures, among them a yarn about the time on the Isle of Pines when he had rushed to aid Mrs. Simpson in the end-of-the-lot privy. Her hysterical screams of "Snakes! Snakes!" had propelled him from the house. But he was brought up short, howling with laughter, when he discovered her frantically trying to club to death the belt he had left beside the open second seat.

There were, however, stories he did not tell—stories of Paris jails. These were not for Ohio ears, and he asked the friends who had heard them (Richard Laukhuff, among others) to keep such tales to themselves. Chagrin Falls was an oasis of order in the swirling disorder through which Crane walked. It was imperative that he be able, in that one place, to be the solid citizen he at heart still remained. It was no accident that Hart and his father wore the same style of overcoat, carried the same type of cane, affected the same tilt to the same gray hats.

There is no telling how long Crane might have stayed in Chagrin Falls—longer, I think, than the two weeks he first intended. For he was making plans to see a great deal of the Rychtariks and to spend several days with Bill Sommer; but suddenly all his plans were altered. He heard through relatives in Warren that his mother was expected in the Cleveland area within a day or two. She would be staying in a little town less than an hour from Chagrin Falls. She was anxious to talk to her son.

Hart went to pieces. The good health he had regained vanished in an hour. He bolted for the station, on the way begging his father to have nothing to do with her. For he could not bring himself to live with his mother again, and he knew that if she were convinced he would never return to her, she would be perfectly capable of carrying out her implicit threat. She might reveal to C.A. the history of homosexuality and drunkenness that had been confessed to her in California. She might attempt a vengeance that could easily destroy his new rapport with his father.

Grace had hoped to spend Thanksgiving with Hart. Hart had hoped to spend Thanksgiving with C.A. All three were cheated out of joy. Embarrassed by Hart's flight and very coldly received by her hosts, Grace quickly departed for Chicago. In New York, Hart spent the emptiest Thanksgiving of his life, dreading to answer the telephone, waiting to hear news of Grace's next move.

Finally, a letter from C.A. arrived.

> I have very little to report to you . . . except that the second morning after arrival . . . she called me on the 'phone and asked me to come there for a conference, which I stoutly refused to do.
>
> Then she asked if I was not interested in her future welfare, and I told her I was not in any particular. That's about all there was to the conversation. . . .
>
> She asked for your address, and I gave it as Patterson, N.Y., thinking to follow out your desire in not having your home molested for the time being, at least.

C.A.'s letter had offered Hart a reprieve. But sooner or later, Hart realized, he would have to come to some decision about Grace —and that it might have to be very soon indeed was strongly implied by the end of C.A.'s note. "I think as matters now stand, she without any money whatever, and a liability to her friends, she should submit to an examination and get in better health, both mentally and physically, and I think you are fully justified in signing such papers as would help clear up the atmosphere." If Grace were really as ill and unstable as Hart and his father had been led to believe, only Hart would be able to take the legal steps to hospitalize her.

Torn by worries over his mother—real concern for her health alternating with nightmare fears that, were he to talk to her, she would persuade him to live with her—Crane nevertheless managed to draft "Quaker Hill" and to set about typing a "final" version of *The Bridge*.

Set down in this fashion, the two weeks between Thanksgiving and December 10, 1929, sound hectic but coherent; but for Crane they were days of ecstasy, pain, and confusion. For his world had become a microcosm of that larger world that in the daily press seemed to be shattering into chaos, the predictable financial world that had become in the eyes of conservative businessmen like Hart's father a lunatic arena where suicidal madmen tore each other to shreds.

Hart's private world now seemed to him intolerable. Only through the love and devotion of close friends did he survive. For orgiastic nights and fiercely driving days piled on one another, Hart rushing back and forth from Patterson to New York, unhappy in both places, incapable of relaxing in either. Possibly it was during these weeks that the painter Peter Blume—briefly a tenant at Mrs. Turner's—wrestled him to the floor. Moments before, stark naked, Hart had been rampaging through the house, smashing everything he could get his hands on. Though they could get *him* down, fallen Crane had shouted, *The Bridge* would soon be on its way to Paris. His back aching for weeks (Crane blamed the backache on his mother's reappearance), he ran full-tilt from party to bar to typewriter and back to party again.

When worry over Grace and *The Bridge*—and far too many drinks—made him incapable of typing, it was friends who saw to it that he was bedded down, ice packs and blankets as needed, until he was able to function. One of the most helpful of these friends was Margaret Robson, the wife of Ernest Robson and a close friend of the Cowleys and the Browns. Convinced that Crane was a great poet and a great human being, she made it her business to see that *The Bridge* was properly prepared for the press. During the better part of three days, she sat at the typewriter in Crane's rooms, working with him through heaps of manuscripts, patiently retyping sections as new revisions made them unfit to send in, gradually accomplishing what Hart, in moments of defeat, had declared hopeless: the final assembly of the poem. The first of the two women he nicknamed "Little Miss Twidget" (Peggy Cowley, in Mexico, would be the second), Margaret Robson became, when needed, hostess, companion, and very close friend.

She was needed, as it turned out, almost immediately. On December 7, Hart gave a party in celebration of his forthcoming book, a party that also served as a farewell for the Crosbys, who had arrived several weeks earlier and whose ship was supposed to leave on December 13. He tried to invite all the people who had aided him with *The Bridge*. In addition to the Crosbys, there were

Peggy and Malcolm Cowley; Walker Evans, whose photographs had finally been selected to illustrate the Black Sun edition; and William Carlos Williams and his wife, invited, I suspect, because Crane had used a passage from *In the American Grain* to link "Ave Maria" and the opening section of "Powhatan's Daughter." There were also, of course, friends invited simply because they were friends—everyone from E. E. Cummings and his wife to a sailor, here anonymous, who had the bad grace to become ill on oysters and gin. Hart, who liked to play host, was flushed with triumph. The faith of his friends had been justified by the poem that was at last completed. There were toasts to Hart, to Brooklyn Bridge itself, and to the Crosbys. When, near dawn, the party broke up, it was really only to adjourn; the next day most of the same people reassembled at a party given by Harry Marks, the American distributor of the Black Sun edition. There, Hart accepted the Crosbys' invitation to join them two days later for dinner and the theater.

When the night of December 10 arrived—the night of the theater party—Caresse Crosby and Harry's mother met Margaret Robson and Crane at the Caviar Restaurant. Harry, who was not given to overlooking appointments, had failed to appear at the Crosbys' hotel and now was missing at the restaurant. Both Caresse and Mrs. Crosby were apprehensive.

There was every reason for them to be concerned. Though she said nothing to the others, Caresse could not forget the events of the morning. Harry, at the open window of their twenty-seventh-floor apartment in the Savoy Plaza Hotel, had turned to her, all excitement, to say: "Give me your hand, Caresse. . . . Let's meet the sun death together." She had managed to dissuade him, but death, she knew, was very much on his mind. Margaret Robson knew it, too; for on the night of Hart's party, she and Harry had volunteered to go off to Pineapple Street to augment the dwindling supply of gin. As they walked through the dark Brooklyn streets, Crosby had talked confusedly of the complicated splendors of love and death, and of a great love that somehow should be fulfilled in his own death.

Nevertheless, Hart and the three women managed to get through dinner, Caresse excusing herself from time to time to telephone friends who might know her husband's whereabouts. One of them —the painter, Stanley Mortimer, Jr.—thought Harry might be at his studio in the Hotel des Artistes at 1 West Sixty-seventh Street. He would walk over to check.

Just as the group was about to leave the restaurant, Stanley Mortimer's call came. The studio door was bolted from inside. Urging Caresse to go on to the theater, he promised he would telephone as soon as he could get into the studio. Harry might, after all, merely have fallen asleep.

When they arrived at the Lyceum Theatre—Leslie Howard starring in *Berkeley Square*—no message was waiting. Hart explained at the box office that an important call was expected for Mrs. Crosby. He left his seat number.

The call came at ten o'clock. Hart took it to learn the details of what he had dreaded. It had been necessary to break down the door; then the police had been called. Harry Crosby was dead, in his arms the body of a young woman. Each had been shot through the temple. The pistol, a .25 Belgian automatic, was still in Harry's hand.

No one has ever learned what happened in that studio. There was no note—only the two bodies, fully clothed, facing each other on the bed, a blanket drawn up to their shoulders. The police medical examiner decided that they had entered into a suicide pact.

But at the time of the theater telephone call there was only confusion and shouting on one end of the phone and, on the other, Hart Crane trying to decide how to break the news to Caresse and to Mrs. Crosby.

"We rushed out," Margaret Robson told me, "and we never saw the end of the play, and went to the Hotel des Artistes. I remember there were policemen there, and everyone wanted to go up but we weren't allowed to. And I remember seeing the dial, showing the floors, going up and stopping on the 9th. Like a movie sequence, you know, of a detective story."

For months Hart would be haunted by that night. "I've been all broken up about Harry," he wrote Allen Tate four days after Crosby's death. "I had just had a party or so for them—and all our friends immediately fell in love with them both. I was with Caresse and Harry's mother the evening of [the] so-called suicide, and had to break the news to them. I haven't been worth much since . . ." Almost two months later, in letters to Cleveland friends, he was still compulsively returning to that night, going over, in almost the same language, the events of "the evening when the disaster occurred." "The terrible shock of Harry Crosby's suicide threw me flat . . . I had just given a big party for him . . . I was with his wife and mother . . . In fact it was I who had to bring the terrible news to those two lovely women."

The following months seemed to Hart nothing more than a mechanical round of activity. Caresse Crosby had told him that she was determined to go on with *The Bridge,* and he promised faithfully to have in her hands by New Year's Day all last-minute revisions. She left for France, as planned, on December 13, Harry's mother accompanying her. Hart sent flowers to the ship.

At this stage, he was dissatisfied with only the "Quaker Hill" section, and he devoted day after day to reworking it. He finished on December 26—a little Christmas present from Hart to Hart. Though he was still not altogether happy with what he had produced, he was certain that the revised version functioned properly in the large design of the poem. He sent it off immediately. "I am hastily enclosing the final version of Quaker Hill, which ends my writing on the Bridge. You can now go ahead and finish it all." He apologized—as he always did—for delays. ("I've been slow, Heaven knows, but I know that you will forgive me.") He talked in a general way about the sort of problems that had cropped up as he had polished the troublesome passages. ("I haven't added as many verses to what you took with you as I had expected. I had several more, roughly, in notes, but think that my present condensation is preferable. Quaker Hill is not, after all, one of the major sections of the poem; it is rather by way of an 'accent mark' that it is valuable at all.") He made a change in a line of the dedicatory section. And he insisted that Walker Evans's photograph of barges and tugs go between "Cutty Sark" and "Hatteras." ("That is the 'center' of the book, both physically and symbolically.")

But Crane was by now tired of working on *The Bridge,* and he was willing to admit it. He had done everything he could do; it was time, he felt, to be "between books." He wanted to coast, to enjoy—for a month or two—a life free from the pressures that for more than five years his great project had subjected him to. He wanted to loaf without feeling guilty.

# 33

L oafing without feeling guilty was no easy project for Hart
Crane. In the eyes of many of his friends he wasted a great
deal of his short life, but Crane was his own severest critic;
his letters are filled, as was his conversation, with self-reproach for
misspent time. "Harried by anxieties," as he told one friend, and
beset by minor ailments—toothaches, boils, hives—he alternately
justified and attacked the sprees that, depending on the day, kept
him going or wore him down.

Much as he wished to relax, he worked so hard at it that he
found himself at day's end physically and spiritually exhausted.
Only with people to whom he did not have to "prove" himself was
Hart able to find brief intervals of calm, as on Christmas Day of
1929, a quiet day spent peacefully in the company of a small
bottle of gin and a handsome young sailor, a cheerful blond boy
whom Crane had met some months earlier and to whom he would
eventually attempt to will such little money as he had. It was for
Crane an idyllic interlude, neither young man demanding more of
the other than affection and good talk, the sailor full of stories of
life aboard the U.S.S. *Milwaukee* and Crane—nearly ten years older
and so a fount of worldly wisdom—full of good advice.

Just what that advice was is now well beyond recovery—but one
suspects it was on the order of the advice Crane would two years
later offer in a note announcing his last will and testament: "I
hope you will happily marry and realize some of the conversations we have had together, sometimes." Many of those conversations must have concerned the pain of the kind of love Crane
experienced and their shared hope that the sailor would lead a
more normal life than Crane had known, that he would find the
"right girl," and that in home and family he would discover a life
as good as—if different from—the one he sometimes joined to
Crane's. Their own unstable world was bound, they knew, to be
compounded of brief meetings, letters that would necessarily be
casual, and much loneliness. (When a week after Christmas the
sailor "sailed away . . . until June," Hart wrote Caresse Crosby
that he was "already missing him a lot." And reports of the sailor's
faithfulness—a faithfulness unanticipated by Crane and conse-

quently valued—punctuated Crane's conversation with Margaret Robson and Sam Loveman and his letters to those persons he felt he could trust: "I had a sweet letter from ——— lately. Says he hasn't used his shore leave since he left N.Y. and won't until he gets back here in May. That's really too good to be true!" For the friends tried to be good for one another, Hart in his letters recommending that the sailor go sightseeing in Jamaica—a little shore leave, after all, would do no harm—and the sailor offering not merely congratulations on the publication of *The Bridge* but admonitions that Hart settle down once more to weekly-paycheck work: "You haven't gotten a job yet. Well I won't say what I think of you, Hart, but I'd like to . . .")

Though a sailor could give Hart a week of happiness during Christmas of 1929 and during a few days in May of 1930 when, back from Cuba, he spent his leave at Hart's apartment, most of Crane's relaxed moments were of far shorter duration. There were parts of evenings with Margaret Robson and her friend Bill Adams, both of whom valued him not so much for his wit, though they admired it, as for the warmth of his affectionate good will. There were wilder evenings with Bob Thompson, a good drinking companion whom Hart in the summer would recommend to Caresse Crosby as "a former sailor who has got tired of office work and expects to hit the deck again for awhile . . ." And there was one most quiet April evening spent with Bill Wright, who, reappearing like a specter of lost boyhood, left Hart for months flooded with echoing memories of clean childhood days impossible to recapture, impossible to forget: memories of a good-luck pat on the back as Hart had years earlier headed in to Miss Peters's German class, his half-finished homework tucked between half-finished poems; of long talks after school as the friends walked, dancing pumps under arms, toward Eleanor T. Flynn's dancing school; of tennis in Wade Park; of secretly shared cigars in Hart's tower bedroom; of the attic discovery, one impossible-to-return-to day, of a bundle of his Grandmother Hart's dusty love letters.

Because such friends demanded nothing of Hart but himself, he was able in their company to escape the pressure many other friends—unintentionally, needless to say—subjected him to. For "literary" friends would soon be judging *The Bridge,* many of them reviewing it, most of them asking Crane that question he had no answer for: "What next?"

When he gave an answer, he did his best to be honest. The brutal work that had gone into finishing *The Bridge* had left him exhausted, and he found himself dissatisfied with every new poem he attempted. Perhaps, he reasoned, it would be best to drop poetry for a while. Perhaps he should try to lead a "commercial" life.

The one poem that in this time he forced himself to finish—"To the Cloud Juggler," which, at Caresse Crosby's request, he had offered for a group of poems dedicated to Harry Crosby's memory —seemed to Hart initially so unsatisfactory that he did his best to withdraw it in the same letter in which he volunteered it: "I'm not at my best right now—so there will be no offence if you do not care to use it in 'transition.'" He was, he explained, "'all sixes and sevens' these days trying to find work and keep my apartment." The remnants of his inheritance were gone; Liveright had paid a small advance on the American edition of *The Bridge*, but that too was gone; $200 of the $250 that was to have been his fee for the Paris edition of *The Bridge* had been spent on passage from Paris to New York, and the remaining $50 would not reach him until early February—when it would serve principally to re-pay debts. There is no wonder, therefore, that at the end of Janu-ary, thoughts other than those about new poems filled his mind. "I've got all I can expect for many months from Liveright—and I don't want to write anything for ages. But we'll see if we can get some chance at ads!"

This revulsion against writing is oddly both supported and be-lied by the poetic fragments begun at this time—phrases scrawled on envelopes, titles jotted down on scraps of paper. For Crane was frightened by the success that—if he were lucky—*The Bridge* might bring him. If the poem were acknowledged to be as great as he hoped it was, he might find himself in the position of the flash-in-the-pan artist whose one effort is unbeatable—not by others but by himself. "I really don't want to write any poetry for a while now, but just the same feel somehow depressed that I haven't some ambitious project on hand to take the place of the Bridge."

This literary dryness was linked, he knew, to fears that *The Bridge* would be attacked by reviewers; consequently, he did every-thing in his power to assist his publishers in "placing" the book well. When Herbert Weinstock wrote to say that he admired Crane's poetry and that he was interested in reviewing the new book, Crane composed an answer that was tactfully grateful for "welcome en-couragement" but that went on to detail some of the uneasiness that he lived with: "I hope The Bridge will not disappoint your expectations. . . . It turned out to be a five-year job, and while I am relieved by its completion I am also left, for the time being, at least, with anything but a fertile viewpoint."

Letters to literary friends—potential reviewers, all—posed even more of a problem in tact, a problem that was frequently com-pounded by temporary financial indebtedness to the same friends. "It was *so* kind of you to have replied so quickly and generously! I feel quite guilty for not having thanked you sooner," one letter to Waldo Frank begins; but soon it turns to the matter that kept Crane from writing and from job hunting: "It was reassuring to know that you got your copy of the Bridge. . . . There's much in it new to your eyes, and I am quite tremulous for your opinion." Crane had staked his future on the success of the poem. Until he knew its fate he could do nothing to force himself into coherent action of any sort: "I've really never known so discouraging a time job-hunting. Insomnia has got me on the rack—and I really can't envisage just what is in store, but perhaps after the reviews of the Bridge come out (Liveright's edition is due out next week) I'll possibly be able to rally my confidence and make a better impression in 'the business world.' "

Through the winter and spring, Crane moved from agonies of disappointment to peaks of optimism and then to new agonies of disappointment. Most frequently, disappointment won out. First there had been delays in the distribution of the Black Sun edition, then the discovery that reviews would be postponed until after the end-of-March publication of the Liveright edition, and finally a very awkward exchange of letters with Caresse Crosby, who, startled to hear of the postponed reviews, wrote to ask exactly what had been the fate of all the handsome copies she had supplied.

"Hart, I am really terribly hurt and upset by what you said about the reviews of 'The Bridge,' " she had written.

> I think that since I sent the review copies six weeks before the Liveright edition appeared and worked so hard over it, didn't object to the Liveright edition so soon, *provided* as you know that *our* book was reviewed first and was told that night by your friends that they would review it if I sent them copies that to have them wait over for Liveright and only give us partial credit is one of the most unkind and disloyal things I've ever heard of—I am *furious* really furious—I suppose they are afraid to get in wrong with Liveright. That is the way the world is run over there, I know, and it makes me contemptuous and disbelieve in human relations.

No easy letter to answer, it cost Hart more sleepless nights. Finally he wrote a long account of the facts of reviewing: no edition of 250 copies could hope for coverage in major periodicals; he could, however, encourage friends to mention the expensive and beautiful Paris edition. Beyond this gesture, he could do little.

> I thought you understood that I would endeavor wherever possible, to have the two editions reviewed together, with yours listed first, and with as much description of *your* edition as I could properly influence the reviewers to attempt within the restrictions of the periodicals they were writing for. This, I have done.
>
> You must realize that, as author of the book, I have certain boundaries of modesty to observe . . . I can decently urge [friends] only about so far, and no farther. I have no right, nor would I exercise it regardless, to attempt to influence other reviewers of the Bridge, whether they have copies of the Paris edition or not. I have done my utmost, wherever it has been permissible to sug-

gest a leading description of the Black Sun edition, and if you persist in lamenting the results I'm afraid you will lead me to regret the whole matter of the de luxe edition, however splendid it is.

Don't mistake me, Caresse, please! I could never lament anything about it except your bitterness or unhappiness, and the fact that you might think me dishonest or ungrateful, as your letter seems to indicate. You ought to know my gratitude for all your interest and Harry's by this time. But it's almost too much, now, that you feel me to have been deceptive and insincere. . . . For our continued friendship's sake, though, Caresse, please don't continue to attribute to me so formidable a control of the press as you apparently imagine me to have!

While Hart waited for reviews to appear, he made sporadic efforts to find work, but in the bleak winter and spring of 1930, jobs were simply not to be found. "Better write me henceforth at Rural Delivery, Patterson, New York," Hart wrote Caresse Crosby. "I haven't enough money to pay for my next month's rent in the city, and the terrible financial depression makes any employment for me extremely improbable during the coming summer. I can retire here, I guess, and listen to the mocking bird awhile." For Hart had entered on a year of aimless wandering, no address good for more than two or three months, a year spent drifting from the Brooklyn Heights basement apartment into which he had moved on January 2, up to Patterson for a two-week April visit, back to New York until the end of June, back to Patterson for a few weeks in July, on to New Hampshire for a few weeks with E. E. Cummings and his wife, then back to Patterson, then back to New York, then an autumn of borrowed rooms and a short stay in a Greenwich Village hotel, and—at the end of the year—a return to Ohio. During all this time, he managed somehow to remain solvent. Every time he seemed certain to starve, someone would pay a debt, volunteer a loan, offer brief and inadequate support, feed him or clothe him. Yet it is extraordinary how little hard cash passed through his hands. There had been several hundred dollars from Liveright early in the year, $50 from Caresse Crosby, a $100 "loan" from Otto Kahn on April 8, several hundred dollars of erratic support from his father during the summer and fall, and the $200 Levinson prize from *Poetry* magazine in October. That, so far as I can determine, comprises Crane's recorded income. There had, of course, been loans from all his friends to tide him over rough spots; but loans had to be repaid, and, in spite of a few slips, Crane was scrupulous to keep track of and ultimately to settle debts.

And yet Crane managed superficially to be the ebullient good companion he had always been. Though his limited cash prevented him from doing much in his own right, he found that the publication of *The Bridge* led to a series of publisher's parties, at most of which he was lavishly wined and dined. "I am still having tremors from the outpouring of whisky at a rip-roaring affair given by Liveright last night," he told Caresse Crosby. "Yes, I met the famous Mr. Hoffenstein—but did not mention what we did to his verses on our taxi ride. Or WAS it Hoffenstein? ! ! ! I really forget. Anyway there were plenty of actresses . . ." Sometimes actresses, sometimes heiresses. At another publication party—this one "a most amusing and successful afternoon party at the Ritz" that had been given to herald the publication of Peggy Hopkins Joyce's *Men, Marriage and Me*—Crane not only met but danced with and finally proposed to the fabulous lady. "I danced with her," he told Sam Loveman, who said in turn, "Do tell?" "Yes. I danced and I danced until finally she said that she had to turn to some of the others and do the courtesy act." Loveman asked what Crane had done then. "Why," Crane answered, "I proposed to her." "What did she say?" " 'Well,' she said, 'Mr. Crane, there are at least two ahead of you. I hope you will have the patience to wait.' "

With no real prospects for work and with insomnia filling his nights, Crane had plenty of time to devote to books, to art galleries, and—when he was invited along by friends—to the theater or to performances of dance or music. Robert Graves's autobiography, *Good-bye to All That*, seemed to him "amazing," and a commentary by Rebecca West on Joyce's progress on *Finnegans Wake* so stimulated him that, stimulated also by hard cider, he got off an exclamatory telegram to Caresse Crosby in Paris. Angna Enters's pantomime was, in his opinion, "wonderful! Humor, pathos, tragedy—the whole gamut of the emotions." At the Museum of Modern Art, he studied the "marvelous collection of modern French painters." And in private galleries, he particularly admired work by Peter Blume, Georgia O'Keeffe, and John Marin.

There was also time for conversation. Crane made a point of looking up friends from earlier days, on at least some occasions bringing with him a set of galleys for *The Bridge*. Dorothy Norman met him at one of these visits. Crane had decided to call on Alfred Stieglitz, his attitude, Miss Norman recalled, both "reverential" and cheerful. She felt that in Stieglitz's presence the extroverted man she had heard about toned down his behavior. Stieglitz, she recalled, was flattered by the visit and grateful to see that Crane—in spite of difficult days—still felt a total commitment to excellence.

It is, indeed, that total commitment to excellence that is most difficult to suggest, though it weaves a significant pattern through Hart's relationships with Gorham Munson, Gene Toomer, Waldo Frank, and with Stieglitz himself. For if Hart was for one audience the "roaring boy" Malcolm Cowley has so effectively captured in his commentaries on Crane, he was also—sometimes for the same audience—one of the most dedicated writers ever to live. "I thought of him," Isidor Schneider told me, "as the most complete artist that I had ever met. By that I mean that I felt that he was an artist to his fingertips, that he was an artist in almost every respect of even his daily living. He was not only interested in literature, he was interested in all the arts; and his interest was always an intimate and an intense one." There was, Schneider felt, a wholeness to the man that transcended momentary crises: "He walked as if he were dancing. There was a grace in his movements. They were those of a dancer . . . There was a certain 'givingness' in the way he spoke which made you feel you were with a gracious and a 'giving' man. . . . Unlike so many other writers, who in their estimates of each other's works were backbiting, were withholding of praise, were competitive, Hart, in his estimate of other people's work, was generous. When I say generous, I don't mean that he overvalued them, I mean that he was glad to pass on a good judgment rather than a bad one. I think if he didn't like anything, he simply didn't say anything." Hart's conversation, Schneider felt, was extraordinary for its eloquence: "He didn't search for the right word. It seemed to come. . . . His conversation was usually very picturesque and vivid, and you felt that he was in his talk re-experiencing and transmitting to you very vivid experiences. I recall that when he came back from the Isle of Pines he spoke principally of the insect life of the island and with such animation, with descriptions that were so life-like, that one almost felt that one was within a world of insects . . ." Yet in spite of such eloquence, Hart was unemployed—and likely to remain so. Like other of Hart's friends, Schneider was concerned for his welfare. What, in the midst of the Depression, could Hart turn to? "I never felt, in the case of Hart," Schneider said, "that he could have been a journalist or a newspaperman or a businessman. I always felt, 'I am in the presence of an artist.' "

We are now well aware how much of an artist Hart Crane was; at the time of the publication of *The Bridge,* however, there was no agreement at all on the quality of his work. Most of Crane's friends —for that matter, most of the men and women he met casually— praised *The Bridge*; but face-to-face praise is one thing, public praise is another.

Hart was realistic. He knew that reviews of his book were bound to be brief, that sales would be small. And yet there is no question that he dreamed of his book's being recognized for the major work it is and that he hoped it would be read not just by poetry lovers but by a significant part of the population. Dreams of this sort—in the soup-kitchen year of 1930—were unrealistic; but they were founded on an essential element in Crane's personality, the very element that drove him to write. For in his own eyes, as Isidor Schneider in his talks with Crane recognized, Crane was a would-be "social poet." He really did want to touch in a most intimate way the life of his country. He wanted, as Schneider told me, really "to affect his fellow human beings."

Perhaps it was for this reason that Crane responded so directly to his reviews. Shortly after the middle of April they began to arrive from the clipping service he had subscribed to. And in an oblique way they shaped his mood. During the six months that they trickled in, they kept Crane on edge, contributing their share to the block against writing that now dominated him.

Not that the reviews were bad. On the whole they were enthusiastic. One of the first to be published, that by Herbert Weinstock, announced in its lead sentence, "The poetry of Hart Crane brings back to American literature a spaciousness which it has lacked since Whitman and Melville," and concluded: "It must be recorded somehow, somewhere, to the credit of our era if it recognizes Hart Crane and rightly praises him instead of leaving his reputation lying about to be resurrected by our descendants." Granville Hicks, reviewing the book for the New York *World* and for *The Nation*, anticipated its future: "Long essays could be, and one trusts will be, written about 'The Bridge.' There is not an angle from which it cannot profitably be scrutinized. Its technique should be studied, to bring out the principles by which the variations of rhythm and rhyme are determined. Its imagery, as even a few quotations show, is sound and amazingly original. The methods of its symbolism should be considered. Its philosophical implications are worthy of comment. Its affirmativeness should be contrasted with the elegiacism of most contemporary poetry." The poem, Hicks made clear, had to be read as a single coherent structure; if it were read that way, it would be recognized as a masterpiece. "It cannot be doubted that 'The Bridge' is as important a poem as has been written in our time. That it will be subjected to careful critical scrutiny is certain, and it is probable that that scrutiny will find in it a greatness beyond the reach of a reviewer's superlatives." Louis Untermeyer, in *The Saturday Review of Literature*, insisted on that same unity: "A set of disparate poems has been integrated by vital figures, the figures having been lifted into the realm of national myth."

Unlike Untermeyer and Hicks, who stressed its coherence, most of the reviewers who praised the poem distinguished between "successful" and "less successful" sections. Horace Gregory, reviewing it for the New York *Herald Tribune*, admired "Cutty Sark" and "The Tunnel" but felt that "in other sections, the design wavers, leaps into consciousness and then falls into darkness." Vincent McHugh, who reviewed it for the New York *Evening Post*, liked "Indiana" (he called it "concrete threnody") and "Virginia" ("a rain-clear and rain-cool instrumentation"). Malcolm Cowley, in *The New Republic*, announced that "The River" section was "one of the important poems of our age" and that it was almost matched in quality by "Cutty Sark," "The Dance," and "Ave Maria." William

Rose Benét, in the second review to be printed in *The Saturday Review of Literature,* complained of "too great haphazardness in the organization of the material" but was impressed by "Harbor Dawn," "The River," and "The Tunnel." Every section, finally, had its champion; but almost all the champions implicitly accepted Benét's charge of haphazard organization. Even Cowley, who described it as "a unified group of fifteen poems," qualified his assertion that "the poem has succeeded" by immediately adding, "—not wholly, of course, for its faults are obvious; but still it has succeeded to an impressive degree." ("The faults of 'The Bridge,' " he charitably added, "I shall leave to other reviewers.")

"Faults"—though not always the same ones—were pointed out by several reviewers, most conspicuous of whom was Percy Hutchinson, who in *The New York Times Book Review* decided that the poem was characterized by a "lack of intelligibility." ("In spite of its glitter and the seeming intellectual importance," he concluded, the poem is "a piece that is in the main spurious as poetry.") Odell Shepard, reviewing it in *The Bookman,* said that the "thought-process" of the poem "begins with false principles and proceeds with frenzy in the wrong direction." For Shepard almost everything about the poem was bad. The poem was little more than "a constant succession of loud noises" that revealed nothing about America; instead it displayed only perverse and pointless "originality": "Mr. Crane lashes and spurs a fancy already jaded. He rejects every natural association of ideas as commonplace; every phrase that might have been written in a normal mood by a normal mind he must torture beyond recognition."

Though reviews of this sort were irritating to Crane, he took them in his stride. Harder to stomach was a long, painfully learned and sometimes pompous critique by Yvor Winters. Hart spoke of it to Isidor Schneider, in a letter thanking him for his own sensitive reception of the poem.

I cannot but realize that these are not easy times for you in a number of respects. That makes me all the more grateful for the evident care which you took in your review of *The Bridge.* Certainly I don't see what more I could ask for—than your generous credit to and recognition of practically all the aspirations implicit in the poem. . . . If you have read Winters' attack in the June issue of "Poetry" you cannot have been more astonished than I was to note the many reversals of opinion he has undergone . . .

Had it not been for our previous extended correspondence I would not, of course, have written him about it. But as things stood I could hardly let silence infer an acceptance on my part of all the wilful distortions of meaning, misappropriations of opinion, pedantry and pretentious classification—besides illogic —which his review presents par excellence. I must read what prejudices he defends, I understand, against writing about subways, in the anti-humanist symposium. Poets should defer alluding to the sea, also, I presume, until Mr. Winters has got an invitation for a cruise!

Crane was disturbed enough by Winters's review to send Allen Tate a carbon of his "answer." Tate's return letter of June 10, 1930, is pertinent; for Tate, whose review of *The Bridge* was about to appear in *Hound and Horn*, had taken a position not altogether dissimilar from that of Winters.

I have read the copy of your letter to Winters, and I intend to get the June Poetry as soon as I can. Your case against Winters seems to be very strong. . . .

I too felt that your tribute to Whitman was, while not excessive, certainly sentimental in places, particularly at the end of Cape Hatteras. But more than this I could not say except that in some larger and vaguer sense your vision of American life comes from Whitman, or from the same sources in the American consciousness as his. I am unsympathetic to this tradition, and it seems to me that you should be too. The equivalent of Whitmanism in the economic and moral aspect of America in the last sixty years is the high-powered industrialism that you, no less than I, feel is a menace to the spiritual life in this country. In the end, this is all I can see in him; though he did write some great poetry.

Winters is a puzzle to me. He is extremely intelligent, and again he can show himself remarkably obtuse. I suppose he has no sense of humor whatever—he has a sort of humorless logic which ignores the very simple and unexplainable elements in human relations, and hence he is very apt to go wrong in his judgments of poetry. Have you ever observed the discrepancy between his particular judgments, his almost incredible admiration for second-rate poets, and the extremely just notions he has of the function of poetry in general? This gets at the problem of Winters somehow. He is just a difficult fellow, with all kinds of qualities. I am sure I couldn't get along with him five minutes; but at the same time I know he has some admirable traits, even a certain nobility of character if I can believe a great variety of testimony about him.

Before Hart answered Tate's letter, he read Tate's own review of *The Bridge*, a review that praised Crane's technical proficiency and the richness of his poetic texture but that went on to be severely critical of the larger structure of the poem. In Tate's eyes it was flawed because it lacked "a coherent plot, whether symbolic or narrative." The Whitmanesque theme of an American destiny was, Tate felt, historically unjustifiable and poetically unworkable: "The episodes of *The Bridge* follow out of no inherent necessity in the

theme, for they are arbitrary, and appear not organically but anal-
ogously. The form is static; each section is a new start, and but
for the broken chronology the poem constantly begins over again."
Viewing *The Bridge* this way, Tate felt free to insist that the poems
comprising it had to be judged independently. "The River" was in
his opinion "a masterpiece of order and style," whereas "Indiana"
was nothing more than "a nightmare of sentimentality and false
writing." The points about the Whitman tradition that Tate had
stressed in his letter were restated in the review. Philosophically,
Crane's poem, Tate said, reduced to "a sentimental muddle of Walt
Whitman and the pseudo-primitivism of Sherwood Anderson and
Dr. W. C. Williams, raised to a vague and transcendental reality."
Such a position Tate regarded as romantic optimism. "In his rejection of a rational and qualitative will," Tate concluded, "Crane
follows the main stream of romanticism in the last hundred years.
. . . If this impulse is dying out, it is as fortunate for its reputation
as it is remarkable that it should be represented at the end by a
poetry so rich, finely wrought, and powerful as Hart Crane's."

Just as he had felt compelled to answer Winters's charges, Crane
felt compelled to answer those Tate made in his review and in his
letter. The letter he wrote Tate has been taken by some Crane
scholars as a confession of failure, a sign that he accepted Tate's
analysis of the structural and philosophical weaknesses of *The
Bridge*. Such an interpretation blurs, I think, argument and polite-
ness. Crane accepted the seriousness of Tate's analysis and he answered it seriously. He knew that Tate was trying to be just, and
he wanted his answer to be equally just.

> Your last good letter and the admirable review of The Bridge
> in the Hound & Horn deserved an earlier response, but time has
> somehow just been drifting by without my being very conscious
> of it. For one thing, I have been intending to get hold of a copy
> of The Hound & Horn and give your review a better reading,
> before replying, than I could achieve at the tables in Brentano's
> when I was in town about two weeks ago. I still haven't a copy
> and consequently may wrong you in making any comments
> whatever. But as I don't want to delay longer I hope you'll par-
> don any discrepancies.
> The fact that you posit the Bridge at the end of a tradition
> of romanticism may prove to have been an accurate prophecy,
> but I don't yet feel that such a statement can be taken as a fore-
> gone conclusion. A great deal of romanticism may persist
> —of the sort to deserve serious consideration, I mean.
> But granting your accuracy—I shall be humbly grateful if the
> Bridge can fulfil simply the metaphorical inferences of its title.
> . . . You will admit our age (at least our predicament) to be
> one of transition. If the Bridge, embodying as many anomalies
> as you find in it, yet contains as much authentic poetry here and

there as even Winters grants,—then perhaps it can serve as . .
a link connecting certain chains of the past to certain chains
and tendencies of the future. In other words, a diagram or
"process" in the sense that Genevieve Taggard refers to all my
work in estimating Kunitz's achievement in the enclosed review.
This gives it no more interest than as a point of chronological
reference, but "nothing ventured, nothing gained"—and I can't
help thinking that my mistakes may warn others who may later
be tempted to an interest in similar subject matter.

Personally I think that Taggard is a little too peremptory in
dispensing with Kunitz's "predecessors." We're all unconscious
evolutionists, I suppose, but she apparently belongs to the more
rabid ranks. . . . Taggard, like Winters, isn't looking for poetry
any more. Like Munson, they are both in pursuit of some cure-
all. Poetry as poetry (and I don't mean merely decorative verse)
isn't worth a second reading any more. Therefore—away with
Kubla Khan, out with Marlowe, and to hell with Keats! It's a
pity, I think. So many true things have a way of coming out all
the better without the strain to sum up the universe in one
impressive little pellet. I admit that I don't answer the requirements. My vision of poetry *is* too personal to "answer the call."
And if I ever write any more verse it will probably be at least
as personal as the idiom of *White Buildings* whether anyone
cares to look at it or not.

This personal note is doubtless responsible for what you term
as sentimentality in my attitude toward Whitman. It's true that
my rhapsodic address to him in the Bridge exceeds any exact
evaluation of the man. I realized that in the midst of the composition. But since you and I hold such divergent prejudices regarding the value of the materials and events that W. responded
to, and especially as you, like so many others, never seem to
have read his Democratic Vistas and other of his statements
sharply decrying the materialism, industrialism, etc. of which
you name him the guilty and hysterical spokesman, there
isn't much use in my tabulating the qualified, yet persistent reasons I have for my admiration of him, and my allegiance to the
positive and universal tendencies implicit in nearly all his best
work. You've heard me roar at too many of his lines to doubt
that I can spot his worst, I'm sure.

It amuses me to see how Taggard takes up some of Winters'
claims against me (I expected this and look for more) . . .

Crane was discouraged by the reception given his poem. Yet he
never repudiated *The Bridge*, the integrity of its design, the validity of its theme. When he was having great difficulty forging its
final tight structure, he sometimes told close friends—Sam Loveman, among others—that his writing seemed to him nothing more
than rhetoric. But these statements came out of frustration and

were more often than not countered moments later when the plan of the poem would again be clear to him and he would be able to work. At such triumphant moments, rhetoric would support vision and he could anticipate the time when, thirty or fifty or a hundred years after his death, readers would discover not "message," or "rhetoric," or "great phrasemaking," or even theme or structure, but rather the visceral impact of a work of art. No longer dismembering it, they would read the poem end to end in the same way that Crane himself had read those works that anticipate it: *Ulysses*, *The Waste Land*, "Crossing Brooklyn Ferry," "The Wreck of the Deutschland." He could anticipate the time when the poem would be accepted in its totality, would become as much a part of its readers as body or soul.

Perhaps we are becoming those readers. For most of the poem's recent critics accept the mosaic plan of the work, discovering beneath its "fragmented" surface an extraordinary coherence. Perhaps, indeed, we are becoming what Crane looked for and could never find: an audience delighted by relationship, by interconnection, by radiant, harmonic wholeness.

# 34

I n the autumn of 1930, Crane could sometimes see his poem as
a coherent form. Yet he could see his recent life only as a
series of "doldrums," listless inactions, fragmented and meaningless. "My summer seems like a blank to me right now," he wrote
Tate early in September. "Perhaps my study of Dante—the 'Commedia' which I had never touched before—will have been seen to
have given it some significance, but that isn't much to boast of."

There had, of course, been correspondence about *The Bridge,*
Crane's grateful letters going out to those who had seemed to
understand it. Paul Rosenfeld had in the spring suggested that
Crane write an explanatory account of the poem for *The New
American Caravan,* a project that fell through when Hart was in-
capable of expanding the notes he had once prepared for Otto
Kahn. The correspondence with Tate about the poem also con-
tinued, Tate trying now to summarize his feelings about all of
Crane's poetry.

> I hope you have had another look at my review. A first read-
> ing emphasizes what we are looking for or don't want to see, and
> I am sure your second reading will convince you of the very
> tentative character of my predictions about the romantic move-
> ment. Many people seem to prefer The Bridge to White Build-
> ings, and think it an "advance" on your old style. I am not sure
> that it is, and I am not sure that, given your particular kind of
> talent and style, an advance was necessary to clinch your posi-
> tion. You have never surpassed certain poems of the first book,
> and I think it is something of a compliment to believe that you
> never will. I am glad therefore to hear that you may return to
> the idiom of that book; you hadn't by any means exhausted it.
> The best of The Bridge is to be found in another form in White
> Buildings—though I don't for a moment say that the poetry in
> the former does not stand up by itself.

Readers other than professional critics were also showing an interest. Eda Lou Walton added *The Bridge* to the course in con-

temporary poetry she taught at New York University and radio station WNYC scheduled Crane for a five-minute reading.

The reading was cancelled, a fact that accidentally provides us with one of the best "external" glimpses of Crane that has survived. For Crane left the studio to visit Sam Loveman, whose other visitor was that indefatigable letter writer, Howard P. Lovecraft. A midnight letter to Lovecraft's aunt focused on Crane.

> I take my pen in hand to relate the events of the day in usual fashion—Saturday, May 24, 1930. . . . About 8 o'clock the bell rang, & there appeared that tragically drink-riddled but now eminent friend of Loveman's whom I met in Cleveland in 1922, & once or twice later in New York—the poet Hart Crane, whose new book, "The Bridge," has made him one of the most celebrated & talked-of figures of contemporary American letters. He had been scheduled to speak over the radio during the evening; but a shipwreck off the coast (demanding the use of the ether for important messages) had cut off all local radio programmes & left him free. When he entered, his discourse was of alcoholics in various phases—& of the correct amount of whiskey one ought to drink in order to speak well in public—but as soon as a bit of poetic and philosophic discussion sprang up, this sordid side of his strange dual personality slipped off like a cloak, & left him as a man of great scholarship, intelligence, & aesthetic taste, who can argue as interestingly & profoundly as anyone I have ever seen. Poor devil—he has "arrived" at last as a standard American poet seriously regarded by all reviewers & critics; yet at the very crest of his fame he is on the verge of psychological, physical, & financial disintegration, & with no certainty of ever having the inspiration to write a major work of literature again. After about three hours of acute & intelligent argument poor Crane left—to hunt up a new supply of whiskey & banish reality for the rest of the night! . . . His case is surely a sad one—all the more so because of his great attainments & of the new fame which he is so ill-fitted to carry for any considerable time. He looks more weather-beaten & drink-puffed than he did in the past, though the shaving off of his moustache has somewhat improved him. . . . Crane, by the way, was interested to hear of my liking for *Charleston*; & though he has never seen it, talked of going there himself as a refugee from a New York he has come to detest.

Crane's detestation of New York City grew more and more obsessive during this time. New York became for him a symbol of his weaknesses—both symbol and temptation—and he tried very hard to locate places in which he would be able to sober up. Patterson seemed for a time an answer ("There's no liquor out here, at any rate," he wrote Paul Rosenfeld), but Patterson could offer no employment and Crane's visits were of short duration. "After a couple of absolutely necessary weeks of relaxation in the country I'm back in town, resuming my apparently timeless quest for employment," he wrote Bill Wright at the end of April; but the letter could have been written at almost any time during the year. For New York City's glamour was gone. "When I visited him in New York," Eugene MacCown told me, "he was living in a tiny Brooklyn basement apartment. . . . What I remember about the place was the gallon of bootleg whiskey that he kept by his bed."

MacCown was full of Paris, and Hart, who had found Paris—indeed, much of France—disappointing, was suddenly irrationally nostalgic for the soft French countryside where a little more than a year earlier he had struggled to shape *The Bridge*. "How I'd love to be with you out at Le Moulin now!" he immediately wrote Caresse Crosby. "New York is so exhausting—and rather loveless, you know. Money-making is its exclusive concern. I want to get away soon if I don't have better prospects here than I seem to be getting —to the Patterson country, at least, for my chances for Europe don't seem very likely for a while."

Each Patterson interval, however, intensified the pain of his return to the "barren . . . harried" pursuit of money, sex, alcohol that Hart's New York days now reduced to. "Have you been out fishing yet?" he wrote Bill Wright after one such return. "Up in the woods recently I went out one day to a nearby stream with Malcolm Cowley and we managed to hook an infinitesimal trout!" The $100 "loan" from Otto Kahn permitted two weeks of country spring, but the escape was too brief to be meaningful. "I remember the primroses in the window boxes last year at this season," he wrote Caresse Crosby from Patterson. "Spring is slower here than in France. There are just a few pussy-willows out here, so far, and a few robins. But the frogs have begun their shrilling in the marshes."

To be forced to abandon springtime and robins for cement, closed agency doors, and city filth was more than Crane was able to take. If he had to starve, he reasoned, why shouldn't he starve in a gracious world? Wildly drunk, he composed a cablegram announcing his immediate departure for Caresse Crosby's French country estate, only to retract the announcement the next morning.

> I'm awfully sorry to have put you to the bother of answering that cable I sent. As a matter of fact I had a serious intention of coming, but only for about three hours, after prolonged tippling with a friend of mine who is sailing on that date and who had persuaded me to accept a passage from him and go along too. For reasons too numerous to mention I couldn't soberly consider the matter, but my cable to you got off before the alcoholic vapors had let go . . .
>
> I suppose you'll be . . . at Cannes, and that would augur well for good company and a pleasant summer. Where I shall be

heaven only knows. . . . An astrologer has just told me that I'm due to be near the water, salt water, and perhaps on it. Purser or deck-swabber, I shouldn't mind either so as to get out of this hot furnace for awhile.

Maybe some job or other will show up next fall; certainly it seems hopeless right now. And so are my brains, preoccupied with the stupidity of the whole business . . .

All through the spring, Hart's sense of disorder, of chaos, had deepened. One of his closest friends in this troubled time was Margaret Robson. Since those days in early winter when she had typed the final draft of *The Bridge*—Alfred Cortot's recording of Franck's *Variations symphoniques* alternating on the phonograph with Sophie Tucker and Marlene Dietrich—they had come to trust each other completely. "I think," Hart told one friend later in the year, "that if things had been different—if I'd led a normal life and had had normal love affairs—that she is a woman I might have wanted to marry." Certainly, they valued each other, did their best to help each other, felt free to be completely honest with each other. She kept on hand in her Bank Street apartment cans of tomatoes and tomato juice, Hart's favorite cure for the hives that plagued him after too much Prohibition rotgut. ("Hives Tomato Juice," he would assure her solemnly, was the only remedy for his ailment.) When he was flush, he would take her to Chumley's for drinks. But more often than not, they would end up in her apartment. "Hart trusted me because he knew I loved him dearly," she told me. "And he would behave very well with me, when he might not with a lot of other people, no matter how drunk he was or rambunctious. He knew he could always call me up and come to the apartment and feel at home. . . . He was the subject of a lot of conversation in the literati crowd. They used to love to expatiate on his wilder episodes, throwing victrolas out of second story windows, and that kind of thing. . . . All of this was deeply disturbing to Hart. He needed to be accepted for himself."

No one at this time had much money. The Wall Street crash had wiped out everybody's reserves. Margaret Robson found herself in the spring of 1930—after the crash and the crash of her marriage to Ernest Robson—the possessor of a bank account reduced to $500. Hart, who had no bank account at all, discussed with her the plan she had for making her money give her, if nothing else, a pleasant summer. She bought a nice new tent, a nice new knapsack, and a nice new set of blue enamel dishes. She bought a gasoline stove. ("Little Miss Campcook," Hart was to christen it.) And she began a summer of weekend campouts on the rolling Patterson acres owned by Eva Parker.

With Margaret Robson away weekends and no prospects of a job, Hart abandoned the pretense of looking for work. He again wrote his father, asking for minimal support, locked the door of his basement apartment, and, on the first weekend in June, joined Peggy as she headed for the hills. "Two days with Peggy Robson in her tent," he wrote Sam Loveman, "long walks and clear skies, have brought me back to something like normalcy, which is more than two days more in that apartment could have done under any conditions! I have my room at Mrs. Turner's to work in, during the day . . . and a tent is better than I thought for sleeping." His plans for the summer were still anything but settled. "I hope to have some other arrangements later on, if I remain up here," he told Loveman. "Since hearing Peter Blume talk about Charleston I don't fancy that idea so much—but Emil may get me a boat job. In which case the horoscope will be justified! I'm not worrying much what happens as yet."

Peggy Robson matched Hart's high spirits. She raced him to the spring in which they attempted to catch frogs (potential frogs' legs as a test for Little Miss Campcook's versatility), joined him in building up the evening campfire before the tent, and talked far into the night about poetry, music, and painting. By mid-week, Hart knew that, for a little while at least, he would stay put. "It's so lovely out here I've decided to stay at least for two weeks—possibly a month," he wrote Loveman. He telephoned Lorna Dietz at her office at the American Book Company, offering her his apartment while he was away, and arranged for Loveman to see that his mail got to him.

For a while Margaret Robson's tent was his Patterson headquarters, though he dropped in on all the neighbors when she was away. "Peggy has been up again this weekend," he wrote Loveman on June 8, "and is mailing this for me in town tonight. . . . It was even hot up here. I spent most of the time over at Bill Brown's. Sue had to be in town for work and that left Bill all alone with an irritable infant, nearly beside himself with eczema. There wasn't much sleep for either of us, but I was glad to be of a little service —and as you know, I always enjoy Bill's company."

As writers from the city gathered for the summer, parties became more frequent, those people who were able to earn a living coming out for weekends. "Are you having those Big Hot City Blues?" Hart was soon writing to Lorna Dietz, who was sweltering in his apartment. "I have looked that malady up in my Brittanica and its truly Roman name is SILENCIA PONDEROSO BOREALIS." She should try to get up for the weekend, join the party: "We all want to see you, Sue, Bill, Gwyllim, Emil, Fitzi, Tiger Titty-Tat, and ——— Buff!"

Toward the end of June, Hart's old room at Mrs. Turner's became available, just in time for the round of parties that had as their excuse the Fourth of July. "There were three great Fourth parties," Crane wrote Tate. "(1) at Schuyler's place, Amawalk, (2) at Peter Blume's, who has rented the abandoned chapel above Fitzi's, and (3) at Brown's. I'm just recovering." Hart's "recovery" followed not only a week of strenuous drinking but also a knock-down, drag-out quarrel with Mrs. Turner. For years the old woman had been Hart's great defender, an apologist for his "weakness," a great one for mothering him through the process of sobering up. This time, Mrs. Turner drew the line. He had stormed from the house one night to buy a refill for his empty "cider" jug. Frightened by the mood he was in, she locked him out. When he returned, Hart smashed in the door, then smashed a window as well. Once he was inside, he picked up an oil lamp and went reeling from room to room, howling for vengeance. His violence was simply too much for her.

"I've been meaning to write you, but much has interfered," Hart wrote Sam Loveman on July 12. "You will note by the above address that I have moved. It is permanent—so far as this country-side is concerned. Mrs. Turner, the old crone with whom I've stayed for years, became impossible. We had a row and I moved lock, stock and barrel with me over here to Fitzi's lovely place, about a 20 minute walk across the state line. . . . I never realized I had so many books to lug. God!"

It was, indeed, permanent—for Hart's books, at least. His desk, the books that during that July week of 1930 he lugged from Mrs. Turner's, many paintings, knickknacks, even odds and ends of clothing would remain at Fitzi's long after his death, even long after hers. "I had to take him in," Eleanor Fitzgerald told a friend. "He couldn't go anywhere else. Everybody else had some excuse for his not staying with them." There were nights during the next months when he would terrorize her, crashing through the house, threatening to burn down the place unless Fitzi would unlock the door behind which she and Buff, her collie, had taken refuge. And there would be other times when he would be an ideal guest, helpful, considerate, full of shamefaced apologies for the bad time he might have given her the drunken night before. "I had to take him," Fitzi said, "because he was a great artist, and because most of the time he was a wonderful man—and because no one else would have him."

"In reading Philip Horton's biography of Hart Crane, generally a very good book and a pioneering book," Malcolm Cowley told me, "I was impressed by the fact that all of Hart's friends sounded like schlemiels. Because the reader would say, 'Why did they put up with this? Was it just their admiration for a poet they thought was superior to themselves?' Well, quite on the contrary, you put up with Hart—you put up with him for a long, long time—because he was so warm and helpful and full of kind attentions when you were sick. I can remember Hart's nursing me when I was sick. . . . He gave you gifts. And then—and then, he would be at a party. He would get into a desperate frame of mind and begin throwing phonographs and records out of the window. And that was the moment when you really got angry at Hart. . . . Then you always got an apology the next morning. But Matty Josephson said he would wake Matty up to give him apologies, and that's what he couldn't forgive."

At first the move to Fitzi's had been marvelous. "Here are a multitude of flowers, an enormous garden and a collie that I may learn to like." His initial stay was very brief, for he and Lorna Dietz were invited almost immediately to visit E. E. Cummings and his wife at Silver Lake, New Hampshire. They would spend the weekend at Fitzi's, they agreed, then go on up to Silver Lake for the celebration of Hart's birthday. "We'll have the neighborhood pretty much to ourselves over the week end," Hart explained, "as nearly everybody is due at Burke's place down in Andover, N.J."

> But that rather suits me. I was invited, but would rather be here with you and Fitzi—being a little tired of big parties, and moreover being very fond of you.
>
> Let's not be dry, however! It's my suggestion that you get two quarts of alky at the French place, 327 West 26th. It's only two bucks per quart there—and I'll halve the cost with you. They sell it by quarts as well as gallons, and last week end the Browns and I bought some of it which proved to be excellent. I'll get ginger ale around here.

When Hart returned from the Cummings' early in August, he returned to a plague of minor discomforts, physical and spiritual. He found waiting for him a birthday letter from his "Aunt Sally" Simpson, whose tight finances matched his own. ("I don't mind my poverty if I don't get helpless," she wrote. "Hoover's continuation of the 'Coolidge prosperity' doesn't look good to me.") She told of her unsuccessful efforts to collect rent from the squatters who were living on what was left of his grandmother's Isle of Pines plantation, of the way the "House House" in which he had accomplished so much only four years earlier was now literally being torn to shreds: "They have stolen everything that could be pulled or pried loose. There is practically nothing to sell but the land and I doubt if anyone would pay $25 per acre for that." She wished him—who would have only one more—"a gloriously happy" birthday "and . . . many more, more happy and more glorious . . . to follow."

He also found waiting for him a birthday letter from his mother. She had moved, now, to Oak Park, Illinois, the town in which she had been born. She had managed, in spite of the Depression and her inexperience, to find work on the staff of a local hotel. Her letter had been difficult to write—and was difficult for Hart to receive. Though she asked for an answer, she probably did not expect one.

> My dear Hart: —
>     This is to convey to you my love and congratulations on your birthday. Last year was the first time you ever failed to receive a

message from me, and that was because I did not know where to address you, but you were in my thoughts just the same.

This time my congratulations are twofold, because of the publication of your book, "The Bridge." I have been reading it as well as some of the reviews and criticisms. You should be happy, proud and highly gratified.

It is a fine achievement, beautifully presented, and I trust you are going to continue right along with more of such work. I am intensely interested in your plans and ambitions, and whenever you feel disposed to write me of them, I shall be greatly pleased. You have never answered my last letter written you sometime in May and addressed to Patterson. Well my dear, your heart will change toward me someday I am sure, and in the meantime I can and shall wait.

I hope there has been some sort of a celebration planned for your birthday, and that there will be lots of fun—and many pleasant things to recall.

My love, and best wishes go with this as well as the enclosed small recent photo which I hope you will be pleased to receive.

I am quite well, pleasantly located and reasonably happy—

Affectionately yours,

Mother—

The letter from his mother was all Hart needed to send him into despair. He added the new photograph to the others of her that he carried about with him always, got roaringly drunk, and insisted to the friends who were with him that he could trace in the photographs progressive evidence of her moral degeneration.

By the end of summer, Hart was emotionally exhausted. And, as always, emotional exhaustion led to physical pain. Hay fever was at its height, hives kept appearing and disappearing with capricious abandon, an outbreak of boils that had begun while he was at Silver Lake refused to be pacified by any of the considerable assortment of patent medicines Hart applied—and a raging toothache raged. His plagues continued well into September, when he told Sam Loveman all about them.

And haven't I been having a time of it! ! ! Ever had boils? ! ? ! ? They started on my visit to the Cummingses—"the royal and *loyal* succession of the Plantaganets" as E.E. named them—and since the throne room (not to mention royal chambers and nursery) are located in my right arm pit I've had an armful and then some! It may be an infected tooth (the one I told you about) or else just bad luck. Certainly that questionable tooth *is* coming out at the first opportunity. Just now Antyphylgistine, or however you spell that detestable mud, is doing considerable good, but the more I hear about boils the more cynical I become.

Suffering is supposed to aid the artist. It did not aid Hart. At the end of six months, he could report only literary sterility. "Nothing," he told Loveman, "not even one lyric, for posterity or for 'Liberty'!" Though several checks from his father permitted him to live "less precariously" from June through September than he had "during the three previous months of job hunting in town," he had been, he told Bill Wright, "so continuously harried by anxieties regarding the immediate future as [to] be in anything but a writing mood." Now that autumn had arrived and Fitzi was closing her house, Hart was forced to return to detested New York.

But there was no place for him to stay. During the summer, he had given up his Brooklyn apartment, a money-saving gesture. When he and Fitzi returned at the end of September, he slept in a spare bed in her apartment at 45 Grove Street, then took a cheap room at the Hotel Albert in Greenwich Village, and finally moved to another cheap room in the Hotel St. George in Brooklyn, the latter two moves made possible when he was awarded *Poetry*'s Levinson prize. But prizes, Hart knew, were one-time-only affairs. He cast about helplessly for more than a month, "looking for the needles in haystacks and jobs in limbo." One late-summer haystack needle was a letter to Otto Kahn, a plea for $25 a week. Kahn, however, was in Europe and Hart's plea was fruitless. Poverty, "the most monotonous and familiar situation of *all*," he wrote Mony Grunberg, "engrosses, nay inundates me . . ."

Yet there were bright patches in Hart's days. *The Bridge* was getting a wider distribution than he had anticipated. When it was first published, he had feared that more copies would reach reviewers than the public. ("From the sales standpoint," he announced several weeks after publication, "the book hasn't much of a chance . . . Nobody seems to be buying a garter, book, Buick, or caramel more than he has to!") But by September the Liveright edition was exhausted. "It's gone into a second printing," he wrote Mony Grunberg, "which means a sale exceeding the first thousand."

There was also his interest in Dante, which, he hoped, might stimulate poetry. (He was careful, however, to announce no plans. He had all too many rueful memories of the "grandiose talk" he had indulged in during the "interrupted progress" of *The Bridge*.) Still, his discovery of *The Divine Comedy* brought the sort of refreshment that earlier discoveries of Hopkins, Donne, Webster, Whitman had brought. He had had, he told Grunberg, "a sudden insight into the values and beauty of Dante's 'Commedia.' "

Not that I've learned Italian, but that I found a decent translation (Temple Classics Edition) thanks to Eliot's inspiring essay on Dante. My recent struggles with a poem of large proportions and intricate framework, I think, gave me a maturer appreciation of the "Commedia" than I could have mustered ten years ago. . . . Of course I now realize how much more than ever I have to work to accomplish anything whatever.

Perhaps as a result of his work on Dante and the vague hope it gave him of writing yet to be done; perhaps as a result of conversations with Waldo Frank and other long conversations with Cummings; perhaps in emulation of Tate or on the strength of the good reviews of *The Bridge*; or perhaps simply as a last desperate bid for survival, Hart had decided early in August to apply for a Guggenheim Fellowship. As soon as he returned from Silver Lake, he sent for forms. The fellowship would give him, he wrote Bill Wright, "a year's study and creative freedom abroad." More important, it would give him a year's guaranteed income. "I . . . hope to God that I'll gain approval."

Hart, who had no real plans, filled in the "plans for work" section of the application by vaguely suggesting that he wanted to contrast classicism and romanticism (in this, he echoed the popular debate that had set the tone for many reviews of *The Bridge*).

My application for a fellowship is prompted by a desire for European study and creative leisure for the composition of poetry. I am interested in characteristics of European culture, classical and romantic, with especial reference to contrasting elements implicit in the emergent features of a distinctive American poetic consciousness.

My one previous visit to Europe, though brief, proved creatively stimulating in this regard, as certain aspects of my long poem, *The Bridge,* may suggest. Modern and medieval French literature and philosophy interest me particularly. I should like the opportunity for a methodical pursuit of these studies in conjunction with my creative projects.

He gave as references Otto Kahn, Waldo Frank, Louis Untermeyer, Henry Seidel Canby, Edmund Wilson, and Paul Rosenfeld. (Perhaps he neglected to name Malcolm Cowley because Cowley was a country neighbor of Henry Allen Moe, the secretary of the Guggenheim Foundation. Allen Tate—also not named—sent in an unsolicited recommendation in November, when he learned that Hart had applied.) Crane mailed his application on August 27 and resigned himself to a long wait; the fellowship winners would be announced in March.

*Waiting, however, was never Hart's long suit. By the time he moved out of Fitzi's apartment, he had fallen into a hopelessness that exceeded anything he had known before. Not only was he worried about money, he was suspicious of the integrity of many friends. Accusations of "betrayal" that he had earlier confined to his father and mother had by now branched out to include almost everyone he knew. (Why, he wanted to know, had a group of sailors ransacked his rooms, carrying off not only his clothing but his "private" address book? Surely some dark plot against him was planned.) By the end of summer, no one was above suspicion. At Silver Lake, Lorna Dietz told me, he once came charging into her bedroom in the middle of the night. He was convinced that Cummings's friendship had cooled, that he wanted Hart to leave. The more Miss Dietz insisted that Cummings and his wife were fond of Hart, the more Hart fretted. Finally he made so much noise that Cummings woke up, overheard the conversation, and shouted enough guarantees of affection to get Hart back to bed.

Without any place he could call his own and with nowhere but a hotel bedroom in which to entertain, Hart's visits with friends became, that autumn, cataclysmic "descents," sudden, often violent. Margaret Robson, Lorna Dietz, Sam Loveman, and Slater Brown were each called on to rescue him from the police—once on a charge of "soliciting," often for drunkenness. One night he appeared at Loveman's apartment very badly beaten up; his assailants, he said, had been two plainclothesmen who had set on him when he approached them during his Sands Street wanderings.

Yet Crane's capacity to bounce back from dissipation and depression was extraordinary, and for much of the month of November—when he was attempting to get in shape two free-lance articles for *Fortune* magazine—he was in good spirits. Especially toward the beginning of his assignments, he found exciting the leg work of professional journalism.

Crane's *Fortune* projects—though they were ultimately to come to nothing—began auspiciously enough. *Fortune* was planning a long article on the George Washington Bridge, at that time nearing completion. What would be better, argued Archibald MacLeish and Russell Davenport, both acquaintances of Crane and both employed by the magazine, than to have the poet of *The Bridge* write the George Washington Bridge article? *Fortune*'s managing editor, Parker Lloyd-Smith, was taken by the idea and agreed to meet with Crane to discuss not only the bridge article but also a biographical piece on J. Walter Teagle, the president of Standard Oil.

Crane set out on the first project with enormous enthusiasm. For much of the first week of November, he could be found prowling among the mountains of machinery and equipment that marked the Manhattan bridge site. He interviewed engineers, workmen, spectators. He arranged to see the design of the bridge from all angles, ascending the towers in elevators, then observing it from the little park at its base and from the tugs and barges that ferried materials from one side of the river to the other. The process that most intrigued him was the spinning of the cables.

The process of writing his article, however, turned out to be almost as difficult as that of writing poetry. He made false start after false start. Finally, in desperation, he called MacLeish. To-

gether, they worked out an outline. But even this did not solve
Crane's problem. The article refused to take shape.

As his deadline for a draft approached, Crane turned down
everything that interfered with writing. When Selden Rodman—
whom he had long wanted to meet—invited him to the Yale-
Harvard football game, he found himself compelled to decline.
"Your generous invitation . . . makes my eyes water—with regrets.
At my present slow progress on some journalistic articles I'm pretty
sure to continue chained to my typewriter for a good two weeks to
come. I'm sorry, but I don't see any chance of attending."

In the meantime—the first article still unfinished—he was faced
with having to begin the second, for an appointment he had made
weeks earlier to interview J. Walter Teagle had come due. And at
the worst possible time. The night before, "relaxing" at a party at
Eda Lou Walton's, Hart had managed to get his eye thoroughly
blackened. When he walked into Teagle's office, he sported a
shiner that was breathtaking.

They talked for several hours, Hart reported to Margaret Robson. Teagle was distinguished, charming, courteous. "Oh, he is
elegant!" Hart kept repeating. Bypassing the black eye, they discussed grouse-hunting in Scotland. "Elegant," Hart murmured ap-
preciatively. "Elegant!" But the article was as hard to write as the
one on the George Washington Bridge.

Hart blamed some of this difficulty on the times—and perhaps
he was right. He had passed soup kitchens on his way to the site
of the George Washington Bridge and bread lines on his way to
interview the Standard Oil millionaire. Hart was in no sense a
"proletarian" writer, but he was in every sense an honest one. His
articles were intended to celebrate America's industrial progress.
Yet grinding poverty stared him in the face. While he worked on
*Fortune* articles, he begged loans from friends to pay his rent. It
was to Bill Wright that he wrote most fully and most frankly.

> New York is full of the unemployed, more every day, and the
> tension evident in thousands of faces isn't cheerful to contem-
> plate. It is a little strange to see the city so "grim about the
> mouth," as Melville might say. Yours truly has been having his
> grim moments, too . . . I am trying to write a couple of articles
> for *Fortune*—that deluxe business-industrial monthly published
> by Time, Inc.—and I am appalled at the degree of paralysis
> that worry can impose on the functioning of one's natural facul-
> ties. One assignment is a "profile" of Walter Teagle, president of
> Standard Oil (N.J.). I managed to keep the oil king talking
> far beyond the time allotted, but when I come to write it up in
> typical *Fortune* style the jams gather by the hundred. . . .
>
> I'll try not to be so remiss in writing again. Would I be
> deemed insensitive in requesting a temporary loan to help carry

me over till a check from *Fortune* can be expected. Please be
very frank. Money is "hard" everywhere these days, and if you
can't spare 25 or 50 dollars, or if you have any scruples against
such transactions, I shall remain as affectionate and as spontaneous a partner to our friendship as ever. In fact I would
prefer to shoulder double my present quandary before exposing you to any stringencies. . . . Meanwhile I'm praying that
I can write well enough on industrial subjects to keep on with
*Fortune*. My room here is surprisingly cheap . . .

His prayers regarding *Fortune* must have been addressed to the
wrong god. Not that he did not struggle! He was sure that once he
got a good start on the Teagle profile, it would write itself. His
only trouble was he could not get that start. Finally, in the middle
of the night, it came to him. Enormously elated, he telephoned Bill
Brown the good news—and then for days kept on telephoning the
same news. "He kept phoning me about this wonderful line that
he'd written," Slater Brown recalled: " 'To the pipeline born.' He
thought for some reason that Mr. Teagle was to the pipeline born.
I don't know why he thought that that was such a wonderful thing.
But I realized then, when he kept phoning me this little wonderful
line that he had written, that he wasn't ever going to finish that
article for *Fortune* magazine!"

Hart did, apparently, get at least one draft finished. Just after
Thanksgiving, he wrote Bill Wright: "The Teagle article is now
awaiting approval. I hope to know more about my immediate fate
early next week. If that doesn't eventuate in a check and another
assignment, then my best bet lies in the direction of book-selling in
one of the many Doubleday-Doran shops in the metropolitan area."

But the Teagle article did not merely fall through. It vanished.
Hart claimed that the rough draft, returned by *Fortune*, was stolen
from his mailbox—as, indeed, it may have been. In any event, he
never attempted to rewrite it. By early December he had also withdrawn from the George Washington Bridge assignment. "As things
turned out with 'Fortune' I might better have surrendered earlier
than I did," he wrote Bill Wright, "but at the time I thought the
chances worth hazarding."

For a week or so, Crane stayed on in New York, making feeble
gestures toward looking for work, spending his evenings with
Brown, or Loveman, or Margaret Robson, or Bill Adams. He was
managing to scrape by on two checks Bill Wright had sent—one
for immediate needs and one to be cashed when and if *Fortune*
failed. With the checks had come Wright's suggestion that Hart,
whom he had always seen as an eloquent, swashbuckling intellectual, should capitalize on his background by going into university teaching. Hart—who might have been a great teacher—knew
all too well that success in teaching depends less on talent or

knowledge than on degrees, decorum, and discreet kowtowing to authority. He thanked Wright for the cash and acknowledged his limitations.

> Your imagination is evidently as magnanimous as your hand is. . . . By ascribing my almost chronic indigence to so Nietzschean a program as the attitude of "living life dangerously" infers, you make me blink a little. For my exposures to rawness and to risk have been far too inadvertent, I fear, to deserve any such honorable connotations;—and my disorderly adventures and peregrinations I regard with anything but complacency. However, it isn't everyone who can lend help with such graceful tolerance of evident shortcomings; and your euphemisms make me doubly grateful.
>
> . . . In normal times, of course, I should have been located with an advertising agency months since. No, teaching isn't a solution for me, Bill. I haven't any academic education whatsoever. You may have forgotten that I left East High without even a diploma—in my junior year. Mirabile dictu! . . . Noblesse oblige! . . . Pax vobiscum! . . . Nunc dimittis est . . . so who am I, therefore, to rule a class!
>
> I'm hoping that I won't need to cash your second check, a contingency which I'll do my best to avoid. You'll hear from me again very soon. Meanwhile I can't tell you how much I appreciate your kindness.

But Hart did cash the second check. He remained in New York through the morning of December 12. Then he telephoned his father in Chagrin Falls, Ohio, to say that he had decided to come home for Christmas. He would like, he said, to help out in C.A.'s stores during the Christmas rush—and after that perhaps look for advertising work in Cleveland. When he reached Chagrin Falls, the fireplaces were blazing; his old room was ready for him, the sheets turned down. A white Christmas snow blanketed the village landscape. He would not write poetry here, Hart knew; he might find momentary peace.

# 35

Hart had gone to Chagrin Falls in search of peace, and for most of the three months he was there, peace seemed enough. To his surprise, it was easy for him to settle into the easy routine that village life offered.

Day after pleasant day drifted by, with Hart helping out in his father's Cleveland stores or painting and polishing woodwork in the huge rooms of Crane's Canary Cottage that on Sundays would fill with Clevelanders out for a drive in the country and a good dinner. Weekdays, Hart, his father, and his father's third wife, Bess, would have time for visits to Garrettsville, where Hart was born and where many of his relatives still lived, or for drives across the snowy country roads to the villages south and east of Cleveland that he had not seen since he was a boy growing up in Warren.

When he thought at all about New York, it was as a place he had escaped from. "New York . . . doesn't quite seem itself these days with its excess of anxiety and tension," he wrote Caresse Crosby, explaining his move. "I was in too melancholy a state those last few days to inflict my presence on anyone . . ."

"I got terribly run down with the worry of it all," he wrote Mony Grunberg, "—and since my father had expected me out here for the holidays anyway I felt I owed him the courtesy of complying, especially since he had been so generous with me for some time past." The "humiliation" of his failure as a *Fortune* writer, he added, though depressing, had led him to his present happy circumstances: "In view of certain recoveries and gains in poise, I don't seriously regret my move."

His "recoveries" had come about largely through good hard work. When he arrived at his father's home, he had asked to be put to work—and put to work he was. It was Christmas. The candy business's one great season was going full blast. "For about ten days I was busy at my father's store on Euclid, near Higbee's," he wrote Sam Loveman. "Driving in from the Falls here, wrapping Xmas parcelpost bundles, and driving back at night, I lived in a veritable whirl of excitement."

For the first time in his life, Hart found it possible both to work for and to get on well with his father—so well, in fact, that he turned down an invitation from Bill Wright to spend the holiday with him in Warren, Pennsylvania. "All sorts of arrangements have already been made to spend the day with my father, aunt, and various other members of the family."

That Christmas Day was for Hart a return to a lost world, a world of tinsel and trimming, turkey and stuffing, hot mince pie, his father's best cigars, carols and courtesy calls, frost on the window and fire in the fireplace.

In a letter to Sam Loveman full of irony and contentment, Hart contrasted the two worlds that claimed him: the one he was trying to abandon, the one he had almost regained.

To make partial amends for my neglect of you, I am, as you see, giving you the full, blazing benefit of the official stationery! Of course, had I been consulted, I should never have permitted so harmless a slogan as "The place to *bring* your guest." The fourth word would still have begun with "b," but there would have been more action implied in the order of the other letters substituted, or I'm no befriender of monks and monkery.

However, that might belie the nights hereabouts. As I have just written to Bill Adams, *la vie sportif* continues its reckless pace hereabouts without any too great abundance of absinthe, gobs, apple-vendors or breadlines. It's too bad that all this drouth and quietude should have produced, so far at least, nothing better than a maidenly complexion and a bulging waist line. Gone is that glittering eye of Sands St. midnights, erstwhile so compelling; and the ancient mariner is facing the new year with all the approved trepidations of the middle west business man, approved panic model of 1931. So much for resignation. It brings me at least a little more sleep than I was getting in New York.

. . . Now that the Xmas "rush" is a memory only, I am casting about for some connection or other with what remains of the direct mail advertising business here. So far it doesn't look promising. But unless I manage to turn a few honest pennies I mayn't get back to your skyline for many months. Of course I knew that when I came out here, but I had borrowed all I felt justified in borrowing and the situation in NY looked, and still looks, hopeless. As you had no doubt observed, it had gotten considerably under my skin.

I have yet to see Bill Sommer, yet to see Gordon, yet to try to see Don B. The Rychtariks asked about you. I hope you got the candy I sent. Please write me all the news from Harlem to the St. George. . . .

After Christmas, Hart thought he might be taken on as assistant to the local photographer, but "apprenticeship to the village baby tickler" was abandoned in favor of work of a more manual sort:

"I've been hammering, waxing, rubbing, painting and repairing—odd jobs—around the place, and work which is rather amusing." Hart did everything from whitewashing Canary Cottage walls to fitting frames to the large reproductions of paintings that his father now sold as a sideline in the candy stores.

He also found himself in a position to give his father good advice. For C.A. had agreed to take a three-week trip to Cuba. "My father and his wife have just left for a vacation in Havana," Hart explained to Sam Loveman, "with extensive notes in their pocket from me as to what French wines to order, where to go, etc. Mrs. Crane #3 has never seen palms and sparkling waters . . ."

Briefly lord of the manor, Hart wrote Loveman about duck dinners and evenings by the fireside. "You'd be delighted by some of the early American pieces though rather embarrassed by some of the paintings. I tune in on WJZ, WEAF and other stations nearly every evening. The Lucky Strike program last night prompted me to some violent demonstrations of the gotzotsky (my Russian steps) besides all sorts of other rhythmical gymnastics. Result: a glowing skin and disposition today!"

When he made his weekly trip to Cleveland, it was to stop by for a few moments at Laukhuff's bookstore, chat for part of an afternoon with one of his aunts, visit the library ("one of [the] best libraries in the country," he told Grunberg, "admirably conducted and with shelves practically wide open"), and—almost always—have dinner with the Rychtariks. With them, he could talk over the books he was reading: Spinoza ("Einstein's grandpop," he wrote Grunberg); Blake (a copy sent on by Lorna Dietz); *Jurgen,* which he had bought more than ten years earlier but was now just getting to ("Don't wonder it was a target for the censors"); *The Story of San Michele* ("it's almost as full of dog sentiment as [Fitzi] is," Hart wrote Lorna Dietz); Russell Davenport's *Through Traffic* ("a good book . . . on a combined business and love theme"); and John Dos Passos's *42nd Parallel* ("good—as far as it goes. But Dos has yet to create a full portrait").

He also attended concerts with the Rychtariks (a Bloch quartet on the evening of January 16) and listened to records on their phonograph. But music brought nostalgia for New York. "When I listen to Roxy's Sunday morning concerts I think of you," he wrote Loveman, "—and imagine us both looking out that window on the harbor. Sundays are nightmares here to me—so many diners around, the endless confabs anent the 'masterpieces' that my father has around the walls,ᵇ no privacy or chance to either relax, concentrate or really be serviceable. No one is to blame; I don't mean that at all. I've really been treated very squarely considering the family prejudices and limited imagination."

With the Rychtariks ("How I do enjoy the Rychtariks! They're the only people I see besides my aunt and [a] few other relatives"),

Hart could escape those "family prejudices" that limited conversation. For in spite of the fact that he was peacefully adjusted, he missed the excitement of talking to people for whom poetry, painting, and music were more than decorative arts—were, in fact, the very reason for living, evidence of the highest good man could accomplish. He wrote Lorna Dietz a long letter in which he contrasted the opposing values held by the Rychtariks and by his father.

> Once a week I generally go into Cleveland and spend some hours with my old friends, the Rychtariks (a Prague painter and his wife whom you must have heard me mention) who really "belong"—and are about the only people in this district that I enjoy seeing. I can be more or less myself with them, and that's a great relief after the unmitigated rigor of the parental regime. (Poetry or anything like that is an offense to mention here, as something belonging in the category with "youthful errors," "wild oats" et cetera, and the "reform" that has been inaugurated has brought me back to just that pleasantly vegetable state of mind that can read Coolidge's daily advice without a tremor of protest.) My father, you can visualize his type, is "enjoying" the depression, or at least his incessant howls about it. Despite the losses personally involved, I think he will actually be disappointed if matters improve in less than five years. . . . All of which makes very stimulating conversation, of course, especially when you are obliged to agree on each and every occasion and reiteration, ad infinitum. . . .

"What a queer winter this has been!" Hart was to write at the end of his Cleveland visit. "But I'm feeling very well indeed—and don't regret a thing."

Hart sometimes satirized the conservative values held by his father, yet they seemed little worse to him than the liberal political ones now being entertained by his New York friends. His father and his newly leftist friends, he decided, had each abandoned reality for an abstraction. "Discussions of Communism," he summarized, had replaced "writing" as the principal activity of all the writers he knew. And though he himself could produce nothing during this time ("No writing is being done yet—or even in prospect. Can't fool myself that way . . ."), he nevertheless refused to be a party to abstract theorizing that seemed meaningless. "These are bewildering times for everyone, I suppose," he wrote Waldo Frank.

> I can't muster much of anything to say to anyone. I seem to have lost the faculty to even feel tension. A bad sign, I'm sure. When they all get it decided, Capitalism or Communism, then I'll probably be able to resume a few intensities; meanwhile

there seems to be no sap in anything. I'd love to fight for—almost anything, but there seems to be no longer any real resistance. Maybe I'm only a disappointed romantic, after all. Or perhaps I've made too many affable compromises. I hope to discover the fault, whatever it is, before long.

What he could do was what he did—read, visit the Rychtariks, go to the movies. "I'm looking forward to Chaplin's 'City Lights' wishing, however, that you were to be seated beside me," he wrote Lorna Dietz. "I don't get the full delight of such spectacles without good company. Weren't Dressler and Beery splendid in 'Min and Bill'! I'm going to see them again here at the village theatre this evening. My father will probably be too devoted to his Jeremiads to budge, but I'd like to get him to come along."

Though Crane was not writing, poetry was seldom far from his thoughts. He read—and carefully—the little magazines, and he continued to write detailed criticism of their poems for those poets with whom he was in correspondence. When *The New Republic* asked him if he could supply a poem, he revised "The Hurricane," previously published in *transition*, and gratefully cashed the consequent check. (It was used for payment of a debt. "I'm enclosing a check for ten dollars as a partial payment on the loan," he wrote Wright a few days after it arrived, "not that I intend to bother you with continued dribblings in the same style, but simply in lieu, for the time being, of the total. It's possible that you can find use for it these days and I don't want to be any more laggard than I'm forced to be.")

His irritation at the adverse criticism leveled at *The Bridge* was now lifting a little. He no longer fretted through his collection of reviews, as he had in the late summer and autumn, or felt driven to compose the sort of letter that, just before Thanksgiving, he had sent Wright.

I am so pleased that you continue to enjoy *The Bridge*. I admit having felt considerably jolted at the charge of sentimentality continually levelled at the "Indiana" fragment, particularly when such charges came from people who acknowledged a violent admiration for Hardy's poetry. For many of his lyrics have seemed to me at least as "sentimental" as this "mawkish" performance of my own. But I approve of a certain amount of sentiment anyway. Right now it is more fashionable to speak otherwise, but the subject (or emotion) of "race" has always had as much of sentiment behind it—as it has had of prejudice, also. Since "race" is the principal motivation of "Indiana," I can't help thinking that, observed in the proper perspective, and judged in relation to the argument or theme of the Pocahontas section as a whole, the pioneer woman's maternalism isn't excessive.

Now his remarks about *The Bridge* were phrased in terms of the changing temper of the times: "Present day America seems a long way off from the destiny I fancied when I wrote that poem. In some ways Spengler must have been right." But the imagery of the poem—the underlying design—still seemed to him entirely valid, both for what he had accomplished and for what the continent had dreamed. When he found in a Chagrin Falls drugstore a postcard of a rock carving done years before by a local blacksmith, Crane was delighted. For the carving remarkably paralleled the imagistic framework of his poem.

> What struck me in the first place was the obvious coincidence of a parallel use of symbols, the serpent and the eagle, with my lines on Pocahontas in the Bridge:
> > "Time, like a serpent, down her shoulder, dark,
> > And space, an eaglet's wing laid on her hair."

He sent copies of the postcard, along with explications, to a number of his friends: "The serpent isn't hard to locate, and you'll see the rather dim outlines of the fore part of an eagle just below where I have indicated in the margin." "A particularly happy parallel use of the snake and eagle as symbols of time and space respectively," Hart explained, represented "identical conceptions of Pocahontas." These "primitive efforts of a local blacksmith" revealed "the same idea as I had thought more or less original to myself."

The blacksmith—a man by the name of Mr. Church—was almost as fascinating to Crane as his rock carving.

> This blacksmith aroused considerable conjecture by his midnight absences, until someone followed his lantern down to this rock where he was busy night after night on this frieze. . . .
> > The blacksmith's character must have been rather Blakian, for he also carved his own tombstone—a lion couchant beside a lamb and a figure of a man walking. And imagine the surprise of his survivors when on the occasion of his obsequies his own voice pronounced his own funeral sermon from the disk of a phonograph!

"Archeological discoveries in Ohio are just rare enough to excite me," Hart wrote, "especially as this one bears such an intimate relation to one of my metaphors . . . Well, Sherwood Anderson didn't quite catch all the incipient Blakes in this middle west! I don't know when anything has more refreshed me than this casual discovery."

Healthy, if not boundlessly happy, Hart might have remained indefinitely in Chagrin Falls. On February 19, he was able to brag to Waldo Frank that he had been "on the water wagon two months now," and in other letters to New York friends he told of improved health and improved spirits. Yet it is also true that almost from the day of his arrival, he had been preparing for the time when he would move on. ("My father, of course, expects me to remain in this locality permanently," he told Grunberg. "I of course keep all contrary plans very much to myself, including the secret of a bank balance sufficient at least to [pay] my carfare east again, whenever my return seems advisable.") There were all sorts of reasons why he was tempted to leave. Letters from Lorna Dietz, from Sam Loveman, from Waldo Frank; a telephone call from Bill Adams— all served to remind him of friends he was hungry to see. He had had a letter from the sailor who had spent the preceding Christmas with him, asking if he would be in New York in March, when the sailor would be discharged from the navy. And there was just the chance, he sometimes felt, that a return to the free living of the city might ignite the creative flame that for over a year had lain dormant. "If abstinence is clarifying to the vision, as they claim, then give me back the blindness of my will. It needs a fresh baptism."

Chances are that had Crane not been awarded a Guggenheim Fellowship, he would have drifted back and forth between Cleveland and New York for some time to come, Cleveland functioning as a place for necessary recoveries. But speculation is pointless, for on March 15 the Guggenheim awards were announced and Hart Crane was among the eighty-one painters, writers, composers, scientists, historians, and anthropologists who were granted awards or who had earlier awards renewed. Hart was jubilant. The award represented, he felt, not just a year's freedom from money worries; it was tangible evidence that his work as a poet was of national importance. The years he had put into *The Bridge*, as well as his integrity as an artist, now seemed justified.

Hart had spoken very little of his application in correspondence with friends, for he was fearful that the award would not come through. (Though he knew nothing of the statistics, there had been 712 applicants from the United States alone, only 53 of whom had been given fellowships.) He had been encouraged, however, when Henry Allen Moe had asked him to send the selection committee copies of *White Buildings* and *The Bridge*. (Hart mailed them on January 24, along with a file of press clippings.) "If I'm lucky," he immediately wrote Caresse Crosby, "you'll see me in Paris . . ." "No, I haven't yet quite decided to remain in chagrin," he wrote Sam Loveman soon after. "I'm planning, at least right now, to return to my darling Babylon within three or four weeks, but am hoping that there will be enough from the Guggenheim millions to launch me on the waters toward the south of France. Anyway and regardless, I shall have to move to save my soul. Physically I am altogether too completely recovered to risk it here another moment." Several weeks later, he made much the same point in a letter to Mony Grunberg.

I admit to a certain tremorousness these days as the date of the Guggenheim fellowships announcement approaches. I'm going back east again midway in March regardless—but I fear I've already exceeded the moderate anticipations of a true stoic in memories of Marseilles, Martigues, Cassis—and anticipations of Spain and Oran, Tunis. But I feel ready for anything beyond a continuance of the compromises necessary here.

By this time, however, he had reason to be encouraged, for on the last day of February Mr. Moe asked him to prepare a tentative budget. Crane, responding, calculated his passage as $400, his living expenses for a year as $1,300, tuition and books as $550, and miscellaneous as $300. The only resources he anticipated were $200 from "possible royalties."

On March 13, Moe wrote again. Fellowships to unmarried men had to be limited to $2,000, but he was sure Hart could live comfortably on that amount; he was pleased to add Hart's name to a distinguished list of Fellows. Hart was elated. The letter he addressed to Henry Allen Moe on March 16 would be the springboard, he was sure, that would lift him again into a life joyous, productive, free.

My appointment as a Fellow of the John Simon Guggenheim Memorial Foundation is appreciated greatly, not only as a welcome opportunity to continue my creative endeavors, but also as a distinguished honor conferred upon me as a poet. In accepting this Fellowship for 1931-32 I feel a stimulating sense of pride and gratitude. Needless to say, this evidence of trust in my abilities and character, alone and quite apart from my instinctive response to such good fortune, would prompt me to my utmost efforts to justify such confidence as the liberal terms and the generous conditions of the Fellowship imply. . . .

As I am at present among the vast horde of the unemployed— and with nothing of consequence to detain me, I should like to situate myself definitely as soon as possible in a favorable environment for constructive work and study. It will therefore be most gratifying to hear from you regarding the propriety and feasibility of taking up my projected foreign residence at an early date. To be specific, I should like to sail for France by the middle part of April, provided such proposal meets the unreserved approval of the Trustees of the Foundation.

Full of good cheer, the local papers announcing the fellowship tucked into his suitcase, Hart on Friday drove to Cleveland with his father and his stepmother. The Rychtariks joined them at the station. Proud that C. A. Crane had at last found a reason to take pride in him, Hart boarded the train, waved, and shouted happy goodbyes. "Goodbye! Write!" Hart shouted. "Goodbye, son! Goodbye!" shouted C. A. Crane, whose death, four months later, would call Hart back from Mexico City to Garrettsville, Ohio, that village where thirty-two years before Hart had been born, and where his father had been born, and where Hart in mid-July would see his father's body consigned to the earth of a little country graveyard.

# 36

When Hart reached New York City, he was still expecting to sail for France. He telephoned Henry Allen Moe at the offices of the Guggenheim Foundation to make an appointment to discuss finances. He then set about the business of gathering his scattered belongings.

Most of his things were at Fitzi's country home, still closed for the winter. Peter Blume and his wife were, however, staying nearby and invited Hart, Malcolm Cowley, and Muriel Maurer to spend the weekend with them.

Hart devoted Saturday morning to choosing the books he would take with him and to collecting his clothes and the most valuable of his art objects. He asked the Blumes to store some of the African carvings and the Lachaise "Sea Gull."

Cowley—who has written a full account of the weekend—recalled Hart's "warmth and thoughtfulness" that afternoon. He selected from his clothing a gift for everyone: for Peter Blume, a suit of evening clothes that had once been his father's; for Mrs. Blume, a pea jacket and a striped French sailor shirt; for Muriel Maurer, a broad red-flannel sash; and for Cowley, a belt embossed with a large brass anchor. "I felt as though we were Roman soldiers casting lots for his garments," Cowley wrote.

The next morning, Crane and Cowley set out on a long walk across the frozen countryside. The sky was gray, and it matched Hart's somber mood. "Hart was thoughtful; he seemed to have acquired the tired wisdom about himself that is sometimes revealed by dissipated men . . . He talked without bitterness about the critics who had condemned *The Bridge* and wondered if they hadn't been partly right; 'But—' he said, and left the word hanging."

He was troubled about his plans to go to France, for he remembered all the lonely wasted time of his earlier trip. Cowley, who had recently returned from Mexico, suggested that country as an alternate; as Cowley talked about Mexican landscapes and Mexican peoples, cigars and spacious houses, Crane began seriously to consider the idea.

There was the poetic drama on Cortez he had once planned to

write—and he quoted four lines of it to Cowley. "Maybe I'll go to Mexico," he said, "if the Guggenheim people don't mind."

At lunch, Hart was animated. "His face, pale that morning, had gone beet red under his now completely grey hair. He talked excitedly about Mexico and then, without a pause, about Marlene Dietrich, whose voice, he said, came straight from Tutankhamen's tomb."

Many of his friends were in the habit, during Hart's visits, of serving one drink and one drink only, as the Blumes had done the night before. It was a form of furniture insurance. Hart's luncheon conversation left no doubt that during the morning he had located and privately relocated the bottle; as the afternoon wore on, Hart—departing now and then for brief intervals—worked through all the stages of drunkenness. At first he was fond of everyone. "He was full of honest warm affection for everyone present and had so many good things to say about each of us that we must have all been blushing." He then went on to praise with the same passion absent friends—among others, dead Harry Crosby, whose poetry Hart declaimed at the top of his lungs.

By midafternoon, he had entered what Cowley described as the "second phase" of his progress through the bottle, "that of brilliant monologue."

> Everything reminded him of something else: landscapes, of musical compositions; poems, of skyrockets or waterfalls; persons, of birds, animals, or piles of grimy snow; he could abstract the smile from a woman's face and make us see it in the design of the mantelpiece. His now immense dark-brown eyes glowed in the first lamplight; they seemed to have burned the vitality from his other features and turned his hair to ashes. Soon he was launched on a stream of words repeated more for their sound than for their meaning.

The "third phase" came shortly before dinner. Hart had by then fallen into patches of silence and his mood had darkened. "I may have heard him mutter the word 'betrayal.' It was the phase at which one might have expected broken furniture, but luckily he was a little afraid of Peter, who had put an end to one of his drunken rages by throwing him down and sitting on his chest . . ."

All through supper Hart was quiet, barely speaking; and his silence continued as they piled into the open touring car that was to take them to the station.

> Hart crouched against Muriel's thick-piled coat and shivered violently, while his eyes followed the headlights as they picked out now a white farmhouse, now a line of heavy white posts at a curve in the road. He began wailing, "Oh, the white fences, oh, the interminable white Connecticut fences"—as if he were giving voice to some inner anguish, buried for years, and as if

the fences were an expression of everything that had hindered him in the task of creating a myth for America.

Hart slept all the way to Grand Central Station, then said goodbye to Cowley on the concourse, a farewell that was spoken "warmly but decisively, while his eyes kept glancing away." This, Cowley felt—the last sight he had of Hart Crane—represented the beginning of "the last phase of his party . . . when he cruised the water front looking for sailors and sometimes ended by being beaten or jailed."

Though Hart did find sailors—and much more alcohol than he had consumed at the Blumes'—he did not forget Cowley's praise of Mexico. Before committing himself to any change of plans, however, he decided to discuss Mexico with the one man he knew who really qualified as a Latin American expert—Waldo Frank. It was Frank who, years before, had helped put into Hart's head the idea of a poetic drama on the Conquest; now it was Frank who warned him of certain aspects of Mexico that he knew Hart would have to beware. "He was drawn to Mexico, there's no doubt," Waldo Frank told me.

> He had read my *America Hispana,* and he wanted to do some-
> thing on Montezuma. I don't say I was responsible for that; but
> I was an agent in it, because I was the one who had opened up
> to him the potentialities . . . of Mexico. . . . And I was afraid.
> I knew Mexico very well, and I knew how strong the death
> wish was in Mexico. I knew there was a dark side to all that
> had come out of the Aztec civilization. And I also knew what
> the climate did to Americans that weren't used to it. . . . I was
> worried about what this winey air, this highly intoxicating air,
> would do to him. So I extracted a promise from him—like a
> papa. I made him promise that he wouldn't drink alcohol for a
> month, my point being that in a month he would get his own
> adjustment. . . . And he promised that he wouldn't drink for a
> month.

Encouraged by Cowley and encouraged but warned by Frank, Hart on March 27 made his way to Henry Allen Moe. The change of plans, as it turned out, was easy to accomplish. He was assigned to a group of about a dozen "Latin American Exchange Fellows." Mr. Moe explained that there were no significant restrictions on Guggenheim Fellows but that they were expected, of course, not to disgrace either themselves or the foundation. Hart—acknowledging past excesses—promised to behave himself. At this meeting, he was given a check for $300 to take care of the trip and a letter of credit for $1,700 ($400 that could be drawn on any time after April 1, another $400 after July 1, a third $400 after October 1, and a final $500 after February 1). If Crane had any difficulties,

Moe told him, he should get in touch with Dr. Eyler Simpson, a sociologist who was in Mexico City as a Fellow of the Institute of Current World Affairs and who acted as secretary to the Guggenheim Foundation's Mexican Selection Committee. When Hart walked out of Henry Allen Moe's office, though momentarily chastened by the discussion of his drinking habits, he walked on air.

Katherine Anne Porter, another Guggenheim Fellow and a casual friend of Hart's, was already in residence in Mexico. That evening Hart wrote her that he would soon be arriving, and in response had an invitation to spend his first week at her house. At last he was free to announce his changed plans. "I am sailing to *Mexico* (damn the gendarmes!) next Saturday," he wrote the Rychtariks. "The change was made without any trouble and I am too happy at change to a *really* (for *me*) creative locality to be anything but pregnant."

He now sent going-away presents to many friends, was interviewed by several New York newspapers, located an English bank in Mexico City and arranged to open an account, paid for his passage on the *Orizaba*, added a few clothes to his depleted wardrobe, and diligently set about paying all the small and not-so-small debts that had piled up during the summer and autumn. Debts and passage money, indeed, consumed all of the $300 Guggenheim advance and bit deeply into the $200 Hart was forced to draw from his first quarter's allotment.

Most of Hart's friends were readily available, of course, to celebrate his good fortune. "Have been having too wonderful a time to breathe," he wrote a few days before leaving, "—and it still goes on." On the night before his sailing, there was a gala party. The next day most of his guests showed up at the dock. Walker Evans —who missed the gathering in Crane's cabin—dropped a note to Margaret Robson a few days later: "I wish I had gone to the boat to see Hart off—I hear you were all there and gai comme les oiseaux. I saw H, spent a very speedy afternoon with him, our stimulating fulminating friend. We fulminated up and down Manhattan buying dungarees. . . ."

But for Hart the voyage was already happily underway. He was prepared for another unknown—or at least as prepared as friends could make him. For he was armed with letters of introduction from Waldo Frank and Hal Smith to several Mexican writers and a letter from the Guggenheim Foundation recommending him to libraries and other educational institutions. There was even, should he need it, a link of a kind between Mexico City and Chagrin Falls: Hazel Hasham—now Mrs. Arthur Cazes—was living in Mexico City with her husband. This was the Hazel Hasham who had worked for C.A. in his New York office and who had helped Hart out of financial jams when at the age of seventeen—a green boy from the Midwest—he had first arrived in New York. "I'm sailing," he explained to Bill Wright, "with contacts there which I feel sure will prove more productive than anything I could meet in Europe. I've wanted to go to Mexico for years. It will match, in some ways, and possibly exceed my earlier Caribbean experiences."

As the ship moved out to the lazy warmth of the Gulf Stream, Hart began to unwind. "It's a nice trip," he wrote Slater Brown, "and I'm gradually 'piping down' after the rush and intensity of the last few days in NY. . . . So—Heigh-ho and Yo-ho, caro hermano! There's good rum on board, and the Captain is very much a Dane! But I'm not depending too much on either."

Though he still, of course, had no notion how he would respond to Mexico, Hart was sure that an acquaintance with native Mexicans—the Indians whom he would find in the back country—would give him clues to character. He was looking for the sort of thing D. H. Lawrence had been looking for. He wanted to discover a primitive Mexico—the world that had existed there before the coming of the white man. If he could make such a discovery, he would feel grounded in the work he hoped to produce. He had insisted to born and bred New Yorkers that *The Bridge* was *not* a poem about Brooklyn and Manhattan—that the "River" sections, the "Indiana" section, the "Van Winkle" section, the "Dance" section represented the spiritual core of the entire American people. His Mexican project, as he initially saw it, was similar. He was after roots. "I'm losing no time getting to work on the Guggenheim Fellowship just rec'd," he wrote Caresse Crosby from the ship.

> As you know, I had expected to go to Martigues or Aix-en-Provence originally, but considering the Aztec theme of the work I have in mind, a drama featuring Montezuma and Cortez, it seemed much more logical to turn to Mexico. Besides, that is something I have been dreaming about for years.
>     . . . I'm going to take a small villa, settle down with a servant and get into one of the greatest themes that I ever heard of.
>     . . . Am feeling as at the beginning of The Bridge,—only fresher and even stronger.

His convictions about the rightness of his approach to Mexico were strengthened as he talked to the Mexicans on board the ship. For Hart wanted to absorb the country before he got there. His curiosity was insatiable. By the time the ship reached Havana, he had all the swagger of an old hand. "There are magnificent people and things ahead," he wrote Lorna Dietz from the Cuban capital. "How valid it all turns out to be!"

One of the Mexicans he talked with on the *Orizaba* was Dr. Maximiliano Ruiz Castaneda, an assistant to the famous bacteriologist Dr. Hans Zinsser. Zinsser, who had been a guest of a guest at Hart's farewell party, had not realized he and Castaneda would be on the same ship with Crane. When the three met on shipboard, they struck up an immediate friendship.

"Zinsser, a product of Heidelberg, the Sorbonne, Pasteur Institute and other places besides American Universities knows and has more interesting ideas about literature than almost anyone I have ever met," Hart wrote Sam Loveman.

> What conversations we had!—He's about 51, bandy legged from riding fast horses, looks about 40 at most, writes damn good poetry (which he claims he'd rather do than excel as he does in the scientific world) and in carelessness and largesse is a thoroughbred if ever I saw one. . . . But I could write ten books about him and his incredible adventures in the war and in various parts of the world. Next year he's going to Abyssinia to fight hook worm and other complaints. . . . I guess I've made a friend who will be a perennial stimulus to the best that I can do.

Zinsser's impression of Crane, written years later in his autobiographical *As I Remember Him*, was of a young man of "much charm." "When—obviously drunk—he walked along the deck with a glass in one hand, a bottle of beer in the other, and smilingly addressed other passengers, he gave no offense. He was rarely entirely sober, but even so his conversation was not only reasonable, but often impressively intelligent; and his literary discrimination and generous taste did not seem to suffer under his alcoholism. The books he had with him consisted almost entirely of critical essays and collections of poetry. He seemed to read immensely and —essentially self-educated—his breadth of literary information was extraordinary."

Crane was intrigued by experiments that Zinsser and Castaneda hoped to perform in Mexico—experiments designed to prove that rats were the interepidemic transmitters of typhus—and was especially intrigued by the rats they had smuggled into Castaneda's cabin. There were a half dozen of them, he wrote Loveman, "loaded with the deadly typhus." These frisky carriers of death seemed to Crane symbolic. "He spent a great deal of time in Castaneda's cabin," Zinsser wrote, "solemnly contemplating the rats."

All the way to Cuba, Crane discussed rats. When the *Orizaba* docked in Havana at about five in the afternoon, Crane, Zinsser, and Castaneda went ashore. They decided to have dinner at the Diane, a café famous for its excellent food and wine. While they waited to be served, Hart wrote postcards, sipped Chablis, and slowly mellowed. ("No more paper dollies to cut with Dr. Zinsser the great bacteriologist from Harvard, also bound for Mexico City," he wrote Lorna Dietz. "A wonderful man—and a happy trip. Am overboard here for a few hours—then to Vera Cruz.") By the time dinner was over, Hart had fortified himself against the world by drinking a second bottle of Chablis. In order to maintain happiness, he borrowed money from Zinsser to buy two quarts of Bacardi.

They got back to the ship at nine-thirty. Crane retired to his cabin with the rum; Zinsser and Castaneda went off to inspect rats. Zinsser's own account tells the rest of the story.

> Two of our rats were lying on their sides, hardly breathing and obviously in their last moments. We decided to throw them overboard and clean out the cages so that we might have some reasonable chance of keeping the others alive. We wrapped the sick ones in paper and carried them to the top deck, hoping that no one would see us. The presence of the rats on board was of course unknown to anyone except to ourselves, Hart Crane, and the well-bribed room steward.
>
> The ship was tied up to the wharf and freight handling was still going on. Lighters were alongside with strong searchlights playing on them. Nevertheless, we threw the rats in, landed them in the sea between two barges but—unfortunately—directly in a strong streak of light. Contact with the cold water revived the animals and we could see their glistening bodies swimming hard against the current, trying to get to one of the outboard ropes that were holding a lighter. It was an anxious moment, because the rats were typhus-infected and, although dangerous consequences were remote, we did not think with easy minds of the possibility of introducing infected animals into the hold of a harbor craft. However, the current won, and to our great relief the weakening animals were carried away and passed out of sight.
>
> While we were concentrated on this spectacle, rather more anxious than the circumstances warranted, Hart Crane had left his cabin and we found him standing beside us, gazing into the water, looking down with horrified eyes—seeing the rats, indeed, long after they had actually disappeared. . . . Considerably excited, he saw rats in every silvery wave that, in the glare of the searchlight, lapped against the sides of the lighter. He began to recite in his deep, loud voice, as though he were scanning lines from his *Bridge* poem: —
>
> "The Doctor has thrown rats into the harbor of Havana.
> The Doctor has thrown typhus rats into the water.
> There will be typhus in Havana.
> The Doctor has thrown rats into the harbor," and so on.
>
> We tried to pull him away, but he was a powerful person, and while we were struggling we heard steps approaching and saw gold lace on a cap; whereupon both Castaneda and I thought it wise to disappear behind a lifeboat. The approaching person was, fortunately, the stolid Scandinavian First Officer, Mr. Jensen. We listened to the following conversation: —

CRANE. "The Doctor has thrown rats into the harbor of Havana. One rat is as big as a poodle."

JENSEN. "What's this about rats? You're soused, man."

CRANE. "No. Look, look! See that rat climbing up the side of the lighter! His eyes shine. He has typhus. The Doctor has thrown typhus rats into the harbor."

JENSEN. "Come, come, man—get to bed," pulling at his arm. . . . But the situation became still more complicated. Out of the shadows stepped a dusky little officer in police uniform, the Cuban Port Officer. In very bad English he asked: —

"What's this about throwing rats into the harbor of Havana? Who's talking about typhus?"

CRANE. "The Doctor has thrown typhus rats into the harbor. See them swimming about. One is as big as a poodle."

JENSEN. "Don't mind him, Mister. He's just one of them drunken Americans."

Castaneda and I slid along the dark deck, found a gangway, and sat in my cabin uncomfortably waiting developments.

After another ten minutes, we heard a group of struggling men clatter along the corridor, and Hart Crane's booming voice: —

"I'm telling the truth! There are rats all over the harbor, and the rats have typhus."

Then we heard him shoved into his cabin, the slam of a door, and the turn of a key. We breathed more easily.

By morning, we were on our way. Crane came out of his cabin, walked the deck as usual with his bottle of beer, and ran slap into the Captain. The Captain was a Bluenose, of the fine-looking fisherman type, whose name—improbable as it may sound—was Blackadder. He had received a report from Officer Jensen and was roaming about with the intention of sizing up the alcoholic passenger. They met face to face, and the Captain engaged Crane in conversation. Fortunately, the rats had been completely forgotten for the moment, and Crane—who could be very charming in his sober intervals—chatted with the Captain about the excellence of the ship and how pleasant the voyage had been.

"And what are you in private life, sir?"—the Captain.

Crane threw back his shoulders and proudly said: "I am a poet, sir!"

The Captain looked at Crane, shook his head, turned on his heel, and walked away.

At Vera Cruz—for the surviving rats, at least—all was well. The Mexican Health Officer arranged for their admission into Mexico. Crane, on the other hand, devoted his "one night in Vera Cruz, . . . not to be repeated if I can help it," to a private tour of waterfront bars.

In the morning, Mexico opened out in front of him. From the moment the train pulled out, Crane was caught up in the country's primitive magnificence. What he saw, he was assured by Zinsser and Castaneda, was the "real Mexico" he had come to investigate. The long, slow trip was a gallery of wonders. But it was the people he focused on. "The peons are the marvel of the place," he wrote Sam Loveman, "just as Lawrence said. So lovable, and although picturesque, not in any way consciously so. What faces, and the suffering in them—but so little evidence of bitterness." Every twist in the track led to new discoveries.

The ride . . . was marvelous, not alone the scenery, but the country people all along the way who swarmed around the train selling fruits, cakes, tortillas, serapes, canes, flowers, pulque, beer and what have you! One rides up, up along incredible ledges over valleys filled with tropical vegetation, waterfalls, etc. for about 5 hours. Then in front of Orizaba everything suddenly begins to change. This is the great plateau that in some ways seems even more splendid. Very austere—and with the mountains rising in the distance on each side, here and there the feudal walls of some old rancho—and the burros and brown natives jogging along dry roads.

At the Mexico City station, Crane said his farewells to Zinsser and Castaneda. Zinsser—who would be there for three more weeks —suggested they meet later in the week at his hotel. Castaneda, who expected to stay at least three months, assured Crane that he could rely on him if problems of any sort arose. "Castaneda being a native Mexican and very much a gentleman has and will continue to do all kinds of favors for me—and one thing is assured: I shall not lack proper attendance here if I ever get sick. 'Max' as I call him, knows everyone from the president down."

It was all so easy, Crane felt, and so gracious. Everyone at the Hotel Panuco, where he settled in until he could get his bearings, was quietly, efficiently helpful. He lolled about the hotel all of the next morning. He wrote a short note to Eyler Simpson. ("As the above is as complete address of yours as I have, I hope you will write or telephone to me here, where I shall be at least for several days. It will afford me great pleasure, I am sure, to meet you.") In the afternoon, he had a leisurely "Sunday dinner a la Mexicano." The "intoxicating air" of Mexico City—nearly a mile and a half above sea level—that Waldo Frank had warned him about was exhilarating, not dangerous. In such congenial surroundings, wine surely would make more open, more relaxed, senses that under New York pressures had threatened to break down. Here, everything would be different. "I begin to feel at home here already," he wrote Loveman, "despite my complete ignorance of the language. But kindly people and generous faces have a way of compensating for one's lack of palabra. . . . Tomorrow I shall go around to the bank to see if any mail has arrived for me as yet. . . . I shall be here in town at least a month as I must get my Spanish somewhat at least before venturing to settle down in any of the smaller native places. . . . God, but I'm glad all the rush is over now—let's hope for a long time to come."

Several days later, when Eyler Simpson came to call, he found Crane waiting for him in his hotel room—totally, spectacularly drunk.

# 37

Hart's progress from the euphoria of Sunday evening, when he had written enthusiastic accounts of his arrival in Mexico, to the alcoholic gloom of Tuesday afternoon, when Simpson found him slumped over a bottle, can be vaguely traced in telegrams and bank statements. On Monday morning, when Hart visited his bank, he realized how very precarious his finances were. Between that morning of April 13 and July 1, he had available exactly $200 in Guggenheim funds. He already owed a little money to Zinsser for shipboard debts. He would soon have to take care of a hotel bill. Even in Mexico, $200 would not stretch indefinitely. He withdrew $75 and then attempted to locate Simpson, obviously in the hope that the local representative of the Guggenheim Foundation might offer practical assistance. All that evening and the next morning, Hart made attempts to reach him. By Tuesday morning, nervousness had translated itself into alcohol. At noon he sent a wire to Henry Allen Moe in New York, demanding Simpson's home address. He then drank steadily until late in the afternoon, when Simpson put in his appearance.

Though jolted by Hart's condition, Simpson did his best to make an "official" welcome—then a quick escape. The next afternoon he sent a letter to the Mexican journalist Rafael Valle, suggesting that Crane, who had "come to Mexico to write poetry and possibly also a play," might provide an interesting newspaper interview.

Hart's recovery from his binge was rapid. Though still concerned about finances, he was reassured to find himself more or less officially installed. He packed up his belongings and set out for the home of Katherine Anne Porter.

Years after his death, Miss Porter would look back on Hart as a man destroyed by the corrupt members of a corrupt society—or at least allowed by them to destroy himself. "I tried to take care of him," she told an interviewer in December 1964.

He said once he wished he had come to Mexico in the first place, when I first told him about it, that he would have done better than to go to Paris. "Here I feel that life is real, people really live and die here. In Paris," he said, "they were just cutting paper dollies." . . . Poor man, what a terrible time we had with him. He was doomed I think. His parasites let him commit suicide. He made such a good show and they had no lives of their own, so they lived vicariously by his, you know. And that of course is the unpardonable sin.

During the two weeks that Hart stayed at Miss Porter's house, he must, indeed, have given her a "terrible time," most terrible of all, perhaps, because his behavior was so unpredictable. Mornings, he was often a delightful companion, joining her in the garden for long chats or helping her with weeding and transplanting. But it was difficult for Miss Porter to predict how an hour or two later he might react to her or to her friends. Mary Doherty, who had been staying with her and who gave up her bed when Hart moved in, got on very well with him. Gene Pressly, on the other hand, who was also staying at Miss Porter's and who Hart felt was "a sourish gentleman of Scotch descent," almost from the beginning rubbed him the wrong way. Pressly, Hart believed, was not only "against" him but also "against" most of Miss Porter's friends. "He can't abide most of her old associates in Mexico (nor they him) any more than I found he could abide me."

Hart's worst moments came during morning-after intervals of self-analysis. "Sober, he tried to analyze his predicament," Miss Porter recalled. This account, set down in the form of notes, was written not long after Hart's death.

. . . he would talk slowly in an ordinary voice, saying he knew he was destroying himself as poet, he did not know why, and he asked himself why, constantly. He said once that the life he lived was blunting his sensibilities, that he was no longer capable of feeling anything except under the most violent and brutal shocks: 'and I can't even then deceive myself that I really feel anything,' he said. He talked about Baudelaire and Marlowe, and Whitman and Melville and Blake—all the consoling examples he could call to mind of artists who had lived excessively in one way or another. Later, drunk, he would weep and shout, shaking his fist, 'I am Baudelaire, I am Whitman, I am Christopher Marlowe, I am Christ' but never once did I hear him say he was Hart Crane. . . . He talked of suicide almost every day. Whenever he read of a suicide in the newspapers, he approved and praised the act. He spoke of Ralph Barton's suicide as 'noble.' He described the suicide of Harry Crosby as 'imaginative; the act of a poet.' Once while he was still stopping at my house he ran out of his room—it was night, and the moon seems to have been shining, again—rushed up to the roof which was only one story high, and shouted that he was going to throw himself off. . . . I called out to him, 'Oh don't. It's not high enough and you'll only hurt yourself.' He began to laugh immediately, a curiously fresh sober humor in the laughter, and came down by way of an apricot tree with branches spreading over the roof. He sat and talked a little while, went in and began to play the piano loudly and incoherently—it was very old and out of tune—and after about an hour of this he left the house, and did not return. He had got into difficulties in town and spent the night in jail. . . .

Hart's "difficulties"—insignificant in the beginning—grew steadily more serious. For he devoted the better part of a week to a careening progress that finally involved not only Miss Porter but a café owner, a taxi driver, a crowd of policemen, a judge, most of the staff of the Mancera Hotel, his father, Hazel Cazes, Eyler Simpson, the American Consul General, and several Vice Consuls at the American Embassy . . . and of course a rather large number of startled Mexicans.

His "bust-out" started on April 24, the night of his "false suicide." When he left Miss Porter's house in the quiet suburb of Mixcoac, he took a taxi to Mexico City. With mechanical precision, he moved from bar to taxi to bar to taxi until cash ran out and the inevitable battle began.

The "informal memorandum" that was prepared several days later for the Consul General of the American Embassy and that was signed by Nathaniel Lancaster, Jr., a Vice Consul, neatly summarizes the initial events.

> About 9:00 A.M., April 25, 1931, a person giving his name as Hart Crane, called Mr. Aguirre [Vice Consul of the American Embassy], stating that he is an American citizen and that he had been confined in la Demarcacion during the previous night.
>
> At 10:00 A.M. I visited la Demarcacion and talked with Mr. Crane, who identified himself as an American citizen. The Chief on duty informed me that Mr. Crane had been arrested the night before for failing to pay a bill for drinks in a bar amounting to pesos 1.80 and a bill for taxi fare for 50 centavos. The Chief also stated that Mr. Crane could not be released until the Judge came at 12 noon and imposed a fine.
>
> Mr. Crane asked me to notify Dr. Simpson of the Guggenheim Foundation in Mexico City of his arrest and to request him to be present when the Judge imposed the fine as he had no money in his possession. Mr. Aguirre located Dr. Simpson and notified him as requested by Mr. Crane.
>
> Dr. Simpson later in the day telephoned Mr. Aguirre that he was present when the Judge imposed a fine of pesos 12.00, that he paid the fine for Mr. Crane and that Mr. Crane was released from la Demarcacion immediately upon the payment of his fine.

The events of the rest of the week fragmented themselves into a parade of bottles and bars, short notes, telegrams, frantic phone calls, and—at the end of it all—a lease on a house around the corner from Miss Porter's, signed by Hart Crane, tenant, and Sr. L. E. Lepine, owner.

When Hart was released from jail, he had gone to the Hotel Mancera, where Zinsser was staying and where Hart's credit was good. ("He used to drop into the Mancera Hotel when I was out," Zinsser remembered, "and introduce himself to the barkeeper, who had orders to give him what he asked for. I had tried to cut down Crane's alcohol, but sobriety never lasted, and made him unhappy. The barkeeper always told me with pride: 'Your friend the great poet was here and had three Bacardis.'") Fortified, Hart returned to Miss Porter's house, on the way stopping to wire his father for money. This may also have been when he set out to examine houses, for the next day he visited his bank and withdrew $75 from his now almost depleted Guggenheim funds. (He would withdraw the rest of the available account the following day.) Since his lease did not begin until the first of May, Hart—still celebrating whatever it was he was celebrating—spent that night with Miss Porter.

But now a new complication intruded. His skin was breaking out in a most uncharacteristic way. This was not hives; Hart knew all about hives. This was something mysterious, a consequence of his wanderings, perhaps, or of the none too sanitary jail. Not even alcohol could dull him into sleep. Groaning, scratching, scrubbing, Hart stumbled about the house half the night. Suddenly there was silence—and the next morning an abrupt message:

DEAR KATHERINE ANNE: HAVE GONE TO THE MANCERA UNTIL THE FIRST. EXCUSE MY WAKEFULNESS PLEASE.

P.S. NO. HAVEN'T BEEN BUSY WITH "LOVERS." JUST YEOWLS AND FLEAS. LYSOL ISN'T NECESSARY IN THE BATHTUB. HAVEN'T GOT "ANYTHING" YET. IF YOU KNEW ANYTHING WHATEVER ABOUT IT, YOU'D KNOW THAT AT LEAST (AND THE LAST THING SYPHILLIS DOES) IT DOESN'T ITCH. OTHER MATTERS DO, SOME-TIMES.

The Mancera Hotel, with its friendly barkeeper, was not the best place for Crane to settle. In two days he consumed an extraordinary quantity of liquor. Emerging from the fog on April 30—six days after the start of his tear—he wrote a short note to Miss Porter: "This is as near as I dare come to you today. Shame and chagrin overwhelm me. I hope you can sometime forgive." On the same day he got an equally short note from Eyler Simpson, who, requesting him to stop in at the Guggenheim Foundation office in the immediate future, mentioned matters of "mutual interest." There was handwriting on the wall. It was time for a reform movement to set in.

Luckily, friends were still willing to help. Katherine Anne Porter forgave him his excesses. Moisés Sáenz, a young Mexican government official who had taken a liking to him, volunteered an excursion to Taxco as a change of pace. "I received your letter late yesterday," Hart wrote Simpson. "Owing to the fact that Sr. Sáenz is taking me to Taxco this morning—not to return until late Sunday —I won't be able to see you as soon as I should wish to. I'll plan, however, on your convenience next Monday afternoon."

Hart waited for Sáenz at his unfurnished new house, number 15 Michoacán, Mixcoac, D.F., Mexico. While he waited, he wrote a second apology to Miss Porter.

> Darling Katherine Anne:
>
> I'm too jittery to write a straight sentence but am coming out of my recent messiness with at least as much consistency as total abstinence can offer.
>
> Your two notes were so kind and gave me so much more cheer than I deserve that I'm overcome all over again. God bless you!!! I've got myself in a fix with a hell of [a] bill at the Mancera—but I'll get out of it somehow. My father is sending me some money—meanwhile Hazel Cazes is going to advance some.
>
> This house is a love—and I'm glad to know that it won't be ruined for me now by any absence on your part—and Gene's. The recent cyclone is my last—at least for a year. Love and a thousand thanks.
>
> Hart.
>
> When I get D.T.'s again I'll just take it out on police . . . They'll have at least a cell for me—or a straitjacket.

The trip to Taxco and the process of setting up housekeeping seemed, for a time, to be all Hart needed to bring him down to earth. Taxco was then far different from the tourist center it now is; a jewel sparkling in the mountains, it was a place of cathedrals and narrow, twisting streets. Here, Hart felt, was his indigenous Mexico. "Guest here recently," he wrote the Rychtariks on a cathedral postcard, "at wonderful villa of Minister of Education. A great *fiesta* in progress. All 10 cathedrals ablaze with candles, songs. My bed heaped with confetti. Dancing, wine, *Courvoisier!* Heavenly! And the drive through the mountains!"

Sáenz was at this time president of the board of directors of the Associated Public Charities of the Federal District of Mexico as well as a member of the Selection Committee of the Guggenheim Foundation's Mexican office. More to the point, he was high-spirited and outgoing. "Moisés has been swell to me," Crane wrote Malcolm Cowley.

> His innate Aztec refinement; his quiet daring; his generosity (one should avoid an *et cetera* in such exceptional cases!) has made me love him very much. He was very instrumental in my accidental possession of a real decoration: an ancient silver pony bridle (bells and all!) from the period of the Conquest . . .

In Taxco, Sáenz had introduced Crane to William Spratling, whose work in rehabilitating the silver industry was already gaining him a reputation. But it was Spratling's collection of pre-Columbian art that was for Crane a revelation. When, several weeks later, Spratling returned to the United States for a month, leaving him in charge of "all his precious collection of timeless, or rather dateless, idols," Crane was proud, delighted, humbled.

He was humbled also—but in a different sense—by his meetings with Mexican writers and by the interviews that had been published in the Mexico City press. For though all had gone well enough in the interviews, and though he felt he had been treated "kindly," he must have recognized—in spite of his dubious Spanish—that there was a good deal of condescension in descriptions of him as a "great Yankee poet" who was a "humble workman of the new literature in the Empire of the Dollar." His experience with the writers was more disconcerting. "A few days after my arrival I took a taxi and delivered the letters of introduction that you so generously provided," he wrote Waldo Frank. "I immediately heard from León Felipe [Camino], and a few days later had an audience with Estrada. The former I saw a couple of times later . . .Camino seemed very cordial, but suddenly 'dropped' me. Latin-Americans, I've been told (and now I *know*) have a way of inviting you out on some specific day, and then 'letting you down' most beautifully —without notice or subsequent apology or explanation. I've got so that I take it quite for granted, and if any other more tempting occasion offers itself in the meantime, I, too, humor my whim."

In 1961, León Felipe wrote out for me some of his recollections of Crane's time in Mexico. He said that from the beginning there had been confusion about their meeting. Crane had left the introductory letter from Waldo Frank in someone else's mailbox, so it was some time before it reached him. On the envelope Crane had indicated that he was living at the Hotel Panuco; though León Felipe went there several times, he was unable to reach Hart. He was told by the hotel staff that Hart saw no one, that he stayed in his room eating and drinking. They exchanged several letters. Finally Hart asked him to come to his house in Mixcoac. It was still unfurnished and León Felipe discovered Hart sprawled on a rumpled bed that was surrounded by empty beer bottles. A keg of liquor was standing in a corner. When León Felipe introduced himself, Hart got up and embraced him affectionately. León Felipe was struck by his "angelic face" and by the large eyes that seemed shadowed by a somber fear, eyes like those of a lost little boy. ("That's what he seemed like to me, a lost boy.") An old phonograph was playing harshly all the time he was there, repeating a song from a Marlene Dietrich film, and León Felipe found it impossible to talk above it. They agreed that Hart would come to his home for their next interview. ("But he never came.")

Crane felt that his visitor had been shocked to find him "relaxed" in his favorite sailor suit. "Since he found me out of the stiff black roundshouldered 'elegance'—in fact in my usual household white sailor pants and shirt—he hasn't been heard from—by mail or otherwise. One must appear in veritable Wall Street gear to impress the Mexican hidalgo!"

Several other Mexican writers to whom Crane had delivered letters of introduction were "unavailable."

The problem with Mexican writers, Hart decided, was that they were trying to be either European or North American; like many of the writers of his own country, they were afraid of a native voice. "What makes me rather indifferent to all of them," he wrote Waldo Frank, "is the fact that not one of them is really interested one iota in expressing anything indigenous; rather they are busy aping (as though it could be done in Spanish!) Paul Valéry, Eliot, —or more intensely, the Parnassians of 35 years ago. And they are all 'bored'—or at least pleased to point the reference." Perhaps Hart had to feel that way. His project, after all, was to accomplish what they had failed in: "I still (to date, at any rate) harbor the illusion that there is a soil, a mythology, a people and a spirit here that are capable of unique and magnificent utterance."

If he was now no longer "frothing over" in his response to Mexico, he was still sure that there was a greater potential for a writer in its primitive interior than anywhere in Europe. "I'm still so fascinated and impressed by the people," he told Frank, "that I want to stay much longer than one year, if I can manage to. You were right, it's a sick country; and God knows if it ever has been, or will be otherwise. I doubt if I will ever be able to fathom the Indian really. It may be a dangerous quest, also. I'm pretty sure it is, in fact. But humanity is so unmechanized here still, so immediate and really dignified (I'm speaking of the Indians, peons, country people—not the average mestizo) that it is giving me an entirely fresh perspective. And whether immediately creative or not, more profound than Europe gave me. . . . This is truly 'another world.' "

Perhaps it was Hart's meeting with Moisés Sáenz, who shared his views about the imperative need for an Indian literature; perhaps it was the fact that he had a house of his own; perhaps merely that he ran out of money or that he became disgusted with the way he had been carrying on; or perhaps that he heeded Eyler Simpson's warning, given on his return from Taxco, that too many trips to jail might jeopardize his fellowship—for whatever reason, Crane did early in May settle down to a little literary activity. It was almost certainly at this time that he wrote the prose poem "Havana Rose," that eloquent testimonial recording "my thoughts, my humble, fond remembrances of the great bacteriologist," "the Doctor" who at Vera Cruz, at Havana, and on shipboard had dealt with death and poetry, with typhus and philosophy. "Tact, horsemanship, courage, were germicides to him," Crane recalled in his poem. But he ended it with Zinsser's analysis of Hart Crane's character: "You cannot heed the negative—so might go on to undeserved doom . . . must therefore loose yourself within a pattern's mastery that you can conceive, that you can yield to—by which also you win and gain mastery and happiness which is your own from birth."

Hart was filled with good resolutions. He talked over his money worries with Simpson, explaining that his father was giving him temporary assistance, that he could probably borrow from Zinsser and Hazel Cazes, but that he would prefer to be on his own. Simpson, an admirer of self-reliance, volunteered to forward to the Guggenheim Foundation Crane's request for $100 of the $400 that would be due him on July 1. In the letter enclosing Hart's note, Simpson mentioned that Crane now seemed to be living modestly. His house rented for approximately $35 a month; he had furnished it cheaply but comfortably with Mexican furniture. By the third week in May, Hart had his advance—more than half of it going for the next month's rent, for the payment of debts, and for the salary of his *mozo*, Daniel, who, with his wife and two children, now moved in to take care of cooking, cleaning, and gardening.

"Let us strip the desk for action—now we have a house in Mexico. . . ." So begins "Havana Rose." And there is no question that in these pleasant days Hart did intend to work. "I am far from having any regrets about Mexico as my choice of a residence during my Fellowship," he wrote Henry Allen Moe. "Indeed my enthusiasm has been a little *too* intense thus far. But now that I have a place entirely to myself I expect to make better progress with my creative project than has ever been possible before. I don't think I have ever had quite such ideal surroundings . . ."

Hart now explored those surroundings: the showplaces of Mexico City. He saw the sweeping work of Diego Rivera and the other muralists; he took leisurely walks through the great parks; he visited, he told his father, "villages, rug factories, museums." In out-of-the-way corners of the city, he watched "wonderful native Mexican dances." He listened to "Saints' Day songs" in front of churches and, in his own courtyard, to popular songs sung to guitar accompaniment by Daniel and his children. "How this city, country and *people* are marvelous!" he wrote the Rychtariks. "Now have a beautiful place—flowers, trees, running water—all my own . . . This city has a park and giant trees dating back to Montezuma —far ahead of the Bois de Boulogne."

Temporarily secure, for the first time in a year and a half working on poetry, Hart again entered into correspondence with editors. He asked Tom Smith, at Liveright, if any of his work had been taken by "the gentle light-fingered anthologists." He sent off to Harriet Monroe at *Poetry* magazine several new poems and gave her permission to use a group of older ones in her revision of the anthology *The New Poetry*. Though she returned the new poems, she asked to see whatever other poetry he might produce. Her letter soon led to an extensive correspondence—most of it between Crane and Morton Dauwen Zabel, associate editor of *Poetry*. Zabel, much more enthusiastic about Crane's work than Miss Monroe had ever been, not only suggested that Crane assemble for *Poetry* the Isle of Pines poems, "presumably with additions or sequel from your present projects," but also guaranteed that the magazine would "publish as much prose as you will let us have during the coming months." For a start, he suggested that Crane review James Whaler's *Green River* and Roy Helton's *Lonesome Water*.

With several poems completed and a number begun, Crane again risked mentioning the project that had brought him to Mexico: "Am planning to do a play, rather Elizabethan, but actable, I hope,—on Cortez and Montezuma," he wrote Selden Rodman, but then added more cautiously, *"Don't spread this detail."* For though he now had definitely settled on the form of drama—and in conversation with a number of friends had talked about the approaches he would make to plot and character—Mexico refused to supply the words he needed.

Still, Mexico gave him "garden, flowers, 2 servants, nightingales, moonlight—my *own home* at last—and all for only $40.00 per month. Mexico beats Europe. *God*, what *people*—especially the poor. I've never been so *really* happy." Letter after letter celebrated the delights of his Mexican home. And though Crane was finally to try to move away from it, for a while it offered him the anchor, the piece of land that, even if rented, he could call his own. "Plenty of roses, lilies, acanthus, etc. besides fleas. But they say you get immune to fleas before you tire of the roses, so my prospects look brighter and brighter."

What Mexico could not give him was the close affection of old friends. While he was still fond of Katherine Anne Porter, he carried a freight of guilty memories of bad behavior. (Once, Mary Doherty told me, Hart—high on tequila—had decided to pay a "surprise visit" to Miss Porter. With elaborate pantomime, and shushing for silence, he climbed onto his own roof and made his way, roof to roof, around the corner to Miss Porter's—from which, howling with delight, he descended into her house. Miss Porter locked herself in the bathroom.)

In Mexico, Hart found drinking companions; but the only person he knew who shared old memories was Hazel Cazes. She did what she could, providing home-cooked meals and recollections of his boyhood, advancing money when he needed it and writing his father reassuring letters.

In the past, Hart had resented such correspondence. He had felt spied on. Now, however, he was grateful for contact with C.A., even if it was roundabout. He might still, after a heavy drinking session, accuse his father of having always wanted to dominate him. But in sober moments he acknowledged that C.A. had done more than many fathers would do to support and encourage a "literary" son. Perhaps he was allowed to see some of the letters his father wrote to Hazel Cazes, letters that showed more affection for Hart than C.A.—trained to be "unsentimental"—could bring himself to spell out directly to Hart. "Your letter was received last Thursday, and I was mighty glad to hear from you, even though the news was not all good," one such letter began. "Harold has since written me a sort of a summary of his conditions and I have sent him another $35.00 to help him along a bit more. He still writes that he loves Mexico and I am hoping that the environment will give him a real inspiration." C.A. always thanked her for "keeping a watchful eye on Harold." "I am very grateful for your kindness to Harold, and I am glad to see that even though God did not bless you with a family, that you evidence strong motherly tendencies." When, at the end of May, Hart once more applied to Mrs. Cazes for aid, C.A. sent a covering check, suggesting that for a while—since the Guggenheim "advance" had just been granted—the two of them hold off any further contributions. But he quickly added: "Of course when I tell you this you understand that it applies only when things are running smoothly and no emergency exists."

His Mexican acquaintances told me that Hart appreciated C.A.'s openness. On the same day that C.A. had written to Mrs. Cazes, he wrote a long, frank letter to his son.

> In this morning's mail I have a letter from Hazel telling me that you have entirely recovered from your illness and that a little American cooking has straightened you out again. . . .
>
> Hazel writes me that she advanced you $50.00 again and I have sent her a check for this. In your previous letter you wrote me that the Guggenheims had given you a drawing account on your next donation and that you felt you could now meet your expenses without further help, so I have written Hazel that she need not advance you more money until she hears from me, for I want you to live within your income now that you are adjusted. This should be very easy to do, as you are in Mexico to work and study and not to entertain. . . .
>
> I write you about what I told Hazel so that you would not be embarrassed. I asked her to do this as I really think you don't need it. I know full well that at the expiration of the time the Guggenheims are supplying you with money you will have need of advances from me which are not apparent to you just now.
>
> We are all well and send our love.

Though Hart's answering letter was vague about writing, it was straightforward enough about money.

> Regarding money—I shall economize and make out probably very well from now on—without any outside help. You know

how grateful I am to you for seeing me installed here, and ultimately with the accepted indispensables. I'm feeling very well,
am getting well into the language study and my work. And—in
a certain way—the less news there is for awhile, the better it
really is.

Hart's was an affectionate letter, full of small talk about C.A.'s
business, about the weather, about the enclosed photograph of Hart
in silver pony bridle and French sailor regalia ("I don't look very
sick, however, do I?"). He even asked about the radio programs
they had listened to together and sometimes parodied: "How is
Sherlock Holmes these days? From over the wall I occasionally hear
American programs from Los Angeles and other stations in California."

If Hart was homesick much of the time—homesick for his "favorite corner of Connecticut," for Sam Loveman and the Columbia
Heights view of Brooklyn Bridge, even for his father and for Chagrin Falls, for trivial radio programs and home-cooked meals and
Midwestern accents—he tried, nevertheless, to make a world for
himself in Mexico and to create a body of friends to whom he
could talk about music and art and poetry. Mary Doherty, Miss
Porter's friend who worked for Eyler Simpson in the Guggenheim
Foundation office, was one such person. When Hart was with her,
with Moisés Sáenz, sometimes when he was with Katherine Anne
Porter, he could escape the sense of being a stranger in a land not
so much hostile as indifferent to him and to the values he lived by.
And yet a vague sense of Mexican hostility troubled him—or rather
a sense of world-wide hostility to those Yankee dollars that had
sent him to Mexico and that his interviewers had stressed in their
newspaper accounts of his arrival. He was not "the rich American,"
but he carried the taint of all the thousands and thousands of bad-
mannered tourists who substitute cash for courtesy, the insensitive
curiosity-seekers who, ignoring local custom and culture, plunder
the countries they visit.

   Though he had established himself in a quiet native quarter of
the city; though his servants and their children and even their dog
were devoted to him and he to them; though Daniel's two brothers,
both local police officers who sometimes joined Hart in his courtyard for games of marbles, assured him that all the natives of the
area admired and respected him—though such assurances came
from dozens of Mexicans, Hart felt himself all too often *different*,
the outsider who, born into another civilization, can never wholly
be accepted by the alien one, no matter how friendly its citizens
might individually be. "Mexico is well enough," he wrote to Morton Dauwen Zabel. "But I'd rather be in my favorite corner of
Connecticut. The first requirement of a scholarship, however, is to
leave the U.S.A. It doesn't matter much whither. It wouldn't so

much matter if the entire outside world didn't positively hate us Americans so much. To create in such an atmosphere isn't so easy however!"

Part of Hart's trouble may have been that he lived in two different Mexicos at the same time: the upper-class Mexico of "correct" writers and journalists and businessmen; and that other Mexico that gathered at the markets to bargain for shoes, for serapes, for bananas. On the one hand were the "pretenders to poesy" who "have just read about orchids in Baudelaire"; on the other were the men and women Hart would have been gossiping with—had his Spanish been adequate—about weather and crops, bullfights and babies. It is no wonder that half the time he was desperate to be home—and the other half, determined to stay not just through his Guggenheim year but well beyond it. "Don't expect much more from me about Mexico for awhile," he wrote Malcolm Cowley.

> Maybe it's the altitude (which *is* a tremendous strain at times), maybe my favorite drink, Tequila; maybe my balls and the beautiful people; or maybe just the flowers that I'm growing or fostering in my garden . . . but it's all too good, so far, to be true. I've been too preoccupied, so far, with furnishing, from every little nail, griddle, bowl and pillow, to look around much outside the fascinating city markets and streets and bars. No chance to stretch pennies—just to spend them. Ran out long ago on my Guggenheim installment. But a house just can't be lived in without a few essentials. And the main "standard American" essentials in Mexico cost like hell. . . . You and Muriel have got to come visit me here before long. I can't dare to think how soon I'll be driven to fight for my little place here—and keep it. But I think I will. And it has an entire guest suite. Not that it's pretentious—anything BUT. BUT—it's the first real home I've ever had. And the devotion of my servants, for $8 total fees per month, and the flowers, and the fleas—well, Malcolm, I don't wanna ever leava!

All through May and most of June, Hart coasted easily along. If he drank too much, he was usually careful to do it when he was alone or with people he trusted.

One person he trusted more than most was a young Irish writer, Ernie O'Malley. O'Malley, Mary Doherty recalled, was the only man in Mexico Hart felt he could talk to as a literary equal. For the two months he and Hart knew each other, they were the best of friends. They were always, Miss Doherty felt, "good influences" on each other. "I have my most pleasant literary moments," Hart wrote Cowley, "with an Irish revolutionary, red haired friend of Liam O'Flaherty, shot (and not missed) seventeen times in one conflict and another; the most quietly sincere and appreciative person, in many ways, whom I've ever met. It's a big regret that he's Dublin bound again after three years from home . . ."

It was unfortunate, Mary Doherty felt, that O'Malley did not stay on a few weeks longer; for his good influence was badly needed toward the end of June when Hart—after nearly two months of good behavior—suddenly erupted into another crescendo of violence. Lonely, hard up for cash in the final week before his July 1 Guggenheim payment, frustrated by his inability to write, he was ready for any imagined insult to set him off.

The beginning of this binge is undocumented, but the middle of it—when he descended on a tea at the American Embassy in such a drunken state he had to be carried off the grounds—and the end, a "final" break with Katherine Anne Porter, are comprehensively recorded.

So far as Crane was concerned, the worst part of the saga was the end of it, the part that took place before Miss Porter's gate. Her account, first printed in Philip Horton's biography, is full of vivid recollection.

The evening before this episode at the gate, I had stopped before his own iron gate and called out to him that his garden already looked like something not made with hands. He came out and we talked for a few minutes. . . . It was just after dark and he had been reading Blake by the light of a single candle. He was drinking somewhat, too, alone in the house. He repeated a few of the vast lines, and added almost in the same voice: 'You can't see them from here, but I have hundreds of little plants that I got at the market this morning.' Holding to the grill he suddenly began to cry and said, 'You don't know what my life has been. This is the only place I ever felt was my own. This is the only place I ever loved.'

The next evening, or rather some time after midnight, he arrived at our gate in a taxicab, and began the habitual dreary brawl with the driver, shouting that he had been cheated, robbed; calling for us to come and pay his fare, as he had been robbed in a café. At times he accused the driver of robbing him. This time he stood there jingling heavy silver coins in his pocket, and as he shouted, he took out half a dozen, looked at them, and returned them to his pocket. I gave the driver the usual fare and sent him away. (Hart always insisted that he could never remember anything of these events, but he never once failed to come or send the next day to return the money I had paid the drivers.) Hart then demanded to come in, but I was tired to death, at the end of my patience, and I told him plainly he must go home. It was then that he broke into the monotonous obsessed dull obscenity which was the only language he knew after reaching a certain point of drunkenness, but this time he cursed things and elements as well as human beings. His voice at these times was intolerable; a steady harsh inhuman bellow which stunned the ears and shocked the nerves and caused the heart to contract. In this voice and with words so foul there is no question of repeating them, he cursed separately and by name the moon, and its light: the heliotrope, the heaven-tree, the sweet-by-night, the star jessamine, and their perfumes. He cursed the air we breathed together, the pool of water with its two small ducks huddled at the edge, and the vines on the wall and the house. But those were not the things he hated. He did not even hate us, for we were nothing to him. He hated and feared himself.

Crane's own recollection of this scene and of the events that had led up to it is contained in a letter to Lorna Dietz. He wrote it about three weeks after he had shouted obscenities in front of Miss Porter's gate.

> To begin with the same subject which you did in your last— and to continue with what has been almost an obsession with me for the last month—I want to say a few words about Katherine Anne Porter. Not that I can possibly give even the outline of the whole queer situation, but since she has done so much announcing, just a hint at the circumstances.

Those circumstances, Crane went on to say, were much concerned with the influence of Gene Pressly, whom he felt was responsible for Miss Porter's coolness toward him. "Maybe you've known like circumstances," Hart wrote.

> . . . Anyway, they're very misleading, eventually in any case. Katherine Anne was quite lovely to me on more than one occasion, and since I have always liked her a lot, it was hard to relinquish her company.
>
> The continuance, however,—and this is the only way I can put it—resulted in some very strained situations and outbreaks on my part—generally at times when I had had too much to drink. Since I have no very clear recollection of everything said during those times I presume I must have been pretty awful. Everything had been going very smoothly for some time, however; Katherine Anne frequently dropping into my place for afternoon chats, beer, etc. when the apparently decisive moment occurred.
>
> I had asked them both to have dinner with me on a certain day at my house. It was well understood, etc. I made extensive preparations—and was left to keep things warm the entire afternoon, nipping at a bottle of tequila meanwhile, and going through the usual fretful crescendo of sentiments that such conduct incurs. Toward evening, having fed most of the natives in the vicinity and being rather upset, I went to town, where more drinks were downed. But in an argument with the taxi driver at my gate later in the evening I challenged him to arbitration at

the local police station. Result: a night in jail; for feeling is so high against Americans in Mexico since the recent Oklahoma affair, that any pretext is sufficient to embarrass one.

K.A.'s place is just around the corner from the house I took, so on the way to the station I passed her gate. She and Mr. Pressly . . . happened to be within speaking distance. I remember having announced my predicament and having said, in anger at her response to the dinner engagement, "Katherine Anne, I have my opinion of you." . . . I haven't seen Katherine Anne since, nor has she ever offered the slightest explanation of her absence. She told a mutual friend that I said something particularly outrageous to her that evening at the gate; but what it may have been beyond what I have just mentioned I don't know. I wrote her a very humble apology a few days later, but there was no response.

It's all very sad and disagreeable. But one imputation I won't stand for. That is the obvious and usual one: that my presence in the neighborhood was responsible for a break or discontinuance of Katherine Anne's creative work. K-A had been in Mexico a full year before I ever arrived without having written one paragraph of the book she had in mind to write when she went there. If her friends don't already know her habit of procrastinating such matters at least I do. If she wants to encumber herself with turkeys, geese, chickens and a regular stock farm for the fun of it then well and good; but I know that she spent many more hours in nursing and talking to them every day than she ever spent in my company. Neither did the slight amount of extra tippling incident to my arrival impair her health. . . . I think there is a great tendency among her friends to sentimentalize and exaggerate her delicate health. She isn't happy, that's true, and is constantly in a nervous flutter, talks more to herself than others lately, and is a puzzle to all her old friends—but those manifestations originated long before my arrival. I'm tired of being made into a bogey or ogre rampant in Mexico and tearing the flesh of delicate ladies. I'm also tired of a certain rather southern type of female vanity. And that's about all I ever want to say about Katherine Anne again personally.

Though this is not quite all Hart said about Miss Porter, it does suggest the general tone of his remarks.

The "very humble apology" he spoke of was just that. He wanted to be sure that they would not have an open break just before the arrival of his friend Peggy Cowley.

Dear Katherine Anne:
My apologies are becoming so mechanical as (through repetition) to savour of the most negligible insincerity. So I have to

leave most of this to your judgment of the potency and mal-
feasance of an overdose of tequila.

Let Theodora [Miss Porter's cook] know—if I have any chance
of talking with you and explaining. Otherwise I'll know that you
don't want to be molested even to that point of endurance.

I spent the night in jail—as Theodora has probably told you.
That was, in its way, sufficient punishment. Besides having
made a fool of myself in Town. . . . However I was arrested for
nothing more than challenging the taxi driver for an excessive
rate. But if it hadn't been for waiting for you—hour on hour,
and trying to keep food warm, cream sweet, and my damnable
disposition—don't suppose I'd have yelled out at you so horribly
en route to doom!

I don't ask you to forgive. Because that's probably past hope.
But since Peggy C. will be here in a few days—I'd rather, for
her sake as well as mine, that she didn't step into a truly
Greenwich Village scene.

Very sincerely and contritely.

Hart.

But Hart's destiny was now rapidly moving out of his control.
Nothing that Katherine Anne Porter did or did not do would make
a great deal of difference.

After his assault on the Embassy tea, his confrontation with
Miss Porter and Mr. Pressly at her gate, and his second night in
a Mexican jail, Crane was more famous than he realized. "Stories
about Hart's escapades were already snowballing," Lesley Byrd
Simpson recalled. Simpson, just arrived in Mexico on a Guggenheim Fellowship, had met Crane only a few weeks earlier in
Eyler Simpson's office. Crane struck him as "a grey-haired, sensitive, boyish sort of man," outgoing and genuine; "I liked him
immediately." A little later, when he met Crane at a bohemian
party, he still seemed a man of great charm, his behavior in
keeping with that of the rest of the crowd. But those who had been
at the Embassy tea had seen a different side of Crane's character—
as had Mr. Pressly and Miss Porter—and demands were soon
made that the offending member of the community be removed.
Sometime between June 21 (when Crane shouted obscenities at
Mr. Pressly and Miss Porter and, earlier in the day, was carted
away from the Embassy party) and June 26 (when Eyler Simpson
reluctantly wrote a letter to Henry Allen Moe), Mr. Jiménez, the
secretary to the Mexican Minister of Education, received an anonymous letter complaining of the behavior of Hart Crane; members of the American Embassy, already concerned over the interrupted tea party, were advised of the concern of the Mexican
officials; and Mr. Pressly brought the Mixcoac "street disturbance"
arrest to the attention of Simpson at the Foundation office.

Eyler Simpson found himself in a very embarrassing position. A

year younger than Crane and by no means sure what their official
relationship was supposed to be, he felt he had to do something
about the "inquiries" from the American Embassy and the Mexican
government. The reports from Mr. Pressly—an associate of Simpson's in the Guggenheim office—were probably even more disturbing than the unhappy notes from men high in public affairs. For
a day or two, Simpson vacillated, then he decided to write to Mr.
Moe in New York, asking for advice. He was worried, he said,
that Crane might be knifed or shot.

Eyler Simpson's letter reached Henry Allen Moe on the morning
of June 29. Moe immediately informed Frank Aydelotte, president
of Swarthmore College and chairman of the Foundation's Advisory
Board for Latin American Exchange Fellowships, and Otto Myers,
treasurer of the Foundation; he asked if they had any specific recommendations. In an effort to get a "warning" to him before he
could pick up his July 1 payment, Moe immediately wrote Crane
a very frank letter, pointing out that Crane was jeopardizing his
fellowship. On the same day, he sent a copy of the letter to Simpson and asked to be kept posted on future developments. "Mr.
Crane can write perfectly grand verse," Moe wrote, "but I don't
think he can do it when he's drunk. I hope he does sober up and
get to work. If he doesn't, he will find his fellowship terminated."

Moe's letter to Crane was explicit.

> As you know, the Foundation is pretty liberal in dealing with
> its Fellows; and I have never before written any one of them
> telling him to drink less and get to work. Those matters
> are ordinarily their own affairs. But no Fellow has ever been
> jailed before either, nor raised public Hell, and that seems to
> me to make all the difference and to justify this letter. It isn't
> interfering with a man's freedom of work to tell him to keep out
> of jail and stay sober.
>
> That's what I am writing this letter to say, and that's, flatly,
> what I mean you will have to do. I am not asking for any
> pledges of total abstinence. I am simply saying you must, and
> I shall insist that (because I don't want any bullet (or other)
> holes in your hide and thereby a diplomatic "incident"; and
> because I am somewhat concerned that the name of the Founda-
> tion continue to stand for high achievement) you stay sober,
> keep out of jail, and get to work.
>
> I thought you and I understood each other pretty well; and
> I still think we do. You will find me on your side every time,
> if you stop the celebrating and get down to business.
>
> There's no use or sense in getting mad at this letter; protests
> have been made in several governmental channels and I cannot
> ignore them, which I have no desire to do anyway. So I put
> my cards on the table and tell you that you are making your-
> self liable to deportation; and, if that happens, your support

from the Foundation must cease. I am far from saying that that is the only incident that would terminate the Fellowship either.

So that's that, and that's flat. The Fourth of July is coming; and that will make a grand occasion for you to go on a *final* bust or quit making a nuisance and fool of yourself and the Foundation. Take your choice and go to it.

But I hardly need to tell you that I should hate to miss the product we bet on you to do.

While Moe was writing to Crane from New York City, C.A. Crane, in Chagrin Falls, was reading the last letter he would receive from his son. That letter has not survived, but its contents can be inferred from C.A.'s answer. Lonely and a little frightened, Hart must have poured out to his father disillusionment, even despair. C.A.'s answer, obviously designed to encourage his son, was written—like Moe's letter—on June 29. It presumably arrived, like Moe's, on July 1 or July 2. C.A., who would be dead within a week of the day Crane read it, seemed in his letter a man who might live forever—gruffly cheerful, concerned with the world around him, full of plans for the future.

My Dear Harold:
After a lapse of three weeks, we are very glad to have your letter this morning. It isn't surprising to me that after a stay of a few months in Mexico that you would find that in this world it isn't all "tit that titters." All of us find out that there are certain illusions that we make and later discover that there are strange conditions in our lives.

We often speak of you at the Cottage. It is wonderful how you are getting along. Drop me a line about once a week.

Friday we had a violent storm that approached a hurricane and did about a million dollars worth of damage in the city and more of that outside. It is the first time in my life that I have ever been stuck on the road. The wind and rain were almost undescribable. . . .

We had 230 at the Cottage yesterday, but we don't know yet that we are more than breaking even because of the reduced prices. It makes a big difference in the revenue.

I am going ahead with a picture deal which I have thought of myself and it promises very well. Whether or not it will come through remains to be seen.

Tell Hazel that I sympathize with her in any trouble which she is enduring . . .

Father [Hart's grandfather Crane] spent Sunday with us at the Cottage and while he fails I think he is a wonderful man for 86 years. . . .

Now try and keep well and when you are through with

Mexico, I am sure you will be glad to come back to the best place on earth. Every morning at breakfast I tell to the girls that there are a lot worse places than Canary Cottage and a lot worse men than your old father. I don't know whether it sinks in or not. . . .

With much love,
Your father
CAC

On July 1, probably before he received either letter, Crane went to his bank to withdraw $75 of the $300 that had just become available to him. A little more than half of this went immediately for rent and for Daniel's salary. Probably on July 2—perhaps on July 3—he came into town to have a talk with Eyler Simpson. There is no way, of course, to recover the conversation, but Simpson seems to have sent Frank Aydelotte a letter that evening, in which he said that Moe's own letter had had a salutary effect on Crane, that it looked as if he would take it to heart.

In New York City, Moe was advised by everyone he consulted that it might be best to attempt to terminate Crane's fellowship. Moe's own feeling, however, was that Crane had to be given a chance to redeem himself. On July 7, unaware that C. A. Crane had died the day before and that Hart had already left Mexico City for Chagrin Falls, Moe sent a short note to Aydelotte and a copy to Simpson. For the time being, he insisted, the Foundation should take no action.

The point about this move is: Crane is already entitled to payment of his 2nd quarter's stipend and it seems to me therefore we might as well try him out to see what happens. If he does not walk the chalk-line from now on there will be plenty of time to make a demand for the return of the letter of credit before the third quarter payment is due on October 1.

My war experiences led me to think that it does not matter what you say to a drunk; but it does matter a great deal how and when you say it, and who says it. I have a hunch that my letter to Crane will do some good. He was a neighbor of mine up near the farm (although I never saw him), and I do not think that Crane would like to go back there and have to admit that his Fellowship was terminated for drunkenness. That is the lever I have under him and, as I say, I have a hunch that it will work.

By now, however, such analysis had lost its meaning. On the morning of July 6, Crane had walked into Eyler Simpson's office with a telegram from his stepmother saying that his father was very ill and that he should return home immediately. For a few moments, when he had first received it, he had thought that it was a "plot" on the part of the Guggenheim officials to lure him home.

His father, in the letter he had just received, had seemed so very well. But by the time he reached Simpson's office he knew the telegram was genuine. He told Simpson he would be gone for at least a month. He went to the bank, withdrew the $225 remaining, and made a plane reservation as far as Albuquerque. When he went home to pack, he found a second telegram announcing his father's death. He left immediately for the airport.

At Albuquerque there were no planes available to fly him to Chicago or Cleveland or even New York. His fastest transportation would be the Santa Fe railroad's Grand Canyon Limited. He got in touch with his stepmother, who decided to delay the funeral until he arrived.

On the train, Hart had plenty of time to review the years of his life and the last year in particular. But I don't know if he did. He may also have written many letters, but I know of only two— both "business" matters of a kind. One, dated July 9, was to Morton Dauwen Zabel.

> Due to the sudden death of my father I've had to come north —before the books for review reached me in Mexico. I hope to get back to Mexico within six weeks—but that is as yet uncertain. And I very much regret my inability to serve you more promptly.
>
> So I'll leave the resolution to you. I'll gladly forward you the cost of the 2 books in case you decide to buy others for review by somebody else.
>
> Until further advice my address will be: Box 604, Chagrin Falls, Ohio.

The other letter was written the day before.

Dear Mr. Moe:

> Due to my Father's sudden death two days ago I cannot yet answer your recent notice beyond expressing my sincere regrets that you felt so wholesale a condemnation was necessary. On my return to Mexico (if I go through New York) it may be possible to have a talk with you—when some rather gross misunderstandings can be explained.
>
> Sincerely yours,
> Hart Crane

Hart reached Chagrin Falls late on the evening of Friday, July 11. His father was buried on July 12, nine days before Hart's thirty-second birthday, nine and a half months before Hart's own death.

# 38

It was hard for Crane to imagine a world without his father. During all the years of his childhood and adolescence, his early years in New York—all his formative years—Grace Crane had shaped an image of C.A. as impetuous, powerful, ruthless, selfish, and domineering; he had been for Hart little more than a source of money, an untrustworthy provider who had to be outwitted. But even before his break with his mother, Hart had gradually seen emerging a different father. In the years immediately before his death, C.A. had seemed human, warm, still unpredictable, but altogether responsive. "He suddenly had a stroke," Hart wrote "Aunt Sally" Simpson later in the year,

> —and probably never knew he was doomed. That was out in Ohio, near Cleveland, where he had established a very beautiful, unique and popular roadside eating-place. I was with him there last winter . . . I got to know him so well, along with his 3rd wife, whom he had married just a year before, that I'm very glad that I had so much time with him. You know already that I completely broke relations with Grace three years ago; and they have never been resumed. That made a big difference in understanding between me and father, and I must add, too, that his new wife is a fine person and did all she could to heal the wounds of the past.

"I'm so glad that I had a chance to *know* him before he died," Hart wrote another friend, "—it left me a lot more self-respect than I had before, and it made him rather happy too . . ." Now, with a "better and truer" picture of his father, Hart could see a person of "fine qualities" who had had for his son "genuine love." "I can say that his character and the impress of it that I lately received will be a real inspiration to me," Hart told Bill Wright. "That is the finest kind of bequest that one can leave, I'm sure."

It is important, I think, in assessing Crane's character to realize that—perhaps no more than most people, but certainly as much as most people—he needed to be needed. He had a great deal to offer in friendship and affection; what he often lacked was the assurance that friendship and affection were desired. In black moments, he would be swept by an intolerable loneliness.

For a while in Chagrin Falls he had a human function to perform. "I'm here for a month or so, at least," he wrote Slater Brown.

> Mrs. Crane wants me to be of what help I can during the settlement of the estate, pending continuance of certain branches of the business and possible suspension of others. As she and I have always been great friends it's only natural that I should comply. Her grief has been genuinely severe; she's been really heroic in facing the burden of so many new responsibilities.

"I'm more impressed by her sincerity and dignity than I can tell you," he wrote Lorna Dietz. "Her feelings toward me make me feel that I have a real home whenever I want to claim it here with her. She had a room and bath all ready for me—and it's to be regarded as permanently mine."

As he and Bess Crane went over C.A.'s business holdings, Hart realized how disastrous the Depression had been. The candy stores, the restaurants, the wholesale candy business all were running at a loss. Only Canary Cottage and the "picture" sideline showed marginal profits.

Nevertheless, it seemed clear that Hart would be fairly well provided for. According to C.A.'s will, his son would receive an immediate payment of a thousand dollars and would be permitted to draw from the profits of the businesses the sum of two thousand dollars a year for four years. At the end of that time, he and Mrs. Crane were to share the estate. "My father's will left very modest provisions for me, but they are as good as an annual Guggenheim, anyway, and that is all I really require," he told Lorna Dietz.

> Quite properly, Mrs. Crane was left with the direction of most of his property and concerns—along with two other executors. The chocolate business will probably be discontinued, as it should have been anyway, as soon as one or two expensive leases can be disposed of. I may or may not take a hand in the picture business—but probably not.

Hart worked hard assisting Bess Crane. "I've been in the habit of driving every day to my father's factory in Cleveland, helping Mrs. Crane out with the correspondence, etc.," he wrote to Margaret Robson. But as the need for his help eased off, he turned again to his own affairs, to the decision that could not be postponed indefinitely: how and where and what to communicate to Henry Allen Moe.

For a little while he hedged: perhaps he would not go back to Mexico City; perhaps he would return, he told friends, only long enough to gather up his things; perhaps, when he returned, he would travel through outlying towns; perhaps he would go on from Mexico to Martinique. He did not say anything about the talk he would have to have with Henry Allen Moe.

But hedging could not go on forever. A week after Hart's arrival in Chagrin Falls there had been another letter from Moe.

> My deep sympathy on the death of your father. I, too, had the experience of being abroad when my father died and I know what distance means in such a case.
>
> As to my letter and yours: I should be most happy to hear that I had grossly misunderstood the facts. But if the facts were right, I can't see what else I could have said or done. So please come to New York and let's have a talk. . . .

In Crane's return letter, he committed himself. He would return to Mexico "within six weeks at the latest." There seemed to him, as he thought it over, very little choice. On the way, he would talk to Moe: "Since it seems so likely that we shall have a chance to talk matters over before I sail I'm deferring any discussion of the subjects mentioned in your 'Fourth of July letter,' if you'll pardon my seemingly flippant, but really serious allusion to same. I think it was very kind of you to suggest our meeting together, in fact."

In the meantime Hart renewed old friendships. He and Sam Loveman, in Cleveland for a short visit, spent one afternoon in Laukhuff's bookstore and another at the country home of Bill Sommer. They saw a great deal of the Rychtariks. And Hart finally went to Warren, Pennsylvania, to see Bill Wright and to meet for the first time Bill's wife, Margaret.

Crane wrote no poetry while he was at Chagrin Falls, but he did correspond with Morton Dauwen Zabel about the reviews he was to do for *Poetry*, Zabel suggesting that he also review Conrad Aiken's *The Coming Forth by Day of Osiris Jones* and Witter Bynner's *Eden Tree*—indeed, that he write a full-length article on any writer who interested him. Though Crane did nothing with the idea, it is easy to determine the author about whom he might have written—for, in a letter to Louis Untermeyer, he mentions him.

> Does anyone know what has happened particularly to Wallace Stevens of late? I miss fresh harmonies from him almost more than I can say. There never was anyone quite like him, nor will there be! I don't think any critic has ever done him full justice, either, and it's a temptation to attempt it sometime oneself. Even I may sometime try. . . .

Untermeyer, who had just anthologized several of Crane's poems, had asked him to select his "best poem" for *The Book of Living Verse*. Crane, flattered to have been consulted, made no bones about ranking his own poetry.

In this regard I can't help thinking that "To Brooklyn Bridge" (Liveright version, *not* Black Sun Press) best answers what I conceive to be the requirements. Barring that, "Voyages II or VI" would be *my* second choice. You are free, of course, to make whatever selection you like. The fee will be the same as for your other anthology: $5.00 for each page or page runover.

As the time for his return to Mexico approached, Hart steadily shortened the interval that he planned to spend in New York City, finally reducing it to "a few days in New York en route just to deliver my customary greetings to Sands St."

He seemed now to be more aimless than ever, not really despondent—merely doubtful of his own feelings, reluctant to say a certain yes to anything. His correspondence also changed character. Hart had always loved to write letters (and to get them), but now he simply stopped writing to many people with whom he had for months been exchanging letters. "I've sent Bill [Adams] my regards . . . but haven't heard from him," Hart wrote Margaret Robson. "Though I like Bill almost as much as ever I somehow haven't any real impulse to communicate with him lately. He doubtless feels the same way regarding me." The trouble was impossible to define— and yet it left Hart spiritually empty.

> Maybe that's general to my attitude towards a good many things and relations in life right now. I feel as though a sort of "full stop" had occurred. I've never been less emotional—and yet never less satisfied, with myself or anything else in general. But really not depressed; and maybe that's the worst of it. Naturally you can't see me waving or brandishing the quill much in such a staid mood.

He could see no future for himself in the Cleveland area, only the possibility of disgrace should he fall into the kind of drinking spree that had nearly caused his ouster from Mexico. Cleveland itself—in spite of the warmth of his welcome in Chagrin Falls—held bitter memories. There had also been recent ominous telephone requests that he stop in to see his mother's lawyer—requests Hart did not honor but that for months afterwards gave him nightmares of a "reconciliation."

There also seemed to be no future in New York City and Patterson. The threat there was rumor. During a brief visit to Chagrin Falls, Lorna Dietz had told him that his old friends were all talking about Katherine Anne Porter's "difficulties" with him; and he was sure that Miss Porter's account of events—an account that had reached everyone—would be accepted rather than his own.

He began to dread even passing through New York; the only people he wanted to see were Sam Loveman, Bobby Thompson, and Margaret Robson. But Margaret Robson turned out to be in Maine. "It's a grief to me that you won't be there," he wrote her.

K. A. Porter so busied herself during my sojourn in her neighborhood by writing every scrap of news about my behavior that I'm already familiar with my altered standing among her audience in New York, most of which consists of that rather tight little circle which you and I know pretty well. I've said about enough to indicate my feelings when I add that I'm growing very tired of so much "concern" about my soul, waggling heads and tongues. And I doubt if I'll bother to provide such a "free" show as formerly. By the time I get back to Mexico Miss Porter will already be on her Guggenheim way to Europe, leaving Peggy Cowley very much to her own devices with a head full of very lively comments on me—to unravel as she wills. I'm not counting much on much future intimacy with Peggy—probably no more than she premeditates right now with me. So CAW! CAW! CAW! for THAT!

His future in Mexico seemed equally meaningless. "I liked it in many ways, but doubt if I'd be returning if I hadn't left with everything (house, servants, possessions, etc.) at such loose ends in order to fly here in time for my father's obsequies." If there were someone in Mexico to whom he might return, then Mexico might be different. "How many times I wished that you were there to share the capacious house that I have for less than $35 per month," he wrote Mrs. Robson. But, of course, she wouldn't be there—and Hart tentatively resigned himself to "traveling around to the villages and places less cosmopolitan than Mexico City." He made no promises to write poetry.

Toward the end of August, Hart reluctantly prepared to pack up and be on his way. He would sail from New York City on August 29 for Vera Cruz. The indecisive life of Chagrin Falls was, in spite of comforts and pleasant times, he wrote Sam Loveman, "getting more and more on my nerves. That vacant feeling midway in the chest! . . . I'm looking forward to the Heights again. Had a dream about it recently. . . ." There was, however, a faint promise of companionship in Mexico. The Danish cavalry officer Hart had known in Europe had been writing and might, he implied, be able to get to Havana if Hart would advance passage money. (A hundred and fifty dollars of Hart's inheritance was contributed—fruitlessly.)

Hart told no one in Patterson that he would be in New York. He wanted—as discreetly as possible—to have his talk with Henry Allen Moe, then be on his way. During his time in New York, he was subdued—troubled by the poverty that now, he felt, scarred the city irremediably. Staying at the Albert in Greenwich Village, he confined his city travels to one Hoboken evening with Bobby Thompson, an evening largely obliterated from Crane's mind by "deadly . . . needle beer."

Yet, one day in Washington Square, Hart did meet a Patterson friend—Slater Brown. "I happened to meet him on the street," Brown told me. "He was hiding away from his friends at that time. . . . I didn't even know that he was in New York. . . . He and I went and had lunch together. He asked me then if I thought he'd ever written anything of permanent value, and he seemed full of doubts about what he had written and full of doubts about whether he could ever write anything more. He seemed very depressed and in a sort of hopeless state of mind at that time. . . . We had a long talk together. I can't remember much of it, but I remember being rather depressed myself—at his attitude toward his work and toward his future work. . . . Then, of course, a few days after that, he returned to Mexico."

Brown had asked Hart why he had failed to get in touch with friends, but Hart had shouldered the question aside. Whether his decision to avoid people was really caused by the "Katherine Anne upset"—which is what he credited it to—or by deeper distrusts can now be only a matter for speculation. Just before the boat sailed, Hart had assured Sam Loveman that he was completely through with all the writers and artists of the Patterson area—but had then excused himself to cross the street to chat with the wife of one of them. And though he explained to Cowley, in a letter written soon after his return to Mexico, that his efforts to hide from old friends must not be taken personally ("As Bill has probably told you, the Katherine Anne upset accounted for my more than diffidence about seeing most of our mutual friends when I passed through N.Y. Sometime I may say more about it, but I'm sick of the subject just now . . ."), he was soon writing more critically to Loveman about those friends and the defenses they had made for his poetry.

I'm not upset about the Eastman and Mencken notices. There *was* a quite serviceable editorial in *The New Republic* on the former a couple of weeks back. And if it provides something for Burke and Cowley to write about—then so much the better. They're bound to be fairly loyal to my *style*, even if not to my "personality." It is even more consoling that a few people like yourself maintain a constancy to both.

The truth about Hart's feelings, however, is more complicated than any letters suggest. For he had become dissatisfied with the whole disordered world, that world the now politically oriented people who had been his close friends loved endlessly to discuss.

New York without friendship seemed to Hart pure hell, and—in spite of the assurances of good behavior that he gave Henry Allen Moe when they met and talked—he drank heavily. Afraid to be discovered drunk, he kept to his hotel room. The day before his ship sailed he was in such bad shape that Walker Evans, who had been invited to join him for dinner, decided that without help Hart would never get away. Evans took on the task of seeing that he bought his ticket, got his luggage to the ship, and got safely into his cabin.

Once back in Mexican isolation, Crane could contrast the frantic life of Manhattan to the drowsy calm of a garden afternoon.

> When I left New York I was pretty much discouraged with everything up north. I think our civilization is on the lurch, to say the least, which isn't, however, a very original thought these days. It will survive, but with considerable pain and a number of economic modifications. Of course all this makes it the hardest time in world (known world history) to write a line of sincere lyricism. . . . At such times it is fortunate to have a place like this, where I never even read the papers, and have developed a great incuriosity regarding most world doings. There's nothing else to do but stuff one's head continually with all that mess while in the States; but my garden (the first time I've ever had the chance to see things grow—and how they GROW here!) keeps me happier, at least right now.

Hart wrote this letter to Mony Grunberg. While there would still be sporadic letters to literary friends—most of them to Cowley, whose wife would become Hart's closest companion—from now until his death Hart would write his fullest, most confidential letters to people who had no literary ax to grind: his stepmother, Loveman, Grunberg, Margaret Robson, Wilbur Underwood, Mrs. Simpson, the Rychtariks, Bill Wright, and that sailor who spent a Christmas with him once and who was now seldom out of his thoughts. These people, Hart felt, loved him unselfishly; it was these people whom he would now try to persuade to come to Mexico.

"I've become so lonely, I could die," Hart had told Sam Loveman just before leaving New York.

All the way to Havana, Hart had looked forward to the meeting that would not take place with the Danish friend to whom he had sent passage money. All through the hot two days between Havana and Vera Cruz and the long train trip up to Mexico City, Hart brooded on loneliness. If there were friends, if there were just ordinary friends—friends he could count on—then perhaps everything might still be well. Exile, then, might become home.

# 39

Hart had arrived in Mexico City filled with loneliness and melancholia, but melancholia gave way to elation, and loneliness to new friendship. For almost immediately Hart found casual acquaintances of earlier days transformed into good friends.

He found also that the large house he had left in charge of servants and had feared would be dismantled was instead in apple-pie order: "The servants had guarded everything beautifully and the garden surprised me with its miraculous growth—sunflowers 14 feet high—profusion of roses, nasturtiums, violets, dahlias, lilies, cosmos, mignonette, etc."

The "awfully diffident" feeling that had been with him when he left the United States evaporated. "I'm beginning to be entirely glad that I came back here after all," he wrote Bill Wright.

> In the first place there was no settling down this time to be accomplished. I found . . . the servants joyful to see me . . . I could begin "living" right away without a moment in a hotel, a blanket or kitchen implement to buy—having spent about three months in such preoccupations on my previous visit. The rainy season is lasting unusually long, but it keeps all the verdure so miraculously green that the countryside will hold its colors all the longer into the long months of drouth to come.

When the rains broke, the climate giving way to a golden Indian summer, Hart enjoyed a voluptuous ease that had come to him only rarely in the past. "A beautiful Sunday it is here," he wrote back to Chagrin Falls on a bright October day. "I hope that it's the same up north with you. I took a good sun bath on the roof this morning, something I always feel the better for, and am settling down to Spanish grammar for the rest of the afternoon."

His Spanish never became good—indeed was never more than bearable to the townspeople he talked to—but it was just funny enough to amuse his servants and their friends and relatives. That spirit he had searched for and seldom found during his first stay turned out to be no further away than his kitchen. "You should see these native Indian people," he was soon writing Grunberg:

> —not the people "in power"—of mixed Spanish and Indian blood. They're dumb as hell in a thousand ways, but wiser, I think, than all our mad, rushing crowd up north. I'm cultivating (as you may observe) the virtues of UN-thought for awhile! The beautiful brown, "it's toasted"-flesh, dark eyes, big white hats, white pyjama suits, sandals, dirt, indigestion, faith, doubt, elation, resignation—but always something fundamental, a contact with the soil and earth and the blue of the mountains hereabouts! I don't know much Spanish, but I get along fairly well with them. Mexico is more foreign than anything remaining in the farthest districts of Europe. I'm glad I didn't go back to France, even though this country is a perfect Calvary in a thousand ways . . .
>
> Every other night or so my servants bring in their friends—and we have a swell time dancing native dances, singing native songs to their guitar music, and clinking glasses of beer and tequila,—a deadly but companionable mixture! Flowers! my dear Mony! I have all I can do to prevent my rooms from resembling mortuary chapels . . . My servant is continually stacking sugar cane and corn stalks, besides hanging myrtle wreaths against the walls. From the garden come stacks of daisies, nasturtiums, roses, calla lilies, violets, heliotrope, cannas, enormous marigolds, mignonette, chrysanthemums, calendulas, buena de noche, cosmos, sun flowers, phlox, iris, geraniums, and a score of other tropical and typically Mexican flowers whose names I do not know. This sounds phoney, but it's true.
>
> The climate here is the same, practically, the year round. Very, very cool at night and early in the morning—with sometimes considerable heat on the sunny side of the street at noon. The altitude accounts for it (I'm something like 8,000 feet above you here on this big plateau) but you can get any temperature you want at any time of the year by going a little more up, or down. The altitude is—especially at first—a strain on the nerves. One is always a little wild, but I doubt if I'm any wilder than usual, after all. I think I'll get used to it, and *maybe* stay here a long, long while. That is, if I find I get to writing poetry again.

Though Crane had not been able to promise Henry Allen Moe never to take a drink again, he had said that he would do his best to stay out of jail. His shield in this respect was, for a while, Daniel, who was assigned the task of carrying coins, bargaining in advance with taxi drivers, and seeing that Crane got home at night. Almost as good a shield was Daniel's family, including the two policemen brothers. "Really, you'd be vastly amused at my house and my servant 'problem'—not that it's really a problem at all, but Mexican, typically Mexican," Hart wrote his stepmother. "Consequently I never look out—*almost* never—without seeing a uniform and gun at my gate. *What* protection!" Entertained by the family life of his servants and fearful of public places, Hart planned to do his drinking at home rather than in bars. Here he could be reasonably sure that neither Mexican poets nor American diplomats would be offended by his behavior. "With a bottle of 'Old Nick' Jamaica rum," he wrote Mony Grunberg,

> here I sit in my spacious salon, twenty feet high, which is only part of my eight-room, old-fashioned Mexican house . . . Houses here are like fortresses, each with a gate, grill, walls etc. around it, and everything under a romantic spell of lock and key.
> . . . I've been in jail twice, but that was only regarding arguments with taxi drivers when I was tight. Nobody but the Guggenheims seemed to mind, which reminds me that I had a right good dream the other night, seeing in headlines that the chief of them all had been murdered by some one named Abernethy!

With a widening circle of friends, Crane found himself playing host. "I've had some nice parties here in my house," he wrote the Rychtariks.

> I know more people than I did before, and as far as space goes I might have sixty here at a time. My servant plays the guitar and sings beautifully. . . . When I have a party it's easy to get him to bring in two or three of his friends, equally gifted, and the result is such music, my friends, as would make your feet dance and your eyes shine brightly all the night! The results were a little too lively, in fact, one day last week when I gave a party to two American boys who are touring down here in a big Lincoln car. One of them suddenly climbed up on my roof, drawing the ladder after him, and began pelting tiles down into the courtyard of my neighbor. I nearly had heart failure before we got him down, since my neighbor is a crack shot, and the provocations for shooting are much less here in Mexico than anywhere I know. The kid had just drunk about a quart of *tequila*, so of course it was only partly due to his response to the music!

When, in these pleasant autumn days, Hart himself had too much tequila, he had little to worry about. There was always Daniel hovering in the background, ready to slip an arm around his waist, help him across the courtyard, and tumble him into bed, where he could dream happily of Guggenheim massacres.

One bed sometimes led to another. Hart's improved Spanish opened up new opportunities for sexual adventures. His sex life in Mexico, he told Mony Grunberg, was more extensive and varied

than ever before. To describe it "would take a book." Hart, who
had always been contemptuous of the effeminate homosexuals he
had watched parade through Greenwich Village and Hollywood,
decided that the Mexican Indian had a much freer, much more
spontaneous kind of sexuality than North Americans—homosexual or heterosexual. The native Indian, Hart believed, might
make love to a woman one night, to a man the next, and might on
the third night take his bride home to a marriage bed. And all
without regrets and without embarrassment. "The nature of the
Mexican Indian, as Lawrence said, isn't exactly 'sunny,'" Hart
wrote Wilbur Underwood,

> but he is more stirred by the moon, if you get what I mean, than
> any type I've ever known. The fluttering gait and the powder
> puff are unheard of here, but that doesn't matter in the least.
> Ambidexterity is all in the fullest masculine tradition. I assure
> you from many trials and observations. The pure Indian type is
> decidedly the most beautiful animal imaginable, including the
> Polynesian—to which he often bears a close resemblance. And
> the various depths of rich coffee brown, always so clear and
> silken smooth, are anything but Negroid. Add to that—voices
> whose particular pitch will make the welkin ring—and you have
> a rather tempting setting for an odd evening. Even Lawrence,
> with all his "blood-fear" of them, couldn't resist some lavish
> descriptions of their fine proportions.

Hart had returned determined to follow the advice of Mary
Doherty and Moisés Sáenz: he should see more of the country than
Mexico City. "We very often speak about you, Mary and I, wishing we were together," Sáenz had written at the time of C.A.'s
death. "And we certainly hope you come back to Mexico, for the
whole year if it were possible but surely long enough to vibrate
to Mexico, or for Mexico to vibrate in you, if you prefer." For
there was a quality in Mexico, Sáenz felt, that no writer from the
States had yet captured and that Hart might well voice. Most of
the writers who were then describing Mexican life were content
to present portraits of idealized peons or tales of revolutionary
violence. Hart, Sáenz hoped, might be able to find poetic equivalents for the fiber of the land, the intensity of a brooding people
that could erupt into ecstatic festivals, and the open, unsophisti-
cated sympathy of men who might in instants of shared affection
swear lifetime brotherhood—and for the duration of their lives
live by those vows.

After Hart's death, Mary Doherty set down what she and Sáenz—
and Hart, too—had dreamed his Mexican year would accomplish.

> Hart's year in Mexico just should *not* have ended as it did. He
> had really gotten a very great deal out of Mexico, had, in far
> less time (which was natural, he being a sensitive person), gotten

far more of the essence of the spirit of this country than many and many another whom we have seen here. . . .

By all of which I mean to say that Hart had touched something very real—and very awful, perhaps, in Mexico, and I had great hopes that he would one day, and perhaps better later than sooner, be able to crystallize into words for us this thing. And that would have been a real contribution. And then, I always felt, what if Hart did not write here? What he wrote later about the streets of New York would be so much the richer for this experience. What a pity we are deprived of it.

We are not, of course, deprived of all of it; for though Hart completed only one important poem in Mexico—a great one—he was able to set down in letters and in fragments of poetry some of his response to that Mexico he and Miss Doherty and Sáenz had hoped to commemorate.

Only four days after his return from the United States he had his first taste of what he soon described as "the most interesting adventure that I think I ever remember." For Hart had located a companion who could lead him both into the Mexican past and into its rural present.

I have had the pleasure to meet a young archeologist from Wisconsin, who is studying in the University here and who thinks he has discovered a buried Aztec pyramid right in the vicinity of my house. Yesterday we took pick and shovel and worked our heads off digging into the side of a small hill, itself on a vast elevation overlooking the entire valley of Anahuac. Except for a few flocks of goats and sheep the entire neighborhood has been abandoned since the Conquest. A marvelous stillness and grassy perfume pervade the district; one sees the two great volcanoes in the distance and a part of the horizon glazed by Lake Texcoco, seemingly below which floats, as in a dream, the City of Mexico. It was an arduous and rich afternoon. I have a lame back today, but also some very interesting chips and pieces of the true Aztec pottery picked up here and there on the surface and from our little excavation. The experience is haunting, melancholy too. But such "first hand" contact beats the more artificial contacts that museums proffer. We also ran across one of those incredibly sharp fragments of obsidian, part of a knife blade used either to carve stone and other materials or human flesh. It is still a mystery as to how they cut obsidian— but this shard was perfectly edged and graded as though it had been as conformable as wood.

Tomorrow morning we are leaving for a four days' visit to Tepoztlan, the town Chase writes about. We shall have to sleep on the floors of schoolhouses or abandoned convents. I'm glad to have the chance to go with R——— (the archeologist) as he speaks Spanish perfectly and also knows a great deal about customs, folklore, etc. He is light, slender, Irish of course . . . If all goes well it may not be our last trip together.

The trip to Tepoztlan, Crane wrote his cousin Helen, "amounted to five of the most absorbing days of my life." The town itself, he explained, "situated about ten miles east of Cuernavaca between tremendous cliffs and crags that rise 800 feet on each side, is rarely visited by anyone but native Indians." When Hart visited it, the modern road that now brings in from Cuernavaca busloads of Yankee tourists, sociologists, and moviemakers was still undreamed of. The only way to reach Tepoztlan was by train and trail. The train would pause briefly several miles from El Porque and the Tepoztlan-bound visitor would begin the scramble down a steep, narrow, cliff-hanging path. "You have to climb down those escarpments by foot to get there, but, though very strenuous, the extreme beauty of the descent, the tropical verdure forming hanging gardens, the waterfalls and the panoramas of the beautiful Valley of Morelos are well worth it." "From the town," he wrote Bess Crane, "these vast palisades look like tremendous citadels." All about him as he descended the cliffs were canyon walls "rising in great and irregular ledges covered with tropical foliage . . . What flowers, ferns, orchids and waterfalls there were! One walked on the edge of an abyss a good deal of the time. . . . I wore the oldest clothes I had—and with a bag of blankets, etc. over my shoulder I certainly looked more like a bum than you have ever seen me."

The descent into the town took Crane and his friend nearly three hours. As they emerged from the jungle of heavy foliage at the bottom of the ravine and made their way along slippery streets, past the low, tiled houses—stone foundations topped by native brick—Crane was struck by the gaiety of the children and the gracious warmth of the adults. Though the town was poor —almost all the houses had dirt floors—the children's clothes were crisp, their eyes sparkling.

> One would think with so much mud (due to the rainy season) and the multitude of pigs running everywhere, that the people were not clean, but I found them very clean and certainly the most polite and hospitable people in the world. . . .
>
> We stayed in the house of a baker—who was, believe it or not—also the town barber and everything else but candlestick maker. He refused to name any fee for his accommodations but we left 4 pesos when we left (about $1.35) and received a very sincere invitation to stay with him when we came back again. It was better than sleeping on the floors of the monastery as we had a bed with bamboo slats, if no mattress. The baker, his wife and two kids all piled into the other bed in the same room.

Well, we took long, long walks every day into the surrounding fields, climbed rocks where wild boars roam and
then returned in the evenings to a coffee bar where the young
men of the town gathered with their guitars to sing together.
And what music! I'll never forget the strange melancholy
tonality, and the plangent accompaniment of their instruments. You can't imagine how picturesque they are with
their dark eyes and faces set in almost complete abstraction
below the great white hats tilted on the backs of their heads.
So simple, unaffected—and so wonderfully polite! That is
their one amusement after the day's work.

If Tepoztlan offered Crane a beautiful people, the experiences of
his second and third days there gave him, he felt, a key to their
souls.

. . . the greatest treat as well as surprise was that we arrived just
a day before their yearly fiesta . . . of the ancient Aztec god
of the district, Tepoztecatl, whose ancient temple, though
partially destroyed, still commands a panorama of the whole
valley from the top of one of the surrounding palisades. We
knew nothing about the feast, however, until after sundown
one evening a light appeared on the roof of the cathedral
where a drum and kind of fife began to sound the most
stirring and haunting kind of savage summons. I rushed
from the bar where I was drinking tequila—up the dark
corridors and the stairways of the church and on to the roof,
expecting to be thrown over when I got there, but still too
excited to resist.

And what a scene it was! Three or four groups of (mostly
the older) Mexicans, totalling not more than 20, were standing with lanterns in their midst, talking together and listening to the music, which continued its pagan and barbaric
beat for over two hours at intervals between the ringing of
the cathedral bells. Can you imagine the strange, strange
mixture, the musicians standing with their faces toward the
high dark cliff surmounted by the temple of the old barbaric
god that they were propitiating, and stopping every 15
minutes while the sextons rang out the call of the Cross over
the same dark valley! Sitting there on top of that church,
with the lightning playing on one horizon, a new moon
sinking on the opposite and with millions of stars overhead
and between and with that strange old music beating in
one's blood—it was like being in the Land of Oz. Then
rockets would be fired from the parapets of the church—and
answering rockets would rise from the dark temple miles
away on the cliff, as some of the old faithfuls had climbed
up there in the afternoon and were holding a wake until
sunrise.

The elders with whom he mingled seemed that night, Crane felt, to have accomplished the spiritual fusion of two antithetical faiths. The "barbaric service" of flute and drum alternated so perfectly with the "loud ringing of all the church bells by the sextons of the church," Hart wrote William Wright, that the "two voices, still in conflict here in Mexico, the idol's and the Cross," became miraculously one. "There really did not seem to be a real conflict that amazing night. Nearly all of these 'elders' I have been describing go to mass!"

The god in whose honor flute, drum, and rockets were dedicated was the god of pulque—and Hart sampled the god's beverage in ceremonial quantities.

> During the day we had found some fragments (perhaps over a thousand years old) of Aztec idols plowed up in the cornfields thereabouts. The Indians were extremely cordial to us, told us legends of the God whose feast day they were celebrating and treated us to many cups of very hot coffee made still "hotter" by the generous infusion of straight alcohol which went into every cup. They were wonderful people, those "elders" who still stuck to their ancient rites despite all the oppression of the Spaniards over nearly 400 years. The fragments of idols that we showed them made a great impression in our favor. The music stopped at nine. We invited them all to a bar for a glass of tequila before retiring and we were urged to attend the resumption of their ceremonies from 3 A.M. until daylight.
>
> I didn't open an eye until nearly five, when I awoke to hear the distant fife and drum again. I poked R——— in the ribs and out we rushed, back to the cathedral in time to have more coffee and see the sun rise over that marvelous valley to such a ringing of bells and wild music as I never expect to hear again.

This time an even rarer opportunity opened to him. The elders had reassembled as before, and again they served coffee with "a generous infusion of pulque, straight pulque alcohol in each cup."

> But most enthralling of all was the addition of another drum —this being the ancient Aztec drum, pre-Conquest and guarded year after year from the destruction of the priests and conquerors, that how many hundreds of times had been beaten to propitiate the god . . . A large wooden cylinder, exquisitely carved and showing a figure with animal head, upright, and walking through thick woods,—it lay horizontally on the floor of the roof, resounding to two heavily padded drum sticks before the folded knees of one of the Indians. The people at the temple had played it up there the night before, and now someone had brought it down to be played to the rising sun in the valley.

Suddenly, as it was getting lighter and lighter and excitement was growing more and more intense, one of the Indians who had been playing it put the drum sticks into my hands and nodded toward the amazing instrument. It seemed too good to be true, really, that I, who had expected to be thrown off the roof when I entered the evening before, should now be invited to actually participate. And actually I did! I not only beat the exact rhythm with all due accents, which they had been keeping up for hours; I even worked in an elaboration, based on the lighter tattoo of the more modern drum of the evening before. This, with such ponderous sticks, was exhausting to the muscles of the forearm; but I had the pleasure of pleasing them so that they almost embraced me. They did, in fact, several of them—put their arms around our shoulders and walk back and forth the whole length of the roof, when at the astronomical hour of six the whole place seemed to go mad in the refulgence of full day. It is something to hear bells rung, but it is inestimably better to see the sextons wield the hammers, swinging on them with the full weight of their entire bodies like frantic acrobats—while a whole bevy of rockets shower into such a vocal sunrise.

"You can't imagine how exciting it was," Hart wrote his stepmother, "—to be actually a part of their ritual . . . That never happened to any American before in Tepoztlan, though two books have been written about the place by American visitors." By comparison, the other events of his visit seemed insignificant. "I went bathing with an Indian friend in a mountain pool, ate beans and tortillas until I nearly burst, and met the vicar of the Church in the privy of the Cathedral." On the climb back to the train, he visited the temple from which earlier he had watched rockets ascend and had first heard sound the ancient drum. The temple, he reported, "still has fragments of remarkable relief and is staunchly and beautifully constructed." But his great experience had been that of being accepted by the whole town. "I never left a town feeling so mellow and in such pleasant relations with everybody in the place."

# 40

A different kind of acceptance—for Hart equal in importance to the acceptance that had been given him on the cathedral roof in Tepoztlan—took place in Taxco, the little town he had first visited with Moisés Sáenz and to which he returned the week after his Tepoztlan trip. For it was in William Spratling's Taxco home—"full of Aztec antiquities"—that Hart met the painter David Siqueiros, and it was in Taxco that he came really to know Lesley Byrd Simpson and ultimately to make love to Peggy Cowley.

During that first autumn visit to Taxco, Hart had been introduced to Siqueiros, then recently out of prison and still under bail on charges of participating in a Communist plot against the Mexican government. Like Spratling, who had commissioned a portrait and purchased a number of drawings, Hart was deeply moved by the financial plight of the artist. Though his own income was barely enough to pay his rent and keep him fed, Hart immediately asked Siqueiros to do a portrait and purchased a small water color from him.

Siqueiros began the portrait at once—an oil, about four feet by two and a half, showing Hart reading, his head bowed, almost as if in prayer. The revelation of character in the painting seemed to Hart "astounding." "When photographs are made I'll have to send you one," he wrote the Rychtariks, "and for heaven's sake don't lose it, whether you like it or not. I don't know yet how I'm going to get the original up north." Hart's portrait and his water color, he assured them, were more characteristically Mexican than a Siqueiros painting they had seen in Cleveland.

I consider [Siqueiros] the greatest of contemporary Mexican painters . . . Siqueiros is the one who painted the picture of that train flying along, that we took particular notice of in the Carnegie exhibit at the Art Amusement last spring. Remember? But that wasn't a fair example of his vast power and scope at all. He's fundamentally a mural painter, and even his smaller paintings have a tremendous *scale*. I bought a small water color of his, a Mexican boy's head, which you will be quite wild about.

I've never seen anything of Gauguin's which was better. . . .
Siqueiros, however, is always *most* Mexican and himself. The
very soil of Mexico seems spread on his canvases.

The portrait would be delivered as soon as the paint was dry.
Crane celebrated its completion by a quick trip to Doña Berta's.

It was probably in this bar—though perhaps not at this time—
that Hart made a close friend of Lesley Byrd Simpson. Simpson,
who had known Hart only casually, now found himself caught
up in a serious discussion. "The first time I had a chance to know
him was in Taxco," Simpson recalled, "in September, 1931."

It was either at Natalie Scott's or at Doña Berta's bar—most
likely both. He told me what he was attempting to do: write
a poem on the Conquest of Mexico. He was up against it, for
he couldn't read Spanish with any fluency and had read precious little about the subject. His notions were mostly
taken from Prescott. I gave him a lecture on bibliography (probably too long, but then we had a good deal to drink) and Hart
got more and more restless and disputatious. His ideas about
the early history of Mexico were completely naïve, according
to my notions. I think I told him he couldn't write a decent
poem on the history of the Conquest without knowing all there
was to know about it. He said to hell with all that and left in
something of a huff. It must have bothered him, for, late that
night, in a blinding storm, he burst into the room I was sharing with Paul Taylor, sopping wet, and sat down on Paul's bed.
Words and rain water were pouring from him. He and Paul got
into a tremendous row over the aesthetic approach to history,
and he damned Paul for a middle-class pedant, which he certainly is *not*. I have only the vaguest recollection of what it was
all about: something about soaking in the traditions of the
country and writing from the spirit. It was the first time I had
seen Hart in one of his roaring moods. I had known enough
drunks to give him his head, but Paul took his roarings seriously and the row lasted until two in the morning. As I led
Hart home he softened considerably—put his arm around
my neck and said: "Lesley, I love you!" Which just about
floored me. I had heard, of course, that Hart was a homo, but
this didn't sound like it. It was more like the cry of a little boy
who had been making a nuisance of himself and felt dreadfully
about it.

Hart came back from Taxco not with the Siqueiros paintings—
he would return for those in a few days—but with some children's
paintings he had bought for twenty cents apiece. Like most of
his treasures, these had to have an audience—and immediately.
He rushed to Mexico City, where Peggy Cowley was living, found
that she was not at home, and left one of the first of the dozens

of notes, telegrams, and letters that would soon be flying back and forth between them.

> Sorry not to find you in. But come out before two if you can, and have lunch with me. If not then later in the day—as soon as convenient.
>
> Just got back from Taxco last night. Have some fascinating children's paintings to show you—as well as puff or so left over from our private—and scandalous—fiesta last Saturday night.

On his return from the States, Hart had had serious qualms about seeing Peggy. She had come to Mexico to arrange for her divorce from Malcolm Cowley, who in the spring had written Crane asking him to be of whatever help he could to her in cashing checks and getting settled. But she had arrived after Crane had gone to Chagrin Falls, and though he left word offering her his fully staffed house, she had decided to stay with Katherine Anne Porter until she could find a place of her own. Hart was sure she was saturated with stories about his jailings, his bad language at Miss Porter's gate, his disaster at the Embassy tea party. Perhaps she would not even want to talk to him.

Yet no sooner had Hart and Peggy met than they were caught up in their shared past. "He and I were delighted to see each other again," Peggy wrote years later. "Hart represented to me the family life I had just lost, making me no longer an exile. And he felt much the same way about me. We were 'home' to each other, and both of us needed 'home.'" By the time of Hart's Taxco visits, they had become indispensable friends. Whenever Peggy fell ill, Hart would read to her, bring her tea and crackers, worry her back to health. Whenever either of them was restless, they would walk through the great parks of Mexico City together, shop in the markets, pay calls on mutual friends.

When Hart came back from a shopping spree to the Toluca market loaded with five serapes ("3 large and 2 small," all of them "of wonderful color, weave and design" and all of them great bargains—"only 21 pesos total . . . about $8.00 at present rate of exchange!"), Peggy was the first to see his purchases. When he planned to return to Taxco, he made sure that Peggy would be among the visitors. "Bill Spratling wired me to bring her along with me to Taxco tomorrow for a few days," Hart wrote Cowley,

> and I think she's planning on joining me since I've had no word to the contrary this afternoon. She was going to ask her doctor about it. . . . I'm glad to be of any help I can to Peggy, love her as always, and enjoy her company (and we see quite a lot of each other) immensely. Old friends are a God-send anywhere! Especially when they're as good sports as Peggy is . . . She's pretty fragile, but I think she's happy here, possibly more so than anywhere else right now.

All through September, October, and early November, Hart and Peggy, often joined by Lesley Simpson, were constant companions. Hart was sure he would soon have the first installment of the two thousand dollars a year he was scheduled to receive from his father's estate—a supplement that would double his Guggenheim income. For the second time in his life, he felt almost prodigal. In imagination, he spent the money six times over; in fact, for these few months, he lived modestly but comfortably. When the inheritance payments began, he wrote to Mony Grunberg, he would be "just extravagant enough to use it all up, month by month; but here in Mexico one sees so many gorgeous and inimitable handicrafts that the purse is always open."

In their tours of the city, Lesley, Hart, and Peggy would invent spectacular professions for passers-by. Passing ordinary people, Peggy Cowley wrote, Hart would clothe them in his own fantasy.

> They were pimps, cutthroats, prostitutes, *femmes fatales*, or princes in disguise.
>
> "Look at that man, Peggy. Look at him, Lesley. See that line of his jaw. It's wonderful, something Leonardo would have put on canvas. God, what form!"
>
> A dull housewife would pass, her shopping bag on her arm.
>
> "Just take a gander at that woman. A typical tart from the word go. Watch her mincing along on her way to a date, swishing her fanny. She's up to no good, you can see that!"

They would try to restrain each other's purchases of blown glass, serapes, and clay figurines.

> Each scolded the others about extravagance, Lesley and I especially joining forces when Hart loaded himself down with an armful of flowers. We reminded him that he had a beautiful flower garden at Mixcoac. He just laughed at us.
>
> "You will admit that I have no tuberoses or orchids, and they both last a long time, so there!"
>
> My room being central, we usually met and returned there with our booty. The men frequently forgot their purchases, until every corner was piled high with knickknacks. "Oh!" Hart would exclaim. "There's that virgin from Cholula. I thought I'd left it on the bus."

After one such expedition, Hart and Simpson went back to Hart's apartment. Hart had had as an intermittent guest the young archaeologist with whom he had visited Tepoztlan, a man one of Hart's more conservative friends dismissed as "a queer, a fuzzy Marxist, and a sponger, all in one." Simpson, who found Hart a better companion when his friend was out, was relieved that the guest was visiting elsewhere. Though the archaeologist was a pleasant enough young man, his Marxist tirades—particularly when fortified by Hart's liquor—could be tiring.

Left to his own devices, Hart was soon talking about his plans for the poem on the Conquest. "I . . . filled him up with some of the grand early chronicles of Mexico," Simpson remembered, "which he swore he'd read at once (and never did)."

We had a long and disconnected conversation about books. I picked up a copy of *Moby Dick* that he had on his desk and began to read aloud one of Captain Ahab's magnificent monologues. Hart took fire. "By God!" he roared. "That is poetry! If I could only write like that!" "But Hart," I replied, "you can." "I did once. *The Bridge* was good, but I'll never do anything like that again. Haven't written a goddam thing since I came to this God-forsaken country."

That conversation degenerated into a long tirade against Mexico, but other conversations about writing gave Simpson glimpses of the poet, the poet who had laboriously fitted together *White Buildings* and *The Bridge* and who would soon be at work on "The Broken Tower." Later that winter, soon after Simpson's wife joined him in Mexico City, Hart and the Simpsons had a particularly fine evening.

One of the most delightful evenings I have ever spent was the night when Hart and Marian and I had planned to see an exhibition of Siqueiros' paintings. Hart came by about eight and we had a highball. . . . He read us *The Bridge* from beginning to end, positively drunk with its rhythms. He had tears in his eyes. The poem took on life and color under his magnificent reading. When he had finished he put the book down and said reverently: "By God, that's great!" It *was* great. It was immense! That was the high point of Hart's year in Mexico, to my way of thinking. In that mood he could have written his epic of the Conquest, or anything else.

So long as Hart was able to travel about—untroubled by money worries or worries over postponed writing or worries that scandalous behavior might lose him friends—he was a joy to be near. When he was ill, or frightened, or badly drunk, however, he was another person. And in November a combination of unpleasant events led to illness, fright, and considerable drunkenness.

It all started with a bad case of the grippe, which he complicated with a home remedy compounded from equal parts of port and brandy. "A sudden cold spell—which is still lingering—was probably responsible," he wrote Bess Crane when the worst of his internal chills were gone. "And since there's hardly a house in all Mexico with any heating arrangements there isn't much to do about it but either run wildly till one's blood is steaming, or else coil up in a large serape. But I'm up today, feeling much better, and it's nice and warm out in the sun."

For a few days he was in good spirits. He went out to observe the Mexican Day of the Dead, walking through cemeteries "full of darkskinned men and women, whole families in fact, sitting on tombstones day and night holding lighted candles to the spirits of the dead." The natives, however, were not melancholy. "Far from being sad, it's very merry. They drink and eat much—and it all ends up by setting off firecrackers made in the image of Judas."

He had gone out too soon and within a day's time a "half relapse" set in—"bad cold, back ache, etc." Again Hart tried his home remedy, but this time it reduced him to a state bordering on paranoia. He became convinced that someone in the post office was opening his mail. After a day of brooding, he sent worried letters and postcards to everyone who hadn't recently written. "Haven't heard since that long letter I wrote you," one postcard began. "And wonder if you got it. Mail is sometimes opened here and not forwarded. I never know. If I'm tampered with any more I intend to object, to the Secretary of State who is a poet and knows me."

Too upset to stay indoors, Hart prepared to do battle with the post office itself. He planted on his head a brand-new sombrero. Mexico City was a town of Spanish businessmen! Hart would show them his respect for the Indian: he'd wear the full regalia. He draped his silver bridle around his neck. One last swig from the bottle of tequila, then off to the wars! Hart charged out to hail a taxi, Daniel tagging after with a bag of coins in each hand. Sometime during that afternoon Hart must have reached the post office. All the cards got to their destinations, neatly postmarked November 10.

Two days later, still drinking heavily, Hart set out once more with Daniel. This time he ended up in front of Peggy Cowley's apartment. She had asked Lesley Simpson to stop by that afternoon for a before-dinner drink. They had just settled down to conversation when "mutterings and shouting began to penetrate from the street, a kind of off-stage mob effect. Peggy looked uneasy," Simpson recalled.

> The tumult grew to a roar. "Jesus!" said Peggy. "That must be Hart!" She had hardly spoken when thunderous footsteps shook the house and Hart burst into the room all decked out in a Mexican outfit: a sombrero two feet wide, gaudy blanket, red sash, white trousers, and sandals. He paid no attention to either of us, but began to damn the country and the people in his best sailor lingo. A lot of thieving sons-of-bitches! Mexico had betrayed him! And a great deal more. There was ten minutes of this before Peggy could find out what the trouble was. It

turned out that Hart had taken a taxi at Mixcoac and driven to town with his Indian boy, and now the goddam taxi driver was trying to hold him up for 4½ pesos. They had a cop out there but he'd be eternally goddamned if he would pay. He'd go to jail first and rot, by God! And so on. I began to get a bit uneasy about the cop and went down to find out what the score was. There were the taxi driver, the cop, and a dozen grinning bystanders. The taxi driver insisted that Hart had been driving about town for two hours and a half. Hart's boy admitted it. So there was nothing to do. Hart came down grumbling and let off a good deal more steam. I told him he'd have to dig up, whereupon he cursed me, along with the Mexicans, for betraying him. But he took nine *tostones* out of his pocket and handed them one by one to the cop, who handed them gravely one by one to the taxi driver.

Peggy Cowley felt that part of the trouble was Hart's costume. "Mexicans would judge that this gringo was satirizing the natives. No one in Mexico City, except the Indians coming in from the country, wears a native costume—which this wasn't. It could easily be looked upon as an insult."

Not only had Hart gotten the police and the taxi driver and the spectators involved; he had also become caught up in a shouting match with the house porter. Peggy decided that she should encourage Hart to move on. Simpson, however, convinced her that Hart had better remain until evening.

In the dusk his costume wouldn't be so noticeable. Finally twilight came and Lesley led the two of them out. They made an unforgettable trio as I watched them through the courtyard— Hart with his sombrero bobbing on his head, a stream of smoke from his cigar, denouncing both me and the government without stopping; Lesley in his impeccable tweeds and Borsalino hat, making placating gestures; little Daniel flitting like a shadow in the rear.

"At the end of the operation," Simpson wrote, "Hart and his Indian boy went off up the street, while vague mutterings came back about thieving bastards."

Next morning Peggy found a note in her mailbox: "Dear Peggy: I don't think you need bother to consider me a friend any more." The morning after that, she had a letter.

I don't know why I felt impelled to write you that gracious note of yesterday, except perhaps on account of the heeby-jeebies—and the fact that when I called with Daniel in the morning I was refused admittance.

Of course, if you really feel that strongly about it, for whatever cause I don't know, then we'll have to remain apart. Please let me contradict that note of yesterday, anyway. And believe me, at least as far as I know, as always,

Your
Hart.

As so often before, Hart decided to reform. He would swear off "dancing, *tequila*, and amor." "I'm on the water wagon for awhile," he wrote Loveman—but found himself almost immediately off it thanks to his own enthusiastic hospitality.

My house is in considerable tumult. David Siqueiros (who is certainly the greatest painter in Mexico) arrived Sunday night from his house in Taxco, with his wife and doctors—so deathly ill from malaria that he had to be carried into the house. No really expert medical attention being available in a town so small as Taxco—and after 8 days of mounting fever—there was nothing to do but rush to Mexico City. . . . Siqueiros is going to pull through all right, but I shall probably have him here with me for a couple of months. Malaria takes a long time. I'm glad to be of help in such a crisis, however, and since I had three rooms which I never used the house really isn't crowded.

It did begin to feel crowded, however, almost immediately. Siqueiros had brought with him not only family and doctors but a great many friends, who, though they did not all stay there, were in and out of the house from dawn until long after dusk. Most of them, like Siqueiros himself, were active propagandists for the extreme left and their impassioned arguments over pinpoint details of Marxist doctrine swirled through the courtyard and overflowed into Hart's own room. Actively participating in the debate was Hart's Marxist archaeologist, who had again taken up residence on a cot in the living room and who joined the turbid ebb and flow of Spanish—now and then pausing to translate juicier passages for Hart's benefit.

At first Siqueiros's visit was exciting and Hart invited in all his own friends to join the endless party. But when food and liquor bills soared, and the general din prevented Hart from so much as writing letters, he began looking for momentary islands of calm. The person he trusted most for such respite was Lesley Simpson. "Hart's attachment to me was a curious and pathetic thing," Simpson felt.

I became a kind of safe-and-sane elder brother, someone to run to when things went wrong. I never scolded him. I was a foil for his magnificent rages and let him blow off steam when he would have burst otherwise. I was so damned sorry for him that I made a stupendous effort not to show it and always treated him as if he were the most normal person in the world. "By God, Lesley," he said to me one night when I had rescued him from his household, "by God, I love you—you're so damned *middle class*! These cockeyed communists have got me down. I'm middle class too. The only people who ever did anything were middle class!"

Finally, after renting a hotel room to get a night's sleep, Hart decided to break and run. He sent a telegram to Peggy Cowley, cancelling plans they had made to join friends in Taxco ("Am fedup and going to tepoztlan for several days. Please tell Simpson caroline anita regarding sunday afternoon. Love. Hart"), and headed for the train. This move, he wrote Bess Crane, was the most sensible he'd made in weeks.

It's been something like Bedlam here for the last ten days. Having serious sickness in the house makes that almost inevitable, of course. David Siqueiros, the painter, whom I've mentioned before, came down with malaria . . . I received a desperate wire asking for the privilege of my house, and of course, there was nothing to do but consent. . . . I didn't even have an extra bed for him, but since his wife had brought along a mattress I let them have my springs . . . But the thousand and one details that ensued, visitors coming and going to say nothing of doctors, and all the extra work and errands put on the servants— all this and more, naturally disorganized the quiet routine of the household completely.

Last Friday the situation got so on my nerves that I bolted for Tepoztlan. It proved to be the best of all remedies. Long strenuous walks over rocks and mountains with my pack on my back, pleasant encounters with some of the natives who remembered me from my former visit, and baths in nearby streams—there's really nothing like getting out in the wilds occasionally to clear one's head.

Hart even managed to have an adventure—nothing really dramatic, but he made it seem so.

Deciding to walk from Tepoztlan to Cuernavaca Sunday I got lost on a false trail through a dense forest and stumbled about, not knowing where on earth I was for hours. Thirsty? ! ! ! And blistered feet? ! ! ! Finally I came upon the railroad track, miles from where I should have been, but was so glad to find something *definite* that I walked the ties for about four hours more until I came to a small station outside Cuernavaca, a filling station for locomotives. And there wasn't much water left in the tank for future trains when I got through drinking there, I can tell you. I didn't attempt any further exploits, but took the next train through to Mexico [City]. I must have walked about 35 miles at least that day. But I've really felt swell ever since. Next time, however, I won't carry so much in my pack!

On Hart's return from Tepoztlan, he found that Siqueiros was up and about.

My "patient" is making a very rapid recovery, is able to eat and walk about again. I was all prepared for a siege of two months at least, but it now looks as though he and his wife would not be here more than a week longer. That prospect relieves the strain immensely . . . I've got about fifty letters to answer, but I'll plunge through them and into my work again in a couple of days, feeling as fit as I do.

The work Hart spoke of was not, of course, poetry. "I must admit that with all my present salutary circumstances my impulses in that direction are surprisingly low," he would soon be writing to Eda Lou Walton. "A beautiful environment and economic security are far from compensating for a world of chaotic values and frightful spiritual depression. And I can't derive any satisfaction in the spinning out of mere personal moods and attitudes."

For a while, Hart felt, the only work he would be capable of would be prose—reviews, perhaps articles. The correspondence with Zabel had grown since the spring, Zabel suggesting subjects that Hart might tackle—a writer's lot in Mexico, Mexico's appeal to the temporary American exile. Crane himself had several projects in mind, each of which Zabel encouraged him to undertake: the critical study of Wallace Stevens that he had earlier mentioned to Untermeyer; a review of James Feibleman's *Death of the God in Mexico*; an article-review that would incorporate William Spratling's *Little Mexico* into a general discussion of the way the poet can draw on a foreign country's resources. In addition to planning these assignments, Crane once again agreed to review James Whaler's *Green River* and also promised to review Phelps Putnam's *The Five Seasons*.

These two books arrived from *Poetry* early in October. Putnam's, Hart felt, was a major accomplishment. ("Putnam is more surprising and magnificent than ever! Am glad to have such a challenge of a review.") Whaler's, however, had been published before Putnam's, and Hart settled down to write about it. A week or so later, he had notes in fairly good order and was beginning to "rip off expletives . . . scratching my head like mad to be impressive." By the last of the month the review was mailed in, its carefully balanced treatment of the poem most interesting for the lines Crane singled out for admiration, lines that in many ways paralleled his own imagery in the "Harbor Dawn" section of *The Bridge*:

With masts and mariners before
Your window, street-cries in your ears,
There lay your bed, there nail your desk,
There leaven all you know with tears.

Though the review would not be published until the April issue, his having accomplished it—and in reasonably good time—gave Hart a great psychological lift. The Putnam review, on the other hand, hovered tantalizingly before Crane for months; all through November, December, and January, he was sure he was going to get it into "final" shape.

One reason, of course, for Crane to put himself to the agony of reviewing was that he did not know from day to day just what his financial situation really was. He had returned to Mexico with a little money in the bank. While he was in Ohio, he had been given $500 of the direct payment from his father's estate. The other $500, he understood, would be deposited in his checking account. The payment of $2,000 a year was somewhat more precarious, and Hart was painfully aware of that. Even before he left Ohio, his uncle Byron Madden, one of the executors of his father's estate, had warned him that he could not count on the payments.

I am hopeful that the revenue of the estate may be sufficient to take care of the annual payments provided for you and Bess both, but I feel that I must write this letter to you in order that you may so regulate your finances as not to be subjected to hardship in case of our inability to make or continue the monthly payments to you, or from any interruption of them which may be necessary.

In the middle of October his uncle told him that there almost certainly would be no payments until the first of the year. He summarized the condition of the businesses, then went on to say:

For all these reasons as well as for the general business depression which still exists we will not know before the first of January whether the various corporations will show any profits out of which dividends may be declared and as your father indicated by his will his desire that the annual payments to be made to you and Bess should be made out of the dividends received upon the stock of these corporations, we do not see how it will be possible to make any such payments until after the first of the year and then only if dividends in a sufficient amount are paid. For this reason I again say to you as I have said before that it will not be advisable for you to place any dependence upon such payments until you know that they have actually been made. When they are made we will advise you.

The day after his uncle wrote this letter—and more than a week before Hart received it—Hart sent an awkward letter to his stepmother. She was the last person in the world he wanted to trouble about finances; but he had just had a note from his bank telling him that he was overdrawn by $350!

> I'm somewhat upset, Bess, that my September statement from the Guaranty Trust showed no deposit from the Estate. Byron wrote me that if such could not be made—"such could not be made" but, I understood that I was to receive notice of same condition at least 30 days in advance. If I can't depend on the monthly division of the annual $2,000 bequest for the last three months (I mean, including the presumable November payment) I'll have to ask you to see that the remaining $500 of the $1,000 outright bequest is credited to my account with Guaranty Trust as soon as possible. If there are any assessment figures available yet I should be glad to know how conditions are. Not that I expect you to undertake any such extensive reports, but there must be, in the course of procedure, some carbon copies of reports, etc.—that is, if any figures have as yet been arrived at. Perhaps it is not my privilege to enquire about this, but I am somewhat mystified that my bank statement was as low as reported.

She answered him immediately, explaining that she had already seen to it that the two checks—the one for $150 he cashed before leaving New York to send passage money to his friend in Europe and the one for $200 for his own passage to Mexico—were covered. The remaining $150 of his inheritance would, she said, immediately be placed in the depleted account. "That is as far as we can go until we know more about things and how they are going to show up. . . . However, I want to know how you are fixed financially." She knew Hart, and she knew how fretful he could be when he owed money; so a few days later, when she had a chance to check the current income of the businesses, she wrote him a tentative summary of conditions. In the candy business, everything—as both she and Hart knew—would depend on Christmas trade. At the beginning of November, all they could do would be to wait and watch—and be grateful that things were no worse off.

> I am hopeful that by January things will show up to better advantage financially than . . . they appear to now. I suppose we should feel grateful, and I do Harold, that C.A. left things in a marvelously clean condition, far more so than one should expect these days. You know it was his boast that he never owed anyone anything at any time that he couldn't take care of. It is a good thing for us that he held to the old-fashioned ideas of honesty or it would be a pretty difficult situation.

Though he explained few of the details to Bess Crane, Hart's immediate problem stemmed from the high cost of the Siqueiros paintings and the expense of housing the Siqueiros entourage for the better part of a month. All September expenses had had to come from what remained of the first inheritance payment. In October, when the third quarter of the Guggenheim payment became available, Hart withdrew $325 of the $400 that was supposed to hold him until the beginning of the year, much of it going to Siqueiros. By the middle of November, the remaining $75 of Guggenheim money was gone. A week after he'd cleaned out the Guggenheim account, he explained his situation to Sam Loveman.

Of course the Siqueiros works cost me *considerably*, so much, in fact, that I've been worried about making ends meet until my next quarterly from the Guggenheims falls due Jan. 1st. For what was my great shock after buying them to be notified that none of the income that I had been assured of from the estate would be paid, and would continue unpaid indefinitely! This meant that the paintings had to be paid for out of the Guggenheim allowance—and in consequence I'm stranded excepting for a few dollars remaining in my personal N.Y. account —until January 1st. And it will be hard to cash personal checks hereabouts. And if business doesn't pick up before next May it probably means that I can't continue to stay in Mexico for awhile longer, as I had hoped to do.

Though Crane did worry about money, Indian customs and the Mexican countryside continued to give him moments that he was sure would ultimately bear fruit in poetry. He might be forced to leave when his Guggenheim ran out, but he really wanted, he told his "Aunt Sally" Simpson, to stay to the last possible minute.

His initial plan of traveling, he now decided, was best after all. If he could dispose of the lease on his house, he might be able to pile his luggage in a convenient corner and be on his way.

I made the mistake of taking a lease on a house here in this suburb of Mexico City when I first came down. Now I'm trying to sublet it for the rest of the term, as I'm anxious to keep traveling about from town to town from now on—and have no real need of it. . . . Mexico is really too beautiful. One can't stop looking at things. And that is a distraction when you want to "get into yourself" and pour out poetry. I haven't done much of any work yet here, and I think I'll have to get bored before I shall. But it's a great experience regardless of that; and maybe when I go back to the States (where I certainly *am* bored) it will all come out of me.

Hart never did sublet, but it was not for lack of trying. His friends supplied him lists of incoming visitors. None of them wanted the Mixcoac house.

Despite house-disposal worries and very little travel, Hart tried to gather material for the projected Conquest idea. The Mexican fiestas, he hoped, would show him the linked Christian-pagan faith that in Tepoztlan he had decided determined the personality of the modern Mexican Indian. Even though the poem was never to be written nor, so far as I have been able to determine, outlined, the design of it was obviously to be much like that of *The Bridge*: a primitive American civilization would be overrun by a modern European one. But whereas in *The Bridge* the design had been Plains Indian giving way to the North American melting pot of nations, in the Conquest poem it would be Mexican Indian absorbing and significantly transforming Spanish Catholicism. Though there is no statement by Crane to this effect, the ceremonies that most affected him and the elements in those ceremonies that most interested him all demonstrate this linkage.

Consider his response to the feast of the Virgin of Guadalupe. As in Tepoztlan, what fascinated him about the ceremonies was the Indian's amalgamation of two antithetical traditions. On the evening of December 12, still keyed up, he wrote Bess Crane about the feast.

There is a distinct smell of powder in the air this evening. But that isn't all! Rockets are whizzing up sporadically for miles around, and the sound of church bells far and near, has been incessant since dawn. All of which is to say that this is an important day in the Mexican calendar—nothing less, in fact, than the annual Feast of the Virgin of Guadalupe, the particular Patroness of all Mexicans. This year's celebration is all the more extravagant, as she is reputed to have "appeared" here (before a humble peon named Juan Diego) just four hundred years ago today.

For weeks the influx of Indians and pilgrims of all types from all the provinces and tribes of Mexico has been in progress. It is probably no exaggeration to say that there are two hundred thousand extra souls, pious and near-pious, who have flocked here to continue the *fiesta* until New Year's. But today—all of them, including the majority of Mexico City's population of one million—went to the little town of Guadalupe Hidalgo, practically a suburb now, of Mexico City, where a great cathedral has been erected near the spot where the Virgin is reputed to have made her first appearance.

I engaged a cab the night before, and got up at four this morning to get an early start, arriving before the Cathedral just at dawn. Even then one couldn't elbow one's way into the church without waiting in line for an hour. I gave that up, having come more to see some of the native Indian dances that take place here and there throughout the town—some, in fact, right in front of the cathedral. The whole business is simply indescribable without ten reams of paper; but suffice to say that the dances were wonderful. Certain people are picked from each district or tribe for their marked ability—and there is quite a rivalry between districts in the excellence of their performance. There are from 24 to 45 in a group, generally in circular formation, with banners, guitars which they play as they sway and turn, and elaborate pantaloons, skirts, feather crests, etc. Death and the Devil weave in and out among them—and other masked figures, like wild boars and old men-of-the-mountain.

I pushed and prodded from one group to another, until by 9:30 I was ready to come home; and did. I had taken Daniel along, and was glad of it, since I just missed causing a riot by attempting to photograph some of the dancers in action, which is, it seems, forbidden. The dancing is all very serious and very set and formal; it generally derives from very ancient tribal rites. It isn't any sort of Mardi-Gras mood at all that the Indians express, despite the flamboyant colors of their costumes.

Well, when I consider that the Indians, all of those, at least, that I saw—had been dancing the same measure for practically all the night before—continued all day after I left—and WILL continue on the same schedule for practically two weeks more —and ALL for the sake of a ritual and *not a cent of money*—I must say I admire their devotion to custom and tradition. The figure of the Virgin of Guadalupe miraculously unites the teachings of the early Catholic missionaries with many survivals of the old Indian myths and pagan cults. She is a typical Mexican product, a strange blend of Christian and pagan strains. What a country and people! The most illogical and baffling on earth; but how appealing! I enclose the authoritative portrait of this Virgin, who, I think, is quite beautiful. She is really the Goddess of the Mexican masses, and you will find her picture or image everywhere, even when you can't see it—as for instance, inside the hat bands of wide *sombreros*. It is rare to escape the sight of her—on a postcard or stencil above the windshield facing half the taxi drivers of Mexico. For protection and good luck!

The feast of the Virgin of Guadalupe is one of the first of a series of Mexican Christmas festivities that begin in mid-December and continue through mid-January. As Hart watched this Christmas activity and as gifts began to arrive from friends in the States, he felt tightening about him the isolation he had committed himself to. A package of candy and cookies ("as aromatic and fresh as though baked yesterday") arrived from Bill Wright's family. From his Aunt Bess Madden had come an announcement that another package was on its way, the announcement itself full of family

news and recollections of Christmases so far back Hart had almost
forgotten them.

My own dear Harold:

If it were not for Christmas, I suppose this letter would still
be put off, for I am such a poor writer and the thought of writing
to a famous poet has quite unnerved me for the task, but I must
think of you still as the little boy who wanted the "Codfish soda,"
and then I will be equal to you, as I was then.

. . . The maple cream was not as nice as I could have sent if
you were not so far away, but I made it hard so it would not be
softened by change of atmosphere. I wish I could see you eating
the ham and I wonder who will share it with you. . . .

From Canary Cottage, he heard, there would be a huge package—the girls at the restaurant joining Bess Crane in sending
contributions. All of Hart's letters to Bess Crane had been full of
recollection of the one home he could still count on. And her
letters to him had been equally affectionate. Now the girls also
sent Christmas notes. "We're going to miss your company this
winter around the fireplace, our Sunday night walks, even to the
searching for the cider," one of them wrote. "Am spending the
day at home and as Bess has not yet arrived home I'll scratch off
a few lines," another wrote, the "few lines" full of news of the
waitresses and customers Crane had known, of the walks and talks
they had shared: "We took a walk the other evening but we stayed
on the main trail—were afraid to go on our old route at night
without a man, so you see we missed you Harold."

Until Christmas, the tone of his letters and those from Bess
Crane was casually breezy. "The girls all insist I send you their
love, you know they wouldn't tell you that," one of her earliest
letters ends. And another one: "All your women send their love,
and wish to say they are still true to you." She had written him
ironically of his Aunt Bess Madden's decision to enter politics;
and Hart had responded in the same tone: "Your jolly letter of
the 3rd was a great treat. I'm glad that things are booming . . .—
and that Bess Madden has become the Mussolini of East Cleveland." He had urged on a project that the girls had instituted—a
chain letter to him; and Bess had renewed the welcome that he
knew would always be his: "You know if it gets too cold down
in Mexico, we have those nice grate fires at the cottage which you
enjoyed so much last winter."

But when Christmas packages arrived—and no snow—Hart
was suddenly conscious of how much he had lost in the loss of a
father. He needed to be reassured that he would not also lose that
father's world. "I haven't heard from you in a long while," he

ended the letter to Bess that had begun with a description of the
feast of the Virgin of Guadalupe:

—no answer yet to my last. But I'm not complaining. I know
the season, the other trials—and how filled your time is. Thank
you very much, by the way, for having arranged the money
payment for me through the Chase Bank. It saved me many
pesos on the "exchange." I won't need to bother you again this
month—nor next. Matters go more smoothly with me as I get
myself more acclimated to Mexico, its habits and the peculiar
strain of the high altitude here. I'm feeling very well, and am
even accused of getting fat.

As Christmas draws near I think much of the Season's loss
in all it can give to you and me this year. Christmas always
probes the deepest memories, and the fondest; and I know what
you will be thinking about this Christmas, and how apt it will
be to make the hearth seem cold. I know your fortitude also,
Bess,—and your natural, spontaneous response to all that is
good and enduring. And I'm sure, therefore, that surrounded
as you are by the loyalty and love of those whose names need
no particular mention, you'll still find many reasons for gratitude
and even a bit of seasonal merriment.

And so—good night. And Merry Christmas to you, to Ethel,
to Anne, to Dorothy—and to all about the cottage who care to
remember me at all. Let me hear from you when you have time.
If you haven't—I can understand.

The past could not, of course, be recaptured—except in memory.
But affection and good will could fight loneliness, bridge the miles
between Mexico's winter-flowering cactus and snow-swept Chagrin
Falls's lighted Christmas trees.

My dear Harold:                                    Dec. 18/31
What a nice letter to read at the breakfast table this morning,
and how much all of us enjoyed it. If you knew the pleasure
derived from your letters you would write every week . . .

Harold I must apologize. I thought I had written you since
sending the money. I guess I just slipped up on that; however
have thought of you so much and said to the girls I couldn't
understand why I hadn't heard from you.

You are right, Harold, this is a hard time of the year for both
of us; just keeping busy has helped me in no small way since
C.A. left, and sometimes I stop and wonder at myself, going
on from day to day, seems he is still here with me, helping and
guiding, else how could it be. I have missed him so. You are
very sweet to say the nice things you do in your letter, and I
want you to know you are very close and dear to me, not only
as C.A.'s son but as a very dear friend, and I am never too busy
to write or think of you.

I do hope you will have a happy day Christmas, and the girls at the office and store and the Cottage all wish to be remembered to you, and Ethel, Ann, and Dorothy join me in sending our love . . .

Lovingly,
Bess.

# 41

Before Hart had a chance to open his Christmas presents—or even to receive Bess Crane's letter—a casual incident drastically changed his life. He helped persuade Peggy Cowley to move to Taxco.

Like Hart, but for very different reasons, Peggy had found Mexico City a difficult place in which to live. The altitude troubled her; she would get rid of one cold only to catch another. Finally, early in December, Hart, Lesley Simpson, and Bill Spratling managed to talk her into moving several thousand feet closer to sea level. Bill found her a house in Taxco, and Hart and Lesley helped her with her packing, Hart promising to join her for a house-warming party during the Christmas holidays.

No sooner had she moved than telegrams began to arrive from Hart. María Luisa and Jesús, the servants she had inherited from the owners of the house, decided that Hart must be desperately in love. No one but a lover, they assured her, would squander that sort of money on telegrams.

Two days before he was expected, Hart arrived. Peggy was taking a bath. But María Luisa—on the look-out for strangers toiling up the steep hill to the house perched just below its summit —was sure that the bright-haired young man she spied in the distance was Peggy's gentleman. "The señor comes! Hurry!" she shouted in to Peggy.

> Sure enough, by the time I got to the veranda, there was Hart coming up the last turn, carrying his suitcase. I rushed down the precipitous steps to meet him. He dropped the suitcase and we embraced as if it had been years since we had seen each other. From the radiant faces of the maid and the gardener I could see it would be a waste of breath to make it clear he wasn't "mine" in their sense of the word.

Hart had arrived full of good intentions. He made Peggy promise that she would install him in front of his typewriter first thing in the morning. The Putnam review, he told her, had to be done—and quickly. Then they went on a tour of the house, Hart exclaiming in admiration as each window offered its own breathtaking view. That evening Bill Spratling arrived to deliver Peggy's Christmas present: a pair of silver earrings, tiny baskets overflowing with flowers.

> The men insisted that I put them on immediately, so I went into my bedroom and changed into a dress that suited them. Hart whirled me around and stepped back to get the full effect.
> "Isn't she wonderful, Bill? I'll fall in love with you," he said jokingly, and then, in a different tone, "Of course I really am already."

All through the visit Hart's good humor led from comedy to gentle gestures of affection to great "displays"—the latter usually staged with the collaboration of María Luisa and Jesús. One of them took place the morning after Hart's arrival.

Long after Spratling's departure, Hart and Peggy had sat up talking. Their conversation had ranged from Mexican modern art to problems of life in a depression economy, but it had ended on the subject of Christmas in Mexico. "I still can't take in that it's Christmas, without the traditional decorations," Peggy had said. "The Christmas holidays need green, piles of it, and a brittle red."

This was the sort of challenge Hart responded to: "I'll find something in the morning. Don't worry. Mexico is wrapped in tinsel. You'll be surprised and satisfied. Just leave it to me."

The next morning Peggy arrived on her porch to find Hart in frantic conversation—all gestures and sputtering Spanish—with María Luisa and Jesús.

> Hart's thick, short-cropped hair gleamed silver in the sun, his cigar in one hand making an arc. He was laughing heartily and, with his free hand, patting first one and then the other on the back. . . .
> "There's your coffee and orange juice, my dear," he said airily, after giving me a kiss. "Maria Louisa, Jesus and I are off to get your decorations. No, I'm not going to tell you what they will be. You can sit here cogitating on the subject. Anyway, it will be something red and green, which is what you asked for."

When they came staggering back up the steps, the effect may not have been Christmas, but the color was surely red and green. Each was loaded down with poinsettias that looked as heavy as cordwood—two hundred of them, about four feet long. In addition, Hart had twenty-five strange yellow blooms.

Hart himself summarized his Taxco visit in letters that he sent out more than two weeks later from his house in Mixcoac. "Well, about Christmas in Taxco!" he wrote Bess Crane:

> I went to visit the former wife of Malcolm Cowley . . . Peggy and I have known each other for years and years, and while

she had about a dozen other guests there for the day, we enjoyed each other's company most, and I was the last one to leave, staying over New Year's—and then some. . . . There were three dogs . . . belonging to Natalie Scott, who owns the house. . . . The dogs alone would have made life tremulous, but there were also two aigrette birds (pets of the house) who were making love continuously to the tune of quack-quack-quack—and craning their necks in the most insinuating manner. . . . "Gretchen" and "Charles," I called them, though I could never distinguish one from the other, except at certain critical moments in their dialogue. They don't (or rather "she" don't) get those expensive tail feathers until the eggs are laid; but I left Taxco with the feeling that feathers were on the way.

I can't say that we had a very "dry" time of it. We were invited to dances in the houses of the Mayor and other city officials—and more brandy poured out to us in various toasts to one thing and t'other than would be needed to sink a battleship. All over Mexico it is customary to go to dances, public, semi-private, and private on the nine evenings before Christmas. These occasions are called "posadas," and the series ends with a great burst on Xmas eve. . . . I attended midnight mass on Christmas eve, and the beauty of the Cathedral, the decorations, singing and service—as well as the touching beauty of the Indian people kneeling about me almost made me bawl. I was pretty well lit anyway—but extremely well behaved, for once, at least.

His stay with Peggy provided him, he wrote Malcolm Cowley, "the pleasantest Christmas and New Year's . . . that I remember for ages."

Peggy's usual mixed crowd appeared for the former date; but I stayed long enough to enjoy a week alone with her. Taxco is so extremely beautiful—and the townsfolk still so affable—that whatever one has to say about the Yankee occupation (and that ultimately seals its doom) it's still one of the pleasantest places to be. Peggy has probably written you about encounters with Brett, Bynner, King, et al. Lewd limericks were shouted from the rooftops—your collection being more than ever in demand. A mad crowd, though. I had enough Duff,—preferring as I do, the nautical variety.

Reading the letters Crane sent friends after his return, the most one can gather is that he had had a very good time. Peggy was a dear friend; he had enjoyed his visit. Nowhere is there any indication that new horizons had opened up. But they had.

For a little while, for friends in the States, Crane would continue in the role in which he and they had cast him. He was the robust, cigar-smoking man who after heavy drinking bouts would comb the waterfront for sailors as desperate and lonely as he. Lovemaking of "the nautical variety" was his preference. In fact, however, he had discovered depths of feeling, intricacies of passion, that two weeks earlier he would have sworn he was incapable of. I do not mean to suggest that Hart did a complete about-face. He did not. He did not abandon his personality. He simply discovered that it was more subtle, more flexible, more "normal" than he had been willing to admit. His discovery was decked with flowers, rung in by cathedral bells, a part and parcel of the fiesta world of the Mexican Christmas. He made love to Peggy Cowley while sky-rockets splintered the sky and all the bells of Taxco hammered their ears.

Afterwards, their love seemed to him as easy, as effortless, as inevitable as sunrise or moonrise. It had begun on Christmas night. They had walked down the hill with the straggle of holiday guests from the housewarming party, seen them to the bus, waved a cheerful goodbye.

> After seeing everyone off . . . Hart and I sat down for a quiet drink in the cantina, deciding that we had had quite enough of the holiday spirit and celebration. We would both stay in our eagle's nest and work hard during the rest of his stay. No more drinking and parties. Making that pre-New Year's resolution, we soberly climbed up to the house.

No sooner had they reached the house than a deafening ringing of bells started. They had heard the intermittent bells in the plaza, of course. But here, perched just above the bell towers, they found town noises strained out; crashing sound rolled everywhere around them. "To me it was terrifying," Peggy wrote. "Maria Louisa proudly told us that the men would be able to keep it up for the next ten days!"

> "It can't last," Hart yelled at me over the dinner table. From then on we communicated mainly by signs. There were to be fireworks and dancing in the Plaza. We might as well go. Anything to get away from the clamor of the cathedral bells. The noise was nowhere near as harsh down in the town, being above us rather than in our ears. The fireworks were gay and exciting. We danced until we could dance no longer, then stopped for a drink and back again. Everything appeared to be spinning off into an infinity of color and music.
>
> "It's all a poem and I shall write it, with us right in the middle of it, darling."
>
> That night, or what was left of it, we slept in my bed, the clamor of the bells our wedding music. The next morning Maria Louisa knocked at my room before bringing us our coffee and orange juice. She had never done this before. Somehow it showed us she put an official seal on our union. The bells were

still monotonously flailing the air. We were so wrapped up in each other, so ludicrously happy, that we hardly noticed. Hart was drunk in the excitement of the moment, a bit awed, but unafraid. He kept looking at me and laughing.

"I don't believe it for a moment, darling, but be good and tell me that it's not a figment of my imagination."

When Hart appeared that afternoon in Doña Berta's bar, he entered with a swagger. Bill Spratling, who was there, remembered him marching up to the little crowd of Americans. He might have been Columbus returning from the New World. Everyone knew his reputation. Now he was out to shatter it in a single gesture. "Boys," he announced. "Boys—I did it!" And then he launched into a graphic account of the delights of heterosexual love. Peggy had performed the miracle. How could he not praise her?

When he came back to Peggy's house, he was full of the poem he had told her he was going to write. For the better part of three days, Peggy remembered, he worked at it, his phonograph roaring an accompaniment to the endless ringing of bells. New Year's Eve, when it arrived, fit into the celebration mood he and Peggy now shared. They came down to the town together, arm in arm. "New Year's Eve with the parades and fireworks of the Indians is past description," Hart wrote Bess Crane. "Imagine a top section of a bull, mounted on a man's shoulders—the bull carrying a kind of tower of fireworks that fly in all directions—and the man carrying the whole shebang and rushing after one after another of the Indians who tantalize him—with the fireworks belching rockets, sizzling pin wheels, etc. flying in all directions."

The slowly emerging poem—Hart would work on it for the next two months—was in part a wedding hymn, and Peggy was as integral to its composition as bells and phonograph.

> He was in love and wanted me with him every moment. . . . His energy seemed inexhaustible. He was keyed to the highest pitch. It was his first experience in loving a woman—somewhat frightening to him. . . . He had found something beyond sensuality, he felt purified of a sense of guilt which he had always had as a homosexual.
>
> Most of his sex life had involved persons whom he picked up when drunk, and the satisfaction of sex was the end of the acquaintance. Still, he had often justified his actions, and sometimes would brag about them. I remembered his telling one night at a party that he happened to be on Brooklyn Bridge when the fleet came up the river. "There I was, looking down, with the entire Navy streaming between my legs!" It was embarrassing to him to find himself so suddenly changed, after living his adult life . . . in the firm conviction that he was a homosexual and could be nothing else.

For a little while, they agreed, Hart and Peggy would keep their secret—not in Taxco, of course; it was public knowledge there. But they would write discreet letters north. Even in Mexico City, where Hart returned at the end of the first week in January, they would be no more than good friends. Yet both of them could think of nothing but their new love, and their daily letters and telegrams were full of it. In private letters, at least, they could revel in sensuality. Peggy's letters are no longer available. (When Grace Crane unpacked them after Hart's suicide, she was horrified. "I can conceive how such things *might* have been said in *private direct* conversation," she wrote to one friend, "but *never* oh *never* be put on paper.") Peggy's words are lost, mislaid, or burned. Hart's, however, have survived; for Peggy kept his letters and telegrams and the scraps of paper on which quick notes were jotted down. The intensity of his feeling, the sense of new life that she had given him, shines through mundane matters, breaks out in rambling stories of his efforts to dispose of his lease. They were now full of plans to travel together, ultimately to settle down together; and their letters were threaded with the passion they had found in each other's arms.

January 6:

Dearest Peggy:

I hope you got the $75. I sent yesterday afternoon. I went first to the Mancera where I ate like a horse; then rushed to the bank in time to get all I wanted. Daniel I found as drunk as usual when I got home, but he did manage to get me a hot bath before eight, after which I really began to enjoy my weariness. Slept fairly well—waking to find old Mizzentop flaunting the colors still in valiant dreams of you. . . .

I'm in such a hectic rush this morning that I can't do more than remind you that you already know the depth of my love for you. The ride back yesterday was psychologically so strange and new a meditation to me that it seemed almost like sheer delirium. When I get more of the pressure of events eased and a moment for a little personal thinking I'll write you a more decent expression of my gratitude. . . .

I'm expecting a letter from you tomorrow, and often afterwards, dear Twidget! Apply yourself well; don't forget the toilet paper, the water wagon, your typewriter, nor your Hart.

Hugs, kisses, and a long upward sigh!

Hart

Thursday [Jan. 7, 1932]:

Dear Twidget:

No letter from you in the first mail today, but perhaps later. I'm hoping. Lesley and I had a delightful afternoon together yesterday, eating heartily and discussing your charms and merits. . . .

I'm already tired—rushing through correspondence this morning. . . .

Off to town again for lunch today. Not drinking, I feel I have a right to better meals. Maybe there'll be a snapshot or so to include with this. I missed your darling hands last night. Old Mizzentop doesn't particularly like air pockets either! Nor standing so long without an occasional tumble . . . Remember me to Gretchen and Charles and Bill and Maria-Luisa.

Love ever, from your<br>Hart

Tuesday [Jan. 12, 1932]:

Dearest Peggy:

It's still early morning, and so cold that I can hardly manipulate my fingers on the keyboard—but you must be immediately informed of my joyful relief at finally hearing from you yesterday. After waiting in vain all last week I began to worry in twenty directions at once. It has been so frigid here—especially o'nights—that Old Mizzentop would surely have all sorts of excuses for a number of meanderings. But excuses don't happen to be in order as he hasn't meandered from home base a second.

. . . I'm so glad that you like the pictures. I've had the extra copies made and will send them as soon as collected. Those of Chapingo were claimed to be "underexposed"! So no prints were made. That was a marvelously ironic comment on what *did* show up on the negatives, however, and I had the blushes allright allright when the clerk at Calpini's held them up to the light! I still have the negatives for your delectation.

According to your letters, life in Taxco is still running rather high. Whatever it might be, it would be preferable to New York, judging by Malcolm's report. I can't see anything ahead but riots before Spring. . . .

Your Saturday and Sunday notes have just arrived. God, it's wonderful to really be "in demand," and it's worse than ever not to be "on hand." I don't know what I'm going to do about it. Daniel, after being absent all day, came home drunk again last night. So drunk he couldn't walk. And right now I feel like packing everything as fast as possible and clearing out for good, regardless of any further obligations to anyone. This can't go on . . . I have been able to work through a lot of necessary correspondence, but I can't get anything done of the Putnam review in such a welter. I'm damned if I want to pay another 100 pesos for another month of this misery here, but I see no hope of renting the place—and, well—HELL! . . .

I'm sorry to hear about your cold in your side; I'm sure I might help a little more than a hot water bottle. What a letter this is! Don't let it depress you; I'm simply in too much of a muddle to do better at the moment: money, plans, "the future" —besides the difficulty of getting or taking any kind of prompt action in such a country as this. Just ask me if I expect to buy any more blankets or gadgets to worry about!

I don't see how I can help coming out to see you before another ten days; but I'd like to have solved a few riddles before that, if possible; otherwise it won't be half as pleasant. Surely you can see how that is . . . Keep on loving me, Peggy, in the meanwhile—even if it "hurts." At least it helps me a lot.

Lovingly,

Hart . . .

Wednesday [probably Jan. 20, 1932]:

Dearest:

In case I don't get off tomorrow morning for Taxco—and hence anticipate this letter by kisses and much contentment—I want you at least to know that it won't be long before we are together again, for I shall be with you certainly before Sunday.

Your letter of this morning makes me ache for you. Why is it you love me so? I don't deserve it. I'm just a careening idiot, with a talent for humor at times, and for insult and desecration at others. But I can, and must say that your love is very precious to me. For one thing it seems to give me an assurance that I thought long buried. You can give me many things besides—if time proves me fit to receive them: the independence of my mind and soul again, and perhaps a real wholeness to my body.

Do you remember me saying that I would *not* fall in love with you, or with anyone again? But I find that though I like to perpetuate that statement, I have really overruled it in a thousand thoughts and emotions. . . .

Since there seems to be such a slight chance of renting the house, and since I really can't welsh on Eyler Simpson (who is equally responsible, since he signed the lease with me) by just walking out—I've decided to pay the $70. odd dollars difference by just keeping it—wherever else I spend my time during the next three months. The family will just have to fork up a loan or something for me, and I feel sure they will. I'm going to try and avoid spoiling my remaining time in Mexico; and much more worry about the house and my few items of possession would succeed in doing so. Don't you think I'm right?

. . . I want you to go to Acapulco with me—and after that I'm going to spend some time up in Michoacan, Morelia, Lake Chapala, etc. I may end up in Jalapa (which is very near Vera

Cruz) but by that time I rather expect you'll be with me. I feel serene and happy in your love today . . .

Your,

Hart

During the two weeks Hart and Peggy were separated, each tried to decide how to handle their new relationship. Peggy was grateful for the interval, for it gave her a chance to make up her mind about the excursions to Indian towns that Hart had planned for the rest of his stay. "I was willing to go as far as Acapulco," she wrote, "but I was very contented where I was and had no desire to ramble uncomfortably around the country. I liked the idea of a short separation. It was hard to keep up with his fierce tempo, charging everything with tremendous energy, drinking, writing, making love, and just enjoying himself. It was like living with an erupting volcano."

For his own part, Hart made ready for travel. He checked to see that his Mexican tourist card was still valid, stopped in at the American consulate to report that he had lost his passport, and visited a doctor to get typhoid shots. He changed his mind about subletting his house literally every day. At first he had hoped that Lesley Simpson might take it. When that fell through, he considered a number of other possibilities, none of which he was able to accept for more than a few hours at a time. His response to pressure of this sort was, of course, predictable: "I went on a kind of tare last Sat night . . . I continue to feel perfectly topsy-turvy without the question of this damned house somehow settled."

The most disturbing element in disposing of the house was what to do about the semi-permanent guest. For the young archaeologist was in a state of near-collapse, Hart and the servants nursing him as best they could.

[R————] is having a return of his jaundice; almost fainted Sunday afternoon and we had to call a doctor. He'd been eating too many of my Xmas sweets and the scrumptious ham that accompanied them. Anita [Brenner] has been very kind to him, assuring him of a place with one of two or more archeological excavations in progress now. He sleeps and sleeps—and never gets enough. That's a feature of the disease he says. Also has lapses of memory—due he says to being struck by an auto during his childhood.

Thanks to Hart's domestic circumstances, the Putnam article fell once more by the wayside: "DAMN that Putnam review! Of all times, now, to sharpen the critical blade! But that's what I get for procrastinating."

Yet Crane was at least thinking in literary terms. He read a group of poems by Ben Maddow that had been forwarded to him by

Malcolm Cowley and wrote a careful commentary on them. He sent on to Morton Dauwen Zabel an article by Anita Brenner that he thought *Poetry* might be able to use. He mailed to a friend on the staff of *Fortune* magazine the outline of an article that Eyler Simpson hoped to write.

There was also a stack of books that had arrived as Christmas presents, Lawrence's *The Man Who Died* being particularly significant to Hart. "Your Christmas gift was a great surprise," he wrote Wilbur Underwood,

> —and an inspiration. Lawrence never wrote a greater story, nor one which provoked less divided feelings. It was a great revelation to me, and I shall read "The Man Who Died" more than once again. In all honesty—it has more to tell me—at least in my present state of mind—than any book in the Bible. It was originally published by the same people in Paris who brought out my *Bridge*—under the title of, "The Escaped Cock"; but I never happened to have read it before. I remember that they had a terrible time with the customs, getting it into this country —and largely on account of that title! Imagine!

There were also occasional requests for him to contribute poems to periodicals, and many warm letters from admirers such as Selden Rodman and Eda Lou Walton. James Oppenheim wrote to say that Horace Gregory had insisted he reread *The Bridge* in book form. Oppenheim, who had not admired the sections of the poem as they had appeared in magazines, was not going to bother with the book. Once forced to read it, however, he was "enthralled" by its "new, authentic American poetry."

Perhaps it was letters of this sort—perhaps his reading of Lawrence—that set Crane to work on his still-fragmented poem. In any event, sometime during his two-week interval away from Peggy, he seems again to have been writing. He returned to Taxco, Peggy remembers, with several stanzas of the poem in hand.

Once more he arrived in the midst of a festival—this time the festival of a local patron saint. On the second day there was a parade of town animals—each elegantly decked out to be blessed by a priest. "One white cat had been dyed pink in blotches," Peggy Cowley remembered, "which she was trying to wash off, cat fashion; she was also unaccustomed to wearing earrings. . . . Not to be outdone, there was Maria Louisa carrying our tomorrow's meal, a turkey, with strands of tiny silvered Christmas beads wound around its neck, at which it was pecking vigorously." Crane judiciously looked over the procession of gaudy animals: "Whores, dressed up for an Easter parade."

Peggy Cowley says that Hart had started "The Broken Tower" during the Christmas festivities and that it was well along by his second visit. Her recollection is probably accurate, for we know enough about Hart's working methods to know that composition was always for him an extraordinarily roundabout affair. He might for weeks, for months, or even for years gather material: words, phrases, fragments of lines. These would be fitted into various trial stanzas—dozens of variants are not uncommon—until he had an area of the poem in something like final shape. He would then work out from this relatively sure center, expanding, cutting, revising until the poem was finished. "Faustus and Helen," "Voyages," and *The Bridge* were, as we know, months and years in composition. He had probably gathered a good deal of material for "The Broken Tower," therefore, when the incident took place that gave him the imagistic form he was looking for. This incident has a definite date, since Lesley Simpson made a note of it. Not long after Hart's death, he wrote:

> I was with Hart Crane in Taxco, Mexico, the morning of January 27, this year, when he first conceived the idea of "The Broken Tower." The night before, being troubled with insomnia, he had risen before daybreak and walked down to the village square. . . . Hart met the old Indian bell-ringer who was on his way down to the church. He and Hart were old friends, and he brought Hart up into the tower with him to help ring the bells. As Hart was swinging the clapper of the great bell, half drunk with its mighty music, the swift tropical dawn broke over the mountains. The sublimity of the scene and the thunder of the bells woke in Hart one of those gusts of joy of which only he was capable. He came striding up the hill afterwards in a sort of frenzy, refused his breakfast, and paced up and down the porch impatiently waiting for me to finish my coffee. Then he seized my arm and bore me off to the plaza, where we sat in the shadow of the church, Hart the while pouring out a magnificent cascade of words. It was . . . an experience I shall never forget.

Hart worked almost without interruption for several days. The poem was falling into shape, and he was confident that at last he had found a theme worth developing: that theme, of course, his earlier experiences of love and loneliness and the contrasting new discovery of the possibility of a healing union, one that depended, as an early draft makes clear, on the "final choice" he had until then evaded. The finished work is not autobiography (the bell-tower dawn becomes dusk and the presence of Peggy Cowley as love's catalyst is no more than hinted), yet the roots of the poem are obviously personal. (Consider the heart/Hart, eye/I puns of the last stanza.) A synthesis of his Mexican experiences (the Tepoztlan night fuses with the Taxco morning), his mystical studies that linked the word of poetry to the Word of God made lovely flesh (Lawrence's Christ hovers over imagery reminiscent

C. A. Crane and his son at Crane's Canary Cottage in Chagrin Falls,
Ohio; December 1930

Overleaf: *A Walker Evans photograph of Hart Crane, taken in New
York, probably in 1930*        *Collection of Richard Rychtarik*

To Charlotte and Richard
from the
"Heart."

*Drafts of portions of the "River" and "Van Winkle" sections of*
**The Bridge**

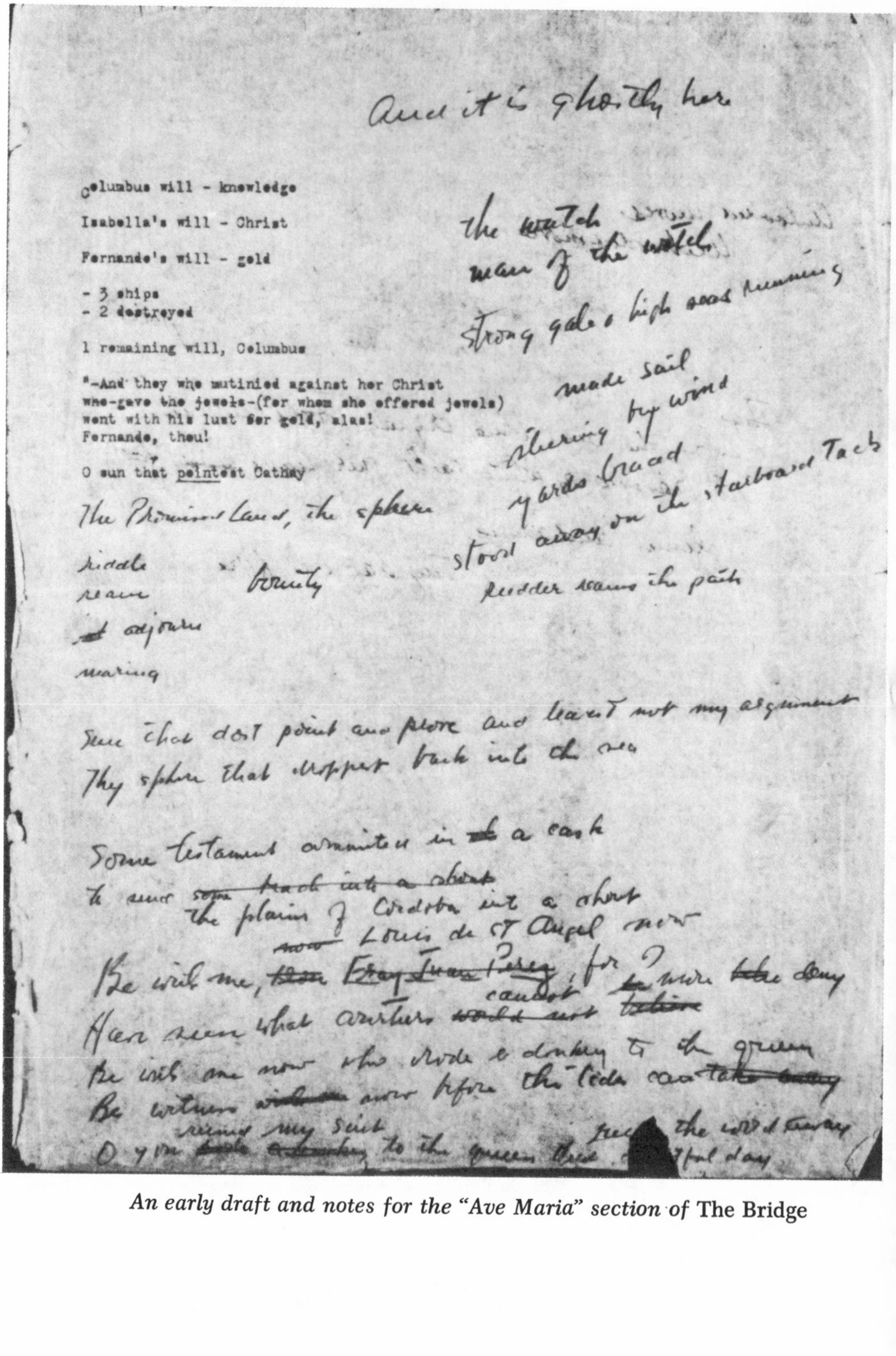

And it is ghostly here

Columbus will - knowledge

Isabella's will - Christ

Fernando's will - gold

- 3 ships
- 2 destroyed

1 remaining will, Columbus

"-And they who mutinied against her Christ
who-gave the jewels-(for whom she offered jewels)
went with his lust for gold, alas!
Fernando, thou!

O sun that pointest Cathay

the watch
man of the watch

Strong gales & high seas running

made sail
steering by wind
yards braced
stood away on the starboard Tack

The Promised Land, the sphere

riddle
ream
adjourn
waning

bounty

Rudder reams the path

Since that dost point and plore and learnt not my argument
Thy sphere that dropped back into the sea

Some testament written in a cask
to send the plains of Cordova in a chart
Louis de St Angel now

Be with me, ~~Fray Juan Perez~~, for I ... more ... deny
Have seen what another cannot ...
Be with me now who rode a donkey to the queen
Be witness now before the ceder can take ...
O ... my suit ... to the queen ... the world away ... ful day

*An early draft and notes for the "Ave Maria" section of* The Bridge

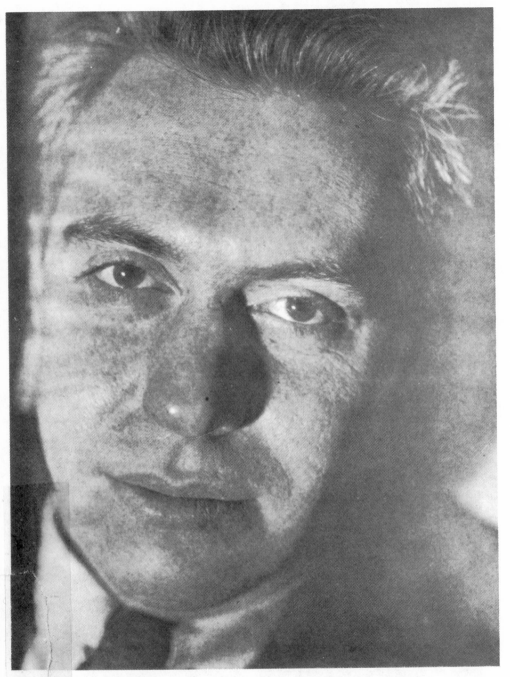

Another Walker Evans portrait, probably made on the same
day as the previous photograph

Above: *Peggy Cowley and Hart Crane. On the back of this photograph, he wrote to the Rychtariks on March 1, 1932: "You might have guessed I'd fall in love again! How do you like our front yard?" Below, left: The Siqueiros portrait* (slightly cropped)

Left and right: *Hart, two months before his death.* Above: *Peggy and Hart, in Mexico*

*This photograph was taken by William Wright during the summer of 1931, when Hart came home from Mexico for his father's funeral*

of Dante and Ouspensky), and the various emotional "wars" that love for mother and for father, for men of the sea and for neighbors had produced leads to the dominant orgasmic image of a tower that is certainly "not stone" but just as certainly not phallus. The poem is about the cleansing "shower" Crane reserves for its last word. But it is also about many other things.

On the evening of January 29, however, the final version of "The Broken Tower" was still distant. After nearly three days of steady work, Hart was ready for a change. He "went down to the town alone," Peggy Cowley wrote.

> Some time later a tiny *mozo* came up the hill and handed me a note. "Your friend got in some kind of scrape and is now in jail." I talked to Bill Spratling, and he told me Hart would simply have to stay in jail for the night. I was angry and hurt; this left me in an unsavory situation. I knew he had been outrageous to many of his friends, but he had insisted that I was the woman he loved and wanted to marry. I didn't go to see him the next day, nor did I see him off on the bus, which he took that afternoon. Bill came over and attempted an explanation.
>
> "Anyone who gets drunk publicly in Mexico is apt to land in jail. It's a means of increasing the town's finances. Because Hart is a foreigner he had to pay nearly three times as much as my house boy. Hart thinks you are acting high hat."
>
> I never did find out what he had done, but it could have been nothing important: a too-loud voice, or solo dancing in the street. From anything worse there would have been reverberations.

But there were reverberations, for Hart at least, and they came from all sides. Some of them are summed up in the telegrams he sent Peggy Cowley, the first two on January 30, the third—I assume in answer to a suggestion from her that he return to Taxco—on January 31.

> Everything all right dear miss you love to lesley and marian
>
> Hart
>
> Have put [R———] out after terrible fight do you care to come in for a few days. Love ever
>
> Hart
>
> Can never enter Taxco again but so need you here for a few days. Will foot all expense thanks darling
>
> Hart

Hart's banishment from Taxco had been a consequence of the "scrape" that sent him to jail—not for making too much noise but for being caught red-handed in an affair with an Indian boy. He would be permitted daytime visits to the town, he was told, but the dangerous evenings were forbidden.

His fight with the young Marxist archaeologist, who at one point had nearly persuaded him to join the campaign for world revolution, had considerably more comic overtones, though they were not apparent to Hart at the time. R——— had been left in charge of Hart's possessions. When Hart returned home suddenly—precipitously expelled from Taxco—he found his house a mess. Hart could forgive disorder, and he could tolerate political wrangling, but there was one sin he could not and would not forgive: an outsider's attack on that typewriter he had himself so often bludgeoned. The archaeologist, Lesley Simpson said, simply had not accurately gauged Hart's passion for his typewriter. He had "made free with that sacred instrument, and Hart came home . . . to find it out of order. He blew up and invited R——— to leave the house. R——— refused to go and Hart threw him out bodily . . . This crisis . . . put Hart squarely back into the middle class."

It also put him out of all but telegraphic communication with the world during the week in which the typewriter was being repaired. But there was consolation: Peggy Cowley took pity on him, agreeing to make a visit for the week of adjustment he assured her he could not do without.

We arranged to meet at the *Broadway*, our favorite restaurant. He met me in high spirits with a corsage of orchids. Sweet peas were on the table and cocktails miraculously appeared as I stepped in the door.

"I'm so glad to have you here, dear. It isn't so bad at the house as I pictured, but I thought if I made it strong enough you'd come armed to the teeth to protect me. The servants are delighted at a visit from the señora. I left Daniel sweeping and dusting like a mad Dutch housewife."

They decided to celebrate their reunion with a trip to the movies. An old Chaplin film was playing in an outlying part of town. Hart, resplendent in a white linen suit, a gardenia in his buttonhole, dashed out into the street to hail a passing taxi. "The taxi," Peggy told me, "drove us to the most miserable part of town . . . It just began getting smellier and more miserable. Most of the houses were only half shacks put together like a quilt, with pieces of tin. Finally the driver said, 'I don't think you want to go there.'" Peggy, however, insisted: they had come all that way; they ought to go in. The garbage-littered streets had been smelly, but the interior of the theater blotted out all external odors. "Pure urine!" was Peggy Cowley's summary. "What a stink of ancient piss!" Hart announced.

The film had not yet begun. As they started down the aisle, every head in the place turned to look at them, Hart in his white linen suit and Peggy loaded down with orchids. "Must have been pretty fantastic, come to think of it," she said. They felt out of place, their finery glaringly conspicuous in the sea of rag-covered people. And yet, when the movie started, differences vanished. "Everybody had been turning around, looking at us, but we no longer became the center of attention. It was simply Charlie Chaplin." Everybody in the theater forgot everything but the film. "Tears streamed down our faces and we clung to each other laughing louder than anyone else in the house. The greatest mime of the century had brought the orchids and rags together in joint appreciation."

Almost immediately after Peggy moved in, Hart came down with a fever; for nearly a week they stayed home, their most strenuous activity the daily climb to the vine-covered roof. There, through blossoms as blue as the sky, they looked off toward Popocatepetl and made plans for the future. Their only social activity was a trip to Mexico City to deliver Hart's portrait to a loan exhibition of Siqueiros's recent paintings.

Peggy returned to Taxco early in February. Hart was sure now that he was in love, that this was not merely an adventure but the beginning of a different kind of life for him. For the first time he risked sending news of it to friends and relatives. "You must tell me more about Peggy," Bess Crane replied, "sounds interesting." Hart's fullest letter, however, was sent to Mony Grunberg, that steadfast friend who through the difficult times after Hart's return from Paris had preached the importance of honest workmanship in art and honest appraisal of one's own character. Though willing to accept Hart as he was, Grunberg had persistently warned him not to underestimate human possibility. When Hart had told him that he wished he could fall in love with Peggy Robson, that he had responded to her with something very close to passion, Grunberg's analysis had been a straightforward one: Hart should accept what happens; he should not try to predict his own behavior, his own feelings. Now it was to Grunberg that Hart wrote at length about a second Peggy, a second "Little Miss Twidget."

> As usual, I'm ignoring all the questions of your last letter. . . . Don't know how long I'm going to remain here, etc. Hate it and love it alternately, but am not, as you surmise, in a constant Bacchic state. Not by any means. However, I happen to be in something approximating it at this present moment, since I've got to work on the first impressive poem I've started on in the last two years. I feel the old confidence again; and you may know what that means to one of my stripe!
> The servants are all asleep—and I'm in that pleasant state of beginning all over again. Especially as I'm in love again—and as never quite before. Love is always much more important than locality; and this is the newest adventure I ever had. I won't say much more than that I seem to have broken ranks with my much advertised "brotherhood"—and a woman whom

I have known for years—suddenly seems to have "claimed her own." I can't say that I'm sorry. It has given me new perspectives, and after many tears and groans—something of a reason for living.

So much for "Mexico." . . . Meantime let me say that you are one of the few heroes I know. I love your steadfastness and uncompromising attitude, Mony. Have we the patience to endure? I say YES!

"I hope you will not be disgusted with me if I say that I had expected that something of the sort would come about," Grunberg answered. "Moreover, what particularly matters is what the 'thing' means to you spiritually." Certainly Crane should not be concerned about his past life or about other ultimately insignificant matters: "physiology—well, that's stale and unprofitable stuff. . . . And again on such matters—when they form a part of another's soul, to quote one of your lines, 'Steps must be gentle.' "

Bess Crane offered good, solid, hardheaded advice. Hart had written her several letters, in one implying that once Peggy's divorce was granted, the two might be married. Yet he was filled with uncertainties. The important thing in marriage, Bess stressed, was sympathy, shared mutual understanding: "Do you know I am so glad you have found someone of whom you are fond? There is nothing like the companionship of the one who understands us. I know that is what I miss now more than I can say, and do you know, Harold, there are really very few who we really feel perfectly at ease with, and who understand all our moods."

With Peggy back in Taxco, Hart hoped to finish "The Broken Tower." But no sooner was she gone than Daniel went on a series of wild binges, wilder even than Hart's. While Daniel was away, the house would be peaceful; but his entrances were cataclysmic. They were also dangerous. For Daniel was by now intimately acquainted with all the complexities of Hart's sex life. He made it explicitly clear that should Hart consider firing him, or even seriously upbraiding him, Hart would find himself a permanent guest at the local jail. He threatened not only Hart but Lisa, a friend of Siqueiros who had stayed on with Hart when Siqueiros returned to Taxco. "Sr. Daniel Hernandez is morose and very threatening indeed," Hart wrote several days after Peggy had left, "despite the fact that I haven't even reprimanded him for his recent drunkenness."

Lisa is scared to death of him, and warns me that there may be all kinds of trouble in store if I fire him, since he knows about half the Police in Mixcoac, knows I have no firearms on the place, etc. Well, neither can I bring myself to endure his insolence and complete disregard of services much more. Sr.

Lepine, my landlord, is going to try to corner and talk to him this afternoon, but Daniel won't be around at the time, as Lepine, who called this morning when D. was out, told his wife the hour when he'd return this afternoon.

Oh Hell! I say. I'm getting so damned tired of the whole problem. Lisa thinks she won't dare remain after Daniel leaves on account of his probably exposing her political affiliations. If you can't find someone from Taxco I shall probably be left here a perfect prisoner—without even a telephone, and afraid to leave the place a minute. Well, don't see how I'm going to get any work done *this* afternoon, nor probably tomorrow. Damned outrageous, I think. Daniel will probably come lurching in about 8 tonight and begin to flirt a knife and pistol about. Such a quiet life in this pretty retreat!

On some days the situation seemed desperate. "I was so tremulous and distracted with the domestic situation as described yesterday to you," he wrote Peggy, "that last night I went on a mild tare with Lisa here in the salon."

I finally came to the decision of packing up and leaving for the States within a week; there just didn't seem to be any other way of proceeding. I certainly felt fed up! Lepine didn't come round until this morning, and if he hadn't offered me a new servant who he swears is reliable, I think I should be sending you the telegram I typed out last night, announcing my departure.

Hart's landlord finally suggested that Daniel and his family continue to live with Hart but that they work full time for his neighbor, "the General." A trustworthy old man whom the landlord had known for years would come in as Hart's houseman; Lisa would stay on as cook. "The combination will be perfect, and will result in little more expense than I have been under right along. . . . I have a notion that this new rearrangement will be satisfactory. Certainly I'm lucky to have Lisa here—so intelligent, generous, neat and efficient in a thousand ways. She doesn't ask for anything but her board and keep, but I shall try to induce her into some sort of salary."

In spite of these difficulties, Hart's poem progressed. When the insomnia that had troubled him for years would become unbearable, he would get out the manuscript and begin the familiar operations that would set him to work. His nights were spent, he told Peggy, "with a little tequila (a very little!) walking back and forth the length of the room to the tune of the records that we enjoyed so together." Almost every day she would receive typed drafts, sometimes only single lines that had been revised, sometimes several stanzas. When she left Mexico, she told me, she had dozens of fragments of "The Broken Tower." "The version of the beginning of The Broken Tower that I sent you early this morning is probably to be changed a good deal yet. But you seemed to hanker for it—and so I let 'er fly." "I worked late on my poem last night despite all the disturbance, and willy-nilly shall get some work accomplished, at least correspondence, today." Though there were many very bad days, on good days Hart was more confident than he had been for years: "I miss you a lot, dear. Somehow we have such a lot to talk about together. I am getting more and more serious and dignified day by day—getting maybe back into myself—as well as into you." "I want things to be smoother than before on your next 'visit' to Mixcoac, besides which I want to get my mind free for work as soon as possible. I'm really in extra-ordinarily good condition and do hope you also feel more settled and industrious. I hope to send you more of the poem in a few days."

Hart was now trying to reestablish that emotional "balance" that he had as a boy talked of with Carl Schmitt, the balance that resulted from an interwoven tension of feelings and that permitted art to accomplish its miracles. Though the process of gaining such balance was infinitely more difficult for the thirty-two-year-old man than it had been for the bright young seventeen-year-old, it seemed just possible. What he needed, he knew, was a combination of affection and freedom, the rarest of combinations; but if he could find a way to assure their linkage, poetry might result. Perhaps if Peggy joined him at Mixcoac, balance could be restored. She would soon have to leave her beautiful, scorpion-infested home; it had been sold and the new owners were expected momentarily. On her last visit, she and Hart had discussed the possibility of her moving in with him. But if she came, Hart tried tactfully to make clear, she would have to respect his independence. He remembered all too well the troubles he had gotten into with the Tates. And he also remembered the sense of entrapment that he had had during his California stay with Grace. Only if both partners could forgo possessiveness would an open, creative love be possible. Hart knew it was what he needed; but was it also what Peggy really needed—or wanted? He thought so. He tried to make certain:

> Of course I'm anxious about your plans after leaving Natalia's. You know you're welcome—more than that, my dear, to make this your future headquarters. I miss you *mucho, mucho, mucho!* But I don't think that either of us ought to urge the other into anything but the most spontaneous and mutually liberal arrangements. I am bound to you more than I ever dreamed of being, and in the most pleasant and deep way. I think I have wandered back to some of my early idealism, and in the proper sort of

way—without any arbitrary forcing or conscious reckoning. You're a great little "rouser," my dear!

Hart's tentative assurance, which almost anything could shatter, was enough, however, for him to try to make plans. "I'm afraid I'm getting 'ingrown' with Mexico and the Indians," he wrote Richard Laukhuff.

They're crafty, childish, delicious, beautiful and horrible—all by turns. And then one is equally seduced by the gorgeous variety of scenery, the climate, etc. I want to stay longer than my scholarship, if I can,—but *quien sabe?* as they say. . . . I'm just really beginning to write again, the first really interesting bit of poetry in two years.

Yet when words started flowing, it hardly seemed worthwhile to worry about house or servants.

Dear Peggy:
   I just can't make up my mind to go traveling or even visiting until I get through some real work here in Mixcoac. Somehow, it seems to me that the time is ripe even though circumstances are difficult; and if I can't do any better I think I'll just try to let the domestic situation here "ride" as best possible—so long as there is no pistol twirling. The place seems to run itself fairly smoothly with Daniel away until 7-8-or-9 at night, and for the moment, at least, relations are back again on a fairly friendly basis. I'm doing my best not to think or worry too much about it. . . .
   I'm going to make a stab again at the Putnam review this afternoon. I'm feeling shabbier and shabbier about my delay. . . . Must send up *something* anyway. And maybe later I'll catch the creative thread of my poem again. . . .

Even when a planned dinner party fell through and Hart went on a private drinking bout, the consequences were relatively happy. Since the guests who had disappointed him were friends of Peggy's, he threatened to punish her by refusing to write to her.

But, really, I find daily communication with you quite irresistible. Especially when your reciprocation is so regular and—need I say? charming. . . .
   True to my word last night, I got very lit. Daniel had come home that way anyhow, and I took the opportunity to talk to him about sobriety—meanwhile pouring him glass after glass of the Tenampa I'd bought for the Kings. The more he drank the more he talked of "his" or "our" Pegguié—accent on the penult;—but you will be able to pronounce that without the acquaintance of Quintilian anyway, I'm sure. You're very popular

around here, and I'm sure that if you care to come and stay with me for awhile you will be regarded as the pet of the place—since Elise and Conrada both dote on you—as well as myself. . . .

Daniel is not drunk tonight; rather he appeared at 6 P.M. with a large bush of *buena de noche*, from the *jardine del general*, as well as a large bouquet of heliotrope. Judge what the sala smells like with a large bunch of tuberoses also, which I purchased yesterday in honor of the Kings! Some times I think this house is the nicest place in the world. It certainly could be—in a not ambitious way. My temperamental reversals of opinion regarding Mexico are a joke. I now regard myself as a confirmed idiot who can't make up his mind about anything whatever any more.

. . . By the way, I don't believe a thing of your wagon wagon, water wagon story. Especially with Luz around, who Lisa says is a great little tanker. I have my own ideas about the sobriety of those nights of yours in such company, and how "lonely" they are. Just as long as you don't let your right hand know what your left hand doeth, as they say. I'll keep the same code, at least with my index finger.

Ahoy and ahoy and AHOY! I'm off for the night! Here comes Elise, after cooking me a scrumptious meal. Wish you were here darling!

Hart devoted his happy days to good-natured "conversation"— if that is what his Spanish could be called—with the servants, and his evenings to long letters to the friends with whom he was still corresponding. The pattern was: letter to Peggy, dinner and "conversation," work on the poem, and an after-midnight letter to a friend in the States, a letter such as this one to Bess Crane.

This room is simply piping with the aroma of tuberoses and heliotrope, from two large bouquets that my servant brought this afternoon from the garden of a Mexican general who lives nearby. My white dog, "Paloma" whose appearance you admired so much in the photograph I sent, lies on the floor beside me, searching for fleas. He insists on lying at the foot of my bed at night; but the pleasure isn't all his. I have to go through about as much scratching as he does. But I wouldn't lose him for the world. There's nothing quite like the devotion and obedience of a dog. This one gets, or seems to get smarter and more accomplished every day. I think I wrote you about my servant problem. They seem to get dumber and dumber every day; but they're very fond of me (it's all like a big family, really) and when I can get the head of the family sober enough to really understand my lame Spanish, I can accomplish wonders—at least for the succeeding 24 hours.

I get so aggravated at times that I swear I'll pack up and leave for the States on the first available boat. Then the next clear and glorious morning comes around, with fresh flowers in the garden, good coffee on the stove—and the renewed vision that sleep brings . . . Then I change my mind all over again. For I know that as soon as I go back I'll regret it—and long and long for Mexico again. Not that I plan on staying here forever; but for the time being the business situation in the States is zero. There's nothing I can really do there. And although I have found that living here is far from being as cheap as it's cracked up to be, it *is* less, on the whole, and when one learns—and how long it takes!—to wade around and learn one's depth and altitude— one can make a good deal of a lame proposition. At least Mexico affords me time and space. I'm not so giddy as I once was about *all* its features; but a very pleasant residue remains. And I'm just getting to know it well enough to get down to work on my poetry and other creative work.

Bess, you certainly have given a demonstration of real heroism in handling the factory rent problem as you have. . . . You're one of the finest people I've ever met or ever expect to meet. I've always been so glad that Father found someone at last who really took the pains to understand him; because he was certainly a difficult person to comprehend. He had many faults, too. I only regret that I was so late in realizing his many virtues.

Life, toward the end of February, seemed very good. It seemed even better when Bess Crane wrote that by the end of March part —perhaps all—of his monthly inheritance payments could probably be sent to him. ("You are right about wanting to stay in Mexico. I can't see very much in the way of something to do here for you at the present time as things are very slow. . . . If you would prefer having your full allowance, it's perfectly alright with me, as long as we are able to give it to you . . .")

Suddenly "The Broken Tower" was developing very well and was being paralleled by some of the Mexican fragments that appear in *The Collected Poems*. Hart now also took time to write for a Mexican publication a short appreciation of David Siqueiros's paintings (Crane's piece, of course, to appear in translation), and managed to convince himself that he was about to turn out the ill-fated Putnam review.

To cap his happiness, Peggy Cowley agreed to move into his house—but not on a "visit." This would be, if not a marriage, the nearest thing to it that would be possible before Peggy's divorce became final. "I'll make you a good husband yet," Hart told her. "Nothing ostentatious. It will be a paltry thing but my own." They posed for photographs before one of the great flowering trees of the garden, then had the photographs made up into postcards.

Mexico, March 1, '32

Dear Lotte & Ricardo—

You might have guessed I'd fall in love again! How do you like *our* front yard? Much love to you both,

Hart

No—she isn't Mexican—but just born on Long Island, N. York. . . .

# 42

When Peggy moved into the house, there was much shift-ing about of furniture, Hart fitting up an extra room for her as a studio for writing and painting.

They made all kinds of resolutions: Hart would moderate his drinking, make a real effort to find reviewing jobs (as soon as he had finished the ones he had taken on), perhaps begin the epic drama on Mexican themes. But first a celebration was in order. They would take a trip, a kind of honeymoon, to the ancient city of Puebla.

Hart went to the bank and withdrew $150, all that remained of his Guggenheim funds. From now on, he would live on the income from his father's estate. ("I don't feel like asking for more than the $125 per month which I mentioned in my last letter," Hart wrote Bess Crane. "However, I'll need all of that, and I think it may be highly important to feel the assurance that I can plan on getting it regularly at monthly intervals.") He used a hundred dollars of the Guggenheim money to open a checking account in a Mexican bank, and planned to deposit the monthly payment from the estate in that account. The remaining fifty dollars went into his pocket.

In Mexico in 1932, fifty dollars could go a long way. "Yesterday in Puebla," he wrote Bess Crane at the end of the trip, "I came back to the hotel with an armful of violets, cornflowers, white carnations and carmine poppies for Peggy,—four bouquets in all, and the total cost not being more than 15 cents in US money. It certainly is delightful to look over the balcony of one's hotel room in the morning and see an Indian walking along with a basket twice the size of any of our laundry baskets full of fresh flowers balanced on his head."

> Puebla is one of the most beautiful places I have ever seen; wide streets, pink, blue and terra cotta houses with balconies of wrought iron; a main plaza with lofty trees of a dozen native varieties; the second largest cathedral on this continent, whose interior blazes with enough gold railings and gold leaf ornament

to pay off Germany's reparation debts. Besides that (believe it or not) the city contains 364 other churches—one for every day in the year. . . . The streets of Puebla would put the average American city to shame with their immaculate cleanliness. And if you could have seen the main market—where not only food but clothing, rugs,.pottery, toys and every conceivable article in the world is sold, you would have raved for weeks! Peggy has an income of her own, and we both bought some of the most beautiful serapes, glass ware (hand blown), pottery and leather work that you ever laid eyes on. Really, Bess, you can't conceive the beauty of the arts and crafts of these Indians. Our house is now a delight to the eyes.

But it was not the trappings of the house that gave Hart his greatest sense of pride. It was the world he and Peggy created within it. "Rather amazing things have happened to me since Xmas," he confessed to Loveman.

Peggy Cowley, whom you certainly remember as Malcolm's wife, and who is getting a divorce here in Mexico, is mainly responsible. You may have heard that we are now living together, and I must admit that I find conjugal life, however unofficial, a great consolation to a loneliness that had about eaten me up. Maybe I am fulfilling some of your theories and predictions. At any rate, if you hear (when you tune in on Mexico City some night) the sound of creaking bed springs—don't fancy it to be just "static."

For with Peggy, Hart felt he had achieved the home that friends took for granted—the kind of home he had tried to become part of in his visits to the Browns, the Rychtariks, the Munsons. It might even resemble—he sometimes felt—that home his father had made for himself in Chagrin Falls, a place where love made work meaningful.

Yes, Bess, I'm really getting to work on one of the strongest pieces of poetry I've yet written. Being with Peggy is doing me a great deal of good. . . . Her companionship is removing that exhausting sense of loneliness that has been a great handicap to me for years. I don't need to tell you what love and devotion mean. You have responded, and how beautifully! to those instincts yourself. You have one of the most beautiful understandings that I know of. And if you ever felt reason to worry about me certainly there is less reason now than ever before. . . . None of you probably realize how often I picture you all by the fireside, the daily program at the Cottage—and how, in spite of all my interest in this vast and exotic country, I always think of your environment as my home. Thanks to you, Bess!

The home that he fitted out for Peggy was Hart's last effort to recapture the middle-class life he had been born into and somehow had drifted away from, a life of neighborliness—uneventful, casual, even humdrum. He and Peggy gave teas for Guggenheim Fellows and attended teas given in return. They went marketing together, fussed in their garden. In the mornings Hart, always an early riser, brought Peggy fresh, steaming coffee; in the afternoons, propped up on pillows, they read together on the porch of the house, a pitcher of beer, Peggy's cigarettes, and Hart's cigars close at hand.

It could have been a good life. But it was a life very much on display, for neither Hart nor Peggy were people who led quiet lives. Hart had all of his reputations trailing in his wake: heavy drinker, homosexual, unpredictable spendthrift, extrovert, introvert —all terms accurate to aspects of his personality, false to the man.

And Peggy, merely by living with him, contributed her share to the gossip that had for almost a year kept American expatriates officially shocked, privately entertained. The gossipers were agreed that Hart's life was disastrous. Their current problem was whether Peggy contributed to the disaster or helped stave it off.

Even before she had left Taxco, speculation of this sort was very much in the air:

> Another guest was already on the scene, the well-known, no-longer-young poet W.B. By now my love affair with Hart was well publicized, and our intention to marry. W.B. made it clear he didn't like Hart personally nor the poetry he had written so far. But, he said at length, if Hart were left to his normal inclinations he might become a real poet. So I was responsible for Hart's dereliction, and I should accept the responsibility for the effects.

One woman—a resident of Taxco who had followed the romance from its inception to the time Hart and Peggy left Mexico on the *Orizaba*—stoutly maintained for years after Hart's suicide that Peggy was responsible for his collapse. But, as Lesley Simpson noted, such an opinion was the "veriest nonsense." Hart, from the middle of March on, Simpson felt, "was ruining himself so fast that [Peggy] couldn't have done more than speed up the process, to some small degree." Hart's dreadful last month in Mexico might have been simpler had Peggy not moved in with him; "Hart could have gone merrily to hell with his Indian boys." Peggy's presence, Simpson felt, contributed only one decibel to the uproar Hart lived in: "Peggy did move in on him, for a fact, and their household would have driven anyone mad. When they weren't quarreling violently with each other they were rowing with the servants."

The most difficult part of being a bystander at their quarrels was listening to Hart's denunciations of the new life that in sober moments seemed so full of possibility.

The first and in some ways the most spectacular of these outbursts came only two weeks after Hart and Peggy had moved her belongings into his house. Though trivial, the quarrel was intense enough for Hart to slam out of the house, race across the street to the telegraph office, and there wire Bess Crane an urgent request for money, a request that was coupled with an attack on Peggy. The next day, after he had made peace with Peggy, he had to write Bess, doing his best to undo the damage.

> Will you please forgive me for that farcical telegram? Explanations follow. . . .
>
> Peggy and I, having imbibed too much tequila, got to wrangling about some money I had borrowed while at Puebla to buy serapes with. I suddenly wanted to pay her back at once . . . and well, you see what happened.
>
> I realize that I unfortunately misunderstood and misinterpreted Peggy's character quite badly. Please put the blame on me entirely. And please accept my apologies.
>
> If it so happens that you have sent the money, it can just as well be substituted for the April allowance. Whatever is in excess of the $125 agreed on I shall return to you with a check from my bank here.

Perhaps it was on this night, before he had patched things up with Peggy, that Hart made one of his descents on the Simpsons.

> One night about ten, as I was getting ready to turn in, the houseboy came up and knocked at my door. There was a man downstairs who wanted to see me. Was it a wild man? Well, he was a little odd. . . . So I put on my clothes and went down, and there was Hart, rigged up in a French sailor's outfit and very merry and noisy. He had just come to tell me that he had made up his mind to move out to "Frisco," which must be a wonderful place, by God, but he promised he wouldn't bother us. So I took him off downtown again and got him something to eat, while he entertained me and the whole restaurant with an account of his adventures with Peggy. "She thinks she can reform me, does she? I'll show her! Why, God damn her, I'd rather sleep with a man any day than with her!" This with a huge guffaw and much pounding on the table. Which told me more about their ménage than if he had written a book. Their continual squabbles invariably ended with Hart moving downtown to a hotel— this half a dozen times to my knowledge. It would have been impossible for him to do any work in such a hurly-burly, but then he hadn't done any work before. So I can't convict Peggy of ruining Hart.

From the middle of March, Hart's alcoholic intake steadily increased. He was worried about his inheritance but even more worried about his literary reputation. He knew "The Broken Tower" was one of his best poems, but he was driven frantic, Peggy told me, by doubts about its reception by editors and friends. "Moroseness and anger against the world possessed him," she wrote. "He became an ugly, sick man in mind and body. Constant tirades against the servants, Mexico, his friends in the States. When he was put in jail for being drunk on the streets, it was a conspiracy to ruin his reputation. He would offer to set me free at one moment and in the next he feared I would take him at his word."

Lesley Simpson, to whom Hart always turned when things were at their worst, still remembers one incident from the many that took place at this time. It was early in April.

Carleton Beals and his wife were dining with us. About nine o'clock a telegram came for me: "In jail in Mixcoac or thereafter. Hart." Which I took to mean a call for help. So I hopped a taxi and drove out to the Mixcoac jail. Did they have a wild man there? Oh yes, señor; that is to say, they had had one, but they had released him an hour before, after he had just about wrecked the place. So I went out to Hart's house. The patio was filled with a mob of Indians and Hart was charging about, shouting. Peggy was clutching him and everybody was talking at once. Hart saw me and said: "Thank God, Lesley, you're here!" He took me by the arm and dragged me into the house, with the mob of Indians on our heels. Hart shut the door in their faces and poured out his story. It was so ridiculous that I had difficulty in keeping a straight face. It seems that Hart had missed his favorite blanket and had accused his boy Daniel of stealing it. (It turned out later that Hart had lent it to Anita Brenner.) Daniel's honor was offended and, according to Hart, he had taken after Hart with a butcher-knife. In the general row, Daniel's brother, the cop, came and hauled Hart off to jail. I may be wrong, but I suspect that Peggy tipped off the cop. Hart was properly outraged and did his best to wreck the jail, throwing all the furnishings out the window.

At this juncture in Hart's story the door burst open and Daniel and Daniel's wife and a swarm of relatives poured into the room and began to tell me *their* story. Daniel was tearful but dignified. *He* was a man of honor and Señor Crane had done very wrong to accuse him. Etc., etc. Daniel's wife was admirable. I told her to take her husband away, that everything would be all right, and so on. So she took Daniel to the kitchen, her baby sleeping the while on her shoulder. I finally persuaded Hart to go downtown with me. . . . I got him into the taxi and started off, but Hart's sense of injury was so strong that he burst out repeatedly in wild ravings about his being betrayed by Mexico. (I never knew just what he meant by being "betrayed.") At every fresh outburst the taxi driver ducked. When we got to town I told Hart that I was hungry and would he have something to eat with me? No, by God, he wouldn't eat. He hadn't eaten anything for forty-eight hours and he wasn't hungry, and so on. I insisted that I was hungry and got him to go into a restaurant with me. I ordered a glass of milk and a ham sandwich and had the waiter put them in front of Hart, who wolfed the sandwich and gulped the milk, and had another sandwich and another glass of milk. And in half an hour he was roaring with laughter over the whole silly business! I walked him around for a while and put him up at a hotel, exacting his solemn promise that he wouldn't stir from the place until I came for him in the morning. Well, while I was eating breakfast a telephone call came from Mixcoac. It was Hart, of course, asking Marian and me out to lunch with him and Peggy!

Though these were, on the whole, terrible days for Hart, it is altogether inaccurate to suggest that there were no good days among them. Once in a while there would be letters from the men to whom he had sent rough copies of his new poem, all uniformly praising it. Letters of this sort came from Mony Grunberg, from Sam Loveman, and from Malcolm Cowley. Hart had a letter from *Contempo* asking for a contribution, and he shipped off the Isle of Pines poem "Bacardi Spreads the Eagle's Wings." By the end of March, "The Broken Tower" had been substantially completed. Hart wrote to Morton Dauwen Zabel saying that he would soon send it to *Poetry*.

It is also inaccurate to suggest that in this difficult time Hart lost either his literary or his critical facility. It is perfectly true that he was afraid he had. But the evidence is to the contrary. "The Broken Tower" is among his finest poems, and the passages of casual criticism that glint through his letters show, as both Zabel and Grunberg recognized, that if Hart wished to set up as a critic, he had the makings of a first-rate one. For Hart read literature with great sensitivity, attentive to the structure of each book he studied. At the end of March, for example, in a letter to Grunberg, Hart answered a question concerning *Moby Dick*.

It has passages, I admit, of seeming innuendo that seem to block the action. But on third or fourth reading I've found that some of those very passages are much to be valued in themselves—minor and subsidiary forms that augment the final climacteric quite a bit. No work as tremendous and tragic as Moby Dick can be expected to build up its ultimate tension and impact without manipulating our time sense to a great extent. Even the suspense of the usual mystery story utilizes that device. In Moby

Dick the whale is a metaphysical image of the Universe, and every detail of his habits and anatomy has its importance in swelling his proportions to the cosmic rôle he plays.

During these days, it is as if at any point Hart might have been able to stop, reverse himself, and regain the security he had known, say, on the Isle of Pines. All through his adult life, he had been able to survive disastrous emotional and alcoholic crises. He had lifted clear from ruinous binges in Paris, New York, Patterson. Now, in Mexico, while some friends looked on in helpless sympathy and others, disgusted, decided that they had best wash their hands of him and his problems, he seemed alternately a hopeless drunk and a figure of gracious charm.

In the last days of March, which he spent watching "all of the gay incidentals of a Mexican Easter," his field of vision was full of "exploding Judases, rockets, flowers, pappas (excuse me, that's the spelling for Mexican potatoes!), mammas, delicious and infinitesimal children wearing masks and firemen's helmets, flowers galore and a sky that carries you ever upward!" He felt that it was a good time in a time of chaos, a time for summing up. His Guggenheim Fellowship would end in a few days, and Hart—who had often studied his past, searching it for meaning and for poetry— once more tried to evaluate what that past, particularly the immediate past, had given him.

Most conspicuously, of course, it had given him Peggy Cowley; and Peggy had given him the masculine assurance that until this year he had never had. He had to brag about it to everyone he met. One day on the street he ran into León Felipe and immediately asked him to pay a visit to the Mixcoac house. When León Felipe arrived a few days later, no sooner were introductions completed than Hart loudly and joyfully announced that he and Peggy were lovers: "I'm very happy because I have discovered that I am not a homosexual!" Peggy was the center of his world. If during drunken moments he doubted the durability of their alliance, he was, when sober, grateful for what she offered him—a "happy relationship" without strings. ("How permanent that will be is far from settled," he wrote, "but we have learned to enjoy the present moment without too much romanticizing—which I think is wisdom.")

Perhaps Hart hoped for the impossible: a whole life without strings, not just a single "happy relationship" but a life in which he would be free to love those people he did love in any way the occasion might offer. He could not see that there was any "disloyalty" to Peggy in his continuing to feel great fondness for those men he had in the past made love to. For he separated yet acknowledged the relationship between Eros and Agape. He was quite capable of loving, like most men, many people at one time. It did not seem "wrong" to make love to an Indian boy one night, to

Peggy the next. There was no need for Peggy to be jealous, since his feeling for her was in no way diminished by satisfactions the boy might offer. Crane was a man who detested deviousness, hypocrisy, deceit, most of all in himself. There is nothing incongruous about a sentimental, cheerful letter to Sam Loveman that shows Hart full of nostalgia for old days at Columbia Heights, full of concern for the welfare of the sailor he had for the past several years loved, and full of delighted surprise in speculating that he might himself some day become a father.

> That last of yours was a bang up letter, Sam. . . . I love to think of . . . Col. Hts. Good lord, but how I jumped to my feet right into a perfect salute yesterday when suddenly—over the neighbor's radio—I caught the chorus of that old favorite of mine, "The Navy Blues" . . . which certainly you can't have forgotten either. Which reminds me that I still haven't heard from B———— S———— since the recent fatal cyclones that swept right across his home town in A————. I wrote immediately for assurances of his welfare and safety. But no word yet. I can never forget that sweet boy; and his letters to me for the last two years have been so consistently affectionate and nostalgic that they sometimes bring tears to my eyes. . . .
>
> Do you know if storks carry cranes—or is it vice versa? We've been a little worried of late, especially as storks have even been known to carry twins, cranes notwithstanding. Please tell us, Dr. Loveman, and not too late. I never studied botany nor numerology neither. Don't say it aint so, even if it aint ever happened before.
>
> . . . There's also a new moon tonight, with a tar "within the nether tip." No, not a tar, a *star*! And a new puppy, so fat he can hardly wobble, has been added to the household. How I wish you could drop in for a month or so. Well, maybe you will before I leave this delightful place. I certainly hope so, Sam. Peggy sends you her best.

What had a year in Mexico amounted to? Hart added it all up for Caresse Crosby.

> My Guggenheim Fellowship terminates today. But I am remaining a while longer in Mexico on the modest income afforded me from my father's estate, since his death last July. At that time I came north for two months, but was very glad to get back here again as soon as possible. Mexico, with its volcanoes, endless ranges, countless flowers, dances, villages, lovely brown-skinned Indians with simple courtesies, and constant sunlight—it enthralls me more than any other spot I've ever known. It *is*—and *isn't* an easy place to live. Altogether more strange to us than even the orient . . . But it

would take volumes to even hint at all I've seen and felt. Have rung bells and beaten pre-Conquistadorial drums in fire-lit circles at ancient ceremonies, while rockets went zooming up into the dawn over Tepoztlan; have picked up obsidian arrows and terra-cotta idols from the furrows of corn fields in far valleys; bathed with creatures more beautiful than inhabitants of Bali in mountain streams; and been in the friendliest jails that ever man got thrown in. There is never an end to dancing, singing, rockets and the rather lurking and suave dangers that give the same edge to life here that the mountains give to the horizon. Harry would have adored it—past expression—and I'm sure you would. I should like to stay indefinitely.

My Spanish is still as lame as my French when I left France. Of the "Epic"—I haven't yet written a line. Only a few lyrics. But then, what did I actually write while in Europe—an environment not half so strange and distractingly new-old curious as this? . . . But I've about made my adjustment now and am beginning to rap the typewriter a good deal lately. With the world all going to hell—what can one gather together with any confidence these days anyway? . . .

Furthermore I've stretched the dominions of Eros a little. Or maybe it should be called "Via Venus" henceforth—with the wife of someone we all know who's here on a mission of divorce. But more's deferred until we meet—or greet again. . . .

# 43

April was for Hart Crane a long downhill descent. It began badly; it ended in death.

His initial concern was money. He had run out during the Easter celebrations and toward the end of March had to start the always painful process of going from friend to friend to ask for small loans. At the same time he sent off a series of wires and letters: Why was his check delayed? He was desperate, etc.

Money fears led to heavy drinking and heavy drinking to the sort of riotous behavior that ended in the Mixcoac jail. Worse, however, than his anxiety about debts was his awareness that he was being judged—and constantly. "There was a maggot in him of unrest, of self-distrust," Lesley Simpson wrote. "He continually tortured himself with thoughts of what his friends and critics back home were thinking of him." But he was also tortured by what friends in Mexico saw and by how they reacted to what they saw. For early in April everyone had the opportunity to see Hart at his worst. There were steadily mounting threats of violence at Mixcoac, abrupt drunken calls to the Simpsons, one sudden, early-morning arrival at the home of Caroline Durieux, his right hand soaked in blood—a barroom-brawl razor cut slashed across the palm.

When he did hear from Bess Crane, he had to live with new guilt feelings that his telegrams and letters had been so demanding. For Bess had been living on the edge of tragedy: one of the women who worked at the Cottage had been killed in an auto accident, a friend who was with her also had been killed, and another woman who worked at the Cottage, one very close to Bess Crane, had been almost fatally wounded. On April 2, Bess wrote him of the "ten terrible days" she had gone through and arranged that day for his check to go out.

In the second week of April, Hart began to recover a little. "I'm in a dull mood today, trying to get back into harness after a couple of feverish weeks," he wrote Mony Grunberg. His check arrived; wallet in hand, he made the rounds of the people he had borrowed from. One of them was Marsden Hartley, who, though he had been in Mexico for only a few weeks, had become, like

Lesley Simpson, a person Hart trusted. Before Hart's heaviest drinking had begun, they had spent quiet afternoons in the Mixcoac patio discussing poetry and painting and had several times taken long walks across the lava-crusted hills.

Perhaps they also discussed what life in the States had become like in the Depression economy of 1932. For there is no doubt at all that Hart was in a very literal way afraid to return north. If he were going to pieces in Mexico—and he knew he was in bad shape —what might happen to him in hostile New York? Would he be able to fit in again with people whose interest seemed focused only on Marxist dogma rather than on art? Could he have any hope of sobering up in a world that had no employment for him, that put no value on his poetry, that saw his middle-class feelings as at best sentimental (the reception that had been given "Indiana" still rankled) and at worst reactionary?

"Peggy and I shall probably stay here at least until next fall," he wrote Grunberg, "and maybe longer."

> We like our isolation from mutual friends there in the north and our domestic life here with a house, servants, garden, pets etc. proves more satisfying every day. If I can avoid drinking too much I'm expecting to get nearer solid earth than I have for several years. Sheer loneliness had nearly eaten me up. Peggy has sufficient sportsmanship, mentality, taste and sensuality to meet one on practically every level. . . .
>
> I had a fine ample letter from Sam not long ago which I must answer soon. He complained of "doldrums," but the tone of his letter betrayed him. At least he could summon up enough jolly good spirits to reassure me of his old cantankerous self. But most all the letters we get from the north are pretty damned blue and dubious in tone. Well, no wonder, of course. I sometimes wonder if I shouldn't go back and wail around the grave of capitalism myself, adopting sackcloth and ashes too, instead of the beautiful bright woolen serape worn around here on cold evenings. All my friends are turning at least a violent pink lately, and I'm almost convinced myself. In fact—by all the laws of logic I *am* convinced. But it goes so against my native grain— seeing nothing but red on the horizon.

Visitors from the States brought tales of conditions in New York. Claire Spenser Smith—for whom Hart had written "Stark Major" but who during a Brookhaven summer had become, he felt, an "enemy for awhile"—appeared one afternoon at their door in the company of William Seabrook's first wife, Katie. "It turned out to be a delightful interlude," Peggy Cowley remembered, "a bit of home fare, and Hart responded to it as such." "We had a great reconciliation," Hart wrote Sam Loveman, "and I've decided that I'm not the only one who has improved since our ancient misunderstandings." Claire and Katie were on their way to Cuernavaca, but they would return to town in a few days. Hart and Peggy would pick them up at their hotel for lunch.

But before that luncheon meeting could take place, Hart fell into a particularly black mood. For one thing, his visitors had asked for a progress report on his writing, and his uncertainties once more set Hart brooding. He was more than troubled about "The Broken Tower," for he had a distinct memory of typing up a copy and sending it off to Zabel. That had been weeks ago, and yet he had not heard a word about it. Peggy tried to reassure him: magazines always dawdle over poetry acceptances. But Zabel had been so insistent in asking for Hart's new poetry that Hart was sure his not reporting on the manuscript meant that the *Poetry* staff considered it a failure. Perhaps the manuscript had been lost in the mails, or Zabel's answer, Peggy suggested. But Hart was quick to counter those suggestions. He got other mail. All sorts. An invitation had just arrived for him to speak at a symposium on "Poetry and Revolution" at the John Reed Club in New York! ("Of all subjects!" Hart had snorted.) No, the failure of a reply from *Poetry* meant that the poem was a failure.

And suddenly there were new money worries. Bess Crane wrote that she had just discovered that in selling a Kansas City business some years earlier, C.A. had personally guaranteed an eight-year lease on a factory building. The new owners were losing so much money they could not make the $600 a month rent payments—and in fact had not made any for the past six months. "Well, Harold, that was just like a bolt from the blue," Bess wrote.

I had not the remotest idea that C.A. had personally guaranteed the lease . . . We are waiting, at least for the present, and not saying much, but you can see, Harold, what that does to the estate. Nothing can be paid from the estate account to you in the way of your bequest, as the executors are liable, and there isn't any income from stocks to speak of. We are not making any money from our different businesses. The only thing we can do is to give you an allowance from my salary each month, and that I have made arrangements to do. You will have to economize, as there isn't any money we can get just for the asking. You can plan on your $125. a month. I know of nothing to interfere with your getting it at this time. Just how this Kansas City matter will turn out nobody can say at this time. We are hopeful we can make some arrangement, and as I am drawing my salary, I will forward your check each month as I did the last. This is I know quite a blow for both of us, but it has to be faced. It upset me so for two or three days, I was just beside myself. The following week came Dorothy's accident. It made me think the Kansas City affair rather insignificant at the time. But we both know if C.A. did guarantee the lease, and I guess he did, some arrangement will have to be made about it. Now it's no use to worry. I find in these problems that it does no good. Be sensible in your expenditures. Time may take care of all of the things which seem so difficult today. We do have a place to live and enough to eat. I guess that's more than many have today.

Fretful about both his art and his income, Hart daily became gloomier, more withdrawn. Peggy was put to all sorts of stratagems to distract him. "He was possessed by a demon that gave him no peace," she wrote.

> One day I decided, in desperation, to ask Mary Doherty and our friend Louise [Howard] to come out for dinner. Hart liked both the girls and it might take his mind off his troubles. . . . Hart was delighted with the idea.
> "Good! You're too much alone with me. I am letting you have my blackest moods. Company is just what we need."

But on the Sunday morning that the two women were to arrive, Hart began drinking before breakfast. By the time Peggy was up, he was already drunk, still in his pajamas, a serape over his shoulder. He hounded Peggy from room to room, giving her no opportunity to telephone the guests to warn them of his condition. When they arrived, Peggy met them at the door to say that Hart was in bad shape, that they had better join her in one of the back rooms. They could hear him rampaging through the house. He was in a towering rage, shouting incoherently. In no time at all he appeared before them, lugging the big Siqueiros portrait. "Look at that piece of trash!" Peggy Cowley remembered him shouting.

> "One of Mexico's greatest painters! What a travesty! Do you think that jackal will be known ten years after he dies? Why, that picture hasn't been painted a year and the paint is already cracking. It's a daub executed with house paint!"

Before the three women could say a word, he had whipped out the straight razor he had brought back from his father's funeral— his father's razor—and slashed the portrait, hacking across the image of his downcast eyes until the painting was reduced to ribbons of pigment and burlap. He threw the razor into a corner and rushed to the courtyard to burn the remains of the portrait.

The women were frightened. But the crashing noises of Hart's progress seemed to halt. Then they heard him shouting for them from the front room. He was sitting at his desk, Peggy recalled; he seemed calm. He told them he was making out his will. Peggy remembers him saying: "I want Mary and Louise to witness this. . . . It is my last will. Read it. I'm leaving everything to Peggy except a few trinkets for Bess and Zell. Peggy is the only person with faith in me and my ability as a poet." She remembered him signing the will and giving it to Mary Doherty, asking her to keep it safe. "There, I wanted to get that done," he announced, "because this afternoon I am going to kill myself." He said it, Peggy recalled, "in an even, steady voice."

Again he disappeared, but they could hear him pacing from room to room. At one point Peggy thought she heard glass breaking. Once he put in an abrupt appearance to announce that he would be dead within three hours. They tried to think what to do. He appeared again, this time with a bottle of iodine. Holding them off with one hand, he yelled that he knew they thought he didn't intend to kill himself, but that this would prove him a man of integrity. "We attempted cajoling him," Peggy wrote, "as if he were a child with a dangerous toy, at the same time relieved it wasn't the razor. He knew we would let him come to no harm, for he could have chosen a different spot, but he held his audience for the melodrama. When he lifted the bottle to his lips, I grabbed his arm. A few drops spilled on his lips, the rest falling on his chin and the serape."

During this performance, Mary Doherty had managed to send Daniel out for a doctor, who arrived almost immediately. He took one look at Crane and announced, "He's drunk." The little iodine that he had consumed would do no harm; at the worst his lips would be slightly burned. He gave Hart a sedative. He told the women to keep an eye on him while he sobered up.

Hart was now much calmer, Miss Doherty told me, but he was still obsessed with making a will. This time he ordered Peggy out of the room.

Because I had seen three completely contradictory accounts of Hart's "will," I asked Miss Doherty to explain the discrepancies. (There are references to a will leaving everything to Peggy, references to a will leaving everything to a sailor, and finally references to the report, after his death, that there had been no will discovered.) "Oh, there were wills, and wills, and wills," she told me. He spent much of the afternoon dictating. Miss Doherty, who had agreed to type up the drafts, remembered that he made revisions as carefully as if he had been working on a poem. Before he was through, there were a number of these drafts, some of them quite different from one another. He wanted a perfect copy, and toward the end he complained bitterly about typing errors. Finally there was a version he approved of. He asked Miss Doherty to retain several copies.

His will finished, Hart then began to compose a letter to the sailor who, he hoped, would inherit the bulk of his estate. This letter—which he also left with Miss Doherty—explained that Hart intended to send his will to his uncle Byron Madden in Cleveland. His father's estate, he wrote, would be tied up for four years, but at the end of that time half of its value would be available. It was this which he wished to bequeath to the sailor with whom he had for years been in correspondence. He hoped, he wrote, that his friend would marry happily, that he would be able to realize some of the dreams for his future that he and Hart had often talked of. Hart told Mary that if the iodine worked—if the doctor were proved wrong—he wanted her to send the letter. "Won't be living at all any more if this ever reaches you," it had begun. "But hope you are all right. . . . I have very willfully killed myself. . . . Dear B———, I remember so many things, and I have loved you always, and this is my only end." Sometime during the afternoon, Crane slipped into the bathroom to drain a bottle of Mercurochrome. When they learned of it, the women again called the doctor, who struggled to clean out Hart's stomach. This time, he gave Hart a heavy dose of morphine. He left some sleeping pills that were to be used if Hart awoke during the night.

The women gathered in the front room to try to make plans. Mary Doherty felt that Hart would have to be returned to the States, preferably by train. The doctor had taken down statements from the women and these, with his report on Hart, would soon be turned over to the police. Peggy might also have to return north. "I am inclined to think the authorities will take this seriously, Peggy remembers Mary saying. "Attempted suicide is a jail offense here—the old Catholic ruling. And you are as good as married to Hart." They agreed to keep news of the suicide attempt as private as possible.

Hart woke only once during the night, Peggy wrote. He asked for water, saying that he was "burning up." She brought the water. He took one of the sleeping pills—"and fell into the first relaxed sleep he had had for days."

In the morning he was hungry. He seemed, on the whole, in good spirits. He was willing to spend the early part of the day in bed. Everything had piled up on him, he said.

Peggy talked about going home. They would have to go, she explained. If they didn't leave of their own accord, there would be trouble. Yes, he agreed, they had better get out of Mexico. He got dressed. He would take a taxi into town to inquire about passage. But first he cleaned up his room. The drafts of the wills, the rough draft of the letter to the sailor were apparently destroyed. Perhaps, had he remembered them, he would have asked for and destroyed the copies of the will that Mary Doherty had taken with her, and the letter he had entrusted to her. But both he and Peggy—and Mary, also, for that matter—were now so caught up in his plans for leaving that the papers were forgotten.

In town, Hart told Lesley Simpson about his suicide attempt as if it were just another incident among the many "comic" episodes of his Mexican career. "Roaring with laughter," Hart capped his story, Simpson said, with the appearance of the doctor, whose pronouncement "He's drunk!" struck Hart as particularly funny.

The story, however, seemed less than funny to Marsden Hartley, who joined Mary Doherty in urging Hart to return to the United States by train rather than ship.

But why should he return by train, Hart argued. Both he and Peggy loved to travel by ship. It would be the only restful way to make the journey. No friend could bring himself to say, "We want you to go by train because you'll have a better chance, that way, of reaching the United States."

While he was waiting for the passage money to come from Bess Crane—he had sent off two importunate telegrams—the luncheon date with Claire Spenser and Katie Seabrook came due. Hart and Peggy arrived at the hotel in high spirits. They had raided their garden and their store of pottery to bring with them, Claire Spenser wrote me, "a lovely black bowl full of red peonies." Though Hart was charming, his nerves, she said, seemed ready to snap. He managed to get her to one side to ask if she would take Peggy to Taxco; he needed to be completely alone, he told her. When that whispered project fell through, he urged the two women to return to the United States with him and Peggy. The *Orizaba*— the ship that had first brought him to Mexico—would be sailing on April 24. Hart had already made a tentative booking. The four of them could share a table in the dining room.

After lunch, the two women went back to their hotel. They had not mentioned it, but they had also booked passage on the *Orizaba*. Katie Seabrook called to cancel those reservations. They would return on a later sailing.

These were not the only friends who found it difficult to be with Hart during his last days in Mexico. "Hart's disintegration during March and April was so apparent and the crises came with such frequency," Lesley Simpson said, "that Marian, who loved him like a brother, could hardly bear it. So I had to take her out of town for a few days while Hart and Peggy were packing up to return to the States."

On April 20, only four days before the ship sailed, the passage money had still not arrived. Frantic, Hart sent off a telegram to his uncle in Cleveland.

BESS INCOMPREHENSIBLE HAVE WIRED TWICE FOR FARE AND MUST LEAVE ON TWENTY-FOURTH SUBJECTING ME TO GREAT CHAGRIN HAVING TO BORROW COSTING ESTATE TWICE AS MUCH WITHOUT GIVING ME CONSIDERATION WIRE MONEY AT ONCE TWO HUNDRED DOLLARS NEEDED NOW

HART CRANE

On the same day he turned to Eyler Simpson—who was already well aware that Hart was once more in trouble with the Mexican authorities. Even though his Guggenheim year was over, would Simpson be willing to help him finance his return trip should no

money be available from Cleveland? Simpson consulted Dr. Aydelotte, who was in Mexico City at the time. They agreed, if need be,
to advance any sum necessary to get Hart out of the country.

Now Hart's preparations began in earnest. "My plans for staying in Mexico have been completely reversed by a suit against the
estate which may cut me off from any income for years," he wrote
Mony Grunberg. "Since I'm having to depend even now entirely
on loans from my stepmother's salary the only thing possible to
do is return to Chagrin Falls and try to work some of it out in service to the organization, several branches of which are approaching
bankruptcy. Not a very happy prospect . . ." He would need money
the moment the ship docked, he told Grunberg. "Could you send
me a small loan of some kind c/o Hotel Lafayette, University Place
& 11th St.?" Notes to the same effect went to Sam Loveman and the
Rychtariks. "PLEASE SAY NOTHING ABOUT THESE MATTERS TO
ANYONE," he cautioned. He left a note with Mary Doherty, asking
that any mail coming either to his Mixcoac address or to the Guggenheim Foundation office be forwarded to Chagrin Falls.

Finally, he did his best to rescue the few literary projects that
might earn some money. He wrote to *Contempo* magazine that he
was delighted they would be printing the "Bacardi" poem and
asked them to assign him some work as a reviewer as soon as he
was settled in Ohio. ("I should love to review MacLeish's *Con-
quistador* for you if you haven't already assigned it elsewhere.")
He also gathered up his courage and wrote to *Poetry*. Perhaps,
after all, the "Broken Tower" manuscript had been lost in the
mail. Perhaps the fretting over its fate had been needless. "About
a month ago I sent you a poem, for possible use in *Poetry*, but
have not as yet heard from you about it. The letter may have gone
astray for all I know, as service isn't any too reliable here." He
asked Zabel to write to him in Ohio.

On the morning of April 21 the passage money arrived. Hart
and Peggy set out for the telegraph office, where it was delivered
to them in silver *tostones*, hundreds and hundreds of them, each
the size of a fifty-cent piece. Elated, Hart hailed a taxi to take the
cash (bundled in canvas sacks) to the Ward Line office. He and
Peggy rode in triumph, their feet propped up on heaps of silver.
When they reached the shipping office, Hart hired half a dozen
children to carry in the loot.

Then chaos set in. Unfortunately, the clerk told them, no more
than twenty *tostones* a day could be changed into foreign currency.
Perhaps they should consult someone at the Bank of Mexico. Another half dozen little boys were engaged to haul the money out to
a taxi, and still another half dozen to drag it to a cashier's window
at the Bank of Mexico. The money made a small heap on the floor.

Since Hart was already on edge, Peggy suggested that he take
care of last-minute shopping. They would meet for lunch.

The bank clerk was not sure the exchange could be made; in any event, the money would have to be counted. Halfway through that process, the bank closed for the long Mexican lunch hour.

Hart was in a good humor at lunchtime, so Peggy suggested that he go back to Mixcoac to wait for her. She would pick up the tickets, then drop in on friends. She would probably not be home for dinner.

When the bank reopened, Peggy realized that she had very little time; the Ward Line office would be closed within two hours. Yet the cashier, with enormous deliberation, counted and recounted the six-hundred-odd *tostones*. Peggy threatened to call the American Embassy. The cashier informed her that the only way to bypass official red tape would be by going to the president of the bank.

Two soldiers conducted me down a long corridor and we stopped at a massive door which, when opened, revealed two new soldiers to whom I was turned over. It felt more like an arrest than an audience. We entered a long, long room covered with a heavy carpet. At the end of the room was a massive desk, to which I was marched. Here were two new, grim warriors, taking the place of my last escorts. It was only then that I realized the man facing me behind the desk, with hard obsidian eyes, was none other than Plutarco Calles, once the President of all Mexico and still the power behind the throne.

Without a word, he handed over a slip of paper, bowed, and smiled slightly at my stammered thanks.

When I handed the cashier the slip of paper from Calles, the money was waiting for me. There was just time to make the Ward Line office.

Peggy then dropped in on Carleton and Betty Beals for late-afternoon cocktails. They really shouldn't leave Hart alone for dinner, they decided, so they took a taxi to Mixcoac. But when they arrived, he was gone. He had written letters for a while, Daniel told them, then he'd had a few drinks. No, he wasn't drunk. He'd just gone into town to report that Peggy had been kidnapped; he shouldn't have let her go out alone with all that money, he and Daniel had agreed.

Before he got through, he had gone not only to the police—who considered locking him up as a public nuisance—but also to one of the attachés at the American Embassy. The Embassy, Hart insisted, had to notify President Hoover of Peggy's abduction. Finally the attaché accompanied Hart to the Mexican government radio station, where a description of Peggy was broadcast. Hart refused to leave the station until he heard the description go on the air. He then returned to Mixcoac to await news of the discovery of the body.

When, long after midnight, he reached home to find Peggy waiting for him, he was furious—chiefly, she recalled, because she was "safe and sound, money, tickets, and virtue intact."

He was too wrought up to sleep. Far into the night he talked on, Peggy remembered. Mexico was destroying him. His friends despised his work. The world despised his work. If proof were needed, there was Zabel's silence about "The Broken Tower." He was a failure as a poet, the laughing-stock of his friends.

The next day, still melancholy, Crane packed his belongings. That evening he wrote a long letter to Bess Crane.

> Pardon me for wiring Byron about money, but so many difficulties came to a head at once here, and with myself weak from a fever and dysentery I had to use every way of impressing on you the urgency of my immediate needs. And I imagine that you well may have been too preoccupied to realize the situation here anyway—even in part.
>
> Altogether I've had a terrible time lately. I can't begin to write the details now in the finalities of packing. I leave for Vera Cruz tomorrow night and sail Sunday morning on the Orizaba for New York. I was planning to return to Ohio even before the shocking news came about the Wilson [lease] matter. But with that having happened I wouldn't have thought of staying here another minute anyway. I may be able to be of some help to you this summer. Anyway I want to make the effort, especially since you must be quite crippled (at least at the Cottage) without Dorothy's help.
>
> You can't imagine how difficult the Mexicans make it for any foreigners to remain here—comfortably. I love the country and the people (Indians) but certainly have had my fill of passport difficulties, servant problems and other complications for awhile. I have been not only ill—but frightened nearly out of my wits because I happened, in all innocence, to put my passport-renewal problem in the hands of a lawyer crook. It's all right; I have clearance papers; but it involved me in a lot of expense, consultations with innumerable people and just endless worry. Then at the last moment my servant got roaring drunk and left, and came back and shook the gate to its foundations, yelling threats against my life, terrorizing us for days, until we had to call on the American Embassy for special police service. Etc. and so on. . . . Do you wonder I've been anxious to get off as soon as possible. Thank God the lease on my house is already expired—and there can be no further complications that I know.
>
> I have hated to draw on you so heavily for money lately, but after all, I had no way of knowing how matters would turn out with the estate; and the expense of coming home now cer-

tainly seems justified in view of the possibility of economizing later on. There are many things highly important for us to discuss together, and besides that I am looking forward to seeing you and the rest of our friends and relatives again. I am bringing back a lot of very interesting things, some very beautiful, that you'll enjoy seeing, I'm sure.

A case of books had to be sent collect (Wells Fargo) direct to the factory. Please be on the watch for it. The other things are all in a large hamper which will go with me on the boat and will be expressed to the factory later on from New York. I'll be in New York a couple of days as I simply must see some of my old friends after so long a time. I'll telephone you on the first night of my arrival around ten o'clock when the rates are reduced.

Please give my love to poor little Dorothy. I haven't had a moment to write to anyone lately or I should have written her long ago. Had to spend all day yesterday running around trying to get the telegraphed money cashed. Wasn't your fault, nor mine. . . . what does a government agency like the telegraph here mean by paying you in currency which the government itself, through its own official bank, turns around and refuses! We finally had to arrange a special interview with the president of the bank himself. I was already to complain to the embassy. So you see how slow things move here and what incessant obstacles one has to fight for the simplest sort of transactions. It certainly has about made a nervous wreck of me. But I'll rest up on the boat.

Lovingly,
Harold

Yet, on the morning of April 23, Hart was full of gaiety. He and Peggy finished packing; they stood beside their baggage where it was piled by the curb. The house was empty. They were on their way. Daniel, tears streaming down his face, thrust an armful of flowers into their taxi.

Their first stop was the train station, where they left the baggage. Then they returned to the heart of Mexico City, for they had arranged a farewell cocktail party at their favorite restaurant, The Broadway. Almost all their friends were there: Lesley Simpson and his wife, the Beals, Eyler Simpson, Mary Doherty, perhaps a dozen others. "Everyone cheered and toasted us," Peggy wrote, "when Hart, in fine good humor, announced we were to be married in New York and would return in two years." After the party Hart and Peggy went off by themselves. "He took me for a farewell sight of our favorite market and he bought me a corsage large enough to satisfy a Hollywood queen."

One of his last stops in Mexico was at the office of the Guggenheim Foundation. Eyler Simpson had ready the loan that would take care of train fare to the ship, tips, and clearance charges. Hart wrote an acknowledgment for the office files, his last Mexico City "correspondence."

April 23, 1932

Dear Dr. Simpson:

This is to acknowledge your kindness in lending me $60.00 (Sixty dollars) for personal expenses for my return to New York. I shall refund this amount to the Guggenheim Foundation as soon as possible.

Yours very sincerely,

Hart Crane

When Hart went out the door, Simpson wrote what he hoped would be his final Hart Crane report to Henry Allen Moe:

April 23, 1932

My dear Mr. Moe:

I will not attempt to explain in detail the reasons for the enclosed letter. Indeed, to do justice to the matter at all would require a literary capacity which unfortunately I do not possess. I will simply say that about a week ago our friend Hart Crane went off the reservation with a bang. He managed to get himself in jail again as a prelude to a number of other difficulties which have been following thick and fast on the heels of one another and requiring the combined efforts of almost everyone in town to rescue him. It soon became apparent to all concerned, including Crane himself, that we must get the gentleman out of the country and that as soon as possible.

. . . Dr. Aydelotte authorized me to advance funds up to the amount of a ticket. Crane was able, however, to obtain some funds from home and it was only necessary for me to supplement those to the extent noted in his letter. He is leaving for Vera Cruz tonight and will sail, God willing, tomorrow morning.

All I've got to say is that I'm going to take a good look at the new poet you are sending down here and if he doesn't present all the earmarks of what we sociologists would call a completely adjusted individual, I'm going to send him back to you on the next boat.

Due to the small amount on hand here in the petty cash fund of the Foundation, it was necessary for me to advance Crane the above mentioned money out of my own personal funds. Will you please be kind enough to reimburse me?

Yours very sincerely,

Eyler N. Simpson

Crane's exit from Mexico City was entirely in character with his life there. His friends had gathered at the cavernous train station. "Quite a crowd of us had collected," Lesley Simpson wrote, "and the train was ready to pull out, and still no Hart. Finally, just as the last warning bell was ringing, here came Hart and Peggy, followed by a gang of *cargadores* and a whole truckload of baggage. They were laughing and greeting us in the jolliest way possible. We were enormously relieved. It looked as though he would get home after all. He even made a date to meet me in New York in June. I can still see him and Peggy standing in the vestibule, waving and blowing kisses."

On the day of the ship's departure, Vera Cruz was hot, humid. Hart and Peggy were grateful to get on board. Since he had traveled on the *Orizaba* before, he knew a number of the officers. He introduced Peggy to each of them: "I noticed some raised eyebrows among the uniformed men when Hart informed them of our marriage in the near future." Once the ship was actually underway, Hart and Peggy relaxed. There were cool breezes. They had a drink in the bar. Then Hart began to tell Peggy of the marvels of Havana.

The night before the *Orizaba* reached Cuba, they made elaborate plans. The ship would be in port all morning and most of the afternoon. Peggy wanted to do a little shopping, then they would meet, they agreed, at a restaurant Hart knew of where English was spoken. Peggy, they planned, would wait there until Hart put in an appearance.

That night they spent in Peggy's cabin.

Hart awoke in the morning refreshed and full of talk about the good times they would have in New York. He announced that the first thing he would do in Havana would be to wire ahead for rooms at the Lafayette.

They went ashore together. The city was sparkling and bright in the morning sun. For a little while Hart acted as guide, recommending stores where Peggy might shop and pointing out the restaurant where they would meet. He warned her to avoid side streets; it was easy to get lost in Havana. Then they parted.

Peggy's shopping loaded her arms with souvenirs. Her last stop was a music store where she bought some records as a surprise for Hart. Then she began to search for the restaurant and finally found what she took to be the right place. It was true that Hart was not there, and it was also true that she could locate no waiter who spoke English. But she remembered having seen a long, cool room exactly like the room she was now in.

She ordered a drink while she waited, then ordered a sandwich. Still no Hart appeared. By this time, the late tropical lunch hour was drawing to an end. The ship was due to sail at 4:30. She was quite upset, and she persuaded the waiter to find a man who spoke English. No, no one answering Hart's description had been in. Yes, she would have to leave immediately if she was to reach the ship before it sailed. The waiter signaled a taxi and gave the driver directions to take her to the pier.

The purser met her at the gangplank. Hart had been on board for over an hour. He was very concerned about her. Several other people also told her he had been searching for her. Someone had seen him arrive carrying a bottle of rum. No, he did not seem to have been drinking.

Peggy was angry, for she was sure Hart had gone off on his own, abandoning her at the restaurant. She went straight to her cabin to dress for dinner, then decided to take the records she had bought to the ship's bar, where she would listen to them over a cocktail. The bartender told her Hart had been in looking for her. He had had a few drinks, the bartender said, then had left to continue the search.

Peggy took a sip of her cocktail, dipped her head to light a cigarette, and struck a match. Suddenly there was an explosion. The whole box of matches was burning in her hand. The flame seemed to circle her hand, race up her arm. "Oh, it was a slight burn compared to these overall burns, you know," she told me, "but it was terrifically painful." The bartender hustled her to the office of the ship's doctor.

It was in the doctor's office that Hart finally found her. He was full of a jumble of feeling—resentment that she had gone to the wrong restaurant, worry over her burn, anger that she had "allowed" the burn to happen. The doctor told him to leave, to come back in an hour. Hart made numerous appearances, each time more glassy-eyed. "The doctor plainly resented his intrusions," Peggy wrote, "as did I." When the doctor permitted her to return to her cabin, Hart tried to carry her. "I resisted this, and groped along the wall."

Hart was now in an agony of resentment, frustration, smoldering violence. "He went on a rampage," Peggy told me. "He hadn't been drinking much of anything. But then he went on this drunken rampage which I knew nothing about—except, twice he got into my room." Hart kept asking questions, demanding answers. Where exactly had Peggy gone in Havana? What was the name of the restaurant she had been in? Why hadn't she come to him when she got back to the ship? Exactly how did the burn happen? Then he would be all tenderness and sympathy. Each time he broke into her room, she begged him to leave. They would have to talk about it in the morning. Pain and the drugs that the doctor had given her made the whole evening nightmarish. Finally, well after midnight, the purser came to say he had locked Hart in his cabin and nailed the door shut. "I said, 'Fine. Why didn't you do it before? Something like that should have been done.' Well, he got out before you could say Jack Robinson. I don't know whether he tore the door down, or what. And then I didn't really see him until the next morning."

Whatever happened to Hart during that night was part and parcel of what had been happening during the long day—and the long nights and days of his entire adult life. But it cannot now be recovered. For Hart's last twenty-four hours are tangled in rumor, blurred in blurred memories. Marsden Hartley later heard a story that Hart had spent part of his time in Havana with a young man from the ship, perhaps a sailor, perhaps a passenger. Hartley felt that Crane's heavy drinking that evening was a form of puritanical recoil from the events of his afternoon. There were other rumors about events that took place between 1 A.M., when Hart escaped from his cabin, and 4 A.M., when, according to the captain's report, he was forcibly returned to it by a steward.

These rumors still circulate. There had been a wild escapade—in one version, with an unidentified member of the ship's personnel; in another version, with a cabin boy; in another, with one of the sailors; and in still another, with several men. Whatever happened, and wherever it happened—in the sailors' quarters, on deck, in Hart's cabin—there was enough violence in it to bring Hart to the deck at about 3:30. The next morning he confessed that he had been beaten and robbed; his wallet was missing, also a ring. His wallet was still missing ten days later when his mother broke the seals on his trunk and his suitcases.

But on deck alone, the night before his suicide, Hart stared with drunken hopelessness into black water. He began deliberately to climb the ship rail. Yet even death was anticipated with anticlimax. He was wrestled back to the deck by the night watch, then quickly escorted back to his cabin.

This time there would be no escape. The second steward, to whom he was handed over, was no man to take chances. He remained in the room until Crane was undressed and in bed. He may also have seen to it that Crane had a sleeping pill, though there is no mention of it in the captain's report. When he left Hart's room, the second steward made a note of the time: exactly 4 A.M.

Peggy awoke the next morning groggy from pain and morphine. She was unable to reconstruct anything that had happened. Hart had sometime during the night been pounding on her door, she remembered. And she vaguely remembered shouts from the corridor. She rang for the stewardess, asking for coffee. Together they went to the ship's doctor, where her burns were dressed. He said nothing about Hart's behavior and Peggy herself asked nothing about Hart.

But as soon as she returned to her cabin, she found Hart waiting to talk to her. He seemed sober but nervous and, she thought, frightened. "He told me he recalled nothing of the previous evening after first seeing me in the doctor's office. His wallet and a ring were missing. I went with him to his room, to see if they could be found, although he was sure they had been stolen." Hart was quite shaky and said he had to have a drink. Then he sat down on the bed beside her. This time, he confessed, he had disgraced himself completely.

> He said, "Everything is lost. I've got to go." And I laughed and said, "Nonsense, let's go and have some breakfast." And he said, "Oh, it's too late for breakfast." I said, "We can have some breakfast." And the purser came in just at that moment, and I said, "Can't we have some breakfast?" He said, "Surely." He went back and they brought in a menu to him, and I don't think he left one item out. Just an enormous meal. He wanted to be filled with something.

While he ate, Hart told her a little about his day in Havana. "He said he had not begun to drink the day before until he got back on the ship. I had been waiting in the wrong restaurant." When Peggy returned to her cabin to be dressed, she was concerned. She knew Hart was troubled about the loss of his wallet. But she also knew that he had often before turned such minor disasters into comedy. Perhaps after a drink or two he would feel more himself.

According to the captain's report, the steward had that morning unlocked Hart's room shortly before ten o'clock. Not long afterwards, he looked in on Hart and found him drinking. At eleven, both the steward and the ship's doctor had called on him. He was then drinking "copiously" from a bottle of whiskey; he was still not dressed.

At a little before twelve, Hart knocked at Peggy's door.

> He was still in his pajamas, wearing a light topcoat for a robe. I asked him to shave and dress.
> "I'm not going to make it, dear. I'm utterly disgraced."
> Perhaps some glimmerings of his actions the night before had come to haunt him, beyond the loss of the ring and the pocketbook. If so, he gave me no hint. . . . He was always immaculate and I kept insisting that he would feel in a calmer mood and more self-possessed once he was dressed in clean clothes.
> "All right, dear. Good-bye."

He leaned over to kiss her, then turned to leave the room. The door closed behind him.

The stewardess helped Peggy brush her hair, then asked what she would want for lunch. "All of a sudden," Peggy told me, "the boat stopped. And I gave a scream, and I said, 'Hart,' and went out to the deck, and they were just letting down the first boats to look for him."

Three days later, Henry Allen Moe added a memorandum to the Hart Crane file of the Guggenheim Foundation.

On April 30, 1932 I had a talk with Mr. M. Seckendorf, Passenger Traffic Manager of the Ward Line, at their offices in New York and Mr. Seckendorf read me a part of the report of the Master of the "Orizaba" concerning the death of Hart Crane.

The report stated that Mr. Crane jumped overboard two minutes before twelve noon on Wednesday, April 27th, 1932 when the vessel was 275 miles north of Havana bound for New York. Mr. Crane was seen to come on deck clad in his pajamas covered by an overcoat. He walked rapidly aft, threw the coat on the deck, climbed up on the rail, and jumped over the side. Life preservers were thrown at once, the ship was manoeuvred and a boat put over the side, but no trace of Mr. Crane was found. He had been seen once after his body struck the water and apparently he made no effort to reach the life preservers thrown him. . . .

Mrs. Cowley was questioned by the Captain and she knew of no other reason for the suicide except Crane's excessive drinking. She further stated that she had expected to marry Mr. Crane when she had obtained her divorce.

Mr. Seckendorf told me that Mr. Crane's stepmother, a representative of Mr. Crane's mother who lives in Oak Park, Chicago, Illinois he said, and Mrs. Cowley were together in Mr. Seckendorf's office last night and that they arranged for the disposition of Mr. Crane's effects.

Four lifeboats had been lowered. For two hours the ship had circled the area, Peggy standing on the bridge beside the captain. The passengers and crew had lined both sides of the ship, their eyes fixed on the bobbing life preservers. Little throngs of people were gathered about those who had met Crane. Those who had seen him leap overboard debated if the hand that had shot to the surface had been clutching for a life preserver or had been signaling goodbye.

A day or two after Hart's death, his "Aunt Sally" Simpson received a card postmarked Havana and dated April 26, 1932. "Off here for a few hours on my way north. Will write you soon. Am going back to Cleveland to help in the business crisis. Permanent address—Box 604, Chagrin Falls, Ohio. Much love. Hart."

A week after his suicide, the slow Mexican mails brought a similar postcard to Lesley Simpson—also from Havana and also dated April 26. "Very pleasant journey. Shall write you when I get in the upper latitudes. Peggy sends *her* love too. Hart."

In Chagrin Falls, there was an unopened letter from Morton Dauwen Zabel of *Poetry* magazine. It had been written on April 24, the day the *Orizaba* sailed from Vera Cruz.

Dear Hart Crane,

I am alarmed to hear that you sent a poem to the POETRY office, for none has reached me . . . Has it been lost in the mails? Nor have we ever received the review you were writing of Phelps Putnam's "Five Seasons," though we looked for it over a space of six months. Was this sent, and lost, too? I hope you can send a duplicate ms of the poem at once, and the review as soon as you can . . .

I have thought frequently of you during these past months. How did the winter go in Mexico? I ached for such country as that during the heavier stretches of sweat and labor since Christmas. I'll be eager to hear of the sort of work you've been doing. . . .

I hope to hear from you directly abt the poem and the review. Diligent search has failed to discover them at the office.

With good wishes,<br>Morton Dauwen Zabel

# 44

Hart Crane died at high noon on April 27, 1932. His body became a part of the sea; his name and the years of his birth and death survive on the stone in Garrettsville, Ohio, that marks his father's grave.

After his death, his friends and relatives searched their hearts and their memories for the "cause" of his suicide. Some of them found easy answers; few of their answers were identical. Certain of his friends blamed themselves for Hart's suicide: had they offered money, love, advice; had they given protection or affection; had they found a way to keep him from drinking—then, perhaps, his death might not have been suicide. Others blamed the world: Hart was a victim of a capitalist economy; he was the victim of a country that rejected his art; he was the victim of a puritanical society that would not let him love or live as he chose. A few blamed his family—and particularly those parents who had shaped his character. A number of his friends blamed other acquaintances —"bad companions"—for his death. And one or two blamed Hart himself: he was bent on self-destruction; nothing could have prevented it.

"Mexico killed Hart, I think," Lesley Simpson wrote some four years after Hart's death. "For him it was a threatening and unfriendly country, and people of Hart's sensitiveness are driven mad by it. It [was] full of crazy Americans, most of them trying to run away from themselves. Hart tried to escape from Mexico via alcohol."

But was it Mexico? If it was, those people on the scene would have had the clearest vision—and their reactions, for the sake of "truth" or for the sake of books like this one, should have been set down quickly, before time had had a chance to dull reality or to distort memory.

Henry Allen Moe—conscious of the importance of such documentation—wrote to Eyler Simpson asking him to encourage Mary Doherty to put down "circumstantially and in detail" everything she could remember about Hart Crane's doings. "She should, I think, project herself a hundred years into the future and ask herself this: 'If I knew Kit Marlowe's life what should I have written?'"

All summer Miss Doherty carried about with her Henry Allen Moe's letter. Finally, on September 11, she tried to explain why she could not write what he had hoped for:

> For the first weeks I puzzled over your letter. I could not decide how to answer it for I wanted to make no promises I might not want to live up to later. And I wanted to be fair—to do what you had suggested, because you had suggested it, and to feel more clearly what I could write that would be a contribution and not just a repeating of details that really are beside the point. From one point of view I hesitated even letting myself think about it—it seems still only so very recent that we (I, at least) have been able to rise above the depressing feeling of frustration and futility Hart's year here and its tragic end had for those of us who came to know him well and to care for him. I was very interested to see that the English journal you quoted used the very words I have repeated over and over in connection with the end—that it was a "wicked, wicked stupidity."

She talked with Moisés Sáenz and with Marsden Hartley about what she might set down. Both of them, she felt, had understood and valued Hart.

> Mr. Hartley . . . feels that enough tawdry writing has been done about Hart and that the public, even the small public, just has no right to the details of Hart's life in Mexico just yet, or ever. I would disagree with Mr. Hartley if, as Mr. Sáenz says, we could decide "how much of Hart's essence as a poet depends on his 'private life.'" Very little, is my belief. Though Hart's mental anguish of the past year as revealed so many times does in my opinion have a great deal to do with the use, lack of use and now loss to humanity of Hart's magnificent gift. The matter seems to me quite apart from Hart himself. I feel so with any artist . . . that he has no personal life, or no right to one. For me, the artist . . . must be ready to face complete revealment at all times, certainly he has little right to secrecy after death. And I suppose the sooner after death those who were placed near that artist record literally what they saw the better. And in complete fashion since who is one to judge what factors in the end will prove the most revealing? And, after all, neither is it one's own to keep. . . .
>
> I am trying to say (in a very involved fashion, I fear) that I fully realize the importance for the future that pretty much all of the details of Hart's year here be written down; that I *have* been at pains to write much of it down or to pass it along in some fashion to the persons I thought should have it because they themselves seemed to be or they were in close touch with those who would be the logical ones to write the weighted ac-

count that was to be left to posterity. I suppose I could try to get these letters back. . . .

Yet, she went on to say, the autumn of 1932 was not "100 years after," and the pain of setting down facts—and the fear of what might be made of them—made such an act unbearable. She could not bring herself to write, though she was well aware that men and women whom Hart had known casually might set down "the truth" that they had heard in gossip. This at least she could discount in advance. "There was, Mr. Moe, an utter absence in the group of friends here last year of anyone whose opinion Hart respected." How could such people be expected to grasp enough of his character to define him?

Whatever the cause of Hart's death, the "causes" that she had already heard advanced were false to the man she had known.

I do want to say that the motive was *not*, even remotely, worries over money matters; it was *not* lost faith in poetry and the place of the poet in this struggling world; and it was *not* some other thing that escapes me at this moment. I don't know why Peggy Cowley said those things. Hart was always bothering about the last five pesos, but who of us aren't? . . . But worried over real money matters to the point of suicide, or his father's business, or his having to go back to it, no. It is ridiculous. And someone has written that Hart lived extravagantly here in Mexico. No, he didn't. He lived extremely simply in his house in Mixcoac and in an entirely Mexican environment. Which was as it should have been. Unless you call drinking too much, and alone, and letting oneself get into a state of utter morbidity extravagant living. To me that would be described by other words. It is being wasteful,—or destructive to one's intuitive qualities, but not necessarily extravagant in one's material living, is it?

Perhaps, she felt, Marsden Hartley might be trusted to set down the Mexican "truth" about Hart. He had said that he was writing an essay on Crane. Miss Doherty gave him what she had—the copies of the "will" and the accompanying letter. Hartley's essay— never published—turned out to be fragmented, a set of vague impressions still kept from publication by the intricate tangle of Hartley's own estate. The one "fact" recorded in it pertains to the carbons of the will—on yellow copy paper—and the accompanying letter. Three years after Crane's death, Hartley had brought them to the attention of Grace Crane—in the absence of a legal will, Hart's only heir. She was grateful, she told him, for his "fine ethical feeling" in offering her a copy of the copy.

Like other people close to Hart, Grace Crane herself had looked for the "cause" of her son's suicide. Though for a short time she was convinced that the immediate cause was his to-her-inexplicable "involvement" with a woman, she soon came to feel that the roots lay further back. Whatever had driven him to leave her in California, she decided, was at the core of his death—that leave-taking, and false rumors about her, and an alcoholism that only she had been able to cope with. If he had known the true story of her life after he had broken with her, their separation and his death, she felt, might have been averted. Soon after his suicide, she set down her version of the four-year period during which Crane had refused to see her or to write to her. She wrote out the story for Sam Loveman.

You know Sam he never needed much persuasion to go on one of his sprees—and when once well started one never knew just how it would end. Don't I well know, from my experiences when he was in California that winter with me! With mother sick unto death and requiring my constant attention night and day and at all times when he was affected, trying to screen his condition from her—for they simply idolized each other. I never allowed myself to chide him when such conditions were evident. I just tried not to notice it, and waded through the scene as calmly and pleasantly as though things were quite normal. I knew perfectly well how "touchy" he was at such times, and upbraiding him would be likely to produce most any kind of scene. It was only in times when things were perfectly normal that I would remonstrate and then *very* gently, mostly casual. The Cranes never knew and will never know very much about the struggles I have had—nor of his emotional perversion of which he calmly told me himself while in California. It was a great shock to me but he never knew it, and it took me a long time to get my mind adjusted to such a condition. I immediately began to read much on the subject and learned much that helped me accept it. Did he ever tell you that he left me out there in the middle of the night after we had all gone to bed and asleep, leaving a note on his pillow which I later found, stating only that he [had] gone but nothing about *where*. Imagine what I had on my hands at that instant with mother still living and scared to death over his actions. It was two weeks before I heard from him—back in Patterson, and during those two weeks I had imagined every conceivable thing —including imprisonment at San Quentin, because of his daily visits to some bootlegger acquaintances he had made. My mother died in the following Sept. and I was so completely prostrated from three years of nursing—besides the ordeal of a second divorce and the publicity attendant to it, worrying over Hart and depleted finances, that I had to stay in bed 3 weeks—. In the midst of this . . . I received a wire from Hart that if I did not send him the trust bequest at once he would immediately start *legal proceedings*. I never was so shocked and incensed in my life and in that state of mind I sent him a very emphatic telegram, which of course I have long since regretted and told him so many times, but to no avail. Although I knew I had by the law at least one year to settle the estate, and no legal proceedings against me could have been brought at that time, I sent word to Mr. Stockwell of the bank to sell at once enough of the most desirable stocks to create [the bequest] —and I have never heard from Hart . . . since. A long nervous breakdown, with secondary anemia immediately followed and kept me in California for over a year—then the financial crash which wiped me out entirely. I sold my beautiful diamonds for a song, to raise the money to get back home and my nurse put me on the train for Ohio, to go to ———, who had previously asked me to come, and whom mother and I had for many years helped financially and kept them at our house for weeks at a time. My intention was to remain there a few days and rest before I went to Warren to bury my mother's ashes. After . . . being there a couple of days, I was literally set out in the street at night in a snow storm—and told that they had been to ——— and conferred with ——— and that she said I was literally eaten up with venereal disease, and that being the case as he believed (God only knows why, as it was a *lie*, and there was no cause for such a thing) he . . . couldn't "run the risk of having his family become contaminated." Sam, can you imagine the shock this was to me—the awful bruise it made to my whole mental being? I still couldn't believe what he said as being truly transmitted to him—so I wired ——— and her reply was "Never set your foot across my doorway again." I walked the floor all night long at the hotel and next day (I will never know how I did it) took the train for Chicago, where I sent for my friend Mrs. Ross. She heard my story and was so incensed that there was a long time that suing for slander was all they talked of. I went through a thorough physical examination which proved the utter falsity of the accusation. I was absolutely certain without it. The only way I could manage to account for it [was] that while in California I had a siege of boils due to my anemic condition and the doctor I employed gave me serum injections twice a week to correct the conditions. Mr. ——— had relatives out there who I disliked and it was mutual and they may have taken this opportunity to damn me. I heard that Hart said he was heartbroken over the downfall of his beautiful mother. Did it ever occur to him, even if it might have been true, that those things can be acquired through no fault of one's own? It was all such a ridiculous fiendish lie that I refused to deny it to any of those who claimed it—and those of them who had circulated the report were in every case persons of very positive shady morals—

I felt that in Hart's case, if even *worse* than that *were* true—

he should have remembered that I was his mother, and one who had always given to him freely of the very best she had—I always loved him better than life itself and *still do*. . . .

Though Grace Crane did continue to love her son—and though she devoted the rest of her long life to the perpetuation of his memory, working with Sam Loveman and Waldo Frank on the manuscripts that went into *The Collected Poems,* then working with Loveman and later with Philip Horton on the first biography, and finally gathering together copies of Hart's letters, assembling the nucleus of the material Brom Weber eventually drew on for the volume of letters he edited in 1952—her feelings about her son were continually assaulted by discoveries of what she took to be betrayals on his part. She heard from Sam Loveman that certain friends of Hart's wanted to have nothing to do with her because of what Hart himself had told them.

Regarding Hart's talking to the ———s . . . about me—all I can say is—that if he did—he was a scoundrel to do such a thing. All my life, I have devoted myself to his interests and ambitions, have sacrificed anything to help him—and gave him far more money than he ever received from his father while he was alive, or through his will. I have no apologies or explanations to make—for my conscience is absolutely clear. Hart's disintegration began when he let go of me—and he went straight to Hell, from then on. To hear that he was brutal enough to condemn me, makes me feel very bitter, I assure you. But my love for him was 1000 per cent, and there are times when I nearly suffocate when I think of not ever seeing him, or knowing his love again. Regardless of anything he has said or done, I shall continue to play my part as a mother, as best I can. I want to see his book through to the end—and I shall not be influenced to neglect it, in any way, or for any cause. As for the approval of his . . . friends—well, that [is] just too bad—but I *can* live without it. I always try to keep in mind that the largest percent of the people in the world are morons—. Unless you have lived and suffered, you are narrow, hypocritical, and totally devoid of understanding. I have learned not to expect much loyalty from anyone. They prefer to believe the lies. It seems to feed their morbidity.

I also have to remember in connection with Hart what his father was. It wouldn't have been possible for him *not* to have inherited some things from that source. But when all is said and done, Hart was his own worst enemy. He was smart enough to analyze the situation, but instead, preferred to shift the responsibilities he should have assumed, to some one else, any one—. With the result that his life was wholly selfish—consequently destructive to his career and happiness. If he had done as he should, showed me consideration and respect, I am sure he would have been alive today, and gaining the goal he wished to achieve. I never asked for much from H. and he knew it. I made *no demands*. The comfort of his letters and love was about all. Do you think that was too much? The more I learn about his recent years, especially his life in Mexico, the more I feel that it is best for us both that he is gone. God only knows what might have happened, if he had kept on at that pace. It might have been much worse.

If such bitter insight sometimes came to Grace Crane, at other times she survived Hart's death in a dream of missed possibilities. "Our estrangement of the last few years, brought on in a moment of great tension for both of us, was nothing but what could have been entirely overcome in a few short weeks," she wrote to Lorna Dietz a few days after she had learned of the suicide.

Hart loved me devotedly and also depended upon me for encouragement to go on with his writing in face of all the opposition and ridicule from his father and his family. I believed in him and fought for his right to do what he so earnestly wanted to do. Out of our mutual struggles grew that marvelous understanding which meant so much to us both.

Hart was off to Europe before I even knew he had even planned to go, leaving me no address and no contacts through which to reach him. I became ill on account of the situation. I wrote several letters to former addresses hoping they would be forwarded, but they never were returned or answered. I did not even know that he was in Mexico, until I read it in the notice of his father's death. . . .

Had I possessed the price of a ticket I would have gone to Mexico and never given up until I had found him. Now I wish I had gone even if on foot. I was working at the time as manager of a hotel, making a modest salary which barely covered my living expenses. Oh, the hours I have spent at night lying awake, wishing, hoping, longing for him. He was my whole life, hope, ambition, everything! I knew he was unhappy—remorseful—and I wanted to release his heart and mind to do the work I fully understood he could not do until he was at peace with me. Knowing that he would likely be returning to New York this summer, I had made a firm resolve to go there and turn heaven and earth, if need be, to see him. And now comes this tragic ending, to us both, for my life has gone out with his—. I am simply crushed, numb, utterly defeated!

It is hard to imagine what Hart's life might have been had he become reconciled with Grace Crane. Mony Grunberg—drawing on his experience as lay psychoanalyst—felt that Hart's relationship to her represented a "horrible involvement of the crudest, of the

most affectionate, of the most indescribable sort." When, just before leaving for California, Hart had questioned Grunberg about
the tangle of emotions he lived with—the creative blocks he experienced—Grunberg had said that he didn't think Hart would
be able to free himself creatively "until he shook off this horrid
hatred for his father . . ." "I explained to him," Grunberg told me,
"that it was not that he hated his father so greatly, but that he also
hated his mother. . . . And, of course, he hated her because there
was no way of pleasing her."

"I . . . see his life as one of those adagios in Beethoven's major
quartets," Grunberg wrote to Sam Loveman when he first heard
of the suicide.

A man's physiology has really no interest for me. I regard a
man's sex life etc. as I do my own—something like a digestive
process, more or less devoid of meaning. We do not excrete in
public. Why we should make the sex functions public was
never something that I could understand. Hart unfortunately
was neurotic—his perversions mere "social" reactions. He used
his sex life, etc. to punish the environment—indirectly his
parents, no doubt. He was really very much in love with his
father—in love, of course, as neurotics are, ambivalently. A
fine messed up life, in other words.

When, almost a year after Hart's death, Grace Crane asked
Grunberg to write to her about Hart, he answered as directly as
he dared. "I have been wondering," he wrote, "how you sustained
Hart's tragic end. It has meant so much to me, and I was not his
mother. He cannot be replaced. I shall never meet his like—and
I never dare to play a certain Beethoven piece when alone, it so
definitely retells his life."

I know a lot about poor Hart—perhaps more than anyone
living knows about him. I knew just what gnawed at his brain—
but [it] was beyond me to help him. You and his father were
never for a half an hour out of his mind. If I had his genius,
I could write something immense about his life. I sometimes
even wonder to what degree you can fathom it—I mean his
lacerating conflicts. God help us all, what a life this is! I hope
to meet you some day soon. We shall then have a lot to talk
about. I feel as if I know you for a very long time.

She answered immediately, with a letter that she asked him to
destroy. He replied within a week.

I am certain that I'll be able to tell you things about Hart
that will be new to you and there is no end of things I should
want to know about him. He was the kind of man one only
meets once in a lifetime and it's a great consolation to me that
I was always aware of that. Both Sam and myself were really
his best and sincerest friends.

Yes, Hart told me enough about his father—and, of course, about you also. I studied him and tried to help him. . . . I even succeeded at one time in convincing him that he was really not abnormal, but that his abnormality was an unfortunate reaction towards you and his father particularly. My theory was sound because his interest in Mrs. C. took place after his father died.

Oh, he was in a dreadful mental mess.

But—he was the only truly civilized man I ever met despite it all—and I am missing him in a manner that can't be described.

Grace Crane lived on until July 30, 1947. The fifteen years that followed the death of her son were for her years of grim hand-to-mouth survival. During the summer following Hart's death, she was forced to sell all the stored Cleveland furniture—including that fourposter bed that had once stood in Hart's tower bedroom and that more than a hundred years earlier had been brought across the country in a covered wagon by his great-grandmother and great-grandfather.

She held catch-as-catch-can jobs—housekeeper, companion, cook, scrubwoman. Her focus, during all that time, was on her son's memory. Thanks to her diligent pursuit of manuscripts and letters, we have an extraordinary record of the man's career—blurred in crucial areas by her equally diligent effort to destroy painful material.

Toward the end, she was supported more than a little by the generosity of Sam Loveman, who followed her as Crane's literary executor, and by Arthur Pell, who had taken over the Liveright Publishing Company. "Should you be hard hit for some money, do not hesitate to call on me and I shall be more than glad to advance it," Pell had written her in the summer of 1945; and he remained true to his word. He anticipated royalties by months, eventually by years. "Sam Loveman telephoned me and told me that you needed some money and I sent him $200.00 on Saturday which he in turn will give you," he wrote her in the summer of 1946, and in the fall of that year wrote again: "I know I have violated all the rules in giving you an advance on the Black and Gold edition as I did but knowing from my sister's case how a broken arm is dragged out, I am enclosing an additional advance check for $50.00. It isn't what you need but it is an awful lot when you have so little and with it goes my sincere wish for better luck in the future."

When she died, her ashes were thrown from the Brooklyn Bridge. Her last words had been of her son.

The significance of Grace Crane's life and death seem clear enough—but what can one make of Hart Crane's death, that death that so obsessed his mother and that still troubles his friends? No single thing, I think.

Was it an "inevitable" suicide? To Richard Rychtarik it seemed more accident than suicide—something that happened, but that might not have happened had circumstances been a fraction different. "Do you think Hart had to commit suicide?" I asked.

"I don't know," Mr. Rychtarik answered. "He was, of course, very much worried about the inheritance and that suit which was pending. . . . Probably this constant worry about a few dollars didn't help him. I still don't know if it was suicide or if it was that he had one drink too many . . .

I put the same question to Charmion von Wiegand. Was Crane's suicide inevitable? "I don't think anything would have been inevitable if somebody had taken care of him," she said. "It was just economically difficult." He needed a way, she felt, "to isolate himself from the stresses of ordinary everyday life in America." Yet she felt too that the combination of economic and emotional difficulties finally proved too much for Hart. "He couldn't make a new beginning. He'd worn himself out. He'd lived himself out. I think that was the trouble. . . . He might have put out another branch if he went somewhere else, but I think he'd lived his life to the full."

I asked my question of Margaret Robson, now Mrs. Babcock, who had faithfully corresponded with Hart in Mexico and who at the end had wired him money for incidental expenses on the way home. Did the suicide seem inevitable? "Yes. I believe so—for psychological reasons. And I think it was foreshadowed, even way back in the 'Voyages.'" "I finally reconciled myself to his death," she told me, though she added, "It knocked me out for a number of years afterwards." There was no "cause" for Hart's death—other than his life.

I asked Waldo Frank about the factors that led up to Hart's suicide. Frank, who had never seen Hart on drunken sprees, who had sometimes played the role of an older brother, sometimes that of a surrogate father, talked to me at length on a number of occasions about these factors. "They were complex," he insisted. "I don't think you can ever get anywhere if you try to seek out one and make it absolute. There isn't any doubt, for instance, that he was deeply humiliated by the fiasco that he had made of his trip to Mexico, that he'd spent his money and not done what he was supposed to do—what he'd promised to do. But he was also troubled about the world situation. This had been growing on him. He'd lost his hope. I think, for a while, he was attracted to the Communists, and then he soured on that—rightly or wrongly. But I do also think . . . that these are diseases which have crises; and if he'd had luck, he could have gotten over it. . . . But I think he just lost heart, and lost faith in himself; and the dismal prospect of New York in 1932—that had a great effect on him."

What final word can one say of the voyager whose death at sea seems an elemental part of his poetry—who accepted the fact that "the bottom of the sea is cruel" but who found in the "vortex of our grave" a place for "the pieties of lovers' hands," for "dark confessions," for "infinite consanguinity"—who turned to the sea as to a lover: "Permit me voyage, love, into your hands . . . ," and who made of it a place

> where death, if shed,
> Presumes no carnage, but this single change,—
> Upon the steep floor flung from dawn to dawn
> The silken skilled transmemberment of song . . .

—what statement can one make more accurate than the last line of "At Melville's Tomb": "This fabulous shadow only the sea keeps"?

"LOST AT SEA." His Garrettsville gravestone makes the statement for us.

My search was for the man. But I found no more of him than Hart Crane himself found of the girl his grandmother had once been, the girl whose love letters had faded in an attic over the course of too many years until they were brown and soft—"And liable to melt as snow."

Like Crane himself, I had tried to play "old keys that are but echoes."

I asked his friends what came to mind when I said the two words *Hart Crane.* "Well, I see the brown eyes, and a very warm and sweet person, really," Charmion von Wiegand said. But she wasn't willing to let it go at that. There was also the "daemonic side." "I mean, sweetness and light alone does not make poetry. I mean, it's the dual aspect of the nature of the unconscious that really fused. Then you get that white heat. And I think he had that. I mean, it was beyond the ordinary experience. And whatever neurosis caused his problems—you can hack it up into psychoanalytical terms—that doesn't matter. The ancients called it the daemon, didn't they?—And he had that."

"What comes to mind—the first thing—when you hear the words *Hart Crane?*" I asked Malcolm Cowley. "What's the first thing that pops into your head?"

"Five-cent cigar."

I asked why, but Cowley went on to search memory. "Five-cent cigar. Hair: bushy hair cropped close to the head. Red face. Rather popping brown eyes. Not a very tall man. I think he was about five feet ten, but he gave an impression of being big, and aggressive, and strangely masculine at all times."

"When I say *Hart Crane,* what comes to mind?" I asked Sam Loveman.

"The best friend I ever had . . . the most charming, the most *alive* human being that life has ever given me, barring none."

I could not put abrupt questions to "Aunt Sally" Simpson or to Bill Wright, for they are long since dead. But their answers survive in letters they wrote after Hart's death.

Bill Wright, who wanted to be remembered as "one of Hart's oldest, I think perhaps the very oldest, friend," who regarded Hart's death as "the most profound shock of my life," and who once considered writing a biography of his friend, felt that everything in Hart Crane's career reduced to "the square question of sincerity, and in this the poems and the man are one. No one who has known Hart Crane very long or very well has failed to feel the silent, terrible sincerity of his purpose."

It was this same sincerity that dominated Mrs. Simpson's view of Hart. "Poor dear Hart," she wrote. "I can't reconcile myself to the thought of suicide, yet I can easily understand how discouraged and despondent he could become over the perfidy of some of his trusted friends! Hart was always so honest and *just*, taking the blame himself when he thought he deserved it. He was a fine likeable person; everyone he met here liked him."

When in the autumn of 1932 Henry Allen Moe received Mary Doherty's letter, her apology for not documenting Hart Crane's last days, he made a final attempt to persuade her to set down everything she knew:

My letter to Dr. Simpson apparently did not make clear what I asked you to do: I hope this will: —

No matter what we think, no matter whether we like it or not, we have and shall have written histories, including literary histories. And history, if it is true history, is a selection and synthesis of that detail which has meaning. Hence, if the Foundation is selecting wisely (and that begs many questions), historically our archives are bound to be important. Let me give you an illustration: Scholars think, and everybody including myself agrees, that the lives of poets illumine their work, and Leslie Hotson for that reason, got great kudos for discovering the facts of Marlowe's death. And I think that I should be doing less than I ought for the Fellows, if I did not make my files the historical source of authentic facts concerning them: if Marlowe had been a Guggenheim Fellow, the *facts* of his life and death ought to have been here! I ought and intend to make the Guggenheim Foundation archives important for literary historians when they are writing the history of this period of American letters.

Hence, I'd gladly give you an undertaking to bury the

"facts" about Hart Crane in Mexico in the files for fifty years, or a hundred, sealed, without seeing them myself or letting anyone see them.

With the above preface, you will understand that I am not, if I may so put it without disrespect, interested for this purpose in your reactions or impressions. What I am interested in may perhaps, by example, be explained thus: Hart Crane on a certain night, I understand, dictated to you his "will." A copy of that document should be here (or elsewhere)—sealed, if you like— with a bald account of what happened that night. There were other epic happenings. What were they? What happened? What was said? Who was concerned? Facts, facts, facts.

This letter is written simply by Henry Moe to Mary Doherty. You have heard about me and I have heard about you—in terms so that we are not strangers. I am not writing as the secretary of the Foundation except insofar as I offer you archives! I have my own thoughts about Hart Crane; you have yours. Some day let's hope we can meet and walk and talk. But now I'm asking only for facts, circumstantially and in detail.

If contemporary estimates of Hart Crane hold through the years, what I am offering you is, in a sense, immortality. History may be interested in what Tate and Frank thought about Hart Crane, but history will also want the facts on which to base its own interpretation.

You may think me hard; but if that be so I plead that these facts seem to me to be close to the main point, secondary only to the poetry. Mr. Sáenz's doubts I share; I don't know; but we may be sure that whether we like it or not, ghouls as well as sound scholars will dig for facts—and only you can leave a record of impeccably accurate detail. Take a year to do it; take two. Do it when you feel you can. But do it. Omit no one. Names, dates, places, happenings, sayings. Deposit it some- where else than in our archives if you find a better place. Do it before you forget.

I am not asking you, please to understand, to do any writing for present publication. Indeed if I were to give you advice, it would be to recall the letters you have written. I am looking at the long future.

Miss Doherty did not answer the letter—though she made available in conversation her recollections of Hart. She helped Philip Horton with his account of Hart's Mexican years. She was of help to me.

That long future of which Henry Allen Moe spoke has already begun. Crane is acknowledged to be one of the greatest American poets of this century. The search for the scraps of paper on which he wrote poetry is the relentless, intense pursuit of librarians and private collectors. His letters, his manuscripts sell for fabulous prices. The man has imperceptibly become a "historical figure." The brown eyes that are gone stare at us—and will continue to stare at us—from the covers of literary studies, from photographs bound up in this book and in the books that will, when more facts have been uncovered, supersede this one.

The man has begun to fade into his legend.

Even if we locate his last letter, even if we wring the memories of all living acquaintances until they are dry, can we hope to discover the "true" Hart Crane? I think not. For the truth of Hart Crane—the truth of any man—lies neither in the events of his life nor in the memories of his friends nor even in his art, if he happens to be—as Hart Crane was—a great artist. Truth is so subtle that it hovers in the flicker of an eyelash, so swiftly changing that it is transformed while a breath of air whispers through the lungs.

> "Are your fingers long enough to play
> Old keys that are but echoes:
> Is the silence strong enough
> To carry back the music to its source
> And back to you again
> As though to her?"

Hart Crane had asked himself that question in the poem about his grandmother's love letters. And he had let the rain provide the answer we must all come to who search a crowded past for lost reality. For finally—no matter how diligent our search for the lonely person: Elizabeth Belden Hart, Harold Hart Crane, whoever—we find ourselves looking into uncomprehending other eyes:

> And so I stumble. And the rain continues on the roof
> With such a sound of gently pitying laughter.

# Notes

In several instances, my transcriptions of published letters differ slightly from the Weber edition. In each of these instances, my variation is based on a reexamination of the original. In unpublished letters by Crane, my policy has normally been to correct spelling but to retain Crane's punctuation, except in those rare cases when an obvious accidental lapse has occurred (a missing period, for example, followed by a capitalized new sentence). I have not regularized his quotation marks and italics but have, rather, followed Crane's text. In letters from his correspondents, on the other hand, I have felt free to regularize spelling and punctuation. Citation is given for the *first words* from a quotation. If the following quotations continue from the same source, no further documentation is given.

The text of the poems is based on *The Complete Poems and Selected Letters and Prose of Hart Crane*, edited by Brom Weber (New York, 1966). The hardbound Liveright edition is identical to the softbound Doubleday Anchor edition. Quoted poetry will be from this edition, unless otherwise indicated, and will not be documented in the notes unless the title of the quoted matter is not clearly indicated in the text. Dates of letters derived from internal evidence or from postmarks are bracketed.

In order to conserve space, the following abbreviations have been used:

L: *The Letters of Hart Crane*, ed. Brom Weber (Berkeley and Los Angeles: University of California Press, 1965).

BL: [Brown Letters] "Hart Crane: The End of Harvest," letters to William Slater Brown and Susan Jenkins Brown, ed. Susan Jenkins Brown, in *The Southern Review*, vol. IV, New Series, No. 4 (October 1968), 947–1014.

CP: *The Complete Poems and Selected Letters and Prose of Hart Crane*, ed. Brom Weber (New York: Liveright Publishing Corp., 1966).

pub.: published.

unpub.: unpublished.

pt.pub.: published in part. (This means that the passage I quote, all or part of which is unpublished, is from a document that has been previously published in an excerpted form.)

SJB: Susan Jenkins Brown.
WSB: William Slater Brown.
CAC: Clarence A. Crane.
GHC: Grace Hart Crane.
HC: Hart Crane.
PBC: Peggy Baird (Cowley).
MC: Malcolm Cowley.
WF: Waldo Frank.
EBH: Elizabeth Belden Hart.
SL: Sam Loveman.
GM: Gorham Munson.
CR: Charlotte Rychtarik.
RR: Richard Rychtarik.
Mrs.S: Mrs. T. W. Simpson.
AT: Allen Tate.
JU: John Unterecker.
WU: Wilbur Underwood.
C von W: Charmion von Wiegand.
WW: William Wright.

CHAPTER I

4. Arthur Crane. Arthur Edward Crane was born Apr. 24, 1846, at Shalersville, Portage County, Ohio; died Mar. 4, 1939, at Cleveland, Ohio. His wife was Ella Melissa, nee Beardsley, born Nov. 7, 1849, at Freedom, Portage County, Ohio; died Dec. 21, 1928, at Cleveland, Ohio. Crane family records that follow are adapted from the manuscripts of Arthur Crane, who had written recollections of the women of his family for the Ohio Federation of Women's Clubs' "records of pioneer women" project. Information on the Hart family is drawn from Philip Horton's *Hart Crane* (New York: Viking Press, Compass Books Edition, 1957; original edition, New York: W. W. Norton & Co., 1937), from the Jethro Robinson papers on deposit in Special Collections of Columbia University, and from conversations with members of the Crane and Hart families.

5. Jason Streator. Jason Streator was also well known as a composer of popular songs, his "When This Old Hat Was New" being a significant element in the Harrison campaign of 1840.

6. Allegheny College. There is some problem in dating the years of C. A. Crane's attendance at Allegheny College. He is listed in the 1894 yearbook as a freshman, a member of the class of 1897. Though records are lacking, it is possible that he may have attended a preparatory division of the college in 1892–1893.

7. If Grace's hesitation . . . Details about his parents' courtship and Hart Crane's early years are reconstructed from interviews with C. A. Crane's sisters—Elizabeth Crane Madden and Alice Crane Williams—and from the account Grace Crane gave to Philip Horton. Mrs. Ida Scott and Mrs. G. H. Raymond, both of Garrettsville, offered recollections of the Crane family. The "pea picking" anecdote comes from Crane's great aunt, Lucy Carnihan.

13. "I have just . . ." HC to GHC, Sept. 28, 1917, pub. L 9.

14. that he was a millionaire. . . . Actually, C. A. Crane was extremely modest in the sums he withdrew from his businesses. His pattern was to return to the companies as much of the profits as possible. Though the companies

had at times a substantial book value, his own personal fortune was small. Hart contributed to the millionaire myth. On first meeting Samuel Loveman, Hart explained his expensive coat by saying, "It's a good coat because my father's a millionaire." Sam was not impressed.

15. "forget C. A. Crane . . ." [postmarked Aug. 21, 1917], unpub.

15. almost to the day . . . The marriage to Frances Kelley took place in Kansas City, Mo., on Aug. 14, 1918.

15. "I did not . . ." Nov. 2, 1926, unpub.

15. "This seems to be . . ." May 19, 1927, unpub.

15. "This turns out . . ." HC to SL [postmarked Nov. 11, 1929], unpub.

16. To his sister. Quotations on this page are drawn from interviews and from the following letters: HC to GHC, July 10, 1919, pub. L 21; HC to GHC, May 28, 1925, pub. L 207; HC to GM, Nov. 13, 1919, pub. L 23; HC to WW, pub. L 377.

17. "Try to see . . ." [postmarked Aug. 5, 1941], unpub.

18. She told Sam. . . . SL interviewed by JU.

CHAPTER 2

19. Warren, Ohio. Details of Crane's life in Warren have been principally supplied by Helen Hart Hurlbert, by Herlin H. Gander, by Mrs. Roscoe Winnagle, and by C. Courtney Denison.

19. "Connais tu le pays . . . ?" from "Porphyro in Akron," CP 144.

20. "had everything . . ." quoted in letter, Mrs. Winnagle to JU.

21. "He was really . . ." interviewed by JU.

21. "My memory . . ." from "Passage," CP 21.

22. . . . his grandmother . . . Elizabeth Belden Hart was born on July 11, 1839, and died Sept. 5, 1928.

23. Christian Science. It is difficult to date the time of Grace's first interest in Christian Science. She may have been reading its literature as early as 1900. On the other hand, she was not an active Christian Scientist until 1908–1909. In the years immediately following her divorce, she increasingly relied on Christian Science practitioners for emotional and spiritual direction.

23. 115th Street. Mr. and Mrs. Arthur Crane's 115th Street prop-

erty was purchased on Apr. 30, 1913, and sold in 1922, after which time C.A.'s parents lived in their apartment house.

24. Both letters quoted on this page are unpub.

25. "I'm too nervous . . ." Alice Crane Williams, interviewed by JU.

26. . . . neighbor's daughter. Crane told this anecdote to Lorna Dietz, who told it to me. In telling it, Crane coupled the story with remarks about his mother's dislike of his playing with girls.

26. . . . first homosexual experience. . . . This is the most likely account of a much-told tale. Crane "confessed" the history of his homosexuality to many people, and their memories are not in agreement as to what he said. My guess is that he did not always tell the same story. According to one recollection, the first contact was with a chauffeur. Grace told a woman for whom she worked late in her life that Hart confessed a "handyman" had seduced him. Horton (79) repeats Hart's one-time bragging account that the other young man had been a "tutor" and that Hart himself was the seducer. Whatever the circumstances of his introduction to homosexual activities, it is

important to keep in mind that not until he was twenty, when he found himself in love with a boy very near his own age, did homosexuality seem a real problem. From that time until his year in Mexico and his affair with Peggy Cowley, he did regard himself as a homosexual. In no way effeminate, he was contemptuous of effeminate men. Perhaps it is significant that his first homosexual love affair followed his parents' divorce and that his first "normal" love affair followed a break with his mother and a reconciliation with his father.

27. January 1914 . . . Horton says that Harold registered in Jan. 1913, after his grandfather's funeral. I think this is an error. His high school records indicate a 1914 registration, and his note to his grandmother that in 1916 he is a junior seems to verify the later date.

28. . . . "Pass" grades . . . His high school record card is mysterious. The office staff at East High School suggested to me that his German and Physics grades are probably off by a column, since Crane dropped out of school before his fourth year had begun. This is a transcript of the record:

|  | FIRST YEAR | SECOND YEAR | THIRD YEAR | FOURTH YEAR |
|---|---|---|---|---|
| Algebra | 85:P | | | |
| English | 90: | 94:71 | w | |
| Geometry | | P:80 | | |
| German | | 77:P | P | 77:w |
| Latin | 75:P | 78:76 | w | |
| Physics | | | 82:w | |
| Physical Tr. | 79:85 | | | |

German was probably a "second year" subject taken in his first year. Perhaps Physics was a "third year" subject taken in his second year.

28. "a Junior . . ." Feb. 10, 1916, pub. L 4.

28. Eleanor Claridge (Mrs. Rodney Sutton) now writes for the Cleveland *Plain Dealer*. Quotations from interview with JU.

29. "his shining . . ." quoted from Horton, 24.

29. "I am going . . ." Apr. 11, 1933, unpub.

30. "It was as if . . ." SL interviewed by JU.

30. "Not a small . . ." WW to GHC, Apr. 11, 1933, unpub.

30. "Do you know . . ." Jan. 9, 1933, unpub.

30. "I am quite sure . . ." WW to GHC, Apr. 11, 1933, unpub.

31. Hazel Brown. Hazel Brown (Mrs. Russell Cate) and Vivian Brown (Mrs. Fred G. New) sup-

plied these recollections of Crane in telephone interviews and in letters to JU.

31. "Hart's 'home room' . . ." WW to GHC, Jan. 9, 1933, unpub.

31. "It must have been . . ." WW to GHC, Apr. 11, 1933, unpub.

32. "I have often . . ." WW to GHC, Jan. 9, 1933, unpub.

32. "For truly . . ." This may have been part of a poem Crane was writing, since he experimented with various punctuations and minor revisions. Crane's books have been in part reassembled at Special Collections of Columbia University, where most of those I refer to are housed.

32. "Simone's death . . ." Though the plot is certainly that of Poe's "Oval Portrait," Poe does not name his character Simone.

33. Kenneth Hurd. Quoted passages that follow are drawn from my interviews and his letters to me, 1961–1968.

33. Socratic *Dialogues.* I have not been able to locate this volume. Horton (31) mentions the underlined passage.

34. Edward J. Noble. Noble, in 1920, changed the name of the company from Mint Products to Life Savers and went on to turn a local candy into a minor national institution. Crane's trademark had been established in the summer of 1913. See Cleveland *Press,* Aug. 7, 1961, for an account of the business transactions.

35. "As long as . . ." Feb. 15, 1915, unpub.

35. "My Dear Girl:—" [Jan. 24, 1915], unpub.

36. "Grace honey . . ." Jan. 30, 1915, unpub.

36. "Your letters . . ." Jan. 30, 1915, unpub.

37. "I've praised . . ." CAC to GHC, Jan. 30, 1915, unpub.

37. "I just about bought . . ." CAC to GHC, Feb. 1, 1915, unpub.

37. "I was *so* . . ." Feb. 6, 1915, unpub.

37. "dreadful letters . . ." Feb. 6, 1915, unpub.

37. "It was two weeks . . ." CAC to GHC, Feb. 7, 1915, unpub.

38. Mrs. Crane never spoke . . . see Horton, 27–28.

38. "Dear: I've just . . ." unpub.

38. "When we are . . ." CAC to GHC, unpub.

38. "It is difficult . . ." interviewed by JU, Jan. 21, 1962 (Oral History files).

39. "Well, we will be glad . . ." authorship uncertain. [Inaccurately dated Jan. 21, 1915 (should be Feb. 21).] The letter, signed "Bess," was written neither by Bess Crane Madden (Hart's aunt) nor by Bess Crane (Hart's stepmother).

39. Hubbard. Horton feels Crane visited Hubbard in 1915. Weber seems to me more likely to be right in dating the visit 1914, the year in which Hubbard had come to Cleveland.

41. "I have a deep . . ." Mar. 23, 1916, unpub.

41. "I am always . . ." unpub.

42. "The Moth that God Made Blind." CP 122. This poem presents a number of problems—not least of which is an inscription on the last page of the manuscript: "(Harold) Hart Crane/ 25 E. 11 St./ N.Y.C./ 1915." For Crane, of course, was not in New York until 1916. The manuscript itself was discovered by Jethro Robinson among Crane's papers. If it is authentic, it represents a poem that was probably written just after Christmas of 1915 and that was perhaps transcribed by Crane after he had reached New York City. The diction resembles that of some of Crane's earliest letters. The poem is itself totally undistinguished.

42. "so lonesome . . ." Jan. 7 [1916, misdated 1915], unpub.

42. "Your letters would . . ." pub. L 3.

42. "It is strange . . ." Feb. 10, 1916, pub. L 4.

43. "We had *English* . . ." HC to EBH, Jan. 26, 1916, pub. L 3.

43. "I have just returned . . ." pt.pub. L 4.

44. "Harold in those days . . ." George Bryan to JU, June 28, 1962, unpub.

45. "Harold was . . ." Mrs. New to JU, July 25, 1961, unpub.

45. tour of the West. Many of his friends recall Crane's descriptions of this trip. My account is based on their recollections and the account Grace Crane gave to Horton.

46. "I am interested . . ." In *The Pagan,* Vol. I, no. 6 (Oct. 1916).

47. Richard Laukhuff . . . I am indebted to Collister Hutchison and Mrs. Richard Laukhuff for much of my information about Mr. Laukhuff and for their careful correction of these pages of my manuscript.

48. "did no physical work . . ." unpub. letter to JU, Aug. 7, 1961.

Other passages from interviews with JU.

49. Though she had . . . My quotations are drawn from the divorce petition and the settlement papers. Copies are included in the Crane papers at Columbia University.

49. "I don't know." quoted in Horton 36. All of Carl Schmitt's letters from Crane were stolen from him in Italy just before the beginning of the Second World War. I have drawn heavily on recollections that Schmitt shared with me in a number of interviews. Quoted passages from the Schmitt letters appear in Horton 36 ff.

CHAPTER 3

52. "a dandy" Jan. 5, 1917, pt.pub. L 5.

53. "write me often . . ." Jan. 5, 1917, unpub.

53. "While I am not home-sick . . ." Jan. 5, 1917, pt.pub. L 5.

53. To his new . . . Material on this and following pages drawn from JU interviews with Kling (1960) and Schmitt (1960, 1961, 1962).

53. "The room I have now . . ." Dec. 31, 1916, pub. L 4. Weber and Horton, misled by Crane's return address, assumed that Schmitt's studio at 308 E. 15 Street was the place of Crane's apartment. Schmitt told me in the summer of 1962 that Crane had all mail sent to the studio because he disliked the room at 139 E. 15 Street so much that he intended immediately to move.

53. "The bath-rooms . . ." Jan. 5, 1917, unpub.

53. "I do most of . . ." pt.pub. L 5.

54. "I have just been out . . ." pub. L 4.

54. "Last night . . ." HC to EBH and GHC, Jan. 2, 1917, unpub. The evening was even more tear-moving for Carl Schmitt, for at the performance, he told me, his overcoat was taken and a "terrible form-fitting one" left in its place.

55. "Well, I haven't . . ." Jan. 2, 1917, unpub.

55. "I took a long ride . . ." Feb. 19, 1917, pub. L 6.

55. "lost identity . . ." Dec. 31, 1916, pub. L 4–5.

56. The diagrams are adapted from those in an unpub. letter from Schmitt to me, July 18, 1962.

56. "Nearly every evening . . ." Jan. 5, 1917, pub. L 5.

57. "Carl is a more . . ." HC to GHC and EBH, Jan. 2, 1917, unpub.

57. "very good to me . . ." Dec. 31, 1916, pub. L 4.

57. "spend the evening . . ." HC to GHC, Jan. 2, 1917, unpub.

58. "A Caution." Poem reprinted by permission of Carl Schmitt, who also recited for me his parody of "Ulalume."

58. "Really," HC to GHC and EBH, Jan. 2, 1917, unpub.

59. "Today has been . . ." unpub.

59. "Things are . . ." unpub.

59. "give an emotional . . ." Mary Colum, *Life and the Dream* (Garden City, New York: Doubleday & Company, 1947), 258. Following quotations are from 257–59, as is the passage on my 62.

59. "a choice volume . . ." HC to GHC and EBH, Jan. 26, 1917, pt.pub. L 5–6.

60. "At this age . . ." Jan. 7, 1917, unpub.

60. "Mrs. Moody gave . . ." unpub.

60. "People here . . ." Feb. 19, 1917, pt.pub. L 6.

61. "Your father sent . . ." unpub.

61. "You must be careful . . ." Feb. 2, 1917, unpub.

61. "Your father's provision . . ." Feb. 4, 1917, unpub.

61. "These kept her in . . ." Jan. 30, 1917, unpub.

61. "fearful of an adhesion," Feb. 19, 1917, unpub.

61. "one of the few . . ." HC to EBH, Jan. 7, 1917, unpub.

62. "I shall think of you." [Jan. 30, 1916], unpub.

62. " 'For *old* love's sake . . ." [Jan. 30, 1916], unpub.

62. "You are in Chicago . . ." HC to GHC and EBH, Jan. 2, 1917, unpub.

62. "You will never know . . ." Jan. 3, 1917, unpub.

63. "Your father is going . . ." Jan. 19, 1917, unpub.

63. "Harold, perhaps . . ." GHC to HC, Jan. 19, 1917, unpub.

63. "I have never done . . ." GHC to HC, Jan. 30, 1917, unpub.

64. "MOTHER AND I . . ." Telegram dated Jan. 22, 1917, unpub.

64. "avowed intent" CAC to HC, Jan. 20, 1917, unpub.

65. "terrible weather . . ." GHC to HC, Feb. 4, 1917, unpub.

66. "I am supposing" Feb. 19, 1917, pt.pub. L 6–7.

67. "Bun-shop food . . ." Jan. 5, 1917, pt.pub. L 5.

67. "Carl and I dine" Jan. 2, 1917, unpub.

67. "Last night I took . . ." Feb. 19, 1917, pt.pub. L 6–7.

67. "Your good letter . . ." Feb. 22, 1917, pub. L 7.
67. "Don't delay" unpub.
67. "I must be . . ." Feb. 19, 1917, unpub.
68. "Harold's room . . ." George Bryan to JU, June 28, 1962, unpub.
68. "a fair amount . . ." Jan. 5, 1917, pt.pub. L 5.
68. "body and mind" GHC to HC, Jan. 5, 1917, unpub.
68. "You can't imagine . . ." Schmitt interviewed by JU, July, 1962.
68. "I am glad . . ." Jan. 29, 1917, unpub.
69. "I was delighted . . ." [Mar. 26, 1917], unpub.
69. "You know Mother . . ." Mar. 23, 1917, unpub.
69. "I was so glad . . ." GHC to HC [Mar. 26, 1917], unpub.
69. "People look too fat . . ." GHC to HC, Mar. 29, 1917, unpub.
70. "Keep the news . . ." Feb. 26, 1917, unpub.
70. "I would prefer," Feb. 19, 1917, unpub.
70. "Please refrain . . ." [Mar. 26, 1917], unpub.
70. "Your telegram . . ." Mar. 23, 1917, unpub.
71. "I have told . . ." GHC to HC [Mar. 26, 1917], unpub.
71. "a boy of 17 . . ." CAC to HC, Mar. 29, 1917, unpub.
71. "My dear Mother," unpub.
72. "Damn good stuff." Nov. 16, 1916, unpub.
72. " 'Others' . . ." Apr. 19, 1917, unpub.
73. "the world such poems" GHC to HC, Mar. 29, 1917, unpub.
73. "I have grown . . ." Feb. 26, 1917, unpub.
74. "If your father . . ." Mar. 29, 1917, unpub.
74. In later years . . . Lorna Dietz, interviewed by JU, 1960. "Fear" and "Annunciation," from the Apr.-May 1917 issue of *The Pagan*, I, 12; II, 1, were signed Harold H. Crane. By November of that year, he had taken to signing his poetry Hart Crane.
75. "Now I want . . ." Apr. 16, 1917, unpub.
75. "How is business?" May 5, 1917, unpub.
76. "Mother and I . . ." May 18, 1917, unpub.
76. "continued communications . . ." CAC to HC, May 16, 1917, unpub.
77. "uncertainties" unpub.
78. "He is looking fine . . ." draft of undated letter, probably written between July 15, 1917, and July 21,

1917. It is interesting that after Grace had spoken of Harold's nervousness she had first written, then heavily scored out, "Otherwise he would not be a poet," recollecting no doubt that it was she rather than CAC who wanted Harold to be a writer.
78. "I have had" CAC to GHC, July 10, 1917, unpub.
78. "I finally had . . ." [probably July 5, 1917, misdated June 5, 1917], unpub.
78. "Your letter of the 7th . . ." June 10, 1917, unpub.
79. "generous" [July 5, 1917, misdated June 5, 1917], unpub.
79. "However, I am glad . . ." GHC to CAC [from an undated draft of a letter composed between June 15, 1917, and June 21, 1917], unpub.
79. "If out of all this . . ." July 10, 1917, unpub.
79. "On Saturday . . ." GHC to CAC [from undated draft of letter composed between June 15, 1917, and June 21, 1917], unpub.
80. "longing for reconciliation" Horton 151.
80. "a perfect understanding" GHC to CAC [from an undated draft of letter composed between June 15, 1917, and June 21, 1917], unpub.
81. "August 1st . . ." CAC to HC, unpub. Copies of many of C.A.C.'s letters have survived thanks to his habit of making carbons of all correspondence. Harold's letters to his father had been sent to C.A.'s office and were often filed in with other correspondence. Harold had himself saved all letters from his father, mother, and grandmother. Most of these have also survived.
82. "I have been . . ." Aug. 8, 1917, pub. L 7–8.
82. "Grace:" [postmarked Aug. 21, 1917], unpub.
83. "When she returned." Horton 52.
83. "forgiveness, tenderness . . ." pt.pub. L 8.
84. "September 23, [191]7." typed draft letter (possibly typed by HC for GHC), unpub.
86. "Forget all the past . . ." Sept. 28, 1917, pt.pub. L 9.
86. "If I have much time . . ." Sept. 28, 1917, unpub.
86. "Its name . . ." Aug. 8, 1917, pt.pub. L 7–8.
87. "I was sorry." Sept. 22, 1917, unpub.
87. "complimented my poetry . . ." HC to GHC, Sept. 28, 1917, pub. L 9.

87. "with the weariness . . ." Kreymborg, *Troubadour*, 251.
87. "through the adverse . . ." HC to GHC, Sept. 28, 1917, pub. L 9.
88. "the equal of any" Horton 56, quoting HC to Schmitt.
88. "I go up there . . ." Kling interviewed by JU, 1960.
89. "It took . . ." *My Thirty Years' War* (New York: Covici, Friede, 1930), 152–153.
89. "Jane's beautiful . . ." Margaret Anderson to JU, Sept. 14, 1961, unpub.
89. "contained a vague . . ." 153.
89. "sometimes leave us . . ." Margaret Anderson to JU, Sept. 14, 1961, unpub.
89. "Dear Hart Crane . . ." Though the unpub. letter is undated, a letter of Sept. 28, 1917, from GHC congratulates HC on his acceptance by the *Little Review* and probably refers to this letter. The underlined "Hart" is an acknowledgment of Crane's recent decision no longer to appear in print as "Harold."
89. "Easter sonnet." The passages from Crane and Pound are quoted in Horton (57–58), and probably based on a now-lost letter from Crane to Schmitt. The original letter from Pound now belongs to Norman Holmes Pearson, who discovered it pasted into Crane's copy of Pound's *Lustra*. It is in rather bad condition, in part illegible, but a good deal of it can be made out. Though similar to, it is phrased differently from Crane's paraphrase. In the copy of *Lustra*, Crane had marked several lines from "Near Perigord" that significantly anticipate his own phrasing of passages in "Voyages."
90. "Success seems . . ." Sept. 28, 1917, pub. L 9.
90. "The plot . . ." Oct. 3, 1917, pub. L 10.
90. "a letter from Walter . . ." Oct. 3, 1917, unpub.
90. "my novel about . . ." Oct. 6, 1917, unpub.
91. "Mrs. Walton . . ." HC to GHC, Oct. 8, 1917, unpub.
91. "O if you knew . . ." Oct. 1, 1917, pub. L 9.

CHAPTER 4
92. "The smallness . . ." [Oct. 1, 1917], pub. L 9.
93. "You mustn't . . ." interviewed by JU.
93. "I have never felt . . ." [Oct. 1, 1917], pt.pub. L 9.

93. "I am alone . . ." [Oct. 3, 1917], L 10.
94. "I do not know . . ." Oct. 3, 1917, unpub.
94. "Your letter of . . ." Oct. 10, 1917, unpub.
95. "I understand," Horton 53–54.
95. "To his mind . . ." Colum, *Life and the Dream*, 257.
96. "However . . ." Horton 53–54.
96. "Dear boy," Oct. 11, 1917, unpub.
96. "Don't write, Mother . . ." Oct. 26, 1917, unpub.
97. "Your letter . . ." Nov. 2, 1917, unpub.
98. "spent some days . . ." Joseph H. Dexter to JU, Dec. 12, 1961, unpub.
98. "no recognizable symptoms," Horton 54–55.
100. "I wrote you . . ." unpub.
102. "My Dear Grace . . ." Monday [Feb. 25, 1918], unpub.
106. "He had a most . . ." Claire Spencer Evans to JU, July 11, 1962, unpub.
107. "all the twentieth century . . ." [postmarked Apr. 12, 1918], unpub.
107. "Such a burst . . ." Horton 58.
107. "white-hot imagination," Alice Chamberlain, "Millionaire's Son Is Clerk In An Akron Drug Store," Akron *Sunday Times*, Dec. 21, 1919.
108. "a picture . . ." *The Pagan*, II, 12; III, 1 (Apr.-May 1918), 55–56.
108. "Delirious with excitement," Charles A. Fenton, *The Apprenticeship of Ernest Hemingway: The Early Years* (New York: Compass Books, 1958), 50.
108. "witnessed the great . . ." HC to GHC, Oct. 5, 1917, unpub.
109. "barely escaped . . ." HC to GHC, Oct. 9, 1917, unpub.
109. "the herald . . ." "The Case Against Nietzsche," CP 197.
110. "I AM SENDING . . ." Mar. 30, 1918, unpub.
110. "which has a mission . . ." Apr. 8, 1918, unpub.
110. "I got a letter . . ." Apr. 23, 1918, unpub.
110. "Once you may . . ." GHC to HC, Tuesday [late Apr. or early May 1918], unpub.
110. "on wet nursing . . ." HC to Carl Schmitt, Horton 58.
110. "at a 'dollar down' . . ." HC to George Bryan, Apr. 23, 1918, unpub.
111. "command" GHC to HC, [May 1918?], unpub.

112. "getting very busy . . ." May 16, 1918, unpub.
113. "I should certainly . . ." May 19, [1918], unpub.
113. "I think of you very often . . ." July 15, 1918, unpub.
113. "I . . . shall spend . . ." July 17, 1918, unpub.
114. "Mood." *The Pagan*, III, 3 (July 1918), 51.
115. "Los Angeles critic" CP 199–200.
116. "The most momentous . . ." Aug. [9], 1918, unpub.
116. "You know, Mother," Decoration Day [May 30] 1919, pub. L 18.
116. "I . . . was not . . ." Aug. 12, 1918, pub. L 11.
117. "I am included . . ." Horton 61.
118. "While they are few . . ." HC to Charles C. Bubb, Nov. 13, 1918, unpub. The "Six Lyrics" have recently been pub. by the Ibex Press as *Seven Lyrics*, in an edition prepared by Kenneth A. Lohf (1966). ("Echoes" had been included in the group sent to Bubb, but it had already appeared in the Oct.-Nov., 1917 *Pagan*. None of the seven is elsewhere published.) As Lohf notes, "Naiad of Memory" anticipates "Legende," and "Meditation" anticipates both "A Persuasion" and "For the Marriage of Faustus and Helen" in some of its lines.
118. "I really feel . . ." Dec. 14, 1918, unpub.
118. "I spent . . ." Jan. 4 [1919], unpub.
118. "The work has . . ." [postmarked Jan. 8, 1919], unpub.
119. "dramatic quality" Crane's review of *The Ghetto and Other Poems* was pub. in the Jan. 1919 issue of *The Pagan*, 55–56. My transcription differs in minor details from that in CP 201–2.
120. "You know . . ." HC to George Bryan, Dec. 14, 1918, unpub.
120. "One night . . ." unpub.
121. "The sky is cleared . . ." Feb. 9, 1919, unpub.
121. "Your letter was . . ." Feb. 15, 1919, unpub.
121. "I am primarily . . ." Feb. 9, 1919, unpub.

CHAPTER 5

123. "Just arrived," unpub.
123. "The city . . ." HC to GHC [Feb. 22, 1919, misdated Feb. 24], pt.pub. L 12.
124. "It must be . . ." Mar. 7, 1919, pub. L 14.
124. "I wrote . . ." pub. L 14.

124. "I think you are . . ." Apr. 2, 1919, pub. L 15.
125. "No:—at present . . ." May 2, 1919, pub. L 16.
125. "How did you like . . ." HC to GHC [Feb. 27, 1919, misdated Feb. 26, 1919], unpub.
125. "Your letter . . ." Mar. 29, 1919, unpub.
126. "Were I in Cleveland . . ." Easter, 1919 [Apr. 20, 1919], unpub.
126. "I must have walked . . ." HC to GHC, Feb. 23 [1919, misdated 1918], unpub.
126. "The landlady . . ." HC to GHC, Mar. 7, 1919, pub. L 13.
127. "practically three rooms . . ." HC to George Bryan, Mar. 17, 1919, unpub.
127. "a lieutenant . . ." HC to GHC, Mar. 7, 1919, pub. L 13.
127. "dozens of movies" interviewed by JU, Oct. 1962.
128. "someone completely" Mar. 21, 1919, unpub.
128. "I see you are displeased . . ." Decoration Day [May 30], 1919, L 17.
128. "to make it a . . ." HC to GHC, Mar. 7, 1919, pt.pub. L 13.
129. "damned lucky" Mar. 17, 1919, unpub.
129. "I have had to buy . . ." HC to GHC, unpub.
129. "The following . . ." enclosed in Mar. 21, 1919, unpub.
129. "I have cashed . . ." L 17–19.
130. "to have a kind . . ." HC to George Bryan, Mar. 2, 1919, unpub.
130. "You have no conception . . ." Mar. 11, 1919, L 14.
130. "Don't give up . . ." Mar. 19, 1919, unpub.
131. "One good thing . . ." Apr. 2, 1919, pt.pub. L 15.
131. "all the great . . ." HC to GHC, Easter [Apr. 20], 1919, unpub.
131. "$4000 . . ." HC to GHC, May 3, 1919, unpub.
131. "looking for . . ." HC to GHC, Decoration Day [May 30], 1919, pub. L 18.
132. "You have no . . ." May 2, 1919, pub. L 16.
132. "Your letter was . . ." Decoration Day [May 30], 1919, pub. L 17–19.
133. "I dined with . . ." Mar. 21, 1919, unpub.
133. "drank beer . . ." HC to GHC, Apr. 12, 1919, unpub.
133. "The play was . . ." HC to GHC [Feb. 27, misdated Feb. 26], 1919, unpub.

133. "up in my room . . ." Apr. 2, 1919, pt.pub. L 15.
133. "Claire and Hal . . ." Apr. 12, 1919, unpub.
134. "Hal rented him . . ." July 11, 1962, unpub.
134. "A Visit to a Poet," *Hints to Pilgrims* (New Haven: Yale University Press, 1921), 92–102. Charles Stephen Brooks (1878–1934) was born in Cleveland and educated at Allegheny and Yale (class of 1900). He wrote several volumes of polite essays as well as a group of plays.
135. "She wore a red . . ." *My Thirty Years' War*, 178, 211.
135. "the Baroness took . . ." letter to JU, autumn 1962, unpub.
135. "He fancied . . ." interviewed by JU, 1961.
136. "are often little . . ." CP 203–4.
136. "The magazine has grown," [Feb. 22, 1919, misdated Feb. 24, 1919], pt.pub. L 12.
136. "Gorham was . . ." interviewed by JU, Sept. 11, 1962 (Oral History files).
137. "I find all . . ." Feb. 25, 1919, unpub.
137. "Stan and Anna . . ." HC to GHC, Easter [Apr. 20], 1919, unpub.
137. "rather diverse" HC to WW, May 14, 1919, pub. L 17.
137. "The last few weeks . . ." Apr. 10, 1919, unpub.
137. "I never dreamed . . ." HC to GHC, Mar. 7, 1919, pt.pub. L 13.
137. "I was Mrs. . . ." HC to GHC, Mar. 21, 1919, unpub.
137. "I being the clothes-model" HC to GHC, May 3, 1919, unpub.
137. "Supped with . . ." HC to GHC, Feb. 23 [1919], unpub.
137. "this afternoon . . ." HC to GHC, Mar. 21, 1919, unpub.
137. "I met Robert Frost's . . ." HC to WW, May 14, 1919, pub. L 17.
137. "She is now . . ." HC to GHC, Mar. 26, 1919, pub. L 14–15.
138. "a terrific . . ." HC to GHC, Mar. 29, 1919, unpub.
138. "crowded metropolis" HC to WW, June 17, 1919, pub. L 19.
138. "I don't plan . . ." May 2, 1919, pt.pub. L 16–17.
138. "a short course . . ." HC to WW, June 17, 1919, pub. L 19.
139. "endless munificence" HC to GHC, July 10, 1919, pt.pub. L 20–21.
140. "We had lots . . ." Claire Spencer to JU, July 11, 1962, and autumn 1962, unpub.

141. "things look so dark" quoted in HC to GHC, July 10, 1919, pt.pub. L 20–21.
142. "very satisfactory," HC to GHC, July 30, 1919, pt.pub. L 21–22. Hart's manuscript contains a marvelous Freudian slip: rather than "an unfriendly or [a] friendly" attitude toward his father, he had written "an unfriendly or unfriendly one."
143. "vast irritations" quoted in Margaret Anderson to HC, Aug. 24, 1919, unpub.
143. "I agree . . ." pub. L 19–20.
144. "Mr. Rheinthal . . ." HC to GHC, Oct. 31, 1919, unpub.
144. "Beyond an expression . . ." CP 205–6.
144. "Some friend . . ." Sherwood Anderson to Hart Crane [Nov. 1, 1919, misdated Oct. 1. Crane refers to the letter as just arrived in a Nov. 5 letter to C von W], unpub.
144. "Knowing your . . ." HC to GM [postmarked Aug. 22, 1919], pub. L 22.
145. "a kind of dumb-animal . . ." Nov. 22, 1919, pt.pub. L 24–25.
145. "You evidently were not . . ." Nov. 13, 1919, pub. L 23.
145. "Josephson's opinions . . ." Nov. 22, 1919, pub. L 24.
146. "Any of the works . . ." HC to C von W, May 6, 1922, pub. L 85–86.
146. "pretentiously," Sept. 22, 1919, unpub.
146. "enthusiastic . . ." HC to GHC, Sept. 22, 1919, unpub.
147. "I leave for Cleveland . . ." pub. L 22.
147. "Thank you . . ." Oct. 31, 1919, unpub.
148. "I am beginning . . ." Nov. 5, 1919, pub. L 22.

CHAPTER 6
149. "The Pagan . . ." Nov. 13, 1919, pub. L 23.
150. *Akron Must Go Forward!* Akron *Beacon Journal*, Wed. Dec. 17, 1919, 10.
151. "about 14 hours . . ." Nov 22 [1919], L 24.
151. "our Portage Drug Store . . ." Akron *Beacon Journal*, Dec. 23, 1919.
152. "I wrote a short . . ." Nov. 22 [1919], pub. L 25.
152. "contact with . . ." HC to GM, Nov. 13, 1919, pub. L 23.
152. "Grandma and her . . ." HC to GM, Nov. 22 [1919], pub. L 25.
152. "I enjoyed . . ." Friday [Nov. 28, 1919], pub. L 25.

152. "Let me speak . . ." Dec. 3, 1919, unpub.
152. "The poem . . ." Dec. 14, 1919, unpub.
153. "New theories . . ." Nov. 22, [1919], pub. L 25.
153. "It should be . . ." Dec. 17, 1919, *Letters of Sherwood Anderson*, ed. by Howard Mumford Jones and Walter B. Rideout (Boston: Little, Brown & Co., 1953), 52.
154. "You might . . ." Dec. 14, 1919, unpub.
154. "Waldo Frank's . . ." Dec. 13, 1919, pub. L 27.
155. "Have you read . . ." Friday [Nov. 28, 1919], pub. L 25.
155. "If you feel . . ." Dec. 14, 1919, unpub.
156. "an agreeable joke . . ." Dec. 27, 1919, pub. L 28.
157. "I expect I will have . . ." Nov. 13, 1919, pub. L 23–24.
157. "About your father," Dec. 3, 1919, unpub.
158. "I hope . . ." Sherwood Anderson to HC, Wednesday [Dec. 17, 1919], pub. Anderson *Letters*, 52.
158. "deplorable." Akron *Sunday Times*, Dec. 21, 1919.
158. "charming with . . ." HC to GM, Dec. 13, 1919, pub. L 26–27.
159. "in Akron exile . . ." HC to GM, Dec. 27, 1919, pub. L 27–29.
160. "I was suddenly . . ." HC to GM, Jan. 9, 1920, pub. L 30.
160. "armed with . . ." Apr. 14, 1920, pub. L 38.
161. "filthy old man." Jan. 9, 1920, pub. L 30.
161. "a lovely . . ." interview with Bert Ginther, 1961.
161. "to hold . . ." Jan. 9, 1920, pub. L 30.
161. "'arrangements,'" "A Note on Minns," CP 207.
162. "I have lately . . ." Dec. 13, 1919, pub. L 26.
162. "I have my . . ." Dec. 14, 1919, unpub.
163. "It is odd . . ." [Dec. 17, 1919], pub. Anderson *Letters*, 52–53.
163. "So many things . . ." pub. L 27–28.
164. "Akron has," Jan. 9, 1920, pub. L 29.
164. "My love affair . . ." undated, pub. L 31. The letter—dated Jan. 15, 1920 by Weber—is more likely a mid-Feb. product, since the "holidays" reference would be meaningless four days after his return from Akron.
165. "My Akron friend . . ." pub. L 35, where "four weeks" is in-

accurately transcribed as "five weeks."
165. "I have gone . . ." Apr. 26, 1920, pub. L 39.

CHAPTER 7

166. "phallic theme," HC to Matthew Josephson, Mar. 15, 1920, pub. L 37, and HC to GM, Apr. 1, 1920, unpub.
166. "the only foundation . . ." May 25, 1920, pub. L 39.
166. "Last night . . ." Mar. 6, 1920, pub. L 34.
166. "Boxing matches . . ." W. A. Widney, interviewed by JU, July 5, 1963.
166. "There is something . . ." Mar. 6, 1920, pub. L 34.
167. "The modern artist . . ." undated [mid-Feb. 1920, misdated Jan. 15, 1920, in L 31, where it is pub.].
167. "I am in truth . . ." [Mar. 2, 1920], unpub.
168. "It is interesting . . ." Apr. 14, 1920, pub. L 37.
168. "The poem fails . . ." HC to GM, Apr. 26, 1920, pub. L 38–39.
168. "I hope . . ." Apr. 24, 1920, unpub.
169. "a set of sketches . . ." HC to GM, June 8, 1920, pub. L 40.
169. "I don't much care . . ." Aug. 18, 1920, pub. L 41.
169. "make something . . ." HC to GM, Apr. 1 [1920], unpub.
169. "The 'Garden Abstract' . . ." Apr. 26, 1920, pub. L 39.
169. "the theme was . . ." HC to GM, June 8, 1920, pub. L 40.
169. "send on . . ." undated [summer, 1920?], unpub.
169. "'Garden Abstract' . . ." undated [Aug. 1920?], unpub.
170. "packing cases . . ." Quotations in this and the following two sentences from HC to GM, Jan. 28, 1920, pub. L 32, and Mar. 6, 1920, pub. L 35.
170. Warshawsky . . . A. G. Warshawsky was born Sharon, Pa., 1883; his brother Xander Warshawsky was born Cleveland, Ohio, 1887.
170. "Of course . . ." Mar. 6, 1920, pub. L 35.
170. "Yes,—whatever . . ." pt.pub. L 33.
171. "impossibly tedious . . ." HC to GM, Jan. 28, 1920, pub. L 32.
171. "long and hypocritical . . ." HC to GM, Mar. 6, 1920, pub. L 35.
171. "seems to be . . ." unpub.
172. "an incipient rupture . . ." HC to GM, Apr. 26, 1920, pub. L 39.

172. "I am beginning . . ." HC to GM, pub. L 32.
172. "Well,—my mother . . ." HC to GM, Mar. 6, 1920, pub. L 33-34.
173. "I read the *Times* . . ." Mar. 15, 1920, pub. L 36.
173. "I cannot write much . . ." Feb. 5, 1920, pub. L 33.
173. "Have been reading . . ." HC to GM, May 25, 1920, pub. L 39-40.
173. "Did I tell you . . ." HC to GM, Aug. 18, 1920, pub. L 41-42.
173. "I like Marianne Moore . . ." HC to GM, Apr. 14, 1920, pub. L 37.
174. "In my limited . . ." Mar. 15, 1920, pub. L 35-36.
174. "beset by two . . ." Apr. 14, 1920, pub. L 38.
175. "You are an old . . ." Feb. 5, 1920, pt.pub. L 32-33.

CHAPTER 8
176. "Monday . . ." unpub.
177. "As the plans . . ." pt.pub. L 40.
178. "the territory . . ." HC to GM, July 30, 1920, pub. L. 40.
178. "I must be a pig . . ." undated [Sept. 1920], unpub.
178. "much better than . . ." HC to GM, July 30, 1920, pub. L 40-41.
178. "a lot of doubts" Aug. 18, 1920, pt.pub. L 41-42.
178. "in an unexceptional . . ." HC to GM, Sept. 13, 1920, pub. L 42.
179. "I am not . . ." Sept. 24, 1920, pt.pub. L 43.
179. "ghastly time." Nov. 9, 1920, pub. L 45, where "ghastly" is mis-transcribed "ghostly."
179. "I dread . . ." Sept. 13, 1920, pub. L 42.
179. "I've been running . . ." Sept. 24, 1920, pub. L 42-43.
179. "postponed July," HC to WW, Sept. 28, 1920, unpub.
179. "I'm proving . . ." HC to GM, Oct. 13, 1920, pt.pub. L 43.
179. "I find agreement . . ." HC to GM, Oct. 20, 1920, pub. L 45.
180. "a terrible vacuity . . ." HC to GM, Sept. 13, 1920, pub. L 42.
180. "Yes, 'Jurgen' . . ." Nov. 9, 1920, pub. L 45.
181. "I am really . . ." Sept. 24, 1920, pub. L 43. The quotation from Rimbaud is from the "Infernal Bridegroom" section of *Season in Hell*, which Crane had just read in the July 1920 *Dial*.
181. "My nights . . ." Oct. 20, 1920, pub. L 44.
181. "I love to walk . . ." interviewed by JU, Aug. 4, 1962 (Oral History files).

182. "But one thing . . ." Emil Opffer interviewed by JU, 1962.
182. "all the official . . ." HC to GM, Sept. 24, 1920, pub. L 43.
182. "The way it was done . . ." Oct. 20, 1920, pub. L 44-45.
183. "NEWS!" HC to WU [Dec. 22, 1920], pt.pub. L 49-50.

CHAPTER 9
185. "He was a wonderful . . ." interviewed 1962.
185. "See that Harold . . ." Louise Howard to JU, Feb. 4, 1962, unpub.
186. "Came Sunday . . ." Bert Ginther to JU, July 15, 1963, unpub.
186. "And I must say," interviewed by JU, Aug. 4, 1962 (Oral History files).
187. "Here is my . . ." Jan. 28, 1921, pub. L 53.
187. "subconscious rioting . . ." pub. L 53-54.
187. "A talk with my father . . ." Jan. 14, 1921, pub. L 50-51.
188. "I'm now keeper . . ." HC to GM, Feb. 11, 1921, pt.pub. L 53-54.
188. . . . in the leisure . . . information from Harley McHugh.
188. "You see," Feb. 24, 1921, pub. L 54.
189. "I don't want . . ." Jan. 31, 1921, unpub.
189. "ran gait" HC to GM, Nov. 23, 1920, pub. L 46-48.
189. "poem on adolescence . . ." HC to GM, Mar. 12, 1921, unpub.
190. "They strike me . . ." HC to GM, Oct. 13, 1920, pub. L 44.
190. "a book for poets . . ." HC to WU, Jan. 31, 1921, unpub.
190. "It seems to me . . ." Apr. 2 [1921], pub. Anderson *Letters*, 73.
190. "The Word . . ." HC to GM, Friday [probably July 1921], pub. L 58.
191. "The Bridge of Estador," For a considerably different reading and a detailed account of Crane's use of the lines of the poem elsewhere, see Brom Weber, *Hart Crane* (New York: Bodley Press, 1948), 102-6.
192. "a poet who . . ." HC to C von W, Aug. 13, 1921, pt.pub. L 64.
192. "He *does* . . ." Nov. 9, 1920, pub. L 46.
192. "What marvelous . . ." Nov. 23, 1920, pub. L 47.
192. "He is all-absorbing . . ." Jan. 28, 1921, pub. L 52-53.
192. "Had I known . . ." Mar. 4 [1921], pub. Anderson *Letters*, 70-71.
192. "It fascinated me . . ." Nov. 23, 1920, pub. L 47.

193. "When a man . . ." Saturday [Nov. 20, 1920], pub. Anderson, *Letters*, 63.
193. "When you get a chance . . ." Nov. 9, 1920, pub. L 46.
193. "I hear . . ." HC to Matthew Josephson, Jan. 14, 1921, pub. L 52.
193. "I read him . . ." Jan. 28, 1921, pub. L 52.
194. "the wet-dream . . ." HC to GM, Feb. 11, 1921, pub. L 53.
195. "I have lately . . ." pt.pub. L 54–55.
195. Sommer. Biographical information concerning Sommer is drawn from obituaries in Cleveland papers, from conversations with his sons, from correspondence with William Zorach, and from the William Sommer Memorial Exhibition catalogue (Cleveland Museum of Art, 1950). The Zorach letter beginning "Bill was always" is from this catalogue. See also "Apples and Dust" by Adelaide Simon, *The Free Lance*, II, 2 (Last Half 1954), 3–6.

CHAPTER 10

199. "April 20th" [1921], pt.pub. L 55.
200. "I am also glad . . ." May 3, 1921, pt.pub. L 55.
200. "Two years thrown . . ." HC to GM, May 16, 1921, pub. L 57.
200. "facing . . ." May 3, 1921, pt.pub. L 55–56.
200. "There is absolutely . . ." May 16, 1921, pub. L 57.
200. "No job in sight . . ." June 12, 1921, pub. L 59.
200. "walked untold . . ." HC to GM, Oct. 6, 1921, pub. L 66.
201. "I feel terribly . . ." pt.pub. L 68–69.
201. "There is nothing . . ." HC to GM, Nov. 21 [1921], pub. L 71.
201. "a diploma . . ." HC to GM, Oct. 1, 1921, pub. L 66.
201. "The great laughter . . ." Kay Kenney Gilmore to JU [postmarked Feb. 4, 1962], unpub. Recollections about Kay Kenney provided in interviews with JU by RR, SL, and Collister Hutchison.
202. "I remember . . ." William Sommer, Jr., to JU, June 10, 1964, unpub. Other information from JU interviews with Ray Sommer and William Sommer, Jr.
202. "mighty talking" Robert Bordner to JU, Sept. 22, 1960, unpub.
204. "Art is no longer . . ." quotations from Memorial catalogue, plates XXXIII, XLII, and V.
204. "under the sidewalk," Kay

Kenney Gilmore to JU [postmarked Feb. 4, 1962], unpub.
204. "We do all kinds . . ." June 12, 1921, pub. L 59.
205. "Well—it has . . ." Saturday midnight [June 25, 1921; postmarked June 27, 1921], pt.pub. L 60.
205. "new wonders," phrases from Crane's 1921 correspondence with Munson.
205. "burgeoning . . ." HC to GM, Dec. 25, 1921, pt.pub. L 74–76.
205. "I have got . . ." HC to GM, May 3, 1921, pt.pub. L 55–56.
206. "I do not . . ." May 21, 1921, pt.pub. L 57–58.
206. "Find out, if you can . . ." June 24, 1921, unpub.
206. "What you say . . ." Saturday midnight [June 25, 1921, postmarked June 27, 1921], pt.pub. L 59–60.
207. "Your letter . . ." unpub.
207. "really a master," pt.pub. L 64.
207. "DeZayas has . . ." Sept. 19, 1921, pt.pub. L 64–65.
208. "just eight months . . ." HC to C von W, Aug. 13, 1921, pt.pub. L 64.
208. "I am to meet . . ." pub. L 66.
208. "We'd sit there . . ." Loveman interviewed by JU, Aug. 4, 1962 (Oral History files).
209. "Tonight I attend . . ." Nov. 3, 1921, pub. L 70.
209. "Lescaze has proved . . ." HC to GM, Oct. 6, 1921, pub. L 66.
209. "It amuses me . . ." May 16, 1921, pub. L 56–57.
210. "I have recently . . ." Nov. 3, 1921, pt.pub. L 69–70.
210. "Perhaps it seems . . ." pub. L 58.
210. "work of distinct . . ." now pub, in CP, 208–13.
211. "reading it . . ." July 22, 1921, pub. L 63.
211. "which, in the original . . ." HC to GM, June 16, 1921, pub. L 60.
211. "suitable" HC to GM, July 8 [1921], pub. L 61.
211. "As a matter of fact," HC to GM, July 22, 1921, pub. L 63.
211. "Sommer said you . . ." June 12, 1921, pub. L 58–59.
212. "They all are . . ." HC to GM, Apr. 11, 1921, unpub.
212. "A friend asked me . . ." Mar. 4 [1921], pub. Anderson, *Letters*, 70. The friend was Paul Rosenfeld.
212. "Citizen of the world!" HC to GM, June 16, 1921, pt.pub. L 59–60.

212. "What a breath . . ." July 14, 1921, pt.pub. L 61–62.
212. "Living *is* at last . . ." July 22, 1921, pt.pub. L 62–63.
213. "Everything must be . . ." HC to GM, Aug. 21, 1921, unpub.
213. "Yes,—we are . . ." HC to GM, Sept. 19, 1921, pt.pub. L 64–65.
213. "Yes," Nov. 1, 1921, pub. L 68–69.
213. "I envy you." HC to GM, Mar. 12, 1921, unpub.

CHAPTER 11

214. "at the mercy . . ." HC to GM, June 12, 1921, pt.pub. L 58.
214. "Life here . . ." June 24, 1921, unpub.
214. "the only place . . ." HC to GM, July 14, 1921, pt.pub. L 61–62.
215. "The 'march of events' . . ." July 22, 1921, pub. L. 62–63.
215. "to regain . . ." HC to GM, June 12, 1921, pub. L 59.
215. "I learn a . . ." Aug. 9, 1921, pub. L 63.
215. "My news is . . ." HC to GM, Aug. 21, 1921, unpub.
216. "My terrible . . ." HC to GM, Oct. 1, 1921, pt.pub. L 65–66.
216. "the arrested climaxes . . ." HC to GM, Nov. 3, 1921, pub. L 69.
216. "Comedy, I may say . . ." HC to GM, Oct. 1, 1921, pub. L 65.
216. "Chaplin may be . . ." Nov. 3, 1921, pub. L 69.
216. . . . letter to Munson. Oct. 6, 1921, pub. L 66.
217. "Oh, yes . . ." interviewed by JU, Aug. 4, 1962 (Oral History files).
217. "I have made that . . ." Oct. 6, 1921, pub. L 66. The Eliot reference is, of course, to "Preludes."
217. "As you did . . ." Oct. 17, 1921, pub. L 67–68.
218. "When I get . . ." Sunday [Oct. 2, 1921], unpub.
218. "animal and earthly life" from article on Sherwood Anderson, CP 209.
218. "more perfectly done" HC to GM, Nov. 3, 1921, pub. L 69.
218. "not nearly so good . . ." HC to GM, Oct. 1, 1921, pt.pub. L 65–66.
218. "The Dada dramas . . ." Nov. 3, 1921, pub. L 70.
218. "verbal richness" HC to GM, Nov. 26, 1921, pub. L 71–72.
220. "I am only interested . . . Oct. 17, 1921, pub. L 67–68.
221. "Two weeks . . ." HC to GM, Dec. 10 [1921], pub. L 72–74.
222. "weary and tormented" HC to GM, Dec. 25, 1921, pub. L 74.

CHAPTER 12

225. "One year of this . . ." Jan. 2, 1922, unpub.
225. "When out of work." Jan. 10 [1922], pub. Anderson, *Letters*, 76.
225. "I grow more pleased . . ." HC to WW, Jan. 25, 1922, unpub.
225. "Never guessed . . ." HC to GM, Jan. 23, 1922, pub. L 77–78.
226. "all ready . . ." Jan. 10 [1922], pub. Anderson, *Letters*, 77.
226. "Ernest Bloch . . ." HC to GM, Mar. 12, 1922, pub. L 82, where it is misdated Mar. 2.
227. "Everyone is suddenly . . ." HC to GM, Mar. 24 [1922], pub. L 82.
227. "There must have been . . ." May 16, 1922, pub. L 86–87.
227. "hopelessly tired . . ." Feb. 25, 1922, pub. L 80.
228. "I have a bone . . ." May 25, 1922, unpub.
229. "I think," 4th of July [1922], pub. L 93. Crane had been given Nelson's set of Nietzsche by Nelson's widow and kept the carefully annotated volumes with him wherever he went.
230. "Bill and I . . ." Dec. 25, 1921, pub. L 75.
230. "In my own work . . ." Jan. 10 [1922], pt.pub. L 77. Crane's quotations from Donne's "Second Anniversary" (lines 296–98) and "The Expiration" (lines 1–12) follow neither the Grierson edition, which he probably did not own, nor the Chambers edition, which was found among his books after his death. He may, of course, have simplified spelling and punctuation for Anderson.
231. "I haven't done . . ." unpub.
231. "at the joint. . . ." Monday, Febrier le 13, '22, unpub.
232. "evident lack . . ." Matthew Josephson, *Life among the Surrealists* (New York: Holt, Rinehart and Winston, 1962), 154. Munson notes that Josephson's reporting of his taste is suspect, since his "Note on Waldo Frank," written for the Nov. 1921 *Gargoyle*, describes Frank's two published novels as "failures." (See Munson, "Annotations on Three Books" [privately published, 1967], 5.)
232. "I met a rather . . ." Gorham Munson, "The Fledgling Years, 1916–1924," *The Sewanee Review*, XL, 1 (Jan.-Mar. 1932), 29.
233. "I labored . . ." Josephson, *Life among . . .* , 155–158.
233. "And now . . ." Jan. 23, 1922, pt.pub. L 78.
234. "Your list . . ." Mar. 12, 1922,

pt.pub. L 81, where letter is misdated.

234. "20 cents," *Secession* announcement (1922), French spellings corrected.

235. "You know I . . ." Mar. 24 [1922], pub. L 82.

235. "perfectly flat" HC to GM, Apr. 19, 1922, pub. L 84.

235. "I am skeptical . . ." May 6, 1922, pub. L 85.

236. "Just now . . ." pub. L 81–82, where it is misdated.

236. "a new pair . . ." Apr. 2, 1922, pt.pub. L 84.

237. "one of those . . ." HC to GM, Mar. 12, 1922, pub. L 82, where it is misdated.

237. "unmellowed ladies" Feb. 11, 1922, pub. L 79.

238. "He once confessed . . ." interviewed by JU, 1960.

238. "I have again . . . Mar. 29, 1922, pub. L 83.

CHAPTER 13

239. " 'investigation . . ." HC to WW, Mar. 2, 1922, pub. L 80.

239. ". . . almost . . ." HC to Harry Candee, Feb. 26, 1922, unpub.

239. "I remember exactly . . ." interviewed by JU, Sept. 11, 1962 (Oral History files).

241. "It is because . . ." May 16, 1922, pub. L 88.

241. "a metaphysical attempt." May 16, 1922, pub. L 87.

241. "quotidian complaints" HC to GM, June 4, 1922, pt.pub. L 89–90.

242. "immersed" June 11, 1922, unpub.

242. "What you say . . ." June 12 [1922], pub. L 90.

243. "Apologies Later!" pt.pub. L 91–92.

245. "I must have . . ." Thurs., June 22 [1922], pub. L 92–93.

245. "I'm interested . . ." [late June, 1922], unpub.

246. "bright" interviewed by JU, 1963.

246. "one of the dozen . . ." Wednesday [July 12, 1922], unpub.

246. "the epic of the age." HC to WU, July 27, 1922, pub. L 94–95.

247. "He was frightened . . ." Material drawn from JU interviews with Munson, 1961, 1963, 1966.

248. "reading poetry . . ." This and following quotations are from P. D. Ouspensky, *Tertium Organum* (New York: Alfred A. Knopf, 1949), 302, 301, 295–296. Crane was familiar with either the first (1920) or the second (1922) edition. The latter is the text on which all subsequent editions have been based.

249. "You cannot," interviewed 1963.

249. "It may be . . ." Jan. 10 [1922], pub. L 76.

249. "It doesn't seem . . ." [Jan. 15, 1922, misdated by Anderson, "Sunday Jan. 13"], unpub.

249. "the first peck . . ." Feb. 11, 1922, unpub.

250. "I just thought . . ." telephone interview, autumn 1963.

250. "I'm sorry indeed . . ." Thursday [July 27, 1922?], unpub.

251. "I sent 27 . . ." Aug. 7, 1922, pub. L 95.

251. "the man's personal . . ." Aug. 15, 1922, pub. L 97.

252. "I got the water colors . . ." undated [late Aug. 1922], unpub.

252. "Let us create . . ." HC to GM, Friday night [late Aug. 1922], pub. L 98.

253. "fresh violences," July 27, 1922, pub. L 95.

253. "vacation," Aug. 7, 1922, pt.pub. L 95–96.

254. "Crane was a good talker," interviewed by JU, 1961.

254. "There are birth pangs . . ." Oct. 9, 1922, pub. L 101.

CHAPTER 14

256. "As for the kind . . ." H. P. Lovecraft to Lillian Clark, Aug. 9, 1922, unpub.

257. "Lately time flies," Aug. 25, 1922, unpub.

257. "Of course . . ." Friday night [late Aug. 1922], pub. L 98.

257. "I'm impatient . . ." HC to GM, Oct. 12, 1922, pub. L 102.

257. "Evidently . . ." HC to GM, Nov. 7, 1922, pub. L 103.

258. "I always . . ." HC to GM, Dec. 7, 1922, pt.pub. L 107.

258. "General Aims and Theories" For problems in dating this work, see page 377. My quotations are from the text printed in Horton 323–24.

259. Ben Jonson's *Alchemist* I am grateful to the poet Michael O'Brien for pointing out to me the extensive use that Crane made of material from Jonson's play. The reader unfamiliar with Jonson is likely to miss much significant allusive material.

260. "good, of course . . ." HC to GM, Nov. 20, 1922, pub. L 105.

260. "most delightful . . ." HC to C von W, May 6, 1922, pub. L 85.

260. "with apologies," HC to GM, Thursday [very late Aug. 1922], pt.pub. L 98–99.

260. "slight reprimand" Tuesday [Sept. 19, 1922], pub. L 100.
261. "out of sheer joy" Monday, Aug. 7, 1922, pub. L 96.
261. "I'm glad . . ." Monday [probably Aug. 28, 1922], pub. L 99.
262. "hastily . . ." Tuesday [Sept. 19, 1922], pt.pub. L 99–100.
262. "He is going . . ." Thursday [probably Aug. 24, 1922], pt.pub. L 98–99.
263. "Am anxious . . ." Saturday [Oct. 7, 1922], unpub.
263. "sipping some . . ." Oct. 9, 1922, pt.pub. L 101–2.
263. "It's as smooth . . ." pt.pub. L 102.
264. "She gave the same . . ." Tuesday, Dec. 12 [1922], pub. L 109.
265. "Hart had a very . . ." interviewed by JU, Aug. 4, 1962 (Oral History files).
265. "I am in great . . ." Tuesday, Dec. 12 [1922], pub. L 110.
266. "However much . . ." Dec. 4, 1922, pub. L 110, where it is misdated Dec. 24, 1922.
266. "I cannot remember . . ." Jan. 5, 1923, pub. L 113.

CHAPTER 15

267. "The snail . . ." quoted in Hunter Ingalls, "Genius of the Everyday—the Art of William Sommer," unpublished Master's essay, Columbia University, 1963, 18. Original in *Tertium Organum*, 100. Other quotations from Sommer that follow are drawn from Ingalls, 19, 20, 21.
268. "bible" William M. Milliken, "William Sommer the Individual," in *The William Sommer Memorial Exhibition* catalogue (Cleveland Museum of Art, 1950), 14.
268. "a beautiful German . . ." HC to C von W, Oct. 9, 1922, pub. L 102.
268. "the most . . ." HC to GM, Oct. 12, 1922, pub. L 102.
268. "He likes . . ." Sept. 15, 1922 [misdated: "Friday, Sept. 14th" by Crane], unpub.
269. "Ye Gods! . . ." [Sept. 19, 1922], unpub.
269. "Williams . . . said . . ." pub. L 102.
269. "If Stieglitz . . ." HC to GM, Thanksgiving Day [Nov. 30] 1922, pt.pub. L 105–106.
270. "never reach . . ." Wednesday, Jan. 10, 1923, pub. L 115.
270. "spiritual events . . ." HC to GM, Jan. 5, 1923, pub. L 113.
271. "Stieglitz voiced . . ." Jan. 5, 1923, pub. L 113–15.

273. "I was not . . ." Joseph Frease to JU, Nov. 15, 1963, unpub.
273. "You see . . ." Feb. 9, 1923, pub. L 122.
273. *Whoops!* July 4 [1922], pt.pub. 93.
274. "an athlete . . ." HC to WU, Sept. 19, 1922, unpub.
274. "But how I . . ." HC to WU, Sept. 2, 1922, unpub.
274. "security against . . ." Feb. 9, 1923, pub. L 122.
275. "Those who have wept . . ." pub. L 126–127.
276. "Passions . . ." HC to GM, Feb. 9, 1923, pub. L 122.
277. "exact and fair" HC to GM, Jan. 10, 1923, pub. L 115.
277. "We never quarrelled," interviewed by JU, autumn 1962.
277. "Waldo Frank wrote . . ." Jan. 5, 1923, pub. L 113.
277. "You are a genuine . . ." Feb. 1 [1923], unpub.
278. "Everyone writes . . ." Feb. 6, 1923, pub. L 118.
278. "S4N," Jan. 20, 1923, pt.pub. L 116–117.
279. "'anointment . . ." *The Little Review*, Winter 1922, 23.
279. "I'm already . . ." pub. L 119–20.
279. "It will be . . ." pub. L 118.
279. "The ads are calling . . ." pt.pub. L 123.
279. "You may be . . ." Feb. 15, 1923, pub. L 124.
280. "I do want . . ." Feb. 18, 1923, pub. L 125.
281. "Such major criticism . . ." Feb. 27, 1923, pub. L 127.
281. "solid, luminous . . ." Feb. 21 [1923], unpub.
282. "And better than all—" Feb. 27, 1923, pub. L 127–28.
282. "an extremely mystic type," Mar. 2, 1923, pt.pub. L 128–30.

CHAPTER 16

285. "an amiable . . ." interviewed by JU, 1962. All following Patno material from same interview.
286. "Your note . . ." Mar. 26 [1923], unpub.
286. "Did you see . . ." Sunday [Mar. 25, 1923], pt.pub. L 130. Crane, of course, gets Munson's wife's name (Lisa) wrong.
286. "Your very interesting . . ." Mar. 29, 1923, unpub.
287. "I wouldn't want . . ." Good Friday [Mar. 30, 1923], unpub.
287. "I shall be very forlorn . . ." Tuesday A.M., Apr. 24, 1923, unpub.
288. "Keeping down . . ." Apr. 4, 1923, unpub.

288. "Preparations for moving . . ." GHC to HC, Apr. 24, 1923, unpub.
288. "The Crane mansion . . ." GHC to HC, May 4, 1923, unpub.
289. "Everybody . . ." Apr. 4, 1923, unpub.
289. "It is a dark . . ." Apr. 13, 1923, pt.pub. L 131.
290. "Crane is a bully chap," GM to Jean Toomer, Mar. 29, 1923, unpub.
290. "Your critique . . ." GM to Jean Toomer, Apr. 17, 1923, unpub.
290. "The copy director . . ." Apr. 19, 1923, unpub.
290. "moderately well" My information concerning Crane's job application at J. Walter Thompson was obtained in telephone conversations with several Thompson personnel executives. Gorham Munson told me, "It took the combined efforts of Waldo Frank, Alyse Gregory, and Evelyn Dewey to land him at Thompson's." GM to JU, Mar. 23, 1969, unpub.
291. "Hart Crane is . . ." undated [late Apr. 1923], unpub.
291. "Crane has completed . . ." Apr. 30, 1923, unpub.
291. "Put an advertisement . . ." Thursday, 2 P.M. [probably May 3 or May 10, 1923], unpub.
291. "I have bids in . . ." May 9, 1923, pub. L 133–34.
291. "Every few days . . ." May 11, 1923, pub. in *The Free Lance*, Vol. 5, No. 1 (First Half 1960), 21–22.
291. "trying to scrape . . ." Thursday [May 24, 1923], unpub.
292. "The other night . . ." May 26, 1923, unpub.
292. "who serve . . ." HC to CR, Apr. 13, 1923, pub. L 131.
292. "the most wonderful . . ." HC to CR and RR, Mar. 30, 1923, unpub.
292. "I'm very much . . ." Apr. 9, 1923, unpub.
292. "There are so many . . ." Apr. 13, 1923, pt.pub. L 131.
293. "It was fine . . ." Wednesday [May 9, 1923? Dated by Weber "ca. May 7."], pt.pub. L 132–33.
293. "Dear great and good . . ." Apr. 15, 1923, pub. L 131–32.
293. "or any one . . ." Apr. 16, 1923, unpub.
294. "Alfred Stieglitz says . . ." Apr. 19, 1923, unpub.
294. "And all felt . . ." Alfred Stieglitz to HC, Apr. 27, 1923, unpub.
294. "Meeting some . . ." Apr. 13, 1923, pub. L 131.
294. "fat-heads." Apr. 16, 1923, unpub.

294. "the beloved . . ." HC to Charles Harris, May 11, 1923, pub. *The Free Lance*, Vol. 5, No. 1, 21–22. Rosenfeld's response is contained in an unpub. letter of July 30, 1923.
295. "quite unsensual." May 9, 1923, unpub.
295. "At LAST!" May 9, 1923, pub. L 113–14.
296. "Please be . . ." May 11, 1923, pub. *The Free Lance*, Vol. 5, No. 1, 21–22.
296. "What I want . . ." Apr. 4, 1923, unpub.
296. "WELL . . ." [postmarked Apr. 23, 1923], unpub.
297. "The children . . ." Apr. 13, 1923, pt.pub. L 131.
297. "stertorous drive" "Eight More Harvard Poets," CP 214.
297. "about the only . . ." May 18, 1923, unpub.
297. "You write with . . ." May 20, 1923, unpub.
297. "It certainly . . ." May 30, 1923, unpub.
298. "It is a warm . . ." May 26, 1923, unpub.
298. "My Dear Hart:" May 27, 1923, unpub.
299. "Please see lots . . ." May 30, 1923, unpub.

CHAPTER 17

300. "They employ . . ." June 10, 1923, pub. L 136. On the same day that Crane had been hired by J. Walter Thompson, he had been offered an editorial post on the trade journal *Machinery*. He chose Thompson's, he told his mother, because of the greater prestige of the latter and because of the possibility of rapid advancement. See unpub. letter of May 23, 1923 (University of Texas collection).
300. "the company . . ." July 2, 1923, unpub.
300. "things look . . ." HC to GHC and EBH, Aug. 18, 1923, pt.pub. L 142–43, where it is misdated Aug. 11, 1923.
300. "I thought . . ." HC to GHC, Aug. 11, 1923, pt.pub. L 142–43.
301. "I have a job . . ." HC to GHC, June 10, 1923, pub. L 135.
301. "I came near . . ." HC to GHC and EBH, Aug. 18, 1923, pub. L 142, where it is misdated Aug. 11, 1923.
301. "I feel . . ." Aug. 24, 1923, pub. L 144.
301. Sue Jenkins. When Hart Crane first met her, "Sue Jenkins" was Mrs. Susan Jenkins Light, though

my text refers to her as "Sue" and "Sue Jenkins." To clarify the text: Susan Light had been living apart from her husband, James Light, since 1921, when he left the U.S. and his wife for France. With Eleanor Fitzgerald's aid, Sue had set up a Connecticut residence to qualify for a divorce for desertion. On his return to the U.S., James Light shared a Patchin Place apartment with the painter-scene designer Harry Gottlieb; then, after some months touring the Midwest in a play, he lived in a furnished room on Washington Square West. Like Hart, he was a frequent dinner guest at 30 Jones Street when he was in New York, and, during 1923–24, when Light was directing plays at the Provincetown Theatre nearby, the core of Light's cast used 30 Jones as a spot to have a quick bite between rehearsals, especially when Paul Robeson was being rehearsed; for, even in Greenwich Village in those years, it was hard to find a decent eating place for a Negro. Hart had become a close friend of Sue's before Light's return to the U.S. He met the Provincetowners at 30 Jones—O'Neill, Robert Edmond Jones, Claire Eames, etc. The Lights' marital separation was known to a few, among them the O'Neills and Fitzi, who also knew what had caused it; it was not generally publicized, as no divorce action could yet be filed.

Mrs. Brown has told me that Hart never stayed at the Jones Street apartment when she lived there, even for one night, though he may have stored some of his belongings there on being evicted from Van Nest Place (Charles Street), before moving them to Columbia Heights; he would not have asked to stay at her apartment, as she was living there alone. When Hart explained to the Browns his financial and sexual predicaments, both Sue and Bill were quick to offer him sympathetic understanding and occasional small loans.

My text does not make it clear that "Sue Jenkins" was granted a decree of divorce from James Light, and that she was Mrs. William Slater Brown when she and Bill Brown bought their Pawling house and moved there in the spring of 1925, four years after her separation from James Light.

302. "Really . . ." HC to GHC, June 10, 1923, pub. L 135.
302. "I am swimming . . ." June 21, 1923, pt.pub. L 136–37.
302. "a body . . ." undated [probably early July 1923], unpub.
302. "I've been trying . . ." July 2, 1923, unpub.
303. "A fine large . . ." HC to GHC and EBH, June 1, 1923, unpub.
303. "all black" HC to CR and RR, June 5, 1923, pub. L 135.
303. "in changing things . . ." June 18, 1923, unpub.
303. "the sweet clean air . . ." HC to EBH, July 19, 1923, unpub.
303. "We took . . ." HC to GHC, July 14, 1923, unpub.
303. "You must plan . . ." July 9, 1923, unpub.
304. "There is . . ." July 8, 1923, pub. in *The Free Lance*, Vol. 5, No. 1 (First Half 1960), 23–24.
305. "This country . . ." July 27, 1923, unpub.
305. "You should have . . ." pub. L 137.
307. "I'm all ready . . ." HC to GHC, June 18, 1923, unpub.
308. "Both you . . ." July 19, 1923, unpub.
308. "the place . . ." July 21, 1923, pt.pub. L 139–42.
311. "I'm only . . ." HC to GHC, June 18, 1923, unpub.
311. "I have been . . ." Sept. 21, 1923, unpub.
311. "My mother is . . ." HC to CR and RR, Aug. 19, [1923], pt.pub. L 143–44.
312. "crooked," etc. These phrases are drawn from the dozens of similar accusations that are scattered through Crane's letters of Aug. and Sept. 1923.
312. "Apparently . . ." Sept. 11, 1923, unpub.
312. "Crane, you see . . ." Oct. 18, 1923, unpub.
313. "Your note . . ." HC to GM, undated [Oct. 18 or Oct. 19, 1923], unpub.
313. "The only . . ." GM to John Brooks Wheelwright, Oct. 27, 1923, unpub.
313. "Cheero, old bird!" Oct. 28, 1923, pub. L 154.
313. "comment" John Brooks Wheelwright note attached to Munson letter of Apr. 14, 1923, unpub.
314. "So I seem," undated [Oct. 18 or Oct. 19, 1923], unpub.
315. "I began . . ." Malcolm Cowley, *Exile's Return* (New York: Viking Press, Compass Books Edition, 1956), 181–82.

315. "The attack . . ." Matthew Josephson, quoted in Harold Loeb, *The Way It Was* (New York: Criterion Books, 1959), 196.
315. "By the end . . ." HC to GHC, Sept. 8, 1923, pub. L 147.
316. "I feel sorry . . ." EBH to HC, Oct. 11, 1923, unpub.
316. "anchorage." HC to GHC and EBH, Sept. 8, 1923, pub. L 146.
317. "I've been in . . ." Aug. 25, 1923, pub. L 145–46.
317. "He remembered . . ." Oct. 5, 1923, pt.pub. L 150. Chaplin's own account of this evening is in *My Autobiography* (New York: Simon and Schuster, 1964), 248–50.
319. "Most of the summer . . ." Oct. 9, 1923, unpub.
319. "Dear Bill . . ." Oct. 11, 1923, unpub.
320. "The situation . . ." Sept. 23, 1923, pub. L 148.
320. "The N.Y. life . . ." undated [Oct. 18 or 19, 1923], unpub.
320. "nerves and insomnia" HC to GHC, Oct. 20, 1923, pub. L 151–53.
321. "It simply had to be," Wednesday, Oct. 24 [1923], unpub.
321. "And if you . . ." Wednesday, Oct. 24, 1923, unpub.
322. "He was assigned . . ." Josephson, *Life among the Surrealists,* 262.
322. "I hardly know . . ." Oct. 26, 1923, pub. L 153.
322. It was a history . . . I have not seen this letter. Horton refers to it (161).
322. "I am not going . . ." HC to GHC, Oct. 26, 1923, unpub.
323. "You must not . . ." HC to GHC and EBH, Nov. 1, 1923, pt. pub. L 155–56.

CHAPTER 18

325. "appalling tragedy" Nov. 3, 1923, unpub.
325. "sad and wondrous." Nov. 4, 1923, unpub.
325. "boat for Antwerp." HC to Jean Toomer, Nov. 23 [1923], unpub.
326. "I think I ought" HC to Jean Toomer, enclosed in letter of Nov. 4, 1923, unpub.
327. "A roisterous time!" Nov. 4, 1923, unpub.
327. "Drunk on cider . . ." HC to CR and RR, Friday evening [Nov. 16, 1923], unpub.
328. "In Woodstock . . ." WSB to JU, undated [postmarked Aug. 5, 1964], unpub.
328. "Long walks . . ." unpub.

328. "Felling trees . . ." pub. L 156–57.
328. "It is a rainy . . ." unpub.
328. "Life is . . ." pub. "Hart Crane: The End of Harvest," by Susan Jenkins Brown, in *The Southern Review,* Vol. IV, New Series, No. 4 (Oct. 1968), 950.
329. "There is much . . ." Friday [Nov. 16, 1923], unpub.
329. "After you have . . ." unpub.
329. "I really am . . ." unpub.
330. "It has not . . ." unpub.
330. "We're about . . ." pub. L 157–58.
330. "It is raining . . ." pt.pub. L 158–59.
330. "The gentle . . ." unpub.
330. "I have just . . ." unpub.
331. "old man Rector" Material in this section is drawn from my 1961 interview with WSB and our subsequent correspondence.
331. "Herr Rector . . ." Nov. 13, 1923, pub. BL 951.
331. "The three of us . . ." Nov. 23 [1923], unpub.
332. "Energy is . . ." dated by Brown: *Woodstock, Winter of 1923,* unpub.
332. "piping" undated and unsigned poem discovered among his papers by WSB, now in Harris Collection, Brown University, unpub.
333. "more metaphysical . . ." Saturday afternoon [Nov. 31, 1923], unpub.
333. "confession" HC to GM, Dec. 10, 1923, pub. L 161.
333. "reflexes and symbolisms" HC to AT, Mar. 1, 1924, pub. L 176.
334. "a deep . . ." Jean Toomer to HC, Sept. 30, 1923, unpub.
334. "to have the most room . . ." HC to GHC, Nov. 27, 1923, unpub.
335. "We had all . . ." HC to EBH, Dec. 5, 1923, pub. L 159.
336. "stayed until nearly midnight." Dec. 20, 1923, pub. L 162–63.
337. "It would be . . ." Dec. 10, 1923, pub. L 161.
337. "I could see . . ." HC to GHC, Dec. 10, 1923 [misdated by Crane, Nov. 10, 1923], unpub.
337. "I'm strongly tempted," Dec. 10, 1923, unpub.
337. "Wouldn't it be . . ." Nov. 21, 1923, unpub.
337. "The folks at Cleveland . . ." Dec. 20, 1923, pub. L 162.
338. "It is now . . ." Oct. 27, 1923, unpub.
338. "much more gratifying" Dec. 10, 1923, unpub.

338. "My father says . . ." Dec. 20, 1923, pt.pub. L 161–63.
339. "You should not . . ." Dec. 10, 1923, pub. L 160.
339. "certain ardors" HC to GHC, Dec. 21, 1923, pub. L 165–67.
341. "Mme. Lachaise . . ." HC to GHC and EBH, Dec. 30, 1923, unpub. The Lachaise drawing of Hart Crane is almost certainly that of a nude dancer, now in the Museum of Modern Art drawing collection. It was reproduced in *Hart Crane: a conversation with Samuel Loveman* (New York: Interim Books, 1964), 22.
341. "lonely and forlorn" Dec. 22, 1923, unpub.
342. "grand dance . . ." HC to GHC, Jan. 4, 1924, unpub.
342. "I hope that . . ." Dec. 20, 1923, pt.pub. L 161–63.

CHAPTER 19
343. "as solitary . . ." Jan. 9, 1924, pub. L 166. Crane misspells Lisa Munson's name.
343. "abristle . . ." Jan. 24, 1924, pub. L 171.
344. "My approach . . ." Jan. 9, 1924, pub. L 167.
344. "Your strange telegram . . ." Monday [Jan. 7, 1924], unpub.
344. "offering . . ." HC to GM, Jan. 9, 1924, pub. L 167.
344. "I see through . . ." Jan. 9, 1924, unpub.
345. "You have never . . ." CAC to HC, Jan. 7, 1924, unpub.
345. "I have written . . ." [probably Jan. 12, 1924, misdated by Crane Nov. 12, 1924], unpub.
345. "kind as it is" HC to CAC, Jan. 12, 1924, pub. L 167–71.
348. "And I want . . ." Jan. 15, 1924, unpub.
349. "I have such . . ." Friday night [Jan. 18, 1924], unpub.
349. "I always get . . ." HC to GHC and EBH, Jan. 29, 1924, pub. L 172.
349. "cheese book" HC to GHC, Feb. 3, 1924, pub. L 173–74.
350. "The man . . ." Feb. 13, 1924, pub. L 175.
350. "on the momentary . . ." HC to GHC and EBH, Apr. 3, '1924, unpub.
350. "My only regret," Feb. 25, 1924, unpub.
350. "I don't know what . . ." Feb. 23, 1924, unpub.
351. "a really sincere . . ." Tuesday [Feb. 26, 1924], unpub.
352. "It has been . . ." Mar. 8 [1924], pub. L 178–79.

353. "He may be . . ." HC to GHC, Mar. 15, 1924, unpub.
353. "CA's silence . . ." HC to GHC, Apr. 3, 1924, unpub.
354. "Still, I am . . ." HC to GHC, Mar. 8 [1924], pt.pub. L 178–79.
354. "dirty NY" HC to GHC, Apr. 3, 1924, unpub.
354. "I have a revived . . ." HC to GHC, Mar. 23, 1924, pub. L 180.
354. "If [my friends] . . ." Apr. 15 [1924], unpub.
354. "Helen says . . ." Tuesday [Nov. 18, 1924], unpub.
355. "I shall never . . ." HC to WF, Apr. 21, 1924, pub. L 182.
355. "There was nothing . . ." interviewed, 1962.
355. "a purity of joy." Apr. 21, 1924, pub. L 181.
355. "It's really . . ." undated [Apr. 20, 1924], unpub.
356. "It is so quiet . . ." Apr. 21, 1924, pub. L 181–83.
356. "I had intended . . ." undated [Apr. 20, 1924], unpub.
357. ". . . right here . . ." GHC to HC, Thursday [Apr. 17, 1924], unpub.
357. "they are also . . ." HC to GHC, Nov. 16, 1924, pub. L 192.
357. "Our group . . ." interviewed by JU, Sept. 11, 1962 (Oral History files).
358. "He wasn't really . . ." interviewed by JU, May 20, 1961.
358. "The work involves . . ." Apr. 21, 1924, pub. L 182.
358. "Things were done . . ." Feb. 3, 1924, pub. L 174. I was misled by Crane into referring to Gurdjieff as "Russian." He was really, as Gorham Munson notes, a Caucasian Greek who attempted to set up a system, in his own words, "for the harmonious development of man." The demonstration Crane attended was at the Neighborhood Playhouse. Sue Brown summarizes her own recollections of it in BL 953–54.
358. "a gratifying sense . . ." HC to GM, July 9, 1924, pub. L 185.
359. "When this came up . . ." HC to GM, Dec. 5, 1924, pub. L 195–96. See also Sue Brown's account, BL 965–66.
359. "Reflecting . . ." HC to GM, Dec. 8, 1924, pub. L 197.
360. "I shall keep . . ." Mar. 23, 1924, pub. L 180–81.
360. "He was . . ." HC to GHC, May 4, 1924, unpub.
360. "Live as much . . ." CAC to HC, June 23, 1924, unpub.

361. "Hay fever . . ." June 29, 1924, unpub.
361. "On going up . . ." HC to GHC, Oct. 21, 1924, pt.pub. L 192.
361. "I have not written . . ." May 28, 1924, unpub.
361. "As for myself . . ." June 19, 1924, pt.pub. L 184.
362. "I do not . . ." June 16, 1924, unpub.
362. "beckonings . . ." HC to Jean Toomer, Aug. 19 [1924], unpub.
362. "I feel very much . . ." June 16, 1924, unpub.
363. "What he really had . . ." interviewed, May 20, 1961.
363. "with occasional . . ." HC to GHC and EBH, May 11, 1924, pub. L 183.
364. "anvil weather" HC to GM, July 9, 1924, pub. L 185.
364. "My happiest times . . ." Sept. 9, 1924, pub. L 190.
364. "His father's death . . ." Oct. 14, 1924, unpub.
364. "There's no stopping . . ." HC to GHC, Nov. 16, 1924, pub. L 192.
365. "The last day . . ." HC to GHC and EBH, Oct. 21, 1924, pub. L 192.
365. "It darkened . . ." HC to GHC, Nov. 16, 1924, pub. L 192–93.
366. "I've been toasting . . ." HC to GHC and EBH, Oct. 21, 1924, pub. L 192.
366. "She absolutely . . ." Emil Opffer interviewed by JU.
366. "well arranged . . ." HC to GHC, Nov. 16, 1924, pub. L 193.
366. "Just now . . ." Nov. 18, 1924, unpub.
366. "Grandmother's . . ." Sept. 4, 1924, unpub.
366. "Mother and Mr. Curtis . . ." Sept. 14, 1924, unpub.
367. "So far . . ." Sept. 14, 1924, pt.pub. L 188–89.
369. "the new aerial mail," HC to GHC, July 4, 1924, unpub.
369. "Your recountal . . ." HC to GHC and EBH, Oct. 14, 1924, unpub.
369. "Your references . . ." Oct. 15 [1924], unpub.
370. "I shall bring . . ." HC to GHC and EBH, Oct. 21, 1924, pt.pub. L 192.
370. "I am counting . . ." Oct. 31, 1924, unpub.

CHAPTER 20

371. "harmless . . . Nov. 16, 1924, pub. L 193.
371. "an egotistical" Howard P. Lovecraft to Mrs. F. C. Clark, Sept. 29, 1924, in H. P. Lovecraft, *Se-*

*lected Letters, 1911–1924* (Sauk City, Wisc.: Arkham House, 1965), 349, 351. My transcriptions are from originals at Brown University.
372. "We found Crane . . ." H. P. Lovecraft to Mrs. F. C. Clark, Nov. 4–5, 1924, Lovecraft, *Selected Letters, 1911–1924*, 358.
372. "I've been just . . ." HC to GHC and EBH, Nov. 9, 1924, unpub.
372. "this is the . . ." pub. L 197–98.
373. "Imagine making . . ." HC to GHC, Feb. 10, 1925, unpub.
373. "quiet and economical . . ." pub. L 199.
373. "usual jamborees . . ." HC to GHC and EBH, May 2, 1925, unpub.
373. "I can see . . ." HC to GHC and EBH, Apr. 21, 1925, unpub.
374. "As you picture . . ." Apr. 9, 1925, pub. L 202.
374. "I . . . never met . . ." HC to Caresse Crosby, Mar. 16, 1930, unpub.
374. "You know . . ." HC to GHC and EBH, Monday [Feb. 22, 1925], pub. L 199.
375. "notably beautiful books" HC to Thomas Seltzer, May 4, 1925, pub. L 203.
375. "I have revised . . ." HC to GHC and EBH, Monday [Feb. 22, 1925], pub. L 199.
375. "experience" June 16, 1924, unpub.
376. "the cloud of fire . . ." Brom Weber, *Hart Crane*, 235.
376. "an 'even so'" HC to WF, Sept. 6, 1924, pub. L 187.
377. "General Aims and Theories," Crane's essay is reprinted in Horton 323–28, and in CP 217–23. I have followed Horton's text.
377. "anything from . . ." GM to Jean Toomer, Mar. 8, 1924, unpub.
378. "There are days . . ." HC to GHC, Sept. 23, 1924, pub. L 191.
379. "I nearly sank . . ." HC to GHC and EBH, Oct. 25, 1924, unpub. I have published this account in a somewhat different form as "'. . . A Piece of Pure Invention': A Hart Crane Episode" in *Columbia Library Columns*, XV, 3 (May 1966), 2–9, and in University of Houston *Forum*, V (Summer 1967), 43–44. In these accounts the full text of a letter of Oct. 21, 1924, is reproduced for the first time.
379. "Knowing how hard . . ." HC to GHC and EBH, Oct. 21, 1924, pt.pub. L 192.
380. "That would suggest . . ." HC to GHC and EBH, May 7, 1925, pub. L 205.

380. "I have been . . ." Mar. 13, 1925, unpub.
380. "Getting that wad . . ." HC to GHC and EBH, Mar. 28, 1925, pub. L 201.
380. "It takes long . . ." May 3, 1925 [misdated by Crane Sunday afternoon—May 2, 1925], pub. L 206.
381. "caught like a rat . . ." Cowley, *Exile's Return*, 222.
381. "It takes this night work . . ." HC to GHC, Mar. 10, 1925, pub. L 200.
381. "it would be . . ." Mar. 21, 1925, unpub.
381. "Just a mile . . ." May 3, 1925, [misdated Sunday afternoon—May 2, 1925], pub. L 205.
382. "Then [Freeman] . . ." May 7, 1925, pub. L 204.
382. "C.A. . . . offered" May 28, 1925, pub. L 207. Emil's account was in a 1961 interview with me.
383. "Gorham, of course . . ." HC to GHC, Mar. 10, 1925, pub. L 201.
383. "But he disappointed . . ." HC to CR and RR, Feb. 28, 1925, pub. L 200.
383. "real turmoil" HC to GHC and EBH, June 4, 1925, pub. L 207.
384. "WELL! . . ." HC to CR and RR, Feb. 28, 1925, pub. L 200.
384. "the great . . ." HC to GHC, Feb. 10, 1925, pub. L 198.
384. "I saw it from . . ." HC to GHC, Jan. 29, 1925, unpub.
384. ". . . have bought . . ." HC to GHC and EBH, Jan. 4, 1925, pub. L 197.
385. Practically everything . . . pt. pub. L 207.

CHAPTER 21

386. "You have no idea . . ." June 17, 1925, pub. L 208. Sue Brown's account of these days, which was published after my book was in type, is required reading for Crane scholars: BL 952–67.
386. "It seems so strange . . ." EBH to HC, June 22, 1925, unpub.
387. "Life has been . . ." HC to GHC and EBH, July 10, 1925, pub. L 209.
387. "I walked over . . ." HC to GHC, Sunday [July 19, 1925], unpub.
387. "We have a bright . . ." June 17, 1925, pt.pub. L 208.
387. "Nothing could beat . . ." July 10, 1925, pub. L 212.
388. "youth and poverty . . ." Cowley, *Exile's Return*, 228 ff.
389. "I've told this story . . ." inter-

viewed, spring 1966 (NET transcription).
389. " 'findrinny' he could never find . . ." *Exile's Return*, 230.
390. "Have a good time . . ." June 4, 1925, pub. L 207–8.
390. "This is . . ." July 10, 1925, pub. L 209–11.
391. "I think the reason . . ." June 12 [1925], unpub.
391. "I left Sweet's . . ." June 27, 1925, unpub.
392. "Someone was telling . . ." Mar. 13, 1925, unpub.
392. "The photos . . ." May 7, 1925, pub. L 203–4.
392. "I would like . . ." HC to GHC, Sunday [July 20, 1925], unpub.
392. "After the quiet . . ." July 23 [1925], pub. L 213.
393. "I can't at present . . ." Friday [July 17, 1925], pub. L 212–13.
393. "I cannot resist . . ." Friday [Aug. 21, 1925?], pub. BL 958.
393. "We rode . . ." undated [before July 10, 1925?], unpub.
394. "This Florida . . ." July 10, 1925, pub. L 209–10.
395. The labors of packing up . . . Recounted in an unpublished statement by Nathan Asch, included in an unpub. July 23, 1961, letter to JU.
395. "I have been trying . . ." Aug. 19, 1925, pub. L 214.
396. "the vanishing . . ." HC to WSB and SJB, Tuesday [July 28, 1925], unpub.
396. "Perhaps you would like . . ." Aug. 6, 1925, unpub.
396. "I only hope . . ." Friday [Aug. 21, 1925?], pub. BL 957.
396. "5 cases . . ." Aug. 27 [1925], pub. BL 959.
396. "one bright afternoon" Aug. 19 [1925], pub. L 214.
397. "at his country place," HC to WSB and SJB, Friday [Aug. 21, 1925?], pub. BL 957.
397. "There are several . . ." SJB to HC, Sept. 4, 1925, unpub. Jennings was not Brown's "landlord," having already sold Brown the "Robbers Rocks" property.
398. "I had expected . . ." Sept. 15, 1925, pt.pub. L 215–16.
398. "A friend of Brown's . . ." Sunday [Oct. 4, 1925?], pub. L 216.
399. "twenty beautiful acres . . ." HC to RR and CR, Oct. 14, 1925, unpub.

CHAPTER 22

400. "spree on . . ." HC to CR and RR, Sept. 15, 1925, pt.pub. L 215–16.

400. "I'm feeling, gradually . . ." Sept. 26, 1925, unpub.
401. "Today it is . . ." HC to CR and RR, Sunday [Oct. 4, 1925?], pub. L 217.
401. "nearly killed me . . ." Oct. 11 [1925], unpub.
402. "At one time . . ." H.P. Lovecraft to Mrs. F.C. Clark, Oct. 14–15, 1925, unpub.
402. "There have been . . ." HC to SJB and WSB, Oct. 21, 1925, pub. L 217, BL 961–62 (with Sue Brown's commentary).
402. "I have been back . . ." HC to William Sommer, Oct. 27, 1925, pt.pub. L 218–19.
403. "I just missed," HC to WSB and SJB, Oct. 21, 1925, pub. L 217–18, BL 961–62.
404. "with the nail keg . . ." Cowley, "The Leopard in Hart Crane's Brow," *Esquire*, Vol. L, No. 4 (Oct. 1958), 257–58.
404. "When Hart pressed . . ." Bert Ginther to JU, Aug. 4, 1963, unpub.
404. "The Dial bought . . ." Dec. 1, 1925, pub. L 220.
405. "Hart Crane complains . . ." *Writers at Work: The Paris Review Interviews, Second Series* (New York: Viking Press, 1963), 80.
406. "We could not but . . ." quoted in HC to WF, Aug. 19 [1925], pub. L 215.
407. "Since the last . . ." HC to SJB and WSB, Oct. 21, 1925, pub. L 218, BL 962.
407. "one has to live . . ." July 10, 1925, unpub.
408. "I am dissatisfied . . ." Friday [July 17, 1925], pub. L 213.
408. "contains some . . ." WF to HC, July 22, 1925, unpub.
408. "some kind of notice" HC to WF, Aug. 19 [1925], pub. L 214.
408. "a preface . . ." HC to CR and RR, Oct. 22, 1925, unpub.
408. "They have lost . . ." Oct. 27, 1925, pub. L 218.
409. "There are men men men . . ." Oct. 16, 1925, unpub.
409. "I, of course . . ." Oct. 24, 1925, unpub.
410. "I hope you will give . . ." unpub.
410. "Tuesday 8 p.m." [postmarked Nov. 4, 1925], unpub. The "Wed. 9 a.m." passage that follows is part of the same letter.
411. "I did not . . ." Nov. 17, 1925, unpub.
412. "I was very glad . . ." HC to CAC, from a transcript of a letter dated Nov. 21, 1925, by transcriber, pt.pub. L 219–20.

413. "It may be . . ." Nov. 25, 1925, unpub.
414. "This filthy mess" HC to CR and RR, Dec. 1, 1925, pt.pub. L 220.
415. "Dear Father" Dec. 3, 1925, pt.pub. L 220–22.

CHAPTER 23

417. "What real writing . . ." Dec. 3, 1925, pub. L 222–23.
418. "AM STILL . . ." Dec. 8, 1925, unpub.
418. "almost six weeks . . ." Dec. 9, 1925 [postmarked Dec. 8, 1925], pub. L 224.
418. "YOUR FIRST . . ." Dec. 11, 1925, unpub.
418. "Dear Hart . . ." Dec. 9 [1925], unpub.
419. "one of the small . . ." HC to EBH, Dec. 29, 1925, unpub.
419. "My pictures . . ." New Year's Eve, 1926 [Jan. 1, 1926], pub. L 225–26.
419. "It is extremely . . ." Dec. 29, 1925, unpub.
419. "Around me always," Jan. 17, 1926, unpub.
420. "I think she was . . ." Caroline Gordon [Tate] interviewed by JU.
420. "a grass widow . . ." "The Leopard . . ." 258.
420. "a New England . . ." interviewed by JU, Sept. 11, 1962 (Oral History files).
421. "From the window . . ." unpub.
421. "Here I am . . ." New Year's Eve, 1926 [Jan. 1, 1926], pub. L 225, 227. Eva Parker interviewed by JU, 1963.
421. "scrumptious . . ." HC to EBH, Jan. 27 [1926], pub. L 234.
421. "despite the amiable . . ." to Charles Harris, Feb. 20, 1926, pub. *The Free Lance*, V, 1, 20.
421. "two mad weeks" [postmarked Jan. 2, 1926], unpub.
422. "my various . . ." Dec. 21, 1925, unpub.
422. "We had an exclamatory . . ." HC to CR and RR, New Year's Eve, 1926 [Jan. 1, 1926], pub. L 226.
422. "One really has . . ." Jan. 5, 1926, pub. L 231–32.
422. "she is getting . . ." Jan. 2, 1926, unpub.
422. "There isn't much . . ." Jan. 7 [1926], pub. L 232.
423. "Yes, it is . . ." Jan. 2, 1926, unpub.
423. "What a tragic . . ." Wednesday [Jan. 13, 1926?], unpub.
424. "the peace and beauty . . ." HC

to GHC and EBH, Jan. 17, 1926, unpub.

424. "My study . . ." Jan. 26 [1926], pub. L 233. WSB and Lorna Dietz recollections from interviews with JU.

424. "was always neat . . ." in "The Leopard . . ." 258.

424. "a little bored . . ." HC to Charles Harris, Feb. 20, 1926, pub. *The Free Lance*, V, 1, 20.

425. "Spring will be . . ." Mar. 2 [1926], pt.pub. L 234.

425. "Charming and imaginative" interviewed by JU.

425. "tramping up and down . . ." Cowley, "The Leopard . . ." 258.

425. "Hart studied . . ." interview.

425. "suddenly spurted . . ." HC to MC, Mar. 28 [1926], pt.pub. L 242–43.

425. "I've been delving . . ." Feb. 20, 1926, pub. *The Free Lance*, V, 1, 20.

426. "is symphonic . . ." Jan. 18, 1926, pub. L 232–33.

426. "I have been reading . . ." Jan. 27 [1926], pub. L 234.

427. "a marvelously illustrated . . ." HC to GM, Mar. 5 [1926], pub. L 235.

427. "incorporate" HC to MC, Mar. 28 [1926], pub. L 242.

427. "the scaffoldings . . ." HC to Charles Harris, Feb. 20, 1926, pub. *The Free Lance*, V, 1, 20.

427. "At times . . ." Mar. 2 [1926], pub. L 235.

427. "In a way . . ." Mar. 5 [1926], pub. L 236.

427. "burlesque" HC to GM, Mar. 17, 1926, pt.pub. L 235–37.

427. "rather diffident" Feb. 2, 1926, unpub.

427. "I saw Liveright . . ." Mar. 1, 1926, unpub.

428. "rummy conversation." HC to GM, Mar. 17, 1926, pub. L 237.

428. "My mother . . ." HC to MC, Mar. 28 [1926], pub. L 243.

428. "dear little note" HC to EBH, Mar. 18 [1926], unpub.

428. "After a perfect . . ." Mar. 28 [1926], pub. L 242.

428. "hideous experience" Mar. 20, 1926, pub. L 242.

429. "I, too, think . . ." Sunday [Mar. 28, 1926], pub. L 243.

429. "You arbitrarily propose . . ." Mar. 17, 1926, pub. L 237–40.

431. "Why he wanted . . ." interview of Sept. 11, 1962 (Oral History files).

431. "lack of a . . ." "Hart Crane" in *The Man of Letters in the Mod-*

*ern World* (New York: Meridian Books, 1955), 286–89.

432. "I have been . . ." Apr. 11, 1926, unpub.

432. "a few 'animations' . . ." HC to GM, Apr. 5 [1926], pub. L 244.

432. "Why this should make . . ." Apr. 18 [1926], pub. L 245–46.

433. "Of course, our quarrel . . ." interview of Sept. 11, 1962 (Oral History files).

433. "What the hell . . ." interviewed by JU.

434. "it's extremely . . ." interviewed by JU, Sept. 11, 1962 (Oral History files).

434. "spread" HC to GHC, Apr. 18 [1926], pub. L 246–47.

434. "Try and not . . ." Apr. 24 [1926], unpub.

434. "You expect . . ." fragment draft of unpub. letter to AT, undated, on Mizzen Top Hotel stationery.

CHAPTER 24

436. "If you feel . . ." Apr. 18 [1926], pub. L 248–49.

436. "made a terrible fuss" Apr. 25, 1926, pub. L 250.

436. "I'm *terribly* . . ." Apr. 24 [1926], unpub.

436. "I realize . . ." Apr. 25, 1926, pub. L 250.

437. "I spose . . ." May 7 [1926], pub. BL 969; pt.pub. L 252.

437. "a dozen penitent . . ." Horton 201.

437. "We had some . . ." May 8 [1926], unpub.

437. "a very dapper . . ." interview.

437. "a wonderful sail . . ." May 3 [1926], unpub.

438. "We didn't visit . . ." May 7 [1926], pub. L 251; BL 968.

439. "trashy bastard people" HC to CAC, May 20, 1926, unpub.

439. "enough Eden" HC to SJB and WSB, May 7 [1926], pub. L 251–52; BL 968–69.

439. "whimsical temper" HC to GHC, Apr. 18 [1926], pub. L 248.

439. "goodness itself," HC to GHC, May 8 [1926], unpub.

439. "really lovable . . ." HC to SJB and WSB, May 7 [1926], pub. L 252, BL 969.

439. "very sociable . . ." HC to GHC, May 8 [1926], unpub.

439. "After Grace's warnings . . ." May 20, 1926, unpub.

439. "Yesterday . . ." May 22 [1926], pub. L 255, BL 974.

440. "and without . . ." HC to GHC, July 8, 1926, pt.pub. L 264–66.

440. "It is, of course . . ." May 14 [1926], pub. L 253.
440. "How I wish . . ." June 1, 1926, pub. L 256.
440. "I feel like . . ." HC to SJB and WSB, May 7 [1926], pub. L 252–53, BL 969–70.
441. "I'm wild . . ." May 26, 1926, unpub.
441. "I am astonished . . ." May 20, 1926, unpub.
441. "the kind the peasants . . ." HC to GHC, May 8 [1926], unpub.
441. "no bigger . . ." HC to SJB and WSB, May 7, 1926, pub. L 252, BL 969.
441. "Nothing 'happens' . . ." HC to WW, July 16, 1926, pt.pub. L 266.
442. "It has been . . ." HC to WU, undated [probably July], pub. L 264, where "touseling" is inaccurately transcribed "tonsiling."
442. "leap in the dark," HC to WW, May 25, 1926, unpub.
443. "By your letter . . ." HC to WW, July 16, 1926, pt.pub. L 266–67.
444. "I have not been . . ." HC to WU, undated [July, 1926?], pt.pub. L 264.
444. "Thursday . . ." HC to GHC, June 1, 1926, pub. L 257.
445. "The motion . . ." June 19, 1926, pub. L 258.
445. "rather toughened . . ." HC to GHC, July 8, 1926, pub. L 266.
445. "double-barrelled . . ." HC to SJB and WSB, July 14, 1926, pub. BL 976.
446. "This man . . ." June 20 [1926], pub. L 260–62.
448. "Yes, I read . . ." Aug. 19, 1926, pub. L 274.
448. "The news . . ." July 24, 1926, pub. L 267.
449. "I'm very glad . . ." July 30 [1926], pub. L 270.
449. "I've meant to write . . ." July 29 [1926], unpub.
449. "I'm feeling quite . . ." July 30 [1926], pub. L 269–70.
450. "One never knows . . ." HC to WF, July 26, 1926, pub. L 268.
450. "I feel . . ." July 24, 1926, pub. L 267.
450. "My plans are soaring . . ." HC to WF, July 26, 1926, pub. L 268.
450. "in the middle . . ." July 29 [1926], pub. L 268–69.
450. "I feel as though . . ." Aug. 3 [1926], pub. L 270–71.
450. "It ends up . . ." HC to WF, Aug. 12 [1926], pub. L 272.
451. "becoming 'divine.'" HC to CR and RR, Aug. 14, 1926, unpub.

451. "Work continues. . . ." HC to WF, Aug. 23 [1926], pub. L 274–75.
451. "Here, too . . ." pub. L 272–73.
452. "Grace,—you naughty . . ." undated [postmarked Aug. 28, 1926], unpub.
453. "fifty dollars . . ." HC to CAC, Sept. 2, 1926, unpub.
453. "Gran Cafe . . ." HC to WF, Sept. 3, 1926, pt.pub. L 275–76.
454. "the most beautiful . . ." HC to WF, Sept. 5 [1926], pt.pub. L 276.
454. "I have no idea . . ." Nov. 1 [1926], pub. L 276–77.
455. "I was awfully . . ." Sept. 6, 1926, unpub.
455. "It's hard to . . ." unpub.
455. "I can warn you," quoted in Horton 213.
456. "You can see . . ." quoted in Horton 214.
456. "I'll confine . . ." Oct. 8, 1926, unpub.
456. "Think I had rather . . ." Mrs. S to HC, Nov. 9, 1926, unpub.
456. "The picture . . ." Mrs. S to HC, Nov. 19, 1926, unpub.
457. "Certain of the actors . . ." HC to Mrs. S, Dec. 5, 1926, pub. L 279.

CHAPTER 25

458. "YOU WILL . . ." unpub.
458. "This is due . . ." Oct. 31, 1926, unpub.
458. "I am overwhelmed . . ." Nov. 1, 1926, unpub.
458. "I heard today . . ." Oct. 29, 1926, unpub.
459. "A telegram . . ." Nov. 6, 1926, unpub.
459. "I am awfully . . ." Nov. 9, 1926, unpub.
459. "My dear Harold . . ." Nov. 2, 1926, unpub. The last paragraph is added in pencil on the back of the typed letter.
460. "My own condition . . ." Nov. 10, 1926, unpub.
460. "Say boy . . ." Nov. 6, 1926, unpub.
461. "Got your nice letter . . ." Nov. 9, 1926, unpub.
461. "Suppose by now . . ." Nov. 19, 1926, unpub.
461. "Mrs. ———" Nov. 6, 1926, unpub.
461. "It made me feel . . ." Nov. 19, 1926, unpub.
462. "I am hoping . . ." Nov. 21 [1926], pub. L 277.
462. "I am so glad . . ." Dec. 5, 1926, unpub.
462. "but I'm not worried . . ." pt. pub. L 278–79.

463. "I remember . . ." Dec. 5, 1926, unpub.
464. "one of the great . . ." Yvor Winters, quoted by Harriet Monroe in *Poetry*, Vol. 29, No. 1 (Oct. 1926), 41.
464. "I'm glad . . ." Nov. 19, 1926, unpub.
464. "a beautiful book" HC to GHC, Dec. 22, 1926, pub. L 280.
465. "Nothing but . . ." pub. L 279–80.
465. "Your letter . . ." Dec. 22, 1926, pt.pub. L 280–81.
466. "Whether I can do it . . ." Dec. 16 [1926], pub. L 280.
466. "A mad year," Dec. 27 [1926], unpub.
467. "Does Mrs. Turner . . ." Dec. 24, 1926 [misdated 1925], unpub.
467. "Dear Sam . . ." HC to SL, undated [Christmas-New Year's, 1926], unpub.

CHAPTER 26

469. "Unable, for various . . ." Jan. 11 [1927], unpub.
470. "The delay . . ." Jan. 23, 1927, pub. L 284–85.
470. "Here is the first . . ." [postmarked Jan. 27, 1927], unpub.
470. "I had heard . . . Jan. 23, 1927, pub. L 283–84.
471. "I suppose . . ." Feb. 28, 1927, unpub.
471. "I took enough . . ." HC to GHC, Mar. 19, 1927, pub. L 292.
471. "Frances Kelley . . ." Fredrica Crane Lewis interviewed by JU, Aug. 20, 1962 (Oral History files).
472. "I'm very much amused . . ." Jan. 23, 1927, pub. L 284.
472. "What you say . . ." Mar. 19, 1927, pt.pub. L 292.
473. "With all your . . ." Oct. 23 [1926], unpub.
473. "Safe and sound . . ." Nov. 15 [1926], unpub.
474. "He was married . . ." Mar. 19, 1927, pt.pub. L 291–93.
474. "I feel very . . ." unpub.
475. "That was a happy . . ." Mar. 19, 1927, pt.pub. L 292.
475. "It's sixteen below . . ." Jan. 28 [1927], pub. L 285.
475. "There is a vague . . ." HC to WSB, Mar. 9 [1927], pub. BL 981–82, where the limerick on the young lady from Thrace is quoted:

There was a young lady from Thrace
Who attempted her corset to lace,
　When her mother said: "Nelly,
　There's more in your belly
Than ever came in through your
　　face."

476. "Spring was really . . ." Mar. 21, 1927, unpub.
476. "I am so glad . . ." Mar. 19, 1927, pub. L 291.
477. "The last two nights" HC to Bill and Sue Brown, Feb. 16 [1927], pub. L 286, BL 979.
478. "B——s and Browns . . ." Mar. 21, 1927, pt.pub. L 293.
478. "The next day," interview, 1966 (NET).
478. "Bill has taken . . ." Mar. 21, 1927, pub. L 293.
478. "I remember . . ." interviewed by JU, 1966 (NET).
478. "It is going . . ." pub. L 284.
479. "wonderful reviews" Jan. 28 [1927], pub. L 285.
479. "immense" Eugene Jolas to HC, Feb. 24, 1927, unpub.
479. "along with several others," Mar. 28 [1927], unpub.
479. "The one quotable . . ." Mar. 14, 1927, pub. L 290–91.
480. *"briefer"* HC to AT, Mar. 27 [1927], pub. L. 294.
480. "what one might call . . ." *The Dial*, Vol. LXXXII (May 1927), 432.
480. "I do not feel" HC to AT, Mar. 27 [1927], pub. L 294.
480. "What strange . . ." HC to AT, Mar. 10 [1927], pt.pub. L 290.
480. "I've had to submit . . ." Feb. 24 [1927], pub. L 289.
480. "I envy . . ." HC to AT, Mar. 14, 1927, pub. L 290.
481. "Altogether . . ." Mar. 30 [1927], pub. L 295.
481. "burning" HC to AT, Mar. 25 [1927], unpub.
481. "promising" HC to AT, Mar. 27 [1927], pt.pub. L 294.
482. "much love," unpub.

CHAPTER 27

484. "I don't want . . ." unpub.
484. "Your splendid . . ." Mar. 12, 1927, unpub.
485. "Nervous crises . . ." Mar. 19, 1927, pub. L 291.
485. "Such stories . . ." GHC to HC, Mar. 20, 1927, unpub.
486. "C.A. was in . . ." interviewed by JU, Aug. 20, 1962 (Oral History files).
487. "Denied Car, She Seeks . . ." Apr. 19, 1927, 16.
487. "Says Mate . . ." Apr. 19, 1927, 17.
487. "as ridiculous . . ." Apr. 24, 1927, unpub.
487. "Complaints by . . ." Apr. 19, 1927, 16.
488. "different . . ." GHC to HC, Apr. 24, 1927, unpub.

488. "Cooled ardor . . ." Apr. 19, 1927, 17.

488. "I *never* put in . . ." GHC to HC, Apr. 24, 1927, unpub.

489. "Am leaving . . ." undated [Apr. 1927], unpub.

489. "with much love," HC to CAC [fragment from a letter probably written on Apr. 23, 1927], unpub.

490. "a summer of 'roses and wine.'" HC to AT, Saturday [Apr. 23, 1927?], unpub.

490. "By this time . . ." Thursday [Apr. 28, 1927], unpub.

491. "Your telegram . . ." Saturday [probably Apr. 30, 1927], unpub.

491. "I think you . . ." HC to WU, unpub.

492. "This tavern . . ." May 3, 1927, unpub.

492. "It has so happened . . ." May 7, 1927, pt.pub. L 296.

493. "If you feel . . ." May 9, 1927, unpub.

494. "Your two nice . . ." May 5, 1927, unpub.

495. "gorgeous" May 9, 1927, unpub.

495. "It is refreshing . . ." May 10, 1927, unpub.

495. "I'm going . . ." unpub. The ———! is Crane's.

495. "I have your . . ." May 19, 1927, unpub.

495. ". . . I brought . . ." May 23 [1927], unpub.

496. "just in time . . ." May 24, 1927, unpub.

496. "Psychoanalysis 'vocationgram.'" GHC to HC, May 21, 1927, unpub.

496. "I should have answered . . ." May 24, 1927, unpub. The poem HC quotes for his father was written by Malcolm Cowley. ("Hart wanted me to do a whole series of them, but Edwardus Rex was as far as I got." MC to JU, May 16, 1969, unpub.)

497. "such prose!" HC to WU, June 6 [1927], unpub.

497. "I'm writing . . ." June 14, 1927, unpub.

497. "I do not want . . ." June 6, 1927, unpub.

498. "practically . . ." HC to GHC, Saturday [June 4, 1927?], unpub.

CHAPTER 28

499. "Edmund Wilson . . ." July 8, 1927, unpub.

499. "curiously vague." Edmund Wilson, "The Muses Out of Work," *New Republic*, vol. L (May 11, 1927), 320.

500. "You need a good drubbing . . ." May 29, 1927, pt.pub. L 298–302.

504. "Sunshine . . ." July 4, 1927, pub. L 302–4.

505. "I received . . ." July 12, 1927, unpub.

505. "The reader . . ." July 4, 1927, unpub.

505. "I wish you would . . ." June 18, 1927, unpub.

505. "I guess . . ." July 8, 1927, unpub.

506. "I don't wonder . . ." June 21, 1927, unpub.

506. "Have almost . . ." July 15, 1927, unpub.

506. "All my activities . . ." Aug. 17 [1927], unpub.

507. "I've had a perfectly . . ." July 9, 1927, unpub.

507. "The check . . ." July 19, 1927, unpub.

507. "I am glad . . ." EBH to HC, July 28, 1927, unpub.

507. "Did you have . . ." July 24, 1927, unpub.

508. "I have been in swimming . . ." July 9, 1927, unpub.

508. "Life goes on here . . ." pt.pub. L 304.

509. "Whatever happens . . ." Aug. 17, 1927, unpub.

510. "It might be better . . ." pub. L 304–9.

511. "Circumstances . . ." Sept. 18, 1927, pt.pub. L 309–10.

CHAPTER 29

513. "This morning . . ." Sept. 21, 1927, unpub.

513. "I have your letter . . ." Sept. 26, 1927, unpub.

514. "I have just had . . ." Oct. 11, 1927, pub. L 310.

515. "In order that . . ." Oct. 13, 1927, unpub.

515. "You can drop . . ." Oct. 17, 1927, unpub.

515. "I was sorry . . ." HC to CAC, Nov. 10, 1927, unpub.

515. "family worries . . ." undated [Oct. 1927], unpub.

516. "My letters . . ." Nov. 3, 1927, unpub.

517. "talk . . . about . . ." HC to WU, Nov. 7, 1927, unpub.

517. "within whistling . . ." Nov. 10, 1927, unpub.

517. "Also, please say nothing . . ." Nov. 3, 1927, unpub.

517. "It is certainly . . ." Nov. 14, 1927, unpub.

518. "I've been having . . ." Nov. 11, 1927, unpub.

518. "Traintime approaches . . ." Nov. 16, 1927, pub. BL 987, pt.pub. L 310–11.

519. "It's humor . . ." HC to WSB,

Dec. 19, 1927, pub. BL 990–91, L 312.

519. "The drives . . ." HC to SL, Dec. 1, 1927, unpub.

519. "flying around" Dec. 15, 1927, unpub.

519. "It is wonderful . . ." Nov. 29, 1927, pt.pub. L 311–12.

520. "read and think some." HC to Isidor and Helen Schneider, Dec. 15, 1927, unpub.

520. "One can't seem . . ." Dec. 19, 1927, pt.pub. BL 988–91, pt.pub. L 312–14.

521. "Dear Hart— . . ." "G" to HC, undated [1929], unpub.

522. "I'll have to save . . ." Feb. 5, 1928, pt.pub. L 316–17.

523. "I am above all . . ." Feb. 22, 1928, pub. BL 992–93, pt.pub. L 317–18. Bert Savoy was the vaudeville and night-club female impersonator whose "Whoops, dearie" is parodied in the Peter Arno cartoons of the time. Crane misquotes —as Sue Brown suggests, probably because he was quoting from memory—Shakespeare's "Ceres' blessing so is on you." What is interesting is that, distorting the text, he keeps the rhythm right.

524. "Writing is next . . ." pt.pub. L 314–15.

525. "From what Hart told us . . ." from a manuscript by Nathan Asch included in a letter to JU (July 23, 1961). Quoted with Mr. Asch's permission.

525. "It has been good . . ." Dec. 19 [1927], pub. L 312, BL 989.

526. "Wise is buying . . ." Feb. 5, 1928, pub. L 316.

526. "God! . . ." Dec. 19 [1927], pub. L 313, BL 989. SJB and Weber assume "Romantist" to be an error for "Romanist." Perhaps they are right, though "Romantic" is as likely. Crane, of course, saw his own orientation as "Romantic" rather than "Classical."

526. "I'm terribly excited . . . Feb. 5, 1928, pub. L 317.

526. "more or less . . ." Yvor Winters, "The Significance of *The Bridge*, by Hart Crane, or What Are We to Think of Professor X?" in *On Modern Poets* (New York: Meridian Books, 1959), 131, 132, 140.

527. "Richards' 'Principles' . . ." Dec. 19, 1927, pub. L 314, BL 990.

527. "damned fine . . ." HC to SL, Feb. 5, 1928, pub. L 316–17.

527. "Every week," Mar. 27, 1928, pub. L 321, BL 997.

527. "my grandmother . . ." Mar.

28, 1928, pt.pub. L 322. Transcribed here from a copy of the original.

529. "rather disappointing experience." June 12, 1928, pub. L 326.

530. "Life is nothing . . ." Mar. 27, 1928, pt.pub. L 319–20, pub. BL 995–96. Emil's version told to me in a 1962 interview.

531. "God bless you . . ." Feb. 5, 1928, pt.pub. L 316–17.

531. "I get terribly . . ." Mar. 27, 1928, pub. L 320, BL 996.

532. "I have been . . ." Nov. 29, 1927, pt.pub. L 311–12.

533. "I see my mother . . ." Feb. 5, 1928, pub. L 316.

534. "in a matter-of-fact . . ." Horton 241.

535. "Yes, I have . . ." Mar. 28, 1928, pt.pub. L 322.

536. "we are still friends . . ." HC to WSB and SJB, Mar. 27, 1928, pt.pub. L 321, pub. BL 997.

537. "The experience . . ." [Apr. 4, 1928, misdated by Crane Mar. 4, 1928], pub. L 318–19. Misled by the inaccurate date on the pub. letter, Sue Brown concludes that Crane left Wise's employment in Feb. In other unpub. Apr. letters of this time, however, Crane repeats the information that is given in the "Mar. 4" letter to WF. All evidence except this misdated letter makes it clear that Hart settled in with his mother late in Mar. of 1928.

537. "As for Hart Crane," HC to GM, Apr. 17, 1928, pub. L 323–24. After my corrected galleys had been returned, an enthusiastic proofreader garbled my text. I had written: "At that time it had seemed to Hart to misrepresent the core of his art; now he was not so sure." The "As for Hart Crane" passage is, of course, written by Crane himself and not, as the proofreader would have it, by Munson.

538. "Since the Fleet . . ." pub. BL 999–1000, pt.pub. L 324–25.

538. "I had a . . ." Mar. 28, 1928, unpub.

539. "If you have . . ." Apr. 10, 1928, unpub.

539. "From what . . ." Apr. 17, 1928, pt.pub. L 323–24.

539. "Your salute . . ." Apr. 27 [1928], pt.pub. L 324–25, pub. BL 999.

540. "intolerable," HC to Isidor and Helen Schneider, July 16, 1928, pub. L 327.

541. "I was desperate . . ." HC to

Zell Deming, quoted in Horton 244, date not given. Sue Brown summarizes a lost letter from HC to the Browns in which he describes one confrontation with his mother, during which he "accused his mother of causing his own financial predicament as well as hers, and renouncing all future responsibility for her. Even worse, he came out with his sexually deviant behavior and blamed her for it—a deed he was regretting, as he wrote, realizing its possible effect on his father." (BL 1000.)

CHAPTER 30

542. "If he had lived," interviewed, 1961.

542. "a coolness," HC to CR and RR, Feb. 26, 1929, pub. L 337.

542. "I . . . was treated . . ." HC to CAC, June 14, 1928, unpub.

543. "The old French . . ." July 16, 1928, pub. L 326. [Inaccuracies in current edition of L; accurately printed in 1948 ed.]

543. "The boat ride . . ." June 14, 1928, unpub.

544. "Write me how . . ." June 18, 1928, unpub.

545. "You are right . . ." July 21, 1928, unpub.

545. "It's nice . . ." June 12, 1928, pub. L 325.

545. "Certainly it sounds . . ." June 21 [1928], unpub.

545. "I hope you are . . ." July 16, 1928, pt.pub. L 326–27.

546. "He had the best . . ." Nathan Asch statement on Crane enclosed in a letter to JU of July 23, 1961.

548. "I'm sorry . . ." July 26, 1928, unpub.

549. "Now, Harold . . ." July 5, 1928, unpub.

550. "Of *course* . . ." July 27, 1928, unpub.

551. "Your check . . ." Aug. 2, 1928, unpub.

551. "His hair was white . . ." interviewed by JU, 1962.

551. "You don't know . . ." Aug. 9, 1928, unpub.

552. "You keep an eye . . ." C von W to JU, interview, 1962.

552. "Suddenly there was . . ." C von W, interviewed by JU (NET transcription), spring 1966. Bessie Breuer interview was conducted by JU in summer of 1962.

552. "When he had been gone . . ." Suzanne Henig to JU, July 28, 1963, unpub.

553. "I've been cooking . . ." Aug. 14, 1928, pub. L 327.

553. "AM SENDING . . ." unpub.

553. "My dear Harold:" Aug. 16, 1928, unpub.

554. "nothing left . . ." HC to WU [Aug. 1928], quoted in Horton 245.

554. "I hope you won't . . ." Aug. 19, 1928, pub. L 327–28.

554. "I've been in the toils . . ." Aug. 20, 1928, unpub.

554. "It looks like . . ." HC to MC, Friday [Aug. 24, 1928?], unpub.

554. "Mother . . ." unpub.

555. "I have your letter . . ." Sept. 12, 1928, unpub.

556. "You couldn't have . . ." Aug. 20, 1928, unpub.

557. "frightfully drunk," interviewed by JU, 1962.

557. "much in common." interviewed by JU, 1961.

558. "an exceptionally . . ." Nov. 5, 1928, unpub.

559. "At times . . ." Sept. 16 [1928], unpub.

559. "COME AT ONCE . . ." unpub.

560. "Sam is in Cleveland . . ." Oct. 23, 1928, pt.pub. L 329.

561. "just a little . . ." July 18, 1928, unpub.

561. "I have it . . ." July 16, 1928, pt.pub. L 326–27.

561. "It has been a pleasure . . ." Dec. 1, 1928, pub. L 330–31.

562. "Since reading . . ." HC to MC, July 3, 1929, pub. L 343.

563. "the 20th . . ." [Oct. 28, 1928], pub. L 329–30.

563. "There's Scott's Emulsion!" Evans, interviewed by JU, winter 1962 and winter 1968.

564. "DON'T WORRY . . ." Zell Deming to HC, unpub.

564. "I've just reread . . ." Nov. 20, 1928, unpub.

565. "I feel very sorry . . ." HC to Zell Deming, quoted in Horton, as "early in November" [1928], 248–49.

566. "If I let . . ." Solomon Grunberg interviewed by JU, Sept. 1960. Following material is drawn from subsequent interviews in 1960, 1961, 1962, and spring 1966 (NET transcription).

568. "Atlantis." see Horton 251.

568. "Grace will . . ." quoted in Horton 250.

568. "I hope . . ." Dec. 1, 1928, pt. pub. L 330–31. Material concerning events of these days also supplied in JU interview with Lorna Dietz, 1961, and Walker Evans, 1961.

569. "The party . . ." SL interviewed by JU, 1961.

570. "First of all . . ." Feb. 26, 1929, pub. L 336-38.

572. "My dear Sam:—" Jan. 24, 1929 [misdated by Grace, Jan. 24, 1928], unpub.

573. "My dear friend Sam:—" Feb. 18, 1929, unpub.

CHAPTER 31

575. "Ahoy Sam!" Dec. 9, 1928, pub. L 331.

575. "all of them . . ." HC to C von W, near Christmas, '28 [probably Dec. 16], pub. L 332.

575. "Some of the people . . ." near Christmas, '28 [probably Dec. 16], unpub.

575. "One old squire," near Christmas, '28 [probably Dec. 16], pub. L 332.

575. "The whiskey . . ." Dec. 9, 1928, pub. L 331.

575. "You must excuse . . ." near Christmas, '28 [probably Dec. 16], pub. L 332.

576. "I *would* be given . . ." HC to SL, Dec. 9, 1928, pub. L 331.

576. "The trip . . ." HC to WSB, near Christmas, '28 [probably Dec. 16], unpub.

576. "My performance . . ." HC to C von W, near Christmas, '28 [probably Dec. 16], pub. L 332.

576. "dress breeches" HC to WSB, near Christmas, '28 [probably Dec. 16], unpub.

576. "Today is like . . ." HC to SL, Monday [Dec. 17, 1928; misdated Dec. 13 in L 332, where it is pub.].

576. "incipient flu" HC to WF, Dec. 28, 1928, pub. L 332-33.

576. "the most unique . . ." [Dec. 25, 1928], unpub.

576. "at Hammersmith . . ." HC to WF, Dec. 28, 1928, pub. L 333.

577. "great affection" see Horton 253 ff.

577. "London, I can still . . ." May 1, 1929, pub. L 341.

577. "No snow here . . ." Dec. 28, 1928, pub. L 333.

577. "Expecting . . ." HC to Isidor Schneider, May 1, 1929, pub. L 341.

577. "dangerous" HC to CR and RR, Feb. 26, 1929, pub. L 338.'

577. "incredibly free . . ." HC to SL, Jan. 8, 1929, unpub.

578. "I've met . . ." Caresse Crosby, interviewed by JU, 1961.

578. ". . . there were people . . ." Harry Crosby, *Shadows of the Sun* (Paris: Black Sun Press, 1930), 6; following passages from 7, 8.

579. "Dinners . . ." Jan. 23, 1929, pub. L 333.

579. *"transition . . ."* Jan. 24, 1929, pub. L 334.

579. "They were both . . ." interview, 1962.

580. "'Teas' are all . . ." Feb. 4, 1929, pub. L 335, where the word "all" is accidentally dropped from this sentence.

580. "Hart was never . . ." interview with JU, 1961.

580. "Hart Crane for luncheon . . ." *Shadows of the Sun*, 10.

580. "Have just returned . . ." HC to MC, Feb. 4, 1929, pub. L 335.

580. "Le Moulin . . ." *Shadows of the Sun*, 12.

581. "new atrocities . . ." HC to MC, Feb. 4, 1929, pt.pub. L 335.

581. "Tuesday afternoon . . ." Gertrude Stein to HC, Feb. 3, 1929, unpub.

581. "One is supposed . . ." HC to WF, Feb. 7, 1929, pub. L 336.

581. "He was always . . ." interviewed by JU, 1961.

581. "Hart Crane came . . ." *Shadows of the Sun*, 13.

581. "For I haven't . . ." Feb. 7, 1929, pub. L 335-36.

582. "Snowstorm . . ." *Shadows of the Sun*, 13.

582. "I'm out here . . ." Feb. 13, 1929, unpub.

583. "Salutations . . ." Feb. 17, 1929, unpub.

583. "Yes, how can one help . . ." Feb. 17, 1929, unpub.

584. "YES AND HOW . . ." Feb. 17, 1929, unpub.

584. "I'm quite mad . . ." Feb. 26, 1929, pt.pub. L 336-39.

584. "Water Boy! . . ." Feb. 19, 1929, unpub.

584. "five days out there . . ." HC to CR and RR, Feb. 26, 1929, pub. L 339.

584. "the blackest . . ." Caresse Crosby, *The Passionate Years* (New York: Dial Press, 1953), 238.

584. "Columbia, loud tone!!!!" HC to Harry Crosby, undated [Feb. 1929], unpub.

585. "I've never been . . ." Feb. 26, 1929, pub. L 338.

585. "Yes, I'm longing . . ." Sunday [Feb. 24, 1929], unpub.

585. "Party on the Boat·. . ." *Shadows of the Sun*, 14.

585. "clean enamel frames of death" transcribed from manuscript presented to Harry Crosby, Feb. 27, 1929. See *transition*, I, 1 (Apr. 1927), 101-2; *Poetry*, Vol. 31, No. 1 (Oct. 1927), 30.

586. "Paris First of March 1929 . . ." unpub.

586. "To-day drank sherry . . ." *Shadows of the Sun*, 15.
587. "I adore . . ." undated [probably late Feb. or early Mar. 1929], unpub.
587. "Stop!" Caresse Crosby interviewed by JU, 1961.
587. "that damned hotel," HC to Harry and Caresse Crosby, Mar. 13 [1929], unpub.
588. "He put an ordinary . . ." Willard Widney interviewed by JU, 1962.
588. "About the poet Burns . . ." I asked Malcolm Cowley if he recalled these as limericks by Crane. He answered: "I *think* Hart wrote them; all his limericks were concerned with literary figures, mostly poets. I also think he wrote a better known limerick:

Said the poetess Sappho of Greece,
"Ah, better by far than a piece
Is to have my pudenda
Rubbed hard by the enda
The little pink nose of my niece."

The difficulty in this case is that the limerick *did* appear in Norman Douglas's anthology of dirty ones, printed in 1928 or thereabouts. But still I'm almost certain that Hart repeated it as his own, which he wouldn't have done if it weren't. Limericks travel fast, and there's no reason why Norman Douglas shouldn't have heard it."
588. "Am feeling too bum . . ." HC to Harry Crosby, undated, unpub.
589. "I hear from Kay Boyle . . ." Apr. 13 [1929], unpub.
589. "Am leaving . . ." Friday [Apr. 19, 1929], unpub.
589. "I wanted to say . . ." Apr. 23 [1929], unpub.
589. "Your suggestion . . ." Apr. 25, 1929, unpub.
590. ". . . I've been late . . ." May 1, 1929, pt.pub. L 340–42.
591. "First impressions . . ." HC to Harry and Caresse Crosby, Apr. 22, 1929, unpub.
591. "Nightingales . . ." HC to SL, Apr. 23, 1929, pub. L 339.
591. "I'm beginning to feel . . ." Apr. 25, 1929, unpub.
591. "Living at . . ." HC to Harry Crosby, May 16, 1929, unpub.
591. "Every nook, corner . . ." Apr. 25, 1929, unpub.
592. "Why the hell . . ." Apr. 25, 1929, pub. L 339, BL 1005.
592. "There has been . . ." Apr. 29, 1929, pub. L 340.
592. "As for Paris . . ." May 1, 1929, pt.pub. L 341–42.

593. "Six bulls . . ." HC to Harry Crosby, May 6, 1929, unpub.
593. "Marseille is . . ." HC to Harry Crosby, May 16, 1929, unpub.
594. Marsden Hartley . . . For details about Hart Crane's relationship with Hartley see Hartley's unpub. "The Spangle of Existence." A copy is on file in the Museum of Modern Art library.
594. "Swimming isn't . . ." June 11, 1929, pub. L 342. Campbell, in his autobiography, mentions that one reason for his soon leaving Martigues was the local reaction to his guest Hart Crane, who had been a bit much for the provincial French citizens. Crane himself, in an unpub. letter to Campbell, recalled their "hectic nights of universal confession." (July 12, 1929, collection of Southern Illinois University library.)
595. "When I come . . ." HC to MC, July 3, 1929, pub. L 343.
595. "Hart Crane back . . ." Harry Crosby, *Shadows of the Sun*, 39.
595. "wonderful," HC to Harry Crosby [postmarked June 7, 1929], unpub.
595. "A thick fog . . ." HC to Harry and Caresse Crosby, July 1 [1929], unpub.
595. "The Crosbys . . ." July 3, 1929, pt.pub. L 343.
596. "I felt toward the end . . ." interview. MacCown's recollection was collected by me in a 1963 interview.
596. "Madame Select," see Horton's account, 258–60. Other information drawn from Harry Crosby, *Shadows of the Sun*, interviews with Eugene MacCown and Willard A. Widney, and from newspaper accounts of the events.
597. "To the Black Sun Press . . ." *Shadows of the Sun*, 41–42.
598. "Want to make . . ." Willard Widney interviewed by JU.
598. "Hart appeared rather . . ." Harry Crosby, *Shadows of the Sun*, 43.

CHAPTER 32

600. "Please ask Harry . . ." Aug. 8, 1929, pub. L 344.
600. "He wasn't any good . . ." SL interviewed by JU, 1962.
600. "I must add . . ." July 7, 1929, unpub.
600. "smooth as castor oil . . ." HC to Harry Crosby, July 23, 1929, unpub.
601. "Hope you didn't . . ." Sept. 30, 1929, unpub.

601. "POET SEES . . ." *The New York Times*, July 11, 1929, 5.
601. "I can't help thinking . . ." Aug. 8, 1929, pub. L 343.
602. "I'm passionately anxious . . ." Aug. 30, 1929, pub. L 344–45.
602. "Machine Age section" Paul Rosenfeld to HC, Sept. 10, 1929, unpub.
602. "two final sections" HC to Caresse Crosby, Sept. 30 [1929], unpub.
602. "I have more . . ." Sept. 6, 1929, pub. L 345.
603. "I forgot to include . . ." HC to Caresse Crosby, Sept. 6, 1929, pub. L 346.
603. "fevers of work" HC to Caresse Crosby, Sept. 6, 1929, pub. L 345.
603. "I sent you . . ." HC to Caresse Crosby, Sept. 17, 1929, pub. L 346.
603. "emergency" interviews with Walker Evans, Lorna Dietz, SL, and WSB, 1961, 1962.
604. "HAVE BEEN ILL . . ." Oct. 17, 1929, unpub.
604. "I was a wreck . . ." Tuesday [Oct. 22, 1929], unpub.
604. "I've been . . ." HC to Lorna Dietz, Wednesday [Oct. 23, 1929], pt.pub. L 347.
605. "You come home . . ." reported to me by Mrs. W. D. Hise (Mrs. Bessie Crane) in 1961 interview.
605. "DEFER PUBLICATION . . ." Oct. 30, 1929, unpub.
605. "I really do want . . ." Oct. 29, 1929, unpub.
606. "This turns out . . ." [postmarked Nov. 11, 1929], unpub.
606. "Father's collection . . ." [postmarked Nov. 11, 1929], unpub.
606. "Girls . . ." Mrs. Hise interviewed by JU, 1961.
607. "I have very little . . ." Nov. 26, 1929, unpub.
608. Peter Blume . . . see Horton 264.
609. "Give me your hand . . ." Caresse Crosby, *The Passionate Years*, 249 ff. The mystery of Harry Crosby's suicide was reported in the New York newspapers for several days. Details concerning it have been assembled from my several interviews with Margaret Babcock (Robson) and Caresse Crosby. See also Cowley, *Exile's Return*, 282 ff.
610. "We rushed out . . ." Margaret Babcock, taped interview with JU, June 12, 1963.
610. "I've been all broken up . . ." Dec. 14, 1929, unpub.
610. "The evening when . . ." HC to CR, Feb. 11, 1930, pub. L 348.

611. "I am hastily . . ." HC to Caresse Crosby, Dec. 26, 1929, pub. L 347.

CHAPTER 33

612. "Harried . . ." HC to WW, Nov. 21, 1930, pt.pub. L 357–58.
612. "I hope you will . . ." HC to B—— ——, Horton 298. Copy of full note at Yale University.
612. "sailed away . . ." Jan. 2, 1930, unpub.
613. "I had a sweet . . ." HC to Caresse Crosby, Feb. 8 [1930], unpub.
613. "You haven't gotten," B—— —— to HC, Mar. 16, 1930, unpub.
613. "a former sailor . . ." HC to Caresse Crosby, May 13, 1930, unpub.
614. "I'm not at my best . . ." HC to Caresse Crosby, Jan. 22, 1930, unpub.
614. "I really don't . . ." HC to CR, Feb. 11, 1930, pub. L 349.
614. "welcome encouragement" Mar. 10, 1930, unpub.
614. "It was *so* kind . . ." Mar. 16 [1930], pub. L 349.
615. "Hart, I am really . . ." Caresse Crosby to HC, Apr. 3 [1930], unpub.
615. "I thought of you . . ." HC to Caresse Crosby, Apr. 19, 1930, unpub.
617. "I am still having . . ." Feb. 8 [1930], unpub.
617. "I danced . . ." SL interviewed by JU, Aug. 4, 1962 (Oral History files).
617. "amazing" HC to Caresse Crosby, Jan. 15, 1930, unpub.
617. "wonderful! . . ." HC to CR, Feb. 11, 1930, pub. L 349.
617. "reverential" interviewed (phone) by JU, 1963.
617. "I thought of him," interviewed 1966 (NET transcription).
619. "The poetry of . . ." Herbert Weinstock, review of *The Bridge*, Milwaukee *Journal*, Apr. 12, 1930.
619. "Long essays could be . . ." Granville Hicks, "The Rediscovery of America," review of *The Bridge* in *The Nation*, Vol. 130, No. 3382 (Apr. 30, 1930), 520–21.
619. "It cannot be doubted . . ." Granville Hicks, "Hart Crane Scales New Poetic Heights in 'The Bridge,' " review in the New York *World, Book World*, 10M.
619. "A set of . . ." Vol. VI (June 14, 1930), 1125.
619. "in other sections . . ." "Far Beyond Our Consciousness," Apr. 20, 1930, Section XI, 4.
619. "concrete threnody" "Crane's

'Bridge' Mighty Symbol of the Nation," Apr. 19, 1930, M11.

619. "one of the important . . ." Vol. 62 (Apr. 23, 1930), 276–77.

620. "too great haphazardness . . ." Vol. 6 (July 5, 1930), 1176.

620. "a unified group . . ." in *The New Republic* review, 276.

620. "lack of intelligibility." Apr. 27, 1930, 2.

620. "thought-process" Vol. 72 (Sept. 1930), 86–87.

620. "I cannot but . . ." June 8, 1930, pt.pub. L 352.

621. "I have read . . ." unpub.

621. "a coherent plot . . ." "A Distinguished Poet," *Hound and Horn*, III, 4 (July-Sept. 1930), 580–85.

622. "Your last good . . ." July 13, 1930, pub. L 352–54.

CHAPTER 34

625. "doldrums" HC to Solomon Grunberg, Sept. 30, 1930, pub. L 356.

625. "My summer seems . . ." Sept. 7, 1930, pub. L 355–56.

625. "I hope you have had," July 16, 1930, unpub.

626. "I take my pen . . ." Howard P. Lovecraft to Mrs. F. C. Clark, unpub.

626. "There's no liquor" Apr. 21 [1930], pub. L 350.

626. "After a couple . . ." Apr. 29, 1930, unpub.

627. "When I visited . . ." interviewed 1962.

627. "How I'd love . . ." Mar. 16, 1930, unpub.

627. "barren . . . harried" HC to WW, Apr. 29, 1930, unpub.

627. "I remember . . ." Apr. 19, 1930, unpub.

627. "I'm awfully sorry . . ." May 13, 1930, unpub.

628. "I think . . ." Solomon Grunberg interviewed by JU. Grunberg's recollection is supported also by similar recollections by WSB and SJB.

628. "Hives Tomato Juice" interviews with Margaret Babcock, 1963 and 1966 (NET transcription of the latter).

629. "Two days with . . ." Sunday [probably June 1, 1930], unpub.

629. "It's so lovely . . ." Tuesday [probably June 3, 1930], unpub.

629. "Peggy has been up . . ." unpub.

629. "Are you having . . ." HC to Lorna Dietz, June 17, 1930, unpub. Buff was a collie dog. The long dash in this quotation is Crane's.

629. "There were three . . ." July 13, 1930, pt.pub. L 352–54.

630. "I've been meaning . . ." July 12 [1930], unpub.

630. "I had to take him in," Pauline Turkel interviewed by JU, 1963; Emil Opffer interviewed by JU, 1963. See also Cowley, "The Leopard . . ." *Esquire* (Oct. 1958), 270.

630. "In reading Philip Horton's . . ." interviewed 1966 (NET transcription).

631. "Here are a multitude . . ." HC to SL, July 12 [1930], unpub.

631. "We'll have the neighborhood . . ." HC to Lorna Dietz, Thursday [probably July 17, 1930], unpub.

631. "I don't mind . . ." July 16, 1930, unpub.

631. "My dear Hart . . ." July 19, 1930, unpub.

632. "And haven't I been . . ." Sept. 7, 1930, unpub.

633. "less precariously" HC to WW, Nov. 21, 1930, pt.pub. L 357–58.

633. "looking for the needles . . ." Sept. 30, 1930, HC to Solomon Grunberg, pub. L 356.

633. "From the sales . . ." HC to WW, Apr. 29, 1930, unpub.

633. "It's gone into . . ." Sept. 30, 1930, pub. L 356.

634. "a year's study . . ." Nov. 21, 1930, pub. L 358.

634. "My application . . ." HC, on application form supplied by the John Simon Guggenheim Memorial Foundation, dated Aug. 27, 1930.

636. "Your generous . . ." Nov. 12, 1930, unpub.

636. "Oh, he is elegant!" Margaret Babcock (Robson) interviewed by JU, 1963.

636. "New York is full . . ." Nov. 21, 1930, pub. L 357.

637. "He kept phoning" interviewed 1966 (NET transcription).

637. "The Teagle article . . ." Nov. 29, 1930, pub. L 359.

637. "As things turned out . . ." Tuesday [probably Dec. 16, 1930], unpub.

638. "Your imagination . . ." Nov. 29, 1930, pub. L 358–59.

CHAPTER 35

639. "New York . . ." Jan. 9, 1931, unpub.

639. "I got terribly . . ." Jan. 10 [1931], pub. L 363.

639. "For about . . ." Dec. 29, 1930, pub. L 360.

640. "All sorts of arrangements . . ." HC to WW, Tuesday [probably Dec. 16, 1930], unpub.

640. "To make partial . . ." Dec. 29, 1930, pt.pub. L 359–60.
640. "apprenticeship . . ." HC to Lorna Dietz, Feb. 10, 1931, pub. L 365.
641. "My father and his wife . . ." Jan. 16, 1931, pt.pub. L 363–65.
641. "one of [the] best . . ." Jan. 10 [1931], pub. L 363.
641. "Don't wonder . . ." HC to SL, Feb. 16, 1931, unpub.
641. "it's almost as full . . ." Feb. 10, 1931, pub. L 366.
641. "When I listen . . ." Feb. 16, 1931, unpub.
642. "Once a week . . ." Feb. 10, 1931, pub. L 365.
642. "What a queer . . ." HC to Solomon Grunberg, Feb. 25, 1931, unpub.
642. "Discussions . . ." HC to Lorna Dietz, Feb. 10, 1931, pub. L 366.
642. "No writing . . ." HC to Solomon Grunberg, Jan. 10 [1931], pub. L 363.
642. "These are . . ." Feb. 19 [1931], pub. L 366.
643. "I'm looking forward . . ." Feb. 10, 1931, pt.pub. L 365–66.
643. "I'm enclosing . . ." Jan. 14, 1931, unpub.
643. "I am so pleased . . ." Nov. 21, 1930, pub. L 357.
644. "Present day America . . ." HC to WF, Feb. 19 [1931], pub. L 366.
644. "What struck . . ." HC to SL, Jan. 16, 1931, pub. L 364.
644. "A particularly . . ." HC to Solomon Grunberg, Jan. 21 [1931], unpub.
644. "identical conceptions . . ." HC to WW, Jan. 14, 1931, unpub.
644. "primitive efforts . . ." HC to Solomon Grunberg, Jan. 21, 1931, unpub.
644. "This blacksmith . . ." HC to SL, Jan. 16, 1931, pub. L 364.
644. "Archeological . . ." HC to WW, Jan. 14, 1931, unpub.
644. "on the water . . ." Feb. 19 [1931], pub. L 366.
645. "My father . . ." Jan. 10 [1931], pub. L 363.
645. "If abstinence . . ." HC to WF, Feb. 19 [1931], pub. L 366.
645. "If I'm lucky," Jan. 9, 1931, unpub.
645. "No, I haven't yet . . ." Feb. 16, 1931, unpub.
646. "I admit . . ." Feb. 25, 1931, unpub.
646. "possible royalties." HC to Henry Allen Moe, Mar. 4, 1931, unpub.
646. "My appointment . . ." pt.pub. L 367.

646. "Goodbye! . . ." reconstructed from recollections of RR and Bess Crane (Mrs. W. D. Hise) in 1962 interviews with JU.

CHAPTER 36

648. "warmth and thoughtfulness" all quotations that follow are from MC, "The Leopard . . ." 270–71.
650. "He was drawn . . ." interviewed 1966 (NET transcription).
651. "I am sailing . . ." Mar. 30 [1931], pub. L 367.
651. "I wish I had . . ." Apr. 29 [1931], quoted to me in a letter from Margaret Babcock of June 13, 1963.
652. "I'm sailing," Apr. 3, 1931, unpub.
652. "It's a nice trip," Apr. 6 [1931], unpub.
652. "I'm losing no time . . ." Apr. 5, 1931, unpub.
652. "There are magnificent . . ." [postmarked Apr. 7, 1931], unpub.
653. "Zinsser, a product . . ." Apr. 12, 1931, pub. L 368.
653. "much charm." Hans Zinsser, *As I Remember Him* (Boston: Little, Brown & Co., 1940), 335.
653. "loaded with . . ." Apr. 12, 1931, pub. L 368.
653. "He spent . . ." Zinsser 335.
653. "No more paper . . ." [postmarked Apr. 7, 1931], unpub.
654. "Two of our . . ." Zinsser 336–39.
655. "one night in Vera Cruz . . ." HC to SL, Apr. 12, 1931, pub. L 368–69.
656. "As the above . . ." Apr. 12 [1931], unpub.
656. "Sunday dinner . . ." HC to SL, Apr. 12, 1931, pt.pub. L 368.

CHAPTER 37

658. "come to Mexico . . ." Apr. 15 [1931], unpub.
658. "I tried to take care . . ." Katherine Anne Porter, "A Country and Some People I Love" [interview with Hank Lopez], *Harper's*, Vol. 231, No. 1384 (Sept. 1965), 67.
659. "a sourish gentleman . . ." HC to Lorna Dietz, July 15, 1931, pt. pub. L 377–79.
659. "Sober, he tried . . ." quoted in Horton 286–87.
660. "informal memorandum" a note prepared by Nathaniel Lancaster, Jr., for the Consul General, copy sent to Eyler Simpson, dated Apr. 27, 1931.
661. "He used to drop . . ." Zinsser 339.
661. "DEAR KATHERINE ANNE . . ."

HC to Katherine Anne Porter [Apr. 28, 1931], pt.pub. L 369.

661. "This is as near . . ." [Apr. 30, 1931], pub. L 369.

661. "mutual interest" Apr. 30, 1931, unpub.

661. "I received your letter . . ." May 1, 1931, unpub.

662. "Darling Katherine Anne . . ." [May 1, 1931], pt.pub. L 369–70.

662. "Guest here recently . . ." [postmarked May 14, 1931], unpub.

662. "Moisés has been . . ." June 2, 1931, pt.pub. L 370.

663. "great Yankee . . ." translated from the interview printed in the Spanish language newspaper *Excelsior*, clipping enclosed in letter of June 13, 1931, HC to WF. I am grateful to Kathleen McGrory for this and all other translations from the Spanish.

663. "A few days . . ." June 13, 1931, pub. L 372.

663. "angelic face" quoted matter translated from a letter, León Felipe to JU, of June 3, 1961.

664. "Since he found me . . ." HC WF, June 13, 1931, pub. L 373, 372, 371.

665. "Let us strip . . ." In the 1966 ed. of *The Complete Poems*, Brom Weber has revised the text to conform to a manuscript that has "horse" rather than "house" in the opening line. I think that the version in the earlier *Collected Poems* (WF ed.) and in *Poetry* (Vol. 41 [Jan. 1933], 180–82) is closer to Crane's intent. Crane was as capable as the next man of making a typographical error. Since everything in the poem is autobiographical, it's worth noting that Crane neither owned nor rented a Mexican horse, though—as we know—he did rent his house, almost certainly just before he wrote this poem. As Crane would probably also note, were he here to comment on the new edition, more desks are in houses than in horses.

665. "I am far from having . . ." May 11, 1931, unpub.

665. "villages, rug factories . . ." June 5, 1931, unpub.

665. "How this city . . ." [postmarked May 14, 1931], unpub.

665. "the gentle light-fingered . . ." May 11, 1931, unpub.

666. "presumably with additions . . ." Morton Dauwen Zabel to HC, June 11, 1931, unpub.

666. "Am planning . . ." May 23, 1931, unpub.

666. "garden, flowers . . ." HC to

Solomon Grunberg [postmarked May 9, 1931], unpub.

666. "Plenty of . . ." HC to Tom R. Smith, May 11, 1931, unpub.

666. "surprise visit" 1962 interview.

667. "Your letter . . ." CAC to Hazel Cazes, May 18, 1931, unpub.

667. "I am very grateful . . ." CAC to Hazel Cazes, June 2, 1931, unpub.

667. "In this morning's . . ." June 2, 1931, unpub.

667. "Regarding money . . ." June 5, 1931, unpub.

668. "favorite corner . . ." HC to Morton Dauwen Zabel, June 20, 1931, pub. L 374.

669. "pretenders to poesy . . ." HC to MC, June 2, 1931, pt.pub. L 370–71.

670. "The evening before . . ." Horton 285–86.

671. "To begin with the same . . ." July 15, 1931, pt.pub. L 377–78.

672. "Dear Katherine Anne . . ." [June 22, 1931], pt.pub. L 375–76.

673. "Stories about Hart's . . ." from a statement prepared for Philip Horton by Lesley Byrd Simpson, dated June 6, 1936, and made available to me by Simpson on Aug. 9, 1961.

674. "Mr. Crane can write . . ." Henry Allen Moe to Eyler Simpson, June 29, 1931, unpub.

674. "As you know . . ." June 29, 1931, unpub.

675. "My dear Harold . . ." June 29, 1931, unpub.

676. "The point about . . ." July 7, 1931, unpub.

677. "Due to the . . ." unpub.

677. "Dear Mr. Moe . . ." unpub.

CHAPTER 38

678. "He suddenly had . . ." Dec. 7, 1931 [misdated 1932], unpub.

678. "I'm so glad . . ." HC to Solomon Grunberg, Oct. 20, 1931, unpub.

678. "better and truer" HC to Lorna Dietz, July 15, 1931, pub. L 379.

678. "fine qualities" HC to WW, July 15, 1931, pub. L 377.

679. "I'm here . . ." July 15 [1931], pub. BL 1010–11.

679. "I'm more impressed . . ." July 15, 1931, pub. L 378–79.

679. "I've been in . . ." July 29, 1931, unpub.

680. "My deep sympathy . . ." July 15, 1931, unpub.

680. "within six weeks . . ." July 22, 1931, unpub.

680. "Does anyone know . . ." July 24, 1931, unpub.

681. "a few days . . ." HC to Margaret Robson [Babcock], July 29, 1931, unpub.

682. "getting more and more . . ." Aug. 14 [1931], unpub.

682. "deadly . . . needle beer" HC to Solomon Grunberg, Oct. 20, 1931, unpub.

683. "I happened to meet . . ." 1966 interview (NET transcription).

683. "Katherine Anne upset" HC to Malcolm Cowley, Oct. 5, 1931, pub. L 383.

683. "I'm not upset . . ." Nov. 17 [1931], pub. L 388.

684. "When I left New York . . ." Oct. 20, 1931, unpub.

684. "I've become . . ." interviewed 1961.

CHAPTER 39

685. "The servants . . ." HC to SL, Sept. 11, 1931, pt.pub. L 379–80.

685. "awfully diffident" Sept. 21, 1931, pub. L 380.

685. "A beautiful Sunday" HC to Bess Crane (Mrs. Hise) [Oct. 4, 1931?], unpub.

686. "You should see . . ." Oct. 20, 1931, unpub.

686. "Really, you'd be . . ." HC to Bess Crane (Mrs. Hise), Oct. 20, 1931, unpub.

687. "With a bottle . . ." Oct. 20, 1931, unpub.

687. "I've had some nice . . ." Nov. 4, 1931, pub. L 385.

688. "would take a book." Oct. 20, 1931, unpub.

688. "The nature of . . ." Nov. 30 [1931], pub. L 390.

688. "We very often speak . . ." Aug. 13 [1931], unpub.

688. "Hart's year . . ." Mary Doherty to Henry Allen Moe, Sept. 11, 1932, unpub.

689. "the most interesting . . ." HC to WW, Sept. 21, 1931, pub. L 380.

689. "I have had . . ." HC to SL, Sept. 11, 1931, pt.pub. L 378–80.

690. "amounted to five . . ." HC to Helen and Griswold Hurlbert, Sept. 20, 1931, unpub.

690. "From the town," HC to Bess Crane (Mrs. Hise) [Sept. 18, 1931?], unpub.

692. "barbaric service" HC to WW, Sept. 21, 1931, pub. L 381.

692. "During the day . . ." HC to Bess Crane (Mrs. Hise) [Sept. 18, 1931?], unpub.

692. "a generous infusion . . ." HC to WW, Sept. 21, 1931, pub. L 382–83.

693. "You can't imagine . . ." HC to Bess Crane (Mrs. Hise) [Sept. 18, 1931?], unpub.

693. "still has fragments . . ." HC to WW, Sept. 21, 1931, pub. L 383.

CHAPTER 40

694. "full of Aztec . . ." HC to Solomon Grunberg [postmarked Sept. 24, 1931], unpub.

694. "astounding" HC to CR and RR, Nov. 4, 1931, pub. L 384–85.

695. "The first time . . ." Lesley Byrd Simpson statement of June 6, 1936, unpub.

696. "Sorry not . . ." HC to Peggy Cowley, Monday [between Sept. 15 and Nov. 15, 1931], unpub.

696. "He and I . . ." Peggy Baird, "The Last Days of Hart Crane," *Venture*, IV, 1 (1961), 21.

696. "3 large" HC to Bess Crane (Mrs. Hise), undated [Oct. 4, 1931?], unpub.

696. "Bill Spratling . . ." Oct. 5, 1931, pub. L 383.

697. "just extravagant . . ." Oct. 20, 1931, unpub.

697. "They were pimps," PBC, "The Last Days . . ." 22–23.

697. "a queer . . ." Lesley Byrd Simpson, statement of June 6, 1936, unpub.

698. "A sudden cold spell . . ." Nov. 5, 1931, unpub.

699. "full of darkskinned . . ." HC to CR and RR, Nov. 4, 1931, pub. L 385.

699. "half relapse" HC to SL, Nov. 17 [1931], pub. L 386.

699. "Haven't heard . . ." HC to Solomon Grunberg [postmarked Nov. 10, 1931], pub. L 386.

699. "mutterings . . ." statement of June 6, 1931, unpub.

700. "Mexicans would judge . . ." PBC, "The Last Days . . ." 22–23.

700. "At the end . . ." statement of June 6, 1936, unpub.

700. "Dear Peggy . . ." HC to PBC, Nov. 13 [probably misdated; following letter suggests this is Nov. 11, 1931], pub. L 386.

700. "I don't know . . ." HC to PBC, Thursday [Nov. 12, 1931], pt.pub. L 386.

701. "dancing, *tequila* . . ." HC to SL, Nov. 17 [1931], pub. L 386–87.

701. "Hart's attachment . . ." statement of June 6, 1936, unpub.

702. "Am fedup . . ." Nov. 20, 1931, unpub.

702. "It's been something . . ." Nov. 23 [1931], pt.pub. L 388–89.

703. "I must admit . . ." Nov. 27, 1931, pub. L 389.

703. "Putnam is more . . ." HC to

Morton Dauwen Zabel [post-marked Oct. 10, 1931], pub. L 384.

703. "rip off expletives . . ." HC to Solomon Grunberg, Oct. 20, 1931, unpub.

704. "With masts . . ." quoted by HC from James Whaler, *Green River: A Poem for Rafinesque* (New York: Harcourt, Brace and Co., 1931), in his review in *Poetry*, Vol. 40 (Apr. 1932), 44–47.

704. "I am hopeful . . ." N. Byron Madden to HC, Aug. 17, 1931, unpub.

704. "For all these . . ." N. Byron Madden to HC, Oct. 19, 1931, unpub.

705. "I'm somewhat upset . . ." Oct. 20, 1931, unpub.

705. "That is as far . . ." Bess Crane (Mrs. Hise) to HC, Oct. 26, 1931, unpub.

705. "I am hopeful . . ." Bess Crane (Mrs. Hise) to HC, Nov. 9, 1931, unpub.

706. "Of course . . ." Nov. 17 [1931], pub. L 387.

706. "I made the mistake . . ." HC to Mrs. S, Dec. 7, 1931 [misdated 1932], unpub.

707. "There is a distinct . . ." pub. L 390–92.

708. "as aromatic . . ." HC to Mrs. Wright, Dec. 7, 1931, unpub.

709. "My own dear Harold . . ." Mrs. N. Byron Madden to HC, undated [Dec., 1931], unpub.

709. "We're going . . ." "Dot" to HC, Dec. 9, 1931, unpub.

709. "Am spending . . ." Ethel Clark to HC, Dec. 16, 1931, unpub.

709. "The girls all insist . . ." Sept. 8, 1931, unpub.

709. "All your women . . ." Oct. 3, 1931, unpub.

709. "Your jolly letter . . ." Oct. 20, 1931, unpub.

709. "You know if it gets . . ." Nov. 9, 1931, unpub. The "chain letter" reference is in her unpub. letter of Oct. 26, 1931.

709. "I haven't heard . . ." Dec. 12, 1931, pt.pub. L 392.

710. "My dear Harold . . ." Bess Crane (Mrs. Hise) to HC, unpub.

CHAPTER 41

712. "The señor comes! . . ." PBC, "The Last Days . . ." 24–26.

713. "Well, about Christmas . . ." Jan. 9, 1932, unpub.

714. "the pleasantest . . ." Jan. 9, 1932, pt.pub. L 393–94.

715. "After seeing . . ." PBC, "The Last Days . . ." 26–27.

716. "Boys," William Spratling interviewed by JU, 1961.

716. "New Year's Eve . . ." Jan. 9, 1932, unpub.

716. "He was in love . . ." PBC, "The Last Days . . ." 28.

717. "I can conceive . . ." GHC to SL, Friday, the thirteenth [May 13, 1932], unpub.

717. "January 6 . . ." pt.pub. L 292–93.

717. "Thursday . . ." unpub.

718. "Tuesday . . ." unpub.

719. "Wednesday . . ." pt.pub. L 394–95.

720. "I was willing . . ." PBC, "The Last Days . . ." 28.

720. "I went" HC to PBC, Tuesday [Jan. 12, 1932], unpub.

720. "DAMN" HC to PBC, Jan. 6 [1932], pub. L 393.

721. "Your Christmas gift . . ." [Jan. 15, 1932], pub. L 395.

721. "enthralled" James Oppenheim to HC, Jan. 15, 1932, unpub.

721. "One white cat . . ." PBC, "The Last Days . . ." 30–31.

722. "I was with . . ." Lesley Byrd Simpson, "The Late Hart Crane," *The New English Weekly*, I, 22 (Sept. 15, 1932), 531.

723. "went down . . ." PBC, "The Last Days . . ." 31.

723. "Everything . . ." all three telegrams unpub.

723. "scrape" information about the jailing from William Spratling, interviewed by JU, 1961.

724. "made free . . ." statement of June 6, 1936, unpub.

724. "We arranged . . ." PBC, "The Last Days . . ." 31–32.

724. "The taxi . . ." 1966 interview (NET transcription).

724. "What a stink . . ." PBC, "The Last Days . . ." 32.

724. "Must have been pretty . . ." 1966 interview (NET transcription).

725. "Tears streamed . . ." PBC, "The Last Days . . ." 32.

725. "You must tell me . . ." Feb. 11, 1932, unpub.

725. "As usual . . ." Feb. 8, 1932, pub. L 395–96.

726. "I hope you will not . . ." Feb. 23 [1932], unpub.

726. "Do you know . . ." Feb. 26, 1932, unpub.

726. "Sr. Daniel . . ." HC to PBC, Feb. 10 [1932], pub. L 396–97.

727. "I was so tremulous . . ." Feb. 11 [1932], pub. L 397–98.

727. "with a little . . ." Feb. 10 [1932], pub. L 396.

728. "I worked late . . ." HC to PBC,

Tuesday [Feb. 23, 1932?], pub. L 401.

728. "I miss you a lot . . ." HC to PBC, Feb. 10 [1932], pub. L 397.

728. "I want things . . ." HC to PBC, Tuesday [Feb. 23, 1932?], pub. L 402.

728. "Of course I'm anxious . . ." HC to PBC, Feb. 11 [1932], pub. L 398.

729. "I'm afraid I'm getting . . ." Feb. 10, 1932, unpub.

729. "Dear Peggy . . ." Feb. 13 [1932], pub. L 398–99.

729. "But, really . . ." HC to PBC, Feb. 16 [1932], pt.pub. L 399–400.

730. "This room . . ." Feb. 17, 1932, pt.pub. L 402–3.

731. "You are right . . ." Feb. 26, 1932, unpub.

731. "I'll make you . . ." PBC, "The Last Days . . ." 34.

732. "Dear Lotte & Ricardo . . ." unpub.

#### CHAPTER 42

733. "I don't feel like . . ." Mar. 8, 1932, unpub.

734. "Rather amazing things . . ." Mar. 10, 1932, pt.pub. L 403.

734. "Yes, Bess . . ." HC to Bess Crane (Mrs. Hise), Mar. 8, 1932, unpub.

735. "Another guest . . ." PBC, "The Last Days . . ." 34.

735. "veriest nonsense." Lesley Byrd Simpson statement of June 6, 1936, unpub.

736. "Will you please . . ." Mar. 15, 1932, unpub.

736. "One night about ten . . ." Lesley Byrd Simpson statement of June 6, 1936, unpub.

737. "Moroseness . . ." PBC, "The Last Days . . ." 36. Her comments on his concern for the reception of "The Broken Tower" from her interviews with me in 1962 and 1966.

737. "Carleton Beals . . ." Lesley Byrd Simpson statement of June 6, 1936, unpub.

738. "It has passages . . ." Mar. 20, 1932, pub. L 404–5.

739. "all of the gay . . ." HC to SL, Easter '32 [Mar. 27, 1932], pub. L 406–7.

739. "I'm very happy . . ." León Felipe to JU, June 3, 1961, unpub.

739. "happy relationship" HC to Solomon Grunberg, Mar. 20, 1932, pub. L 404.

740. "That last of yours . . ." Apr. 13, 1932, pt.pub. L 409.

740. "My Guggenheim . . ." Mar. 31, 1932, pt.pub. L 405–6.

#### CHAPTER 43

742. "There was a maggot . . ." Lesley Byrd Simpson statement of June 6, 1936, unpub.

742. "ten terrible days" Apr. 2, 1932, unpub.

742. "I'm in a dull mood . . ." Apr. 12, 1932, pt.pub. L 407–8.

743. "enemy for awhile" HC to SL, Apr. 13, 1932, pub. L 409.

743. "It turned out . . ." PBC, "The Last Days . . ." 35.

743. "We had a great . . ." Apr. 13, 1932, pub. L 409.

744. "Poetry and Revolution" Oakley Johnson to HC, Apr. 11, 1932, unpub.

744. "Well, Harold . . ." Apr. 12, 1932, unpub.

745. "He was possessed . . ." PBC, "The Last Days . . ." 36–38.

746. "He's drunk." Lesley Byrd Simpson statement of June 6, 1936, unpub.

746. "Oh, there were wills . . ." interviewed 1961.

747. "Won't be living . . ." HC to B—— S——, undated, quoted in Horton 298. Copy of full letter at Yale University.

747. "I am inclined . . ." PBC, "The Last Days . . ." 38–39.

747. "Roaring with laughter," Lesley Byrd Simpson statement of June 6, 1936, unpub.

748. "a lovely black bowl . . ." Claire Spencer Evans to JU, undated [1962], unpub.

748. "Hart's disintegration . . ." Lesley Byrd Simpson statement of June 6, 1936, unpub.

748. "BESS INCOMPREHENSIBLE . . ." HC telegram to N. Byron Madden, Apr. 20, 1932, unpub.

749. "My plans . . ." Apr. 20 [1932], pub. L 409–10.

749. "PLEASE . . ." HC to CR and RR, Apr. 20, 1932, unpub.

749. "I should love to . . ." Apr. 20, 1932, pub. L 411.

749. "About a month . . ." HC to Morton Dauwen Zabel, Apr. 20, 1932, pub. L 410.

750. "Two soldiers . . ." PBC, "The Last Days . . ." 40–41.

751. "Pardon me . . ." Apr. 22, 1932, pt.pub. L 411–12.

752. "Everyone cheered . . ." PBC, "The Last Days . . ." 41.

753. "Dear Dr. Simpson . . ." unpub.

753. "My dear Mr. Moe . . ." unpub.

754. "Quite a crowd . . ." statement of June 6, 1936, unpub.

754. "I noticed . . ." PBC, "The Last Days . . ." 41.

755. "Oh, it was a slight burn . . ." interviewed 1966 (NET transcription).

755. "The doctor . . ." PBC, "The Last Days . . ." 43.

755. "He went on a rampage," interviewed 1966 (NET transcription).

756. Marsden Hartley later heard . . . see Hartley's unpub. "The Spangle of Existence," 167.

756. "He told me . . ." PBC, "The Last Days . . ." 44. Events of the night before the suicide reconstructed from Horton's account, newspaper reports, PBC's recollections in print and in conversation, the captain's report on the suicide, material in Guggenheim Foundation files, and frequently garbled secondhand accounts from passengers and crew of the *Orizaba*.

757. "He said 'Everything . . .'" PBC, interviewed 1966 (NET transcription).

757. "He said he had not . . ." PBC, "The Last Days . . ." 44.

757. "copiously" quoted in Henry Allen Moe memorandum of Apr. 30, 1932, unpub.

757. "He was still . . ." PBC, "The Last Days . . ." 44-45.

757. "All of a sudden," interviewed 1966 (NET transcription).

758. "On April 30, 1932 . . ." Henry Allen Moe memorandum for Hart Crane file of Guggenheim Foundation, dated Apr. 30, 1932.

In a letter to me dated September 27, 1969, Mrs. C. G. Vogt provided what I had been unable to uncover during my years of research on *Voyager:* an eyewitness account of Crane's suicide. I am grateful in this second edition to print her account of that morning:

Dear Prof. Unterecker:

I have read your splendid biography of Hart Crane with an increasing feeling of sadness. I bought it because of my particular interest in Crane: I was one of those who saw him commit suicide. . . .

On that ill-fated morning, one of the ship's officers told us that Crane had been in the sailors' quarters the previous night, trying to make one of the men, and had been badly beaten. Just before noon, a number of us were gathered on deck, waiting to hear the results of the ship's pool—always announced at noon. Just then we saw Crane come on deck, dressed, as you noted, in pajamas and topcoat; he had a black eye and looked generally bat-

tered. He walked to the railing, took off his coat, folded it neatly over the railing (not dropping it on deck), placed both hands on the railing, raised himself on his toes, and then dropped back again. We all fell silent and watched him, wondering what in the world he was up to. Then, suddenly, he vaulted over the railing and jumped into the sea. For what seemed five minutes, but was more like five seconds, no one was able to move; then cries of "man overboard" went up. Just once I saw Crane, swimming strongly, but never again. It was a scene I am unable to forget, even after all these years, and now I am glad to know why that tortured man made such a decision. Thank you for your book.

Sincerely,
Gertrude E. Vogt

758. "Off here . . ." HC to Mrs. S. [postmarked Apr. 26, 1932], pub. L 412.

758. "Very pleasant journey . . ." quoted in Lesley Byrd Simpson statement of June 6, 1936, unpub. According to Simpson the card was dated Apr. 26, 1932.

759. "Dear Hart Crane . . ." unpub.

CHAPTER 44

760. "Mexico killed . . ." statement of June 6, 1936, unpub.

760. "circumstantially and in detail" Henry Allen Moe to Eyler N. Simpson, undated, received in Mexico July 25, 1932, unpub.

761. "For the first weeks . . ." letter to Henry Allen Moe, unpub.

762. "fine ethical feeling" GHC to Marsden Hartley, undated, unpub. See Hartley's unpub. "The Spangle of Existence."

763. "You know Sam . . ." Friday the thirteenth [May 13, 1932], unpub.

765. "Regarding Hart's . . ." GHC to SL, Thursday [Sept. 8, 1932], unpub.

766. "Our estrangement . . ." May 3, 1932, unpub.

766. "horrible involvement . . ." interviewed by JU, 1966 (NET transcription).

767. "I . . . see his life . . ." Thursday [1932], unpub.

767. "I have been wondering," Mar. 27, 1933, unpub.

767. "I am certain . . ." Apr. 4, 1933, unpub.

768. "Should you be hard hit . . ." Arthur Pell to GHC, Aug. 1, 1945, unpub.

768. "Sam Loveman . . ." Arthur Pell to GHC, July 22, 1946, unpub.
768. "I know I have . . ." Arthur Pell to GHC, Sept. 19, 1946, unpub.
769. "I don't know . . ." interviewed 1966 (NET transcription).
769. "I don't think . . ." interviewed 1966 (NET transcription).
769. "Yes. I believe so . . ." interviewed 1966 (NET transcription).
769. "They were complex," interviewed 1966 (NET transcription).
770. "the bottom of . . ." quotations drawn from "Voyages," CP 35, 36, 37.
770. "Well, I see . . ." interviewed 1966 (NET transcription).

770. "Five cent cigar." interviewed 1966 (NET transcription).
771. "The best friend . . ." interviewed 1966 (NET transcription).
771. "one of Hart's oldest . . ." WW to GHC, May 17, 1932, unpub.
771. "the square question . . ." WW in an undated and unpub. manuscript written shortly after Crane's death.
771. "Poor dear Hart," Mrs. S to GHC, Oct. 22, 1932, unpub.
771. "My letter . . ." Henry Allen Moe to Mary Doherty, Sept. 28, 1932, unpub.

# Bibliography

The bibliography that follows is not in any sense a comprehensive list of Crane's works or of the many fine works that have been written about him. It is, rather, a list of the works actually quoted from in the body of this book. I have excluded from it all works—including one of my own essays—that are referred to without quotation or that are not referred to at all. The best up-to-date bibliographical tool for the Crane scholar is *The Literary Manuscripts of Hart Crane*, compiled by Kenneth A. Lohf and published by Ohio State University Press (1967). A good bibliography of Crane's work is very much needed, as is a good historical bibliography of the works about him. A number of interesting full-length literary studies have recently been published, the most helpful of which are those by Herbert Leibowitz, L. S. Dembo, Vincent Quinn, Samuel Hazo, and R. W. B. Lewis. For a short study on Crane, the reader might wish to consult Monroe K. Spears, *Hart Crane* (Univ. of Minnesota pamphlet). A collection of critical articles on Crane is being prepared by David Clark for 1970 publication.

[Aiken, Conrad?]. unsigned review, *The Dial*, Vol. LXXXII (May, 1927), 432.

Anderson, Margaret. *My Thirty Years' War*. New York: Covici, Friede, 1930.

Anderson, Sherwood. *Letters of Sherwood Anderson*, Edited by Howard Mumford Jones and Walter B. Rideout. Boston: Little, Brown & Co., 1953.

Baird, Peggy. "The Last Days of Hart Crane," *Venture*, IV, 1 (1961), 21–46.

Benét, William Rose. "Round about Parnassus," *The Saturday Review of Literature*, Vol. 6 (July 5, 1930), 1176.

Brooks, Charles. "A Visit to a Poet." *Hints to Pilgrims*. New Haven: Yale University Press, 1921, 92–102.

Campbell, Roy. *Light on a Dark Horse*. Chicago: Henry Regnery Co., 1952.

Chamberlain, Alice. "Millionaire's Son Is Clerk In An Akron Drug Store," Akron *Sunday Times*, Dec. 21, 1919.

Chaplin, Charles. *My Autobiography*. New York: Simon and Schuster, 1964.

Colum, Mary. *Life and the Dream*. Garden City, N.Y.: Doubleday & Co., 1947.

Cowley, Malcolm. *Exile's Return*. New York: Viking Press, Compass Books Edition, 1956.

———. "The Leopard in Hart Crane's Brow," *Esquire*, L, 4 (Oct. 1958), 257–71.

———. Review of *The Bridge*, *The New Republic*, Vol. 62 (Apr. 23, 1930), 276–77.

Crane, Hart. *The Collected Poems of Hart Crane*, edited by Waldo Frank. New York: Liveright Publishing Corp., 1933. (Paperback edition titled *The Complete Poems of Hart Crane*. Anchor Books, 1958.)

———. *The Complete Poems and Selected Letters and Prose of Hart Crane*, edited by Brom Weber. New York: Liveright Publishing Corp., 1966. (Paperback edition: Anchor Books, 1966.)

———. "Hart Crane: The End of Harvest" [Hart Crane's letters to William Slater Brown and Susan Jenkins Brown. Edited with an Introduction and Reminiscence by Susan Jenkins Brown.] *The Southern Review*, Vol. IV, New Series, No. 4 (Oct. 1968), 947–1014.

———. "Letter," *The Pagan*, I, 6 (Oct., 1916).

———. *The Letters of Hart Crane*, edited by Brom Weber. Berkeley and Los Angeles: University of California Press, 1965. (Original edition: New York: Hermitage House, 1952.)

———. "Letters of Hart Crane," *The Free Lance*, Vol. 5, No. 1 (First Half 1960), 17–24.

——. *Seven Lyrics*, edited by Kenneth A. Lohf. Ibex Press, 1966.
——. Theatre review, *The Pagan*, II, 12; III, 1 (April-May 1918), 55–56.
Crosby, Caresse. *The Passionate Years.* New York: Dial Press, 1953.
Crosby, Harry. *Shadows of the Sun.* Paris: Black Sun Press, 1930.
Fenton, Charles A. *The Apprenticeship of Ernest Hemingway: The Early Years.* New York: Compass Books, 1958.
Gregory, Horace. "Far Beyond Our Consciousness." *New York Herald Tribune Books*, Apr. 20, 1930, Section XI, 4.
Hartley, Marsden. "The Spangle of Existence." Unpublished manuscript deposited in Museum of Modern Art (New York) library.
Hicks, Granville. "The Rediscovery of America," *The Nation*, Vol. 130, No. 3382 (Apr. 30, 1930), 520–21.
——. "Hart Crane Scales New Heights in 'The Bridge'," *New York World, Book World*, May 6, 1930, 10M.
Horton, Philip. *Hart Crane.* New York: W. W. Norton & Co., 1937; reprinted New York: Viking Press, Compass Books edition, 1957.
Hutchinson, Percy. "Hart Crane's Cubistic Poetry in 'The Bridge'." *New York Times Book Review*, Apr. 27, 1930, 2.
Ingalls, Hunter. "Genius of the Everyday—the Art of William Sommer." Unpublished Master's essay, Columbia University, 1963.
Josephson, Matthew. *Life Among the Surrealists.* New York: Holt, Rinehart and Winston, 1962.
Kreymborg, Alfred. *Troubadour.* New York: Boni & Liveright, 1925.
Loeb, Harold. *The Way It Was.* New York: Criterion Books, 1959.
Lovecraft, Howard P. *Selected Letters, 1911–1924.* Sauk City, Wisc.: Arkham House, 1965.
Loveman, Sam. *Hart Crane: a Conversation with Samuel Loveman.* New York: Interim Books, 1964.
McHugh, Vincent. "Crane's 'Bridge' Mighty Symbol of the Nation." *New York Evening Post*, Apr. 19, 1930, M11.
Milliken, William M. "William Sommer the Individual," *The William Sommer Memorial Exhibition* catalogue. The Cleveland Museum of Art, 1950.
Monroe, Harriet. "A Discussion with Hart Crane," *Poetry*, Vol. 29, No. 1 (October 1926), 34–41.
Moore, Marianne. Interview, *Writers at Work: The Paris Review Interviews, Second Series.* New York: Viking Press, 1963.
Munson, Gorham. "Annotations on Three Books." Privately published, 1967.
——. "The Fledgling Years, 1916–1924." *The Sewanee Review.* XL, 1 (Jan.-Mar., 1932), 24–54.
Ouspensky, P. D. *Tertium Organum.* New York: Alfred A. Knopf, 1949.
Porter, Katherine Anne. "A Country and Some People I Love" [interview with Hank Lopez]. *Harper's*, Vol. 231, No. 1384 (Sept. 1965), 58–68.
Schmitt, Carl. "A Caution," *The Pagan*, III, 7 (Nov. 1918), 54–55.
Shepard, Odell. Review of *The Bridge*, *The Bookman*, Vol. 72 (Sept. 1930), 86–87.
Simon, Adelaide. "Apples and Dust," *The Free Lance*, II, 2 (Last Half 1954), 3–6.
Simpson, Lesley Byrd. "The Late Hart Crane," *The New English Weekly*, I, 22 (Sept. 15, 1932), 531.
Sommer, William. *The William Sommer Memorial Exhibition* catalogue. Cleveland Museum of Art, 1950.
Tate, Allen. "A Distinguished Poet," *Hound and Horn*, III, 4 (July-Sept. 1930), 580–85.
——. "Hart Crane," *The Man of Letters in the Modern World.* New York: Meridian Books, 1955, 283–94.
——. "Crane: The Poet as Hero," *The Man of Letters in the Modern World.* New York: Meridian Books, 1955, 295–98.
Unterecker, John. " '. . . A Piece of Pure Invention': A Hart Crane Episode," *Columbia Library Columns*, XV, 3 (May 1966), 2–9; also published in University of Houston *Forum*, V (Summer 1967), 43–44.
Untermeyer, Louis. "Prophetic Rhapsody," *The Saturday Review of Literature*, Vol. VI (June 14, 1930), 1125.
Weber, Brom, *Hart Crane.* New York: Bodley Press, 1948.
Weinstock, Herbert. Review of *The Bridge*, Milwaukee *Journal*, Apr. 12, 1930.
Whaler, James. *Green River: A Poem for Rafinesque.* New York: Harcourt, Brace and Co., 1931.

Wilson, Edmund. "The Muses Out of Work," *New Republic*, L (May 11, 1927), 319–21,

Winters, Yvor. "The Significance of *The Bridge*, by Hart Crane, or What Are We to Think of Professor X?" *On Modern Poets*. New York: Meridian Books, 1959, 120–43.

Wright, William H. "Mood," *The Pagan*, III, 3 (July, 1918), 50.

Zinsser, Hans. *As I Remember Him*. Boston: Little, Brown & Co., 1940.

# Index

*About Catherine de Medici* (Honoré Balzac), 32

Acapulco (Mexico), 719–20

Adams, John, 4

Adams, William (Bill), 613, 637, 640, 645, 681

*Aesthete, 1925*, 358

"Again," 404

Aiken, Conrad, 60, 480

"Air Plant, The," 444, 452, 464, 506, 528

Akron (Ohio), 6, 21–2, 79, 150–2, 155–62, 164–5, 169–70, 176, 178, 182, 193, 202, 205, 247

Akron *Beacon Journal*, 150, 155

Akron *Sunday Times*, 156, 158

Albuquerque (N.M.), 677

*Alchemist, The* (Ben Jonson), 259

Aldington, Richard, 592

Allegheny College, 6, 76

Altadena (Calif.), 519, 530, 534–5

*America Hispana* (Waldo Frank), 650

*American Caravan, The*, 476, 506, 580–1, 602, 625

"America's Plutonic Ecstasies," 278

*Anarchy Is Not Enough* (Laura Riding), 527

Anderson, Margaret, 88–9, 131, 135, 143, 160–1, 169, 178, 205, 209, 246, 279, 334

Anderson, Maxwell, 552

Anderson, Sherwood, 88, 144, 152–5, 157–9, 162–4, 167–8, 170, 174, 190, 192–4, 210–12, 217–18, 222–3, 225–6, 230, 237, 245–6, 249–52, 255, 390, 622, 644

Apollinaire, Guillaume, 146, 228, 233, 235

*Appius and Virginia* (John Webster), 231

Aragon, Louis, 233, 235

Arden, Elsie, 587

*As I Remember Him* (Hans Zinsser), 653

Asch, Lysel, 546

Asch, Nathan, 30, 525, 546–8, 559–560

"At Melville's Tomb," 191, 407, 463, 770

"Ave Maria," 449–50, 470, 510, 609, 619

Aydelotte, Frank, 674, 676, 749, 753

Aztecs, 650, 652, 662, 689, 691–2, 694

Babcock, Margaret, *see* Robson, Margaret

"Bacardi Spreads the Eagle's Wings," 738, 749

*Back to Methuselah* (G. B. Shaw), 216

Bacon, Francis, 425

Baird, Peggy (Peggy Baird Cowley), 22, 164, 271, 343, 357, 372, 382, 389, 424, 432, 437, 442, 450, 460, 524–5, 546, 553, 558, 563, 569, 608–9, 672–3, 682, 684, 694–7, 699–702, 712–41, 743–58, 762, 768

Baldwin, Charles, 287

Baltzly, Alex, 127–8, 145, 177

Barnes, Djuna, 160, 178

Barney, Alice *and* Nathalie Clifford, 538

Barton, Ralph, 659

"Bathers, The," 88

Baudelaire, Charles, 115, 173, 209, 243, 272, 659, 669

Beals, Betty *and* Carleton, 737, 750, 752

Beardsley, Orsa, 6, 7

Belden, Mattie, 6

Bell, Clive, 194, 203, 207, 210, 270, 275

"Belle Isle," 262

Benét, William Rose, 620

Biggers, Earl Derr, 60

Binet, Jean, 208, 210, 287

Black Sun Press, 578, 590–1, 609, 615–16, 681

"Black Tambourine," 188–90, 210, 219, 228, 231

Blake, William, 194, 272, 333, 446, 503, 528, 586, 641, 644, 659, 670
Bloch, Ernest, 208, 226, 283, 641
*Blue Juniata* (Malcolm Cowley), 561-2, 578, 580
Blum, Jerome, 60
Blume, Peter, 608, 617, 629, 648-50
Bodenheim, Maxwell, 87-8, 136, 247, 481
Boni and Liveright, *see* Liveright Publishing Company
*Book of Living Verse, The* (Louis Untermeyer), 680
*Bookman, The*, 327, 620
Booth, Fred, 158
Bordner, Bob, 202-3
"Bottom of the Sea Is Cruel, The," 216, 218, 261
Boyd, Ernest, 359
Boyle, Kay, 527, 580-1, 585, 589, 592
Braithwaite, William Stanley, 260
Brenner, Anita, 720-1, 737
Breton, André, 233, 235
Breuer, Bessie, 552
*Bridge, The*, 19, 22, 45, 119, 137, 191, 226, 258, 260-1, 265, 267, 276, 279, 283, 296, 302, 304-5, 307-10, 318, 320, 326, 336, 357, 363-5, 374, 376, 378, 405-6, 417, 419, 422, 425-9, 431-2, 438, 443, 446-52, 455-7, 459-62, 465, 467, 469-70, 475-6, 480-1, 485, 492, 495-7, 504-6, 508-511, 514, 528, 536-7, 543, 545, 551, 555-6, 558, 561, 566, 571, 573, 578-84, 586-90, 594-5, 598-9, 601-605, 608, 610-11, 613-23, 625-8, 632-5, 643-5, 648, 652, 654, 698, 703-4, 707, 721-2
"Bridge of Estador, The," 168, 191, 199, 232
"Broken Tower, The," 22, 271, 698, 721-3, 726-7, 731, 737-8, 744, 749, 751
Brookhaven (L.I.), 139-43, 146, 743
Brooks, Charles, 69, 74-6, 86, 97, 106, 123, 129, 134-5
Brooks, Van Wyck, 153, 158, 476
*Broom*, 233-4, 249, 258, 260, 277-8, 304, 312, 314, 318, 357, 377
Brown, Hazel, 31, 44-5
Brown, William Slater, 234, 271, 294-297, 301-4, 307, 312, 314, 320, 322, 325, 327-9, 331-2, 334-5, 338-9, 341, 357, 363, 377, 382-3, 386-7, 389-93, 395-8, 400-2, 404, 418-19, 421-5, 430, 432, 437-8, 440, 442, 460, 462, 465-6, 469, 475-8, 490, 514, 518-20, 522-3, 525-7, 530-1, 536, 538-40, 546, 561, 568-9, 575,

591-2, 601, 603, 606, 608, 629, 631, 635, 637, 652, 679, 683, 734
Brown, Sue, *see* Jenkins, Susan
Brown, Vivian *and* Hazel, 31, 39, 44-5
Browning, Elizabeth Barrett, 220-1, 588
Bruno, Guido, 52, 107
*Bruno's Bohemia*, 107
*Bruno's Weekly*, 46-7
Bryan, George, 44-5, 50, 68, 87, 97, 99, 107, 110-11, 113, 118, 120-1, 123, 129-30, 137, 141
Bubb, Charles C., 118
Bullus, Leonard, 475
Burchfield, Charles, 47
Burke, Kenneth, 258, 261, 272, 294, 304, 312, 314, 343, 357-8, 372, 377, 382, 405, 631, 683
Burnett, Whit, 597-8
Bynner, Witter, 88, 714
Byron, Lord, 221

"C 33," 46
*Calendar, The*, 478, 500, 576
"Calgary Express," 450
Calhoun, Alice, 137
Calles, Plutarco, 477-8, 750
Camino (León Felipe), 663-4, 739
Campbell, Roy, 594-5, 599
Canby, Henry Seidel, 602, 634
Candee, Harry, 159-60, 162, 182, 247, 290, 292
*Cane* (Jean Toomer), 289
Cannell, Kitty, 597
Cape, Jonathan, 527
"Cape Hatteras," 582-3, 585, 590, 602-3, 611, 621
"Carmen de Boheme," 107
"Carrier Letter," 108
Castaneda, Maximiliano Ruiz, 652-6
Catullus, 159, 171
Cavalcanti, Guido, 221
Cazes, Hazel, 651, 660, 662, 665-7, 675; *see also* Hasham, Hazel
Cerf, Bennett, 529
Cézanne, Paul, 194, 268, 594
Chagrin Falls (Ohio), 14-16, 497, 508, 539, 605-7, 638-9, 644, 651, 668, 675-7, 679-82, 685, 696, 710, 734, 749, 758
Chamberlain, Alice, 156
Chaplin, Charlie, 216-18, 260, 317-319, 345, 529, 643, 724-5; *City Lights*, 643; *The Kid*, 216-17
"Chaplinesque," 216-18, 228, 260, 318, 521
*Chartreuse de Parma* (Stendhal), 173
Chatterton, Thomas, 221

Chaucer, Geoffrey, 137, 234
Chautauqua (N.Y.), 44–5
Chicago (Ill.), 5–7, 9–10, 13–14, 19, 24, 40–1, 47, 61–3, 79, 88, 147, 157, 235, 300, 390–1, 485, 490–1, 493, 496, 607, 677, 758, 764
Chirico, Giorgio di, 374
Church Head Press, 118
*City Block* (Waldo Frank), 279–80, 283
Claridge, Eleanor, 28–9
Clark, Donald, 475
Clark, Donald B., 234
Cleveland (Ohio), 7, 9, 14–16, 19, 21–3, 27–8, 30, 34–5, 39–42, 44, 46–7, 50, 52, 54, 60–1, 63, 65–7, 69–71, 73–6, 78–80, 83, 86–9, 93, 96, 98–9, 106–7, 109–14, 117, 120, 125–6, 128, 137–8, 147, 149–50, 152, 155, 157–8, 160, 163–5, 170–1, 173–4, 176–8, 180–1, 185, 188–91, 194, 200, 202, 204, 207–8, 212–17, 222, 226, 228, 230, 234, 238–9, 243–5, 247–8, 250–1, 253, 255–7, 260, 263–4, 266, 273, 280, 282–3, 285–7, 289–90, 292, 297–8, 300, 307–9, 311–12, 315–16, 321, 337–9, 344, 351, 353–4, 356, 360, 362, 366, 370–2, 374, 382, 391–8, 400, 402, 404–5, 407, 409, 413–14, 416, 418–19, 422–3, 428, 442–3, 459–61, 463, 465–72, 474–5, 477, 482–5, 487–8, 490, 492–3, 498, 506–7, 512–514, 532, 554, 558, 560, 562, 567, 574, 607, 610, 626, 638–9, 641–2, 645–6, 677–81, 694, 709, 746, 748, 758, 768
Cleveland *News*, 487–8, 490
Cleveland *Plain Dealer*, 118, 120, 131
Cleveland *Press*, 47, 487–8
Cocteau, Jean, 219, 597
Coleridge, Samuel Taylor, 221, 527, 594
*Collected Poems, The* (Crane), 17, 405, 585, 731, 765
Collioure (France), 588–9, 591–3
Colum, Mary, 58–60, 63, 69, 95, 389
Colum, Padraic, 41, 58–60, 69, 210, 223, 318
Columbia University, 52, 64, 70, 77, 96, 137–9, 146, 154, 162, 170, 292
Conrad, Joseph, 155, 173
*Contempo*, 738, 749
"Contract, The" (Sherwood Anderson), 249
*Conversations* (Walter Landor), 173
Coolidge, Calvin, 631, 642
Corday and Gross, 223, 225, 231, 239, 253, 290, 382

Corn Products Refining Company, 9, 19, 23
"Cornhuskers" (Carl Sandburg), 156
Cortez, Hernando, 648, 652, 666
Cortot, Alfred, 628
*Counterfeiters, The* (André Gide), 527
Cowley, Malcolm, 234–5, 297, 306, 312, 314–15, 330, 337, 343, 357–8, 363, 372, 381–2, 388–9, 404, 420, 424, 427–8, 430, 432, 437, 442, 450, 456, 460, 476, 524–5, 527, 540, 546, 552–4, 558, 561–3, 568–9, 580, 590, 595–6, 608–9, 617, 619–20, 627, 630–1, 634, 648–50, 662, 669, 683–4, 696, 713–14, 718, 720, 734, 738, 770
Cowley, Peggy, *see* Baird, Peggy
Craig, Gordon, 209
Crane, Alice (Mrs. Loring Williams), 6, 25–7, 43, 472, 486, 488
Crane, Alma, 472
Crane, Arthur *and* Ella, 4–6, 9–10, 23–4, 236, 285, 288, 311, 396, 492, 550, 675
Crane, Bess (Aunt Bess), *see* Madden, Bess Crane
Crane, Bessie Meacham, 15–16, 605, 607, 639, 641, 646, 676–9, 684, 687, 690, 693, 698–9, 702–5, 707, 709–714, 716, 725–6, 730–1, 733–4, 736, 742, 744–5, 748–9, 751–2, 758
Crane, Cassius (Cash), 4
Crane, Clarence (C.A.), 6–16, 19, 20, 23–4, 26–7, 34–44, 48–54, 56–7, 61–87, 92–106, 110–13, 116–17, 120, 122, 125–8, 130, 132, 138, 141–2, 144–5, 147–51, 153, 156–7, 160, 164–7, 170–3, 177–80, 185–9, 194, 196–200, 214, 217, 222, 236, 248, 272–3, 277, 285, 287–90, 311, 322, 338, 344–54, 360–1, 372, 382–3, 390–1, 395, 399, 411–17, 421, 423, 439, 441, 443, 453, 455, 458–62, 470–2, 476, 481–3, 486–98, 504–9, 513–15, 517–18, 531, 538–40, 543–5, 548–51, 553–6, 559, 562, 566–8, 570–1, 573, 590, 605–8, 616, 628, 634, 638–43, 645–8, 651, 660–2, 665–8, 675–9, 688, 697, 704–5, 709–710, 731, 740, 744, 746, 760, 765–8
Crane, Edward Manley, 5
Crane, Frances Kelley, 15, 111, 288, 352, 459, 470–2, 482, 486
Crane, Frederic, 4–6
Crane, Fredrica, 471–2, 482, 486, 493
Crane, Grace Hart, 6, 7, 8–20, 23–9, 31–2, 34–45, 48–53, 55, 57–87, 90–1, 93–113, 116–17, 121–33, 136, 138–

142, 146–9, 155, 164–5, 171–4, 177,
  184–8, 196–200, 209, 214–15, 222,
  235–6, 246, 248, 251, 253, 256, 263–
  266, 272–3, 277, 285–9, 291–2, 297–
  301, 307–12, 315–18, 321–3, 325,
  328–31, 334–5, 337–41, 343–6, 349–
  358, 360–61, 363–4, 366–72, 375,
  379–85, 387–95, 397, 399, 401, 408–
  411, 413–15, 418–19, 421–4, 428–9,
  432–4, 436–7, 439, 442–4, 449, 452,
  454–5, 458–62, 465–7, 469–72, 474–
  476, 478–9, 481–91, 493–9, 504–5,
  507–8, 513–17, 519–20, 530–5, 537–
  538, 540–5, 548–50, 554–60, 562–74,
  590, 604–5, 607–8, 631–2, 634, 678,
  681, 717, 728, 758, 760, 762–8
Crane, Simeon, 5
Crane, Sylvina, 5
Crane Brothers's store, 4, 6, 7
Crane Candy Company, 14, 52, 345,
  347.
Crevel, René, 592
*Criterion, The*, 404, 407, 506, 578
*Crome Yellow* (Aldous Huxley), 237
Crosby, Caresse, 374, 578–81, 585–91,
  593, 595–6, 600–5, 608–10, 612–17,
  627–8, 639, 645, 652, 740–1
Crosby, Harry, 578–82, 584–90, 593–
  605, 608–10, 614, 616, 649, 659,
  741
"Crossing Brooklyn Ferry" (Walt
  Whitman), 624
Croton-on-Hudson (N.Y.), 545, 551,
  556
Cuernavaca (Mexico), 690, 702, 744
Cummings, Anne, 518, 539, 569, 609,
  616, 631–2, 635
Cummings, E. E., 234, 294–5, 327,
  343–4, 358, 372, 393, 439, 518, 527,
  569, 597, 609, 616, 631–2, 634–5
Curtis, Charles, 366–7, 369–71, 383,
  393, 409, 414, 424, 437, 452, 454–5,
  460–1, 466, 470, 484–5, 487–8, 507
"Cutty Sark," 449–50, 511, 603, 605,
  611, 619

Dada, 193–4, 218–19, 228, 234, 241,
  306
Daly, James, 256, 287, 292, 472
"Dance, The," 480, 504, 511, 605,
  619, 652
Dante, 58, 115, 221, 451, 625, 633–4,
  703; *The Divine Comedy*, 240, 625,
  633
*Dark Mother* (Waldo Frank), 250
Davenport, Russell, 635
Da Vinci, Leonardo, 501–2, 697
*Death of the God in Mexico* (James
  Feibleman), 703

*Decline of the West, The* (Oswald
  Spengler), 446
Deming, Will, 48
Deming, Zell, 20, 48–9, 51, 65, 77, 99,
  100, 137, 289, 291, 329, 341, 367,
  379, 390, 397–8, 475, 532, 541,
  559–60, 563–5, 568, 573, 745
Denison, C. Courtney, 20
*Destinations* (Gorham Munson), 537
DeZayas, 206–7
*Dial, The*, 131, 152, 169, 171, 188,
  195, 199, 205, 210, 216, 218, 223,
  232, 240, 244, 249, 251, 257–8, 261,
  269, 272, 279, 303, 313, 329, 372,
  404–5, 407, 478, 480, 485, 506,
  528, 561, 578
Dietrich, Marlene, 628, 649, 663
Dietz, Lorna, 74, 424, 553, 557–8,
  569, 603–5, 629, 631, 635, 641–3,
  645, 652–3, 671, 679, 681–2, 766
Doherty Co., Henry L., 562–3
Doherty, Mary, 659, 666, 668–70,
  688–9, 745–9, 752, 760–2, 771–2
Donne, John, 209, 219, 221, 271, 336,
  503, 510, 529, 602, 633; *quoted*,
  230–1, 333
Dos Passos, John, 294, 334, 393, 641
Dostoevsky, Fyodor, 184, 192
Doubleday, Doran and Co., 561, 637
*Double-Dealer*, 169, 210–11, 216, 236,
  239, 241, 277–8
Drayton, Michael, 234, 477
Dreiser, Theodore, 46, 154, 156, 232
Duncan, Isadora, 264–5
Durieux, Caroline, 742

East Aurora (N.Y.), 39–40
East High School, 27–9, 31, 33, 44,
  49, 638
"East of Yucatan," 506
"Echoes," 88
Eddy, Mary Baker, 23, 468
*Eden Tree* (Witter Bynner), 680
"Egyptian Sonnets" (Charmion von
  Wiegand), 145
Eliot, T. S., 88, 158, 160, 167, 173,
  189–90, 209, 217, 219–20, 240–2,
  254, 259–60, 270, 272, 278, 336,
  344, 404, 407, 431, 434, 446–7, 450,
  464, 506, 510, 517, 526–7, 537, 602,
  633, 664
Éluard, Paul, 233, 235
Ely, Mr., 100, 103–6, 123–4
"Emblems of Conduct," 336
Emerson, Ralph Waldo, 221
*Enormous Room, The* (E. E. Cum-
  mings), 253
Enters, Angna, 617

"Episode of Hands," 166–7, 169, 191, 375
Epstein, Jacob, 193
*Erik Dorn* (Ben Hecht), 221
Ermenonville (France), 580–1
"Eternity," 464
"Euthanasia" (Allen Tate), 239
Evans, Walker, 562–3, 569, 603, 609, 611, 651, 683–4
*Exile's Return* (Malcolm Cowley), 314, 363; *quoted*, 315, 388

Fawcett, James Waldo, 144–5
"Fear," 136
Felipe, León, *see* Camino (León Felipe)
Fetzer, Herman (Jake Falstaff), 170, 202
Field, Eugene, 159
Figueras (Spain), 593
Fisher, William, 269, 329, 335–6
Fiske, Agnes *and* Sybil, 437
Fitts, Norman, 262, 278
Fitzgerald, Eleanor, 327, 357, 400, 417, 466, 516–17, 546, 548, 550, 558, 569, 629–31, 633–4, 648
*Five Seasons, The* (Phelps Putnam), 703, 759
Fletcher, Herbert, 151, 159–60
Fletcher, John Gould, 88
"Flower in the Sea, The" (Malcolm Cowley), 428
Flynn, Bina, 398–400, 402, 437–8, 445, 477
Flynn, Eleanor T., 30–1, 474, 613
"For the Marriage of Faustus and Helen," 107, 169, 189, 191, 226, 241–2, 244, 246, 252–4, 256–9, 262, 266–7, 277–81, 283–4, 294, 297, 309, 312–14, 356, 374, 405–7, 431, 464, 503, 722
Ford, Ford Madox, 587, 592
"Forgetfulness," 115, 136
*Fortune*, 635–7, 639, 721
*42nd Parallel* (John Dos Passos), 641
France, Anatole, 108
Franck, César, 363, 628
Frank, Waldo, 17, 153–5, 158, 232, 247, 249–51, 276–84, 286, 289–91, 294, 302–6, 309, 314–15, 317–18, 320, 339, 345, 353, 355–9, 363, 372–3, 380–3, 390, 392–3, 395–7, 406, 408, 417, 426, 428, 431–2, 437–9, 442, 445–8, 450–4, 462, 464, 475, 478–9, 482, 528–9, 531, 537, 539, 543, 545, 564, 568, 577, 581, 583–4, 614, 617, 634, 642–5, 650–1, 656, 663–4, 765, 769, 772

Frease, Hurxthal *and* Joseph, 272–3
Frease-Green, Rachel, 272, 369
*Freeman, The*, 169, 211, 278
Freeman, William, 382
Frost, Robert, 137, 154, 186
Fry, Roger, 194, 203, 207, 210
*Fugitive, The*, 387. 403–4

Galpin, Alfred, 247, 256–7
Garden, Mary, 34, 186
"Garden Abstract," 166, 169
Garfield, Lucretia, *see* Rudolph, Lucretia
*Gargoyle*, 260
Garrettsville (Ohio), 4–10, 19, 23, 472, 639, 647, 760, 770
Gaudier-Brzeska, Henri, 135, 195, 267
Gauguin, Paul, 195, 695
Gauthier, Eva, 578
"General Aims and Theories," 258, 377
*Ghetto and Other Poems, The* (Lola Ridge), 119
Gide, André, 146, 209, 523, 597
Ginther, Bert, 186, 192, 201, 404
*Golden Ass, The* (Apuleius), 183
Goldman, Emma, 592
*Good-bye to All That* (Robert Graves), 617
Gordon, Caroline, *see* Tate, Caroline
Gottschalk, Laura, *see* Riding, Laura
Gourmont, Remy de, 209, 222, 234, 243
Grand Cayman, 445–7, 585
*Grandmothers, The* (Glenway Westcott), 527
Graves, Robert, 576, 617
"Great Western Plains, The," 260
*Green River* (James Whaler), 666, 703
Greenberg, Samuel, 335–6, 376
Gregory, Horace, 619, 721
Griffin, Johnson & Mann, 554
Grunberg, Solomon (Mony), 429, 566–7, 569, 575, 633, 639, 641, 645–6, 684, 686–7, 697, 725–6, 738, 742–3, 749, 766–7
Guadalupe Hidalgo (Mexico), 707
*Guardian, The*, 407
Guardian Trust Company, 564, 567–8, 570–1
Guest, Edgar, 221, 544
Guggenheim Foundation, 634, 645–6, 648–52, 658, 660–2, 665, 667–70, 673–6, 679, 682, 687, 697, 706, 733, 735, 739–40, 748–9, 752–3, 757, 771–2
Gurdjieff Institute, 358, 500

Habicht, Hermann, 146-7, 212, 292, 545
Hager, Fred, 195
"Hamlet" (Archibald MacLeish), 591
Hampden, Walter, 182
Hanfstaengl, Putzi, 127
"Harbor Dawn," 326, 365, 510-11, 605, 620, 703-4
Harcourt, Brace & Co., 380, 407
Hardy, Thomas, 502, 643
Harper, Allanah, 578
Harris, Charles, 208, 256, 281, 287, 290-2, 294, 296, 304, 308, 397, 422, 425
Harris, Frank, 58, 184
Hart, Clinton, 5, 9, 19, 23, 27, 436, 555, 564, 570
Hart, Elizabeth Belden, 19, 21-4, 27-8, 30, 32, 35, 37-8, 42-4, 59-62, 64-6, 71, 73-8, 81-3, 90, 98, 100-6, 110, 112-13, 116-17, 123, 128, 141, 148-9, 152, 155, 165, 172, 185, 214, 235-6, 246, 250, 256, 263, 272, 285-9, 298-9, 307-9, 311, 315-16, 321, 323, 328-30, 337-41, 350-1, 366-7, 370, 380, 383, 386-7, 390-5, 397, 408-11, 413-15, 418-24, 426, 428-9, 439-41, 443, 449, 452, 466-7, 469-71, 474, 484-5, 494, 498, 507, 513-15, 527, 531-7, 540-1, 544, 549-50, 554-6, 558-60, 564, 570, 572-4, 590, 613, 763-4, 770, 773
Hart, Frank, 48
Hart, George, 544
Hart, Grace, *see* Crane, Grace Hart
Hart, Stephen, 5
Hartley, Marsden, 161, 594, 742-3, 748, 756, 761-2
Hasham, Hazel, 52, 70-1, 76, 82, 84; *see also* Cazes, Hazel
Hatfield, Gordon, 210
Havana (Cuba), 90, 438-9, 445, 452-5, 458, 641, 652-5, 664, 682, 685, 754-8
"Havana Rose," 664-5
Hayes, Arthur, 568
Heap, Jane, 88-9, 131, 260, 279, 417
Heine, Heinrich, 219
Hemingway, Ernest, 108, 477, 587
Henig, Suzanne, 552
Hernandez, Daniel, 665, 676, 686-7, 699, 700, 718, 724, 726-7, 729-30, 737, 746, 750, 752
Hicks, Granville, 619
*him* (E. E. Cummings), 539
*History of Charles XII, King of Sweden* (Voltaire), 32
*History of the Reign of Ferdinand and Isabella, The* (William H. Prescott), 426
*Hit the Deck*, 363
"Hive, The," 55, 73-4
Hoffenstein, Samuel, 617
Hollywood (Calif.), 318, 516, 519-521, 525, 530-2, 534-5, 538-9, 541-3, 558, 573, 688
*Homeric*, 598, 600
Hoover, Herbert, 631, 750
"Hope" (Waldo Frank), 277
Hopkins, Gerard Manley, 58, 526, 528-9, 633
Horton, Philip, 17, 38, 80, 83, 98, 198, 377, 437, 534-5, 630, 670, 765, 772
*Hound and Horn*, 621-2
Howard, Alan, 185
Howard, Louise, 745
Hubbard, Elbert, 39, 40
Huebsch, B. W., 237, 249, 350
Hurd, Kenneth, 33-4, 48, 50, 287
Hurlbert, Helen Hart, 20, 354, 475, 690
"Hurricane, The," 643
Hutchison, Collister, 201
Hutchinson, Percy, 620

"I Want to Know Why" (Sherwood Anderson), 167
Ibsen, Henrik, *quoted*, 92
"Idiot, The," 451-2
*Ile* (Eugene O'Neill), 108
"In Shadow," 89
*In the American Grain* (William Carlos Williams), 609
"Indiana," 511, 603-5, 619, 622, 643, 652
Ingalls, Hunter, 267
"Interior," 145
"Interludium," 334
Isle of Pines (Cuba), 28, 34-5, 38, 42, 88, 90, 165, 172, 320-3, 337, 353, 381, 392, 395, 410-11, 413, 426, 436-41, 443, 445-6, 449, 453-4, 456-7, 459, 461-2, 469-71, 476, 488, 504-5, 508, 514, 533, 561, 580, 600, 602, 606, 618, 631, 666, 738-9
Izant, Mary, 20

*Jack's House* (Alfred Kreymborg), 108
Jacobs, Samuel, 375, 379-80
James, Henry, 137, 161, 173
Jamestown (N.Y.), 44, 239
Jenkins, Susan, 301-2, 327-8, 331, 351, 354-5, 357-8, 372, 389, 391, 393, 397, 402, 422, 424-5, 437-8, 440, 460, 462, 466, 469, 475-8, 490,

514, 518–20, 523, 530–1, 536, 546, 569, 608, 629, 631, 734
Jennings, Charles (Uncle Charlie), 397, 442, 477
Jolas, Eugène, 479, 578, 582, 592
Jones, R. Edmond, 343
Jonson, Ben, 219, 231, 234, 283
Josephson, Matthew, 139, 145, 147, 152–3, 158–9, 162, 166, 173–4, 194, 212, 218–19, 223, 226–8, 230, 232–5, 258, 272, 304–6, 312, 315, 322, 343, 358, 404–5, 478–9, 546, 631
*Journal of Christopher Columbus*, 426
*Journeys to Bagdad* (Charles Brooks), 69
Joyce, James, 115–16, 133, 136, 209, 211, 222, 246, 254, 273, 305, 332, 617
Joyce, Peggy Hopkins, 617
"Joyce and Ethics," 115
*Jurgen* (James Branch Cabell), 641

Kahn, Otto, 417–18, 422, 424, 431, 434, 436, 438, 442, 445, 448, 453, 455–9, 481, 509–11, 513–14, 536, 586, 616, 625, 627, 633–4
Kansas City (Missouri), 14–15, 117, 147, 157, 471, 744
Kantor, Louis, 303, 353
Keats, John, 192, 221, 623
Keisogloff, Peter, 201
Keller, George Henry, 47
Kelley, Frances, 112; *see also* Crane, Frances
Kenney, Kay, 201, 204, 287, 296, 443, 472
King, Clinton, 714, 729–30
"King of the Strange Marshes, The" (Gorham B. Munson), 136
"King's Henchmen, The" (Edna St. Vincent Millay), 499
Kirk, George, 371
Kirkham, Hall, 475
Kling, Joseph, 46–7, 52–3, 58, 88, 106–7, 123, 135–6, 144, 177, 194, 205, 246
*Kora in Hell* (William Carlos Williams), 190
Korner and Wood, 49, 79, 221
Kreymborg, Alfred, 60, 72, 87, 108, 137, 212, 476
"Kubla Khan" (Samuel Taylor Coleridge), 586, 623

Lachaise, Gaston, 319, 329, 334–5, 341, 345, 357, 381, 424, 437, 445, 476, 531, 539, 648

"Lachrymae Christi," 336, 375–6, 404
*Lady Windermere's Fan* (Oscar Wilde), 32
Laforgue, Jules, 146, 219, 221, 236, 336, 447
Lancaster, Nathaniel Jr., 660
Landor, Walter, 221
Laukhuff, Richard, 47–8, 88, 109, 118, 149, 173, 176, 185–6, 192–3, 201, 208, 247, 254, 455, 465, 606, 641, 680, 729
Lawrence, Carroll, 256
Lawrence, D. H., 137, 213, 425, 652, 656, 688, 721–2
Lazare, Edward, 256
Lebègue, Eugénie, 93, 123
"Legend," 403
"Legende," 145
Lepine, L. E., 661, 726–7
Lescaze, William, 208–11, 229, 243–4, 247, 250, 256, 260, 262, 287, 292, 303
Lewis, Sinclair, 133
Lewis, Wyndham, 88, 136, 195, 207, 267, 270, 526, 528, 537
*Liberator, The*, 205, 243
*Life Among the Surrealists* (Matthew Josephson), 232
Light, James, 315, 327, 343, 354–5, 358, 393, 417, 448–9
Light, Sue, *see* Jenkins, Susan
*Limbo* (Aldous Huxley), 173
Lindbergh, Charles, 506
Lindsay, Vachel, 40, 60, 88, 481
Li Po, 221
*Little Mexico* (William Spratling), 703
*Little Review*, 88–9, 106–7, 115, 128–132, 134–6, 139, 142–4, 146–9, 152, 161, 169, 178, 205, 219, 222, 234–5, 260–1, 279, 333–4
Liveright, Horace, 380, 408, 414–15, 427–8, 448–9, 476, 478
Liveright Publishing Company, 222, 380, 408, 493, 590, 601–2, 614–17, 633, 665, 681, 768
*Lives* (Plutarch), 32
Lloyd, John, 48, 87
Lloyd-Smith, Parker, 635
Loeb, Harold, 233, 258, 312, 315
London (England), 212, 347, 509, 521, 568, 571, 576–8, 582
*Lonesome Water* (Roy Helton), 666
Loringhoven, Baroness Elsa von, 134–5, 149, 160, 178, 193, 215
Los Angeles (Calif.), 514, 517, 520, 536, 543, 668
Lovecraft, H. P., 256, 371–2, 401, 621
Loveman, Sam, 16–18, 30, 181, 186,

191–4, 201, 208–9, 217, 222, 229, 238, 243, 247, 256, 263–5, 281, 287, 311, 357, 366–7, 371, 382, 393, 401–2, 467, 511, 514, 522, 526–7, 531–4, 553, 558, 560–1, 566, 569, 572–6, 578–9, 584, 603–4, 606, 613, 617, 623, 626, 629–30, 632–3, 635, 637, 639–41, 645, 653, 656, 668, 680–4, 701, 706, 734, 738, 740, 743–4, 749, 763–5, 767–8, 770–1
Lowenfels, Walter, 592
Lucretius, 144

McAlmon, Robert, 194
MacCown, Eugene, 343, 584, 587–8, 592, 595–8, 627
McHugh, Harley, 185–6
McHugh, Vincent, 619
MacLeish, Archibald, 478–9, 635
McPherson, Aimee Semple, 524
Madden, Bess Crane, 6, 8–10, 16, 288, 472, 482, 488, 505, 555, 708–9
Madden, N. Byron, 6, 482, 505, 704–5, 746, 748, 751
Maddow, Ben, 720
Majorca (Spain), 508, 511, 563, 585
*Man Who Died, The* (D. H. Lawrence), 721
"Mango Tree, The," 441, 450, 452, 580
*Maniken and Minikin* (Alfred Kreymborg), 108
Mann, Klaus, 592
"March," 506
Marco Polo, 427
"Marginalia on Poe and Baudelaire" (Remy de Gourmont), 216
Marin, John, 269, 294, 617
Marks, Harry, 597, 609
Marlowe, Christopher, 219, 221, 486, 501, 623, 659, 760, 771
Marseilles (France), 571, 593–5, 599, 646
Martigues (France), 594, 646, 652
Martinique, 403, 508, 514, 680
Massis, Henri, 526
Masters, Edgar Lee, 88, 144, 156, 481
Matisse, Henri, 269, 343, 591
Maupassant, Guy de, 144, 151
Maurer, Muriel, 648–9, 669
Maurras, Charles, 526
*Measure, The,* 210
Melchers, Julius *and* Gari, 195
Melville, Herman, 427, 441, 575, 619, 659; *quoted,* 637
Mencken, H. L., 155, 173, 683
"Mermen, The," 561
*Messages* (Ramon Fernandez), 523, 528, 537

Mexico City, 21, 647, 651, 653, 656, 660, 663, 665, 676, 679, 682, 684–5, 688–9, 695–6, 699–701, 703, 706–7, 712, 717, 725, 734, 749, 752–3
Miami (Fla.), 394–5, 408–10, 415, 418
Millay, Edna St. Vincent, 220, 247
Miller, Catherine, 475
Milliken, William, 268
Milton, John, 221
*Minna and Myself* (Maxwell Bodenheim), 136
Minns, H. W., 161–2, 169, 186, 193
Mississippi River, 504–5, 543, 556
Mitchell, Stewart, 334, 384, 398, 526–7
Mixcoac (Mexico), 660, 662–3, 673, 700, 706, 728–9, 737, 739, 742–3, 749–50, 762
*Moby Dick* (Herman Melville), 237, 389, 427, 445, 698, 738–9
"Modern Craft," 107
*Modern School, The,* 131
*Modernist, The,* 144, 149; *quoted,* 145
Moe, Henry Allen, 634, 645–6, 648, 650–1, 658, 665, 673–7, 679–80, 682–3, 686, 753, 757–8, 760–2, 771–2
"Moment Fugue," 580
Monroe, Harriet, 463–4, 561, 665–6
Montezuma, 650, 652, 665–6
"Mood" (William Wright), *quoted,* 114
Moody, Harriet, 40–2, 44, 46, 59–60
*Moon and Sixpence, The* (Somerset Maugham), 160
Moore, Marianne, 173, 232, 234, 294, 404, 406–7, 417, 480; *quoted,* 405
Moore, Thomas, 221, 232
Morgan, Ed, 187, 482, 492–3
Morris, William, 40, 576
Mortimer, Stanley, 609
*Mosses from an Old Manse* (Nathaniel Hawthorne), 32
"Moth that God Made Blind, The," 42
Moulin, Le, 580–1, 584, 586–7, 593–4, 627
Munson, Lisa, 286, 289, 295, 304, 316, 343, 351, 358, 553, 569, 734
Munson, Gorham B., 136, 145–7, 149–50, 152–71, 174, 177–83, 186–190, 192–5, 199, 200, 203–18, 222–8, 230–6, 238–41, 243–7, 249–53, 257–258, 260–6, 268–71, 273–4, 276–83, 285–6, 289–91, 293–5, 297, 302, 304–7, 312–16, 320–1, 329, 333, 336–8, 342–4, 351, 358–60, 363, 377, 383, 393, 396, 417, 427–30,

500, 531, 537–9, 553, 561, 569, 617, 623, 734
Murray, J. Middleton, 192
"My Grandmother's Love Letters," 3, 148, 152–3, 169, 171, 773
*My Heart and Flesh* (Elizabeth Madox Roberts), 527
*My Thirty Years' War* (Margaret Anderson), 89
Myers, Otto, 674

Nagle, Edward, 271, 303, 312, 322, 325, 328–9, 331–2, 334–5, 338–9, 341, 377
"Name for All, A," 561
*Nation, The*, 131, 211, 479, 527, 619
"National Winter Garden," 594
Naumberg, Margaret, 343
Nelson, Ernest, 229–32, 318–9
*New Masses*, 243
New Orleans (La.), 504, 541–3
*New Poetry, The*, 665
*New Republic, The*, 131, 169, 211–212, 464, 471, 478–9, 499, 503, 527, 619, 643, 683
*New Testament, A* (Sherwood Anderson), 153
New York City, 14, 21, 44, 47–8, 51–7, 64–9, 71–5, 79–84, 86, 88, 92, 95–7, 99, 100, 103, 107, 110–11, 113–14, 117, 120, 122–3, 132, 136–9, 141–2, 145, 147, 149–50, 157–9, 161–4, 166, 170, 172–3, 177–8, 193–6, 199, 205, 207, 209, 223, 226–7, 235, 239, 246, 249–51, 253, 261, 263, 265–6, 268, 271, 285–90, 294–9, 301–4, 308, 311, 313, 315–17, 320–1, 324–5, 327, 331, 333–4, 336, 338–9, 343, 347, 351, 353–4, 360–1, 364, 366–7, 371–4, 382, 387, 390–3, 397–8, 400–1, 421–4, 428, 434, 436–7, 442–3, 449, 454, 458, 464, 466, 469, 474, 476, 478, 483–4, 487, 489–91, 493, 497, 507–8, 511–515, 526, 532, 539, 541–4, 546–7, 551–3, 559, 563, 576, 590, 595–6, 598, 601, 603, 607–8, 613–14, 616, 626–7, 633, 636–40, 642, 644–5, 648, 651–2, 656, 658, 674–7, 680–4, 689, 705–6, 718, 739, 743–4, 751–4, 758, 766, 769
New York *Evening Post*, 619
New York *Evening Sun*, 59, 479
New York *Herald Tribune*, 303, 478–479, 527, 597–8, 619
*New York Times, The*, 54, 173, 291, 479, 620
New York *World*, 619
*New Yorker, The*, 481

Nietzsche, Friedrich, 209, 220
*1924*, 334
Noble, Edward J., 34
"Nocturne," 41
Norman, Dorothy, 617
"North Labrador," 88–9, 145
*Nouvelle Revue Française*, 597

"O Carib Isle," 452, 463–4, 479, 581, 585–6
Obermeyer, Martha, *see* Sommer, Martha
"October–November," 49, 136
O'Flaherty, Liam, 669
O'Keeffe, Georgia, 271, 293, 319, 617
"Old Song," 506
O'Malley, Ernie, 669–70
O'Neill, Eugene, 327, 343, 345, 351, 357, 372, 377, 381, 383, 390, 393, 398, 408, 415–17, 427, 448–9
Opffer, Emil, 327, 355–8, 360–4, 366, 376, 378, 380–3, 392–3, 400, 402, 529–31, 539, 604, 629
Opffer, Emil Sr., 356, 358, 363–4, 393
Opffer, Ivan, 327, 356, 364
Oppenheim, James, 87, 721
*Ordeal of Mark Twain* (Van Wyck Brooks), 153
*Oresteia* (Aeschylus), 426
*Orizaba*, 651–3, 656, 735, 748, 751, 754, 758
Orr, Elaine, 333
*Others*, 60, 67, 72, 87
*Our America* (Waldo Frank), 153, 155
Ouspensky, P. D., 247–9, 270, 275, 358, 723
"Oval Portrait, The" (Edgar Allan Poe), 32

*Pagan, The*, 47, 49, 55, 58, 60, 73–4, 77, 88, 107–9, 112–15, 119, 136, 144, 149, 194, 205; *quoted*, 46
"Paraphrase," 403
Paris (France), 166, 196, 208, 212, 226–8, 234, 416, 538, 558, 577–82, 584–5, 587, 590, 592, 595–8, 606, 609, 614–15, 617, 627, 645, 658, 725, 739
*Paris Review, The, quoted*, 405
Parker, Eva, 421, 628
Parrish, Maxfield, 34, 79, 142, 147
Pasadena (Calif.), 516, 522, 548
"Passage," 326, 404–7
"Pastorale," 218–19
*Paterson* (William Carlos Williams), 305
Patno, Stanley, 253–6, 285, 371
Patterson (N.Y.), 402–3, 419–21, 424,

428, 434, 436, 442, 444, 446, 448,
450, 457, 460, 464, 474, 484–5,
489–90, 495, 497, 513, 525, 539,
543, 551, 570, 592, 602–4, 607–8,
616, 627–9, 632, 681–3, 739, 763;
*see also* Pawling (N.Y.)
*Pavannes and Divisions* (Ezra
Pound), 151
Pawling (N.Y.), 382, 386, 402; *see
also* Patterson (N.Y.)
*Pearsons*, 58
Pell, Arthur, 768
"Persuasion, A," 210
Peters, Miss M., 28, 613
*Phaedrus* (Socrates), 355
*Physique d'Amour* (Remy de Gour-
mont), 222, 243
Picasso, Pablo, 195, 207, 293, 343,
581, 592
"Pied Beauty" (Gerard Manley
Hopkins), 529
Plato, 137, 430
*Plumed Serpent, The* (D. H. Law-
rence), 426
Poe, Edgar Allan, 221, 336, 480;
*quoted*, 575
*Poetical Works of Percy Bysshe
Shelley* (Dowden), 32
*Poetry*, 34, 463–4, 478–80, 506, 616,
620–1, 633, 665–6, 680, 703, 721,
738, 744, 749, 758–9
Polytype Press, 375
*Poor White* (Sherwood Anderson),
192, 218
"Porphyro in Akron," 159, 167, 169,
216
Portapovitch, Anna *and* Stanislaw,
92–3, 96–7, 107, 110–11, 114, 131,
137
Porter, Katherine Anne, 651, 658–62,
666, 668, 670–3, 681–3, 696
*Portrait of the Artist as a Young
Man, A* (James Joyce), 115, 133
"Possessions," 334, 362
"Poster," 218, 262
"Postscript," 108
Pound, Ezra, 88–90, 133, 136, 160,
173, 209, 211, 222, 247, 253, 267,
464
"Powhatan's Daughter," 449–50, 485,
510–11, 601, 605, 609, 644
"Praise for an Urn," 191, 230–2, 234,
240, 260
Pratt and Lindsey, 349–50
"Preludes" (T. S. Eliot), 153, 242
Pressly, Gene, 659, 662, 671–4
*Principles of Literary Criticism* (I. A.
Richards), 527
"Proem," 119, 449

*Prophetic Books* (William Blake),
240
Proust, Marcel, 209, 527
*Prufrock and Other Observations*
(T. S. Eliot), 151, 242, 263
Puebla (Mexico), 733–4, 736
Putnam, Phelps, 703–4, 712, 718,
720–1, 729, 731

"Quaker Hill," 481, 603–4, 608, 610–
611

Rabelais, 155, 167, 209
Rauh, Ida, 160
Ravel, Maurice, 208–9, 388, 594
Ray, Man, 193–4, 207
"Recitative," 22, 326, 333–4, 405, 407
Reeck, Emil, 237
"Rest, The" (Ezra Pound), *quoted*,
183
"Return, The," 464
Rheinthal and Newman, 142–4, 146–7
Rickword, Edgell, 478, 576
Ridgefield (Conn.), 212, 327, 351,
357, 398
Riding, Laura, 402, 421, 527–8, 576–7
Rimbaud, Arthur, 146, 173, 181, 203,
240, 242, 336, 441, 446–7, 451, 523
"River, The," 45, 260, 490, 504–6,
551, 619–20, 622, 652
Rivera, Diego, 665
Robeson, Paul, 576
Robinson, Boardman, 195
Robinson, Ted, 287
Robson, Ernest, 608, 628
Robson, Margaret (Margaret Bab-
cock), 608–10, 613, 628–9, 635–7,
651, 679, 681–2, 684, 725, 769
Rodin, Auguste, 193
Rodman, Selden, 636, 666, 721
Roebling, John Augustus, 481, 485
Roger Williams Company, 253, 290
Rosenfeld, Paul, 153, 250–2, 269,
279, 294, 343, 417, 476, 602, 625–6,
634
Ross, Mildred *and* Verna, 63, 390,
491
"Royal Palm," 452
Rudolph, Lucretia, 5
Rychtarik, Charlotte, 257, 281, 286–9,
292, 294, 296–7, 299, 302–3, 307–
311, 320, 329, 339, 341, 354, 357,
366, 374, 383–4, 389, 393, 396,
398, 400, 404, 407, 418–19, 421,
424, 427, 432, 436, 438, 446, 451,
454, 465, 507–8, 514, 519–20, 532–3,
558, 560, 570–1, 584–5, 607, 640–3,
646, 651, 662, 665, 680, 684, 687,
694, 732, 734, 749

Rychtarik, Richard, 257, 277, 281, 286–9, 291–3, 295–7, 299, 302–3, 307–11, 314, 320, 329, 339, 341, 354, 357, 366, 374, 383–4, 393, 396, 398, 400, 404, 407, 414, 418–19, 421, 424, 427, 432, 436, 438, 446, 451, 465, 507–8, 514, 519–20, 532–3, 558, 570–1, 584–5, 607, 640–3, 646, 651, 662, 665, 680, 684, 687, 694, 732, 734, 749, 769

*S4N*, 278, 297
*Sacred Wood, The* (T. S. Eliot), 219
Sáenz, Moisés, 661–4, 668, 688–9, 694, 761, 772
Saltus, Edgar, 159, 173, 183, 192
San Francisco (Calif.), 45, 147, 157, 531, 736
San Pedro (Calif.), 519, 525, 530–1
Sanborn, Robert, 312
*Saturday Evening Post*, 133, 290
*Saturday Review of Literature*, 602, 619–20
*Satyricon* (Petronius), 183, 186
Schmitt, Carl, 48–53, 56–60, 64, 67–71, 86–9, 92–3, 95–7, 99, 107, 114, 117, 305, 728
Schneider, Helen *and* Isidor, 312, 476, 481, 518–20, 527–9, 535–6, 539–40, 545–6, 561, 569, 577, 590, 592, 617–21
*Science and the Modern World* (Alfred North Whitehead), 426
*Scientific American*, 450
Scott, Natalie, 695, 714, 728
Seabrook, Katie, 743–4, 748
*Secession*, 218, 232–4, 245, 251, 258, 260, 262, 268, 297, 312–14, 318, 357
Seldes, Gilbert, 257–8
Seltzer, Thomas, 380
Service, Robert, 221
*Seven Arts, The*, 87
*Seven Keys to Baldpate* (Earl Derr Biggers), 60
*Sewanee Review, The*, 357
*Shadowland*, 211
Shakespeare, William, 221, 240, 283, 476, 500–2, 589
Shelley, Percy, 221
Shepard, Odell, 620
*Show Boat*, 569, 578
Silver Lake (N.H.), 631–2, 634–5
Simpson, Eyler, 651, 656–8, 660–2, 664–5, 668, 673–4, 676–7, 719, 721, 748–9, 752–3, 760, 771
Simpson, Lesley Byrd, 673, 694–5, 697–702, 712, 717, 720, 722–4,

735–8, 742–3, 747–8, 752, 754, 758, 760
Simpson, Marian, 698, 723, 736–8, 742, 748, 752
Simpson, Sally, 439–41, 444–5, 449, 451–3, 456–65, 467, 469, 481, 504, 507, 531, 533, 545, 564–5, 600–1, 606, 631, 678, 684, 706, 758, 771
*Since Cézanne* (Clive Bell), 253, 268
Siqueiros, David, 29, 694–5, 698, 701–3, 705–6, 725–6, 731, 745
Sitwell, Edith, 190
*1601* (Mark Twain), 155
Skeel, George, 87
*Smart Set, The*, 90–1, 167
Smith, Claire Spencer, *see* Spencer, Claire
Smith, Harrison (Hal), 106, 123, 128–9, 133–5, 139–40, 143, 146–7, 290, 380, 407–8, 417, 651
Smith, Joseph Frease, 272, 369
Smith, Leonard, 253
Smith, Tom, 665
Sommer, Edwin, 202
Sommer, Martha, 195–6, 202
Sommer, Ray, 21, 202, 307
Sommer, William (Bill), 21, 47, 190, 194–6, 201–8, 211–12, 219–20, 222–4, 226, 229–31, 244, 247, 250–253, 256, 260–1, 267–72, 274, 279, 281, 291–2, 295, 297, 303, 305, 307, 319, 393, 396–7, 402, 408, 424, 465, 556, 607, 640, 680
Soupault, Philippe, 233, 235, 578, 592
Spear, Zilla, 20
Spencer, Mrs., 106, 112, 123–4, 129, 133, 139
Spencer, Claire, 106–7, 110–12, 114, 123, 128–9, 133–5, 139–41, 143, 146–7, 162, 164, 279, 389, 444, 743–4, 748
Spencer, Marjorie, 334
Spengler, Oswald, 446, 448, 517, 526, 528, 537, 644
Spinoza, Baruch, 641
Spratling, William, 21, 683, 694, 696, 712–14, 723
"Springs of Guilty Song, The," 258
Squarcialupi, John, 357, 372, 383
Standard Oil Company, 635–6
"Stark Major," 277–9, 743
*Starved Rock* (Edgar Lee Masters), 160
Stein, Gertrude, 343–4, 581, 592–3
Stella, Joseph, 261, 556, 579, 595
Stevens, Emily, 182
Stevens, Wallace, 153, 157, 173, 219, 234, 336, 464, 680, 703

Stevenson, Hazel, 202
Stieglitz, Alfred, 251, 269, 271, 293–4,
  305–8, 315, 317, 319–20, 322, 330,
  339, 343, 345, 357, 466, 476, 583,
  617
*Story of San Michele, The* (Axel
  Munthe), 641
Stravinsky, Igor, 383
Streator, Charity, 5
Streator, Elizabeth, 5
Streator, Jason, 5
Streator, John, 5
Sullivan, John J., 49, 59, 70–1, 74,
  85, 100, 103–4, 128–30, 187
*Sun Also Rises, The* (Ernest Heming-
  way), 474
"Sunday Morning Apples," 261
Sweet's Catalogue Service, 353, 357–8,
  381–2, 389, 391
Swinburne, Algernon Charles, 46,
  115, 137, 192, 576
Sykes, Jessie, 7
Symon, Arthur, 59
Symonds, John Aldington, 46, 55
Synge, John Millington, 219
Szold, Bernadine, 592

Taggard, Genevieve, 623
Tagore, Rabindranath, 40, 46
*Tales of Mystery and Imagination*
  (Edgar Allan Poe), 32–3
*Tamburlaine* (Christopher Marlowe),
  580
Tanner, Alan *and* Florence, 587–8
*Taras Bulba* (Nikolai Gogol), 237
*Tarr* (Wyndham Lewis), 221
Tate, Allen, 38, 136–7, 239–42, 245,
  276–9, 285–6, 289, 292, 294, 333–4,
  357–9, 372, 387–8, 402–4, 407,
  417–25, 428, 430–5, 442, 448–9,
  467, 478–81, 490, 493, 526–7, 546,
  582, 586, 592, 594–5, 610, 621–3,
  625, 634, 728, 772
Tate, Caroline (Caroline Gordon),
  402, 418–21, 424–5, 427, 432–5,
  442, 444, 467, 490, 493, 546, 592,
  595, 728
Taxco (Mexico), 661–4, 694–7, 701–2,
  712–15, 717–19, 721–7, 735, 748
Taylor, Paul, 695
Tchelitchew, Pavel, 587–8
Teagle, J. Walter, 635–7
Teasdale, Sara, 220
*Tempest, The* (William Shakespeare),
  523
Tennyson, Alfred Lord, 221
Tepoztlan (Mexico), 21, 689–91,
  693–4, 697, 702–3, 707, 722, 741

*Tertium Organum* (P. D. Ouspensky),
  203, 247; *quoted*, 248, 267
Thayer, Scofield, 405
Thomas, Edward, 186, 219
Thomas, Harold, 67
Thompson, Basil, 211
Thompson, Francis, 221
Thompson, J. Walter, Agency, 201,
  289–91, 300, 320, 338–9, 346, 381
Thompson, Robert, 613, 681–2
"Three Songs," 594
*Through Traffic* (Russell Davenport),
  641
*Time and Western Man* (Wyndham
  Lewis), 523, 537
"To Brooklyn Bridge," 681
"To Emily Dickinson," 506
"To Portapovitch (du Ballet Russe),"
  93
"To the Cloud Juggler," 613
"To Zell, Now Bound for Spain," 379
*Tom Jones* (Henry Fielding), 502
Toomer, Jean, 203, 249, 289–91, 302,
  304, 314–15, 320, 325–9, 331, 334,
  339, 343, 358, 361–3, 372, 375, 377,
  393, 531, 558, 617
Torrence, Ridgely, 60, 137
*transition*, 479, 506, 527–8, 540,
  578–9, 585, 614, 643
Tucker, Sophie, 628
*Tulips and Chimneys* (E. E. Cum-
  mings), 375
"Tunnel, The," 451, 506, 619–20
Turner, Addie, 402, 419–22, 425,
  432–4, 457, 460, 466–7, 469, 475–8,
  483, 485, 490–1, 495, 506, 519, 525,
  531, 546, 548, 550–1, 554, 608,
  629–30
Turner, W. J., 563
*Tuscania*, 575–6
Twain, Mark, 137, 154–5, 167
*Two Slatterns and a King* (Edna St.
  Vincent Millay), 108
Tzara, Tristan, 233, 235

"Ulalume" (Edgar Allan Poe), 57;
  *quoted*, 58
*Ulysses* (James Joyce), 88, 136, 222,
  246, 253–4, 262, 282, 292, 305, 312,
  624
*Un Coeur Virginal* (Remy de Gourmont), 222
Underwood, Wilbur, 182–4, 189, 229,
  246, 253, 273–6, 295, 325, 442,
  444, 465–6, 469, 476, 490–1, 495,
  497, 506–7, 515, 518, 538, 554,
  684, 688, 721
Untermeyer, Louis, 260, 278, 294,
  619, 634, 680, 703

Vail, Laurence, 578, 581, 585
Valéry, Paul, 501, 538, 586, 664
Valle, Rafael, 658
*Valley, The* (Nathan Asch), 546
Van Doren, Mark, 479
*Vanity Fair*, 393, 427, 602
"Van Winkle," 504, 510–11, 652
Varèse, Edgar, 578–9, 592
Vaughan, Henry, 503
Vera Cruz (Mexico), 653, 655, 664, 682, 684, 719, 751, 753–4, 758
Vildrac, Charles, 173, 211, 597–8
Villefranche (France), 578, 581
Villon, François, 173
*Virgin Spain* (Waldo Frank), 318, 426, 448
"Virginia," 450, 619
"Visit to a Poet, A" (Charles Brooks), 134
"Voyages," 182, 216, 218, 258, 261, 326, 336, 357, 361–3, 374, 376–8, 389, 406–7, 425, 428, 681, 722, 769

Wagner, Richard, 140, 196
Walton, Eda Lou, 509, 552, 625–6, 636, 703, 721
Walton, Mrs., 90–1, 93–7, 100–1, 114, 123, 126
Warner, Marian Wright, 28–9
Warren, Robert Penn, 527
Warren (Ohio), 4, 5, 9, 10, 12–13, 16, 19–21, 24, 34, 48–9, 65, 89, 99, 475, 556, 564, 573, 607, 639, 764
Warren (Penn.), 266, 473–4, 640, 680
Warren *Tribune*, 48, 65, 379
Warshawsky, Abe, 196
Washington, D.C., 66, 178–82, 186, 229, 314, 459, 490, 538
*Waste Land, The* (T. S. Eliot), 260, 270, 282, 450–1, 624
Watson, Sibley, 257, 269–70
*Way of All Flesh, The* (Samuel Butler), 173
Weber, Brom, 46, 375–7, 765
Webster, John, 219, 221, 231, 284, 633
Weinstock, Herbert, 619
Wells, H. G., 469, 537
West, Rebecca, 617
West Englewood (N.J.), 139, 146
Westcott, Glenway, 312, 315, 343, 377, 527, 578, 592
Western Reserve University, 22, 201, 290, 486

Wheelright, John Brooks, 258, 297, 312–14
*White Buildings*, 137, 167, 210, 325–327, 333, 336, 374, 377, 383, 403, 405, 407–8, 414, 427, 438, 443, 448, 455, 462, 464–5, 472, 474, 476, 478–9, 481, 499, 508, 529, 561, 578, 602, 623, 625, 645, 698
*White-Jacket* (Herman Melville), 427
Whitman, Walt, 221, 248, 264, 283, 336, 431, 447–8, 479–80, 583, 590, 619–22, 633, 659
Widney, Willard, 587–8, 596–8
Wiegand, Charmion von, 145–9, 177, 207, 212, 235, 237, 251, 254, 263, 268, 278, 292, 389, 545, 551–2, 554, 556–8, 569, 575, 579, 769–70
Wilcox, Walter, 90
Wilde, Oscar, 46, 58, 115, 183
Wilkinson, Marguerite, 220
Williams, William Carlos, 72, 173, 190, 268–71, 305, 559, 609, 622
Wilson, Edmund, 499, 500, 503, 634
"Wine Menagerie, The," 404–6
*Winesburg, Ohio* (Sherwood Anderson), 144, 156, 167, 192, 249
Winters, Yvor, 462, 464, 478–80, 499–504, 526–8, 620–3
Wise, Herbert, 516–17, 519, 525–6, 529–31, 534–6, 569–70
Wishart and Company, 478
Woodstock (N.Y.), 233, 271, 314, 322–3, 325, 327–8, 331, 334, 337–8, 341–2, 386, 401
"Wreck of the Deutschland, The" (Gerard Manley Hopkins), 529, 624
Wright, Margaret, 443, 473–4
Wright, William, 16, 28–33, 38, 47, 50, 54, 87, 113–17, 121, 125, 132, 137–9, 143, 146–7, 152, 154–5, 162, 170, 173–7, 179, 217, 220, 231, 236–7, 239, 242, 245–6, 257, 265, 292, 441–3, 460, 472–5, 570, 582–3, 613, 627, 633–4, 636–8, 640, 643, 652, 678, 680, 684–5, 692, 708, 771

Yeats, William Butler, 40, 55, 88–9, 136, 363, 502

Zabel, Morton Dauwen, 666, 668–9, 677, 680, 703, 721, 738, 744, 749, 751, 758–9
Zinsser, Hans, 652–6, 658, 661, 664–5
Zorach, William, 108, 196
Zucker, Roger, 137, 146